PROCEEDINGS

SUPERCOMPUTING '93

SUPERCOMPUTING '93

Portland, Oregon
November 15 – 19

Sponsored by

IEEE Computer Society Technical Committees on
Supercomputing Applications and Computer Architecture
ACM SIGARCH

IEEE Computer Society Press
Los Alamitos, California

Washington • Brussels • Tokyo

The Association for Computing Machinery
1515 Broadway
New York, NY 10036

IEEE Computer Society Press Order Number 4340-02
ACM Order Number 415932
IEEE Catalog Number 93CH3342-3
ISBN 0-8186-4340-4 (paper)
ISBN 0-8186-4341-2 (microfiche)
ISBN 0-8186-4342-0 (case)
ISSN 1063-9535

Additional copies may be ordered prepaid from

ACM Order Department
P.O. Box 12114
Church Street Station
New York, NY 10257

Phone: 1-800-342-6626 (U.S. and Canada)
1-212-626-0500 (All other countries)
Fax: 1-212-944-1318
E-mail: ACMPUBS@ACM.ORG

Additional copies can be ordered from

IEEE Computer Society Press	IEEE Service Center	IEEE Computer Society	IEEE Computer Society
Customer Service Center	445 Hoes Lane	13, avenue de l'Aquilon	Ooshima Building
10662 Los Vaqueros Circle	P.O. Box 1331	B-1200 Brussels	2-19-1 Minami-Aoyama
P.O. Box 3014	Piscataway, NJ 08855-1331	BELGIUM	Minato-ku, Tokyo 107
Los Alamitos, CA 90720-1264			JAPAN

To order IEEE Computer Society Press books, call: 1-800-CS-BOOKS, or
Fax: 714-821-4641. E-mail: CS.BOOKS@COMPUTER.ORG

Production Editor: Robert Werner
Cover design by Mo Viele
Artwork production by Joseph Daigle/Schenk-Daigle Studios
Printed in the United States of America by Braun-Brumfield, Inc.

 The Institute of Electrical and Electronics Engineers, Inc.

Preface

The Supercomputing '93 conference, sponsored by the Computer Architecture and Supercomputing Applications Technical Committees of the IEEE Computer Society, and ACM SIGARCH, features both a forum for sharing ideas and research results, as well as an exhibition that showcases commercial and experimental research hardware and software.

The role of the program committee has expanded considerably since the inception of the conference. With a balance of academia, industry, and government institutions among its members, the committee is responsible for all aspects of the technical program, including contributed papers, invited speakers, panels, minisymposia, research exhibits, poster and video poster sessions, networking programs, and the Visualization Theatre. The tutorial committee is responsible for the content of the tutorials and the conference workshops.

These proceedings contain the full text of the contributed papers, as well as abstracts for the invited speakers, panels, and minisymposia. Research exhibit and poster session abstracts are included in the final program. After the success of last year's CD-ROM version of the proceedings, we are producing half of the proceedings in the CD-ROM format this year, and the other half in paper hardcopy. Conference attendees are given their choice of formats.

There were over 300 submissions of technical papers to the conference. Papers were assigned to the following tracks: 1) applications, 2) algorithms/numerical analysis, 3) systems, 4) visualization, 5) networking/communications, and 6) architectures. (It is sometimes very difficult to properly categorize a paper, since the content often overlaps several areas of the computing environment.) Each paper was reviewed by three persons knowledgeable in their field, and was given an overall ranking within its assigned track. Ultimately, 72 were selected for presentation, an acceptance rate of 24 percent.

The conference is committed to involvement by students, from the high school level through graduate school. Accordingly, a set of education sessions, aimed primarily at high school teachers, is featured in this year's program. In addition, to obtain more consistency in the designation and selection of student papers, all student authors were required to verify their status as students and their role as primary contributors to an accepted paper. Thirty-three such verifications were received. Of these, five finalists were chosen by a further review process, to compete for the Best Student Paper award, which is determined by presentation of the papers at the conference. The winner of this award becomes a member of next year's program committee, and is in charge of the selection process for the next conference.

There were 12 invited speakers, 4 panels, and 12 minisymposia at this year's conference. The invited speakers were selected by the program committee on the basis of acknowledged expertise in their particular field and their presentation skills. A wide variety of talks, ranging from molecular manufacturing to global warming to computer-generated dinosaurs for the motion picture *Jurassic Park* is the result of the selection efforts of the committee. Talks by the finalists in the Gordon Bell Prize category and the winners of the Forefronts Award and the Sid Fernbach Award are again featured.

The panels and minisymposia this year reflect current industry concerns and include sessions comparing and contrasting the concepts of MPP versus vector computers along with the future of parallel architectures. Observing supercomputing efforts from countries around the world, and exploring the emerging language "battles" upon entering the parallel computing era are other timely topics on the program.

A special day of additional sessions is included, designated "Environmental Day." Three panels cover various topics of computing concerns in the environmental profession. Environmental professionals and researchers are specifically invited to attend these sessions.

Much work goes into the making of a conference of this size and caliber. The technical program is the result of the work of the various committees, the authors, the reviewers, those who implement the network on the floor, and many others on the committee staff. These proceedings are meant to sum up the flavor of this year's conference. We hope you will find it useful in your future work.

Enjoy Supercomputing '93!

Bob Borchers
SC '93 General Chair

Dona Crawford
Program Chair

List of SC '93 Reviewers

Vikram Adve, *University of Wisconsin*

Borislav Agapiev

Anant Agarwal

Sriniva Aluru, *Ames Lab, Iowa State University*

Gail A. Alverson, *Tera Computer Company*

Susan Amarasinghe, *Stanford University*

Bean Anderson, *Silicon Graphics, Inc.*

Jennifer Anderson, *Stanford University*

Boon S. Ang, *MIT Lab for Computer Sci.*

Bill Appelbe, *Georgia Tech*

Arvind, *MIT Lab for Computer Science*

Cleve Ashcraft, *Boeing Computer Services*

Jonathan Babb, *MIT*

Scott B. Baden, *University of California*

Richard Bahr, *Silicon Graphics*

David H. Bailey, *NASA/Ames Research Center*

Mike Bailey, *SDSC*

Prith Banerjee, *University of Illinois*

Jesse L. Barlow, *Pensylvania State University*

Frank R. Barriuso, *Cray Research Park*

Eric Barszcz, *NASA Ames Research Center*

Jim Barton, *Silicon Graphics, Inc.*

John Barton

Mike Barton, *Intel Corp.*

Marti Baucroft, *Cray Research Inc.*

Michael J. Beckerle, *Motorola*

Robert Bedall, *Boeing*

R.K. Belew, *University of California*

R.J. Bergeron, *NASA Ames Research Center*

Wes Bethel, *Lawrence Berkeley Lab*

Sandeep Bhatt

Christian Bischof, *Argonne National Laboratories*

Bill Boas, *Essential Communications*

Bob Boothe, *University of California*

Andy Boughton, *MIT*

David Bowen, *Cray Research, Inc.*

Ralph G. Brickner, *Los Alamos National Laboratory*

Mark Bromley, *Thinking Machines Corp.*

Eugene Brooks, *Lawrence Livermore National Laboratory*

Ingrid Bucher, *Los Alamos National Laboratory*

F. Warren Burton, *Simon Fraser University*

Russel Caflisch, *University of California, Los Angeles*

David Callahan

Tim Callahan, *University of California, Berkeley*

Michael Campbell, *The Aerospace Corporation*

Roy Campbell, *University of Illinois*

Tom Canfield, *Argonne National Laboratory*

Jon Cargille, *University of Wisconsin*

Paul R. Carini, *IBM T.J. Watson Research Center*

John R. Carlson, *SGI*

Andrea Carnevali, *Motorola Cambridge Research Center*

Enrique Castro-Leon, *Intel Corp.*

David Chaiken, *MIT*

Siddhartha Chatterjee, *NASA Ames Research Center*

Doreen Y. Cheng, *NASA Ames Research Center*

Geoff Chesshire, *IBM T.J. Watson Research Center*

Greg Chesson, *Silicon Graphics, Inc.*

Alex Cheung, *Sandia National Laboratories*

Andrew Chien

Derek Chiou, *MIT*

Fred Chong, *MIT*

A. Chronopoulos, *University of Minnesota*

Bob Ciotti, *NASA Ames Research Center*

Gerardo Cisneros

Grant Cook, *Lawrence Livermore National Laboratory*

Mark E. Crovella, *University of Rochester*

Lawrence Crowl, *Oregon State University*

P. Culler, *McGill University*

Jan Cuoy, *University of Massachusetts*

Eduardo F. D'Azevedo, *Oak Ridge National Laboratory*

Bill Dannevik, *Lawrence Livermore National Laboratory*

Fredenzo Darema, *IBM T.J. Watson Research Center*

B. Davie, *Bellcore*

Jim Dehnert

David des Jardins, *IDA/CER*

Andre Detton, *MIT Al Laboratory*

Inderjit S. Dhillon, *University of California*

David C. DiNucci, *NASA Ames Research Center*

June Donato, *Oak Ridge National Laboratory*

Jack Dongarra, *University of Tennessee*

Craig C. Doughas, *Yale University*

David C. Douglas, *Thinking Machines Corp.*

John B. Drake

Todd F. Dupont, *University of Chicago*

Alan Edelman, *University of California*

Susan Eggers, *University of Washington*

Doug Elias, *Cornell University*

Gary Elsesser, *Cray Research*

Perry Emrath, *University of Illinois*

Mary M. Eshaghian, *NJIT University Heights*

Chien Fang, *Sandia National Laboratories*

Jeanne Ferrante, *University of Colorado*

Samuel A. Fineberg, *NASA Ames Research Center*

Charles Fineman, *Sun Microsystems*

Gregory Fischer

Stuart Fiske, *MIT*

John Forrest, *IBM*

Paul O. Frederickson, *Cray Research Inc.*

R. Stockton Gaines, *University of Southern California*

Mike Galles, *Silicon Graphics*

E. Gallopoulos, *University of Illinois*

J.L. Gaudiot

Al Geist

Al Gerrish

Douglas Gharmley, *University of California*

Laurie Gibson, *Fortesque Corp.*

John Gilbert, *Xerox PARC*

Harvey Glass, *University of South Florida*

Stephen Goldschmidt, *Stanford University*

Seth C. Goldstein

Steve Gossage, *Sandia National Laboratory*

R. Govindarajan, *McGill University*

Ananth Y. Grama

Tom Green, *Supercomputer Compuations Res. Inst.*

David Greenberg, *Sandia National Laboratories*

Bob Greiner

A. Grimshaw, *University of Virginia*

William Griswold, *University of California at San Diego*

Bill Gropp

Robert Grossman

Dirk Grunwald, *University of Boulder*

John Gustafson, *NASA Ames Research Laboratory*

Fred Gustavson, *IBM T.J. Watson Research Center*

Jim Hack, *NCAR*

Robert Halstead, *Digital Corporation*

Chuck Hansen

Marius C. Hasegan, *Purdue University*
Omar Hassaine
Stuart Hawkinson, *Intel Corp.*
Michael T. Heath, *University of Illinois*
Wendy Heffner, *University of California*
Dick Hessel, *Silicon Graphics, Inc.*
Markus Hitz, *Rensselaer Polytechnic Institute*
Ching-Tien Ho, *IBM Almaden Research Center*
Robert H. Holibaugh, *Carnegie-Mellon University*
Jeff Hollingsworth
Frank Honose, *MIT*
Robert T. Hood
Thomas P. Hughes, *Mission Research Corp.*
Don Heller, *Shell Development Co.*
Kai Hwang
Yuan-Shin Hwang
Bob Iannucci
M. Ashraf Iqbal, *University of Southern California*
Bruce Irvin, *University of Wisconsin-Madison*
Nayeem Islam, *University of Illinois*
Verne L. Jacobs, *Naval Research Laboratory*
Chris Joerg, *MIT*
Darin Johnson, *CSE, VCSD*
Kirk Johnson, *MIT Laboratory for Computer Science*
Lennart Johnsson, *Thinking Machines Corp.*
Jeff A. Jones, *University of California*
Merritt E. Jones, *IBM/Federal Systems Co.*
Robert R. Jones, *University of Michigan*
Harry Jordan, *University of Colorado*
Wayne Joubert, *Los Alamos National Laboratory*
F. Kaashoek, *MIT LCS*
W. Kahan, *University of California*
Alan Kaplan, *Bell Laboratories*
Alan Karp, *Hewlett-Packard Company*

George Karypis, *University of Minnesota*
Stephen Keckler, *MIT*
Kimberly Keeton, *University of California*
Peter Keleher, *Rice University*
Charlie Kennedy, *University of California*
David Keyes, *Yale University*
Jae H. Kim, *Digital Computer Lab.*
Doug Kimelman, *IBM T.J. Watson Research Center*
David Kincaid, *CNA*
Adrian King, *Sandia National Laboratories*
Tom Kitchens, *U.S. Dept. of Energy*
Edward W. Knightly
Charles Koelbel, *Rice University*
James A. Kohl, *University of Iowa*
Richard E. Korf, *University of California*
David Kranz, *MIT*
Ulrich Kremer, *Rice University*
Michael F. Krogh, *Los Alamos National Laboratory*
Tony Kubalak, *Cray Research, Inc.*
Helene E. Kulsrud, *IDA, Center for Comm. Research*
K.G. Kumar, *IBM T.J.Watson Research Center*
Ed Kushner, *Intel Corp.*
Bradley C. Kuszmaul, *MIT Lab for Computer Science*
Thomas Kwan, *National Center for Supercomputing Applications*
Thomas W. Laneatella, *Cray Research, Inc.*
Mark LaPolla
James Larus
Corinna Lee, *University of Toronto*
Craig A. Lee, *The Aerospace Corporation*
Meemong Lee
W.J. Lennon, *Lawrence Livermore National Laboratory*
Joseph W.H. Leu, *York University*

Michael R. Leuze, *Oak Ridge National Laboratory*

David Levine, *Argonne National Laboratory*

John G. Lewis, *Boeing Computer Services*

Ted Lewis

Kai Li, *Princeton University*

Cheng Liao, *Silicon Graphics, Inc.*

Beng-Hong Lim, *MIT*

Kevin R. Lind, *Lawrence Livermore National Laboratory*

Miron Livny, *University of Wisconsin*

Ginnie Lo

Bei Lu, *Syracuse University*

Olaf Lubeck, *Los Alamos National Laboratory*

Steve Lumetta, *University of California*

Steve Luna, *University of California*

Bryan Lyles, *Xerox PARC*

Eva Ma

Tom MacDonald, *Cray Research*

Ken Mackenzie, *MIT*

David Malon, *Argonne National Laboratory*

Allen D. Malony, *University of Oregon*

Tom Malzbender

William R. Martin, *University of Michigan*

Margaret Martonosi, *Center for Integrated Systems*

Stephen P. Masticola, *Rutgers University*

Peter M. Maurer, *University of South Florida*

Dror Maydan, *IBM Israel-Science & Technology Ltd.*

Alan Mayer

Michael McConnell, *Cray Research, Inc.*

Carolyn McCreary, *Auburn University*

Michael McGowen, *Essential Communications*

Nathaniel McIntosh, *Rice University*

Nick McKeown, *University of California*

Kathryn S. McKinley, *ENSMP (CRI)*

Larry Meadows, *The Portland Group*

Ali Mechentel

Pankaj Mehra, *NASA Ames Research Center*

Piyush Mehrotra, *ICASE*

John Mellor-Crummey, *Rice University*

Michael Merchant, *Cray Research, Inc.*

J. Mesirov, *CCR — LaJolla*

David Meyerhafer, *University of Rochester*

Bart Miller, *University of Wisconsin*

Ron Minnich, *SRC*

Daniel Miranker, *University of Texas at Austin*

E. Miya, *NASA Ames Research Center*

Bernd Mohr, *University of Oregon*

Gary Montry, *Southwest Software*

Reagan W. Moore, *SDSC*

Jose Moreira, *University of Illinois*

John Morrison, *Los Alamos National Laboratory*

Charles C. Mosher, *ARCO Exp. & Prod. Tech.*

Masato Motomura, *System VLSI Research Laboratory*

Todd C. Mowry

Brian Murphy

Leonard Napolitano, *Sandia National Laboratories*

Rob Netzer, *Brown University*

Esmond Ng, *Oak Ridge National Laboratory*

Tung M. Nguyen, *IBM Corp.*

David Nicol

Rishiyur S. Nikhil, *Digital Corp.*

Bill Nitzberg, *NASA Ames Research Center*

Michael Noakes, *MIT*

Mark Nodina, *MIT*

Victor T. Norman, *Purdue University*

Rod Oldehoeft, *Colorado State University*

Susan Owicki, *DEC SRC*

J. Pallis

Richard Palmer, *Sandia National Laboratories*

G. Papadopoulos, *Cornel University*

Manish Parasher, *Syracuse University*

Dave Pase, *Cray Research*

George Paul, *IBM T.J.Watson Research Center*

David K. Paulsen, *University of Illinois*

Barry Peyton, *Oak Ridge National Laboratory*

John Pezaris, *MIT Lab for Computer Science*

R.L. Phillips, *Los Alamos National Laboratory*

Lyndon Pierson, *Sandia National Laboratories*

Robert Plemmons, *Wake Forest University*

Mark J. Potts, *Cray Research Inc.*

A. Powell

Gill Pratt, *MIT*

Jeff Prisner, *Inst. for Defense Analysis*

William Pugh, *University of Maryland*

Michael J. Quinn, *Oregon State University*

M. Raghunath, *University of California*

Aruna Ramanan

Sanjay Ranica, *Syracuse University*

Bob Rau, *Hewlett Packard Laboratories*

Lawrence Rauchwerger, *University of Illinois*

Steve Reinhardt, *University of Wisconsin-Madison*

Stephen Remondi, *Exa Corp.*

John Renwick, *NetStar Inc.*

Luis G. Reyna, *IBM T.J. Watson Research Center*

David Robertson, *Lawrence Berkeley Laboratory*

Gerals Roth, *Rice University*

Diane T. Rover, *Michigan State University*

Tom Rowan, *Oak Ridge National Laboratory*

Chris Rowen, *Silicon Graphics*

John Rowlan, *Argonne National Laboratory*

Paul R. Rupert, *Lawrence Livermore National Laboratory*

John Ruttenberg, *Silicon Graphics*

Jeff Rutter

Barbara G. Ryder, *Rutgers University*

Rafael H. Saavedra, *University of Southern California*

Ali A. Sadjadi, *Cray Research Inc.*

Vikram Salelore, *Oregon State University*

Joel Saltz, *University of Maryland*

Ahmed Sameh, *CSRD, University of Illinois*

David Sanders, *Cray Research Inc.*

Vivek Sarkar, *Compiler Tech. Institute*

Sekhar Sarukkai, *NASA Ames Research Center*

Richard K. Sato, *NCAR*

Dan Scales

Klaus E. Schauser, *University of California*

Brian Schmidt, *Stanford University*

David Schneider, *University of Illinois*

Edith Schonberg, *IBM Research*

Rob Schreiber, *NASA*

David Scott

Jeffrey S. Scraggs, *North Carolina State University*

Steven R. Seidel, *Michigan Technological University*

Naveen Sharma

Andrew Shaw, *MIT Lab for Computer Science*

Dennis G. Shea, *IBM Research*

Margaret Simmons, *Computer Research Group*

Horst D. Simon, *NASA Ames Research Center*

Jaswinder Pal Singh, *Stanford University*

Milan Singh, *MIT*

Robert Skeel, *University of Illinois*

Thomas Skibo, *Silicon Graphics*

Richard D. Smith, *Los Alamos National Laboratory*

D. Sorensen, *Rice University*

Mark S. Squillante, *IBM T.J.Watson Research Center*

Dan Stevenson, *MCNC*

James M. Stichnoth, *CMU/SCS/CSD*

Table of Contents

Keynote

Session 1: Algorithms for Applications
Chair: John Gustafson

Session 1: Computational Physics
Chair: Randy Christensen

Session 1: Workshop

Session 1: Invited Presentations

Session 2: Partitioning
Chair: Frederica Darema

Session 2: Networks
Chair: Bill Boas

Session 2: Workshop

Session 2: Workshop: Education

Session 2: Invited Presentations

Session 3: Matrix Library Issues
Chair: Bob Ward

Session 3: Evaluation of Real Machines
Chair: David Culler

Session 3: Minisymposium: Networking

High Performance Internetworking
Speaker: C. Partridge

Session 4: Applications I
Chair: Rick Stevens

Session 4: Parallel Languages
Chair: Carl Kesselman

Session 4: Workshop

Session 4: Invited Presentations

Session 4: Minisymposium: Advent of ATM
Chair: Don Tolmie

Session 5: Applications II
Chair: Wilf Pinfold

Session 5: Data Parallel Compilers
Chair: Ray Cline

Session 5: Minisymposium

Session 5: Panel

Session 6: Parallel I/O I
Chair: Helene Kulsrud

Session 6: Optimizations for High-Performance Compilers
Chair: Doug Pase

Session 6: Workshop

Session 6: Invited Presentations
Allen Hammond
Bob McGaughey
Christine Shoemaker

Session 6: Panel

Session 7: Parallel I/O II
Chair: Helene Kulsrud

Session 7: Sparse Matrices
Chair: Bob Ward

Session 7: Minisymposium
Chair: Don Heller

Session 7: Minisymposium: EDS/NIIT

Session 8: Visualization Environments
Chair: Allan Tuchman

Session 8: Run-Time Support for Parallelism
Chair: Doreen Cheng

Session 8: Workshop

Session 8: Minisymposium

Session 9: Super Micros
Chair: David Culler

Session 9: Communication Intensive Algorithms
Chair: Vineet Singh

Session 9: Invited Presentations
Dave Dixon
Dennis Gannon

Session 9: Minisymposium: Mass Storage
Chair: Dick Watson

Session 10: Parallel Rendering
Chair: John Hart

Session 10: Cache Coherence
Chair: Jim Barton

Session 10: Workshop

Session 10: Invited Presentations
Dennis Muren
Margaret Simmons

Session 10: Minisymposium

Session 11: Interconnection/Networks
Chair: Greg Papadopoulos

Session 11: Scheduling and Allocation
Chair: Fran Berman

Session 11: Minisymposium: Fernbach and Forefronts Awards

Session 11: Minisymposium: Clustered Workstations
Chair: Ray Cline

Session 12: Performance Measurement and Debugging
Chair: Bart Miller

Session 12: Panel

Session 12: Minisymposium

Session 12: Workshop
Chair: Jack Dongarra

Session 13: Performance Bottlenecks
Chair: Mike Quinn

Session 13: Panel
Moderator: Gary Montry

Session 13: Minisymposium: Gbit Testbeds
Chair: Charlie Catlett

Supercomputing '94, the next conference in the series on high performance computing and communications, will take place November 14-18, 1994, at the Washington D.C. Convention Center.

In addition to serving its traditional purpose of advancing the science and application of supercomputing technology, the conference will focus on research and education in computational science and engineering. Particular emphasis will be given to applications in biology and medicine, design and manufacturing, and environmental issues. Educational activities at Supercomputing '94 will span the spectrum from K-12 through graduate school.

Supercomputing '94 will be held at the Washington D. C. Convention Center, just five blocks from the White House. The Center, which features state-of-the-art design and engineering accommodations, is located on a 9.7 acre site bounded by New York Avenue, 9th, H and 11th Streets, N. W. It is convenient to commercial, historic and cultural sites and can be approached from several nearby Metrorail subway stations serving the city and suburbs. You can become involved in Supercomputing '94

through the technical program, tutorials, workshops, or exhibits. The technical program will cover applications in several disciplines — with emphasis on biology and medicine, design and manufacturing, and environmental issues — and will feature invited and contributed technical and education papers, panels, posters, and research exhibits. The tutorials and workshops will feature experts on the application of high performance computing and communications. The industry exhibit will feature the latest in hardware, software, applications, systems, and services.

We invite you to submit a proposal for a paper, panel, workshop, tutorial, research exhibit, or poster, and become a part of Supercomputing '94. For more information or to find out how you can participate, refer to the Call for Participation in your registration bag, or stop by the Supercomputing '94 booth and ask one of our committee members.

SUPERCOMPUTING '94

Washington D.C.

November 14-18

Session 1:
Algorithms for Applications
Chair: John Gustafson

A Massively Parallel Adaptive Finite Element Method with Dynamic Load Balancing

Karen D. Devine[1,2] and Joseph E. Flaherty[1]
Department of Computer Science
Rensselaer Polytechnic Institute
Troy, NY 12180
kddevin@cs.sandia.gov
flaherje@cs.rpi.edu

Stephen R. Wheat[1]
Massively Parallel Computing
Research Laboratory, Dept. 1424
Sandia National Laboratories
Albuquerque, NM 87185-5800
srwheat@cs.sandia.gov

Arthur B. Maccabe[2,3]
Department of Computer Science
The University of New Mexico
Albuquerque, NM 87131
maccabe@cs.unm.edu

Abstract

We construct massively parallel adaptive finite element methods for the solution of hyperbolic conservation laws. Spatial discretization is performed by a discontinuous Galerkin finite element method using a basis of piecewise Legendre polynomials. Temporal discretization utilizes a Runge-Kutta method. Dissipative fluxes and projection limiting prevent oscillations near solution discontinuities. The resulting method is of high order and may be parallelized efficiently on MIMD computers. We demonstrate parallel efficiency through computations on a 1024-processor nCUBE/2 hypercube. We present results using adaptive p-refinement to reduce the computational cost of the method, and tiling, a dynamic, element-based data migration system that maintains global load balance of the adaptive method by overlapping neighborhoods of processors that each perform local balancing.

1. Introduction

We are studying massively parallel adaptive finite element methods for solving systems of d-dimensional hyperbolic conservation laws of the form

$$\mathbf{u}_t + \sum_{i=1}^{d} \mathbf{f}_i(\mathbf{u})_{x_i} = 0, \ \mathbf{x} \in \Omega, \ t > 0, \qquad (1a)$$

subject to the initial conditions

$$\mathbf{u}(\mathbf{x}, 0) = \mathbf{u}^0(\mathbf{x}), \ \mathbf{x} \in \Omega \cup \partial\Omega, \qquad (1b)$$

and appropriate well-posed boundary conditions on $\partial\Omega$. High-order methods and the combination of mesh refinement and order variation (hp-refinement) have been shown to produce effective solution techniques for elliptic [16] and parabolic [1, 2, 3] problems. It is, thus, natural to

determine whether or not they will be as efficient when applied to hyperbolic systems. High-order Total Variation Diminishing (TVD) [19, 21] and Essentially Non-Oscillatory (ENO) [17] finite difference schemes for (1) use a computational stencil that enlarges with order. The wide stencil inhibits efficient implementation near irregular boundaries and complicates processor communication on massively parallel computers. Finite element methods, however, can easily model problems having complex geometries and have stencils that are invariant with method order.

With a motivation to explore adaptive high-order parallel methods, we use a local discontinuous Galerkin method [8, 9, 10] rather than the traditional finite element formulation. Spatially, the solution is approximated by a basis of piecewise continuous Legendre polynomials that may have discontinuities at interelement boundaries. By not enforcing global continuity, we can approximate discontinuous solutions of (1) more accurately. Fluxes at element boundaries are computed by solving an approximate Riemann problem with a projection limiter applied to keep the average solution monotone near discontinuities [21]. An adaptive limiting procedure maintains high-order accuracy near smooth extrema while improving global monotonicity near discontinuities relative to other techniques [7, 10]. Time discretization is performed by an explicit Runge-Kutta method.

Nearly perfect scaled parallel speed-up [11] on an nCUBE/2 hypercube degrades substantially when adaptive p-refinement is incorporated into the local finite element method due to processor load imbalance. Parallel finite element methods often use *static* load balancing [12, 13] as a precursor to obtaining a finite element solution. Adaptive methods, however, require *dynamic* load balancing to adjust changing processor loads as the computation proceeds. In our work, we have developed a dynamic, fine-grained, element-based data migration algorithm called *tiling* that maintains global load balance by overlapping neighborhoods of processors that each perform local load balancing. The tiling system supports a

---

1. This work was partially supported by Sandia National Laboratories under Research Agreement #67-8709.

2. This work was performed at Sandia National Laboratories, operated for the U.S. Department of Energy under contract #DE-AC04-76DP00789.

3. On Faculty Sabbatical to Sandia National Laboratories.

large class of finite element and finite difference applications. Its effectiveness has been demonstrated for standard finite difference and finite element methods whose geometries and boundary conditions create load imbalance [22]. We incorporate the adaptive p-refinement method into the tiling system to recover the parallel efficiency lost to load imbalance during order enrichment, and demonstrate the tiling system's effectiveness with several experiments on an nCUBE/2.

2. The Discontinuous Galerkin Method

To simplify the presentation, consider a one-dimensional ($d = 1$) system of conservation laws (1), and partition Ω into subintervals (x_{j-1}, x_j), $j = 1, 2, ..., J$. Construct a weak form of the problem by multiplying (1a) by a test function $\mathbf{v} \in L^2(x_{j-1}, x_j)$ and integrating the result on (x_{j-1}, x_j) while integrating the flux term by parts to obtain

$$\frac{d}{dt} \int_{x_{j-1}}^{x_j} \mathbf{v}^T \mathbf{u}\, dx + \mathbf{v}^T \mathbf{f}(\mathbf{u}) \Big|_{x_{j-1}}^{x_j} - \int_{x_{j-1}}^{x_j} \mathbf{v}_x^T \mathbf{f}(\mathbf{u})\, dx = 0, \quad (2)$$

for all $\mathbf{v} \in L^2(x_{j-1}, x_j)$. Use a linear transformation to map (x_{j-1}, x_j) onto a "canonical element" $-1 \leq \xi \leq 1$ and approximate $\mathbf{u}(\xi, t) \in L^2(-1, 1)$ by the pth-degree polynomial $\mathbf{U}_j(\xi, t)$ expressed in terms of a basis of Legendre polynomials as

$$\mathbf{u}(\xi, t) \approx \mathbf{U}_j(\xi, t) = \sum_{k=0}^{p} \mathbf{c}_{jk}(t) P_k(\xi), \; \xi \in (-1, 1). \quad (3)$$

Substituting the polynomial approximation (3) into (2), selecting $\mathbf{v}$ to be proportional to $P_k(\xi)$, and using the orthogonality properties of Legendre polynomials [20], we determine $\mathbf{c}_{jk}$, $j = 1, 2, ..., J$, $k = 0, 1, ..., p$, as

$$\frac{d}{dt} \mathbf{c}_{jk} = -\frac{2k+1}{\Delta x_j} (\mathbf{f}(\mathbf{U}_j(1, t)) - (-1)^k \mathbf{f}(\mathbf{U}_j(-1, t))$$

$$\quad (4)$$

$$- \int_{-1}^{1} P_k'(\xi) \mathbf{f}(\mathbf{U}_j) d\xi).$$

The $\mathbf{c}_{jk}$ are initialized by L^2 projection of the initial data (1b) onto the space of Legendre polynomials. Integral terms in (4) are evaluated exactly for linear problems, using the properties of Legendre polynomials [20], or numerically using $(p + 1)/2$-point Gauss-Legendre quadrature. The boundary flux $\mathbf{f}(\mathbf{U}_j(1, t))$ is approximated by a numerical flux function $\mathbf{h}(\mathbf{U}_j(1, t), \mathbf{U}_{j+1}(-1, t))$ [10, 19]. Runge-Kutta integration of order p is used for temporal integration.

In regions where the solution of (1) is smooth, the scheme (3, 4) produces the $O(\Delta x^{p+1})$,

$$\Delta x = \max_{j = 1, 2, ..., J} \Delta x_j,$$

convergence expected for a pth-degree approximation [10]. When $p > 0$, projection limiting is needed to prevent spurious oscillations near solution discontinuities. With projection limiting, the solution $\mathbf{U}_j(\xi, t)$, $j = 1, 2, ..., J$, is restricted after each Runge-Kutta stage to eliminate oscillations. Cockburn and Shu [10] describe a procedure for the projection limiting of scalar problems that prevents $U_j(\xi, t)$ from taking values outside of the range spanned by the neighboring solution averages. While preserving monotonicity of the average numerical solution, this limiting scheme flattens solutions near smooth extrema so that first-order accuracy is obtained there. To overcome this deficiency, we developed a limiting scheme [7] that maintains monotonicity of solution moments on neighboring elements. Using the orthogonality properties of Legendre polynomials and (3), solution moments of a scalar problem are given by

$$\int_{-1}^{1} U_j(\xi, t) P_k(\xi) d\xi = \frac{2}{2k+1} c_{jk}(t), \quad (5a)$$

$$k = 0, 1, ..., p-1, \quad j = 1, 2, ..., J.$$

Thus, to keep the kth moment monotone, we keep c_{jk} monotone on neighboring elements by limiting $c_{j,k+1}$ as

$$(2k+1) c_{j, k+1} =$$
$$minmod((2k+1) c_{j, k+1}, \quad (5b)$$
$$c_{j+1, k} - c_{j, k}, c_{j, k} - c_{j-1, k}),$$

where

$$minmod(a, b, c) =$$

$$\begin{cases} \text{sgn}(a) \min(|a|, |b|, |c|), & (5c) \\ \qquad \text{if } \text{sgn}(a) = \text{sgn}(b) = \text{sgn}(c), \\ 0, \text{ otherwise.} \end{cases}$$

The limiter (5) is applied adaptively. First, the highest-order coefficient is limited. Then the limiter is applied to successively lower-order coefficients when the next higher coefficient on the interval has been changed by the limiting. In this way, the limiting is applied only where it is needed, and accuracy is retained in smooth regions.

For vector systems, the scalar limiting (5) can be applied component-wise; however, Cockburn et al. [9] showed that this approach does not have a total variational bounded

(TVB) theory and can produce spurious oscillations even for linear problems. To improve accuracy at the price of additional computation, we apply the limiter to the characteristic fields of the system [9, 14]. The diagonalizing matrices $\mathbf{T(u)}$ and $\mathbf{T^{-1}(u)}$ (consisting of the right and left eigenvectors of the Jacobian $\mathbf{f_u}$) are evaluated using the average values $\mathbf{c}_{0j}$ of $\mathbf{U}_j$, $j = 1, 2, ..., J$. The scalar limiter (5) is applied to each component of the characteristic vector. The result is projected back to the physical space by post-multiplication by $\mathbf{T^{-1}(U}_j)$.

The two-dimensional method is a direct extension of the one-dimensional method. Restricting Ω to be rectangular, partition it into rectangular elements

$$\Omega_{ij} = \{ (x, y) \,|\, x_{i-1} \leq x \leq x_i, y_{j-1} \leq y \leq y_j \},$$

$$i = 1, 2, ..., I, j = 1, 2, ..., J.$$

Representing $\mathbf{u}(x, y, t)$ on Ω_{ij} by a basis of tensor products of Legendre polynomials on the canonical element $\Omega_C = \{ (\xi, \eta) \,|\, -1 \leq \xi, \eta \leq 1 \}$,

$$\mathbf{u}(\xi, \eta, t) \approx \mathbf{U}_{ij}(\xi, \eta, t) =$$

$$\sum_{k=0}^{p} \sum_{m=0}^{p} \mathbf{c}_{ijkm}(t) P_k(\xi) P_m(\eta), (\xi, \eta) \in \Omega_C, \quad (6)$$

and constructing a weak form of (1) yields a system of ODEs similar to (4) for $\mathbf{c}_{ijkm}$. Following Biswas et al. [7], we apply the one-dimensional projection limiter (5) along each of the two spatial directions. Experimental results [6, 7] support this approach; however, a more rigorous analysis is necessary.

Example 1. Consider the periodic initial value problem for Burgers' equation

$$u_t + (\frac{u^2}{2})_x = 0, t > 0, \quad (7a)$$

$$u^0(x) = \frac{1}{2} + \frac{1}{2} \sin(\pi x). \quad (7b)$$

Solutions of (7) at time $t = 1.1$, obtained on a 32-element mesh for $p = 0$, 1, and 2 using an upwind numerical flux and moment limiting (5), are shown in Figure 1. The improved solution accuracy when p is increased from 0 to 2 can easily be seen. With $p = 2$, the limiter (5) maintained third-order accuracy in smooth regions of the solution (see Table 1), produced a sharp shock, and preserved average as well as global monotonicity on all but one subinterval.

Example 2. The one-dimensional Euler equations of gas dynamics can be written in the form (1), with $\mathbf{u}(x, t) = [\rho, m, e]^T$, and

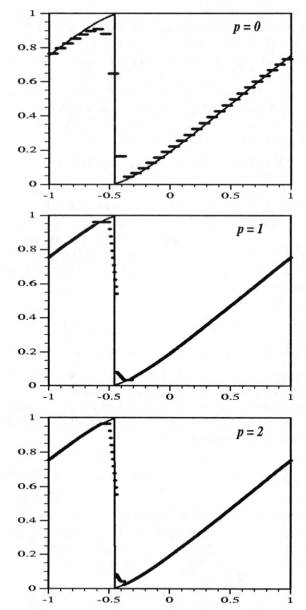

Figure 1. Exact (line) and numerical (■) solutions of Example 1 for p=0, 1, and 2 using the moment limiter (5). (Finite element solutions are shown at eleven points per element.)

$\mathbf{f(u}(x, t)) = [\rho q, mq + P, eq + Pq]^T$, where ρ, P, m, q, and e are the density, pressure, momentum ($m = \rho q$), velocity, and energy, respectively. The system is completed with the ideal equation of state

$$P = (\gamma - 1)(e - \frac{1}{2}\rho q^2)$$

where γ is the ratio of specific heats, taken here as 1.4. We consider Sod's shock tube Riemann problem [18]

Number of Elements	Error in L^1 Norm	Order
32	2.39585e-05	
64	1.64509e-06	3.86
128	1.68787e-07	3.28
256	1.79387e-08	3.23
512	1.90090e-09	3.23

Table 1. Convergence of (7) with $p = 2$ and limiter (5) in smooth regions of Example 1. Error was measured for $x \in (-1, -0.5675) \cup (-0.375, 1)$ using (8).

$$[\rho^0, q^0, P^0]^T = \begin{cases} [1, 0, 1]^T, & \text{if } x \le 0.5, \\ [0.125, 0, 0.1]^T, & \text{if } x > 0.5, \end{cases}$$

which we solve using a piecewise quadratic approximation ($p = 2$) on a 64-element mesh. In Figure 2, we show the density, pressure, and velocity at time $t = 0.1$ using limiter (5). The solution method sharply captures shocks, contact discontinuities and expansions. The high-order coefficients are determined to preserve average and, to a large extent, global monotonicity.

3. Adaptive p-Refinement

We have developed an adaptive p-refinement version of the two-dimensional method using a method-of-lines approach. A spatial error estimate is used to control order variation procedures that attempt to keep the global L^1-error

$$\left\| \mathbf{u}(\bullet, \bullet, t) - \mathbf{U}(\bullet, \bullet, t) \right\|_1 =$$

$$\left\| \int\int_\Omega |\mathbf{u}(x, y, t) - \mathbf{U}(x, y, t)| \, dxdy \right\|_\infty \quad (8)$$

less than a specified tolerance by maintaining

$$E_{ij}(t) \le \text{TOL} = \frac{\text{tolerance}}{IJ}, \quad (9)$$

$$i = 1, 2, ..., I, \quad j = 1, 2, ..., J,$$

where E_{ij} is the maximum local L^1-error estimate of the solution vector on element Ω_{ij}. We initialize $\mathbf{U}_{ij}$, $i = 1, 2, ..., I$, $j = 1, 2, ..., J$, to the lowest-degree polynomial satisfying

$$\left\| \int\int_{\Omega_{ij}} |\mathbf{u}^0(x, y) - \mathbf{U}_{ij}(\xi(x), \eta(y), 0)| \, dydx \right\|_\infty \le \text{TOL}. \quad (10)$$

After each time step, we compute E_{ij}, $i = 1, 2, ..., I$, $j = 1, 2, ..., J$, and increase the polynomial degree of $\mathbf{U}_{ij}$ by one if $E_{ij} > \text{TOL}$. The solution $\mathbf{U}_{ij}$ and the error estimate are recomputed on enriched elements and the

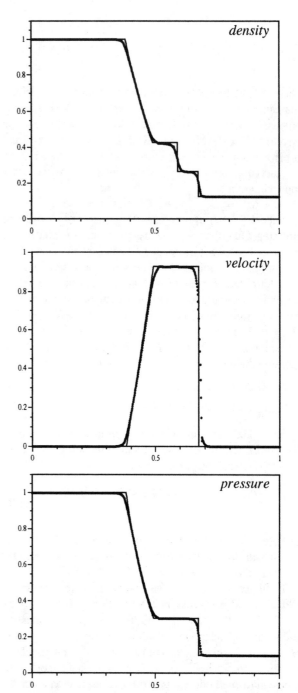

Figure 2. Density, pressure, and velocity at $t=0.1$ for Example 2 with $p = 2$ using the moment limiter. (Finite element solutions are shown at eleven points per element.)

degree is increased until $E_{ij} \le \text{TOL}$ on all elements when the time step is accepted.

For these experiments, we use a p-refinement spatial error estimate:

$$E_{ij}(t) = \left\| \int_{-1}^{1} \int_{-1}^{1} \left| \mathbf{U}_{ij}^{p+1}(\xi, \eta, t) - \mathbf{U}_{ij}^{p}(\xi, \eta, t) \right| d\xi d\eta \right\|_{\infty} \quad (11)$$

where $\mathbf{U}_{ij}^{p}$ is the pth-degree approximation of $\mathbf{u}$. While this estimate is computationally expensive, it is still less expensive than mesh-refinement techniques and can be used to reduce the effort involved in recomputing $\mathbf{U}_{ij}$ and its error estimate when enrichment is needed. Thus, instead of recomputing $\mathbf{U}_{ij}(t + \Delta t)$ when a higher-order approximation is needed, set $\mathbf{U}_{ij}(t + \Delta t) = \mathbf{U}_{ij}^{p+1}(t + \Delta t)$, initialize the new error estimate $\mathbf{U}_{ij}^{p+2}(t)$ at time t, and compute $\mathbf{U}_{ij}^{p+2}$ over the time step. Other less expensive error estimation procedures are described by Biswas et al. [7], and Bey and Oden[4].

Additional computational savings are possible by predicting the degree of the approximation needed to satisfy the accuracy requirements during the next time step. After a time step is accepted, if $E_{ij} > H_{max}\text{TOL}$, $H_{max} \in (0, 1]$, we increase the degree of $\mathbf{U}_{ij}(t + \Delta t)$ for the next time step. If $E_{ij} < H_{min}\text{TOL}$, $H_{min} \in [0, 1)$, we decrease the degree of $\mathbf{U}_{ij}(t + \Delta t)$ for the next time step.

Example 3. We solve

$$u_t + 2u_x + 2u_y = 0, \, 0 \le x, y \le 1, \, t > 0, \quad (12a)$$

by both fixed-order and adaptive p-refinement methods on $0 < t \le 0.1$ with initial and Dirichlet boundary conditions specified so that the exact solution is

$$u(x, y, t) = \frac{1}{2}(1 - \tanh(20x - 10y - 20t + 5)),$$
$$0 \le x, y \le 1. \quad (12b)$$

In Figure 3, we show the exact solution of (12) at time $t = 0$ and the adaptive 16×16-element mesh generated to satisfy the initial data for $TOL = 1.0 \times 10^{-5}$.

In Figure 4, we show the global L^1-error versus the CPU time for fixed-order methods with $p = 0, 1$, and 2 on 8×8, 16×16, 32×32, and 64×64-element meshes, and the p-adaptive method with $H_{max} = 0.9$, $H_{min} = 0.1$, and local error tolerances TOL ranging from 5×10^{-9} to 5×10^{-4} on a 16×16-element mesh. The p-adaptive method requires more computation than the fixed-order methods for large error tolerances, but because of its faster convergence rate, it requires less work than the fixed-order methods to obtain small errors.

4. Parallel Implementation

The Discontinuous Galerkin method is well suited to parallelization on massively parallel computers. The computational stencil involves only nearest-neighbor communication regardless of the degree of the piecewise polynomial approximation and the spatial dimension.

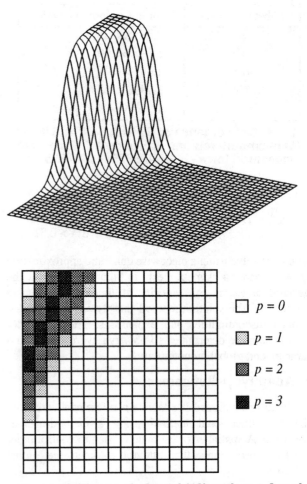

Figure 3. Exact solution of (12) at time $t=0$ and the adaptive p-refinement initial mesh generated for a local error tolerance 0.00001.

Additional storage is needed for only one row of "ghost" elements along each edge of a processor's uniform subdomain. Thus, the size of the problems solved can be scaled easily with the number of processors.

We measure performance on an nCUBE/2 hypercube computer by considering the method's *scaled parallel efficiency*, the ratio of uniprocessor execution time for a problem of size W to execution time on N processors for a problem of size NW [11]. Thus, the amount of work per processor is kept constant as processors are added, and we expect the solution time to be constant for each trial. In two dimensions,

$$W = \text{number of elements} \times \text{number of timesteps} \times (p+1)^2. \quad (13)$$

Example 4. In Table 2, we show the execution time for the two-dimensional spatially periodic problem

$$u_t + u_x + u_y = 0, \, t > 0, \quad (14a)$$

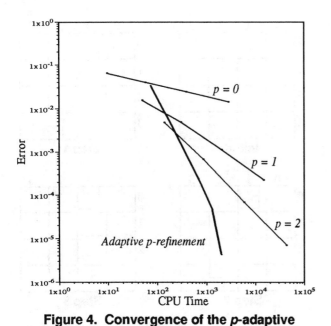

Figure 4. Convergence of the *p*-adaptive method compared with fixed-order methods for Example 3.

Number of Processors	Work (W)	Execution Time (secs.)	Parallel Efficiency	Avg/Max Processor Work Ratio
1	52,992	268.96		1.000
2	105,984	276.39	97.3%	.998
4	211,968	276.77	97.2%	.992
8	423,936	276.79	97.2%	.998
16	847,872	276.80	97.2%	.997
32	1,695,744	276.80	97.2%	.996
64	3,391,488	276.80	97.2%	.988
128	6,782,976	276.84	97.2%	.995
256	13,565,952	276.80	97.2%	.995
512	27,131,904	276.80	97.2%	.993
1024	54,263,808	276.80	97.2%	.995

Table 2. Scaled parallel efficiency for Example 4. Times were measured on an nCUBE/2.

$$u(x, y, 0) = \sin(\pi x)\sin(\pi y), \qquad (14b)$$

using various numbers of processors and a standard method with p fixed at 2. Each processor's subdomain contained 128 elements, and the problem was solved for 46 time steps. As indicated, the solution times increase only slightly with the dimension of the hypercube, demonstrating the high parallel efficiency of the basic method. We also show the ratio of the average execution time on all the processors to the maximum execution time among the processors. The average/maximum processor work ratio is above 0.98 for all hypercube dimensions due to the natural load balance of the standard method.

5. Dynamic Load Balancing via Tiling

While the standard method exhibits near-perfect scaled parallel efficiency, processor load imbalances degrade the parallel performance of the adaptive p-refinement method. Non-uniform and changing processor work loads make dynamic load balancing necessary. Tiling is a modified version of a technique developed by Leiss and Reddy [15] which uses balances performed within overlapping processor neighborhoods to achieve a global load balance. Work is migrated from a processor to others within the same neighborhood.

Leiss and Reddy define a neighborhood as a processor at the center of a circle of some predefined radius and all other processors within the circle along the *hardware* interconnections. Each processor may be a neighborhood center and individual processors may belong to several neighborhoods. In tiling, a neighborhood is defined as a center processor and all processors that share subdomain boundaries with the center processor and, thus, require interprocessor communication with it in the application. Every processor is a neighborhood center. In Figure 5, we show examples of 12 processors in 12 neighborhoods using the Leiss/Reddy and tiling definitions.

Processors within a given neighborhood are balanced with respect to each other using local performance measurements. A processor's load depends on the number of elements in its local subdomain and the per-element processing cost. When each processor has the same number of elements and all elements have the same degree, as in Example 4, global load balance results; however, an imbalance occurs when one processor has a higher per-element load due, for example, to adaptive p-refinement.

In Figure 6, we illustrate an example of the dynamic balancing provided by tiling. Without *a priori* knowledge, the data set is divided evenly among 16 processors. After some period, processors (0,1) and (3,2) are discovered to be more heavily utilized than their neighbors. At this time, processor (0,0) receives some of the data originally allocated to processor (0,1), and processor (3,2) gives processor (3,3) some of its data, as shown in Step 1 of the figure. Processors (0,0) and (0,1) are now equally balanced yet out of balance with other processors. Thus, in Step 2, some data are migrated from processor (0,1) to processor (1,1). The ripple effect continues to move through processors (2,1) and (3,1) in subsequent balancing steps.

6. The Tiling Algorithm

Programs to be integrated into the tiling environment are partitioned into (*i*) a computation phase and (*ii*) a

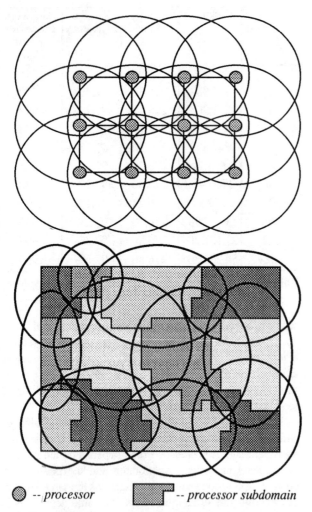

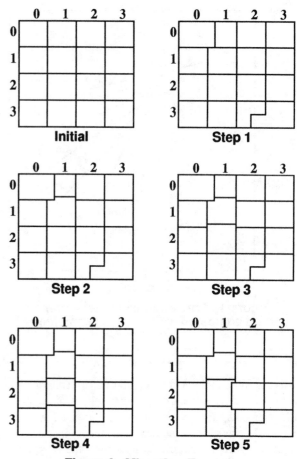

Figure 6. Migration Example

Figure 5. Examples of 12 processors in 12 neighborhoods using the Leiss/Reddy (top) and the tiling definitions (bottom).

balancing phase. The *computation phase* corresponds to the application's implementation without load balancing. Each processor operates on its local data, exchanges inter-processor boundary data, and processes the boundary data. A balancing phase follows a given number of computation phases in order to restore load balance. Each *balancing phase* consists of the following operations:

i. **Determine work loads.** Each processor determines its work load as the time to process its local data since the previous balancing phase less the time to exchange inter-processor boundary data during the computation phase. Neighborhood average work loads are also calculated.

ii. **Determine processor work requests.** Each processor compares its work load to the work load of the other processors in its neighborhood and determines which processors have greater work

loads than its own. If any are found, it selects the one with the greatest work load (ties are broken arbitrarily) and sends a request for work to that processor. Each processor may send only one work request but may receive several work requests.

iii. **Determine which work requests to satisfy.** Each processor prioritizes the work requests it receives in order of size and satisfies requests until its work load equals the neighborhood average.

iv. **Select export elements.** Within the exporting processors, each element is assigned an export priority, initially zero. The priority is increased by 2 for each neighboring element in the importing processor, decreased by 1 for each neighboring element in its own processor, and decreased by 2 for each neighboring element in a foreign processor other than the importing processor (see the example in Figure 7). In this way, elements are "peeled" off the processor boundary in an attempt to prevent the creation of "narrow, deep holes" in the tile. Priority determination is completely local through pointers within an element's data structure to neighboring and ghost cells.

v. **Notify and transfer elements.** Importing processors and those processors with ghost cells for the migrating elements are notified. Importing processors allocate space for the incoming elements, and the elements are transferred.

Each processor knows how many computation phases to perform before entering the balancing phase. Synchronization guarantees that all processors will enter the balancing phase at the same time.

		Non-importing Processor	
Exporting Processor		-2+2-1-1 = -2	
		-1+2+2-1 = +2	
	-1+2-1-1 = -1		
	-1+2-2-1 = -2	Importing Processor	
		Non-importing Processor	

		Non-importing Processor	
Exporting Processor		-2+2+2-1 = +1	
	-1+2-1-1 = -1		
	-1+2-1-1 = -1		
	-1+2-2-1 = -2	Importing Processor	
		Non-importing Processor	

Figure 7. Element distribution and migration priorities (with the contributions from the north, east, south, and west neighboring elements, respectively) of exportable (shaded) elements before (top) and after (bottom) migration.

Example 5. We solve (12) using the adaptive p-refinement method and tiling on a 32×32-mesh using 16 processors of the nCUBE/2 hypercube. In Figure 8, we show the processor domain decomposition after 10 time steps using tiling. The shaded elements have higher-degree approximations and thus, higher work loads. Initially, each processor is assigned an 8×8-element subdomain. The tiling algorithm redistributes the work so that processors with high-order elements have fewer elements than those processors with low-order elements. The total processing time was reduced 25.9% from 29.49 seconds to 21.86 seconds by balancing once each time step. The

average/maximum processor work ratio without balancing was 0.353, and with balancing, it was 0.609.

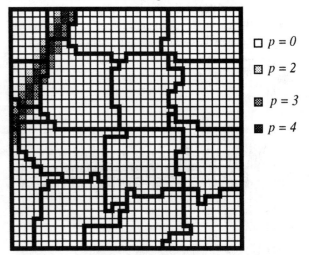

	$p = 0$
	$p = 2$
	$p = 3$
	$p = 4$

Figure 8. Domain decomposition after 10 time steps for Example 5 using adaptive *p*-refinement and tiling on 16 processors. Shaded squares are high-order elements; dark lines represent processor subdomain boundaries.

Example 6. We solve (12) for 225 time steps using all 1024 processors of the nCUBE/2 without balancing and with balancing once each time step. With balancing, the maximum computation time (exclusive of communication and balancing time) was reduced by 58.0% (see Table 3). The irregular subdomain boundaries created by the tiling algorithm increased the average communication time by 48.3%. Despite the extra communication time and the load balancing time, however, we see a 35.6% improvement in the total execution time.

	Without Balancing	With Balancing
Max. Execution Time	871.42 secs.	561.62 secs.
Max. Computation Time	801.95 secs.	336.49 secs.
Avg. Communication Time	68.54 secs.	101.66 secs.
Max. Balancing Time	0.0 secs.	38.55 secs.
Avg./Max. Work Ratio	0.392	0.934
Parallel Efficiency	36.04%	55.95%

Table 3. Performance comparison for Example 6 without and with load balancing each time step.

In Figure 9, we show the unit standard deviation curves of the maximum computation time for each time step. Initially, the deviation is large, indicating that the processors are far from a global balance. The deviations quickly become smaller, indicating that the processors rapidly approach balance. In Figure 10, we show the 5th,

35th, median, 65th, and 95th-percentile processor loads, where the 95th-percentile load, for example, is greater than or equal to 95% of the loads. The large negative slope of the 95th-percentile curve indicates significant improvement in the load balance early in the program's execution.

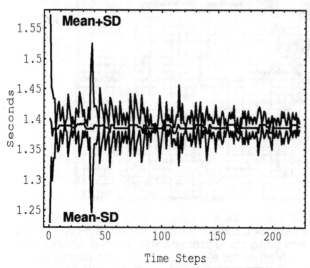

Figure 9. Processor work load mean and standard deviation for each time step.

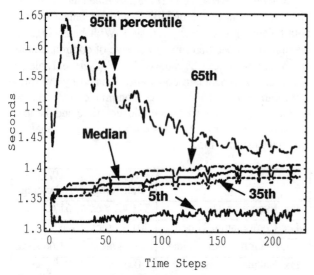

Figure 10. Sampled processor loads for each time step.

In Figure 11, we show the maximum processing costs per time step, including the computation and balancing times. The dashed and solid lines represent the maximum cost per time step without and with balancing, respectively. The balanced computation's maximum cost per time step is significantly lower than that without balancing. The spikes in both curves occur when the adaptive p-method's error tolerance was not satisfied during the time step, and the step had to be repeated using a higher-order approximation

on the high-error elements. Since computation occurs on relatively few elements during this "back tracking," the work load is extremely unbalanced. Balancing immediately after back tracking would remove too much work from those processors that had to repeat a step. The tiling algorithm ignores back tracking when determining work loads, avoiding thrashing where elements are repeatedly assigned and removed from a processor's domain.

In Figure 12, we show the cumulative maximum processing times with and without balancing. The immediate and sustained improvement of the application's performance is shown.

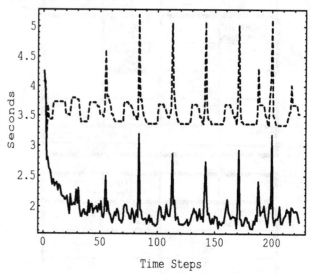

Figure 11. Maximum work load in each time step with (solid) and without (dashed) balancing.

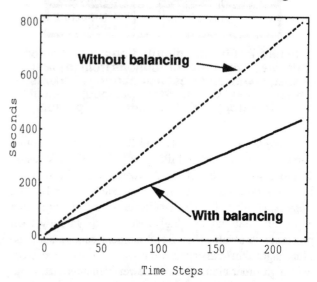

Figure 12. Cumulative maximum loads with (solid) and without (dashed) balancing.

7. Conclusion

We have shown the viability of the discontinuous finite element method for solving systems of hyperbolic conservation laws on massively parallel computers. By not enforcing continuity at inter-element boundaries, we can accurately model problems with discontinuities. A moment-based projection limiter eliminates oscillations near solution discontinuities while maintaining high-order accuracy near smooth extrema. Because of the compact stencil, the method can be parallelized on MIMD computers with scaled parallel efficiencies exceeding 90%. Adaptive p-refinement is used to solve problems to a prescribed accuracy with less computational expense than fixed-order methods. Using tiling to migrate data between processors, we can recover the parallel efficiency lost to the adaptive p-refinement method.

The basic method (4) readily extends to non-rectangular geometries and unstructured meshes; however, it remains to determine whether the moment limiting (5) is likewise extensible. Inexpensive and, apparently, asymptotically correct error estimates of Biswas et al. [7] show promise, but need further examination and testing on rectangular and unstructured meshes.

We plan to combine adaptive mesh (h-) refinement with p-refinement techniques to obtain an adaptive hp-refinement technique that can optimize computational effort in both smooth and discontinuous solution regions. The hp-method will present a serious challenge to the tiling algorithm, as the processor work loads and communication patterns are much more complex.

As seen in Example 6, back tracking when a time step is rejected is a very expensive and unbalanced computation. To reduce the amount of back tracking, we propose to use pattern matching ideas similar to those of Bieterman et al. [5] to predict regions that will need enrichment during the next time step. The predicted mesh and order information can also be used to estimate processor work loads in the next time step, and detect potential load imbalance. The tiling algorithm could migrate data prior to performing the actual computation, thus reducing load imbalance.

8. References

[1] Adjerid, S., and J. E. Flaherty. "Second-Order Finite Element Approximations and a posteriori Error Estimation for Two-Dimensional Parabolic Systems." *Numer. Math.*, **53** (1988), 183-198.

[2] Adjerid, S., J. E. Flaherty, P. K. Moore, and Y. Wang. "High-Order Adaptive Methods for Parabolic Systems." *Physica D*, **60** (1992),. 94-111.

[3] Arney, D.C. and J. E. Flaherty. "An Adaptive Local Mesh Refinement Method for Time-Dependent Partial Differential Equations." *App. Num. Math.*, **5** (1989), 257-274.

[4] Bey, K.S. and J.T. Oden. "An A Posteriori Error Estimate for Hyperbolic Conservation Laws." in preparation.

[5] Bieterman, M., J. Flaherty, and P. Moore. "Adaptive Refinement Methods for Non-Linear Parabolic Partial Differential Equations." *Accuracy Estimates and Adaptive Refinements in Finite Element Computations.* I. Babuska, et al., Eds. Wiley & Sons, (1986) 339-358.

[6] Biswas, R. "Parallel and Adaptive Methods for Hyperbolic Partial Differential Systems." Ph.D. Dissertation. Dept. Comp. Sci., Rensselaer Polytechnic Institute, Troy, 1991.

[7] Biswas, R., K. Devine, and J. Flaherty, "Parallel, Adaptive Finite Element Methods for Conservation Laws." *Applied Numerical Mathematics*, (1993), to appear.

[8] Cockburn, B., S. Hou, and C.-W. Shu. "The Runge-Kutta Local Projection Discontinuous Galerkin Finite Element Method for Conservation Laws IV: The Multidimensional Case." *Math. Comp.*, **54** (1990), 545-581.

[9] Cockburn, B., S.-Y. Lin, and C.-W. Shu. "TVB Runge-Kutta Local Projection Discontinuous Galerkin Finite Element Method for Conservation Laws III: One-Dimensional Systems." *Jrnl. of Comp. Phys.*, **84** (1989), 90-113.

[10] Cockburn, B., and C.-W. Shu. "TVB Runge-Kutta Local Projection Discontinuous Galerkin Finite Element Method for Conservation Laws II: General Framework." *Math. Comp.*, **52** (1989), 411-435.

[11] Gustafson, J., G. Montry, and R. Benner. "Development of Parallel Methods for a 1024-Processor Hypercube." *SIAM Jrnl. Sci. Stat. Comp.* **9** (1988), 609-638.

[12] Hammond, S. *Mapping Unstructured Grid Computations to Massively Parallel Computers.* Ph.D. Dissertation. Rensselaer Polytechnic Institute, Dept. Comp. Sci., Troy, 1992.

[13] Hendrickson, B., and R. Leland. "Multidimensional Spectral Load Balancing." Sandia National Laboratories Tech. Rep. SAND93-0074.

[14] Lafon, F. and S. Osher. "High-Order Filtering Methods for Approximating Hyperbolic Systems of Conservation Laws." *ICASE* Report No. 90-25, March 1990.

[15] Leiss, E., and H. Reddy. "Distributed Load Balancing: Design and Performance Analysis." *W.M.Keck Research Computation Laboratory.* **5** (1989) 205-270.

[16] Rank, E. and I. Babuska. "An Expert System for the Optimal Mesh Design in the hp-Version of the Finite Element Method." *Intl. Jrnl. Num. Meth. in Engng.*, **24** (1987), 2087-2106.

[17] Shu, C.-W., and S. Osher. "Efficient Implementation of Essentially Non-oscillatory Shock-Capturing Schemes, II." *Jrnl. of Comp. Phys.*, **83** (1989), 32-78.

[18] Sod, G. "A Survey of Several Finite Difference Methods for Systems of Nonlinear Hyperbolic Conservation Laws." *Jrnl. of Comp. Phys.*, **27** (1978), 1-31.

[19] Sweby, P.K. "High Resolution Schemes Using Flux Limiters for Hyperbolic Conservation Laws." *SIAM J. Numer. Anal.*, **21** (1984), 995-1011.

[20] Szabo, B. and I. Babuska. *Introduction to Finite Element Analysis*, Wiley, New York, 1990.

[21] Van Leer, B. "Towards the Ultimate Conservative Difference Scheme. IV. A New Approach to Numerical Convection." *Jrnl. of Comp. Phys.*, **23** (1977), 276-299.

[22] Wheat, S. *A Fine Grained Data Migration Approach to Application Load Balancing on MP MIMD Machines.* Ph.D. Dissertation. Dept. Comp. Sci., Univ. of New Mexico, Albuquerque, 1992.

A Parallel Hashed Oct-Tree N-Body Algorithm

Michael S. Warren*
Theoretical Astrophysics
Mail Stop B288
Los Alamos National Laboratory
Los Alamos, NM 87545

John K. Salmon
Physics Department
206-49
California Institute of Technology
Pasadena, CA 91125

Abstract

We report on an efficient adaptive N-body method which we have recently designed and implemented. The algorithm computes the forces on an arbitrary distribution of bodies in a time which scales as $N \log N$ with the particle number. The accuracy of the force calculations is analytically bounded, and can be adjusted via a user defined parameter between a few percent relative accuracy, down to machine arithmetic accuracy. Instead of using pointers to indicate the topology of the tree, we identify each possible cell with a key. The mapping of keys into memory locations is achieved via a hash table. This allows the program to access data in an efficient manner across multiple processors. Performance of the parallel program is measured on the 512 processor Intel Touchstone Delta system. We also comment on a number of wide-ranging applications which can benefit from application of this type of algorithm.

1 Introduction

N-body simulations have become a fundamental tool in the study of complex physical systems. Starting from a basic physical interaction (e.g., gravitational, Coulombic, Biot-Savart, van der Waals) one can follow the dynamical evolution of a system of N bodies, which represent the phase-space density distribution of the system. N-body simulations are essentially statistical in nature (unless the physical system can be directly modeled by N bodies, as is the case in some molecular dynamics simulations). More bodies implies a more accurate and complete sampling of the phase space, and hence more accurate or complete results. Unfortunately, the minimum accuracy required to model systems of interest often depends on having N be much larger than current computational resources allow.

Because interactions occur between each pair of particles in a N-body simulation, the computational work scales asymptotically as N^2. Much effort has been expended to reduce the computational complexity of such simulations, while retaining acceptable accuracy. One approach is to interpolate the field from a lattice with resolution h, where it can be computed in time $O(h^{-3})$ (using multigrid) or $O(h^{-3} \log h^{-3})$ (using Fourier transforms). The N-dependence of the time complexity then becomes $O(N)$. The drawback to this method is that dynamics on scales comparable to or smaller than h cannot be modeled. In three dimensions, this restricts the dynamic range in length to about one part in a hundred (or perhaps one part in a thousand on a parallel supercomputer), which is insufficient for many calculations.

Over the past several years, a number of methods have been introduced which allow N-body simulations to be performed on arbitrary collections of bodies in time much less than $O(N^2)$, without imposition of a lattice. They all have in common the use of a truncated expansion (e.g., Taylor expansion, Legendre expansion, Poisson expansion) to *approximate* the contribution of many bodies with a single *interaction*. The resulting complexity is usually cited as $O(N)$ or $O(N \log N)$, but a careful analysis of what dependent variables should be held constant (e.g., constant per-timestep error, constant integrated error, constant memory, constant relative error with respect to discreteness noise) often leads to different conclusions about the scaling. In any event, the scaling is a tremendous improvement over $O(N^2)$ and the methods allow accurate computations with vastly larger N.

The basic idea of an N-body algorithm based on a truncated series approximation is to partition an arbitrary collection of bodies in such a manner that the series approximation can be applied to the pieces, while maintaining sufficient accuracy in the force (or other quantity of interest) on each particle. In general, the methods represent a system of N *bodies*[1] in a hierarchical manner by the use of

---

*Department of Physics, University of California, Santa Barbara

[1] We refer to both bodies and particles, which should both be understood to be general "atomic" objects which may refer to a mass element, charge, vortex element, panel, or other quantity subject to a multipole approximation.

12

© 1993 ACM 0-8186-4340-4/93/0011 $1.50

a spatial *tree* data structure. Aggregations of bodies at various levels of detail form the internal nodes of the tree, and are called *cells*. Generally, the expansions have a limited domain of convergence, and even where the infinite expansion converges, the truncated expansion introduces errors of some magnitude. Making a good choice of which cells to interact with, and which to reject as being too inaccurate is critical to the success of these algorithms. The decision is controlled by a function which we shall call the multipole acceptance criterion (MAC). Some of the multipole methods which have been described in the literature are briefly reviewed in the next section.

2 Background

2.1 Multipole Methods

Appel was the first to introduce a multipole method [1]. Appel's method uses a binary tree data structure whose leaves are bodies, and internal nodes represent roughly spherical cells. Some care is taken to construct a "good" set of cells which minimize the higher order multipole moments of the cells. The MAC is based on the size of interacting cells. The method was originally thought to be $O(N \log N)$, but has more recently been shown to be $O(N)$ [2].

The Barnes-Hut (BH) algorithm [3] uses a regular, hierarchical cubical subdivision of space (an oct-tree in three dimensions). A two-dimensional illustration of such a tree (a quad-tree) is show in Fig. 1. Construction of BH trees is much faster than construction of Appel trees. In the BH algorithm, the MAC is controlled by a parameter θ, which requires that the cell size, s, divided by the distance from a particle to the cell center-of-mass be less than θ (which is usually in the range of 0.6–1.0). Cell-cell interactions are not computed, and the method scales as $N \log N$.

The fast multipole method (FMM) of Greengard & Rokhlin [4] has achieved the greatest popularity in the broader population of applied mathematicians and computational scientists. It uses high order multipole expansions and interacts fixed sets of cells which fulfill the criterion of being "well-separated." The FMM has a well-defined worst case error bound, ϵ, which is guaranteed to be met when multipole expansions are carried out to order $p = -\log_2(\epsilon)$. In two dimensions, when used on systems which are not excessively clustered, the FMM is very efficient. It has been implemented on parallel computers [5, 6]. The crossover point (the value of N at which the algorithm becomes faster than a direct N^2 method) with a stringent accuracy is as low as a few hundred particles. On the other hand, implementations of the FMM in three dimensions have not performed as well. Schmidt and Lee have implemented the algorithm

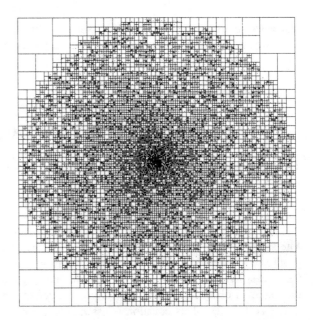

Figure 1: A representation of a regular tree structure in two dimensions (a quad-tree) which contains 10 thousand particles which are centrally clustered.

in three dimensions, and find a crossover point of about 70 thousand particles [7]. The reason is that the work in the most computationally intensive step scales as p^2 in two dimensions, and p^4 in three dimensions. It is possible to obtain much better performance by using a smaller p [8, 9], but the worst-case error can become uncomfortably large in this case. The major advantage of the FMM over the methods such as that of Barnes & Hut is that the error bound is rigorously defined. However, this deficiency has been remedied, as is shown in the following section.

2.2 Analytic Error Bounds

Recently, we have analyzed the performance of the Barnes-Hut algorithm, and have shown that the worst case errors can be quite large (in fact, unbounded) for commonly used values of the opening criterion, θ [10]. We have developed a different method for deciding which cells to interact with. By using moments of the mass or charge distribution within each cell, the method achieves far better worst case error behavior, and somewhat better mean error behavior, for the same amount of computational resources.

In addition, the analysis provides a strict error bound which can be applied to any fast multipole method. This error bound is superior to those used previously because it makes use of information about the bodies contained within a cell. This information takes the form of easily computed moments of the mass or charge distribution (strength) within the cell. Computing this information takes place in the tree construction stage, and takes very little time compared with the later phases of the algorithm. The exact form of the error bound is:

$$\Delta a_{(p)}(r) \leq \frac{1}{d^2} \frac{1}{(1 - \frac{b_{max}}{d})^2}$$
$$\left((p + 2) \left(\frac{B_{(p+1)}}{d^{p+1}} \right) - (p + 1) \left(\frac{B_{(p+2)}}{d^{p+2}} \right) \right) . \quad (1)$$

The moments, $B_{(n)}$ are defined as:

$$B_{(n)} = \int_{\mathcal{V}} d^3x \, |\rho(x)| \, |\vec{x} - \vec{r}_0|^n = \sum_{\beta} |m_\beta| \, |\vec{x}_\beta - \vec{r}_0|^n . \quad (2)$$

The scalar $d = |\vec{r} - \vec{r}_0|$ is the distance from the particle position $\vec{r}$ to the center of the multipole expansion, p is the largest term in the multipole expansion, and b_{max} is the maximal distance of particles from the center of the cell, (see Fig. 2). This equation is essentially a precise statement of several common-sense ideas. Interactions are more accurate when:

- The interaction distance is larger (larger d).

- The cell is smaller (smaller b_{max}).

- More terms in the multipole expansion are used (larger p).

- The truncated multipole moments are smaller (smaller $B_{(p+1)}$).

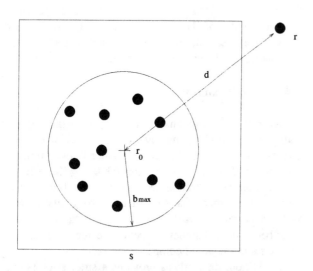

Figure 2: An illustration of the relevant distances used in the error bound equation.

Having a per-interaction error bound is an overwhelming advantage when compared to existing multipole acceptance criteria, which assume a worst-case arrangement of bodies within a cell when bounding the interaction error. The reason is that the worst-case interaction error of an *arbitrary* strength distribution is usually many times larger than the error bound on a *particular* strength distribution. This causes an algorithm which knows nothing about the strength distribution inside a cell to provide *too much* accuracy for most multipole interactions. This accuracy is wasted, however, because of the few multipole interaction errors which do approach the worst-case error bound that are added into and pollute the final result. A data-dependent per-interaction error bound is much less prone to this problem, since the resulting error *bound* is much tighter, even though the actual error in the computation is exactly the same.

The implementation of an algorithm using a fixed per-interaction error bound poses little difficulty. One may simply solve for r_c in,

$$\Delta a_{(p)}(r_c) \leq \Delta_{interaction}, \quad (3)$$

where $\Delta_{interaction}$ is a user-specified absolute error tolerance. Then, r_c defines the smallest interaction distance allowed for each cell in the system. For the case of $p = 1$, the critical radius can be analytically derived from Eq. 1 if we use the fact that $B_3 \geq 0$:

$$r_c \geq \frac{b_{max}}{2} + \sqrt{\frac{b_{max}^2}{4} + \sqrt{\frac{3B_2}{\Delta_{interaction}}}}. \quad (4)$$

B_2 is simply the trace of the quadrupole moment tensor. In more general cases (using a better bound on B_3, or with $p > 1$), r_c can be computed from the error bound equation (Eq. 1) using Newton's method. The overall computational expense of calculating r_c is small, since it need only be calculated once for each cell. Furthermore, Newton's method need not be iterated to high accuracy. The MAC then becomes $d > r_c$ for each displacement d and critical radius r_c (Fig. 3). This is computationally very similar to the Barnes-Hut opening criterion, where instead of using a fixed box size, s, we use the distance r_c, derived from the contents of the cell and the error tolerance. Thus, our data dependent MAC may replace the MAC in existing algorithms with minimal additional coding.

3   Computational Approach

Parallel treecodes for distributed memory machines are discussed in [11, 12], and their application to the analysis of galaxy formation may be found in [13, 14]. Further analysis and extensions of the computational methods may be found in [15, 16, 17]. The MAC described above is problematical for these previous methods because the parallel algorithm

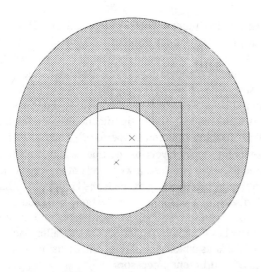

Figure 3: The critical radii of a cell and one of its daughters are shown here as circles. For the specified accuracy, a particle must lie outside the critical radius of a cell. The shaded region shows the spatial domain of all particles which would interact with the lower left daughter cell. Those particles outside the shaded region would interact with the parent cell, and those within the unshaded region would interact with even smaller cells inside the daughter cell.

requires determination of locally essential data before the tree traversal begins. With the data-dependent MAC it is difficult to pre-determine which non-local cells are required in advance of the traversal stage. The problem becomes particularly acute if one wishes to impose error tolerances which vary from particle to particle.

It is for this reason that the algorithm described here was developed. It does not rely on the ability to identify *a priori* locally essential data; instead it provides a mechanism to retrieve non-local data as it is needed during the tree traversal. The decision to abandon our previous parallel N-body algorithm was also motivated by the desire to produce a more "friendly" code, with which a variety of research could be performed in computational science as well as physics. The old code, which was the result of porting a previously existing sequential algorithm, was a maze of complications, brought about by the haphazard addition of pieces over several years. We took full advantage of the opportunity to start over with a clean slate, with the additional benefit of several years of hindsight and experience.

When one considers what additional operations are necessary when dealing with a tree structure distributed over many processors, it is clear that retrieval of particular cells required by one processor from another is a very common operation. When using a conventional tree structure, the pointers in a parent cell in one processor must be somehow translated into a valid reference to daughter cells in another

processor. This required translation led us to the conclusion that pointers are not the proper way to represent a distributed tree data structure (at least without significant hardware and operating system support for such operations).

Instead of using pointers to describe the topology of a tree, we use keys and a hash table. We begin by identifying each possible cell with a *key*. By performing simple bit arithmetic on a key, we are able to produce the keys of daughter or parent cells. The tree topology is represented implicitly in the mapping of the cell spatial locations and levels into the keys. The translation of keys into memory locations where cell data is stored is achieved via hash table lookup. Thus, given a key, the corresponding data can be rapidly retrieved. This scheme also provides a uniform addressing mechanism to retrieve data which is in another processor. This is the basis of the hashed oct-tree (HOT) method.

3.1 Key construction and the Hashing Function

We define a key as the result of a map of d floating point numbers (body coordinates in d-dimensional space) into a single set of bits (which is most conveniently represented as a vector of integers). The mapping function consists of translating the floating point numbers into integers, and then interleaving the bits of the d integers into a single key (Fig. 4). Note that we place no restriction on the dimension of the space, although we are physically motivated to pay particular attention to the case of $d = 3$. In this case, the key derived from 3 single precision floating point numbers fits nicely into a single 64 bit integer or a pair of 32 bit integers.

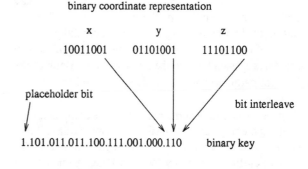

Figure 4: An illustration of the key mapping. Bits of the coordinates are interleaved and a place-holder bit is prepended to the most significant bit. In this example, the 8-bit x, y and z values are mapped to a 25-bit key.

Apart from the trivial choice of origin and coordinate system, this is identical to Morton ordering (also called Z or N ordering, see Chapter 1 of [18] and references therein, and also [19]). This function maps each body in the system to a unique key. We also wish to represent nodes of the tree using this same type of key. In order to distinguish the higher level internal nodes of the tree from the lowest level body nodes, we prepend an additional 1-bit to the most significant bit of every key (the place-holder bit). We may then represent all higher level nodes in the tree in the same key space. Without the place-holder bit, there would be an ambiguity amongst keys whose most significant bits are all zeroes. The root node is represented by the key 1. A two-dimensional representation of such a tree is shown in Fig. 5.

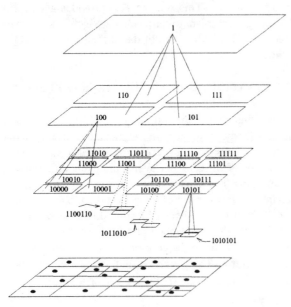

Figure 5: A quad-tree shown along with the binary key coordinates of the nodes. At the bottom is a "flat" representation of the tree topology induced by the 20 particles. The rest of the figure demonstrates the relation of the key coordinates at each level to the tree topology. Many of the links from parent to daughter cells are omitted for clarity.

In general, each key corresponds to some composite data describing the physical data inside the domain of a cell (the mass and center-of-mass coordinates, for example). To map the key to the memory location holding this data, a hash table is used. A table with a length much smaller than the possible number of keys is used, with a hashing function to map the k-bit key to the h-bit long hash address. We use a very simple hashing function, which is to AND the key with the bit-mask $2^h - 1$, which selects the least significant h bits.

Collisions in the hash table are resolved via a linked list (chaining). The incidence of collisions could degrade performance a great deal. Our hashing scheme uses the simplest possible function; a one instruction AND. However, it is really the map of floating point coordinates into the key that performs what one usually would consider "hashing." The structure of the hierarchical key space and selection of the least significant bits of the key performs extraordinarily well in reducing the incidence of collisions. For the set of all keys which contain fewer significant bits than the hash mask, the hashing function is "perfect." This set of keys represents the upper levels of the tree, which tend to be accessed the most often. At lower levels of the tree (where the number of bits in a key exceeds the length of the hash mask), distinct keys can result in the same hash address (a collision). However, the map of coordinates into the keys keeps these keys spatially separated. On a parallel machine, many of the keys which would results in collisions become distributed to different processors.

The key space is very convenient for tree traversals. In order to find daughter nodes, the parent key is left-shifted by d bits, and the result is added (or equivalently OR'ed) to daughter numbers from 0 to $2^d - 1$. Also, the key retrieval mechanism is much more flexible in terms of the kinds of accesses which are allowed. If we wish to find a particular node of a tree in which pointers are used to traverse the tree, we must start at the root of the tree, and traverse until we find the desired node (which takes of order $\log N$ operations). On the other hand, a key provides immediate ($O(1)$) access to any object in the tree.

An entry in the hash table (an hcell) consists of a pointer to the cell or body data, a pointer to a linked list which resolves collisions, the key, and various flags which describe properties of the hcell and its corresponding cell. In order to optimize certain tree traversal operations, we also store in each hcell 2^d bits that describe which daughters of the cell actually exist. This redundant information allows us to avoid using hash-table lookup functions to search for cells which don't exist.

The use of a hash table offers several important advantages. First, the access to data takes place in a manner which is easily generalized to a global accessing scheme implementable on a message passing architecture. That is, non-local data may be accessed by requesting a key, which is a uniform addressing scheme, regardless of which processor the data is contained within. This type of addressing is not possible with normal pointers on a distributed memory machine. We can also use the hash table to implement various mechanism for caching non-local data and improving memory system performance.

3.2 Tree Construction

The higher level nodes in the tree can be constructed in a variety of ways. The simplest is analogous to that which was described in [3]. Each particle is loaded into the tree by starting at the root, and traversing the partially constructed tree. When two particles fall within the same leaf node, the leaf is converted to a cell which is entered into the hash table, and new leaves are constructed one level deeper in the tree to hold each of the particles. This takes $O(\log N)$ steps per particle insertion. After the topology of the tree has been constructed, the contents (mass, charge, moments, etc.) of each cell may be initialized by a post-order tree traversal.

A faster method is possible by taking advantage of the spatial ordering implied in the key map. We first sort the body keys, and then consider the bodies in this list in order. As bodies are inserted into the tree, we start the traversal at the location of the last node created (rather than at the root). With this scheme, the average body insertion requires $O(1)$ time. We still require $O(N \log N)$ time to sort the list in the first place, but keeping the body list sorted will facilitate our parallel data decomposition as well.

3.3 Parallel Data Decomposition

The parallel data decomposition is critical to the performance of a parallel algorithm. A method which may be conceptually simple and easy to program may result in load imbalance which is unacceptable. A method which attempts to balance the work precisely may take so long that performance of the overall application suffers.

We have implemented a method which can rapidly domain decompose a d-dimensional set of particles into load balanced spatial groups which represent the domain of each processor. We take advantage of the properties of the mapping of spatial coordinates to keys to produce a "good" domain decomposition. The idea is to simply cut the one-dimensional list of sorted body key ordinates (see Fig. 6) into N_p (number of processors) equal pieces, weighted by the amount of work corresponding to each body. The work for each body is readily approximated by counting the number of interactions the body was involved in on the previous timestep. This results in a spatially adaptive decomposition, which gives each processor an equal amount of work. Additionally, the method keeps particles spatially grouped, which is very important for the efficiency of the traversal stage of the algorithm, since the amount of non-local data needed is roughly proportional to the surface area of the processor domain. An illustration of this method on a two-dimensional set of particles is illustrated in Fig. 7 for a highly clustered set of particles (that which was shown in Fig. 1) with $N_p = 16$. One source of inefficiency in the Morton ordered decomposition is that a processor domain can span one of the spatial discontinuities. A possible solution is to use Peano-Hilbert ordering for the domain decomposition, which does not contain spatial discontinuities.

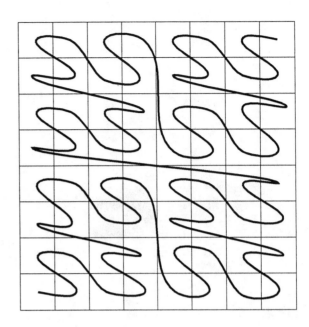

Figure 6: The path indicates the one-dimensional symmetric self-similar path which is induced by the map of interleaved bits (Morton order). The domain decomposition is achieved by cutting the one-dimensional list into N_p pieces.

3.4 Parallel Tree Construction

After the domain decomposition, each processor has a disjoint set of bodies. The initial stage in parallel tree building is the construction of a tree made of the local bodies. A special case occurs at each processor boundary in the one-dimensional sorted key list, where the terminal bodies from adjacent processors could lie in the same cell. This is taken care of by sending a copy of each boundary body to the adjacent processor, which allows the construction of the proper tree nodes. Then, copies of *branch* nodes from each processor are shared among all processors. This stage is made considerably easier and faster since the domain decomposition is intimately related to the tree topology (unlike the orthogonal recursive bisection method used in our previous code [12]). The branches make up a complete set of cells which represent the entire processor domain at the coarsest level possible. These branch cells are then globally communicated among the processors. All processors can then "fill in" the missing top of the tree down to the branch cells. The address of the processor which owns each branch cell is passed to the destination processor, so the hcell created is marked with its origin. A traversal routine can then immediately determine which processor to request data from when it needs access to the daughters of a branch cell. The daughters received from other processors are also marked in the same fashion. We have

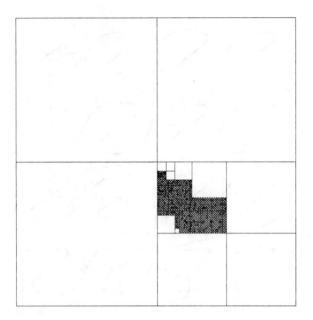

Figure 7: A processor domain for one of 16 processors in a data decomposition for the clustered system of bodies shown in Fig. 1. The domain shown is a result of the decomposition strategy outlined in the text.

also tried implementing the branch communication step in a more computationally clever manner which does not globally concatenate the branches, but its complexity has tended to outweigh its benefit. This does not rule out the possibility of finding a better method for this stage of the algorithm, however.

3.5 Tree Traversal

A tree traversal routine may be cast in recursive form in a very few lines of C code:

```
Traverse(Key_t key, int (*MAC)(hcell *),
        void (*postf)(hcell *)) {
  hcell *pp;
  unsigned int child;

  if ((pp=Find(key)) && MAC(pp)) return;
  key = KeyLshift(key, NDIM);
  for (child = 0; child < (1<<NDIM); child++)
    Traverse(KeyOrInt(key, child), MAC, postf);
  postf(pp);
```

This code applies an arbitrary MAC to determine whether to continue traversing the children of a cell. If the children are traversed, than another function, postf, is called upon completion of the descendants. By appropriate choice of the MAC and postf one can execute pre-order or post-order traversals with or without complex pruning strategies (i.e., multipole acceptability criteria).

On a parallel machine, one may add additional functionality to the Find function, in order to handle cases where the requested node is in the memory of another processor. The additional code would request non-local data, wait to receive it, and insert it into the tree. This allows the same traversal code fragment to work without further modification on a distributed memory computer. However, the performance of such an approach is bound to be dismal. Each request of non-local data is subject to the full interprocessor communication latency. Computation stalls while waiting for the requested data to arrive.

It is possible to recast the traversal function in a form which allows the entire *context* of the traversal to be stored. In this case, when a request for non-local data is encountered, the request is buffered, and the computation may proceed. Almost all of the latency for non-local data requests may be hidden, by trading communication latency for a smaller amount of complexity overhead.

The traversal method we have chosen is breadth-first list based scheme. It does not use recursion, and has several useful properties. We shall discuss the plain sequential method first, and then show the additions to allow efficient traversals on a parallel machine.

The input to the list-based traversal is a *walk list* of hcell nodes. On the first pass, the walk list contains only the root hcell. Each daughter of the input walk list nodes is tested against the MAC. If it passes the MAC, the corresponding cell data is placed on the *interaction list*. If a daughter fails the MAC, it is placed on the output walk list. After the entire input list is processed the output walk list is copied to the walk list and the process iterates. The process terminates when there are no nodes remaining on the walk list. This method has an advantage over a recursive traversal in that there is an opportunity to do some vectorization of the intermediate traversal steps, since there are generally a fair number of nodes which are being tested at a time. It also results in a final interaction list which can be passed to a fully vectorized force calculation routine. The details are too intricate to allow us to present real C code, so we present the algorithm in pseudocode instead:

```
ListTraverse((*MAC)(hcell *))
{
  copy root to walk_list;
  while (!Empty(walk_list)) {
    for (each item on walk_list) {
      for (each daughter of item) {
        if (MAC(daughter))
          copy daughter to interact_list;
        else
          copy daughter to output_walk_list;
      }
    }
    walk_list = output_walk_list;
  }
}
```

When the traversal is complete, the `interact_list` contains a vector of items that must undergo interactions (according to the particular MAC). The interactions themselves may be computed separately, so that code may be vectorized and optimized independently of the tree traversal method.

3.6 A Latency Hiding Tree Traversal

On a parallel machine, the traversal will encounter hcells for which the daughters are not present in local memory. In this case we add some additional lists which allow computation to proceed, while the evaluation of the non-local data is deferred to some later time. Each hcell is labeled with a HERE bit. This bit is set if the daughters of the hcell are present in local memory. This bit is tested in the traversal before the attempt to find the daughters. If the HERE bit is not set, the key and the source processor address (which is contained in the hcell) are placed on the *request* list, and another copy of the key is placed on a *defer* list. We additionally set a REQUESTED bit in the hcell, to prevent additional requests for the same data. This allows processing to continue on the hcells in the input walk list. As the traversal proceeds, additional requests will occur, until a final state is reached, where as much progress as possible has been made on the given traversal (using only data in local memory). In this state, there are a number of keys and processor addresses in the request list, and an equal number of keys in the defer list, which require non-local data to be received before the traversal may continue.

The request list is periodically translated into a series of interprocessor messages which contain requests for data. Upon receipt of such a message, the appropriate hcells are packaged into a reply, and the answer is returned via a second interprocessor message. When a reply is received, an appropriate entry is made in the hash table, and subsequent Find requests will return the data. It is possible to implement this request/reply protocol either loosely synchronously or asynchronously. The decision is governed by the level of support and relative performance offered by the hardware and operating system.

Upon receipt of some replies (it is not necessary to wait for all replies to arrive), the defer list can be renamed as the `walk_list`, and the traversal can be restarted with the newly arrived data. Alternatively, one can begin an entirely separate traversal to compute, e.g., the force on another particle. With appropriate bookkeeping one can tolerate very long latencies by implementing a circular queue of active traversals (with a shared request list). We have used a circular queue with 30 active traversals, so that after 30 traversals have been deferred, we restart the first traversal by copying its defer list to its walk list. The requested data has usually arrived in the interim.

4 Performance

Here we provide timings for the various stages of the algorithm on the 512 processor Intel Touchstone Delta installed at Caltech. The timings listed are from an 8.8 million particle production run simulation involving the formation of structure in a cold dark matter Universe [14]. During the initial stages of the calculation, the particles are spread uniformly throughout the spherical computational volume. We set an absolute error bound on each partial acceleration of 10^{-3} times the mean acceleration in the system. This results in 2.2×10^{10} interactions per timestep in the initial unclustered system. The timing breakdown is as follows:

computation stage	time (sec)
Domain Decomposition	7
Tree Build	7
Tree Traversal	33
Data Communication During Traversal	6
Force Evaluation	54
Load Imbalance	7
Total (5.8 Gflops)	114

At later stages of the calculation the system becomes extremely clustered (the density in large clusters of particles is typically 10^6 times the mean density). The number of interactions required to maintain the same accuracy grows moderately as the system evolves. At a slightly increased error bound of 4×10^{-3}, the number of interactions in the clustered system is 2.6×10^{10} per timestep.

computation stage	time (sec)
Domain Decomposition	19
Tree Build	10
Tree Traversal	55
Data Communication during traversal	4
Force Evaluation	60
Load Imbalance	12
Total (4.9 Gflops)	160

It is evident that the initial domain decomposition and tree building stages take a relatively larger fraction of the time in this case. The reason is that in order to load balance the force calculation, some processors have nearly three times as many particles as the mean value, and over ten times as many particles as the processor with the fewest. The load balancing scheme currently attempts to load balance only the work involved in force evaluation and tree traversal, so the initial domain decomposition and tree construction work (which scales closely with the particle number within the processor) becomes imbalanced.

Note that roughly 50% of the execution time is spent in the force calculation subroutine. This routine consists of a few tens of lines of code, so it makes sense to obtain the maximum possible performance through careful tuning. For the Delta's `i860` microprocessor we used hand coded assembly language to keep the three-stage pipeline fully filled, which results in a speed of 28 Mflops per processing node in this routine.

If we count only the floating point operations performed in the force calculation routine as "useful work" (30 flops per interaction) the overall speed of the code is about 5–6 Gflops. However, this number is in a sense unfair to the overall algorithm, since the majority of the code is not involved in floating point operations at all, but with tree traversal and data structure manipulation. The integer arithmetic and addressing speed of the processor are as important as the floating point performance. We hope that in the future, evaluation of processors does not become over-balanced toward better floating point speed at the expense of integer arithmetic and memory bandwidth, as this code is a good example of why a balanced processor architecture is necessary for good overall performance.

5   Multi-purpose Applications

Problems of current interest in a wide variety of areas rely heavily on N-body and/or fast multipole methods. Accelerator beam dynamics, astrophysics (galaxy formation, large-scale structure), computational biology (protein folding), chemistry (molecular structure and thermodynamics), electromagnetic scattering, fluid mechanics (vortex method, panel method), molecular dynamics, and plasma physics, to name those we are familiar with, but there are certainly more. In some of these areas, N^2 algorithms are still the most often used, due to their simplicity. However, as problems grow larger, the use of fast methods becomes a necessity. Indeed, in the case of problems such as electromagnetic scattering, a fast multipole method reduces the operation count for solving the second-kind integral equation from $O(N^3)$ for Gaussian elimination to $O(N^{4/3})$ per conjugate-gradient iteration [20]. Such a vast improvement allows one to contemplate problems which were heretofore simply impossible. Alternatively, one can use a workstation to solve problems that had previously been in the sole domain of large supercomputers.

We have spent substantial effort in this code keeping the data structures and functions required by the "application" away from those of the "tree". With suitable abstractions and ruthless segregation, we have met with some success in this area. We currently have a number of physics applications which share the same tree code. In general, the addition of another application only requires the definition of a data structure, and additional code is required only

with respect to functions which are physics related (e.g., the force calculation).

We have described the application of our code to gravitational N-body problems above. The code has also been indispensable in performing statistical analyses and data processing on the end result of our N-body calculations, since their size prohibits analysis on anything but a parallel supercomputer. The code also has a module which can perform three-dimensional compressible fluid dynamics using smoothed particle hydrodynamics (with or without gravity). We have also implemented a vortex particle method [21]. It is a simple matter to use the same program to do physics involving other force laws. Apart from the definition of a data structure and modification of the basic force calculation routine, one only need derive the appropriate MAC using the method described in Salmon & Warren [10].

6   Future Improvements

The code described here is by no means a "final" version. The implementation has been explicitly designed to easily allow experimentation, and inclusion of new ideas which we find useful. It is perhaps unique in that it is serving double duty as a high performance production code to study the process of galaxy formation, as well as a testbed to investigate multipole algorithms.

Additions to the underlying method which we expect will improve its performance even further include the addition of cell-cell evaluations (similar to those used in the fast multipole method) and the ability to evolve each particle with an independent timestep (which improves performance significantly in systems where the timescale varies greatly). We expect that the expression of the algorithm in the `C++` language will produce a more friendly program by taking advantage of the features of the language such as data abstraction and operator overloading. The code is very portable to other parallel platforms, and we currently have code running on the Intel Paragon, the CM-5, the IBM SP-1, and networks of workstations. The bulk of the remaining improvements are in the area of processor specific tuning, such as `CDPEAC` coding of the inner loop of the force-evaluation routine to obtain optimal floating point performance on the CM-5.

7   Conclusion

In an overall view of this algorithm, we feel that these general items deserve special attention:

- The fundamental ideas in this algorithm are, for the most part, standard tools of computer science (key mapping, hashing, sorting). We have shown that in combination, they form the basis of a clean and efficient parallel algorithm. This type of algorithm does not evolve from a sequential method. It requires starting anew, without the prejudices inherent in a program (or programmer) accustomed to using a single processor.

- The raw computing speed of the code on an extremely irregular, dynamically changing set of particles which require global data for their update, using a large number of processors (512), is comparable with the performance quoted for much more regular static problems, which are sometimes identified as the only type of "scalable" algorithms which obtain good performance on parallel machines. We hope we have convinced the reader that even difficult irregular problems are amenable to parallel computation.

We expect that algorithms such as that described here, coupled with the extraordinary increase in computational power expected in the coming years, will play a major part in the process of understanding complex physical systems.

Acknowledgments

We thank Sanjay Ranka for pointing out the utility of Peano-Hilbert ordering. We thank the CSCC and the CCSF for providing computational resources. JS wishes to acknowledge support from the Advanced Computing Division of the NSF, as well as the CRPC. MSW wishes to acknowledge support from IGPP and AFOSR. This research was supported in part by a grant from NASA under the HPCC program. This research was performed in part using the Intel Touchstone Delta System operated by Caltech on behalf of the Concurrent Supercomputing Consortium.

References

[1] A. W. Appel, "An efficient program for many-body simulation," *SIAM J. Computing*, vol. 6, p. 85, 1985.

[2] K. Esselink, "The order of Appel's algorithm," *Information Processing Let.*, vol. 41, pp. 141–147, 1992.

[3] J. Barnes and P. Hut, "A hierarchical O(NlogN) force-calculation algorithm," *Nature*, vol. 324, p. 446, 1986.

[4] L. Greengard and V. Rokhlin, "A fast algorithm for particle simulations," *J. Comp. Phys.*, vol. 73, pp. 325–348, 1987.

[5] L. Greengard and W. D. Gropp, "A parallel version of the fast multipole method," *Computers Math. Applic*, vol. 20, no. 7, pp. 63–71, 1990.

[6] F. Zhao and S. L. Johnsson, "The parallel multipole method on the connection machine," *SIAM J. Sci. Stat. Comp.*, vol. 12, pp. 1420–1437, Nov. 1991.

[7] K. E. Schmidt and M. A. Lee, "Implementing the fast multipole method in three dimensions," *J. Stat. Phys.*, vol. 63, no. 5/6, pp. 1223–1235, 1991.

[8] J. A. Board, J. W. Causey, J. F. Leathrum, A. Windemuth, and K. Schulten, "Accelerated molecular dynamics simulation with the parallel fast multipole algorithm," *Chem. Phys. Let.*, vol. 198, p. 89, 1992.

[9] H.-Q. Ding, N. Karasawa, and W. Goddard, "Atomic level simulations of a million particles: The cell multipole method for coulomb and london interactions," *J. of Chemical Physics*, vol. 97, pp. 4309–4315, 1992.

[10] J. K. Salmon and M. S. Warren, "Skeletons from the treecode closet," *J. Comp. Phys.*, 1993. (in press)

[11] J. K. Salmon, *Parallel Hierarchical N-body Methods*. PhD thesis, California Institute of Technology, 1990.

[12] M. S. Warren and J. K. Salmon, "Astrophysical N-body simulations using hierarchical tree data structures," in *Supercomputing '92*, IEEE Comp. Soc., 1992.

[13] M. S. Warren, P. J. Quinn, J. K. Salmon, and W. H. Zurek, "Dark halos formed via dissipationless collapse: I. Shapes and alignment of angular momentum," *Ap. J.*, vol. 399, pp. 405–425, 1992.

[14] W. H. Zurek, P. J. Quinn, J. K. Salmon, and M. S. Warren, "Large Scale Structure after COBE: Peculiar Velocities and Correlations of Dark Matter Halos in a CDM Universe," *Nature*, 1993. (submitted)

[15] J. P. Singh, J. L. Hennessy, and A. Gupta, "Implications of hierarchical N-body techniques for multiprocessor architectures," Tech. Rep. CSL-TR-92-506, Stanford University, 1992.

[16] J. P. Singh, C. Holt, T. Totsuka, A. Gupta, and J. L. Hennessy, "Load balancing and data locality in hierarchical N-body methods," *Journal of Parallel and Distributed Computing*, 1992.

[17] S. Bhatt, M. Chen, C. Y. Lin, and P. Liu, "Abstractions for parallel N-body simulations," Tech. Rep. DCS/TR-895, Yale University, 1992.

[18] H. Samet, *Design and Analysis of Spatial Data Structures*. Reading, MA: Addison-Wesley, 1990.

[19] J. E. Barnes, "An efficient N-body algorithm for a fine-grain parallel computer," in *The Use of Supercomputers in Stellar Dynamics* (P. Hut and S. McMillan, eds.), (New York), pp. 175–180, Springer-Verlag, 1986.

[20] N. Engheta, W. D. Murphy, V. Rokhlin, and M. S. Vassiliou, "The fast multipole method (FMM) for electromagnetic scattering problems," *IEEE Transactions on Antennas and Propagation*, vol. 40, no. 6, pp. 634–642, 1992.

[21] J. K. Salmon, M. S. Warren, and G. S. Winckelmans, "Fast parallel tree codes for gravitational and fluid dynamical N-body problems," *International Journal of Supercomputing Applications*, 1993. (submitted)

Distributed Computation of Wave Propagation Models Using PVM

R. E. Ewing
Institute for Scientific Computation
Texas A&M University
College Station, TX 77843

D. Mitchum and P. O'Leary
Institute for Scientific Computation
University of Wyoming
Laramie, Wyoming 82071

R. C. Sharpley
Department of Mathematics
University of South Carolina
Columbia, SC 29208

J. S. Sochacki
Department of Mathematics
James Madison University
Harrisonburg, VA 22807

Abstract

PVM is an inexpensive, but extremely effective tool which allows a researcher to use workstations as nodes in a parallel processing environment to perform large-scale computations. The numerical approximation and visualization of seismic waves propagating in the earth strains today's largest supercomputers. We present timings and visualization for large earth models run on a ring of IBM RS/6000's which illustrate PVM's capability of handling large-scale problems.

1 Introduction

Specialized computer architectures provide a way for simulating large-scale problems. Although supercomputers with shared memory architectures such as Cray and Convex, MIMD distributed memory architectures as implemented by Intel and NCube, SIMD distributed memory architectures exemplified by Maspar and Thinking machines, and emerging architectures such as the Kendall Square ring, can attack most of today's large-scale computing problems, these comptutational resources are usually inaccessible to the average researcher. The Parallel Virtual Machine (PVM) tool was developed in a joint effort at Emory University, the University of Tennessee, and Oak Ridge National Laboratory [2, 9, 22] to implement networked UNIX-based workstations into a distributed computational environment.

We will show that PVM can effectively compete with traditional supercomputers. Any researcher with accounts on UNIX-based workstations can corral unused CPU cycles to solve large-scale problems. Significant computational speedups can be achieved, but are algorithm-dependent.

The computational power and cost effectiveness of PVM will be demonstrated on the problem of simulating the propagation of seismic waves in the earth. The equations used to model seismic wave propagation will be the acoustic and elastic wave equations. The acoustic wave equation is used to simulate pressure changes and the elastic wave equation is used to simulate particle displacement. We present results for large-scale two-dimensional (2D) problems, but these results extend naturally to the three-dimensional (3D) case. The seismic problem is also of computational interest because of surface conditions, absorbing boundary conditions, and the associated inverse problem. The model equations may also be used to solve problems occurring in medical imaging, sonar, and nondestructive testing of materials.

The remainder of this paper proceeds as follows: A conceptual description of PVM and the associated working environment is presented in Section 2. In Section 3 the governing equations and numerical simulator are described and their important features are discussed. Section 4 describes our PVM implementation of the numerical schemes, while Section 5 presents sample results from 2D acoustic and elastic wave simulations in the PVM environment. In section 6, we provide the particular model parameters for our acoustic and elastic experiments and conclude the paper with timings of the two model formulations and a discussion of future investigations.

© 1993 ACM 0-8186-4340-4/93/0011 $1.50

2 Parallel Virtual Machine

PVM is a distributed computing software utiliuty for developing and executing distributed computations. PVM can connect various hardwares in a relatively inexpensive parallel computing environment. Such hardware is frequently abundant at most locations, so that little or no hardware costs are associated with the implementation of PVM.

PVM was developed to be flexible and has many desirable features: (1) it runs on several workstation platforms, mini-supercomputers, and specialty machines, (2) it utilizes existing communication networks (i.e., ethernet or fiber) and remote procedural libraries, (3) both C and Fortran procedural programming languages are available to the application programmer, and (4) it may be used to emulate several commercially available architectures such as hypercubes, meshes, and rings.

PVM, however, also has disadvantages. For example, PVM cannot take advantage of nearest neighbor communication algorithms. Since PVM depends on existing networks, communications must follow network package protocols. Thus, a message may be processed by several machines before it eventually reaches its desired destination. A second disadvantage is that the network could become a significant bottleneck. For many applications, speedups will be less significant as processors are added and the network communication becomes saturated. Finally, PVM may not be suitable for some algorithms in a heterogeneous computing environment due to incompatible processors and inaccuracies in their math libraries. These drawbacks to PVM, however, may be less significant as network technologies improve, as the Open Systems Foundation addresses system compatibility, and as PVM undergoes continued development.

The PVM software was developed in a simple and straightforward manner consisting of two primary components, a controlling daemon and a procedural library. The controlling daemon *pvmd* institutes distributed control by requiring that each processing unit involved in the distributed calculation initiates execution of this daemon. This enables each processing unit to absorb any master/slave overhead. As the controlling daemons exchange information, interprocessor communication is facilitated through a resident lookup table of enrolled subprocesses. Finally, the *pvmd* daemon allows for and facilitates point-to-point data transfer, message broadcasting, mutual exclusion, process contol, shared memory emulation, and barriers.

The procedural library is the user's link to the *pvmd* daemon. A set of simple subroutine calls allow the application programmer to interact with the *pvmd* daemon in a relatively transparent manner. Therefore, parallelization of a specific application in this environment requires few subroutine calls and provides an unprecedented flexibility.

3 Governing Equations and Numerical Discretization

Geophysicists produce vibrations (through controlled explosions or vibroseis trucks) at or near the surface of the earth in an attempt to determine the substructure of the earth. Substructure properties of interest are the density, sound speed, and Lamé parameters of the materials comprising the section of the earth in a volume surrounding the location of the explosion. Typical measurements from these events include: (1) the pressure distribution at the surface of the earth caused by the explosion, i.e., the *pressure seismogram* and (2) the vertical displacement of the surface of the earth, referred to as the *displacement seismogram*. The synthetic pressure seismogram is obtained from the acoustic wave equation and the synthetic displacement seismogram is obtained from the elastic wave equation. From these seismograms the geophysicist attempts to determine the substructure characteristics. Determining the effects of a particular wave source on a specified substructure configuration is termed the *forward problem* while determining the substructure and its parameters is referred to as the *inverse problem*. In this paper we address the forward problem. Since we are dealing with the 2D problem, we let x_1 or x represent distance along the surface of the earth and x_2 or z represent depth into the earth.

The equations describing the pressure distribution in a fluid come from Euler's equation and are

$$
\begin{aligned}
\rho_t + \nabla \cdot (\rho \vec{v}) &= 0, \\
(\rho \vec{v})_t + \nabla \cdot (\rho v_i \vec{v}) + \nabla p &= \vec{F}(x_1, x_2, t)
\end{aligned}
\tag{1}
$$

where ρ is the density, $c = c(x_1, x_2)$ is the speed of sound in the medium, $\vec{v} = (v_1, v_2)$ is the fluid particle velocity, p is the pressure, and $\vec{F}$ is the interior disturbance. By using the adiabatic condition $p' = c^2 p'$ where $p = p_0(x_1, x_2) + p'$, $\rho = \rho_0(x_1, x_2) + \rho'$, and p_0, ρ_0 are the equilibrium pressure and density, respectively. Upon linearization, this system reduces to

$$
\begin{aligned}
\frac{1}{c^2} p_t + \rho_0 \nabla \cdot (\vec{v}) &= 0, \\
(\rho_0 \vec{v})_t + \nabla p &= \vec{F}(x_1, x_2, t).
\end{aligned}
\tag{2}
$$

In this paper we solve the equation

$$u_{tt} - \rho_0 c^2 \nabla \cdot \left(\frac{1}{\rho_0} \nabla u \right) = g(x_1, x_2, t), \qquad (3)$$

and note that if $p = -u_t$ and $\vec{v} = \frac{1}{\rho_0} \nabla u + \vec{G}$, where $g(x, t) = c^2 \rho_0 \nabla \cdot (\vec{G})$, and $\vec{G}_t = \frac{1}{\rho_0} \vec{F}$, then p and $\vec{v}$ solve Equation (2). The condition at the surface of the earth is $p(x_1, 0, t) = -u_t(x_1, 0, t) = S(x_1, t)$, where S is a surface excitation ($S = 0$, if there is no surface source). Equation (3) along with the surface conditions will be the acoustic wave equation used in this paper to simulate the pressure seismogram.

The 2D elastic wave equation used to simulate the displacement seismogram is

$$\rho u_{tt} = \frac{\partial}{\partial x}[(\lambda + 2\mu)u_x + \lambda w_z] + \frac{\partial}{\partial z}[\mu(u_z + w_x)]$$
$$+ F_1(x, z, t)$$
$$\rho w_{tt} = \frac{\partial}{\partial x}[\mu(u_z + w_x)] + \frac{\partial}{\partial z}[\lambda u_x + (\lambda + 2\mu)w_z]$$
$$+ F_2(x, z, t),$$
$$(4)$$

where $\rho = \rho(x, z)$ is the equilibrium density, $\lambda = \lambda(x, z), \mu = \mu(x, z)$ are the Lamé parameters, $c = \alpha = \sqrt{\frac{\lambda 2\mu}{\rho}}, \beta = \sqrt{\frac{\mu}{\rho}}$ are the P and S wave velocities, respectively, u is the horizontal particle displacement, w is the vertical particle displacement, and F_1, F_2 are the interior sources. The surface of the earth is handled using free surface boundary conditions which are formulated as

$$\mu(u_z + w_x) = S_1(x, t),$$
$$(\lambda + 2\mu)w_z + \lambda u_x = S_2(x, t),$$

where, again, S_1 and S_2 are the surface excitation sources.

The forward acoustic problem consists of solving Equation (3), given ρ_0, c, $\vec{F}$, and S, while the forward elastic problem consists of solving Equation (4), given α, β, ρ, F_1, F_2, S_1, and S_2. In our model for the earth there are idealized curves of discontinuity for the parameters ρ, c, and β which describe the *interfaces* between layered media. Geophysicists are interested in determining the location of these interface curves and the parameter values of the layers. In forward problems, these parameters and interfaces are, of course, specified and there are many numerical methods available for providing solutions, each with their own strengths and weaknesses. A sampling of these include finite difference [11], finite element [13], Fourier methods [14, 25], and pseudo-spectral methods [8]. In

this paper we use a finite-difference method, developed in [19], which consists of discretizing the region of interest and integrating the equations at each spatial grid point. In time, we use centered differences to keep second order accuracy. The integration scheme forces continuity of the pressure and the normal velocity at the interfaces in Equation (3), and the particle displacements, normal, and tangential stresses at the interfaces in Equation (4). This method is naturally parallel since the integration scheme is uniform at each node and may be handled independently.

Since typically there are no physical boundaries in the region surrounding the location of the explosive sources, the numerical simulator should attempt to minimize artificial reflections off the numerical boundary. These reflections are usually termed spurious in the literature and numerical boundary conditions devised to eliminate or reduce these spurious reflections are called absorbing boundary conditions. Since boundary conditions are calculated only by processors handling the outer edges of the model, this presents load balancing problems in a multi-processor environment.

To address this problem, we use the damping method introduced in [20] and note that, to our knowledge, all reported absorbing boundary conditions are at best approximately absorbing. This method requires that we solve the modified equation

$$u_{tt} + 2Au_t = \rho_0 c^2 \nabla \cdot \left(\frac{1}{\rho_0} \nabla u \right) + g(x_1, x_2, t) \quad (5)$$

for Equation (3) and

$$u_{tt} + 2Au_t = \frac{1}{\rho} \left(\frac{\partial}{\partial x}[(\lambda + 2\mu)u_x + \lambda w_z] + \lambda w_z] \right.$$
$$\left. + \frac{\partial}{\partial z}[\mu(u_z + w_x)] \right) + \vec{F}_1(x, z, t),$$
$$w_{tt} + 2Aw_t = \frac{1}{\rho} \left(\frac{\partial}{\partial x}[\mu(u_z + w_x)] \right.$$
$$\left. + \frac{\partial}{\partial z}[\lambda u_x + (\lambda + 2\mu)w_z] \right) + \vec{F}_2(x, z, t)$$
$$(6)$$

for Equation (4), where $A = A(x, z)$ incorporates the lateral and bottom boundary conditions and vanishes on the interior of the model. Therefore, each node solves similar equations and "load balancing" of the calculations is automatic. Of course, this requires more calculations at the interior points, but most of the known absorbing boundary conditions are computationally intensive.

The difference approximation to the acoustic equation (3) without damping is given by

$$
\begin{aligned}
u_{j,k}^{n+1} \\
= 2u_{j,k}^n - u_{j,k}^{n-1} + M_{j,k} \left(\frac{1}{\Delta x^2} \left(b_{j+\frac{1}{2},k} u_{j+1,k}^n \right. \right. \\
\left. - \left(b_{j_{\frac{1}{2}},k} + b_{j-\frac{1}{2},k} \right) u_{j,k}^n + b_{j-\frac{1}{2},k} u_{j-1,k}^n \right) \\
+ \frac{1}{\Delta z^2} \left(b_{j,k+\frac{1}{2}} u_{j,k+1}^n - \left(b_{j,k+\frac{1}{2}} + b_{j,k-\frac{1}{2}} \right) u_{j,k}^n \right. \\
\left. \left. + b_{j,k-\frac{1}{2}} u_{j,k-1}^n \right) \right) + \Delta t^2 g_{j,k}^n,
\end{aligned}
$$

(7)

where

$$
M_{j,k} = \frac{9 \Delta t^2}{\sum_{n=j-1}^{j+1} \sum_{m=k-1}^{k+1} \frac{1}{c(x_n, z_m)^2 \rho_0(x_n, z_m)}}
$$

and $b_{j,k} = \frac{1}{\rho_0(x_j, z_k)}$. The corresponding scheme for (5) which includes the absorbing boundary conditions is obtained by

$$
u_{j,k}^{n+1} = \frac{v_{j,k}^{n+1} + A_{j,k} \Delta t u_{j,k}^n}{1 + A_{j,k} \Delta t}
$$

(8)

where $v_{j,k}^{n+1}$ denotes the expression computed in Equation (7) and $A_{j,k}$ denote the damping weights. This is easily seen to be a five point star for u. Although the difference equations for system (6) are similar, they include mixed differences for the cross derivative terms and the difference stencil becomes a nine point star.

The free surface boundary conditions for the elastic equation are difficult to solve when using finite differences. We use the implicit method presented in [20, 23], which gives rise to the resulting difference equations:

$$
\frac{1}{\Delta z} u_{j,0} + \frac{1}{2\Delta x} w_{j-1,0} - \frac{1}{2\Delta x} w_{j+1,0} = \frac{1}{\Delta z} u_{j,1} - G_{1,j},
$$

(9)

$$
-\frac{1}{2\Delta x} u_{j-1,0} + \frac{1}{2\Delta x} u_{j+1,0} + c_j w_{j,0} = c_j w_{j,1} + G_{2,j},
$$

(10)

where $c_j = -\frac{1}{2\Delta z} \left[\left(\frac{\lambda+2\mu}{\lambda} \right)_{j+1} + \left(\frac{\lambda+2\mu}{\lambda} \right)_{j-1} \right]$ and G_1, G_2 are the surface sources. The resulting symmetric system that arises from these equations has four bands and must be solved at each time iteration. Directly inverting this matrix is essentially a sequential algorithm, so iterative methods for solving this system should be used in order to keep the code parallel and will be discussed in more detail in the following section. We note that in the 3D case the matrix may fail to be symmetric.

4 PVM Implementation

In the parallelization of our 2D acoustic wave propagation simulator, we have followed the host/node (H/N) paradigm. The host program performs input/output (I/O) and dictates the domain decomposition to the node program. The node program gathers and scatters information needed for and produced by the calculations of the explicit finite difference scheme, and communicates iterative interprocessor boundary solutions to neighboring nodes with respect to the problem's domain decomposition.

This implementation provides a 2D domain decomposition of the problem. Therefore, the domain can be divided into strips to take advantage of available vector processors or patches to reduce the size of the communication packets. Our timings have shown this flexibility can prove to be significant in achieving optimal speedups.

The node program calculates communication pathways by assigning node values from 0 to $n-1$ to the processors. This maintains a nearest neighbor communication paradigm although no computational advantage is obtained in PVM. The communication of the iteration interprocessor boundary solutions synchronizes the node programs, while requirements for output synchronize the H/N programs. The parallelization of the 2D elastic wave propagation simulator is similar, but with the addition of the implicit scheme to incorporate the stress-free surface conditions. Since these particular calculations occur only at the surface nodes, load balancing and node program synchronization become issues.

We note however, that reorganization of the data structure among the nodes is not necessary because this implicit scheme uses the same finite difference stencil. On the other hand, our choice of the conjugate gradient squared algorithm (CGS) [21] as a solver yields five barriers to parallelization, involving both inner products and a matrix multiply. The inner products require a global sum across surface nodes, but we note that the associated communication packet is small. For the matrix multiply, all the necessary components of the matrix are locally available, but the components of the vector that correspond to the off-diagonal bands are not resident and must be gathered using nearest neighbor communication between surface nodes.

Our particular implementation was performed on an isolated ethernet ring consisting of an IBM RS/6000 550 as the host and 6 IBM RS/6000 320H's as the nodes.

5 Sample Model Descriptions

We now present two models that are of importance to geophysicists. The elastic model contains a fully saturated salt dome to test the S wave propagation. We present the model descriptions (both geophysical and numerical), visual I/O, and timings for elastic and acoustic models in the PVM environment. The visual snapshots of the elastic model illustrate the generation of S waves which are not present in the acoustic simulations.

The acoustic model is shown in Figure 1a. We have a salt dome lying under three layers of different homogeneous materials. The model dimensions are 1000 m × 1000 m while the density and sound speed values are as shown in Figure 1a. These three layers are separated at 200 m and 400 m and the subsurface dome lies between 500 m and 1000 m as shown.

The source is a surface explosion set off at 400 m and is a casual source with frequencies from 3 to 7 Hertz. The pressure distribution (wave propagation) is shown in Figure 1b at 0.2, 0.3, 0.4, and 0.5 seconds. The remaining parameters for the acoustic model are $dt = 0.001$ sec, $dx = dz = 10$ m.

The elastic model is shown in Figure 2a. This model, except for the fluid saturated dome from 600 m to 800 m and the outcropping at the surface, is the same as the acoustic model. As mentioned, the dome is used to demonstrate the added features of the elastic equations for S waves while the slanted interface at the surface is to show the importance of accurate surface boundary conditions for the elastic model.

The source in this model is interior to the model and is located at $x = 600$ m, $z = 200$ m and has the form of a compressional spherical source with amplitude in time given by the derivative of a Gaussian, $3(t - .25)e^{-1000(t-.25)^2}$. The energy of the particle motion (wave propagation) is shown at 0.2, 0.3, 0.4, and 0.5 seconds in Figure 2b. The remaining parameters in this case are the same for the acoustic model.

6 Computational Results

Computational experiments of 10 runs of each model were performed with the number of processors varying from one to six for a total of sixty runs per model. Figures 3–5 are plots which indicate various measures of speedup and performance for the acoustic model and elastic model with and without surface boundary conditions imposed, respectively. Figure 3 consists of four subplots of timings for the acoustic

model runs with speedup plotted against the number of processors. In Figures 3.a–c, the solid line represents perfect parallelism, while the dashed lines correspond to worst, average, and best performance tests, respectively. Figure 3.a is a plot of total execution times, including initialization, H/N I/O, discrete model computations on each processor, and the interprocessor communication to allow the time-evolution of the model. Figure 3.b is the ideal time which excludes initialization, H/N I/O, and the interprocessor communication, and is just short of linear speedup, which indicates the overhead cost incurred with the master/slave interaction between the PVM daemon and the subprocessors. Figure 3.c is a plot of execution timings which includes iteration computations and interprocessor communication, but excludes initialization and H/N I/O, while Figure 3.d is a plot of the timings in seconds of the interprocessor communication alone.

In these figures, the tight grouping of the worst to the best runs indicates that the runs were statistically consistent and that significant speedups of approximately 5.6 for total execution time and for the iteration time were achieved. In Figure 3.d, with the exception of adding the sixth processor, the communication time becomes asymptotic to 250 seconds due to the limiting communication that each processor must perform as the problem size remains fixed.

Figures 4.a–d and 5.a–d are similar plots for the elastic models with and without surface boundary conditions imposed, respectively, where the subplots of each model are the same as described above for the acoustic case. Figure 4 shows that speedup of the elastic equation without a surface solve is very similar to that of the acoustic case since both are direct finite difference methods with more intense calculations (corresponding to Equation (6)) on each processor in this case. On the other hand, speedups degradate to approximately 5.1 for the elastic model with the surface matrix solve since, as described in Section 4, there are barriers in the form of a matrix multiply and dot products which must be iterated until convergence at each time iteration. This significant, approximately double, increase in interprocessor communication is the major contributor to the corresponding decrease in speedup.

7 Future Directions

To address the free-surface computations, the system of equations generated by (9) and (10) looks very much like a matrix arising from an elliptic differential equation. One way to parallelize this computation is to precondition this system with a diagonal preconditioner and to then parallelize the matrix multiply part of a preconditioned conjugate-gradient type iterative procedure. This method also requires parallelization of the scalar product and a global sum. Techniques are available for these parallel computations.

As the size of the application increases and the discretiation sizes decrease, the conditioning of the matrix described above will increase significantly, and the diagonal preconditioner will be less effective. For this reason, we are developing better parallelization methods based on domain decomposition algorithms. A general Additive-Schwartz, overlapping domain code has been written for domain decomposition applications. Parallelization is accomplished by physically splitting the domain up while communication is controlled by the size of the overlapping region, an input parameter. Multigrid methods can then be applied locally to give good local preconditioning. The code is briefly described in [6] while the underlying domain decomposition theory comes from [3].

We have demonstrated the potential of PVM for two types of large-scale seismic application codes and have briefly indicated how the implementations might change in 3D. The major differences between the performance on the two codes was the communication overhead caused by the free-surface constraints required for the elastic model. However, we have identified bottlenecks to parallelization of the codes that can now be addressed more carefully. The corresponding development for elliptic solvers in our other research indicates avenues for future improvements. Since the calculations were performed on a homogeneous network of IBM RS/6000 machines on an isolated network, we expect performance to degrade somewhat with a heterogeneous environment or using a network with heavy or bursty traffic. The heterogeneous system will cause some additional load-balancing problems. In any case, this work illustrates that PVM can build a very powerful machine from available workstations and that realistic applications can be treated effectively.

Acknowledgments

The authors would like to thank Patrick K. Malone, Christian Turner, and Phillip Crotwell for their help and the University of South Carolina and Westinghouse Savannah River Laboratory for the use of the IBM RS/6000 computing ring. This work was supported in part by the National Science Foundation under grants EHR–910–8774, EHR–910–8772, and INT–89–14472.

References

[1] R.M. Alford, K.R. Kelly, and D.M. Boore, Accuracy of finite-difference modeling of the acoustic wave equation, *Geophysics* **39(6)** (1974), 834–842.

[2] A. Beguelin, J. Dongarra, A. Geist, B. Manchek, and V.S. Sunderam, A user's guide to PVM parallel virtual machine, *ORNL Technical Report, TM-1126*, 1991.

[3] J.H. Bramble, J.E. Pasciak, J. Wang, and J. Xu, Convergence estimates for product iterative methods with applications to domain decomposition, *Math. Comp.* **57** (1991), 23–45.

[4] C. Cerjan, D. Kosloff, R. Kosloff, and M. Reshef, A non-reflecting boundary condition for discrete acoustic and elastic wave equations, *Geophysics* **50(8)** (1985), 705–708.

[5] B. Enquist and A. Majda, Absorbing boundary conditions for the numerical simulation of waves, *Math. Comp.* **31(139)** (1977), 629–651.

[6] R.E. Ewing, M.A. Celia, P. O'Leary, J.E. Pasciak and A. Vassilev, Parallelization of multiphase models for contaminant transport in porous media, *Parallel Processing for Scientific Computing* **1** (R. Sincovec, D. Keyes, M. Leuze, L. Petzold, and D. Reed, eds.), 1993, 83–91.

[7] W.M. Ewing, W.S. Jardetzky, and F. Press, *Elastic Waves in Layered Media*, McGraw Hill, 1957.

[8] B. Fornberg, The pseudo spectral method: Accurate representation of interfaces in elastic wave equations, *Geophysics* **53(5)** (1988), 625–637.

[9] G.A. Geist and V.S. Sunderam, Network based concurrent computing on the PVM system, *Concurrency: Practice and Experience*, (to appear).

[10] T. Ha-Duong and P. Joly, A generalized principle of images for the wave equation with absorbing boundary conditions and applications to fourth order schemes, *Math. Comp.*, (submitted).

[11] K.R. Kelly, R.W. Ward, S. Treitel, and R.M. Alford, Modeling – The forward method, *Concepts and Techniques in Oil and Gas Exploration* (K.C. Jain and R.J.P. de Figueiredo, eds.), Soc. Expl. Geophys., 1982.

[12] A.R. Levander, Fourth-order finite-difference P-SV seismograms, *Geophysics* **53(11)** (1988), 1425–1436.

[13] K.J. Marfurt, Accuracy of finite-difference and finite-element modeling of the scalar and elastic wave equation, *Geophysics* **49(5)** (1984), 533–549.

[14] M. Reshef, D. Kosloff, M. Edward, and C. Hsiung, Three dimensional acoustic modeling by the Fourier method, *Geophysics* **53(9)** (1988), 1175–1183.

[15] A.C. Reynolds, Boundary conditions for the numerical solution of wave propagation problems, *Geophysics* **43(6)** (1978), 1099–1110.

[16] R.D. Richtmeyer and K.W. Morton, *Difference Methods for Initial Value Problems*, Interscience Publishers, New York, 1967.

[17] J.S. Sochacki, Absorbing boundary conditions using regions with exponential decay, *Proceedings of First International Conference on Mathematical and Numerical Aspects of Wave Propagation Phenomena*, Strasbourg, France, April 23–26, 1991, 293–302.

[18] J.S. Sochacki, R.E. Ewing, P. O'Leary, C. Bennett, and R. Sharpley, Seismic modeling and inversion on the NCUBE, *The Fifth Distributed Memory Computing Conference* **1** (D. Walker and Q. Strout, eds.), IEEE Computer Society Press, 1990, 530–535.

[19] J.S. Sochacki, J.H. George, R.E. Ewing, and S.B. Smithson, Interface conditions for acoustic and elastic wave propagation, *Geophysics* **56(2)** (1991), 161–181.

[20] J.S. Sochacki, R. Kubichek, J.H. George, W.R. Fletcher, and S.B. Smithson, Absorbing boundary conditions and surface waves, *Geophysics* **52(1)** (1987), 60–71.

[21] P. Sonneveld, CGS, a fast Lanczos-type solver for nonsymmetriclinear systems, *SIAM J. Stat. Comput.* **10** (1989), 36–52.

[22] V.S. Sunderam, A framework for parallel distributed computing, *Concurrency: Practice and Experience* **2(4)** (1990), 315–339.

[23] J.E. Vidale and R.W. Clayton, A stable free-surface boundary condition for two-dimensional elastic wave propagation, *Geophysics* **51(12)** (1986) 2247–2249.

[24] J. Virieux, SH-wave propagation in heterogeneous media: Velocity-stress finite-difference method, *Geophysics* **49(11)** (1984), 1933–1957.

[25] J. Wen, G.A. McMechan, and M.W. Booth, Three dimensional modeling and migration of seismic data using Fourier transforms, *Geophysics* **53(9)** (1988), 1194–1201.

Figure 1a

Acoustic Wave

Figure 1b

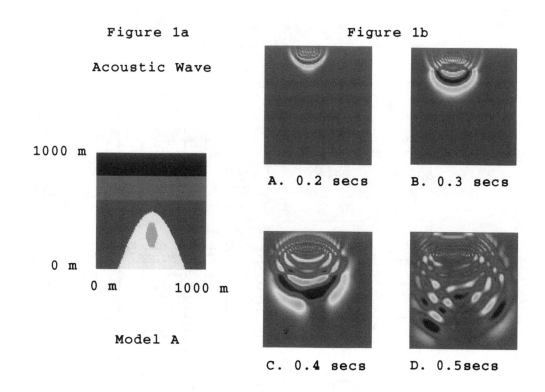

1000 m

0 m

0 m   1000 m

Model A

A. 0.2 secs   B. 0.3 secs

C. 0.4 secs   D. 0.5secs

Figure 2a

Elastic Wave

Figure 2b

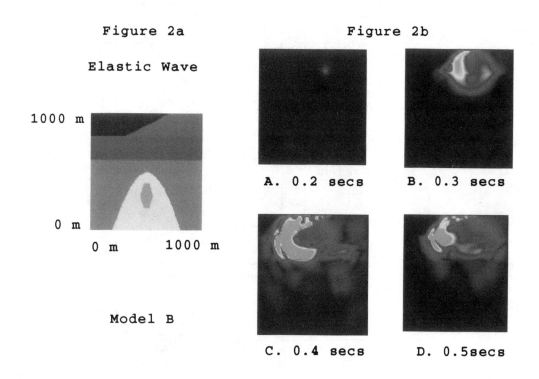

1000 m

0 m

0 m   1000 m

Model B

A. 0.2 secs   B. 0.3 secs

C. 0.4 secs   D. 0.5secs

[For color plate see page 924]

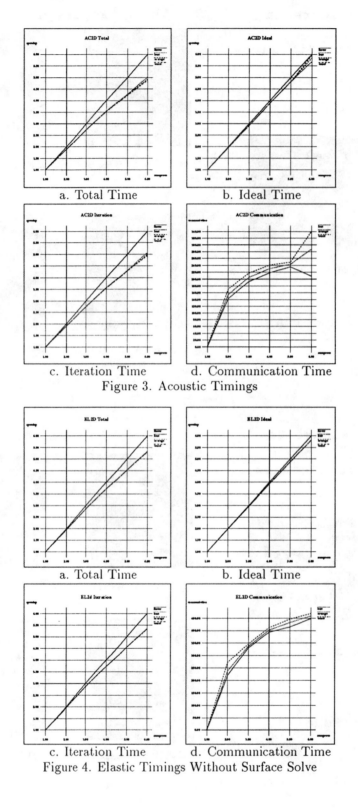

a. Total Time   b. Ideal Time

c. Iteration Time   d. Communication Time

Figure 3. Acoustic Timings

a. Total Time   b. Ideal Time

c. Iteration Time   d. Communication Time

Figure 4. Elastic Timings Without Surface Solve

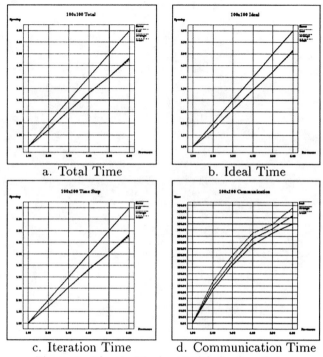

a. Total Time   b. Ideal Time

c. Iteration Time   d. Communication Time

Figure 5. Elastic Timings With Surface Solve

Session 1:
Computational Physics
Chair: Randy Christensen

Monte Carlo Simulations of Quantum Systems on Massively Parallel Supercomputers

Hong Q. Ding[†]

Concurrent Supercomputing Facilities
California Institute of Technology
Pasadena, California 91125

Abstract

A large class of quantum physics applications uses operator representations that are discrete integers by nature. This class includes magnetic properties of solids, interacting bosons modeling superfluids and Cooper pairs in superconductors, and Hubbard models for strongly correlated electrons systems. This kind of application typically uses integer data representations and the resulting algorithms are dominated entirely by integer operations. We implemented an efficient algorithm for one such application on the Intel Touchstone Delta and iPSC/860. The algorithm uses a multispin coding technique which allows significant data compactification and efficient vectorization of Monte Carlo updates. The algorithm regularly switches between two data decompositions, corresponding naturally to different Monte Carlo updating processes and observable measurements such that only nearest-neighbor communications are needed within a given decomposition. On 128 nodes of Intel Delta, this algorithm updates 183 million spins per second (compared to 21 million on CM-2 and 6.2 million on a Cray Y-MP). A systematic performance analysis shows a better than 90% efficiency in the parallel implementation.

1 Introduction

High performance computers are now increasingly used in a wide variety of applications in physics sciences. A particular application area is two-dimensional(2D) strongly correlated electronic systems[1], which has attracted enormous attention in recent years, prompted by the recent discovery of high temperature superconductivity. This area of quantum physics also includes magnetic properties of solid

crystals, interacting bosons modeling superfluids and Cooper pairs in superconductors. This class of 2D quantum many-body systems rarely admits reliable analytical treatments; good understanding of them is lacking. However, numerical simulations of these quantum systems using the advanced computer architectures has proven to be very fruitful[2]. Besides revealing qualitative features of these systems, numerical simulations in some cases provide quantitative information that can be directly compared with experimental results, leading to conclusive and specific descriptions about what is happening in these delicate materials.

These applications are characterized by operator representations of the quantum system, which are discrete integers by nature. This kind of applications typically uses integer data representations and the resulting algorithms are entirely dominated by integer operations on a computer. For these applications, vector or pipelined processors perform poorly. On the other hand, the regularity of the data and program structures makes the algorithms highly scalable and thus best suited for massively parallel architectures. In this paper, we describe one such application. We describe in detail the algorithm and its implementation on a class of distributed-memory parallel supercomputers which includes the Intel iPSC/860 and Intel Touchstone Delta, Connection Machine CM-5, nCUBE/2, Meiko Computers, etc. Unlike many other cases where existing sequential codes (often on vector computers) are re-implemented on parallel computers, the code for this problem is written from scratch and takes full advantage of the parallel architecture. We show that a multi-spin coding technique (Sec.5) is particularly effective for these systems of discrete representations. We devised a two-decomposition parallel implementation (Sec.6) that avoids complicated global communications for global Monte Carlo moves

© 1993 ACM 0-8186-4340-4/93/0011 $1.50

by dynamically switching between primary and secondary data decompositions, thus achieving higher efficiency and simpler programming structures. By using a small number of carefully chosen communications routines (the entire algorithm uses only two: exchange and broadcast), the code is easily portable to different communications systems and to different computers. A systematic performance analysis (Sec.7) is presented that indicates a high (90%) parallel efficiency. Using 128 nodes of the Intel Delta (while the rest 384 nodes of the 512-node Delta are running other applications), the algorithm updates 183 million spins per second. For comparison, a similar algorithm for a one-dimensional quantum system[3] (simpler in algorithm structure and requiring about half calculations per spin compared to our 2D algorithm) implemented on CM-2 updates 21 million spins and a highly vectorized code on Cray YMP updates 6.2 million spins. Thus this class of quantum systems is best suited for the parallel architectures. (Over 98% calculations in the algorithm are integer operations, due to the multispin coding technique.)

The extensive simulations of this algorithm for various magnetic properties of the undoped superconductors[4-7] were carried out first on the Caltech/JPL MarkIIIfp, and later on the Intel iPSC/860 and Intel Touchstone Delta. Results of these simulations resolved several outstanding issues and physical parameters are extracted from the comparison with experiment[2,4-7]. We will briefly discuss some of them in Sec.8. For more details, we refer readers to an editorial article in *Nature*[8] which gives a vivid discussion of some of our simulation results with proper perspective.

2   Physical System

Soon after the first high temperature superconductor $La_{1.85}Ba_{0.15}CuO_4$ (obtained by doping La_2CuO_4 with Ba) is discovered in 1986, several families of copper oxides containing yttrium, bismuth and thallium were discovered with critical temparetures exceeding the all-important boiling tempareture of liquid nitrigen at 77 Kelvin. The highest critical tempareture to date reaches 125 Kelvin for the "thallium 2223" material $Tl_2Ba_2Ca_2 Cu_3O_{10}$. Since these superconductors can be cooled economically by liquid nitrigen, they are expected to have a wide range of technological applications, such as power transmissions, sensitive instruments, etc.

A common feature of all these new materials is the presence of copper-oxygen planes in their crystal struc-

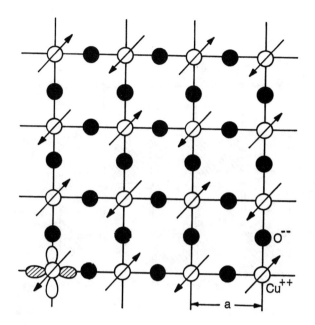

Figure 1: The Copper-Oxygen layer in high temperature superconductors. The Oxygen 2p shell are filled. There is a hole in the Cu 3d shell, leading to the Heisenberg spin coupling through superexchange.

tures. It is widely accepted that dominant electronic and magnetic properties, especially the superconductivity, are due primarily to these copper-oxygen planes (see Fig.1). At present, a great number of theoretical studies are focusing on various aspects of this two-dimensional system. A good understanding of this strongly correlated electron system represents a great chanllenge. Because of the many differences in structure and property between these new materials and the conventional (low temparature) superconduuctors, it is generally believed that a new theory is needed to explain superconductivity at these high temparetures[1].

This numerical study is focused on the magnetic properties of these materials. When the material is undoped, such as the parent compound La_2CuO_4, it exhibits strong antiferromagnetism. These magnetic properties are modeled by the quantum Heisenberg model

$$H = \sum_{\langle ij \rangle} J[S_i^x S_j^x + S_i^y S_j^y + (1 - \lambda)S_i^z S_j^z] = \sum_{\langle ij \rangle} Jh_{ij},$$
$$(1)$$

where $\langle ij \rangle$ goes over all the nearest neighbor pairs on the square lattice and S_i is the quantum spin-$\frac{1}{2}$ operator. This seemingly simple model in fact describes a quite complicated quantum system. Our goal is to simulate various properties of this model. In particu-

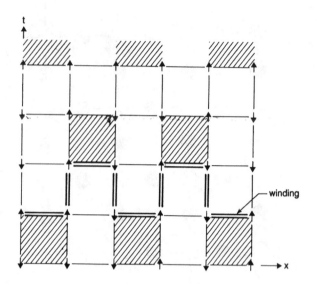

Figure 2: A slice from the 3-dimensional spin lattice. The shaded plaquettes are interacting plaquettes. Also shown is the global loop that changes the winding number.

lar, we wish to calculate some model properties which can then be directly compared to experimental data.

We mention that besides describing a variety of magnetic systems, this model also describes[9] a class of bosonic particle systems, such as

$$H = \sum_{\langle ij \rangle} [-t(\psi_i^\dagger \psi_j + \psi_i \psi_j^\dagger) + U n_i n_j]$$

after a simple transformation: the creation operator $\psi_i^\dagger \rightarrow S_i^x + i S_i^y$, and the density operator $n_i \rightarrow S_i^z + 1/2$. This interacting boson model describes the dynamics of the superfluids, (e.g., Helium film) and of the superconductors when the coherence length of the Cooper pairs are less than lattice spacing. In fact, the quantum Monte Carlo simulation method used is best described in this bosonic picture. However, to keep with our starting motivation of studying magnetic property of superconductors, we shall use the magnetic spin language throughout this paper, and comment briefly when the boson representation is appropriate.

3 Quantum Monte Carlo

In statistical theory, most of useful informations are derived from the partition function $Z = \mathrm{Tr}(e^{-H/kT})$,

where the trace is over all possible quantum states. The quantum Monte Carlo method follows a path-integral formulation. We break the partition function into m pieces so that $\Delta\tau \equiv J/mkT$ is small. One has the following identity:

$$Z = \mathrm{Tr}(e^{-\Delta\tau H} e^{-\Delta\tau H} \cdots e^{-\Delta\tau H}) =$$

$$\sum_{\{C\}} \langle C_1|e^{-\Delta\tau H}|C_2 \rangle \langle C_2|e^{-\Delta\tau H}|C_3 \rangle \cdots \langle C_m|e^{-\Delta\tau H}|C_1 \rangle$$

$$(2)$$

where we have inserted complete sets C_i of states (eigen-states of S_i^z). Now, since $\Delta\tau$ is small, we have the important Suzuki-Trotter[10] factorization:

$$e^{-(H_1+H_2+H_3+H_4)\Delta\tau} \simeq e^{-H_1\Delta\tau} e^{-H_2\Delta\tau} e^{-H_3\Delta\tau} e^{-H_4\Delta\tau},$$

$$(3)$$

where $H = H_1 + H_2 + H_3 + H_4$ is a decomposition of the Hamiltonian into four parts[4] such that each H_i contains only terms commuting among themselves. This step is crucial; it allows us to further decompose each of the $4m$ Boltzmann factors $\langle C_t|e^{-\Delta\tau H_i}|C_{t+1} \rangle$ into a product of $\frac{1}{2}N_x N_y$ factors:

$$W = \langle S_{i,t}^z S_{j,t}^z |e^{-\Delta\tau h_{ij}}| S_{i,t+1}^z S_{j,t+1}^z \rangle.$$

Labeling the four states of the spin pair as $1 = (\uparrow\uparrow), 2 = (\uparrow\downarrow), 3 = (\downarrow\uparrow), 4 = (\downarrow\downarrow)$, the Boltzmann factor connecting spin-pair state α at time slice t to the spin-pair state β at time slice $t+1$ can be written explicitly as (after a unitary transformation which changes the sign of XY parts)

$$|W_{\alpha\beta}| = \begin{vmatrix} D & 0 & 0 & 0 \\ 0 & D^{-1}cosh(2K) & D^{-1}sinh(2K) & 0 \\ 0 & D^{-1}sinh(2K) & D^{-1}cosh(2K) & 0 \\ 0 & 0 & 0 & D \end{vmatrix}$$

$$(4)$$

with $K = \Delta\tau/4 = J/4mkT$ and $D = exp[K(1-\lambda)]$. Since the matrix elements are all non-negative, they can be interpreted as transition probabilities, which allows an evaluation by Monte Carlo process. Due to the conservation of magnetization (the spin S^z component), many elements of the transfer matrix are zero. The quantum system, under this transformation, becomes a general 3-dimensional Ising spin system with plaquette (4-spin square) interactions. A slice of the lattice in the x-t plane is shown in Fig.2. This algorithm, often called World-line Monte Carlo after Hirsch et al.[11], in one-dimension has been recently described in detail[12] and implemented on Connection Machine[3]. In two dimensions, the geometry becomes quite more complicated due to increased interactions, as described in the next section.

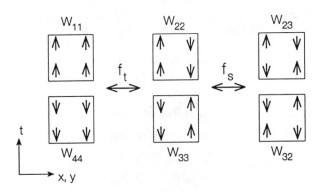

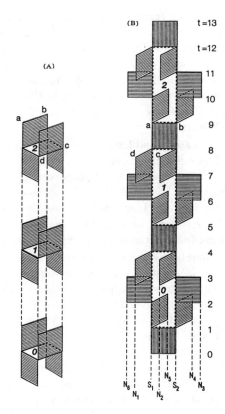

Figure 3: The six allowed 4-spin states. There are only two types of spin flips: f_t flips two spins along t-direction, while f_s flips two spins in x-y plane.

4 Monte Carlo Moves

We simulate the system using the Metropolis algorithm which for this 2-state problem, is equivalent to the Heatbath algorithm. A simple, single-spin flip violates the conservation law and its acceptance probability is zero. To avoid generating trial states with these zero transfer probabilities and thus wasting CPU time because they would never be accepted, two spins in each interacting plaquette are flipped together, as indicated in Fig.3. In this way, the conservation law is built into the Monte Carlo moves. Since each grid point on the lattice has two associated interacting plaquettes, the links between the flipped spins on a plaquette should form a closed loop. The procedure is then (1) to locate a loop C of L spins, and (2) check for each of the interacting plaquettes on the loop, if the flipping of the two spins belongs to one of the two types indicated in Fig.3. If this is so, we compute the probability that the present configuration remains unchanged:

$$P_i = \prod_{k=1}^{L} W_{C_k,C_k}^{(k)},$$

where $W_{C_k,C_k}^{(k)}$ are the diagonal elements of the transfer matrices [cf. Eq.4] along the loop C. The probability that all the spins on the loop are flipped is

$$P_f = \prod_{k=1}^{L} W_{C_k,C_{k+1}}^{(k)},$$

where $W_{C_k,C_{k+1}}^{(k)}$ are the off-diagonal elements of the transfer matrices. The Metropolis algorithm is to ac-

Figure 4: Space-like local loop that contains four spins and (b) time-like local loop that contains eight spins (spins on every grid point are not shown explicitly here). The objects in (a) and (b) can be patch together by matching the four grid points denoted as a,b,c,d. Space loops $0,1,2,\cdots$, are independent, since no interacting plaquettes connect them. Time loops $0, 2, 4,\cdots$, are independent, as are time loops $1, 3, 5,\cdots$. Independent loops are updated in a vectorized fashion.

cept the flip according to the probability

$$P = P_f/P_i. \tag{5}$$

If the flip is not accepted, we keep the initial configuration and go on to the next loop of spins.

On the $(2+1)$ dimensional lattice (the extra t-direction is introduced in the path-integral formulation, Eq.2), there exist very large number of closed loops such that flipping all the spins on the loop satisfies the conservation law. We chose a set of four elementary loops such that all other loops can be built as successive application of these elementary loops. Two of the loops are local loops. A time-like loop consists of eight spins of a rectangle extending in t-direction, bordering eight interacting plaquettes (see Fig.4). A flip is attempted only when all four spins on a vertical edge are up and all the four spins on the other edge are down (or vice versa). Either all eight spins are flipped or none of them is flipped. A space-like loop consists of four spins on a plaquette in the x-y plane (Fig.4). A flip is attempted only when all four spins are in a Néel state.

Two loops are global loops. One of these is a single straight line extending from $t = 0$ to $t = 4m$ along the it t-direction (periodic boundary condition makes it a closed loop). Either all of the $4m$ spins are flipped or none are flipped. This move changes the magnetization of the system: at finite temperature, there are always some fluctuations in the magnetization. (In the corresponding boson system, this amounts to density fluctuations in a grand canonical system.) Another global loop extends in either the x-direction or the y-direction and includes $2N_x$ spins (see Fig.2). This changes the winding number of the system, which is related to spin modulus (superfluid density in boson systems). The inclusion of global updates also speeds up the thermal relaxation (sampling rate in the phase space). In the simulations, periodic boundary conditions are imposed in all directions to preserve the translation invariance in spatial directions and to satisfy the trace requirement in the time direction.

5   Multi-spin Coding

The discrete representations of these quantum systems is naturally represented by integers. Each spin has two states, either up or down. In the boson case, each grid point is either occupied by a boson or empty.

To achieve a high level of speed and efficiency, we implemented this algorithm via a multi-spin coding technique. The idea is that a finite number of state can be most effectively represented by individual "bits" in the integers. In the present case, each spin on a grid point is a single bit, and 32 spins along the imaginary time direction are packed into an 4-byte integer. The algorithm is most efficient if the integers are completely packed, which means that the number of time slices has to be a multiple of 32 (or, alternatively, the Trotter number, m, should be an integer multiple of eight).

All the necessary checks and updates can be implemented through bitwise logical operations on integers. The same principles are applied for both local and global moves, but it is easier to illustrate them for local moves, as shown in Fig.4.

A pair of adjacent integers S_1, S_2 contains eight "time" loops. These eight loops of spins are updated in the following vectorized fashion. We first compute

$$F = S_1 \text{ XOR } S_2,$$

$$E_1 = S_1 \text{ XOR } N_1,$$

$$E_5 = S_1 \text{ XOR } N_5,$$

$$E_6 = S_1 \text{ XOR } N_6,$$

$$E_2 = S_2 \text{ XOR } N_2,$$

$$E_3 = S_2 \text{ XOR } N_3,$$

$$E_4 = S_2 \text{ XOR } N_4,$$

$$H_1 = S_1 \text{ XOR } (S_1 \text{ RIGHTSHIFT } 1),$$

where N_1, N_5, N_6 are for the determination of the three interacting plaquettes extending horizontally out of S_1, and N_2, N_3, N_4 are for those extending out of S_2. H_1 is for determining the plaquettes above and below the loops. Now we are ready to update loops $i = 0, 2, 4, 6$, since they are independent from each other. If

$$F \text{ AND } \text{MASK}(i) = \text{MASK}(i),$$

and

$$[S_1 \text{ AND } \text{MASK}(i) = 0] \text{ OR } [S_2 \text{ AND } \text{MASK}(i) = 0],$$

i.e., all four spins on S_1 are up and all four spins on S_2 are down, or vice versa, the flip of these eight spins are allowed. Here

$$\text{MASK}(0) = 0....001111,$$

$$\text{MASK}(i + 1) = \text{MASK}(i) \text{ LEFTSHIFT } 4,$$

etc. Now using the information contained in $N_1 - N_6$, we can easily determine by a few logical operations the six f_t type flips for the six horizontal interacting plaquettes (see Fig.3) and the two f_s type flips in the upper and lower plaquettes. The result is a 8-bit integer which is then used as index to find the Metropolis ratio [cf. Eq.5] in a pre-calculated lookup table. Notice that the only floating point operations in these updates are random number generations and comparisons, required for the Metropolis accept/reject test. If the trial is accepted, we flip the eight spins by

$$S_1 = S_1 \text{ XOR } \text{MASK}(i),$$

$$S_2 = S_2 \text{ XOR } \text{MASK}(i),$$

and go on to the next loop. If the trial is rejected, we simply go on to the next loop. Once the 0,2,4,6 loops are finished, we keep $F, N_1 - N_6$, recalculate only H_1, and repeat the same procedure for loops $i = 1, 3, 5, 7$.

Four adjacent integers contain eight "space" loops, which can be even more easily vectorized. They can be updated without alternating even and odd ones, since they are decoupled.

The global move in time direction is very easy to implement with this type of spin packing. We can only attempt a flip if either all $4m$ bits on this t-line are 0s or all of them are 1s. If so, we XOR this integer with four neighboring integers to get the transition probability. The same principles are used to implement the global flip in spatial directions, although the actual procedure is more complicated. It is desirable to have the simplest possible spin interaction in order to minimize the complexity of the various tests needed to determine the transition probability. For this reason, we believe that our "bond-type" decomposition is preferable due to the simplicity of spin interactions, although the spin packing could be done with any other decomposition, such as "cell-type" breakup, which leads to more complicated 8-spin interactions [13].

To summarize, the spins are compacted into integers and are updated in a vectorized fashion. A single logical operation on an integer calculates energy information for all eight time/space loops and the use of the lookup table essentially eliminates all the floating point evaluations of the transfer matrices. This multi-spin coding and vectorized update algorithm is thus very efficient.

6   Parallel Implementation

Using the multi-spin coding technique, the data is very compact and does not occupy a large memory storage. However, the simulation is computation intensive, due to the high statistics required at low temperatures when the correlations are strong. Typically order of 10^5 Monte Carlo sweeps through the lattice are necessary. This requires many processors to compute simultaneously on different domains of the physical space to speedup the calculation in a coarse-grained parallelism. The Monte Carlo nature of the calculation allows simple data decompositions[14]; each processor updates the spins in its subdomain almost independently, but pays careful attention to the interactions with spins on other nodes.

Two data decompositions are used in the parallelism (see Fig.5). In the y-decomposition, the 2D physical space is partitioned into strips (subdomains)

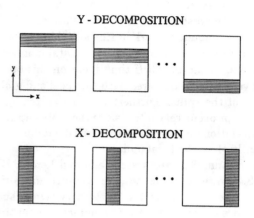

Figure 5: Two data decompositions used in the algorithm. Processor nodes are configured as a 1D ring in both decompositions.

along x-direction and each subdomain is mapped onto a node. The processor nodes in a parallel computer are configured as a 1D ring. This is the primary decomposition in which most of the simulation is carried out. During the simulation, each node updates the spins of local loops in its subdomain. This sometimes requires spins on neighbor node which are brought in with simple nearest-neighbor communications. The global loop along the time direction (magnetization fluctuation) and along the x-direction (winding number fluctuation) are entirely local and its environment is also obtained by nearest-neighbor communications. The communications are quite efficient because each call shifts $N_y \times N_t$ spins instead of just N_t spins if a 2D decomposition has been used. The communication overhead is reduced by a factor of N_y in the 1D decomposition compared with a 2D decomposition.

In the y-decomposition, the global loop that changes winding numbers along the y-direction requires a true global communication because it involves spins on all nodes. In addition, we need to compute the correlation functions and other properties that also require the same global communications along the y-direction. For these operations, we used the x-decomposition (Fig.5), where strips along y-directions are mapped onto a processor-node. The processors are still configured as a 1D ring. The switching between the y-decomposition and the x-decomposition is accomplished in a loosely synchronous pipelined fashion by shifting the data to the left node along the 1D ring and each node only picks up the corresponding portion for its subdomain (much like a matrix transpose operation on the distributed memory environment). Although the amount of work in this switching between different decompositions scales as the total number of processors, the actual CPU time spent on this operation is very small, compared with the local and global updates of the spins. Furthermore, the switching itself does not occur very often, since the global updates and correlation measurement are carried out much less frequently than the local updates.

The communications system adopted here is EXPRESS. However, due to the two-decomposition scheme, the communication pattern is significantly simplified so that only two communication routines (*exchange* and *broadcast*) are used in the entire algorithm. Because such a small number of simple, carefully chosen communication routines are used in this algorithm, the code is easily portable to other communication systems and even to different computers. In the simulation, we use a parallel version of the legged Fibonacci additive random number generator which has a period larger than 2^{127}[15].

In short, the main ideas we finally used in this parallelization are (1) rather than designing a complicated communication pattern for the global moves, we switch between different data decompositions, each of which corresponds to different global moves; and (2) use only a small number of carefully chosen communication routines.

7   Performance Analysis

This algorithm was first implemented on the Caltech/JPL MarkIIIfp parallel computer[14]. Later it was further refined and implemented on the Intel iPSC/860 and Touchstone Delta. On the 32-node MarkIIIfp, the largest problem size is 128x128 due to memory limitations (4MB/node). On the 64-node Intel iPSC/860, the largest problem we have run is 1024x1024, a factor of 64 larger. The largest problem we can run on the 512-node Intel Delta is 8192x8192, which is almost a macroscopic scale!

On 128 nodes of the Delta, switching between the primary and secondary decompositions requires 131 seconds for a quantum cluster 2048x2048 ($m = 80$). The compacted data in this case is 168MB. Thus the effective data transfer rate is 1.3MB/sec which includes pure data transmission and a simple sorting (data indexing is different in the two decompositions).

This rate is about 30% higher than that on the Intel iPSC/860 due to the specially-designed routing chip for communication in the Delta.

In this multi-spin coding implementation of the quantum simulation, the calculation is dominated by vectorized updates, which are mostly bit-wise logical operations. The entire code is written in C, and the communications are written in EXPRESS in the loosely synchronous mode. Performance of this code on the Intel Delta (and iPSC/860) is about four times faster than on the nCUBE/2, and two times faster than on MarkIIIfp on per node basis.

As a benchmark, on the Delta (128 nodes are used, the rest 384 nodes are busy doing other work), for quantum system 4096 x 4096 ($m = 24, T = 0.5J$), 183 millions of Monte Carlo steps were made on each spin per second. (An application of all possible time-like local loops visit every spin. So does each of the other local/global loops). Although a straight comparison to other implementations is not possible at present, we can compare with the published results[3] of the same algorithm in 1D case as listed below[16]:

Computers	spin/second
Intel Delta (128 node used)	183×10^6
Connection Machine CM-2 (64K)	21×10^6
Cray YMP 8/128 (one proc used)	6.2×10^6

On the Connection Machine (64K CM-2) (implemented in C/Paris) the rate is 21 million spins per second (it would be nice to see the results on the CM-5). On a Cray YMP 8/128 system (one processor is used), a highly vectorized code updates 6.2 million spins per second; this slow rate is probably due to the relative slower integer manipulations on the Cray, since in this algorithm the overwhelming portions are integer operations (see Section 5).

In Fig.6, we plotted the parallel speedup, t_1/t_M (t_i is the time for the same cluster run on i nodes), on up to 64 Intel Delta nodes for various cluster sizes. As the figure clearly illustrates, the speedup is 59.7 for the largest cluster size, which is quite close to the ideal speedup of 64. In general, the speedup (or the parallel efficiency) is higher for larger clusters, simply because the surface to volume ratio becomes smaller as cluster size increases. Evidently, this quantum simulation problem is well suited for parallel computers.

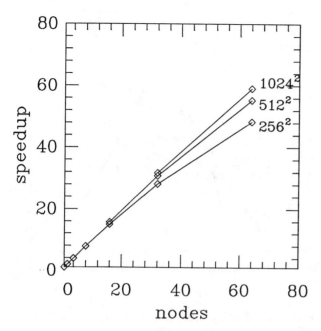

Figure 6: Speedups of the parallel algorithm for different cluster sizes.

8 Physics Results

Using this algorithm, we have carried out extensive simulations for modeling various magnetic properties of the emerging superconducting materials. (At the level of abstraction of the 2D model, only the common features due to the copper-oxygen planes are captured; the model does not distinguish between different materials yet. However, the model property should be quite close to those materials like La_2CuO_4 whose electronic/magnetic structure are quite close to pure copper-oxygen planes.) Many of the simulation results provided new understanding of magnetic characteristics of these materials and have been presented elsewhere[4-7]. Here we briefly discuss some of them. For the pure Heisenberg model $\lambda = 0$, our simulation has firmly established that the spin correlation length behaves as

$$\xi(T)/a = 0.276e^{\rho J/kT}$$

at low temperature, where a is the Cu-Cu distance and the spin stiffness constant is determined by our simulation results to be $\rho = 1.25 \pm 0.01$. Correlation length can be directly measured in neutron scattering experiments. In Fig.7, the inverse correlation length obtained in our simulations is directly compared with neutron scattering experiments. The agreement is excellent. This in turn determines another important physical parameter, the spin exchange coupling con-

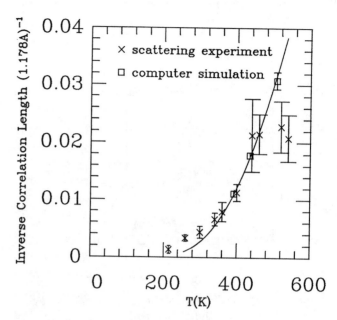

Figure 7: Inverse correlation lengths of the undoped material La_2CuO_4 measured in neutron scattering experiments as compared with our simulation results. This determines $J = 1450K$. Two experimental data points at $T \gtrsim 500K$ are not relevant for this comparison, because La_2CuO_4 undergoes a structural transition there. From Ref.4.

stant J:

$$J = 1450 \pm 30K.$$

This results agrees well with $J = 1480 \pm 70K$ obtained from Raman scattering experiments. Raman scattering probes short-distance physics and the correlation length describes the large-distance phenomenon. Thus, the agreement on J between Raman scattering and correlation length provides solid evidence that the Heisenberg model is a good theoretical model for the undoped superconductors[4,8]. The value of J obtained in our simulation is now widely quoted in the literature.

In Fig.7, at very low temperature $T \simeq 200K$, the theoretical curve deviates from the experimental curve. This is attributed to the small anisotropy $\lambda \sim 10^{-4}$ present in the real material. With this tiny in-plain XY-anisotropy our simulation results indicates the appearance of the long range order at $T_c = 210-280K$ in the undoped materials[5], as shown in the phase diagram in Fig.8. Such a long range order at this temperature range does exist experimentally (although many people consider it as the results of the very week coupling between the 2D layers), our simulation therefore provides new insight into this long range order[5].

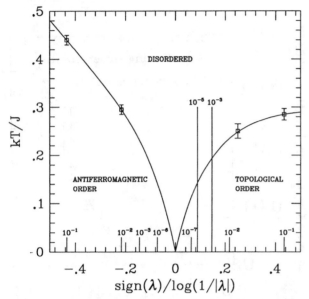

Figure 8: Phase diagram of the spin-$\frac{1}{2}$ antiferromagnet near the isotropic limit. The scale of λ is also directly indicated in the figure. The two vertical lines sandwich the experimental limits on this class of materials: $T_c = (0.14 - 0.19)J = 210 - 280K$. This agrees with experiments on a variety of materials, both hole-based La_2CuO_4, $YBa_2Cu_3O_6$, and electron-based Nd_2CuO_4, Pr_2CuO_4. From Ref.5.

In other materials, the crystal field effects and the spin-orbital coupling introduce the Ising-like anisotropy $\lambda < 0$. This situation is also shown in Fig.8, where a second-order phase transition separates the disordered phase from the antiferromagnetically ordered phase. As shown in Fig.9, the specific heat capacity diverges as the quantum cluster sizes increase, clearly indicating a second-order transition[6].

Finally, for $\lambda = 1$, the quantum model has the complete $O(2)$ symmetry and exhibits clearly the Kosterlitz-Thouless scaling behaviors (Fig.10), similar to those in classical models. In fact, our extensive simulations confirm the general universality arguments that, near the critical temperature, scaling behaviors are determined by the symmetry of the interaction. Quantum effects, although particularly strong in the spin-$\frac{1}{2}$ case, appear to be properly accounted by renormalizing some the parameters and the overall scaling behaviors remain unchanged.

9   Concluding Remarks

We have presented in detail a parallel implementation of a 2D quantum Monte Carlo algorithm. From

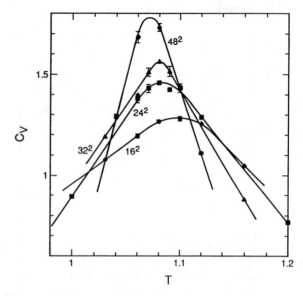

Figure 9: The specific heat varies as a function of temperature for several different cluster sizes for the Ising-like anisotropy $\lambda = -1$. This indicates a divergent behavior at the transition point. From Ref.6.

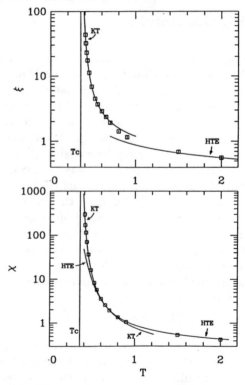

Figure 10: (a) correlation length and (b) transverse susceptibility as a function of T. The theoretical Kosterlitz-Thouless scaling curve (KT) and high temperature expansion (HTE) curve are also shown. Note the very rapid growth near the transition point T_c. From Ref.7.

the implementation and performance analysis, we demonstrated that this algorithm is particularly suited for parallel architectures. The discrete representation in this class of quantum system leads naturally to the multi-spin integer representation. The use of a lookup table for transition probabilities leaves the algorithm entirely dominated by integer operations. This character makes the algorithm perform poorly on all vector/pipelined processors (which explains why Cray also performs poorly on this algorithm). On the other hand, the regularity of this problem makes the algorithm highly scalable, as confirmed in a systematical performance analysis. For this type of application, massively parallel computers perform far better than conventional vector supercomputers.

Many of the techniques and design ideas used in this algorithm such as multi-spin coding for discrete representations, multiple data decomposition scheme to simplify the data communications, the use of minimal set of communication routines for code portability, etc., are quite general and can be applied in many other parallel supercomputer applications. For architecture and hardware designers, this application emphasizes the importance of coarse-grained parallelism which not only scales well, but also greatly simplified the programming efforts. In addition, the dominant integer processing requirements in this class of application emphasizes the need of a balanced approach to processor design: simply increasing the floating point capabilities will not improve performance on these applications.

Acknowledgments. I wish to thank Miloje Makivic for a collaboration in the early stage of this project and Geoffrey Fox for much encouragement. I thank Roy Williams and Tina Mihaly for careful proofreading of this manuscript. This work began as a project in the Caltech Concurrent Computation Program and is now supported by the Concurrent Supercomputing Consortium adminstrated through Caltech and the Caltech Concurrent Supercomputing Facility. I thank Paul Messina and Mary Maloney for their support which made the present work possible.

† Present address: Jet Propulsion Laboratory, California Institute of Technology, 169-315, Pasadena, CA 91109.

References

[1] P.W. Anderson, *Science*, **235**, 1196 (1987). P.W. Anderson and J.R. Schrieffer, *Physics Today*, **44**, 55 (June 1991).

[2] Two reviews are given by S. Chakravarty, in *High Temperature Superconductivity Proceedings, Los Alamos Symposium 1989*, ed. K.S.Bedell, et al., Addison-Wesley, Reading, MA, 1990, and by T. Barnes, Int.J.Mod.Phys.**C2**, 659 (1991).

[3] W.R. Somsky and J.E. Gubernatis, *Comput. Phys.* **6**, 178 (1992). This paper also contains the Cray YMP results obtained by H.Q.Lin.

[4] H.Q. Ding and M.S. Makivic, Phys.Rev.Lett. **64**, 1449 (1990). M.S. Makivic and H.Q. Ding, *Phys.Rev.* **B43**, 3562 (1991). H.Q. Ding, *Phys.lett.* **A159**, 355 (1991).

[5] H.Q. Ding *Phys.Rev.Lett.* **68**, 1927 (1992).

[6] H.Q. Ding, J. Phys: Condens Matter, **2**, 7979 (1990).

[7] H.Q. Ding *Phys.Rev.* **B45**, 230 (1992).

[8] "Towards Explaining Superconductivity", J. Maddox, *Nature*, **344**, 485 (1990)].

[9] E. Loh, D.J. Scalapino and P.M. Grant, Physica Script **32**, 327 (1985); Phys.Rev. B31, 4712 (1985).

[10] M. Suzuki, J. Stat. Phys. **43**, 883 (1986).

[11] J.E. Hirsch, D.J. Scalapino, R.L. Sugar, and R. Blankenbecler, Phys. Rev. B **26**, 5033 (1982).

[12] J. Tobochnik, G. Batrouni, and H. Gould, *Comput. Phys.* **6**, 673 (1992).

[13] J. D. Reger and A. P. Young, Phys. Rev. B **37**, 5978 (1988). Y. Okabe and M. Kikuchi, J. Phys. Soc. Jpn **57**, 4351 (1988). M. Gross, E. Sanchez-Velasco, and E. Siggia, Phys. Rev. B **39**, 2484 (1989).

[14] G.C. Fox et al., "Solving Problems on Concurrent Processors", Prentice Hall, Englewood Cliffs, New Jersey (1988).

[15] H.Q. Ding, Caltech Report C3P-629, unpublished.

[16] Here we have not taken into account the fact that due to the increased number of interactions in the 2D case, the cost per site is roughly doubled in 2D as compared with 1D.

The Quantum Structure of Matter Grand Challenge Project: Large-scale 3-D Solutions in Relativistic Quantum Dynamics

J. C. Wells[1,2], V. E. Oberacker[1,2],
A. S. Umar[1,2], C. Bottcher[1], M. R. Strayer[1]

[1] Physics Division,
Oak Ridge National Laboratory,
Oak Ridge, TN 37831-6373; and
[2] Department of Physics & Astronomy,
Vanderbilt University, Nashville, TN 37235

J. Drake and R. Flanery

Engineering Physics &
Mathematics Division,
Oak Ridge National Laboratory,
Oak Ridge, TN 37831

Abstract

We describe the numerical methods used to solve the time-dependent Dirac equation on a three-dimensional Cartesian lattice. Efficient algorithms are required for computationally intensive studies of nonperturbative relativistic quantum dynamics. Discretization is achieved through the lattice basis-spline collocation method, in which quantum-state vectors and coordinate-space operators are expressed in terms of basis-spline functions on a spatial lattice. All numerical procedures reduce to a series of matrix-vector operations which we perform on the Intel iPSC/860 hypercube, making full use of parallelism. We discuss our solutions to the problems of limited node memory and node-to-node communication overhead inherent in using distributed-memory, multiple-instruction, multiple-data stream parallel computers.

1 Introduction

In this paper, we focus on the time-dependent Dirac equation in three space dimensions and its lattice representation on a distributed-memory hypercube multicomputer. Over the past several years, we have developed a new approach to strong-field relativistic quantum dynamics which combines advanced techniques for solving boundary-value differential equations with supercomputer technology.[1] The Dirac equation is one of the most fundamental equations of nature: it is the relativistic analogue of the Schrödinger equation and describes the quantum dynamics of fermions, i.e. spin-1/2 elementary particles such as leptons and quarks. The lepton family consists of three generations: the well-known electron and its associated neutrino, the muon and muon-neutrino, and the tau-lepton and tau-neutrino. Similarly, the quarks come in three different generations: up/down, charmed/strange, and top/bottom. In the following, we will consider the dynamics of leptons only; however, we believe that our computational methodologies will also have application to the quark sector.

1.1 Physics background

During the collision of highly charged heavy ions at velocities near the speed of light, extremely large time-dependent electromagnetic fields are produced which lead to a variety of effects. These electromagnetic fields are up to 10 billion times stronger than today's strongest laser fields. One of the most interesting effects of these fields is the sparking of the vacuum, i.e. production of matter-antimatter pairs from empty space as the heavy ions pass near each other. In particular, at Oak Ridge National Lab (ORNL), we have studied the vacuum production of lepton pairs, i.e. electrons, muons, and tauons, as well as other exotic particles. Collisions such as these are currently performed at experimental facilities around the world such as Brookhaven National Laboratory on Long Island, and CERN, the European Center for Nuclear Research, in Geneva, Switzerland. During the last nine years, much study has been devoted to the problem of vacuum production of lepton-pairs in anticipation of new experimental opportunities at the Relativistic Heavy-Ion Collider (RHIC), currently under construction at Brookhaven. This facility will provide colliding beams of ions as heavy as gold with all of the ion's atomic electrons removed, fully exposing the large charge of the atomic nucleus.

Lepton-pair production from nuclear processes has been widely discussed as a possible signal for the formation of a quark-gluon plasma phase of matter, which is thought to have existed in the initial phases of the Big Bang. The recreation of this phase of matter in the laboratory is the primary goal of the RHIC project. Electromagnetic electron-pair production from the vacuum by highly stripped heavy ions in relativistic motion is the dominant background process for these signatures. Furthermore, an accurate description of electromagnetic electron-pair production is important for both the design of experimental detectors for RHIC and the performance of the colliding-beam accelerator. In particular, electron and muon pair production, with subsequent atomic capture of the negatively charged lepton, changes the charge state of a participant heavy ion, leading to a decrease in the beam lifetime of the collider [3]. In addition to these practical matters, lepton-pair production is of interest because it allows physicists to test quantum electrodynamics – the fundamental theory of the interaction of light with the subatomic world – in a new energy regime.

Traditionally, processes such as lepton-pair production have been studied using perturbation theory, which is extremely successful in predicting phenomena associated with weak fields. However, this approach fails to describe the physics of the most intense collisions. In order to understand these non-perturbative effects for the important electron-capture problem, we explicitly solve the time-dependent Dirac equation coupled to the strong, time-dependent external fields produced by the heavy ions.

Another application of the lattice Dirac equation is a study of the fission dynamics of actinide nuclei. In this case, muons are captured by actinides and form excited muonic atoms. By nonradiative transitions (inverse internal conversion), sufficient atomic excitation energy is transferred to the nucleus to give a high probability that the nucleus will fission. Through the dynamics of a muon in the presence of the fissioning nucleus one expects to gain a deeper understanding of the energy-dissipation mechanism in large-amplitude nuclear collective motion.[4]

1.2 Dirac equation

In discussing the solution of the Dirac equation, we use natural units, i.e. $\hbar = c = m = 1$. This implies that energies are measured in units of the lepton rest mass, mc^2, and that our length and time units are the lepton Compton wavelength $\lambda_c = \hbar/m_c$ and

Compton time $\tau_c = \lambda_c/c$, respectively. We solve the time-dependent Dirac equation in a reference frame in which one nuclei, henceforth referred to as the target, is at rest. The target nucleus and the lepton interact via the static Coulomb field, A_T^0. The only time-dependent interaction, $(\vec{A}_P(t), A_P^0(t))$, arises from the classical motion of the projectile. Thus, it is natural to split the Dirac Hamiltonian into static and time-dependent parts. Accordingly, we write the Dirac equation for a lepton described by a spinor $\phi(\vec{r}, t)$ coupled to an external, time-dependent electromagnetic field as

$$[H_S + H_P(t)]\phi(\vec{r}, t) = i\frac{\partial}{\partial t}\phi(\vec{r}, t), \qquad (1)$$

where the static Hamiltonian, H_S, which describes a stationary lepton in the presence of the strong, external Coulomb field of the target nucleus, is given by

$$H_S = -i\vec{\alpha} \cdot \nabla + \beta - eA_T^0, \qquad (2)$$

and the time-dependent interaction of the lepton with the projectile is

$$H_P(t) = e\vec{\alpha} \cdot \vec{A}_P(t) - eA_P^0(t), \qquad (3)$$

where α_x, α_y, α_z, and β are the 4×4 Dirac spin matrices. The stationary states of the system, i.e. the eigenstates of the static Hamiltonian H_S in Eq. (2), are defined

$$H_S\chi_i(\vec{r}) = E_i\chi_i(\vec{r}), \qquad (4)$$

which are also proper ingoing and outgoing states for asymptotic times $|t| \to \infty$, where the interaction $H_P(t)$ is zero.

2 Numerical implementation

We solve the time-dependent Dirac equation using a lattice approach to obtain a discrete representation of all Dirac spinors and coordinate-space operators on a three-dimensional Cartesian mesh. We implement our lattice solution using the basis-spline collocation method, which is discussed in detail in Refs. [1, 5], and briefly summarized in Section 2.1. We limit this discussion to the special case of cubic lattices with uniform spacing in all three directions and periodic boundary conditions. However, the basis-spline collocation method is equally well suited for nonuniform lattice spacings and fixed-boundary conditions [1]. Both the applications previously introduced require the solution of the lowest-energy static bound state and subsequent evolution of this state in time. We describe the algorithms used for these tasks in Sections 2.2 and 2.3, respectively.

2.1 Lattice basis-spline collocation

Splines of order M are functions $S^M(x)$ of a single, real variable belonging to the class $\mathcal{C}^{(M-2)}$ with continuous $(M-2)$th derivatives. These functions are piecewise continuous, as they are constructed from continuous polynomials of $(M-1)$th order joined at points in an ordered set $\{x_i'\}$ called knots. Basis-splines are the subset of the spline functions with minimal support in that they are zero outside the range of $M+1$ consecutive knots $x_i', \ldots, x_{i+M}'$, and non-negative otherwise. We label these functions with the index of their first knot from the left as $B_i^M(x)$.

Consider a region of space with boundaries at $x_{\min}$ and $x_{\max}$ containing $N+1$ knots, including the knots on the boundaries. For a set of Mth-order basis-splines to be complete, M of the functions must be nonzero on each knot interval $[x_i', x_{i+1}']$ within the physical region. For this to occur, $M-1$ basis-splines must extend outside each boundary. Therefore, to construct a complete set of basis-splines requires $N+M+1$ functions naturally numbered as $B_1^M(x), \ldots, B_{N+M-1}^M(x)$.

For purposes of illustration, we seek to approximate a continuous function $f(x)$, defined in the interval $[x_{\min}', x_{\max}']$, which is the solution of the differential equation

$$\mathcal{O}f(x) = 0 , \qquad (5)$$

subject to periodic boundary conditions, where $\mathcal{O}$ is a coordinate-space differential operator. We introduce an approximate solution f^a in terms of the complete set of basis-spline functions $\{B_i^M(x)\}$ which is required to satisfy periodic boundary conditions exactly, i.e. $f^a(x_0) = f^a(x_0 + L)$. We do this in two steps: first we form a closed space by requiring $x_{\min} = x_{\max}$, and then we wrap the last $M-1$ splines in the basis set, which extend beyond the upper physical boundary, so that they enter the space from the lower boundary [5]. With this construction, $M-1$ basis-spline functions are redundantly labeled [5], resulting in the following expansion for f^a

$$f^a(x) = \sum_{i=1}^{N} B_i^M(x) c^i , \qquad (6)$$

so that $R(x) \equiv \mathcal{O}f^a(x)$, where the quantities $\{c^i\}$ denote the expansion coefficients, and $R(x)$ denotes the residual in the interior of the region.

To obtain a set of equations for the expansion coefficients $\{c^i\}$, we apply the collocation method in which inner products of the residual weighted with Dirac-delta functions are required to be zero, where the set $\{x_\alpha\}$ contains the collocation points. Using Eqs. (6), the trivial integrals of the weighted residual are evaluated to obtain

$$R(x_\alpha) = \sum_{i=1}^{N} [\mathcal{O}B]_{\alpha i} c^i = 0 , \qquad (7)$$

where $[\mathcal{O}B_i^M(x)]$ is the function resulting from the operation of $\mathcal{O}$ on the basis-spline function $B_i^M(x)$, and $[\mathcal{O}B]_{\alpha i} \equiv [\mathcal{O}B_i^M(x_\alpha)]$. In obtaining Eq. (7), we approximate the differential equation Eq. (5) for the function $f(x)$ by a set of linear equations for the expansion coefficients. This is done in a manner so that the coefficients require the residual $R(x)$ to be zero at the collocation points with the basis-splines providing an accurate interpolation to other values of x.

The solution of the linear system (Eq. (7)) for the expansion coefficients c^i provides, upon substitution into Eq. (6), the solution at all values of x within the boundaries. However, the essence of the lattice method is to eliminate the expansion coefficients c^i from the calculation in favor of a representation of the functions only on the collocation points. To implement this transformation, we create a linear system of equations by evaluating Eq. (6) at the collocation points x_α, which we invert to isolate the expansion coefficients, i.e.

$$c^i = \sum_{\alpha=1}^{N} B^{i\alpha} f_\alpha^a , \qquad (8)$$

where $B^{i\alpha} \equiv [B^{-1}]_{i\alpha}$. Using Eq. (8) to eliminate the expansion coefficients from the linear system in Eq. (7), one obtains

$$\sum_{i=1}^{N} [\mathcal{O}B]_{\alpha i} c^i \equiv \sum_{\beta=1}^{N} O_\alpha^\beta f_\beta^a = 0 , \qquad (9)$$

where we define the collocation-space or lattice representation of the operator $\mathcal{O}$ as

$$O_\alpha^\beta \equiv \sum_{i=1}^{N} [\mathcal{O}B]_{\alpha i} B^{i\beta} . \qquad (10)$$

The most important applications of Eq. (10) are to local functions of the coordinates, and to spatial differential operators. Local operators such as potentials simply become diagonal matrices of their values at the collocation points, i.e. $V(x) \rightarrow V_\alpha$. Also, for example, the lattice representation of the first-derivative operator in the basis-spline collocation method is

$$D_\alpha^\beta \equiv \sum_{i=1}^{N} B_{\alpha i}' B^{i\beta} , \qquad (11)$$

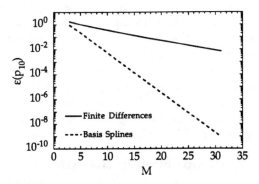

Figure 1: Errors in basis-spline and finite-difference representations of a single linear-momentum eigenvalue as a function of the order of the representation in a periodic space. Discrete values are shown as lines to guide the reader's eye.

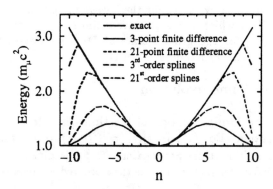

Figure 2: Depicted are the positive branches of the energy spectra for basis-spline and finite-difference representations of the free Dirac equation in one dimension.

where $B'_{\alpha i} \equiv \frac{dB_i^M(x)}{dx}|_{x=x_\alpha}$. In Fig. (1), we demonstrate the accuracy of the basis-spline collocation method, as compared to traditional finite-difference schemes, by computing the error in lattice representations of a single eigenvalue of the linear-momentum operator $\hat{p} \equiv -i(d/dx)$. Figure 2 demonstrates that the use of high-order spline representations of the momentum operator avoids the notorious energy-spectrum doubling problem for lattice representations of the Dirac equation [5].

We generalize the above procedure to functions in three-dimensional space by expanding in terms of products of basis-spline functions, i.e. $B_i^M(x)B_j^M(y)B_k^M(z)$. For example, using Eq. (10), consider the collocation-lattice representation of the gradient operator in Cartesian coordinates

$$\vec{D}_{\alpha\beta\gamma}^{\mu\nu\xi} = \hat{e}_1 D_\alpha^\mu \delta_\beta^\nu \delta_\gamma^\xi + \hat{e}_2 D_\beta^\nu \delta_\alpha^\mu \delta_\gamma^\xi + \hat{e}_3 D_\gamma^\xi \delta_\alpha^\mu \delta_\beta^\nu , \quad (12)$$

where and $\hat{e}_j$ is a unit vector in the jth coordinate direction. In matrix notation, we denote Eq. (12) as

$$\vec{D} = \hat{e}_1 \mathbf{D}_1 + \hat{e}_2 \mathbf{D}_2 + \hat{e}_3 \mathbf{D}_3 , \quad (13)$$

with the obvious definitions of the matrices $\mathbf{D}_1$, $\mathbf{D}_2$, and $\mathbf{D}_3$. Using Eq. (13), the lattice representation of the static Hamiltonian, Eq. (4), may be written

$$\mathbf{H}_S = -i\vec{\alpha} \cdot \vec{\mathbf{D}} + \beta - e\mathbf{A}_T^0 . \quad (14)$$

In summary, the collocation points define the lattice on which the calculations are performed; neither the splines nor the knots appear explicitly again once the lattice representation of the operators has been obtained at the beginning of the calculation. We have reduced the partial differential equation (Eq. (4)) to a set of matrix equations which may be solved using iterative techniques. As a consequence of eliminating

the expansion coefficients from the theory, $\mathbf{H}_S$ has a blocked sparse representation which is self-adjoint for periodic boundary conditions and uniform meshes.

2.2 Lowest-energy bound state

The complete eigensolution of $\mathbf{H}_S$, providing its full spectrum of stationary states, currently approaches the state-of-the-art in computational capabilities due to the size of $\mathbf{H}_S$, which is equivalent to a rank $8N^3$ real matrix. We believe convergent calculations will be achieved for $N \approx 100$, based on the length and momentum scales involved, and experience with one-dimensional calculations. For this reason, we compute the lowest energy bound state (1s) needed as the initial state for our time-dependent problems by a partial eigensolution of $\mathbf{H}_S$.

Standard methods for partial eigensolution of large matrices, which are designed to converge to the lowest energy eigenstate of the spectrum, are not directly applicable for computing the 1s state of $\mathbf{H}_S$ because its spectrum extends to negative energies. The analytic operator H_S has positive and negative continua, $E > mc^2$ and $E < mc^2$, as well as bound states $|E| < mc^2$; the spectrum of $\mathbf{H}_S$ has the same branches though all the eigenvalues are discrete. The 1s state has been computed using a damped relaxation method [2]. This algorithm is constructed to remove the high-frequency components from the residual, and does not depend on the spectrum of $\mathbf{H}_S$ being bounded from below.

For larger lattice sizes discussed in this paper, we have developed a more efficient iterative Lanczos algorithm to compute the initial state [2]. The Lanczos algorithm proves attractive for our purposes as the memory requirements are relatively small and the method approximates extremal eigenvalues in the spectrum very well. Since convergence is most rapid for extremal eigenvalues, we solve for the lowest energy eigenstate of $H_S{}^2$, which has a positive-definite spectrum. By solving for the ground state of $H_S{}^2$, we obtain the lowest-energy bound state of H_S.

2.3 Time evolution

The formal solution of the time-dependent Dirac equation (Eq. (1)) is $\phi_j(t) = \hat{U}(t, t_0)\phi_j(t_0)$, where the unitary time propagator $\hat{U}(t, t_0)$ is given in the Schrödinger picture by the time-ordered exponential

$$\hat{U}(t, t_0) = \text{Texp}\left(-i \int_{t_0}^{t} dt' \left[H_S + H_P(t')\right]\right) . \quad (15)$$

We discretize time in the sense that the electromagnetic interactions are taken as constant in successive small intervals of possibly varying size Δt_ℓ, i.e. $t_{\ell+1} = t_\ell + \Delta t_{\ell+1}$, $\ell = 0, 1, \ldots, L$, and express the evolution operator in successive factors $\hat{U}(t, t_0) = \hat{U}(t, t_{L-1}), \ldots, \hat{U}(t_1, t_0)$.

A number of different methods have been used to approximate the time-evolution operator

$$\hat{U}(t_{\ell+1}, t_\ell) = \exp\left(-i\left[H_S + H_P(t_{\ell+1})\right]\Delta t_{\ell+1}\right) , \quad (16)$$

particularly in studies of the time-dependent Hartree-Fock method applied to atomic and nuclear collisions. The choice of a method usually depends on the dimensionality and structure of the Hamiltonian matrix. Several methods which work well in one- and two-dimensional problems are impractical for unrestricted three-dimensional problems because they require the inversion of part or all of the Hamiltonian matrix. In our three-dimensional solution of the Dirac equation, the exponential operator, Eq. (16), is implemented as a finite-number of terms of its Taylor series expansion.

In conclusion, all of the numerical procedures discussed for implementing our lattice methods reduce to a series of matrix-vector operations which can be executed with high efficiency on vector or parallel supercomputers without explicitly storing the matrix in memory.

3 Hypercube implementation

The iPSC/860 at ORNL is a distributed-memory, multiple-instruction, multiple-data-stream multicomputer containing 128 processors with 8 MBytes of memory per processor connected via a hypercube topology. The details of our implementation of the lattice representation of the Dirac equation on this computer are discussed in detail in Ref. [2] and briefly discribed here. As with many parallel implementations, we face the problems of limited memory per node and the optimization of the algorithm to minimize the communication between nodes. We discuss these issues for our implementation of the Dirac equation in Sections 3.1 and 3.2. Section 3.3 contains a brief analysis of the floating-point performance of the i860 processor.

3.1 Decomposition of the lattice

As discussed in Section 3, Dirac spinors are represented on a three-dimensional Cartesian lattice in our numerical solution of the Dirac equation

$$\phi(x, y, z) \longrightarrow \begin{pmatrix} \phi_{\alpha,\beta,\gamma}^{(1)} \\ \phi_{\alpha,\beta,\gamma}^{(2)} \\ \phi_{\alpha,\beta,\gamma}^{(3)} \\ \phi_{\alpha,\beta,\gamma}^{(4)} \end{pmatrix} , \quad (17)$$

where x_α, y_β, and z_γ denote the collocation lattice points in the x, y, and z directions, respectively. Indices in parentheses denote the Dirac spinor component. In the following, we denote the number of lattice points in the three Cartesian directions by N_x, N_y, and N_z.

We choose to parallelize the time-dependent Dirac equation by data decomposition. In practice, we partition the y and z dimensions of the lattice into subblocks while maintaining the full x dimension on each node. These subblocks are distributed onto the processors using a two-dimensional Gray-lattice binary identification scheme.[2]

To maximize the occurrence of nearest-neighbor communication, the number of lattice points in the y and z directions are chosen to be powers of two. If the number of allocated nodes, p, is an exact square, we allocate $p_z = \sqrt{p}$ and $p_y = \sqrt{p}$ nodes in y and z directions, respectively. This results in a square Gray lattice. For intermediate powers of two, the partition is performed by $p_z = \sqrt{2p}$, $p_y = \sqrt{p/2}$, thus resulting in a rectangular Gray lattice. We determine the number of lattice points kept on each node by $m_y = N_y/p_y$, and $m_z = N_z/p_z$. Thus, all local arrays have a spatial dimension of $N_x m_y m_z$ on each node.

The lattice subblock maintained on a particular node is established using the row and column indices of that node as obtained from the Gray lattice. For y_β and z_γ, the indices β and γ are offset by

$$1 + m_y(i_c - 1) \leq \quad \beta \quad \leq m_y + m_y(i_c - 1)$$
$$1 + m_z(i_r - 1) \leq \quad \gamma \quad \leq m_z + m_z(i_r - 1) , \quad (18)$$

where $1 \leq i_c \leq p_y$ and $1 \leq i_r \leq p_z$ denote the column and row location of the node in the Gray lattice.

3.2 Ring algorithm

All of our iterative algorithms for the solution of the Dirac equation make use of the operation of the Dirac Hamiltonian matrix multiplying a Dirac spinor, $\phi' = (\mathbf{H}_S + \mathbf{H}_P(t))\phi$. Furthermore, most of the computational effort needed is required in computing this generalized matrix-vector product. In our lattice representation, the action of the Hamiltonian on a spinor is given schematically in Eq. (19). Using Cartesian coordinates, this product naturally decomposes into four parts, one for each coordinate direction (x, y, z), and a diagonal part. This separability makes it easy to define this product implicitly in a storage-efficient way. The explicit Hamiltonian matrix is never created in memory, reducing our memory requirements from order N^6 to order N^3.

The Dirac Hamiltonian matrix contains local potential terms, which are diagonal matrices, and nonlocal derivative terms, which are dense matrices. Performing matrix-vector multiplications with the nonlocal summations in the y and z dimensions requires node-to-node communication as these dimensions of the lattice are distributed across the processors. These terms which require communication are shown in brackets in Eq. (19),

$$
\begin{aligned}
\left(\phi^{(s)}\right)'_{\alpha,\beta,\gamma} = \\
- \ i \sum_{\alpha'=1}^{n_x} D_\alpha^{\alpha'} \sum_{s'=1}^{4} \alpha_x^{(ss')} \phi_{\alpha',\beta,\gamma}^{(s')} \\
- \ \sum_{i_c=1}^{p_y-1} \left[i \sum_{\beta'=1+m_y(i_c-1)}^{m_y+m_y(i_c-1)} D_\beta^{\beta'} \sum_{s'=1}^{4} \alpha_y^{(ss')} \phi_{\alpha,\beta',\gamma}^{(s')} \right] \\
- \ \sum_{i_r=1}^{p_z-1} \left[i \sum_{\gamma'=1+m_z(i_r-1)}^{m_z+m_z(i_r-1)} D_\gamma^{\gamma'} \sum_{s'=1}^{4} \alpha_z^{(ss')} \phi_{\alpha,\beta,\gamma'}^{(s')} \right] \\
+ \ eA_x(i,j,k) \sum_{s'=1}^{4} \alpha_x^{(ss')} \phi_{\alpha,\beta,\gamma}^{(s')} \\
+ \ eA_y(i,j,k) \sum_{s'=1}^{4} \alpha_y^{(ss')} \phi_{\alpha,\beta,\gamma}^{(s')} \\
+ \ eA_z(i,j,k) \sum_{s'=1}^{4} \alpha_z^{(ss')} \phi_{\alpha,\beta,\gamma}^{(s')} \\
+ \ \sum_{s'=1}^{4} \left([\beta]^{(ss')} - eA^0(i,j,k)\delta_{ss'} \right) \phi_{\alpha,\beta,\gamma}^{(s')} \ . \quad (19)
\end{aligned}
$$

In the execution of the y and z nonlocal sums in Eq. (19), we use a ring algorithm, in which each sub-block of the Dirac spinor visits each node once to perform the nonlocal matrix-vector operations economically [6]. This is achieved by having loops over the number of y and z nodes performed on each node as shown in lines 3 and 4 of Eq. (19). All the derivative matrices are stored in full on each node.

3.3 Computational kernel

The inner loops of Eq. (19) may be written as daxpy operation, i.e. $\mathbf{y} = a\mathbf{x} + \mathbf{y}$, where $\mathbf{x}$ and $\mathbf{y}$ are vectors and a is a scalar. To optimize the utilization of the high-performance features of the i860 processor, such as dual-instruction, pipeline, and quad-load modes, we have written an implementation of the daxpy in assembler language [2]. Figure 3 shows the performance results for the daxpy on the i860 for our assembler language routine. The vector length is measured in 64-bit words. The execution rate shown is obtained using timing tests that make 10^5 successive calls of the basic routine, using a stride of 1, and using the same argument list for each call. We see that the real performance of the daxpy saturates at about 25 Mflops. Because of memory constraints on the iPSC/860 hypercube, we currently realize modest vector lengths of 8 to 64 words in our solution of the Dirac equation. The performance of the daxpy over this range varies significantly due to pipelining.

3.4 Scaling model

In discussing the performance of our application, we will consider only the matrix-vector product discribed in Eq. (19), as this operation consumes more than 95% of the CPU time needed in solving the time-dependent Dirac equation. We will develop a simple

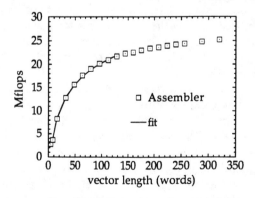

Figure 3: Execution rates as a function of vector length for the daxpy operation on the Intel i860.

scaling model of Eq. (19) for the time needed for useful calculation and internode communication in terms of the number of lattice points, the number of nodes, and the particular performance characteristics of the iPSC/860.

To execute Eq. (19) once, the total predicted time per node needed to perform floating-point operations (T_{calc}) is the number of floating-point operations required, multiplied by the time $t_{\mathrm{flop}}(N)$ required to perform a single 64-bit floating-point operation within a vector of length N words. Assuming that the lattice has an equal number of points in the three coordinate directions, $N_x = N_y = N_z = N$, the estimated calculation time for Eq. (19) is

$$T_{\mathrm{calc}} = (48N + 448)\frac{N^3}{p}t_{\mathrm{flop}}(N) . \qquad (20)$$

The dependence of $t_{\mathrm{flop}}(N)$ on N is caused by the pipelined floating-point units of the i860 processor. From the performance of the assembler-coded daxpy operation shown in Fig. 3, we determine that $t_{\mathrm{flop}}(N)$ varies with N as the inverse of a logarithmic function

$$t_{\mathrm{flop}}(N) \approx \frac{1}{(15.1\log(N) - 9.9) \times 10^6} \text{ seconds} \qquad (21)$$

over N ranging from 8 to 128.

Empirically, the communication time for a one-hop node-to-node message is a linear function of the size of the message [2]. In performing the nonlocal summations in Eq. (19), we are required to pass $p_y + p_z$ messages of length $8N^3/p$ 64-bit words. Passing these subblocks of the Dirac spinor around the two-dimensional Gray lattice ideally consumes the time

$$T_{\mathrm{pass}} = (p_y + p_z)\left(8\frac{N^3}{p}t_{\mathrm{comm}} + t_{\mathrm{start}}\right) , \qquad (22)$$

where t_{comm} is the typical time needed to actually transmit a single 64-bit word of data between two nodes, and t_{start} is the startup time for a single communication request. Typical times for the iPSC/860 are $t_{\mathrm{comm}} = 3.2 \times 10^{-6}$ sec, and $t_{\mathrm{start}} = 1.36 \times 10^{-4}$ sec [2].

Other overheads associated with communication add to the total communication time and are difficult to quantify. For example, since the nonlocal operations of Eq. (19) are dominated by communication, as we shall see in Section 5, a node must occasionally pause from performing useful computation until it receives the next subblock of the Dirac spinor. This waiting leads to additional delays caused by loss of synchronization between the nodes during message

Table 1: Presented are execution times in seconds for 2004 iterations of Eq. (19) for $p = 1$ and $p = N$ processors using various lattice sizes. Extrapolated values are denoted by an asterisk. Speedup and parallel efficiency are computed using these values.

N	$T(p = N)$	$T(p = 1)$	$S(p = N)$	$\epsilon(p = N)$
8	48.4	90.5	1.9	0.24
12	-	257.4	-	-
16	239.5	718.5	3.0	0.19
20	-	1580.2	-	-
32	1269.0	6375.9*	5.0	0.16
64	6421.0	55816.8*	8.7	0.14

passing. We denote these overheads in useful computation as T_{ohead}, and include this in our overall estimate of the communication time needed to perform Eq. (19)

$$T_{\mathrm{comm}} = (p_y + p_z)\left[8\frac{N^3}{p}t_{\mathrm{comm}} + t_{\mathrm{start}}\right] + T_{\mathrm{ohead}} . \qquad (23)$$

We will adjust T_{ohead} to fit the measured communication time.

4   Timing results

Table 1 presents the time in seconds consumed by 2004 iterations of Eq. (19) on the iPSC/860 for lattice sizes of N^3, where $N = 8$, 16, 32, and 64 using one and $p = N$ nodes, respectively, and the corresponding values of the speedup and parallel efficiency. The total execution time for Eq. (19) on one i860 processor, which is necessary for computing the speedup and the efficiency, cannot be measured directly for our application for $N > 20$ because of memory constraints. However, we obtain estimates for Eq. (19) for lattice sizes $N = 32$ and 64 by extrapolation using a power law fit to the measured dependence on problem sizes for $N = 8$, 12, 16, and 20.

To distinguish accurately the time spent in communication from the time spent performing useful calculations in a realistic parallel algorithm such as Eq. (19) is a difficult task. Since we are only interested in understanding, in general terms, the balance between communication and computation in Eq. (19), we will use a simple, indirect approach to obtain communication and calculation times. Our method is based on the fact that node-to-node communication occurs only in the nonlocal summations in the y and z dimensions, namely, lines 3 and 4 of Eq. (19). Also, if $N_x = N_y = N_z = N$, each of the three nonlocal

Table 2: Execution times in seconds for 2004 operations with Eq. (19) on a lattice with N^3 points using an Intel iPSC/860 hypercube with $p = N$ nodes.

N	T_{xprd}	T_{yprd}	T_{zprd}	T_{calc}	T_{comm}	f_c
8	6.1	10.9	23.9	25.6	22.6	0.88
16	22.3	102.9	96.1	84.2	154.5	1.84
32	97.7	422.0	702.4	349.6	929.0	2.66
64	479.7	3006	2963	1659	5010	3.02

operations performs the same amount of useful work. We give these x, y, and z dimensional summations the names xprd, yprd, zprd, respectively, and the full operation of Eq. (19) is named hdprd. We attribute the difference in time needed to execute xprd and yprd, or xprd and zprd to node-to-node communication, and, thus, estimate this time as

$$T_{\mathrm{comm}} \equiv T_{\mathrm{yprd}} + T_{\mathrm{zprd}} - 2T_{\mathrm{xprd}} , \qquad (24)$$

where T_{xprd} is the time spent in xprd, and so on. To obtain our estimate of the time T_{hdprd} spent performing useful calculations in Eq. (19), we simply subtract T_{comm} from the total time needed to compute Eq. (19),

$$T_{\mathrm{calc}} = T_{\mathrm{hdprd}} - T_{\mathrm{comm}} . \qquad (25)$$

Execution times for xprd, yprd, and zprd are presented in Table 2 for 2004 iterations of Eq. (19). Calculation and communication times are determined using Eqs. (24) and (25) and are also presented in Table 2 along with the fractional communication overhead, $f_c = T_{\mathrm{comm}}/T_{\mathrm{calc}}$. In order to perform the larger size calculations presented here, we are constrained by memory to increase the number of nodes used as the lattice size increases. We choose to increase the number of nodes in such a way that $p = N$.

We observe good agreement between our model for the calculation time and the measured result. The overhead T_{ohead} is fit by a power law so that Eq. (23) reproduces the measured communication time. The predicted fractional communication overhead obtained using Eqs. (20) and (23), and the measured values of this quantity listed in Table 2 are compared in Fig. 4. Notice that the predicted and measured values for this quantity agree well throughout the range of problem sizes, $8 \leq N \leq 64$, and that the communication overhead increases rapidly up to $N = 64$. This initial increase in overhead with problem size at first seems counterintuitive, but is explained by pipelining. Increasing floating-point performance with problem size causes the fractional communication overhead to initially increase.

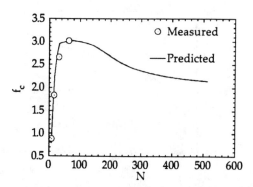

Figure 4: Plotted is the fractional communication overhead f_c as a function of the lattice size N obtained from the predictions in Eqs. (20) and (23) and from the measurements given in Table 2.

The large communication overheads in Table 2 and the small efficiencies in Table 1 indicate a poor balance between computation and communication for current problem sizes. There are two main reasons for our program being communication-bound. The first results from the slow speed of node-to-node communication relative to the speed for performing floating-point operations on the iPSC/860. The ratio of the time to communicate one node-to-node message of length 64 bits to the time to perform one double-precision floating-point operation, Eq. (21), in large, i.e.

$$\frac{t_{\mathrm{comm}}}{t_{\mathrm{flop}}} = 48.3 \log N - 31.7 . \qquad (26)$$

Another reason for the low efficiency of our application is its large memory requirement resulting is large messages being passed from node to node. The number of these messages passed increases roughly as $2\sqrt{p}$ with the number of processors used.

In Fig. 5, we compare the performance of our solution of the time-dependent Dirac equation on the iPSC/860 with its performance on two other computers to which we have access: a Cray-2 supercomputer and an IBM RS/6000 320H workstation. In computing the floating-point performance of the i860 for the purposes of this comparison, we use the overall time T_{hdprd} for Eq. (19) without factoring the communication. In this case, floating-point performance can be considered proportional to CPU time. We optimize our implementation of Eq. (19) on the Cray-2 machine using the cf77 Fortran compiler with default vectorization, loop unrolling, and no autotasking. For the IBM workstation, we use the IBM AIX XL Fortran Compiler/6000 version 2.2 with full optimization. We see that for $N = p = 64$, the iPSC/860 performs better than the Cray-2 by a factor of 2.2, with the trend for larger problem sizes clearly in favor of the hypercube.

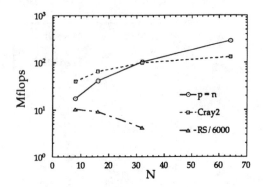

Figure 5: A comparison of the performance of implementations of Eq. (19) on the Intel iPSC/860 with $p = N$ processors, on a Cray-2, and on an IBM RS/6000 320H.

5 Numerical results

We present preliminary results for muon-pair production with capture into the ground state in collisions of $^{197}Au + ^{197}Au$ at energies of 2 GeV per nucleon in a collider frame of reference. In Fig. 6, we show the time-evolution of the muon-position probability density plotted as a negative logarithm for a grazing impact parameter. In the lower part of Fig. 6, we show the scalar-component $(A^0(\vec{r}, t))$ of the interaction of the muon with the time-dependent electromagnetic field. The contribution to this interaction from the target is the relatively small bump in the center of the lattice. The contribution from the projectile is the large, negative spike moving across the lattice.

When the projectile is very far away from the target, the initial density of the ground state is spherical. As the projectile passes the target, this spherical density deforms, expands, and develops both positive and negative energy continuum (free) components. This time-evolved spinor is required to compute the probability for muon-pair production with capture. We have reported preliminary results for these calculations in Ref. 3. Larger numerical boxes with more lattice points are needed for convergent calculations.

In Fig. 7, we present results for prompt fission of ^{238}U induced by the $E2 : (3d \rightarrow 1s, 9.6 MeV)$ nonradiative muonic atom transition. In the upper part of Fig. 7 we show the time-development of the muon position probability density during fission. The lower part of the figure displays the Coulomb interaction energy between the muon and the fission fragments. Initially, the muon is bound to a deformed ^{238}U nucleus. We can see that the muonic wave function tends to follow the two Coulomb wells of the fission fragments

in motion. The deeper well on the right is generated by the heavy fission fragment. For a fragment mass ratio of $A_H/A_L = 1.40$, we observe that the muon sticks predominantly to the heavy fragment; the muon attachment probability to the light fragment is represented by the small bump on the right. Preliminary results for the muon attachment probability to the light fission fragment, P_L, as a function of the dissipated nuclear energy have been published in a recent Letter journal [4]. We are currently in the process of performing a quantitative comparison between the theory and all the available experimental data.

Acknowledgements

This research was sponsored in part by the U.S. Department of Energy under contract No. DE-AC05-84OR21400 managed by Martin Marietta Energy Systems, Inc., and under contract No. DE-FG05-87ER40376 with Vanderbilt University. The numerical calculations were carried out on the Intel iPSC/860 hypercube multicomputer at the Oak Ridge National Laboratory, and the CRAY-2 supercomputers at the National Energy Research Supercomputer Center at Lawrence Livermore National Laboratory, and the National Center for Supercomputing Applications in Illinois.

References

[1] A. S. Umar, J.-S. Wu, M. R. Strayer, and C. Bottcher, *J. Comp. Phys.* **93** (1991) 426.

[2] J. C. Wells, V. E. Oberacker, A. S. Umar, C. Bottcher, M. R. Strayer, J.-S. Wu, J. Drake, and R. Flanery, *Int. J. Mod. Phys. C* **4** (1993) 459.

[3] J. C. Wells, V. E. Oberacker, A. S. Umar, C. Bottcher, M. R. Strayer, J.-S. Wu, and G. Plunien, *Phys. Rev. A* **45** (1992) 6296.

[4] V. E. Oberacker, A. S. Umar, J. C. Wells, C. Bottcher, and M. R. Strayer, *Phys. Lett.* **B293**, (1992) 270.

[5] J. C. Wells, V. E. Oberacker, M. R. Strayer, and A. S. Umar, submitted to *Int. J. Mod. Phys. C* (1993).

[6] G. Fox, M. Johnson, G. Lyzenga, S. Otto, J. Salmon, and D. Walker, *Solving Problems on Concurrent Processors, Vol. I* (Prentice-Hall, Englewood Cliffs, N.J., 1988), p. 261.

[For color plate see page 925]

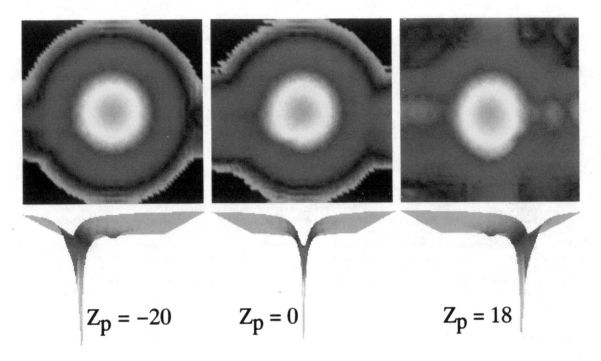

Figure 6: Plotted is the negative logarithm of the muon-position probability density (*top*) and the scalar-component $A^0(\vec{r}, t)$ of the muon's interaction with the time-dependent electromagnetic field (*bottom*) for projectile positions of $z_p = -20, 0$, and $18\lambda_c$. The muon density was computed for a grazing impact parameter collision of $^{197}Au + ^{197}Au$ at energies of $2GeV$ per nucleon in the collider frame of reference.

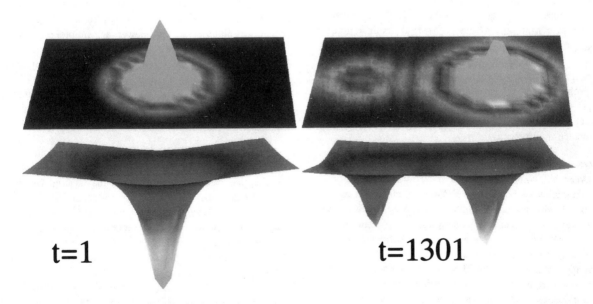

Figure 7: Coulomb potential (*bottom*) and muon-position probability density (*top*) at times $t = 1$, 901, and $1301\tau_c$ and internuclear distance $R = 2.5$, 19.9, and $52.9fm$.

A Parallel Adaptive Fast Multipole Method

Jaswinder Pal Singh, Chris Holt,
John L. Hennessy and Anoop Gupta

Computer Systems Laboratory
Stanford University
Stanford, CA 94305

Abstract

We present parallel versions of a representative N-body application that uses Greengard and Rokhlin's adaptive Fast Multipole Method (FMM). While parallel implementations of the uniform FMM are straightforward and have been developed on different architectures, the adaptive version complicates the task of obtaining effective parallel performance owing to the nonuniform and dynamically changing nature of the problem domains to which it is applied. We propose and evaluate two techniques for providing load balancing and data locality, both of which take advantage of key insights into the method and its typical applications. Using the better of these techniques, we demonstrate 45-fold speedups on galactic simulations on a 48-processor Stanford DASH machine, a state-of-the-art shared address space multiprocessor, even for relatively small problems. We also show good speedups on a 2-ring Kendall Square Research KSR-1. Finally, we summarize some key architectural implications of this important computational method.

1 Introduction

The problem of computing the interactions among a system of bodies or particles is known as the N-body problem. Examples of its application include simulating the evolution of stars in a galaxy under gravitational forces, or of ions in a medium under electrostatic forces. Many N-body problems have the properties that long-range interactions between bodies cannot be ignored, but that the magnitude of interactions falls off with distance between the interacting bodies. The hierarchically structured Fast Multipole Method (FMM) [7] is an efficient, accurate, and hence very promising algorithm for solving such problems. Besides being very efficient and applicable to a wide range of problem domains—including both classical N-body problems as well as others that can be formulated as such [7]—the FMM is also highly parallel in structure. It is therefore likely to find substantial use in applications for high-performance multiprocessors.

There are two versions of the FMM: The *uniform* FMM works very well when the particles in the domain are uniformly distributed, while the *adaptive* FMM is the method of choice when the distribution is nonuniform. It is easy to parallelize the uniform FMM effectively: A simple, static domain decomposition works perfectly well, and implementations on different architectures have been described [19, 8, 12]. However, typical applications of the FMM are to highly nonuniform domains, which require the adaptive algorithm. In addition, since these applications simulate the evolution of physical systems, the structure of the nonuniform domain changes with time. Obtaining effective parallel performance is considerably more complicated in these cases, and no static decomposition of the problem works well.

In this paper, we address the problem of obtaining effective parallel performance in N-body applications that use the adaptive FMM. We propose and evaluate two partitioning techniques that simultaneously provide effective load balancing and data locality without resorting to dynamic task stealing. One is an extension of a recursive bisection technique, and the other (which we call *costzones*) is a new, much simpler approach that performs better, particularly as more processors are used. Using these techniques, we demonstrate that N-body applications using the adaptive FMM can be made to yield very effective parallel performance, particularly on multiprocessors that support a shared address space. Finally, we summarize some of the key implications of the FMM for multiprocessor architecture.

Section 2 of this paper introduces the gravitational N-body simulation that is our example application in this paper, and the adaptive Fast Multipole Method that is used to solve it. Section 3 describes the available parallelism, the goals in exploiting it effectively, and the characteristics that make these goals challenging to achieve. Section 4 describes the execution environments in which we perform our experiments. In Section 5, we describe the two approaches we use to partition and schedule the problem for data locality and load balancing, and present results obtained using these schemes. Finally, Section 6 summarizes the main conclusions of the paper and the implications for multiprocessor architecture.

54

2 The Problem and the Algorithm

Our example N-body application studies the evolution of a system of stars in a galaxy (or set of galaxies) under the influence of Newtonian gravitational attraction. It is a classical N-body simulation in which every body (particle) exerts forces on all others. The simulation proceeds over a large number of time-steps, every time-step computing the net force on every particle and updating its position and other attributes.

By far the most time-consuming phase in every time-step is that of computing the interactions among all the particles in the system. The simplest method to do this computes all pairwise interactions between particles. This has a time complexity that is $O(n^2)$ in the number of particles, which is prohibitive for large n. Hierarchical, tree-based methods have therefore been developed that reduce the complexity to $O(n \log n)$ [3] for general distributions or even $O(n)$ for uniform distributions [2, 9], while still maintaining a high degree of accuracy. They do this by exploiting a fundamental insight into the physics of most systems that N-body problems simulate, an insight that was first provided by Isaac Newton in 1687 A.D.: Since the magnitude of interaction between particles falls off rapidly with distance, the effect of a large group of particles may be approximated by a single equivalent particle, if the group of particles is far enough away from the point at which the effect is being evaluated.

The most widely used and promising hierarchical N-body methods are the Barnes-Hut [3] and Fast Multipole [9] methods. The Fast Multipole Method (FMM) is more complex to program than the Barnes-Hut method, but provides better control over error and has better asymptotic complexity, particularly for uniform distributions (although the constant factors in the complexity expressions are larger for the FMM than for Barnes-Hut in three-dimensional simulations). In addition to classical N-body problems, the FMM and its variants are used to solve important problems in domains ranging from fluid dynamics [4] to numerical complex analysis, and have recently inspired breakthrough methods in domains as seemingly unrelated as radiosity calculations in computer graphics [10, 18].

The FMM comes in several versions, the simplest being the two-dimensional, uniform algorithm. This is itself far more complex to program than the Barnes-Hut method, but is considerably simpler than the adaptive two-dimensional version and the three-dimensional versions. Since we are interested in nonuniform distributions, and since the parallelization issues are very similar for the two- and three-dimensional cases, we use the adaptive two-dimensional FMM in this paper. Let us first describe the sequential algorithm.

2.1 The Adaptive Fast Multipole Method

To exploit Newton's insight hierarchically, the FMM recursively subdivides the computational space to obtain a tree-structured representation. In two dimensions, every subdivision results in four equal subspaces, leading to a quadtree representation of space; in three dimensions, it is an octree. A cell is subdivided if it contains more than a certain fixed number of particles (say s). For nonuniform distributions, this leads to a potentially unbalanced tree, as shown in Figure 1 (which assumes $s=1$). This tree is the main data structure used by the FMM.

A key concept in understanding the algorithm is that of *well-separatedness*. A point or cell is said to be well-separated from a cell C if it lies outside the domain of C and C's colleagues (colleagues are defined as the cells of the same size as C that are adjacent to C). Using this concept, the FMM translates Newton's insight into the following: If a point P is well-separated from a cell C, then C can be represented by a multipole expansion about its center as far as P is concerned. The force on P due to particles within C is computed by simply evaluating C's multipole expansion at P, rather than by computing the forces due to each particle within C separately. The same multipole expansion, computed once, can be evaluated at several points, thus saving a substantial amount of computation. The multipole expansion of a cell is a series expansion of the properties of the particles within it (expansions of nonterminal cells are computed from the expansions of their children). It is an exact representation if an infinite number of terms is used in the expansion. In practice, however, only a finite number of terms, say m, is used, and this number determines the accuracy of the representation.

Representing cells by their multipole expansions is not the only insight exploited by the FMM. If a point P (be it a particle or the center of a cell) is well-separated from cell C, then the effects of P on particles within C can also be represented as a Taylor series or *local expansion* about the center of C, which can then be evaluated at the particles within C. Once again, the effects of several such points can be converted just once each and accumulated into C's local expansion, which is then propagated down to C's descendants and evaluated at every particle within C. The mathematics of computing multipole expansions, translating them to local expansions, and shifting both multipole and local expansions are described in [7].

To exploit the above mechanisms for computing forces, the adaptive FMM associates with every cell C a set of four lists of cells. The cells in a list bear a certain spatial relationship to C with respect to well-separatedness. Some of these lists are defined only for leaf cells of the tree, while others are defined for internal cells as well. The lists for a leaf cell C are described in Figure 3, and their role is discussed in more detail in [7, 15]. Using these lists, the adaptive FMM proceeds in the following steps:

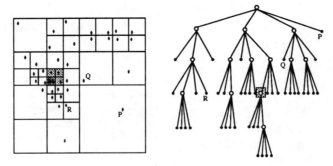

Figure 1: A two-dimensional particle distribution and the corresponding quadtree.

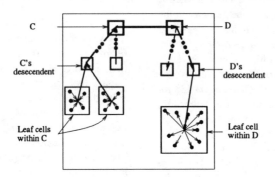

Figure 2: Computing forces on particles in cell D due to particles in cell C in the FMM.

1. **Build Tree**: The tree is built by loading particles into an initially empty root cell.

2. **Construct Interaction Lists**: The U, V and W lists are constructed explicitly. The X list is not constructed, since it is the dual of the W list.

3. **Upward Pass**: The multipole expansions of all cells are computed in an upward pass through the tree. Expansions of leaf cells are computed from the particles within them, and expansions of internal cells from those of their children.

4. **Compute List Interactions**: For every cell C, the relevant list interactions are computed. First, if C is a leaf, interactions between all particles in C are computed directly with all particles in C's U list. Second, the multipole expansions of all cells in the V list of C are translated and accumulated into local expansions about the center of C. Third, if C is a leaf, the multipole expansions of the cells in the W list of C are evaluated at the particles in C. Since the X list is the dual of the W list and does not need to be constructed explicitly, X list interactions are computed at the same time as the W list interactions in our implementations. That is, for every cell W_i in its W list, C first computes the W list interaction and updates the forces on its own particles accordingly, and then computes the X list interaction and updates the local expansion of W_i. Since X list interactions are thus computed by leaf cells, internal cells compute only their V list interactions.

5. **Downward Pass**: The local expansions of internal cells are propagated down to the leaf cells in a downward pass through the tree.

6. **Evaluate Local Expansions**: For every leaf cell C, the resulting local expansion of the cell (obtained from the previous two steps) is evaluated at the particles within it. This resulting force on each particle is added to the forces computed in steps 3 and 6.

The direct computation of interactions among internal cells is the key factor that distinguishes the FMM from the Barnes-Hut method, the other major hierarchical N-body method. In the Barnes-Hut method, forces are computed particle by particle. The tree is traversed once per particle to compute the forces on that particle, so that the only interactions are between a particle and another particle/cell. The use of cell-cell interactions allows the FMM to have a better asymptotic complexity, but is also responsible for complicating the partitioning techniques required to obtain good performance, as we shall see.

Our example application iterates over several hundred time-steps, every time step executing the above steps as well as one more that updates the velocities and positions of the particles at the end of the time-step. For the problems we have run, almost all the sequential execution time is spent in computing list interactions. The majority of this time (about 60-70%) is spent in computing V list interactions, next U list (about 20-30%) and finally the W and X lists (about 10%). Building the tree and updating the particle properties take less than 1% of the time in sequential implementations.

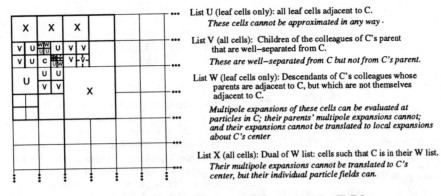

List U (leaf cells only): all leaf cells adjacent to C.
These cells cannot be approximated in any way ·

List V (all cells): Children of the colleagues of C's parent that are well–separated from C.
These are well–separated from C but not from C's parent.

List W (leaf cells only): Descendants of C's colleagues whose parents are adjacent to C, but which are not themselves adjacent to C.
Multipole expansions of these cells can be evaluated at particles in C; their parents' multipole expansions cannot; and their expansions cannot be translated to local expansions about C's center

List X (all cells): Dual of W list: cells such that C is in their W list.
Their multipole expansions cannot be translated to C's center, but their individual particle fields can.

Figure 3: Interaction lists for a cell in the adaptive FMM.

3 Taking Advantage of Parallelism

3.1 The Available Parallelism

All the phases in the FMM afford substantial parallelism., which we exploit in parallel programs written for a machine that supports a shared address space. We exploit parallelism only within a phase. Fine-grained overlap across phases can be exploited by synchronizing at the level of individual cells, but this can incur a lot of overhead without hardware support and is unlikely to be beneficial. Although the basic entities in the N-body problem are particles, the above description makes it clear that the preferred units of parallelism are cells in all phases of the FMM other than tree-building.

The tree-building, as well as the upward and downward passes to transfer expansions, clearly require both communication and cell-level synchronization, since different processors may own a parent and its child. The cell-level synchronization required includes mutual exclusion in the tree-building phase, and event synchronization to preserve dependences between parents and their children in the upward and downward passes. These upward and downward passes also have limited parallelism at higher levels of the tree (close to the root), which may become an important performance limitation on very large-scale machines when the number of processors becomes large relative to the problem size.

Some of the list interactions may require synchronization for mutual exclusion. For example, in a straightforward implementation a processor writes the U list and X list interaction results of cells that may not belong to it. This locking can be eliminated for the U list interactions, and can be reduced for X list interactions as follows: Instead of writing the X list interaction results into the cumulative local expansion of the target cell (which the owning processor of that cell also writes), a separate per-cell X list result data structure is maintained so that both it and the local expansion updates can be written without locking; this array is then accumulated into the local expansion only during the downward pass. In any event, the communication in the interaction phase has the important prop-

erty that the data read are not modified during this phase, but only later on in the update or upward pass phases, a property that can be taken advantage of by coherence and data transfer protocols, particularly since the interaction phase is the most time-consuming. Finally, the update phase can be performed without synchronization or communication.

3.2 Goals and Difficulties in Effective Parallelization

In general, there are six major sources of overhead that inhibit a parallel application from achieving effective speedups over the best sequential implementation: inherently serial sections, redundant work, overhead of managing parallelism, synchronization overhead, load imbalance and communication. As in many scientific applications, the first four are not very significant here. Let us therefore define the goals of our parallel implementations in the context of the last two sources.

Load Balancing: The goal in load balancing is intuitive: Cells should be assigned to processors to minimize the time that any processor spends waiting for other processors to reach synchronization points.

Data Locality: Modern multiprocessors are built with complex memory hierarchies, in which processors have faster access to data that are closer to them in the hierarchy. Exploiting the locality in data referencing that an application affords can increase the fraction of memory references that are satisfied close to the issuing processor, and hence improve performance. While we make all reasonable attempts to exploit locality within a processing node, we restrict our discussion of data locality to reducing the interprocessor communication in the application by scheduling tasks that access the same data on the same processor. We do not examine several other, more detailed issues related to locality[1] or the impact of locality in a network topology.

Many scientific applications operate on uniform problem domains and use algorithms which directly require only local-

---

[1] Such as prefetching data with long cache lines or in software, false-sharing of data, and cache mapping collisions.

ized communication (see, for example, [17]). This application, however, has several characteristics that complicate the task of obtaining effective parallel performance. In particular:

- Direct, relatively *unstructured, long-range communication* is required in every time-step, although the use of hierarchy causes the amount of communication to fall off with distance from a particle/cell.

- The physical domain in galactic simulations is typically highly *nonuniform*, which makes it difficult to balance the computation and the communication across processors. For example, the work done per unit of parallelism (cell) is not uniform, and depends on the entire spatial distribution.

- The *dynamic nature* of the simulation causes the distribution of particles, and hence the cell structure and work/communication distributions, to change across time-steps. There is no steady state. This means that no static partitioning of particles or space among processors is likely to work well, and repartitioning is required every time-step or few time-steps. In fact, the natural units of parallelism (cells) do not even persist across times-steps—since both the bounding box and the particle distribution change—and therefore cannot be partitioned statically anyway.

- The fact that communication falls off with distance equally in all directions implies that a processor's partition should be spatially contiguous and not biased in size toward any one direction, in order to minimize communication frequency and volume.

- The different phases in a time-step have different relative amounts of work associated with particles/cells, and hence different preferred partitions if viewed in isolation.

Before we discuss the techniques we use to obtain both data locality and load balancing despite these characteristics, let us first describe the multiprocessor environments we use in our experiments.

4 The Execution Platforms

We perform experiments to evaluate the performance of our schemes on two parallel machines that provide a cache-coherent shared address space: the Stanford DASH multiprocessor, and the Kendall Square Research KSR-1. In addition, we use a simulated multiprocessor to extend our results to more processors and to obtain quantitative support for some of our architectural implications (such as inherent communication to computation ratio and working set size).

The Stanford DASH Multiprocessor The DASH multiprocessor is a state-of-the-art research machine [13]. The machine we use has 48 processors organized in 12 clusters. A cluster comprises 4 MIPS R3000 processors connected by a shared bus, and clusters are connected together in a mesh network. Every processor has a 64KB first-level cache memory and a 256KB second-level cache, and every cluster has an equal fraction of the physical memory on the machine. All caches in the system are kept coherent in hardware using a distributed directory-based protocol. A hit in the first level cache is satisfied in a single cycle, while references satisfied in the second

level cache and in local memory stall the issuing processor for 15 and 30 cycles, respectively. Misses that go remote take about 100 or 135 cycles, depending on whether or not the miss is satisfied on the node in which the memory for the referenced datum is allocated.

The Kendall Square Research KSR-1 The KSR-1 is a commercial example of a new kind of architecture called an ALL-CACHE or Cache-only Memory Architecture (COMA). Like in more traditional cache-coherent architectures, a processing node has a processor, a cache and a "main memory". The difference is that the main memory on the node is itself converted into a very large, hardware-managed cache, by adding tags to cache-line sized blocks in main memory. This large cache, which is the only "main memory" in the machine, is called the attraction memory (AM) [6]. The location of a data item in the machine is thus decoupled from its physical address, and the data item is automatically moved (or replicated) by hardware to the attraction memory of a processor that references it.

A processing node on the KSR-1 consists of a single 20MHz custom-built processor, a 256 KB instruction cache, a 256 KB data cache, and a 32MB attraction memory [4]. The machine is configured as a hierarchy of slotted, packetized rings, with 32 processing nodes on each leaf-level ring. We use a two-ring machine, with 64 processors. Since a couple of the processors on each ring have to perform system functions and are therefore slower than the others, we present results on only upto 60 processors. Reference latencies are as follows: 2 cycles to the subcache, 20 cycles to the AM, 150 cycles to a remote node on the local ring, and 570 cycles to another ring. The line size in the data subcache is 64 bytes, while that in the AM (which is the unit of data transfer in the network) is 128 bytes. The unit of data allocation in the AMs, called a page, is 16KB.

The processor on the KSR-1 is rated lower than the DASH processor for integer code, but is much faster in peak operation on floating point code (40 MFlops versus 8 MFlops). KSR-1 also has higher interprocessor communication latency (both in processor cycles and in actual time, see above), but higher peak communication bandwidth owing to its longer cache line size.

The Simulated Multiprocessor The real multiprocessors that we use have the limitations of having only a certain number of processors, and of distorting inherent program behavior owing to their specific memory system configurations. To overcome these limitations we also run our programs on a simulator of an idealized shared-memory multiprocessor architecture [6]. The timing of a simulated processor's instruction set is designed to match that of the MIPS R3000 CPU and R3010 floating point unit. Every processor forms a cluster with its own cache and equal fraction of the machine's physical memory. A simple three-level non-uniform memory hierarchy is assumed: hits in the issuing processor's cache cost a single processor cycle; read misses that are satisfied in the local memory unit stall the processor for 15 cycles, while those that are satisfied in some remote cluster (cache or memory unit) stall it for 60 cycles; since write miss latencies can be hidden more easily by software/hardware techniques, the corresponding numbers for write misses are 1 and 3 cycles, respectively.

5 Obtaining Effective Parallel Performance

We have seen that it is not straightforward to obtain both load balancing and data locality simultaneously in this application. Whatever the technique used to partition cells for physical locality, the relative amounts of work associated with different cells must be known if load balancing is to be incorporated in the partitioning technique without resorting to dynamic task stealing (which has its own overheads and compromises locality). Let us therefore first discuss how we determine the work associated with a cell, and then describe the techniques we use to provide locality.

5.1 Determining the Work Associated with Cells

There are two problems associated with load balancing in this application. First, the naive assumption that every cell has an equal amount of work associated with it does not hold. Different childless cells have different numbers of particles in them, and different cells (childless or parent) have interaction lists of different sizes depending on the density and distribution of particles around them. The solution to this problem is to associate a cost with every cell, determined by the amount of computation needed to process its interactions.

The second problem is that the cost of a cell is not known a priori, and changes across time-steps. In fact, even the cells themselves do not persist across time-steps, since both the bounding box and the tree structure change. Let us first ignore the latter problem and see how we would determine the changing cell costs if cells did persist across time-steps, and then take care of the lack of cell persistence.

There is a key insight into N-body application characteristics that allows us to estimate cell costs even though the costs change across time-steps. Since N-body problems typically simulate physical systems that evolve slowly with time, the distribution of particles changes very slowly across consecutive time-steps, even though the change from the beginning to the end of the simulation may be dramatic. In fact, large changes from one time-step to the next imply that the time-step integrator being used is not accurate enough and a finer time-step resolution is needed. This slow change in distribution suggests that the work done to process a cell's interactions in one time-step is a good measure of its cost in the next time-step. All we therefore need to do is keep track of how much computation is performed when processing a cell in the current time-step.

In the Barnes-Hut method, the interactions that a particle computes are very similar, so that it suffices to count the number of interactions and use that count as an estimate of the particle's cost. In the FMM, however, a cell computes different types of interactions with cells in different interaction lists. It doesn't suffice to measure cost as simply the number of interactions per cell, or even the number of interactions of different types. Instead, for each type of interaction, we precompute the costs—in cycle counts—of certain primitive operations whose costs are independent of the particular interacting entities. Since the structure of every type of interaction is known, the cycle count for a particular interaction is computed by a very simple function for that type of interaction, parametrized by the number of expansion terms being used and/or the number of particles in the cells under consideration. The cost of a leaf cell is the sum of these counts in all interactions that the cell computes. The work counting is done in parallel as part of the computation of cell interactions, and its cost is negligible.

Let us now address the problem that cells not persist across time-steps, so that it doesn't really make sense to speak of using a cell's cost in one time-step as an estimate of its cost in the next time-step[2]. To solve this problem, we have to transfer a leaf cell's cost down to its particles (which do persist across time-steps) and then back up to the leaf cell that contains those particles in the next time-step. We do this as follows. The profiled cost of a leaf cell is divided equally among its particles. In the next time-step, a leaf cell examines the costs of its particles, finds the cost value that occurs most often, and multiplies this value by its number of particles to determine its cost. Since internal cells only compute V list interactions in our implementations (see Section 2.1), and since the cost of a V list interaction depends only on a program constant (the number of terms used in the expansions) and not on the number of particles in any cell, the cost of an internal cell is simply computed from the number of cells in its V list in the new time-step.

5.2 Partitioning for Locality and Load Balancing

As mentioned earlier, the goal in providing locality is that the cells assigned to a processor should be close together in physical space. Simply partitioning the space statically among processors is clearly not good enough, since it leads to very poor load balancing. In this subsection, we describe two partitioning techniques that try to provide both locality and load balancing, both of which use the work-counting technique of the previous subsection. The first technique partitions the computational domain space directly, while the second takes advantage of an insight into the application's data structures to construct a more cost-effective technique. Since the particle distribution and hence the cell structure changes dynamically, the partitioning is redone every time-step.

5.2.1 Partitioning Space: Orthogonal Recursive Bisection

Orthogonal Recursive Bisection (ORB) is a technique for providing physical locality in a problem domain by explicitly partitioning the domain space [5]. The idea here is to recursively divide space into two subspaces with equal costs, until there is one subspace per processor (see Figure 7). Initially, all processors are associated with the entire domain space. Every time a space is divided, half the processors associated with it are assigned to each of the subspaces that result. The Cartesian direction in which division takes place is usually alternated with successive divisions, and a parallel median finder is used to determine where to split the current subspace in the direction chosen for the split. ORB was first used for hierarchical N-body problems by Salmon [14], in a message-passing implementation of a galactic simulation using the Barnes-Hut

---

[2]This is a problem that the Barnes-Hut method does not have, for example, since work is associated with particles rather than cells in that case, and particles persist across time-steps.

method. The partitioning in that case was made simpler by the fact that work in the Barnes-Hut method is associated only with particles and not with cells. Particles are naturally represented by points, and can be partitioned cleanly by ORB bisections since they fall on one or the other side of a bisecting line. Further details of implementing ORB are omitted for reasons of space, and can be found in [15, 14]. ORB introduces several new data structures, including a separate binary ORB tree of recursively subdivided subdomains.

The fact that work is associated with internal cells as well in the FMM (rather than just leaves) requires that we include internal cells in determining load balancing, which is not necessary in Barnes-Hut. Also, besides the leaf or internal cell issue, the fact that the unit of parallelism is a cell rather than a particle complicates ORB partitioning in the FMM. When a space is bisected in ORB, several cells (leaf and internal) are likely to straddle the bisecting line (unlike particles, see Figure 4). In our first implementation, which we call *ORB-initial*, we try to construct a scheme that directly parallels the *ORB* scheme used in [14] for Barnes-Hut (except that internal cells are included among the entities to be partitioned). Cells, both leaf and internal, are modeled as points at their centers for the purpose of partitioning, just as particles are in the Barnes-Hut method. At every bisection in the ORB partitioning, therefore, a cell that straddles the bisecting line (called a *border cell*) is given to whichever subspace its center happens to be in.

As our performance results will show, this treatment of border cells in the *ORB-initial* scheme leads to significant load imbalances. It is not difficult to see why. Given the fact that cells are always split in exactly the same way (into four children of equal size), the centers of many cells are likely to align exactly with one another in the dimension being bisected. These cells are in effect treated as an indivisible unit when finding a bisector. If a set of these cells straddles a bisector, as is very likely, this entire set of border cells will be given to one or the other side of the bisector (see Figure 4(a)), potentially giving one side of the bisector a lot more work than the other.[3] The significant load imbalance thus incurred in each bisection may be compounded by successive bisections.

To solve this problem, we extend the ORB method as follows. Once a bisector is determined (by representing all cells as points at their centers, as before), the border cells that straddle the bisector are identified and repartitioned. In the repartitioning of border cells, we try to equalize costs as far as possible while preserving the contiguity of the partitions (see Figure 4(b)). A target cost for each subdomain is first calculated as half the total cost of the cells in both subdomains. The costs of the border cells are then subtracted from the costs of the subdomains that *ORB-initial* assigned them to. Next, the border cells are visited in an order sorted by position along the bisector, and assigned to one side of the bisector until that side reaches the target cost. Once the target cost is reached, the rest of the border cells are assigned to the other side of the bisector. We call this scheme that repartitions border boxes *ORB-final*.

---

[3]This situation is even more likely with a uniform distribution, where many cells will have their centers exactly aligned in the dimension along which a bisection is to be made.

5.2.2 A Simpler Partitioning Technique: Costzones

Our *costzones* partitioning technique takes advantage of another key insight into the hierarchical N-body methods, which is that *they already have a representation of the spatial distribution encoded in the tree data structure they use*. We therefore partition the tree rather than partition space directly. In the *costzones* scheme, the tree is conceptually laid out in a two-dimensional plane, with a cell's children laid out from left to right in increasing order of child number. Figure 5 shows an example using a quadtree. The cost of (or work associated with) every cell, as counted in the previous time-step, is stored with the cell. Every internal cell holds the sum of the costs of all cells (leaf or internal) within it plus its own cost[4]. In addition, it holds its own cost separately as well.

The total cost in the domain is divided among processors so that every processor has a contiguous, equal range or zone of costs. For example, a total cost of 1000 would be split among 10 processors so that the zone comprising costs 1-100 is assigned to the first processor, zone 101-200 to the second, and so on. Which cost zone a cell belongs to is determined by the total cost up to that cell in an inorder traversal of the tree.

Code describing the *costzones* partitioning algorithm is shown in Figure 6. Every processor calls the *costzones* routine with the `Cell` parameter initially being the root of the tree. The variable `cost-to-left` holds the total cost of the particles that come before the currently visited cell in an inorder traversal of the tree. Other than this variable, the algorithm introduces no new data structures to the program. In the traversal of the planarized tree that performs costzones partitioning, a processor examines cells for potential inclusion in its partition in the following order: the first two children (from left to right), the parent, and the next two children[5]. The algorithm requires only a few lines of code, and has negligible runtime overhead, as we shall see.

The *costzones* technique yields partitions that are contiguous in the tree as laid out in a plane. How well this contiguity in the tree corresponds to contiguity in physical space depends on the orderings chosen for the children of all cells when laying them out from left to right in the planarized tree. The simplest ordering scheme—and the most efficient for determining which child of a given cell a particle falls into—is to use the same ordering for the children of every cell. Unfortunately, there is no single ordering which guarantees that contiguity in the planarized tree will always correspond to contiguity in physical space.

The partition assigned to processor 3 in Figure 7 illustrates the lack of robustness in physical locality resulting from one such simple ordering in two dimensions (clockwise from the bottom left child for every node). While all cells within a tree cell are indeed in the same cubical region of space, cells (subtrees) that are next to each other in the linear ordering from left to right in the planarized tree may not have a common ancestor until much higher up in the tree, and may therefore not be anywhere near each other in physical space.

---

[4]These cell costs are computed during the upward pass through the tree that computes multipole expansions.

[5]Recall that we use a two-dimensional FMM, so that every cell has at most four children.

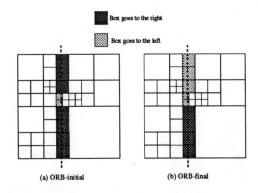

Figure 4: Partitioning of border cells in *ORB* for the FMM.

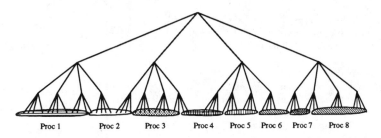

Figure 5: Tree partitioning in the *costzones* scheme.

There is, however, a simple solution that makes contiguity in the planarized tree always correspond to contiguity in space. In this solution, the ordering of children in the planarized tree is not the same for all cells. However, the ordering of a cell C's children is still easy to determine, since it depends on only two things: the ordering of C's parent's children (i.e. C's siblings), and which child of its parent C is in that ordering.

Consider a two-dimensional example. Since every cell has four children in two dimensions, there are eight ways in which a set of siblings can be ordered: There are four possible starting points, and two possible directions (clockwise and anticlockwise) from each starting point. It turns out that only four of the eight orderings need actually be used. Figure 8(a) shows the four orderings we use in our example, and illustrates how the ordering for a child is determined by that for its parent. The arrow in a cell represents the ordering of that cell's children. For example, if the children are numbered 0, 1, 2, 3 in a counterclockwise fashion starting from the upper right, then in case (1) in Figure 8(a) the children of the top-level cell are ordered 2, 1, 0, 3, and in case (2) the children are ordered 2, 3, 0, 1. The ordering of the children's children are also shown.

Figure 8(b) shows the resulting partitions given the same distribution as in Figure 7. The bold line follows the numbering order, starting from the bottom left cell. All the partitions are physically contiguous in this case. The three-dimensional case is handled the same way, except that there are now 32 different orderings used instead of 4. A discussion of the extension to three-dimensions can be found in [15]. We use this more robust, nonuniform child ordering method in the partitioning scheme we call *costzones*.

5.3 Results

Figure 9 shows the performance results on DASH for a simulation of two interacting Plummer model [1] galaxies that start out slightly separated from each other. The results shown are for 32K particles and an accuracy of 10^{-10}, which translates to $m=39$ terms in the expansions. Five time-steps are run, of which the first two are not measured to avoid cold-start effects that would not be significant in a real run over many hundreds of time-steps.

Clearly, both the *ORB-final* and *costzones* schemes achieve very good speedups. The *ORB-initial* scheme is significantly worse than the *ORB-final* scheme, which shows that the extension to handle border boxes intelligently—rather than treat them as particles at their centers—is important. To demonstrate that it is also important to take the cost of internal cells into account when partitioning, the figure also shows results for a scheme called *costzones-noparents*, in which only the cost of leaves is taken into account during partitioning and internal cells are simply assigned to the processor that owns most of their children for locality.

While both the *ORB-final* and *costzones* schemes perform very well upto 32 processors (*ORB* requires the number of processors to be a power of two and therefore cannot be used with 48 processors), we can already see that *costzones* starts to outperform *ORB*. This difference is found to become larger as more processors are used, as revealed by experiments with more processors on the simulated multiprocessor. Closer analysis and measurement of the different phases of the application reveals the reasons for this (see Figure 10). One reason is that the *costzones* scheme does provide a little better load balancing and hence speeds up the force-computation a little better. However, the main reason is that the *ORB* partitioning phase

```
Costzones (Cell,cost-to-left)
{
    if (Cell is a leaf) {
        if (Cell is in my range)
            add Cell to my list
    }
    else {
        for (first two Children of Cell) {
            if (cost-to-left < max value of my range) {
                if (cost-to-left + Child cost >= min
                    value of my range)
                    Costzones (Child,cost-to-left)
                cost-to-left += Child cost
            }
        }
        if (cost-to-left is in my range) {
            add Cell itself to my list
            cost-to-left += cost of Cell itself
        }
        for (last two Children of Cell) {
            if (cost-to-left < max value of my range) {
                if (cost-to-left + Child cost >= min
                    value of my range)
                    Costzones (Child,cost-to-left)
                cost-to-left += Child cost
            }
        }
    }
}
```

Figure 6: *Costzones-final* partitioning for the FMM

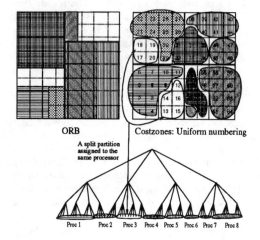

Figure 7: *ORB* and *costzones* with uniform numbering.

itself is more expensive than *costzones* partitioning (as the descriptions earlier in this section should show), the difference in partitioning cost increasing with the number of processors. The cost of *costzones* partitioning grows very slowly with n or p, while that of *ORB* grows more quickly. Thus, the *costzones* scheme is not only much simpler to implement, but also results in better performance, particularly on larger machines.

In addition to the nonuniform distribution described above,

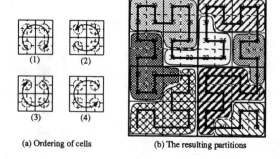

(a) Ordering of cells   (b) The resulting partitions

Figure 8: *Costzones* with nonuniform numbering.

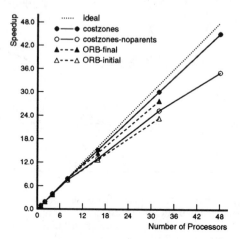

Figure 9: Speedups for the FMM application on DASH (n = 32k, $\epsilon = 10^{-10}$).

we have also measured results for other distributions, including a uniform one. The results were similar to those discussed above (with the uniform cases performing a little better than the nonuniform cases). Finally, Figures 11 and 12 show the results for the best costzones scheme for different problem configura-

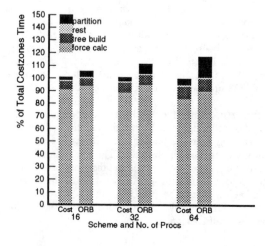

Figure 10: Execution Profiles of *Costzones* and *ORB* on DASH.

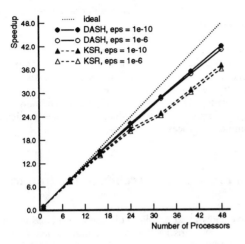

Figure 11: Speedups for the FMM application on DASH and KSR-1 (n = 64k).

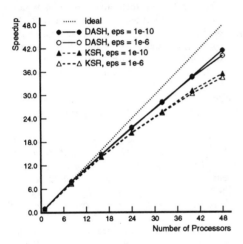

Figure 12: Speedups for the FMM application on DASH and KSR-1 (n = 32k).

tions on both DASH and KSR-1. As expected, higher numbers of particles and greater force-calculation accuracies lead to slightly better speedups, particularly since both these lead to relatively more time being spent in the well-balanced phase of computing interactions. The difference between costzones and ORB partitioning is also emphasized as the force-calculation accuracy decreases (results not shown), since the impact of partitioning cost (which is independent of accuracy) becomes greater relative to the cost of computing interactions. Finally, we find that the speedups on DASH are consistently better than those on KSR-1. This is because the communication latencies are higher on KSR-1, and its ALLCACHE nature gives it no real advantages since the important working set of the application is very small and fits in the cache on DASH as well. Uniprocessor performance is also better on DASH by about 25%, primarily since there is a lot of integer code in the tree and list manipulations, and the processor on DASH does better on these. A more detailed discussion of DASH versus KSR-1 can be found in another paper in these proceedings [11].

5.3.1 The Parallel Tree-Building Bottleneck

Figure 10 also reveals a potential bottleneck to performance on large parallel machines, which is that the tree-building phase does not speed up as well in parallel as force-computation. If the number of particles per processor stays very large, tree building is not likely to take much time relative to the rest of the time-step computation. However, under the most realistic methods of time-constrained scaling, the number of particles per processor shrinks as larger problems are run on larger machines [16], and tree-building can become a significant part of overall execution time.

The obvious way to parallelize the tree-building algorithm is to have processors insert their particles into the shared tree concurrently, synchronizing as necessary. This can lead to substantial locking overhead in acquiring mutually exclusive access whenever a processor wants to add a particle to a leaf cell, add a child to an internal cell, or subdivide a leaf cell.

Because the *costzones and* ORB partitioning techniques give every processor a contiguous partition of space, they effectively divide up the tree into distinct sections and assign a processor to each section. This means that once the first few levels of the tree are built, there is little contention for locks in constructing the rest of the tree, since processors then construct their sections without much interference. Most of the contention in the initial parallel tree-building algorithm outlined above is due to many processors simultaneously trying to update the first few levels of the tree.

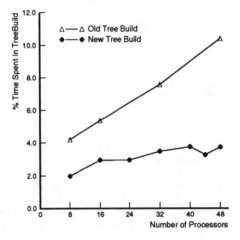

Figure 13: Percentage of total execution time spent building the tree on DASH.

Fortunately, the same physical locality in our partitions that helps the intial parallel tree-building algorithm also allows us to construct a better algorithm. It is possible to substantially reduce both the contention at the upper levels of the tree and the amount of locking of cells that needs to be done, by splitting the parallel tree construction into two steps. First, every processor builds its own version of the tree using only its own particles. The root of this local tree represents the whole computational domain, not just a domain large enough to hold the local particles. This step is made more efficient by having a processor remember where in its tree it inserted its last particle, and start traversing the tree from there for the next particle, rather than from the root. No locking is needed in this step. Second, these individual trees are merged together into the single, global tree used in the rest of the computation.

Since the root cells of all the local trees represent the entire computational domain, a cell in one tree represents the same subspace as the corresponding cell in another tree. This fact allows the merge procedure to make merging decisions based on the types of the cells in the local and global trees only (i.e. whether the cell is internal cell or a leaf etc.).

The merge procedure starts at the root of both trees, comparing the type of cell (body, cell, or empty) from each tree, and taking an appropriate action based on the two types. There are six possible cases:

1. *local cell is internal, global cell is empty*: The local cell is inserted into the tree.

2. *local cell is internal, global cell is a leaf*: The global cell is removed from the tree. Then the global particle is inserted into the subtree with the local cell as the root. The parent of the global cell is relocked, and the local cell is inserted into the tree.

3. *local cell is internal, global cell is internal*: A spatial equivalent to the local cell already exists in the global tree, so nothing is done with the local cell. The merge algorithm is recursively called on each of the local cell's children and their counterparts in the global tree.

4. *local cell is a leaf, global cell is empty*: Same as Case 1.

5. *local cell is a leaf, global cell is a leaf*: Same as Case 2.

6. *local cell is a leaf, global cell is internal*: The local cell is subdivided, pushing the particle one level deeper in the local tree. Since the local cell is now internal, Case 3 applies.

Details of the algorithm and pseudocode can be found in [15]. The algorithm greatly alleviates the problem of too much contention at the early levels of the tree. When the first processor tries to merge its tree into the global tree, it finds the global root null. By case 1, it sets the global root to its root. The processor's local tree has now become the global tree, and its size reduces contention at any one cell. Just as important, it only took one locking operation to merge the entire first local tree. Since large subtrees are merged in a single operation, rather than single particles, the amount of locking required (and hence both the overhead of locking as well as the contention) is greatly reduced.

The reduction in locking overhead and contention comes at a cost in redundant work. There is some extra work done in first loading particles into local trees and then merging the local trees, rather than loading particles directly into the global tree (as in the old tree building algorithm). When the partitioning incorporates physical locality, this extra work overhead is small and the reduction in locking overhead is substantial, since large subtrees are merged in a single operation. Of course, if the partitioning does not incorporate physical locality, this new tree-building algorithm has no advantages over the old one,

and the extra work overhead it introduces will make it perform significantly worse.

To compare the old and new tree-building algorithms, Figure 13 shows the percentage of the total execution time of the application on the DASH multiprocessor that is spent in building the tree. The problem size used is the same as the one for which speedups are presented in Figure 9. The new algorithm clearly performs much better than the old one, particularly as the number of processors increases.

6 Summary and Architectural Implications

We have shown that despite their nonuniform and dynamically changing characteristics, N-body simulations that use the adaptive Fast Multipole Method can be partitioned and scheduled for effective parallel performance on shared-address-space machines. We described a method for obtaining load balancing without resorting to dynamic task stealing, and proposed and evaluated two partitioning techniques, both of which use this load balancing method but use different techniques for providing data locality. We showed that our *costzones* partitioning technique provides better performance than an extended recursive bisection technique—particularly on larger numbers of processors—by taking advantage of an additional insight into the Fast Multipole Method. Using the *costzones* technique, we demonstrated 45-fold speedups on the Stanford DASH multiprocessor, even for a relatively small problem size.

In addition to understanding how to parallelize important classes of applications, it is also important to understand the implications of application characteristics for the design of parallel systems. We have studied several of these implications for the FMM. Our methodology and detailed results can be found in [16, 15]. Here, we summarize the main results.

We found that exploiting temporal locality by caching communicated data is critical to obtaining good performance, and that hardware caches on shared-address-space machines are well-suited to providing this locality automatically and efficiently. On the other hand, data distribution in main memory, to allocate the particle/cell data assigned to a processor in that processor's local memory unit, is both very difficult to implement and not nearly as important. We also found that the nonuniform, dynamically changing nature of the application causes implicit communication through a shared address space to have substantial advantages over explicit communication through message-passing in both ease of programming and performance.

Finally, we examined how some important application characteristics scale as larger problems are run on larger parallel machines. We showed that scaling to fill the memory on the machine in unrealistic since it increases the execution time too much, and that the following results hold under the most realistic, time-constrained scaling model: (i) the main memory requirements (or number of particles) per processor become smaller, (ii) the communication to computation ratio increases slowly, but is small enough in absolute terms to allow good performance even on large-scale machines, and (iii) the working set size per processor, which helps determine the ideal cache size for the computation, also grows slowly but is very small.

In fact, the important working set holds roughly the amount of data reused from one cell's list interactions to another's, and is therefore independent of the number of particles and the number of processors; it depends only on the number of terms used in the multipole expansions, which grows very slowly with problem and machine size. As a result, unless overheads and load imbalances in the phases of computation (such as the tree building phase, discussed earlier, and the load-imbalanced upward and downward passes through the tree) that are not significant on the problem and machine sizes available today become significant on much larger machines, machines with large numbers of processors and relatively small amounts of cache and main memory per processor should be effective in delivering good performance on applications that use the adaptive Fast Multipole Method.

Acknowledgements

We would like to thank Leslie Greengard for providing us with the sequential program and for many discussions. This work was supported by DARPA under Contract No. N00039-91-C-0138. Anoop Gupta is also supported by a Presidential Young Investigator Award, with matching grants from Ford, Sumitomo, Tandem and TRW.

References

[1] S.J. Aarseth, M. Henon, and R. Wielen. *Astronomy and Astrophysics*, 37, 1974.

[2] Andrew A. Appel. An efficient program for many body simulation. *SIAM Journal of Scientific and Statistical Computing*, 6:85–93, 1985.

[3] Joshua E. Barnes and Piet Hut. A hierarchical O(N log N) force calculation algorithm. *Nature*, 324(4):446–449, 1986.

[4] A. J. Chorin. Numerical study of slightly viscous flow. *Journal of Fluid Mechanics*, 57:785–796, 1973.

[5] Geoffrey C. Fox. *Numerical Algorithms for Modern Parallel Computer Architectures*, chapter A Graphical Approach to Load Balancing and Sparse Matrix Vector Multiplication on the Hypercube, pages 37–62. Springer-Verlag, 1988.

[6] Stephen R. Goldschmidt and Helen Davis. Tango introduction and tutorial. Technical Report CSL-TR-90-410, Stanford University, 1990.

[7] Leslie Greengard. *The Rapid Evaluation of Potential Fields in Particle Systems*. ACM Press, 1987.

[8] Leslie Greengard and William Gropp. *Parallel Processing for Scientific Computing*, chapter A Parallel Version of the Fast Multipole Method, pages 213–222. SIAM, 1987.

[9] Leslie Greengard and Vladimir Rokhlin. A fast algorithm for particle simulation. *Journal of Computational Physics*, 73(325), 1987.

[10] P. Hanrahan, D. Salzman, and L. Aupperle. A rapid hierarchical radiosity algorithm. In *Proceedings of SIGGRAPH*, 1991.

[11] John L. Hennessy Jaswinder Pal Singh, Truman Joe and Anoop Gupta. An empirical comparison of the ksr-1 all-cache and stanford dash multiprocessors. In *Supercomputing '93*, November 1993.

[12] Jacob Katzenelson. Computational structure of the N-body problem. *SIAM Journal of Scientific and Statistical Computing*, 10(4):787–815, 1989.

[13] Dan Lenoski, James Laudon, Kourosh Gharachorloo, Anoop Gupta, and John Hennessy. The directory-based cache coherence protocol for the DASH multiprocessor. In *Proceedings of the 17th Annual International Symposium on Computer Architecture*, pages 148–159, May 1990.

[14] John K. Salmon. *Parallel Hierarchical N-body Methods*. PhD thesis, California Institute of Technology, December 1990.

[15] Jaswinder Pal Singh. *Parallel Hierarchical N-body Methods and their Implications for Multiprocessors*. PhD thesis, Stanford University, February 1993.

[16] Jaswinder Pal Singh, Anoop Gupta, and John L. Hennessy. Implications of hierarchical N-body techniques for multiprocessor architecture. *Submitted to ACM Transactions on Computer Systems*. Early version available as Stanford Univeristy Tech. Report no. CSL-TR-92-506, January 1992.

[17] Jaswinder Pal Singh and John L. Hennessy. *High Performance Computing II*, chapter Data Locality and Memory System Performance in the Parallel Simulation of Ocean Eddy Currents, pages 43–58. North-Holland, 1991. Also Stanford University Tech. Report No. CSL-TR-91-490.

[18] Jaswinder Pal Singh, Chris Holt, Takashi Totsuka, Anoop Gupta, and John L. Hennessy. Load balancing and data locality in hierarchical N-body methods. *Journal of Parallel and Distributed Computing*. To appear. Preliminary version available as Stanford Univeristy Tech. Report no. CSL-TR-92-505, January 1992.

[19] Feng Zhao. An O(n) algorithm for three-dimensional N-body simulations. Technical Report 995, MIT Artificial Intelligence Laboratory, 1987.

Session 1:
Workshop
Uses of Videoconferencing in the Supercomputing Environment

Uses of Videoconferencing in the Supercomputing Environment

Mary Stephenson, MCNC; Larry Brandt, NSF; Eric Sills, MCNC; Alex Ropelewski, PSC; Bruce Loftis, MCNC; and Bill Buzbee, NCAR

MCNC, National Science Foundation (NSF), National Center for Atmospheric Research (NCAR), and Pittsburgh Supercomputing Center (PSC)

Abstract

Discussion will focus on the role of videoconferencing in conducting training courses and in promoting collaboration among researchers at widely dispersed locations. Participants will offer an overview of how video networks can contribute to the high performance computing environment, describing recent experiences with a statewide network (North Carolina's CONCERT) and the NSF supercomputing centers' videoconferencing network (HPCCVC).

Anyone interested in seeing how such a network can be used in a supercomputing environment is encouraged to attend as well as persons who will be involved in operating or using a video network.

Videoconferencing refers to the use of interactive audio and video communication links between individuals or institutions. In this workshop, the uses of such technology for researchers in the High Performance Computing and Communications (HPCC) arena will be addressed.

The growth of videoconferencing has been created by HPCC technology, the need for collaboration and resource sharing among HPCC researchers, and the need for face-to-face communications. Increasingly tight budgets have spurred institutions to look for ways to reduce travel costs. A videoconferencing network greatly reduces travel expenses for researchers by eliminating the need to travel to other institutions for meetings, conferences, training events, or collaboration with colleagues. The growth of high performance computing has been accompanied by a dramatic increase in the amount of information that needs to be communicated with colleagues in a timely manner. Communication technologies such as electronic mail and conference calls are not enough to provide the real time interaction necessary for today's HPCC researchers. The ability to talk face-to-face, view visualizations of data simultaneously, plan and prepare joint proposals, and truly interact as though you were in the same room, is provided via today's videoconferencing technologies.

The national scientific computing community has recognized this need and addressed it by forming the High Performance Computing and Communications Video Collaboratory (HPCCVC). The HPCCVC is a videoconferencing network among the National Science Foundation, the four NSF supercomputer centers, and a statewide videoconference network in North Carolina, as shown in figure 1. The four NSF supercomputing centers are: Cornell Theory Center (CTC), the National Center for Supercomputing Applications (NCSA), the Pittsburgh Supercomputing Center (PSC), and the San Diego Supercomputing Center (SDSC). The statewide videoconference network is operated by MCNC, a nonprofit organization that provides high performance computing, communications, and microelectronics resources to North Carolina.

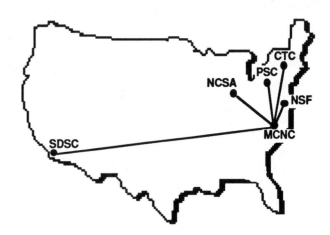

Figure 1. HPCC video collaboratory network topology

The HPCCVC is just the beginning of a national videoconferencing infrastructure. The HPCCVC was started in 1992 and is used for training on HPCC technology and collaboration among HPCC researchers at the national centers. The videoconferencing facilities at the four national supercomputing centers use

© 1993 ACM 0-8186-4340-4/93/0011 $1.50

commercially available video equipment. The network is implemented with 384Kbps dedicated telecommunication links. When the videoconferencing facilities are not being used for HPCCVC events, they can be used to connect to other videoconferencing networks for programs with other sites. One goal of the HPCCVC is to further research in packet video, which many see as the future of videoconferencing over the Internet.

MCNC has had a long history in videoconferencing, including designing, implementing, and operating the first statewide videoconferencing network, CONCERT (Communications for North Carolina Education, Research, and Technology), shown in figure 2. CONCERT has been operating in the state of North

computing resources at MCNC, such as the Cray Y-MP and the KSR1-48. MCNC's video conference rooms are equipped with overhead cameras to display hard copy notes and an IBM RS/6000 workstation whose display can be sent over the video network through a scan converter, as shown in figure 3.

The MCNC Scientific Support and Training group reserves a block of time on CONCERT on a chosen day of every week. While this block of time changes each semester due to scheduling demands on the network, this regularly scheduled time helps users remember training presentations. The training presentations over CONCERT are typically one to two hours long with a lecture format using slides on plain paper and some

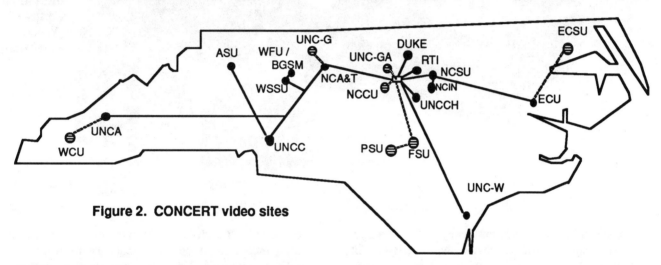

Figure 2. CONCERT video sites

Carolina since 1985 and is used primarily for accredited coursework, as well as meetings, remote collaboration, seminars, and training events. It currently connects 14 universities and research institutions in the state with two duplex video channels. Funding for six additional sites has been approved. An additional duplex video channel connects the state's four medical schools. Additional video capability is achieved via compressed video. The interactive video channels provide two-way fully interactive communications capabilities among all institutions. CONCERT is in use more than 100 hours per week.

In addition to its CONCERT facilities, MCNC also provides high performance computing resources to academic and corporate researchers throughout North Carolina.

Training and education

CONCERT has proven to be a valuable tool for providing training for users of the high performance

workstation demonstrations. The Scientific Support and Training group presents a regular two-part introduction to MCNC high performance computing resources over CONCERT on consecutive weeks approximately every four months. The majority of the other presentations are one-time presentations on special interest topics in high performance computing, such as overviews of various third-party software packages and a series of computational chemistry presentations.

Materials for training over video networks are best prepared in landscape format using a large, bold, sans serif font (such as 18 point bold Helvetica). Notes made on the slides during the presentation should be done clearly with a felt tip pen (like an overhead pen). To use workstation demonstrations, the font sizes used in the applications also need to be considered. Depending on the frame rate of the video network being used, the workstation demonstrations should not involve rapid motion. MCNC usually places a compressed PostScript file containing the lecture slides in an anonymous ftp account prior to the presentation so that those planning to

Figure 3. The MCNC videoconference room

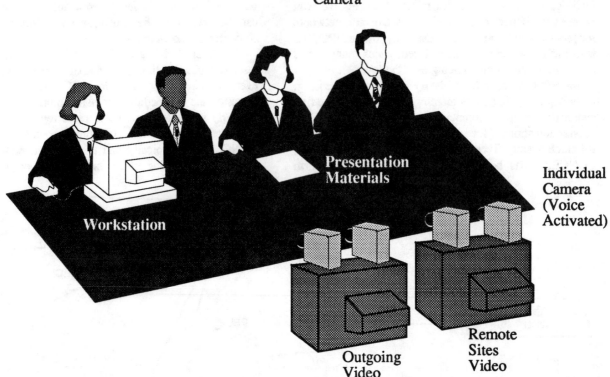

Overhead Graphics Camera

Presentation Materials

Individual Camera (Voice Activated)

Workstation

Outgoing Video

Remote Sites Video

attend can download and print a copy of the materials.

The video networks provide the benefit of virtual proximity, allowing geographically distant students to participate together in a training presentation. However, there are also drawbacks. The experience at MCNC has been that while student interactivity is possible, it is challenging to make the students feel like involved participants rather than spectators. Also, the instructor is seated and unable to move around, which may differ considerably from the instructor's normal presentation style. MCNC rarely gives long or multiday presentations due to difficulty in scheduling these presentations. The training presentations also rarely contain laboratory components due to equipment and laboratory instructor limitations. Advance preparation can help overcome these difficulties as was demonstrated in the case study of a class taught over CONCERT by the Pittsburgh Supercomputing Center.

PSC Protein Sequence Analysis course

In April, 1992 instructors from PSC came to MCNC and taught their Protein Sequence Analysis (PSA) course

on CONCERT to over 100 students and researchers at ten campuses. Prior to the class, laboratory instructors from each campus attended a full day training session at MCNC to prepare them to assist with the exercises.

Groundwork for the course began months in advance with MCNC staff contacting relevant department heads on various campuses to identify a contact person for the class at each campus. This contact was responsible for registration on their campus, assistance with publicity for the class, and distribution of course materials for their campus.

For this workshop, videoconferencing provided several benefits over the traditional method of presentation. Videoconferencing allowed more researchers to attend the course at the same time and enabled instructors to cover more material than could have been presented by visiting each site individually.

The format of the five-day class was 2.5 hours of morning lecture on CONCERT followed by laboratory time at each site. A second CONCERT session was conducted each afternoon to answer any questions on the exercises that the local laboratory instructors had not been able to answer.

Although the initial planning, preparation, and laboratory instructor training sessions were very staff intensive, the remote broadcast of this class made it extremely successful in increasing class size and attendance.

Research collaboration

There is always a need for effective communication between collaborating researchers. With the growing importance of global scale problems, there has been an increase in the size and complexity of the problems to be studied. Solving complex problems often requires the formation of interdisciplinary teams at different universities and laboratories. All of the talent is rarely available at a single site. The importance of removing barriers to remote collaboration will continue to increase for the future.

Videoconferencing provides opportunities for more effective communication between large and small teams of remotely-based researchers. The CONCERT video network is routinely used by teams of collaborating North Carolina researchers. Our experience has been that the videoconference is often as effective as a meeting for planning and brainstorming.

When the collaborators are as geographically dispersed as the NSF supercomputer centers, the value of videoconferencing is even more apparent. The national centers and NCAR have used the HPCCVC for planning the submission of metacenter proposals and discussing proposal content.

The HPCCVC and CONCERT represent the upper end of virtual proximity technology. We are also beginning to see the development of hardware and software tools that support lower cost virtual proximity options. For example, CuCme from Cornell University uses a camera device (a small desktop gooseneck model or home video camera) to send a packetized video image to another workstation via an internet connection. XTV from MCNC and Collage from NCSA are other tools that enable real-time collaborative sessions using a variety of workstations. Remote collaborators are able to share, modify, and control windows of text, commands, and graphics.

Session 1:
Invited Presentations
J.A. Sethian
Robert Coyne
Harry Hulen
Richard Watson

Computational Fluid Mechanics and Massively Parallel Processors

J. A. Sethian
Department of Mathematics
and
Lawrence Berkeley Laboratory
University of California
Berkeley, California 94720

Abstract

We report on work devising massively parallel implementations of vortex methods for computing turbulent flow in highly complex geometries. In this paper, we discuss the challenges involved in fitting evolving compilers, hardware, and I/O to non-traditional fluid mechanics techniques, N-body solvers, and interactive real-time visualization environments. Our results describe algorithms to compute two and three-dimensional inside chambers and around bluff bodies. As conclusions, we discuss some issues involved in developing intuition about parallel implementation of complex codes.

Introduction

In this paper, we describe the current state of an on-going project in computational fluid mechanics and parallel processing. There are two goals of this work. The first is to devise algorithms that can shed light on some of the delicate fundamentals issues in the computation of high Reynolds numbers flow. On the engineering side, one would like to calculate such quantities as the wake structure, eddies, drag forces, and pressures in flows past bodies, over wings, and in chambers. On the mathematical side, the goal is to understand such key issues as vortex merger, vortex breakdown, stretching, and mixing transport.

The second goal is one in parallel processing, namely, to report on our experiences trying to write an experimental CFD code under evolving architecture, hardware, compilers, and I/O. Here, there are opposing desires; on one hand, the wish to take advantage of the latest advances, no matter how unstable the computing platform and environment, and on the other hand, the (understandable) strategy of not committing too much time and energy until one has some confidence that a particular computing view will survive.

The outline of this paper is as follows. In order to explain the underlying numerical techniques, we begin with a brief explanation of vortex methods for computing turbulent flow, describing both their parallel implementation and reporting on some previous results. In the second section, we then focus on two particular aspects of the computational fluid dynamics simulation, namely the N-body solver required to compute the velocity field from a distribution of particles every time step, and techniques for parallel visualization of the evolving flow. In this section, we present timing results for various ways to program N-body solvers under different compilers, global vs. message-passing environments, etc. Finally, we discuss some of our experiences so far in massively parallel programming, and make some comments on what we perceive to be the current state of affairs.

There are a large number of collaborators who should be mentioned at the outset. The parallel two-dimensional piston calculation on the CM-2 was performed joint work with J-P. Brunet, A. Greenberg, and J.P. Mesirov. The three-dimensional serial vortex code for flow past airfoils and wings is joint work with J. Grant, S. Huyer, and J. Uhlman. The parallel three-dimensional vortex code is joint work with A. Greenberg and J. Grant. The work on parallel N-body solvers is joint with A. Greenberg and J. P. Mesirov. The two-dimensional parallel flow visualization environment is joint work with J. Salem. The three-dimensional parallel flow visualization environment is joint work with K. Lowther and J. Salem.

I. Vortex Methods and Parallel Processing

A. Vortex Methods for Two-Dimensional Flow

Vortex methods, (see [8]), offer an attractive alternative to the traditional, finite difference based techniques for the calculation of viscous, incompressible, turbulent flow. The critical flow quantity in this approach is the *vorticity*, which is the curl of the velocity and represents the amount of rotation at a point in the flow. Instead of an Eulerian finite difference mesh, a Lagrangian approach is taken in which the initial vorticity field is discretized into a large number of vortex elements whose ensuing motion describes the evolution of the flow. At any time, the velocity of the fluid may be recovered from the positions and strengths of the vortex elements.

In more detail, in two dimensions, we have (see [8]).

$$\frac{D\xi}{Dt} = \frac{1}{R} \nabla^2 \xi \qquad (1)$$

Here, the vorticity ξ is the curl of the velocity, that is, $\xi = \nabla \times \mathbf{u}$, R is the Reynolds number, and (D/Dt) is the material derivative, The appropriate boundary conditions are that both the normal and tangential velocity must vanish on solid walls.

In order to "close" this equation, we must recover $\mathbf{u}$ from the vorticity. Given that $\nabla \cdot \mathbf{u} = 0$ and $\xi = \nabla \times \mathbf{u}$, we know that there exists a vector function $\mathbf{\psi}(\mathbf{x})$ such that $\mathbf{u} = \nabla \times \mathbf{\psi}$ and $\nabla^2 \mathbf{\psi} = -\xi$. This will form the basis for the vortex method. Recall that the solution to the Poisson equation is given by the fundamental solution to the Laplace operator as

$$\mathbf{\psi}(\mathbf{x},t) = \int L(\mathbf{x} - \mathbf{z}) \xi(\mathbf{z}) d\mathbf{z} \qquad (4)$$

where $L(x) = \frac{-1}{2\pi} \log |x|$. Since $\mathbf{u} = \nabla \times \mathbf{\psi}$, we have that

$$\mathbf{u}(\mathbf{x},t) = \int K(\mathbf{x} - \mathbf{z}) \xi(\mathbf{z}) d\mathbf{z} \qquad (6)$$

where the kernel K is defined by

$$K(x) = \frac{1}{2\pi} \frac{(-x_2, x_1)}{|\mathbf{x}|^2} \qquad (7)$$

Thus, we have the following closed system for the evolution of the vorticity, namely,

$$\frac{D\xi}{Dt} = \frac{1}{R} \nabla^2 \xi \qquad (8)$$

$$\mathbf{u}(\mathbf{x},t) = \int K(\mathbf{x} - \mathbf{z}) \xi(\mathbf{z}) d\mathbf{z} \qquad (9)$$

where K is given above.

We envision the initial condition $\xi(\mathbf{x},0)$ as describing the vorticity of the particle initially located at $\mathbf{x}$, and ask for the ensuing motion of particles located at all possible starting points. This leads to a Lagrangian formulation for the particle trajectories. The central idea behind vortex methods, due to Chorin [3], is to discretize the initial vorticity into a finite number of particles carrying vorticity, and integrate them along their particle trajectories using a discrete time ordinary differential equation solver. In addition, Chorin smoothed the singularity in the kernel by convolving K with a smoothing function. This guaranteed that the velocities induced by the neighboring vortex elements remained bounded, regardless of how close the elements came together. For more information about various how smoothing affects the convergence properties of the algorithm, see [6]. At each time step, in order to advance the vortex elements, an N-body problem must be solved to evaluate the Biot-Savart interaction.

The advantage of this technique is two-fold. First, since no grid is introduced, this Lagrangian approach avoids the introduction of numerical viscosity which swamps the real physical viscosity. Second, the method is dynamically adaptive: computational elements are naturally clustered in regions of high vorticity where flow gradients are large and accuracy is required. As such, vortex methods have proven to be a powerful technique for modeling much of the intricate, complex behavior of turbulent flow (see [8,9,11]).

The addition of boundary conditions adds considerable complexity to the algorithm. On solid walls, we typically require that both the normal and tangential components of the velocity vanish. We may consider these two conditions separately. The normal boundary condition can be met by superposition of a potential flow on top of that induced by the vortex elements. This potential flow "confines" the motion of the flow to the flow geometry by exactly canceling the normal velocity component of the vorticity field on solid walls. Mathematically, the potential flow amends the Green's function for the stream function so that the normal component vanishes on the boundary of the region.

The presence of viscosity in the flow and the imposition of the no-slip condition complicates matters further. Vorticity is created on the boundary in response to the no-slip condition. Algorithmically, we must add computational elements at solid walls which cancel the tangential component and then diffuse into the flow. To provide accuracy near the boundary, we employ the Prandtl boundary layer equation, which suggests a different type of vortex elements with a significantly more complicated interaction mechanism. Finally, vorticity diffusion in the body of the flow is modeled by a random walk imposed on the vortex trajectories.

To summarize, at each time step we must:

(1) Calculate two N-body problems (interior and boundary)
(2) Solve a potential flow for the no-flow condition
(3) Dynamically create vortex elements for the no-slip boundary condition

A large number of calculations have been performed using vortex methods to compute turbulent flow in two space dimensions. For example, serial versions of the two-dimensional method have been used to compute flow in closed chambers [9], and flow over a backwards facing step [8]. For a review, see [8].

B. Parallel Implementation of the Two-Dimensional Method

In general, it might seem that the above method is not particular well-suited to a parallel implementation. There is no fixed grid, the problem lacks a simple nearest neighbor structure, and computational elements are created adaptively when and where necessary to resolve gradients. As such, it serves as a good testbed example of the challenges involved in building a parallel implementation of a complex algorithm. In order to do so, issues of processor allocation for geometry, processor allocation for vortex elements, parallel solutions of N-body problems, parallel elliptic solvers, and parallel visualization must be tackled.

In [10], a parallel version of the above method was implemented on a CM2, a data-parallel computer containing up to 65,536 1-bit processors, each with 1 megabit of local memory. The processor connection topology is essentially a hypercube, however, a general purpose communications system called the "router" allows messages to be sent from any processor to any other while the exact route is hidden from the user. Each processor is also directly connected to one of eight possible 75 Mbyte/sec internal I/O channels. The CM2 is a single-instruction multiple-data (SIMD) computer, programmed in a data-parallel language such as CMFortran. Each physical processor simulates a number of "virtual" processors by segmenting its memory and time multiplexing the processor hardware. Its implementation is transparent to the user, and the number of virtual processors may be changed dynamically. For graphics purposes, a 1280 x 1024 framebuffer with 24 bits per pixel display can be directly connected to the internal I/O BUS.

To begin, in the parallel implementation we wished to accommodate arbitrary rectilinear geometries. Thus, to initialize the geometry and the flow conditions on input, we configured the processors as a two-dimensional rectangular grid. The bounding confinement geometry is then draw on grid lines, with those processors corresponding to points within the flow geometry being active. In a different view of the machine, the vortex elements are stored as arrays with the processors configured as a one-dimensional grid. The number of elements in this array can rise and fall as vortex elements are both created at solid walls and destroyed as they leave the computational domain. This can leave "holes" in the array as processors corresponding to exiting elements are turned off. To efficiently utilize this array, we perform "garbage collection" which removes these holes and collapses the list to include only the active processors.

The N-body problem for the computational vortex elements was solved by a parallel implementation of the direct method. Thus, we evaluate all possible pairwise interactions using the exact Biot-Savart force law. There are several reasons why we chose a direct method, rather than the fast summation techniques. First, we wanted to perform a careful study of the speed-up that would result from a parallel implementation of the direct method, to provide comparison with a serial implementation. Second, the interaction between computational elements in the boundary layer is extremely complex, including several Heaviside functions and switches, unlike the straightforward inverse distance force law in the interior. These switches locate nearby computational elements, which are the only ones that contribute in the boundary force law expression. The original boundary layer algorithm by Chorin, evaluated these switches by computing the distance between all pairs of elements, which is an $O(N^2)$ operation, see [8]. Other options, such as a bin mechanism, attempt to efficiently locate nearby elements, but this may become intractable for the highly complex geometries under consideration here. On the other hand, while a multi-pole type expansion might be appropriate in the interior, to the best of our knowledge the intricate boundary force law cannot be easily cast in such a framework. Consequently, we chose a different approach, namely to pass *all* the computational elements to the N-body solver, and rely on the efficiency of the parallel N-body solver to calculate the appropriate interactions. The N-body problem was solved by means of a replicated orrery; which is a version of the algorithm presented in the next section on N-body solvers. For details of the N-body solver, see (2).

The associated elliptic flow that satisfies the no-flow condition is obtained using a parallel red-black overrelaxation with Chebyschev acceleration. Finally, the results are visualized using a real-time interactive flow visualization environment developed for the CM2, see [13]. Starting from a pre-computed discrete set of time-dependent flow quantities, such as velocity and density, this environment allows the user to interactively examine the data on a framebuffer using animated flow visualization diagnostics that mimic those in the experimental laboratory. For example, the user may study fluid velocity by injecting color-coded dye that is passively advected as the animation unfolds. Because the animation is both interactive and in real-time, moving eddy structures can be tagged and tracked with dye as they form. Different colored dyes can be used to watch regions merge or diffuse, and mixing mechanisms may be studied.

Complete details of this parallel implementation may be found in [10]. Using this parallel code, a wide variety of two-dimensional high Reynolds numbers flow simulations have been performed, including flow in an expanding/contracting nozzle, around islands, air flow through a two-dimensional cross-section of a Connection Machine, and around a piston/valve. These and other studies are discussed in detail in [8].

C. Three-Dimensional Vortex Methods and Their Parallel Implementation

The extension of vortex methods to three dimensions is complicated by the presence of vortex stretching in the vorticity transport equation. This is manifested by an additional term in the vorticity transport equation, namely

$$\frac{D\xi}{Dt} - (\xi \cdot \nabla)\mathbf{u} = \frac{1}{R}\nabla^2\xi$$

Once again, vorticity is described by discrete vortex elements, only this time thin sticks are used to carry the three-dimensional vorticity vector. A Biot-Savart law is again used to advect the vortex elements, and vortex stretching is accomplished by differentially moving the

ends of the sticks. Because the length of any individual stick may increase significantly, an adaptive control mechanism is used by which a stick is split up into smaller sticks if necessary. The no-flow boundary condition is again met through the addition of potential flow, this time found through the use of a panel method on the tessellated boundary, and the no-slip condition is satisfied through vortex creation on the boundary. A serial version of this technique is presented in [4]. Here, the method was used to compute flow past pitched airfoils and flow past spheres at several different Reynolds numbers; the resulting drag and pressure on the bodies was then computed.

A parallel version of this code has been developed on the CM5, see [12]. The CM5 is a multiple-instruction-multiple-data MIMD machine with hardware synchronization support for SIMD usage. It is programmable using either message passing on a node or from a high-level using a data parallel language such as CMFortran. Each node contains a 32 MHz Sun Sparc processor, as well as 4 vector units. There are 128 MBytes of memory per node, with a peak speed of 128 Mflops (double precision). A CM5 can range from 32 to 16,384 processing nodes, arranged in a fat-tree topology. Parallel I/O is supported, and graphics are performed through a coupling of the Application Visualization System (AVS) to the CM5. The essential guidelines of the serial code have been followed. Three issues stand out in the parallel implementation of this code; the parallel N-body solvers and visualization, which are both addressed in the next section, and the parallel elliptic solver, which computes the panel source influence matrix using a parallel QR factorization library routine from package CMSSL.

II. Two Components of a Parallel Implementation: A. The Parallel Implementation of N-Body Solvers

In this section, we discuss in some detail the implementation of an N-body solver on a massively parallel machine. Complete details of this work may be found in [5]. Once again, we focus on direct methods, which perform the full N^2 operations to compute all possible pairwise interactions. To be sure, in recent years a collection of approximation techniques have been developed, including cloud-in-cell techniques, local corrections, and multipole approaches. In this section, we will focus on the direct method to demonstrate how parallel programming style and approach can cause wide variation in performance, even for such a straightforward method. The point here is that under evolving architecture, hardware, and compilers, developing the proper intuition for even a very simple algorithm is not necessarily an easy task.

The basic direct N-body algorithm is as follows. We imagine that we are given N bodies, each described by a position $\vec{x}$ and a strength C. The goal is to compute the total force exerted on each body, which consists of the superposition of the individual forces exerted by all other bodies. More precisely, Let $F(I,J)$ be the force exerted on body I by body J. Then the following serial algorithm computes the total force $Force(I)$ on each body:

N-Body Algorithm:
```
Do I=1,N
Force(I) = 0.0
    Do J=1,N
        Force(I) =  Force(I) + F(I,J)
    Enddo
Enddo
```

As written, this is an $O(N^2)$ algorithm. A somewhat faster algorithm may be obtained by noting that it is more convenient to compute both $F(I,J)$ and $F(J,I)$ when I and J are in place, which then suggests the following "triangular" N-body algorithm:

Triangular N-Body Algorithm:
```
Do I=1,N
    F_Static  = 0.0
    F_Dual  = 0.0
Enddo

Do I=1,N-1
F_Static(I) = F_Static(I) + F(I,I)
    Do J=I+1,N
        F_Static(I)  = F_Static(I) + F(I,J)
        F_Dual(J) = F_Dual(J) + F(J,I)
    Enddo
Enddo

F_Static(N)  = F_Static(N) + F(N,N)

Do I=1,N
    Force(I)  =  F_Static(I)  +  F_Dual(I)
Enddo
```

The important thing to notice in the above algorithm is that the J index now runs from I+1 to N, rather than from 1 to N as it does in the previous algorithm. The reason that this algorithm may run faster is because the calculation of F(I,J) may contain quantities that may be used in the calculation of F(J,I) without recomputing. For example, a typical force law may require the evaluation of a square root to compute the distance between body I and body J, and need to be calculated only once for both F(I,J) and F(J,I).

There are several possible parallel implementation of the above two algorithms.

Using CSHIFTS:

Here, we consider a static and dynamic copy of the vortex elements, containing the position and strengths. The data is always laid out in one-dimensional arrays. For the full N-body algorithm, the dynamic copy is rotated through $N-1$ CSHIFTS, and between shifts the forces of the dynamic copy on the static copy are computed. This algorithm is referred to in the literature as the digital orrery, (see [1]).

Using SPREADS:

Here, we consider a static and dynamic copy of the vortex elements, containing the position and strengths. For the full N-body algorithm, the dynamic copy is created by spreading each element from the fixed copy to form the entire dynamic copy, Here, a "spread" is a broadcast of the data from an N-dimensional set to an N+1 dimensional set. Between each SPREAD, we compute the influence of the dynamic copy on the static copy. After N such SPREADs, the complete interaction has been summed.

A Few Ways To Program an N-Body Solver

```
DO J=1,N
DO I=1,N
    U(J)=U(J)+F(I,J)
ENDDO
ENDDO
```

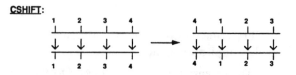

CSHIFT:

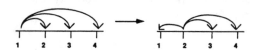

SPREAD:

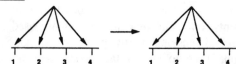

BROADCAST:

Using BROADCASTS:

Here, we again use a static and dynamic copy of the vortex elements, containing the position and strengths. For the full N-body algorithm, the dynamic copy is created by sending each body in turn to the front-end (in the CM-2) or the control processor (in the CM-5) and then broadcasting it out to fill the entire dynamic copy, Between each broadcast, we compute the influence of the dynamic copy on the static copy. After N such broadcasts, the complete interaction has been summed. Schematics of the cshift, spread, and broadcast techniques are given below.

Using FILLS:

If the number of bodies is not exactly matched with the layout of the array on the CM, the compiler uses masking, which flags the processors that do not contain actual bodies. While this is transparent to the user, it unfortunately means that operations such as CSHIFT become significantly slowed while the mask is checked. A simple fix is to determine the number of processors (here, processors means virtual processors) that the machine will allocate for a given number of bodies, and initially load the "extra" processors with bodies of zero strength. Adding these extra bodies of zero strength does not affect the forces calculated on the "live" bodies. We call this an "N-body algorithm with fill". First, we note that this approach does not require any extra memory, since those processors are automatically allocated during compile time. Second, by filling the "extra" processors with bodies of zero strength, the masking is turned off, and hence the speed of such operations as CSHIFT is increased. We get better performance even though more computation is being done.

Determining the number of bodies to add to reach the size of array allocated during compilation depends on the particular machine. Let P be the number of processing nodes on the machine (by a processing node on a CM-2, we mean a floating point unit). A CM-2 will allocate an array with an across-processor axis of length a multiple of $4P$, while a CM-5 with vector units will allocate an array with an across-processor axis of length a multiple of $8P$, and a CM-5 without vector units will allocate an array with an across-processor axis of length a multiple of P. (We note that the "current" version of the compiler (2.1) does not pad if so instructed). The idea of an "N-body problem with fill" is to make sure that the number of bodies is always equal to an integral multiple of this across-processor axis length.

A Message Passing Code:

The various CM Fortran techniques presented in previous sections share a common feature: they move the bodies as independent entities. They do not use block transfer of data thus amortizing latency and overhead in communication. This is a consequence of the limited control of data layout. Instead, one would like to configure the vortex array as a two-dimensional array (in actuality, three-dimensional, since the x, y, c, u, v elements are included), where one axis is purely physical (across processors) and the other purely serial. Then, for both the CSHIFT and SPREAD algorithms, a block move variant would move blocks from node to node and then vectorize serial operations in these blocks. While such capabilities are not yet available at this time in a global data parallel language such as CMFortran, such a code can easily be written using the message passing library available on the CM-5; where such commands as CSHIFT are replaced by explicit CMMD_send_and_receive calls. We have written such a code as part of our test codes.

Results

In the tables below, we give the results of timing runs to evaluate the various algorithms described above. We perform the CSHIFT, triangle-CSHIFT, SPREAD, and broadcast/broadcast-bit-blit algorithms, both with and without fill, for a 256 floating point node CM2, a 256 Sparc node CM-5, and a 128 pn (512 vector unit) CM-5, and some associated CMMD trials on a CM5.

It is important to note a seemingly minor change in coding style can make a major impact in timings. For example, in the implementation of the simple SPREAD algorithm, we note that it is unnecessary to spread the stored velocities from the static copy to the dynamic copy. Thus the static copy is of serial dimension 5, whereas the dynamic copy has serial dimension 3. In the implementation given in the text, the x and y positions and strength are each spread separately, that is,

$$\text{dynamic}(1,:) = \text{spread}(\text{static}(1,i),1,n)$$
$$\text{dynamic}(2,:) = \text{spread}(\text{static}(2,i),1,n)$$
$$\text{dynamic}(3,:) = \text{spread}(\text{static}(3,i),1,n)$$

However, if one were to replace this with the single SPREAD

$$\text{dynamic} = \text{spread}(\text{static}(1:3,i),1,n)$$

the resulting code is **fifteen** times slower.

Comparative 2-D Direct N-body Kernel Timings (in seconds)

10^5 Bodies

	CM-2 256 Welteks	CM-2 Fill 256 Welteks	CM-5 Sparc 256 Nodes	CM-5 Sparc Fill 256 Nodes	Inititally		1 Year Later	
					CM-5 VU 128 Nodes (512VU)	CM-5 VU Fill 128 Nodes (512VU)	CM-5 VU 128 Nodes (512VU)	CM-5 VU Fill 128 Nodes (512VU)
CSHIFT	2873	610.0	744.6	505.2	170.2	227.4	66.0	78.5
CSHIFT TRIANG	2300	637.7	637.3	409.4	113.3	159.5	45.5	103.5
SPREAD	325.5	325.6	246.3	252.0	91.01	116.1	63.0	63.81
BROAD-CAST	327.6	325.5	242.0	252.5	119.7	110.7	65.0	63.85
BC - BITBLT	307.0				66.53			

CMMD

Bodies	10^5
CMMD Sparc 128 Nodes Initially	210.4
CMMD Sparc 128 Nodes 1 Year Later	177.0
CMMD 128 Sparc VU CMF on a Node	45.0

{27 Mflops per node}

The above techniques for programming direct N-body solvers are by no means the only possible ways. However, what is clear is that coding modifications can have significant performance effects, even though the algorithm, language, and machine have remained more or less constant. On the one hand, each new version of the compiler brought an improvement in performance, on the other hand, the relative positions of the different approaches changed. Thus, the preferred approach for one compiler version is not necessarily the best for the next release. Nonetheless, we can make two observations. First, the variation in times between the different algorithms has markedly decreased. Second, the best global CMF code approaches the message-passing times. Ultimately, significant understanding of a changing compiler/machine interface is required to pick the best approach at any given time.

B. The Parallel Implementation of a Real-Time Visualization Environment

As discussed earlier, a real-time visualization environment was built on the CM2 (see [13]) using the attached frame buffer. Unfortunately, no such frame buffer is provided with the CM5. Consequently, none of our graphics software functioned. We thus rebuilt the real-time visualization environment on the CM5 using AVS modules coupled to the CM5, see [7]. In terms of AVS modules, three fields are read from disk: the boundary, the velocity data, and the object description. A "sampler" module uses the boundary data to create a suitable list of points from which particles can be injected. These points as well as the boundary and velocity data are passed to the "CM Particle Advector" module, which performs the advection on the CM5 and passes the new particle positions back to AVS. The "Points to Geometry" module combines this information with a color map created by the "Generate Colormap" module to build a set of colored three-dimensional spheres representing particles. Finally, the three-dimensional particles, the polygons defining the object, the original particle positions, and a bounding box are passed to the "Geometry Viewer" module, which renders the image. A connect map of the module is given below.

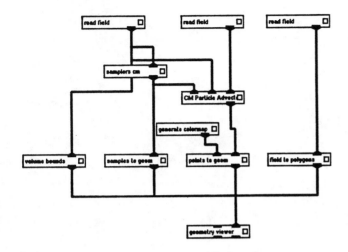

obtained by relatively little work, and then significant speedup obtained through a major conversion effort. Indeed, as shown in the middle graph, there may be a period in which the curve turns down, which might correspond to time spent rewriting code, changing programming models, changing machines, or rethinking the algorithm. Such a downturn is acceptable, as long as some positive results are obtained early on. Ultimately, to move parallel processing into the mainstream, one needs both some success for some work, and lots of success for lots of work.

Because so many elements of the system are provided by AVS, there is significantly less programming required to assemble a usable environment. The tradeoff is that some desired customizations may be harder to implement if they conflict with the design provided by AVS.

A far more serious problem with the CM5 implementation is the degradation in speed over the CM2 version. The speed obtained by the direct connection of the framebuffer to the CM2 is hard to match, and we have found that the CM5/AVS version is two to three times slower because of the overhead involved in going to a remote graphics device, since a framebuffer is not available on the CM5. This slowdown is noticeable and disturbing, and an unfortunate consequence of trying to stay abreast of evolving technologies.

III. Some Observations

The above illustrates that the work involved in implementing a parallel version of a code is significant. It also illustrates that the path to obtaining good performance is not always either clear or intuitive, even if one is willing to invest considerable energy. A suggestive drawing of the situation is given below. On the one hand, obtaining real performance requires considerable investment before any real speedup can be obtained over conventional serial/vector machines; makers of exotic architectures routinely expect users to invest such time (the speedup vs. invested time plot corresponding to the "fantasy user"). On the other hand, the bulk of users hope that little work (code change) will be required to obtain significant speedup; and, better yet, that beyond a certain point, additional work will yield little improvement (plot corresponding to the "user's fantasy"). In between the two lies a reasonable path; some speedup

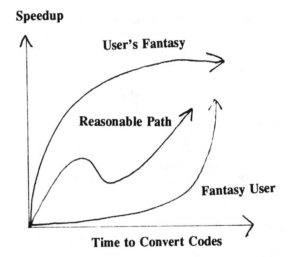

Acknowledgements: This work was supported in part under contract N66604-93-M-LC10 from the Office of Naval Research.

References

1) Applegate, J.F., M.R. Douglas, Y. Gursel, P. Hunter, C. Seitz, and G.J. Sussman, *IEEE Trans. Comput.*, **84,** pp. 822, (1985).

2) Brunet, J-Ph., Edelman, A., and Mesirov, J.P., *An optimal hypercube direct N-body solver on the Connection Machine*, Proceedings of Supercomputing '90, IEEE Computer Society Press (1990), 748--752

3)   Chorin, A.J., *Numerical Study of Slightly Viscous Flow*, J. Fluid Mech., **57,** pp. 785-796, (1973).

4)   Grant, J.R., Huyer, S., Sethian, J.A., and Uhlman, J., *Three-Dimensional Vortex Methods Past Bluff Bodies,* in preparation

5)   Greenberg, A., Mesirov, J., and Sethian, J.A., *Programming Direct N-body Solvers on Connection Machines,* Thinking Machines Technical Report, 1993.

6)   Hald, O.H., *Convergence of Vortex Methods,* in Vortex Methods and Vortex Motion, Eds. K. Gustafson and J.A. Sethian, SIAM Publications, Philadelphia, 1991.

7)   Lowther, K., Salem, J.B., and Sethian, J.A., *An Interactive, Animated Visualization Environment for Three-dimensional Fluid Flow,* to appear, Int. Jour. Super. Appl., 1993

8)   Sethian, J.A, *A Brief Overview of Vortex Methods,* in Vortex Methods and Vortex Motion, Eds. K. Gustafson and J.A. Sethian, SIAM Publications, Philadelphia, 1991.

9)   Sethian, J.A., *Turbulent Combustion in Open and Closed Vessels,* J. Comp. Phys., **54,** pp. 425-456, (1984).

10) Sethian, J.A., J.P. Brunet, A. Greenberg, J. Mesirov, *Two-Dimensional, Viscous, Incompressible Flow on a Massively Parallel Processor,* J. Comp, Phys. **101,** 1, pp. 185-206 (1992).

11) Sethian, J.A., and Ghoniem, A.F. *Validation Study of Vortex Methods,* J. Comp. Phys., **74,** pp. 283-317, (1988).

12) Sethian, J.A., Greenberg, A., Pryor, D., and Grantm, J.R., *A Parallel Implementation of Three-Dimensional Vortex Methods for Turbulent Flow,* in preparation.

13) Sethian, J.A., Salem, J.B., *Animation of Interactive Fluid Flow Visualization Tools on a Data Parallel Machine,* Int. Jour. Super. Appl., **3.2,** pp. 10-39, (1988).

The High Performance Storage System

Robert A. Coyne
Harry Hulen

IBM Federal Systems Company
3700 Bay Area Blvd., Houston, TX 77058

Richard Watson

Lawrence Livermore National Laboratory
P.O. Box 808, Livermore, CA 94550

Abstract

The National Storage Laboratory (NSL) was organized to develop, demonstrate and commercialize technology for the storage systems that will be the future repositories for our national information assets. Within the NSL four Department of Energy laboratories and IBM Federal Systems Company have pooled their resources to develop an entirely new High Performance Storage System (HPSS). The HPSS project concentrates on scalable parallel storage systems for highly parallel computers as well as traditional supercomputers and workstation clusters. Concentrating on meeting the high end of storage system and data management requirements, HPSS is designed using network-connected storage devices to transfer data at rates of 100 million bytes per second and beyond. The resulting products will be portable to many vendor's platforms. The three year project is targeted to be complete in 1995.

This paper provides an overview of the requirements, design issues, and architecture of HPSS, as well as a description of the distributed, multi-organization industry and national laboratory HPSS project.

1: Storage system requirements and challenges

The National Storage Laboratory (NSL) has initiated a project to develop a next generation High Performance Storage System (HPSS). Participants in the HPSS project are IBM Federal Systems Company, Lawrence Livermore National Laboratory, Los Alamos National Laboratory, Sandia National Laboratories, and Oak Ridge National Laboratory.

There are many requirements and challenges motivating the need for a new generation of storage system such as HPSS [4,5]. The requirements are driven both by the pull of applications and the push of technology. Today's storage systems can move one to ten million bytes of information per second, but current needs call for systems that can move data at 100 million bytes per second. Future needs will almost certainly reach 500 million to one billion bytes per second and beyond. On the technological front, the successful commercialization of parallel computers and disks has accelerated the already brisk rate of growth in the underlying hardware capabilities. The NSL was organized to develop, demonstrate, and commercialize high-performance storage system technologies to meet these challenges [9]. These new technologies will help meet the storage requirements of the Department of Energy and other government agencies as well as the private sector.

While the immediate objective of HPSS is to meet the individual and collective needs of the participating Department of Energy laboratories, the longer range objectives include participating in a national information infrastructure and transferring the technology to the commercial sector. The HPSS project leverages Department of Energy applications and expertise with that of industry to accelerate the development of U.S. technology for local and nationwide storage system architectures and to facilitate the availability of improved systems for the government and US industry.

Recognizing the importance to the nation's future of communicating, storing and manipulating large quantities of information, both the House of Representatives and the Senate have proposed legislation to create a national information infrastructure to facilitate broad-based access to information [25,26]. The Department of Energy, for example [27,28], has information on the global ecosystem, environmental remediation, petroleum reservoir modeling, the structure of novel materials, and plasma physics, to name only a few of its data resources that are of value to education, research, and industry. Many other government agencies, universities and commercial enterprises also have information assets whose potential economic value can only be fully realized if a national information infrastructure is created.

1.1: Requirement for storage systems to be part of an information infrastructure

To participate in a national information infrastructure, storage systems must become invisible components embedded in and supporting digital libraries of text and graphic information, scientific data, and multimedia data. Users will want to browse, access, and store data using a language and tools that are tied to the application domain, not the storage domain. The interface to the storage system must support appropriate primitives required by application domains such as education, science, and business. These requirements include the need for multiple levels of storage and mechanisms for migration and caching of data between storage levels, with explicit control by the application domain as well as implicit or automatic controls that are the rule in today's storage systems. They include mechanisms for efficient organization such as clustering, partitioning and explicit placement of data under the control of the application domain.

1.2: Requirements for scalability

A fundamental requirement of HPSS is that it must be scalable. There are several important dimensions to the scalability requirement:

- *Size*. The projected storage requirements are for billions of datasets, each potentially terabytes in size, for total storage capacities in petabytes. In addition the file naming environment must support millions of directory entries for thousands of users.

- *Data transfer rate*. The I/O architecture must scale, using parallel I/O mechanisms, to support individual application data transfers in the range of gigabytes per second and total system throughput of several gigabytes per second.

- *Topology*. Scalable parallel processors and parallel storage devices must be supported, as well as parallel data transfer at all levels. In the general case, the

number of nodes at either end and the number of paths between can all be different.

- *Geography*. Multiple storage systems located in different geographical areas must be integratable into a single logical system accessible by client systems as wide ranging as personal computers, workstations, and supercomputers.

The scalability requirements for HPSS are driven by applications and the distributed high performance computing environments necessary to run them. For example, large grand challenge applications such as three dimensional hydrodynamics, global climate modeling, lattice gas theory, materials processing, plasma modeling, and magnetic fusion reactor modeling currently generate datasets of the order of magnitude of tens to hundreds of gigabytes. When these models are scaled to take advantage of massively parallel computers, they will generate storage requirements of terabytes of data. Similarly data gathered by experimental devices and sensor based systems in the oil and gas industry, medical field, high energy physics, planetary space probes and earth observing satellites will create terabyte storage requirements. Digitized libraries, educational and other multimedia resources, and databases in commercial enterprises such as insurance companies also represent very large datasets.

1.3: Requirement for an industry standard infrastructure

Large storage systems live and evolve over decades. In order for such systems to have a long useful life, they need to be highly portable, adaptable to new applications, and accommodate new devices, storage system modules, policies and algorithms. A central requirement is that HPSS be implemented using industry standards wherever possible, including for its architecture, function, distributed environment, communications protocols, system management, and security. While standards in some of these areas are firmly established, many are emerging or are only now beginning to be discussed. Others, particularly in the parallel I/O area are at best in early research stages. The standards selected for HPSS are discussed in Section 2 of this paper.

1.4: Requirement for storage system management

Storage system management is the collection of functions concerned with control, coordination, monitoring, performance and utilization of the storage system. These functions are often interdependent, involve human decision making, and span multiple servers. The need for a separate, identifiable storage system management architecture arises from the requirement to exchange management information and to provide control in a consistent, predictable manner between components of the storage system. There is also a requirement for storage system management to be built around system management standards.

2: HPSS architecture, design and implementation considerations

HPSS is an evolving system designed to take advantage of current and future hardware and software technology. While many of the design features of HPSS are comfortably within the state-of-the-art for distributed, client-server, standards-based software projects, many features of HPSS, such as scalable parallel I/O, stake out positions at the leading edge of storage system technology. In this section we discuss the main architectural features and issues of HPSS. Figure 1 illustrates the system architecture that HPSS supports. Note that the architecture is network-centered, including a high speed network for data transfer and a separate network for control. In actual implementation, the control and data transfer networks may be physically separate as shown or may be combined. The data transfer network may also have parallel connections to storage subsystems such as disk arrays and tapes. The disk and tape servers are compatibility mechanisms that provide data network transfer interfaces for devices that cannot be directly network attached.

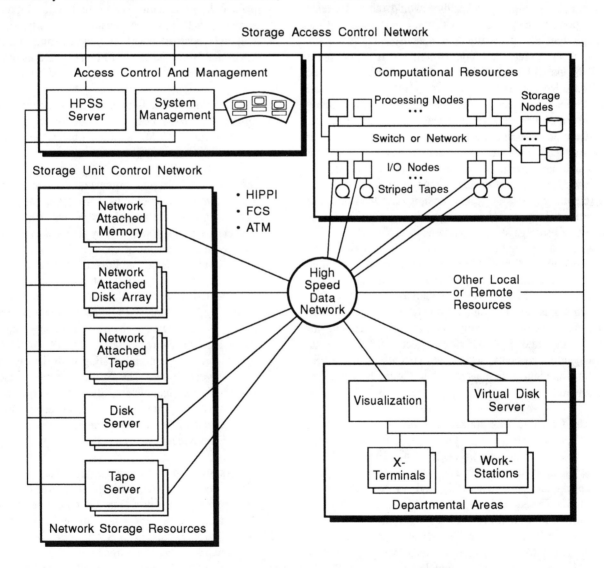

Figure 1. System architecture supported by HPSS

2.1: Modularity based on the Mass Storage Reference Model, Version 5

The basic architecture and modularity of HPSS have benefited from the nearly three years of collaborative work on the Version 5 of the Mass Storage Reference Model [8,16]. This new version of the Reference Model represents the work of over 50 experienced developers and users of storage systems from universities, industry, and government. The Reference Model details those components for which there are plans for developing standard interfaces and services and also recognizes other components and functionality needed in a complete system. The advantages of a design approach based on the Reference Model is four-fold. First, by basing the design on the Reference Model it was possible to complete the system design much quicker than would otherwise have been possible and to do so with the expectation that the design would be internally consistent. Second, by staying close to the Reference Model structure, it is hoped that it will be possible to provide and receive interchangeable software components to and from other vendors and development projects in the future. Third, since many members of the HPSS design team have participated in the Reference Model development, it provides a basis for communication between them and a basis on which to organize the project. Fourth, work on HPSS will provide an opportunity to obtain experience in working with the Reference Model in a new design and feedback our experience into the Model's ongoing evolution, as well as associated storage system standards work.

Recognizing that storage systems will increasingly be embedded in digital libraries and data management systems, the approach of the IEEE Storage System Standards Working Group, and therefore of HPSS, is to design storage systems in such a way as to provide layers of function with application interface points suitable for use by separate digital library, object storage and data management systems. Major components of the HPSS architecture and design, as shown in Figure 2, include the following:

- The Client is the application interface to the storage system. HPSS initially presents clients with a file system abstraction in which the files, and the application interface libraries that operate on the files appear similar syntactically and semantically to the POSIX file and I/O libraries. For historical reasons, the initial file system abstraction is supported by a server called a Bitfile Server. The client interface has been extended to support parallel data transfer interfaces and application level parallel I/O libraries. A POSIX Virtual File System interface is also planned. Initial

file system daemons will be provided to support client interfaces to IBM's Vesta parallel file system [7], to Sun's Network File System (NFS) [23], and to the Open Software Foundation's Distributed Computing Environment (DCE) Distributed File System [20]. As HPSS becomes a foundation for digital libraries, large object stores and data management systems, additional application interfaces will be developed.

- The Name Server is recognized by the Reference Model as being a necessary component but one that is outside the boundaries of the model. The purpose of the Name Server is to map a name known to the client to a bitfile id known to the storage system. The initial HPSS Name Server provides a POSIX view of the name space. The strategic Name Server for HPSS is planned to be a name server under development at Cornell, that has the desired characteristics of scalability, performance efficiencies, and reliability. Additional Name Servers will be provided as new data management name spaces are introduced by users.

- The Location Server is planned for future releases to be scalable and keep track of the billions of distributed and replicated HPSS storage objects expected in mature usage.

- The Storage Server organizes physical storage volumes into virtual volumes. Virtual volumes can also span multiple physical volumes that have characteristics not found in physical volumes such as striping and replication groups. In HPSS, the storage server implements an additional storage abstraction called storage segments. Storage Segments are implemented over virtual volumes and provide a volume independent byte stream view of storage. Storage server clients using storage segments are relieved of the chores of allocating and deallocating virtual volume space and dealing with data migration and recovery issues. The Storage Server, based on type-of-service parameters, determines the parallel data transfer organization. It also determines the optimum use of parallel data transfer paths and parallel storage components such as disks and tapes.

- Movers are responsible for copying data to and from storage media as well as requesting transmission of data from a source to a sink. Of particular interest in HPSS is a type of Mover that implements third party data transfer, discussed in Section 2.6, that is key to the network-centered architecture of HPSS. Parallel I/O Movers also execute the parallel data transfer plan determined by the Storage System.

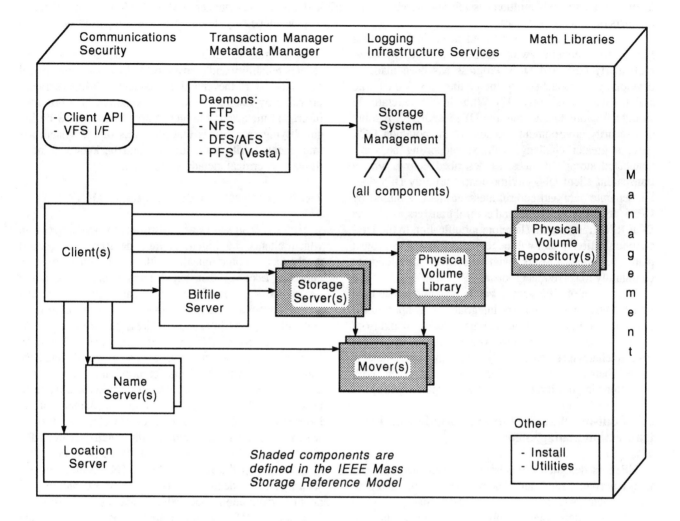

Figure 2. HPSS design is based on the IEEE Mass Storage Reference Model

- The Physical Volume Repository is responsible for storing removable physical volumes contained in cartridges and mounting these volumes onto physical drives, employing either robotic or human operators.

- The Physical Volume Library (PVL) integrates multiple Physical Volume Repositories into a distributed media library across an entire enterprise, similar to a distributed tape management system. The PVL in HPSS is responsible for atomic mounts of parallel tape cartridges.

In HPSS, each component has a well-defined application program interface. The APIs define the operations that may be performed on the objects owned

by each component. Each API is therefore available directly to any application with proper authorization, setting the stage for the use of HPSS as an embedded storage system in data management, object store and digital library applications.

2.2: Distribution and multitasking based on DCE

One of the requirements of HPSS is that it be possible to distribute, replicate, and multiprocess its servers and clients. Further, it is required that HPSS provide concurrent access to hundreds of applications. The basic server architecture of HPSS is built on the Open Software Foundation's DCE. In particular, HPSS is based on DCE's remote procedure call (RPC) services for control messages and DCE threads for multitasking [20]. The latter is vital to both multiprocessing and serving large numbers of concurrent requests.

One of the requirements outlined earlier is the need for HPSS to integrate with distributed file services, particularly NFS and DFS. Progress has been made in developing approaches to integrating distributed file systems with mass stores [19]. While it will be relatively straight forward to integrate the HPSS and DFS naming and security environments because of the common DCE base, a greater challenge will be supporting network-connected storage devices, as described below, with a transparent client DFS environment. Currently DFS does not separate data and control messages as is required by HPSS. It performs all data and control transfers within the DCE RPC framework. Therefore modification to the DFS communication model will be required. The HPSS project plans to work closely with the DFS development community to solve this problem.

In the case of NFS access we are planning to use high speed NFS frontend servers integrated with appropriate automatic migration and caching mechanisms to and from the large hierarchical storage system. This will present several challenges, particularly when the same data is shared between multiple NFS frontends, given NFS limitations in providing full location transparency [23].

2.3: Built-in reliability through metadata and transaction management

HPSS is designed around a distributed metadata and transaction manager, an idea borrowed from database management systems. The metadata manager is a distributable entity that reliably stores the metadata each server requires for each of its abstract objects. This manager supports the concept of distributed atomic transactions involving multiple servers, that is, a set of actions that must be treated as a single operation and whose suboperations either all complete or no data is changed. Transaction management allows HPSS to provide facilities to commit or abort a transaction across multiple servers, thus providing assurance that metadata updates will not be left in a partially completed state. Transaction management guards against leaving data without pointers or pointers without data in the event a failure occurs in the midst of an update. For example, transaction management protects against having a name space entry without a corresponding file or vice versa, that has been a problem in previous storage systems. Transaction management is difficult to retrofit into an existing system. The requirement for transaction management is therefore one of the principal motivators for developing HPSS as a new system rather than as a derivative of an existing storage system. The metadata and transaction manager used in HPSS is Encina [12], that was developed by Transarc and is supported on several vendors' platforms.

In addition to use of transaction management, HPSS assures reliability and recoverability by replicating critical metadata and the naming database using services provided by Encina. Periodic backups are also provided of critical metadata. Another feature of the HPSS design simplifying recovery is that all levels of the system are implemented with both forward and backward pointers throughout critical metadata structures.

2.4: Built-in security through use of DCE

HPSS is designed to be a distributed storage system in which clients, intelligent storage devices, and control mechanisms communicate with each other over a network. Like all distributed architectures, this raises security issues. How, for example, can a server know that a request from a client or a storage server is an authorized, authentic request? In order to address this problem, HPSS is designed around DCE Security [20], that is based on Kerberos which originated at MIT's Project Athena. By using DCE, the mechanisms for providing security in a distributed environment are moved outside the domain of proprietary HPSS design and into the domain of an industry standard environment. The mechanism through which security is invoked is the DCE secure RPC mechanism. All of the control interfaces between HPSS modules are in the form of RPCs. The requirement for security and the decision to use a DCE infrastructure was another motivation that helped drive the decision to implement HPSS from the ground up, as it did not appear practical to retrofit such a capability into an existing design.

2.5: Multiple dynamic hierarchies

A concept pioneered at the NSL is multiple dynamic hierarchies. Current storage systems generally provide a single, simple, predefined hierarchy of storage media [4]. In the conventional hierarchy, frequently used data is kept on disk, less frequently used data is kept in an automated tape library, and infrequently used data is kept in tape vaults. With the availability of new media, such as solid state disk, disk arrays, and helical scan tape; and the wide range of devices offering different levels of cost, capacity, and performance, there is a need for more complex hierarchies that can be defined and dynamically redefined by a system administrator. The need for multiple hierarchies is based on such factors as location, reliability, data type, cost, performance and project affiliation. Each hierarchy must be adaptable to meet specific application and system configuration requirements and must be able to change over time under the control of a system administrator. The approach used in the initial storage system at NSL, which is based on UniTree [13] and adopted for HPSS was originated by NSL participants Buck and Coyne [3].

2.6: Network-connected storage concepts

The NSL has successfully demonstrated the concept of a network-connected storage system architecture in which network-attached storage devices communicate directly with supercomputers and other clients under the control of a storage system management and control entity [5,9]. Using a network-connected architecture, the NSL has shown, in its work with NSL UniTree, more than a tenfold increase in throughput over the former processor-centered architecture in use at the National Energy Research Supercomputer Center. NSL UniTree is an extension of the UniTree storage system from OpenVision [13]. The network-centered architecture is shown in Figure 1, which depicts processing nodes and storage devices connected by a high speed network such as HIPPI, FCS, or ATM.

Most operational storage systems at national laboratories and supercomputer centers use general purpose computers as storage servers. These storage servers connect to storage units such as disks and tapes and serve as intermediaries in passing data to compute-intensive nodes [4]. As data rates increase for storage devices and communications links, it becomes necessary to increase the size of the storage server to provide the required memory and data bandwidth. The alternative, that has been the subject of much of the work at NSL, is to attach storage devices directly to the network [6,9,15,17,24]. This network-centered alternative supports higher data rates than can be supported in the traditional processor-centered storage server configuration and does not require the storage server to be as large, thus reducing its cost. HPSS will extend the network-connected storage architecture to use Parallel I/O, discussed below.

2.7: Support for parallel clients and scalable parallel I/O

Most of the work in parallel computing has focused on processing and associated programming models. Very little work has gone into thinking about the equally important issues associated with parallel I/O, particularly parallel I/O involving a hierarchy of storage systems [2]. There have been important developments in RAID disk systems and striping I/O systems that have transfer rates

in the range of 60 to 100 megabytes per second [10,11,14,22], but what is needed is another order of magnitude or more increase in performance, only possible through parallel transfers to parallel RAID disk and tape systems.

To meet its scalability requirements, the HPSS design is addressing many issues from simply providing adequate size fields in its data structures to complex issues such as fast recovery after a crash and efficient resource management algorithms for very large stores. One of the most challenging areas will be meeting the scalabilty requirements for I/O rates. This requires support for parallel I/O at all levels of the system architecture from application libraries and compilers down through the servers and the movers. The HPSS project plans to work closely with other research projects in the parallel I/O area [2].

The HPSS project is working to develop an application driven, scalable, parallel I/O model and architectures that provide the needed support. In parallel processing algorithms, a single large logical data object, such as a matrix, linked list, or other data structure, is broken into pieces that are distributed among the memories of various processors and storage devices to maximize overall algorithm performance. The pieces may form a non-overlapping partition of the object, or they may overlap slightly, where the redundancy of the overlapping may help reduce communication between processors. The programmer, the parallel libraries, and the compiler work to distribute the data in such a way as to increase parallel computation while at the same time decreasing the amount of costly interprocessor exchanges of data.

Parallel I/O services must minimize the time to write or read such distributed data objects to or from secondary and tertiary storage by making use of multiple storage devices and parallel data paths. The result is that a single logical object will have to be spread out (mapped) over many devices in such a way that the high-level structure of the data object, as seen at the application program level, can be reconstructed from the many pieces. This is complicated by the fact that the application may read or write the separate blocks of data in quite unpredictable order from any of the processors. Furthermore, a parallel data object may be stored with a distribution structure that is near optimal for the way the data set was produced but which may be very inefficient for subsequent patterns of access. The parallel I/O system needs to interact with whatever data partitioning methodologies are employed by client applications.

Figure 3 illustrates the problem of moving data between parallel nodes. The convention is that the data moves from the source nodes to the sink nodes. The source and sink nodes may be parallel processors or striped I/O devices. In Figure 3, four parallel source nodes are shown moving twelve blocks of data to three parallel sink nodes. The plan by which the data is moved is negotiated between the source and sink movers and the storage server. Then, the storage server manages the transfer.

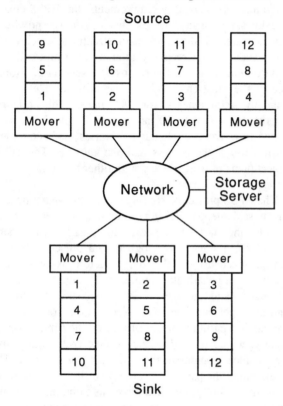

Figure 3. An example of moving data in parallel

Figure 3 could just as easily show interconnected parallel computer systems between which data transfer is desired. A project has been initiated under sponsorship of the NSL, DOE national laboratories, IEEE Storage System Standards Working Group in collaboration with the parallel computer vendor and research communities to define and prototype strategies for parallel data transfer interface with the intent of developing a standard for parallel data exchange [1]. HPSS will support clients that are either parallel or sequential computers. The initial implementation will interface to IBM Research Division's Vesta parallel file system [7]. Later versions will interface to any vendor's parallel computing system that supports the parallel data exchange protocols referenced above.

2.8: Storage system management

In a distributed storage system such as HPSS, the need for a storage system management architecture is much greater than in previous centralized systems. In the current prototype storage system at the National Storage Laboratory, some significant proof of concept work has been done using a storage management system with a graphical user interface [18]. For HPSS the decision was made to clearly identify during system design all system management functions and managed objects and to provide a common management system interface. The management system itself is still being designed, but the intent is to use, to the extent possible, an industry standard base such as the OSF Distributed Management Environment [21].

HPSS plans are to define the managed objects for storage systems in a manner consistent with the ISO/OSI Guidelines for the Definition of Managed Objects (GDMO) [29]. This structure will permit the HPSS storage system management framework to be standardized around the emerging technology from the OSF Distributed Management Environment.

3: Project methodology and status

The HPSS project began in 1992 as a series of requirements meetings. The initial goal was to determine if two or more organizations could converge on a single set of high level requirements called Level A requirements. A composite Level A requirements document was agreed to by representatives from the four DOE laboratories and IBM. In addition, Argonne National Laboratory, the National Center for Atmospheric Research, and Pacific Northwest Laboratory provided requirements and helpful input and review.

The next step was to expand the requirements into a more detailed Level B requirements specification for each of the modules and functional areas outlined in Section 2. This was accomplished, with the results cross-referenced to the Level A requirements, in March, 1993.

Once the requirements were completed, a project organization was created. The basic project organization consists of an Executive Committee, a Technical Committee and Development Teams. The Executive Committee has a member from each participating organization and handles policy level issues. The Technical Committee is led by the HPSS project leader and has a member from each of the participating organizations, who are also members of the Development Teams. The Technical Committee meets at least once a week by teleconference to deal with resource allocation, scheduling and technical issues spanning the Development Teams. The Technical Committee is responsible for setting coding, documentation and other development standards for the project. The project is following high standards of software engineering. This is essential not only for system quality but to facilitate the distributed development nature of the project.

The Development Teams are organized around the modularity of the system and infrastructure areas. To the extent possible, the Teams are organized to take advantage of geographical closeness. The Teams interact frequently by teleconference, email and when necessary at a participant's site for design sessions and design reviews with the Technical Committee. Each Development Team submits a weekly progress report to the Technical Committee. A central on-line repository of project documentation, designs, schedules, and source code, is maintained. Computer systems are located at each site for development and there is shared access to certain systems as necessary to reduce software license fees. Subsystem integration is distributed, but system integration will be at one site. Our experience with the distributed development process is very positive.

By using the IEEE Reference Model as the starting point, a design for HPSS was achieved which consists of well-defined modules that could be developed relatively independently. This was an important factor considering that HPSS is being developed at five sites across the country. A design document was developed for each server along with interface definitions between servers. These designs were reviewed by the other server teams and the Technical Committee. By July, 1993, the design of the first release was formalized.

At this point, implementation of the first release is well under way. Staffing is up to 24 individuals, some part time, at five sites. Discussions are also in progress with other possible DOE laboratory and industrial participants. By the end of the first quarter of 1994, it is expected that the first release will be developed, integrated, and undergoing system test. The test plan then calls for the individual laboratories and IBM to each set up a pilot project to test the first release in as realistic an operational environment as possible. A second and third release are planned, that will follow the same design, development, and test methodology as the first release.

The expectation is that HPSS will, at the appropriate stage of development, be licensed by the developers for commercial use. This will include a source license so the system can be ported. It is anticipated that by the time of the second release, that should be toward the end of 1994 or early 1995, there will be sufficient functionality and maturity in HPSS to allow HPSS to be ported to other platforms and installed at other computer centers. The schedule for offering HPSS for use outside the sponsoring organizations has not been established, but will come shortly after HPSS has stabilized and proven itself in operation at the participating government laboratories.

4: The National Storage Laboratory

HPSS is a project of the National Storage Laboratory. The NSL collaboration, launched in 1992, has grown in just under two years into a major collaboration of governmental, industrial, and academic partners. The DOE laboratory partnership includes Lawrence Livermore, (LLNL) Los Alamos (LANL), Sandia (SNL), and Oak Ridge (ORNL) national laboratories, with planned participation of other DOE laboratories in the future. Industrial participants include IBM Federal Systems Company, IBM ADSTAR, Ampex Systems Corporation, Maximum Strategy Incorporated, Network Systems Corporation (NSC), OpenVision, Zitel Corporation, PsiTech, CHI Systems, Cray Research Inc., IGM, and Kinesix. University and supercomputing center participants include Cornell Office of Information Technologies and the San Diego Supercomputing Center. Discussions with other potential industrial, academic, and government agency participants are ongoing.

The approach of the NSL is based on the premise that no single company, government laboratory, or research organization has the ability to confront all the system-level issues that must be resolved before there is significant advancement in the storage systems technology needed for a national information infrastructure and for local high performance computing environments.

The NSL's primary prototype equipment site is located within the National Energy Research Supercomputer Center at LLNL. The NSL's collaborative software development projects are distributed across the DOE laboratories and other members sites. Work is performed under Cooperative Research and Development Agreements (CRADAs), with all participants funding their own participation. In particular, the DOE laboratories are supported by DOE Defense Programs Technology Transfer Initiative and DOE Energy Research funding.

Acknowledgments

We wish to acknowledge the many discussions and shared design, implementation, and operation experiences with our colleagues in the National Storage Laboratory collaboration, the IEEE Mass Storage Systems and Technology Technical Committee, the IEEE Storage System Standards Working Group, and in the storage community. Specifically we wish to acknowledge the people on the HPSS Technical Committee and Development Teams. At the risk of leaving out a key colleague in this ever-growing collaboration, the authors wish to acknowledge Dwight Barrus, Ron Christman,

Danny Cook, and Tyce McLarty from LANL; Larry Berdahl, Jim Daveler, Dave Fisher, Mark Gary, Steve Louis, and Norm Samuelson from LLNL; Rena Haynes, Sue Kelly, Hilary Jones, and Bill Rahe from SNL; Randy Burris, Dan Million, and Vicky White from ORNL; and Paul Chang, Jeff Deutsch, Kurt Everson, Rich Ruef, Danny Teaff, and Terry Tyler from IBM Federal Systems Company and its contractors.

This work was, in part, performed by the Lawrence Livermore National Laboratory, Los Alamos National Laboratory, Oak Ridge National Laboratory, and Sandia National Laboratories, under auspices of the U.S. Department of Energy, and by IBM Federal Systems Company under Independent Research and Development and other internal funding.

References

1. Berdahl, L., ed., "The Parallel Data Exchange", working document in progress, available from Lawrence Livermore National Laboratory, Sept. 1993.

2. Bershad, B., et al, "The Scalable I/O Initiative", White paper, available through the Concurrent Supercomputing Consortium, CalTech, Pasadena, CA, Feb. 1993.

3. Buck, A. L. and R. A. Coyne, Jr., "Dynamic Hierarchies and Optimization in Distributed Storage System," Digest of Papers, Eleventh IEEE Symposium on Mass Storage Systems, Oct. 7-10, 1991, IEEE Computer Society Press, pp. 85-91.

4. Coleman, S. and R. W. Watson, "The Emerging Paradigm Shift in Storage System Architectures," Proceedings of the IEEE, April 1993.

5. Coleman, S. S., R. W. Watson, R. A., Coyne, H. Hulen, "The Emerging Storage Management Paradigm", Proceedings of the Twelfth IEEE Symposium on Mass Storage Systems, Monterey, CA., April 1993.

6. Collins, B., et al., "Los Alamos HPDS: High-Speed Data Transfer" Proceedings of the Twelfth IEEE Symposium on Mass Storage, IEEE Computer Society Press, April, 1993.

7. Corbett, P. F., D. G. Feitelson, S. J. Baylor, J. Prost, "Parallel Access to Files in the Vesta File System," Proceeding of Supercomputing '93, IEEE Computer Society Press, November, 1993.

8. Coyne, R. A. and H. Hulen, "An Introduction to the Storage System Reference Model, Version 5," Proceedings of the Twelfth IEEE Symposium on Mass Storage, IEEE Computer Society Press, April, 1993.

9. Coyne, R. A., H. Hulen, and R. W. Watson, "Storage Systems for National Information Assets," Proceedings of Supercomputing 92, Minneapolis, IEEE Computer Society Press, Nov. 1992.

10. DeBenedictus, E., and S. Johnson, "Extending Unix for Scalable Computing", to appear in IEEE Computer, Nov. 1993.

11. Dibble, P. C., "A Parallel Interleaved File System", Ph.D. Thesis, Univ. of Rochester, 1989.

12. Dietzen, Scott, "Distributed Transaction Processing with Encina and the OSF/DCE", Transarc Corporation, September 1992.

13. DISCOS, "UniTree, the Virtual Disk System, An Overview," available from OpenVision, 1991.

14. Ghosh, J. and B. Agarwal, "Parallel I/O Subsystems for Distributed Memory Multicomputers", Proceeding of the Fifth International Parallel Processing Symposium, May 1991.

15. Hyer, R., R. Ruef, and R. W. Watson, "High Performance Direct Network Data transfers at the National Storage Laboratory" Proceedings of the Twelfth IEEE Symposium on Mass Storage, IEEE Computer Society Press, April, 1993.

16. IEEE Storage System Standards Working Group, "Mass Storage Reference Model Version 5," IEEE Computer Society Mass Storage Systems and Technology Committee, unapproved draft, August 5, 1993.

17. Katz, R. H., "High Performance Network and Channel-Based Storage," Proc. of IEEE, Aug. 1992.

18. Louis, S., and S. W. Hyer, "Applying IEEE Storage System Management Standards at the National Storage Laboratory" Proceedings of the Twelfth IEEE Mass Storage Symposium, IEEE Computer Society Press, April, 1993.

19. Nydict, D. et al., "An AFS-based Mass Storage System at the Pittsburgh Supercomputer Center" Digest of Papers Eleventh IEEE Symposium on Mass Storage Systems, Oct., 1991, pp. 117-122.

20. Open Software Foundation, Distributed Computing Environment Version 1.0 Documentation Set. Open Software Foundation, Cambridge, Mass. 1992.

21. Open Software Foundation Distributed Management Environment (DME) Architecture, Open Software Foundation, Cambridge, Mass., May 1992.

22. Peterson, D. G., and R. Katz, "A Case for Redundant Arrays of Inexpensive Disks (RAID)," Proc. SIGMOD Int. Conf. on Data Management, Chicago 1988, pp. 109-116.

23. Sandberg, R., et al., "Design and Implementation of the SUN Network Filesystem," Proc. USENIX Summer Conf., June 1989, pp. 119-130.

24. Sloan, J. L., B.T. O'Lear, D. L. Kitts, and E. E. Harano, "The MaSSIVE Project at NCAR" Proceedings of the Twelfth IEEE Symposium on Mass Storage, IEEE Computer Society Press, April, 1993.

25. U.S. Congress, "National Information Infrastructure Act of 1993, - H.R. 1757," Washington, DC, April 21, 1993.

26. U.S. Congress, "National Competitiveness Act of 1993 - S.4," Washington, DC, January 21, 1993.

27. U.S. Department of Energy, Office of Energy Research, Office of Scientific Computing, "Requirements for Supercomputing in Energy Research: The Transition to Massively Parallel Computing," National Technical Information Service, Publication DOE/ER-0587, February, 1993.

28. U.S. Department of Energy, Office of Energy Research, Office of Scientific Computing, "The DOE Program in High Performance Computing and Communications Energy Transition," National Technical Information Service, Publication DOE/ER-0536, March, 1993.

29. "Information Technology - Open Systems Interconnection - Structure of Management Information - Part 4: Guidelines for the Definition of Management Objects," ISO/IEC 10165-4, 1991.

Session 2:
Partitioning
Chair: Frederica Darema

AUTOMATIC PARTITIONING OF UNSTRUCTURED GRIDS INTO CONNECTED COMPONENTS

Leonardo Dagum
Computer Sciences Corporation
NASA Ames Research Center
Moffett Field, CA 94035-1000

Abstract

This paper presents two partitioning schemes that guarantee connected components given a connected initial grid. Connected components are important for convergence of methods such as domain decomposition or multigrid. For many of the grids tested, the schemes produce partitions as good (in terms of number of cut edges) or better than spectral partitioning and require only modest computational resources. This paper describes the two schemes in detail and presents comparison results from a number of two and three dimensional unstructured grids.

Introduction

Automatic partitioning of unstructured grids is important to many problems in computer science and numerical analysis. The partitioning problem arises naturally from trying to solve, on multiprocessor architectures, large scale computational problems based on unstructured computational domains. Mapping such problems onto a multiprocessor generally requires partitioning the computational domain into a number of subdomains and assigning these subdomains to the different processors. The increased attention recently given to multiprocessor architectures has sparked greater interest in the partitioning problem, and a number of different algorithms have been investigated. Algorithms motivated by the physics underlying the computational problem include simulated annealing as used by Williams [13] and Nour-Omid, Raesfky and Lyzenga [7]; and a greedy algorithm used by Farhat [2]. Algorithms based on geometric considerations include straight coordinate bisection, discussed by Simon [9]; a coordinate bisection type algorithm but employing the principal axes of inertia

---

[1] Employee of Computer Sciences Corp, Work sponsored under NASA contract NAS-2-12961

for bisection directions used by Farhat and Lesoinne [3]; and stereoscopic projection investigated by Teng [10]. Graph based algorithms include a graph bisection scheme employing rooted level structures and a Kerninghan-Lin algorithm [6] applied to structures problems by Vaughan [11]; and spectral partitioning proposed by Pothen, Simon and Liou [8] and further developed by Simon [9] and Barnard and Simon[1].

A primary consideration in evaluating the various partitioning schemes is the number of cut edges resulting from the partitioning. These are the edges of the original graph which are connecting the different subgraphs induced by the partitioning. One would like to choose a partitioning that minimizes the amount of communication between processors, and a first order approximation of the communication cost is given by the number of cut edges in a partition [12]. Recursive spectral partitioning is perhaps most notable amongst the many schemes for consistently yielding partitions with low numbers of cut edges [9]. A fundamental drawback of spectral partitioning, however, is that it does not guarantee connected components. Disconnected components are undesirable in various numerical techniques which make use of partitioning. In particular, multigrid methods require connectivity between points in a coarse grid and the associated children in the finer grid. Also, domain decomposition methods will converge faster with connected subdomains than with disconnected subdomains [3]. Furthermore, on a parallel or distributed system, connected components usually lead to a smaller number of of neighbors and therefore a smaller number of messages between processors. Since the communication cost is also a function of the number of neighboring subdomains, this also can be an important metric in evaluating the effectiveness of a partitioning. These advantages of connected subdomains has been the motivating factor in the development of the two bisection schemes based on spanning trees described in this paper.

The remainder of this paper is organized as follows. Section 2 gives a formal description of the partitioning problem using graph theoretical notation. Section 3 describes a single spanning tree graph bisection algorithm. Section 4 describes a dual spanning tree graph bisection algorithm similar to the rooted level structures algorithm described by Vaughan [11]. Section 5 provides a quantitative comparison of the two algorithms with recursive spectral partitioning as implemented by Barnard and Simon in [1]. Finally, section 6 will present conclusions from this work.

The Partitioning Problem

The partitioning algorithms presented in this paper, as with spectral partitioning, are recursive. That is, the computational domain is first divided into two subdomains by some method, and the same method is then applied to each subdomain such that in k applications one gets $p = 2^k$ subdomains, or partitions. Therefore, for the purposes of this paper, the partitioning problem is defined in terms of the graph bisection problem. The graph bisection problem can be stated as follows: Given an undirected graph, G, with the set of vertices V and the set of edges E, such that $G = (V, E)$, partition V into two subsets V_1 and V_2 where $V = V_1 \cup V_2$ and $V_1 \cap V_2 = \vee$, such that the size of the cut set, $|E_c|$, defined as

$$|E_c| = \{e | e \in E; e = (v_1, v_2); v_1 \in V_1; v_2 \in V_2\} \quad (1)$$

is minimized subject to some constraint on the partition. In general, the constraint applied is for the two partitions be approximately equal in size, that is, $||V_1| - |V_2|| \leq \epsilon|V|$ where $\epsilon \ll 1$. However, the requirement for connected components adds a further constraint, namely that $K_v(G_1) \geq 1$ and $K_v(G_2) \geq 1$, where $K_v(G)$ is the minimum number of vertices whose removal will disconnect G and $G_1 = (V_1, E_1)$ and $G_2 = (V_2, E_2)$.

It is worth noting that recursive partitioning schemes based on graph bisection are by definition greedy, in the sense that all such schemes strive for an optimal partition on every bisection. It is not necessary, however, to go through a series of optimal bisections in order to ultimately produce an optimal partitioning. Furthermore, recursive bisection is not the only approach to partitioning; many of the algorithms mentioned in section 1 are based on "bottom-up" approaches for which the problem definition above does not apply. Finally, it should be noted that for prov-

ably optimal solutions, the graph bisection problem requires exponential work.

Recursive Single Tree Bisection (STB)

The idea behind recursive single tree bisection (STB) is to build a spanning tree of the graph, then bisect the graph by removing a single branch from the tree. By definition, a graph is connected if it can be spanned by a single tree. It is clear that the removal of a single branch will disconnect the tree into exactly two subtrees, and since nodes in the tree correspond uniquely to vertices in the graph this approach guarantees two connected subgraphs (assuming an initially connected graph). This approach does not, however, guarantee that each component is equal in size nor does it guarantee an "optimal" bisection. These requirements can be met to some degree through an appropriate choice of root node and/or type of spanning tree.

There are many different types of spanning trees but of particular importance are breadth first and depth first spanning trees (algorithms for their construction may be found in any elementary graph theory textbook, c.f. Gibbons [4]). A breadth first spanning tree is built by visiting all the vertices in the graph with a breadth first search. This proceeds by visiting first all the vertices directly connected to the root, and then in turn visiting all the vertices directly connected to the vertices directly connected to the root (that have not already been visited), and so on. As a result the nodes in the tree get organized in levels of increasing distance from the root. In other words, level i of the tree will include all the vertices in the graph that are a minimum distance i from the root node. Breadth first trees tend to maximize branching and span the graph in a minimum number of levels.

A depth first spanning tree, on the other hand, is built by visiting all the vertices in the graph with a depth first search. This proceeds by visiting the first vertex directly connected to the root, and then visiting the first vertex directly connected to that vertex (that has not already been visited), and so on until no directly connected unvisited vertex can be found. At this point the search goes back up the tree trying to restart at each node. The search ends when it reaches the root and cannot find a directly connected unvisited vertex. The resulting trees tend to have a very large number of levels and very little branching. Both breadth first and depth first trees can be built in linear time (i.e. they have complexity $O(\max(|V|, |E|))$).

Intuitively one expects that a breadth first tree will be most effective in terms of minimizing the number of edge cuts since it arranges the vertices of the graph by proximity to the root. This arrangement persists, to some extent, when the tree is bisected. Not all such trees, however, will bisect well (i.e. split into two subtrees of approximately equal size) through removal of a single branch because of the high degree of branching and small number of levels. This becomes especially true for smaller trees with very few levels. Therefore for smaller graphs it often becomes necessary to use a depth first spanning tree in order to obtain an even bisection.

The basic bisection algorithm proceeds as follows:
Single Tree Bisection (STB)

1. Pick root vertex.

2. Build breadth first spanning tree.

3. Compute "weight" for each node in the tree.

4. Find branch which comes closest to splitting the tree.

5. Split the tree (bisect the graph).

6. Determine size of partitions and number of cut edges in the graph.

In the simplest case, the "weight" of a node refers simply to the number of nodes (inclusive) below it. This corresponds to vertices in the graph all having uniform weight. Sometimes, however, vertices in the graph may have some variable weight associated with them (e.g. computational cost). In such instances the "weight" of a node is the total weight of the vertices associated with the nodes (inclusive) below it.

The best bisection which can be produced by this algorithm may always be found by trying all the vertices in the graph as a root. In practice this is slow and unnecessary. Consider that for a bisection to be useful, the tree must be evenly divisible to some acceptable tolerance (the test cases presented in section 5 used $\epsilon = 0.005$). Most of the vertices in a typical graph will not produce even bisections. Furthermore, those vertices that do give even bisections tend to appear in clusters. These observations lead to the following heuristic algorithm for picking root vertices:
Picking Root Vertices for STB

1. Find two vertices on a pseudo-diameter of the graph.

2. Build a breadth first tree from one of the vertices in step 1.

3. Select every $(|V|/\log_2 |V|)^{th}$ node from this tree in order to create a list of $\log_2 |V|$ starting roots.

4. For each starting root in the list do:

   (a) Execute STB with current root.

   (b) If the bisection is even (to some tolerance), mark root as "good".

   (c) Pick next root with breadth first search around last "good" root.

   (d) Repeat until $\log_2 |V|$ "good" roots are found without improvement in the current minimum number of cut edges.

The first step in this algorithm is carried out with a simple but effective heuristic algorithm due Gibbs *et al* [5] and outlined below.
Finding Vertices on Pseudo-diameter

1. Pick any vertex in the graph as current root.

2. Build breadth first spanning tree with current root.

3. Determine distance to furthest vertex from root and select this vertex as current root.

4. Repeat steps 2 and 3 until there is no increase in distance.

The algorithm for picking roots strives to accomplish several things. It divides the graph into $\log_2 |V|$ regions and uses locality to improve the hit ratio for finding even bisections in each region. Furthermore, it limits the search for the best (i.e. minimum number of cut edges) even bisection by stopping the search within a region if no better bisection is found after some number of hits. Note that there is nothing special about $\log_2 |V|$ other than that it makes a reasonable bound on the number of regions to search. Also, rather than use a spanning tree to create regions, a maximal independent set of vertices could have been used.

Recursive Dual Tree Bisection (DTB)

Breadth first search visits the vertices in a graph in a manner analogous to a wave front propagating from the root. The idea behind the recursive dual tree bisection (DTB) algorithm is to concurrently construct two breadth first spanning trees of the graph and bisect the graph where the two "wave fronts" meet. In practice it is necessary only to carry out concurrent breadth first searches without actually constructing trees. The process then is to pick two vertices as roots for the searches, and concurrently breadth first search around each root until all the vertices have been visited by one or the other of the two searches. As vertices are visited, they get tagged to one or the other partition. The resulting components are always connected since the breadth first search guarantees that each vertex tagged is directly connected to a vertex that was previously tagged. Any two vertices may be picked as roots and the algorithm is applied iteratively with different pairs of roots to obtain good partitions. The method gives best results when the two root vertices are some distance (but not necessarily the pseudo-diameter) apart in the graph. For root vertices on a pseudo-diameter the method is similar to the graph based algorithm described by Vaughan [11] and also the recursive graph bisection algorithm described by Simon [9]. Those schemes, however, do not guarantee connected components, and in particular may produce disconnected components on graphs with two pseudo-diameters which share an endpoint. The method here is referred to as dual tree bisection to emphasize that it is a tree based bisection which makes use of two roots. The bisection algorithm goes as follows:

Dual Tree Bisection (DTB)

1. Create a list of $3 \log_2 |V|$ pairs of vertices some distance apart in the graph.

2. For each pair in step 1 do:

   (a) Carry out two concurrent breadth first searches.

   (b) Tag each vertex to the partition corresponding to the search which first found it.

   (c) Determine size of partitions and number of cut edges in the graph.

3. Use best pair from step 2 as graph bisection.

The list of pairs is constructed as follows:
Finding Suitable Root Pairs

1. Arbitrarily pick $\log_2 |V|$ vertices.

2. For each vertex do:

   (a) Build a breadth first tree from current root vertex.

   (b) Pair the current root with a vertex randomly selected from either the last or the second to last level of the tree.

   (c) Repeat three times using the selected vertex in (b) as the current root.

The two searches are carried out concurrently by alternately adding an unvisited vertex to each search. Although this usually results in an even bisection, sometimes one search can surround the other before all the vertices have been visited resulting in a disproportionate or uneven bisection.

One can purposely construct bisections of disproportionate size by letting one search proceed faster than the other (e.g. one search is allowed to tag three vertices for every two tagged by the other). This is useful if the algorithm is to be applied to partitioning some initially disconnected graph. The procedure then is to order all the disconnected components by size, assign each component alternately to one or the other partition, and bisect the last (largest) component in a disproportionate manner to give an even bisection overall. Disproportionate bisections also are useful for partitioning graphs into other than power of two partitions. This is important for mapping unstructured grid problems to mesh based parallel architectures like the Intel Paragon which has a non-power of two number of processors. Note also that in many problems the computational cost is only very roughly associated with the number of vertices in a partition. If one can associate a computational cost with each vertex, then the partitioner should bisect the graph in order to split the total cost rather than the total number of vertices. With DTB this can be implemented by keeping track of the current total cost of each tree and always adding a node to the tree with the smaller value.

Comparison

In this section the two partitioning algorithms are compared with recursive spectral bisection (RSB) for a number of two and three dimensional unstructured grids. The metric for comparison is the number of cut edges induced by the partitioning, and will be called E_c. Also presented for each grid is the CPU time required to generate the partitioning. The two partitioning algorithms of this paper were implemented in C and compiled with full optimization. The RSB algorithm was implemented in Fortran by Barnard and Simon [1] and uses a multi-level approach to computing the Fiedler vector used for partitioning. This implementation is much faster than the original unfactored Lanczos implementation, however it does require the user to specify the coarsest level to be used by the code. In all the cases studied this was set to 10% of the original grid. The partitioners were run on a Silicon Graphics Indigo workstation with a 50 MHz MIPS R4000 CPU and corresponding FPU.

Table 1 describes the grids used for comparison of the three partitioning schemes. The first two grids are the same four element airfoil grid examples discussed in [9]. Each grid is a dual of a two dimensional unstructured grid used for computational fluid dynamics; the second grid being a more refined version of the first. Both the original grids were Delauney triangulations therefore the duals have an average connectivity very close to 3. The dual grid is used for partitioning here because it is well established (see [12]) that the communication cost for the solver is directly related to the edges cut in the dual grid. For a multigrid application, one expects that the best partitioning (at least in terms of speeding convergence and satisfying stability bounds) will be the one that induces the shortest perimeter. To some extent this should correlate with minimizing the number of cut edges in the dual, however the extent (if any) of such a correlation is not yet established.

The next two grids are three dimensional finite element grids and therefore have a much greater average connectivity than the first two. "Wing/body" is a grid used for structural analysis of a wing/body configuration and "moving point source" is the last in a series of adapted grids used for studying the fluid dynamics of a moving point source. It is not clear how minimizing the number of edges cut in partitioning these grids correlates either to minimizing communication in a parallel solver or improving convergence in a multigrid or a domain decomposition method. For domain decomposition one prefers subdomains with good aspect ratio (see [3]), and the same probably applies to multigrid. This should correlate with minimizing the cut edges, but again it is not clear to what extent.

Table 2 presents the number of cut edges and the CPU time for partitioning the unrefined airfoil grid up to 2048 subdomains using recursive STB, recursive DTB and recursive spectral bisection (RSB). Also included for RSB is the number of components in the partitioning. For this grid, STB produces less cut edges than either DTB or RSB. DTB produces about the same number of cut edges as RSB for up to 512 partitions, and is slightly better for over 256 partitions. This is attributed to RSB performing poorly when disconnected components are induced. At 512 partitions RSB has about 5% more components than partitions, and this fraction grows with each partitioning. A partition with disconnected components will

generally have many more cut edges than one with a single connected component. Thus algorithms that produce connected components should perform better at this stage.

Table 3 presents the cut edges and CPU time for partitioning the refined airfoil grid. Again STB produces less cut edges than either DTB or RSB. In this case, DTB produces some bad partitions (in particular, the first and third) and in general performs worse than RSB up to 256 partitions. After this, DTB shows improvement over RSB. Again this is attributable to the disconnected components induced by RSB.

Table 4 presents the results from partitioning the wing/body grid. STB performs poorly for all but the first partition. STB was found to perform poorly in general for three dimensional grids. The higher connectivity of these grids induces a large amount of branching in the breadth first spanning tree, consequently, it is difficult to find a branch that will evenly bisect the tree. A better approach probably would be to generate quadsections or some higher order sections than bisections, but this has not been investigated.

DTB performs respectably well on this grid producing about the same number of cut edges as RSB for most of the partitions. This is a very encouraging result since RSB did not generate as many disconnected components on this grid as on the first two grids. The airfoil grids have "holes" for each element of the airfoil, therefore they are more likely to disconnect and as such will be more difficult for RSB.

Finally, table 5 presents the results from partitioning the moving point source grid. Again, DTB does better than STB because the higher connectivity gives STB greater difficulty. RSB however is clearly superior than DTB for this grid. This grid leads to very few disconnected components with RSB so it does well for all partitions.

The above discussion has concentrated on number of cut edges as a metric for good partitioning. One should not lose sight of the purpose of the algorithms developed in this paper, which is to guarantee connected components in a partitioning. That the algorithms also produce "low" numbers of cut edges (that is, within 10-20% of RSB) is important because it indicates that the quality of partitioning is good. Therefore not only do the algorithms generate partitions with connected components, the components themselves will have a good shape for multigrid and domain decomposition methods.

The CPU times are presented in tables 2-5 in order to provide some idea of the computational requirements of the various schemes. In general one can say

Grid description	Application	Dim	$|V|$	$|E|$	avg conn
airfoil	fluids	2	11451	16880	2.95
airfoil, refined	fluids	2	30269	44929	2.97
wing/body	structures	3	2851	15093	10.59
moving point source	fluids	3	10556	76109	14.42

Table 1: Description of grids tested with three partitioners.

Partns	STB $(|E_c|)$	Time (sec)	DTB $(|E_c|)$	Time (sec)	RSB $(|E_c|)$	Time (sec)	Compns
2	69	139.2	71	11.3	83	2.2	2
4	170	238.9	183	20.6	175	5.5	4
8	252	316.3	307	29.0	325	8.3	8
16	400	372.1	471	36.8	460	13.4	16
32	616	431.8	770	45.0	723	23.0	32
64	939	486.4	1178	54.5	1157	30.1	65
128	1468	543.9	1768	67.1	1745	35.7	131
256	2238	612.6	2552	85.6	2550	40.2	265
512	3339	702.4	3687	128.0	3727	43.1	537
1024	4801	822.0	5138	190.5	5353	49.2	1105
2048	6878	977.4	7079	275.2	7580	57.5	2362

Table 2: Edges cut $|E_c|$ and CPU time for airfoil grid ($|V| = 11451, |E| = 16880$).

Partns	STB $(|E_c|)$	Time (sec)	DTB $(|E_c|)$	Time (sec)	RSB $(|E_c|)$	Time (sec)	Compns
2	83	798	144	40.4	88	6.4	2
4	244	1261	294	68.2	280	16.8	4
8	393	1558	623	92.9	491	31.9	8
16	618	1785	910	127.0	838	49.9	16
32	960	2004	1329	151.4	1220	87.7	32
64	1497	2232	2012	183.1	1815	114.8	64
128	2314	2484	2940	222.5	2810	134.0	128
256	3493	2785	4267	281.1	4206	150.4	258
512	5164	3179	6171	370.6	6178	166.0	528
1024	7551	3721	8724	530.0	8897	185.2	1067
2048	10939	4485	12168	796.3	12647	208.9	2198

Table 3: Edges cut $|E_c|$ and CPU time for refined airfoil grid ($|V| = 30269. |E| = 44929$).

Partns	STB ($\|E_c\|$)	Time (sec)	DTB ($\|E_c\|$)	Time (sec)	RSB ($\|E_c\|$)	Time (sec)	Compns
2	255	31.0	278	4.2	259	0.4	2
4	525	53.8	586	8.0	471	1.1	4
8	959	70.1	866	11.5	832	1.7	8
16	1669	83.2	1498	19.2	1474	2.4	17
32	2568	93.0	2320	22.3	2399	3.7	33
64	3834	101.5	3544	25.5	3519	4.8	66
128	5639	110.1	5543	40.6	5108	5.4	130
256	7764	119.6	7500	47.1	7267	6.1	260
512	10200	130.7	10017	56.4	9923	7.0	517

Table 4: Edges cut $\|E_c\|$ and CPU time for wing/body structure ($\|V\| = 2851, \|E\| = 15093$).

Partns	STB ($\|E_c\|$)	Time (sec)	DTB ($\|E_c\|$)	Time (sec)	RSB ($\|E_c\|$)	Time (sec)	Compns
2	2787	389	2566	33	1995	8.5	2
4	6966	846	6464	61	5158	14.4	4
8	10752	1228	10581	85	8530	16.0	8
16	15572	1465	14472	108	12016	21.8	16
32	21095	1607	19309	129	16178	32.3	32
64	28110	1703	24801	150	21198	40.2	64
128	35431	1782	31001	174	27624	46.7	128
256	42629	1865	38154	204	35010	52.5	258
512	49144	1968	45417	242	43061	57.2	523
1024	55203	2100	53000	305	51771	63.0	1045
2048	61318	2265	60783	404	60488	70.8	2089

Table 5: Edges cut $\|E_c\|$ and CPU time for moving point source grid ($\|V\| = 10556, \|E\| = 76109$).

that STB is more demanding than DTB which is itself more demanding than the multilevel implementation of RSB. For both STB and DTB, however, most of the cost is in searching for the best root or root pair and this can easily be parallelized. The multilevel RSB, on the other hand, is difficult to parallelize and may not gain much from a parallel implementation.

Conclusions

This paper presents two partitioning algorithms that guarantee connected components given a connected initial grid. The algorithms have been implemented and tested on a number of two and three dimensional unstructured grids. For many of the grids tested, the algorithms produce partitions as good (in terms of number of cut edges) or better than spectral partitioning and require only modest computational resources. It has been found that grids leading to many disconnected components under spectral partitioning are most suitable for partitioning with these new algorithms. The new algorithms do not perform as well on grids leading to only a few disconnected components under spectral partitioning, however, number of cut edges is only one metric for quality of a partition, and methods like domain decomposition and multigrid may benefit more from connected components.

Acknowledgments

I wish to thank Horst Simon and V. Venkatakrishnan (NASA Ames) for many useful discussions on graph theory and partitioning, and thanks again to Horst and to Steve Barnard (Cray Research) for providing me with their multilevel spectral partitioning code.

References

[1] S.T. Barnard and H.D. Simon, "A Fast Multilevel Implementation of Recursive Spectral Bisection for Partitioning Unstructured Problems", *Concurrency: Practice and Experience,* (to appear) 1994, also Tech Report RNR-92-033, NAS Division, NASA Ames Research Center, Moffett Field, CA, November 1992.

[2] C. Farhat, "On the Mapping of Massively Parallel Processors onto Finite Element Graphs", *Computers and Structures*, vol. 32, no. 2, pp. 347-353, 1989.

[3] C. Farhat and M. Lesoinne, "Automatic Partitioning of Unstructured Meshes for Parallel Solution of Problems in Computational Mechanics", *Int J Numerical Methods in Engineering*, vol. 36, pp. 745-764, 1993.

[4] A. Gibbons, *Algorithmic Graph Theory*, Cambridge Univ Press, Cambridge, Great Britain, 1985.

[5] N.E. Gibbs, W.G. Poole Jr., and P.K. Stockmeyer, "An Algorithm for Reducing the Bandwidth and Profile of a Sparse Matrix", *SIAM J Numer Anal*, vol. 13, no. 2, pp. 26-250, 1976.

[6] B.W. Kerninghan and S. Lin, "An Efficient Heuristic Procedure for Partitioning Graphs", *The Bell System Technical J.*, vol. 49, pp. 291-307, 1970.

[7] B. Nour-Omid, A. Raefsky, G. Lyzenga, "Solving Finite Element Equations on Concurrent Computers", in A.K. Noor editor, *Parallel Computations and Their Impact on Mechanics*, pp. 209-227, ASME, New York, 1986.

[8] A. Pothen, H. Simon and K.-P. Liou, "Partitioning Sparse Matrices with Eigenvectors of Graphs", *SIAM J Mat Anal Appl*, vol. 11, pp. 430-452, 1990.

[9] H.D. Simon, "Partitioning of Unstructured Problems for Parallel Processing", *Computing Systems in Engineering*, vol. 2, no. 2/3, pp. 135-148, 1991.

[10] S. H. Teng, *Points, Spheres, and Separators, A Unified Geometric Approach to Graph Partitioning*, Ph.D. thesis, School of Computer Science, Carnegie Mellon Univ., Pittsburgh, PA, August 1991.

[11] C. Vaughan "Structural Analysis on Massively Parallel Computers" *Computing Systems in Engineering*, vol. 2, no. 2/3, pp. 261-267, 1991.

[12] V. Venkatakrishnan, H. Simon, and T. Barth, "A MIMD Implementation of a Parallel Euler Solver for Unstructured Grids", *J of Supercomputing*, vol. 6, no. 2, pp 117-127, 1992.

[13] R.D. Williams, "Performance of Dynamic Load Balancing Algorithms for Unstructured Mesh Calculations", *Concurrency: Practice and Experience*, vol. 3, pp. 457-481, 1991.

Efficient Implementation of a 3-Dimensional ADI Method on the iPSC/860

Rob F. Van der Wijngaart

MCAT Institute

NASA Ames Research Center, Moffett Field, CA, 94035

Abstract

A comparison is made between several domain decomposition strategies for the solution of three-dimensional partial differential equations on a MIMD distributed memory parallel computer. The grids used are structured, and the numerical algorithm is ADI. Important implementation issues regarding load balancing, storage requirements, network latency, and overlap of computations and communications are discussed. Results of the solution of the three-dimensional heat equation on the Intel iPSC/860 are presented for the three most viable methods. It is found that the Bruno-Cappello decomposition delivers optimal computational speed through an almost complete elimination of processor idle time, while providing good memory efficiency.

1 Introduction

Implicit numerical algorithms for the solution of multi-dimensional partial differential equations (PDE's) are usually more efficient computationally than explicit methods, when implemented on conventional (vector) computers. However, they are harder to program efficiently on parallel computers due to a more global data dependence than is exhibited by explicit methods. Numerical solution of PDE's typically involves more or less the same operations for all the points in a computational grid used to discretize the problem space. Consequently, domain decomposition is the natural way of creating separate tasks for a parallel computer: a roughly equal number of grid points is assigned to each processor. Depending on the type of implicit algorithm chosen, some domain decompositions perform better than others. Efficiency is also affected by hardware parameters (e.g. network latency and bandwidth, and processor memory) and operating model (e.g. MIMD, SIMD). In this paper we compare three viable domain decompositions for the solution of

three-dimensional PDE's using ADI (Alternating Direction Implicit) on the Intel iPSC/860 MIMD parallel computer. The results of this study also apply to other line-based solution strategies, such as line-relaxation, when multiple sweep directions are used during each iteration.

As an example, we solve the time-dependent three-dimensional heat equation. Since the aim is to assess parallel efficiency, the problem is kept as simple as possible (i.e. Cartesian grid, constant mesh spacing, Dirichlet boundary conditions, constant material properties, no source term). As a result, the computational program is simple and easy to analyze, and the computations per grid point are at a bare minimum. No effort was made to use the simplifying assumptions to reduce communication, so a relatively bad balance results between computation and communication time; a worst-case parallel performance analysis is obtained.

2 Problem formulation

The equation to be solved is:

$$\rho c T_t = \nabla \cdot (\mathbf{k} \nabla T), \tag{1}$$

where T is temperature, t time, ρ density, c specific heat, and $\mathbf{k}$ the conduction tensor. Assuming $\mathbf{k}$ to be a constant scalar, i.e. $\mathbf{k} = k\mathbf{I}$, we get

$$\rho c T_t = k\left(\frac{\partial^2}{\partial x^2} + \frac{\partial^2}{\partial y^2} + \frac{\partial^2}{\partial z^2}\right)T. \tag{2}$$

Equation (2) is subsequently discretized using central differencing in space and the θ-method in time:

$$(1 - \frac{h\theta k}{\rho c}[(\delta_x^c)^2 + (\delta_y^c)^2 + (\delta_z^c)^2])\Delta T =$$
$$\frac{hk}{\rho c}[(\delta_x^c)^2 + (\delta_y^c)^2 + (\delta_z^c)^2]T. \tag{3}$$

Here $\delta_{x_i}^c$ signifies the central difference operator in the x_i-direction, T is the temperature, ΔT its temporal increment, and h is the size of the time step. The

© 1993 ACM 0-8186-4340-4/93/0011 $1.50

parameter θ controls the 'implicitness' of the problem ($\theta = 0$ yields Euler explicit, $\theta = 1$ gives Euler implicit, and $\theta = 1/2$ defines the second-order-accurate Crank-Nicholson scheme). Equation (3), which is said to be in delta form, defines a matrix equation with a very large bandwidth due to the three-dimensionality of the discrete operator. Approximate factorization reduces this operator to a product of three one-dimensional operators with a bandwidth of only three each (e.g. [7]). So equation (3) is approximated by:

$$(1 - \frac{h\theta k}{\rho c}(\delta_x^c)^2)(1 - \frac{h\theta k}{\rho c}(\delta_y^c)^2)(1 - \frac{h\theta k}{\rho c}(\delta_z^c)^2)\Delta T =$$

$$\frac{hk}{\rho c}[(\delta_x^c)^2 + (\delta_y^c)^2 + (\delta_z^c)^2]T. \qquad (4)$$

An outline of the numerical algorithm is:

1. Compute rhs, the right hand side of equation (4).

2. Solve the system $(1 - \frac{h\theta k}{\rho c}(\delta_x^c)^2)A = rhs$ along lines in the x-direction.

3. Solve the system $(1 - \frac{h\theta k}{\rho c}(\delta_y^c)^2)B = A$ along lines in the y-direction.

4. Solve the system $(1 - \frac{h\theta k}{\rho c}(\delta_z^c)^2)\Delta T = B$ along lines in the z-direction.

5. Update T for all interior grid points.

3 Domain decomposition

The Intel iPSC/860 computer on which the problem is solved is of the MIMD (Multiple Instruction Multiple Data) distributed memory type. Data is owned by the individual processors in the processor array, which is structured as a hypercube. The only way that data can be shared among processors is by message passing. Sending or receiving a message takes communication time, which goes at the expense of the computing efficiency. Moreover, synchronization and load balancing are an issue; processors should not be allowed to idle because they are out of work or are waiting for data to be prepared by other processors. The following sections discuss three different domain decomposition strategies and the associated numerical implementations. Although many more such strategies are conceivable, these appear the most viable, for they all have a good load balance and attempt to minimize data communication in some sense.

3.1 Static block-Cartesian decomposition

In the static block-Cartesian case, each processor owns one contiguous Cartesian-product subspace—a block—of the whole grid for the duration of the entire computation. This decomposition assumes a very small latency, relatively low communication bandwidth, and limited storage. The grid blocks are as close to cubical as possible in order to minimize surface area, which in turn minimizes the amount of data to be communicated between blocks. It also minimizes storage of an extra layer of points around the grid block, a common and convenient vehicle in domain decomposition strategies for sharing information with neighboring processors.

A serious drawback is, however, that no single block-Cartesian decomposition is efficient for all line solves in steps 2 through 4. Consider step 2, for example. Here a matrix equation is formed for each line in the x-direction across the whole grid. If this line is contained completely in a single processor (which means that the block is of the width of the grid in the x-direction), then all processors can solve their matrix equations independently, and complete parallelism is obtained. However, since the grid is divided into multiple blocks, there must be at least one coordinate direction, say y, that runs across several blocks. That means that in step 3 no whole y-line can be formed within one processor, and a processor must wait to receive information from neighboring blocks before it can do its part of the forward elimination or the back-substitution; communication is needed during line solves.

When using the Thomas algorithm for solving the tri-diagonal matrix equations, the information to be passed to the next processor during the forward elimination consists of the updated right hand side and the upper and diagonal matrix elements at the end of each line (the matrix elements are not strictly needed in the current constant-coefficient case, but we pass them for generality's sake to reflect the communication requirements of curvilinear (section 5) and fully nonlinear algorithms). If the latency is very large, one can collect all such triplets of values for all the line segments in the current grid block and send them to the next processor as one message. On arrival, they can be unpacked and used by the next processor to advance further along the line in the forward elimination step. But this leads to a severe load imbalance, since only one layer of grid blocks perpendicular to the line solve direction is active at any given time. Instead, we send each triplet individually, giving the next processor something to chew on already before starting on the next line segment of the forward elimination within the current processor. This process, called Pipe-lined Gaussian Elimination (PGE) [4], has a much better load balance, provided each grid block contains many more line segments than there are consecutive grid blocks in any coordinate direction. However, it does require sending many small messages. An alternative to PGE that avoids the latter problem is offered by variants of the cyclic reduction algorithm [4], called substructuring methods. These rely on eliminating as many off-diagonal matrix elements as possible within each grid block in parallel before communicating with processors containing neighboring blocks. Substructuring methods are very similar in appearance to solution methods for periodic problems, and they require a comparable number of arithmetic operations, which is almost twice as many as are needed by PGE. Due to this added computational expense, substructuring methods are not considered in this study.

3.2 Dynamic block-Cartesian decomposition

In the dynamic block-Cartesian case, each processor again owns a contiguous grid block, but this time the decomposition changes between the different line solve stages. This decomposition assumes a large latency, relatively high communication bandwidth, and abundant storage. The dynamic redecomposition (also called Mass Reorganization [5] or Complete Exchange [1]) enables the data lay-out to be tailored to the line solve step it supports. Before solution in the x_i-direction (i= 1, 2, 3), the Cartesian blocks are made to be of the width of the grid in that same direction. The extra expense incurred is the communication needed to redecompose the domain, but no data needs to be transferred *during* any of the three solution stages.

The optimal dynamic subdivision is found as follows. The whole grid contains $n_x \times n_y \times n_z$ points. Let $np_{x_j}^{x_i}$ signify the number of processors (blocks) in the x_j-direction during the x_i-line solves, the total number of blocks being np. Some useful identities are:

$$np_{x_i}^{x_i} = 1, \quad \prod_{j=1}^{3} np_{x_j}^{x_i} = np, \quad (i = 1, 2, 3). \quad (5)$$

In between the x- and y-line solves the intermediate solution A on a processor has to be communicated to all other processors that need it. The only information that does not need to be communicated lies in the intersection of the Cartesian blocks of the successive decompositions that reside on the same processor during both line solve stages. The size of the intersection region on a single processor is at most:

$$\frac{n_x}{\max(np_x^x, np_x^y)} \cdot \frac{n_y}{\max(np_y^x, np_y^y)} \cdot \frac{n_z}{\max(np_z^x, np_z^y)} =$$

$$\frac{n_x n_y n_z}{np_x^y np_y^x \max(np_z^x, np_z^y)}. \quad (6)$$

The total number of grid points in a block is $\frac{n_x n_y n_z}{np}$, which makes the total amount of grid point data communicated equal to:

$$n_x n_y n_z \left(\frac{1}{np} - \frac{1}{np_x^y np_y^x \max(np_z^x, np_z^y)} \right). \quad (7)$$

Similar expressions can be derived for communications between y- and z-line solves, and before the final temperature update (step 5). Assuming all inter-processor data transfer can happen without conflicts, the total communication time t_c is:

$$t_c = n_x n_y n_z c \left[\frac{3}{np} - \frac{1}{np_x^y np_y^x \max(np_z^x, np_z^y)} - \right.$$

$$\left. \frac{1}{np_y^z np_z^y \max(np_x^y, np_x^z)} - \frac{1}{np_x^z np_z^x \max(np_y^x, np_y^z)} \right], \quad (8)$$

with c the time to send one floating point number. Using the identities (5), t_c can be simplified to:

$$t_c = \frac{n_x n_y n_z c}{np} \left[3 - \frac{1}{\max(np_x^y, np_y^x)} - \right.$$

$$\left. \frac{1}{\max(np_y^z, np_z^y)} - \frac{1}{\max(np_x^z, np_z^x)} \right]. \quad (9)$$

It is not easy to see how this expression can be minimized for a certain choice of the $np_{x_j}^{x_i}$. Therefore, two extreme cases are considered.

First, map the planes perpendicular to each line solve direction to a *square* processor array, i.e. $np_{x_i}^{x_{(i+1)\bmod 3}} = np_{x_i}^{x_{(i+2)\bmod 3}} = \sqrt{np}$, $(i = 1, 2, 3)$. This leads to a small aspect ratio of the blocks in the plane perpendicular to the line solve direction. The corresponding communication time t_c^{sq} is:

$$t_c^{sq} = \frac{n_x n_y n_z c}{np} \left[3 - \frac{3}{\sqrt{np}} \right]. \quad (10)$$

Second, map the planes perpendicular to each line solve direction to a *linear* processor array, i.e. $np_{x_i}^{x_{(i+1)\bmod 3}} = np$ or $np_{x_i}^{x_{(i+2)\bmod 3}} = np$, $(i = 1, 2, 3)$. This leads to a large aspect ratio of the blocks in the plane perpendicular to the line solve direction; the domain is dissected into *slices* stretching across the entire width of the grid in two coordinate directions. Equation (9) shows that the corresponding communication time t_c^{lin} is, in general:

$$t_c^{lin} = \frac{n_x n_y n_z c}{np}\left[3 - \frac{3}{np}\right].$$ (11)

An additional gain is obtained by selecting one particular coordinate direction x_{j_0} and requiring $np_{x_{j_0}}^{x_i} = 1$, $(i = 1, 2, 3)$. Then one of the terms on the right hand side of equation (9) is 1, and the communication time drops to:

$$t_c^{lin} = \frac{n_x n_y n_z c}{np}\left[2 - \frac{2}{np}\right].$$ (12)

Now there is one pair of solution steps between which no communication is necessary at all. For example, suppose that $j_0 = 2$, then the grid dissection chosen for either the x-line solves or the z-line solves will also be adequate for the y-line solves. Coordinate direction x_{j_0} is called the *pile*-direction of the decomposition (see below). A comparison of the communication times for the square and the linear decompositions yields:

$$t_c^{lin}/t_c^{sq} = \frac{2}{3}\left[1 + \frac{1}{\sqrt{np}}\right], (np \neq 1).$$ (13)

For $np > 4$ the linear decomposition is superior, with gains increasing as np grows.

3.3 Bruno-Cappello multi-cell decomposition

In the Bruno-Cappello case ([5], [2]), each processor owns a collection of grid blocks, called *cells*. This decomposition supports a large latency and a relatively low bandwidth, and requires somewhat more memory than the static but a lot less than the dynamic block-Cartesian decomposition. The arrangements of the equally-sized cells is such that every coordinate plane that cuts the grid intersects with exactly one cell of each processor. The number of cells is the smallest possible to satisfy the above requirement. If the number of processors is again np, then each processor owns $\sqrt{np}$ cells. Consequently, the total number of cells is $np\sqrt{np}$, which are laid out in a $\sqrt{np}\times\sqrt{np}\times\sqrt{np}$ three-dimensional array. No two cells belonging to the same processor abut, so that no complete lines in any coordinate direction can be formed within one processor; communication is again necessary during line solves, but now we do not have to worry about load balancing the algorithm. Therefore, each cell can finish all its

line segments during forward elimination before sending a packet of consolidated data to the adjacent cell for processing.

3.4 Right hand side evaluation

So far the cost of assembling the right hand side of equation (4) has been ignored. Whereas the computing cost of that assembly depends only weakly on the decomposition chosen, the communication cost is proportional to the surface area of each block. The surface area is smallest for the static and largest for the dynamic block-Cartesian decomposition. In the latter case the surface area does not scale with the number of processors; the communication overhead of evaluating the right hand side appears to grow indefinitely. But in all three cases the right hand side can be computed for points interior to the blocks or cells owned by each processor while boundary information is being sent to other processors. Experiments with the AIMS performance monitoring system [10] show that this communication does not lead to processor idle time for grids of reasonable size (more interior points than interface points).

4 Implementation issues

All cases are programmed in C. This language provides the flexibility and convenience of mixed-type data structures that keep parameter lists short and clean. It also has the advantage that functions are built in for computing the length of system- or user-defined data types (important for sending messages), that dynamic memory allocation is supported, and that interfaces with Fortran subroutines are possible. Tests on the iPSC/860 show that Fortran77 and C have the same computational efficiency. What seems to be a drawback of C is that it does not allow multi-dimensional arrays of variable size in parameter lists, which forces the programmer to map them into one-dimensional arrays with explicit computation of indices. But this can be done easily and efficiently, with no performance degradation. In fact, having explicit control over array lay-out obviates the need for the auxiliary arrays reported in [5].

4.1 Static block-Cartesian

In the static block-Cartesian approach each grid block has dimensions augmented by one in all directions to account for block interface information. The blocks themselves are arranged in a three-dimensional array such that communication between neighboring blocks is also between neighboring processors (Hamming distance of 1). This can be achieved using binary reflected gray codes (see e.g. [3]). The processor number p of a block with indices (i, j, k) in the three-dimensional array of size $(I_{size}, J_{size}, K_{size})$ is given by $p = \mathrm{gray}(i) + I_{size} * (\mathrm{gray}(j) + J_{size} * \mathrm{gray}(k))$. Experiments using gray codes show a performance improvement of about 5% over the canonical numbering $p = i + I_{size} * (j + J_{size} * k)$ for medium-sized grids ($60 \times 60 \times 30$ to $80 \times 80 \times 40$ grid points) on a 32-processor hypercube.

As was mentioned earlier, the computation of the right hand side vector for points interior to the grid block can concur with the exchange of boundary face information between neighboring grid blocks. This requires the use of asynchronous message passing. Extra speed-up is obtained by using so-called *forced* messages, which bypass system wait buffers and get copied immediately into the application space of the receiving processor. Once the boundary data has been received, the right hand side for points on the edge of the grid block can be evaluated. This strategy offers a significant increase in efficiency, although there is a hidden cost; since the computation of the right hand side is split in two (interior and boundary points), the vector length for each of these steps—most notably for the boundary points—is reduced, which leads to a loss of performance on the iPSC/860 vector processors.

The left hand side matrices for the simple Cartesian-grid case are constant, so they need not be constructed explicitly. Consequently, there is no computational work that can be done when transferring information between neighboring cells during the line-solve phases of the algorithm, and simple synchronous message passing is used.

4.2 Dynamic block-Cartesian

In the linear dynamic block-Cartesian approach each processor owns a *slice* of the whole grid, whose orientation depends on the phase of the solution process. Each processor contains a number of slice variables—one for each physical variable defined on its part of the grid—that hold the data in an array of function values. That array is distributed over a number of *pile* data structures, each of which contains a block of data that can be transferred monolithically to other processors during the change of decomposition direction (Figures 1 and 2). A pile stretches across the grid in the x_{j_0}-direction (see section 3.2). No rearrangement of the values within a pile is necessary after transfer.

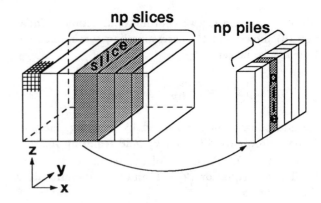

Figure 1: Storage of slice variable in terms of piles of data

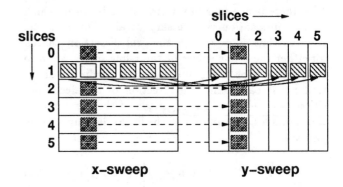

Figure 2: Exchanging piles of data during change of decomposition

During the redecomposition phase, each processor needs to send a (different) pile of data to every other processor in the allocated hypercube. These cannot all be nearest neighbors, so there is a danger of *edge contention* [1]; two messages cannot normally share the same data path—*edge*—between two processors in the hypercube, so if communication requires the paths of several messages to overlap (partially), then they will have to wait for each other until the contended edge is freed.

In Figure 2 the data transfer needed for changing the decomposition direction between the x-line solves and the y-line solves is depicted, assuming the pile is aligned with the z-axis. The hatched piles sitting on processor 1 during the x-line solves have to be distributed among processors 0, 2, 3, 4, 5 for use during the y-line solves. Note that pile 1 (open box) need not be communicated, since it stays on processor 1. This is generally true for pile i on processor i. Conversely, processor 1 also receives piles (shaded) from processors 0, 2, 3, 4, 5 for use during the y-line solves. It obviously does not receive information from itself.

It is found in [1] and [9] that this type of communication, called *complete exchange*, suffers from significant edge contention if programmed in a naive way, i.e.:

for pile = 0, np-1 **do**: **if** pile ≠ mynumber **then**
    send-pile-to-processor(pile)

Communication conflicts are avoided by using Bokhari's *linear* algorithm [1]:

for pile = 1, np-1 **do**:
    send-pile-to-processor((pile+mynumber) mod np)

This is the strategy employed in this study. It is on a par with the stable method and the pairwise-synchronized method with forced messages also described in [1], while outperforming all other algorithms for the global exchange of medium to large-size messages on medium-size hypercubes. Again, asynchronous communication and forced message types are used, which has the advantage that no delay is caused by placing the sizable messages associated with each pile on the network.

In order to compute the right hand side vector, each processor needs to have access to temperature values on adjacent slices; these are stored in buffer zones. Buffer zones are not included in the slices themselves—as was the case with the static block-Cartesian decomposition—since this would necessitate a certain repacking of pile data during the complete exchange. Instead, interface data is stored in two buffer arrays on each node, one for either side of a slice. The thickness of each buffer is one, because a seven-point-star stencil is used for computing the right hand side. Buffers are shipped to neighboring processors as single messages. In order to keep these communications as efficient as possible, they are overlapped with the computation of the right hand side vector for points interior to the slices. In addition, the slices are numbered using gray codes such that neighboring slices are on neighboring processors, i.e. $p = \text{gray}(slice)$.

4.3 Bruno-Cappello multi-cell

In the Bruno-Cappello approach each cell has dimensions augmented by one in all directions to account for cell interface information. Many lay-outs are conceivable that satisfy the requirement that each coordinate plane cutting across the whole grid intersect with exactly one cell of each processor. In addition, we demand that for a given communication direction all cells belonging to a certain processor send information to only one other processor. For example, suppose a cell on processor 0 has neighbors on processors as indicated in Figure 3, then all the other cells owned by processor 0 exhibit the same configuration.

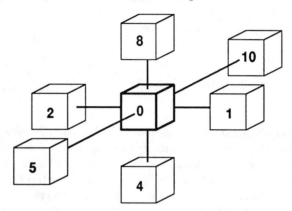

Figure 3: Neighbors of a cell on processor 0

Such a lay-out of cells can be constructed as follows; starting with a certain assignment of cells in the 'ground' plane ($k = 0$), every subsequent plane has the same relative assignment of cells to processors—save boundary effects—and is shifted in both the i- and j-directions. In order to preserve the neighbor relation in the z-direction, the (periodic) shift for plane k should be of the form $(a * k, b * k)$. Bruno and Cappello show [2] that it is not possible to construct a hypercube mapping of cells to processors that results in nearest-neighbor communication only, but that it is possible to have a maximum communication distance of 2 in one coordinate direction while preserving nearest-neighbor relations in the other two directions. This mapping is constructed easily using gray-code mappings for the assignment of cells to processors in the ground plane, and by applying either the $(k, -k)$ or the $(-k, k)$ shift to subsequent z-planes. In the latter case, cell (i, j, k) lies on node number $p = \text{gray}\left((i + k) \mod \sqrt{np}\right) + \sqrt{np} * \text{gray}\left((j - k) \mod \sqrt{np}\right)$. This mapping requires only one message per processor in each of the six coordinate directions (east, west, north, south, top, bottom) when exchanging boundary information with neighboring cells, regardless how many cells there are per node. Again, we can overlap this copying action with computation of the new right hand side vector for interior points of all cells.

An additional advantage of the Bruno-Cappello decomposition is that all processors have exactly one cell face on each of the six faces of the global grid. That means that boundary effects are the same for all processors, yielding a perfect load balance automati-

	static	dynamic	Bruno-Cappello
communication	$18\dfrac{n^2}{\sqrt[3]{np^2}}$	$2n^2 + 2\dfrac{n^3(np-1)}{np^2}$	$18(\sqrt{np}-1)\dfrac{n^2}{np}$
# messages	$6 + 6\dfrac{n^2}{\sqrt[3]{np^2}}$	$2np$	$6\sqrt{np}$
storage	$\left(\dfrac{n}{\sqrt[3]{np}} + 2\right)^3$	$n^2\left(\dfrac{n}{np} + 2\right)$	$\sqrt{np}\left(\dfrac{n}{\sqrt{np}} + 2\right)^3$

Table 1: Storage and communication for all three decompositions

cally. In the static and dynamic block-Cartesian cases, processors owning interior grid blocks have a different work load than those that face a grid boundary. It should be noted that the Bruno-Cappello method described here is a special case of the more general class of multi-partition methods described in detail in [6]; it is tailored towards a scalable implementation on a binary hypercube topology.

4.4 Resources summary

In Table 1 we summarize the number of messages and the amount of communication (8-byte words) needed during one time step of each of the three implementations, as well as the amount of storage (8-byte words) per grid variable. All numbers are for one processor. The grid contains $n \times n \times n$ points, and the total number of processors is np.

It should be stressed that one third of the communication cost in the dynamic and Bruno-Cappello decompositions is hidden by computations, whereas the static decomposition offers hardly any savings in this regard. That is because most messages in the latter case are sent during the line solve stage, when no overlap of computation and communication is possible. The amount of storage required is just for one variable. What makes the dynamic algorithm memory-inefficient is the fact that certain variables have to be stored multiple times because of the different decompositions. This is especially true when generalized coordinates or nonuniform material properties are used, in which case multiple versions of properties and metrics data need to be stored.

5 Comparison

Three sets of computations were done in order to assess the impact of the different domain decompositions on the parallel performance ϕ, the results of which are presented in Tables 2-4. ϕ, also called the

efficiency, relates the time to execute a certain problem on np processors ($time(np)$) to the time it takes to solve the same problem on just one processor, i.e.

$$\phi(np) = \frac{time(1)}{np\, time(np)} \ . \qquad (14)$$

It should be noted that $time(1)$ is the true serial execution time on one processor, stripped of all the parallel overhead.

For each case are also listed the computing speed *Mflops* (millions of double precision floating point operations per second). Mflops were computed by multiplying the total number of grid points by the number of floating point operations per point (41 in this case), and dividing the result by the total elapsed time during one time step. The elapsed time is wall-clock time averaged over 50 time steps. Only the smallest grid will fit on a single processor, so efficiencies for larger grids are computed by comparing with the Mflops for that smallest grid.

The numerical problem solved is the same for each case; the time integration is fully implicit ($\theta = 1$), and the initial values are $T(x,y,z,0) = \sin(\pi x)\sin(\pi y)\sin(\pi z)$ on the unit cube. If the boundary values are kept at zero (Dirichlet boundary conditions), the analytical solution is easily found through separation of variables, i.e. $T(x,y,z,t) = \exp(-\pi^2 t)T(x,y,z,0)$.

From the three sets of computations (Tables 2-4) it is concluded that the parallel performance of the algorithms generally improves—as expected—when the total grid size increases. It is also clear that the dynamic block-Cartesian decomposition is almost twice as efficient as the static one. The Bruno-Cappello multi-cell decomposition, in turn, is significantly faster than the dynamic block-Cartesian approach, even when only half the number of available nodes is utilized (Bruno-Cappello requires the number of nodes to be a square). Moreover, the grids chosen favor the dynamic block-Cartesian decomposition, which is most efficient for grids that have some small aspect

	Number of processors								
Grid	1	2	4	8	16	32	64	128	
$48^2 \times 24$	1.00	0.53	0.50	0.28	0.20	0.15	.091	.066	ϕ
	2.94	3.12	5.75	6.55	9.22	14.8	17.2	24.7	Mflops
$96^2 \times 48$					0.24	0.25	0.17	0.13	ϕ
					11.4	23.4	31.3	49.0	Mflops
$192^2 \times 96$							0.22	0.19	ϕ
							41.5	71.8	Mflops

Table 2: **Parallel performance of static block-Cartesian decomposition**

	Number of processors								
Grid	1	2	4	8	16	32	64	128	
$48^2 \times 24$	1.00	0.83	0.72	0.58	0.44	0.27			ϕ
	2.94	4.87	8.43	13.7	20.8	25.2			Mflops
$96^2 \times 48$				0.69	0.60	0.49	0.29		ϕ
				16.3	28.1	46.0	55.3		Mflops
$192^2 \times 96$							0.47	0.28	ϕ
							89.0	104.	Mflops

Table 3: **Parallel performance of dynamic block-Cartesian decomposition**

	Number of processors			
Grid	1	4	16	64	
$48^2 \times 24$	1.00	0.94	0.60	0.23	ϕ
	2.94	11.0	28.0	42.9	Mflops
$96^2 \times 48$			0.85	0.54	ϕ
			40.2	101.	Mflops
$192^2 \times 96$			0.77		ϕ
			144.		Mflops

Table 4: **Parallel performance of Bruno-Cappello decomposition**

ratio, whereas Bruno-Cappello performs best on a cubic grid. We therefore conclude that the last method is best suited for ADI-type applications.

6 Curvilinear algorithm

Now that the optimal algorithm has been selected for the high-communication ADI-algorithm on a simple rectangular grid, we also apply the Bruno-Cappello decomposition to the solution of the heat equation on a curvilinear grid. It is a straightforward exercise to rewrite equation (2) using the coordinate transformation $(x, y, z) = (x(\xi, \eta, \zeta), y(\xi, \eta, \zeta), z(\xi, \eta, \zeta))$. The resulting equation is subsequently discretized again, using central differences for all derivatives. In order to enable approximate factorization, mixed second derivatives are all moved to the right hand side, leading to the following (factored) difference scheme:

$$
(1 - \frac{h\theta k}{\rho c}\delta_\xi g^{\xi\xi}\delta_\xi)(1 - \frac{h\theta k}{\rho c}\delta_\eta g^{\eta\eta}\delta_\eta)
$$
$$
(1 - \frac{h\theta k}{\rho c}\delta_\zeta g^{\zeta\zeta}\delta_\zeta)\Delta T \; = \; \frac{hk}{\rho c}\,(\delta_\xi g^{\xi\xi}\delta_\xi T +
$$
$$
\delta_\eta g^{\eta\eta}\delta_\eta T + \delta_\zeta g^{\zeta\zeta}\delta_\zeta T + \delta_\xi(g^{\xi\eta}\delta_\eta T + g^{\xi\zeta}\delta_\zeta T) +
$$
$$
\delta_\eta(g^{\eta\xi}\delta_\xi T + g^{\eta\zeta}\delta_\zeta T) + \delta_\zeta(g^{\zeta\xi}\delta_\xi T + g^{\zeta\eta}\delta_\eta T)), (15)
$$

where g is the metric tensor divided by the determinant of the Jacobian of the transformation.

This scheme involves 150 floating point operations per grid point per iteration, provided g is stored for every grid point. The algorithm for doing one time step has to be modified slightly to account for the fact that the difference stencil is no longer a seven-point star, but a $3 \times 3 \times 3$-cube with the eight corners excluded. Thus, in order to evaluate a new right hand side, points on the corner of a cell need information from six other processors, instead of just three in the Cartesian-grid case. In order to exchange all necessary boundary data a communication scheme similar to the one outlined in [8] is used, whereby the face data transfer is broken up into three pairs (east-west, north-south, top-bottom). After the third transfer, all boundary data of the augmented cells has been updated. While each pair is being sent, one third of the right hand side for interior points is computed. This strategy is not as efficient as the one in the Cartesian grid case, where all face data was sent at the same

Number of processors

Grid	1	4	9	16	25	36	49	64	81	100	121	
36^3	1.00	0.88	0.76	0.67	0.53	0.43	0.34	0.30	0.23	0.18	0.16	ϕ
	5.91	20.7	40.3	63.2	77.6	92.3	99.3	112.	109.	109.	114.	Mflops
56^3		0.89	0.83	0.74	0.70	0.63	0.56	0.52	0.44	0.37	0.32	ϕ
		21.1	44.3	70.4	103.	135.	162.	195.	209.	217.	232.	Mflops
74^3			0.86	0.82	0.76	0.72	0.66	0.63	0.57	0.50	0.45	ϕ
			45.6	77.6	112.	153.	191.	240.	271.	294.	325.	Mflops
89^3				0.83	0.80	0.76	0.72	0.68	0.64	0.59	0.55	ϕ
				78.2	118.	161.	208.	258.	307.	350.	390.	Mflops
102^3					0.80	0.78	0.73	0.72	0.66	0.63	0.55	ϕ
					118.	165.	211.	273.	318.	375.	394.	Mflops
113^3						0.78	0.76	0.72	0.71	0.65	0.64	ϕ
						166.	221.	272.	339.	382.	455.	Mflops
124^3							0.67	0.75	0.71	0.69	0.66	ϕ
							196.	282.	339.	410.	474.	Mflops
138^3								0.75	0.74	0.70	0.69	ϕ
								282.	354.	415.	494.	Mflops
149^3									0.72	0.71	0.70	ϕ
									347.	421.	500.	Mflops
160^3										0.74	0.71	ϕ
										438.	508.	Mflops
170^3											0.74	ϕ
											526.	Mflops

Table 5: Parallel performance of Bruno-Cappello decomposition for curvilinear case

time and the whole right hand side for interior points was computed in one loop, but it still takes advantage of the overlap of communication and computation.

The left hand side matrices for the different approximate factors are recomputed each time step in order to save memory. Here the Bruno-Cappello decomposition offers yet another advantage; during the forward elimination phases the communication of end-of-line data to the next cell can be overlapped with the computation of the next left hand side matrix. This cannot be done in the static block-Cartesian approach, because the messages to be sent are many and small. So in the Bruno-Cappello case the only communication that is not overlapped with computation is that of the solution as it is passed on during the back-substitution phases. This involves only one data item per point of each cell face, as opposed to three during the forward elimination phases.

An additional computational gain is obtained by writing the line solve routines such that the inner loops always run over the first array index of the (intermediate) solution; since all partial line solves within a cell are completely independent, it does not matter if we first finish one line segment and then proceed to the next, or if we do one computation at a time for each line segment within a cell in the direction of increasing first index while keeping the others fixed. This again is not possible using the static block-Cartesian approach, because Gaussian-elimination pipe-lines have to be filled one line segment at a time.

The results of computations done with the thus generalized scheme are presented in Table 5. The program was modified such that some processors were allowed to idle within a hypercube, so that the program could be run on any square number of processors smaller than 128. Performance figures refer to the actual number of active processors. If the number of processors is not a power of 2, no useful cell-to-processor mapping can be constructed using gray codes. Consequently, some performance degradation occurs, although this effect is minimized through the overlap of communication and computation. The cases run are selected such that they constitute the biggest grid possible on some number of processors (e.g. a 56×56×56 grid on 4 processors). Interestingly, the increase of the problem size on a fixed number of processors does not always yield a monotonically increasing performance. This may be due to a degeneration of the cache utilization and the increase of memory strides as the problem size grows.

Table 5 shows that the parallel performance of the Bruno-Cappello decomposition degrades relatively slowly for increasing numbers of processors, and that an efficiency of about 75% is feasible on any number of processors, provided the grid is large enough. A maximum performance of 526 Mflops is attained for a 170^3 grid on 121 processors, at an efficiency of 74%.

7 Discussion, summary, and conclusions

Three methods have been investigated for solving ADI-type problems on a MIMD distributed memory parallel computer. The most efficient uses the Bruno-Cappello multi-cell decomposition, which automatically ensures a near-perfect load balance and is easily amenable to overlap of computations and communications —the most important source of reduction of parallel overhead. It also sends the smallest number of messages per iteration, which minimizes communication cost due to high latency, and allows high computational efficiency on individual processors. Solution of the three-dimensional unsteady heat equation in curvilinear coordinates shows good scalability, and performance figures of up to 526 Mflops (double precision) on 121 processors of the Intel iPSC/860 for a large enough grid, even though only 150 floating point operations per grid point are carried out per iteration. The current implementation in C has been extended to include more complex boundary conditions (e.g. adiabatic wall, prescribed time-varying wall temperature or heat flux, wrap-around C-grid, etc.), and it was found that the use of high-level data structures kept the programming complexity as low as that of the static or dynamic block-Cartesian decompositions.

The multi-cell method is expected to offer an even larger relative benefit on the new generation of ring-, mesh- and torus-connected MIMD computers, since their connectivity is weaker than that of a hypercube, which means that communication distances will increase. Contention-free implementation of the dynamic block-Cartesian decomposition is virtually impossible on these machines, and the static block-Cartesian decomposition will suffer due to increased lengths of message paths of non-overlapped communications.

References

[1] S.H. Bokhari, *Complete exchange on the iPSC-860*, Technical Report 91-4, ICASE, NASA Langley Research Center, Hampton, VA, 1991

[2] J. Bruno, P.R. Cappello, *Implementing the Beam and Warming method on the hypercube*, Proceedings of 3rd Conference on Hypercube Concurrent Computers and Applications, Pasadena, CA, Jan. 19-20, 1988

[3] T.F. Chan, *On gray code mapping for mesh-FFTs on binary N-cubes*, Technical Report 86.17, RIACS, NASA Ames Research Center, 1986

[4] S.L. Johnsson, Y. Saad, M.H. Schultz, *Alternating direction methods on multiprocessors*, SIAM Journal of Scientific and Statistical Computing, vol. 8, No. 5, pp. 686-700, 1987

[5] P.J. Kominsky, *Performance analysis of an implementation of the Beam and Warming implicit factored scheme on the NCube hypercube*, Proceedings of the Third Symposium on the Frontiers of Massively Parallel Computation, College Park, MD, October 8-10, 1990, IEEE Computer Society Press, Los Alamitos, CA

[6] N.H. Naik, V.K. Naik, M. Nicoules, *Parallelization of a class of implicit finite difference schemes in computational fluid dynamics*, International Journal of High Speed Computing, Vol. 5, No. 1, pp. 1-50, 1993

[7] T.H. Pulliam, D.S. Chaussee, *A diagonal form of an implicit approximate factorization algorithm*, Journal of Computational Physics, Vol. 29, p. 1037, 1975

[8] S.J. Scherr, *Implementation of an explicit Navier-Stokes algorithm on a distributed memory parallel computer*, AIAA Paper 93-0063, 31st Aerospace Sciences Meeting & Exhibit, Reno, NV, January 11-14, 1993

[9] S. Seidel, M-H. Lee, S. Fotedar, *Concurrent bidirectional communication on the Intel iPSC/860 and iPSC/2*, Computer Science Technical Report CS-TR 90-06, Michigan Technological University, Houghton, MI, 1990

[10] J.C. Yan, P.J. Hontalas, C.E. Fineman, *Instrumentation, performance visualization and debugging tools for multiprocessors*, Proceedings of Technology 2001, vol. 2., pp. 377-385, San Jose, CA, December 4-6, 1991

A Data-parallel Algorithm for Three-dimensional Delaunay Triangulation and its Implementation

Y. Ansel Teng [*]   Francis Sullivan [†]   Isabel Beichl [‡]   Enrico Puppo [§]

Abstract

In this paper, we present a parallel algorithm for constructing the Delaunay triangulation of a set of vertices in three-dimensional space. The algorithm achieves a high degree of parallelism by starting the construction from every vertex and expanding over all open faces thereafter. In the expansion of open faces, the search is made faster by using a bucketing technique. The algorithm is designed under a data-parallel paradigm. It uses segmented list structures and virtual processing for load-balancing. As a result, the algorithm achieves a fast running time and good scalability over a wide range of problem sizes and machine sizes. We also incorporate a topological check to eliminate inconsistencies due to degeneracies and numerical errors. The algorithm is implemented on Connection Machines CM-2 and CM-5, and experimental results are presented.

1 Introduction

In the last decade, with the advent of commercial parallel computers, parallel processing has evolved essentially from a theoretical stage to a practical stage. However, widespread application of parallel processing is impeded by the fact that most parallel programs achieve satisfactory performance only for a very limited range of problems. It is especially true for discrete algorithms whose data are usually organized in an irregular structure.

Delaunay triangulation is a basic example of such an irregular structure that has applications in many fields of computing. It is particularly useful in mesh generation for solving fluid dynamics problems using finite element methods. Delaunay triangulation in two

dimensions has been studied extensively in the field of computational geometry. Algorithms, both sequential and parallel ones, have been designed and carefully implemented. However, in three-dimensional space, much less has been studied due to the difficulty in analyzing the properties of three dimensions, and even fewer algorithms are implemented. Because 3-d Delaunay triangulation is as useful as its 2-d counterpart in practice, we take on the task of designing a practical parallel algorithm for three-dimensional Delaunay triangulation.

The goals in our design of this algorithm include not only a good asymptotic complexity in terms of both time and work, but also efficiency and scalability in its implementation. Additionally, it should be robust in the face of numerical errors and degeneracies.

We will review some of the basics in the next section and then describe our algorithm in Sections 3 to 6. The algorithm is implemented on Connection Machines CM-2 and CM-5 and experimental results are presented in Section 7.

2 Basics

2.1 Geometric definitions

Let S be a set of points in $\mathcal{R}^3$, called sites. The *Delaunay triangulation* of S is a partition of their convex hull by a set of tetrahedra T whose vertices are the sites, S, and such that the circumsphere of every tetrahedron contains no sites in its interior.

Discussion of these geometric objects is usually under the general position assumption, that is, we assume no four sites are co-planar and no five sites are co-spherical. Under this assumption, a unique set T exists for every point set S, which is also the dual structure of the Voronoi diagram.

In this paper, we consider the problem of constructing T for a given S in parallel. Throughout the paper, n and k denote the sizes of S and T respectively. We first assume general positions for simplicity in the discussion, and later we will show how to accommodate

---

[*]Center for Automation Research, University of Maryland, College Park, MD 20742.

[†]Supercomputing Research Center, Bowie, MD 20715.

[‡]Computing and Applied Mathematics Laboratory, National Institute of Standard and Technology, Gaithersburg, MD 20899.

[§]Istituto per la Matematica Applicata, Consiglio Nazionale delle Ricerche, Via L.B. Alberti, 4 - 16132 Genova, ITALY.

situations where this assumption does not hold.

2.2 Previous work

Due to its importance in both theory and practice, there are numerous publications on Delaunay triangulation and Voronoi diagram. See [1] for an extensive survey.

The method we will be using falls into the class of incremental construction methods. This is probably the most popular method that has been implemented so far due to its relative ease of implementation. The basic idea is to construct the structure by adding one point at a time and to modify the triangulation accordingly. Two different approaches exist under this general method:

- Interpolation: in this approach, the points are added to the *interior* of an existing simplex. The simplex is split and an operation called "flipping" is employed to update the structure so that it is again a Delaunay triangulation for the points inserted so far. 3-d algorithms [9, 11] and a 2-d parallel algorithm [12] are implemented based on this idea. However, it is not clear how to insert points in parallel for the 3-d case.

- Extrapolation: extrapolation differs from interpolation in that partial results are always a subset of the final structure. New points are chosen to expand the structure toward its *exterior*. There are a few algorithms for 3 or higher dimensions in this class, such as [3, 6]. Saxena and others [13] proposed a parallel 3-d algorithm with VLSI implementation under this approach, which has a control framework similar to ours.

Other powerful methods exists mainly for the 2-d case, such as divide-and-conquer, plane-sweeping, and local improvement. However, their generalization to 3-d is mostly unclear, and the implementations are complicated or subject to numerical instability.

Since the number of tetrahedra in a 3-d Delaunay triangulation is $\Theta(n^2)$ in the worst case, an $O(n^2)$ algorithm will be worst-case optimal, and it has been achieved in [2]. However, for most input data, there will only be $O(n)$ tetrahedra in the triangulation. Therefore, an algorithm with better expected complexity and/or output-sensitive complexity is still desirable. It has been proven, in particular, that $O(n)$ is the expected number of tetrahedra for uniformly distributed random points independently by Bernal and Dwyer [4, 6]. They both proposed sequential algorithms that achieve expected linear time complexity for random points.

2.3 Data-parallelism

The algorithm we propose is designed under the data-parallel paradigm [10] in which parallelism is expressed by applying a single operation to a set of data objects in parallel. For the computational primitives, we use the *scan-vector model* by Blelloch [5]. The scan-vector model is defined as a set of primitives that operate on arbitrarily long vectors of atomic values. These primitives include elementwise arithmetics, permutation among elements, and scan operations.

The scan-vector model is distinguished by the set of scan primitives that perform a prefix operation with a wide class of operators, such as addition, multiplication, maximum, minimum, and all the binary logic operators. A simple variation of the add-scan will provide the copy and enumerate operations along the vector. The scan operations can also be conducted in a segmented fashion, where the segments are defined using a flag vector whose values are set to 1 at the head of each segment.

A set of high-level data-parallel operations can be implemented using these primitives as the building blocks. These composite operations, including *pack, append, distribute, sort, union,* and *concurrent read/write,* will be extensively used in our algorithm, and we refer the reader to [5] for their implementations. When an operation involves several vectors of equal length, these vectors will be considered as a list of data objects each consisting of a few variables. A mechanism called context indicates the active/inactive status of each data object. Contextualization is performed by **where** statements, and only the selected data objects will execute the instructions in the scope of the where statements. In this model, we apply operations to vectors of arbitrary length but in reality the machine size is fixed. We assume a virtual processing mechanism in the implementation such that the machine will automatically partition each vector among its physical processors.

The scan-vector model provides a set of powerful operations for the algorithm designer while maintaining simplicity and flexibility in the instruction set so that it can be implemented efficiently on different machine topologies. The complexity of an algorithm for a specific topology is incorporated through the cost of the implementation of these primitives.

2.4 Terminology and Representation

Throughout the paper, we assume that the input sites are normalized in a unit cube. We use the term *face* to refer to a *facet* with an associated orientation.

Input sites are stored in a list where each element contains the three coordinates of a site. A d-simplex is represented as a d-tuple of vertices, but only the indices of the site list are actually stored. For a face f in the form of $\langle a, b, c \rangle$, orientation is defined by the vector product $ab \times ac$, and the positive half-space, $H_P(f)$ is defined as the half-space on this side of the face.

3 Parallel incremental extrapolation

Our algorithm is based on the idea of incremental extrapolation. In the sequential case of such algorithms, an initial Delaunay facet is usually found by *gift wrapping*; that is, start with a site a, usually the one nearest the center of the unit cube, and find the site b that is nearest to a. $\langle a, b \rangle$ is a Delaunay edge. Then find the site c that forms the smallest circumcircle with $\langle a, b \rangle$. By properties of the Voronoi diagram, $\langle a, b, c \rangle$ is a Delaunay facet. We refer to the *expansion* of a face as the operation that searches for a site on the positive side of the face to form a Delaunay tetrahedron. A null vertex is returned if there are no vertices on its positive side, making this a boundary face. A face is an *open face* if it is a Delaunay face but has not been expanded; it is a *dead face* otherwise.

The algorithm maintains an open face list which is initialized to both sides of the first facet. Then it proceeds by expanding the faces in the open face list into tetrahedra and inserting new open faces back to the open face list until the list becomes empty. If we start with only one site, the algorithm will exhibit only a limited degree of parallelism due to the limited degree of face-adjacency among the tetrahedra. We observe that, under the general position assumption, the input sites should determine a unique Delaunay triangulation and we should obtain this triangulation no matter where we start the construction. Therefore, we can start the triangulation from **all** sites and achieve a very high degree of parallelism by expanding all open faces at the same time. Let OFL be the open face list, and TL be the tetrahedron list. Both lists are maintained as sets, i.e., there are no duplicate items in the lists. The control structure of the algorithm is outlined as follows:

Algorithm Parallel Extrapolation
begin
  for each vertex
    find the first Delaunay facet by gift wrapping;
    initialize OFL to the initial faces;
    while OFL is not empty
      expand all open faces into tetrahedra;

      append the new tetrahedra to TL;
      append the new outward faces to OFL;
      purge OFL: delete opposite-duplicates;
  end while
end Algorithm

Let T be the set of tetrahedra in the Delaunay triangulation. Consider the face-adjacency graph G induced by T, that is, the graph whose nodes correspond to the tetrahedra in T, and whose edges connect pairs of tetrahedra that share a common facet. Let I be the set of initial faces and define the depth function for a tetrahedron t

$$d_T(t) = \begin{cases} 1 & \text{if } t \text{ has a face in } I \\ min(d_T(u) + 1) & \text{otherwise} \end{cases}$$

where u is a neighbor of t in the face-adjacency graph. It is easy to shown that the algorithm performs a breadth-first search in G: in the i-th iteration, all tetrahedra with depth i will be traversed. Since the induced face-adjacency graph is finite and connected, $d_T(t)$ is finite for all $t \in T$. Therefore, all tetrahedra will be discovered in a finite number of iterations, and each tetrahedron should appear only once in the tetrahedron list.

4 Face expansion

The key to the performance of this algorithm is the search in face expansions. We describe the details of face expansions in this section. A similar technique can also be applied to the gift-wrapping.

4.1 Fundamental calculation

There are two numerical primitives in a face expansion: the Orientation test and the InSphere test. Orientation determines whether a fourth point is on the positive side of a triple $\langle a, b, c \rangle$ and InSphere tests if a fifth point is inside the sphere determined by 4 given points, $\langle a, b, c, d \rangle$. Both primitives can be formulated as matrix evaluations, which are costly if performed directly. We follow the formulation in [3] and show that both primitives can be implemented with one QR decomposition per face so that the computation in the inner loop is minimized.

For the Orientation primitive, a point d is in $H_P(\langle a, b, c \rangle)$ if the determinant of the 3×3 matrix

$$A = [b - a, c - a, d - a]$$

is positive, where the vectors $b - a$, $c - a$ and $d - a$ are column vectors. Using the QR decomposition [14], we

may write:
$$A = QR$$

where $Q = [q_1 \ q_2 \ q_3]$ is an orthogonal 3×3 matrix with columns $q_i \ \{i = 1, 2, 3\}$ and R is an upper triangular 3×3 matrix, that is:

$$R = \begin{bmatrix} r_{1,1} & r_{1,2} & r_{1,3} \\ 0 & r_{2,2} & r_{2,3} \\ 0 & 0 & r_{3,3} \end{bmatrix}$$

Then $\{q_1, q_2, q_3\}$ is an ordered orthonormal basis for $\mathcal{R}^3$ having the following properties:

1. $\{q_1, q_2\}$ is an orthonormal basis for the plane spanned by $\{b - a, c - a\}$.

2. q_3 is orthogonal to this plane.

3. The determinant of A is $r_{1,1} * r_{2,2} * r_{3,3}$.

For the InSphere primitive, instead of computing whether a fifth point is in the circumsphere of four points, we compute a signed distance function. For a face $\langle a, b, c \rangle$, let ξ_{circ} be the center of the circumcircle determined by these three points. A fourth point d, together with $\langle a, b, c \rangle$ will determine a circumsphere. Let ξ_d be the center of this sphere. Define the signed distance function of d with respect to $\langle a, b, c \rangle$, as

$$SD(d) \overset{\text{def}}{=} (\xi_d - \xi_{circ}) \cdot \frac{ab \times ac}{\|ab \times ac\|}$$

It can be shown that finding a site d in $H_P(\langle a, b, c \rangle)$ that forms an empty sphere is equivalent to finding the d that minimizes $SD(d)$. To get a convenient expression for $SD(d)$, we arrange the sphere equation in a matrix form:

$$\begin{bmatrix} 1 & a_1 & a_2 & a_3 \\ 1 & b_1 & b_2 & b_3 \\ 1 & c_1 & c_2 & c_3 \\ 1 & d_1 & d_2 & d_3 \end{bmatrix} \begin{bmatrix} \mu \\ -2p \\ -2q \\ -2s \end{bmatrix} = - \begin{bmatrix} \|a\|^2 \\ \|b\|^2 \\ \|c\|^2 \\ \|d\|^2 \end{bmatrix}$$

where p, q, s are the coordinates of the center ξ_d and μ is the quantity $p^2 + q^2 + s^2 - r^2$. Subtracting row 1 of this equation from the other rows gives:

$$R^T Z = - \begin{bmatrix} \|b\|^2 - \|a\|^2 \\ \|c\|^2 - \|a\|^2 \\ \|d\|^2 - \|a\|^2 \end{bmatrix}$$

where

$$Z = [Z_1 \ Z_2 \ Z_3]^T = -2Q^T \xi_d$$

Since Q is an orthogonal matrix, once the first two columns are computed, the third column, q_3, is

uniquely determined. Hence, in the equations above, Z_1 and Z_2 are determined by a, b, and c and only Z_3 depends on d. In fact,

$$\xi_d = -\frac{Z_1}{2} q_1 - \frac{Z_2}{2} q_2 - \frac{Z_3}{2} q_3$$

In the affine plane containing a, b, c, the center of the circle determined by these vertices is

$$\xi_{circ} = -\frac{Z_1}{2} q_1 - \frac{Z_2}{2} q_2 + \langle q_3, a \rangle q_3$$

Hence, the signed distance of ξ_d from ξ_{circ} is just

$$SD(d) = sign(r_{1,1} * r_{2,2} * r_{3,3}) * (\frac{Z_3}{2} + \langle q_3, a \rangle),$$

Therefore, for the face expansion, a QR decomposition is performed in the beginning for the matrix $[b-a, c-a]$ of each face. Then, for each site considered, we only carry out the necessary computation to obtain $r_{3,3}$ for the Orientation primitive and Z_3 for the InSphere primitive.

4.2 Bucketing

A bucketing technique is employed in our algorithm to reduce the search complexity. Although in the worst case it may be necessary to check all sites in order to expand a face, in most cases the tetrahedron can be found by just looking at sites near the face. If we arrange the sites so that we can find all the sites near a given point immediately, the search will be very efficient. This notion of closeness has been exploited by using bucketing in several previous works [3, 6]. All these works use a regular partition for simplicity, and we adopt this scheme for the same reason. The unit cube is partitioned into sub-cubes of the same size, or cells. The number of cells is proportional to the size of the input so that the expected number of sites in each cell is constant. The cell in which each site is located is computed in the initialization step and the sites are reordered so that each cell contains sites with consecutive indices. Therefore, the bucketing structure is simply a list of index pairs each recording the range of site indices for a cell.

A cell is *opened* if all the sites in the cell are searched. For each face, the idea of face expansion with bucketing is performed by first opening the cell in which ξ_{circ} is located and then iteratively opening cells that are most likely to contain the best site. The search terminates when all cells intersecting the best circumsphere or the positive half-space are opened. With an appropriate strategy to determine the cell to be opened in each iteration, this routine should perform very well for most faces. However, if we applied this routine in parallel directly to expand all open faces, we would encounter load-balancing problems twofold: first, each face may need to search a different number of cells, which would cause a variation in the number of iterations before the search terminates; second, each cell may contain a different number of sites, which would cause a variation in the time needed to complete a search iteration.

The general strategy in dealing with these problems is to convert the time variation into a resource variation and use virtual processing to balance the load of each physical processor. That is, we evaluate the load for each component of the problem and allocate the resources proportionally. The algorithm is modified so that several cells may be opened for a face at one iteration. We take the strategy that allows more cells to be opened as the search iterates, and open all cells once a preset limit is exceeded. This enables the amount of work to be adaptive to the different needs of each face while it guarantees a limit on the number of iterations.

Two auxiliary structures are employed to cope with the two levels of imbalance. In order to balance the variation in the number of cells to be opened among the faces, a number of *requests* are allocated for each face, each being responsible for opening a cell for the given face and each request is thus identified by a face-cell pair; similarly, in order to balance the variation in the number of sites in each cell, a number of *warrants* are allocated for each request. It is the warrant that actually performs the search for the fourth vertex using the formulation in Section 4.1. For efficiency, a warrant will perform the search over several sites for the same face. The number of sites for which a warrant is responsible is determined in advance and it is usually set to the expected number of sites in a cell. Therefore, each warrant is identified by its corresponding face and the range of site indices that will be searched by this warrant.

These structures are implemented by segmented lists using the distribute operation described in Section 2.3. Figure 1 illustrates the relation among these structures. In the request list, a segment of requests is allocated for each face; likewise, in the warrant list, a segment of warrants is allocated for each request and the warrants corresponding to the same face occupy consecutive segments and thus form a super-segment. These super-segments enable fast computation of the minimal signed distance over all sites for the same face using the scan primitives.

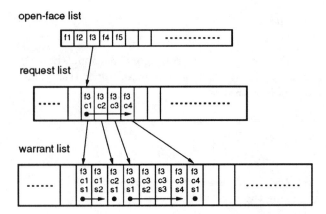

Figure 1: Implementing the auxiliary structures using segmented lists. In this example, four cells are to be searched for the open face f3. A segment of four elements is allocated for f3 in the request list. Each request is identified by the face id and a cell id. Then, a segment of warrants is allocated for each request, whose length depends on the number of sites in the corresponding cell. The heavy dots indicate the heads of segments, while the arrowed line emitting from each dot marks a segment.

Now we need a strategy to determine the cells to be opened in the initial step and the subsequent iterations in order to achieve good performance using these structures. Since a face may open $O(n)$ cells in one iteration, it is very important to make sure that the corresponding cell of each request can be computed efficiently. Therefore, we maintain the volume searched after each iteration as a *box*, which, in the following discussion, is defined as a set of cells forming a parallelepiped. A box can be represented by the ranges of coordinates along the three axes, thus has a constant-size representation in spite of its volume. We define *dead box* of a face as the box whose constituent cells are already opened for that face, and *new box* as the box whose constituent cells will have been opened after the next search. The difference between the new box and the dead box are the cells to be opened in the next search. Initially, we set the dead box of a face to empty and the new box to the *containment box* of the face and ξ_{circ}. The containment box of a set of points is defined as the minimal box that contains these points and is obtained by finding the extremal coordinates among the given points. After each iteration, we compute the center and the radius of the circumsphere determined by the face and the best site using the formula in Section 4.1. The containment box of the circumsphere is then computed and compared with the dead box. If further search is necessary, the new box is obtained by extending the dead box in the directions where the gaps between the boxes are large.

The face expansion scheme using bucketing is summarized as follows:

Algorithm Face Expansion
begin
  for all open faces
    $newbox := containment\_box(\{a, b, c, \xi_{circ}\})$;
    $deadbox := \emptyset$; $done := false$;
    $min\_sd := \infty$; $d := null$;
    while not globally $done$, **where** not $done$
      compute the number of cells to open;
      allocate the request list;
      for each request
        compute its corresponding cell;
        obtain the range of site indices of the cell;
        allocate the warrant list;
        for each warrant
          $WS :=$ the range of its site indices;
          $w\_min\_sd :=$
            $min\{SD(p) \mid p \in WS \bigcap p \in H_P\}$;
        end for each
      end for each
      $min\_sd := min\{min\_sd, w\_min\_sd\}$ for all
        warrants of the face;
      $d := p$ that contributes to this minimum;
      $deadbox := newbox$;
      $newbox := containment\_box($
        $circumsphere(\langle a, b, c, d \rangle))$;
      if $newbox \subseteq deadbox$
        or $(unit\ cube \bigcap H_P) \subseteq deadbox$
        $done := true$;
      else
        adjust $newbox$;
    end while
  end for all
end Algorithm

5 Robustness

Robustness is a serious issue in geometric algorithms due to degeneracies and numerical errors. In their primitive form, many geometrical algorithms simply assume that there is neither degeneracy nor numerical error. As a result, when these methods are used on data that is degenerate or nearly degenerate, they either fail completely or else give incorrect results. Another problem that may occur in a parallel algorithm is the inconsistency among the partial results obtained by different processors. In the degenerate cases, a Delaunay cell may be partitioned into tetrahedra in many ways, and each processor may independently decide to take a different one. This will not only generate intersecting tetrahedra, but may also lead the algorithm into infinite loop by repeatedly generating the same tetrahedra.

Our approach in obtaining robustness while maintaining efficiency consists of three elements. Besides using the numerically stable methods, such as the QR decomposition, we also apply a perturbation to the input points to resolve ambiguities in the InSphere primitive, and a topological check is employed to detect and eliminate the inconsistency among the distributed results.

5.1 Resolving ambiguities

One simple method to resolve the ambiguities is to add a small amount of random noise to the sites. However, this is not a good way to eliminate degeneracies, because the added noise generates many extra tetrahedra, even where there is no ambiguity. A better approach is to perturb the input only when necessary. An important method of this type, called Simulation of Simplicity, has been devised by Edelsbrunner and Mücke [7]. Here perturbations are applied when degeneracies are detected, and symbolic methods are used. Fewer false features are introduced and there is usually no after-the-fact removal of zero volume tetrahedra. Detection of degeneracy is implemented by using extended-precision integers to achieve the effect of exact arithmetic. This, in addition to the fact that the order of the sites must be fixed for the test, results in costly computations.

In order to resolve the ambiguities in the InSphere primitive while maintaining efficiency, we perform a random linear transformation: a single perturbation matrix $A = I + \eta M$ is computed, where M is a random matrix and η is a small constant. and the input points v are replaced by points $x = Av$. Since matrix A is the same for all input points, all the affine relations implied by the original data are preserved.

It is proved in [3] that with probability 1, degeneracy exists after the transformation only if all input points are co-planar or the matrix A is singular. In practice, the entries of M are chosen at random in [0,1], and the probability that A is singular is very small with a small η. As the ambiguities of the InSphere primitive are resolved by the perturbation, Delaunay cells with more than four points will be partitioned consistently among the processors. Since coplanarity is preserved in our perturbation, the Orientation primitive will prevent the generation of zero-volume tetrahedra. Therefore, the algorithm should output a desirable triangulation of the space.

5.2 Consistency check

The perturbation eliminates degeneracies in real arithmetic. But in the case of floating point arithmetic, there is a finite probability that there will still be degeneracies with respect to the precision of the arithmetic. It is very difficult to detect and eliminate such degeneracies by checking geometric properties since such computation will also be subject to numerical errors. Therefore, topological consistency is checked to further reduce the impact of such problems.

The consistency check is based on the following topological property of a triangulation: each face of the triangulation should have at most one tetrahedron on each side of the face. In a degeneracy involving five co-spherical points, there are two different ways to partition the convex hull of these five points. Two tetrahedra from the two different partitions will always coincide on one face. By detecting that two tetrahedra are coincident on the same side of a face, we can detect such degeneracy and eliminate it by discarding all but one tetrahedron that are coincident on the same side of a face.

For degeneracies involving only five points, it suffices to check only the faces of the new tetrahedra. If more than five points are involved in such degeneracy, the situation will be much more complicated. In such cases, intersecting tetrahedra may be generated without violating the topological consistency. However, as the different ways of partitioning should agree on the convex hull, the inconsistency will at least be detected at a later iteration and localized within the convex hull if we check all the faces in the triangulation. Although the degeneracy will not be eliminated by discarding the extra tetrahedra, we will see that these situations rarely occur with double-precision floating-point arithmetic.

Based on the above discussion, we check the topological consistency after each face expansion by maintaining a dead face dictionary. The dictionary is initialized as empty. After each face expansion iteration, new dead faces are inserted into the dictionary. Duplicates in the dictionary will be detected and the corresponding tetrahedra will be eliminated.

6 Complexity analysis

The complexity of the algorithm is determined by two factors: the number of face expansion iterations and the number of sites searched in face expansion steps.

Using the graph distance function, $d_T()$, defined in Section 3, the number of face expansion iterations is $max\{d_T(t) \mid t \in T\}$. According to [13], if the algorithm terminates after m steps, there will be $\Omega(m^2)$ tetrahedra in the final structure. Since the output size of a 3-d Delaunay triangulation can be $O(n^2)$ in the worst case, the algorithm may need $O(n)$ iterations to generate all the tetrahedra.

However, such worst cases rarely happen in practice. We observed empirically that if the input sites are uniformly distributed random points, the number of tetrahedra incident to a site has a distribution similar to a normal distribution with mean 24. If we consider only tetrahedra incident to a site and start the face expansion from one initial face, the expected number of iterations should be a small constant close to four. In the Parallel Extrapolation algorithm, a tetrahedron can be generated through a path from any initial face, thus it is very unlikely that $d_T(t)$ is large for any t. We can randomize the choice of initial faces (instead of the one whose circumcircle is smallest) to ensure this low probability even if the output size is larger than $O(n)$.

As for the cost of face expansion, we conjecture that each face will search only an expected constant number of sites for uniformly distributed random points. Although we will not give a rigorous proof, Dwyer [6] has proved linear expected time for a sequential algorithm that performs face expansion in a similar fashion. The major differences between his work and ours are:

1. Dwyer's complexity analysis is done with sites uniformly distributed in a unit ball instead of a unit cube. However, since the difference between a unit ball and a unit cube is a small percentage of both in 3 dimensions, we conjecture that his result can apply to our problem space.

2. His algorithm uses a priority queue to arrange the order in which the cells are opened. When a Delaunay tetrahedron is discovered, all cells that intersect the circumsphere and the positive half-space must have been opened. Our algorithm basically opens all cells in the containment box of the cells his algorithm opens. Again, in 3-d, the ratio between the number of extra cells and the number of necessary cells is bounded by a constant.

Based on the above discussion, a face expansion in our algorithm should search only an expected constant number of points for uniformly distributed random input, and it should only take a small number of face expansion iterations. Considering the costs of the scan-vector primitives, our algorithm should have an expected time complexity poly-logarithmic in n using $O(n)$ processors for such input sets in many scalable network models.

7 Experimental result

Our algorithm has been implemented in the C* language and tested on Connection Machines CM-2 and CM-5. For the CM-2, it is compiled using the Version 6.0.3 compiler and tested on a 16K-processor model. Single-precision floating point arithmetic is used due to the lack of double-precision hardware support in the tested machine. For the CM-5, it is compiled using the Version 7.0 beta compiler and tested on a 32-node system. Double-precision floating-point arithmetic is used on the CM-5 unless specified otherwise. According to the vendor, this compiler is a test version that does not utilize the vector units. It has not had the benefit of optimization or performance tuning and, consequently, is not necessarily representative of the performance of the full version of this software.

Table 1 shows the CM-5 running time and other information for several 3-d data sets. The data sets are divided into three groups: 1. uniformly-distributed random points, which are named by the prefix "rand" and a suffix indicating the sizes of the sets; 2. points sampled from 3-D objects, as indicated by their names. Some of these files are also used in [8]; 3. polymer data, which are named by the prefix "polymer" and a suffix indicating the sizes of the sets. Among the columns, n and k are the number of input points and the number of output tetrahedra respectively: the column "time" shows the running time of the main loop, and "time/k" is the cost per tetrahedron.

Figure 2 shows the running time for uniformly distributed random points. The figure is drawn in double logarithmic scale, and a reference curve is plotted to shown the slope of a linear relation in such scale. The running times for the random points in Table 1 are plotted as the "CM-5 double precision" curve. The slope is indeed very close to that of the linear relation curve. As a contrast, a "CM-5 brute-force" curve is plotted for which exhaustive search is used in all face expansions without the auxiliary processor structures. It illustrates a curve with quadratic growth rate. The break-even point for bucketing is about 500 sites. Also the running time using a 16K-processor CM-2 is plotted. Its growth rate is even slower than the linear relation since the machine is not fully utilized with most of the problem sizes. This curve illustrates the

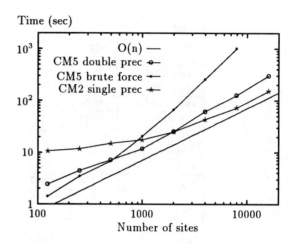

Figure 2: The running times for random points.

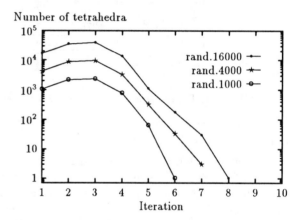

Figure 3: The number of tetrahedra generated at each iteration.

achievement of a poly-logarithmic time bound with unlimited resources.

In the complexity analysis, we conjectured the low likelihood that $d_T(t)$ is large for any tetrahedron t. The column entitled "depth" in Table 1 shows the number of face expansion iterations performed for each data set, i.e., the largest $d_T(t)$. None of the data sets requires more than 10 iterations and most of them are done after 6 or 7 iterations. Figure 3 shows the distribution of $d_T(t)$ for random points. It is confirmed that most tetrahedra are discovered by the fourth iteration and the maximal $d_T(t)$ seems to grow in a logarithmic rate with the minimal-circle initialization. It is also interesting to notice that, for all the input sets, the total number of tetrahedra is roughly six times the

Data set	n	k	depth	time (sec)	time/k (ms)	FE	search/FE (sites)
rand.125	125	676	6	2.42	3.5	1095	81.7
rand.250	250	1489	6	4.40	2.9	2311	69.2
rand.500	500	3037	6	7.14	2.3	4693	65.4
rand.1000	1000	6361	7	11.84	1.8	9732	73.5
rand.2000	2000	12947	7	26.10	2.0	19717	85.3
rand.4000	4000	26252	8	61.17	2.3	39812	80.1
rand.8000	8000	52895	8	125.31	2.4	80120	88.6
rand.16000	16000	106693	9	299.77	2.8	161060	88.6
dodecahedron	20	40	5	0.65	16.3	104	20.0
torus	256	1328	6	4.34	3.2	2346	140.7
m1	318	1967	6	7.91	4.0	2974	134.0
cube	343	1296	5	6.54	5.0	2417	133.7
tori	800	5889	7	17.87	3.0	9150	156.3
spiral	1248	8799	7	28.62	3.2	13818	182.0
m2	1366	8938	7	27.58	3.1	13571	121.7
bust	2630	17249	6	91.33	5.2	26338	324.3
fract2	2704	16909	10	182.56	10.7	26323	724.4
liss-5-8	4200	27550	6	113.22	4.1	43084	246.0
teapot	4668	27081	6	246.37	9.0	43778	617.4
phone1	6070	39429	8	371.19	9.4	59739	645.7
polymer.278	278	1670	6	5.15	3.1	2538	97.0
polymer.500	500	2904	7	6.64	2.2	4516	61.1
polymer.932	932	5424	6	16.82	3.1	8524	141.9

Table 1: Experimental results for 3D data sets on 32-node CM-5 using double precision arithmetic.

number of the sites.

The last two columns in Table 1, labeled "FE" and "search/FE", are the number of face expansions performed by the algorithm and the average number of points searched in each face expansion respectively. The number of face expansions is usually 50% more than the number of the tetrahedra due to the convex hull faces and those tetrahedra that are discovered by several open faces in the same iteration. In these experiments, the unit cube is partitioned in a way such that the computation cost of the site search and the overhead of managing the intermediate structures are balanced. The number we obtained is an average of eight sites per cell. Therefore, according to the column "search/FE", an average of 10 cells are opened in each face expansion for the random points. This means that most face expansions are completed after the second search iteration, and it confirms our conjecture that a constant number of searches are expected in a face expansion.

Another important goal of our algorithm is good scalability over a wide range of machine sizes. We tested our algorithm on the CM-5 at the Army High

#PE	rand.4000		rand.16000	
	time	speedup	time	speedup
32	55.03	1.0	266.9	1.0
128	15.31	3.59	77.83	3.43
256	11.63	4.73	43.89	6.08

Table 2: Scalability over different machine sizes. The times are in seconds.

Performance Computing Center using various number of processors. Table 2 lists the running time and the speedup with respect to the 32-node running time. Substantial speedup is obtained with increased number of processors, although it is limited by the scalability of the network connecting the processors as well as the constant overhead such as resource allocation and instruction decoding.

As for the robustness of the program, it has not encountered any inconsistency while using double-precision arithmetic. With single-precision arithmetic, the consistency checking helps to overcome the degeneracies in all cases involving random points and

Data set	n	k	inconsistency
rand.4000	4000	26239	2
rand.16000	16000	106879	5
torus	256	1351	27
cube	343	–	too many
spiral	1248	8795	8
bust	2630	–	too many
fract2	2704	–	too many
liss-5-8	4200	27545	19
teapot	4668	–	too many
phone1	6070	–	too many
polymer.932	932	5432	10

Table 3: Robustness with the consistency check in single-precision arithmetic.

polymer data. For some highly degenerate data sets that involve hundreds of points symmetrically sampled from a sphere or a circle, the single-precision arithmetic is unable to localize the inconsistency and therefore unable to finish within a reasonable amount of time. The result is shown in Table 3.

8 Conclusion

In this paper, we presented a parallel algorithm for constructing Delaunay triangulation of a set of points in three-dimensional space. The algorithm achieves a high degree of parallelism by starting the construction from every vertex and expanding over all open faces thereafter. In the expansion of the open faces, the search is made faster by using a bucketing technique. The algorithm is designed under a data-parallel paradigm. It uses segmented list structures and virtual processing for load-balancing. As a result, the algorithm achieves a fast running time and good scalability over a wide range of problem sizes and machine sizes. We incorporated a topological check for eliminating inconsistencies due to degeneracies and numerical errors. The algorithm is implemented on Connection Machines CM-2 and CM-5 and the experimental results confirmed our prediction of a good performance over a wide variety of input data sets.

Acknowledgement

The first author would like to thank Larry Davis and David Mount for their valuable discussions and suggestions during the project development. We also like to thank E.P. Mücke for his help in obtaining some of the test data sets.

References

[1] F. Aurenhammer. Voronoi diagram — a survey of a fundamental geometric data structure. *ACM Computing Survey*, 23(3):345–405, 1991.

[2] F. Aurenhammer and H. Edelsbrunner. An optimal algorithm for constructing the weighted Voronoi diagram in the plane. *Pattern Recognition*, 17:251–257, 1984.

[3] I. Beichl and F. Sullivan. Fast triangulation via empty spheres. manuscript, 1992.

[4] J. Bernal. On the expected complexity of the 3-dimensional Voronoi diagram. Technical Report NISTIR-4321, National Institute of Standards and Technology, 1990.

[5] G. Blelloch. *Vector models for data-parallel computing*. MIT Press, 1990.

[6] R. A. Dwyer. Higher-dimensional Voronoi diagrams in linear expected time. *Discrete and Computational Geometry*, 6:343–367, 1991.

[7] H. Edelsbrunner and E. Mücke. Simulation of simplicity: a technique to cope with degenerate cases in geometric algorithms. *ACM Transactions on Graphics*, 9(1):66–104, 1990.

[8] H. Edelsbrunner and E. Mücke. Three dimensional alpha shapes. Technical Report UIUCDCS-R-92-1734, Dept. of Computer Science, University of Illinois at Urbana-Champion, 1992.

[9] H. Edelsbrunner and N. Shah. Incremental topological flipping works for regular triangulations. In *Proc. 8th ACM Symposium on Computational Geometry*, pages 43–52, 1992.

[10] W. Hillis and G. Steele. Data parallel algorithms. *Communications of the ACM*, 29:1170–1183, 1986.

[11] H. Inagaki, K. Sugihara, and N. Sugie. Numerically robust incremental algorithm for constructing three-dimensional Voronoi diagrams. In *Proc. Fourth Canadian Conference on Computational Geometry*, pages 334–339, 1992.

[12] E. Puppo et al. Parallel terrain triangulation. In *Proc. Fifth International Symposium on Spatial Data Handling*, pages 632–641, 1992.

[13] S. Saxena, P. Bhatt, and V. Prasad. Efficient VLSI parallel algorithm for Delaunay triangulation on orthogonal tree network in two and three dimensions. *IEEE Trans. on Computers*, 39(3):400–404, 1990.

[14] G. Stewart. *Introduction to Matrix Computations*. Academic Press, New York, 1973.

Session 2:
Networks
Chair: Bill Boas

A Programmable HIPPI Interface for a Graphics Supercomputer

Raj K. Singh   Stephen G. Tell   Shaun J. Bharrat
David Becker   Vernon L. Chi

Department of Computer Science
University of North Carolina
Chapel Hill, NC 27599-3175

Abstract

As networks approach gigabit performance, supercomputer host interfaces are becoming the communication bottleneck. The Network Interface Unit (NIU) is a high-performance host interface for Pixel Planes 5, a custom graphics supercomputer. The design offers both performance and programmability through a balance of data-marshaling hardware and an embedded processor. In this paper, we describe the NIU hardware and firmware architecture. We present some preliminary performance measurements and assess the applicability of this design for the targeted environment. We also comment on its suitability for other environments and outline plans for the future work.

1: Introduction

Metacomputing, where a large number of heterogeneous computing resources are networked together and operate in tandem, is emerging as a means to solve computational problems beyond the scope of any one computer. In this model of computing, the network is no longer simply a means of communication but serves as the "backplane" of a supercomputer, the *metacomputer*. For effective metacomputing, the network must approximate the high-bandwidth, low-latency characteristics of a backplane. The emerging public B-ISDN standards promise networks which meet these characteristics. A necessary component is then a high-performance host interface for each computer in the network. A particular requirement for the VISTAnet project [1-3] is a host interface for the custom graphics supercomputer called Pixel Planes 5 [4].

This paper describes the Network Interface Unit (NIU) [5]. The NIU serves two purposes: (1) it is the host interface for Pixel Planes 5 and must, therefore, be capable of sustaining high-bandwidth data transfer with minimal latency; and (2) it serves as a platform for protocol research and must be sufficiently programmable to process a wide range of upper-layer network protocols. These two requirements are conflicting and, to meet both, the NIU partitions the tasks between hardware and software. To meet the throughput requirements, all data movement is performed by hardware. To satisfy the programmability, a microprocessor directs and initiates the data movement and performs the protocol processing.

Section 2 gives an overview of the VISTAnet project and the Pixel Planes 5 graphics supercomputer. Sections 3 and 4 detail the NIU hardware and system software architectures, respectively. Section 5 describes the system firmware program. Preliminary performance results are presented in section 6. A summary of present and future work is given in section 7.

2: Overview

2.1: The network

The VISTAnet network [1] is based on the emerging B-ISDN standards and uses SONET (Synchronous Optical Network) framing to transmit Asynchronous Transfer Mode (ATM) cells. The infrastructure consists of an ATM switch at the BellSouth Chapel Hill Central Office (CO) and a GTE cross-connect switch at the GTE Durham CO connected with a 2.488 Gbps Synchronous Digital Hierarchy transmission facility and extended with 622 Mbps access lines to the user sites. The network is terminated at each user site with a Network Terminal Adapter (NTA) which provides an ANSI X9T3 HIPPI [6] interface. Currently, three computers - a Cray Y-MP at the North Carolina Supercomputing Center, the Pixel Planes 5 graphics multicomputer, and a Silicon Graphics 340 VGX workstation at the University of North Carolina - are connected to the network.

The NTA provides a HIPPI interface to the network. The NIU serves as a HIPPI interface for the Pixel Planes host, thus, allowing it to be network-sharable resource. The NTA and NIU together function as an ATM interface for Pixel Planes. However, the NIU alone can be used to directly connect Pixel Planes to a HIPPI network and, in fact, it is being used in this manner for locally sharing Pixel Planes.

2.2: The application

The target application for the VISTAnet project, Dynamic Radiation Therapy Planning, assists physicians in the planning of radiation therapy for cancer patients. The need to perform 3D radiation dose profiling in real-time results in overwhelming computational complexity. This task is handled effectively by partitioning the application among several machines: the workstation serves as the user interface, the Cray computes radiation dosages, and Pixel Planes 5 renders the images. Using joystick control, the physician can modify the beam parameters, rotate the image, or select different areas of detail. Changes are reflected in new images in real-time. The throughput requirements for the application, illustrated in Fig. 1, place severe demands on all components of the underlying network, including the NIU.

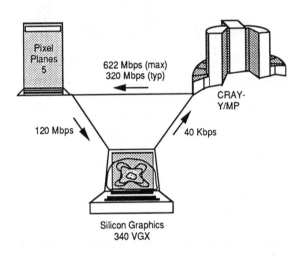

Fig. 1: VISTAnet application throughput rates

2.3: The pixel planes 5

Pixel Planes 5 [4] is a custom multicomputer optimized for interactive graphics applications. The multicomputer consists of heterogeneous processing nodes interconnected by an internal ring network. The network is a 32-bit wide synchronous ring organized into eight 640 Mbps channels. Access to the ring is through bidirectional ports. The transfer unit is the *message*, which can range in size from one 32-bit word to a receiver dependent maximum between 1024 and 16384 words. The transfer latency is a minimum of a few μs; the maximum latency is unbounded. Each message header contains a 32-bit Ring Address Word (RAW). Each RAW contains a unique 7-bit device address and a specific 12-bit mailbox address within a particular device. The device addresses are based on the physical location of the board on the ring.

2.4: Related work

Several similar high-performance host interfaces have been reported in the literature. To achieve the high performance, some of these interfaces use a purely hardware approach. Kanakia and Cheriton's [12] VMP Network Adapter Board uses a hardware solution for a specific transport protocol, the Versatile Message Passing (VMP) protocol. Abu-Amara et. al. [10] take a more general, but still a hardware-based approach. Using their Psi compiler, any protocol can be implemented. First, the protocol is specified using a symbolic language, and then the Psi compiler is used to generate hardware mask descriptions. These masks are then used to create custom hardware.

Other interfaces split tasks between hardware and software for the interface as well as the host. Banks and Prudence describe their Medusa FDDI interface for the HP Apollo Series 700 workstation in [14]. Traw and Smith [7] detail an ATM interface that is to be used in the AURORA testbed. This interface allows the connection of an IBM RS/6000 workstation to a SONET STS-3c line carrying ATM cells. Another interface, also designed for the AURORA testbed, is detailed by Davie in [8]. This ATM interface connects a DECstation 5000 to a SONET/ATM network through the DEC TURBO channel I/O bus. All of these interfaces focus on the physical and link-level communications and leave the protocol processing to the host computer. In contrast, the Nectar Communications Accelerator Board (CAB) [11] includes protocol processing as one of its main tasks. The CAB functions as an outboard protocol processor for the host machine and communicates with the host memory directly.

The NIU shares many characteristics with these other interfaces. Many of the concepts used are common among most high-performance interfaces and the primary difference lies in the choice of lower layer protocol (e.g. HIPPI, ATM, proprietary, etc.), the level of protocol processing supported (i.e. link and data layers only, or transport layer also), and their implementations. For example, the need for data movement in hardware is also reflected in the designs of [7,8,10,12,14], the use of a processor control subsystem for flexibility is shared with [8,11], and the ability to handle outboard protocol processing is similar to that of [11].

The NIU is particularly similar in function to the CAB [11]. They both connect a host to a network. Both support outboard processing of various upper layer protocols and run additional application code. The main difference between the NIU and the CAB lies in the generality of the interface. The CAB connects a host to a special purpose network whereas the NIU provides a standard HIPPI interface. Hence, while the CAB allows a host to communicate with other CAB-connected hosts, the NIU allows Pixel Planes to communicate with any device with a HIPPI interface.

The NIU differs from the other interfaces in several respects, the most significant of which is that the NIU is a host interface for a supercomputer, not a workstation. This has three ramifications. First, there is ample bandwidth to the host, so the network interface is truly the bottleneck. Any limitation in the NIU, therefore, directly degrades the overall performance. Second, while it may be acceptable to use host CPU cycles to do protocol processing on a workstation, it is not acceptable to use the Pixel Planes CPUs for anything but graphics processing. This dictates that all protocol processing must be handled by the NIU. Third, while the Pixel Planes internal ring can be considered a backplane in some respects, it is actually a network connecting independent devices. Hence, the NIU must also perform some functions more characteristic of a gateway than of an interface. These include tasks such as data reformatting, stripping and replacing protocol headers, and address translation.

3: NIU hardware architecture

3.1: Organization

The NIU consists of five subsystems as shown in Fig. 2: the HIPPI subsystem, the ringbound buffers, the ring subsystem, the netbound buffers, and the control processor. The source module of the HIPPI subsystem, the netbound buffers, and the receive module of the ring subsystem constitute the Network-Bound pipeline. The destination module of the HIPPI subsystem, ringbound buffers, and the transmit module of ring subsystem similarly comprise a Ring-Bound pipeline. The control processor oversees the operation of the other modules. It determines the destination of data, handles protocol processing, and initiates all data transfers.

3.2: Control processor

The processor module consists of a 25 MHz Cypress SPARC CY7C611 RISC processor with 1 MByte of zero-wait-state memory and 64 KBytes of bootstrap EPROM. The processor executes one instruction every 1.25 to 1.5 clock cycles and has an interrupt latency of between 4 and 7 clock cycles. The bootstrap code monitors the command FIFO to load and initialize program code through Port 0 of the ring subsystem. The NIU, like other parts of the Pixel Planes, is fully reset and loaded with a new program at the start of each application.

A real-time clock is implemented with a hardware counter of 40 ns period. The fine-grained time stamps from this counter have proven extremely useful in profiling the firmware. The processor subsystem interfaces to the other hardware subsystems through 25 I/O registers and 6 prioritized interrupts.

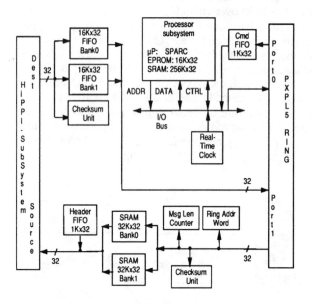

Fig. 2: NIU hardware architecture

3.3: Ring subsystem

The ring interface subsystem provides two communication links between the NIU and the Pixel Planes 5 internal ring network. The NIU occupies an entire slot in the Pixel Planes card cage and makes use of both ring ports on the board. Port 0 is reserved for software-controlled messages to and from the control processor. It is designated as the command port, and is used for system initialization, testing, and monitoring.

Port 1, called the data port, is used to transfer ring messages to and from the network. The receive (Network-Bound) module of the port is the simpler of the two; it accepts a single message each time the processor indicates that a netbound buffer is available. The transmit (Ring-Bound) data port terminates a protocol layer called RingP, which encapsulates Pixel Planes messages transmitted across the network. We expected the network throughput to increase with larger packets, and hence created RingP to allow multiple ring messages to be assembled into larger network packets. The

RingP state machine can be operated in a streaming mode, in which messages span across HIPPI packets, or in a packet mode where messages do not cross packet boundaries. The former is used when RingP is sent within a stream-based transport protocol, such as TCP, while the latter is used with datagram-oriented protocols.

3.4: HIPPI subsystem

The HIPPI interface consists of two simplex channel; one each for transmit (source module) and receive (destination module). At the destination port, the differential ECL signals from the HIPPI cable are converted to TTL signals. Data parity and LLRC are checked, HIPPI bursts are reassembled into packets, and the data is sent to the ringbound buffer subsystem. Similarly, the source port accepts a stream of data from the netbound buffer subsystem and breaks it into bursts. LLRC and parity are computed, and the signals are translated to ECL levels.

At both the source and destination port, the setup and tear down of HIPPI logical connections is controlled by the processor with minimal hardware support. We expected that these events would be relatively infrequent, and thus appropriate for software handling. We have since found that some HIPPI interfaces prefer to break and reestablish this logical connection on every packet, causing a severe reduction in performance. (The Cray HIPPI interface is one such example). In retrospect, additional hardware support for connection management is desirable.

3.5: Ringbound buffer subsystem

Incoming data from the HIPPI destination subsystem is placed in a ringbound buffer composed of FIFO memories. Usage of the two FIFO banks is interleaved on a packet basis; while one buffer is being filled by the HIPPI subsystem, the ring subsystem empties the other. As soon as the first word is received, the FIFO controller will signal the processor that a packet is arriving so it can begin reading and processing the packet's header. A pair of dedicated 16-bit ALUs compute a ones-complement checksum over arriving data for use by protocol software in implementing reliable transport protocols.

FIFOs were chosen to implement the ringbound buffer for several reasons. The ATM network guarantees that if packets are delivered at all, they will be in order, so packets need not be reordered before being sent to the ring. We desired that the processor be able to start processing a packet's header before the packet had fully arrived; FIFOs provide a simple means of achieving a dual-ported memory. A FIFO-based design is independent of the FIFO length; we have recently upgraded the FIFOs from the original 16 KByte size to 64 KBytes. Finally, the available board area was too small to implement a dual-ported buffer with separate RAM and the associated control logic.

3.6: Netbound buffer subsystem

Data arriving from the ring is placed into a buffer in the netbound buffer subsystem. The buffer system RAM is organized into two banks, each with eight 16 KByte buffers. Multiple buffers are provided for use in implementing acknowledge/retransmit reliable protocols. Data must be stored on the NIU until acknowledgment is received since the rest of Pixel Planes system assumes that ring message delivery is reliable. No provision is made for combining ring messages into long packets. The complex logic that would be required for this feature is not justified because the ring devices that will be sending data to the network in our application can be programmed to send long ring messages. Furthermore, the outgoing bandwidth required by most Pixel Planes applications, including VISTAnet, is lower than the incoming bandwidth.

The buffer management scheme is designed to allow maximum possible overlapping of operations. As soon as the ring address word arrives, it is stored in a separate register and the protocol processor is informed. As the remainder of the ring message arrives, a pair of ALUs computes a ones-complement checksum on it. While the remainder of the message from the ring is being written into the netbound buffer, the microprocessor can begin constructing the upper layer protocol header, which is written into the header FIFO. When the packet is ready for transmission, the buffer subsystem first sends the contents of the header FIFO and then the contents of the selected data buffer to the HIPPI source subsystem.

An important overall design constraint was the physical size of the interface. This limited the amount of functionality that could be accommodated in hardware. The resulting printed circuit board is 14"x15" in size with 10 layers and 232 ICs.

4: NIU system software

The NIU system software follows a microkernel architecture. The microkernel only provides functions for multitasking and basic synchronization with the hardware. Other operating system facilities, namely semaphores and shared buffers, are layered on top of the microkernel.

4.1: The Microkernel

The NIU runs a custom multitasking operating system. All tasks are implemented as threads, which are based on the Mach C threads [13]. The context of a thread consists of its local stack space and the contents of the processor's register set. There is no memory protection, and all threads share the same physical address space. A thread is defined as a C function taking no parameters and returning type void. This defining function may call any number of other functions with no restrictions on the call depth (providing that the stack does not overflow), and when this function returns, the thread is terminated.

The kernel is implemented as a C++ class, and every NIU program contains a single global instance of this class. This operating system object provides functions for dynamic thread creation and destruction, scheduling, and context-switching. Thread creation and destruction both involve rather few instructions (less than 40 SPARC instructions) so programs which rely on rapid thread creation and destruction are possible. Scheduling is first-in, first-out among the ready threads. Currently, the operating system uses a model of cooperating threads and, hence, does not preempt. Therefore, scheduling only occurs when a thread blocks or voluntarily relinquishes control.

In addition to thread manipulation, the kernel provides for synchronization with the hardware. Each of the interrupts is associated with an event, and when a thread waits for an event, the kernel checks whether that event was posted (i.e. its flag bit set); if it was, the thread is allowed to continue. Otherwise, the thread is moved to the wait queue associated with that event. When an interrupt is raised, the interrupt handler posts the associated event, and the kernel moves the threads waiting on that event back onto the run queue.

The kernel also implements a software event facility. Software events are used for inter-thread communications and are analogous to their hardware counterparts. They differ in that they may be dynamically created as needed.

4.2: Semaphores

Instantiations of the semaphore C++ class may also be used for inter-thread synchronization. The class is an implementation of a general semaphore with the standard atomic p and v operations. While it is difficult, or at least error-prone, to solve some critical section problems using semaphores, the synchronization problems encountered in NIU code are easily solved using this simple construct. Future NIU programs may necessitate implementation of more elaborate synchronization mechanisms.

4.3: Shared buffer

Because of the single address space, the shared memory model of inter-thread communication is most efficient. Threads communicate with each other through instantiations of the shared buffer class. A shared buffer can be used to exchange messages of arbitrary format and length. Of course, the length of a single message cannot exceed the length of the buffer. Reading from and writing to a shared buffer are mutually exclusive operations. A thread reading from a buffer is guaranteed of either receiving the specified number of bytes or blocking. A thread writing a message is guaranteed that the entire message will be written; if sufficient space is not available, the thread is blocked until the message can be saved. No time-out mechanism is implemented so the requesting thread remains indefinitely blocked until the request can be satisfied.

The shared buffer construct can be used to organize threads into "software pipelines". Each thread in such a grouping is a stage of the pipeline, and it accepts messages from the preceding stage through a shared buffer and sends messages to the succeeding stage through another shared buffer. Since, both a read attempt on an empty buffer and a write attempt to a full buffer will cause the requesting thread to block, the shared buffers will eventually equalize the rates of each thread in the pipeline. This model of threads organized into software pipelines is used in the NIU firmware, which is described next.

5: NIU firmware

The NIU control program consists of four main threads organized into two software pipelines. The Netbound software pipeline controls data flow from the Pixel Planes 5 ring to the B-ISDN network and consists of the RingIn and Source threads. The Ringbound software pipeline controls data in the opposite direction. It also consists of two threads, the Destination and RingOut threads.

The RingIn thread accepts packets from the ring and buffers them in the netbound buffers. First, the thread indicates to the ring interface into which buffer the next packet should be placed. It then directs the hardware to accept the next packet and goes to sleep awaiting the arrival of the packet. When the thread is awakened, it maps the Ring Address Word of the incoming packet to the destination I-field address, constructs the appropriate header and places it into the header FIFO, and then writes a message into a shared buffer to signal the Source thread.

The Source thread forwards packets from the netbound buffers onto the B-ISDN network. When it receives a message from the RingIn thread indicating that a packet should be transmitted, the Source thread directs the HIPPI source hardware to set up a connection, if necessary, and initiates the transfer.

The Destination thread accepts packets from the B-ISDN network and buffers them in one of the ringbound FIFOs. After a connection has been established, the thread sleeps until the packet starts arriving. When awakened, it reads and processes the HIPPI-FP header from the ringbound FIFO and sleeps until the rest of the packet has been received. Finally, when awakened again, the Destination thread processes the rest of the header and signals the RingOut thread by writing a message into another shared buffer.

The RingOut thread forwards packets from the ringbound FIFOs onto the ring. When it receives a message from the Destination thread indicating that a packet should be forwarded, the thread extracts the location and length of the packet to be transmitted from the message and relays that information to the ring interface. It then directs the ring interface to commence transmission.

6: Performance

6.1: Upper bounds on hardware performance

To get upper bounds on the performance of the hardware, we developed a small control program which first placed a packet into a netbound buffer and then repeatedly looped the packet across the HIPPI ports. This test setup is shown in Fig. 3. The program was single-threaded, so no context-switching occurred, and interrupts were disabled, so no interrupt handling was involved. The HIPPI loopback cable was short (less than 2 m) and, hence, there was negligible latency through the cable. Approximately 500 MBytes of data was transmitted using several different packet sizes and the throughputs collected.

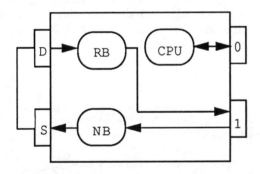

Fig. 3: Hardware performance test setup

As shown in the Fig. 4, the hardware is capable of sustaining near maximum HIPPI throughput of 800 Mbps when using large packet sizes. For the smaller packets, however, throughput was more than 200 Mbps short of the maximum. The shortfall was not caused by interrupt handling since interrupts were disabled. Profiling of the test code indicated that the processing amounted to approximately 80 processor instructions and, using values of 1.5 clock cycles/instruction and a 40 ns clock cycle time, this amounts to a per packet overhead of 4.8 μs and a theoretical overall maximum of

544 Mbps for 1 KByte packets. Hence, even this minimal per packet processing severely reduces the throughput for small packets.

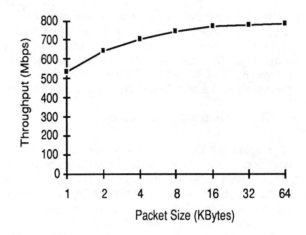

Fig. 4: NIU hardware performance

6.2: A multi-threaded control program

The next program used the same test setup but was organized as two threads, with one thread controlling the HIPPI source hardware and the other the destination hardware. All interrupts were enabled and the synchronization and communication mechanisms described in section 4 were used. Since the physical setup was identical to that of Section 6.1, this test highlights the interrupt handling and context-switching, i.e. software overhead. The results are shown in Fig. 5.

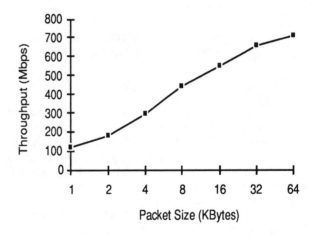

Fig. 5: Performance of multi-threaded program

In this configuration, several interrupts and context switches occur. The combined interrupt processing amounts to a per packet overhead of 56 μs. The exact number of context switches per packet processed is probabilistic but is either 1 or 2, and the context switch time is highly variable with typical measured values between 30 and 60 μs. The context switch overhead per packet is therefore between 30 and 120 μs. The observed throughputs fall within the bounds predicted by these parameters.

6.3: The standard NIU firmware

The setup for this test is shown in Fig. 6. Eight graphics processors (GPs) on the Pixel Planes 5 and the NIU are used. The NIU ran the standard NIU firmware described in Section 5, the four of the GPs ran a source program, and the other four ran a sink program. The packets generated by the sources were directed to the NIU which sent them around the HIPPI loopback and then back onto the ring to the sinks. The combined throughputs for several packet sizes were collected and plotted in Fig. 7.

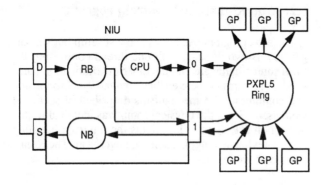

Fig. 6: Standard firmware performance measurement setup

In this configuration, there are between 2 and 4 context switches per packet and, hence, a context switch overhead of between 60 and 240 μs per packet. The total interrupt handling time per packet is now 63.5 μs. This program is significantly more complex than the test programs, and the average packet processing code amounts to over 400 SPARC instructions. However, the actual amount of code executed for a particular packet is highly variable and ranges from a low of 100 to a high of 550 instructions. The high variance of per packet overhead results in loose throughput bounds which are not useful in evaluating the observed values.

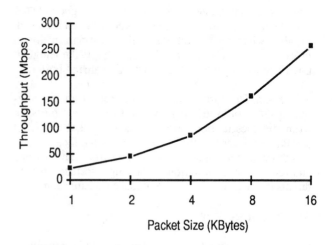

Fig. 7: Performance of standard firmware

6.4: Unidirectional traffic

The traffic on the VISTAnet network is decidedly asymmetric. A very high volume of data flows from the Cray to Pixel Planes 5 with a smaller amount leaving Pixel Planes 5. The final test exercised the NIU in the direction of anticipated heavy load. The setup is shown in Fig. 8. Eight GPs are used as sinks. The NIU under test runs the standard NIU control program, but the threads controlling the netbound pipeline are idle. The other NIU generates the traffic. The throughputs for several different packet sizes are plotted in Fig. 9.

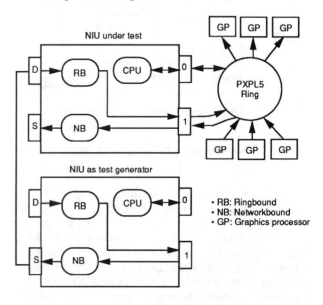

Fig. 8: Unidirectional performance measurement setup

The packet processing in this setup is identical to that of the previous section. The only difference is that the netbound pipeline, which is minimally utilized in the real application, is idle. Like the previous test, the high variance in per packet overhead makes the computed throughput bounds too loose for useful comparison with the empirical results. However, the observed throughputs approach the rates that the final network connection can sustain.

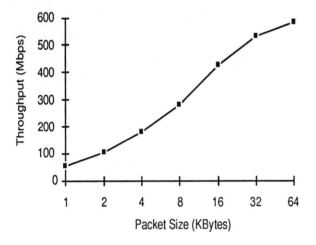

Fig. 9: Performance of unidirectional traffic

7: Summary and future work

We have described the design and implementation of the Network Interface Unit (NIU), a high-performance host interface for a custom graphics supercomputer. The system was customized to meet the needs and specifications of the VISTAnet network, its computing resources, and the driving application. The design decisions were primarily influenced by the two conflicting requirements of performance and programmability.

The primary goal of the NIU was to support the high-bandwidth transmission of radiation dosage data sets, which are sent as 64 KByte packets, from the Cray to Pixel Planes 5. This motivated such choices as the size and number of buffers, the use of interrupts, and the amount of packet processing done in software. Early results indicate that the system meets its predicted performance goals: when large packet sizes are used, the architecture can sustain data transfers near the maximum HIPPI throughput. While we feel that the NIU has satisfied its primary objective, we did not anticipate such severe throttling of throughput for small packets. Clearly a different approach is needed if the primary application is the transmission of small packets (such as ATM cells).

We have identified two impediments to efficient transmission of small packets in the current NIU architecture. The first is the interrupt-driven packet handling. In this case, two interrupts are generated by each ringbound HIPPI packet: one when the packet starts arriving and another when the packet has completely arrived. The second interrupt can be easily eliminated. However, since the number of ready pulses to be sent is computed in software, removing the first interrupt would require that this function be moved entirely into hardware. The second impediment is the context-switch overhead. Since the context-switch time cannot be appreciably reduced, reducing the context-switch overhead will require handling a group of packets at a time. The number of packets per group is variable and will have to be optimized based on the packet sizes, throughput, and latency requirements. Note, that this task is easier if the packet sizes are fixed (e.g. ATM cells).

Future work will focus on incorporating protocol processing. The NIU is highly programmable and can be used as a platform for implementing various protocol stacks. Although no experimental results with the use of protocol stacks are available at this time, the framework for incorporating protocol processing is in place. The lower layers of the protocol stack, consisting HIPPI-FP/HIPPI-LE/IEEE 802.2LLC, are complete. UDP/IP has been implemented and is being tested; since the additional protocol processing overhead for this stack is small (less than 1600 SPARC instructions), we expect minimal degradation in performance compared to no protocol stack. TCP/IP is currently being implemented. Since much of the overhead of this protocol stack is associated with checksum computation, the NIU's hardware based checksum unit is immensely helpful. However, we are hampered by the constraints of the ringbound buffer architecture. Specifically, with only two inbound FIFOs, we are unable to resequence packets that are out of order by more than one packet. Normally, this would result in an unacceptable TCP implementation, but fortunately the NTA guarantees that packets are delivered in order. The resequencing problem, therefore, does not surface in our environment, but we are nevertheless investigating the requisite changes for overcoming this limitation.

Work is also proceeding in profiling the traffic patterns in the network. The traffic in our environment is heterogeneous but the different "streams" have distinct characteristics. We intend to study the individual streams and suitably adapt different protocol stacks to provide maximal performance. We anticipate that UDP/IP and TCP/IP will suffice for the bulk of these streams. However, it is likely that some form of UDP with sequencing will also be implemented for streams that require packet loss detection but no recovery (i.e. application layer recovery).

Acknowledgments

The work undertaken for the VISTAnet project is supported, in part, by NSF and DARPA under cooperative agreement NCR 8919038 with CNRI. Support is also provided by BellSouth Services and GTE Corp.

References

[1] B. E. Basch et al, "VISTAnet: A B-ISDN Field Trial," IEEE-LTS, Aug. 1991, pp. 22-30.

[2] D. Stevenson and J. Rosenman, "VISTAnet Gigabit Testbed," IEEE J. Selected Areas in Communications, Vol. 10, No. 9, Dec. 1992, pp. 1413-1420.

[3] Special Report, "Gigabit Network Testbeds," IEEE Computer, Vol. 23, No. 9, Sep. 1990, pp. 77-80.

[4] H. Fuchs et al, "Pixel Planes 5: A Heterogeneous Multiprocessor Graphics System Using Processor Enhanced Memories," Computer Graphics, Vol. 23, 1989, pp. 79-88.

[5] R. K. Singh, S. G. Tell, and D. Becker, "VISTAnet Network Interface Unit: Prototype System Specifications," TR91-017, Department of Computer Science, University of North Carolina at Chapel Hill, 1991.

[6] ANSI Systems, "HIPPI Mechanical, Electrical and Signaling Protocol Specifications (HIPPI-PH)," X3T9.3/88-023 Rev 7.2, Aug. 1990.

[7] B. Traw and J. Smith, "Hardware/Software Organization of a High Speed Host Interface," IEEE J. Selected Areas in Communications, Vol. 11, No. 2, Feb. 93, pp. 240-53.

[8] B. Davie, "The Architecture and Implementation of a High Speed Host Interface," IEEE J. Selected Areas in Communications, Vol. 11, No. 2, Feb. 93, pp. 228-39.

[9] P. Steenkiste, "Analyzing Communication Latency using the Nectar Communication Processor," in Proc. SIGCOMM 1992, Baltimore (Aug. 17-20), pp. 199-209.

[10] H. Abu-Amara, T. Balraj, T. Barzilai, and Y. Yemini, "Psi: A Silicon Compiler for Very Fast Protocol Processing," in Protocols for High Speed Networks, ed. R. C. Williamson, North-Holland (1989).

[11] E. Arnould, F. Bitz, E. Cooper, R. Sansom, and P. Steenkiste, "The design of Nectar: A network backplane for heterogeneous multicomputers," in Proc. ASPOLS-III (Apr. 1989), pp. 205-216.

[12] H. Kanakia and D. Cheriton, "The VMP Network Adapter Board (NAB): High Performance Network Communication for Multiprocessors," in Proc. SIGMETRICS' 88 (1988).

[13] E. Cooper and R. Draves, "C Threads," Tech. Rep., CMU-CS-88-154, Computer Science Department, Carnegie-Mellon University, Jun. 1998.

[14] D. Banks and M. Prudence, "A High-Performance Network Architecture for a PA-RISC Workstation," IEEE J. Selected Areas in Communications, Vol. 11, No. 2, Feb. 93, pp. 191-192.

Experiments with a Gigabit Neuroscience Application on the CM-2

Thomas T. Kwan*   Jeffrey A. Terstriep†

National Center for Supercomputing Applications
University of Illinois
Urbana, Illinois 61801

Abstract

Recently, there has been considerable interest in high performance networks. To help evaluate the high-speed-networking-related performance of supercomputers, we selected a computational neuroscience simulation program that has a bandwidth requirement in excess of 1.5 Gigabits per second. The simulation runs on the Thinking Machines CM-2 and the target visualization engine is the Convex C3880. We benchmarked the various operations required to transmit data from the CM-2 to the Convex C3880. Our results show that the parallel to serial data transformation operation on the CM-2 and the network interfaces are the major bottlenecks.

1 Introduction

The recent National Information Infrastructure initiatives envisioned by the Clinton-Gore administration as well as the federal High Performance Computing and Communication Program have generated great interest in gigabit-per-second networks. As members of the Blanca national gigabit testbed, we have been working closely with scientists to explore the utility of gigabit networks. The potential gigabit application reported here was originally developed by a computational neuroscientist. The application is a neural simulation program that runs on the Thinking Machines CM-2; the program generates new data at a rate of 1.8 Gigabits per second. To avoid performing the necessary, but expensive, visualization calculation on the CM-2, we examined the possibility of transferring the visualization calculation to a Convex C3880 and sending the data to it from the CM-2. This would require the use of a high speed network that connects the two supercomputers.

To date, there is little published literature on distributing computation among supercomputers connected together by high speed networks. Although earlier work of Mechoso *et al* [8] and Malevsky *et al* [7] have explored the decomposition of applications among supercomputers, little is known about the interaction of the machines and the applications that require the transport of very high speed data streams. Previous high speed network tests performed by Clinger [4] and Beach [1] did not include the CM-2 and the Convex C3880, the machines we are using for our experiments. Krystynak [6] and Bryson *et al* [2], respectively, have timing data for the CM-2 and the Convex C3240. However, the nature of their applications and the bandwidth requirements are very different.

In [6, 2], the numerical computation and visualization calculations are carried out on the same supercomputer. The output of the visualization calculation is then transferred to an SGI graphics workstation for rendering. As reported in [2], the bandwidth is limited by the SGI to about 13 Mbytes/second. On the other hand, we are interested in moving the visualization calculation to another supercomputer. In other words, we are interested in the high speed link between supercomputers rather than the link between a supercomputer and a graphics workstation. The objective of our work is to evaluate the high-speed-networking-related performance of the host supercomputers. Based on the captured performance data, we can then obtain insights into the characteristics of the gigabit application.

*Supported in part by a Research Assistantship from the National Center for Supercomputing Applications.

†This work is supported by the National Science Foundation and the Advanced Research Projects Agency under Cooperative Agreement NCR-8919038 with the Corporation for National Research Initiatives.

133

1.1 Overview

The remainder of this paper is organized as follows. In §2, we briefly describe the neuroscience simulation code. The benchmarks used to measure the network-related performance of the CM-2 are described in §3. In §4, we describe the results and in §5, we elaborate on the significance of our findings. Finally, in §6, we conclude with a summary of our effort.

2 Neuroscience Application

Our gigabit application is a neural simulation code that has been used to advance the understanding of special structures, called visual maps, in the brain. These maps are formed as a result of visual experience which led to changes in the synaptic connection strengths between the receptors in the eyes and the cortical nerve cells in the brain. The simulation models the development of the visual map by adjusting the synaptic strengths accordingly.

The neural simulator is written in C/Paris and runs on the CM-2. The use of virtual processors on the CM-2 enables the large number of neurons to be mapped onto the limited number of physical processors available on the machine. Each virtual processor represents a cortical nerve cell in the brain and each virtual processor has an array (i.e. serial dimension) that represents connections to the receptors. In a typical simulation, there are about 33 thousand cortical nerve cells each connected to 1800 receptors. Thus, about 59 million connections are modeled in the simulation.

The simulated cortical visual map can be visualized by color-coding the map and displaying it on the CM-2 frame buffer. These images can then be compared to actual images obtained from applying voltage-sensative dyes to the visual cortex of macaque monkeys. Using a particular mathematical model, Obermayer *et al* [10] found that the color map obtained from the simulation closely resembles the actual color map obtained from the visual cortex of the macaque monkeys. In other words, visualization of the cortical map is an indispensable part of the science.

Visualization of the color map *during* the simulation is also important because it enables neuroscientists to observe the development of the map and to correct mistakes in the model if the images are anomalous [9]. Unfortunately, on the CM-2, it is very expensive to perform the visualization calculation at every timestep. Our timing of the application code indicated that it takes 29 seconds to perform the visualization calculation on the data obtained from one timestep.

However, it takes only one second to update all the connections and advance one timestep of the simulation. Thus, it would be advantageous to off-load the expensive visualization calculation to another supercomputer while allowing the simulation to proceed at high speed on the CM-2.

Running the visualization computation and the numerical simulation on separate supercomputers will require a high speed network to support communication between the hosts. A closer look at the simulation code reveals that new data are being generated at a rate of 59,000,000 connections × 32 bits per connection / 1 second per timestep ≈ 1.8 Gigabits per second. Thus, we conjecture that, with the use of a gigabit-per-second network, we could enhance the productivity of neuroscientists by enabling them to interact with the image on another supercomputer while allowing the numerical simulation to continue at high speed on the CM-2.

3 Benchmark Methodology

To evaluate the rate at which data can be transferred from the CM-2 to the Convex C3880[1], we identified the various steps involved in the data transfer process. To send data out of the CM-2, the data in the CM-2's memory must first be byte swapped to convert them from little-endian ordering to big-endian ordering [13]. Then, the data need to be converted from the internal CM parallel format to the regular serial format. The serial data can then be sent to the Convex C3880. Below, we first describe the test configuration used and then describe the individual benchmarks.

3.1 Dedicated Test Configuration

Figure 1 shows the machine and network configuration of the dedicated test system used here at the National Center for Supercomputing Applications (NCSA). The CM-2 has 32K bit-serial data processors and one Gigabyte of memory. There are four sequencers; each sequencer controls a partition of 8K processors and 256 Megabytes of memory. Each partition is connected to the CM-HIPPI via a CMIO bus. There are four CMIO buses in total; each CMIO bus is rated at 400 Mbits/second. See [12] for additional details about the CMIO bus and [5] for additional information about the general performance of the CM-2.

---

[1] We selected the Convex C3880 for the visualization computation because of its large memory capacity and vector processing capability.

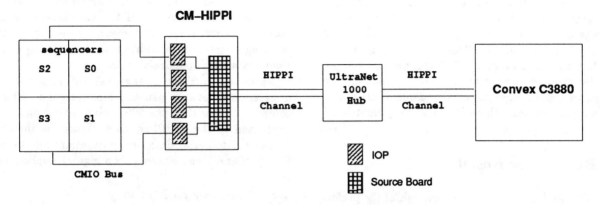

Figure 1: The Dedicated Test Configuration

The CM-HIPPI consists of a Sun-4 CPU, a number of IOP boards (each connected to a CMIO bus), a source board for sending data out the HIPPI channel, and a destination board (not shown) for receiving data from the HIPPI channel. The CM socket server runs on the CM-HIPPI. The CM-HIPPI is connected to the UltraNet 1000 Hub via a HIPPI channel. The HIPPI channel and the UltraNet 1000 Hub are rated, respectively, at 800 Mbits/second and 1 Gbit/second. See [14] for additional details on the CM-HIPPI and [1] for additional details on the UltraNet.

As shown in Figure 1, the UltraNet 1000 Hub is connected to the Convex C3880 via another HIPPI channel. The Convex C3880 has eight 60 MHz vector processors and four Gigabytes of memory. It is rated at 1.92 Gflops (32-bit floating point arithmetic).

3.2 Byte Reordering

The first test measured the byte-reordering speed of the CM-2 as a function of virtual processor ratio. (The virtual processor ratio determines the size of the data buffer.) The byte reordering operation converts floating point data from little-endian ordering (CM ordering) to big-endian ordering (standard Sun ordering).

To assess the scalability of the CM-2, we varied the number of physical processors by using one, two, and four sequencers. We also investigated the effect of grid organization by using one-dimensional, two-dimensional, and three-dimensional geometries. (On the CM-2, a *geometry* specifies the grid organization in *n*-space.) The byte-reordering time was recorded for each combination of the benchmark.

3.3 Parallel to Serial Data Transformation

The second test measured the parallel to serial data transformation speed of the CM-2 as a function of virtual processor ratio. This operation converts data from the internal CM parallel format to the regular serial format. Again, we timed the transformation speed using a combination of one, two, and four sequencers, and one-dimensional, two-dimensional, and three-dimensional geometries. The transformation time was recorded for each combination of the benchmark.

3.4 Memory to Memory

The third test measured the speed at which data can be moved from the memory of the CM-2 to the memory of the Convex C3880. The data rate was measured as a function of virtual processor ratio. For this test, we used the standard cm_tsock utility on the CM-2 and the tsock utility on the Convex C3880. The cm_tsock utility is a program that uses CM sockets to send fixed size buffers from the CM-2 to the destination host via the UltraNet. The matching Convex program tsock merely receives the data sent by cm_tsock. We measured the data rates for the cases of one, two, and four sequencers. The timing statistics generated by cm_tsock were recorded.

3.5 Application to Application

The final test evaluated the data transfer rate at the application level. We measured the time taken to complete the whole sequence of operations: byte reordering, parallel to serial data transformation, and data transmission from the source to the destination. This synthetic application uses the Data Transfer Mechanism [11], a socket based interprocess communication package developed at NCSA, to send the data from the CM-2 to the Convex C3880. Again, we measured the data rate as a function of virtual processor ratio. We also measured the data rate using a combination of one, two, and four sequencers, and one-dimensional, two-dimensional, and three-dimensional geometries.

4 Benchmark Results

In this section, we present an analysis of the performance data obtained using the benchmarks described in §3. All experimental data are shown with 95 percent confidence intervals. We found that, at the application level, the effective data rate is roughly fifteen percent of the corresponding theoretical peak rate of the HIPPI channel.

4.1 Byte Reordering

Figures 2a, 2b, and 3 show the results for the byte reordering benchmark using one-dimensional, two-dimensional, and three-dimensional geometries respectively. The corresponding asymptotic data rates are shown in Table 1. In these figures, we observe that as the virtual processor ratio increases, the data rate also increases. At higher virtual processor ratios, the data buffers are larger; the startup cost is amortized and hence an increase in the data rate.

Comparing Figures 2 and 3, we observe that the speed of byte reordering is independent of the geometry. Moreover, the byte reordering speed scales with the number of sequencers. With four sequencers, the maximum byte reordering speed is about 49 Gbits/second. Clearly, the byte reordering operation is not the bottleneck for a gigabit application.

4.2 Parallel to Serial Data Transformation

Figures 4a, 4b, and 5 show the results for the parallel to serial data transformation benchmark using one-dimensional, two-dimensional, and three-dimensional geometries respectively. The corresponding asymptotic data rates are shown in Table 2. Again, we observe that as the virtual processor ratio increases, so does the data rate.

Figures 4 and 5 also show that the speed of data transformation scales with the number of sequencers.

However, Table 2 shows that as the geometry's dimension increases, the data rate decreases. At higher dimensions, the efficiency of the transformation decreases because of the extra overhead involved in the ordering of the axes in addition to the ordering of the elements along a particular axis.

As shown in Table 2, the peak rates for four sequencers are between 520–653 Mbits/second. This is somewhat lower than the 800 Mbits/second data rate supported by the HIPPI channel. Hence, on the CM-2, parallel to serial data transformation will be the first bottleneck encountered by a gigabit application.

4.3 Memory to Memory

The results for the cm_tsock benchmark are shown in Figure 6; Table 3 shows the corresponding asymptotic data rates. Recall that each sequencer is connected to an individual CMIO bus rated at 400 Mbits/second. Hence, the rates shown in Table 3 can be directly compared to the theoretical peak rates of the CMIO buses. From Table 3, we observe that the measured data rate for one CMIO bus (i.e. one sequencer) is $\frac{135}{400} = 34\%$ of the theoretical peak rate. This can be attributed to software overhead. However, as shown in Table 3, the measured cm_tsock data rate for two and four CMIO buses are, respectively, only 22% and 11% of the corresponding theoretical peak rates. Even with four sequencers, the measured data rate is only $\frac{180}{800} = 23\%$ of the rate supported by the HIPPI channel. The limited data rate observed here is not due to the Convex C3880 nor the link between the UltraNet and the Convex because other internal studies [3] have shown them to be capable of sustaining above 200 Mbits/second. Thus, it appears that the limitation is due to a combination of the network interfaces and protocol processing capabilities of the CM-HIPPI and the UltraNet Hub.

4.4 Application to Application

Figures 7a, 7b, and 8 show the results for the application-to-application data transfer benchmark using one-dimensional, two-dimensional, and three-dimensional geometries respectively. The corresponding asymptotic rates are shown in Table 3. Figures 7 and 8 show that the data rate increases with the number of sequencers. However, as in the case of memory-to-memory data transfer, the data rates do not scale with the number of sequencers. Table 3 also shows that the data rate decreases slightly with an increase in the number of dimensions of the geometry. Again,

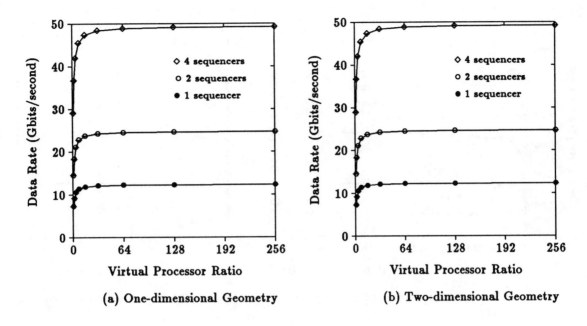

(a) One-dimensional Geometry   (b) Two-dimensional Geometry

Figure 2: Byte Reordering

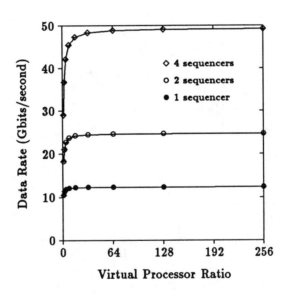

Figure 3: Byte Reordering (Three-dimensional Geometry)

Number of Sequencers	Asymptotic Data Rate		
	One-dimensional Geometry	Two-dimensional Geometry	Three-dimensional Geometry
1	12.34	12.34	12.34
2	24.67	24.67	24.67
4	49.34	49.34	49.34

Table 1: Byte Reordering (Rates in Gbits/second)

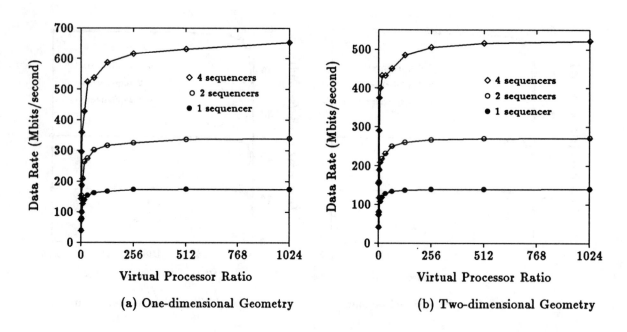

(a) One-dimensional Geometry   (b) Two-dimensional Geometry

Figure 4: Parallel to Serial Data Transformation

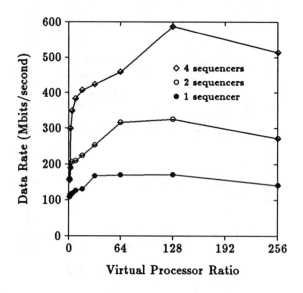

Figure 5: Parallel to Serial Data Transformation (Three-dimensional Geometry)

Number of Sequencers	Asymptotic Data Rate		
	One-dimensional Geometry	Two-dimensional Geometry	Three-dimensional Geometry
1	174.6	140.0	139.9
2	338.1	270.6	269.4
4	653.0	521.0	520.9

Table 2: Parallel to Serial Data Transformation (Rates in Mbits/second)

Number of Sequencers	Asymptotic Data Rate			
	Memory to Memory	Application to Application		
	cm_tsock	One-dimensional Geometry	Two-dimensional Geometry	Three-dimensional Geometry
1	134.5	70.5	64.0	64.0
2	172.0	102.0	94.6	94.4
4	180.3	123.8	118.1	118.0

Table 3: Application to Application Data Transfer (Rates in Mbits/second)

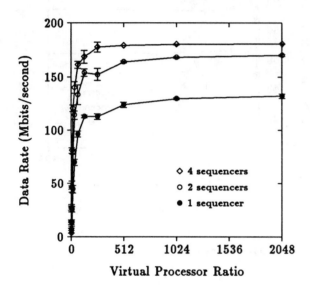

Figure 6: Data Transfer using cm_tsock

Operation	Peak Data Rate
Neural simulation	1.8
Byte reordering	50483
Data transformation	653
Memory to memory	180
Net throughput	124

Table 4: Summary of Peak Data Rates (Rates in Mbits/second)

this is due to the overhead associated with axes ordering.

As shown in Table 3, the data rates for the application-to-application benchmarks are generally less than 70% of those for cm_tsock. This is because the timing statistics returned by cm_tsock does not include the time spent in parallel to serial data transformation.

The data from Table 3 indicate that, at the application level, the measured data rate is about $\frac{124}{800} = 15\%$ of that available on the HIPPI channel. This is considerably lower than what we expected.

5 Discussion

Table 4 summarizes the data rates for the neural simulation and the various benchmarks. Based on the benchmarking results, we can estimate the time taken by the application to transfer data from the CM-2 to the Convex C3880.

In the neural simulation code, the 32K cortical cells are implemented as a two-dimensional geometry (256 × 128) with a serial dimension of 1800 words. With four sequencers, this geometry has a virtual processor ratio of one. From Table 4, we see that data are generate at a rate of 1.8 Gbits/second. From Figure 7b, we observed that with a two-dimensional geometry and a virtual processor ratio of one, the measured data transfer rate for four sequencers is 95.2 Mbits/second. Hence, it will take this application $\frac{1.8 \times 1024}{95.2} = 19$ seconds to transfer the data from the CM-2 to the Convex C3880. Recall that it originally took about 29 seconds to perform the visualization calculation on the CM-2. Thus, just transferring the data will take more than 65% of the time needed to do the actual calculation. In other words, even if the visualization calculation can be performed on the Convex with a speedup of $\frac{29}{29-19} = 2.9$, it will just break even with doing everything on the CM-2. Since data transfer is so costly, we conclude that, at the moment, it is not cost effective to distribute the visualization computation to the Convex.

As shown in Table 4, the data transformation rate is 653 Mbits/second. This is slightly higher than 622 Mbits/second, the data rate of the XUNET-3 wide-area network in the Blanca testbed. Thus, it appears that data transformation would not be a bottleneck for the wide-area network. In reality, data transformation will still be a bottleneck. The reason is that the CM-2 requires all the data in the buffer to be trans-

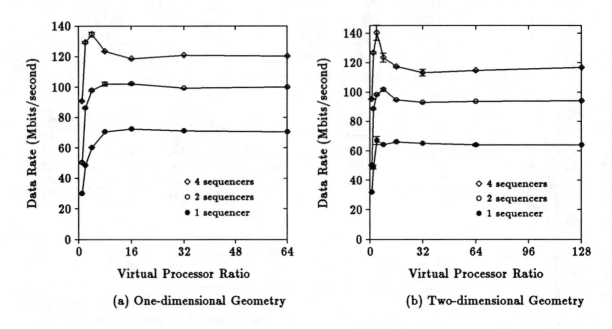

(a) One-dimensional Geometry   (b) Two-dimensional Geometry

Figure 7: Application to Application Data Transmission

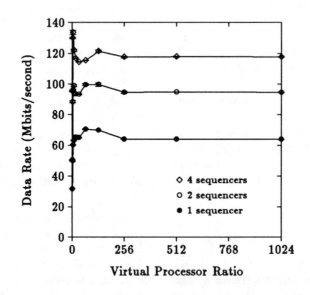

Figure 8: Application to Application Data Transmission (Three-dimensional Geometry)

formed at the same time. This prohibits the communication phase from overlapping with the data conversion phase. In essence, data conversion and data transmission cannot be pipelined.

Although we studied a particular gigabit application in the context of a specific architecture, namely the CM-2, we can nevertheless obtain insights into issues related to gigabit applications in general. These issues are discussed below.

To begin with, the gigabit application itself needs to be designed with the use of a high speed network in mind. For example, if we use a virtual processor ratio of one and use one sequencer to execute the current neural simulation code, the parallel to serial data transformation rate will be 40 Mbits/second (obtained from Figure 4b). However, if the code's two-dimensional geometry along with the serial dimension were remapped into a three-dimensional geometry, the parallel to serial data transformation rate (obtained from Figure 5) would have been 108 Mbits/second. With respect to data transformation, implementing the data structure as a three-dimensional geometry would have provided a speedup of 2.7. Therefore, it is important to keep these machine trade-offs in mind when designing a distributed application.

On the other hand, the use of high dimensional arrays may also effect the speed of data transformation. As illustrated earlier in Table 2, switching from a one-dimensional geometry to a two-dimensional geometry decreases the data conversion speed by about 20%. As explained earlier, this is due to the effect of axes ordering. However, this problem is not specific to the CM-2. Rather, it is a general problem associated with distributed memory parallel systems. To balance the work load on a distributed memory parallel machine, data is typically decomposed and distributed among the processing nodes. Unfortunately, the data must first be rearranged into a serial format (e.g. column major format for FORTRAN arrays) before they can be transmitted across the network and get reassembled on the target machine. Thus, massively parallel system designers need to address the performance of data transformation to enable users to take advantage of high speed networks.

6 Conclusion

In this paper, we have evaluated the CM-2 in terms of its capability to support gigabit applications. We have benchmarked the performance of the byte reordering operation, the parallel to serial data transformation operation, and the effective data transfer rate

from the CM-2 to the Convex C3880 via the Ultra-Net 1000 Hub. We observed that the parallel to serial data transformation operation of the CM-2, and the network interfaces and protocol processing capabilities of the CM-HIPPI and the UltraNet 1000 Hub are the major bottlenecks to achieving high data transfer rates. We believe that improvements are need in both network interface and application design in order to take full advantage of the bandwidth available on a gigabit-per-second network.

Acknowledgments

We thank Klaus Obermayer for help on all matters related to the neural simulation code. We thank Joe Godsil, Von Welch, and Randy Butler for help with using the CM-HIPPI and the UltraNet. We are grateful to Sue Lewis and Mike Pflugmacher for arranging dedicated time on the CM-2 and the Convex C3880. Rick Kufrin, Charlie Liu, and Mike D'Mello helped clarify technical details about the CM-2. We also thank Dan Reed for providing valuable suggestions at various stages of the project.

References

[1] BEACH, B. Ultranet: An Architecture for Gigabit Networking. Tech. rep., Ultra Network Technologies, 101 Daggett Drive, San Jose, CA 95134.

[2] BRYSON, S., AND GERALD-YAMASAKI, M. The Distributed Virtual Windtunnel. In *Proceedings of Supercomputing 1992* (Nov 1992), pp. 275–284.

[3] BUTLER, R. L., GODSIL, J. M., AND WELCH, V. S. Host Network Performance Measurements on the NCSA UltraNet Network. Tech. rep., National Center for Supercomputing Applications, April 1993.

[4] CLINGER, M. Very High Performance Networking for Supercomputing. In *Proceedings of the 4th International Conference on Supercomputing* (May 1990), pp. 160–168.

[5] HELIN, J. Performance Analysis of the CM-2, a Massively Parallel SIMD Computer. In *Proceedings of the International Conference on Supercomputing* (July 1992).

[6] KRYSTYNAK, J. High Speed Network Issues in a Distributed Visualization Application. In

Proceedings of Supercomputing 1992 (Nov 1992), pp. 267–274.

[7] MALEVSKY, A. V., YUEN, D. A., AND JORDAN, K. E. Simulation of Particle Mixing by Turbulent Convective Flows on the Connection Machine. In *Proceedings of Supercomputing 1992* (Nov 1992), pp. 294–300.

[8] MECHOSO, C. R., MA, C., FARRARA, J., SPAHR, J. A., AND MOORE, R. W. Distribution of a Climate Model Across High-Speed Networks. In *Proceedings of Supercomputing 1991* (Nov 1991), pp. 253–260.

[9] OBERMAYER, K. Personal Communication.

[10] OBERMAYER, K., RITTER, H., AND SCHULTEN, K. A Principle for the Formation of the Spatial Structure of Cortical Feature Maps. In *Proceedings of the National Academy of Sciences* (1990), vol. 87, pp. 8345–8349.

[11] TERSTRIEP, J. A. Data Transfer Mechanism (DTM). Tech. Rep. ND-104, National Center for Supercomputing Applications, Jan 1991.

[12] THINKING MACHINES CORPORATION. Connection Machine CM-2 Technical Summary, May 1989. Version 5.1.

[13] THINKING MACHINES CORPORATION. The Connection Machine I/O System Programming Guide, October 1991. Version 6.1.

[14] THINKING MACHINES CORPORATION. The CM-HIPPI User's Guide for the CM-2, May 1992. Version 6.1.

Distributed Computing Feasibility
in a
Non-Dedicated Homogeneous Distributed System

Scott T. Leutenegger   Xian-He Sun

Institute for Computer Applications in Science and Engineering
NASA Langley Research Center
Hampton, VA 23681-0001

Abstract

The low cost and availability of clusters of workstations have lead researchers to re-explore distributed computing using independent workstations. This approach may provide better cost/performance than tightly coupled multiprocessors. In practice, this approach often utilizes wasted cycles to run parallel jobs. In this paper we address the feasibility of such a non-dedicated parallel processing environment assuming workstation processes have preemptive priority over parallel tasks. We develop an analytical model to predict parallel job response times. Our model provides insight into how significantly workstation owner interference degrades parallel program performance. A new term **task ratio**, *which relates the parallel task demand to the mean service demand of non parallel workstation processes, is introduced. We propose that* **task ratio** *is a useful metric for determining how large the demand of a parallel applications must be in order to make efficient use of a non-dedicated distributed system.*

1 Introduction

Most early parallel processing research focused on using distributed systems to speedup computations. The basic approach was to utilize many computers connected via a local area network (LAN) to execute a parallel job. We will refer to this environment as *distributed computing*. With the advent of multiprocessor architectures the majority of the focus shifted from distributed computing to multiprocessing, the major distinction being the tightly coupled architecture allowing more finely grained parallelism.

Recently, a significant portion of the parallel community has returned to the distributed processing approach. Several commercial and noncommercial tools have been developed to support distributed computing. One widely used tool is the *Parallel Virtual Machine* (PVM) project [9, 5, 1, 2]. According to the authors, PVM is now being used at more than 100 sites. A major driving force behind the reevaluation of distributed computing is the high cost of parallel computers. Using a group of workstations connected via a LAN may provide better cost/performance, or may be the only way to achieve high performance within budget constraints for some organizations. Another factor in favor of distributed computing is the availability of many lightly loaded workstations. These otherwise wasted idle cycles can be used by a distributed computation to provided speedups and/or to solve large problems that otherwise could not be tackled.

It is clear that many problems are amenable to the distributed computing approach [3]. However, for some applications, the inherent synchronization requirements, communication/computation ratio, and the granularity of parallelism may limit the obtained performance. Even for the "good" applications, a tacit

*This research was supported by the National Aeronautics and Space Administration under NASA contract NAS1-19480 while the authors were in residence at the Institute for Computer Applications in Science and Engineering (ICASE), NASA Langley Research Center, Hampton, VA 23681-0001.

assumption of the expected high performance is that a system of *dedicated* workstations are used, which may not be true in practice. In this paper we study the performance of distributed computing in a *non-dedicated* system assuming workstation owner processes have preemptive priority over parallel tasks

We assume the parallel application considered belongs to the class of programs that can run efficiently in a dedicated distributed computing environment. We do not consider the effects of synchronization, communication, or granularity of parallelism. Given the program executes efficiently in a dedicated system, we wish to determine whether we can achieve good performance in a non-dedicated system.

One factor that must be considered in a non-dedicated system is how intrusive the parallel programs are to the owners of the workstations and vice versa. The priority of the parallel tasks relative to the priority of processes initiated by the owner of the workstation can have a significant impact on the performance of both the parallel job and the owner's serial jobs. We assume that a workstation owner is not tolerant of other people using their workstation, and hence surmise the most appropriate model of such a system is to assume workstation owner processes have preemptive priority over processes belonging to a parallel job. Hence, use of the workstation will interfere with parallel program performance. The major goal of this paper is to provide insight into how significantly workstation owner interference degrades parallel program performance. We seek to answer the question, "When is distributed computing in a non-dedicated environment where workstation owner processes have preemptive priority over parallel tasks a viable approach?"

An analytical model is developed to predict the performance under the non-dedicated assumption. The new term *task ratio* is introduced along with new metrics that incorporate the utilization of workstations by owner processes. We find that the task ratio plays an important role in the overall performance, possibly as important as the communication/computation ratio in a dedicated system. The analytical model

provides the relationships between the identified parameters and shows how these parameters influence the overall response time.

In addition to our analysis, a hypothetical local computation [11] problem is implemented with PVM on systems with 1 to 12 homogeneous workstations. These initial experimental results confirm the qualitative results from the analytical model.

This paper is organized as follows. In Section 2 we present the analytical model and introduce new parameters and metrics for non-dedicated distributed computing. The results from our analysis are presented in Section 3. Experimental results with PVM on 12 homogeneous workstations are presented in Section 4, and our conclusions are in Section 5.

2 Model Description, Analysis and Simulation

In this section we describe our system model, our analysis technique, and simulation model. We make simplifying assumptions that favor the distributed computing approach. In particular, we assume a parallel job is composed of W tasks (one per workstation), and the computation is perfectly balanced among these tasks. In addition, the parallel job is composed of one single parallel phase with no communication or synchronization requirements other than the final synchronization which occurs when all of the tasks have completed. Hence, we are assuming perfect parallelism of the problem. This model is simplistic, but provides the best case scenario for a distributed computing environment. In addition, by not incorporating communication or synchronization requirements into the model we are able to attribute all degradation of parallel program performance to workstation process interference. Since our assumptions are always optimistic, the model predictions provide an upper bound on expected performance.

We assume there are W homogeneous workstations in the system and that there is one owner per workstation. Workstation owners are in a continuous cycle

Table 1: Notational Definitions

$\mathcal{J}$	Total demand of the parallel job.
$\mathcal{W}$	Number of workstations in the system.
$\mathcal{T}$	Demand of one parallel task $= \mathcal{J} / \mathcal{W}$.
$\mathcal{O}$	Time a owner process uses the workstation.
$\mathcal{U}$	Utilization of a workstation by owner.
P	Probability of the owner requesting the processor during a given time step.
E_t	Mean expected task completion time.
E_j	Mean expected job completion time.

of thinking (idle time) and then use time. We assume there is one parallel job being executed on the system at a time.

In table 1 we define our notation used through out the paper. The demand of a job is the total computing cycles (time) needed for the job.

2.1 Model Description

Our model is a discrete time model. We assume a geometric distribution with mean $\frac{1}{P}$ for the owner think time, i. e. at each time unit the owner requests the processor with probability P. When an owner process starts execution an executing parallel task is suspended and the owner process is immediately started. The owner process executes for $\mathcal{O}$ units. Once the owner processes completes execution, the parallel task restarts execution and is guaranteed to complete at least one unit of work before the owner may issue another process requesting the processor.

The model guarantees the parallel task will complete in at most $\mathcal{T} + (\mathcal{T} \times \mathcal{O})$ units. Task execution time at a single workstation is thus the sum of task demand plus the time to complete any owner processes that occur during the tasks tenure in the system, i. e.

$$task\ time = \mathcal{T} + (n \times \mathcal{O}), \qquad (1)$$

where n equals the number of owner process requests. The owner process can make a request after each unit of time the parallel task uses the processor, hence the number of owner requests is binomially distributed:

$$Bin(\mathcal{T}, n, P) = \left(\begin{array}{c} \mathcal{T} \\ n \end{array} \right) P^n (1 - P)^{\mathcal{T}-n}. \qquad (2)$$

Thus, expected task execution time is equal to

$$E_t = \mathcal{T} + \sum_{i=0}^{\mathcal{T}} \mathcal{O} \cdot i \cdot Bin(\mathcal{T}, i, P). \qquad (3)$$

The job execution time is the time until the last of the parallel tasks completes execution. Thus, job completion time is at least $\mathcal{T}$ units and at most $\mathcal{T}+(\mathcal{T} \times \mathcal{O})$ units. We first derive the probability that job execution time equals i and then from these probabilities get the expectation.

Let S[n] equal the probability that an individual task is interrupted by at most n owner processes.

$$S[n] = \sum_{i=0}^{n} Bin(\mathcal{T}, i, P). \qquad (4)$$

Let C[W,n] equal the probability that all parallel tasks are interrupted by at most n owner processes. By independence,

$$C[W, n] = (S[n])^{W}. \qquad (5)$$

Let Max[W,n] equal the probability that the maximum number of owner process interferences over all the parallel tasks is equal to n.

$$Max[W, n] = C[W, n] - C[W, n - 1]. \qquad (6)$$

Using these functions, expected job execution time is calculated as:

$$E_j = \mathcal{T} + \sum_{i=0}^{\mathcal{T}} \mathcal{O} \cdot i \cdot Max[W, n]. \qquad (7)$$

Owner utilization ($\mathcal{U}$) can be calculated as:

$$\mathcal{U} = \frac{\mathcal{O}}{\mathcal{O} + 1/P} \qquad (8)$$

For the purposes of analysis we were forced to make some simplifying assumptions. Our model makes assumptions that favor the distributed computing approach, hence the model provides a lower bound on expected response time. In particular, the model is optimistic with regards to the three following points:

- We assume parallel task times are deterministic. Although this is one of the goals of parallel algorithm design, in practice there is often some imbalance of load.

- Variance of owner process service demands. We have assumed a deterministic owner process service demand when in fact typical processes experience a much larger variance [7]. Assuming a distribution with more variance could cause some parallel tasks to be delayed much longer than $\mathcal{T} + (\mathcal{T} \times \mathcal{O})$.

- Guaranteeing the parallel task at least one unit of execution between requests. In a real system owner processes may be reissued in less time, thus parallel tasks could be delayed longer than $(\mathcal{T} \times \mathcal{O})$.

These assumptions together clearly show that our results are optimistic, and hence actual performance could be worse than predicted by our observations.

2.2 Simulation Description

We have simulated the system using the CSIM simulation language [8]. The purpose of the simulation is solely to validate the coding of our analysis. We intend to use our simulation in future work to explore other service demand distributions.

All results have confidence intervals of 1 percent or less at a 90 percent confidence level. Confidence intervals are calculated using batch means [4] with 20 batches per simulation run and a batch size of 1000 samples. We duplicated the experiment found in figure 1 of this paper and the simulation results were identical to the analysis thus verifying the correctness

of analysis code. We did not plot the results since they are indistinguishable from the analysis.

3 Analysis Results

In this section we present the results from our analysis. All results in this section assume an owner process has preemptive priority over a parallel task. We first present results for a fixed size problem, and then discuss the impact of scaling problem size with the number of workstations.

3.1 Fixed-Size Speedup

We first address the benefit of the distributed computing approach for a fixed-size job. In this case, the desired goal of parallelizing the program is to achieve faster execution times, hence we use expected speedup as our primary metric. Since the standard definition of speedup does not take into consideration the cycles consumed by the (higher priority) owner processes, we also define the metric *weighted-speedup*. We also consider the metrics efficiency and *weighted-efficiency* to illustrate more concretely the achieved percent of optimal performance. Specifically, once again let $\mathcal{J}$ equal the total job demand, $\mathcal{W}$ equal the number of workstations, E_j equal the expected job completion time, and $\mathcal{U}$ equal the owner process utilization of the workstations. Then:

$$
\begin{aligned}
\text{Task Ratio} &= \frac{\mathcal{T}}{\mathcal{O}} \\
\text{Speedup} &= \frac{\mathcal{J}}{E_j} \\
\text{Weighted-Speedup} &= \frac{\mathcal{J}}{(1-\mathcal{U})\,E_j} \\
\text{Efficiency} &= \frac{\mathcal{J}/\mathcal{W}}{E_j} \\
\text{Weighted-Efficiency} &= \frac{\mathcal{J}/\mathcal{W}}{(1-\mathcal{U})\,E_j}
\end{aligned}
$$

The expected speedup and efficiency metrics are of interest if a user wishes to determine the benefit of parallelizing the job relative to running the program on a single dedicated machine. The weighted metrics incorporate utilization to clearly demonstrate how effectively the parallel program is able to use the idle system cycles. We focus primarily on the weighted metrics since they provide a better metric for determining how well the distributed computing approach can utilize idle cycles.

In figure 1 we plot speedup versus the number of workstations for workstations utilizations of 1%, 5%, 10%, and 20% assuming a parallel job demand ($\mathcal{J}$) equal to 1000 units, and an owner processes demand ($\mathcal{O}$) equal to 10 units. For a given utilization we assume all workstations have the same owner process utilization. The top curve is the theoretical optimal speedup, i.e. unitary linear. The speedup curves are concave increasing, i.e. the benefit of adding more nodes decreases as nodes are added, despite ignoring overhead for parallelizing the program (synchronization, communication, non-balanced load, etc). At 100 nodes the speedup for a system with only 1% utilization is only 61% of the optimal speedup, for a 20% utilization the speedup is only 32.5% of the optimal speedup.

To present the efficiency of the system, i.e. how close to optimal speedups are achieved, we plot efficiency versus number of nodes in figure 2.

In both of the preceding plots we compare the performance of the parallel program executed on a system of workstations with a given owner utilization to that of the same program executed on a single node with no owner utilization. To focus on the how effective distributed computing utilizes wasted cycles we consider the weighted-speedup and weighted-efficiency metrics. In figures 3 and 4 we plot weighted-speedup and weighted-efficiency versus the number of nodes for the same parameters as in figures 1 and 2. Note the weighted-efficiency is still only 61.5% (41%) for a utilization of 1% (20%). Hence, even once owner utilization is taken into consideration achieved performance is significantly worse than optimal.

One cause for the degradation of performance is that the probability of one of the workstations experiencing a transient period of high utilization increases as the number of nodes increases. Since the parallel job must wait for each task to complete execution, just one workstation experiencing a transient high utilization will slow down the entire computation, hence performance degrades as the number of workstations increases.

A second more subtle cause of performance degradation results from a decrease in the ratio of parallel task time to owner process task time (*task ratio*). To demonstrate this effect consider what happens if we increase the parallel job demand from 1K units to 10K units. In figure 5 and 6 we plot the weighted-speedup and weighted-efficiencies for the same experiment as in figures 3 and 4, except job demand equals 10K. The weighted-speedups and weighted-efficiencies for a job demand of 10K units are much higher than their counterparts in figure 3 and 4. For $\mathcal{J}$ equal to 10K, $\mathcal{T}$ equals 100 units for a 100 workstation system, whereas $\mathcal{J}$ equal to 1K results in a $\mathcal{T}$ equal to 10 units for a 100 workstation system. Tasks of demand 10 units experience a proportionally larger delay by owner processes than tasks requiring 100 units.

To more clearly illustrate the point, we plot weighted-efficiency versus the task ratio for a system with 60 workstations in figure 7. (The plot for weighted-speedups is identical except the y-axis is scaled from 0 to 60 instead of 0 to 1.) From the figure we conclude that in order to achieve acceptable efficiencys, and thus good speedups, we must ensure that the parallel task demand is sufficiently large relative to the average demand of owner processes, i. e. we must ensure a large task ratio.

In the previous experiment we fixed the number of workstations equal to 60. In figure 8 we plot the weighted-efficiency versus task ratio for various system sizes for an owner utilization of 10%. Sensitivity to the task ratio increases with system size.

One of the main conclusions from these experiments is that in order to achieve good speedups for fixed size problems, it is essential that the task ratio be sufficiently large. Similar to the computation to communication ratio being an important consideration for parallel computations, the task ratio is an important factor in non-dedicated distributed computing.

3.2 Scaled Problem Size

We now consider the effect of scaling the problem size with the number of nodes. We assume job demand scales linearly with the number of workstations. This type of scaling has been called *memory-bounded scaleup* [10]. With memory-bounded scaleup and perfect parallelism, ideally, we may be able to complete W times the amount of work in the same time as the original problem on a single workstation by using a system with W nodes [12]. In figure 9 we plot job execution time versus the number of workstations assuming job demand is equal to 100 units times the number of workstations. Since the problem size scales, the parallel task demand is a constant 100 units, and hence, the task ratio is fixed at 10. Initially there is a sharp increase in response time as system size increases, but the increase diminishes as system size becomes large. For system utilizations of 1, 5, 10, and 20%, the response time for a problem using 100 workstations increases by 14, 30, 44, and 71% relative to the response time for a problem using one workstation with the same owner utilization. In other words, the distributed computing approach offers the potential to increase the problem size by a factor of 100 and only increase response time by 44% assuming all workstations have a utilization of 10%.

Memory-bounded scaleup exhibits better performance than fixed-size computing since the task ratio is fixed, while the task ratio in fixed-size computing decreases with an increase in the number of workstations. We also considered larger job demands and found the increase in response time to be even less. Hence, we conclude that the distributed computing approach offers significant potential for scaling of problems even if workstation owner processes are granted preemptive priority over parallel tasks.

4 Experimental Validation

In this section we present preliminary results from experimental studies to validate the analysis. In these initial studies we focus only on fixed size problems. We have chosen to implement our parallel program using the PVM package. We chose the PVM package based on the package being well known and highly available. We made no attempt to compare the PVM package with any other distributed computation packages.

To isolate the effects of workstation owner interference we assume the parallel program is a local computation problem [11]. That is, the problem has perfect parallelism and no interprocess communication. The parallel program forks W parallel tasks, one for each workstation in the system, and each task executes independently. Each parallel task is "niced" (runs at low priority) granting workstation owner processes preemptive priority over the parallel tasks.

Our primary metrics are maximum task execution time and speedup. The most common metric for a study such as this is job response time, i. e. the time from the parallel job is started until it completes. This metric is influenced by the overhead of the parallel computing package for initiating the processes and collecting the results. We want to focus only on the interference of workstation owner processes and thus rejected defining response time in this standard way. Instead, we focus on the maximum task execution time. This time was obtained by having each task record the system time when it started computation and noting the system time immediately when completing computation. Each of the parallel tasks then return their task execution time to the master process which selects and reports the maximum. By considering the maximum task execution time we isolate the impact of workstation owner process interference.

We report the results from one experiment. Further experiments are currently being conducted. The system studied is composed of at most 12 Sun ELC Sparcstations. We varied the number of workstations from 1 to 12, first ensuring that none of the workstations are executing long running jobs. In general the only interference is from more trivial usage such as editing files, reading mail, news, etc. For each number of workstations considered we ran the parallel program 10 times for each parameter value and calculated the mean of these 10 runs as our metric. Given the number of workstations, the input parameter to our parallel program is the problem size. We consider five different problem sizes; 1,2,4,8, and 16 minutes are the service demands of these problems on a single dedicated machine. No attempt has yet been made to provide confidence intervals or more detailed statistical analysis.

If figure 10 we plot the maximum task execution time versus the number of workstations for the five different job demands assuming a fixed problem size. The solid lines are the measured values from our experiment. The dashed lines are predictions from our analytical model where the input parameter for workstation owner utilization is set to 3%. We obtained the 3% value by computing the mean of the machine utilizations (by using the unix uptime command) over two working days when no PVM programs were executing. The models qualitative and quantitative predictions are in close agreement with the measured results.

In figure 11 we plot the speedup versus the number of workstations. The values plotted were obtained from measurement of the system. In this case we define speedup as the ratio of the maximum task execution time using one workstation over the maximum task execution time using W workstations. The utilization of the machines is very low and thus there is not significant degradation of parallel program performance. In a more heavily loaded system we would expect much more degradation. Focusing on the 8 and 12 workstation cases we see that the speedup decreases as the job demand decreases, i.e. the speedup for a job demand of 1 is lower than the speedup for a job demand of 16. This is because the task ratio is smaller for a job demand of 1 than it is for a job demand of 16. This experiment thus qualitatively validates the analysis. Note that the analysis shows a more significant drop in speedup as system size increases. Unfortunately we only have 12 homogeneous workstations with which to validate our results and hence can not experimentally validate this result.

5 Conclusions and Discussion

In this paper we have developed an abstract model of a distributed computing system to determine the feasibility of using distributed computing in a non-dedicated system assuming workstation owner processes have preemptive priority over parallel tasks. The model is an abstraction of a parallel program ignoring communication and synchronization overheads. We assume the targeted parallel programs execute efficiently on a dedicated distributed system, hence we can ignore these overheads and focus on the impact of a non-dedicated environment. The purpose of considering a non-dedicated system is to determine if idle (wasted cycles) workstations can be utilized to reduce execution time and to solve large problems.

For fixed-size problems we have found that good speedups can be achieved, but only if the amount of work allocated to each machine is sufficiently large compared to the mean service demand of workstation processes. Hence, for non-dedicated systems where the workstation owner processes have preemptive priority over parallel tasks, the parallel task demand to owner task demand ratio (*task ratio*) is a determining factor in performance of the parallel program. In particular, we find that the task ratio should be at least 8 for a parallel job to achieve 80 percent of the possible speedup, even adjusting for system utilization, for a system in which each homogeneous workstation has a utilization of 5 percent. In addition, the task ratio needed to achieve 80 percent of the possible speedup increases with system utilization. At a utilization of 10 percent the task ratio must be 13 or higher, and at a utilization of 20 percent the task ratio must be 20 or greater.

The model proposed in this paper assumes local

workstation processes have deterministic service requirements. This assumption implies that results presented in this paper is conservative. Hence, even larger task ratios are likely to be necessary to achieve good performance. Thus, based on our study, distributed computing in a non-dedicated environment where workstation owner processes have preemptive priority over parallel tasks is a viable approach only if the task ratio is sufficiently large. The exact size of the ratio needed is both application and environment dependent.

For scaled problems under a non-dedicated environment, we have found that distributed computing offers significant potential for the efficient execution of scaled problems. In particular, assuming each workstation in the system has a utilization of 5 percent (20 percent), mean job response time is only increased by 30 percent (71 percent) when comparing the response time of a scaled problem using 100 workstations relative to that of problem using one workstation with a 5 percent (20 percent) utilization. The performance difference between fixed-size and scaled problems is due to the fact that the task ratio of scaled problems is fixed, while the task ratio of fixed-size problems decreases as the number of workstation increases. Note that the results are based on our idealized assumption and hence are optimistic. The actual response time of these problems would be dependent on communication bandwidth requirements which are ignored in our model.

We assume the workload of the non-dedicated environment is light and the effect of long running workstation owner jobs is not considered. How to provide reasonable execution times for parallel jobs in a nondedicated system with long running workstation owner jobs must be solved if distributed computing is to be feasible in a non-dedicated environment. Currently our model only provides some initial insights into the general problem of distributed computing in a nondedicated system. In the future we intend to extend the model to handle more complex workloads. In addition, we are currently pursuing further experimental validation of our model.

References

[1] Beguelin, A., Dongarra, J.J., Geist, G.A., Mancheck, R., and Sunderam, V.S., "A Users' Guide to PVM Parallel Virtual Machine," Technical Report ORNL/TM-11826, Oak Ridge National Laboratory, July 1991.

[2] Beguelin, A., Dongarra, J.J., Geist, G.A., Mancheck, R., Moore, K., and Sunderam, V.S., "Tools for Heterogeneous Network Computing", Proc. 6th SIAM conf. on Parallel Processing For Scientific Computing, Vol 2, March 1993.

[3] G. Fox and et. al., *Solving Problems on Concurrent Processors*, Prentice-Hall Inc., 1988.

[4] Kobayashi, *Modeling and Analysis*, Addison-Wesley, 1978.

[5] Geist, G.A., and Sunderam, V.S., "Experiences With Network Based Concurrent Computing on the PVM System", Technical Report ORNL/TM-11760, Oak Ridge National Laboratory, January 1991.

[6] J.L. Gustafson and G.R. Montry and R.E. Benner, "Development of Parallel Methods for a 1024-processor Hypercube", SIAM J. on SSTC, Vol. 9, No. 4, 1988.

[7] Sauer, C.H., Chandy, K.M., *Computer System Performance Modeling*, Prentice-Hall, 1981, page 16.

[8] Schwetman, H.D., "CSIM: A C-Based Process-Oriented Simulation Language", Proc. of the 1986 Winter Simulation Conference, December, 1986.

[9] Sunderam, V.S., "PVM: A Framework for Parallel Distributed Computing", Concurrency: Practice and Experience, Vol. 2, No. 4, December 1990.

[10] Xian-He Sun and L. Ni, "Another View on Parallel Speedup", Proc. of Supercomputing '90, Nov. 1990.

[11] Xian-He Sun and L. Ni, "A Structured Representation for Parallel Algorithm Design on Multicomputers", Proc. of the Sixth Conf. on Distributed Memory Computing, April, 1991.

[12] Xian-He Sun and L. Ni, "Scalable Problems and Memory-Bounded Speedup", J. of Parallel and Distributed Computing, Vol. 19, Sept. 1993.

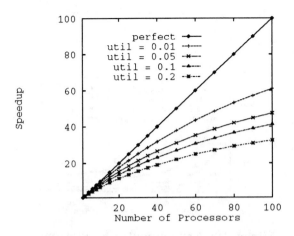

Figure 1: Speedup. J = 1000 units

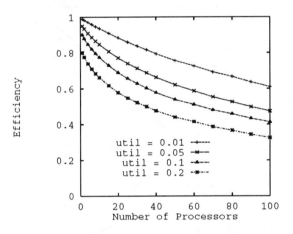

Figure 2: Efficiency, J = 1000 units

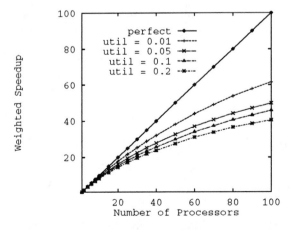

Figure 3: Weighted Speedup, J = 1000 units

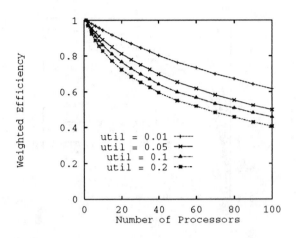

Figure 4: Weighted Efficiency, J = 1000 units

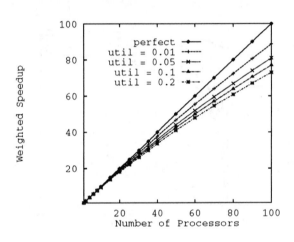

Figure 5: Weighted Speedup, J = 10,000 units

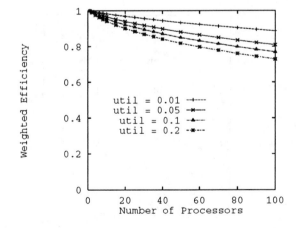

Figure 6: Weighted Efficiency, J = 10,000

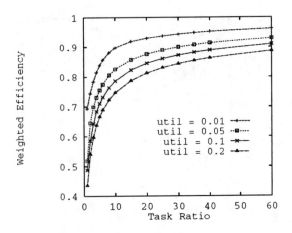

Figure 7: Effect of Task Ratio, 60 Workstations

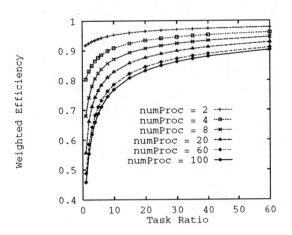

Figure 8: Effect of Task Ratio, Number Workstations Varied, Owner Utilization = 0.1

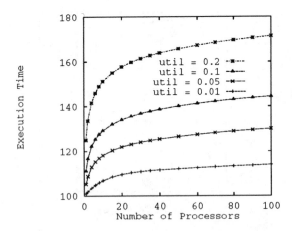

Figure 9: Effect of Scaling Problem

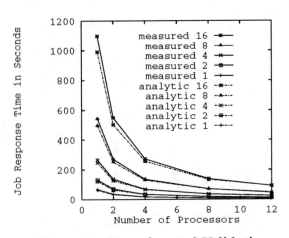

Figure 10: Experimental Validation: Response Time

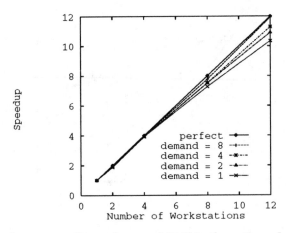

Figure 11: Experimental Validation: Speedups

Session 2:
Workshop
Integrating Task and
Data Parallelism

Integrating Task and Data Parallelism

Ian Foster

Mathematics and Computer Science Division
Argonne National Laboratory
Argonne, IL

Carl Kesselman

Computer Science Department
California Institute of Technology
Pasadena, CA

Abstract

The increased computational power of massively parallel computers and high bandwidth low latency computer networks will make a wide range of previously unpractical problems feasible. This will inevitably result in the need to develop parallel software whose complexity far exceeds that of parallel programs being developed today. These programs will combine task and data parallelism within a single application.

In this workshop, we will discuss multi-paradigm parallel programs and programming languages to support their development. We will introduce the parallel programming languages Fortran M and Compositional C++. Fortan M is a small set of extensions to Fortran 77; Compositional C++ is a small set of extensions to C++. We will demonstrate how these languages can be used to develop parallel programs that contain both task and data parallelism and how these languages are well suited to writing reusable parallel program libraries.

1 Paradigm Integration

The need for paradigm integration is driven by several factors:

Code reuse. The advantages of reusing software components are widely recognized. Code reuse is inhibited when the component places restrictions on its execution environment. In parallel programs, this implies that the user of a parallel library might be a parallel program: task or data parallel programs should be able to reuse task and data parallel components. Consequently, integration of parallel programming paradigms is a prerequisite if general reuse of parallel software components is to be achieved.

Heterogeneous Models. The computing power of MPPs will result in heterogeneous applications becoming more commonplace. Heterogeneity can be introduced into an application in different ways.

- As parallel machines get larger, numerical simulations will become more realistic and entire systems will be modeled rather than individual subsystems. For example, global climate models will contain separate models for ocean currents and atmospheric circulation. Ocean models and circulation models are data parallel applications. The climate model would therefore consist of two data parallel computations executing in task parallel mode.

- With increased computational resources, engineering design problems will extend their scope, hence multi-disciplinary optimization. For example, rather than just looking at the aerodynamic properties of an airplane wing, a more useful design would optimize the cost of production, structural and aerodynamic properties simultaneously. As with the climate model, each optimization problems can be solved in parallel with the overall control of the optimization being a parallel program.

Heterogeneous Computing Systems Parallel computers will interconnected via high speed networks, such as HPPI or ATM. Different parts of a computation will run on different machines: large scale distributed memory MPPs will perform numerical simulations while specialized shared memory visualization workstations visualize the results. It is unrealistic to expect that the same type of parallelism will be appropriate to the entire system.

Each of the above applications results in more than two or more different types of computations being executed in parallel. Heterogeneity in an application implies heterogeneity in the types of parallelism that can be exploited in the application. Paradigm integration is a natural consequence of heterogeneity.

Most current parallel programming languages and parallel programming environments such as HPF, PVM an NX work best when the application can be expressed as a data parallel algorithm. However, these languages tend to fall short in applications that require task level or functional parallelism and multi-paradigm applications.

Multi-paradigm programs will require a programming language in which:

- Both task and data parallelism can be expressed

- Task and data parallel components can interact with one another

- A range of data structures can be conveniently expressed

- Libraries of code can be developed and used in a variety of situations. For example, a library routine that utilized data parallelism should be callable from a task parallel computation

To meet these challenges, we have identified a core set of concepts which will facilitate the integration of parallel programming paradigms. Additionally, these concepts provide a framework on which portable, reusable program libraries can be build. Based on these concepts, we have designed and implemented a small extensions to Fortran and C++ that meet the requirements outlined above. These extended languages, called Fortran M and Compositional C++ (CC++) are currently being used to solve a wide range of complex parallel programming problems.

This workshop will introduce Fortran M and CC++. With examples, we will show how to how to design and build programs that integrate both task and data parallelism and how to engineer reliable, portable parallel programs by composing program components.

Session 2:
Workshop
Education

Session 2:
Invited Presentations
Eric Drexler
Tom Leighton

Session 3:
Matrix Library Issues
Chair: Bob Ward

LAPACK++: A Design Overview of Object-Oriented Extensions for High Performance Linear Algebra

Jack J. Dongarra [§‡], Roldan Pozo[‡] , and David W. Walker[§]

[§]Oak Ridge National Laboratory
Mathematical Sciences Section

[‡]University of Tennessee
Department of Computer Science

Abstract

LAPACK++ is an object-oriented C++ extension of the LAPACK (Linear Algebra PACKage) library for solving the common problems of numerical linear algebra: linear systems, linear least squares, and eigenvalue problems on high-performance computer architectures. The advantages of an object-oriented approach include the ability to encapsulate various matrix representations, hide their implementation details, reduce the number of subroutines, simplify their calling sequences, and provide an extendible software framework that can incorporate future extensions of LAPACK, such as ScaLAPACK++ for distributed memory architectures. We present an overview of the object-oriented design of the matrix and decomposition classes in C++ and discuss its impact on elegance, generality, and performance.

1 Introduction

LAPACK++ is an object-oriented C++ extension to the Fortran LAPACK [1] library for numerical linear algebra. This package includes state-of-the-art numerical algorithms for the more common linear algebra problems encountered in scientific and engineering applications. It is based on the widely used LINPACK [5] and EISPACK [13] libraries for solving linear equations, linear least squares, and eigenvalue problems for dense and banded systems. The current

LAPACK software consists of over 1,000 routines and 600,000 lines of Fortran 77 source code.

The numerical algorithms in LAPACK utilize block-matrix operations, such as matrix-multiply, in the innermost loops to achieve high performance on cached and hierarchical memory architectures. These operations, standardized as a set of subroutines called the Level 3 BLAS (Basic Linear Algebra Subprograms [6]), improve performance by increasing the granularity of the computations and keeping the most frequently accessed subregions of a matrix in the fastest level of memory. The result is that these block matrix versions of the fundamental algorithms typically show performance improvements of a factor of three over non-blocked versions [1].

LAPACK++ provides a framework for describing general block matrix computations in C++. Without a proper design of fundamental matrix and factorization classes, the performance benefits of blocked codes can be easily lost due to unnecessary data copying, inefficient access of submatrices, and excessive run-time overhead in the dynamic-binding mechanisms of C++.

LAPACK++, however, is not a general purpose array package. There are no functions, for example, to compute trigonometric operations on matrices, or to deal with multi-dimensional arrays. There are several good public domain and commercial C++ packages for these problems [4], [9], [11], [12]. The classes in LAPACK++, however, can easily integrate with these or with any other C++ matrix interface. These objects have been explicitly designed with block matrix algorithms and make extensive use of the level 3 BLAS. Furthermore, LAPACK++ is more than just a shell to the FORTRAN library; some of the key routines, such as the matrix factorizations, are actually implemented in C++ so that the general algorithm can be applied to derived matrix classes, such as distributed memory matrix objects.

---

*This project was supported in part by the Defense Advanced Research Projects Agency under contract DAAL03-91-C-0047, administered by the Army Research Office, the Applied Mathematical Sciences subprogram of the Office of Energy Research, U.S. Department of Energy, under Contract DE-AC05-84OR21400, and by the National Science Foundation Science and Technology Center Cooperative Agreement No. CCR-8809615.

LAPACK++ provides speed and efficiency competitive with native Fortran codes (see Section 2.2), while allowing programmers to capitalize on the software engineering benefits of object oriented programming. Replacing the Fortran 77 interface of LAPACK with an object-oriented framework simplifies the coding style and allows for a more flexible and extendible software platform. In Section 6, for example, we discuss extensions to support distributed matrix computations on scalable architectures [2].

The motivation and design goals for LAPACK++ include

- Maintaining competitive performance with Fortran 77.

- Providing a simple interface that hides implementation details of various matrix storage schemes and their corresponding factorization structures.

- Providing a universal interface and open system design for integration into user-defined data structures and third-party matrix packages.

- Replacing static work array limitations of Fortran with more flexible and type-safe dynamic memory allocation schemes.

- Providing an efficient indexing scheme for matrix elements that has minimal overhead and can be optimized in most application code loops.

- Utilizing function and operator overloading in C++ to simplify and reduce the number of interface entry points to LAPACK.

- Providing the capability to access submatrices by **reference**, rather than by value, and perform factorizations "in place" – vital for implementing blocked algorithms efficiently.

- Providing more meaningful naming conventions for variables and functions (e.g. names no longer limited to six alphanumeric characters, and so on).

LAPACK++ also provides an object-oriented interface to the Basic Linear Algebra Subprograms (BLAS) [6], allowing programmers to utilize these optimized computational kernels in their own C++ applications.

2 Overview

The underlying philosophy of the LAPACK++ design is to provide an interface which is simple, yet powerful enough to express the sophisticated numerical algorithms within LAPACK, including those which optimize performance and/or storage. Programmers who wish to utilize LAPACK++ as a black box to solve $Ax = B$ need not be concerned with the intricate details.

Following the framework of LAPACK, the C++ extension contains **driver routines** for solving standard types of problems, **computational routines** to perform distinct computational tasks, and **auxiliary routines** to perform certain subtasks or common low-level computations. Each driver routine typically calls a sequence of computational routines. Taken as a whole, the computational routines can perform a wider range of tasks than are covered by the driver routines.

Utilizing function overloading and object inheritance in C++, the procedural interface to LAPACK has been simplified: two fundamental drivers and their variants, LaLinSolve() and LaEigenSolve(), replace several hundred subroutines in the original Fortran version.

LAPACK++ supports various algorithms for solving linear equations and eigenvalue problems:

- Algorithms

    - LU Factorization

    - Cholesky (LL^T) Factorization

    - QR Factorization (linear least squares)

    - Singular Value Decomposition (SVD)

    - Eigenvalue problems (as included in LAPACK)

- Storage Classes

    - rectangular matrices

    - symmetric and symmetric positive definite (SPD)

    - banded matrices

    - tri/bidiagonal matrices

- Element Data Types

    - float, double, single and double precision complex

In this paper we focus on matrix factorizations for linear equations and linear least squares.

2.1 A simple code example

To illustrate how LAPACK++ simplifies the user interface, we present a small code fragment to solve linear systems. The examples are incomplete and are meant to merely illustrate the interface style. The next few sections discuss the details of matrix classes and their operations.

Consider solving the linear system $Ax = b$ using LU factorization in LAPACK++:

```
#include <lapack++.h>

LaGenMatDouble A(N,N);
LaVectorDouble x(N), b(N);

// ...

LaLinSolve(A,x,b);
```

The first line includes the LAPACK++ object and function declarations. The second line declares A to be a square $N \times N$ coefficient matrix, while the third line declares the right-hand-side and solution vectors. Finally, the `LaLinSolve()` function in the last line calls the underlying LAPACK driver routine for solving general linear equations.

Consider now solving a similar system with a tridiagonal coefficient matrix:

```
#include <lapack++.h>

LaTridiagMatDouble A(N,N);
LaVectorDouble x(N), b(N);

// ...

LaLinSolve(A,x,b);
```

The only code modification is in the declaration of A. In this case `LaLinSolve()` calls the driver routine `DGTSV()` for tridiagonal linear systems. The `LaLinSolve()` function has been **overloaded** to perform different tasks depending on the type of the input matrix A. There is no runtime overhead associated with this; it is resolved by C++ at compile time.

2.2 Performance

The elegance of the LAPACK++ matrix classes may seem to imply that they incur a significant runtime performance overhead compared to similar computations using optimized Fortran. This is not true. The design of LAPACK++ has been optimized for

performance and can utilize the BLAS kernels as efficiently as Fortran. Figure 1, for example, illustrates the Megaflop rating of the simple code

```
C = A*B;
```

for square matrices of various sizes on the IBM RS/6000 Model 550 workstation. This particular implementation used GNU g++ v. 2.3.1 and utilized the Level 3 BLAS routines from the native ESSL library. The performance results are nearly identical with those of optimized Fortran calling the same library. This is accomplished by *inlining* the LAPACK++ BLAS kernels. That is, these functions are expanded at the point of their call by C++ compiler, saving the runtime overhead of an explicit function call.

In this case the above expression calls the underlying DGEMM BLAS 3 routine. This occurs at *compile* time, without any runtime overhead. The performance numbers are very near the machine peak and illustrate that using C++ with optimized computational kernels provides an elegant high-level interface without sacrificing performance.

Figure 2 illustrates performance characteristics of the LU factorization of various matrices on the same architecture using the LAPACK++

```
LaLUFactorIP(A,F)
```

routine, which overwrites **A** with its LU factors. This routine essentially inlines to the underlying LAPACK routine `DGETRF()` and incurs no runtime overhead. (The **IP** suffix stands for "In Place" factorization. See Section 4.1 for details.)

3 LAPACK++ Matrix Objects

The fundamental objects in LAPACK++ are numerical vectors and matrices; however, LAPACK++ is **not** a general-purpose array package. Rather, LAPACK++ is a self-contained interface consisting of only the minimal number of classes to support the functionality of the LAPACK algorithms and data structures.

LAPACK++ matrices can be referenced, assigned, and used in mathematical expressions as naturally as if they were an integral part of C++; the matrix element a_{ij}, for example, is referenced as `A(i,j)`. By default, matrix subscripts begin at zero, keeping with the indexing convention of C++; however, they can be set to any user-defined value. (Fortran programmers typically prefer 1.) Internally, LAPACK++ matrices

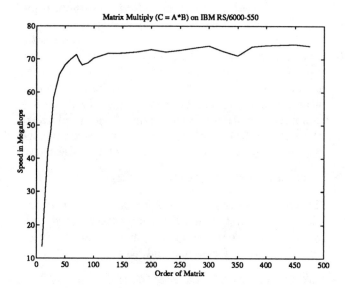

Figure 1: Performance of matrix multiply in LA-PACK++ on the IBM RS/6000 Model 550 workstation. GNU g++ v. 2.3.1 was used together with the ESSL Level 3 routine **dgemm**.

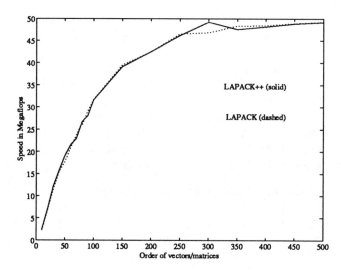

Figure 2: Performance of LAPACK++ LU factorization on the IBM RS/6000 Model 550 workstation, using GNU g++ v. 2.3.1 and BLAS routines from the IBM ESSL library. The results are indistinguishable between the Fortran and C++ interfaces.

are typically stored in column-order for compatibility with Fortran subroutines and libraries.

Various types of matrices are supported: banded, symmetric, Hermitian, packed, triangular, tridiagonal, bidiagonal, and non-symmetric. Rather than have an unstructured collection of matrix classes, LA-PACK++ maintains a class hierarchy (Figure 3) to exploit commonality in the derivation of the fundamental matrix types. This limits much of the code redundancy and allows for an open-ended design which can be extended as new matrix storage structures are introduced.

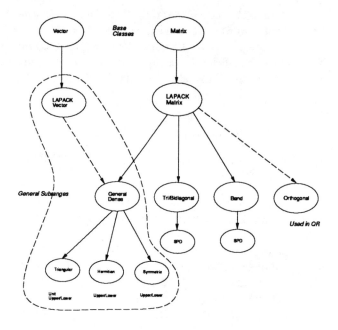

Figure 3: The Matrix Hierarchy of LAPACK++. Rectangular and Vector classes allow indexing of any rectangular submatrix by reference.

Matrix classes and other related data types specific to LAPACK++ begin with the prefix "**La**" to avoid naming conflicts with user-defined or third-party matrix packages. The list of valid names is a subset of the nomenclature shown in Figure 4.

3.1 General Matrices

One of the fundamental matrix types in LA-PACK++ is a general (nonsymmetric) rectangular matrix. The possible data element types of this matrix include single and double precision of real and complex numbers. The corresponding LAPACK++ names are given as

LaGenMat*type*

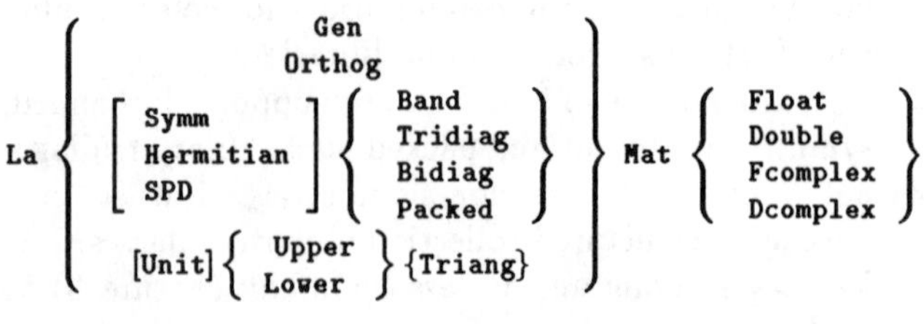

$$La \begin{Bmatrix} & \text{Gen} \\ & \text{Orthog} \\ \begin{bmatrix} \text{Symm} \\ \text{Hermitian} \\ \text{SPD} \end{bmatrix} \begin{Bmatrix} \text{Band} \\ \text{Tridiag} \\ \text{Bidiag} \\ \text{Packed} \end{Bmatrix} \\ [\text{Unit}] \begin{Bmatrix} \text{Upper} \\ \text{Lower} \end{Bmatrix} \{\text{Triang}\} \end{Bmatrix} Mat \begin{Bmatrix} \text{Float} \\ \text{Double} \\ \text{Fcomplex} \\ \text{Dcomplex} \end{Bmatrix}$$

Figure 4: LAPACK++ matrix nomenclature. Items in square brackets are optional.

for Lapack General Matrix. The *type* suffix can be **float**, **double**, **fcomplex**, or **dcomplex**. Matrices in this category have the added property that submatrices can be efficiently accessed and referenced in matrix expressions. This is a necessity for describing block-structured algorithms.

3.1.1 Declarations

General LAPACK++ matrices may be declared (constructed) in various ways:

```
#include <lapack++.h>
float d[4] = {1.0, 2.0, 3.0, 4.0};

LaGenMatDouble      A(200,100) = 0.0; // 1
LaGenMatDComplex    B;                // 2
LaGenMatDouble      C.ref(A);         // 3
LaGenMatDouble      D(A);             // 4
LaGenMatFloat       E(d, 2, 2)        // 5
```

Line (1) declares **A** to be a rectangular 200x100 matrix, with all of its elements initialized to 0.0. Line (2) declares **B** to be an empty (uninitialized) matrix. Until B becomes initialized, any attempt to reference its elements will result in a run time error. Line (3) declares **C** to share the same elements of **A**. Line (4) illustrates an equivalent way of specifying this at the time of a new object construction. Finally, line (5) demonstrates how one can initialize a 2x2 matrix with the data from a standard C++ vector. The values are initalized in column-major form, so that the first column of **E** contains $\{1.0, 2.0\}^T$, and the second column contains $\{3.0, 4.0\}^T$.

3.1.2 Submatrices

Blocked linear algebra algorithms utilize submatrices as their basic unit of computation. It is crucial that submatrix operations be highly optimized. Because of this, LAPACK++ provides mechanisms for accessing rectangular subregions of a general matrix. These regions are accessed by *reference*, that is, without copying data, and can be used in any matrix expression.

Ideally, one would like to use familiar colon notation of Fortran 90 or Matlab for expressing submatrices. However, this modification of the C++ syntax is not possible without redefining the language specifications. As a reasonable compromise, LAPACK++ denotes submatrices by specifying a subscript range through the **LaIndex()** function. For example, the 3x3 matrix in the upper left corner of **A** is denoted as

```
A( LaIndex(0,2), LaIndex(0,2) )
```

This references $A_{ij}, i = 0, 1, 2$ $j = 0, 1, 2$, and is equivalent to the **A(0:2,0:2)** colon notation used elsewhere. Submatrix expressions may be also be used as a destination for assignment, as in

```
A( LaIndex(0,2), LaIndex(0,2) ) = 0.0;
```

which sets the 3x3 submatrix of A to zero. Following the Fortran 90 conventions, the index notation has an optional third argument denoting the stride value,

```
LaIndex(start, end, increment)
```

If the **increment** value is not specified it is assumed to be one. The expression **LaIndex(s, e, i)** is equivalent to the index sequence

$$s, \quad s+i, \quad s+2i, \quad \ldots \quad s + \lfloor \frac{e-s}{i} \rfloor i$$

The internal representation of an index is not expanded to a full vector, but kept in its compact triplet format. The increment values may be negative and allow one to traverse a subscript range in the opposite direction, such as in **(10,7,-1)** to denote the sequence $\{10, 9, 8, 7\}$. Indices can be named and used in expressions, as in the following submatrix assignments,

```
LaGenMat<double> A(10,10), B, C; // 1
LaIndex I(1,9,2),                // 2
LaIndex J(1,3,2);                // 3

B.ref(A(I,I));                   // 4
B(2,3) = 3.1;                    // 5
C = B(LaIndex(2,4,2), J);        // 6
```

In lines (2) and (3) we declare indices $I = \{1, 3, 5, 7, 9\}$, and $J = \{1, 3\}$. Line (4) sets B to the specified 5x5 submatrix of **A**. The matrix B can used in any matrix expression, including accessing its individual elements, as in line (5). Note that **B(2,3)** is the same memory location as **A(5,7)**, so that a change to B will also modify the contents of A. Line (6) assigns the 2x2 submatrix of B to C. Note that C can also be referenced as `A( LaIndex(5,9,2), LaIndex(3,7,2))`.

Although LAPACK++ submatrix expressions allow one to access non-contiguous rows or columns, many of the LAPACK routines only allow submatrices with unit stride in the column direction. Calling an LAPACK++ routine with a non-contiguous submatrix columns *may* cause data to be copied into contiguous submatrix and can optionally generate a runtime warning to advise the programmer that data copying has taken place. (In Fortran, the user would need to need to do this by hand.)

4   Driver Routines

This section discusses LAPACK++ routines for solving linear a system of linear equations

$$Ax = b,$$

where A is the **coefficient matrix**, b is the **right hand side**, and x is the **solution**. A is assumed to be a square matrix of order n, although underlying computational routines allow for A to be rectangular. For several right hand sides, we write

$$AX = B,$$

where the columns of B are individual right hand sides, and the columns of X are the corresponding solutions. The task is to find X, given A and B. The coefficient matrix A can be of the types show in Figure 4.

The basic syntax for a linear equation driver in LAPACK++ is given by

`LaLinSolve(`*op*`(A), X, B);`

The matrices `A` and `B` are input, and `X` is the output. `A` is an $M \times N$ matrix of one of the above types. Letting *nrhs* denote the number of right hand sides in eq. 4, `X` and `B` are both rectangular matrices of size $N \times nrhs$. The syntax *op*`(A)` can denote either `A` or the transpose of `A`, expressed as `transp(A)`.

This version requires intermediate storage of approximately $M * (N + nrhs)$ elements.

In cases where no additional information is supplied, the LAPACK++ routines will attempt to follow an intelligent course of action. For example, if `LaLinSolve(A,X,B)` is called with a non-square $M \times N$ matrix, the solution returned will be the linear least square that minimizes $||Ax - b||_2$ using a QR

factorization. Or, if A is declared as SPD, then a Cholesky factorization will be used. Alternatively, one can directly specify the exact factorization method, such as `LaLUFactor(F, A)`. In this case, if A is non-square, the factors return only a partial factorization of the upper square portion of A.

Error conditions in performing the `LaLinSolve()` operations can be retrieved via the `LaLinSolveInfo()` function, which returns information about the last called `LaLinSolve()`. A zero value denotes a successful completion. A value of $-i$ denotes that the ith argument was somehow invalid or inappropriate. A positive value of i denotes that in the LU decomposition, $U(i,i) = 0$; the factorization has been completed but the factor U is exactly singular, so the solution could not be computed. In this case, the value returned by `LaLinSolve()` is a null (0x0) matrix.

4.1   Memory Optimizations: Factorizing in place

When using large matrices that consume a significant portion of available memory, it may be beneficial to remove the requirement of storing intermediate factorization representations at the expense of destroying the contents of the input matrix A. For most matrix factorizations we require temporary data structures roughly equal to the size of the original input matrix. (For general banded matrices, one needs slightly more storage due to pivoting, which causes fill in additional bands.) For example, the temporary memory requirement of a square $N \times N$ dense non-symmetric factorization can be reduced from $N \times (N+nrhs+1)$ elements to $N \times 1$. Such memory-efficient factorizations are performed with the `LaLinSolveIP()` routine:

`LaLinSolveIP(A, X, B);`

Here the contents of A are overwritten (with the respective factorization). These "in-place" functions are intended for advanced programmers and are not recommended for general use. They assume the programmer's responsibility to recognize that the contents of `A` have been destroyed; however, they can allow a large numerical problem to be solved on a machine with limited memory.

5   Programming Examples

This code example solves the linear least squares problem of fitting N data points (x_i, y_i) with a dth

```
void poly_fit(LaVector<double> &x,
    LaVector<double> &y, LaVector<double> &p)
{
    int N = min(x.size(), y.size());
    int d = p.size();

    LaGenMatDouble P(N,d);
    LaVectorDouble a(d);
    double x_to_the_j;

    // construct Vandermonde matrix
    for (i=0; i<N; i++)
    {
        x_to_the_j = 1;
        for (j=0; j<d; j++)
        {
            P(i,j) = x_to_the_j;
            x_to_the_j *= x(i);
        }
    }
    // solve Pa = y using linear least squares
    LaLinSolveIP(P, p, y);

}
```

Figure 5: LAPACK++ code example: polynomial data fitting.

degree polynomial equation

$$p(x) = a_0 + a_1 x + a_2 x^2 + \ldots + a_d x^d$$

using QR factorization. It is intended for illustrative purposes only; there are more effective methods to solve this problem.

Given the two vectors x and y it returns the vector of coefficients $\mathbf{a} = \{a_0, a_1, a_2, \ldots, a_{d-1}\}$. It is assumed that $N \gg d$. The solution arises from solving the overdetermined Vandermonde system $Xa = y$:

$$\begin{bmatrix} 1 & x_0^1 & x_0^2 & \ldots & x_0^d \\ 1 & x_1^1 & x_1^2 & \ldots & x_1^d \\ \vdots & & & & \vdots \\ 1 & x_{N-1}^1 & x_{N-1}^2 & \ldots & x_{N-1}^d \end{bmatrix} \begin{bmatrix} a_0 \\ a_1 \\ \vdots \\ a_d \end{bmatrix} = \begin{bmatrix} y_0 \\ y_1 \\ \vdots \\ y_{N-1} \end{bmatrix}$$

in the least squares sense, i.e., minimizing $\|Xa - y\|_2$. The resulting code is shown in figure 5.

6   ScaLAPACK++: an extension for distributed architectures

There are various ways to extend LAPACK++. Here we discuss one such extension, ScaLA-PACK++ [2], for linear algebra on distributed memory architectures. The intent is that for large scale problems ScaLAPACK++ should effectively exploit the computational hardware of medium grain-sized multicomputers with up to a few thousand processors, such as the Intel Paragon and Thinking Machines Corporation's CM-5.

Achieving these goals while maintaining portability, flexibility, and ease-of-use can present serious challenges, since the layout of an application's data within the hierarchical memory of a concurrent computer is critical in determining the performance and scalability of the parallel code. To enhance the programmability of the library we would like details of the parallel implementation to be hidden as much as possible, but still provide the user with the capability to control the data distribution.

The design of ScaLAPACK++ includes a general two-dimensional matrix decomposition that supports the most common block scattered encountered in the current litertature. ScaLAPACK++ can be extended to support arbitrary matrix decompositions by providing the specific parallel BLAS library to operate on such matrices.

Decoupling the matrix operations from the details of the decomposition not only simplifies the encoding of an algorithm but also allows the possibility of postponing the decomposition scheme until runtime. This is only possible with object-oriented programming languages, like C++, that support *dynamic-binding*, or *polymorphism* – the ability to examine an object's type and dynamically select the appropriate action [10]. In many applications the optimal matrix decomposition is strongly dependent on how the matrix is utilized in other parts of the program. Furthermore, it is often necessary to dynamically alter the matrix decomposition at runtime to accommodate special routines. The ability to support dynamic run-time decomposition strategies is one of the key features of ScaLAPACK++ that makes it integrable with scalable applications.

The currently supported decomposition scheme defines global matrix objects which are distributed across a $P \times Q$ logical grid of processors. Matrices are mapped to processors using a block scattered class of decompositions (Figure 6) that allows a wide variety of matrix mappings while enhancing scalability and maintaining good load balance for various factor-

0	1	2	3	0	1	2	3	0	1	2	3
4	5	6	7	4	5	6	7	4	5	6	7
0	1	2	3	0	1	2	3	0	1	2	3
4	5	6	7	4	5	6	7	4	5	6	7
0	1	2	3	0	1	2	3	0	1	2	3
4	5	6	7	4	5	6	7	4	5	6	7
0	1	2	3	0	1	2	3	0	1	2	3
4	5	6	7	4	5	6	7	4	5	6	7
0	1	2	3	0	1	2	3	0	1	2	3
4	5	6	7	4	5	6	7	4	5	6	7
0	1	2	3	0	1	2	3	0	1	2	3
4	5	6	7	4	5	6	7	4	5	6	7

Figure 6: An example of block scattered decomposition over an 2x4 processor grid.

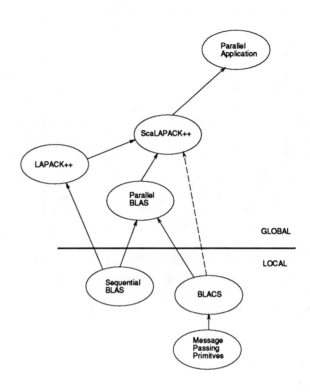

Figure 7: Design Hierarchy of ScaLAPACK++. In an SPMD environment, components above the horizontal reference line represent a global viewpoint (a single distributed structure), while elements below represent a per-node local viewpoint of data.

ization algorithms. Each node of the multicomputer runs a sequential LAPACK++ library that provides the object oriented framework to describe block algorithms on conventional matrices in each individual processor.

We can view the block scattered decomposition as stamping a $P \times Q$ processor grid, or template, over the matrix, where each cell of the grid covers $r \times s$ data items, and is labeled by its position in the template (Figure 6). The block and scattered decompositions may be regarded as special cases of the block scattered (SBS) decomposition. This scheme is practical and sufficiently general-purpose for most, if not all, dense linear algebra computations. Furthermore, in problems, such as LU factorization, in which rows and/or columns are eliminated in successive steps, the SBS decomposition enhances scalability by ensuring processor load balance. Preliminary experiments of an object-based LU factorization algorithm using an SBS decomposition [2] suggest these algorithms scale well on multicomputers. For example, on the Intel Touchstone Delta System, a 520 node i860-based multicomputer, such algorithms can achieve nearly twelve Gflops (figure 8).

Parallelism is exploited through the use of distributed memory versions of the Basic Linear Algebra Subprogram (BLAS) [6] [3] that perform the basic computational units of the block algorithms. Thus,

at a higher level, the block algorithms look the same for the parallel and sequential versions, and only one version of each needs to be maintained.

The benefits of an object oriented design (Figure 7) include the ability to hide the implementation details of distributed matrices from the application programmer, and the ability to support a generic interface to basic computational kernels (BLAS), such as matrix multiply, without specifying the details of the matrix storage class.

7 Conclusion

We have presented a design overview for object oriented linear algebra on high performance architectures. We have also described extensions for distributed memory architectures. These designs treat

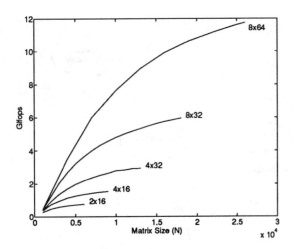

Figure 8: Performance of distributed LU factorization using an Square Block Scattered (SBS) matrix decomposition on the Intel Touchstone Delta system. Results are provided for various processor-grid configurations.

both conventional and distributed matrices as fundamental objects.

In both the parallel and sequential aspects of LAPACK++, decoupling the matrix algorithm from a specific data decomposition provides three important attributes: (1) it results in simpler code which more closely matches the underlying mathematical formulation, (2) it allows for one "universal" algorithm, rather than supporting one version for each data decomposition needed, and (3) it allows one to postpone the data decomposition decision until runtime.

We have used the **inheritance** mechanism of the object oriented design to provide a common source code for both the parallel and sequential versions. Because the parallelism in embedded in the parallel BLAS library, the sequential and parallel high level matrix algorithms in ScaLAPACK++ look the same. This tremendously simplifies the complexity of the parallel libraries.

We have used **polymorphism**, or dynmanic binding mechanisms to achieve a truly portable matrix library in which the data decomposition may be dynamically changed at runtime.

We have utilized operator and function **overloading** capabilities of C++ to simplify the syntax and user interface into the LAPACK and BLAS functions.

We have utilized the **function inlining** capabilities of C++ to reduce the function-call overhead usually associated with interfacing Fortran or assembly kernels.

In short, we have used various important aspects of object oriented mechanisms and C++ in the design of LAPACK++. These attributes were utilized not because of novelty, but out of necessity to incorporate a design which provides scalability, portability, flexibility, and ease-of-use.

References

[1] E. ANDERSON, Z. BAI, C. BISCHOF, J. W. DEMMEL, J. J. DONGARRA, J. DU CROZ, A. GREENBAUM, S. HAMMARLING, A. MCKENNEY, S. OSTROUCHOV, AND D. SORENSEN, *LAPACK User's Guide*, SIAM, Philadelphia, 1992.

[2] J. CHOI, J. J. DONGARRA, R. POZO, D. W. WALKER, *ScaLAPACK: A Scalable Linear Algebra Library for Distributed Memory Concurrent Computers*, Frontiers of Massively Parallel Computing, McLean, Virginia, October 19-21, 1992.

[3] J. CHOI AND J. J. DONGARRA AND D. W. WALKER, *PB-BLAS : Parallel Block Basic Linear Algebra Subroutines on Distributed Memory Concurrent Computers*, Oak Ridge National Laboratory, Mathematical Sciences Section, in preparation, 1993.

[4] R. DAVIES, *newmat07, an experimental matrix package in C++*, robertd@kauri.vuw.ac.nz, 1993.

[5] J. J. DONGARRA, J. R. BUNCH, C. B. MOLER, AND G. W. STEWART, *LINPACK Users' Guide*, SIAM, Philadelphia, PA, 1979.

[6] J. J. DONGARRA, J. DU CROZ, I. S. DUFF, AND S. HAMMARLING, *A set of Level 3 Basic Linear Algebra Subprograms*, ACM Trans. Math. Soft., 16 (1990), pp. 1–17.

[7] J. J. DONGARRA, R. POZO, D. W. WALKER, *LAPACK++: Object Oriented Extensions for High Peformance Linear Algebra*, in preparation.

[8] J. J. DONGARRA, R. POZO, D. W. WALKER, *An Object Oriented Design for High Performance Linear Algebra on Distributed Memory Architectures*, Object Orriented Numerics Conference (OONSKI), Sunriver, Oregon, May 26-27, 1993.

[9] DYAD SOFTWARE CORPORATION, *M++ Class Library*, Bellevue, Washington, 1991.

[10] M. A. ELLIS, B. STROUSTRUP, *The Annotated c++ Reference Manual*, Addison-Wesley, 1990.

[11] K. E. GORLEN, S. M. ORLOW, P. S. PLEXICO, *Data Abstraction and Object-Oriented Programming in C++*, John Wiley & Sons, Chichester, England, 1990.

[12] ROGUE WAVE SOFTWARE, *Math.h++*, Corvallis, Oregon, 1992.

[13] B. T. SMITH, J. M. BOYLE, J. J. DONGARRA, B. S. GARBOW, Y. IKEBE, V. C. KLEMA, AND C. B. MOLER, *Matrix Eigensystem Routines – EISPACK Guide*, vol. 6 of Lecture Notes in Computer Science, Springer-Verlag, Berlin, 2 ed., 1976.

Reducing Synchronization on the Parallel Davidson method for the Large, Sparse, Eigenvalue Problem

Andreas Stathopoulos and Charlotte F. Fischer

Computer Science Department
Vanderbilt University
Nashville, TN 37235

Abstract

The Davidson method is extensively used in quantum chemistry and atomic physics for finding a few extreme eigenpairs of a large, sparse, symmetric matrix. It can be viewed as a preconditioned version of the Lanczos method which reduces the number of iterations at the expense of a more complicated step. Frequently, the problem sizes involved demand the use of large multicomputers with hundreds or thousands of processors. The difficulties occurring in parallelizing the Davidson step are dealt with and results on a smaller scale machine are reported. The new version improves the parallel characteristics of the Davidson algorithm and holds promise for a large number of processors. Its stability and reliability is similar to that of the original method.

1 Introduction

The eigenvalue problem, $Ax = \lambda x$, is central to many scientific applications. In these applications it is common for A to be real, symmetric, and frequently very large and sparse. Examples abound both in engineering and in science [15, 7, 8, 4]. Following the recent advances in High Performance Computing technology, the demands for even higher order matrices have increased. Numerous large matrix methods have been developed that solve only for a few extreme eigenpairs, and do not modify the matrix since usually it cannot be stored in memory or on disk in full.

The Lanczos [16] and the Davidson [3] methods are amongst the most widely used methods. The Lanczos iteration builds an orthogonal basis for the Krylov subspace, $\mathcal{K}(A, g, m) = \text{span}\{g, Ag, \ldots, A^m g\}$, from which the required eigenvectors are approximated through a Rayleigh-Ritz procedure. The attraction of the Lanczos method is that the orthogonal basis is built through an easy-to-compute three-term

recurrence and the projection of A onto $\mathcal{K}(A, g, m)$ is a tridiagonal matrix of order m. The Davidson method builds a subspace that deviates from the Krylov subspace. In each iteration the Rayleigh-Ritz procedure is solved and the residual of the current approximation is preconditioned $((M - \lambda I)^{-1}(A - \lambda I)x)$ before it enters the basis. Therefore, the new vector should be explicitly orthogonalized to all previous basis vectors. The Davidson method can be considered a preconditioned version of the Lanczos method [12, 13, 18]. The convergence is much faster but the work per iteration is increased. In quantum chemistry and atomic physics calculations the size and structure of the matrix justifies the extra work per step, even with a preconditioner as $M = Diag$, where $Diag$ is the diagonal of A.

In the last ten years, considerable effort has been put into transporting the Lanczos method to parallel computers. This effort has been fruitful in machines that offer vectorization and coarse grain parallelism. For medium and fine grain parallelism more difficulties had to be faced because of the iterative nature of the method. However, due to the simplicity of the recurrence, good performance was achieved on these architectures by reducing the synchronization overheads. The Davidson method has been optimized for vector and coarse grain machines [1, 18, 21, 22], but there are no previous attempts to transport the Davidson to a medium grain machine (tens or a few hundreds of processors). A reason for this is the more complicated nature of the algorithm and the increased synchronization requirements.

In this paper the original algorithm is restructured so that it requires only one synchronization per iteration. In some cases the numerical stability of the restructured algorithm is relaxed but in quantum chemistry and atomic physics applications shifting the matrix with the extreme diagonal element restores most of the lost numerical accuracy. Moreover, when used with frequent restarting, the two algorithms are prac-

172

© 1993 ACM 0-8186-4340-4/93/0011 $1.50

tically equivalent. The gain in time and speedup is significant when the number of processors is large.

In Section 2 the original Davidson algorithm is outlined. In Section 3, the distribution issues and the synchronization needs of a parallel Davidson are addressed. The restructured algorithm is presented in Section 4. Sections 5 and 6 cope respectively with time and numerical behavior of the new algorithm. Concluding remarks and future directions are given in Section 7.

2   The Original Davidson Method

The Davidson method is similar to the Lanczos method. If no preconditioning is used, the space created by Davidson is identical with the Lanczos space. In this case the Davidson method becomes an expensive way of implementing the Lanczos procedure; explicit orthogonalization is used, the Rayleigh-Ritz is applied in each step, and the projection matrix is full [2, 18, 12, 10, 22].

If preconditioning is used instead of the residual as the next basis vector, a better estimate can be chosen from perturbation theory: $b = (M - \lambda I)^{-1} Res(x)$, where M is a good approximation to matrix A, λ very close to the eigenvalue and $Res(x)$ the residual of the current approximation x [5]. Davidson proposed the diagonal of A as the preconditioner M. In applications where the eigenvectors have only one dominant component this choice is sufficient to provide extremely rapid convergence. Applications in quantum chemistry and atomic physics demonstrate the benefits [5, 22]. The same preconditioner is considered hereafter because of its excellent parallel properties.

Assuming that the K lowest eigenpairs are required, a brief description of the original algorithm follows:

The Original Algorithm

Step 0: Set $m = K$. Compute initial Basis $B = \{b_1, \ldots, b_m\} \in \Re^{N \times m}$, also $D = AB = \{d_1, \ldots, d_m\}$, and the projection of size $m \times m$, $S = B^T A B = B^T D$.

Repeat until converged steps 1 through 8:

1. Solve $SC = C\Lambda$, with $C^T C = I$, and Λ diagonal.

2. Target one of the K sought eigenpairs, say (λ, c).

3. If the basis size is maximum truncate:
   $D \leftarrow DC$, $B \leftarrow BC$, $C = I_K$, $S = \Lambda$, $m = K$.

4. Compute $R = (Diag - \lambda I)^{-1}(Dc - \lambda Bc)$.

5. Orthogonalize: $b_{new} = R - \sum b_i b_i^T R$, normalize: $b_{new} \leftarrow b_{new}/\|b_{new}\|$.

6. Matrix vector multiply: $d_{new} = Ab_{new}$

7. Compute the new column of S:
   $S_{i,m+1} = b_i^T d_{new}$, $i = 1, \ldots, m+1$.

8. Increase m.

The above algorithm can be extended in several useful ways that improve its functionality and its run-time behavior [22, 5].

3   Transporting to a Parallel Computer

Previous results have shown that the Davidson algorithm can be implemented efficiently on parallel-vector computers (both shared and distributed memory) when the number of processors is small [18, 21]. The necessity of using more processors is evident, not because of the intolerably long execution of the algorithm but because of the increasing storage demands. Large applications can easily saturate the memory of hundreds of processors with the auxiliary vectors, without even storing the matrix. Care should be taken when this transition is made, so that the algorithm does scale up with the processors. Specifically, considerations about the distribution of the work arrays and the matrix, and about the synchronization-communication bottlenecks of the algorithm are in order.

3.1   Distribution Issues

The distribution of the matrix A onto the processors is the most compelling need. The matrix A affects the algorithm only through the user provided matrix-vector multiply. The distribution of A can be also left to the user so as to suit the specific multiplication routine. In many applications the matrix is large enough to be stored only on disc or recomputed each time it is needed [14]. The only assumption used in this paper about the matrix vector multiply is that it accepts and returns vectors in the following specified format.

The arrays D and B are the only "long" arrays needed in the algorithm, and their distribution can be performed in either of their two dimensions. The Davidson method was designed to cope with problems of large order. Thus, the number of columns in D and B is small, because of resource limitations. In parallel computers with several tens or hundreds of processors the number of vectors is not large enough to allow every vector to reside on one processor, hence distribution along the long dimension is considered.

Distribution can be performed in a wrap-around row fashion, or in terms of blocks of contiguous rows. The second option is followed in this implementation. If *nodes* is the number of processors, each processor stores $\lfloor \frac{N}{nodes} \rfloor$ rows, except the first $\text{mod}(N, nodes)$ ones that store $\lfloor \frac{N}{nodes} \rfloor + 1$ rows. The same distribution is also assumed for the elements of the diagonal of the matrix, *Diag*, used in the preconditioning step. The load imbalancing ratio is then limited to $\frac{min(mod(N,nodes),1)}{N/nodes} \le \frac{nodes}{N}$, which is negligible for large matrices. The two arrays S and C are very small (size $m \times m$) and they are duplicated in all processors.

3.2 Synchronization Needs

The above choice of distribution facilitates the parallel execution of vector updates like addition and scaling (daxpy and dscal operations). Each processor simply updates the local piece of the vector. Reduction operations (ddot) require two steps. First, a parallel computation of the local dot-products and second, a global addition of the partial results (log *nodes* step). Besides the communication costs, the second step introduces a synchronization point that serializes the processors preventing them from exploiting later parallelism.

The Lanczos algorithm can be given in a form where only one synchronization point is necessary per iteration. The same can not be easily achieved with the Davidson algorithm. Synchronization stemming from dot products appears in the following points in the Davidson algorithm:

1. The inner products $b_i^T R$, $i = 1, \ldots, m$ in orthogonalization.

2. The computation of the norm $\|b_{new}\|^2 = b_{new}^T b_{new}$.

3. The computation of the new column: $S_{i,m+1} = b_i^T d_{new}$, $i = 1, \ldots, m+1$.

Data dependencies prohibit any postponement of global addition of inner products to some common synchronization point: Point (3) depends on Point (2) which depends on Point (1). The existence of three well separated synchronization points in one iteration, places strict limits on the efficient parallelization of the algorithm.

The solution of the Rayleigh-Ritz small system (step 1) could introduce additional synchronization if a parallel algorithm was used. Because of the small size of this system, the benefits from a parallel execution do not account for the additional overheads. Consequently, step 1 of the algorithm is executed identically by all processors.

4 The Restructured Davidson Method

In each iteration a new basis vector is computed from the current information. Since the information is distributed through the processors, the need of at least one synchronization point is obvious if the new vector is to contain the new Davidson direction. An alternative way of proceeding is the s-step methodology which is not considered in this paper [11]. To achieve only one synchronization point in each iteration, the above dependencies must be removed.

4.1 Removing the dependencies

The objective is to carry out all necessary inner products independently. After a single global addition, their values can be used to compute the new basis vector, the new column of S, and d_{new}. Since b_{new} is not available before the synchronization, the computation of $\|b_{new}\|$, S and D without an additional synchronization requires the use of the equivalent form:

$$b_{new} = R - \sum_{i=1}^{m} b_i b_i^T R. \tag{1}$$

By substituting (1) for b_{new} whenever b_{new} is needed, the dependencies disappear. The following formulae present this approach.

$$\begin{aligned} \text{If} \quad V &= AR, & (2) \\ \text{and} \quad rar &= R^T V & (3) \\ rr &= R^T R & (4) \\ t_i &= b_i^T R & (5) \\ g_i &= b_i^T V, \quad i = 1, \ldots, m & (6) \end{aligned}$$

then the new vectors are given by:

$$\|b_{new}\| = \sqrt{rr - \sum_{i=1}^{m} t_i^2} \tag{7}$$

$$S_{i,m+1} = \frac{g_i - \sum_{j=1}^{m} S_{ij} t_j}{\|b_{new}\|}, \quad i = 1, \ldots, m \tag{8}$$

$$S_{m+1,m+1} = \frac{rar - \sum_{i=1}^{m} t_i(g_i + S_{i,m+1}\|b_{new}\|)}{\|b_{new}\|^2} \quad (9)$$

$$b_{new} = (R - \sum_{i=1}^{m} b_i t_i)/\|b_{new}\| \quad (10)$$

$$d_{new} = (V - \sum_{i=1}^{m} d_i t_i)/\|b_{new}\| \quad (11)$$

Since the four inner products (3–6) are independent, one synchronization point is enough to compute their values. These values can be used later for the updates (7–11). The "long" updates (10–11) can be computed in parallel.

4.2 The Restructured Algorithm

The following algorithm is a restructured version of the Davidson algorithm that uses the above formulae to compute the elements of the next iteration. It requires only one synchronization point per iteration.

Step 0: Set $m = K$. Compute initial Basis $B \in \Re^{N \times m}$, also $D = AB$, and the projection of size $m \times m$, $S = B^T AB = B^T D$.

Repeat until converged steps 1 through 14:

1. Solve $SC = C\Lambda$, with $C^T C = I$, and Λ diagonal.

2. Target one of the K sought eigenpairs, say (λ, c).

3. If the basis size is maximum truncate:
   $D \leftarrow DC$, $B \leftarrow BC$, $C = I_K$, $S = \Lambda$, $m = K$.

4. Compute $R = (Diag - \lambda I)^{-1}(Dc - \lambda Bc)$.

5. Matrix vector multiply: $V = AR$.

6. Locally compute $t_i = b_i^T R$, $g_i = b_i^T V$, $i = 1, \ldots, m$ and $rar = R^T V$, $rr = R^T R$.

7. Synchronize: Globally sum the corresponding t_i, g_i, rar, rr.

8. Set $\|b_{new}\| = \sqrt{rr - \sum_{i=1}^{m} t_i^2}$.

9. Set $S_{i,m+1} = (g_i - \sum_{j=1}^{m} S_{ij} t_j)$.

10. Set $S_{m+1,m+1} = rar - \sum_{i=1}^{m} t_i(g_i + S_{i,m+1})$.

11. Scale $S_{i,m+1} \leftarrow S_{i,m+1}/\|b_{new}\|$, $i = 1, \ldots, m + 1$.

12. Set $b_{new} = (R - \sum_{i=1}^{m} b_i t_i)/\|b_{new}\|$.

13. Set $d_{new} = (V - \sum_{i=1}^{m} d_i t_i)/\|b_{new}\|$.

14. Increase m.

The original and the restructured algorithm have the same first four steps. The matrix-vector multiplication is also common although it appears in different steps. Table 1 gives a comparison of the arithmetic involved in each iteration for the non-common steps. The amount of work per iteration is slightly increased compared to the work of the original algorithm. The restructured algorithm requires two less dot products but m more daxpy operations. Since the daxpy is an update operation, it can be performed fully in parallel and for a large number of processors the extra work is insignificant.

	Original	Restructured
dot	$2m + 4$	$2m + 2$
daxpy	m	$2m$
other (flops)	-	$\mathcal{O}(2m^2)$

Table 1: Comparison of the iteration work for the non-common steps of the two algorithms.

5 Timing Results

The two versions of the algorithm have been implemented on a iPSC/860 hypercube, with 8Mb of memory per node. The large network latency and low computation-to-communication ratio of the iPSC/860 suggest the use of coarse grain parallelism [6]. However, the high processor speed is achievable in optimal situations, thus medium grain applications may perform equally well on the iPSC/860. The major advantage of using a hypercube architecture for the above iterative methods is the node topology which permits the global addition-synchronization in $\log nodes$ steps without channel contention.

The matrix used in the timing experiments is a single diagonal matrix with elements $A_{ii} = i$, except the initial block $A_{ij} = -1$, $i, j \leq 30$ and $i \neq j$. This form facilitates a fully parallel execution of the matrix vector multiply and it is economical to compute. It requires a vector update operation and a small matrix-vector multiply, operations that consist a small percentage of the iteration-work of the algorithm. In this way the algorithm timings are affected neither by extra communication on the multiplication routine nor by the dominating parallelizing properties of a large matrix. The sizes of matrices tested are varied from small cases, $N = 5000$, up to a moderately large case $N = 10^6$. In the latter case, the memory requirements

impose the use of at least 16 processors. For all the
experiments the lowest eigenpair is required, the algorithm is restarted every 7 iterations, and it is run from
twenty to forty iterations depending on the size of the
matrix. Results are reported in node configurations
from 1 to 64 nodes.

The objective is to reduce synchronization on the
Davidson algorithm and hence improve the speedup
for a large number of processors. This is important
when a bigger number of processors is needed to compensate for the increased memory needs of large applications. Figures 1 and 2 illustrate the speedup curves
for both versions applied on seven different sizes of the
above test matrix and for all node configurations.

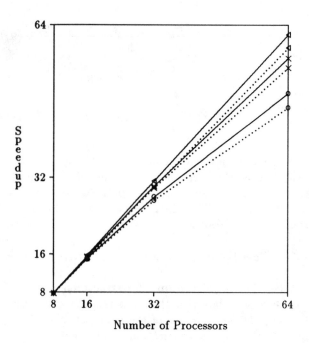

Figure 2: Speedup curves for the test matrix and
sizes:(o) : $N = 60000$, ($\times$) : $N = 200000$, and
($\triangleleft$) : $N = 10^6$. The original version is depicted by
dotted lines.

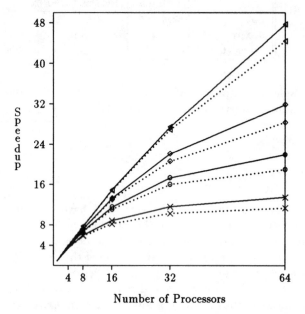

Figure 1: Speedup curves for the test matrix and
sizes:($\times$) : $N = 5000$, (o) : $N = 10000$, ($\diamond$) : $N =
20000$, ($\triangleleft$) : $N = 50000$. The original version is depicted by dotted lines.

In both figures the speedup increases with the size
of the cube and the size of the matrix. For some small
cases in Figure 1 the speedup levels off but does not
decline, at least for the cube-sizes used, and for the
large cases in Figure 2 it is close to linear. In addition, most of the small cases demonstrate an ascending
speedup character which is promising for execution in
multiprocessors with hundreds of nodes. On the other
hand, the "leveling off" is justified by the fact that
all of the small cases in Figure 1 have execution times
close or much lower than 1 sec.

The comparison of the restructured with the original method verifies what is theoretically expected.
There is a consistent improvement over the older ver-

sion that increases with the number of processors.
This is the consequence of the reduction on synchronization. In the original algorithm the more processors
there are, the more time is wasted in synchronization
and communication. The new version allows the processors to run independently until the following iteration, exploiting more of the available parallelism. The
speedup increase over the older version varies from
5% to 18%. Projecting the experience from 64 nodes
onto hundreds of nodes, the restructured algorithm
should present significant improvements on the Davidson method. As the size of the matrix grows, there is
an slight decrease in the difference between the two
versions because each processor is assigned more work
and this diminishes the effect of the synchronization
overheads. However, the superiority of the restructured algorithm is obvious even for the case $N = 10^6$.

In view of the increased arithmetic on the restructured algorithm, execution timings are also important
to show the actual benefits. The restructured algorithm is slower on one node by 0.7% to 2.6%. This
is due to the additional vector updates and the extra
operations for calculating $S_{i,m+1}$. The better parallel
properties offset the overhead after 8 or 16 processors
and the new version steadily reduces the time. With
64 nodes the new algorithm is faster by 2.6% to 9%

and execution times show descendent tendencies while the original ones level off. For large cases, the break even point can increase to 16 or 32 processors, but this is only a small percentage of the processors required by these sizes. Figure 3 shows the differences in these execution times for some of the test cases.

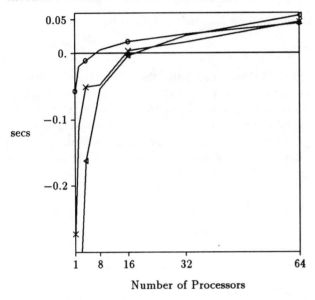

Figure 3: Time differecnce between the restructured and the original algorithm ($T_{orig} - T_{rest}$) for various node configurations and for the sizes: (o): N=10000, (×): N=50000, (◁): N=60000.

Finally, it should be mentioned that since communication consists a $\log nodes$ step, synchronization is the bigger bottleneck for a large number of processors. When more complicated matrix vector multiplies are introduced, the larger load imbalances and delays favor the version with fewer synchronization points. In addition, the restructured version is also favored if smaller dimension topologies (as the mesh) are used.

6   Numerical Behavior

The restructured algorithm makes extensive use of values computed in previous steps to remove the dependencies from the same step. The results of this methodology have generally been regarded as numerically unstable [19]. Numerical instabilities are also observed for the restructured method when run without restarting, i.e., without step 3. However, these instabilities are not severe and the algorithm converges to a low residual threshold (see Figure 4) for the atomic physics test problems appearing on Table 2, [17, 7]. The original method improves the residual about two orders of magnitude. For the same test problems, the accuracy can be improved significantly if the matrix is shifted by the extreme diagonal element corresponding to the extreme required eigenvalue (see Figure 5). When restarting is used (usually every 15-20 iterations), the original and the restructured methods perform in a similar way (Figure 6). A brief explanation of the observed behavior appears below.

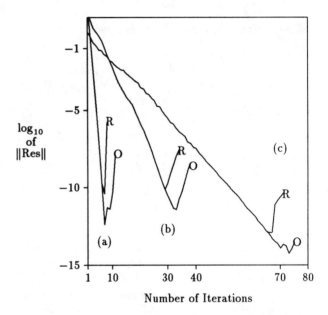

Figure 4: Convergence of the residuals of the restructured (R) and original (O) versions for the three cases in Table 2 with no restarting.

The numerical errors introduced from the use of old entries of S and D for computing the new columns in equations (8) and (11) are first considered. For comparison purposes and without loss of generality it is assumed that g_i and t_i are accurate since they are computed in the current step by simple dot products and matrix vector multiplies. These operations appear in the original Davidson as well. Assume that for every (i, j) S-element, the computed value, $S_{i,j}$, and the theoretically correct value $S_{i,j}^{real}$, satisfy:

$$S_{i,j}^{real} = S_{i,j} + \delta S_{i,j} \tag{12}$$

$$S_{i,j}^{real} = g_i - \sum_{k=1}^{j-1} S_{i,k}^{real} t_k \tag{13}$$

$$S_{i,j} = g_i - \sum_{k=1}^{j-1} S_{i,k} t_k \tag{14}$$

Case	Program	Description	Size	Nonzero
(a)	(MCDF)	Lithium-like Uranium.	410	31087
(b)	(MCDF)	A complete active space calculation with n up to 4 for Beryllium-like Xenon.	2149	335416
(c)	(MCHF)	Li, 2S; by n method; n=6.	862	120735

Table 2: Description of the atomic physics test cases.

Substituting (13) and (14) to (12) yields:

$$\delta S_{i,j} \;=\; -\sum_{k=1}^{j-1} \delta S_{i,k} t_k \qquad (15)$$

$$\Rightarrow \quad |\delta S_{i,j}| \;\leq\; \sum_{k=1}^{j-1} |\delta S_{i,k}||t_k| \qquad (16)$$

Under the initial assumptions a similar formula for the error of the D vectors can be found:

$$\|\delta D_j\| \;\leq\; \sum_{k=1}^{j-1} \|\delta D_k\||t_k| \qquad (17)$$

Formulae (16) and (17) suggest the intuitive result that the errors from previous steps are accumulated to create unstable later steps. If the crude upper bound $|t_k| \leq \|R\| < 1$ is assumed, the error on both S and D is bound by the exponential form $\mathcal{O}(u2^j)$, where u is the error in the first step. Since t_k are the overlaps of the new vector with the old basis vectors, t_k are usually several orders of magnitude less than one in early iterations. Without the preconditioning, t_k would be exactly zero. As the algorithm proceeds, the basis fills up with meaningful vectors. When preconditioning is applied to the new residual, the improvement in the direction causes unavoidable larger overlaps with existing vectors. If the t_k are bounded by some very small number T, $|T| \ll 1$, the error grows like $\mathcal{O}(u(1+T)^j)$. The bound is still exponential but it requires hundreds of steps to become large.

When the basis is truncated after a number of steps, the restarting vectors for D and B as well as the new projection S, are computed from the step 3 in both algorithms. As a result, the errors introduced in the previous iterations in calculating S, C and D are now propagated to the new restarting vectors and matrices. If the restarting takes place before the errors in formulae (16) and (17) become large, the two versions of the algorithm become effectively equivalent and this explains the convergence behavior in Figures 4 and 6. In Figure 6 the test case (a) is not included because it converges before restarting occurs. In some

ill-conditioned problems the restructured algorithm could demonstrate numerical instability. Fortunately, encountering such an instability would also imply a good basis and signify a quite close convergence.

Ideally, to avoid error propagation from restarting, step 3 of both algorithms should be performed explicitly, by the alternative steps:

(3.1) $B \leftarrow BC$

(3.2) reorthonormalize B

(3.3) $D = AB$

(3.4) $S = B^T D$

(3.5) solve $SC = C\Lambda$ for C.

This is an expensive procedure that introduces extra synchronization and additional matrix-vector multiplies. Practically, this procedure should be performed only near convergence or when the monitored error reaches a specified threshold [22].

Shifting the spectrum of the matrix is a widely used technique to improve numerical stability. Applications that benefit from the Davidson algorithm have large diagonal-dominance ratio [1], i.e., very small off-diagonal elements compared with the changes in magnitude between diagonal elements [10, 12, 22]. It is expected that some digits will be lost if arithmetic involves both the large and the small elements. The purpose of shifting is to reduce the norm of A which is an important factor in error bounds. For example, the matrices S and D are not normalized and their norm is bounded by $\|A\|$. Reducing $\|S\|$ and $\|D\|$ can substantially improve the method's numerical stability. The appropriate shift for optimally reducing $\|A\|_2$ is $(Diag_{min} + Diag_{max})/2$. However, this choice is not necessarily beneficial for the Davidson algorithm.

The shift to be chosen is one that brings the required eigenvalue very close to zero. In atomic

---

[1] The term is used to refer to the ratio $d = \min_{i,j} |(A_{ii} - A_{jj})/A_{ij}|$

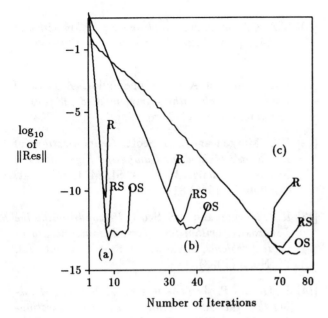

Figure 5: Convergence of the residuals of the restructured (R), the restructured with shift (RS), and the original with shift (OS) versions with no restarting.

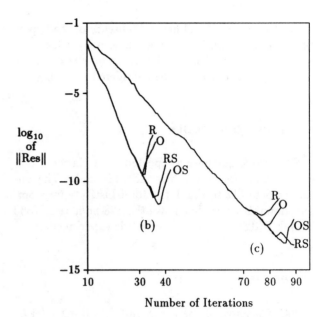

Figure 6: Convergence of the residuals of the restructured (R), the original (O), restructured with shift (RS), and original with shift (OS) with restarting.

physics and quantum chemistry applications the matrices have large diagonal-dominance ratio and therefore the eigenvectors have one dominant component. From the Gershgorin Circles theorem [9] it falls that the required eigenvalue is very close to the diagonal element corresponding to the dominant eigenvector component. This diagonal element is thus a good shift. Such a shift does not reduce $\|A\|$ in general. Since the goal in iterative algorithms is to find one eigenpair rather than the whole eigensystem, it is desirable to make the problem most stable near the solution. Therefore, the magnitude of the required eigenvalue and the eigenvalues close to it should be minimized. This is satisfied by the choice of the corresponding diagonal element as a shift. Figure 5 illustrates the gains of this strategy, by comparing it with the unshifted restructured and the shifted original version. The shifted version is better than the unshifted original method and similar to the shifted original version. The improvements are obvious even for the test case (c), which has the lowest diagonal dominance ratio of the three cases in Table 2.

In most of the current applications, the Davidson method is used with frequent restarting. If shifting is applied in addition, the numerical stability of the restructured algorithm is enchanced and it is proved as reliable as the original method. Results from the two test cases in Figure 6 demonstrate the similarity of the two versions.

7 Conclusions

The Davidson method is a useful tool for finding a few extreme eigenpairs of large symmetric matrices appearing in quantum chemistry and atomic physics. The large diagonal-dominance ratio and the very large size of these matrices advocate the use of the Davidson instead of the Lanczos method and the large sizes necessitate the use of hundreds of processors in todays multicomputers.

The three distinct synchronization points arising from dot products in the original Davidson algorithm are reduced to one by restructuring the algorithm. The new version demonstrates better speedups and faster execution times even on a fairly low number of processors. The experiments show that the benefits are expected to increase with the number of processors.

In some ill-conditioned problems the new version can exhibit numerical instability. However, the nature of the matrices where the Davidson is used, as well as the employment of simple and necessary techniques as restarting and shifting, alleviate the problem. Convergence close to working accuracy is observed for several atomic structure matrices.

The above results are encouraging, and further experiments have to be carried out in multicomputers with more processors and faster interconnects. Candidates include the CM-5 and the Intel Paragon. It is interesting to see if and how the absence of the hypercube topology can be counterbalanced by a fast network. Parallel implementation of the many extensions of the algorithm needs to be considered as well.

Acknowledgements

This work has been supported by a National Science Foundation grant No. ASC-9005687. The authors would like to thank the Joint Institute for Computational Science that make the 128-node iPSC/860 in Oak Ridge available for scientific experiments.

References

[1] G. Cisneros, M. Berrondo and C.F. Bunge, *DVD-SON: A Subroutine to Evaluate Selected Sets of Eigenvalues and Eigenvectors of Large Symmetric Matrices*, Compu. Chem. 10 (1986) 281.

[2] M. Crouzeix, B. Philippe and M. Sadkane, *The Davidson Method*, Tech. Rep., Report TR/PA/90/45, CERFACS, Toulouse, 1990.

[3] E.R. Davidson, *The Iterative Calculation of a Few of the lowest Eigenvalues and Corresponding Eigenvectors of Large Real-Symmetric Matrices*, J. Comput. Phys. 17 (1975) 87.

[4] E.R. Davidson, in: Methods in Computational Molecular Physics, eds. G.H.F. Diercksen and S. Wilson (Reidel, Dordrecht, 1983) p. 95.

[5] E.R. Davidson, *Super-Matrix Methods*, Comput. Phys. Commun. 53 (1989) 49.

[6] T.H. Dunigan, *Performance of the Intel iPSC/860 and NCUBE 6400 Hypercubes*, Report ORNL/TM-11790, Oak Ridge National Laboratory, 1991.

[7] C.F. Fischer, *The MCHF atomic-structure package*, Comput. Phys. Commun. 64 (1991) 369.

[8] C.F. Fischer, The Hartree-Fock Method for Atoms: A Numerical approach, (J. Wiley, New York, 1977).

[9] G.H. Golub and C.F. Van Loan, Matrix Computations, 2nd ed. (Johns Hopkins Univ. Press, Baltimore, 1989).

[10] T.Z. Kalamboukis, *Davidson's algorithm with and without perturbation corrections*, J. Phys. A 13 (1980) 57.

[11] S.K. Kim and A.T. Chronopoulos, *A class of Lanczos-like algorithms implemented on parallel computers*, Parallel Computing 17 (1991) 763.

[12] R.B. Morgan and D.S. Scott, *Generalizations of Davidson's Method for Computing Eigenvalues of Sparse Symmetric Matrices*, SIAM J. Sci. Stat. Comput. 7 (1986) 817.

[13] R.B. Morgan and D.S. Scott, *Preconditioning the Lanczos Algorithm for Sparse Symmetric Eigenvalue Problems*, SIAM J. Sci. Stat. Comput. Vol. 14, No. 3 (1993).

[14] J. Olsen, P. Jørgensen and J. Simons, *Passing the One-Billion Limit in Full Configuration-Interaction (FCI) Calculations*, Chem. Phys. Lett. 169 (1990) 463.

[15] B.N. Parlett, *The Software Scene in the Extraction of Eigenvalues from Sparse Matrices*, SIAM J. Sci. Stat. Comput. 5 (1984) 590.

[16] B.N. Parlett, The Symmetric Eigenvalue Problem (Prentice-Hall, Englewood Cliffs, New Jersey, 1980).

[17] F.A. Parpia, I.P. Grant and C.F. Fischer, *GRASP2*, 1990.

[18] B. Philippe and Y. Saad, in: Proceedings of International Workshop on Parallel Algorithms and Architectures, eds. M. Cosnard at al. (North-Holland, Amsterdam, 1989) p. 33.

[19] Y. Saad, *Krylov Subspace methods on Supercomputers*, SIAM J. Sci. Stat. Comput. 10 (89) 1200.

[20] D.S. Scott, *Implementing Lanczos-like Algorithms on Hypercube Architectures*, Comput. Phys. Commun., 53 (1989) 271.

[21] A. Stathopoulos and C. F. Fischer, *A Hypercube Implementation of Davidson's Algorithm for the Large, Sparse, Symmetric Eigenvalue Problem*, Intel Supercomputer Users' Group, 1991 Annual Users' Conference, (1991) 343.

[22] A. Stathopoulos and C. F. Fischer, *A Davidson program for finding a few selected extreme eigenpairs of a large, sparse, real, symmetric matrix*, Comput. Phys. Commun., submitted.

Issues in Scalable Library Design for Massively Parallel Computers*

Lionel M. Ni, Hong Xu and Edgar T. Kalns

Department of Computer Science
Michigan State University
East Lansing, MI 48824-1027
{ni,xuh,kalns}@cps.msu.edu

Abstract

This paper examines some critical issues raised in the design of libraries for MPCs, such as scalability, portability, recompilation, and flexibility. We advocate a layered structure of library design, comprising a high-level language layer, a machine-independent node layer, a machine-dependent node layer, and an object code layer for different demands and requirements. We discuss the impact of various data decomposition strategies on program performance and the computation and communication analysis techniques employed at different layers. We also propose the concept of the range of scalability as a metric for selecting the most appropriate implementation. A linear system solver based on the Gaussian elimination method is used as an example to illustrate various design alternatives.

1   Introduction

Massively parallel computers (MPCs), characterized by their scalable architectures, are a viable platform on which to solve the so-called grand-challenge problems. These distributed-memory systems are expandable and can achieve a proportional performance increase without changing the basic architecture. In order to take full advantage of scalable hardware, the application software must also be scalable to exploit the increased computing capacity.

The data-parallel or SPMD programming model based on a single name space provides an easier and familiar programming style for users. In order to provide high-level language support for data-parallel programming, several data-parallel Fortran extensions have been proposed, such as Fortran D [1]. In an effort to standardize data parallel Fortran programming, HPF (High Performance Fortran) [2] is being proposed as a standard by the High Performance For-

tran Forum led by Rice University for distributed-memory machines. In this paper, we shall use HPF to illustrate the salient issues in the design of scalable libraries. However, these issues also apply to other parallel languages supporting the SPMD programming model.

In addition to supporting various data decomposition strategies and parallel constructs, a number of intrinsics and libraries are defined in HPF in addition to the rich set of intrinsics and libraries inherited from Fortran 90. Most of these libraries involve various global data movement operations on data arrays, such as replication, reduction, segmented scan, and permutation. Efficient implementation of these operations is crucial to the performance of data parallel programs.

Providing a rich set of libraries is becoming increasingly popular in programming MPCs because libraries offer some unique advantages.

- Providing a library with a uniform interface further enhances the portability of programs among various parallel architectures.

- Although a library provides a uniform interface to programs, the design and implementation of the library can explicitly exploit machine specific features to provide better performance.

- The program development cycle can be shortened as the correctness of libraries can be independently verified and some low-level programming details can be hidden from programmers.

- The existence of libraries can reduce the burden of optimizing compilers.

Several libraries are being developed for MPCs. The ScaLAPACK being developed at University of Tennessee and Oak Ridge National Laboratory attempts to provide a scalable LAPACK package for dense and banded matrix computations [3]. The ComPaSS library being developed at Michigan State University attempts to provide a set of scalable communication

*This work was supported in part by NSF grants CDA-9121641 and MIP-9204066, and DOE grant DE-FG02-93ER25167.

primitives which have been proven optimal for a class of MPC architectures [4].

However, designing libraries for MPCs is quite different from designing traditional libraries. Many issues have arisen from our experience in the design of ComPaSS and other parallel programs. For example, how can libraries handle different data decomposition patterns? should libraries be provided in the form of source code or object code? what is the role of compilers vis-à-vis libraries? should the number of processors be considered in the design of libraries? and should the problem size be considered in the design of libraries? The last two issues also relate to the scalability concern of libraries. This paper attempts to address the above issues.

The paper is organized as follows. Section 2 presents an overview of HPF and a typical structure of the compilation process for HPF. A linear system solver based on Gaussian elimination is presented. This algorithm is used throughout this paper as an example to illustrate various issues in the design of a scalable library. Section 3 gives an overview of the issues involved in scalable library design and discusses the layered library structure and its interaction with the compilation process. Section 4 describes the impact of data decomposition strategies and the evaluation of different decomposition patterns at different layers. Section 5 discusses the concept of range of scalability for algorithms and how this knowledge can be incorporated into the library. Section 6 concludes the paper.

2 HPF and Compilation Process

The data-parallel or SPMD programming model based on a single address space provides an easier and familiar programming style for users. Due to their non-uniform memory access architecture, determining an appropriate data decomposition among different memories is critical to the performance of data-parallel programs. Thus, data parallel languages, such as HPF, provide a mechanism to specify data decomposition patterns, which greatly affect the design of libraries. To understand the role of libraries, we have to understand the compilation process of data parallel programs.

The data decomposition problem involves *data distribution*, which deals with how data arrays should be distributed, and *data alignment*, which deals with how data arrays should be aligned with respect to one another. The goal of data decomposition is to maximize the system performance by balancing the load and by minimizing remote memory accesses (or communication messages). Data distribution and alignment are accomplished by `!HPF$ DISTRIBUTE` and `!HPF$ ALIGN` primitives, respectively. Four regular data distribution patterns: *block, cyclic, block(b),* and *cyclic(c)* are defined in HPF. These distribution patterns are applied to each dimension of a data array. The choice of an efficient data decomposition should consider data reference patterns which dictate the required data movement operations in an HPF program. Thus, an appropriate distribution and alignment for one phase of an algorithm may not be good, in terms of performance, for a subsequent phase. Therefore, HPF supports data realignment and redistribution, `!HPF$_REALIGN` and `!HPF$_REDISTRIBUTE`. There is a performance tradeoff between the higher efficiency of a new decomposition and the communication cost of data redistribution among nodes.

Another salient feature of HPF is the **FORALL** construct which expresses parallel computation. In support of data parallel programming, the construct enables simultaneous assignment to large groups of data elements. For a detailed description of HPF, please refer to [2].

Figure 1 is an example HPF program for solving systems of linear equations, $Ax = b$, using Gaussian elimination and subsequent backward substitution. The basic idea of this algorithm is to reduce the matrix A to upper triangular form and then to use backward substitution to diagonalize the matrix. In our program, A is declared as an $n \times (n + 1)$ array, where the $(n + 1)$st column of A stores the constant vector b. Following the array declarations are a set of compiler directives, including alignment and distribution primitives described earlier. The two **ALIGN** directives (s7-s8) align the solution vector x and the index vector $xindx$ to rows of A. This has the effect of replicating these vectors when rows of A are distributed among processors. The vector *intrm* holds intermediate values computed during backward substitution, which is aligned to the $(n+1)$st column of A. The matrix, along with its aligned data, is distributed *(block, *)*. The **INDEPENDENT** directive asserts the independence of the **FORALL** loop iterations. The call to **MAXLOC**, a reduction operation, is an example of HPF library support. Note that this algorithm will be used for illustration in the design of a scalable library and is by no means the most efficient algorithm.

Typically, MPC vendors provide a compiler to translate the message-passing code of each node to the corresponding object code for the node. One way to compile an HPF program is to generate the underlying message passing code first, such as the Fortran D compiler [5]. Figure 2(a) illustrates a typical compilation process from a high-level language source code, such as F90/HPF, to absolute object code.

The first phase of the compiler performs global analysis including data dependence analysis, data decomposition analysis, partitioning analysis, and communication analysis. Various parallelization and optimization techniques may be used to further exploit the parallelism of the program.

The optimized HPF code is then input to the second compilation phase, the generation of fully portable message passing code. During this phase, machine-independent message-passing source code for each node is generated. The advantage of this phase is that its output is fully portable to any MPC which supports the machine-independent message passing primitives, such as MPI [6]. Various message-level optimization techniques may be applied in this phase.

```
s1:   SUBROUTINE LINSYS(A,x,n)
s2:   REAL INTENT (IN) :: A(:,:)
s3:   REAL INTENT (OUT) :: x(:)
s4:   INTEGER INTENT (IN) :: n
s5:   INTEGER xindx(n)
s6:   REAL intrm(n), temp(n)
s7:   !HPF$ ALIGN x(:) WITH A(*,:)
s8:   !HPF$ ALIGN xindx(:) WITH A(*,:)
s9:   !HPF$ ALIGN intrm(:) WITH A(:,n+1)
s10:  !HPF$ DYNAMIC, DISTRIBUTE A(BLOCK,*)
s11:  FORALL (i = 1:n) xindx(i) = i
s12:  DO i = 1, n
s13:      maxloc = MAXLOC(A(i,i:n))
s14:      maxval = A(i,maxloc)
s15:      temp = A(:,maxloc)
s16:      A(:,maxloc) = A(:,i)
s17:      A(:,i) = temp
s18:      tempx = xindx(maxloc)
s19:      xindx(maxloc) = xindx(i)
s20:      xindx(i) = tempx
s21:      A(i,i:n+1) = A(i,i:n+1) / maxval
s22:  !HPF$ INDEPENDENT (j,k)
s23:      FORALL (j = i+1:n, k = i+1:n+1)
s24:          A(j,k) = A(j,k) - A(j,i) * A(i,k)
s25:  END DO
s26:  !HPF$ REDISTRIBUTE A(CYCLIC, *)
s27:  intrm(n) = 0
s28:  DO i=n, 1, -1
s29:      x(xindx(i))=(A(i,n+1)-intrm(i))/A(i,i)
s30:      FORALL (j = i-1:1:-1)
s31:          intrm(j)=intrm(j)+(A(j,i)*x(xindx(i)))
s32:  END DO
```

Figure 1. A Linear System Solver in HPF code.

The next phase transforms the machine independent message passing code into the underlying machine-specific message-passing code. Several machine-specific features, such as hardware multicast and hardware barrier synchronization, may be used to further optimize the program. Note that depending on the support available in individual MPCs, one of the first two phases may be skipped. In the last phase, the relocatable object code is generated, linked, and loaded creating an executable module.

An important issue in the compilation process is whether the number of processors is known. If the number of processors is known, the compiler can gen-

erate more efficient code, e.g., one based on a more appropriate data decomposition pattern which minimizes remote data references. However, this also implies that the program has to be recompiled for different numbers of processors. Ideally, a good compiler should generate a generic code which can accommodate the number of processors during run-time to follow an efficient execution flow. Note that there are many open research issues involved in the compilation process. However, these issues are not within the scope of this paper. Interested readers may refer to [5] for details.

3 Layered Structure of Library Design

Figure 2(b) shows a layered structure of library design and its interaction with the compilation process. However, we shall first address several desirable features of libraries.

3.1 Desired Library Features

There are a number of features which influence the design of a library. Each is discussed below.

Scalability

Ideally, a library can be used for different number of processors and different problem sizes. Furthermore, as the number of processors increases, it will provide a corresponding increase in performance. However, it is known that for a given problem size, as the number of processors increases, the ratio between computation and communication will decrease. Except for embarrassingly parallel algorithms, the performance of an algorithm will decrease when the number of processors is increased beyond a certain limit. Thus, the range of scalability is a function of problem size and the number of processors.

Given a problem, there may exist several parallel algorithm solutions. For example, in addition to Gaussian elimination, the Gauss-Jordan algorithm can also be used to solve a system of linear equations. Different algorithms may exhibit different degrees of parallelism. For an algorithm, there may exist numerous implementations. For example, data decomposition strategies and various programming tricks, such as message pipelining, may greatly affect the performance. Furthermore, the performance of different implementations may be machine dependent and each implementation possesses a unique range of scalability. In the design of a library for an algorithm, we may have to provide different implementations for different ranges of scalability. Ideally, it is the responsibility of the compiler to select the most appropriate implementation. A more detailed study of the range of scalability will be presented in Section 5.

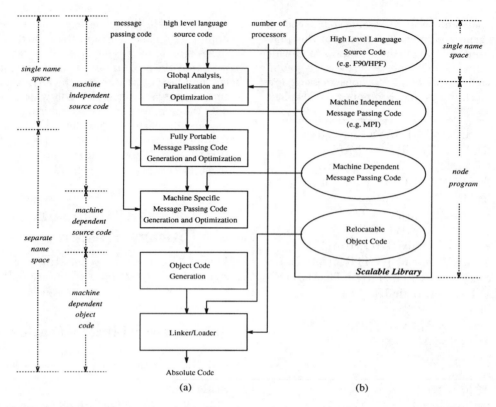

message passing code	high level language source code	number of processors	

Figure 2. The layered structure of scalable libraries and their interaction with the compilation process

Portability

It is desirable that a library can be easily ported to different parallel architecture platforms. However, different parallel architectures may have quite different interconnect topologies and other hardware features. Certainly, the implementation of a library is machine dependent in order to achieve the best performance. The tradeoff between portability and performance should be considered.

Flexibility

A library must provide a flexible, yet consistent interface. The functionality of the library must be complete with respect to the needs of the programmer or compiler. Furthermore, a library should exploit different numbers of processors and offer good performance among varying problem sizes. As indicated in Section 2, a data array has many potential distribution and alignment patterns. It is practically impossible for a library to handle all possible patterns. Thus, the library must determine the most appropriate subset of distributions and alignments for the given task and provide these in the library. This may or may not require data redistribution and realignment. Such decisions must be made on a case by case basis.

Recompilation

Traditionally, a library is provided as a set of executable routines. This protects the vendor since they may not be willing to release the source code, reduces

the cost of the library to the user, saves compilation time, and further reduces the burden of compilers. Since the performance of a scalable library is a function of the problem size and the number of processors, it may be beneficial in terms of performance to allow recompilation of library routines. It is desirable that without recompilation, a library still can achieve its best performance.

There are some other features that are desirable in the design of libraries, such as *robustness* and *maintainability*.

3.2 Layered Structure

Ideally, a library should possess all of the above features. However, some of the features are contradictory. For example, in order to support portability, we may have to sacrifice performance and scalability. Depending on the needs of users, a layered structure of library design shown in Figure 2(b) can meet different demands and requirements. In order to provide the compiler maximal flexibility, the library provides four, mutually exclusive, services. The compiler or programmer must decide which level of service is most appropriate for the given program.

High-Level Language Library

At the highest level, a library is provided in the form of high-level languages, such as F90/HPF code. For example, a programmer's call to a linear system solver would invoke an HPF code implementation as shown in Figure 1. Such high-level language libraries may be locally parallelized and optimized. The code is provided to the compiler prior to the first analysis phase, thus enabling possible global code optimization. This level of service offers the most flexibility in terms of data decomposition. The HPF code is written for a single name space, thus the alignment and distribution declarations are independent of the code which follow them. The library is portable and could be exported using whatever decomposition the programmer decided appropriate offering great flexibility and alleviating redistribution. Conversely, the library may tailor the implementation to a particular decomposition known to offer the best performance. Redistribution may be beneficial in order to use the distribution-specific high-level language code. A library at this layer requires compilation when it is invoked and its performance is highly dependent on the compiler.

Machine-Independent Node Library

The next level of service provides SPMD node programs, built upon machine-independent message-passing code (e.g., MPI). A library at this level is easy to port and is flexible for different number of processors and problem sizes. Since the message-passing code is quite different for different data decompositions, a library usually implements a particular set of data decomposition patterns. However, using performance analysis techniques to be discussed in Section 4, the most appropriate decompositions for each algorithm are determined and implemented. Given the limited set of decompositions offered by a library, data redistribution or realignment may be necessary when the library is invoked. If the performance benefit resulting from redistribution is overshadowed by the cost of redistribution, then the library will recommend using the high-level library service instead.

A machine-independent node library can be locally optimized. Compilation is necessary. However, it is invoked and compiled after the first phase (Fig. 2). The compiler still has the opportunity to perform global message passing code optimization. Thus, this approach potentially provides a better performance than that offered by the high-level language library.

Machine-Dependent Node Library

The third level of service is targeted for specific machine architectures, providing non-portable SPMD node programs. This layer is provided primarily for machines which do not use an accepted message passing interface standard and to exploit machine-specific features. In addition to applying machine-dependent message-passing code optimization, many machine-specific features should be considered to further optimize the performance. These machine-specific features include physical processor topology, network interconnect, processor technology, and memory hierarchy.

Object Code Library

The last layer of service provides relocatable object code and requires no compilation. This layer does not allow any global optimization since the code is passed directly to the linker, and the performance is highly dependent on the flexibility of its internal implementation. However, there is a cost benefit since object code is typically much more inexpensive than providing source.

In summary, the two higher library layers are portable, while the two lower ones can better exploit machine-specific features to provide better performance. From the high-level language, such as F90/HPF, programmer's point of view, the highest layer is provided in the form of intrinsics and the lower three layers are in the form of extrinsics. The actual performance that can be achieved at the top three layers, especially the highest layer, is highly dependent on the capability of the compiler. In the next two sections, we will discuss two critical issues to the design of libraries: the impact of different data decomposition patterns on performance, and the range of scalability of an algorithm.

4 Data Decomposition Issues

As shown in Fig. 1, there are many possible alignments and distributions for A, x, $xindx$, and $intrm$. Data objects should be distributed and aligned in a way so that the interprocessor communication can be minimized and the processor load can be maximally balanced. Automatic data distribution and alignment is an area of current research. This is not within the scope of this paper. It is impractical for a library to support all possible data decomposition patterns; however, a library should support some good data decompositions. This section will address techniques and information available at different layers in order to evaluate and determine appropriate data decomposition strategies.

4.1 High-Level Language Library

At this layer, the compiler should exploit maximum parallelism, for example, converting loops into FORALL constructs when program semantics are unaffected. There are two major criteria in determining a good data decomposition: one is to balance the load of computation among processors and the other is to minimize communication among processors.

The *owner-computes rule* is typically used in the SPMD programming model [2]. This rule suggests that the workload assigned to each processor should be proportional to the number of times that array elements owned by that processor have been written. A good load balancing can be attained when the left-hand-side array elements can be evenly distributed to all processors. However, it is difficult to determine such an optimal array decomposition when the FORALL index space is varied in different iterations of the outermost sequential loop, such as statement s23 in Figure 1. In s23, the index space is a subrectangle, $[i + 1 : n] \times [i + 1 : n + 1]$ for a given i (note that the $(n + 1)$st column of A contains the vector b). Figure 3(a) shows different index spaces with different values of i for the FORALL statement in s23 when the size of array A is 5×6. In Figure 3(a), each circle represents an array element and a shaded circle represents the array element which is written, i.e., $A(j, k)$ in s24.

Based on such a pattern of writable array elements in the index space, it is obvious that a cyclic distribution will achieve a better load balancing than a block distribution as shown in Figures 3(b) and (c) assuming there are two processors p_1 and p_2. When $i = 3$, both p_1 and p_2 are assigned the same amount of workload in the (cyclic,*) distribution, while p_1 is idle in the (block,*) distribution. The performance in terms of computation would be approximately the same with different cyclic distributions, namely, (cyclic,cyclic) and (*,cyclic).

From the communication point of view, a good data decomposition scheme should minimize remote data references or interprocessor communication. At the high-level language layer, an intuitive approach to measure the amount of remote data references is to count the number of remote data elements that a local processor needs to read. Consider the FORALL statement (s23) in Figure 1, which dominates both computation and communication in the program. The vector $A[i, i : n + 1]$ has to be replicated to all other processors at each step of the outermost loop if A is distributed in (cyclic,*) or (block,*). If A is distributed in (*,cyclic) or (*,block), the vector $A[i : n, i]$ has to be replicated to all other processors too. As a result, selecting any of (cyclic,*), (block,*), (*,cyclic) and (*,block) distributions makes no difference in terms of the amount of remote data references for the FORALL statement in s23. For the FORALL statement in s30, both (cyclic,*) and (block,*) offer the least amount of remote data references as x is the only vector that has to be broadcast.

From the above communication analysis, either (cyclic,*) or (block,*) makes no difference. From the computation analysis, either (cyclic,*), (*,cyclic), or (cyclic,cyclic) provides a better load balancing. Thus, (cyclic,*) is selected as the best distribution pattern for the implementation of the linear system solver library at the high-level language layer. However, this analysis is incomplete for the following two reasons.

- The computation and communication analysis may not be accurate without knowing any machine-specific parameters. For example, the amount of remote data references may not accurately reflect the amount of messages generated, and the amount of computation will be skewed by special architectural features, such as pipelining, cache memory, and superscalar design.

- The computation and communication analysis may impose conflicting requirements on the decomposition of various arrays. It is difficult to resolve these conflicts.

Although designing a library using a high-level language limits the ability of determining an appropriate data decomposition strategy, it does provide a high degree of portability and allows a parallelizing compiler to perform global program optimization and data decomposition analysis.

4.2 Machine-Independent Node Library

A common approach to determine data decomposition at this layer is to use a static performance estimator or cost function [7, 8]. The cost considers both computation and communication overhead. Computation cost can be calculated based on the number of integer or floating-point operations involved in a particular implementation. The amount of computation can be further normalized by converting the number of integer operations to the equivalent number of floating-point operations. Suppose each floating-point operation takes t_f execution time. The computation cost equals the product of t_f and the normalized amount of computation.

Consider the FORALL statement (s23) again. Using the cost function model, the difference of computation cost can be calculated between (cyclic,*) and (block,*) distributions. For simplicity, suppose all floating-point operations take the same unit of execution time, t_f. Assume that the number of available processors is p. The total computation cost for the (block,*) distribution is about:

$$2t_f \times \left(\Sigma_{m=\frac{n-p}{p}+1}^{n} \frac{m(m + 1)}{p} + \Sigma_{m=\frac{n-2p}{p}+1}^{\frac{n-p}{p}} \frac{m(m + 1)}{p - 1} \right.$$
$$\left. + \ldots + \Sigma_{m=\frac{n-kp}{p}+1}^{\frac{n-(k-1)p}{p}} \frac{m(m + 1)}{p - k + 1} + \ldots + 2 \right)$$

When A is distributed (cyclic,*), no processor becomes idle until the last $p - 1$ iterations. Therefore, the total computation cost for (cyclic,*) distribution is about: $2t_f \times (\Sigma_{m=1}^{n} \lceil \frac{m}{p} \rceil \times (m + 1))$. Thus, the cost difference between (cyclic,*) and (block,*) is approximately $6t_f \times \frac{n^2}{p}$.

The communication cost is usually estimated based on a set of message passing primitives. To accurately measure the unicast message transmission time, the formula $t_u(\ell) = \alpha + \beta \times \ell$ can be used assuming wormhole routing, where α is the message transmission start-up latency, β is the network latency, and ℓ is the length of the message. The start-up latency α can be further divided into the sending latency α_s, the software overhead involved at the sender, and receiving latency α_r, the software overhead involved at the receiver. Similarly, the broadcast message transmission time can also be formalized as $t_b(\ell) = \gamma + t_u(\ell)$ where γ is the broadcast cost and $t_u(\ell)$ is the unicast latency.

In MPCs, message sending is usually performed in a non-blocking mode, which implies a potential overlap of computation and communication; also known as message pipelining [5]. Figure 3 is used to illustrate the effect of message pipelining in the library implementation of the linear system solver. Figure 3(d) shows the timing diagram in the implementation using the (cyclic,*) distribution. In the case of (cyclic,*), the computation of the current pivot element cannot start until the message carrying the previous pivot element has been received by the local processor. The elapsed time during each of phases $i = 1$, $i = 2$, and $i = 3$ is $\alpha_s + \gamma + \beta \times \ell + \alpha_r$. However, this is not true in the implementation using the (block,*) distribution as shown in Fig. 3(e). In Fig. 3(e), due to the block distribution, the computation of the current pivot element can start right after the non-blocking send of the previous pivot element is done, as long as both the previous and current elements are owned by the same processor. As shown in Figure 3(e), the elapsed time during each phase of $i = 2$ and $i = 3$ is only $\alpha_s + \gamma + \beta \times \ell$, and the receiving latency α_r is overlapped[1]. Overall, for p processors and an $n \times (n+1)$ array, there are approximately $n - \frac{n}{p}$ receiving latencies overlapped in the implementation using (block,*). In other words, the difference in communication cost between these two implementations is approximately $\left(n - \frac{n}{p}\right) \times \alpha_r$.

Based on both computation and communication analysis, the best data distribution of the linear system solver based on Gaussian elimination and backward substitution can be concluded as follows.

- (block,*): when $\left(n - \frac{n}{p}\right) \times \alpha_r \leq 6t_f \times \frac{n^2}{p}$.

- (cyclic,*): when $\left(n - \frac{n}{p}\right) \times \alpha_r > 6t_f \times \frac{n^2}{p}$.

The actual values of parameters α_r and t_f are dependent on the underlying machine architecture. From the view-point of library design, both implementations using (block,*) and (cyclic,*) have to be provided due to different ranges of scalability (to be discussed in Section 5). The MPI-like [6] code for the linear system solver can be found in [9]. A more detailed study to evaluate computation and communication costs of different distribution patterns can be found in [8].

4.3 Machine-Dependent Node Library

Although the computation and communication analysis at the machine-independent node library layer provides a more accurate estimation than that at the

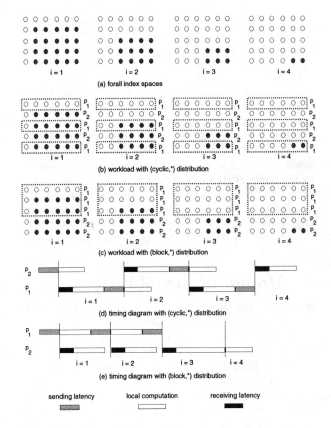

Figure 3. Computation and communication patterns of the linear system solver.

high-level language layer, the cost functions used cannot capture or model many machine-specific characteristics. The traditional computational complexity based on operation counts is no longer valid as the traditional approach does not consider those characteristics, such as multiple instruction issuing and scheduling, instruction pipelining, vector processing, memory hierarchy, and cache capacity. The impact of these machine-specific characteristics on the performance analysis is further amplified as new processor technology, such as superpipelining and superscalar, continues to evolve.

The communication analysis is also complicated by various machine-specific hardware and software implementations. Some MPCs have hardware support for broadcast, such as the nCUBE-2/3 and CM-5, and some MPCs have separate computation and communication processors, such as the Intel Paragon. The start-up latency is critical to the evaluation of message transmission time. Some MPCs can shorten this latency to a few microseconds, such as the nCUBE-3 and MIT J machine, while some other MPCs have latencies measured in the hundreds of microseconds. The underlying switching mechanism, such as wormhole routing and store-and-forward switching, makes a great difference in evaluating the communication cost. This is further complicated by the dynamics

---

[1] Usually, the sending latency α_s is a little bit greater than the receiving latency α_r.

of network load which will introduce additional and unpredictable network latency. Effectively quantifying and then incorporating these factors is a difficult problem and requires further analysis on each specific machine architecture.

The object code library layer is similar to the machine-dependent node library layer. However, it does not allow source level global optimization. In general, it is the responsibility of the library designers to decide, either automatically or manually, the most appropriate data decomposition strategies and to fine-tune their designs to provide the best performance. This is likely to be performed on a case by case basis. It is the responsibility of programmers, ideally compilers, to select among those supported data decomposition patterns the most appropriate implementation.

5 Range of Scalability

It is desirable that a library be scalable, i.e., the library will provide a corresponding performance improvement as the number of processors increases. We use *absolute execution time* to represent the performance metric, which is more meaningful than using *speedup*. As more processors are used, the execution time will decrease. However, due to the decreased ratio between computation and communication, the execution time will increase when more processors are used. We define the *range of scalability* of an implementation of an algorithm as follows.

Definition 1 *For an implementation, β, of an algorithm, α, the range of scalability of a given problem size, C, is represented by $\mathcal{R}_\beta(C) = [P_\ell, P_u]$, where P_ℓ is the minimum number of processors required to run it and P_u is the optimal number of processors to achieve the minimum execution time.*

Due to memory constraints, P_ℓ may not be 1 for a given problem size. Obviously, the range of scalability is between P_ℓ and P_u. For an implementation of an algorithm, the range of scalability is dependent on many machine-specific parameters, such as processor technology, interconnection network topology, switching and routing mechanisms, and memory capacity.

For an algorithm, there are many different implementations. The performance or range of scalability of different implementations may vary depending on many factors, such as data decomposition strategies, programming tricks, and underlying machine specific communication support. Among these factors, the data decomposition strategy has a great impact on the performance as indicated in the previous section. Although a library's interface is machine independent, its performance or range of scalability is machine dependent. Thus, a good library should provide more detailed information concerning the range of scalability for different implementations as a function of problem size and the number of processors for each machine. This information will help the compiler or the programmer to select an appropriate implementation to use.

Consider k different implementations, β_i for $1 \leq i \leq k$, of an algorithm α. We have $\mathcal{R}_{\beta_i}(C_j) = [P_\ell(\beta_i, C_j), P_u(\beta_i, C_j)]$ for $1 \leq i \leq k$ with respect to the problem size C_j.

Definition 2 *Given a problem size C and k implementations, β_i for $1 \leq i \leq k$, of an algorithm, α, where $\mathcal{R}_{\beta_i} = [P_{\ell_i}, P_{u_i}]$, the range of scalability of the algorithm, $\mathcal{R}_\alpha$, in terms of these k implementations is represented as $\mathcal{R}_\alpha(C) = [\cup_{i=1}^k \beta_i(P'_{\ell_i}, P'_{u_i})]$, where the range of processors covered by each implementation is disjoint.*

Given two implementations of an algorithm, depending on the executions times and the range of scalability of each implementation, the range of scalability of the algorithm can be derived by considering all possible cases. Figure 4 shows four typical examples. In Fig. 4(a), Implementation 1 has a narrower range of scalability than Implementation 2. However, Implementation 1 provides better performance when the number of processors is less than 96. The combined range of scalability, or the range of scalability for the algorithm, is shown on top of the figure, which suggests a better choice of implementations for different numbers of processors. In Fig. 4(b), clearly Implementation 1 is superior to Implementation 2 for all range of processors. In Fig. 4(c), when the number of processors is between 64 and 140, the performance is worse than using less than 64 or more than 140 processors. Thus, there is a gap in the range of the scalability of the algorithm. Again, in Fig. 4(d), there is no need to support Implementation 2. For a given problem size and a known number of allocated processors, $\mathcal{R}_\alpha(C)$ suggests an appropriate implementation method. If the required number of processors is not covered by any implementation, then the closest implementation method which requires fewer processors may be used.

Obviously, it is impractical to provide $\mathcal{R}_\alpha(C)$ for different problem sizes. One approach is to obtain $\mathcal{R}_\alpha(C_i)$ for some problems sizes (C_i). For each implementation, β_i, we can estimate its range of problem size as $f_i(\beta_i) = [f_{\ell_i}(P), f_{u_i}(P)]$. Note that $f_i(\beta_i)$ consists of two functions and each of them is a function of the number of processors, P. Based on some measured pairs of P and C, each function can be estimated. Thus, for a given problem size, C, we can use $f_i(\beta_i)$'s to derive $\mathcal{R}_\alpha(C)$. Then the above procedure can be used to select the most appropriate implementation. Note that along the boundary of two different implementations, the difference in terms of execution time is usually small. Thus, it is unnecessary to make a precise selection near the boundary of two implementations.

The above description provides a theoretical basis for deriving the range of scalability of an algorithm.

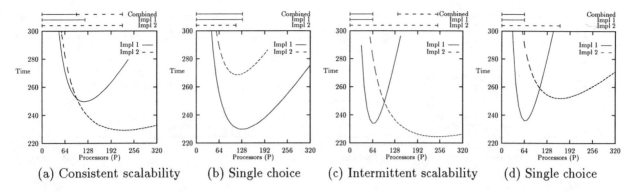

(a) Consistent scalability   (b) Single choice   (c) Intermittent scalability   (d) Single choice

Figure 4. Possible Scalability Ranges

In practice, some modifications have to be made in order to tailor some machine- and algorithm-specific constraints. For example, in hypercube machines, the number of processors allocated is a power of 2. Also, the upper bound P_u may not be obtained if the machine does not have a sufficient number of processors to measure it. In this case, we may use the maximum number of available processors to represent P_u, or we may estimate P_u based on some performance prediction models. It is also possible that the performance improvement is negligible when more processors are added (i.e, the execution time stays along a flat valley). In this case, P_u may be chosen so that the execution time decrease from $P_u + k$ to P_u is less than a small ϵ for a given k. P_ℓ is dependent on the available memory capacity. If a machine supports virtual memory, then P_ℓ is also a function of the disk size. Such scalability information should be provided by library designers, who are supposed to have the best knowledge of the algorithm and the architecture, for each target machine configuration.

Here we shall use the two implementations, (block,*) and (cyclic,*), of the Gaussian elimination algorithm to illustrate its range of scalability. Our experiments are conducted on a 64-node nCUBE-2. Four different problems sizes are considered: $n = 256, 512, 768$ and 1024. Figures 5(a-d) show the measured execution time versus the number of processors with respect to two different implementations.

The range of scalability of the algorithm for four different problem sizes is shown in Fig. 6. Note that the results from our measurements are quite consistent with what we derived in the previous section based on our cost model.

Based on the results from Fig. 6, Fig. 7 shows the range of scalability as a function of the problem size, n, and the number of processors, p. The memory requirement in the implementation of Gaussian elimination is $O(N^2/p)$ per processor. Depending on the number of bytes per data item (in nCUBE2 each floating point datum is 4 bytes), the size of the matrix, and the number of processors, there is an upper bound as to the size of problem that can be solved for a

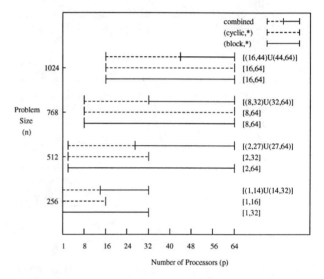

Figure 6. Various ranges of scalability of Gaussian elimination algorithm for different problem sizes measured on a 64-node nCUBE-2.

particular processor configuration. Thus, when the problem size increases, P_ℓ is no longer 1 as shown in Fig. 7. Since the nCUBE-2 we used has only 64 processors, P_u is bounded by 64 when the problem size is large. In this example, the selection between two implementations can be distinguished by a linear function $n = 25.6p - 102.4$, i.e., if $\frac{n+102.4}{25.6} > p$, then the (cyclic,*) distribution should be used. With a good static performance estimator or cost function, the information of the range of scalability can be theoretically generalized to a larger problem size and to a greater number of processors. However, such an analysis must be performed on a case by case basis. More research is needed along this direction.

6   Concluding Remarks

Providing a rich set of libraries to programmers in MPCs is a highly demanded, but non-trivial, task. This paper discussed four major features: scalability,

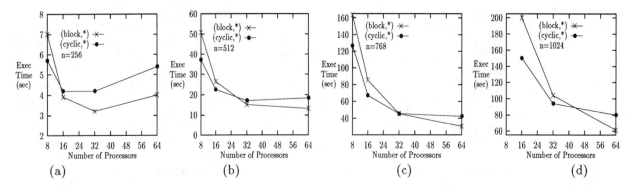

Figure 5. Absolute execution time for implementations (cyclic,*) and (block,*).

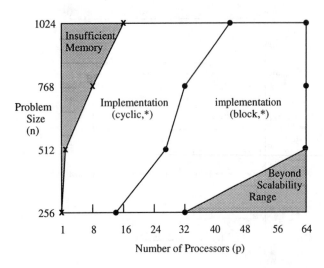

Figure 7. The range of scalability as a function of the problem size and the number of processors.

portability, recompilation, and flexibility, required in the design of scalable libraries. We advocate a layered structure of libraries to meet different demands and requirements from different perspectives. In general, the higher two layers provide more flexibility and the lower two layers provide better performance. However, as compiler technologies mature, the higher layers may also provide better performance.

Both the number of processors and the problem size have a great impact on the library performance. However, a good library design should accommodate these varying factors in a user transparent manner. Both data decomposition strategies and the range of scalability are critical to the performance of a library, which are also affected by the number of processors and the problem size. There are many open issues to be resolved in the design of high performance scalable libraries. Nevertheless, this paper provides our initial thought and experience in the design of scalable libraries for MPCs.

References

1. G. Fox, S. Hiranandani, K. Kennedy, C. Koelbel, U. Kremer, C.-W. Tseng, and M.-Y. Wu, "Fortran D language specification," Tech. Rep. COMP TR90-141, Rice University, Department of Computer Science, Dec. 1990.

2. High Performance Fortran Forum, "High Performance Fortran Language Specification (version 1.0, draft)," Jan. 1993.

3. J. Choi, J. J. Dongarra, R. Pozo, and D. W. Walker, "ScaLAPACK: A scalable linear algebra library for distributed memory concurrent computers," in *Proceedings of the Fourth Symposium on the Frontiers of Massively Parallel Computation (FRONTIERS'92)*, (McLean, Virginia), pp. 120–127, Oct. 1992.

4. P. K. McKinley, H. Xu, E. T. Kalns, and L. M. Ni, "ComPaSS: Efficient communication services for scalable architectures," in *Proceedings of Supercomputing'92*, pp. 478–487, Nov. 1992.

5. S. Hiranandani, K. Kennedy, and C.-W. Tseng, "Compiling Fortran D for MIMD distributed-memory machines," *Communications of the ACM*, vol. 35, pp. 66–80, Aug. 1992.

6. J. J. Dongarra, R. Hempel, A. J. G. Hey, and D. W. Walker, "A Proposal for a User-Level, Message Passing Interface in a Distributed-Memory Environment," Tech. Rep. TM-12231, Oak Ridge National Laboratory, March 1993.

7. J. Li and M. Chen, "Compiling communication-efficient programs for massively parallel machines," *IEEE Transactions on Parallel and Distributed Systems*, vol. 2, pp. 361–376, July 1991.

8. E. Kalns, H. Xu, and L. M. Ni, "Evaluation of data distribution patterns in distributed-memory machines," in *Proceedings of the 1993 International Conference on Parallel Processing*, vol. II, pp. 175–183, Aug. 1993.

9. L. M. Ni, H. Xu, and E. T. Kalns, "Issues in scalable library design for massively parallel computers," Tech. Rep. MSU-CPS-ACS-82, Department of Computer Science, Michigan State University, Mar. 1993.

Session 3:
Evaluation of Real Machines
Chair: David Culler

Communication and Computation Performance of the CM-5

Thomas T. Kwan*   Brian K. Totty†   Daniel A. Reed‡

Department of Computer Science
University of Illinois
Urbana, Illinois 61801

Abstract

The Thinking Machines CM-5 is one of the first of a new generation of massively parallel systems. To assess the scalability of the CM-5's computation and interprocessor communication rates, we used a series of benchmarks to measure the performance of the CM-5 data and control networks, the node vector units, and the balance of computation and communication. At the application level, we found the achievable communication bandwidth and processing rates to be roughly fifty percent and forty percent, respectively, of the corresponding theoretical peak rates. Our early assessment is that the CM-5 is scalable but that a better balance of communication and processing rates would increase its effectiveness.

1 Introduction

The Thinking Machines CM-5 is a member of the new generation of massively parallel systems. Although the CM-5 was announced in 1991, only recently have large CM-5 configurations appeared with vector units, compilers that allow Fortran programs to execute independently on each node, and enhanced libraries that provide active messages [14], virtual channels, and asynchronous interprocessor communication. Hence, there are many open performance questions, and relatively little is known about the interactions of

these features and the achievable processor and communication performance.

Preliminary performance measurements by Bozkus et al [1], Ponnusamy et al [8, 9] and Lin et al [7] exposed the limitations of an early version of the CM-5 communication library. Since then, the library has been re-implemented using active messages as the base layer. The goal of our work is to re-evaluate the CM-5's computation and communication performance and the interaction of the two.

1.1 Overview

The remainder of this paper is organized as follows. In §2, we briefly describe the architecture of the CM-5. The benchmarks used to measure its performance are described in §3, and the results[1] are described in §4. In §5, we discuss the implications of our findings. Finally, in §6, we conclude with a summary of our observations and describe our ongoing benchmarking efforts.

2 Overview of the CM-5 Architecture

The CM-5 is a MIMD, distributed memory system composed of interconnected processing nodes. Each processing node (see Figure 1) contains a 32 MHz SPARC processor, four floating point vector units with an aggregate, peak rate of 128 Mflops, four memory banks controlled by the vector units, and a network interface (NI) chip. Each of the vector units supports an interface to a single memory bank (i.e., the SPARC

*Supported in part by a Research Assistantship from the National Center for Supercomputing Applications.

†Supported in part by an IBM Graduate Fellowship and by the National Science Foundation under grant NSF CDA87-22836.

‡Supported in part by the National Science Foundation under grant NSF CDA87-22836, by the National Aeronautics and Space Administration under Contract NAG-1-613, by the Advanced Research Projects Agency under Contract DABT63-91-C-0004, and by a research agreement with the Intel Supercomputer Systems Division.

[1] Thinking Machines Corporation has requested the display of the following disclaimer: the results presented here are based upon a test version of the system software where the emphasis was on providing functionality and the tools necessary to begin testing the CM-5 with vector units. This software release has not had the benefit of optimization or performance tuning and, consequently, is not necessarily representative of the performance of the full version of the software.

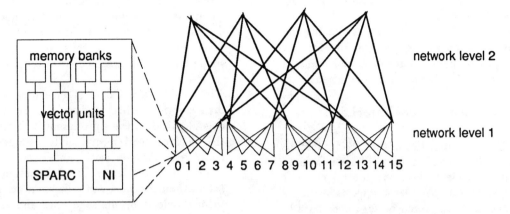

network level 2

network level 1

0 1 2 3 4 5 6 7 8 9 10 11 12 13 14 15

Figure 1: 16 Node CM-5 Partition

processor's access to memory is via the vector units), as well as a set of internal scalar registers, vector registers, arithmetic-logic units, and floating point units [11]. Finally, the node network interface supports all accesses to the interconnection network; see [12] for additional details on the processing node architecture.

The CM-5 interconnection network is actually three separate networks: a data network, a control network, and a diagnostic network. The data network, which is responsible for application data motion, connects the processing nodes in a fat tree topology [6]. Figure 1 illustrates a fat tree for a group of sixteen nodes. As the figure shows, processors in the same group of four communicate with one another via only the first level of the fat tree. Similarly, processors at the second level, the group of sixteen in this case, communicate via the second level network. By increasing the bandwidth of higher level links and providing redundant paths, the design of the fat tree topology avoids many of the bottlenecks inherent in ordinary k-ary trees.

The other two CM-5 networks, which also interconnect all the processors, have binary tree topologies; however, they are dedicated to specific, lower bandwidth tasks. As the name suggests, the diagnostic network supports system diagnostics; it will not be considered here. The control network is responsible for various global operations (e.g., reduction and summation). The control network can be viewed as a combination of three subnetworks: a broadcast subnetwork, which is responsible for broadcast operations, a combining subnetwork, which is responsible for global operations like reduction and summation, and a global subnetwork, which supports interprocessor synchronization. Each subnetwork has its own message queues. See [6, 12] for additional details on the three CM-5 interconnection networks.

3 Benchmark Methodology

All the experiments described below were conducted on the 512 node CM-5 at the National Center for Supercomputing Applications. Each node is equipped with four vector units and 32 Mbytes of memory. The machine is configured with four partitions: two 64 node partitions, one 128 node partition, and one 256 node partition; all the partitions are timeshared. Our measurements used the CM Fortran compiler (Version 2.1 Beta 0.1 Patch 1), the CMMD communication library (Version 3.0.1 Final), C compiler (Version 2.1), and the CMOST operating system (Version 7.2 Beta 2 Patch 2). Unless otherwise noted, all experimental data are shown with 95 percent confidence intervals.

3.1 Virtual Timer Characteristics

The CM-5 provides a *virtual*, rather than a physical clock, with one microsecond resolution. Intuitively, the timer is active only when the application is eligible to execute. To assess the overhead for the virtual timer and to verify that performance measurements were consistent and repeatable, we first investigated the effect of context switching on the CM-5 virtual timer.

We constructed a simple program to record and analyze virtual clock timestamp values. The program contained two, nested loops – the inner null loop spins for a fixed number of iterations, and the outer loop repeats the execution of the inner loop enough times to observe the potential effects of operating system time slices. We found that at 0.5 second intervals, the time slice quantum of the operating system, about 1.5 milliseconds was added to the execution time of the spin loop. Thus, a portion of the context switching overhead is reflected in the timing values returned by the CM-5 virtual timer.

To remove the effects of context switching on the virtual timer, in all subsequent experiments, we scanned the captured performance data and removed all instances of the 1.5 millisecond perturbations.

3.2 Communication Benchmarks

To explore the characteristics of the CM-5 interconnection networks, we identified a set of benchmarks to measure specific aspects of data and control network performance. We then applied least squares linear regression analysis to the captured performance data to determine communication latency and bandwidth.

3.2.1 Data Network Benchmarks

The benchmarks used to measure the performance of the fat tree data network, except those for active messages and virtual channels, were derived from work by Grunwald and Bradley [4, 2] on Intel systems. We ported the benchmarks to the CM-5 by replacing the Intel message passing calls with equivalent CMMD calls.

Unlike on the Intel iPSC/860 or Paragon XP/S, the CM-5 data network is hierarchical. Hence, measuring the effects of spatial and temporal communication locality necessarily involves considering message transmissions across network levels. In the communication benchmarks, we selected message source and destination nodes such that communication between them would require the use of links at a particular network level. The individual benchmarks are described briefly below.

1. *Simple Send* This test measures the message transmission latency and bandwidth between a pair of nodes. Messages of various sizes were sent from the source node to the destination node, and the transmission time was recorded. In this test, we used blocking send and receive calls.

2. *Send-Reply* This test is identical to the simple send test except the destination node returns the message to the source node. In this test, we recorded the round trip transmission time. After performing a least-squares fit, we normalized the results, allowing us to compare them directly with those of the simple send benchmark. This comparison assesses potential link simultaneity (i.e., bi-directional transmission) and software overlapping of message preparation and receipt.

3. *Exchange* This test measures the speed of exchanging data values between two nodes. This test is identical to the send-reply test except separate send and receive calls were replaced by a single CMMD_send_and_receive call [13].

4. *Virtual Channel* This test measures the performance of the CMMD read and write channel calls; it is identical to the simple send test except that the blocking send/receive calls were replaced by read/write channel calls. Intuitively, a channel is a connection-oriented communication protocol, rather than the more common connectionless protocol provided by message send and receive. In our measurements, we excluded the overhead for channel open and close, but included the overhead for polling the channel status for each message transmission.

5. *Active Request* This test measures the latency to send a request active message. This primitive uses the "left" data network interface to transmit data. Note that an active message is a single network packet that triggers a function call at the receiving node.

6. *Active Reply* This test measures the latency to send a reply active message. This primitive uses the "right" data network interface for data transmission.

7. *Active Serial Copy* This test measures the performance of the active message primitive used for serial array transfer. Arrays of various sizes were transferred from the serial memory of the source node to that of the destination node, and the transmission time was recorded.

8. *Spatial Locality* This test measures the performance of link simultaneity and the importance of locality. In this experiment, each node in a set of sixteen nodes sent fifty fixed length messages to destinations randomly selected from the set of sixteen. Message sends were asynchronous and all receives were blocking. For various message sizes, we measured the time needed for all nodes to complete their message transmission and receipt.

3.2.2 Control Network Benchmarks

Because the CM-5 control network can be viewed as three subnetworks (broadcast, combine, and global), we measured the performance of each subnetwork separately with benchmarks tailored to the specific features of each subnetwork function.

1. *Native Broadcast* This test measures the performance of the broadcast subnetwork using the CMMD broadcast intrinsics. One node broadcasts a message to all other nodes within the partition. We measured the performance of the broadcast operation as a function of message size.

2. *Reduction* This test measures the performance of the combining subnetwork by gathering a data value from each node, applying some global operation on all the values (e.g., summation or maximum), and returning the result to all the nodes. For this test, we measured the time to find the minimum and maximum value of a set of integers, single precision floating point values, and double precision floating point values.

3. *Synchronization* Finally, this test measured the performance of the global subnetwork. In this test, we measured the delay to synchronize all the nodes in a partition.

3.3 Processor Benchmarks

To evaluate the performance of the CM-5 vector units, we measured the execution time of several common arithmetic operations when expressed in data parallel CM Fortran. Specifically, the benchmarks included the following:

- single precision vector add ($Z = X + Y$),

- double precision vector add ($Z = X + Y$),

- SAXPY (single precision $Z = aX + Y$),

- DAXPY (double precision $Z = aX + Y$), and

- DOTPRODUCT (a CM Fortran intrinsic).

Each benchmark was tested in two configurations, involving both single and multiple node execution. In the first configuration, the benchmark executed on a single node, and the vectors were distributed only among the four vector units on that node. In the second case, the vectors were distributed across all the 256 vector units in a 64 node partition. Together, these two configurations capture the base hardware performance of the vector units and the potential performance of the entire system, involving the CM-5 vector units and the networks.

3.4 Computation and Communication

Although the dot product involves both computation and communication, it provides only a limited test of processor and communication network interactions. To assess the balance of the CM-5, we measured the execution time of a two-dimensional, first-order Laplace solver with varying mesh sizes on a single node, on 64 nodes, and on 256 nodes. The code was written in CM Fortran and used CSHIFTs to access and iteratively compute the average of four neighboring values. No convergence checking occurred; the code executes for a fixed number of iterations.

Although there are many potential definitions of system balance, and balance varies across applications (i.e., a system may be balanced for one application and imbalanced for another), the common definition is that a system is balanced if it is neither computation nor communication limited [5, 3]. By measuring the execution time of the Laplace solver t_{total}, and the time needed for the computation alone, t_{comp}, we obtain the balance factor $b = t_{comm}/t_{comp}$, where $t_{comm} = t_{total} - t_{comp}$. A system is not communication limited if $b < 1$. Thus, the balance factor captures the effects of both communication and computation.

4 Benchmark Results

Below, we present a detailed analysis of the performance data obtained using the benchmarks described in §3. At the application level, we found the achievable communication bandwidth and processing rates to be roughly fifty percent and forty percent, respectively, of the corresponding theoretical peak rates. Our early assessment is that the CM-5 is scalable but that a better balance of communication and processing rates would increase its effectiveness.

4.1 Communication Benchmarks

In general, the communication benchmarks show that the data network has a latency of 2–70 microseconds and a bandwidth of 8–10 Mbytes/second; the control network has a latency of 5–19 microseconds, but has a bandwidth much lower than that of the data network. The communication protocol, message size, and locality are all important in determining the message transmission time. Below, we present the results from the data and control networks, respectively.

Machine		Simple Send	Send-Reply	Exchange	Virtual Channel	Active Request	Active Reply	Serial Copy
Partition Size	Network Level	Latency	Normalized Latency	Normalized Latency	Latency	Latency	Latency	Latency
64	1	57.68	66.62	38.93	32.53	2.03	1.90	7.21
64	2	58.02	67.98	41.50	33.63	2.04	1.88	5.90
64	3	59.64	68.23	43.31	33.81	2.04	1.85	3.86
128	1	63.98	70.77	44.38	32.83	2.01	1.90	7.21
128	2	57.88	71.46	45.57	33.89	2.02	1.89	5.90
128	3	61.91	72.98	45.97	34.85	2.03	1.82	3.90
128	4	60.19	74.65	45.73	36.13	2.02	1.74	1.27
256	1	57.12	66.48	40.34	32.75	2.04	1.90	7.15
256	2	60.75	67.93	42.09	33.24	2.03	1.89	5.91
256	3	60.84	69.75	43.42	34.73	2.04	1.81	3.92
256	4	62.20	71.95	43.32	35.23	2.03	1.74	1.31

Table 1: Data Network Latencies (Times in Microseconds)

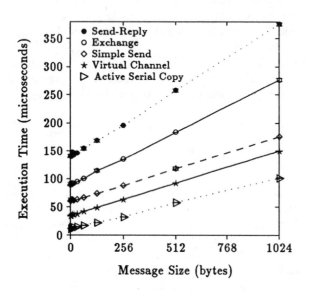

Figure 2: Data Network Benchmarks (256 Nodes)

4.1.1 Data Network Benchmarks

Table 1 shows the latencies for the simple send, send-reply, exchange, virtual channel, and active message benchmarks; Table 2 shows the bandwidths.[2]

The simple send and virtual channel benchmarks show that there is little difference in the achievable bandwidth with the two approaches to message transmission; the bandwidth for the virtual channel benchmark is marginally higher because there is less overhead for identifying the message destination. However, the connection-oriented, virtual channels have substantially lower latency, favoring their use if, as is most common, there is repeated communication between a pair of nodes.

Table 1 shows that the normalized latency for the exchange benchmark is smaller than that of simple send and send-reply. This can be attributed to savings from software overlapping of message preparation and receipt. Table 1 also shows that the latencies for active messages are lower than those for virtual channels. Because active messages are never buffered on arrival [13], the overhead required to do buffering can be eliminated. The average latency for the active message request and reply primitives are comparable to the latencies observed in the Berkeley implementation of active messages [14].[3]

Table 2 contains one seeming anomaly: the normalized bandwidth for the exchange benchmark is higher than for all other cases. Here, the normalized bandwidth reflects the use of two communication links, one in each direction, rather than just one link, as is the case for the other benchmarks.

Tables 1 and 2 also show that message transmission latencies and bandwidths are independent of the partition size and vary only slightly with the number of network levels crossed. Reflecting modern communication transport mechanisms, the "time of flight"

[2]Recall that the normalized latencies and bandwidths for the send-reply and exchange benchmarks have been obtained by dividing the raw latencies by two and multiplying the raw bandwidths by two, reflecting the cost of two message transmissions. This permits direct comparison with the simple send benchmark.

[3]The Berkeley CMAM and the CMMD active message layer are independent implementations.

Machine		Simple Send	Send-Reply	Exchange	Virtual Channel	Serial Copy
Partition Size	Network Level	Bandwidth	Normalized Bandwidth	Normalized Bandwidth	Bandwidth	Bandwidth
64	1	8.256	8.169	10.29	8.382	8.434
64	2	8.230	8.187	10.40	8.405	8.437
64	3	8.197	8.146	10.39	8.396	8.447
128	1	8.278	8.139	10.28	8.380	8.433
128	2	8.277	8.168	10.39	8.384	8.437
128	3	8.262	8.164	10.40	8.389	8.445
128	4	8.273	8.174	10.40	8.388	8.481
256	1	8.257	8.128	10.25	8.378	8.434
256	2	8.274	8.169	10.35	8.398	8.438
256	3	8.275	8.173	10.39	8.399	8.448
256	4	8.258	8.150	10.39	8.397	8.483

Table 2: Data Network Bandwidths (Rates in Megabytes/second)

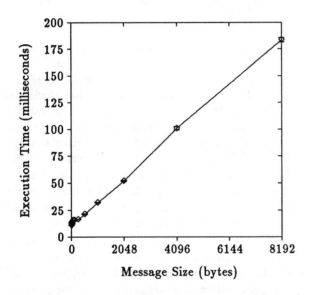

Figure 3: Spatial Communication Locality

Partition Size	Native Broadcast	
	Latency (microseconds)	Bandwidth (KBytes/second)
64	2.01	803.1
128	1.75	803.1
256	1.93	799.9

Table 3: Broadcast Network Benchmarks

Partition Size	Reduction					
	int		float		double	
	Min	Max	Min	Max	Min	Max
64	5.4	6.0	18.2	15.0	18.3	14.2
128	5.5	6.0	18.1	15.2	17.1	14.2
256	5.5	6.1	18.5	15.2	17.4	14.2

Table 4: Combining Network (microseconds)

delay for message transmission is, in an otherwise quiescent network, essentially independent of the distance between the sender and receiver. Given these small differences, Figure 2 shows detailed data for only one case, a 256 node partition using links at network level four; other cases are similar.

Figure 3 shows the result of the spatial locality benchmark when sixteen nodes each send fifty, fixed size messages to randomly selected destinations. From the data in Figure 3, about 101 milliseconds are required to send and receive fifty, 4096 byte messages. Therefore, the average time to transmit a 4096 byte

message is $\frac{101 \times 10^3}{50} = 2020$ microseconds. However, measured data for the normalized send-reply benchmark show that only 562 microseconds should be required to transmit a 4096 byte message. Network contention increases the mean message transmission time by a factor of 3.5. Simply put, message transmission locality remains important. Greater locality decreases the mean distance of message transmission, lessening network contention.

4.1.2 Control Network Benchmarks

Table 3 shows the latencies and bandwidths for the

Partition Size	Global Synchronization
64	5.0
128	5.0
256	5.1

Table 5: Global Network (microseconds)

Operation	One Node		64 Nodes
	$n_{1/2}$ (vector length)	r_∞ (MFlops)	Peak Rate (GFlops)
Vector addition (single precision)	34	9.19	0.58
Vector addition (double precision)	45	13.61	0.89
SAXPY	45	17.25	1.10
DAXPY	77	25.21	1.64
DOTPRODUCT	337	20.30	1.27

Table 6: Simple Processor Benchmarks

native broadcast benchmark. Comparing Table 3 with Table 2 reveals that, not surprisingly, the bandwidth of the data network is much higher than that of the broadcast subnetwork. This is not a debilitating limitation; the broadcast subnetwork is special purpose, is used much less frequently, and typically transmits only small amounts of data (e.g., scalars).

Tables 4 and 5 contain the results for the reduction and synchronization experiments respectively; execution times for these operations vary little with changing partition size. Interestingly, the latency for global synchronization is less than that for reduction. Reduction requires more data (i.e., a 32 or 64 bit quantity) and an arithmetic operation on each data pair. In contrast, a single bit suffices for global synchronization.

4.2 Processor Benchmarks

Generally, for our set of processor benchmarks, the asymptotic processing rate is under twenty percent of the theoretical peak rate. There is also a noticeable difference between single and double precision processing rates. Below, we present the results of each individual benchmark.

Figure 4 shows the result of the simplest possible vector performance measurement, a double precision vector addition on one node. The staircase pattern is an artifact of stripmining. Recall that on the CM-5

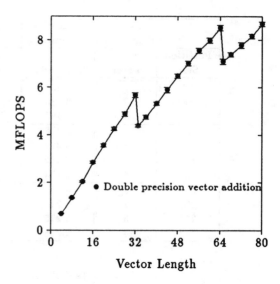

Figure 4: Vector Addition (One Node)

there are four vector units per node. Each vector unit has reconfigurable vector registers (e.g., one can increase the number of vector registers while decreasing their lengths). Currently, the registers are configured to contain eight, 64-bit words. Hence, the effective vector register length per node is $4 \times 8 = 32$ words. Thus, local minima occur when the vector size is a multiple of the node's effective vector register length.

Figure 5 shows the performance of the remaining processor benchmarks. Table 6 summarizes the asymptotic processing rate r_∞ and the vector length $n_{1/2}$ needed to achieve one half of r_∞.

Note that although DAXPY and SAXPY have the same number of arithmetic operations, DAXPY is substantially faster than SAXPY. Similarly, double precision vector add and single precision vector add have the same number of operations but the former is faster than the latter. In both cases, the reasons are the same. The datapath from the CM-5 vector units to the memory modules is 64 bits wide. Smaller, single precision 32-bit memory stores require a load-modify-store operation to write a half word. Hence, extra processor and memory cycles are needed to process single precision data.

Although they both have the same number of arithmetic operations, the performance of DOTPRODUCT falls short of that for DAXPY. For the DOTPRODUCT, the CM Fortran compiler must also generate the code needed to compute the global sum; this requires use of the combine subnetwork. As the vector length increases, the amount of computation per node

Partition Size	Maximum Mesh Size	Processing Rate		Execution Time		Balance Factor
		Computation Only (Mflops)	Computation & Communication (Mflops)	Computation Only (milliseconds)	Computation & Communication (milliseconds)	
1	512 x 512	49	17	95.57	285.1	1.98
64	4096 x 4096	3162	1013	95.52	298.3	2.12
256	8192 x 8192	12652	4064	95.48	297.2	2.11

Table 7: Laplace Code Times and Balance Factors

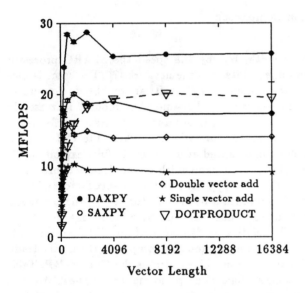

Figure 5: Processor Performance (One Node)

Mesh Size	t_{comp}	t_{total}	Balance Factor
64 x 64	0.08	1.2	14.38
128 x 128	0.09	1.3	13.96
256 x 256	0.15	1.7	10.14
512 x 512	0.42	2.8	5.63
1024 x 1024	1.53	7.2	3.71
2048 x 2048	5.93	22.8	2.85
4096 x 4096	23.71	79.1	2.34
8192 x 8192	95.48	297.2	2.11

Table 8: 256 Node Laplace Code (milliseconds)

increases faster than the cost of global summation, and the computation rate for the DOTPRODUCT approaches that for SAXPY.

4.3 Computation and Communication

Table 7 summarizes the performance of one, 64, and 256 nodes on the Laplace benchmark described in §3.4.[4] Figure 6 and Table 8 show detailed data for a 256 node partition; the other cases are similar. Recall that this code iteratively solves the Laplace equation using CSHIFTs to access four neighboring values in a grid; because this was a test, convergence checking was omitted. Hence, the only communication among vector units and nodes is due to CSHIFTs.

As Table 7 shows, the peak processing rates for one, 64, and 256 nodes are roughly 17 Mflops, 1 Gflops, and 4 Gflops, respectively. The corresponding raw floating point rates, excluding all communication, were 49 Mflops, 3 Gflops, and 13 Gflops, about forty percent of their peak values.

Table 8 show that even for extremely large grid sizes, the CM-5 remains communication limited for this algorithm — the balance factor is only near two even when each node contains 256K grid points. Note that the data is laid out in memory with node zero containing the subgrid [1:256,1:1024], node one containing the subgrid [1:256,1025:2048], and so on. Thus, communication is optimized along the Y-dimension but costly along the X-dimension. Hence, even on a single node, there is enormous overhead for accessing all the neighboring elements in the 5-point stencil.

5 Machine Comparisons

It is instructive to compare the performance of the CM-5 to other previous and current generation parallel systems. Table 9 summarizes the normalized elapsed time and throughput for the send-reply benchmarks for the CM-5 and three generations of Intel's distributed memory parallel systems.[5]

---

[4]Communication for the single node case is defined as data movement between vector units on a single node.

[5]Like the CM-5, the message passing software for the Intel Paragon XP/S is still an early release, and the numbers are

Message Size (bytes)	Send-Reply (Normalized)							
	Elapsed Time (microseconds)				Throughput (Mbytes/second)			
	CM-5	Paragon XP/S	iPSC/860	iPSC/2	CM-5	Paragon XP/S	iPSC/860	iPSC/2
0	65	147	69	278	0	0	0	0
32	69	148	86	352	0.46	0.22	0.37	0.09
128	80	188	219	662	1.60	0.68	0.58	0.19
1024	184	194	572	991	5.57	5.28	1.79	1.03
8192	1038	500	3159	3565	7.89	16.38	2.59	2.30
32768	3891	1696	11939	12386	8.42	19.32	2.74	2.64

Table 9: Communication Comparison

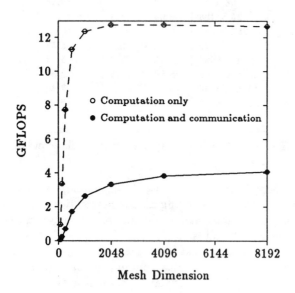

Figure 6: 2-D Laplace Solver (256 Nodes)

As shown in Table 9, the elapsed time of the CM-5 compares favorably with that of the previous generations of Intel systems. However, for large messages, the Paragon XP/S is superior due to its higher bandwidth. Observe that the effective throughput of the data network is only a factor of three greater than that for the iPSC/2 and is less than half of the theoretical, 20 Mbytes/second peak for the first level of the fat tree. In contrast, the observed 19.3 Mbytes/second Paragon XP/S bandwidth is far from the 200 Mbytes/second theoretical peak. On the CM-5, the effective data rate is limited not by the link

bandwidth, but by the speed the SPARC processor can inject data into the network [7]. The same is true for the Paragon XP/S; software overheads dominate.

In contrast to the somewhat modest increases in communication performance, processor performance has improved dramatically. Thus, the CM-5 might well be imbalanced even if it could fully exploit the 20 Mbytes/second bandwidth of the data network. This hypothesis is supported by the balance factors of Table 8. To approach a balance factor of one, the communication costs must decrease by a factor of two.

The relative performance of the CM-5 vector units can best be understood by comparing them with traditional vector machines such as the Cray Y-MP. Table 10 shows single node performance for the CM-5 and single processor performance for the Cray Y-MP on three common arithmetic benchmarks.[6] As Table 6 illustrates, the aggregate performance for the CM-5 is high. However, as Table 10 shows, $n_{1/2}$ for the CM-5 generally remains higher than that for the Cray Y-MP.

In summary, the CM-5 offers substantially higher performance than the earlier generation of distributed memory parallel systems, but based on our experiments, may be communication limited for some classes of applications.

6 Conclusion

Based on a communication and processor benchmark study of the CM-5, we observed that communication latency can be reduced by using active messages and connection oriented virtual channels rather than the connectionless send/receive model. However, optimizing communication remains important on the CM-5; the data network communication bandwidth is modest and must be used carefully. We believe the

---

subject to change. The performance data reported here were captured on a 32 node Paragon XP/S system with R11 node boards running OSF/1 R1.0C with compiler icc Release 4.1.2.

[6]The data for the Cray Y-MP are from [5].

Benchmark	$n_{1/2}$ (Vector Length)		r_∞ (MFLOPS)	
	Cray Y-MP	CM-5	Cray Y-MP	CM-5
Vector add (double precision)	35	45	135	13.61
DAXPY	20	77	216	25.21
DOTPRODUCT	490	337	271	20.30

Table 10: Vector Computation Comparison

CM-5 can be scaled to somewhat larger numbers of nodes, but further improvements are needed to bring the system closer into balance.

At present, we are instrumenting CM-5 application codes, using the Pablo instrumentation library [10], to capture application dynamics, message passing, and input/output patterns. This data will provide the basis for a comparison of applications and an analysis of hardware/software interactions.

References

[1] BOZKUS, Z., RANKA, S., AND FOX, G. Benchmarking the CM-5 Multicomputer. In *Proceedings of 4th Symposium on the Frontiers of Massively Parallel Computation* (Oct 1992), pp. 100–107.

[2] BRADLEY, D. K. First and Second Generation Hypercube Performance. Master's thesis, University of Illinois at Urbana–Champaign, Department of Computer Science, Sept 1988.

[3] FOX, G., JOHNSON, M., LYZENGA, G., OTTO, S., SALMON, J., AND WALKER, D. *Solving Problems on Concurrent Processors*, vol. I. Prentice-Hall, Englewood Cliffs, N.J., 1989.

[4] GRUNWALD, D. C., AND REED, D. A. Benchmarking Hypercube Hardware and Software. In *Hypercube Multiprocessors* (1987), M. T. Heath, Ed., Society for Industrial and Applied Mathematics, pp. 169–177.

[5] HELIN, J. Performance Analysis of the CM-2, a Massively Parallel SIMD Computer. In *Proceedings of the International Conference on Supercomputing* (July 1992).

[6] LEISERSON, C. E., ET AL. The Network Architecture of the Connection Machine CM-5. In *Proceedings of Parallel Algorithms and Architectures Symposium* (May 1992), pp. 272–285.

[7] LIN, M. J., TSANG, R., DU, D. H. C., KLIETZ, A. E., AND SAROFF, S. Performance Evaluation of the CM-5 Interconnection Network. In *Proceedings of Spring COMPCON 93* (Feb 1993).

[8] PONNUSAMY, R., CHOUDHARY, A., AND FOX, G. Communication Overhead on CM5: An Experimental Performance Evaluation. In *Proceedings of 4th Symposium on the Frontiers of Massively Parallel Computation* (Oct 1992), pp. 108–115.

[9] PONNUSAMY, R., THAKUR, R., CHOUDHARY, A., AND FOX, G. Scheduling Regular and Irregular Communication Patterns on the CM-5. In *Proceedings of Supercomputing '92* (Nov 1992), pp. 394–402.

[10] REED, D. A., OLSON, R. D., AYDT, R. A., MADHYASTHA, T. M., BIRKETT, T., JENSEN, D. W., NAZIEF, B. A. A., AND TOTTY, B. K. Scalable Performance Environments for Parallel Systems. In *Proceedings of the Sixth Distributed Memory Computing Conference* (Apr 1991), pp. 562–569.

[11] THINKING MACHINES CORPORATION. CM-5: Programming the Connection Machine System, Dec 1992.

[12] THINKING MACHINES CORPORATION. Connection Machine CM-5 Technical Summary, Nov 1992. Revised Edition.

[13] THINKING MACHINES CORPORATION. CMMD Reference Manual Version 3.0, May 1993.

[14] VON EICKEN, T., CULLER, D., GOLDSTEIN, S., AND SCHAUSER, K. Active Messages: a Mechanism for Integrated Communication and Computation. In *Proceedings of the 19th International Symposium on Computer Architecture* (May 1992), pp. 256–266.

Micro Benchmark Analysis of the KSR1[§]

Rafael H. Saavedra

Computer Science Department
University of Southern California
Los Angeles, California 90089-0781
saavedra@pollux.usc.edu

R. Stockton Gaines and Michael J. Carlton

USC/Information Sciences Institute
4676 Admiralty Way
Marina del Rey, CA 90292
{gaines,carlton}@isi.edu

ABSTRACT

A new approach, micro benchmarks, has recently been developed. Using this technique, we have analyzed the KSR1, and in particular the "ALLCACHE" memory architecture and ring interconnection. We have been able to elucidate many facets of memory performance. The technique has enabled us to identify and characterize parts of the memory design not described by Kendall Square Research. Our results show that a miss in the local cache can incur a penalty ranging from 7.5 microseconds to 500 microseconds (when a dirty "page" in the local cache must be evicted). The programmer must be very careful in placement and accessing of data to obtain maximum performance from the KSR1; the data presented here will help in understanding the performance actually obtained.

1. Introduction

The KSR1 from Kendall Square Research is a novel new parallel computer. It is the first commercial machine embodying a scalable all cache form of shared memory architecture. In addition, there are a number of other interesting features of the machine.

We report our observations of the KSR1, obtained by means of a suite of small benchmarks that expose the details of the machine characteristics. We refer to these small benchmarks as micro benchmarks. In section 2 we briefly describe the micro benchmark approach, and its application to parallel machines. The micro benchmark suite has been developed and used to analyze the performance of uniprocessor machines [11, 12]. We describe the architecture of the KSR1 as we understand it in section 3. We have run our standard micro benchmark suite for processor performance, and included the results together with comparative results from two other CPUs of interest. The main focus of our work has been to understand and measure the performance of the KSR1's novel "ALLCACHE" memory, which we have extensively analyzed with a new set of micro benchmarks. This work and the results are described in section 5. Section 6 analyses a set of experiments used to measure the effect of contention in the interconnection network.

2. The Micro Benchmark Approach

Recently, one of us (Saavedra) has explored a new approach to benchmark analysis of computers. This approach has been documented in several papers [11, 12, 13]. The approach was

§ This research was supported by the Advanced Research Projects Agency under Rome Laboratories Contract F30602-91-C-0146.

developed in reaction to the use of large applications as benchmarks. Though it is hoped that large applications will be more representative of real workloads than synthetic benchmarks or small kernels, it is not clear what features of a particular system they exercise, or what actually accounts for the differences in the performance of these benchmarks on different machines.

The micro benchmark approach returns to the idea of measuring specific features of the machine. But in contrast to measuring only a few parameters, such as floating point multiply, the approach consists of (1) measuring every observable feature of the machine, and (2) making use of the collected set of data in an integrated way. For uniprocessors, one of the most powerful ways of using the micro benchmarks is to predict the performance of a program on a new computer without first porting the program and measuring the results. This is done by analyzing the program to determine how much use is made of each of the machine features measured by the micro benchmarks, and then using the results of the execution of only the micro benchmark suite on the new computer to predict the running time of the program. Using the approach, it has proven possible to estimate accurately the performance of a wide range of programs, including standard benchmark suites such as Spec and Perfect [15, 3]. Further, the analysis of these programs in terms of the features measured by the micro benchmark suite gives insight into the reasons for the observed performance differences for the programs on different computers.

An important factor in machine performance is cache, memory, and network interconnect behavior. A test has been developed that reveals a great deal about the memory hierarchy behavior (including the network), and a way of displaying the data from this test using a set of diagrams that we have named *Physical and Performance Profiles* (or P^3 diagrams) has been developed. We will explain this test, and the main characteristics of the P^3 diagrams, below. The data thus obtained, together with information about the rate of misses in a program, is factored into the other micro benchmark results as part of the prediction methodology.

This paper reports results of the micro benchmark analysis of the KSR1. The machine contains many features (described below) not found in other machines. To understand the performance implications of these features, it has been necessary to develop additional micro benchmarks beyond the initial, general purpose suite. These are described later.

An open and interesting question is the analysis of parallel programs, and the prediction of their performance through the use of micro benchmarks. This involves developing new tests for synchronization, access to shared variables, and probably features provided in run time libraries for parallel machines.

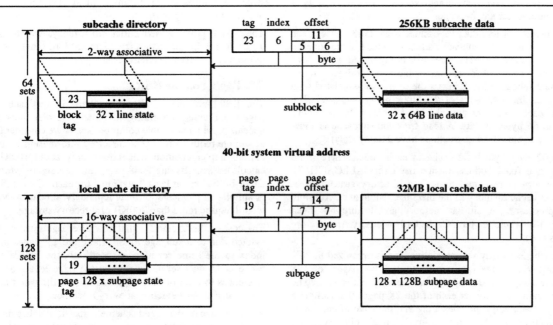

Figure 1: KSR1 cache and subcache organization.

However, it is not clear at this point which factors are relevant to take into account in building a reasonable model of program execution which can produce predictions about the execution time of parallel programs. Furthermore, we believe that a substantial experimental understanding about the performance regimes exhibited by shared memory machines is required before any such model can be developed. We will report separately our results for message passing machines, and for other shared memory machines such as the Stanford DASH [8], for which we have also developed new micro benchmarks.

As will be seen below, our approach reveals a great deal of interesting information about the KSR1. There is much more work to be done, however, to extend the approach into the area of prediction.

3. Architecture of the KSR1.

The KSR1 is a new architecture for parallel machines, and one that attempts to solve the problem of scalability in shared memory multicomputers. The problem is that as the number of processors increases, the average cost of access to memory goes up. One approach has been to design faster memory interconnects, together with highly interleaved memory. This approach appears to be limited to at most a few hundred processors.

An alternate approach, explored by both Kendall Square and the Stanford DASH project, is to use a directory-based caching scheme with a relatively large amount of memory close to each individual processor. Both of these machines use a "message-passing" interconnect mechanism rather than more typical memory interconnect methods. In the case of the KSR1, it is a ring of rings [6], while the Stanford DASH uses a 2 dimensional mesh interconnection [8].

The KSR1 is organized as a ring of rings, with up to thirty two processors connected to each lowest level ring, called ring:0. Ring:0 rings are interconnected by another ring, ring:1. Each node consists of a CPU, a 512-KByte subcache, 32 MBytes of cache

memory, a cache directory, a ring interface, and an I/O interface. The directory supports the cache coherency protocol between processors and between rings. A total of 1088 processors can be connected as 34 ring:0 rings interconnected by one ring:1 ring. Kendall Square Research intends to extend the hierarchy so as to connect even more processors in future designs.

The processing component has four functional units: integer, floating point, control, and an I/O unit. Instructions are issued in pairs: an integer or floating point instruction paired with a control or I/O instruction. The machine is a load/store architecture, with loads and stores issued by the control unit. Some floating point instructions result in two floating point operations. There are 32 integer registers, 64 floating point registers, and 32 addressing registers. The integer and floating point registers hold 64 bits, the addressing registers are 40 bits. The machine operates at 20 megahertz and is fully pipelined, with two branch delay slots.

The user view of memory (called the *Context Address* - CA) is a segmented address space. Segments can range from 2^{22} to 2^{40} bytes (in the current implementation) in length. The processor produces 40 bit addresses, interpreted as a segment number and offset. The processor contains an instruction segment table, with 8 entries, and a data segment table of 16 entries.

The addresses generated by the processor are translated into *System Virtual Address* (SVA) space. The segment tables include the base location of the segment in SVA, the segment's length, and access permissions. Presumably, the segment tables are fully associative.

3.1. KSR1 ALLCACHE Memory Architecture

The memory in each processor is organized as a two-level cache hierarchy. There is a large *local cache* that combines the functions of memory and a second level cache, and a *subcache* that is the first level cache. Both caches are managed by a directory structure consisting of a large unit of allocation in the cache directory, and a smaller unit of data transfer, as shown in Figure 1. This is in contrast with more common cache organizations in which the units of allocation and transfer are the same.

There are instruction and data subcaches, each 256K bytes. Each subcache is managed by a subcache directory with 128 blocks each containing 32 subblocks. The directory is organized as 64 two-way associative sets with a random replacement policy. A reference to a new subcache block incurs the overhead associated with invalidating all the subblocks of the block being displaced. The subcache is cache coherent with the local cache. The subblocks each contain 64 bytes of data. A read from the subcache is satisfied in 3 clock cycles (load instructions have 2 delay slots).

There is a 32 megabyte local cache in each node. There is no memory with a fixed address (hence the term "ALLCACHE"). Instead, memory is managed through a directory structure that makes all the cache memory in the machine visible and accessible to every processor. A similar memory architecture has been described in [5], where the term Cache Only Memory Architecture (COMA) is used.

The local cache is 16-way set associative, and is organized in 16K byte "pages". Each page is divided into 128 "subpages" of 128 bytes. These subpages are the unit of memory coherence. The directory contains an entry for each of the 2K pages that comprise the memory. Each entry includes a tag and the state of each subpage, of which the visible states are invalid, read-only, exclusive, and atomic. Exclusive means that this is the only copy in any processor's local cache. Atomic is exclusive and locked.

Neither the whole 32 MBytes nor the 16-way associativity is accessible from a user program. The OS sets aside a significant number of pages (close to 30% of the total memory) for its own use and these cannot be displaced out of the cache. We discuss in detail the effective associativity experienced by user programs in section 5.5.

A consequence of this design is that if the processor references a subpage from a new page, all the lines from another page present in the cache may need to be evicted. In order to keep at least one copy of all pages currently being referenced, each page is assigned a "home" node. The home page provides space for every subpage, even if there are no valid subpages at the home node. Having a home node greatly simplifies evicting a subpage, as there is guaranteed to be a node with room for the subpage. If the home node must evict a page, the operating system will swap the page to disk or to another node's local cache to make room for the new page. A significant fraction of the node's memory is set aside by the operating system to be used as home pages [2].

The instruction set includes instructions to prefetch and poststore subpages. A prefetch allows the processor to read a subpage from another node without having to stall while the request is serviced. There can be up to four prefetches outstanding at any time. If this limit is reached, then additional prefetches are either discarded or the processor is forced to block until one of the four pending prefetches completes. A field in the prefetch instruction determines the action to follow. An additional field indicates the state of the subpage that is to be read: exclusive or read-only. A poststore instruction causes the local cache to broadcast a read-only copy of a subpage. All nodes with the subpage's page allocated in their cache will read it, provided the cache directory is not busy.

A multi-ring machine contains a ring interface in each ring:0 ring that is a directory for the entire ring (that is, it contains an entry for every page that is in any processor cache in the ring).

The data rate of ring:0 is 1 gigabyte/second. Ring:1 supports a "fat" structure with multiple rings to provide 1.2, 2.4, or 4.8 Gbytes/s bandwidth. Increasing the number of subrings in a ring:1

structure reduces the total number of available nodes that can be used for processing in ring:0.

The KSR1 provides sequential consistency, which implies that writes to a subpage cannot complete until all other copies present in the machine have been invalidated [7].

3.2. Paging on the KSR1

The KSR1 scheme of allocating space in the caches in large, page-sized units and filling in units of cache lines (subpages) appears to be a reasonable compromise. If we consider the amount of storage required for cache directory information we see that the current implementation will require only about 100KB. This is calculated from having 2048 page entries, each of which includes an 19-bit tag and at least 3 state bits for each of the 128 subpages. A simpler implementation that separately allocated each subpage would require more than 700KB of directory storage.

The cost of this method is that an entire page must sometimes be evicted due to a subpage miss. There are 2^{19} pages in SVA that index to the same set of page positions (see Figure 1), and the cache is 16 way set associative at the page level. So sequential references to a set of only 17 pages can (in the worst pathological case) cause a page eviction at every reference.

An advantage of the paged scheme is that it matches disk accesses well. When accessing a disk, a system wants to get big chunks from the disk since it's slow. With local cache pages, KSR1 can quickly clear a page's state to make room, especially since the disk page is the same size. Without cache pages a system would have to clear each block individually. This is likely to be done serially, since the tags would be in sequential RAM locations.

The KSR1 implementation saves a significant amount of storage per node. This also greatly affects the ring interface node which must duplicate the entire state information of all 32 nodes on a ring:0. This is an important consideration when looking at larger configurations of the KSR1, as the ring directory must not become a bottleneck if the system is to be scalable. More important than the amount of storage in the ring directory is the time and cost to search it: it requires checking each of the 512 (32 caches * 16-way associativity) entries which might have a copy of the referenced page.

3.3. Comments on COMA and NUMA

The COMA organization of the KSR1 contrasts with a more traditional directory-based NUMA (non-uniform memory access) machine such as the Stanford DASH by treating all of its main memory as a cache. NUMA machines treat a memory address as having a static, known location. The distance between a processor and the various main memory modules differs, leading to the non-uniform access distances. Both architectures commonly use the cache block as the coherency unit (i.e. sharing occurs on a block basis). Note that the KSR1 and Stanford DASH both include caches below the level of main memory to improve performance. The DASH has first and second-level caches, while the KSR has its subcache.

One important difference in the architectures occurs when accessing shared data. When a NUMA misses in its cache for consistency reasons, it will initiate a transaction to a node which is functioning as the "home" for this address. However, a COMA machine cannot direct its transaction to a specific location, instead it issues a request that will search the caches of the system until it finds the requested data. Determining which organization will faster for a particular access depends upon the relative locations of shared data and the coherency protocol implemented.

Factor	KSR1	Alpha	DASH
Integer Add	44.0 ns	6.1 ns	33.9 ns
Integer Multiply	92.5 ns	98.1 ns	360.5 ns
Integer Divide	4968.8 ns	198.9 ns	1023.2 ns
F-Point Add	52.5 ns	22.9 ns	88.2 ns
F-Point Multiply	22.1 ns	20.0 ns	147.2 ns
F-Point Divide	1760.6 ns	171.9 ns	702.4 ns
Complex Arith.	3199.1 ns	182.7 ns	780.3 ns
Intrinsic Func.	7969.6 ns	1134.3 ns	2683.0 ns
Logical Ops.	148.5 ns	27.2 ns	106.7 ns
Branch/Switch	148.2 ns	15.0 ns	36.4 ns
Proc. Calls	757.2 ns	62.0 ns	379.6 ns
Array Indexing	47.3 ns	39.7 ns	111.4 ns
Loop Overhead	101.6 ns	19.5 ns	105.6 ns

Table 1: Single CPU Performance of the KSR1, DEC Alpha 4000/610, and DASH.

4. Summary of KSR1 CPU Micro Benchmark Measurements

As mentioned above, a micro benchmark suite that measures CPU performance has previously been developed and used to obtain measurements on a variety of uniprocessor machines. Results for many systems have been reported in [11, 12]. We have run the same suite on the KSR1 CPU.

The CPU micro benchmarks are machine-independent, so instead of measuring machine instructions they measure operations defined in a high level abstract machine. The abstract machine is based on the Fortran programming language, so applications written in Fortran compile directly into the abstract machine code. The number and type of operations is directly related to the kind of language constructs present in Fortran. Most of these are associated with arithmetic operations and trigonometric functions. In addition, there are parameters for procedure call, array index calculation, logical operations, branches, and do loops.

In Table 1 we present the results we obtained, together with the results of running the same micro benchmarks on the Stanford DASH and a DEC Alpha 400 model 610 system running at 160 MHz. The processor in the Stanford DASH is the MIPS R3000 running at 33 MHz. In future work, we plan to use these benchmarks and provide a comparison of the KSR1 with a number of other parallel machines.

5. Analysis of the KSR1 Memory Architecture

As discussed above, a general methodology for analyzing the memory behavior of machines with caches has been described in [12]. We have extended this methodology with additional benchmarks that measure the memory hierarchy behavior of shared memory multiprocessors. Here, we give a brief explanation of the approach, and present the results we have obtained for the KSR1.

5.1. Methodology

There are many specific measurements one can make of a memory system. In general, there may be several levels of cache in addition to the main memory in the system. The main memory may be a single global module or distributed among the nodes. If the memory is distributed, the processors may treat each module as local memory, or may share the memory of all modules in a global, shared address space. The properties of the memory interconnect, including bandwidth and latency under a variety of loads, are

of interest. There may also be a write buffer associated with each level of cache. There may be separate cache coherency directories as well as the cache itself. It is a challenge to simply measure the performance of all of these mechanisms in a way that shows what happens under a variety of conditions. It is clear that a few simple numbers are far from sufficient to characterize memory behavior.

Beyond the issue of obtaining measurements that characterize the behavior of the memory architecture under a full range of conditions, there is the problem of presenting the results in a more meaningful form than a large table of measurements, or reducing the results to a few average numbers. Most useful would be a presentation of the results that allows a programmer with a specific application to understand what the memory performance of his program would be. We have developed a method of displaying the results that captures a significant amount of information in graphical form. We called these diagrams *Physical and Performance Profiles* (P^3 diagrams) of the memory subsystem as they contain the physical characteristics of each memory structure in addition to the performance characteristics.

5.2. The Structure of the Physical and Performance Profiles

Because of the complexity of the memory architectures of interest, the P^3 diagrams require some effort at interpretation, but they have a great advantage as compared with a set of tables of results, and provide far more information than averages which summarize the measurements. The P^3 diagrams are a set of plots representing the average execution time needed to read, modify and write (a R-M-W cycle) a single element in a sequence of locations (not necessary contiguous) taken from a region of memory as a function of the size of the region (R) and the distance (stride S) between consecutive elements. An alternative experiment consists of reading elements without changing their values. We refer to this type of experiment as read-use cycle (R-U cycle).

The access times are measured by timing the execution of a Fortran loop. Each data point on a curve is the mean time per iteration calculated from performing a fixed number of accesses to an array of the given size, using that stride. The clock resolution of the machine is 20 μsec. By factoring out loop overhead and averaging over a large number of iterations, we believe that the error in our results is generally less than a clock cycle.

Depending on the relative magnitudes of R and S of a R-M-W experiment with respect to the size, width, and associativity of the structures forming the memory hierarchy a distinctive value for the average execution time is obtained. All results are depicted as a set of curves, where each curve corresponds to a particular value of R, with all values of $S = 2^n$ from 1 to $R/2$ plotted. In this section we briefly explain how to read these diagrams. A more extensive discussion can be found in [13].

For explanatory purposes, the discussion will focus in the effects of our experiments on a memory hierarchy consisting of a single cache. The explanation extends trivially to more complex hierarchies and in what follows we provide some comments in this respect. Depending on the values of R and S with respect to the size of the cache C, the line (block) size b and associativity a, we can observe one of four basic regimes. Furthermore, the response of a more complex memory hierarchy is just the superposition of the memory structures' individual responses, which always fit one of the four basic regimes.

In the presentation we assume that all variables take values that are powers of two. However, if one of the physical dimensions of a memory structure happens not to be a power of two, it will be necessary to use different sequences of values for R and S.

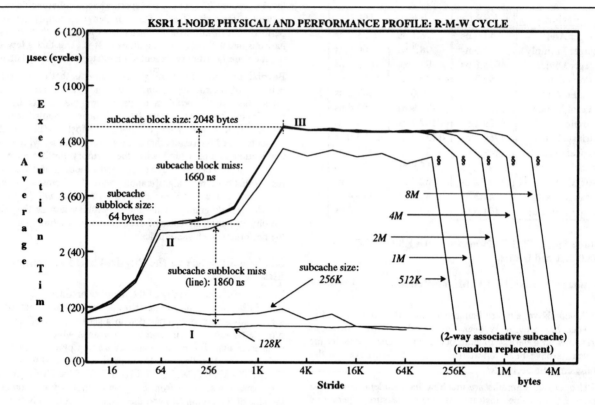

Figure 2: KSR1 single node Read-Modify-Write cycle physical and performance profile.

Each micro benchmark consists of making multiple passes over an array of size R, accessing every S^{th} element. The first pass (at stride 1) over region R will incur some cold misses, but this error is negligible due to the length of the micro benchmark. Micro benchmarks at larger strides will incur no cold misses, as they touch a smaller set of elements.

The simplest regime (regime 1) occurs when $R \leq C$. Here, independently of the stride, all elements accessed by the experiments fit in the cache, so there are no cache misses in the steady-state phase of the experiment. Therefore, the average time of the R-M-W cycle as a function of S is a constant line. Curve $128K$ in Figure 2 is a clear example of regime 1[1].

When $R > C$, misses start to occur, and depending on S we can observe one of three regimes (2.a, b, c). Regime 2.a occurs when $S < b$. Here, there are several consecutive accesses to each cache line in between corresponding misses, so the cache miss penalty is amortized amongst the accesses. As S grows, the average time for the R-M-W cycle increases in proportion to S. All curves in Figure 2 where $R \geq 512K$ and $S \leq 64$ correspond to regime 2.a. Regime 2.b represents the situation where each reference falls into a different cache line and it always generates a miss. Formally, this is true only if the cache replacement policy is either FIFO or

---

[1] Figure 2 represents the superposition of the effects of two memory structures: the subcache subblock and block organizations. All four regimes, however, are clearly identifiable in the figure and we make reference to it to illustrate the regimes.

LRU. For a random replacement policy, the effect rapidly converges to that of LRU and FIFO as the number of lines mapping to a set increases above the degree of associativity. Regime 2.b occurs when $b \leq S < R/a$. Here, each experiment touches a subset of all cache sets, but the number of cache lines mapping to a set is greater than the associativity. This result follows from the following argument. There are C/ab sets in a cache. In general, an experiment touches $R/(b\lceil S/b\rceil)$ cache lines which are mapped into $C/(ab\lceil S/b\rceil)$ sets if $S \leq C/a$ or into a single set if $S > C/a$. In regime 2.b, $S \geq b$, so S/b is always a whole number greater than one. Therefore, the number of lines touched are R/S and these are mapped into either C/aS sets or a single one. In both cases, each set receives Ra/C or R/S lines, respectively, and it follows from condition $R > C$ that $Ra/C > a$ and $R/S > a$.

Therefore, in regime 2.b, the average time for the R-M-W cycle as a function of S is constant, assuming there are no other effects produced by the other memory structures. In Figure 2, regime 2.b corresponds to the two plateaus present in all curves in the regions $R \geq 512K$ and $64 \leq S \leq 256$, and $R \geq 512$ and $2K < S < R/4$. The last regime (2.c) occurs when the number of different cache lines mapping into the same set is less than or equal the set-associativity. This situation is characterized by condition $R/a \leq S < R$. For this regime, the R-M-W cycle average time drops to the level of regime 1. Furthermore, the ratio R/S at which the drop occurs gives the set-associativity of the memory structure. In Figure 2 all curves where $R \geq 512K$ exhibit this behavior at their rightmost point, indicating that the set-associativity is two.

In the next section, we discuss some specific performance characteristics of the KSR1 that are observable from the P^3 diagrams our

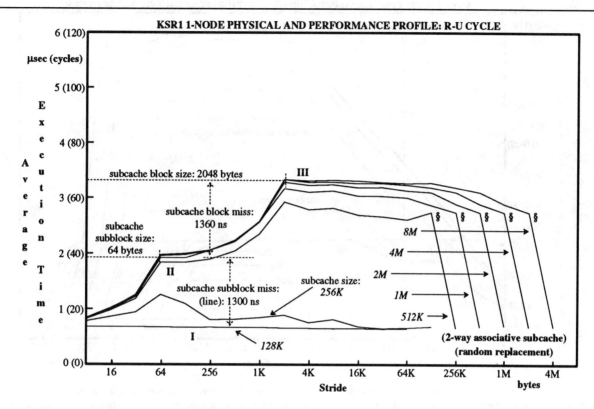

Figure 3: KSR1 single node Read-Use cycle physical and performance profile.

experiments generate. In the diagrams we identify the KSR1 regimes regimes by using roman numerals instead of the basic regime numbers. We do this to avoid confusion, because most of the KSR1 regimes represent the superposition of several basic regimes affecting different memory structures in the memory hierarchy.

5.3. KSR1 Single Ring, Single Node Performance Results

In Figure 3 we show the performance of a single KSR1 node while reading data from the cache. The figure consists of curves for regions of size $R=128K$ to $8MB$, with strides of 8 bytes, 16 bytes, ..., R/2 bytes. The KSR1 word size is 64 bits, so 8 bytes is the smallest stride.

When the data set being accessed is smaller than the size of subcache (regime 1) there will be no cache misses and we can read the base time per iteration. The flat curve for the 128KB data set in Figure 3 shows this case, and we see that the average time per iteration of the loop for all strides used was about 650 nanoseconds. This is the time to perform one iteration of the loop with a floating point add and multiply.

The size of the largest such curve with no misses tells us the size of the subcache. In this case we see that the subcache is 256KB. The line is not completely flat due to interference from other data used by the process — the data set is the same size as the cache and any accesses to other data will cause cache misses.

The 512KB and larger curves show us what happens in regimes 2.a, 2.b, and 2.c. The data is initially not in the subcache and the first reference to a subblock will cause a cache miss; succeeding

references to the same subblock will hit. At stride 8, there will be one miss and 7 hits. At stride 16, there will be one miss and only 3 hits to each subblock. As we increase the stride, we decrease the number of hits and the cost of the miss is amortized over fewer accesses. At a stride of 64 bytes, the curve flattens out, as every reference is made to a different subblock. This indicates the transition from regime 2.a to 2.b and we are able to conclude that the subblock size for the subcache is 64 bytes.

We can also read the time taken to satisfy a miss to a subblock by measuring the difference in times between the case with a miss on every access (a data set of 512KB and stride of 64) and the case with no misses (a data set of 128KB). We see on the KSR1 that this is approximately 1300 nanoseconds.

Between stride 64 and 2048 the curves repeat the same pattern of rising access times. This regime shows the effect of accessing a new block in the subcache. There is a second major inflection in the curve at a stride of 2048 bytes; this corresponds to the case in which every reference is to a new block of the subcache. From these curves, we are able to deduce that there is a directory structure with blocks and subblocks which manages the subcache (which we call the subcache directory - Kendall Square Research has not published any information about this aspect of the architecture).

At a stride of 256K bytes, the 512K byte curve shows that the cost of a read is the same as the cost when there are no subcache misses. In contrast, if the stride is 128K bytes, the cost of a read includes the cost of a subcache page miss. From this, we can conclude that the subcache is two-way set associative because at a stride of 256K bytes only 2 different subblocks are being accessed

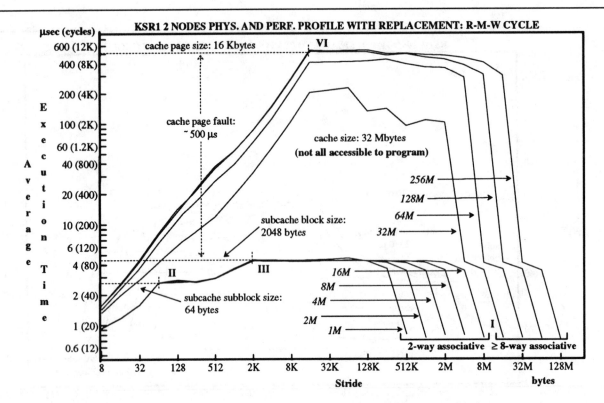

Figure 4: Physical and performance profiles of the KSR1 subcache and cache structures obtained using 2 competing nodes running R-M-W based experiments. Each regime identifies the mean execution time for a particular combination of subcache and cache miss penalties. For array sizes smaller then 16MB, there is no contention between the nodes.

and they map to a single set in the cache.

Figure 2 shows the case of a loop that reads a word, modifies it, and writes the result back to memory. Compared with the read case shown in Figure 3, there are extra costs because the blocks of the subcache have been modified. This increases the subcache sub-block miss penalty by about 560 nanoseconds (approximately 11 clock cycles), and the cost of a subcache block miss increases by about 300 nanoseconds (6 clock cycles). We note that the base case is 650 nanoseconds, as it was for the read case. From this we conclude that the write is completely overlapped with the loop branch and other operations.

5.4. Subcache Random Replacement Policy

In Figure 3 we can also observe the fact that the subcache replacement policy is random. This manifests itself in the height of curve 512K which reaches a lower height than the other curves in regime **III**. Regime **III** corresponds to basic regime 2.b. This basic regime assumes either an LRU or FIFO replacement discipline to enforce that every reference generates a miss (a subcache subblock and block misses in this case). With random replacement, however, some subset of the references will not cause misses.

As mentioned in section 5.2, in a cache of size C and associativity a, an experiment covering a region R will map $Ra/C > a$ cache block into the same set. Now, in a random discipline, the probability p_{surv} that a cache block will remain in the cache after a pass through all elements in the experiment is

$$p_{surv} = \left[1 - \frac{1}{a}\right]^{\frac{aR}{C} - 1}. \tag{1}$$

Consequently, the average execution time per R-M-W cycle in regime **III** (T_{III}) should be:

$$T_{III} = T_{no-miss} + (1 - p_{surv}) \cdot D_{miss}. \tag{2}$$

where $T_{no-miss}$ and D_{miss} are, respectively, the average execution time without misses and the miss delay penalty. Now, if we replace the KSR1 parameters in eqs. (1) and (2) we get that the effective subcache miss delay penalty for curve $512K$ should be $7/8 = 0.875$ of D_{miss}. The results in Figure 3 for curve $512K$ exhibit an effective delay penalty in the range .86 to .88.

A more subtle manifestation of the random replacement policy in Figures 2 and 3 is the decrease in the effective delay penalty for the points $S > C/a$ (128K) in curves $1M$ and higher. In all these points there are R/S cache lines mapping to a single set and as S increases fewer lines are mapped to the set. A similar argument to that given above applies, except that now the exponent is $R/S - 1$. We can see that the second point from the right (identified by symbol §), which corresponds to stride $S = R/4$, should also have an effective delay penalty $7/8$. Figure 3 shows that the miss penalty drops to the same value of curve $512K$.

The previous discussion illustrates how effective the P^3 diagrams are in capturing the complex performance space exhibited by shared memory machines.

5.5. KSR1 Single Ring, Two Nodes Performance Results

It is fairly expensive to use data that resides in another node on the same ring in the KSR1. Figure 4 (*see also Figures C-3 and C-4 shown on the color plate page*) shows a set of curves for read-

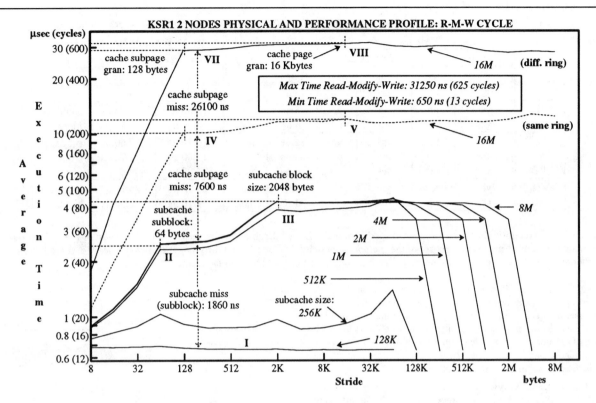

Figure 5: Physical and performance profiles of the KSR1 subcache and cache structures obtained using 2 competing nodes running R-M-W based experiments. Each regime identifies the mean execution time for a particular combination of subcache and cache miss penalties. For array sizes smaller then 16MB, there is no contention between the nodes.

modify-write (as was the case for Figure 2), when the data sets are as large or larger than the local cache. The 32 MByte line is particularly interesting. Not all the data can fit in the local cache at one time, since some space is needed for the program, and perhaps for the operating system or other pages for which the executing node is the home cache. But clearly there is enough reuse of blocks that even at large strides (8K to 2M), the average cost of the memory accesses is somewhat less than the cost of large strides for larger data sets.

As we mentioned in section 2, the KSR1 local cache is 32 MBytes and 16-way associative. However, some pages are "wired" by the operating system, so they cannot be selected as victims. In addition, the local cache acts as home of some fraction of the user's pages. Hence, the effective cache size that a program sees is significantly less than the 32 MBytes and the effective set associativity is less than 16.

Both of these characteristics are clearly present in Figure 4. For example, the 32*M* curve, which in principle should fit in the cache, clearly shows the presence of page misses with replacement. If the entire 32 MBytes were available, the curve's shape should be the same as the 16 MByte curve. The reason why the curve reaches its highest point between strides 16K and 64K and then drops, is because the total number of pages touched by a particular experiment is constant for all strides less than 16K and then it decreases in proportion to the stride.

With respect to the set associativity, the three rightmost points of all curves having regions greater than 16 MBytes indicate that the cache associativity is 8-way. We can see this by noting that when

the larger curves have a stride of 1/8 their size (e.g. 4MB stride in 32MB data set), their access time drops back to the subcache block miss level. This occurs because we are referencing only 8 different local cache pages and they map to a single set in the local cache. This value is less than the expected 16-way. Because our experiments change *R* and *S* only in powers of two, we detect 8-way associativity, while its real value can be any number between 8 and 16. We have performed more detailed experiments and have found that the effective associativity varies from set to set in the range from 3 to 12.

Finally, from Figure 4, we observe that the cost of removing and replacing a page in the cache is quite large (about 500 μsec). It should be borne in mind that one or more blocks in each page being replaced have been modified (are in the exclusive state), and must be evicted before a new block of the new page can be retrieved. This is a form of page swapping or thrashing between memories in the same ring, and does not require that the pages being evicted be written to disk.

5.6. KSR1 Two Rings, Two Nodes Performance Results

So far, we have discussed the performance of a single node in accessing data, though the data may reside on more than one node. We now turn our attention to the case in which multiple nodes are writing to the same set of data. Figure 5 (*see also Figures C-1 and C-2 shown on the color plate page*) shows an experiment in which two nodes in the same ring access data. This figure is like Figure 3, but with two additional curves labeled "16M", for a 16 MByte data set. Two processes on different nodes are simultaneously

Summary of the KSR1 Micro Benchmark Results Using One and Two Nodes

Regime	Misses				Rings?	Evict dirty page	R-M-W Cycle Iteration Time		
	Sub Cache		Local Cache				Total Time	Residual Time	
	subblock	block	subpage	page			time	time	Miss
I	no	no	no	no	n.a.	n.a.	0.65 μs	——	baseline
II	yes	no	no	no	n.a.	n.a.	2.50 μs	1.85 μs	subblock
III	yes	yes	no	no	n.a.	n.a.	4.20 μs	1.70 μs	block
IV	yes	no	yes	no	same	n.a.	10.10 μs	7.60 μs	subpage
V	yes	yes	yes	no	same	no	11.80 μs	1.70 μs	block
VI	yes	yes	yes	yes	same	yes	520.00 μs	508.00 μs	page
VII	yes	yes	yes	no	diff	n.a.	28.60 μs	26.10 μs	subpage
VIII	yes	yes	yes	yes	diff	no	31.10 μs	2.50 μs	block

Table 2: Mean execution time for a single read-modify-write iteration. Each regime represents a combination of R and S producing a particular pattern of misses to a subset of the memory hierarchy. Column "Evict dirty page" shows the delay involved in moving a dirty page out of a cache after a cache miss. The dirty page has to be sent back to the "home" node.

accessing the data set in read-modify-write mode, for different strides. In one case, the two nodes are on the same ring, and in the second case, they are on different rings. The figure shows that the cost of a miss in the local cache is about 7.6 μsec (at stride 128, the size of a subpage, every read misses), if the subpage is in another cache on the same ring. Note that the total cost of the access is the sum of all the misses, about 10.1 μsec.

The cost of accessing smaller data sets will be the same as shown in the 16M curve, since the two processors will be invalidating each others' cache subpages. The experiment was designed so that the starting point for each processor was separated by 1/2 the size of the data set (i.e., 8 megabytes apart). In this way, the processors are not competing for the same data at the same time except at large strides.

From the curve for the case of two processes located in nodes on different rings, the subpage miss penalty is 27.8 μsec. The machine used for the experiment had two ring:0 rings interconnected by a ring:1 ring. We assume that there were only two ring interfaces in ring:1. If traversal time in ring:0 is about 7.5 μsec for 33 nodes (including the ring interface), then about 13 μsec are consumed in the ring interfaces and in traversing ring:1. Since the per link data rate in ring:1 is the same as ring:0 for this machine, the cost of the directory operations and ring insertions would appear to be consuming most of this time.

The results displayed in Figures 4 and 5 show eight performance regimes (indicated by roman numerals in the figures). Each regime is determined by the number the misses it triggers in a number of enclosing levels of the hierarchy. Different regimes also identify the locations from which a miss can be satisfied.

Regime I (Figure 5) represents the baseline time; the case when no misses are triggered by the micro benchmark. Regime II adds to the baseline the delay due to subcache subblock misses, while regime III includes both subblock and block miss delays. Regimes IV and VII contain the effect of local cache subpage misses. The first captures the case when the miss is satisfied by a node in the same ring, while the second represents reading the data from a remote ring. In all regimes, except VI, the region of data covered by the micro benchmarks is less than the size of the local cache. Hence, all subpage misses occurring in these regimes are only the result of mutual invalidations between the nodes, because both nodes need exclusive rights over the subpage.

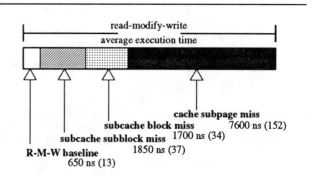

Figure 6: Components of regime V (ring:0 latency).

In regime **VI**, on the other hand, satisfying a miss requires either evicting a dirty page if the micro benchmark is based on the R-M-W cycle or detecting that the page is not dirty and just dropping it if it is based on the R-U cycle. In the former case the complete dirty page has to be sent to the "home" node. In both situations there is a significant extra penalty involved. The results just discussed are summarized in Table 2.

Figure 6 shows the component times of a memory access in regime **V**.

6. Communications Performance of the KSR1

The performance of the interconnection network has a significant effect on the overall performance of parallel computations and greatly affects the granularity achievable. The experiments reported in the previous section which measured the performance of the memory hierarchy were carefully designed to minimize the effects of loading of the communications network. For real applications, both memory performance and communications network performance will affect the overall rate of computation. In this section, we report on our experiments to investigate the performance of the KSR1 ring interconnection network.

The experiments are similar to our memory experiments. A single shared array is accessed by several nodes. The array is divided into equal portions, with each portion accessed in a read-modify-

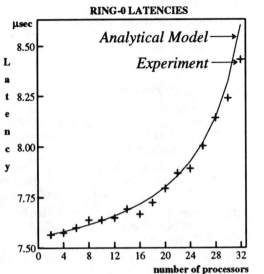

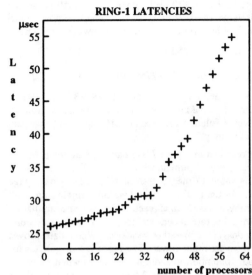

Figure 7: Communication latency as a function of the number of nodes communicating.

write cycle by only two nodes. The placement of the nodes and the assignment of portions of the array to nodes is carefully designed so that all nodes execute their portion of the experiment in in about the same amount of time. (This requires care; it is easy to construct experiments in which the performance of some of the nodes is much worse than other nodes, even though all are doing the same amount of work).

6.1. Contention on a Single Ring: Analytic Model

Here we present a simple model for the extra delay in latency due to contention in the ring in the case when all communication is local to ring:0. We then compare the model against experimental results. In our experiments, the time per iteration t_{iter} can be broken into two components: time of computation (t_{comp}) and time for communication (t_{comm}). Term t_{comm} has two additional components: the communication time without contention ($t_{no-cont}$) and the extra delay due to contention ($t_{penalty}(n_{nodes})$). The later term is a function of the number of communicating nodes (n_{nodes}). Let n_{slots} be the number of slots in ring:0. On the average, when a node wants to drop a packet into the ring, there are $(n_{nodes} - 1) \cdot t_{no-cont} / t_{iter}$ other messages occupying slots. The probability that a random slot is empty is given by

$$p_{empty} = 1 - \frac{(n_{nodes} - 1) t_{no-cont}}{n_{slots} \cdot t_{iter}}.$$

Now, the number of consecutive occupied slots passing through a node before an empty slot is found follows the geometric distribution with parameter p_{empty}. Hence, the expected number of consecutive occupied slots is $(1 - p_{empty})/p_{empty}$[2]. Given that the time between successive slots is $t_{no-cont}/n_{slots}$, we can compute the expected extra delay in latency due to contention as

_____
[2] The mean number of slots passing through a node, including the empty one, is given by

$$\frac{1}{p_{empty}} = \frac{1 - p_{empty}}{p_{empty}} + 1.$$

$$t_{penalty}(n_{nodes}) = \frac{t_{no-cont}}{n_{slots}} \left[\frac{1 - p_{empty}}{p_{empty}} \right]. \qquad (3)$$

Eq. (3) does not apply to the case when nodes in different rings communicate. Unfortunately, we do not have enough information about ring:1 and the interfaces between ring:0 and ring:1 to produce a realistic analytical model in this case.

6.2. Experimental Results

The graphs in Figure 7 shows the experimental values for $t_{comm} + t_{penalty}(n_{nodes})$ for various numbers of nodes. The figure labeled "**RING-0 LATENCIES**" also shows the latency predicted by eq. (3) in the single ring case.

The ring-0 results in Figure 7 clearly show that in the case of a single ring, even when the latency tends to increase with the number of nodes, this increase is relatively modest. In fact the total increase in latency going from 2 to 32 nodes is less than 15% of the original t_{comm}. There is a small error between the analytical and experimental results which increases with the number of nodes. The maximum error observed is less than 11%[3]. This is because eq. (3) overestimates $t_{penalty}$ by assuming that t_{iter} is independent of the number of nodes in the experiment. In actuality the time per iteration is given by

$$t_{iter}(n_{nodes}) = t_{comp} + t_{no-cont} + t_{penalty}(n_{nodes}).$$

Considering this new term in (1) reduces the error between the experimental and analytical results to approximately less than 5 percent.

The contention penalty when node communication requires sending messages through ring:1 shows a more interesting behavior. Figure 7.b distinctly shows two performance regimes, one for less than 32 nodes and another for more than 32 nodes. In the former case increasing the number of nodes by one, on the average

_____
[3] The 11% error in $t_{penalty}$ represents only a 2% error in terms of the total communication latency.

increases latency by 152 ns (~ 3 cycles), while in the later case, the increment is as large as 1000 ns (~ 20 cycles). A simple model based on linear fit of both regimes gives the following formulas:

$$L(n) = \begin{cases} 152\,\text{ns} \times n + 25200\,\text{ns} & \text{for } n \leq 32 \\ 1004\text{ns} \times (n-32) + 27500\,\text{ns} & \text{for } n > 32. \end{cases} \quad (4)$$

with respective correlation coefficients of 0.9713 and 0.9116. When the number of active nodes increases from two to 32 and 60, then eq. (4) gives a relative increase of 21% and 110% respectively in the total latency.

From the data presented in Figure 7, we can estimate the data rate per node under various communications loads. The conflict-free rate for a node is about 17 megabytes/second (a 128 byte subpage every 7.6 µsec). As the load gets heavy within a single ring, with the ratio between requests for data (cache misses) and computation of our experiments, the rate declines to about 15 megabytes/second when all 32 nodes are generating requests. When data moves between rings, rates are much lower. The range is 5 megabytes for one node without contention to about 4 megabytes when 32 nodes are active, and declining to less than 2.5 megabytes per second per node with a load of 60 nodes.

7. Related Work

Recently several other researchers have been investigating the performance of the KSR1. Boyd et. al [1] show a method of measuring communications performance on multiprocessors using a synthetic workload based on matrix multiplication of generated matrices. Other researchers [10, 9] have also reported on experiments to measure the performance effects of specific features of the KSR1. The communication and synchronization performance of the KSR1 has been analyzed by Dunigan [4]. Singh et. al [14] present performance results of several kernel codes and some of the SPLASH benchmark suite on the KSR1 and DASH machines. Finally, analytic model comparing the potential benchmark performance of NUMA and COMA machines has been developed by Hagersten [5].

8. Conclusions

Based on our measurements, it appears that the KSR1 ALLCACHE memory architecture should gracefully extend to a large number of processors. It indeed fulfills its promise of a scalable shared memory architecture. As with any parallel machine, the performance of parallel applications will depend on the degree and form of interactions between computations running on separate nodes of the machine. From our results, it is clear that there are types of shared access that are expensive, and that the programmer should be aware of the costs of accessing data, especially at larger strides, that reside on a different node from the accessing node.

The overall performance of any machine is a combination of its many features. The ALLCACHE memory is only one component of the KSR1. In addition to the processor, the ring of rings interconnect is a major element. The architecture is interesting and effective. Our results do not permit us to give a relative evaluation of the machine in comparison with other architectures, but our data will, we believe, help potential users in deciding whether to use the machine, and how to use it effectively.

9. Acknowledgements

We want to thank Tom Dunigan at Oak Ridge for giving us access to the KSR1 and to Eric Boyd who made useful suggestions.

10. References

[1] Boyd, E., Wellman, J.D., Abraham, S., and Davidson, E., "Evaluating the Communication Performance of MPPs Using Synthetic Sparse Matrix Multiplication Workloads", *Proc. of the 7th ACM Int. Conf. on Supercomputers*, Tokio Japan, July 1993.

[2] Bryant, C., *Personal communication*, April 1993.

[3] Cybenko, G., Kipp, L., Pointer, L., and Kuck, D., *Supercomputer Performance Evaluation and the Perfect Benchmarks*, University of Illinois Center for Supercomputing R&D Tech. Rept. 965, March 1990.

[5] Dunigan, T.H, "Kendall Square Multiprocessor: Early Experience and Performance", Oak Ridge National Laboratory Tech. Rept. No. ORNL/TM-12065, April 1992.

[6] Hagersten, E., Landin, A., and Haridi, S., "DDM -- A Cache-Only Memory Architecture", *Computer*, September 1992, pp. 44-54.

[7] Kendall Square Research, *KSR Parallel Programming*, KSR1 Documentation, February 1992.

[8] Lamport, L. "How to Make a Multiprocessor Computer That Correctly Executes Multiprocess Programs", *IEEE Transactions on Computers*, Vol.C-28, No.9, September 1979, pp. 690-691.

[9] Lenoski, D., Laudon, J., Gharachorloo, Gupta, A., and Hennessy, J., "The Directory-Based Cache Coherence Protocol for the DASH Multiprocessor", *Proc. of the 17th Int. Symp. on Comp. Arch.*, May 28-31 1992, Seattle, Washington, pp. 148-159.

[10] Ramachandran, U., Shah, G., Ravikumar, S., and Muthukumarasamy, J., "Scalability Study of the KSR-1", 22nd Int. Conf. on Parallel Processing, St. Charles, August 1993.

[11] Rosti, E., Smirni, E., Wagner, T., Apon, A., and Dowdy, L., "The KSR1: Experimentation and Modeling of Poststore", *Proc. of the 1993 ACM Sigmetrics Conf. on Meas. & Modeling of Comp. Sys.*, Santa Clara, California, May 1993, pp. 74-85.

[12] Saavedra-Barrera, R.H., Smith, A.J., and Miya, E. "Machine Characterization Based on an Abstract High-Level Language Machine", *IEEE Trans. on Comp.* Vol.38, No.12, December 1989, pp. 1659-1679.

[13] Saavedra-Barrera, R.H., *CPU Performance Evaluation and Execution Time Prediction Using Narrow Spectrum Benchmarking*, Ph.D. Thesis, U.C. Berkeley, Tech. Rept. No. UCB/CSD 92/684, February 1992.

[14] Saavedra, R.H., Gaines, R.S., and Carlton, M.J., "Characterizing the Performance Space of Shared Memory Computers Using Micro-Benchmarks", USC Tech. Rept. No. USC-CS-93-547, July 1993.

[15] Singh, J.P., Truman, J., Hennessy, J., and Gupta, A., "An Empirical Comparison of the Kendall Square Research KSR-1 and Stanford DASH Multiprocessors", *Supercomputing'93*, November 1993.

[16] SPEC, "*SPEC Newsletter: Benchmark Results*", Vol.2, Issue 1, Winter 1990.

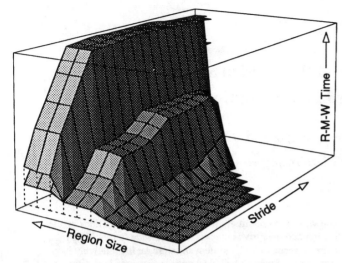

Fig. C-1: KSR1 2-Node Physical and Performance Profile (Fig. 5).
The projection is taken from point {-2.5, -1.7, +0.5}.

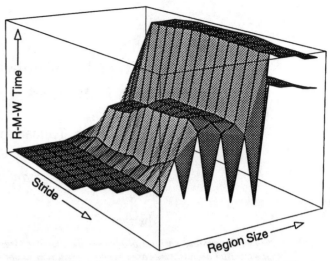

Fig. C-2: KSR1 2-Node Physical and Performance Profile (Fig. 5).
The projection is taken from point {-2.5, +1.7, +0.5}.

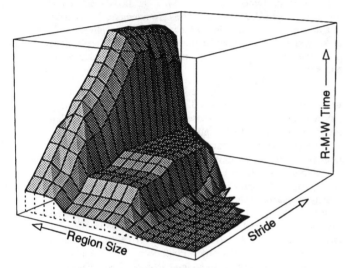

Fig. C-3: KSR1 1-Node Physical and Performance Profile (Fig. 4).
The projection is taken from point {-2.5, -1.7, +0.5}.

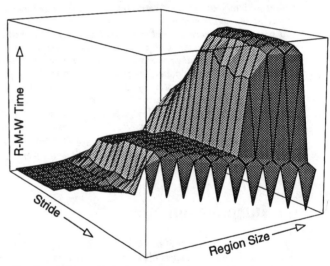

Fig. C-4: KSR1 1-Node Physical and Performance Profile (Fig. 4).
The projection is taken from point {-2.5, +1.7, +0.5}.

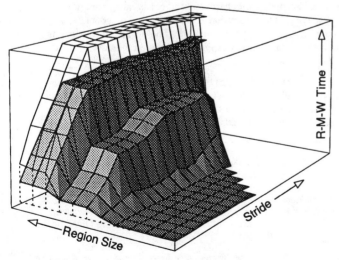

Fig. C-5: KSR1 2-Node Physical and Performance Profile (Fig. 5).
Cache misses satisfied in local ring:0 are shown.

213

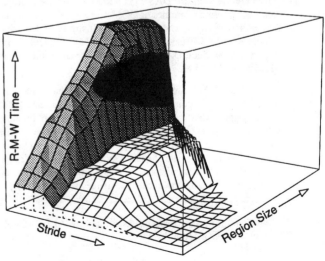

Fig. C-6: KSR1 1-Node Physical and Performance Profile (Fig. 4).
The effect of misses with page replacement is shown.

An Empirical Comparison of the Kendall Square
Research KSR-1 and Stanford DASH Multiprocessors

Jaswinder Pal Singh, Truman Joe, Anoop Gupta and John L. Hennessy

Computer Systems Laboratory
Stanford University

Abstract

Two interesting variants of large-scale shared-address-space parallel architectures are cache-coherent non-uniform-memory-access machines (CC-NUMA) and cache-only memory architectures (COMA). Both have distributed main memory and use directory-based cache coherence. While both architectures migrate and replicate data at the cache level automatically under hardware control, COMA machines do this at the main memory level as well. Previous work had discussed the general advantages and disadvantages of the two types of architectures, and presented results comparing the performance of small problems on simulated architectures of the two types. In this paper, we compare the parallel performance of a recent realization of each type of architecture—the Stanford DASH multiprocessor (CC-NUMA) and the Kendall Square Research KSR-1 (COMA). Using a suite of important computational kernels and complete scientific applications, we examine performance differences resulting both from the CC-NUMA/COMA nature of the machines as well as from specific differences in system implementation.

1 Introduction

Large-scale multiprocessors with a single address-space and coherent caches offer a flexible and powerful computing environment. Two interesting variants of these architectures have recently emerged: (i) CC-NUMA (cache-coherent non-uniform memory access machines) and (ii) COMA (cache-only memory architectures[1]). Examples of CC-NUMA machines are the Stanford DASH [9] and MIT Alewife multiprocessors [1], while examples of COMA are the Kendall Square Research KSR-1 [4] and the Swedish Institute of Computer Science's Data Diffusion Machine (DDM) [6]. KSR-1 is a commercial product, DASH is an experimental prototype, and Alewife and DDM are in implementation.

CC-NUMA and COMA architectures have many important features in common, including a shared address space with physically distributed memory, a scalable interconnection network, and directory-based cache coherence. However, they have important differences. A processing node on a CC-NUMA machine consists of a processor, a cache, and a fraction of the machine's main memory. The allocation, movement and coherence of data in the caches is managed automatically by

hardware at the relatively fine granularity of cache lines, while that in main memory is managed by software (explicitly by the user or transparently by system software) at the relatively large granularity of pages. A COMA processing node is similar, except that the main memory on the node is itself converted into a very large, hardware-managed cache by adding tags to cache-line sized blocks in main memory. This large cache, which is the only "main memory" in the machine, is called the *attraction memory* (AM)[2] [6]. As a result of this arrangement, the location of a data item in the machine is decoupled from its physical address, and the data item is automatically moved (or replicated) by hardware to the attraction memory of a processor that references it.

The main advantage of COMA machines is that the user does not have to *explicitly* distribute and move data among physical memories. In this sense, the user is presented with a programming model that is quite close to the familiar model of a centralized shared-memory machine with caches. The migration/replication in "main memory" is also managed at a finer granularity (typically a cache line) than an operating system can manage efficiently in software on a CC-NUMA machine. Finally, reusable replicated data are not likely to be replaced easily from a large attraction memory, even if they are replaced from a processor cache and may thus require recommunication on a CC-NUMA machine. On the other hand, COMA machines also have several disadvantages. First, decoupling the location of a datum from its physical address requires a mechanism to locate the datum on a miss. Current COMA machines accomplish this by using a hierarchical directory structure and/or snooping on a ring interconnect, both of which lead to somewhat larger communication latencies than on CC-NUMA machines. Second, the coherence protocol is more complex because it needs to ensure that at least one copy of a data item remains in some attraction memory. The attraction memory is also more complex to design than the main memory of a CC-NUMA machine.

A previous paper [16] described the relative advantages and disadvantages of COMA and CC-NUMA architectures in detail (in the context of running a single parallel application at a time), and discussed the application characteristics that are

---

[1] Kendall Square Research uses the term ALLCACHE™ to refer to its COMA architecture.

[2] The term "attraction memory" is used by the DDM designers to refer to the "main memory" and the term "cache" refers to the cache memory closest to the processor. Kendall Square Research refers to the "main memory" as the "cache" and refers to the cache memory closest to the processor as the "subcache". To avoid confusion, we will adopt the DDM nomenclature in this paper.

likely to make one perform better than the other. That paper also presented performance comparisons for a variety of applications on the two styles of architecture. Because there was no COMA machine available at the time, the performance evaluation was done through execution-driven simulation of the architectures. The use of simulation led to several limitations: (i) simplifying assumptions were made in the architectural model, (ii) only very small problem sizes could be run, and (iii) the machine organizations (especially cache sizes) needed to be artificially adjusted to try to approximate the performance of a real-sized problem on a real-sized machine.

Today, there is a real COMA machine: the Kendall Square Research KSR-1. We have access to this as well as to a CC-NUMA machine: the Stanford DASH multiprocessor. We can therefore run full-scale problems on real hardware. We do that in this paper, using important computational kernels and complete applications to compare both the absolute performance as well as the parallel speedups obtained on the two machines (although we focus primarily on speedups). Our goals are twofold. First, we want to understand how important the primary advantage (managing locality in main memory automatically) and disadvantage (typically higher communication cost) of COMA machines are for these applications. Second, we want to evaluate performance differences between the two specific machines we use, since these are both important machines in their own right and also the only existing examples of their types. Both the machines have hardware performance monitors, which allow us to explore detailed reasons for performance differences. As in [15], our focus is on a single application running on a parallel machine: COMA machines may have advantages in flexibility when running multiprogramming workloads or in the presence of process migration, but that is beyond the scope of this paper.

The rest of the paper is organized as follows. The next section discusses the differences between CC-NUMA and COMA machines in general, and the two machines we use in particular. It also reasons qualitatively about the impact of application characteristics on the relative performance of the two machines. In Section 3, we describe our experimental methodology and our choice of kernels and application programs, many of which are from the SPLASH application suite [15]. Section 4 describes the kernels and provides detailed analyses of the results obtained with them. Results for the complete applications are provided in Section 5. Finally, Section 6 discusses the overall results and summarizes the paper.

2 CC-NUMA and COMA Machines

The advantage of a COMA machine is obvious: by handling locality in main memory automatically, it requires little programmer effort to ensure that capacity misses in the processor cache will be satisfied in the local attraction memory. Let us explain the reasons underlying the disadvantages a little more.

Both the CC-NUMA and COMA architectures we consider use directory-based cache-coherence. For each memory line (an aligned memory block that has the same size as a cache line), the directory memory records the identities of nodes (or groups of nodes) that currently cache that line, and the state in which they cache it. CC-NUMA and COMA machines differ in how they find the directory information and the actual data for a line on a cache miss.

In a CC-NUMA machine, every physical memory line and its directory information have a *home node,* which is the processing node from whose main memory that line (page) is allocated. The home node is usually determined by the physical address of the line. The result is that a processor knows exactly which processing node to go to for directory information upon a cache miss. The directory then sends the request directly to the node where the valid line resides.

In a COMA machine, there is no home node for a line. We therefore need a mechanism to find the directory information and data upon a miss in the local AM. Current COMA machines use a *hierarchical directory scheme* for this purpose. Processing nodes are typically at the leaves of the hierarchy. Every node in the hierarchy (leaf or internal) has a directory memory, which maintains state information about all memory lines stored in the subsystem below that node.

Upon a COMA read miss, for example, a request propagates up the hierarchy to the closest ancestor that has a directory entry for that line. Then, the request propagates down the hierarchy to a node that has a copy of the line. This node returns the line along the same path as the request. A directory access needs to be done to update the state at each intermediate directory along the path, both in the forward and return directions. The result is that a cache miss that cannot be satisfied locally is likely to incur a significantly larger latency in a COMA machine than in a CC-NUMA machine, unless the remote miss is satisfied very close to the issuing node in the hierarchy.

As mentioned earlier, an additional complication of COMA machines is the need to ensure that the last copy of a line is not purged from the memory system. When a line that is the last copy (i.e. is held in exclusive mode) is replaced, it must be transferred to another attraction memory, potentially replacing a line there. KSR-1 solves this problem by maintaining a home for every 16KB block of memory, called a page, to which the memory lines from that page are returned if they are replaced in an AM. (This is not have the same function as a home in the CC-NUMA sense, however, and it can cause greatly increased memory requirements since the memory for the page is reserved at the home). Alternatively, one would have to let the line propagate up the hierarchy until a directory finds an empty or non-exclusive line in its subsystem that can host the line.

2.1 CC-NUMA: Stanford DASH Multiprocessor

The prototype DASH multiprocessor [9] consists of 16 processing nodes or clusters, each with 4 processors, for a total of 64 processors. Each processor is a 33MHz MIPS R3000, and has a 64 Kbyte first-level cache, and a 256 Kbyte second-level cache. Due to address space limitations each cluster has 14 MB of main memory. With 8 or fewer clusters, each cluster can have 28 MB of main memory. The cache line size is 16 bytes. The network connecting these clusters is a wormhole routed 2-D mesh. The access latencies for a cache hit, local memory access, and remote memory access are approximately 1, 30, and 100 or 135 (depending on whether the miss is satisfied at the home node or not) processor clocks respectively.

Table 1: Benchmark programs.

	Benchmark	Description	Lines of Code
Kernels	MatIncr	Increments every element of a matrix	100
	SOR	5-point nearest-neighbor computation on a 2-d grid	100
	MatMult	Blocked dense matrix multiplication	250
	FFT	1-dimensional FFT using a radix $\sqrt{n}$ method	500
	LU	Blocked dense LU decomposition	700
	Cholesky	Sparse Cholesky factorization	2000
Complete Applications	Water	Molecular dynamics code: Water	1500
	Barnes-Hut	N-body problem solver O(NlogN)	2750
	Ocean	Ocean basin simulation	3300
	LocusRoute	VLSI standard cell router	6400

2.2 COMA: Kendall Square Research KSR-1

A processing node on the KSR-1 consists of a single 20MHz custom-built processor, a 256 KB instruction cache, a 256 KB data cache, and a 32MB attraction memory [4]. The machine is configured as a hierarchy of slotted, packetized rings, with 32 processing nodes on each leaf-level ring. Reference latencies are as follows: 2 cycles to the cache, 20 cycles to the AM, 150 cycles to a remote node on the local ring, and 570 cycles to another ring. We use a 32-processor KSR-1, which means that we use only a single ring *with no hierarchy*. The line size in the data subcache is 64 bytes, while that in the AM (which is the unit of data transfer in the network) is 128 bytes. The unit of data allocation in the AMs, called a page, is 16KB.

Our results in this paper use up to 28 processors on each machine. This is because on the 32-processor single-ring KSR-1 we use, 2 or 3 processors are designated to handle system functions and are therefore effectively slower than the rest. We shall report on multiple-ring KSR-1s and larger DASH configurations in the future.

2.3 Key Implementation Differences

For our purposes, the main implementation-level distinctions of the KSR-1 from DASH are:

- *The ring interconnect*: This implies that every remote request has to go around the entire ring before it returns to the requestor. Thus, even though the 32-processor KSR-1 has no directory hierarchy, it does have higher communication latency than DASH. The interconnect latency is approximately 2 times longer in absolute time while only 25%-50% worse in terms of processor clocks.

- *The substantially larger cache line size*: This has prefetching advantages as well as false-sharing disadvantages. It also means that although KSR-1 has higher latency to access a remote cache line, the communication bandwidth in cycles per byte is actually larger on KSR-1 (1.2 cycles per byte on KSR-1 versus 7.2 on DASH).

- *A different processor*: The KSR-1 processor has lower integer performance, but a higher floating point perfor-

mance rating. While the peak floating point rating is 8 double precision MFlops on DASH, it is reported to be 40 MFlops on KSR-1 [4] (these are, of course, peak numbers).

- *More memory*: While the KSR-1 has 32MB of memory per processor, DASH has 28MB per 4-processor cluster.

- *The use of clusters*: Some coherence (communication) misses on DASH might be satisfied in the cache of another processor on the same cluster. This phenomenon, called cache-to-cache sharing, makes the latencies of these misses much smaller (30 cycles) than the latency of going off-cluster (100-135 cycles). On a large KSR-1, each 32-processor ring may be viewed as a cluster. However, we use only a single ring here.

- *A Different Memory Consistency Model*: KSR-1 uses the sequential consistency model while DASH uses a weaker consistency model (processor consistency). These weaker models have the advantage that a write does not stall the processor unless there is not enough buffering in the memory system to accept the write. Under typical sequential consistency implementations, writes stall the processor until they are globally performed. Because of the limited buffering of writes in the prototype, weak consistency does not buy too much performance on DASH

General performance expectations: For floating-point intensive programs, therefore, we expect KSR-1 to have better uniprocessor performance than DASH. Parallel applications with very low cache miss rates should produce roughly the same speedups on both machines, since it is the handling of cache misses that distinguishes parallel performance on the two machines. Applications in which capacity misses dominate in the processor cache are expected to perform better on KSR-1 (unless we are able to distribute data appropriately in main memory on DASH), while those in which coherence misses dominate are expected to speed up better on DASH (unless the remote data prefetched by the long cache lines on KSR-1 are used effectively). Part of our goal, therefore, is to understand the relative importance of capacity and coherence misses in the applications we study. The effects of false-sharing are expected to be worse on KSR-1, due to both longer cache lines and larger communication latencies.

3 Experimental Methodology

3.1 Choice of Programs

We use two groups of programs in our study, as listed in Table 1. The first group comprises computational kernels, and the second group complete scientific applications. The first two kernels we discuss (MatIncr and SOR), as well as the problem sizes we choose for them, are selected primarily because they very cleanly expose the advantages of one or the other machine. Kernels like these, however, are also found very commonly in grid-based scientific applications (such as Ocean later in this study). The other more complex kernels are included because they are found in important scientific applications but are not represented in the complete applications we study. The Cholesky factorization kernel and most of the complete applications are taken from the SPLASH application suite [15]. The Ocean program is modified from that in the SPLASH suite: It is written in C rather than Fortran, and it uses a multigrid equation solver rather than simple successive over-relaxation (SOR). We do not consider PThor and MP3D from the SPLASH suite because these applications are expected to perform poorly on both machines.

3.2 Running the Programs

All our programs are written in C. They were written with a centralized-memory cache-coherent shared-address-space architecture in mind, and are not specifically tuned to either the KSR-1 or DASH. The only tuning we do in our study is for appropriate initial data distribution in physical memory on DASH where appropriate. Examining the programmer effort required for and the performance benefits of this data distribution is an integral part of the study, and we discuss all cases explicitly. We do not perform low-level optimizations such as unrolling loops by hand or using other techniques to obtain better uniprocessor performance. Rather, the codes are written in a natural but performance-sensitive way in C, the same source code is run on both machines (with some compile-time flags for setting up machine-specific environments and for controlling data distribution on DASH). All of the codes were compiled with the optimization flag on (-O2).

From the hardware performance monitors on both machines, we obtain the number of cache misses incurred by the program and the number of misses that have to go off the processing node or cluster to be satisfied. While we rarely report the detailed information obtained from the performance monitors directly due to space limitations, we use this information to understand and explain performance differences.

For every program, our first implementation on DASH does not use any explicit effort on the user's part to distribute data appropriately. The program simply partitions the computation for load balancing and cache locality, as on a COMA or centralized shared-memory machine, and the system distributes memory in some default manner. On DASH, our first version distributes the memory pages of the application data round-robin (rr) among the clusters that the program runs on. Our second version allocates a page on the cluster that contains the processor which first touched (ft) that page. In highly regular codes with coarse-grained data sharing, this has the poten-

tial for actually doing the memory allocation correctly—with almost no programmer effort—as long as the initialization of the main data structures is done in parallel (so that the part of a data structure that a processor references most in the computation is first touched by that processor). Other versions employ increasing levels of user knowledge and effort to distribute pages appropriately.

3.3 Choosing Problem Sizes

Since the choice of problem size can often have a substantial impact on the relative importance of capacity and communication misses in the application, it is important that we choose problem sizes carefully in our experiments. For the kernels, it makes sense to examine results for different data set sizes, number of processors, and the sizes of different levels in the machines's memory hierarchies. For many of our kernels (MatIncr, SOR and FFT), an important working set for each processor is its entire partition of the data set, since the computation simply sweeps through its partition of data in every phase. For the kernels, we therefore use four data set sizes, each of which fits one of the following categories:

1. The entire data set of the problem is smaller than the size of a single processor's cache (on DASH, we use the second-level cache, which is as large as the data subcache on the KSR-1, to make this determination). Capacity misses are therefore negligible (in the absence of cache conflict problems), so that memory allocation is not important on DASH after cold-start and the performance differences are dominated by communication behavior.

2. The data set does not fit in a single cache, but fits in a single local memory and in some number of caches less than the maximum number of processors we use. As more processors are used, at some point a processor's partition of the data set fits in its cache.

3. The data set never fits in cache for all the numbers of processors we use, but fits in a single local memory. There are thus still no remote references in a uniprocessor run on either KSR-1 or DASH.

4. The data set does not fit in a single local memory, so that even a uniprocessor run incurs remote misses.

For the complete applications, we choose problem sizes that are likely to actually be run on machines of these sizes. By using different problem sizes, we examine the relative importance of capacity and communication misses in these applications, as well as how the relative importance is likely to change as larger problems are run on larger machines.

4 Performance of the Kernels

We study the performance of the kernels in this section, and that of the complete applications in the next section. We examine the first two kernels in some detail, since they are very simple and yet highlight all the points of contrast in the two machines.

4.1 MatIncr

The MatIncr kernel, which we use for illustrative purposes, iterates over a two-dimensional grid, incrementing every element of the grid by a constant. This computation is repeated

16 times. The computation is completely parallel, with no inherent communication. The grid is partitioned into subgrids that are as close to square as possible. This is done because although this particular computation is free of inherent communication, kernels like it are often found in applications that use near-neighbor grid iterations (see the SOR kernel or the Ocean application, for example), for which square partitions minimize the inherent communication to computation ratio. Every processor traverses its subgrid in row-major order (in C). The natural way to code this computation on a shared-address-space machine is to represent the grid data structure as a 2-d array (as would be done on a uniprocessor).

We use four versions of this code. The first version, called MatIncr-2d-rr, employs the above 2-d array data structure with round robin (rr) page distribution among processing nodes. The second version, MatIncr-2d-ft, also uses a 2-d array, with first-touch (ft) distribution of pages (see Section 3.2). All the user does in MatIncr-2d-ft is ensure that the data in a processor's partition are touched by that processor first.

While a 2-d array is the natural data structure to use for 2-d grid computations in a shared address space, this data structure is difficult to distribute well at the granularity of pages when the grid is partitioned in roughly square subgrids. The reason is that since a 2-d array is allocated row-major in C, successive subrows in a processor's square partition are not contiguous in virtual memory. Unless each subrow is large enough, most pages constituting the array are likely to hold data from different processors' partitions. By an artifact of the number of processors we use, the number of processors in a DASH cluster, and how we assign partitions to processors, this is not a problem for our grid kernels on DASH. However, the page boundaries can pose problems for larger machine sizes. To get rid of the artifact and thus show the impact of poor first touch memory allocation with 2-d arrays, our third version of MatIncr assigns the *p* subgrid partitions randomly to *p* processors. We call this scheme MatIncr-2d-ft-rnd.

Our final version of MatIncr represents a robust solution to the data distribution problem. This version represents the 2-d grid by a different data structure, namely a 4-d array, which ensures that a processor's 2-d subgrid partition is contiguous in virtual memory. The first two dimensions of the 4-d array designate the partition number in the 2-d grid of partitions, and the last two dimensions are used to index into the specified partition. The 4-d array clearly makes the programmer's task more difficult when accessing nonlocal data. We call this version MatIncr-4d-ft. (A 3-d array can be used as well, with the first dimension specifying the partition number, but this makes the arithmetic needed to access nonlocal data even more difficult).

Speedups for a 128-by-128 problem (128KB of data), which fits in a single processor's cache, are shown in Figure 1. The first interesting result is that the speedups on KSR-1 are much worse than those on DASH when 2-d arrays are used, despite the fact that there is no inherent communication in the program and the problem always fits in cache. This is primarily due to false-sharing of data and the resulting unnecessary communication, and demonstrates a disadvantage of the long cache lines on KSR-1. The false-sharing is caused by the same problem that makes allocating pages appropriately given a 2-d array data structure difficult: Grid elements from different partitions

may often be collocated on the same cache line at column-oriented partition boundaries. This leads us to the second result, which is that even though capacity misses and hence memory placement (the main reason for using 4-d arrays) are not important, using 4-d arrays improves performance on both machines over 2-d arrays, simply because it reduces false-sharing. DASH experiences superlinear speedups going from 1 to 2 processors, since with 2 processors the problem fits in each processor's 64KB primary cache. The speedups on DASH are better than on KSR-1 even without this superlinearity.

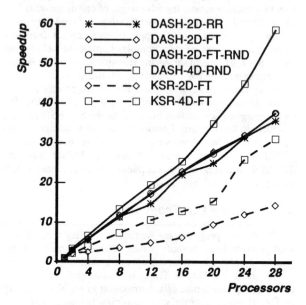

Figure 1: MatIncr Speedup for 128x128 Grid.

The results for the 512-by-512 problem, shown in Figure 2, use 2MB of data, which doesn't fit in a single cache but fits in a single local memory and in about 8 caches. All the versions speed up quite well up to 4 processors, particularly since the bigger partitions reduce the impact of false-sharing. The results become more interesting in going from 4 to more processors (i.e. to more than one cluster on DASH). First, this larger problem shows the impact of capacity misses and poor memory allocation on DASH. The round-robin allocation scheme (dash-2d-rr) does very poorly compared to the first-touch scheme (dash-2d-ft). This is true until 16 processors are used, at which point a processor's partition mostly fits in the cache, even modulo cache conflicts. From this point on, the round-robin scheme is almost as good as first-touch. The 2-d first touch method on DASH does better than the 2-d version on KSR-1, both because data allocation works out right on DASH due to the cluster artifact and because the false-sharing effects are worse on KSR-1.

The second notable result is that the 4-d array version once again performs much better than the 2-d version, both on DASH and even on KSR-1. Because of the cluster artifact, the difference on DASH is not due to data distribution. Nor is it due mostly to false-sharing for this problem size. Rather, the performance monitor shows that a lot more *local* misses occur with a 2-d array, due to cache mapping conflicts across subrows of a processor's partition (which are not contiguous in memory in a

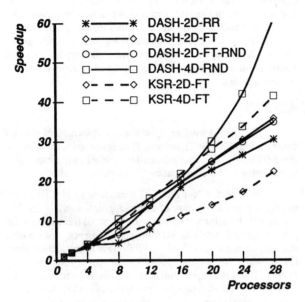

Figure 2: MatIncr Speedup for 512x512 Grid.

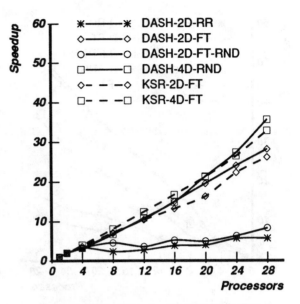

Figure 3: MatIncr Speedup for 1024x1024 Grid.

2-d array). With a 4-d array, a processor's partition is contiguous in memory, and fits neatly in the cache at 8 processors. In fact, this causes superlinear speedups (on both DASH and KSR-1) when going from 4 to 8 processors with the 4-d array version.

On a single processor, KSR-1 performs only about 20% faster than DASH on the 512-by-512 problem (despite the much higher peak floating point performance of the KSR-1 processor and the prefetching advantage of long cache lines). In both the 2-d and 4-d array cases, however, DASH speeds up better (in the 4-d case primarily because conflict misses improve more significantly on DASH), and becomes better than KSR-1 at 8 processors with 2-d arrays and at 24 processors with 4-d arrays.

The 1k-by-1k problem never fits in cache. Once again, round-robin page placement and the random binding of processors to partitions lead to terrible parallel performance when going beyond one cluster. As shown in Figure 3, the performance of these versions stays bad even up to 28 processors, since the problem never fits in cache. 4-d arrays still perform better than 2-d arrays due to fewer local conflict misses, particularly for larger numbers of processors on DASH. Since the problem never fits in cache, however, the differences and the superlinearity effects are smaller.

The 2k-by-2k problem does not fit in a single local memory on DASH or a single attraction memory on KSR-1. As shown in Figure 4, the uniprocessor performance of KSR-1 is much better (by a factor of 2.4) than that of DASH. This is primarily because there are now many misses to data not in local memory, and the prefetching effect of long cache lines substantially reduces the number of these misses on KSR-1. Up to 4 processors (1 cluster) the relative performance of DASH gets worse since the problem now fits in local memories on KSR-1 but not on DASH. With round-robin placement or random processor binding, the relative performance of DASH keeps get-

ting worse. However, with first-touch 2-d arrays (with row-major processor binding) or with 4-d arrays, DASH relative performance gets a lot better going from 1 to 2 clusters, and ends up worse by only a factor of 1.4 from 8 processors onward. This is because a strong superlinearity effect returns when going from 1 cluster to 2 (on DASH, or 1 processor to 2 on KSR-1), not because of the problem fitting in the cache, but because of it fitting in the local memories. Since KSR-1 was better at handling the remote accesses that resulted from the problem not fitting in local memory, the impact of this superlinearity is much larger, and the speedups over a single processor therefore much greater, on DASH.

4.2 SOR

The SOR kernel is very similar in structure to MatIncr, except that it sets the value of every grid point to the average of its nearest neighbors—rather than just increment it by a constant—and therefore has inherent communication at partition boundaries. We therefore discuss the results only to the extent that they differ from the results for MatIncr.

On the small, 128-by-128 problem that fits in a single cache, the superiority of speedups on DASH is quite dramatic, since the inherent communication is cheaper than on KSR-1 and because of the difference in memory consistency models (which shows up substantially when writes at interpartition boundaries generate invalidations, see Section 2.3). Speedups on both machines saturate at some point owing to the increasing rate of communication as processors are added. However, the KSR-1 saturates much earlier than DASH and at a much lower speedup. In this kernel, speedups with 2-d arrays are somewhat better than with 4-d arrays for this small problem. This is because in the 2-d array implementations, line sizes longer than a word often prefetch the nonlocal element that the processor needs. This does not happen with 4-d arrays. In terms of absolute performance, DASH starts out about 20% slower

219

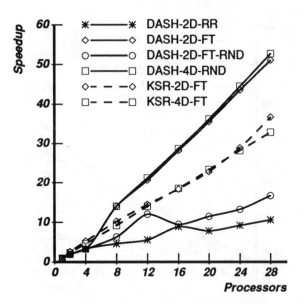

Figure 4: MatIncr Speedup for 2048x2048 Grid.

than KSR-1 with a single processor (just as in MatIncr), but ends up about a factor of 10 faster with 28 processors.

The results for the 512-by-512 problem are what we might expect from our results for a 512-by-512 MatIncr and the above results for the 128-by-128 SOR. As long as allocation works right or the problem fits in cache, DASH speedups are better than KSR-1 (albeit by a lesser extent than for the 128-by-128 problem owning to the relatively smaller impact of communication). DASH starts out about 10% slower than the KSR-1 on a single processor, but quickly becomes better.

On the 1024-by-1024 and 2048-by-2048 problems, the results are similar to those for MatIncr, except that the speedups are generally lower for SOR. On the latter problem, which does not fit in local memory, DASH's uniprocessor performance relative to KSR is significantly better than it was for MatIncr, since there is some reuse of data across grid points in the nearest-neighbor calculations.

Thus, for the above grid kernels, whether capacity or communication misses dominate depends on whether each processor's partition is bigger or smaller than its cache. For a problem that fits in cache, DASH performs much better than the KSR-1, owing to the expensive inherent communication and/or false-sharing on the latter. While capacity misses can be important for larger problems, they can be satisfied locally if the programmer uses slightly more complex data structures such as 4-d arrays. These data structures are not difficult to implement, and are in fact substantially motivated by other reasons anyway, such as reducing conflict misses and false-sharing. There is no need for dynamic memory migration/replication in these simple kernels. When capacity misses are satisfied locally, communication misses dominate and DASH has better parallel performance than KSR-1 even for large problems

An interesting issue that extends to all applications concerns how the relative importance of capacity and communication misses will scale as larger problems are run on larger

machines. We shall address this issue in section 6. We shall see that while capacity misses dominate when large problem sizes are run on small numbers of processors for some applications (including those that are dominated by kernels such as the above), they may not dominate when the applications are scaled in an appropriate, time-constrained manner to run on larger machines.

4.3 FFT

Our FFT kernel computes a one-dimensional n-point complex Fast Fourier Transform. It does not use a standard radix-2 (butterfly) FFT, but rather uses a higher radix (radix $\sqrt{n}$) to minimize the communication to computation ratio.

We use the "6-pass" FFT described in [2]. This FFT treats the n-point 1-d array of complex points as a 2-d $\sqrt{n}$-by-$\sqrt{n}$ matrix. It performs the following steps: (i) transpose the input $\sqrt{n}$-by-$\sqrt{n}$ matrix to order the points correctly for the next step; (ii) compute a standard 1-d FFT on each row of the matrix; (iii) multiply the resulting points by the appropriate "twiddle" factors [2]; (iv) transpose the matrix again; (v) perform a standard 1-d FFT on each row; (vi) transpose the matrix back to reorder the points correctly. The inherent communication in the program is contained in doing the transposes. In each transpose, every processor reads a subset of the columns of a source matrix and writes them into the corresponding subset of the rows of a destination matrix. Even on a NUMA machine like DASH, this means that first-touch data allocation naturally allocates data in the appropriate memories, so that the rowwise FFTs are entirely local and the transpose is essentially the only communication in the program. (There is also some communication in read-sharing the twiddle factors when they don't fit in the cache).

Figure 5 and Figure 6 show the results for this FFT for different problem sizes, one that fits in a single cache and one that does not. Round-robin data placement is worse than first-touch placement for the larger problems on DASH, since it causes more remote misses. The difference is not very large because there are many remote misses incurred in doing the transposes in any case. If the problem is large enough, an FFT performs better on KSR-1 than on DASH. Since allocation of the main data structures works out correctly on DASH under a first-touch rule, the reason for better performance on KSR-1 is not the better handling of capacity misses due to COMA (except to some extent in handling the array of twiddle factors, which are difficult to allocate appropriately). Rather, the reason is the nature of the communication in the program and how it interacts with the long cache lines on KSR-1.

As mentioned in Section 2.3, while the latency of communication is higher on KSR-1 than on DASH, the peak bandwidth for moving data is much higher on KSR-1 as well. This is because KSR-1 has larger cache lines, and communicates 128 bytes in 150 cycles, while DASH communicates only 16 bytes in a little over a 100 cycles on average. In a computation like SOR, only 8 bytes of remote data are useful at any remote access. The rest of the fetched line is therefore useless. In an FFT, however, as long as a processor is assigned enough rows of a matrix (8 in this case), so that it transposes enough columns into rows, the prefetching provided by the longer cache lines is helpful. Even if the prefetched data don't stay in the processor cache while the processor writes a row of the matrix, they do

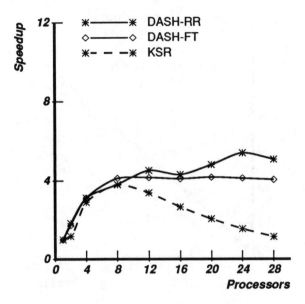

Figure 5: FFT Speedup for 2^{12} point input.

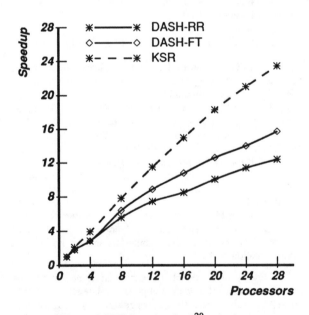

Figure 6: FFT Speedup for 2^{20} point input.

stay in the attraction memory. This ability to move contiguous data more rapidly causes KSR-1 to do the transpose communication faster than DASH. As the number of rows/columns assigned to a processor decreases (to less than 8), the bandwidth advantage of the larger cache lines diminishes and only the latency disadvantage remains. This is why the speedups for the smallest FFT (2^{12} points, or 64 points per row) are actually worse on KSR-1 than on DASH beyond 8 processors. Thus, the performance advantage of the KSR-1 can be attributed mainly to its longer cache lines rather than its COMA architecture.

4.4 Linear Algebra Kernels (LU, Cholesky)

In addition to the above kernels, we have also examined the performance of some important linear algebra kernels. For space reasons, we will not present the results themselves, but will summarize them qualitatively.

Our blocked dense linear algebra examples are a blocked matrix multiplication and a blocked dense LU factorization. Blocking reduced the miss rate to a point where both machines perform very well, and COMA affords no noticeable advantage.

The sparse Cholesky code is taken from the SPLASH suite. It uses a column-oriented, supernodal factorization technique, and incurs a lot of capacity misses for large matrices. In the version in the SPLASH suite, processors obtain supernodes dynamically from a task queue. Given the dynamic scheduling, there is not much one can do about data distribution on DASH, other than to do it round-robin to prevent hot-spots. Speedups are better on DASH up to 4 processors (i.e. within a single cluster), but are significantly better on KSR-1 once we get off a single DASH cluster.

We also have a static version of the code, which assigns supernodes to processors statically, based on work estimates computed during the preprocessing, symbolic factorization phase. This involves a substantial overhaul of the data structures, and is essentially a whole new code. The static version allows good data distribution, and DASH now yields somewhat better speedups than KSR-1. It also provides better temporal locality, and hence improves performance on both CC-NUMA and COMA machines. However, the main reason to go through the code overhaul is to allow proper data distribution, and we can argue that the COMA nature of KSR-1 makes it easier to obtain good performance on column-oriented Cholesky factorization.

Two points are worthy of note in this context. First, column-oriented Cholesky factorization (even supernodal) does not yield good speedups beyond a relatively small number of processors anyway. Second, obtaining more scalable performance requires going to block-oriented Cholesky factorization, which is in many respects similar to blocked dense linear algebra problems and therefore does not afford COMA much advantage due to capacity misses.

5 Performance on Complete Applications

5.1 Hierarchical N-body Methods: Barnes-Hut

This Barnes-Hut application performs an N-body simulation of stars in interacting galaxies. The classical N-body problem is to simulate the evolution of a system of bodies (e.g. stars in a galaxy) under the forces exerted on each body by the whole system. Hierarchical algorithms have recently attracted a lot of attention in many scientific computing domains, N-body and other, since they take advantage of fundamental insights into the nature of physical processes. The two most prominent hierarchical N-body methods are the Barnes-Hut and Fast Multipole methods, of which we use the former [14].

The computation in N-body problems proceeds over a number of time-steps. Every time-step computes the forces experienced by all bodies, and uses these forces to update the positions and velocities of the bodies. The main data structure used by the Barnes-Hut method is an octree which represents the computational domain space. Internal cells of this tree represent recursively subdivided space cells, and the leaves represent individual particles (bodies). The tree is traversed once per particle to compute the net force acting on that particle. The force-calculation starts at the root of the tree and conducts the following test recursively for every cell it visits. If the center of mass of the cell is far enough away from the particle (as defined by a user-defined accuracy parameter), the entire subtree under that cell is approximated by a single particle at the center of mass. Otherwise, the cell must be "opened" and each of its subcells visited.

Since the physical domain is highly nonuniform and dynamically changing, the application is repartitioned among processors every time-step. The particles and tree cells are stored in shared arrays. Since the particles/cells assigned to a processor in a time step are not likely to be contiguous in these arrays, it is both difficult to allocate data appropriately at the coarse granularity of memory pages on a NUMA machine, and also expensive since partitions change with time. However, the correct allocation of data in main memory is not very important to the performance of this application. What is important is caching communicated data to exploit temporal locality.

In both the Barnes-Hut and Fast Multipole methods, the important working sets are relatively small and grow very slowly as larger problems are run on larger machines [11]. Reasonably small cache sizes therefore suffice to ensure that capacity misses are not important to performance. The communication miss rate is also very small. Thus, both COMA and CC-NUMA machines perform well, as shown in Figure 7. Since communication latencies are larger on KSR-1 than on DASH, and since the long lines of KSR-1 provide some benefit but not too much, the speedups are somewhat better on DASH. Uniprocessor performance is about 30% better on KSR-1 for Barnes-Hut, and about 25% better on DASH for the Fast Multipole method.

5.2 Molecular Dynamics with Cutoff Radius: Water

The Water application [15] is a molecular dynamics code modelling water molecules in liquid state. It uses an $O(n^2)$ algorithm with a fixed cutoff radius to compute the interactions among n molecules (a cutoff radius is acceptable since long-range interactions are not important). Like Barnes-Hut, this application also has very low miss rates. It has even smaller cache requirements, so that it achieves good speedups on both machines without any attempts at data placement (we do not show the results for reasons of space). The same is true of algorithms that use a spatial directory to keep track of which particles are within the cutoff radius; these algorithms have O(n) complexity and are therefore attractive for large calculations. Capacity misses are therefore not likely to be important for N-body applications. In the case of Water, DASH actually performs better

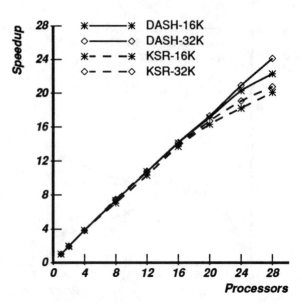

Figure 7: Barnes Speedup for 16K & 32K body input.

by about a factor of 2 with a single processor, and therefore performs much better overall.

5.3 Regular Grid-based P.D.E.'s: Ocean

This application studies the role of eddy and boundary currents in influencing large-scale ocean movements. It is a regular grid-based computation, and uses many kernels similar to MatIncr and SOR. A cuboidal ocean basin is simulated, using a discretized quasi-geostrophic circulation model. Wind stress from atmospheric effects provides the forcing function, and the impact of friction with the ocean walls and floor is included. The application proceeds over thousands of time-steps. The work done every time-step essentially involves setting up and solving a set of spatial partial differential equations on two-dimensional fixed-size grids, which represent cross sections of the ocean basin [12]. A W-cycle multigrid solver is used to solve the equations. Other than the solver, all the computations involve either nearest neighbor communication or no inherent communication at all.

Owing to the details of our multigrid solver, we can only use numbers of processors that are an integer power of 2. Since 32-processor performance is poor on KSR-1 (see Section 2), we focus on the results up to 16 processors. As in the MatIncr and SOR kernels, we use both 2-d and 4-d array data structures. Using the DASH cluster artifact referred to in Section 4.1, we assign processors correctly for good data placement even with 2-d arrays.

Speedup for two grid sizes (130-by-130 and 514-by-514) are shown in Figure 8 and Figure 9. With 130-by-130 grids, DASH has much better speedups, owing to false-sharing and high communication latencies on KSR-1. For various reasons that we shall not go into here, including the use of nine-point stencils and the multigrid solver, 4-d arrays are more difficult to implement in this application than in SOR. The implementation difficulties lead to high performance overheads on

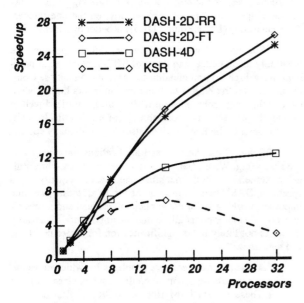

Figure 8: Ocean Speedup for 130x130 grid input.

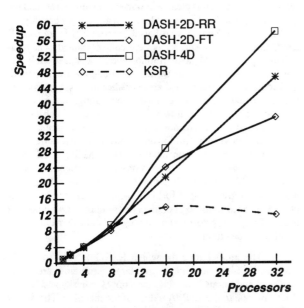

Figure 9: Ocean Speedup for 514x514 grid input.

small grids, which is why the speedups on DASH 4D grids are not as good as for the 2D grids. On larger grids, DASH's advantage over KSR-1 diminishes since the communication to computation ratio and the false-sharing effects are smaller. However, the advantages are still substantial (even without the superlinear speedup artifacts on DASH) since each grid is still not very large. An important difference between Ocean and the SOR kernel is that Ocean has a lot of conflict misses even across the different tasks in the application each task accessing some small subset of the 25 grids used by the application. With proper allocation, these conflict misses are local; without, most of them go remote and can hurt performance dramatically.

While capacity/conflict misses and hence data distribution are therefore important, the data distribution is not difficult to do on DASH. Interestingly enough, although the code is highly floating-point dominated, DASH is faster by a factor of 2 even on a uniprocessor, and therefore performs much better in our experiments.

5.4 VLSI Routing: LocusRoute

LocusRoute is a standard cell router from VLSI CAD, taken from the SPLASH benchmark suite. The program proceeds over a number of iterations, in each iteration ripping up and rerouting the wires in a circuit until the routing "converges". A *cost array* data structure is used to keep track of the occupancies of the channels in the circuit, and hence the costs of routing a new wire through them. We use two versions of LocusRoute on DASH. One, called DASH-R, allocates all the data round-robin, including the cost array. The other, called DASH-S (for Smart), tries to allocate the cost array based on the geographic partitioning used. There is not much difference in performance between the two (see Figure 9 and Figure 10), since wires can be long and since it is difficult to allocate the 2-d cost array appropriately in page-sized units.

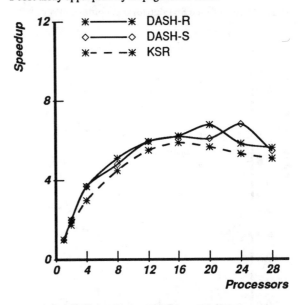

Figure 10: LocusRoute Speedup for input problem Primary1.

DASH is about 3 times faster on a uniprocessor, since this is integer code. On the smaller input circuit, speedups are low due to the high volume of communication, but are about the same on both machines (DASH is a little better). On the larger circuit, KSR-1 is significantly better. This may be because there are a lot of wires in a big circuit that remain mostly within a processor's partition of the cost array but incur capacity misses, which are kept local dynamically at cache-line granularity by KSR-1 much more effectively than statically at page granularity on DASH. (Or it may at least partially be due to the fact that the computation is much slower on a uniprocessor on KSR-1.) Thus, while speedups are not very large or scalable for most

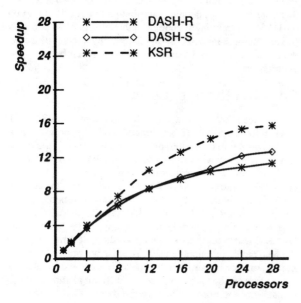

Figure 11: LocusRoute Speedup for input problem Primary2.

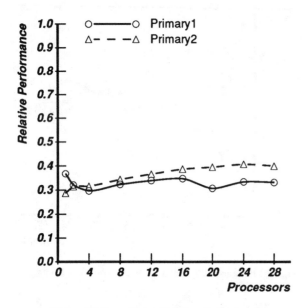

Figure 12: LocusRoute Relative Performance.

circuits with this application, the COMA nature of KSR-1 gives it performance advantages.

6 Discussion and Conclusions

Uniprocessor Performance: For many of the floating-point intensive kernels and codes, DASH uniprocessor performance is worse than KSR-1, ranging between 10% for SOR to 20-30% (for MatIncr, Barnes, Cholesky) to 50% (for Cholesky). In some of the floating point codes (Ocean and Water), DASH actually does substantially better on a uniprocessor

(60-100%), despite the much better peak floating point performance of the KSR-1 processor[3]. Finally, on the one integer-dominated code (LocusRoute), DASH is better by a factor of 3.

Speedups: For small problems, DASH speedups are invariably much better than those of KSR-1, since small problems have high communication-to-computation ratios. Communication on the KSR-1 communication incurs higher latency, and the long cache lines on KSR-1 are not utilized well to provide higher effective communication bandwidth. In addition, the long cache lines lead to false-sharing in many codes.

Some of our kernels and applications have very low miss rates (e.g. Water, Barnes, and the blocked dense linear algebra kernels) so both machines yield about equally good speedups, DASH being a little bit better. In all these cases, the important working set of the application is small and grows either very slowly or not at all, so that the importance of capacity misses is not likely to be significant even for larger problems and machines.

At the other extreme are problems for which capacity/conflict misses are important when the problem sizes are large enough. These include the MatIncr and SOR kernels, Cholesky, Ocean and LocusRoute. Grid-based iterative codes such as Ocean are an interesting example in which the working set is equal or proportional to a processor's entire partition of the data set. Data distribution is clearly important in these cases, and the question is how hard it is to do the distribution correctly on DASH. For the regular grid-based problems (MatIncr, SOR and Ocean), the data sharing is very coarse grained, which facilitates appropriate data distribution even at a page granularity. The use of clusters helps as well. However, data structure modifications (such as using 4-d arrays rather than 2-d arrays) are needed to make a processor's partition contiguous in virtual memory, and hence ensure robustness in data distribution. These modifications are not difficult in regular applications, and are in fact very useful for other purposes besides data distribution (e.g. reducing conflict misses and making good use of long cache lines). In fact, they improve performance substantially on KSR-1 as well. It is not clear, therefore, whether the increased programming effort in CC-NUMA should be attributed to the need to for explicit data distribution, or whether it is needed for good performance anyway and data distribution is a beneficial side effect.

The applications for which KSR-1 is seen to clearly have a speedup advantage for large problems are FFT, Cholesky and LocusRoute. Of these, only Cholesky and Locus-Route are due to the COMA nature of the machine. The higher performance on FFT is simply due to the higher communication bandwidth for moving chunks of contiguous data. Cholesky requires a whole new design of data structures and a new partitioning approach to get the data distribution right. The new partitioning approach is also useful to get good reuse of data and hence good performance on KSR-1, and is therefore useful in any case. Still, most of the new data structure design is needed solely to improve data distribution, and hence KSR-1 has an advantage here. Finally, LocusRoute shares data at a fine granularity, which makes it difficult to allocate data appropriately on DASH. It is not clear whether the better speedups

---

[3]One operation that KSR-1 is much faster at is a multiply-accumulate, which our codes did not use much.

on KSR-1 for LocusRoute are due to better handling of capacity misses or simply due to the fact that uniprocessor performance on KSR-1 is much worse and the impact of communication therefore smaller.

Absolute Overall Performance: In terms of absolute performance using 28 processors (uniprocessor and speedup combined), DASH does better for most of the programs using small input problems (up to 80% faster) with the exception of Barnes (13.9% slower) and Cholesky (33.1% slower). For large problems, KSR-1 performs better on 28 processors for MatIncr (27.1%), SOR (17.6%), Cholesky (42.8%), Barnes-Hut (13.1%) and FFT (17.8%). DASH performs better on 28 processors for Locus (60.0%), Ocean (43.8% on 16 processors; 72.3% on 32 processors), and Water (50.0% faster). As we go to larger machines, KSR-1 communication latencies increase drastically since we go from one ring to a hierarchy. We therefore expect our results to slant more toward DASH in 48-processor comparisons that we are currently performing.

Implications for Larger Machines: A useful way to look at the implications of application characteristics for large-scale CC-NUMA and COMA architectures is in terms of working sets, communication to computation ratios, and how these scale as applications are scaled to run on larger machines. If the important working sets are large compared to reasonable cache sizes, capacity misses are likely to be important and COMA machines advantageous. This is particularly true for applications which both have large working sets and exhibit fine-grained data sharing (if such applications indeed exist). If communication to computation ratios are large, CC-NUMA machines are expected to be advantageous. It has been shown that the important working sets of many important classes of scientific applications are actually quite small [10]. It is also increasingly accepted that time-constrained scaling is a more useful scaling model for scientific applications than memory-constrained scaling (in which case memory requirements per processor remain constant but execution time grows too rapidly). Under time-constrained scaling, the important working sets grow either very slowly or not at all [10]. Also, since the data set per processor shrinks under realistic time-constrained scaling, the communication to computation ratio increases [13]. All of these trends point toward diminishing advantages for COMA as machines become larger.

Acknowledgments

We would like to thank Ed Rothberg for providing and helping with some of the codes. We would like to thank Steve Woo for assisting with and providing a version of the Ocean code which uses a multigrid solver. We would also like to thank the University of Michigan and the Cornell University Theory Center for providing us access to their KSR-1 machines. This work has been supported by DARPA contract N00039-91-C-0138. Truman Joe is also supported by an IBM Graduate Fellowship. This support is gratefully acknowledged.

References

[1] Anant Agarwal et al. APRIL: A processor architecture for multiprocessing. In *Proceedings of the 17th Annual International Symposium on Computer Architecture*, pages 104-114, May 1990.

[2] David H. Bailey. FFTs in External or Hierarchical Memories. In *Journal of Supercomputing*, 4: 23-25, 1990.

[3] Gordon Bell. Ultracomputers: A Teraflop Before Its Time. In *Communications of the ACM*, 35(8): 26-47, August 1992.

[4] Henry Burkhardt III et al. Overview of the KSR1 Computer System. Technical Report KSR-TR-9202001, Kendall Square Research, Boston, February 1992.

[5] Alan Gottlieb et al. The NYU Ultracomputer - Designing a MIMD, shared memory parallel machine. IEEE Transactions on Computers, 32(2):175-189, February 1983.

[6] Erik Hagersten, Seif Haridi, and David H.D. Warren. The cache-coherence protocol of the data diffusion machine. In Michel Dubois and Shreekant Thakkar, editors, *Cache and Interconnect Architectures in Multiprocessors*. Kluwer Academic Publishers, 1990.

[7] Erik Hagersten, Anders Landin, and Seif Haridi. DDM -- A Cache-Only Memory Architecture. *IEEE Computer*, pages 44-54, September 1992.

[8] Monica Lam, Edward Rothberg and Michael Wolf. The cache performance and optimizations of blocked Algorithms. In *Proceedings of the 4th International Conference on Architectural Support for Programming Languages and Operating Systems*, pages 63-74, 1991.

[9] Daniel E. Lenoski et al. The directory-based cache coherence protocol for the DASH multiprocessor. In *Proceedings of the 17th Annual International Symposium on Computer Architecture*, pages 148-159, 1990.

[10] Edward Rothberg, Jaswinder Pal Singh and Anoop Gupta. Working sets, cache sizes, and node granularity for large-scale multiprocessors. In *Proceedings of the 20th Annual International Symposium on Computer Architecture*, 1993.

[11] Jaswinder Pal Singh and John L. Hennessy. Finding and exploiting parallelism in an ocean simulation program: experiences, results, implications. In *Journal of Parallel and Distributed Computing*, 15(1): 27-48, May 1992.

[12] Jaswinder Pal Singh, John L. Hennessy, and Anoop Gupta. Scaling parallel programs for multiprocessors: methodology and examples. *IEEE Computer*, July 1993.

[13] Jaswinder Pal Singh et al. "Load balancing and data locality in parallel hierarchial N-body methods", Technical Report CSL-TR-92-505, Stanford University, February 1992.

[14] Jaswinder Pal Singh, Wolf-Dietrich Weber, and Anoop Gupta. SPLASH: Stanford parallel applications for shared-memory. *Computer Architecture News*, 20(1):5-44, March 1992.

[15] Per Stenström, Truman Joe and Anoop Gupta. Comparative performance evaluation of cache-coherent NUMA and COMA architectures. In *Proceedings of the 17th Annual International Symposium on Computer Architecture*, pages 80-91, 1992.

[16] Joseph Torrellas, Monica S. Lam, and John L. Hennessy. Shared data placement optimizations to reduce multiprocessor cache miss rates. In *Proceedings of the International Conference on Parallel Processing*, pages 266-270, 1990. Vol. II.

Session 3:
Minisymposium
Networking

Session 4:
Applications I
Chair: Rick Stevens

Latency and Bandwidth Considerations in Parallel Robotics Image Processing

Jon A. Webb
School of Computer Science
Carnegie Mellon University
Pittsburgh, PA 15213-3890

Abstract

Parallel image processing for robotics applications differs in a fundamental way from parallel scientific computing applications: the problem size is fixed, and latency requirements are tight. This brings Amdhal's law in effect with full force, so that message-passing latency and bandwidth severely restrict performance. In this paper we examine an application from this domain, stereo image processing, which has been implemented in Adapt, a niche language for parallel image processing implemented on the Carnegie Mellon-Intel Corporation iWarp. High performance has been achieved for this application. We show how a I/O building block approach on iWarp achieved this, and then examine the implications of this performance for more traditional machines that do not have iWarp's rich I/O primitive set.

1 Introduction

A typical system for mobile robot control is illustrated in Figure 1. It consists of a series of steps: the capture of sensory data from a camera, processing of that data and the generation of a planned action from it, and finally the generation of the robot actions. The important characteristic of this system is that no step can begin before the last step completes. For example, it does the robot no good to begin processing a new image before the last image is acted upon; doing so can cause the robot to doubly compensate for an inaccuracy in steering, and lead to instability in the control algorithm.

We would like to speed up this cycle through the use of parallel computers. This paper addresses the perceptual issues, namely capturing and processing sensory data. This tends to be a major bottleneck in such systems, since images are large and often sig-

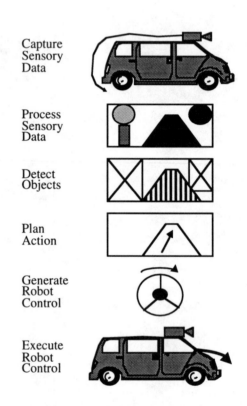

Figure 1: Mobile robot control system.

nificant processing is required before the sensory data can be useful for control.

Because the robot must sense the results of each action before the next can take place, it is the total execution time of sensory processing that is important (its latency), not the number of sensory actions completed per second (its throughput).

Parallel systems are widely recognized to be increasing in message passing bandwidth, but latency is not decreasing as rapidly. As we apply more and more processors to a particular problem, message passing latency plays a greater role in limiting overall speed

230

since, with more processors, messages are shorter (because the data set is divided into more, hence smaller, pieces) and there are more of them (because more processors must communicate). Two approaches for dealing with increasing latency are pipelining and data set scaling.

In pipelining, we process multiple data sets at the same time. There is no communication except for the input and output of the data set; thus, relatively small demands are placed on the message passing system. However, while the total number of data sets processed per unit time increases with this method, the time to process any one data set stays the same. Thus, pipelining is useless for increasing the speed of the system illustrated in Figure 1. The same observation applies to functional pipelining, where we divide a processing operation into a number of stages, each of which processes a complete data set.

As data set sizes increase, for many important scientific computing applications the processing time increases faster than communication time and other overheads. Hence if we increase the problem size as we add more processors, the increase computation time balances the increased communication time imposed by the extra processors. But this does not apply in sensory tasks, for two reasons. First, the problem size (in this case, the image size) is determined by the problem requirements, for example robot motions must occur to a certain precision. We do not need to sense more accurately than this, but we would like to sense more quickly. Therefore the problem size is fixed. Second, even in cases where more accurate sensing is desirable, there are a number of technical obstacles to achieving this. For example, increasing image size requires designing new cameras.

Because pipelining cannot be applied and the problem size cannot be scaled, Amdhal's law applies with full force. The consequence of this is that in order to add more processors to the system to increase performance we must have sufficiently low message passing latency and high enough bandwidth to keep the extra communication time from dominating the shorter processing time created by the extra processors.

This paper examines a successful application of parallel computers to an image processing task, namely an implementation of multi-baseline stereo on the Carnegie Mellon-Intel iWarp. The performance achieved (62 ms for recovering 16 depth levels from three 240×256 images, exceeding 15 Hz), is the fastest stereo time ever reported, and even the fastest depth measurement time for systems of this resolution. Two things were essential to achieving this performance:

1. The implementation of the I/O functions in the stereo vision system in terms of the basic I/O operations on iWarp.

2. Tight coupling between the iWarp parallel computer and the video I/O, This is achieved using an I/O board that brings the video input directly into the memory of the iWarp cell.

In addition to describing this, this paper discusses the implication of this performance for parallel computers with communication based on send and receive. It turns out that by using a simple model of communication time we can derive strong constraints on send and receive performance if we are to achieve the same overall communication time as we did on iWarp.

2 The stereo vision algorithm.

The algorithm used is Kanade-Okutomi multi-baseline stereo vision[2]. We do not describe the algorithm or its justification here. The key elements of the implementation of the algorithm are that

- It is correlation-based, requiring a computation at every pixel of the image. The result of the algorithm is a depth image, with a depth value calculated at every pixel of the image.

- It partitions naturally into two steps, which are performed at every depth level over the entire image. The two steps are *difference* and *minimize*. The *difference* step calculates a difference image, which is the pixel-by-pixel error between the corresponding pixels at the given depth level. The *minimize* step sums the difference image over a rectangular window around each pixel, and compares this error value with the best error so far at that pixel, updating the depth image at that pixel to have the current depth value if the new sum is less than the best error so far.

- Because the images are fairly small (240×256) and the rectangular window is fairly large (e.g., 13×13), it is necessary to perform the *difference* step in parallel on all processors, then communicate the difference image among processors before performing the *minimize* step. This means that communication is an important part of the total execution time, being performed for each depth value.

Function	Assembly	C
Difference	22.0 ms (257 MFLOPS)	36.0 ms (157 MFLOPS)
Maximize	17.3 ms (369 MFLOPS)	40.7 ms (156 MFLOPS)
Total	39.3 ms	76.7 ms

Table 1: Stereo computation times

3 Adapt implementation of the stereo vision algorithm

The algorithm is implemented in Adapt[3], a niche language for image processing on parallel architectures. The Adapt implementation on iWarp partitions the computation between two processor classes: the *master* processor (implemented on iWarp on a special processor called the SIB, for Sun Interface Board), which runs the user's program and controls the overall computation; and the *slave* processors (implemented in a 64-cell iWarp on the 8×8 processor array), which do all image processing functions using code generated from the user's Adapt program.

Images are block-partitioned across the slave processors by rows, and are allocated and de-allocated explicitly by the user's program on the master processor. Special Adapt I/O functions allow the user to distribute and collect images between the master processor and the slave processors.

After obtaining the input images the stereo vision program first *distributes* them to the slave processors. Then, for each depth value, the program calls *difference* and *minimize*. The resulting depth image is then *collected* back to the master processor's memory, and then displayed.

The execution time for the stereo vision system divides into two parts: computation and communication. Of these, communication is of more interest and will be described in greater detail.

4 Computation Issues

Table 1 summarizes the performance of the computation in the stereo program and compares the performance of the assembly-language routines used with C-generated code.

There are two primary reasons why the assembly code is significantly faster than the C code:

1. Across-basic block optimizations. The compiler optimizes code primarily within a basic block. In assembly coding, there is no such restriction. This is particularly evident in the minimize routine, in which the inner loop is an if statement. In the assembly version, some of the calculation from the then clause of the if is merged with the calculation of the conditional expression, leading to greater overlap of computation.

2. Avoiding machine bugs. There are two important bugs in the C-step implementation of the iWarp component, both of which impact the performance of the compute-and-access instruction, which allows floating point add and multiply operations to proceed in parallel with access memory operations. The first bug makes it unsafe to do an access memory operation of any type in a compute-and-access if an event (interrupt) can occur, and the second makes it unsafe to fully use the load memory capabilities of compute-and-access if a spooling (DMA to or from memory to the network) operation can occur. The existence of these bugs makes it difficult for the C compiler to fully use compute-and-access, since it cannot guarantee the absence of memory or spooling operations in general. However, within Adapt these operations either cannot occur or can easily be disabled. Hence the assembly code can make full use of the compute-and-access, while the C code cannot.

5 iWarp Communications Structure

Before discussing communications issues in the stereo program, we first briefly discuss the communication capabilities of the iWarp computer; more detail is available elsewhere[1]. It is a two-dimensional torus of processors, each of which is connected physically to its nearest neighbor by input and output ports, each of which can transfer data at 40 MB/s. Cells (0,0) and (0,7) are connected to the SIB. The SIB can communicate with the outside world across a VME bus; all data processed by the iWarp array must pass through the SIB.

iWarp supports a three level communications structure. At the highest level there are connections, which define communications routes among processors. Connections are created by sending a connection header from one processor to another; the header causes physical buffers to be allocated that will be used to pass data along the route traversed by the header. These buffers stay allocated until a connection trailer is sent. Connections are generally allocated for the life of the program. Within connections messages can be used to allow more than two processors to communicate on a single connection. As with connections, messages are created by sending a message header, followed by data, followed by a message trailer. The message header identifies a certain processor that is to receive the data, from among those processors that share the connections. Messages can be sent and received from the memory of one processor to another, or individual words of data may be sent or received from the network. Word-based communication is called *systolic* because the words of data may be processed directly without being stored in the processor's memory, making it possible to efficiently implement many systolic algorithms.

6 Communications Issues

As described in Section 3 images must be distributed from the SIB to the slaves, and collected from the slaves to the SIB. Additionally, two other communications functions are needed:

- *Broadcast.* This operation is used to transfer data from the iWarp SIB to all processors. The maximum bandwidth achievable is 40 MB/s, because this is the maximum physical bandwidth along any one path.

- *Create working copy.* This operation transfers data within the array among adjacent cells. Between any two adjacent cells there is a maximum bandwidth of 80 MB/s. If we transfer across both sides of the cells the maximum bandwidth achievable is 160 MB/s.

The maximum I/O bandwidth for *distribute* and *collect* is 80 MB/s, because there are two physical paths between the SIB and the array, each with a maximum bandwidth of 40 MB/s. (We can use both paths with distribute and collect, but not with broadcast, because the cells can be divided into two groups, each of which is to receive or send half the image to the SIB. In broadcast, each cell receives the identical data, so that data cannot be partitioned in this way.)

In order to ensure maximum bandwidth for Adapt I/O operations, a collection of primitive I/O operations that operate with maximum bandwidth is first defined. The above operations are then constructed from these primitive operations. Since the primitives achieve maximum bandwidth, so will any operations we construct from them, and they will therefore be implemented as efficiently as possible.

The primitive I/O operations available depend on the capabilities of the machine. The iWarp processor is capable of doing the following at maximum bandwidth, i.e. feeding data at 40 MB/s on each physical pathway:

1. *Receive.* Data is taken from the pathway and stored in memory. This can be done in two ways: under explicit program control (systolically) or in the background using a DMA-like operation called spooling. Spooling involves some overhead for setup, but up to four spools can be run at the same time.

2. *Send.* Data is taken from memory and sent to the pathway Again, the operation can be done either systolically or with spooling, using up to four spools.

3. *Pass.* Data is passed from one pathway to another. This can be done either systolically or by manipulation of the communications agent, with some startup overhead. If the pass is done by the communications agent the termination of the pass operation is under control of the sender of the data; if it is done systolically, termination is under control of the processor doing the pass.

4. *Receive and pass.* Data is be passed from one pathway to another and simultaneously copied into memory. This operation can be done only systolically.

5. *Receive and pass twice.* Data is be copied into memory and also sent to two other pathways. This operation can be done only systolically.

The above discussion distinguishes between "systolic" and "spooling" operations. iWarp's systolic capabilities allow it to take data from the pathway and process it directly, or send it back to the pathway, without the data having to pass through memory first. This allows the construction of maximum bandwidth primitive operations not otherwise supported, as in receive and pass and receive and pass twice above. However, only oneof the above primitive operations can occur at a single time, while multiple spools can be executing at once.

These primitive operations are illustrated graphically in Figure 2. We now consider how to implement each of the Adapt I/O functions using these primitive operations.

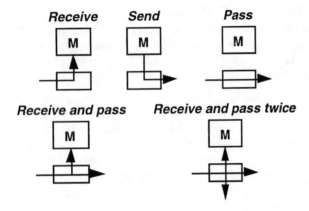

Figure 2: iWarp I/O Primitives.

6.1 Broadcast

Broadcast can be implemented in a variety of ways, some of which are illustrated in Figure 3. The SIB is connected to the processor array at two points, so data can be sent either entirely from one connection (either systolically or using spooling) as in methods (a) and (c), or over both connections simultaneously (using spooling) as in method (b). Once the data is inside array it can be transferred from cell to cell in a pipeline using receive and pass as in methods (a) and (b), or in a tree fashion by also using receive and pass twice as in method (c).

All of these methods achieve the same maximum bandwidth (40 MB/s). The only difference between them is in latency. In method (a) data is passed through all processors before reaching the final cell. In method (b) data travels through half the processors. If in method (c) we organize the tree so that one branch extends down the first column of processors and the other branches extend along the rows then data will travel down the first column and across the last row before reaching the final processor.

These differences in latency lead to a significant difference in performance, as illustrated in Figure 4. (The time for the message to be sent was calculated by first synchronizing the cells, then measuring the time at which the last cell received data.) All methods achieve the same maximum bandwidth on large messages, but with messages of, for example, 256 bytes the three methods give bandwidths of 3.9, 6.1, and 8.0 MB/s, respectively. Significantly, spooling seems to have little overhead; it is used in method (b) but not in (a) or (c) with little evident cost.

Adapt uses method (c) for broadcast, sending the data down the first column and across all rows. Using

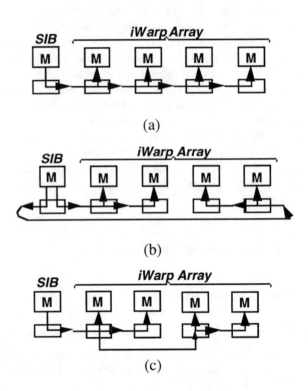

Figure 3: Methods of Implementing Broadcast.

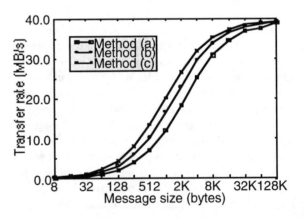

Figure 4: Broadcast performance.

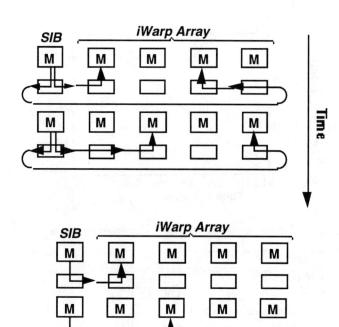

Figure 5: Implementing *distribute*.

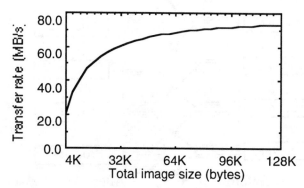

Figure 6: Performance of *distribute*.

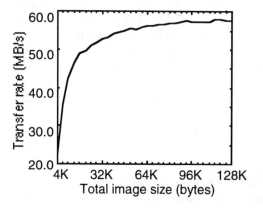

Figure 7: Performance of *collect*.

a modification of method (c) that does broadcast with a binary tree instead of by rows would yield approximately 15 ms additional savings per broadcast or 480 ms overall.

6.2 Distribute

In contrast to broadcast, which has many different methods of implementation, there are really only two different methods of implementing distribute, shown in Figure 5. In the first method, data is sent systolically from the SIB over one pathway; each cell executes a receive followed by a pass. In the second method data is sent from the SIB over two pathways, one that goes in a forward direction through the processors and the other that goes in a reverse direction. Processors in the forward pathway act as before, while processors in the reverse pathway execute at pass followed by a receive.

The method that uses two pathways has a potential bandwidth of 80 MB/s, while the first method has a maximum bandwidth of only 40 MB/s. The only disadvantage of the second method is that it uses spools. We therefore examine the transfer rate for images of various sizes in Figure 6. From this graph we observe

that even for small images of 8K bytes, the transfer rate exceeds the maximum that can be expected from using just one pathway. We therefore adopt the two pathway method.

6.3 Collect

Collect can be implemented using either one or two pathways, similarly to *distribute*. The performance of the two pathway method is shown in Figure 7. As with distribute, the graph rapidly exceeds the maximum bandwidth with a single pathway (at 12K bytes the bandwidth is 42 MB/s), so this method is chosen. However, the maximum bandwidth achievable in collect seems to be 60 MB/s, which is less than the theoretical maximum of 80 MB/s.

This discrepancy is due to a bug in the current iWarp hardware implementation. When data is sent to a cell over a pathway that extends across the board

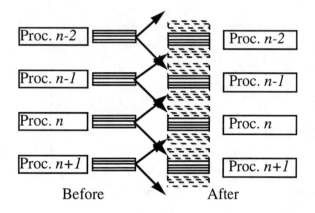

Figure 8: Create working copy.

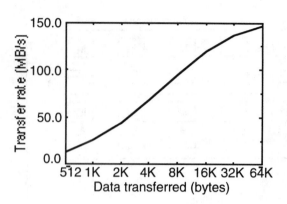

Figure 9: *Create working copy* performance.

Function	Time
Broadcast	1.92 ms
Distribute	3.00 ms
Create working copy	
Difference image	8.76 ms
Sum image	4.90 ms
Collect	4.16 ms
Total	22.7 ms

Table 2: Stereo I/O times

boundary, and the data is received using spooling, the maximum bandwidth achievable is 30 MB/s instead of 40 MB/s. Since the SIB is a single cell on a board, all pathways sending data to the SIB extend across the board boundary and carry at most 30 MB/s This bug did not manifest itself with distribute because the data was being sent, instead of received, at the SIB and all receives in the processor array were done systolically.

6.4 Create working copy

In create working copy each cell initially has several rows of data, and will obtain some rows of data above and below its rows from adjacent cells. The functional behavior is shown in Figure 8. From this figure, it is clear that create working copy can be implemented as two shift operations, in which processor i sends its rows of data to the next or previous processor in the array, depending on whether the shift is in a forward or reverse direction. Create working copy consists of one shift in the forward direction and one shift in reverse. (If more rows are needed on a processor than can be supplied by the processors immediately adjacent then the shift operations are repeated as necessary.)

Each shift operation can be implemented with send and receive operations in the obvious way. If these operations are done systolically, the maximum bandwidth of each will be 40 MB/s; but if spooling is used instead, then each processor can be sending and receiving data for both shifts simultaneously, giving a maximum bandwidth of 160 MB/s.

The performance of the I/O within create working copy is shown in Figure 9. This figure shows the rate that data was transferred from one processor to adjacent processors (counting all four spooling operations), divided by the elapsed time on the proces-

sor. The transfer rate seems to peak at 150 MB/s, instead of the expected 160 MB/s; some of this difference must be due to the limited transfer rate using spooling to a processor whose pathway extends across the board boundary, as was noted with collect. Also, create working copy does not attain maximum bandwidth as quickly as other operations; this is probably due to the use of multiple spools in create working copy, as well as the need for synchronization in two different directions through the processor array when doing the two shift operations.

6.5 I/O times within stereo

Table 2 summarizes the I/O times within stereo. The times for distribute and create working copy were measured directly, and the times for broadcast and collect were estimated from the work earlier in this section (these times could not be estimated directly in a running system since they are overlapped with other computation; thus, the times reported here are overestimates in terms of the impact of these times on total execution time.)

The times for create working copy are larger than would be expected purely from the I/O necessary. This is because create working copy must do other operations in addition to I/O. For example, in the small

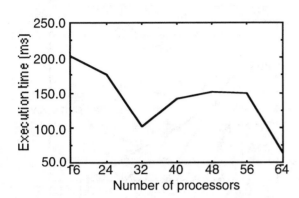

Figure 10: Scaling of performance with number of processors.

stereo test, create working copy for the difference image must obtain eight rows above and seven rows below each processor's rows, for a total data transferred of 30720 bytes (repeated 16 times); 8.76 ms gives a transfer rate of only 56 MB/s. But in addition to the I/O, create working copy also has to copy the processor's own data to a new memory area, and do other initialization.

7 Scaling with number of processors

Figure 10 gives the scaling of the stereo vision algorithm (for three 240×256 images with a 13×13 summation window) from 16 to 64 processors. The execution time does not decrease smoothly with increasing numbers of processors as might be expected. This is because the program is sensitive to the match between the number of rows in the image and the number of processors. The *minimize* function is optimized by forming a partial sum image in the *difference* function; this partial sum image is the sum of four rows at a time of the difference image. As a result, when the processor array size does not nearly evenly divide the image size divided by four, create working copy must do extra work in difference (it realigns the data to fit the largest processor array that evenly divides into the image height divided by four). This occurs with processor numbers of 40, 48, and 56.

8 External I/O

So far we have considered computation and communication within the stereo program running on iWarp. In order to demonstrate high-speed processing, however, we must also address the issue of external I/O,

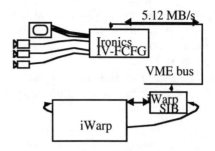

Figure 11: I/O with Ironics IV-FCFG

i.e., the provision of the video input to the processor array and the taking of the video output from the processor array and display on a monitor.

In developing the high-speed stereo vision system reported here, we went through several different system designs. The first system is shown in Figure 11. This uses a standard commercial framebuffer (an Ironics IV-FCFG), which delivers a fairly high VME transfer rate (5.12 MB/s).

Using this design, we were only able to achieve an 8-10 Hz processing rate. The bottleneck is the VME bus. Both the input and output images are transferred via this bus. The input image (from three cameras) is stored in the Ironics framebuffer as three bytes in a 32-bit word of data; thus, for a 240×256 input we must transfer $240 * 256 * 4 = 245760$ bytes of data, taking 48 ms. The output image is stored one byte per word; thus we must transfer 245760 bytes again for display, taking another 48 ms. Since we cannot overlap input and output on the VME bus, the minimum time is 96 ms or 10 Hz., which can be overlapped with processing on the iWarp. In practice, problems with using the Ironics at high speed prevented us from achieving more than about 8 Hz.

In seeking to overcome these problems we developed a high-speed video input board, which interfaces directly to iWarp's memory. The design of this board is extremely simple; it simply does A/D conversion, and sync detect. The inputs from four (synchronized) cameras are packed by the board and packed into a 32-bit word, which can be read from memory by the iWarp cell. At 20 MHz, an iWarp cell is just fast enough to read a full 480×512 image (read as two successive 240×512 fields) at 30 Hz. (In the present system, we use only one field at half horizontal resolution, and process only every third field.)

As the iWarp cell reads the video input data it immediately sends it to the systolic pathway, where it is spooled by another cell into that cell's memory. This intermediate cell in turn spools the image to the SIB, which distributes it to the slave processors as needed. Thus there is almost no delay between the time the pixel is sent in analog from the camera and the time the pixel is processed by the iWarp.

The system reported here uses this and a similar video output board to achieve the 15 Hz processing rate reported.

9 Using Send and Receive

iWarp has a fairly rich communication model; it addition to send and receive, it has pass, receive and pass, etc. Most parallel computers do not have this rich communication model. In this section we consider the implications of our results for such machines.

To do this, we will adopt a very simple model of send and receive and use it to derive the performance requirements necessary to achieve the same I/O times achieved on iWarp. Our model will be described by two parameters: l, for latency, and b, for bandwidth. To simplify the analysis, we will allow no overlap between successive sends or receives between processors. That is, when a processor executes a send, it will wait until the data is completely received before going on to the next operation. While there are parallel computers that work in this way, it must be admitted that a more realistic model, e.g., the postal model, would be preferable. But this model is useful as a first step.

9.1 Broadcast

In broadcast we distribute data in a binary tree. The SIB sends its data to the first cell, then that cell and the SIB send to two other cells, and so on.

Stereo has 32 broadcasts, half with 32 bytes, half with 36 bytes. Seven stages are needed to reach 64 processors. The total time is $32*7(l+34/b) = 1.94$ ms.

9.2 Distribute

Distribute is implemented simply by having the SIB send the appropriate portion of the image to each of the 64 processors. In each cycle of stereo, three images are distributed, with each cell receiving 1024 bytes. The equation relating latency and bandwidth to observed time is $3*64(l + 1024/b) = 3.00$ ms.

9.3 Collect

In collect each cell sends its data directly back to the SIB, in sequence. There is one collect in stereo; each cell sends 4096 bytes. The equation for collect is $64(l + 4096/b) = 4.16$ ms.

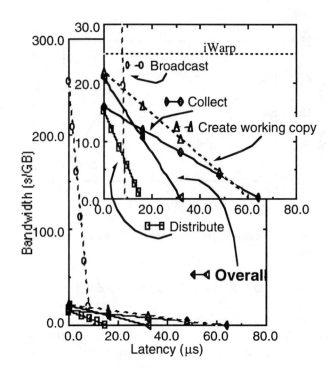

Figure 12: Latency-bandwidth trade-off.

9.4 Create Working Copy

Adapt create working copy is already implemented using send and receive; the only difference here is that no overlap is allowed. Stereo vision does 32 create working copies in all. Half transmit 4096 bytes each time, half 1024. The first does four send/receives twice, the other does four the first time and two the second. Total time is $16(8(l + 4096/b)) + 16(6(l + 1024/b)) = 13.7$ ms.

9.5 Results

Figure 12 gives the latency/bandwidth trade-off needed to achieve the same performance in stereo as on iWarp, using this send/receive model. Note that the vertical axis is in terms of seconds/Gigabyte, the inverse of the usual measure; this makes all the curves straight lines.

Several curves are given, one for each of the Adapt communications functions taken individually, and one for them all taken together. We see that

Overall, there is a fairly strong constraint on latency and bandwidth; latency must be less than approximately 30 μs, and bandwidth less than 20 s/GB (greater than 50 MB/s). Most modern parallel computers have little problem with achieving this bandwidth (at least in peak) but the latency criterion is much more difficult.

The most strongly constraining I/O functions are broadcast and distribute. It is here that the iWarp communications primitives receive and pass and receive and pass twice are used to best advantage. We can relax the requirement for low latency somewhat if these functions are implemented in special ways, perhaps taking advantage of low-level hardware features as on iWarp.

10   Conclusions and Future Work

Achieving the high performance reported here required particular attention to Adapt I/O:

- Many optimizations were made, culminating in the introduction and use of the primitive I/O operators discussed in Section 6. Thinking of the I/O in iWarp in terms of a collection of primitive operators that could be assembled to get the Adapt I/O functions was the key to efficiency. Previous implementations of the Adapt I/O functions made apparently reasonable choices (e.g., using a binary tree and message-passing to implement broadcast) but because there was no systematic approach to getting maximum efficiency performance was poor, and, more importantly, it was impossible to determine whether the implementation was as good as possible. In the work reported here we can be reasonably certain that the Adapt I/O functions are as efficient as possible.

- Most parallel computers support only message passing, and have no systolic communication facilities. This limits the primitive operators to receive and send. Using just these operators, it is possible to build the Adapt I/O functions, but with great loss of efficiency. Perhaps by analysis of the primitive I/O functions the machine is capable of as it is being constructed, increased flexibility can be introduced, resulting in greater efficiency for common program communications functions.

- The rich set of iWarp communications primitives gives significant benefit in terms of being able to tolerate longer latency and lower bandwidth. Since it is very difficult to achieve low message passing latency, perhaps attention should be turned to efficiently implementing a richer set of communications primitives as an alternative.

Our current work focusses on using the stereo system described here as a basis for a more accurate, high-speed stereo vision system that will deliver 1 mm accuracy in a 0.5 m cube.

Acknowledgments

The video I/O boards were designed and built by Thomas Warfel and Luke Tuttle of the iWarp and parallel computer vision projects at Carnegie Mellon.

The work on stereo vision was started by Hans Thomas and Bill Ross of the Vision and Autonomous Systems Center at Carnegie Mellon. The Adapt I/O library was originally written by Doug Smith of the Adapt project. Michael Mills of the iWarp project did some of the early work on the iWarp implementation of multi-baseline stereo. The support of several other members of the iWarp group, in particular Thomas Gross, Dave O'Hallaron, and Susan Hinrichs, is gratefully acknowledged.

This research was supported by the National Science Foundation under Grant MIPS 8920420 and by the Defense Advanced Research Projects Agency and monitored by U. S. Army Training and Doctrine in Fort Huachuca, Arizona under Contract DABT63-91-C-0035.

The Government has certain rights in this material. Any views, opinions, findings, and conclusions or recommendations expressed in this material are those of the author and do not necessarily reflect the views of the National Science Foundation. They should also not be interpreted as representing the official policies, either expressed or implied, of the U.S. Government.

References

[1] Borkar, S., Cohn, R., Cox, G., Gleason, S., Gross, T., Kung, H. T., Lam, M., Moore, B., Peterson, C., Pieper, J., Rankin, L., Tseng, P. S., Sutton, J., Urbanski, J., and Webb, J. (1988). iWarp: An Integrated Solution to High-Speed Parallel Computing. In *Proceedings of Supercomputing '88*, (pp. 330-339). Orlando, Florida.

[2] Okutomi, M., and Kanade, T. (1991). A Multiple Baseline Stereo. In *IEEE Computer Society Conference on Computer Vision and Pattern Recognition*, (pp. 63-69). Lahaina, Maui, Hawaii: IEEE Computer Society.

[3] Webb, J. A. (1992). *Steps Toward Architecture Independent Image Processing.* IEEE Computer, 25(2), 21-31.

Decentralized Optimal Power Pricing:
The Development of a Parallel Program *

S. Lumetta

L. Murphy   X. Li
D. Culler   I. Khalil

University of California at Berkeley
Berkeley, CA 94720

Abstract

For MPP's to solve new and interesting problems, they must support the development of sophisticated algorithms on very large data sets. Successful development depends strongly on the speed of the execute-fix cycle. Sequential machines cannot provide sufficiently fast execution of large problems, but many programming systems available on MPP's today neglect the significance of time spent fixing an algorithm during development. Those systems which do address the fix time commonly demand drastic sacrifices in execution speed. Between these two extremes is the middle ground where development must occur. We have implemented a new algorithm to solve an optimization problem for an electrical power system, a problem large enough to require significant computational resources. To help abstract the communication and layout requirements of the problem away from the main algorithm, we have developed a small object system library. The results are an efficient and easily modifiable solution to the problem and a general approach to solving this class of problems.

1   Introduction

Use of MPP's divides into two classes: the brute force acceleration of simple numeric kernels and the development of novel solution techniques for problems large enough to require significant computational resources. The former demands only efficient execution, but the latter requires the ability to abstract away from the issues of layout and communication and the ability to quickly modify the algorithm under development. We have implemented a new algorithm to solve one of these latter problems—a large-scale optimization problem for an electrical power system.

The power system optimization problem is stated as follows: given a power network represented by a tree, with the power plant at the root and the customers at the leaves, use local information to determine the prices which will optimize the benefit to the community. In an operational system, the problem must be solved in a few seconds, and a simulation must demonstrate that these constraints are reasonable. The size of the network—10,000 customers served from a single plant or substation—is typical of realistic systems. To solve the problem, we implemented a novel strategy of iterative optimization put forth in [7]. The size of the problem, coupled with the real-time constraints, convinced us that solution on a workstation would be neither productive nor worthwhile.

Prior to our implementation, the algorithm had only been tested on toy systems three orders of magnitude smaller than our own. We expected difficulties to arise both in implementing the algorithm itself and in adjusting the algorithm to work on the larger system. As with any large problem, we wanted to divide the problem into smaller subproblems which could be solved independently. Specifically, we hoped to isolate the layout and communication problems from the main algorithm. We found, however, that the abstractions available to us were insufficient to allow easy segmentation. To meet the need for flexible but efficient code, we designed and implemented a system for fine-grained synchronization of data objects between

---

*This material is based upon work supported under a National Science Foundation Graduate Research Fellowship and National Science Foundation Infrastructure Grant number CDA-8722788. Any opinions, findings, conclusions, or recommendations expressed in this publication are those of the authors and do not necessarily reflect the views of the National Science Foundation.

processors. After encapsulating the layout and communication problems of the program within our object system, the remaining code became much cleaner and easier to modify.

Our implementation runs on the Connection Machine-5 at Berkeley. The CM-5 connects 64 Sparc processors with private local memories in a fat-tree network, providing a SPMD, message-passing paradigm with which to program (note that these 64 processors are not enhanced with vector capabilities as are some CM-5 installations). The CM Active Message layer[9] insulates the application from the private nature of the processor memory, allowing any processor to access memory on any other processor without the latter explicitly recognizing the former.

The remainder of this paper is organized as follows: Section 2 describes the problem and algorithm; Section 3 explains the goals of the object system and how they were met; Section 4 discusses the interactive process of development and the results obtained from the work. Section 5 summarizes the project, gives our conclusions, and suggests avenues for further research.

2 Pricing of Electric Power

Electric power distribution systems almost always have a tree structure, with a unique point of supply at the root (the *substation*) and the customers at the leaves. Intermediate nodes represent switches, tap-points, and transformers, where the path of electrical power is split. The tree structure for this application is shown in Figure 1. Ten main feeders run from the root, each branching off twenty lateral nodes. Each lateral node is the head of a line of five branch nodes, and each branch node has ten leaves. In total, there are 1,201 internal nodes and 10,000 customers. This system is a typical size for medium-to-large distribution systems.

The pricing problem is to set the price for each customer's power consumption so that the economic efficiency of the whole community is maximized. Customers are assumed to act locally to maximize their own benefits, based on the prices currently offered to them. The local information used by a customer to determine their maximum benefit is *private* to that customer. On the other hand, customers are not concerned with the operation of the power system. They are only exposed to the effects of their actions on the system through the prices sent to them by the root. Thus, the pricing problem is inherently decentralized.

Previous pricing schemes either ignored the decentralized nature of the problem by assuming all the in-

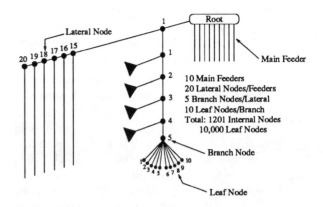

Figure 1: Power Distribution Tree

formation necessary for solution was available in one location, or attempted to learn this information by using past behavior or by 'probing' the system. In [7], a pricing scheme was presented which sets the prices in such a way that individual benefit maximization by the customers also results in maximization of community benefits. This scheme addresses the issue of decentralized knowledge by using a new distributed pricing algorithm, emphasizing local computations.

The algorithm requires a number of parameters to be chosen beforehand. These include the local optimization conditions for the leaves (customer benefit functions and constraints), the power loss parameters for each line, the electrical constraints imposed by the power system, and the cost of supply of electrical power at the substation.

2.1 Problem Formulation

We formulate the pricing problem as an optimization problem at two levels, those of the customer and of the community.

	Partial list of variable names
P_i	Real power demanded by i^{th} customer
Q_i	Reactive power demanded by i^{th} customer
π_{iR}	Price for real power demand P_i
π_{iX}	Price for reactive power demand Q_i
P_r^{out}	Real power flow out of line r (sum of flows to children)
Q_r^{out}	Reactive power flow out of line r (sum of flows to children)
P_r^{loss}	Real power loss in line r
Q_r^{loss}	Reactive power loss in line r
P_r^{in}	Real power flow into line r (before loss)
Q_r^{in}	Reactive power flow into line r (before loss)
θ_R	Lagrange multiplier for the global real power

equality constraint

θ_X Lagrange multiplier for the global reactive power equality constraint

First, for each customer i, the cost of consumption is the price of electricity multiplied by the demand : $\pi_{iR} \cdot P_i$ for the real power consumed, and $\pi_{iX} \cdot Q_i$ for the reactive power. The problem is to find the real and reactive power demands P_i and Q_i which maximize individual benefit minus cost of consumption, for given prices π_{iR} and π_{iX}. There is a linear equality and a quadratic inequality constraint associated with each customer. Individual benefit maximization thus consists of solving 4 simultaneous nonlinear equations for each i.

The benefit of electricity consumption to the community is the sum of the individual benefits. The substation cost of supply is a negative benefit to the community. Hence the net benefit to the community is the sum of the individual benefits, minus the cost of supply.

This net benefit is maximized, subject to balance constraints on the flow of power in each lossy line. For a lossy line r, the balance constraints take the form:

$$P_r^{in} = P_r^{out} + P_r^{loss}$$
$$Q_r^{in} = Q_r^{out} + Q_r^{loss}$$

The power losses in r are quadratic functions of the power flows into r; i.e., P_r^{loss} is a quadratic function of P_r^{in} and Q_r^{in}, and similarly for Q_r^{loss}. Thus, given the values of P_r^{out} and Q_r^{out}, these balance constraints are coupled quadratic equations in P_r^{in} and Q_r^{in}. In our application, there are $1,200$ pairs of power balance constraints.

Since the optimal values of the prices are not known in advance, we send prices down the tree from the root, compute the customer responses to these prices at the leaves, and propagate the effects of these responses on the system back up the tree to the root. The pricing algorithm is *iterative*, where each iteration consists of a downward sweep followed by an upward sweep.

Each P_r^{out} and Q_r^{out} is the sum of the flows to descendant nodes of r. The upward sweep begins by calculating demand at the leaves, where downstream flows are defined to be zero. Once the demands of all children of an internal node have been calculated, the demand of that node may be calculated to satisfy the balance constraints on the line above. This process leads to an upward sweep, propagating up the tree until it reaches the substation, where a convergence check is applied. If this check fails, the prices are updated, and propagated down the tree to the leaves

(customers), which compute new demands. Then the upward sweep begins again.

The outline of the algorithm, broken into four steps, is shown below.

1. **Initialization**
   $k \leftarrow 0$
   Guess initial values of the multipliers associated with the substation convergence check, $\theta_R(0)$ and $\theta_X(0)$.

2. **Pass prices down and compute demand**
   (a) Compute the prices for customer i, using $\theta_R(k)$ and $\theta_X(k)$.
   (b) Compute customer i's demand, $P_i(k)$ and $Q_i(k)$, by solving the 4 simultaneous nonlinear equations associated with i.
   (c) Begin upward sweep at the leaves.
   (d) When $P_r^{out}(k)$ and $Q_r^{out}(k)$ have been calculated for r, compute $P_r^{in}(k)$ and $Q_r^{in}(k)$ by solving 2 coupled quadratic equations.
   (e) Propagate the computed power flows towards the root.

3. **Convergence test (done at the root node)**
   Compute the new values of total system demand.
   Use the new total demands to check for convergence of θ_R and θ_X.
   If converged, stop. Otherwise, go to step 4.

4. **Update the multipliers (done at the root node)**
   Use an update rule to generate $\theta_R(k+1)$ and $\theta_X(k+1)$.
   $k \leftarrow k + 1$
   Go to step 2

The algorithm is described graphically in Figure 2.

3 Object System

Traditional message-passing systems present more trouble to programmers than do sequential or shared memory machines because of the need to design and implement message-passing protocols for communication and synchronization on a per-problem basis. The most efficient implementations require that this communication code be fully integrated with the rest of the program, but for development one must be capable of easily modifying the algorithm without redesigning the communication pattern. One needs abstractions which are general enough to allow separation of the code sections and yet close enough to the hardware communication primitives that a reasonable efficiency is maintained. We began to work out a model for these abstractions, keeping in mind that while an object system needs to make correct and efficient programming easy, it need not make misuse impossible.

The central goal of the object system is to separate the problem of data layout from the algorithm itself

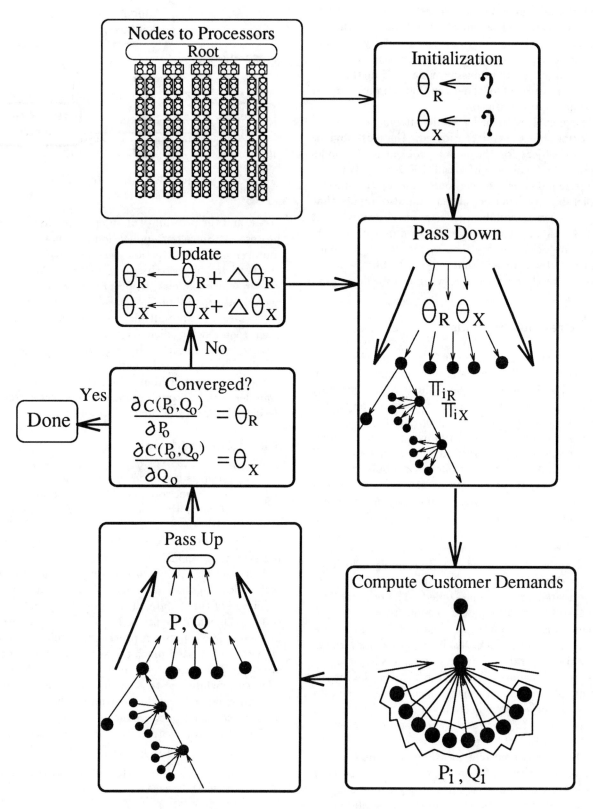

Figure 2: Algorithm to Iteratively Optimize an Electrical Power System

by providing a global object space abstraction, yet to allow an optimized layout to be reflected in the execution time of the program. Data locality occupies a crucial position in efficient programming of MPP's, and the object system must provide good methods for the common case of local data so that the programmer is capable of optimization.

Design choices for such systems often depend on the particular objects being considered. The most obvious choice of object for the power problem is the node, each of which consists of about 100 bytes. This fine grain-size puts fairly strong constraints on the amount of tolerable overhead per object, but also implies that several accesses will be made to an object when it is used, making it more efficient to duplicate remote objects in local memory than to repeatedly reference them remotely. In addition, we would like to access objects directly on reference, without introducing extra levels of indirection.

3.1 Previous Systems

Several systems have already been developed for distributed parallel programming, including Ivy [4], Linda [3] and Tarmac [1] [5]. Shared virtual memory systems such as Ivy move entire memory pages between processors, clearly inappropriate for a problem in which an object averages 100 bytes. Linda is based on the tuple space abstraction, and requires that all shared data be encoded as tuples. The application has no say in placement of data or communication patterns, however, so the programmer can not optimize the program with an appropriate data layout.

The Tarmac system came closest to meeting the goals of our system. Tarmac provides a model of shared global state called mobile memory, which allows uniquely-identified and arbitrarily-sized objects to be created, moved, and copied. The original Tarmac abstraction [5] made no attempt to provide synchronization capabilities, but the CM-5 implementation [1] corrects this lack. However, the extra overhead involved in several of Tarmac's design decisions interferes with the goals of our system: under the mobile memory abstraction, Tarmac objects are not bound to any processor—each object can reside and be moved from processor to processor. When a processor wishes to access an object, it must follow a chain of 'hints' as to the object's current location (i.e., one or more levels of indirection). Keeping with this model, only a single copy of an object exists at any time—copying an object results in the creation of a new, uniquely-identified object. The object in Tarmac is thus inherently consistent, but at the cost of inefficiency in

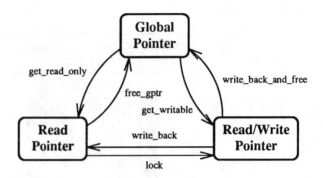

Figure 3: Gptr state model

access and the possibility of objects thrashing between processors. Since our application does not require the mobile memory abstraction, we do not wish to pay the overhead to support these abstractions. We prefer a system which exploits the programmer's knowledge of access patterns by binding each object to a processor and which allows multiple copies of objects to exist when required for efficiency.

After reviewing the object systems mentioned, we decided that none came sufficiently close to meeting the goals presented above for our program. The remainder of this section describes the object system we designed to meet our goals more effectively.

3.2 Pointer Model

The system is based on the *global pointer*, consisting of a home processor number and a pointer in the address space of the home processor.[1] The user is provided with routines to allocate data objects of arbitrary size and to access them asynchronously for reading and synchronously for writing.

When an object is created using **gmalloc**, a structure called a *gptr* is returned. A gptr structure can be in one of three states, including the global pointer state, as shown in Figure 3. In this state, the gptr can be passed freely between processors, copied, stored in objects, and treated much the same as any other type of data. The data object itself, however, cannot be referenced while a gptr is in the global pointer state. The gptr can be transformed into either of the two other states via object system procedures.

The other two states of the gptr are used when a local copy of a data object is present on the proces-

---

[1]The reader familiar with Split-C [2] will recognize the similarity to the Split-C memory model—the main difference here is that our code is completely at the user level. Without compiler support, some concepts are difficult to implement as elegantly as one would like. We hope to port our system to Split-C in the near future.

sor. The first provides only the capability to read the data, and is called a *read pointer*. The second provides the additional capability to write to the data object, and is called a *read/write pointer*. While in either of these states, the gptr should only be used to reference the data; the gptr in these states has no significance to other processors, and may be corrupt even for the same processor at a later time. Thus, read pointers and read/write pointers can not be stored in objects or passed between processors.

Synchronized accesses can be accomplished by means of the read/write pointer. At most one gptr referring to a particular object can be in this state at any time, and the object itself is considered to be locked. Requests to change state from a global pointer to the object are denied while the object is locked, but no attempt is made to invalidate or update older *versions* of the object which may be present on other processors. Since managing data consistency at the library level must be general enough to provide consistency models for every program, and since this generality implies overhead not only for what is used but also for what is not, we felt that implementing a data consistency model was best left to the programmer. We encountered no problems in building an appropriate model for the power problem using the object system.

The object system library provides procedures to transform gptrs in any given state into any of the other states. Obtaining either a read pointer or a read/write pointer from a global pointer is done with the **get_read_only** and **get_writable** procedures. If the object is local to the processor requesting the state change, the gptr is simply changed (assuming the request was successful), and the data object itself is used as a virtual local copy. If the object is remote, the data is copied into local memory and the gptr is changed to reference this copy. Since most objects will be referenced more than once in a short period of time, it is more efficient to make a copy of a small object than to repeatedly request data from a remote processor.

A read pointer may be returned to the global pointer state by a call to **free_gptr**, or a read/write pointer for the object may be obtained by a call to **lock**. To avoid sending unnecessary messages, the latter does not obtain the latest version of the object. If the latest version is needed, one must first release the version being held with **free_gptr**.

Read/write pointers must write the modified data back to the data object to change to another state. **write_back** simply writes back the data and maintains a local copy of the object with a read pointer. **write_back_and_free** writes the data back and discards the local copy, returning the gptr to the global pointer state.

By direct modification of the gptr, the system avoids the expense of lookup for each reference. Macros are provided to determine the state of a given gptr, although in most cases the programmer will already know.

3.3 Implementation

A gptr consists of two 32-bit fields, one indicating the processor number of the processor on which the global data object is located, and the second field pointing to the object in the home processor's address space. The scheme used to differentiate between gptr states relies on the home processor (*pnum*) field. If the pnum is greater or equal to 0, the gptr is the global pointer state. Recall that no direct access is possible from this state. The constants READ and READ_WRITE are used in place of the processor for the read and read/write states. In both cases, the address field of the gptr becomes a local pointer to the data (or a copy of the data if the object was remote). Figure 4 shows the structures used for objects and local copies along with a global pointer and a read pointer.

In addition to the user-visible gptr structure, the library uses a second structure internally to manage synchronization and local caching of data objects. The global header, or *gheader*, structure is appended to the front of each data object as it is created, and also appears on the front of each local copy. The actual pointer value in both global and local gptrs points beyond this header.

The gheader structure contains four 32-bit fields. The first field holds the size of the data object, and is used to simplify requests for state changes which might require data transfers. Only a single bit is used in the second field, a flag for locking the object. The flag in the global object is set whenever a gptr is changed to the read/write state and cleared when the gptr is returned to the global pointer state. The lock bit in the local copy mirrors that of the global object and is used to efficiently prevent more than one gptr on the same processor from entering the read/write state (see caching below). The third and fourth fields of the gheader form a global pointer which points to the global data object. When a routine changes the state of a gptr from global pointer to either read or read/write, it must store the global pointer for later use. The fields in the global object are self-referencing, and allow the system to change a global pointer into a local pointer for objects on the

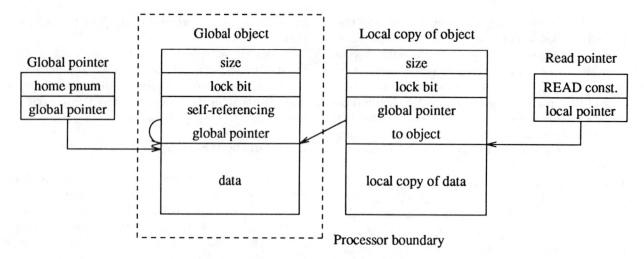

Figure 4: Global and local data objects

same processor by merely changing the pnum field to READ or READ_WRITE and to avoid relatively high cost of copying the data.

The other internal device used by the system is a hash table mapping global pointers to local copies. Because of the possibility of several gptrs on a single processor referencing the same data object, a mapping with reference counts is maintained, ensuring that only a single local copy of any object will ever exist. Any time a read or read/write pointer is requested, the routines first search the hash table to determine if a local copy already exists. If a copy is present, it is used, preventing costly communication with the data's home processor. Requests to obtain a read/write pointer must still contact the home processor for the lock, of course, but may not need to receive the data, just an approval. Again, if another gptr on the same processor already possesses the lock, refusal is automatic and requires no communication because the lock bit in the local copy will be set.

3.4 Example of Use

To demonstrate how the object system simplifies the code in the program, this section presents a portion of the code used to compute demand at the leaves. Figure 5 shows the code executed for each leaf owned by a processor. The leaves are linked in a list by gptrs, and the processor traverses the list and calculates the demand for each node, adding it to the downstream demand of the parent. If all of the children for a parent node have been processed, the parent node is added to the queue on its home processor (not shown).

Note that the only differences apparent between this code and code one would write for a uniproces-

```
/* Obtain a writeable copy of the leaf node */
/* and read the gptr to the next leaf node.  */

while (get_writable (&current));
next=LEAF_NODE (current)->next_leaf;

/* Calculate the demand at the leaf */

optimize_node (&NODE_P (current), &NODE_Q (current),
               LEAF_NODE (current)->pi_R,
               LEAF_NODE (current)->pi_I);
if (NODE_P (current) < 0)
    NODE_P (current)=NODE_Q (current)=0;

/* Duplicate the gptr to the parent of the */
/* leaf, then modify the parent node to    */
/* indicate that another child's           */
/* calculations have been completed.       */

parent=LEAF_NODE (current)->parent;
while (get_writable (&parent));
NODE_P (parent)+=NODE_P (current);
NODE_Q (parent)+=NODE_Q (current);
done=++CHILDREN_DONE (parent);

/* Write the modified data back */
/* and free the local copies.   */

write_back_and_free (&parent);
write_back_and_free (&current);
```

Figure 5: Code segment for calculation of leaf demand

sor are the calls to get and write back local copies of data, and the duplication of the parent's gptr. These calls can be likened to declaration of variables—the programmer declares which data he intends to read and which he intends to write, performs the actions, and then declares that he has finished with the data. Because it is modified directly, the local gptr is fully equivalent to a uniprocessor pointer.

4   Implementation and Results

After designing and implementing the object system to help break apart the electrical power network problem, we began to attack the problem itself. This section discusses the various stages of development, first with the structure of the program and the optimal solution for lossless power lines, and then with the development of the algorithm to solve the problem with typical loss rates.

4.1   Algorithm Implementation

The first part to be written was the code to distribute the network across the processors. The network used in the problem is fixed, so we avoided the issues of dynamic load-balancing and simply allocated the nodes to processors to roughly balance the load. The division of the tree is shown in Figure 6—the small boxes represent processors and each circle represents a lateral node and associated branch and leaf nodes. The root node is owned by one of the processors along the top row. After building the lateral nodes and passing a gptr to the next processor, each processor builds the nodes below each lateral node it owns. Node initialization is performed as each node is created.

Once the tree structure had been set up, other sections of code could treat the tree as if it were completely local, with the object system handling any implicit communication. For example, see Figure 5 for a sample segment of code for computation of customer demand.

The iteration of the algorithm became a simple loop relying on two procedures to perform the work. The first procedure corresponds to the 'Pass Down' frame of Figure 2 and computes the path-dependent price information for each customer. The second corresponds to the 'Compute Customer Demands' and 'Pass Up' frames, which find customer demand and calculate line losses, passing information upward to determine the power demand at the root. The 'Converged?' and 'Update' frames were coded directly into the main loop

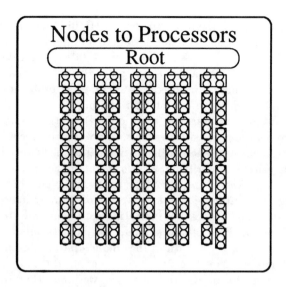

Figure 6: Distribution of the tree across processors

since only the owner of the root node need perform these actions.

4.2   Lossless Solution

Working with the simpler problem of a lossless system, we debugged the code and found that the basic algorithm did work as expected. Although we can not directly verify that our solution to the lossless problem is indeed correct, predictions based on smaller systems agree with our results, and scaling is reliable with lossless systems.

Recall now the real-time constraints on the problem: the substation will perform this algorithm with a period of between 10 and 30 minutes. Prices must not be allowed to vary for more than a small fraction of this period to ensure reliable costs to the customers. With these limits in mind, we proceeded to time our first results.

Timing with the 33MHz processor clock on one of the processors (after processor synchronization), the solution of the lossless network takes a total of 5.436 seconds, most of which is spent building the tree. The iterations take between 107 and 691 milliseconds, depending on how close the leaf nodes start to the solution of the demand optimization. The previous solution of demand from a leaf node is used as initial values in the subsequent solution, and computation time decreases monotonically as the algorithm progresses. The iterations are computationally intensive, with only about 10 milliseconds needed to pass prices down the tree and, presumably, a similar amount to pass information back up. Clearly the CM-5 meets the constraints of the problem, demonstrating that the algorithm can meet the needs of actual power networks.

Initial timing results on a workstation indicated that solution of a single customer demand problem required about 6 milliseconds. Scaling the problem to 10,000 nodes, we expect that the problem will take about one minute per iteration. Even the lossless problem requires six iterations, so a workstation could well require one-half of the pricing period just to settle the prices. To verify our beliefs, we built the tree on a single processor and solved the lossless problem. Finding the solution required an average of 48 times longer than did 64 processors, indicating approximately 75% efficiency. Part of this speedup can be attributed to the cache size—1/64th of the tree fits into the cache, while the entire tree does not. Running the code on the workstation mentioned above, we found that the solution in fact took twice as long as predicted—a total of 12 minutes for the lossless problem. Neither the single CM-5 processor nor the workstation is capable of meeting the real-time constraints of the problem. An adequately fast solution requires the computational power of the CM-5.

4.3 Code Development

After our initial success with the lossless problem, we set the line impedances to what we believed to be typical values (these values turned out to be an order of magnitude too large). The algorithm broke down trying to solve such a high-loss problem—demand oscillated wildly between almost nothing and about twice that of the lossless solution. Reducing the line impedances, we found that the algorithm converged for impedances of up to 1/10th of the proposed values. Table 1 shows the solutions for various impedances, scaled to actual typical impedances. Noting that the total demand at the root decreases almost linearly in impedance over the range measured, with real demand dropping by 2.4 units at $1/100^{th}$, 23.4 units at $1/10^{th}$, and 216.7 units at full impedance, we were able to guess at the solution to the high-loss problem.

Over the next few weeks we directly verified our ideas about reducing modification time as we passed hundreds of times through the execution-fix cycle. The time invested in development of the object system was more than returned in the time saved in later modification. The global memory abstraction insulated the necessary changes from the communication schemes, allowing us to concentrate on the algorithm itself.

After many failed attempts to eliminate the oscillations, we tested the system to determine the amount of power being lost in the lines. The line impedances proposed initially for the system proved far too high—over 16% of the power was lost near equilibrium. Since no actual system would allow the total losses to exceed 2-3% of demand at the root, we probed the system with successively higher line impedances to determine the percentage of power loss for which the algorithm broke down. The results are shown in Table 2. The algorithm breaks down at about four times the typical line impedance, when the power lost in the system is roughly three times the nominal value of 2-3%.

5 Conclusions and Future Work

Using the CM-5 as a development tool, we have successfully implemented a new algorithm to solve the problem of optimal pricing for electrical power networks. Because of the problem's size, solution by a workstation would be unproductive. Because of the real-time constraints imposed on the problem for use with actual power networks, such a solution would also fail to be worthwhile. An adequate solution to the problem requires the computational power of the CM-5.

We approached the problem by first separating out the requirements of communication and layout from the algorithm. Through the abstraction provided by our object system, we removed the complexity of integrating communication patterns into the main code. As a result, the code became more flexible and easier to modify. The overhead cost of the simplification was not unreasonable, with processors operating at approximately 75% efficiency. We feel that our approach could be profitably extended to many problems.

Although we have made progress in understanding optimal power pricing in distribution networks, many avenues remain for exploration. Realistic power systems might reconfigure the network, for example, so a simulation must be capable of redistributing nodes to processors in a short time. The addition of direct power flow constraints on internal lines would also increase realism, perhaps requiring iteration over each subtree to arrive at a valid solution. Also, some of the equations used in our solution were simplified versions of the actual optimization equations—the precise equations may introduce further complications in the algorithm. Furthermore, customers in realistic systems would have distinct benefit and inequality functions, whereas each of the customers in our example used the same functions.

We also hope to further develop the object system by integrating it into the Split-C library[2]. Split-C is

Fraction of Typical Impedance	Number of Iterations	θ_R	θ_X	P_0	Q_0
0	6	0.72527	0.14505	7252.7	1450.5
$1/100^{th}$	6	0.72504	0.14502	7250.3	1450.2
$1/10^{th}$	12	0.72293	0.14472	7229.3	1447.2
Typical	19	0.70360	0.14192	7036.0	1419.2

Table 1: Results for Various Loss Rates

Multiple of Typical Impedance	Number of Iterations	Demand at Root	Demand at Leaves	% Loss
Typical	18	7034.7	6862.9	2.44
2	21	6848.9	6535.1	4.58
3	48	6686.8	6252.5	6.49
3.5	107	6612.5	6124.4	7.38

Table 2: Power Lost for Various Loss Rates

an extension to the C language which provides efficient support for the shared memory, message passing, and data parallel programming paradigms. Making the system available for use by others at Berkeley will provide valuable feedback about its features, drawbacks, and general usefulness.

Acknowledgements

The authors would like to thank Professor Felix Wu for helpful discussions about the material presented here.

References

[1] D. F. Bacon and S. E. Lucco, "Tarmac: A Mobile Memory System for the Connection Machine CM-5," Draft

[2] D. E. Culler, A. Dusseau, S. C. Goldstein, A. Krishnamurthy, S. Lumetta, T. von Eicken, K. Yelick, "Introduction to Split-C," to be published in *Proceedings of Supercomputing*, 1993.

[3] D. Gelernter, "Parallel Programming in Linda," *Proceedings of the International Conference on Parallel Processing*, pp. 255-263, Aug. 1985.

[4] K. Li and P. Hudak, "Memory Coherence in Shared Virtual Memory Systems," *Proceedings of the 5th Annual ACM Symp. on ACM Conf. on Principles on Distributed Computing*, pp. 229-239, 1986.

[5] S. E. Lucco and D. P. Anderson, "Tarmac: a Language System Substrate Based on Mobile Memory," UCB Report CSD 89/#525, November 1989.

[6] D. G. Luenberger, *Linear and Nonlinear Programming*, 2nd. Ed., Addison-Wesley, 1989.

[7] L. Murphy, R. J. Kaye and F. F. Wu, "Distributed Spot Pricing in Radial Distribution Systems," Paper 93 WM 148-7 PWRS, presented at the IEEE Power Engineering Society 1993 Winter Meeting, Columbus, OH, Jan 31 - Feb 5, 1993.

[8] P. Stenström, "A Survey of Cache Coherence Scheme for Multiprocessors," IEEE Computer, pp. 12-24, June 1990.

[9] T. von Eicken, D. E. Culler, S. C. Goldstein, K. E. Schauser, "Active Messages: a Mechanism for Integrated Communication and Computation," UCB Report CSD 92/#675, March 1992.

DAYLIGHTING DESIGN VIA MONTE CARLO WITH A CORRESPONDING SCIENTIFIC VISUALIZATION

Roland Schweitzer[1], Jonathan McHugh, Patrick J. Burns and Charles Zeeb
Department of Mechanical Engineering Colorado State University
Fort Collins, CO 80525
schweitzer@yuma.ACNS.ColoState.EDU,
jmchugh@carbon.LANCE.ColoState.EDU,pburns@yuma.ACNS.ColoState.EDU and czeeb@carbon.-LANCE.ColoState.EDU

ABSTRACT

A brief history of Monte Carlo methods is presented, with emphasis on uses in engineering. An overview of daylighting design is then presented, exploring both quantity and quality of light. Various strategies for achieving effectively daylit enclosures are examined, with heavy emphasis upon computation. Monte Carlo methods are the only ones which are sufficiently robust to handle specular surfaces and properties which vary with incident angle (such as for glass). A general purpose computer code, DAY3D, is developed and applied to the calculation of luminous intensities in general enclosures. Due to the requirement for huge computing resources, we perform an architectural study of photon tracing on a Cray Y/MP and a CM-2, illustrating the promise of a small CM-2 architecture for this problem. Next, we explore various strategies for visualizing both field results and the discrete Monte Carlo processes.

1. HISTORY OF MONTE CARLO

The Monte Carlo method was formalized in the 1940's. Uses of the method have been diverse and varied since that time. However, due to computer limitations, the method has not yet fully lived up to its potential as discussed by Metropolis [Metropolis, 1985]. Indeed, this is reflected in the stages the method has undergone in the fields of engineering. In the late 1950's and 1960's the method was tested in a variety of engineering fields. At that time, even simple problems were compute-bound. Since that time frame, attention was focused upon much-needed convergence enhancement procedures. Many complex problems still remained intractable through the 1970's.

With the advent of gather/scatter vector hardware and masks in massively parallel hardware, we today have a synthesized approach to vectorizing Monte Carlo problems. In his Ph.D. dissertation, Brown introduced the concept of the "event step" [Brown, 1981], enabling efficient

---

1. Member, ACM, presently at University of Nevada, Reno

vectorization of Monte Carlo algorithms where the particles do not interact. This approach was later successfully exploited by several investigators. Martin et al. [Martin et al., 1986] reported speedups of a factor of five on an IBM 3090 with vector units. Nearly linear speedup was reported [Sequent Computer Systems, 1985] on a parallel architecture for photon tracing. Bobrowicz et al. [Bobrowicz et al., 1984a; Bobrowicz et al., 1984b] obtained speedups of factors from five to eight in an algorithm where particles are accumulated in queues until efficient vector lengths are obtained. Even physics algorithms such as the Los Alamos benchmark GAMTEB can be effectively vectorized [Burns et al., 1988]. Such advanced coding techniques have enabled much bigger problems to be attacked, with improved accuracy. However, there are still a host of problems which are intractable, even with an effectively vectorized algorithm. Kalos [Kalos, 1985] addresses architectural issues, including the importance of shared memory, the difficulty of load balancing, the small granularity and the high degree of logical complexity.

We now contrast transport Monte Carlo methods with the continuum approach. Transport Monte Carlo methods follow natural stochastic processes. As such, Monte Carlo methods offer the advantage of giving "fidelity to nature, to experiments, and to engineering requirements" [Kalos, 1985]. In many implementations, there is no natural time scale, to wit enough particles must be traced to achieve stationary answers, which no longer vary (at least to some small statistical tolerance) upon further increase in number of particles traced. That is, the answers must be "converged." Maltby [Maltby, 1989] has shown for a broad class of Monte Carlo algorithms entailing Bernoulli trials, that convergence is assured. The convergence rate is proportional to the inverse square root of the number of particles traced. Thus, accuracy is assured, if the user can afford the CPU time to finish the run. This is an important distinction between Monte Carlo methods and continuum methods, which are oft subject to divergence.

However, the "inverse root N" convergence rate is slow, and many have investigated convergence enhancement algorithms. Among the most popular is splitting, where particles approaching a "target" are partitioned into multiple particles, each of which is then traced separately. This increases the number of samples which reach the target, thereby increasing statistical accuracy. This methodology is usually applied together with Russian Roulette, where particles which travel away from the "target" volume are dealt with in the converse, i.e. a random half have their characteristics doubled while the remainder are destroyed and tracing ceases for these. Heifetz [Heifetz, 1987] gives a particularly lucid explanation of these strategies. Of course, this approach is only possible where there exists a well-defined and localized target. Where accurate answers are required for entire geometries, Maltby and Burns [Maltby and Burns, 1991] have employed "inverse sampling," where only enough particles are traced from each surface to obtain a preset level of accuracy. Thus, the emission of new particles dynamically evolves with the simulation. This method holds promise for large reductions in CPU time when tracing particles in complex geometries.

Our particular focus here is the tracing of photons in typical room geometries to provide daylighting, which displaces electrical lighting. This particular application emphasizes large-scale aspects, for which visualization is an almost essential component of debugging. To aid in our debugging process, we desire to extend the extension of "standard" visualization packages to problems of Monte Carlo type. Most if not all standard visualization packages are designed to display continuum fields. By contrast, Monte Carlo particle transport involves action at a distance. Thus, our experience was a bit like "trying to fit a square peg into a round hole." We desired to prepare a visualization that would help to validate the model. At the same time we needed to be able to communicate the results to people both familiar and unfamiliar with the computational technique. We desired to visualize the position of the photons in the room over many event steps. In addition, we wished to color the object representing the photon according to a particular characteristic. This process needed to be easily automated to view the positions for many event steps. Additionally, we wanted to be able to see the geometry of the room along with the objects that represented the photons. We also needed advanced rendering techniques to enhance the perception of the three-dimensional nature of the geometry and to see through some parts of the room geometry.

At the time that we started this project, there had been some preliminary work done for Monte Carlo visualization using the apE package, from the Ohio Supercomputing Center (now commercially available from Taravisual). We found that apE required a great deal of computer time and memory to render a sequence of event steps with only a few photons represented. Soon after the project started, we obtained the Advanced Visualizer from Wavefront Technologies. The Advanced Visualizer is a very general purpose animation environment. Because of its generality, we were able to adapt it to our task. Doubtless there are other software environments that could be adapted to the job (including perhaps the commercial version of apE), but the final factor was that we already had the Wavefront software in house, and it had proved to be much faster and more parsimonious of memory than apE.

Finally, as extensive CPU resources are required, we explore the suitability of traditional vector architectures and massively parallel architectures for the particular problem of interest. Large-scale problems can take many minutes, or even hours per emitting surface. Often, many design excursions are required to achieve a near optimal design. Note that we are embarking upon a design problem. In particular, we are not exploring ways to generate images, such as is typical in the field of Computer science. Rather, we are instrumenting a design tool to assist in the debugging process, and to impart physical intuition to the designer. Thus, this is an applications paper, and should be viewed in this context.

2. INTRODUCTION TO DAYLIGHTING

From time immemorial, sunlight has been used to illuminate interior spaces of shelters [Butti and Perlin, 1980; Moore, 1985]. With the advent of electric lighting, modern architecture has been freed of the constraint of placing work areas near windows. This has allowed buildings of thick cross-section to be built, providing a high ratio of internal volume to exterior surface area.

Windows are now perceived as liabilities in conventional building design: heat is easily transferred across their relatively low thermal resistance; bothersome glare and solar gains also result. Despite these drawbacks, few commercial buildings are built without windows. Windows provide a view to the outside; promoting employee morale [Ne'eman et al., 1984; Robbins, 1986]. The color of daylight is so pleasing to the eye, that a premium is placed on light bulbs with a high Color Rendering Index, a measure of how closely the "color" of the emitted light matches the spectrum of sunlight [Kaufman and Haynes, 1981].

The amount of internal heat gain generated by different sources of light may be evaluated by comparing the luminous efficacy of different sources of light in the conditioned space. Luminous efficacy is the ratio of lumens in the beam (i.e., the physiological "brightness" of light), to the radiant power in the beam over a spectrum that includes visible light. In other words, luminous efficacy is the weighted average value of k_λ in equation (1). Since radiant power is proportional to the amount of heat generated when this beam is absorbed, a beam of high luminous efficacy will generate less heat per unit of perceived light (lumen) than a beam of low luminous efficacy.

As illustrated in Figure 1, except for buildings equipped with the latest in fluorescent light technology, the

Figure 1 Efficacy of Various Light Sources

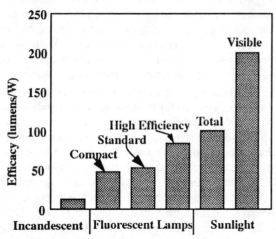

efficacy of electric lighting is approximately 2/3 that of daylight. Furthermore, if one can filter solar radiation so that only wavelengths between 0.38 and 0.77 micrometers are admitted into the conditioned space, daylight would have an efficacy of approximately 200 lumens/W, triple the efficacy of standard fluorescent lights, and more than double the efficacy of state of the art fluorescent lighting. (Note that filtering a fluorescent fixture does not increase the overall efficacy of the fixture since all of the heat still remains in the conditioned space.)

3. DAYLIGHTING DESIGN OF AN ULTRA-LOW ENERGY BUILDING

As part of the design of an ultra-low energy usage, multistory commercial office building for Colorado, we examine reducing electrical lighting loads as much as possible. To do this, we illuminate most of the interior zones of the building with daylight and provide the remainder of the lighting with photosensor controlled, dimmable, high efficiency fluorescent lighting. Since we seek to daylight a multistory building, skylights are inappropriate as the only design option; thus any design tool that we use must model inter-reflections as light from the perimeter windows bounces several times to penetrate to the rear of the room. Additionally, the skies of Colorado are extremely clear; the majority of the solar resource is direct beam radiation. As light travels from the south windows to the north side of the room via reflection, a specular reflector possesses a distinct advantage over a diffuse reflector in preserving directionality. Thus our approach requires sufficient fidelity to model specular reflectance. Similarly, transmittance of the glazing is dependant on incident angle; thus any accurate transmittance model must include a dependance upon incident angle.

Mathematical simulation is essential to provide the fidelity necessary to model specular (mirrorlike) reflections. Fortunately, a 3-D photon tracing program with the required capabilities has been developed and refined at Colorado State University. This Monte Carlo radiative exchange factor program, MONT3D, uses the efficient Maltby [Maltby and Burns, 1991] formulation to model thermal radiative transport. This program was altered to model the behavior of daylight and renamed DAY3D. To our knowledge, we are the first to employ a sophisticated Monte Carlo approach in performing daylighting design. (Recall the adage that, "if one is proficient with a hammer, then everything begins to look like the head of a nail.")

4. THEORETICAL FORMULATION

We begin by discussing the tracing of "individual" photons. We define a single surface of the enclosure as the emitting surface, and emit photons uniformly over the area of the surface. Each is then traced from "birth" at the emission surface, to "death" on an absorbing surface, through possibly many intermediate reflections. Upon egress from a surface, the photon is traced along its trajectory to the nearest surface, whence the photon strikes, and a photon/surface interaction occurs. Using weighted probabilities that vary with incident angle for diffuse and specular reflectance and for transmittance, the disposition of the photon is determined. If reflected, its direction is changed appropriately (according to an outgoing directional distribution, either diffuse or specular - i.e. mirrorlike), and tracing continues. If absorbed, it dies, and the process is repeated for the next photon emitted. Our interest here is to count those photons passing through a fictitious work surface, located 3 feet above the floor. This work surface is used solely for tallying those photons passing downwards through it, as a measure of luminous flux, which is related to the flux of sunlight entering the enclosure (i.e. crossing the emission plane). In each wavelength band k, we trace N^k photons from the single emitting surface, and tally the number which pass through the discretized work surfaces j. This ratio is then multiplied by the incident luminous flux I^k_T to yield, in wavelength band k:

$$I^k_j = \frac{N^k_j}{N^k} I^k_T A = F^k_j I^k_T A \qquad (1)$$

where

I_j^k = one-way flow of light in wavelength band k from source surface to surface j (lumens)

N_j^k = number of photons from source surface in wavelength band k passing through work surface j

N^k = total number of photons in wavelength band k traced from source surface

I_T^k = luminous flux in wavelength band k emanating from source surface (lumens/m^2)

A = area of source surface (m^2)

F_j^k = illumination factor in wavelength band k from source surface to surface j

Due to the properties of most building materials not being readily available with respect to wavelength, we perform our simulation in a single wavelength band (k=1), and hereinafter drop all superscripts k.

If a large enough sample population is employed, the overall bulk behavior of the photons accurately represents solar radiative exchange from the environment to inside surfaces. An analytical solution to the number of photons required to achieve a given level of accuracy was formulated by Maltby [Maltby, 1990]:

$$c_j = z\sqrt{\frac{1 - F_j}{N F_j}} \qquad (2)$$

where

C_j = confidence interval (as a fraction of F_j) for exchange fraction to surface j

Z = standard random variable of the normal probability function (Z = 1.96 for 95% confidence)

DAY3D is designed to loop through successive emissions from the source surface until a prescribed accuracy level is attained or a maximum number of photons are emitted. The prescribed accuracy is formulated for the exchange fractions from the single source surface to a "work" surface. Note that emitting more photons improves the accuracy of all results. As rule of thumb for fairly simple geometries (around 20 surfaces), approximately 200,000 photon-bundle emissions are required to achieve answers accurate to within 2%.

5. SOLUTION PROCEDURE

The geometry is defined by triangular or quadrilateral planes. These planes are described by the 3-D Cartesian coordinates of their vertices. Optical properties of each surface are specified versus incident angle. Both transmission and reflection are modelled with an outgoing directional dependence that may be diffuse, specular, or a convex combination of diffuse and specular. A lookup table describing the material properties is generated from the data set given. Specifically for this simulation, windows are modelled as specular transmitters and reflectors with properties varying with the incident angle, while all other surfaces are opaque and are either totally specular or totally diffuse reflectors, with properties that are constant with the incident angle.

Sunlight is modelled as radiation emitted from a plane outside the room. Direct normal (or beam) radiation is modelled as a plane wave, incident in the direction aligned with the vector from the center of the sun to the center of the earth. Diffuse radiation is modelled as isotropic, i.e. a photon has an equal probability of emission in any solid angle (weighted by projected area). Thus for each hour of the day, the program traces to all surfaces in the enclosure many photons representing incident direct beam radiation having an initial direction vector opposite to the solar azimuth and altitude. Diffuse solar radiation is modelled by one run of photons diffusely emitted weighted accordingly for each hour of the day to the diffuse solar intensity at that hour. Illuminance of the emission plane is calculated the same way as one would calculate the solar flux on a planar surface [Duffie and Beckman, 1991; Kreith and Kreider, 1978]. Here, we use Typical Meteorological Year (TMY) data, representing the 12 average months of the weather data collected over the past 23 years [National Climatic Center, 1981].

A completely transmitting "work" surface at a height of 3 ft. (1 meter) above the floor is subdivided into a 10 X 10 grid. The number of photons which pass through each element of the work surface are tallied. The ratio of photons which pass through the work surface to the number of photons emitted from the "environment" provides the illumination factor, F_j, as compared to the illumination at the emission plane. (N.b., due to multiple reflections, the sum of illumination factors for the "work" surface may, in rare instances, exceed 1.) This illumination factor is multiplied by the luminous intensity at the source plane to obtain a corresponding light level for the section of the work surface tallied. These concepts are illustrated for a south room light-shelf geometry in Figure 2.

6. GEOMETRY

Additional detail is appropriate on the geometry of Figure 2. A lower view window 3' in height is located 4' above the floor. The light shelf begins 8' above the floor and is about 2" thick (a suspended ceiling). The height above the light shelf is 3', making the total height of the room 11' - suitable for running ductwork in the space (11' heights are common in commercial construction). Except for the specular light duct (top ceiling, sides and top of the light shelf), modelled as aluminized mylar with a reflectance of 0.8 , all surfaces are diffuse - with a reflectance of 0.7 for the white-painted walls (including the underside of the specular light shelf) and 0.25 for the floor (brown carpet) [Gubaref et al., 1960]. Glass properties were modelled using manufacturers data for the normal transmittance [Hurd Glass, 1991] and the results of Stoke's equations for transmittance of multiple layers of glazing (two sheets of glass and two sheets of mylar) [Kreith and Kreider, 1978]

Figure 2 Daylighting Geometry

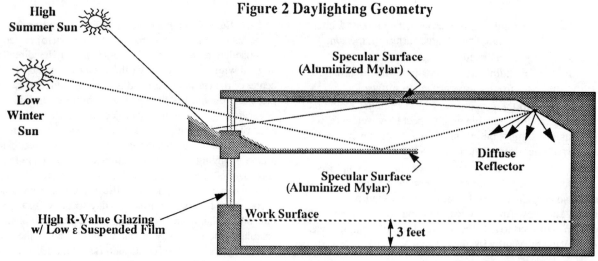

In Figure 3, we provide a computer generated plot of the geometry. The view is from the top rear, outside the geometry, and shows the large emitting surface in addition to all building surfaces. This picture was constructed using the special purpose program MPLOT [Shivaswamy et al., 1992], which we have devised solely to display data associated with our Monte Carlo codes. MPLOT is capable of displaying the geometry simulated (including translations, rotations and scalings), plots of material properties, trajectories of "lost" particles, and a variety of other information useful in debugging input decks. With hundreds of surfaces, we have found it essential to access information visually. Of particular interest is locating "leaks" or "holes" in the geometry, which result in biased answers. MPLOT runs interactively under Open Windows using the X11R5 graphical library.

Figure 3 MPLOT Representation of Geometry

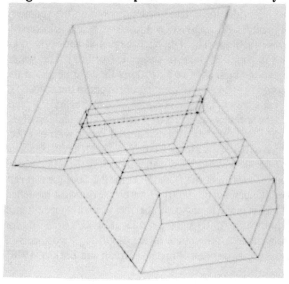

7. SCIENTIFIC VISUALIZATION - IMPLE-MENTATION

7.1 Technology

Contour plots, although a good quantitative tool, represent old technology for visualization, and are uninteresting except as a base case with which to compare other visualization techniques. They are done "off line" on a personal computer under MS/DOS after the Monte Carlo results are obtained (i.e., post-processed). Although it is possible to implement a contouring package under X11, we have sufficient experience with contouring packages that we consider this task too daunting even to attempt.

The grey-scale plots we implemented under X11 using a Gouraud shading algorithm effected in software. Although these too are done "off line," there is no reason we could not do them in real time as the code is executing (in fact, as these display *output* quantities, we could dynamically observe convergence). This technology is relatively recent, using a raster device to provide qualitative field information. Incidentally, we found a grey-scale implementation more pleasing and illustrative than a full color shading. The MPLOT program also utilizes raster technology, and has enough special-purpose requirements that we found it necessary to construct our own program. However, the implementation provides only "skeleton" views of the geometry, with no hidden line removal - this makes it appear as if the display were a stroke device.

Finally, we also generated the event-based videotape "off line." This represents our principal contribution, and consumed most of our effort in visualization. It coincidentally produced the best results physically, as we were able to observe directly physical interactions. Additionally, it was the only we had of assessing whether the details of the code were in fact correct (it is difficult to divine through the field results whether the answers are physically realistic, but it is easy to observe whether individual physical interactions are in error). Currently, we are exploring establishing a socket between computers on the Internet to perform this in real time. We feel as if this represents state of the art technology. We now embark upon a description of production of the videotape.

7.2 Event-Based Videotape

The room geometry was translated into the appropriate object file format using a simple text editor. A faceted sphere was used to represent the photons. Only thirty-two polygons were used in the definition of the spheres to cut down on the memory requirements for the 960 photons to be traced.

The Advanced Visualizer allows a user to import the motion data as an x,y,z position. The software maintains the data in the user defined coordinate system, so the flight of the photons corresponds correctly to the room geometry. Because of the relatively small memory size of our machine, 16 MBytes, and the correspondingly large number of objects (960), only 18 frames of animation date could exist in memory at any time. To overcome this, we divided the output from the Monte Carlo simulation into files of 10 frames each. The same program that reformatted the Monte Carlo data also output a Wavefront script file that automatically cycles through the sets of frames and objects that were in memory, and read in the data set of the corresponding motion.

Included with the x,y,z position was a fourth parameter that is used to color the photons. The photons change color as they move through the geometry. Initially, all the photons are colored yellow. Photons that enter the light shelf turn pink. Photons that traverse the mini-blinds turn green. All photons turn red the instant before being absorbed.

The Advanced Visualizer does not have a facility for directly animating the color of an object. This forced us to maintain a separate object file for each of our 960 photon objects. We included special command sequences in each of these files to allow the value for the color to be substituted as the object file was read in for rendering. This procedure also required a material file with a material entry for each photon object. Each of the separate object files and the material file was created via custom Unix shell scripts. We understand that future versions of the software will allow direct animation of the material properties of an object. This will allow us to maintain only one sphere object file to be used in all 960 positions.

We choose several camera positions and rendered the file images. Each sequence (with the exception of the close-up) has 90 frames. The rendering was done without shadows or reflections. In many cases shadows and reflec-tions can be used to improve the viewer's perception of the three-dimensional nature of the picture. In our case, due to the fact that the light shelf is a highly specular surface and the large number of photon objects, we found reflections and shadows to be distracting to the viewer. Since shadows and reflections were turned off, each frame only required about 15 minutes of rendering time.

Naturally, we made compromises about several aspects of the visualization. In addition to the coarseness of the photon objects to save memory, we compromised on the photon's interaction with the walls. Surfaces in the Monte Carlo simulations are modeled as planes, and the positions of the photons are calculated for objects of zero radius.

7.3 Videotape Description

Here, we describe the sequence of "shots" we shall show via videotape at the conference. First, we show a perspective view from the outside the upper rear of the geometry. In this view and those following, we have made some surfaces transparent so that we may "see into" the geometry, and observe the photon interactions. This first view is intended solely to establish perspective and to illustrate the geometry.

Next, we show a view from the side of the geometry. It is appropriate to now begin discussing the details of the photon trajectories and interactions. Photons (960 in number) are released from the emitting surface in a direction coincident with the incoming beam of sunlight. The ones which strike exterior building surfaces interact in accordance with their probabilities of reflectance and transmittance. In particular, some are transmitted through the two glazings, and some are reflected from the exterior of the light shelf (and then make it through the upper glazing). Note that the ones which make it through the glazings change color from yellow to green. Of those which enter the upper light shelf, 80% are reflected specularly upon each bounce until they strike the tilted diffuse white surface at the rear of the room. Of these, 70% are diffusely reflected and backscattered into the room. Of those which enter the bottom of the room, most strike the floor where 25% are reflected diffusely into the room. Of those photons which strike the diffuse, white walls, 70% are reflected and backscattered into the room. It is easy to perceive the chaotic interactions occurring in the lower portion of the room, when compared to the orderly reflections within the light shelf.

Next, we show a close-up view of photons interacting with the mini-blinds. Here, we use 42 mini-blinds to span the space behind the window. The mini-blinds are modelled with outside surface specular, and inside surface diffuse. This is typical of the higher quality products, as it is desirable to preserve directionality in the incoming daylight with a specular reflection, and the inside surface should act much like a wall. However, we model the mini-blinds as flat when, actually, they are convex to "fan out" the incoming

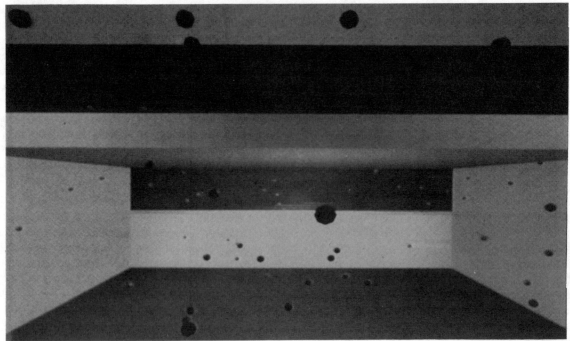

(a) View from the Rear

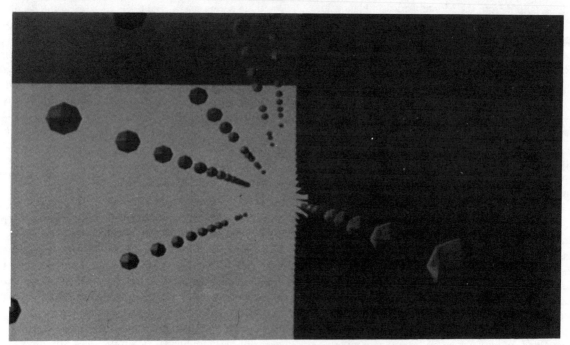

(b) View from the Side including Mini-Blinds
FIGURE 4 Photon Trajectories from the Videotape

light. The most effective strategy for the use of mini-blinds, after using them to control the amount of light entering the space, is to use them to reflect the incoming daylight onto the underside of the light shelf - a diffuse, white surface. This, then, lights the front third of the room. The light shelf is used to light the rear two-thirds of the room. An important aspect of an effective design will be the ability to maintain a uniform spatial distribution of light - i.e., will the intensity of light diminish near the middle of the room?

We observe a variety of interactions with the mini-blinds. First, a small number of photons are transmitted straight through the mini-blinds without interaction (there are small slits open to the sunlight). Next, some bounce once and enter the room (these are reflected onto the underside of the light shelf). Additionally, some bounce twice, and are reflected onto the floor. Finally, some are absorbed. It is very apparent in this view that the spheres are modelled of finite radius, and the trajectories are modelled as point motion - the photon objects sink into the surfaces before undergoing an interaction.

Next, we show a view from above, depicting the photon transport in the light shelf. Subsequent to that, we show a view from the bottom, depicting the interactions occurring in the room. In these views, the light shelf is opaque, so as to isolate the photon interactions in the light shelf and room.

Next, we show a wide-angle view from the back of the room at the height of the light shelf, but for the first time from inside the geometry. Then we show a similar view, but from lower. In these views, the photons pass through the viewing plane - first becoming circles, then disappearing, and finally reappearing if reflected to the space in front of the camera. We conclude with the first view presented, from above and outside the rear of the geometry.

8. COMPUTATIONAL ASPECTS

Although each run consumes only a fraction of an hour, many runs must be done to effect an optimal design. An optimal design here is characterized by acceptable lighting levels over the entire work surface. To achieve this, the geometry must be varied, including location and size of the light shelf, location and size of the windows, geometry of the overhang/outside reflector, etc. To achieve the "optimal" design shown in Figure 2 (not to scale) required 45 variations on the geometry, 4 parametric variations of the material properties, 28 variations in incident angle of direct normal radiation (representing one run for each window for each hour of representative half-days in the seasons of winter, summer, and spring/fall, and two single runs involving diffuse radiation - one for each window). Taken all together, this required over 5,040 total runs - requiring over 1,600 hours of CPU time on a Sun Sparc 10. It is obvious that a supercomputer would aid greatly in performing parametric design studies.

The problem exhibits parallelism at various levels. In fact, this type of problem has been referred to as "embarrassingly parallel." As the tracing of photons is CPU intensive, and many photons must be traced to achieve acceptable accuracy, simulating large problems via Monte Carlo is a daunting process. As mapping photon tracing algorithms to supercomputing architectures entails significant effort, we restrict our efforts to a subset of the photon tracing code. That is, we have not mapped our pro-

duction algorithm to a supercomputing architecture. Rather, we strip shading, reflections and grid tracing from the code, and trace photons from emission to the first surface of intersection only, where they are absorbed. Further, we trace them in a two-dimensional, prismatic Cartesian geometry, where the tracing algorithm is simpler than it is in an axisymmetric geometry. If the approach appears to "prove out," we can then consider taking additional steps which would relax these simplifications.

We implement our reduced algorithm on a single processor of a Cray Y/MP, and on an 8,192 node (8K) Connection Machine, Model CM-2. The Cray Y/MP is a traditional vector register machine, with hardware scatter/gather. Burns and Pryor [Burns and Pryor, 1988] have discussed vectorization of photon tracing algorithms based upon the "event step" of Brown [Brown, 1981]. In such an approach, photons in the form of vectors are passed through logical "sieves" which are formulated to filter out those photons which do not pass the requisite tests. At each stage in the multilevel sieve, a hardware gather of indices is generated using the Cray SCILIB routines WHENFLT, etc. [Cray, 19xx]. These operations are purely overhead, as no useful work results from the generation of indices, and the ensuing gathers/scatters. However, subsequent vector operations are performed on reduced vector lengths. This offers some flexibility not generally available on massively parallel architectures, where masking must be done (thus, there is no savings effected). Generally, speedup factors of around ten can be achieved from vectorization of photon tracing on Cray architectures.

An alternative architecture is the CM-2, a massively parallel architecture. The CM-2 is a data parallel architecture, where the same identical operation is performed on all of the 8K processors. On a CM-2, data are passed to and from the processors by a front end scalar machine (here, a Sun 4). On the CM-2, FORTRAN 90 is used as the language to effect parallelism via array operations. Each processor performs the same operation on its element of the array. Where logical operations are to be performed, a masking array is created (either explicitly or implicitly). Then, all processors process the data; however, on processors where the masking array is FALSE, the data for that processor are not stored. Thus, where the truth density decreases, inefficiency results. For problems of this type, FORTRAN 90 is an extremely convenient language, due to its ability to perform array operations without do loops - each data element is mapped to an individual processor.

Normally, over 90% of the CPU time is consumed in tracing photons. As the problem is scaled up in numbers of surfaces, the photon tracing time grows as the cube of the number of surfaces, while all other times (emission, surface interaction) grow only as the square of the number of surfaces. Therefore, it is critically important to effect maximum performance on the photon tracing. The present "stripped down" algorithm is representative of emission, tracing, and absorption. During tracing, the surfaces are handled sequentially, and the photons are handled in parallel. Viz., attention is focused upon an individual emitting surface, where photons are emitted ("birth") in parallel. Then, all photons are traced to all surfaces in the enclosure, where they are absorbed ("death"). The surfaces are handled sequentially, and the photons are again handled in parallel.

On the Cray, the surface loop is the outer, non-vector loop. The inner loops are vectorized, over photons. It is important that vector lengths be kept long, to amortize the overheads of: (1) vector start-up, (2) generation of indices, and (3) data motion. On a Cray architecture, due to the fact that the generation of indices must be done in a subroutine, this exacerbates the overhead. Tests indicate that vector lengths must be greater than about 1,000 to achieve near asymptotic speedup. Thus, for these types of problems, the Cray begins to look like a long vector machine (shades of the Cyber 205!). Further, there are some efficiencies to be gained on a Cray by compressing the photons which pass the succession of tests for intersections with surfaces into new, smaller vectors. Viz., one can eliminate up to 1/2 of the photons with simple conditionals based on the direction of flight (dot products between photon direction and surface normal direction). It is essential that the smallest vector lengths be long (i.e., for the last filter in the sieve). We began with vector lengths of 16,384 to ensure this for our problem.

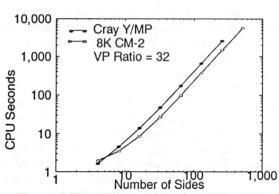

Figure 5 Total Time vs. Number of Surfaces

On a CM-2, only the surface arrays are front-end arrays, with all photon arrays spread out over the CM-2 processors. Thus, all surface quantities are broadcast from the front end to the CM-2. Furthermore, since there are no efficiencies to be gained from eliminating only a portion of the photons from the computation (in this initial algorithm, we have not explored seeding inactive processors), we eliminate the dot product test. The algorithm was indeed much easier to map to the CM-2 due to the array structure of FORTRAN 90. There is a one to one correspondence to photon arrays and FORTRAN 90 arrays, lending itself to a direct, intuitive implementation

CPU timings are shown in Figure 5 for both the Cray Y/MP and the CM-2. After considerable tuning, we are confident that the timings are nearly optimal for this problem on both architectures. The 8K CM-2 performs the problem in about 1/2 the time of a single processor of the Cray Y/MP. However, as shown in Figure 6, to achieve this performance, we found it necessary to increase the VP Ratio to 32. This results in the tracing of 256K photons per side - about 10 times the number required to achieve acceptable accuracy in ordinary radiative transfer applications, but about 1/10 the number required to achieve acceptable in daylighting calculations. Measured speedups on the Cray Y/MP fell into the range of between a factor of 9 and a factor of 10.

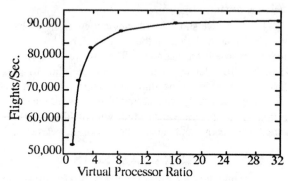

Figure 6 Performance on CM-2 vs. VP Ratio

9. SUMMARY AND RECOMMENDATIONS

We have visualized both continuum field results of a Monte Carlo simulation, and the discrete events of the simulation process. The contour plots nicely complement the grey-scale plots, providing both quantitative and qualitative information. The logarithmic scale implemented for the grey-scale plots is more consistent with the physiological response of the eye. The event-based videotape is very effective at both adding new insight to the physical process. In spite of the compromises necessitated by the Advanced Visualizer, we have produced a visualization that accomplishes the original goals of helping to validate the model and to communicate the results to others.

Future work in this area will allow us to improve the photon wall interaction. Another technique that might be effective would be to assign a low intensity light to each position where a photon is absorbed. A large number of photons could be visualized and the final spatial distribution of points of light would illustrate the light intensity field. It would be beneficial were the developers of visualization packages to take cognizance of the special requirements imposed by a Monte Carlo particle simulation.

Finally, both the Cray Y/MP and the CM-2 are viable architectures for effective parallelization. In our reduced test problem, the CM-2 outperformed the Cray Y/MP by a factor of two. However, the specific test problem was chosen so as to offer the maximum relative advantage to the CM-2, to assess whether it is worthwhile to proceed with an in depth study, including reflections and grid tracing. Based upon these promising results, we conclude that it is worthwhile to proceed.

Acknowledgment

We are indebted to the Public Service Company of Colorado for support of this effort, and to Mr. Narayanan Pagaldipti for his assistance with the graphics.

REFERENCES

Bobrowicz, F. W., Lynch, J. E., and Fisher, K. J., 1984a, "Vectorized Monte Carlo photon transport," *Parallel Computing 1*.

Bobrowicz, F. W., Fisher, K. J., and Lynch, J. E., 1984b, "Vectorized Monte Carlo neutron transport," LA-UR-84-1269, Los Alamos National Laboratory report.

Brown, T. B., 1981, *Vectorized Monte Carlo*, Ph.D. Dissertation, Department of Nuclear Engineering, University of Michigan.

Burns, P., Christon, M., Schweitzer, R., Wasserman, H., Simmons, M., Lubeck, O., and Pryor, D., 1989, "Vectorization of Monte Carlo particle transport - an architectural study using the LANL benchmark GAMTEB" *Proceedings, Supercomputing '89*, Reno, NV.

Burns, P. J., Maltby, J. D., and Christon, M. A., 1990, "Large-scale Monte Carlo surface transport in engineering," *Computing Systems in Engineering, 1*(1), pp. 92-109.

Butti, K., and Perlin, J., 1980, *A Golden Thread - 2500 Years of Solar Architecture and Technology*, Cheshire, Palo Alto.

Gubaref, G., Janssen, J., and Torberg, R., 1960, *Thermal Radiation Properties Survey*, 2nd ed. Honeywell Research Center, Minneapolis.

Haji-Sheikh, A., 1988, "Monte Carlo Methods," Ch. 16 in *Handbook of Numerical Heat Transfer*, Wiley Interscience, New York, pp. 673-722.

Heifetz, D. B., 1987, "Vectorizing and macrotasking Monte Carlo neutral particle algorithms," Princeton Plasma Physics Laboratory Report PPPL-2427.

Helms, R., and Belcher, M.C., 1980, *Lighting for the Energy Efficient Luminous Environments*, Prentice Hall, Englewood, NJ.

Hurd Glass, 1991, "Insol-8 The New Performance Leader," Window Selection Guide.

Kalos, M. H., April 1985, "Monte Carlo methods and the computers of the future," Ultracomputer Note #83.

Kleinjnen, J. O. C., 1974, *Statistical Techniques in Simulation, Part 1*, Marcel Dekker, New York, NY.

Kreith, F., and Kreider, J., 1978, *Principles of Solar Engineering*, Hemisphere, New York.

Maltby, J. D., 1987, *Three-dimensional Simulation of Radiative Heat Transfer by the Monte Carlo Method*, Master's Thesis, Department of Mechanical Engineering, Colorado State University.

Maltby, J. D., 1990, *Analysis of Electron Heat Transfer via Monte Carlo Simulation*, Ph.D. Dissertation, Department of Mechanical Engineering, Colorado State University.

Maltby, J., and Burns, P., 1991,"Performance, Accuracy, and Convergence in a Three- Dimensional Monte Carlo Radiative Heat Transfer Simulation," *Numerical Heat Transfer, Part B*, Vol. 19, pp.191-209.

Martin, W. R., Nowak, P. F., and Rathkopf, J. A., 1986, "Monte Carlo photon tracing on a vector supercomputer," *IBM Journal of Research and Development 30*(2).

Metropolis, N., 1985, "Monte Carlo - in the beginning and some great expectations," Monte Carlo Methods and Applications in Neutronics, Photonics and Statistical Physics, Cadarache Castle, France.

Metropolis, N., 1987, "The beginning of the Monte Carlo method," *Los Alamos Science 15*.

Miller, B., et al., 1992, "Initial Energy Conserving Design of a Low Energy Office Building," *Proceedings, ASME Solar Energy Conference*, Maui, April 5-9, 1992.

Moore, F., 1985, *Concepts and Practice of Architectural Daylighting*, Van Nostrand, New York.

Ne'eman, E., Sweitzer, G., and Vine, E. 1984, "Office Worker Response to Lighting and Daylighting Issues in Workspace Environments: a Pilot Survey," *Energy and Buildings, 6*, pp. 159-171.

Robbins, C., 1986, *Daylighting Design and Analysis*, Van Nostrand.

Sequent Computer Systems, 1985, "Parallel ray tracing study," TN-85-09(rvp), Rev. 1.0.

Session 4:
Parallel Languages
Chair: Carl Kesselman

Parallel Programming in Split-C

David E. Culler, Andrea Dusseau, Seth Copen Goldstein, Arvind Krishnamurthy,
Steven Lumetta, Thorsten von Eicken, and Katherine Yelick
Computer Science Division
University of California, Berkeley *

Abstract

We introduce the Split-C language, a parallel extension of C intended for high performance programming on distributed memory multiprocessors, and demonstrate the use of the language in optimizing parallel programs. Split-C provides a global address space with a clear concept of locality and unusual assignment operators. These are used as tools to reduce the frequency and cost of remote access. The language allows a mixture of shared memory, message passing, and data parallel programming styles while providing efficient access to the underlying machine. We demonstrate the basic language concepts using regular and irregular parallel programs and give performance results for various stages of program optimization.

1 Overview

Split-C is a parallel extension of the C programming language that supports efficient access to a global address space on current distributed memory multiprocessors. It retains the "small language" character of C and supports careful engineering and optimization of programs by providing a simple, predictable cost model. This is in stark contrast to languages that rely on extensive program transformation at compile time to obtain performance on parallel machines. Split-C programs do what the programmer specifies; the compiler takes care of addressing and communication, as well as code generation. Thus, the ability to exploit parallelism or locality is not limited by the compiler's recognition capability, nor is there need to second guess the compiler transformations while optimizing the program. The language provides a small set of global access primitives and simple parallel storage layout declarations. These seem to capture most of the useful elements of shared memory, message passing, and data parallel programming in a common, familiar context. Split-C is currently implemented on the Thinking Machines Corp. CM-5, building from GCC

and Active Messages[17] and implementations are underway for architectures with more aggressive support for global access. It has been used extensively as a teaching tool in parallel computing courses and hosts a wide variety of applications. Split-C may also be viewed as a compilation target for higher level parallel languages.

This paper describes the central concepts in Split-C and illustrates how these are used in the process of optimizing parallel programs. We begin with a brief overview of the language as a whole and examine each concept individually in the following sections. The presentation interweaves the example use, the optimization techniques, and the language definition concept by concept.

1.1 Split-C in a nutshell

Control Model: Split-C follows an SPMD (single program, multiple data) model, where each of PROCS processors begin execution at the same point in a common code image. The processors may each follow distinct flow of control and join together at rendezvous points, such as barrier(). Processors are distinguished by the value of the special constant, MYPROC.

Global Address Space: Any processor may access any location in a global address space, but each processor owns a specific region of the global address space. The local region contains the processor's stack for automatic variables, static or external variables, and a portion of the heap. There is also a spread heap allocated uniformly across processors.

Global pointers: Two kinds of pointers are provided, reflecting the cost difference between local and global accesses. *Global pointers* reference the entire address space, while standard pointers reference only the portion owned by the accessing processor.

Split-phase Assignment: A split-phase assignment operator (:=) allows computation and communication to be overlapped. The request to *get* a value from a location (or to *put* a value into a location) is separated from the completion of the operation.

---

*Send e-mail to: Split-C@boing.CS.Berkeley.EDU

Signaling Store: A more unusual assignment operator (:-) signals the processor that owns the updated location that the store has occurred. This provides an essential element of message driven and data parallel execution that shared memory models generally ignore.

Bulk Transfer: Any of the assignment operators can be used to transfer entire records, *i.e.*, structs. Library routines are provided to transfer entire arrays. In many cases, overlapping computation and communication becomes more attractive with larger transfer units.

Spread Arrays: Parallel computation on arrays is supported through a simple extension of array declarations. The approach is quite different from that of HPF and its precursors because there is no separate layout declaration. Furthermore, the duality in C between arrays and pointers is carried forward to spread arrays through a second form of global pointer, called a *spread pointer*.

1.2 Organization

Section 2 describes a non-trivial application, called EM3D, that operates on an irregular, linked data structure. Section 3 gives a simple parallel solution to EM3D, begins a sequence of optimizations on the program, showing how unnecessary remote accesses can be eliminated. Sections 4 and 5 show how to make the remaining remote accesses more efficient using split-phase assignments and signaling stores. Section 6 discusses bulk transfers and applies them to EM3D. Section 7 illustrates the use of spread arrays and how various array layouts are achieved. Section 8 explores how disparate programming models can be unified in the Split-C context, and Section 9 summarizes our findings.

2 An Example Irregular Application

To illustrate the novel aspects of Split-C for parallel programs, we use a small, but rather tricky example application, EM3D, that models the propagation of electromagnetic waves through objects in three dimensions [13]. A preprocessing step casts this into a simple computation on an irregular bipartite graph containing nodes representing electric and magnetic field values.

In EM3D, an object is divided into a grid of convex polyhedral cells (typically nonorthogonal hexahedra). From this primary grid, a dual grid is defined by using the barycenters of the primary grid cells as the vertices of the dual grid. Figure 1 shows a single primary grid cell (the lighter cell) and one of its overlapping dual

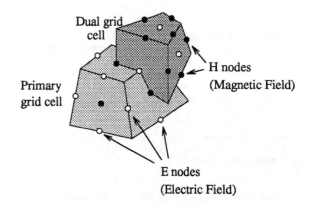

Figure 1: *EM3D grid cells.*

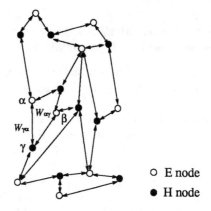

Figure 2: *Bipartite graph data structure in EM3D.*

grid cells. The electric field is projected onto each edge in the primary grid; this value is represented in Figure 1 by a white dot, an *E node*, at the center of the edge. Similarly, the magnetic field is projected onto each edge in the dual grid, represented by a black dot, an *H node*, in the figure.

The computation consists of a series of "leapfrog" integration steps: on alternate half time steps, changes in the electric field are calculated as a linear function of the neighboring magnetic field values and *vice versa*. Specifically, the value of each E node is updated by a weighted sum of neighboring H nodes, and then H nodes are similarly updated using the E nodes. Thus, the dependencies between E and H nodes form a bipartite graph. A simple example graph is shown in Figure 2; a more realistic problem would involve a non-planar graph of roughly a million nodes with degree between ten and thirty. Edge labels (weights) represent the coefficients of the linear functions, for example, $W_{\gamma\alpha}$ is the weight used for computing α's contribution to γ's value. Because the grids are static, these weights are constant values, which are calculated in a preprocessing step [13].

```
1 typedef struct node_t {
2     double          value;      /* Field value */
3     int             edge_count;
4     double          *coeffs;    /* Edge weights */
5     double          *(*values); /* Dependency list */
6     struct node_t *next;
7 } graph_node;
8
9 void compute_E()
10 {
11    graph_node *n;
12    int i;
13
14    for (n = e_nodes; n != NULL; n = n->next)
15      for (i = 0; i < n->edge_count; i++)
16        n->value = n->value
17            - *(n->values[i]) * (n->coeffs[i]);
18 }
```

Program 1: *Sequential EM3D, showing the graph node structure and E node computation.*

A sequential C implementation for the kernel of the algorithm is shown in Program 1. Each E node consists of a structure containing the value at the grid point, a pointer to an array of weights (coeffs), and an array of pointers to neighboring H node values. In addition, the E nodes are linked together by the next field, creating the complete list e_nodes. E nodes are updated by iterating over e_nodes and, for each node, gathering the values of the adjacent H nodes and subtracting off the weighted sum. The H node representation and computation are analogous.

Before discussing the parallel Split-C implementation of EM3D, consider how one might optimize it for a sequential machine. On a vector processor, one would focus on the gather, vector multiply, and vector sum. On a high-end workstation one can optimize the loop, but since the graph is very large, the real gain would come from minimizing cache misses that occur on accessing n->values[i]. This is done by rearranging the e_nodes list into chunks, where the nodes in a chunk share many H nodes. This idea of rearranging a data structure to improve the access pattern is also central to an efficient parallel implementation.

3 Global Pointers

Split-C provides a global address space and allows objects anywhere in that space to be referenced through global pointers. An object referenced by a global pointer is entirely owned by a single processor.[1] A global pointer can be dereferenced in the same manner as a standard C pointer, although the time to dereference a global pointer is considerably greater

---

[1] The term *object* corresponds basic C objects, rather than objects in the sense of object-oriented languages.

```
1 typedef struct node_t {
2     double          value;
3     int             edge_count;
4     double          *coeffs;
5     double          * global (*values);
6     struct node_t *next;
7 } graph_node;
8
9 void all_compute_E()
10 {
11    graph_node *n;
12    int i;
13
14    for (n = e_nodes; n != NULL; n = n->next)
15      for (i = 0; i < n->edge_count; i++)
16        n->value = n->value
17            - *(n->values[i]) * (n->coeffs[i]);
18
19    barrier();
20 }
```

Program 2: *EM3D written using global pointers. Each processor executes this code on the E nodes it owns. The only differences between this Split-C kernel and the sequential C kernel are: insertion of the type qualifier* global *to the list of* value *pointers and addition of the* barrier() *at the end of the loop.*

than that for a local pointer. In this section, we illustrate the use of the Split-C global address space on EM3D and explain the language extension in detail.

3.1 EM3D using global pointers

The first step in parallelizing EM3D is to recognize that the large kernel graph must be spread over the machine. Thus, the structure describing a node is modified so that values refers to an array of global pointers. This is done by adding the type qualifier global in line 5 of Program 2. The new global graph data structure is illustrated in Figure 3. In the computational step, each of the processors performs the update for a portion of the e_nodes list. The simplest approach is to have each processor update the nodes that it owns, *i.e., owner computes*. This algorithmic choice is reflected in the declaration of the data structure by retaining the next field as a standard pointer (see line 6). Each processor has the root of a list of nodes in the global graph that are local to it. All processors enter the electric field computation, update the values of their local E nodes in parallel, and synchronize at the end of the half step before computing the values of the H nodes. The only change to the kernel is the addition of barrier() in line 19 of Program 2.

Having established a parallel version of the program, how might we optimize its performance on a multiprocessor? Split-C defines a straight-forward cost model: accesses that are remote to the request-

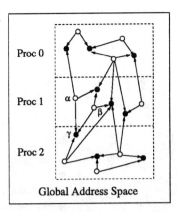

Figure 3: *An EM3D graph in the global address space with three processors. With this partitioning, processor 1 owns nodes α and β and processor 2 owns node γ. The edges are directed for the electric field computation phase.*

ing processor are more expensive than accesses that are owned by that processor. Therefore, we want to reorganize the global kernel graph into chunks, so that as few edges as possible cross processor regions[2]. Additionally, each processor should be responsible for roughly the same amount of work. For a given machine, we could estimate the cost of the kernel loop on a processor for a given layout as $L + XR$, where L is the number of edges to local nodes, R is the number of edges that cross to other processors, and X is the relative cost of a remote access. On the CM-5, the local accesses and floating point multiply-add cost roughly $3\mu s$ and a remote access costs roughly $14\mu s$. There are numerous techniques for partitioning graphs to obtain an even balance of nodes and a minimum number of remote edges, *e.g.*, [11, 14]. Thus, for an optimized program there would be a separate initialization step to reorganize the global graph using a cost model of the computational kernel. Load balancing techniques are beyond the scope of this paper, but the global access capabilities of Split-C would be useful in expressing such algorithms.

3.2 Language definition: Global Pointers

Global pointers provide access to the global address space from any processor.

DECLARATION: A global pointer is declared by appending the qualifier `global` to the pointer type declaration (*e.g.*, `int *global g;` or `int *global garray[10];`). The type qualifier `global` can be used

with any pointer type (except a pointer to a function), and global pointers can be declared anywhere that standard pointers can be declared.

CONSTRUCTION: A global pointer may be constructed using the function `toglobal`, which takes a processor number and a local pointer. It may also be constructed by casting a local pointer to a global pointer. In this case, the global pointer points to the same object as the local pointer on the processor performing the cast.

DECONSTRUCTION: Semantically, a global pointer has a component for each of the two dimensions in the global address space: a processor number and a local pointer on that processor. These values can be extracted using the `toproc` and `tolocal` functions. Casting a global pointer to a local pointer has the same effect as `tolocal`: it extracts the local pointer part and discards the processor number.

DEREFERENCE: Global pointers may be dereferenced in the same manner as normal pointers, although the cost is higher.

ARITHMETIC: Arithmetic on global pointers reflects the view that an object is owned entirely by one processor: arithmetic is performed on the local pointer part while the processor number remains unchanged. Thus incrementing a global pointer will refer to the next object on the same processor[3].

COST MODEL: The representation of global pointers is typically larger than that of a local pointer. Arithmetic on global pointers may be slightly more expensive than arithmetic on local pointers. Dereferencing a global pointer is significantly more expensive than dereferencing a local pointer. A local/remote check is involved, and if the object is remote, a dereference incurs the additional cost of communication.

The current Split-C implementation represents global pointers by a processor number and local address. Other representations are possible on machines with hardware support for a global address space. This may change the magnitude of various costs, but not the relative cost model.

3.3 Performance study

The performance of our EM3D implementation could be characterized against a benchmark mesh with a specific load balancing algorithm. However, it is more illuminating to work with synthetic versions of

---

[2]Some of the optimizations we use here to demonstrate Split-C features are built into parallel Grid libraries like the Parti system [1].

[3]There is another useful view of the "next" object: the corresponding object on the "next" processor. This concept is captured by spread pointers, discussed in Section 7.

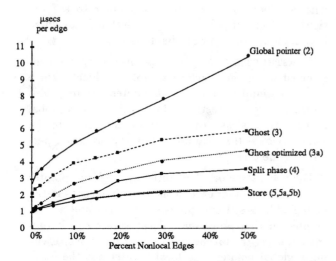

Figure 4: *Performance obtained on several versions of EM3D using a synthetic kernel graph with 320,000 nodes of degree 20 on 64 processors. The corresponding program number is in parentheses next to each curve. The y axis shows the average number of microseconds per edge. Because there are two floating point operations per edge and 64 processors, 1 μsec per edge corresponds to 128 Mflops.*

the graph, so that the fraction of remote edges is easily controlled. Our synthetic graph has 5,000 E and H nodes on each processor, each of which is connected to twenty of the other kind of nodes at random. We vary the fraction of edges that connect to nodes on other processors to reflect a range of possible meshes.

Figure 4 gives the performance results for a number of implementations of EM3D on a 64 processor CM-5 without vector units. The x axis is the percentage of remote edges. The y axis shows the average time spent processing a single graph edge, i.e., per execution of lines 16–17 in Program 2. Each curve is labeled with the feature and program number used to produce it. The top curve shows the performance of Program 2, the first parallel version using global pointers. The other curves reflect optimizations discussed below. For Program 2, 2.7 μs are required per graph edge when all of the edges are local. As the number of remote edges is increased, performance degrades linearly, as expected.

3.4 Eliminating redundant global accesses

Reorganizing the EM3D graph in the global address space does not necessarily minimize the the number of remote accesses, because some remote accesses may be redundant. For example, in Figure 3, two nodes, α and β on processor 1 reference a common node γ

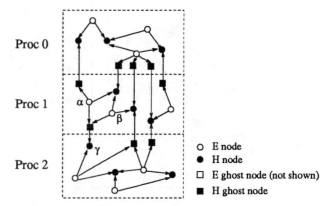

Figure 5: *EM3D graph modified to include ghost nodes. Local storage sites are introduced in order to eliminate redundant remote accesses.*

on processor 2. Eliminating the redundant references requires a more substantial change to the global graph data structure. For each remote node accessed by a processor, a local "ghost node" is created with room to hold a value and a global pointer to the remote node. Figure 5 shows the graph obtained by introducing the ghost nodes. The ghost nodes act as temporary storage sites, or caches, for values of dependent nodes that are remote in the global address space.

The resulting EM3D program is shown in Program 3. A new structure is defined for the ghost nodes and a new loop (lines 21–22) is added to read all the remote values into the local ghost nodes. Notice that the node struct has returned to precisely what it was in the sequential version. This means that the update loop (lines 24–27) is the same as the sequential version, accessing only local pointers. The Program 3 curve in Figure 4 shows the performance improvement.

In practice, the performance of parallel programs is often limited by that of its sequential kernels. For example, a factor of two in EM3D can be obtained by carefully coding the inner loop using software pipelining. The performance curve for this optimized version is called Program 3a in Figure 4. The ability to maintain the investment in carefully sequential engineered software is an important issue often overlooked in parallel languages and novel parallel architectures.

The shape of both Program 3 curves in Figure 4 is very different from our initial version. The execution time per edge increases only slightly beyond the point where 30% of the edges refer to remote nodes. The reason is that as the fraction of remote edges in the synthetic kernel graph increases, the probability that there will be multiple references to a remote node increases as well. Thus, the number of remote nodes referenced remains roughly constant, beyond some threshold. In other words, with an increasing number of remote edges, there are approximately the same number of ghost nodes; more nodes will depend upon these ghost nodes instead of depending upon other local nodes. The graphs obtained from real meshes exhibit a similar phenomenon.

4   Split-Phase Access

Once the redundant remote accesses have been eliminated, we want to perform the remaining remote accesses as efficiently as possible. The global read operations in line 22 of Program 3 are unnecessarily inefficient. Operationally, a request is sent to the processor owning the object and the contents of the object are returned. Both directions involve transfers across the communication network with substantial latency. The processor is simply waiting during much of the remote access. We do not need to wait for each individual access, we simply need to ensure that they have all completed before we enter the update loop. Thus, it makes sense to issue the requests one right after the other and only wait at the end. In essence, the remote requests are pipelined through the communication network.

Split-C supports overlapping communication and computation using split-phase assignments. The processor can initiate global memory operations by using a new assignment operator :=, do some computation, and then wait for the outstanding operations to complete using a sync() operation. The initiation is separated from the completion detection and therefore the accesses are called split-phase.

4.1   Split-phase access in EM3D

We can use split-phase accesses instead of blocking reads to improve the performance of EM3D, where we fill the values in the ghost nodes. We replace = by := in line 8 of Program 4 and use the sync operation to ensure the completion of all the global accesses before starting the compute phase. By pipelining global accesses, we hide the latency of all but the last global access and obtain better performance, as indicated by the Program 4 curve in Figure 4.

4.2   Language definition: Split-Phase Access

GET: The get operation is specified by a split-phase assignment of the form: l := g where l is a local l-value and g is a dereference of a global l-value. The right hand side may contain an arbitrary global pointer expression (including spread array references

```
1   typedef struct node_t {
2       double          value;
3       int             edge_count;
4       double          *coeffs;
5       double          *(*values);
6       struct node_t *next;
7   } graph_node;
8
9   typedef struct ghost_node_t {
10      double              value;
11      double *global      actual_node;
12      struct ghost_node_t *next;
13  } ghost_node;
14
15  void all_compute_E()
16  {
17      graph_node *n;
18      ghost_node *g;
19      int i;
20
21      for (g = h_ghost_nodes; g != NULL; g = g->next)
22          g->value = *(g->actual_node);
23
24      for (n = e_nodes; n != NULL; n = n->next)
25          for (i = 0; i < n->edge_count; i++)
26              n->value = n->value
27                  - *(n->values[i]) * (n->coeffs[i]);
28
29      barrier();
30  }
```

Program 3: *EM3D code with ghost nodes. Remote values are read once into local storage. The main computation loop manipulates only local pointers.*

discussed below), but the final operation is to dereference the global pointer. Get initiates a transfer from the global address into the local address, but does not wait for its completion.

PUT: The put operation is specified by a split-phase assignment of the form: g := e where g is a global l-value and e is an arbitrary expression. The value of the right hand side is computed (this may involve global accesses) producing a local r-value. Put initiates a transfer of the value into the location specified by expression g, but does not wait for its completion.

SYNC: The sync() operation waits for the completion of the previously issued gets and puts. It synchronizes, or joins, the thread of control on the processor with the remote accesses issued into the network. The target of a split-phase assignment is undefined until a sync has been executed and is undefined if the source of the assignment is modified before executing the sync.

By separating the completion detection from the issuing of the request, split-phase accesses allow the communication to be masked by useful work. The EM3D code above overlaps a split-phase access with other split-phase accesses, which essentially pipelines the transfers. The other typical use of split-phase accesses is to overlap global accesses with local computation. This is tantamount to prefetching.

Reads and writes can be mixed with gets and puts; however, reads and writes do not wait for previous gets and puts to complete. A write operation waits for itself to complete, so if another operation (read, write, put, get, or store) follows, it is guaranteed that the previous write has been performed. The same is true for reads; any read waits for the value to be returned. In other words, only a single outstanding read or write is allowed from a given processor; this ensures that the completion order of reads and writes match their issue order [7]. The ordering of puts is defined only between sync operations.

5 Signaling Stores

The discussion above emphasizes the "local computation" view of pulling portions of a global data structure to the processor. In many applications there is a well understood global computation view, allowing information to be *pushed* to where it will be needed next. This occurs, for example in stencil calculations where the boundary regions must be exchanged between steps. It occurs also in global communication operations, such as transpose, and in message driven programs. Split-C allows the programmer to reason at the global level by specifying clearly how the global address space is partitioned over the processors. What is remote to one processor is local to a specific other processor. The :- assignment operator, called *store*, stores a value into a global location and signals the processor that owns the location that the store has occurred. It exposes the efficiency of one-way communication in those cases where the communication pattern is well understood.

5.1 Using stores in EM3D

While it may seem that the store operation would primarily benefit regular applications, we will show that it is useful even in our irregular EM3D problem. In the previous version, each processor traversed the "boundary" of its portion of the global graph getting the values it needed from other processors. Alternatively, a processor could traverse its boundary and store values to the processors that need them.

The EM3D kernel using *stores* is given in Program 5. Each processor maintains a list of "store entry" cells that map local nodes to ghost nodes on other processors. The list of store entry cells acts as an anti-dependence list and are indicated as dashed

```
1  void all_compute_E()
2  {
3    graph_node *n;
4    ghost_node *g;
5    int i;
6
7    for (g = h_ghost_nodes; g != NULL; g = g->next)
8      g->value := *(g->actual_node);
9
10   sync();
11
12   for (n = e_nodes; n != NULL; n = n->next)
13     for (i = 0; i < n->edge_count; i++)
14       n->value = n->value
15              - *(n->values[i]) * (n->coeffs[i]);
16
17   barrier();
18 }
```

Program 4: *EM3D with pipelined communication*

lines in Figure 6. The all_store_sync() operation on line 19 ensures that all the store operations are complete before the ghost node values are used. Note also that the barrier at the end the routine in Program 4 has been eliminated since the all_store_sync() enforces the synchronization. The curve labeled "Store" in Figure 4 demonstrates the performance improvement with this optimization. (There are actually three overlapping curves for reasons discussed below.)

Observe that this version of EM3D is essentially data parallel, or bulk synchronous, execution on an irregular data structure. It alternates between a phase of purely local computation on each node in the graph and a phase of global communication. The only synchronization is detecting that the communication phase is complete.

A further optimization comes from the following observation: for each processor, we know not only where (on what other processors) data will be stored, but how many stores are expected from other processors. The all_store_sync() operation guarantees globally that all stores have been completed. This is done by a global sum of the number of bytes issued minus the number received. This incurs communication overhead, and prevents processors from working ahead on their computation until all other processors are ready. A local operation store_sync(x) waits only until x bytes have been stored locally. A new version of EM3D, referred to as Program 5a, is formed by replacing all_store_sync by store_sync in line 19 of Program 5. This improves performance slightly, but the new curve in Figure 4 is nearly indistinguishable from the basic store version–it is one of the three curves labeled "Store."

```
 1 typedef struct ghost_node_t {
 2   double value;
 3 } ghost_node;
 4
 5 typedef struct store_entry_t {
 6   double *global ghost_value;
 7   double *local_value;
 8 } store_entry;
 9
10 void all_compute_E()
11 {
12   graph_node *n;
13   store_entry *s;
14   int i;
15
16   for (s = h_store_list; s != NULL; s = g->next)
17     s->ghost_value :- *(s->local_value);
18
19   all_store_sync();
20
21   for (n = e_nodes; n != NULL; n = n->next)
22     for (i = 0; i < n->edge_count; i++)
23       n->value = n->value
24             - *(n->values[i]) * (n->coeffs[i]);
25 }
```

Program 5: *Using the store operation to further optimize the main routine.*

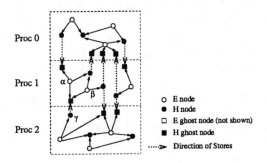

Figure 6: *EM3D graph modified to use stores*

5.2 Language definition: Signaling Stores

STORE: The store operation is specified by an assignment of the form: g :- e where g is a global l-value and e is an arbitrary expression. The value of the right hand side is computed producing a local r-value. Store initiates a transfer of the value into the location specified by expression g, but does not wait for its completion.

ALL_STORE_SYNC: The all_store_sync is a form of global barrier that returns when all previously issued stores have completed.

STORE_SYNC(N) The store_sync function waits until n bytes have been stored (using :-) into the local region of the address space. It does not indicate which data has been deposited, so the higher level program protocol must avoid potential confusion, for example

by detecting all the stores of a given program phase.

The completion detection for stores is independent from that of reads, writes, gets and puts. In the current implementation, each processor maintains a byte count for the stores that it issues and for the stores it receives. The all_store_sync is realized by a global operation that determines when the sum of the bytes received equals the sum of that issued and resets all counters. The store_sync(n) checks that the receive counter is equal or greater than n and decrements both counters by n. This allows the two forms of completion detection to be mixed; with either approach, the counters are all zero at the end of a meaningful communication phase.

6 Bulk Data Operations

The C language allows arbitrary data elements or structures to be copied using the standard assignment statement. This concept of bulk transfer is potentially very important for parallel programs, since global operations frequently manipulate larger units of information. Split-C provides the natural extension of the bulk transfers to the new assignment operators. An entire remote structure can be accessed by a read, write, get, put, or store in a single assignment. Unfortunately, C does not define such bulk transfers on arrays, so Split-C provides a set of functions: bulk_read, bulk_get, and so on. Many parallel machines provide hardware support for bulk transfers. Even machines like the CM-5, which support only small messages in hardware,[4] can benefit from bulk transfers because more of the packet payload is utilized for user data.

Again, there is a small performance improvement with the bulk store version of EM3D (called Program 5b), but the difference is not visible in the three store curves in Figure 4. The overhead of cache misses incurred when copying the data into the buffer costs nearly as much time as the decrease in message count saves, with the final times being only about 1% faster than those of the previous version.

We have arrived a highly structured version of EM3D through a sequence of optimizations. Depending on the performance goals and desired readability, one could choose to stop at an intermediate stage. Having arrived at this final stage, one might consider how to translate it into traditional message passing style. It is clear how to generate the sends, but generating the receives without introducing deadlock is much trickier, especially if receives must happen in

---

[4]On the CM-5, each Split-C message can contain 16 bytes of user data. Four bytes of the 20 byte CM-5 network packet is used for header information.

the order data arrives. The advantage of the Split-C model is that the sender, rather than receiver, specifies where data is to be stored, and data need not be copied between message buffers and the program data structures.

7 Spread Arrays

In this section we shift emphasis from irregular, pointer-based data structures to regular, multidimensional arrays, which are traditionally associated with scientific computing. Split-C provides a simple extension to the C array declaration to specify *spread arrays*, which are spread over the entire machine. The declaration also specifies the layout of the array. The two dimensional address space, associated cost model, and split phase assignments of Split-C carry over to arrays, as each processor may access any array element, but "owns" a well defined portion of the array index space.

Most sequential languages support multidimensional arrays by specifying a canonical linear order, *e.g.*, 1-origin column-major in Fortran and 0-origin row-major in C. The compiler translates multidimensional index expressions into a simple address calculation. In C, for example, accessing `A[i][j]` is the same a dereferencing the pointer `A + i*n + j`. Many parallel languages eliminate the canonical layout and instead provide a variety of layout directives. Typically these involve mapping the array index space onto a logical processor grid of one or more dimensions and mapping the processor grid onto a collection of processors. The underlying storage layout and index calculation can become quite complex and may require the use of run-time "shape" tables, rather than simple arithmetic. Split-C retains the concept of a canonical storage layout, but extends the standard layout to spread data across processors in a straight-forward manner.

7.1 "Regular" EM1D

To illustrate a typical use of spread arrays, Program 6 shows a regular 1D analog of our EM3D kernel. The declarations of E and H contain a *spreader* (`::`), indicating that the elements are spread across the processors. This corresponds to a cyclic layout of n elements, starting with element 0 on processor 0. Consecutive elements are on consecutive processors at the same address, except that the address is incremented when the processor number wraps back to zero. The loop construct, `for_my_1d`, is a simple macro that iteratively binds `i` to the indexes from 0 to n-2 that are owned by the executing processor under the

```
1  void all_compute_E(int n,
2                      double E[n]::,
3                      double H[n]::)
4  {
5    int i;
6    for_my_1d(i,n-1)
7      if (i != 0)
8        E[i] = w1*H[i-1] + w2*H[i] + w3*H[i+1];
9    barrier();
10 }
```

Program 6: *A simple computation on a spread array, declared with a cyclic layout.*

canonical layout, *i.e.*, processor p computes element p, then $p + $ PROCS and so on. Observe, that if $n = $ PROCS this is simply an array with one element per processor.

In optimizing this program, one would observe that with a cyclic layout two remote references are made in line 8, so it would be more efficient to use a blocked layout. Any standard data type can be spread across the processors in a wrapped fashion. In particular, by adding a dimension to the right of the spreader, *e.g.*, `E[m]::[b]`, we assign elements to processors in blocks. If `m` is chosen equal to PROCS, this corresponds to a blocked layout. If `m` is greater than PROCS, this is a block-cyclic layout. The loop statement `for_my_1d(i,m)` would be used to iterate over the local blocks. One may also choose to enlarge the block to include ghost elements at the boundaries and perform the various optimization described for EM3D.

7.2 Language definition: Spread Arrays

DECLARATION: A spread array is declared by inserting a single spreader to the right of an array dimensions.

ADDRESSING: All dimensions to the left of the spreader are spread across processors, while dimensions to the right define the per processor subarrays. The spread dimensions are linearized in row major order and laid out in a wrapped fashion starting with processor zero.

SPREAD POINTERS: A second form of global pointer, qualified by the keyword `spread`, provides pointer arithmetic that is identical to indexing on spread arrays.

Figure 7 shows some declarations (with element types omitted for brevity) and their corresponding layouts. The declaration of X produces a row-oriented layout by spreading only the first dimension. Because Split-C inherits C's row-major array representation, a column layout is not as simple. However, the effect can be obtained by spreading both dimensions and rounding the trailing dimension up to a multiple of PROCS.

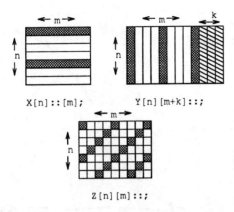

X[n]::[m];   Y[n][m+k]::;

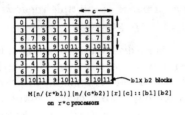

Z[n][m]::;

Figure 7: *Spread array declarations and layouts, with processor zero's elements highlighted. Assumes* n *is 7,* m *is 9,* k *is 3, and there are 4 processors.*

M[n/(r*b1)][m/(c*b2)][r][c]::[b1][b2]
on r*c processors

Figure 8: *A declaration for a blocked/cyclic layout in both dimensions. Each block shows the number of the processor that owns it. Shown for n=8, m=9, r=4, c=3, where there are 12 processors.*

The declaration of Y shows such a matrix, assuming that k is the computed constant such that m + k is a multiple of PROCS. The Z array is blocked, but has its elements scattered across processors.

To see how spread arrays can achieve other layouts, consider a generic declaration of the form

M[n/(r*b1)][m/(c*b2)][r][c]::[b1][b2].

Logically, we may think of this as a two dimensional matrix of size n by m. Physically, it has blocks of size b1 by b2. A special property holds if we choose r*c to be a multiple of PROCS: the dimensions r and c act as an r by c processor grid. The layout becomes blocked-cyclic in both dimensions. Figure 8 shows a particular case of this for 12 processors, where r is 4 and c is 3. The number in each block is the number of the processor that owns that block. In each column there are 8 blocks spread across only 4 distinct processors; in each row there are 9 blocks spread across 3 distinct processors.

Since the data layout is well-defined, programmers can write their own control macros (like the for_my_1d macro) that iterate over arbitrary dimensions in arbitrary orders. They can also encode subspace iterations, such as iterations over lower triangular, or

diagonal elements, or all elements to the left of an owned element. Spread arrays are sometimes declared to have a fixed number of elements per processor, for example, the declaration int A[PROCS] will have a single element for each processor.

The relationship between arrays and pointers in C is carried over to spread arrays in Split-C *spread pointers*. Spread pointers are declared with the word spread, *e.g.* int *spread p, and are identical to global pointers, except with respect to pointer arithmetic. Global pointers index the memory dimension and spread pointers index in a wrapped fashion in the processor dimension.

7.3 Matrix Multiply in Split-C

In many cases it is critical that blocking be employed to reduce the frequency of remote operations, but not so critical how the blocks are actually laid out. For example, in matrix multiplication a block size of b will reduce the number of remote references by a factor of b. However, the three matrices may have very different aspect ratios and not map well onto the same processor grid. In the blocked matrix multiply shown in Program 7, C is declared (in line 2) as a n by m matrix of b by b blocks and a blocked inner-product algorithm is used. The call to matrix_mult in line 17 invokes a local matrix multiply, which is written to operate on conventional C arrays. Observe that the layouts for the three arrays may be completely different, depending on the aspect ratios, but all use the same blocking factor. The iterator for_my_2d is used to bind i and j to the appropriate blocks of C under the owner-computes rule.

Figure 9 shows the performance of four of matrix multiply versions. The lowest curve, labeled "Unblocked" is for a standard matrix multiply on square matrices up to size 256×256. The performance curves for the blocked multiply are shown using $\frac{n}{8} \times \frac{n}{8}$ blocks: "Unopt" gives the results for a straightforward C local multiply routine with full compiler optimizations, whereas "Blocked" uses an optimized assembly language routine that pays careful attention to the local cache size and the floating point pipeline. A final performance curve in Figure 9 uses a clever systolic algorithm, Cannon's algorithm, which involves first skewing the blocks within a square processor grid and then cyclic shifts of the blocks at each step, *i.e.*, neighbor communication on the processor grid. All remote accesses are bulk stores and the communication is completely balanced. It peaks at 413 MFlops which on a per processor basis far exceeds published LINPACK performance numbers for the Sparc. This

```
1  void all_mat_mult_blk(int n, int r, int m, int b,
2                        double C[n][m]::[b][b],
3                        double A[n][r]::[b][b],
4                        double B[r][m]::[b][b])
5  {
6    int i,j,k,l;
7    /* Local copies of blocks */
8    double la[b][b], lb[b][b];
9
10   for_my_2D(i,j,l,n,m) {
11     double (*lc)[b] = tolocal(C[i][j]);
12
13     for (k=0;k<r;k++) {
14       bulk_get(la, A[i][k], b*b*sizeof(double));
15       bulk_get(lb, B[k][j], b*b*sizeof(double));
16       sync();
17       matrix_mult(b,b,b,lc,la,lb);
18     }
19   }
20   barrier();
21 }
```

Program 7: *Blocked matrix multiply.*

comparison suggests that the ability to use highly optimized sequential routines on local data within Split-C programs is as important as the ability to implement sophisticated global algorithms with a carefully tuned layout.

8 Fusion of Programming Models

Traditionally, different programming models, *e.g.*, shared memory, message passing, or data parallel, were supported by distinct languages on vastly different architectures. Split-C supports these models by programming conventions, rather than enforcing them through language constraints.

Split-C borrows heavily from shared memory models in providing several threads of control within a global address space[10, 12]. Virtues of this approach include: allowing familiar languages to be used with modest enhancements[6, 3, 2], making global data structures explicit, rather than being implicit in the pattern of sends and receives, and allowing for powerful linked data structures. This was illustrated for the EM3D problem above; applications that demonstrate irregularity in both time and space[4, 18] also benefit from these features.

Split-C differs from previous shared memory languages by providing a rich set of memory operations, not simply read and write. It does not rely on novel architectural features, nor does it assume communication has enormous overhead, thereby making bulk operations the only reasonable form of communication [16, 9]. These differences arise because of differences in the implementation assumptions. Split-C

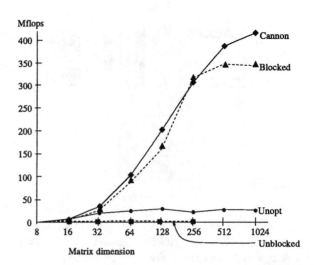

Figure 9: *Performance of multiple versions of matrix multiply on 64 Sparc processor CM-5.*

is targeted toward distributed memory multiprocessors with fast, flexible network hardware, including the Thinking Machines CM-5, Meiko CS-2, Cray T3D and others. Split-C maintains a clear concept of locality, reflecting the fundamental costs on these machines.

Optimizing global operations on regular data structures is encouraged by defining a simple storage layout for global matrices. In some cases, the way to minimize the number of remote accesses is to program the layout to ensure communication balance[5]. For example, an n-point FFT can be performed on p processors with a single remap communication step if $p^2 \leq n$ [5]. In other cases, *e.g.*, blocked matrix multiplication, the particular assignment of blocks to processors less important than load balance and block size.

The approach to global matrices in Split-C stems from the work on data parallel languages, especially HPF [8] and C* [15]. A key design choice was to avoid run-time shapes or dope vectors, because these are inconsistent with C and with the philosophy of least surprises. Split-C does not have the ease of portability of the HPF proposal or of higher level parallel languages. Some HPF layouts are harder to express in Split-C but some Split-C layouts are very hard to express in HPF. The major point of difference is that in Split-C, the programmer has full control over data layout, and sophisticated compiler support is not needed to obtain performance.

9 Summary

This paper has introduced Split-C, a new parallel extension to C which is designed to allow optimization of powerful algorithms for emerging large-scale multiprocessors. It supports a global address space with a clear notion of local and global access and a simple data layout strategy to allow programmers to minimize the frequency of remote access. It provides a rich set of assignment operators to optimize the remote accesses that do occur and to integrate co-ordination among processors with the flow of data. With these simple primitives, it captures many of the best aspects of shared memory, message passing, and data parallel programming avoiding many of the drawbacks of each. It retains a "small language" philosophy, so program performance is closely related to the program text. The languages concepts and optimization techniques have been illustrated by a simple example, which we believe will prove challenging for other available language systems.

Acknowledgements

We would like to thank Ken Stanley for optimizing the local matrix multiply code, and Randy Wang and Su-Lin Wu for writing the original EM3D code.

This work was supported in part by the National Science Foundation as a PFF (number CCR-9253705), RIA (number CCR-9210260), Graduate Research Fellowship, and Infrastructure Grant (number CDA-8722788), by Lawrence Livermore National Laboratory, by the Advanced Research Projects Agency of the DOD monitored by ONR under contract DABT63-92-C-0026, by the Semiconductor Research Consortium and by AT&T. The information presented here does not necessarily reflect the position or the policy of the Government and no official endorsement should be inferred.

References

[1] H. Berryman, J. Saltz, and J. Scroggs. Execution Time Support for Adaptive Scientific Algorithms on Distributed Memory Multiprocessors. *Concurrency: Practice and Experience*, pages 159–178, June 1991.

[2] J. Boyle, R. Butler, T. Disz, B. Glickfeld, E. Lusk, R. Overbeek, J.Patterson, and R. Stevens. *Portable Programs for Parallel Processors*. Holt, Rinehart, and Winston, 1987.

[3] E. Brooks. PCP: A Parallel Extension of C that is 99% Fat Free. Technical Report UCRL-99673, LLNL, 1988.

[4] S. Chakrabarti and K. Yelick. Implementing an Irregular Application on a Distributed Memory Multiprocessor. In *Principles and Practice of Parallel Programming*, San Diego, CA, 1993.

[5] D. Culler, R. Karp, D. Patterson, A. Sahay, K. Schauser, E. Santos, R. Subramonian, and T. von Eicken. LogP: Towards a Realistic Model of Parallel Computation. In *Principles and Practice of Parallel Programming*, May 1993.

[6] F. Darema, D. George, V. Norton, and G. Pfister. A Single-Program-Multiple Data Computational Model for EPEX/FORTRAN. *Parallel Computing*, 7:11–24, 1988.

[7] M. Dubois and C. Scheurich. Synchronization, Coherence, and Event Ordering in Multiprocessors. *IEEE Computer*, 21(2):9–21, February 1988.

[8] High Performance Fortran Forum. High Performance Fortran language specification version 1.0. Draft, Jan. 1993.

[9] S. Hiranandani, K. Kennedy, and C.-W. Tseng. Compiler optimziations for Fortran D on MIMD distributed-memory machines. In *Proceedings of the 1991 International Conference on Supercomputing*, 1991.

[10] B. A. C. Inc. TC2000 Technical Product Summary. 1989.

[11] B. W. Kernighan and S. Lin. An Efficient Heuristic Procedure for Partitioning Graphs. *Bell System Technical Journal*, 49:291–307, 1970.

[12] D. Lenoski, J. Laundon, K. Gharachorloo, A. Gupta, and J. L. Hennessy. The Directory Based Cache Coherance Protocol for the DASH Multiprocessor. In *In Proceedings of the 17th International Symposium on Computer Architecture*, pages 148–159, 1990.

[13] N. K. Madsen. Divergence Preserving Discrete Surface Integral Methods for Maxwell's Curl Equations Using Non-Orthogonal Unstructured Grids. Technical Report 92.04, RIACS, February 1992.

[14] A. Pothen, H. D. Simon, and K.-P. Liou. Partitioning Sparse Matrices with Eigenvectors of Graphs. *Siam J. Matrix Anal. Appl.*, 11(3):430–452, July 1990.

[15] J. Rose and G. Steele Jr. C*: An Extended C Language for Data Parallel Programming. In *Proceedings of the Second International Conference on Supercomputing, Vol. 2*, pages 2–16, May 1987.

[16] A. Skjellum. Zipcode: A Portable Communication Layer for High Performance Multicomputing – Practice and Experience. Unpublished draft, March 1991.

[17] T. von Eicken, D. E. Culler, S. C. Goldstein, and K. E. Schauser. Active Messages: a Mechanism for Integrated Communication and Computation. In *International Symposium on Computer Architecture*, 1992.

[18] C.-P. Wen and K. Yelick. Parallel Timing Simulation on a Distributed Memory Multiprocessor. In *International Conference on CAD*, Santa Clara, California, November 1993. To appear.

Fortran-S: A Fortran Interface for Shared Virtual Memory Architectures

F. Bodin L. Kervella T. Priol
IRISA-INRIA
Campus de Beaulieu
35042 Rennes Cedex - France

Abstract

In this paper we present a new programming environment for distributed memory parallel computers consisting of a Fortran 77 compiler enhanced with directives to specify parallelism. These directives are used to specify shared data structures and parallel loops. Shared data structures are implemented using the KOAN shared virtual memory that is available on an Intel iPSC/2 computer. Preliminary results obtained with the first prototype of the compiler are presented.

1 Introduction

The current generation of parallel architectures tends toward MIMD distributed memory parallel computers (DMPCs). However, the success of these parallel architectures will depend on the availability of programming environments that help users design parallel algorithms. The previous generation was characterized by the lack of software; users had to take into account the underlying architecture in the design of their parallel algorithms including data distribution among the local memories, processes mapping, etc. Since then, researches have undertaken the task of providing parallel extensions to sequential languages such as C or Fortran to hide the distributed nature of these architectures. Several prototypes have been built, including Fortran-D [10], Vienna Fortran [3], Pandore [2]. Recently, a coalition of industrial and academics group founded the High Performance Fortran Forum to propose extensions to Fortran (HPF). All these approaches provide the user with a global address space and the compilers are in charge of generating processes and communications. Data management is also carried out by the compiler. Because the compiler is in charge of everything, its design and implementation

become intricate. Moreover, when data access patterns are unknown at compile time, the generation of efficient parallel code must rely on runtime techniques [24].

There is another alternative based on the use of both a data management service available within an operating system of a DMPC and an ad hoc compiler that could drastically simplify the design of a programming environment for DMPCs. This approach, which is the one explored here, takes advantage of a Shared Virtual Memory (SVM) implemented within the operating system. The basic idea of this concept is to hide the underlying architecture of DMPCs by providing the user with a virtual address space. Locality is achieved by a page caching mechanism. Thus, a DMPC can be programmed as a conventional shared memory parallel computers. The compiler is then responsible for generating parallel processes and communications are handled by the operating systems. Consequently, the compiler design is simplified in comparison to those approaches based on explicit data distribution. Unfortunately, few experiments have been done to show the effectiveness of such an approach on message-passing parallel architectures. The KOAN project [14, 19] has been established to to investigate the use of the SVM paradigm on DMPCs and to validate this programming model for DMPCs. We propose a Fortran-77 code generator based on a directives set called Fortran-S. It is intended to be a testbed for studying code generation and optimizations for SVM architectures. This paper gives an overview of Fortran-S and performance results are provided for some parallel algorithms. These results were obtained with an iPSC/2 running the KOAN shared virtual memory.

The paper is organized as follows. Section 2 sketches the KOAN SVM runtime system. Section 3 describes the Fortran-S fundamentals. Section 4 presents a description of the Fortran-S directive set.

Section 6 gives performance results, followed by conclusions in Section 7.

2 KOAN SVM Runtime

The KOAN SVM is embedded in the operating system of the iPSC/2. It allows the use of fast and low-level communication primitives as well as a Memory Management Unit (MMU). It differs from SHIVA described in [17] in that it is an operating system based implementation. The KOAN SVM implements the fixed distributed manager algorithm as described in [16] with an invalidation protocol for keeping the shared memory coherent at all times (strong coherency). This algorithm offers a suitable compromise between ease of implementation and efficiency. We now summarize the basic functionality of the KOAN SVM runtime system [1].

KOAN SVM provides the user several memory management protocols for efficiently handling some particular memory access patterns. One of these is when several processors have to write into different locations of the same page. This pattern involves a lot of messages because the page has to move from processor to processor (this is called the *ping-pong effect* or *false sharing*). KOAN provides a weak cache coherence protocol to let processors concurrently modify their own copy of a page. At a synchronization point, all the copies of a page which have been modified are merged into a single page that reflects all the changes. This technique is similar to the one presented in [13] by Karp et al. However, in order to speedup the merging process, our implementation of this form of weak coherency has some restrictions : each processor must only access a memory regions that are not overlapping. Hence, the starting and the ending addresses specified by each processor are used to carry out the merging process.

A drawback of shared virtual memory on DMPCs is its inability to run efficiently parallel algorithms that contain a producer/consumer scheme, i.e. when a page is modified by one processor and then accessed by the other processors. KOAN SVM can efficiently manage this memory access pattern by using the broadcast facility of the underlying topology of DMPCs (hypercube, 2D-mesh, etc). All pages that have been modified by the processor in charge of running the producer phase are broadcast in parallel to all other processors that will run the consumer phase.

Last of all, KOAN SVM provides a page locking mechanism to implement atomic updates and special synchronization schemes. Page locking allows a processor to lock a page into its cache until it decides to release it. Page locking is very efficient and minimizes the number of critical sections within a parallel code.

We have performed measurements in order to determine the costs of various basic operations for both read and write page faults (the size of a page is 4 *Kbytes*) of the KOAN shared virtual memory. For each type of page fault (read or write), we have tested the best and worst possible situation on different numbers of processors. For a 32-processor configuration, the time required to solve a read page fault is in the range of 3.412 *ms* to 3.955 *ms*. For a write page fault, timing results are in the range of 3.447 *ms* to 10.110 *ms* depending on the number of copies that have to be invalidated. These results can be compared with the communication times of the iPSC/2. The latency is roughly 0.3 *ms*. Sending a 4 *Kbytes* message (a page) costs between 2.17 *ms* and 2.27 *ms* depending on the number of intermediate routing steps.

3 Fortran-S Fundamental Concepts.

Fortran-S is a code generator targeted for shared virtual memory parallel architectures. One of our goals was to respect the Fortran-77 standard since it is widely used in the scientific community. Therefore no extension to the language syntax has been made. A set of annotations provides the user with a simple programming model based on shared array variables and parallel loops. One of the unique features of Fortran-S is its SPMD (Single Program Multiple Data) execution model that minimizes the overhead due to the management of parallel processes. The Fortran-S code generator creates a process for each processor for the entire duration of the computation. There is no dynamic creation of processes during the execution. In the following subsections, we present both the user programming and the execution models.

3.1 User Programming Model

The Fortran-S programming model is based on parallel loops and shared variables. As a default, variables are not shared. Non-shared variables modified in a parallel loop have undefined value at the end of the execution of the loop. The value of a variable is said to be undefined when at some point in the program the variable can have different values on different processors. Except for parallel loops, the semantics of the

---

[1] A more detailed description of the KOAN SVM can be found in [14]

program is identical to the semantics of the sequential program.

In the sequential parts of programs, shared variables behave identically to non-shared variables. However since shared variables are accessible by the processors, computation of these variables can be done in parallel.

Alternatively, all the variables in a program could be shared by default and this would make a DMPC look like a shared memory architecture. This solution was not chosen because it could lead to very inefficient programs because of the unnecessary data movement and synchronization. Taking into account communication costs, it is usually more efficient to compute the value of a variable redundantly on all the processors than globally accessing a single set of values. On the other hand, data structures which are to be computed within a parallel loop need to be shared. Restricting shared variables to some data structures in programs constraints parallelism to the computation of those variables. For example, if we consider the following parallel loop:

do in parallel $i = 1, n$
    $temp = 0.$
    do $k = ia(i), ia(i+1) - 1$
        $temp = temp + a(k)*x(ja(k))$
    enddo
    $y(i) = temp$
enddo

Variables **a**, **ia**, **x**, **ja** can be either shared or non-shared variables. If a variable is not shared it will be replicated on each processor (this remains transparent to the users). The programmer must take this point into account when deciding which variable should be shared. The choice is a tradeoff between efficiency and the amount of memory used. For example, note that in the previous loop the variable **y** has to be shared since it is modified in the loop. If such variable is not declared as shared each processor will see a different value of the variable **y** at the end of the loop execution. The case of variable **temp** is different. The variable is defined at the beginning of each iteration, and that value is only used in the iteration. So not only can it not be shared, it must be local. Subject to these previous constraints, the program will behave similarly on a sequential computer and on an DMPC.

We believe that the programming model is easy to understand and use. Since Fortran-S is a full implementation of Fortran-77, an application can be quickly ported to a DMPC. However efficiency and scalability frequently rely on finding a better parallel algorithm than original. (For example, block algorithms instead of column approaches for numerical algorithms).

Declaring parallel loops and shared variables is done using directives. An overview of the main directives is given in section 4.

Because SPMD execution model (see section 3.2), there is only one process per processor and we do not support nested parallelism [2]. However, perfectly nested loops can be easily implemented through loop collapsing. If loops are not perfectly nested, only the outermost loop is executed in parallel. To illustrate this let us consider an example:

```
        program myprog
        ..........
C parallel loop 1
        do in parallel
C subroutine call 1
            call myfunction(x,y,z)
        enddo
        ..........
C subroutine call 2
        call myfunction(i,j,k)
        end

        subroutine myfunction(t,u,v)
        ..........
C parallel loop 2
        do in parallel
        .........
        enddo
        ..........
        end
```

In the above example we have: two parallel loops 1 and 2 and two calls (1 and 2) to subroutine **myfunction**. When execution reaches parallel loop 1, iterations of that loop are distributed over the processors. However, parallel loop 2 will be executed sequentially for that call. When the program execution reaches the second call to the subroutine, the second parallel loop is then executed in parallel. This is decided at runtime.

There is no constraint on the parameters to subroutines; they can be shared or non-shared variables and the same parameter can be a shared variable at one call site and a local variable somewhere else. It is not required that the program be in the same file because Fortran-S accepts full separate compilation.

3.2 SPMD Execution Model

The SPMD execution model has been widely used to program distributed memory parallel computers with a message passing programming style since it allows a low-overhead parallel execution during both the

---

[2]Nested parallelism is currently under investigation

loading and the running of parallel programs. With an SPMD execution model, a process is created on each processor at the beginning of the program execution and then executed. These processes remain alive until the end of the program. This execution model has been widely investigated in the design of programming environments that exploits data parallelism [2, 3, 10]. However, few work has been done to combine both control parallelism and SPMD code generation. This idea has been investigated within the EPEX project [9, 21] but the user programming model is more complicated than ours because users have to work with several types of code sections: uniprocessor section (that is performed by a single processor), independent section (each processor executed the same section in parallel) and shared section (a parallel loop distributed among the processors). The basic synchronization primitives are implemented by shared variables (locks, barrier, etc...). The user is responsible for adding, within his program, macros that indicate to a preprocessor the boundaries of the uniprocessor, independent and shared sections. Adding these macros is a difficult task since the user has to know perfectly the control flow of his program.

The SPMD execution model we implemented simulates a kind of fork&join paradigm. During the execution of a parallel loop, each process running on a processor accesses non-shared variables. Most of the overhead associated with a true fork&join implementation comes from this heritage. To avoid this extra-cost, sequential code sections are duplicated on each processor. Hence, if a parallel loop is executed, each processor has the same view of the contents of the non-shared variables. The iteration space of the parallel loop is then distributed and the execution continues. Since sequential code sections are duplicated, the code generator has to manage some instructions and library subroutines. Indeed, in a sequential code section, we cannot let several processors to write into the same shared variables. The code generator has to insert properly extra code to allow only one processor to modify a shared variable to avoid memory contention and race conditions. A similar problem arises when shared and non-shared variables are involved in I/O routine calls executed in a sequential code section. For reading operations in a sequential section, only one processor is allowed to execute the I/O routine; for non-shared variables, the read value has to be broadcast to every processor. Similarly, writing operations in a sequential section is carried out by only one processor.

To ensure the correctness of these code generation rules, the code generator adds synchronization barriers when entering or leaving a parallel loop as well as when a processor is elected for executing an I/O routine or for updating a shared variables. Generating efficient SPMD code from control parallelism requires that several optimizations be carried out by the code generator to remove these synchronization barriers.

4 Fortran-S directives

The compiler's main function is to translate a Fortran-S program into a Fortran SPMD program. Parallel loops and shared variables are declared using directives. In this section we present the main directives available in Fortran-S. Section 5 gives an overview of the code generation scheme performed by the first prototype of compiler.

4.1 Shared Variables

A variable is declared as shared using the directive:

real V(N,N)
C\$ann[Shared(v)]

Presently, shared variables can only be declared in the main program. Strong coherency is applied by default to shared variables. However in many cases this can lead to false sharing. The KOAN SVM allows shared variable to be managed using a weak cache coherence protocol in some parts of the program, as explained in section 2. The following paragraph shows parallel loop directives and how weak coherency can be used in Fortran-S.

4.2 Parallel Loops

A parallel loop is declared using the directive:

C\$ann[DoShared("BLOCK")]
    do *nel* = 1, *nbnel*
        sounds(nel) = sqrt(gama*p(nel)/ro(nel))
    enddo

The string **"BLOCK"** indicates the scheduling strategy of the iterations. The strategies available are the following:

1. **"BLOCK"**: chunks of contiguous iterations are assigned over the processors.

2. **"CYCLIC"**: iterations are distributed over the processor according to a "modulo-p" scheme. The first iteration is affected to the first processor, the second to the second processor, and so on.

3. **"ALTERNATE"**: identical to cyclic distribution but uneven processors execute the sequence of iterations in the reverse order. Depending on data accesses, this scheduling may help to reduce the amount of "false-sharing".

4. **"AFFINITY"**: the affinity scheduling allows the system to map iterations onto processors in order to exploit temporal locality and, consequently, best use of the local cache. Before using this kind of scheduling, the user must first specify a virtual iteration space by adding the annotation `C$ann[Affinity("DIST",low,up,step)]` in his program. DIST indicates the loop distribution strategy and the remaining parameters are the starting, the ending and the stride of a 1D iteration space. The affinity scheduling will refer to this virtual distribution in order to assign to a processor the same index value whatever the parameters of the loop to be distributed.

5. **User defined**: in that case the user defines how the iterations are distributed. This is useful for instance to solve some load balancing problem. This can, for instance, be used in sparse matrix computations. After examination of the structure of the matrix, at run-time, the iteration space can be distributed according to the number of nonzero elements per row there is in the matrix.

Weak cache Coherency The following annotation, when applied to a parallel loop, establishes weak coherency for a shared variable, and thusly, may greatly reduce the number of conflicts that may arise on pages that own the variable:

$$C\$ann[WeakCoherency(y)]$$

Where **y** is a shared variable. For example, in the following loop the variable **y** is written simultaneously by many processors, so there will be false sharing on pages where the variable **y** is stored. The weak coherence protocol removes that phenomenon, by merging modification of pages only at the end of the loop.

```
C$ann[DoShared("BLOCK")]
C$ann[WeakCoherency(y)]
    do i = 1, n
        temp = 0.
        do k = ia(i), ia(i + 1) − 1
            temp = temp + a(k)*x(ja(k))
        enddo
        y(i) = temp
    endddo
```

Reduction operations Fortran-S provides two annotations for making reduction operations either on a scalar or a vector variable more efficient. The annotations are

```
C$ann[SGlobal(OP,v)]
C$ann[VGlobal(OP,v,n)]
```

where **OP** is an associative and commutative operator such as SUM, PROD, MIN, MAX. The parameter **v** is a scalar when it appears in **SGLOBAL**, and it is a vector in **VGLOBAL**. In the later case, **n** specifies the number of elements in the vector. For this latter directive, the reduction operator is applied to every element of the array. The following example illustrates the use of a reduction operation (global maximum):

```
        real u(N,M)
C$ann[Shared(u)]
.........
C$ann[DoShared("BLOCK")]
C$ann[SGlobal(SMAX,rmax)]
    do j = 1, 63
        do i = 3, 128 − 1, 2
            uold = u(i,2*j+1)
            u(i,2*j+1) = omega * ((2*u(i-1,2*j+1)
                        +2*u(i+1,2*j+1)
                    ....
                    omega1*u(i,2*j+1)
            r = DABS(uold - u(i,2*j+1))
            if (r .gt. rmax) rmax = r
        enddo
    enddo
```

For instance, in order to get a global maximum in the previous example, it is more efficient to compute the maximum over each processor (stored in a non-shared variable) and then to merge the results using the `C$ann[SGlobal(SMAX,rmax)]` directive. Several DMPCs have such reduction operations implemented efficiently with message passing techniques. Fortran-S is able to exploit them transparently.

4.3 Page broadcast

When a shared variable is modified within a sequential code section and then used within a parallel loop, every processor will send requests for the same page to the processor that ran the sequential code section. To avoid this potential contention, it is possible to broadcast pages that stored the shared variable to every processor, before they start to access it. This is done using the following directives:

```
C$ann[BeginBroadcast(var)]
C$ann[EndBroadcast()]
```

where **var** is a shared variable. These directives cannot appear in a parallel loop. For example, in the following code segment, the directive **BeginBroadcast(v)** is used to indicate that modification, done within the sequential code section, to the shared array **v** must be recorded. The directive **EndBroadcast()** indicates that the recorded modifications must be broadcast to all the processors.

```
          do i = 1, m
C$ann[BeginBroadcast(v)]
          tmp = 0.0
          do k = 1, n
            tmp = tmp + v(k,i)*v(k,i)
          enddo
          xnorm = 1.0 / sqrt(tmp)
          do k = 1, n
            v(k,i) = v(k,i) * xnorm
          enddo
C$ann[EndBroadcast()]
C$ann[DoShared("BLOCK")]
          do j = i + 1, m
            tmp = 0.0
            do k = 1, n
              tmp = tmp + v(k,i)*v(k,j)
            enddo
            do k = 1, n
              v(k,j) = v(k,j) - tmp*v(k,i)
            enddo
          enddo
        enddo
```

The broadcasting reduces contention when several processors want to access the same part of a shared variables (computed sequentially) and improves the performance of the parallel loop. The value of non-shared variables modified between a **BeginBroadcast(v)** and a **EndBroadcast()** are undetermined after the broadcasting. This is because only one processor executes the sequence of code delimited by the broadcast directives.

4.4 Directives for synchronization

When programming with shared variables, it is sometimes necessary to synchronize processors when they have to write to the same memory address. In the following example, the do loop could be parallelized unless we ensure that several processors will not write to the same array element at the same time. Unfortunately, the value of index k is only known at runtime.

```
          do i = 1, n
            k = idx(i)
            v(k) = v(k) + a(i)
          enddo
```

Fortran-S provides two ways for synchronizing parallel computations: critical section and atomic update.

```
C$ann[BeginCritical()]
C$ann[EndCritical()]
```

With a critical section, the previous example could be rewritten as follows:

```
C$ann[DoShared("BLOCK")]
          do i = 1, n
            k = idx(i)
C$ann[BeginCritical()]
            v(k) = v(k) + a(i)
C$ann[EndCritical()]
          enddo
```

With an atomic update, the previous example could be rewritten as follows:

```
C$ann[DoShared("BLOCK")]
          do i = 1, n
            k = idx(i)
C$ann[AtomicUpdate()]
            v(k) = v(k) + a(i)
          enddo
```

This annotation has to be inserted before an assignment statement that modifies a shared variable within a parallel loop. It ensure that the page that contains the address to be accessed is locked in the memory until the assignment is completed. The main difference between these two synchronization techniques is the cost of synchronization. Critical sections are implemented thanks to a distributed algorithm based on the sending a token around a ring of processors [22]. It has to be used to synchronize large grain computations whereas atomic update can be to synchronize small grain computations as shown in the previous example. Experiments we have done on a matrix assembling in a numerical application [4] have shown this type of page locking as a synchronization tool is efficient.

4.5 The Escape Mechanism

In some case, to achieve efficiency, the user may want to take control of parallelism management and data structure distribution. This is possible by adding a C$ann[Escape()] directive that tells to the compiler which subroutines are not to be modified. In these subroutines, programmers can freely exploit the SPMD execution model. The programmer has access to shared variables but he or she cannot declare parallel loops. This escape mechanism is similar to the one found in HPF [1].

5 Implementation of a Prototype Fortran-S Compiler

The compiler is implemented using the Sigma system developed at Indiana University [11]. Sigma has a Fortran parser, libraries to write program transformations and support for program annotations. The Fortran-S Compiler is a source to source compiler. The function of the compiler is to generate the appropriate SPMD code for the following statements:

- Allocating shared variable: the compiler generates subroutine call to the KOAN system to allocate the shared variables.

- Access to the shared variable in sequential region (i.e. that part of the code that simulates the sequential execution of the program in SPMD execution) of the program. When a shared variable is updated in a sequential region of the program it must be ensured that only one processor will update the variable, all the other processor having to synchronize on that store operation. One of the optimizations the compiler performs is to decrease the number of these synchronizations by moving them out of loop bodies. Deciding if a variable is shared or non-shared is done at run-time except for those variables for which this can be determined at compile-time.

- Parallel loops. At the beginning of a parallel loop the compiler generates a call to a function that decides the allocation of the iteration to the processors. A barrier is also generated at the end of the parallel loop. The processor also sets a flag which indicates the entry in a parallel loop.

- Function bodies: The body of each function is duplicated. The decision as to which routine body to execute is done at run-time according to a flag that indicates if the call to the function is done in a parallel loop or not. Indeed depending on whether the call to the function is done in a parallel loop or in a sequential region, synchronizations must be done or not. So the compiler generates two bodies for the function:

  1. A body identical to the original one to be used if the function is called from within a parallel loop. Parallel loops are left sequential in this body.

  2. A body with synchronizations and parallel loops. This body is executed when the function is called in a sequential region of the code. This body contains synchronization for updating shared variables and managing the distribution of the iteration space of parallel loops.

6 Preliminary Results

In this section we present the first results obtained using Fortran-S on an Intel iPSC/2 with 32 nodes. The goal of these experiments was to port sequential Fortran 77 programs to Fortran-S and to measure the performance obtained. In these early performance measurements, it was not intended that there be extensive modifications to the applications. Rather, the desire was to measure the performance of Fortran-S when applied in a straight forward manner to Fortran 77 code. Very few modifications have been done to the original programs. The primary modification was to expose parallel loops in the programs. However no modification of the data structure used in the programs was made. Also they were no major modification to the algorithms, so the scalability of some application is not limited by Fortran-S but by the algorithm used in the application. The problem of false-sharing that appears in many applications was solved using a weak coherence protocol.

6.1 Jacobi loops

The code used for the Jacobi experiment is shown in Figure 1. Table 1 gives the speedups and efficiencies for different problem sizes when using either a strong

```
C$ann[DoShared("BLOCK")]
C$ann[WeakCoherency(a)]
    do j = 2, n − 1
        do i = 2, n − 1
            a(i, j) = (b(i − 1, j)
            + ... + b(i + 1, j) + b(i, j − 1)
            + ... + b(i, j + 1)) / 4
        enddo
    enddo
C$ann[DoShared("BLOCK")]
C$ann[WeakCoherency(b)]
    do j = 2, n − 1
        do i = 2, n − 1
            b(i, j) = a(i, j)
        enddo
    enddo
```

Figure 1: Fortran-S code for the Jacobi loop.

P	With strong coherency					
	100 x 100			200 x 200		
	Times (ms)	S	E %	Times (ms)	S	E %
1	3112	-	-	12933	-	-
2	1927	1.61	80.75	7323	1.77	88.30
4	1280	2.43	60.78	3975	3.25	81.34
8	1322	2.35	29.43	2284	5.66	70.78
16	3882	0.80	5.01	1446	8.94	55.90
32	5339	0.58	1.82	1928	6.71	20.96
	With weak coherency					
1	3112	-	-	12933	-	-
2	1972	1.58	78.90	7323	1.77	88.30
4	1311	2.37	59.34	4016	3.22	80.51
8	923	3.37	42.15	2305	5.61	70.14
16	921	3.38	21.12	1567	8.25	51.58
32	1151	2.70	8.45	1244	10.40	32.49

Table 1: Performance results for the Jacobi loop.

or a weak cache coherence protocol. For a matrix size set to 100 × 100, we got a "speed-down" when the number of processors is greater than 16. False sharing could be avoided by using our weak cache coherence protocol. For the same problem size, this cache coherence protocol improves the speedups a little but the remain flat. For a larger problem size (200 × 200) we did not observe this phenomena. however when the number of processors is set to 32, the efficiency is bad (20.71%). The weak cache coherence protocol increases the efficiency to 32.49%. This behavior is observed only for small matrices while for large matrices the efficiency is close to the maximum.

P	With strong coherency					
	100 x 100			200 x 200		
	Times (ms)	S	E %	Times (ms)	S	E %
1	15694	-	-	127657	-	-
2	7920	1.98	99.08	64037	1.99	99.67
4	4056	3.87	96.73	32292	3.95	98.83
8	2206	7.11	88.93	16522	7.73	96.58
16	3393	4.63	28.91	8982	14.21	88.83
32	4379	3.58	11.20	5196	24.57	76.78
	With weak coherency					
1	15694	-	-	127657	-	-
2	7923	1.98	99.04	64036	1.99	99.68
4	4048	3.88	96.92	32276	3.96	98.88
8	2202	7.13	89.09	16521	7.73	96.59
16	1287	12.19	76.21	8972	14.23	88.93
32	884	17.75	55.48	5206	24.52	76.63

Table 2: Performance results for the matrix multiply.

6.2 Matrix multiplication

Table 2 gives timing results for small matrices (100 × 100 and 200 × 200). For larger matrix size, speedups are near to the maximum. This can be seen in this table; for a 32 nodes configuration, speedups increase from 3.58 to 24.57 when the number of matrix elements was quadrupled. However, for small matrices, the results can be improved by using the weak cache coherence protocol. Indeed, the poor performances are always due to the same effect: "false-sharing". The same table provides timing results when the parallel loop is executing with weak coherency. For the small matrix, the gain in performances is impressive. When the number of processors is set to 32, speedup augments from 3.58 to 17.75.

6.3 Modified Gram-Schmidt

Given a set of independent vectors $\{v_1, ..., v_n\}$ in R^m, the Modified Gram-Schmidt (MGS) algorithm produces an orthonormal basis of the space generated by these vectors. The basis is constructed in steps where each new computed vector replaces the old one. We added annotations to improve the efficiency of the parallel MGS algorithm. The source code is shown in section 4.3. The vector, which is modified in the sequential section, is broadcast to every processor, since it will be accessed within the parallel loop. This is done by using the C$ann[BeginBroadcast(v)]. A weak cache coherence protocol is also associated with the inner loop to avoid false sharing. A detailed study of this algorithm can be found in [19, 20]. Table 3 summarizes the results we obtained with different strate-

P	Strong		Weak		Weak+Broadcast		MP
	Times (s)	S	Times (s)	S	Times (s)	S	S
200 X 200							
1	125.99	-	125.99	-	125.99	-	-
2	79.34	1.59	66.34	1.90	66.69	1.89	1.97
4	64.20	1.96	37.07	3.40	37.09	3.40	3.82
8	61.59	2.05	23.99	5.25	23.04	5.47	7.22
16	65.49	1.92	20.61	6.11	16.85	7.48	13.98
32	78.79	1.60	23.62	5.33	14.88	8.47	23.79
500 X 500							
1	1986.81	-	1986.81	-	1986.81	-	-
2	1029.11	1.93	1007.51	1.97	1013.20	1.96	1.97
4	562.52	3.53	517.57	3.84	522.38	3.80	3.90
8	339.23	5.86	276.17	7.19	278.72	7.13	7.74
16	233.10	8.52	163.98	12.12	158.97	12.50	14.81
32	205.75	9.66	124.71	15.93	101.62	19.55	28.87

Table 3: Performance results for the MGS algorithm.

gies. The last column shows the speedup with a hand-coded message passing version of the MGS algorithm. As the problem size increases, the performances of the two versions tend to draw closer since the SVM version generates less false-sharing. This phenomenon appears very frequently in the experiments we have carried out.

6.4 Because 2.5.1

The benchmark program BECAUSE BBS 2.5.1 is based on the matrix assembly that occurs in the Everest semiconductor device modeling system. Only the Poisson's equation solver has been studied here. It consists of a simplified matrix assembly loop over a quasi realistic mesh. A performance analysis of a version of this benchmark written in Fortran-S is described in [7]. With 10648 nodes, we achieved a speedup of 11.39 with 16 processors and 15.71 with 32 processors.

6.5 Ordinary Differential Equation

An ordinary differential equation solver [8] has been written with Fortran-S. The main parallel loop in that application is limited to 8 iterations. A speedup of 5.8 has been obtained with 8 processors.

6.6 Sparse Matrix-Vector product

A performance study of a sparse matrix-vector product is described in [6]. We have shown that computations involved in a sparse matrix vector multiply can be easily distributed by using the user defined loop scheduling strategy provided by Fortran-S. Concerning data locality, the overhead induced by reading the matrix comes from an initial system distribution that is unrelated to the loop distribution. But these page moves become negligible as soon as the number

of iterations calling the sparse matrix vector multiply becomes sizable.

7 Conclusion

The approach presented in this paper could be seen as a complementary approach to HPF when the latter is not able to generate efficient code (sparse computations). By using a shared virtual memory, the design of the Fortran-S compiler has been simplified. Our first prototype, which has been designed and implemented in few months. is able to generate efficient parallel code and we have seen encouraging speedups for various applications. Our main objective in designing Fortran-S has been to provide a set of directives to the Fortran language to help the user with parallelizing applications. Because it took very little time rewriting sequential algorithm in Fortran-S, we feel that this object has been achieved. However, this code generator must be be considered a research tool for evaluating new optimizations that will be added either into the compiler or into the SVM. For example, we plan to add and test optimizations such as those described in [5, 12, 15, 18, 23]. As we further investigate applications and gain experience as to what is required, the set of directives will no doubt grow. We will also carry out experiments on new, commercially available parallel machines such as the Paragon XP/S, which will have a Shared Virtual Memory.

Acknowledgment

The authors wish to thank Pr D. Gannon for his careful reading and helpful suggestions and comments for improving this paper. This work is supported by Intel SSD under contract no. 1 92 C 250 00 31318 01 2 and Esprit BRA APPARC.

References

[1] High performance fortran language specification. May 1993.

[2] Françoise André, Jean-Louis Pazat, and Henry Thomas. Pandore : A System to Manage Data Distribution. In *International Conference on Supercomputing*, ACM, June 11-15 1990.

[3] S. Benkner, B. Chapman, and H. Zima. Vienna fortran 90. In *Scalable High Performance Computing Conference*, pages 51–59, IEEE Computer Society Press, April 1992.

[4] R. Berrendorf, M. Gerndt, Z. Lahjomri, T. Priol, and P. d'Anfray. Evaluation of numerical applications running with shared virtual memory. July 1993. APPARC ESPRIT deliverable.

[5] F. Bodin, C. Eisenbeis, W. Jalby, and D. Windheiser. *A Quantitative Algorithm for Data Locality Optimization*. Springer Verlag, 1992.

[6] F. Bodin, J. Erhel, and T. Priol. Parallel sparse matrix vector multiplication using a shared virtual memory environment. In *Proceeeding of the Sixth SIAM Conference on Parallel Processing for Scientific Computing*, March 1993.

[7] F. Bodin and T. Priol. Overview of the KOAN programming environment for the iPSC/2 and performance evaluation of the BECAUSE test program 2.5.1. In *Because Workshop*, October 1992.

[8] Philippe Chartier. L-stable parallel one-block methods for ordinary differential equations. In *Proceedings of the Sixth SIAM Conference on Parallel Processing*, March 1993.

[9] F. Darema-Rodgers, V.A. Norton, and G.F. Pfister. *Using A Single-Program-Multiple-Data Computational Model for Parallel Execution of Scientific Applications*. Technical Report RC11552, IBM T.J Watson Research Center, November 1985.

[10] G. Fox, K. Kennedy S. Hiranandi, C. Koebel, U. Kremer, C. Tseng, and M. Wu. *Fortran D language specification*. Technical Report TR90079, Department of Computer Science, Rice University, March 1991.

[11] Dennis Gannon, Jenq Kuen Lee, Bruce Shei, Sekhar Sarukaiand Srivinas Narayana, Neelakantan Sundaresan, Daya Atapattu, and François Bodin. Sigma II: a tool kit for building parallelizing compilers and performance analysis systems. *To appear in* Elsevier, 1992.

[12] E.D. Granston and H. Wijshoff. Managing pages in shared virtual memory systems: getting the compiler into the game. In *Proceedings of the International Conference on Supercomputing*, ACM, July 1993.

[13] A.H. Karp and V. Sarkar. Data Merging for Shared-Memory Multiprocessor. In *Proc. Hawaii International Conference on System Sciences*, pages 244–256, January 1993.

[14] Z. Lahjomri and T. Priol. KOAN: A Shared Virtual Memory for the iPSC/2 Hypercube. In *CONPAR/VAPP92*, September 1992.

[15] M. Lam, E. Rothberg, and M. Wolf. The cache performance and optimizations of blocked algorithms. In *Proceedings of the Fourth ACM ASPLOS conference*, pages 63–75, 1991.

[16] Kai Li. *Shared Virtual Memory on Loosely Coupled Multiprocessors*. PhD thesis, Yale University, September 1986.

[17] Kai Li and Richard Schaefer. A hypercube shared virtual memory system. *Proceedings of the 1989 International Conference on Parallel Processing*, 1:125–131, 1989.

[18] K. S. McKindley. *Automatic and Interactive Parallelization*. PhD thesis, Rice University, 1992.

[19] T. Priol and Z. Lahjomri. Experiments with Shared Virtual Memory on a iPSC/2 Hypercube. In *International Conference on Parallel Processing*, pages 145–148, August 1992.

[20] T. Priol and Z. Lahjomri. *Trade-offs Between Shared Virtual Memory and Message-passing on an iPSC/2 Hypercube*. Technical Report 1634, INRIA, 1992.

[21] J.M. Stone. *Nested Parallelism in a Parallel FORTRAN Environment*. Technical Report RC11506, IBM T.J Watson Research Center, November 1985.

[22] I. Suzuki and T. KASAMI. An optimality theory for mutual exclusion algorithms in computer networks. In *Conf on Distributed Computing Systems*, oct 1982.

[23] M. Wolf and M. Lam. *An algorithm to generate sequential and parallel code with improved data locality*. Technical Report , Stanford University, 1990.

[24] J. Wu, J. Saltz, S. Hiranandanu, and H. Berryman. Runtime compilation methods for multicomputers. In *Proceedings of the 1991 International Conference on Parallel Processing*, pages 26–30, 1991.

DYNAMIC DATA DISTRIBUTIONS IN VIENNA FORTRAN*

Barbara Chapman[a]   Piyush Mehrotra[b]   Hans Moritsch[a]   Hans Zima[a]

[a]*Institute for Software Technology and Parallel Systems,*
University of Vienna, Brünner Strasse 72, A-1210 VIENNA AUSTRIA
E-Mail: zima@par.univie.ac.at

[b]*ICASE, MS 132C, NASA Langley Research Center, Hampton VA. 23681 USA*
E-Mail: pm@icase.edu

Abstract

Vienna Fortran is a machine-independent language extension of Fortran, which is based upon the Single-Program-Multiple-Data (SPMD) paradigm and allows the user to write programs for distributed-memory systems using global addresses. The language features focus mainly on the issue of distributing data across virtual processor structures. In this paper, we discuss those features of Vienna Fortran that allow the data distributions of arrays to change dynamically, depending on runtime conditions. We discuss the relevant language features, outline their implementation and describe how they may be used in applications.

1 Introduction

High-level language extensions to Fortran, which enable users to design programs for massively parallel computers much as they are accustomed to on a sequential machine, have been the subject of intense discussion and research activity in recent months. Vienna Fortran [3, 4] is one of several proposals put forth for such a set of language extensions [5, 6, 9, 12, 13]. A number of features of Vienna Fortran have since been adopted by the High Performance Fortran Forum. One of these is the concept of static and dynamic distributions of arrays in a program, although the details of these features are not the same in High Performance Fortran (HPF).

The language extensions provided by Vienna Fortran allow the user to explicitly control and specify the mapping of arrays across the underlying set of processors. The computation, however, is still specified using a global address space which is independent of the distribution of the data. That is, the programmer writes code using a single thread of control just as when writing a sequential program. It is the compiler's responsibility to produce code suitable for parallel execution.

The Vienna Fortran Compilation System generates code based on the *SPMD* (Single Program Multiple Data) model, in which each processor executes essentially the same code, but on a local data set. The mapping specification provided by the user determines the *ownership of data*: a processor owns the data which is distributed to it, and stores it in its local memory. In general, the compiler distributes work based upon the *owner computes* rule: the processor performs the computation that defines data elements owned locally. The compiler satisfies any non-local references required for this computation by inserting communication statements to transfer the data.

The performance of the generated code is critically dependent on the data distribution used for the program. A distribution is selected with the aims of spreading the workload as evenly as possible across the processors, while preserving the locality of computation. The appropriate distribution for a given code will depend on the characteristics of both the program itself and that of the target architecture. The former includes factors such as the data access patterns exhibited by the code, and the size of the data structures relative to the number of processors used for a particular execution. The hardware factors include the communication latency and bandwidth, the computation/communication ratio, and the cache behavior of the machine.

If these factors can be determined statically, then the user can choose the "best" data distribution at compile time. However, in situations where the program behavior is dependent on runtime values, the choice of the appropriate distribution may be made at runtime if there is language support for dynamic distributions. Major uses of dynamic distribution of data in programs are to:

- improve the locality of data accesses in codes with identifiable computation phases,

- write highly portable code in which the data dis-

*The work described in this paper was supported by the Austrian Research Foundation (FWF) and by the Austrian Ministry for Science and Research (BMWF). This research was also supported by the National Aeronautics and Space Administration under NASA contract NAS1-18605 while the authors were in residence at ICASE, Mail Stop 132C, NASA Langley Research Center, Hampton, VA 23681-0001. The authors assume all responsibility for the contents of the paper.

tributions are selected on the basis of input data and/or characteristics of the executing machine,

- maintain a good load balance throughout the execution of a program for which the workload varies significantly during the computation.

There are significant costs associated with using dynamic distribution of data. At run time, this includes the cost of performing the actual data transfers and the cost of maintaining runtime information about the current distribution. At compile time, a more rigorous analysis must be performed to determine the distributions associated with a particular data reference. In particular, the compiler has to generate code which allows for the possibility that several data distributions may reach some statements. Despite these costs, the judicious use of dynamic distribution features can reduce the overall communication costs of the program while improving the load balance. Thus, the overall performance of the code may improve even in the presence of the runtime overheads.

In this paper, we present the language features of Vienna Fortran which support dynamic distribution of data. Section 2 describes the distribution facilities along with some control constructs required for expressing code in the presence of redistribution of data. The compiler and runtime support required for implementing these features is discussed in Section 3 while their usefulness for scientific codes is considered in Section 4. The paper concludes with a discussion of related work and some final remarks.

2 Distribution and Alignment in Vienna Fortran

The Vienna Fortran language extensions include features for the specification of the **processors** which execute the program, the **distribution** of arrays to subsets of processors, **alignment** between arrays, flexible mechanisms for the transfer of arguments to **procedures**, and explicitly parallel asynchronous **forall loops** [4, 16]. In this section, we focus only on the aspects relevant in the context of dynamic array distributions.

2.1 Basic Notation and Terminology

Each array A is associated with an **index domain** which we denote by $\mathbf{I}^A$. An **index mapping** from an index domain $\mathbf{I}$ to an index domain $\mathbf{J}$ is a total function $\iota : \mathbf{I} \to \mathcal{P}(\mathbf{J}) - \{\phi\}$, where $\mathcal{P}(\mathbf{J})$ denotes the powerset of $\mathbf{J}$.

A **distribution** of an array maps each array element to one or more processors which become the **owners** of the element and, in this capacity, store the element in their local memory. We model distributions by mappings between the associated index domains:

Definition 1 *Let A denote an array, and R a processor array. An index mapping δ_R^A from $\mathbf{I}^A$ to $\mathbf{I}^R$ is called a **distribution** for A with respect to R.*

An **alignment** establishes a relationship between elements of different arrays such that corresponding elements are guaranteed to reside in the same processor:

Definition 2 *Let A, B denote arbitrary arrays. An index mapping α_B^A from $\mathbf{I}^A$ to $\mathbf{I}^B$ is called an **alignment** for A with respect to B.*

Given δ_R^B, δ_R^A is determined as follows: For each $\mathbf{i} \in \mathbf{I}^A$:

$$\delta_R^A(\mathbf{i}) := CONSTRUCT(\alpha_B^A, \delta_R^B) = \bigcup_{\mathbf{j} \in \alpha(\mathbf{i})} \delta_R^B(\mathbf{j})$$

2.2 Specification · of Distribution and Alignment

Distributions are specified in a program by **distribution expressions**. Each distribution expression, for example *(BLOCK,CYCLIC(K))*, determines a class of distributions which is called a **distribution type**. The application of a distribution type to a (data) array and a processor section yields a distribution.

Simple distribution expressions specify mappings between one array dimension and one processor dimension; they include the intrinsic distribution functions *BLOCK*, *CYCLIC*, *S_BLOCK*, and *B_BLOCK*. *BLOCK* distributes one array dimension to one processor dimension in evenly sized segments. *CYCLIC* maps elements of an array dimension in a round-robin fashion to a dimension of the processor array. *S_BLOCK* and *B_BLOCK* permit the specification of contiguous irregular blocks, introducing the concept of *general block* distributions.

Distribution expressions associated with multi-dimensional arrays may be specified as a list of simple distribution expressions, each one corresponding to exactly one array dimension. The **elision symbol** ":" in such a list prevents the associated array dimension from being distributed.

Alignments are expressed in a Vienna Fortran program by **alignment specifications**. We illustrate their use – together with distribution expressions – by a simple example:

Example 1 Distribution and Alignment

```
PARAMETER (M=2)
PROCESSORS R(1:M,1:M)
REAL C(10,10,10) DIST (BLOCK,BLOCK,:) TO R
REAL D(10,10,10) ALIGN D(I,J,K) WITH C(J,I,K)
```

R denotes a two-dimensional processor array. The distribution of array C is specified by the distribution expression (BLOCK,BLOCK,:) *which indicates that the first two dimensions are distributed by BLOCK, while the third dimension is not distributed. More precisely, $\delta^C(i,j,k) = \{R(\lceil \frac{i}{5} \rceil, \lceil \frac{i}{5} \rceil)\}$ for all $k, 1 \le k \le 10$. The alignment specification for D transposes the first and second dimensions of C, i.e., the resulting alignment function maps each index triplet (i,j,k) in $\mathbf{I}^D$ to the index triplet (j,i,k) in $\mathbf{I}^C$.*

2.3 Dynamically Distributed Arrays

The language distinguishes between statically and dynamically distributed arrays, depending on whether or not the association between an array and its distribution is invariant in a given scope[1]. This distinction is made syntactically in the declaration of the array. The arrays shown in Example 1 were statically distributed.

We define an equivalence relation, **connect**, in the set of dynamically distributed arrays within a given scope. This relation satisfies the following conditions:

1. Each equivalence class consists of one distinguished member, the **primary array**, B, of the class, and 0 or more **secondary arrays**. We denote the class associated with primary array B by $\mathcal{C}(B)$.

2. The distribution of each secondary array $A \in \mathcal{C}(B)$, if any, is defined in the declaration of A by referring to B in a *secondary array annotation*, which specifies a *connection* by distribution extraction [16] or alignment.

3. Distribute statements are explicitly applied to primary arrays only; their effect is to redistribute all arrays in the associated equivalence class so that the *connection* is maintained.

4. The distributions of arrays in different equivalence classes are independent of each other.

5. The connect relation does not extend across procedure boundaries.

An annotation specifying $B_1, \ldots, B_r$ as *primary arrays* has the form

REAL $B_1(\ldots), B_2(\ldots), \ldots, B_r(\ldots)$ **DYNAMIC**
[*,distribution-range*] [*,initial-distribution*]

A **distribution range** determines the set of all distribution types (or a superset thereof) which can be associated with the arrays B_i during the execution of the procedure in which the declaration occurs. The distribution range is specified by the keyword **RANGE**, followed by a parenthesized list of *distribution expressions* (see Section 2.2). The "*" can be used as a "don't care" symbol. Distribute statements applied to the B_i must respect the restrictions imposed by this attribute.

If no distribution range is specified, then there is no restriction on the distributions that can be associated with a primary array.

An **initial distribution** is evaluated and associated with each B_i each time the array is allocated. An array for which an initial distribution has not been specified cannot be legally accessed before it has been

---

[1]If no ambiguity is possible, we simply refer to *static* or *dynamic* distributions.

explicitly associated with a distribution by the execution of either a distribute statement or a procedure call.

A *secondary array annotation*, for the arrays $A_1, \ldots, A_s$, has the form

REAL $A_1(\ldots), \ldots, A_s(\ldots)$ **DYNAMIC**,
CONNECT *connection*

The *connection* can be either a *distribution extraction* [16], or an *alignment specification*. In both cases, all secondary arrays A_j are **connected** to a primary array B. As a result of this declaration, the A_j are entered into the equivalence class $\mathcal{C}(B)$.

Example 2 Dynamic array annotations

> **REAL** B1(M) **DYNAMIC**
> **REAL** B2(N) **DYNAMIC, DIST**(*BLOCK*)
> **REAL** B3(N,N), B4(N,N) **DYNAMIC**,
> & **RANGE** ((*BLOCK,BLOCK*),(**,CYCLIC*)),
> & **DIST**(*BLOCK,CYCLIC*)
>
> **REAL** A1(N,N) **DYNAMIC, CONNECT**(=B4)
> **REAL** A2(N,N) **DYNAMIC, CONNECT**
> & A2(I,J) **WITH** B4(I,J)

All arrays declared here are dynamically distributed; B1 through B4 are primary, A1 and A2 secondary arrays. For B1, no distribution range and no initial distribution are given. For B2, no distribution range is given, and $(BLOCK)$ is specified as initial distribution. For B3 and B4, a distribution range as well as an initial distribution are specified. A1 is connected to B4 via distribution extraction while A2 uses an (identity) alignment to specify the connection. As a consequence, $\mathcal{C}(B4) \supseteq \{B4, A1, A2\}$; the connections specified ensure that the distribution type of A1 and A2 will be always the same as that of B4.

2.4 Distribute Statements

A *distribute-statement* has the form

DISTRIBUTE B:: *da* [*notransfer-attribute*]

where B is an array name associated with a primary array, and *da* is either a *distribution expression*, possibly associated with a processor section, or an *alignment specification*.

The distribute statement is executed as follows: First, a set $NOTRANSFER$ is determined as the set of all names specified in the *notransfer-attribute*, or the empty set in the default case. All names in $NOTRANSFER$ must be secondary arrays in $\mathcal{C}(B)$. Secondly, *da* is evaluated; its result is used to determine a distribution, δ^B, for array B. Thirdly, for each secondary array A in $\mathcal{C}(B)$, its distribution, δ^A, is determined from the distribution type associated with *da*, $\mathbf{I}^A$, and the *connection* between A and B, as established in the associated secondary array annotation. If A is a member of $NOTRANSFER$, then only the access function for A is changed and the elements of the array are not physically moved.

Example 3 Distribute Statement

We refer to the declarations in the previous example. It is assumed that the statements below are executed unconditionally in the order of their appearance in the text.

> **DISTRIBUTE** B1 :: (*BLOCK*)
> $\cdots$
> K = *expr*
> **DISTRIBUTE** B1,B2 :: (*CYCLIC*(K))
> $\cdots$
> **DISTRIBUTE** B3 :: (*BLOCK,CYCLIC*)
> **DISTRIBUTE** B4 :: (=B1, *CYCLIC*(3))
> $\cdots$

In the first statement, the array B1 is distributed by ($BLOCK$).

In the second statement, B1 and B2 (both of which are currently distributed by ($BLOCK$)) are redistributed as ($CYCLIC(k')$), where k' denotes the value assigned to the variable K in the assignment K = expr.

The third statement redistributes B3 as ($BLOCK,CYCLIC$); in the next statement, B4 and the associated secondary arrays A1 and A2 are distributed as ($CYCLIC(k'),CYCLIC(3)$).

2.5 Control Constructs

The capability to redistribute data at an arbitrary position in a Vienna Fortran program, including within conditionals, implies that

- an array reference in the program may, at run-time, be reached by more than one distribution for the array, and

- the compiler may not be able to determine precisely the set of all distributions reaching such a reference, no matter how much analysis is performed.

Thus, *control-constructs* have been included in the language to alleviate the problems arising from this situation: first, they allow the user to formulate an algorithm, depending on the actual distribution type of one or more arrays; secondly, they provide the compiler with information about the distribution of arrays. They include the *dcase-construct*, which is modeled after the Fortran 90 CASE construct, and the *if-construct*, which is based on a generalized form of *logical expressions*, and the related Fortran if statements.

2.5.1 The DCASE Construct

The *dcase-construct* has the form

> **SELECT DCASE** $(A_1, \ldots, A_r)$
> $cap_1, \ldots, cap_m$
> **END SELECT**

where

- $r \geq 1$ and all A_i, $1 \leq i \leq r$, are array names. The A_i are called **selectors**. At the time of execution of the *dcase construct*, each selector must be allocated and associated with a well-defined distribution.

- $m \geq 1$ and each cap_j, $1 \leq j \leq m$, is a *condition-action-pair*, where the *condition* is either a *query-list* or the keyword **DEFAULT**, and the *action* is a *block*. A *block* is a sequence of *executable_statements*, including the statements of the language extension, except for the distribute statement. None of the statements in a block may be the target of a branch from outside of that block. It is permissible to branch to an *end-select-statement* only from within the *dcase construct*.

The *dcase construct* selects at most one of its constituent blocks for execution. It is evaluated as follows:

1. The distribution of each selector, and its type, are determined.

2. Let $(c_1, a_1), (c_2, a_2), \ldots$ denote the sequence of condition action pairs in the *dcase construct*. Then $c_1, c_2, \ldots$ are sequentially evaluated until either a $j, 1 \leq j \leq m$ is reached such that c_j **matches**, or no match occurs.

   If c_j matches, then the associated action a_j is executed. This completes the execution of the *dcase construct*. If no match occurs, the execution of the construct is completed without executing an action.

A condition c_j **matches** iff either c_j is the keyword **DEFAULT**, or c_j is a list of queries, each of which matches. Each query tests the distribution of one selector array. Query lists may be either **positional** or **name-tagged**. In a positional query list, the queries are associated with the selectors $A_1, A_2, \ldots$ in this order. In a name-tagged query list, the selector associated with each query is explicitly specified by a *name-tag*. The order in which the queries occur in such a list is semantically irrelevant. A query list need not contain a query for every selector. In such a case, an implicit "*" is inserted for every selector which is not represented.

Full details of the matching process are given in [16].

Example 4 The dcase construct

> **REAL** B1(M) **DYNAMIC**
> **REAL** B2(N) **DYNAMIC, DIST**(*BLOCK*)
> **REAL** B3(N,N), **DYNAMIC,**
>   &   **RANGE** ((*BLOCK,BLOCK*),
>   &   *(CYCLIC, CYCLIC(*)),(*,CYCLIC))*,
>   &   **DIST**(*BLOCK,CYCLIC*)
> $\cdots$

```
SELECT DCASE(B1,B2,B3)
   CASE
&      ( BLOCK),(BLOCK),(CYCLIC(2),CYCLIC)
            a₁
   CASE B1: ( CYCLIC), B3:( BLOCK,*))
            a₂
   CASE B3:( BLOCK,CYCLIC)
            a₃
   CASE  DEFAULT
            a₄
   END SELECT
```

In the following, let t_i denote the distribution type associated with B_i.

The first query list is positional; it matches if $t_1 = t_2 = (BLOCK)$, and $t_3 = (CYCLIC(2), CYCLIC)$.

The second list is name-tagged; it matches if $t_1 = (CYCLIC)$, $t_3 = (BLOCK, t')$, where t' is arbitrary, and t_2 is any distribution type.

The third query list matches if $t_3 = (BLOCK, CYCLIC)$. t_1, t_2 are irrelevant in this case.

Finally, the fourth query list is always matched. Thus, if none of the first four query lists match, then a_4 will be executed.

2.5.2   The IF Construct

The *if-construct* of Vienna Fortran is based upon a **generalized logical expression**, which is a Fortran *logical_expression* that in addition may contain references to the intrinsic function *IDT*. This function performs a test of the distribution types associated with their arguments and, optionally, of the processor sections to which the arguments are distributed; it yields a logical value. For example, the second clause in the *dcase construct* above can be explicitly expressed as

```
   IF ( IDT(B1,( CYCLIC)))
&     .AND.( IDT(B3,( BLOCK(*)))) THEN
         a₂
```

3   Implementation

In this section, we briefly describe, at an abstract level, the support for dynamic data distributions in the Vienna Fortran Compiler System (VFCS). More details of the compilation strategy used in VFCS are given in [7, 17]. Some of the issues discussed here are also being handled in other systems [1, 2, 8, 14].

The features required to manage dynamic data distribution comprise both *compile time* and *run time* elements. Most of these features are actually required to handle other aspects of Vienna Fortran: in particular, many of the problems posed by run time redistribution of data structures are the same as, or similar to, those posed by the redistribution of arrays at subroutine boundaries, and those posed by the fact that in any code, several arrays, with possibly distinct distributions, may be bound to the same formal argument of a subroutine.

3.1   Compiler Support

There are two major phases in the compiler: analysis and code generation. The most important task in the analysis phase is solving the reaching distribution problem: that is, the compiler must determine the *range* of distribution types which may reach a specific array access in the code, by intra- and inter-procedural analysis. This is performed both for declared (and explicitly distributed) arrays as well as for formal subroutine arguments. The system constructs pairs consisting of a distribution type and a target processor array. We call the set of all such pairs which is valid for a specific array at a specific position in the program the set of *plausible distributions*. The information computed may not be precise, since some of the distributions may not actually be assumed at run time. If the full code is not available, the compiler will have to rely on range specifications provided by the user, or make worst case assumptions.

An extensive communication analysis provides not only information on the communication associated with each plausible distribution for an array, but also the memory requirements of the array under that distribution. The details of this analysis are outside the scope of this paper.

The compiler also performs a partial evaluation of distribution queries (both IDT and the dcase construct), by checking whether there is a plausible distribution which will match.

The compiler must perform many related tasks during code generation. In particular, it generates code to create and maintain data structures describing the distributions and other attributes of arrays, such as the associated overlap areas. The compiler also inserts calls to run time routines to perform communication as necessary and to routines which perform the redistribution of data.

3.2   Run Time Support

The **run time** support required may be described as the **Vienna Fortran Engine (VFE)**, an *abstract machine* that executes Vienna Fortran object programs. VFE is a machine at a higher level of abstraction than the vendor-supplied hardware/operating system interface. It is realized by a set of run time libraries which provide the required functionality on a specific target architecture. In particular, these provide complex data organization and access schemes, and high-level operations:

- The **memory management scheme** of the VFE is inherently dynamic. Even without dynamic distributions, the actual allocation of an array to the processors' memories may not be known. Redistribution requires, in addition, the possibility of reallocation.

- The **data organization and access features** provided by the VFE include:

  1. Data access functions for Vienna Fortran distributions (including the implementation of irregular accesses via translation tables

and sophisticated buffering schemes for accesses to non-local objects, as implemented in the PARTI routines [15]).

2. An interface for external distribution generators and specifiers.

3. Run time optimization of communication related to dynamic array references.

- A run time library of communication routines for transferring single array elements and array sections, including specialized routines for handling reductions.

- Routines to perform the tasks associated with **DISTRIBUTE**, construct access functions, to modify descriptors associated with arrays (this information may be modified when the distribution is changed, or on entry to a subroutine), and test information stored in these as required for the implementation of IDT and the dcase construct.

3.2.1 Run-Time Representation of Arrays

Some of the relevant components of the information related to an array stored locally in each processor are the data structures and access functions listed below. Here, A denotes an array name, and p a processor.

Data Structures:

- $index\_dom(A)$ specifies the *index domain* of A.

- $dist(A)$ characterizes the distribution of A, which includes a distribution type, and a specification of the target processors. For certain complex distributions, a pointer to a translation table is required[2].

- $connect\_class(A)$ determines the set of secondary arrays *connected* to a primary array.

- $alignment(C)$ specifies, for each array C in $connect\_class(A)$, the alignment of C with respect to A.

- For every $\mathbf{i}$ such that $A(\mathbf{i})$ is owned by processor p, $loc\_map_p^A(\mathbf{i})$ specifies the offset of $A(\mathbf{i})$ in the local memory of processor p.

- For regular and irregular BLOCK distributions, $segment_p^A$ specifies the sequence of the local lower and upper bounds in each dimension.

Access Functions

- Access in processor p to *local* array element $A(\mathbf{i})$ is performed by evaluating $loc\_map_p^A(\mathbf{i})$.

---

[2]For dummy arguments, the description may include a pointer to another array representation and/or sectioning operations.

- Access in processor p to a *non-local* array element $A(\mathbf{i})$ is performed by determining a processor q owning $A(\mathbf{i})$ from $dist(A)$, and inserting message passing operations that send the required element from q to p.

3.2.2 Implementation of DISTRIBUTE

Consider the statement

DISTRIBUTE B:: da [notransfer-attribute]

where da is a distribution expression or an alignment specification, and the *notransfer-attribute* determines the set $NOTRANSFER=\{C_1, \ldots, C_m\}$ (see Section 2.4). The realization of this statement is handled by a run-time routine executed on each processor which is passed the array and its current set of descriptors and returns new descriptors. Each processor determines the new locations of current local data, sends it to the new locations, and receives data from other processors. Data motion is suppressed where data flow analysis, or a NOTRANSFER specification, permits.

This corresponds to executing the following sequence of steps on each processor:

- **Step 1: Evaluate the new distribution and the associated access functions**

  1. Evaluate the new distribution: $dist(B):=eval(da)$

  2. Determine the functions loc_map and $segment$ from $dist(B)$

- **Step 2: Determine the distributions of the arrays** *connected* to B:

  for every $C \in connect\_class(B) - \{B\}$ **do**
      $dist(C):= CONSTRUCT(alignment(C), \delta^B)$
  endfor

  Here, the application of the function *CONSTRUCT* to the alignment function associated with C and the new distribution of B yields the new distribution of C.

- **Step 3: Communicate**

  for every C **such that**
  $(C \in connect\_class(B) - NOTRANSFER) \wedge$
  (the previous distribution of C is $old\_dist(C)$) **do**
      $COMMUNICATE(C, old\_dist(C), dist(C))$
  endfor

4 Applications

In this section, we discuss the benefits of dynamic distribution of data for scientific codes. We present several examples in which using dynamic data distributions allows the user to choose the appropriate data distribution based on the runtime behavior of the program.

```
    PARAMETER (NX = 100, NY = 100)

    REAL U(NX, NY), F(NX, NY) DIST (:, BLOCK)
    REAL V(NX, NY) DYNAMIC,
    &          RANGE( (:, BLOCK), ( BLOCK, :)),
    &          DIST (:, BLOCK)

    CALL RESID( V, U, F, NX, NY)

C Sweep over x-lines
    DO J = 1, NY
       CALL TRIDIAG( V(:, J), NX)
    ENDDO

    DISTRIBUTE V :: ( BLOCK, : )

C Sweep over y-lines
    DO I = 1, NX
       CALL TRIDIAG( V(I, :), NY)
    ENDDO
```

Figure 1: ADI iteration in Vienna Fortran

Consider first the case in which a runtime value determines the choice of the best distribution. For example, in a grid based computation, such as smoothing, the value at a grid point is based on its 4 nearest neighbors. A column distribution of the $N \times N$ grid will give rise to 2 messages per processor, each of size N, per computation step. On the other hand, if the grid is distributed by blocks in two dimensions across a p^2 processor array, then each computation step requires 4 messages of size N/p each on each processor. Thus, given the startup overhead and cost per byte of each message of the target machine, the ratio N/p will determine the most appropriate distribution. If the code has been written such that the size of the grid is an input parameter, then the user can use the dynamic distribution facilities of Vienna Fortran to set the distribution of the grid[3].

Another class of codes which can benefit from dynamic distributions are codes which exhibit different data access patterns in different phases of the program. Dynamic data distributions can be used to control the locality of data access in such codes. For example, consider ADI (Alternating Direction Implicit) codes [11] used for solving partial differential equations in computational fluid dynamics and other areas of computational physics. The name ADI derives from the fact that "implicit" equations, usually tridiagonal systems, are solved in both the x and y directions at each step. In terms of data structure access, one step of the algorithm can be described as follows: an operation (a tridiagonal solve here) is performed in-

dependently on each x-line of the array and the same operation is then performed, again independently, on each y-line of the array. The tridiagonal solve has a recurrence and thus generates data dependencies along the columns in the first phase and along the rows in the second phase.

There are two broad choices in such situations [4]. We could choose a single distribution for the whole program so that data accesses are satisfied locally in one phase while paying the communication costs in the other phase. On the other hand, we could dynamically redistribute the data so that data accesses in all phases are satisfied locally.

In Figure 1, we present a Vienna Fortran code fragment which employs the latter strategy. The tridiagonal solves are performed by a sequential routine *TRIDIAG* (not shown here) which is given a right hand side and overwrites it with the solution of a constant coefficient tridiagonal system. The array V is declared as **DYNAMIC** and is initially distributed by block in the second dimension. Thus, in the first loop which performs the sweep over columns (representing x-lines), each column is local to a processor and causes no communication. The array is then explicitly remapped to be distributed by block in the first dimension. This allows the second loop, a sweep over y-lines, to also be executed without any communication. Thus, all the communication is confined to the redistribution operation, with only local accesses during the computation.

If the array is not explicitly redistributed between the two loops, then the argument to the second call to *TRIDIAG* is distributed across a set of processors and it becomes the responsibility of the compiler to embed the required communication in the generated code. The efficiency of the resulting code will depend on various factors including, in particular, the analysis capabilities of the compiler. The dynamic distribution facilities of Vienna Fortran make it easy for the user to restrict the communication to the redistribution operation which, at least in the above code, can be implemented by an efficient pre-compiled routine.

For the examples given above it is possible to write the code without using explicit redistribution statements. For example, one could declare two or more arrays with different static distribution and use array assignments to produce the effect of redistribution. This approach, clearly, wastes storage space since only one of the arrays would be fruitfully used in any single computation phase.

Another approach is to use procedure boundaries for implicit redistribution of data. Vienna Fortran allows procedure arguments to be declared with a specific distribution. When the procedure is called, it is the compiler's responsibility to redistribute the actual argument to match the specified distribution. Thus, the ADI example could be rewritten such that it calls a different subroutine in the second loop, one which specifically declares its argument to be distributed by block in the first dimension. Similarly, the grid example could be written such that a different subroutine is called, depending on the ratio of the size of the grid and the number of executing processors. The prob-

---

[3]Vienna Fortran supports an intrinsic function **$NP** which returns the number of processors being used to execute the program and can be used to compute the ratio N/p.

lem, however, is that this approach may lead to an explosion of subroutines which are different only in the distribution specified for their arguments.

Another problem with using either assignment or procedure boundaries for implicit redistribution is that the approaches are particularly awkward and cumbersome to use if there is an outer iterative loop around the phases requiring redistribution. Further, it is not always feasible to write a program such that distributions change only at procedure boundaries. For example, in applications such as adaptive mesh codes or particle-in-cell (PIC) codes, the work distribution changes as the computation progresses. In such codes, the data needs to be redistributed dynamically in order to rebalance the workload.

Consider a simulation code based on the particle-in-cell method, which can be used to study the motion of particles in a given domain, such as plasmas for controlled nuclear fusion, or stars and galaxies. The computation at each time step can be divided into two phases. In the first phase, a global force field is computed using the current position of particles. In the second phase, given the new global force field, new positions of the particles are computed. The program can be structured by dividing the underlying domain into cells with each cell owning a set of particles. The particles move from one cell to another as they change positions across the domain. Since the computation in each cell is dependent on the number of particles in the cell, the workload across the domain changes as the computation progresses.

Figure 2 shows the outermost level of a simplified version of a PIC code as expressed in Vienna Fortran. The code omits details irrelevant to the discussion here. In this code, the cells are represented by the first dimension of the array *FIELD*. There are a maximum of *NCELL* cells and each cell is restricted to have a maximum of *NPART* particles.

The main goal here is to distribute the cells across the processors such that the work per processor is approximately equal. In this code, we use the generalized block distribution to distribute the cells in irregular (but contiguous) blocks to the processors. The block sizes (i.e., the number of contiguous cells) are selected so that each processor has roughly the same number of particles on its local part of the domain.

The array *FIELD* is declared to be **DYNAMIC** with the first dimension initially distributed into regular blocks. The procedure *initpos* determines the initial position of the particles and places them in the appropriate cells. Using the number of particles in each cell, the procedure *balance* computes the block sizes to be assigned to each processor. It stores these in the array *BOUNDS*, which is then used to redistribute the array *FIELD* via the the intrinsic distribution function *B_BLOCK)*.

In each time step (represented by one iteration of the outer loop), the procedure *update_field* computes the new force field based on the current particle positions. Then, the procedure *update_part* is called to update the positions of the particles. Based on the new positions, the new owner cell for each particle is determined. If a particle has moved from one cell to

another, it is explicitly reassigned. This obviously requires communication if the new cell is on a different processor. Since this communication is based on the locations of the current and the new cell, it is highly irregular in nature. Thus, the compiler will have to generate runtime code using the inspector/executor paradigm [10, 15] to support this particle motion.

If the number of particles on each processor remains roughly equal for the duration of the simulation, then load balance will be maintained. Some problems of this kind display sufficient uniformity such that a simple block distribution will suffice to provide a reasonable load balance. For other problems, the motion of particles during the simulation may lead to a severe load imbalance. The code, as shown here, checks on every 10th iteration (by calling function *rebalance*) whether rebalancing is required. If so, a new *BOUNDS* array is computed and the cells redistributed to balance the workload.

The redistribution needed for such load balancing is based on the current values of some data structure, for example, in the above case it is based on the number of particles per cell. Thus, this kind of redistribution cannot be expressed using either array assignment or procedure boundaries and requires language support for dynamic distributions.

5 Related Work

Kali [12] was the first language to introduce dynamic data distribution in a data parallel language aimed at distributed memory machines. It provided indirect mapping and user defined distribution functions which could depend on runtime values. A distribute statement allowed the user to dynamically change the distribution of an array at runtime. The design of Kali has greatly influenced the development of Vienna Fortran.

The DINO language, which extends C by constructs for specifying virtual processors to which data may be mapped, and whose compiler is targeted to distributed memory computers, supports redistribution of data at procedure boundaries, but does not extend these mechanisms to handle other forms of user-specified run-time distribution ([14]).

An executable *DISTRIBUTE* statement which performed run-time redistribution of arrays was formulated by Marc Baber and implemented in his *Hypertasking* compiler for block distributions of arrays; the system attempted to optimize the communication required for redistribution. This system did not permit procedure calls with distributed data. It has been implemented on the Intel iPSC hypercubes [2].

The Fortran D language proposal [6] suggests a set of features for enabling the portable specification of code to run on a variety of parallel architectures, including a dynamic *DISTRIBUTE* statement. Fortran D does not, however, provide a means for static distribution of arrays, and does not include any additional constructs which might enable the user to control or structure the use of dynamic distributions. As far as we are aware, the Fortran D implementation does not yet provide for dynamic data distributions.

```
      PARAMETER (NCELL = ..., NPART = ...)

      INTEGER BOUNDS($NP)
      REAL FIELD(NCELL, NPART, ...) DYNAMIC, DIST( BLOCK, :, :)

C     Compute initial position of particles
      CALL initpos(FIELD, NCELL, NPART, ...)

C     Compute initial partition of cells
      CALL balance(BOUNDS, FIELD, NCELL, NPART, ...)
      DISTRIBUTE FIELD :: B_BLOCK (BOUNDS)

      DO k = 1, MAX_TIME
C        Compute new field
         CALL update_field(FIELD, NCELL, NPART, ...)
C        Compute new particle positions and reassign them
         CALL update_part(FIELD, NCELL, NPART, ...)

C        Rebalance every 10th iteration if necessary
         IF ( MOD(k,10) .EQ. 0 .AND. rebalance() ) THEN
            CALL balance(BOUNDS, FIELD, NCELL, NPART, ...)
            DISTRIBUTE FIELD :: B_BLOCK (BOUNDS)
         ENDIF

      ENDDO
```

Figure 2: High level PIC code in Vienna Fortran

The High Performance Fortran proposal [9] includes static and dynamic distributions in much the same way that Vienna Fortran does and has included a small set of distribution queries in the language constructs. It has *REALIGN* and *REDISTRIBUTE* directives to permit independent redistribution and realignment of arrays during execution. These are both subsumed by the *DISTRIBUTE* statement in Vienna Fortran. In contrast to Vienna Fortran, if an array is redistributed in a procedure, HPF does not permit the new distribution to be returned to the calling procedure.

6 Conclusions

Dynamic data distributions are essential for a variety of real applications, which are characterized by large variations in the size or structure of input data sets, the need to perform dynamic load balancing, or the necessity to execute the code on several different architectures or different configurations of one machine. In all these cases, the decision on how to map the data arrays to the executing processors might have to be deferred until run time.

However, the deferment of such decisions makes it difficult for the compiler to generate efficient code. This problem can be alleviated by a combination of enhanced language support, extensive intra- and interprocedural compiler analysis, and careful structuring of the program by the user so that in all critical code sections the distribution is known at compile time.

References

[1] F. André, J.-L. Pazat, and H. Thomas. PAN-DORE: A system to manage data distribution. In *International Conference on Supercomputing*, pp. 380–388, June 1990.

[2] Marc Baber. Hypertasking support for dynamically redistributable and resizeable arrays on the iPSC. In *Proceedings of the Fifth Distributed Memory Computing Conference*, 59-66, 1990.

[3] S. Benkner, B. Chapman, and H. Zima. Vienna Fortran 90. In *Proceedings of the SHPCC Conference 1992*, 51–59, April 1992.

[4] B. Chapman, P. Mehrotra, and H. Zima. Programming in Vienna Fortran *Scientific Programming* 1(1):31-50, Fall 1992.

[5] M. Chen and J. Li. Optimizing Fortran 90 programs for data motion on massively parallel systems. Technical Report YALE/DCS/TR-882, Yale University, January 1992.

[6] G. Fox, S. Hiranandani, K. Kennedy, C. Koelbel, U. Kremer, C. Tseng, and M. Wu. Fortran D language specification. Department of Computer Science Rice COMP TR90079, Rice University, March 1991.

[7] H. M. Gerndt. *Automatic Parallelization for Distributed-Memory Multiprocessing Systems.* PhD thesis, University of Bonn, December 1989.

[8] S. Hiranandani, K. Kennedy, and C. Tseng. Compiling Fortran D for MIMD distributed mem-

ory machines. *Communications of the ACM*, 35(8):66–80, August 1992.

[9] High Performance FORTRAN Language Specification. Technical report, Rice University, May 1993.

[10] C. Koelbel and P. Mehrotra. Compiling global name-space parallel loops for distributed execution. *IEEE Transactions on Parallel and Distributed Systems*, 2(4):440–451, October 1991.

[11] G. I. Marchuk. *Methods of Numerical Mathematics*. Springer-Verlag, 1975.

[12] P. Mehrotra and J. Van Rosendale. Programming distributed memory architectures using Kali. In A. Nicolau, D. Gelernter, T. Gross, and D. Padua, editors, *Advances in Languages and Compilers for Parallel Processing*, pp. 364–384. Pitman/MIT-Press, 1991.

[13] D. Pase. MPP Fortran programming model. In *High Performance Fortran Forum*, Houston, TX, January 1992.

[14] M. Rosing, R. W. Schnabel, and R. P. Weaver. The DINO parallel programming language. Technical Report CU-CS-457-90, University of Colorado, Boulder, CO, April 1990.

[15] J. Saltz, K. Crowley, R. Mirchandaney, and H. Berryman. Run-time scheduling and execution of loops on message passing machines. *Journal of Parallel and Distributed Computing*, 8(2):303–312, 1990.

[16] H. Zima, P. Brezany, B. Chapman, P. Mehrotra, and A. Schwald. Vienna Fortran – a language specification. ICASE Internal Report 21, ICASE, Hampton, VA, 1992.

[17] H. Zima and B. Chapman. Compiling for Distributed Memory Systems. *Proceedings of the IEEE, Special Section on Languages and Compilers for Parallel Machines*, February 1993.

Session 4:
Workshop
Scientific Visualization of
Chemical Systems

Scientific Visualization of Chemical Systems

Richard E. Gillilan and Bruce R. Land

Visualization Group
Cornell Theory Center
Ithaca, NY 14853-380

Abstract

Within the past few years, computer graphics has played a decisive role in transforming the field of molecular modeling into an international industry. While computer scientists are conversant in the language of their own discipline, they are often unfamiliar with the terminology and unique graphical constructs of physical scientists. Similarly, physical scientists are often unfamiliar with the latest paradigms and technological advances in graphical computing. The successful marriage of Chemistry and Computer Graphics is an outstanding model of technology transfer and cross-disciplinary fertilization. Drawing on chemistry visualizations performed at the Cornell Theory Center, this workshop covers some of the terminology, tools and current problems that have evolved at the boundary between these two fields.

1 Introduction

Chemistry is a field with a long history of modeling and graphical representation. Nearly every student of Organic Chemistry learns the story of August Kekulé, who was puzzling over why carbon, of all atoms, could form so many compounds. According to his own account [1], one summer evening in 1854, he dozed off while riding on an omnibus. In his dream, he saw myriads of atoms "whirling in a giddy dance" before his eyes, forming ever longer chains. This was the beginning of a series of visions that would eventually lead him to the discovery of the structure of Benzene and other landmark principles of Organic Chemistry. Molecules by their nature are complex moving geometrical objects unseen to the naked eye. Because this microscopic world eludes our direct experience, models offer a visual language of sorts, which allows us to formulate questions, make statements and, in general, communicate.

Modern computer graphics technology allows researchers to share the experience and visions that were once trapped in the minds of the privileged few. Ideally, it extends our natural capabilities and frees our creativity from technical limitations of expression. Too often, however, computer graphics enters research at a late stage, mainly for purposes of presentation. Although chemists have been particularly good about developing practical research tools, there still exists a gap between tools of presentation and tools of discovery. Chemistry is nonetheless a model field in which computer graphics methodology has reached a high state of development. The unique constructs that have evolved have shed light on complex problems and yielded dramatic insights that might otherwise have gone long unnoticed. We provide a brief overview of rendering principles relevant to molecular graphics with emphasis on the new data-flow paradigm for graphical computing. Basic chemical terminology is then introduced, followed by a discussion of several of the most widely used graphical constructs in chemistry and their role in the discovery process. In the final section, we outline the steps that a researcher might take in developing their own scientific visualization using the IBM Visualization Data Explorer software as a tool.

2 Graphics principles and techniques

A great deal of what is now established interactive graphics technique for Chemistry can be traced back to the days of vector graphics machines when points and lines were the only renderable objects. It is remarkable just how much can be achieved with these simple forms and a rudimentary lighting model. The reason why chemists adopted this technology at such an early stage may be that molecules are represented quite well as simple stick figures. Even today, this is the default representation in most software packages.

High-speed workstations with specialized graphics engines have greatly expanded the realism of models, the primary tool available today being the polygon surface. When three vertex points, for example, define a triangular surface, one can model the effect of lighting by assigning the color of points interior to the triangle on the basis of incident light angles. The surface can also have an intrinsic color obtained by interpolation of colors defined at vertices. Advanced graphics systems are even capable of mapping raster images to polygon faces. This process is called *texture mapping*. One can just as well define solid volumes by specifying how points are connected together into a three-dimensional network. A connection list of this type is necessary for *volumetric rendering*, a method which is capable of rendering gas-cloud-like objects where each point of a three-dimensional volume has a data value. *Ray-tracing* and *radiosity rendering* have the greatest level of realism and the greatest demand for computing power and are capable of creating shadows and reflections. Few scientific visualization packages have implemented these methods since they are far too slow for interactive work; most professional animation software, however, has some capability for ray-tracing.

The most important component that realism has to offer scientific visualization is improved sense of depth. Depth cues are critical to understanding complex geometrical objects like an enzymes. The major depth cues, perspective, atmospheric effects (often called depth cueing), stereopsis, and rotational motion were all available in early vector machines, but surprisingly some are commonly neglected in contemporary visualization. Atmospheric effects, for example, make objects close to the viewer brighter [2]. Figure 1 shows the same molecule rendered with and without this effect. Note how the deep tunnel to the active site at center and two other recessed regions are essentially invisible without this effect. Stereopsis, rendering a different viewpoint for each eye, requires special hardware and doubles the rendering time, but many chemists use it regularly [3]. Rotational motion also contributes to depth-cueing since points closer to the viewer appear to move faster. This is easy to achieve in animation but fast rotation for interactive work requires a special rendering engine.

3   Chemical systems

One of the things that makes Chemistry visualization interesting and nontrivial is that atoms are so small that Newton's familiar principles of motion are no longer always valid. The atom lives in a gray area of our understanding, halfway between the classical world of Newtonian motion and the novel, but reasonably well understood, world of quantum mechanics. Contrary to the impression many receive in introductory courses, the connection between classical and quantum-mechanical behavior in this regime is still not well understood and is the subject much recent research and controversy [4]. Nevertheless, atoms are basically hard spheres that sometimes stick together, and much useful chemistry can be understood in these terms!

An important example is the polypeptide. Amino acids are some of the basic building blocks of life. Each of the 22 common acids has an amino group on one end and an acid group on the other, allowing them to form long chains. Amino acids differ only in the particular molecule groups that hang off to the side of the chain (sidechains). Figure 2 highlights one amino acid in the middle of a long chain. Chemists are highly interested in the making and breaking of the *bonds* that hold atoms together so we usually represent bonds as lines or tubes.

There are times when the Newtonian description of molecules as balls and sticks is simply not appropriate. In computing the quantum-mechanical distribution of electrons, for example, it is more useful to view them as a continuous distribution rather than a set of points. This density of electrons is something like a ripple on a pond, only three dimensional. In graphics terminology this is a *scalar field*. The density value is sampled at various positions to create a set of points that can be connected for interpolation and rendering. The position and motion of atoms can also be represented quantum mechanically, though, being much heavier than electrons, atoms are accordingly more Newtonian in behavior. The lightest of atoms, Hydrogen and Helium, can participate in the strangest of quantum mechanical behavior: tunneling and diffraction. The simulation of atomic motion using Newton's equations is known as *molecular dynamics*. Quantum-mechanical simulation of this same motion is known as *quantum dynamics*, a much more difficult computational task.

In summary, there is no "real" representation for a molecule, only models designed to bring out important features.

3.1   Molecular graphics techniques

Perhaps one of the best and most dramatic illustrations of how simplified representations have enhanced our understanding of chemistry is the ribbon model. We have discussed how amino acids join together in long chains to form polypeptides. Many larger polypeptides, however, appear as featureless blobs when displayed as ball-and-stick or space-filling models. The mass of tangled atoms and bonds is overwhelming to the eye and of little help in recognizing important structural features. Part of the confusion is simply due to the fact that amino acids have so many types of side chains which hang off in all directions. The underlying molecule itself is actually just a long repeating chain: α-Carbon, Carbon, Nitrogen, α-Carbon, Carbon, Nitrogen, $\cdots$ with short sidechains connected to the alpha Carbons. One additional feature of this backbone is that while the α-Carbon-Nitrogen bond can rotate freely, the Carbon-Nitrogen bond cannot. As a result, the α-Carbon, Oxygen, Carbon, Nitrogen, the next α-Carbon, and accompanying Hydrogen are often coplanar. The series of planes thus defined makes the amino acid chain behave more like a ribbon with the Carbon-Oxygen double bond parallel to the ribbon surface (see Figure 2). Early computer algorithms of this type were pioneered by Richardson [5] and further developed by Carson and Bugg [6]. An otherwise featureless protein blob so rendered becomes a recognizable collection of recurring structural motifs: the alpha helix, the beta sheet and so on. Incidentally, the problem of consistent ribbon orientation is an example of a common problem solved independently by chemistry and computer graphics researchers [7].

The molecular surface is another geometrical construction that has gained widespread popularity. Like the ribbon model, molecular surfaces are simplified representations that leave out information irrelevant or even confusing to the problem. Of all the atoms in a protein, usually only a few are actually exposed to the solvent. The rest remain buried deep within the molecule, completely inaccessible from the outside due to the close proximity of other atoms. Though select in number, the solvent-exposed atoms play a major role in the behavior of the protein in solvent as well as defining the overall shape.

A number of models have been proposed to study this aspect of protein structure, but one given by Richards [8] has been particularly successful. The actual implementation was worked out by Connolly [9] and is now in widespread use. Geometrically, the idea is straightforward. A sphere the size of a solvent molecule is used as a probe to determine which points can and cannot be reached subject to steric constraints. Mathematically, the surface is constructed in a piecewise fashion from hemispheres and portions of

tori. The different types of surface patches are created by the probe being in contact with different numbers of atoms simultaneously. The actual implementation is rather involved and will not be presented here but the advantages are clear: one obtains only the exposed "skin" of the molecule. Figure 3 is a cross section of the acetylcholinesterase molecule [10] showing the molecular surface, several important sidechains and a molecule of acetylcholine at the active site. This type of surface is used not only as a general guide to the shape of the molecule, but as an analytical tool for evaluating solvent effects and as a manifold for electrostatic potential calculations [11].

The technique of mapping a three-dimensional function, such as electric potential to a surface, is a recent invention which is gaining popularity. The fact that we can interpolate functions defined on a three-dimensional grid and find their value at any vertex of a polygon surface means that surface features such as folds and gorges can be correlated with property values though the use of color mapping. This aids in the identification of sites of interaction and molecular function. In electronic structure calculations, for example, the density of the lowest unoccupied molecular orbital (LUMO) can be mapped onto the surface of constant overall electron density to give an indication of the accessibility of sites for nucleophilic attack. In biophysics, electrostatic potential can be mapped to the molecular surface and color coded as has been done in Figure 3.

Surfaces of constant functional value, isosurfaces, have been in use for quite a long time. Originally constructed from stacks of contour plots, these surfaces are heavily used in X-ray structure determinations to guide the placement of atoms. Electronic structure computations have also long used this method. The discovery of the marching cubes algorithm [2] has only recently made it convenient to compute a renderable set of polygons on such a surface.

Visualization techniques invented for the study of fluid flow have proven valuable in other fields as well. The negative gradient of an electric potential is a vector field that can be treated much like the velocity field of a flowing fluid. Streamlines are simply the paths taken by particles flowing in the field. We have used this technique to study how charged substrate molecules might drift to enter the active site of the acetylcholinesterse enzyme [10]. The dramatic convergence of lines illustrates how the electric field may serve to funnel and concentrate charged species near the mouth of the active site (Figure 4). The effects of solvent on, and the detailed internal structure of the charged species has been left out of the model as well as the motion of the enzyme. These effects are probably important but the principle physics of interest is captured.

As simulation technology improves, the number of new problems of representation will increase. Quantum dynamics simulations, for example, are now routinely carried out for systems of up to three variables, but four and more will soon be the norm. How can these functions of many variables evolving in time be visualized? As chemists simulate actual reactions more often, tools for examining the time-evolving electron densities will need to be developed [12]. On the biological and material science fronts, simulations are getting larger and larger in number of atoms included. Much of the mechanics of life takes place on a vast scale in comparison to the atom. Visualization techniques will be challenged with very large memory requirements. On all of these frontiers, the key to developing effective scientific visualization will ultimately be in understanding what should be left out and determining how best to represent what remains.

4 Building a scientific visualization

This section describes the four basic stages a researcher might use to develop a scientific visualization: *importation*, *exploration*, *customization* and *presentation*. Though IBM Data Visualization Data Explorer is used as an example throughout, we feel these stages are a good model for any visualization environment.

The process usually starts with the import of data from external sources. *Importation* is, in our experience, often the more frustrating and difficult part of the whole visualization process. To this end, any visualization environment should have one or more of the following components:

- specialized modules or options for convenient import of the most common data types encountered.

- general data-description language with graphical "point and click" interface to facilitate the the import of generic tabular and tagged data formats.

- ability to send and receive data from external processes and to serve as a graphical front end to another program.

- ability to write customized import modules in a low-level language.

Since data arrives from multiple sources and is often expressed in different units or even different coordinate systems, some minor preparatory computations are usually required. In programs like IBM Visualization Data Explorer, these kinds of computations are easily implemented through the use of general compute modules.

Preliminary graphical display of the data is made with the default program settings. At this point, the researcher needs to identify how program settings and simulation variables, such as positions of cutting planes and values of isosurfaces, should be modified to provide a clearer view of the phenomenon. This is the *exploration* phase. Control and interaction need to be added to refine the simulation, extract useful information and explore newly discovered features. Good visualization environments will include advanced interactivity such as 3D cursors, picking and navigation controls. Easy manipulation of objects are critical in order for the researcher to translate the data set into a complete mental picture which can be used as a foundation on which chemical reaction scenarios are envisioned and tested.

Once familiar with the data set, users may write specialized macros or modules to make future visualizations with the same kind of data simpler and more convenient. This is the *customization* phase. Prior to the data-flow paradigm, a researcher had to choose between high-level applications, which were often rigid and problem-specific, and low-level programming, which is highly flexible but time-consuming and not always easy to modify and document. Data-flow pograms such as IBM Visualization Data Explorer are modular in nature and have the power and generality of a language but are easier to use.

The final phase is *presentation*. The researcher has a story to tell, with all the traditional elements: the setting, the nature of the problem, the progression of success and failure leading to solution and finally, the solution. Few scientific graphics packages are designed, however, to control the flow of images in progression in the way that a professional animation package does. Scientific packages frequently do not have strong annotation and lettering capabilities, especially when it comes to video production. Graphics must also be presented in a medium suitable for larger audiences. Each medium has its own particular requirements and limitations but video is especially restrictive. Graphics that looks good on a computer screen invariably looks poor and illegible on a video monitor.

5 Summary

In many ways, Chemistry is a field primed for scientific visualization. The already established use of graphical representations and the intrinsic geometrical nature of the fundamental problems in the field paved the way for the adoption of new technology. The use of early primitive rendering types (point and line) were highly effective, so much so that they are still in use today. Both realism and speed are important factors that add to the researchers' ability to recognize shapes and spatial relationships. In our examination of two popular molecular graphics constructs, the ribbon and the molecular surface, we see that what is left out of a model is often as important as what is left in. The fact that molecules can exhibit both classical and quantum-mechanical behavior provides interesting challenges in visual representation. As more sophisticated theories of chemistry are realized in simulation, scientific visualization will play a key role in both interpreting results and giving form to ideas.

Acknowledgements

Special thanks to Wendy J. Bacon for editorial help and to Martin Berggren for technical assistance. We gratefully acknowledge the National Institutes of Health who support biomedical computing and visualization at the Cornell Theory Center. This work was conducted using the the Cornell Theory Center, which is funded in part by the National Science Foundation, New York State, IBM, and members of the Theory Center's Corporate Research Institute.

References

[1] R.T.Morrison and R.N.Boyd, *Organic Chemistry*, 3rd Ed. Allyn and Bacon, Inc., Boston (1979)

[2] J.D. Foley, A. van Dam, S.K. Feiner and J.F. Hughes, *Computer Graphics: Principles and Practice*, Addison-Wesley, New York (1990).

[3] Larry F. Hodges, "Tutorial: Time-Multiplexed Stereoscopic Computer Graphics", *IEEE Computer Graphics and Applications*, March (1992)

[4] M.-J.Giannoni, A. Voros and J.Zinn-Justin editors, *Chaos and Quantum Physics* Les Houches session LII , North Holland (1989)

[5] J.S. Richardson, "The anatomy and taxonomy of protein structure', *Advances in Protein Chemistry" 34 167 (1981)*

[6] M. Carson and C.E. Bugg, "Algorithm for ribbon models of proteins",*Journal of Molecular Graphics* 5 (2) 103 (1987)

[7] Jules Bloomenthal, "Calculation of Reference Frames Along a Space Curve", in *Graphics Gems*, edited by Adrew S. Glassner, Academic Press, New York (1990).

[8] F.M. Richards, *Annual Reviews in Biophysics and Bioengineering* 6, 151 (1977)

[9] M.L. Connolly, "Analytical Molecular Surface Calculation", *Journal of Applied Crystallography* 16 548 (1983)

[10] J.L. Sussman, M.Harel, F. Frolow, C. Oefner, A. Goldman, L. Toker and I. Silman, "Atomic Structure of Acetylcholinesterase from Torpedo Californica: a prototypic acetylcholine-binding protein", *Science* 253, 872, (1991).

[11] R.J. Zauhar and R.S. Morgan, "Computing the Electric Potential of Biomolecules: Application of a New Method of Molecular Surface Triangulation", *Journal of Computational Chemistry*, 11 (5) 603 (1990)

[12] R.H. Wolfe, M. Needels and J.D. Joannopoulos, "The Electronic Structure of Oxygen in Silicon as Revealed by Volume Visualization of Ab Initio Calculations", *IEEE Visualization '91 Proceedings'* p17 (1991)

[For color plate see page 927]

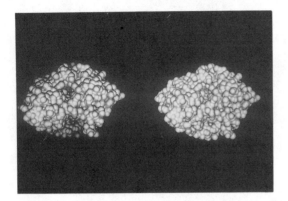

Figure 1: Molecule rendered with (left) and without (right) depth cueing.

Figure 3: Cross section of acetylcholinesterase enzyme in molecular surface representation.

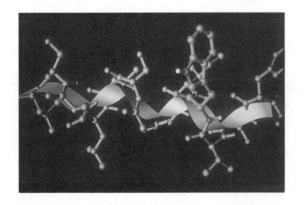

Figure 2: Typical polypeptide segment with one amino acid residue colored and a ribbon model superimposed.

Figure 4: Streamlines of the electric field of acetylcholinesterase converging near the entrance to the active site.

Session 4:
Invited Presentations
Warren Washington
T. Dietterich

Computer Modeling of the Global Warming Effect

Warren M. Washington

National Center for Atmospheric Research*
Boulder, Colorado 80307-3000

ABSTRACT

The state of knowledge of global warming will be presented and two aspects examined: observational evidence and a review of the state of computer modeling of climate change due to anthropogenic increases in greenhouse gases. Observational evidence, indeed, shows global warming, but it is difficult to prove that the changes are unequivocally due to the greenhouse-gas effect. Although observational measurements of global warming are subject to "correction," researchers are showing consistent patterns in their interpretation of the data.

Since the 1960s, climate scientists have been making their computer models of the climate system more realistic. Models started as atmospheric models and, through the addition of oceans, surface hydrology, and sea-ice components, they then became climate-system models. Because of computer limitations and the limited understanding of the degree of interaction of the various components, present models require substantial simplification. Nevertheless, in their present state of development climate models can reproduce most of the observed large-scale features of the real system, such as wind, temperature, precipitation, ocean current, and sea-ice distribution.

The use of supercomputers to advance the spatial resolution and realism of earth-system models will also be discussed.

*The National Center for Atmospheric Research is sponsored by the National Science Foundation.

Session 4:
Minisymposium
Advent of ATM
Chair: Don Tolmie

Session 5:
Applications II
Chair: Wilf Pinfold

Multi-CPU Plasma Fluid Turbulence Calculations on a CRAY Y-MP C90

V. E. Lynch, B. A. Carreras, and J. N. Leboeuf

Oak Ridge National Laboratory

Oak Ridge, Tennessee 37831

B. C. Curtis and R. L. Troutman

National Energy Research Supercomputer Center

Livermore, California 94551

Abstract

Significant improvements in real-time efficiency have been obtained for plasma fluid turbulence calculations by microtasking the nonlinear fluid code KITE in which they are implemented on the CRAY Y-MP C90 at the National Energy Research Supercomputer Center (NERSC). The number of processors accessed concurrently scales linearly with problem size. Close to six concurrent processors have so far been obtained with a three-dimensional nonlinear production calculation at the currently allowed memory size of 80 Mword. With a calculation size corresponding to the maximum allowed memory of 200 Mword in the next system configuration, we expect to be able to access close to ten processors of the C90 concurrently with a commensurate improvement in real-time efficiency. These improvements in performance are comparable to those expected from a massively parallel implementation of the same calculations on the Intel Paragon.

1: Introduction

To predict the size, expense and performance of magnetic fusion reactors, it is critical to know the scaling of particle transport and losses across the magnetic field with machine and plasma parameters. The mechanism for transport across magnetically confined plasmas is not yet known. However, at the plasma edge of the TEXT tokamak, a type of toroidal magnetic confinement device, losses larger than those predicted by classical theory have been shown to be induced by fluctuations [1]. Numerical calculations of plasma edge turbulence are expected to lead to the identification of the transport scaling parameters [2].

At the plasma edge, the dynamics of the plasma can be modeled by fluidlike equations. A possible model for the turbulence at the edge of tokamaks like TEXT is collisional drift waves destabilized by atomic physics sources such as line radiation cooling caused by light impurities [3-4]. These impurity radiation-driven drift waves are adequately described by five nonlinear fluid equations for plasma density, vorticity, potential, parallel velocity, and temperature, with impurity radiation sources introduced in the latter. These equations are solved as an initial value problem in the nonlinear fluid computer code KITE [5], which treats the linear terms implicitly and the nonlinear terms explicitly. The implicit treatment of the linear terms requires the inversion of block-tridiagonal matrices. The calculation of the nonlinear terms is usually done by convolutions.

High resolution is needed to resolve all scale lengths in a turbulence problem [2], requiring the use of large amounts of memory. To study the development of steady-state turbulence, the plasma evolution must be followed for many time steps. Therefore, these calculations also require large amounts of computing time. With present computers, the parameter regime that can be studied is still limited.

To improve the real-time efficiency of plasma turbulence calculations using the KITE family of fluid computer codes, we have explored two main avenues: massively parallel numerical schemes on the Intel iPSC/860 and Touchstone Delta and multiprocessing on the CRAY IIs and the CRAY Y-MP C90. Improvements in performance on the Intels have been reported elsewhere [6-8], and we concentrate here on the multi-CPU implementation of the KITE code on the CRAY Y-MP C90.

Multiprocessing of the KITE family of codes [9] for the CRAY IIs started upon their arrival at the National Energy Research Supercomputer Center (NERSC) in the mid 1980s. At that time, use of more than one processor was achieved via software multitasking calls inserted in

308

the Fortran programs [10]. Given the small number of processors (four to eight), the Cray TIme Sharing System (CTSS) operating system environment, and the large amount of code modifications required, the experience was less than satisfactory.

The situation has changed substantially with the recent arrival of the CRAY Y-MP C90 at NERSC. Its 16 processors with peak aggregate speed of 16 Gflop, its 268 *Mword* of shared memory, the UNICOS 7.C operating system, its efficient CF77 compiling system, and associated autotasking and microtasking software make the C90 very attractive for multiprocessing. Autotasking has the advantage of simplicity because it only requires one option of the CF77 compiler to be activated for it to analyze the code and insert compiler directives. Autotasking does, however, often parallelize loops that do not account for much of the running time and leaves the important loops as serial code. Fortunately, microtasking is an alternative to autotasking that can produce better performance [11] . Microtasking involves analyzing the code by hand or using parallelizing tools and inserting directives where parallelism is found.

Here we present the results of the multi-CPU implementation of our plasma edge turbulence model on the CRAY Y-MP C90. These results are compared with the corresponding serial implementation on the C90 and with the massively parallel implementation on the Intel parallel computers. In Section 2, the equations used in the present studies are described, and the algorithm is briefly summarized. The multiprocessor implementation of this scheme on the C90 is discussed in Section 3. The timing results for serial, autotasked, and microtasked modes of operation and different problem sizes are presented in Section 4. In Section 5, we give our conclusions.

2: Equations and numerics

In the study of collisional drift wave-type instabilities driven by impurity radiation at the plasma edge, we assume cylindrical geometry and use fluidlike model equations. The system of equations consists of the continuity equation, coupled to the parallel and perpendicular momentum balance or vorticity equations, and the electron temperature equation, including impurity radiation effects [3]:

$$\frac{d\tilde{n}}{dt} = -V_{*_n}\frac{1}{r}\frac{\partial\tilde{\phi}}{\partial\theta} - c_s\nabla_{\parallel}\tilde{V}_{\parallel} - \chi\nabla_{\parallel}^2(\tilde{\phi} - \tilde{n} - \alpha\tilde{T})$$
$$+ D\nabla_{\perp}^2\tilde{n}. \tag{1}$$

$$\frac{d\tilde{V}_{\parallel}}{dt} = -c_s\nabla_{\parallel}(\tilde{n} + \tilde{T}) + \mu_{\parallel}\nabla_{\parallel}^2\tilde{V}_{\parallel} + \mu_{\perp}\nabla_{\perp}^2\tilde{V}_{\parallel}. \tag{2}$$

$$\frac{d\tilde{U}}{dt} = -\chi\nabla_{\parallel}^2(\tilde{\phi} - \tilde{n} - \alpha\tilde{T}) + \mu\nabla_{\perp}^2\tilde{U}. \tag{3}$$

$$\frac{d\tilde{T}}{dt} = -V_{*_T}\frac{1}{r}\frac{\partial\tilde{\phi}}{\partial\theta} - \frac{2}{3}c_s\nabla_{\parallel}\tilde{V}_{\parallel} - \frac{2}{3}\alpha\chi\nabla_{\parallel}^2(\tilde{\phi} - \tilde{n} - \alpha\tilde{T})$$
$$+ \chi_{\parallel}\nabla_{\parallel}^2\tilde{T} + \chi_{\perp}\nabla_{\perp}^2\tilde{T} + \gamma_T\tilde{T} - \gamma_n\tilde{n}. \tag{4}$$

An auxiliary time-independent equation is also solved to determine the electrostatic potential, ϕ from the vorticity U:

$$\tilde{U} = \rho_s^2\nabla_{\perp}^2\tilde{\phi}. \tag{5}$$

The total time derivative in Eqs. (1–4) is such that

$$\frac{d}{dt} = \frac{\partial}{\partial t} - c_s\rho_s(\vec{\nabla}\tilde{\phi} \times \zeta) \cdot \vec{\nabla}, \tag{6}$$

where the second term in Eq. (6) is the convective nonlinearity.

Here, the electrostatic potential, density n, parallel velocity $V_{\parallel}$, and temperature T, fluctuations have been normalized to

$$\tilde{\phi} = \frac{|e|\phi}{T_{e0}}, \quad \tilde{n} = \frac{n}{n_0}, \quad \tilde{V}_{\parallel} = \frac{V_{\parallel}}{c_s}, \quad \tilde{T} = \frac{T}{T_{e0}}, \tag{7}$$

where T_{e0} is the equilibrium electron temperature, n_0 is the equilibrium density, and $c_s = \sqrt{T_{e0}/M_i}$ is the sound speed. In Eqs. (1) to (6), $V_{*n} = c_s\rho_s/L_n$ and $V_{*T} = c_s\rho_s/L_T$ are the diamagnetic drift velocities for the density and the temperature with gradient scale lengths L_n and L_T, respectively; $\rho_s = c_s/\omega_{ci}$ is the sound Larmor radius; $\chi_{\parallel} = 2\kappa_{\parallel}/3n_o$ is the normalized parallel thermal conductivity; $\chi = \chi_{\parallel}/1.07$ is the normalized resistivity; $\chi_{\perp}$ is the normalized perpendicular thermal conductivity; D is the particle diffusivity; μ is the classical fluid viscosity; $\mu_{\parallel}$ and $\mu_{\perp}$ are the parallel and perpendicular ion viscosities; and the parameter α is such that $\alpha = 1.71$. The symbol $\parallel$ means parallel to the total magnetic field, which is expressed as

$$\vec{B} = B_0(\vec{\zeta} - \frac{r}{R}\frac{1}{q}\vec{\theta}), \tag{8}$$

where the safety factor $q = rB_0/(RB_p)$, with B_0 the toroidal magnetic field in the ζ direction, Bp the poloidal magnetic field in the θ direction, the major radius R, and radial variable r. The symbol $\perp$ indicates the direction perpendicular to the toroidal magnetic field. For periodic perturbations proportional to $\cos(m\theta + n\zeta)$ or $\sin(m\theta + n\zeta)$, with m the poloidal mode number and n the toroidal mode number, $\nabla_{\parallel} = 0$ at the radial position for which $q(r) = m/n$. The radial position is called the resonant or singular surface for this perturbation.

Impurity radiation manifests itself in the electron temperature equation, Eq. (4), through the terms $\gamma_T = -2/3n_z \, dI_z/dT_{e0}$ and $g_n = n_z I_z/T_{e0}$ multiplying temperature and density fluctuations, respectively, with n_z the impurity density and I_z the low-z impurity cooling rate. Both can act as sources of fluctuations at the plasma edge of magnetic confinement devices such as tokamaks. The impurity radiation strength causes the fluctuations with low-to-moderate m numbers to grow exponentially in time in the linear phase. A turbulent, saturated, steady state is obtained through coupling to damped modes with higher m numbers and generation of a mean poloidal sheared flow velocity via the convective nonlinearity. The impurity radiation strength and profile, as well as the equilibrium temperature and density profiles, are held fixed throughout the calculation; we are, therefore, in a driven turbulence situation.

The edge turbulence model represented by Eqs. (1)–(5) has been implemented in the computer code KITE [5]. To maximize resolution, Eqs. (1)–(5) are solved within a cylindrical annulus that extends from $r_{\min}$ to the minor radius a of the cylinder. The fluctuating fields are written as expansions in sines and cosines:

$$\tilde{f}(r,\theta,\zeta) = \sum_{m,n} \left[f_{mn}^c(r)\cos(m\theta + n\zeta) + f_{mn}^s(r)\sin(m\theta + n\zeta) \right], \qquad (9)$$

in the poloidal (θ) and toroidal (ζ) angles.

The boundary conditions are such that the radial components of the velocity are zero at conducting walls placed at $r = r_{\min}$ and $r = a$, and so are density, temperature, and parallel velocity perturbations. That is, for all fields,

$$f(r_{\min},\theta,\zeta) = f(a,\theta,\zeta). \qquad (10)$$

To complete the numerical representation of the fields, we use finite differences in r. First and second radial derivatives are calculated with three-point, finite-difference formulas. Derivatives in θ and ζ are performed analytically. All quantities are stored in spectral form and are never transformed to a finite-difference grid in θ and ζ.

These nonlinear equations are solved as an initial value problem. The numerical scheme presently used in the computer code KITE treats all linear terms in the perturbation implicitly. This requires the inversion of a block-tridiagonal matrix for each Fourier component, with the size of the blocks given by the number of equations (ten here, five each for the sine and cosine components) and the number of blocks set by the number of grid points. The matrix inversion problem is solved with the block-tridiagonal linear system solver of Hindmarsh [12]. The blocks of the matrix and the corresponding rows of the right-hand side vector are stored in memory. The solver uses block Gauss elimination. Partial pivoting is done within block rows only. These routines (SOL and SOLBT) are vectorized over the number of equations only, which leads to short vector lengths, because pivoting makes it difficult to vectorize the matrix inversion over the number of modes, which would lead to longer vector lengths. The nonlinear terms are explicit and accurate to first order in time. They lead to convolutions over poloidal and toroidal modes that are performed analytically rather than using fast Fourier transforms because only modes within a narrow helicity band are of interest. The subroutine (MULT) performing the mode convolutions is fully vectorized with do-loop unfolding [13].

3: Multi-CPU implementation

For the KITE family of codes, the matrix operations and mode convolutions are the most time-consuming parts of the calculations. This is so not only in serial implementation on the CRAYs but also in massively parallel implementation on the Intel iPSC/860 and Touchstone Delta [8]. Most of the effort has, therefore, been put into achieving efficient multiprocessing of the matrix operations and convolutions on the C90.

Compared to the algorithm development and extensive code modifications necessary to obtain efficient massively parallel code for the Intel parallel computers, few changes are required for the code to multiprocess effectively on the C90. We did restructure the code so that the matrix and right-hand side were stored in memory for all the modes. Previous codes read the matrix from disk one mode at a time each time step and calculated the right-hand side with each mode overwriting the right-hand side for the last one. This I/O bound version was preferred on the CRAY IIs to circumvent the scheduling and charging scheme in effect at NERSC, at the expense of slower turnaround, more than to save memory storage.

On the C90, the autotasked version of the code is produced automatically by the CF77 compiling system when the -zp option is used on the compiler line with no further changes made to the serial version. The microtasked version was produced by first profiling the code to assess which modules account for most of the computational time. The automatic parallelizer tool FORGE was then applied to these modules to detect parallelism, and compiler directives were inserted where parallelism was found. To microtask the matrix inversion, only the following three lines were required:

```
CMIC\$ DOALL
CMIC\$*SHARED (index,nmatx,mjml,ampls,bmpls)
CMIC\$*SHARED (cmpls,y,impls)
CMIC\$*PRIVATE (l)
      do 21 l=2,index+1
      call solbt(nmatx,mjml,ampls(1,1,1,l),
   &   bmpls(1,1,1,l),cmpls(1,1,1,l),y(1,1,l),
```

```
        impls(1,1,l))
   21 continue
```

The parallelization is performed over the number of modes. Each variable in the do-loop over modes must be declared to be shared with all the processors or private to each processor. To microtask the convolutions over modes, the following four lines of compiler directives were inserted in the subroutine MULT:

```
CMIC\$ DOALL
CMIC\$*SHARED (mj,lmax,l0,k1max,l1max,l1h,k1h)
CMIC\$*SHARED l1g,k1g,h,g,f)
CMIC\$*PRIVATE (kp,lp1,lp,j,fs,l)
CMIC\$*SAVELAST

        do 1999 l=1,lmax
        do 1897 j=0,mj
   1897 fs(j)=0.
        do 1898 lp=l1max(l-1)+1,l1max(l),4
        if(l1max(l)-lp.lt.4) go to 100
        do 98 j=0,mj
        fs(j)=(((((fs(j)+g(j,l1g(lp)*h(j,l1h(lp)))
   1              +g(j,l1g(lp+1)*h(j,l1h(lp+1)))
   1              +g(j,l1g(lp+2)*h(j,l1h(lp+2)))
   1              +g(j,l1g(lp+3)*h(j,l1h(lp+3)))
   98   continue
        go to 1898
  100   do 150 lp1=lp,l1max(l)
        do 150 j=0,mj
  150   fs(j)=fs(j)+g(j,l1g(lp1))*h(j,l1h(lp1))
 1898   continue
        do 1998 kp=k1max(l-1)+1,k1max(l)
        do 1998 j=0,mj
        fs(j)=fs(j)-g(j,k1g(kp))*h(j,k1h(kp))
 1998   continue
        do 1999 j=0,mj
 1999   f(j,l)=0.5*fs(j)
```

The convolution routine is highly optimized. Each inner loop is vectorized over the number of radial grid points and has do-loop unfolding with four terms written out explicitly. With unfolding the array fs needs to be accessed and stored only one-fourth as frequently. The outer loop is performed in parallel over the number of modes. One other subroutine was microtasked, with parallelization over the number of modes. It is a simple tridiagonal solver over radial grid points (TRDG) that is called for all modes when the potential is calculated from the vorticity [Eq. (5)].

With these modifications, the KITE profile displayed as a pie chart in Fig. 1 is obtained for our plasma edge turbulence model run for 100 time steps with 385 grid points and 539 modes. The matrix operations (SOL/SOLBT) account for 47% of total CPU time, the convolutions (MULT) for 41%, and the tridiagonal solver (TRDG) for 3%, for a total of 91%. It is clear from Fig. 1 that all parts of the calculations that matter are the

ones that have been microtasked save for 9% of the computational burden, which is made up of the startup serial routines. This startup overhead would be much lower if a calculation over thousands of steps had been profiled.

ORNL-DWG 93M-3416 FED

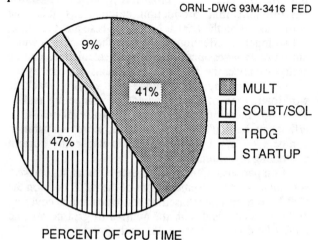

PERCENT OF CPU TIME

Figure 1: **Profile of the plasma fluid turbulence calculations with the microtasked computer code KITE on the CRAY Y-MP C90. The pie chart indicates the breakdown of the computational burden for 100 time steps, with MJ = 385 grid points and Nmodes = 539 modes between matrix operations (SOLBT/SOL), the mode convolutions (MULT), the tridiagonal solver (TRDG), and the serial startup routines.**

4: Results

The arbitrary memory limit currently in effect on the C90 at NERSC is set at 80 $Mword$. For the KITE implementation of the plasma edge turbulence model given by Eqs. (1)–(5), the memory size, $Msize$, is dominated by the matrices and by varying the number of modes, $Nmodes$, and grid points, MJ; and we have obtained the following scaling:

$$Msize(Mword) = 0.66 + 3.76$$
$$\times 10^{-4}(MJ \times Nmodes). \qquad (11)$$

The present studies have, therefore, been limited to grid sizes and numbers of modes that result in a memory size ≤ 80 $Mword$, with the largest size calculations attempted having $MJ = 385$ and $Nmodes = 539$ for $Msize = 79$ $Mword$. We have refrained from using the Solid-State Storage Device (SSD), which would enable us to accommodate larger system sizes, because it is incompatible with autotasking and microtasking. Even if it were compatible, access to the arrays on the SSD would be single threaded, creating a severe performance bottleneck. We point out that the calculations reported here were not carried out in single-user or dedicated mode but in the usual, competitive, multiuser batch environment that production calculations must be performed in on the C90 at NERSC. These are, therefore, not so much a reflection of the best the machine can do but more an assessment of how well calculations can be performed under the day-to-day constraints imposed by the system (swapping, scheduling) and varying machine workload (time of day, hundreds of competing tasks). They do, therefore, give a true measure of real-time efficiency, particularly since all tasks, serial and parallel, compete on a roughly equal basis under the current scheduling algorithm.

Comparisons of the performance of serial, autotasked, and microtasked implementations of the KITE code on the C90 have been made based on test calculations covering 100 time steps, and with the number of grid points and modes held fixed at $MJ = 385$ and Nmodes = 539. The results of these comparisons are shown in Fig. 2, where connect seconds and wallclock seconds are displayed as bar charts for all three modes of operation. Connect seconds are used on the C90 as a measure of the average time spent in concurrent CPUs. Figure 2 shows that good overlap is obtained with autotasking, and even better overlap is achieved by microtasking, with 4.12 processors accessed concurrently in microtasked mode compared to 2.55 processors in autotasked mode. The wallclock time is within 7% of the connect time for all three modes of operation. The improvement of performance with microtasking and autotasking over serial operation is directly proportional to the number of CPUs accessed concurrently, with the best real-time efficiency or lowest wallclock time for fastest turnaround obtained in microtasked mode. Autotasking is slower than microtasking because it cannot make loops with subroutine calls parallel. For instance, in the case of the matrix solver, calls to SOLBT are made in parallel under microtasking, as shown in Section 3. However, autotasking can only make loops inside the solver itself parallel. From now on, we, therefore, concentrate on results obtained with the microtasked version of KITE.

Tests of the KITE code in microtasking mode have been carried out in which the number of CPUs requested on the C90 was varied from 2 to 16 by setting the environment variable NCPUS to the appropriate value and the average number of concurrent CPUs achieved was recorded. As shown in Fig. 3, after 8 CPUs requested up to the maximum of 16, the average number of CPUs accessed is almost constant and hovers around 4.3. These tests were carried out for 100 time steps, $MJ = 385$, and Nmodes = 539. For production calculations with 5000 time steps or more, we average 5.9 processors when we request 16 processors. In either case, the number of CPUs accessed concurrently varies slightly depending on the

machine workload at the time the calculations are performed.

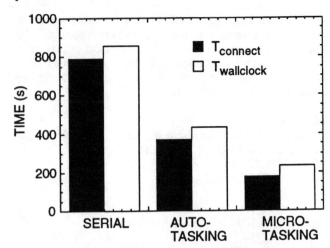

Figure 2: Timings of KITE for 100 time steps, 385 grid points, and 539 modes on the C90 in serial, autotasked, and microtasked modes. Wallclock seconds in light shading and connect seconds in dark shading (average time spent in CPU) are displayed in a bar chart for all three modes of operation. Microtasking provides the best real-time efficiency.

ORNL-DWG 93M-3418 FED

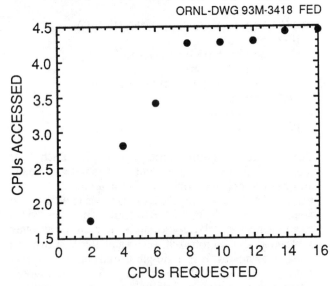

Figure 3: Average number of CPUs accessed in microtasking mode as a function of number of CPUs requested for runs of KITE with 385 grid points and 539 modes on the C90 for 100 time steps.

Calculations have been performed in microtasked mode for 100 time steps with varying numbers of grid points and modes. All 16 processors were requested for these tests. Results of these studies are shown in Fig. 4, where the average number of concurrent CPUs obtained, $Ncpus$, is displayed as a function of the size of the calculation, $MJ \times Nmodes$. The upper and lower set of data are for $Nmodes = 539$ and 201, respectively, and different MJs. The middle set of data is for $MJ = 385$ and different $Nmodes$ up to a maximum of 539. The number of CPUs accessed concurrently depends linearly on both the number of modes and the number of grid points, with a much stronger dependence on the number of modes. A global fit to the data yields the following scaling for the number of CPUs accessed concurrently:

$$Ncpus = 0.835 + 5.3 \times 10^{-3} Nmodes$$
$$+ 1.4 \times 10^{-3} MJ. \qquad (12)$$

The stronger dependence of the number of concurrent CPUs on the number of modes just reflects the fact that parallelization is done over modes in the C90 version of KITE.

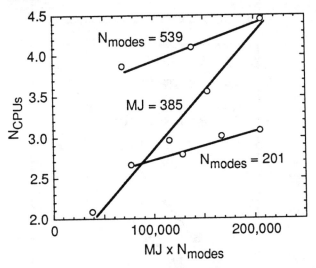

Figure 4: Average number of concurrent CPUs in microtasking mode as a function of calculation size MJ × Nmodes for calculations over 100 time steps with KITE on the C90. The upper and lower data points are for Nmodes = 539 and 201 and varying MJ. The middle data points are for MJ = 385 and varying Nmodes.

For these same calculations with varying numbers of grid points and modes, we have also plotted in Fig. 5 the average time spent in CPU or connect seconds, $T_{Connect}$, and the wallclock seconds, $T_{wallclock}$, as a function of the size of the calculation, $MJ \times Nmodes$. In marked contrast to the three distinct dependencies observed in Fig. 4 for the number of concurrent CPUs as a function of calculation size, the data points for the connect seconds

and wallclock seconds lie on a straight line; a very good fit to the data is

$$T_{connect}(\text{seconds}) = 0.38 + 7.21$$
$$\times 10^{-6}(MJ \times Nmodes), \qquad (13)$$

and

$$T_{wallclock}(\text{seconds}) = 0.43 + 8.61$$
$$\times 10^{-6}(MJ \times Nmodes). \qquad (14)$$

The linear dependence on MJ is expected because the number of operations in KITE scales as the number of grid points. However, while the number of operations is proportional to $MJ \times Nmodes$ for the matrix operations, it does scale as $MJ \times (Nmodes)^2$ for the convolutions. This is indeed what is obtained in serial mode for problem sizes, such as the ones considered here, with $Nmodes > MJ$. However, as shown in Fig. 4, the concurrent CPUs scale as $Nmodes$ so that more processors work simultaneously on the calculation as the number of modes increases, with the net effect that the connect seconds and wallclock seconds scale linearly with $Nmode$ as well as MJ.

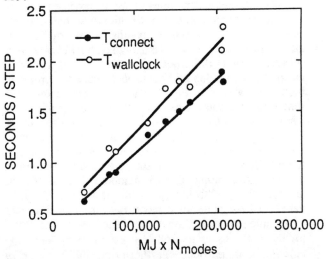

Figure 5: Connect seconds (solid circles) and wallclock seconds (open circles) as a function of calculation size MJ × Nmodes for calculations over 100 time steps with KITE in microtasking mode on the C90.

In performing production calculations, we have observed that better real-time efficiency can, in fact, be obtained. More concurrent CPUs can be accessed, and connect seconds per time step go down by a commensurate amount. Results of tests over 5000 time steps are displayed in Fig. 6(a) for concurrent CPUs and Fig. 6(b) for connect seconds as a function of number of modes. For reasons of affordability, we have kept the number of grid points fixed at 385. The results of Fig. 6(a) show that the average number of CPUs accessed concurrently is larger for these calculations than for those with 100 steps, with 5.9 concurrent processors obtained for the largest calculations with $MJ = 385$ and Nmodes = 539. We have been able to perform one calculation for 100 steps in dedicated mode with a memory size of 196 $Mword$, corresponding to 1325 modes and 385 grid points. We have achieved 8.5 concurrent CPUs for this calculation. A reasonable fit to the data of Fig. 6(a) is $Ncpus$ (5000 steps) = $Ncpus$ (100 steps) + 1.6. It is also clear from Fig. 6(b) that the connect seconds per time step are lower for the 5000 time step calculations than for those with 100 steps. A good fit to the data of Fig. 6(b) is $T_{connect}$ (5000 steps) = $T_{connect}$ (100 steps) - (0.35 + 5 ×10^{-4} Nmodes). These improvements are partly due to a better averaging of system performance with more steps, but also because the serial initialization is reduced over 5000 steps to much less than the 9% of the computational burden it accounted for over 100 steps as shown in Fig. 1. In fact, as shown in Fig. 6(b), when the data for 100 time steps are corrected for the serial setup, the connect seconds per step reduce to the values obtained from the calculations with 5000 time steps.

Microtasked calculations on all 16 processors of the C90 have been compared to identical calculations performed with the massively parallel version of KITE on all 128 processors of the Oak Ridge National Laboratory (ORNL) Intel iPSC/860 [8]. The results of these calculations with 385 grid points and a varying number of modes are shown in Fig. 7, where connect seconds per time step are displayed as a function of number of modes. Timings from tests over 5000 time steps were used for the C90 data. Real-time efficiency as measured by connect time is better by a factor of 10 on the C90 as compared to the iPSC/860. These comparisons are for the best version of the code running on each machine. Because of the memory limit of 8Mbyte per node on the iPSC/860, its version of the code must recalculate the matrix blocks every time step as they are needed. The C90 version stores all the matrices in its 268-$Mword$ memory and only calculates them once. Furthermore, the number of processors is kept fixed on the iPSC/860, whereas the number of accessible processors on the C90 increases with the number of modes. Earlier extrapolations [8] of results obtained with KITE on the Intel iPSC/860 and Delta to the Intel Paragon, with its faster communications between processors, its better compiler optimization, and its 2048 processors show that it will be possible to obtain a gain in real-time efficiency equivalent to the C90 on the Paragon.

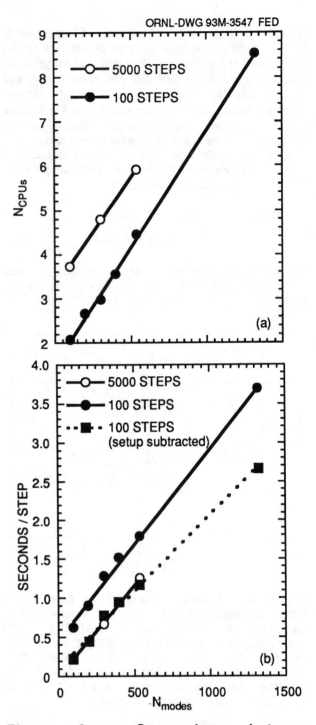

Figure 6: Comparison between microtasked C90 KITE calculations for 100 (solid circles) and 5000 (open circles) time steps: a) average number of concurrent CPUs as a function of number of modes and b) connect seconds per time step as a function of number of modes. The connect seconds for 100 steps with startup substracted are plotted as solid squares.

[For color plate see page 928]

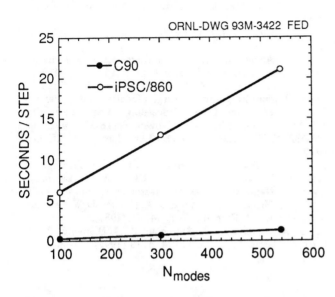

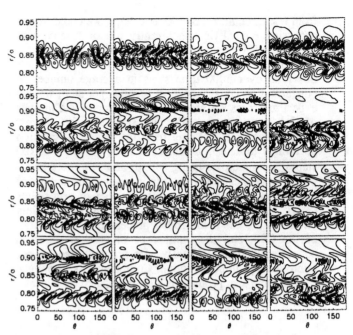

Figure 7: Connect seconds per time step for identical calculations with the microtasked version of KITE on the 16 processors of the C90 and with the massively parallel version of KITE on all 128 processors of the Intel IPSC/860.

Figure 8: Color contours of the plasma density as a function of radius (vertical axis in each frame) and poloidal angle (horizontal axis) are shown as the nonlinear production calculation advances in time.

Production calculations of impurity radiation-driven drift waves as a model of turbulence at the edge of the TEXT tokamak have been performed on the C90 with the microtasked version of the computer code KITE. These calculations had 385 grid points and 539 modes. The time evolution of Eqs. (1)–(5) has been followed for 40,000 steps deep into the nonlinear saturated steady state. Even though these calculations were performed in the usual multiuser batch operation of the C90, we have been able to complete 20,000 contiguous steps over one weekend and have routinely completed 5000 steps overnight. As a measure of comparison, we were able to complete only 1000 steps every 2 or 3 days, depending on machine load, for the same size calculations in serial mode on the CRAY IIs and C90. This improvement in turnaround in microtasked mode on the C90 is due to the fact that these production calculations have been able to access an average of 5.9 processors concurrently. Because of this improvement in real-time efficiency, we are now able to achieve a nonlinear saturated steady state within a few days instead of a few weeks. Results of these production calculations are illustrated in the color plate displayed in Fig. 8. Color contours of the plasma density as a function of radius (vertical axis in each frame) and poloidal angle (horizontal axis) are shown as the nonlinear calculation advances in time.

We have concentrated for this paper on results from the KITE code because it is one of our most mature and computationally intensive production codes when applied to plasma edge turbulence calculations. However, the best microtasking performance that we have obtained to date on the C90 is with the DTEMFAR code, which solves a paradigmatic one-equation model of dissipative trapped electron mode (DTEM) turbulence in slab geometry [14]. It uses an algorithm identical to KITE as far as matrix operations and mode convolutions are concerned, with the matrix solver accounting for 70% of the computational burden. In multiuser mode, we were able to access 7.42 concurrent CPUs, as compared to 1.65 processors for the autotasking version, for a calculation over 100 time steps with 534 grid points and 439 modes, corresponding to a memory size of 11 $Mword$.

5: Conclusions

In the next system configuration on the C90 at NERSC, the memory size available to users will be set to a maximum of 200 $Mword$. This will enable us to perform experimentally relevant calculations of plasma edge turbulence with higher radial resolution and including more modes to increase mode couplings and radial mixing. Using Eq. (11), we will be able to fit 500 grid points and 1000 modes in memory, for a memory size of $Msize = 190$ $Mword$, only slightly below the maximum allowed. Using the scalings of Eqs. (12) and (13) obtained from test calculations of 100 time steps, we could expect accessing 6.8 CPUs concurrently out of a maximum possible of 16 and respectable timings of 4 connect seconds per time step. With the additional improvements observed over 5000 time steps in average number of concurrent CPUs and connect seconds per step, we can expect to access 8.5 processors concurrently and timings of 3.1 connect seconds per step for the largest calculations. Extrapolating from the largest calculation performed to date in dedicated mode (196 *Mword*, 100 steps), we anticipate being able to access more than 10 processors concurrently by only increasing the number of modes (up to 1325) with a fixed number of grid points (385). These anticipated improvements in real-time efficiency are due to the 16 fast processors, large memory of the C90, and the number of processors accessed concurrently scaling linearly with problem size for our microtasking implementation. Comparable performance for the same size problem is also anticipated on the Intel Paragon.

Acknowledgments

We thank Drs. J. Sheffield and R. A. Dory of ORNL and Dr. C. W. McCurdy of NERSC for their support and encouragement in carrying out this project.

This research was sponsored by the Office of Fusion Energy, U. S. Department of Energy, under contract DE-AC05-84OR21400 with Martin Marietta Energy Systems, Inc.

References

1. Ch. P. Ritz, R. V. Bravenec, P. M. Schoch, R. D. Bengtson, J. A. Boedo, J. C. Forster, K. W. Gentle, Y. He, R. L. Hickcok. Y. J. Kim, H. Lin, P. E. Phillips, T. L. Rhodes, W. L. Rowan, P. M. Valanju, and A. J. Wootton, Phys. Rev. Lett. **62**, 1844 (1989).

2. B. A. Carreras, N. Dominguez, J. B. Drake, J. N. Leboeuf, L.A. Charlton, J. A. Holmes, D. K. Lee, V. E. Lynch and L. Garcia, Int. J. Supercomput. Appl. **4**, 97 (1990).

3. A. S. Ware, P. H. Diamond, B. A. Carreras, J. N. Leboeuf and D. K. Lee, Phys. Fluids B **4**, 102 (1992).

4. J. N. Leboeuf, D. K. Lee, B. A. Carreras, N. Dominguez, J. H. Harris, C. L. Hedrick, C. Hidalgo, J. A. Holmes, J. R. Ruiter, P. H. Diamond, A. S. Ware, Ch. P. Ritz, A. J. Wootton, W. L. Rowan, and R. V. Bravenec, Phys. Fluids B **3**, 2291 (1991).

5. L. Garcia, H. R. Hicks, B. A. Carreras, L. A. Charlton, and J. A. Holmes, J. Comput. Phys. **65**, 253 (1986).

6. J. B. Drake, B. F. Lawkins, B. A. Carreras, H. R. Hicks, and V. E. Lynch, "Implementation of a 3-D Nonlinear MHD Calculation on the Intel Hypercube," ORNL-6335, Martin Marietta Energy Systems, Inc., Oak Ridge National Laboratory, Oak Ridge, Tennessee, 1987.

7. V. E. Lynch, B. A. Carreras, J. B. Drake, J. N. Leboeuf, and J. R. Ruiter, Comput. Sys. Eng. **2**, 299 (1991).

8. V. E. Lynch, B. A. Carreras, J. B. Drake, J. N. Leboeuf, and P. Liewer, "Performance of a Plasma Fluid Code on the Intel Parallel Computers," Proceedings of Supercomputing '92, Minneapolis, Minnesota, November 16-20, 1992, pp. 286-293, IEEE Computer Society, Los Alamitos, California, 1992.

9. H. R. Hicks, and V. E. Lynch, J. Comput. Phys. **63**, 140 (1986).

10. D. V. Anderson, "Parallel Algorithms for Plasma Physics Calculations," Computer Physics Reports **11**, 117 (1989).

11. F. F. Young and C. H. Wu, "A Fully-Vectorized Code for Nonequilibrium RF Glow Discharge Modeling and its Parallel Processing on a Cray X-MP," Proceedings of Supercomputing '92, Minneapolis, Minnesota, November 16-20, 1992, pp. 424-432, IEEE Computer Society, Los Alamitos, California, 1992.

12. A. C. Hindmarsh, "Solution of Block-Tridiagonal Systems of Algebraic Equations," UCID-30150, Lawrence Livermore National Laboratory, Livermore, California, 1977.

13. H. R. Hicks, B. A. Carreras, J. A. Holmes, D. K. Lee, and B. V. Waddell, J. Comput. Phys. **44**, 46 (1981).

14. B. A. Carreras, K. L. Sidikman, P. H. Diamond, P. W. Terry, L. Garcia, Phys. Fluids B **4**, 3115 (1992).

An Interactive Remote Visualization Environment for an Electromagnetic Scattering Simulation on a High Performance Computing System

Gang Cheng[†‡], Yinghua Lu[†], Geoffrey Fox[†‡], Kim Mills[†] and Tomasz Haupt[†]

[†]Northeast Parallel Architectures Center
[‡]School of Computer and Information Science
Syracuse University, Syracuse, NY 13244

Abstract

Electromagnetic scattering(EMS) simulation is an important computationally intensive application within the field of electromagnetics. Advances in high performance computing and communication (HPCC) and data visualization environment(DVE) provide new opportunities to visualize real-time simulation problems such as EMS which require significant computational resources. In this work, an integrated interactive visualization environment was created for an EMS simulation, coupling a graphical user interface(GUI) for runtime simulation parameters input and 3D rendering output on a graphical workstation, with computational modules running on a parallel supercomputer and two workstations. Application Visualization System(AVS) was used as integrating software to facilitate both networking and scientific data visualization. Using the EMS simulation as a case study in this paper, we explore the AVS dataflow methodology to naturally integrate data visualization, parallel systems and heterogeneous computing. Major issues in integrating this remote visualization system are discussed, including task decomposition, system integration, concurrent control, and a high level DVE-based distributed programming model.

1 Introduction

Scientific visualization has traditionally been carried out interactively on workstations, or in post-processing or batch on supercomputers. With advances in high performance computing systems and networking technologies, interactive visualization in a distributed environment becomes feasible. In a re-mote visualization environment, data, I/O, computation and user interaction are physically distributed through high-speed networking to achieve high performance and optimal use of various resources required by the application task. Seamless integration of high performance computing systems with graphics workstations and traditional scientific visualization is not only feasible, but will be a common practice with real-time application systems [18, 16, 15].

Electromagnetic scattering(EMS) simulation represents an important computationally intensive application in industry, and is an area of emphasis in the national high performance computing initiative[5]. In previous work, an electromagnetic scattering(EMS) problem was used as an application problem in a benchmark suite for the Fortran-90D/High Performance Fortran development at Northeast Parallel Architectures Center(NPAC) at Syracuse University, to evaluate parallel algorithm and programming language issues of this application on parallel systems [14]. To further develop this application and provide engineers with visual insights into EMS simulation problem, an interactive remote visualization environment was developed. Over a Ethernet-based local network, this environment combines a graphical user interface of runtime system control and 3D graphics rendering on a graphical workstation with parallel and sequential computational modules running on a parallel supercomputer Connection Machine CM5 and two SUN Sparc stations. Application Visualization System(AVS) was used in this real-time simulation system as a data visualization environment(DVE), enabling high level 3D data visualization and networking capabilities.

In this paper, we address a number of issues encountered in building an interactive visualization environment for EMS, including decomposition of computation, system integration, interstage communication and concurrent control, and a high level DVE-based distributed programming model.

2 The Electromagnetic Scattering Problem

Electromagnetic scattering is a widely encountered problem in electromagnetics [7, 10, 21], with important applications in industry such as microwave equipment, radar, antenna, aviation, and electromagnetic compatibility design. Figure 1 illustrates the EMS problem we are modeling. Above an infinite conductor plane, there is an incident EM field in free space. Two slots of equal width on the conducting plane are interconnected to a microwave network behind the plane. The microwave network represents the load of waveguides, for example, a microwave receiver. The incident EM field penetrates the two slots which are filled with insulation materials such as air or oil. Connected by the microwave network, the EM fields in the two slots interact with each other, creating two equivalent magnetic current sources in the two slots. A new scattered EM field is then formed above the slots. We simulate this phenomena and calculate the strength of the scattered EM field under various physical circumstances. The presence of the two slots and the microwave load in this application requires simulation models with high performance computation and communication. Visualization is very important in helping scientists to understand this problem under various physical conditions.

In previous work, data parallel and message passing algorithms for this application were developed to run efficiently on massively parallel SIMD machines such as Connection Machine CM-2 and DECmpp-12000, and MIMD machines such as the Connection Machine CM-5 and iPSC/860. The data parallel algorithms run approximately about 400 times faster than sequential versions on a high-speed workstation [11]. Parallel models on high performance systems provides a unique opportunity to interactively visualize the EMS simulation in real-time. This problem requires response time of a simulation cycle that is not possible on conventional hardware.

3 Parallization of the EMS Simulation Model

3.1 A Distributed Computing Model

In [3], a simple and feasible performance model of a remote visualization environment for a financial modeling application was developed. This model can be generalized as follows, shown in Figure 3 in which distributed I/O is not considered. A simulation cycle is started from a GUI module running on the local machine, with simulation parameters are represented as slide buttons and dials to provide real-time instrumentation of the simulation's progress as well as simulation steering (changing simulation parameters before a new simulation cycle). Source data for the simulation can also be read in by the GUI module from databases or data files. The computational task of the simulation is decomposed into a set of computationally relatively independent subtasks, which are represented as computing modules distributed to different remote machines. Input data are collected from the GUI by user runtime interaction, from disk files, or both sources, and broadcasted to computing modules on the remote machines. There is no data transfer among modules on different remote machines. A remote machine may be a workstation or a supercomputer, whichever architecture and computational power best suited to the decomposed subtask. The simulation ends with some kind of GUI rendering/viewing modules that run on the local machine and use results generated from remote modules. Fundamentally, this is a dataflow (data-driven) programming model, in which activation of a module process is triggered solely by availability of input data from another module process on either the same or a different machine.

This general model is well suited to rapid-prototyping certain simulation and modeling applications that require both scientific data visualization and high performance computing. At the software environment level, this model only requires support of high level data visualization and networking facilities. Most importantly, this dataflow based model is well supported by most commercially available DVEs, such as AVS[1] from AVS Inc. and Explorer[17] from Silicon Graphics Inc..

Components of our distributed model for simulation and visualization are:

1. Decomposition of visualization computation,

2. Selection of simulation parameters,

3. Design of a graphical user interface,

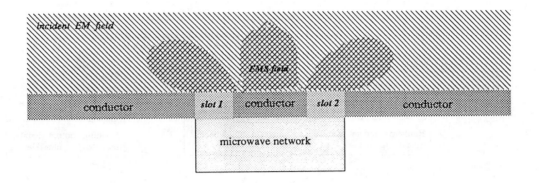

Figure 1: Profile of the electromagnetic scattering problem

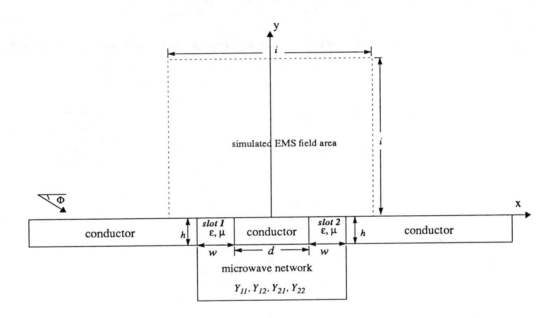

Figure 2: Physical parameters of the EM scattering problem

4. System integration and synchronization, and

5. Interstage communication and performance analysis.

Using the EMS simulation, we next examine decomposition of visualization computation and selection of simulation parameters. The remaining components are discussed in later sections.

3.2 Computational Task Decomposition

Control parallelism and data parallelism are used to target at the distributed computing model illustrated in the preceding section and a MIMD parallel machine along with a number of high-speed workstations. We use the following guidelines for the decomposition of our model's control parallelism:

1. Hardware architecture and computational power best suited to decomposed subtasks.

2. Logical components of the application's computational model.

3. Performance balance among decomposed modules, and

4. Communication requirements.

The moment method [8, 9, 12] is used as the numerical model for the EMS problem, which can be

319

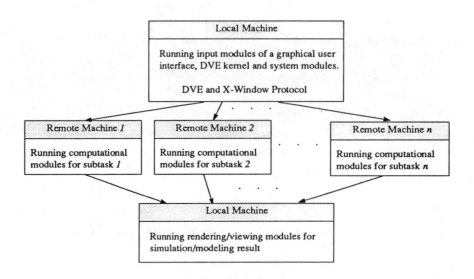

Figuse 3: A general performance model for a remote visualization enviroment

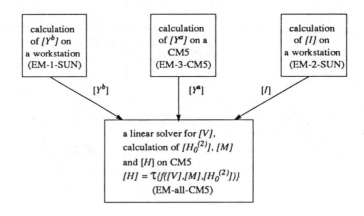

Figuse 4: Decomposition of the simulation task

represented as:

$$\{[\ Y^a\ ] + [\ Y^b\ ]\}\vec{V} = \vec{I}$$

$$[\ H\ ] = \mathcal{L}\{f\ (\vec{V}, \vec{M}, [\ H_0^2\ ])\}$$

where,

$[\ Y^a\ ]$: equivalent admittance matrix of the free space;

$[\ Y^b\ ]$: equivalent admittance matrix of the microwave network;

$\vec{V}$: coefficient vector;

$\vec{I}$: the excitation vector;

$\vec{M}$: a vector of mode functions;

$[\ H_0^2\ ]$: matrix of Hankel functions;

f : a function;

$\mathcal{L}$: a linear operator on f;

$[\ H\ ]$: final matrix of the simulated EMS field strength.

From the previous parallel algorithm design, we observed that:

1. Calculations of $[\ Y^a\ ]$, $[\ Y^b\ ]$, $\vec{I}$, $\vec{M}$, and $[\ H_0^2\ ]$ can be done independently;

2. Computation of $[\ Y^a\ ]$, $[\ H_0^2\ ]$, and the linear solver for $\vec{V}$ have significant communication requirements and are computationally intensive;

3. $\left[Y^b \right]$ is a sparse matrix and calculation of $\vec{M}$ requires little time. Calculation time for $\left[Y^a \right]$, $\left[Y^b \right]$ and $\vec{I}$ are relatively balanced.

Thus, we partition computations of this application into four loosely coupled computing modules(they are named as 'EM-1-SUN', 'EM-2-SUN', 'EM-3-CM5' and 'EM-all-CM5' in the AVS module network of Figure 6). Three modules can run simultaneously in the distributed computing environment(see Figure 4).

At the second level, i.e., data decomposition, because most computations of $\left[Y^a \right]$, $\vec{V}$(a linear solver), $\left[H_0^2 \right]$, and $\left[H \right]$ are matrix manipulations, data parallel algorithms are developed in Fortran90 and tailored to run on the Connection Machine 5, to take the advantages of CM5's balanced data network and control network. The CM Scientific Subroutine Library (CMSSL) is used in the data parallel implementation[13].

At a more general level, we can view the entire system a 'metacomputer' that makes use of both functional parallelism and pipelining. In this application, functional parallelism consists of graphical I/O (i.e., user interaction, 3D rendering) and decomposed simulation computations which are handled concurrently by different components of the metacomputer. Pipelining combines calculations and communications among different processors or groups of processor(e.g. the CM5) that are carried out simultaneously in consecutive stages of the simulation. We will discuss pipelining execution of the system in later sections.

3.3 Selection of Simulation Parameters

Simulation parameters are implemented as control widgets within a graphical user interface to provide a visual medium for the user to interact with the simulation and visualization at runtime. We choose parameters representing the physical foundation of the EMS problem and the computational model that the user can manipulate in order to visually understand the problem.

As shown in Figure 2, the following parameters are graphically represented to allow user's runtime input:

1. Φ : angle of the incident EM field(wave);

2. i : $i \times i$ is the simulated area of the EMS field;

3. w : width of the slot;

4. d : distance between the two slots;

5. ϵ : permittivity of the media in the slot;

6. μ : permeability of the media in the slot;

7. h : height of the slots;

8. $y_{11}, y_{12}, y_{21}, y_{22}$: admittance parameters of a given microwave network.

In addition, there are four parameters representing characteristics of the equivalent magnetic current originally formed by the penetrating incident EM field. These parameters are used as mode function expansions and the number of pulse functions in the moment method. Another parameter used for visualization purposes is the number of grid points for discretizing the visualized EMS area. All the five parameters have direct impact on the computational requirements and simulation resolution of the moment method. Using different combinations of the parameters, we can visualize the EMS simulation under a large number of real application circumstances. We also use visualization of typical parameters to verify the EMS computational model and some well-known theories about this physical phenomena.

4 Implementation of the Remote Visualization Environment

4.1 System Configuration and Integration Using AVS

Figure 5 illustrates the system configuration and module components distributed over the network to three high-end workstations and a supercomputer Connection Machine 5. The network is a 10 MBit/s Ethernet-based local network. Commercially available AVS software is used to provide sophisticated 3D data visualization and system control functionality required by the simulation. We use AVS to facilitate high level networking and data transfers among visualization and computational modules on different machines in the system. AVS provides a data-channel abstraction that transparently handles type-conversion and module connectivities. This software system is optimized for data movement by using techniques such as shared memory message passing among modules on the same machine. Message passing occurs at a high level of data abstraction in AVS. This approach helps to make optimal use of both the high performance computing resources and the rendering capabilities of the local graphical workstation. The transparent networking capabilities of AVS open up possibil-

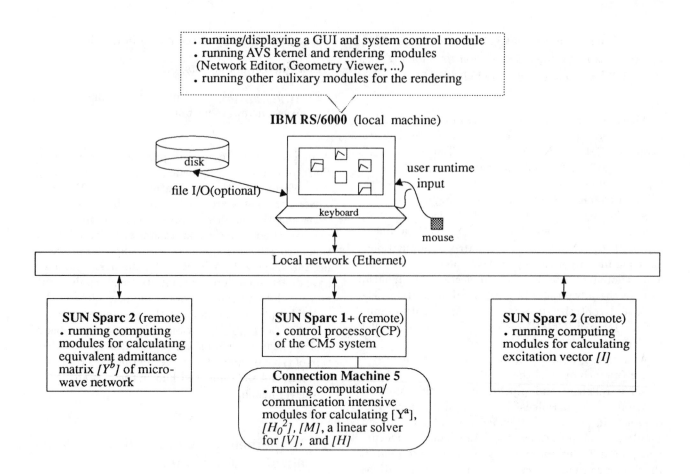

- running/displaying a GUI and system control module
- running AVS kernel and rendering modules (Network Editor, Geometry Viewer, ...)
- running other aulixary modules for the rendering

IBM RS/6000 (local machine)

disk

file I/O(optional)

keyboard

user runtime input

mouse

Local network (Ethernet)

SUN Sparc 2 (remote)
- *running computing modules for calculating equivalent admittance matrix $[Y^b]$ of microwave network*

SUN Sparc 1+ (remote)
- control processor(CP) of the CM5 system

Connection Machine 5
- running computation/ communication intensive modules for calculating $[Y^a]$, $[H_0^2]$, $[M]$, a linear solver for $[V]$, and $[H]$

SUN Sparc 2 (remote)
- *running computing modules for calculating excitation vector $[I]$*

Figure 5: System configuration and distributed components

ities for visualization far beyond traditional graphics capabilities[1, 2].

The local machine in our system is a IBM RS/6000 with a 24-bit color GTO graphics adaptor. An AVS coroutine module (in C) on the local machine serves as a graphical input and system control interface to monitor and collect user runtime interaction with the simulation through keyboard, mouse and other I/O devices. The AVS kernel also runs on the local machine, coordinating data flows and control flows among AVS (remote) modules in the network.

We use an AVS system module called 'geometry viewer' along with other system modules('generate colormap', 'color range' and 'field to mesh') for 3D rendering operations.

The computationally intensive modules of this application are distributed to the CM5[20], a MIMD supercomputer which is configured 32 processing nodes at NPAC. Each processing node(PN) of the CM5 consists of a SPARC processor for control and non-vector computation, four vector units for numerical compu-

tation and 32 MB of RAM. It also includes a Network Interface chip which gives the node access to the CM5 internal Data Network and Control Network. The two internal networks connect all the PNs with a control processor(CP) which runs a custom version of SunOS on a SPARC host.

Two Sun SPARC workstations are used in our distributed visualization environment to run the computational modules with modest communication requirements.

All modules other than those on the local machine are implemented as AVS remote modules. Their input/output ports are defined by specific AVS libraries for receiving/sending data from/to other (remote) modules via socket connections. This configuration allows the interrupt driven user interface input mechanisms and rendering operations to be relegated to the graphical workstation, while the computationally intensive components run on the CM5 coupled with the two workstations. This distributed simulation environment implemented in AVS provides a transparent mechanism for using distributed computing resources along with a sophisticated user interface component that permits a variety of interactive, application-specified inputs.

The flow-chart diagram in Figure 6(lower right) is a module network configured by the AVS Network Editor for this application.

4.2 The Graphical User Interface

The graphical user interface includes a main control panel, three individual input panels, and a 3D rendering window.

The main control panel provides the user parameters input and simulation control at runtime. There are seven dial widgets representing simulation parameters used by all computing modules on the three remote machines, and a control button for starting a new simulation cycle(see lower left in Figure 6). The rest of simulation parameters discussed in Section 3.3 are implemented as dial widgets in individual panels associated with the modules only requiring them, to minimize redundant data transfers between the input interface module on the local machine and computational modules on remote machines. They can also be turned on from the AVS Network Control Panel(not shown in Figure 6).

Using the AVS Geometry Viewer, 3D simulation data can be rendered in various forms such as move, rotate, scale, move the eye point and perspective view, and with sophisticated rendering techniques such as lighting and shading, multiple camera, Z-buffering, 2D and 3D texture mapping, automatic removal of hidden surfaces, sphere rendering, etc. The geometry viewer also takes advantage of the hardware rendering capabilities of the GL library and the GTO graphics adaptor of the IBM RS/6000. Figure 6(upper) shows a typical AVS Geometry Viewer window with two cameras from two different angles.

In addition, the AVS Network Editor provides a visual programming interface enabling the user to interactively reconfigure and reuse network modules. The Layout Editor in AVS allows easy and complete customization of the control panels in the GUI. Figure 6 illustrates this interface.

4.3 Interstage Communication and Synchronization

Using the data-flow programming model in AVS, message passing among modules on the same machine and on different machines are identical and completely transparent to module programmer. AVS ker-

nel(protocol) supervises data transfer which is eventually carried out by TCP/IP at a lower level. The module programmer needs only to define module input and output ports in AVS predefined data types. Message passing among AVS modules occurs only through I/O ports. A set of routines for initializing and describing modules to AVS, as well as parameter handling, accessing data, error handling and coroutine event handling are provided. Data sources and destinations can be flexibly defined by visually connecting module input and output ports using the Network Editor.

In most cases, we use an AVS 'field' as the transferred data type which is actually a C structure. In the module network shown in Figure 6, data transmissions are overlapped with simulation computations(pipelining). For example, the computation of 'EM-3-CM5' can be pipelined with the data transfer between 'Input-interface-IBM' and 'EM-2-SUN' or 'EM-1-SUN'. Message passing within a machine is implemented in AVS by copying pointers to the same memory (shared memory). Thus, there is no network communication cost for transferring the matrix $\begin{bmatrix} Y^b \end{bmatrix}$ between the two modules, i.e.,'EM-3-CM5' to 'EM-all-CM5', on CM5's control processor. Instead of generating a complete 3D data on the CM5 and sending them to rendering modules on the local machine, we use a computing module 'EM-3D-IBM' on the local machine to generate the X-Y coordinate data. Only the Z-coordinate data(i.e., $\begin{bmatrix} H \end{bmatrix}$) and two scalar parameters for defining the X-Y data are transferred from the CM-5 to the local machine.

Simulation parameters are defined as input ports and connected to widgets on control panels supervised by the X-window manager on the local machine. By distributing parameter only to the modules that require them, we minimize recomputation of modules in a new simulation cycle. For example, changing of a parameter on the control panel of 'EM-1-SUN' will not activate the 'EM-3-CM5' and 'EM-2-SUN'.

This system is designed to work under a complete resource and time sharing environment(shared Ethernet, CM5 and all remote workstations) thus wall-clock time for computation and communication of all modules is difficult to predict. Concurrent control in the module network plays an extremely important role in assuring correctness, robustness and reliability. We issue concurrent controls in three different places:

1. In the main control panel of the GUI, a one-shot control button is set to allow the end-user to control the start of a new simulation cycle.

2. Broadcast of parameters from the module 'input-interface-IBM' to the computing modules on the

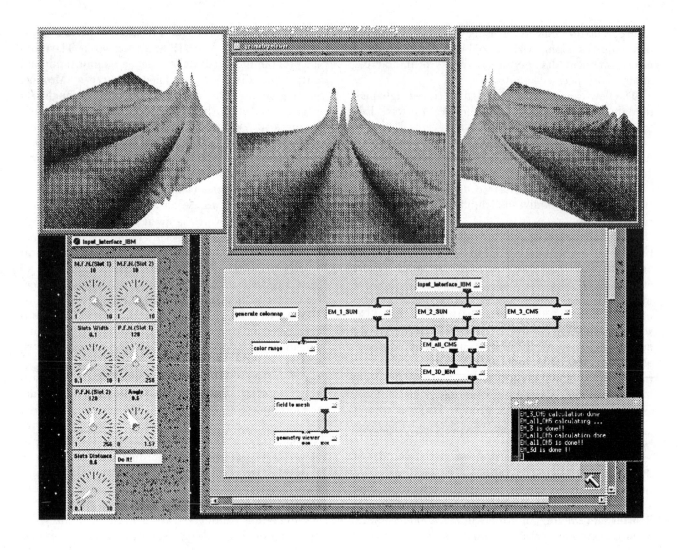

Figure 6: The Graphical User Interface on the Local Machine

remote machines is performed only when all the other module processes in the network are inactive.

3. Module 'EM-all-CM5' is implemented as a coroutine such that computations of the linear solver for $\vec{V}$ and $[\,H\,]$ will not be activated until all the required input data for $[\,Y^a\,]$, $[\,Y^b\,]$ and $\vec{I}$ have been recieved ($[\,Y^a\,]$ if only parameters on control panel of 'EM-1-SUN' are changed).

4.4 Experimental Results

A preliminary performance requirement analysis of this general performance model shown in Figure 3 can

be found in [3]. Our experiments show that under a typical working environment(only 0.5 MBits/s of the Ethernet's 10 MBits/s capacity are available), a complete simulation cycle for a set of typical EMS parameters takes about 8 seconds. This response time is quite satisfactory for this application. Table 1 lists timing data of major system components. For comparison, timings of sequential implementation on a SUN4 workstation of the two parallel modules are also given in the table.

Table 1: Timings of calculations and communications (in second)

Module name	Calculation time	Communication time with 'Input-interface-IBM'	Communication time with 'EM-all-CM5'	Communication time with 'EM-3D-IBM'
EM-1-SUN	0.1 (Sun)	0.02	0.045	
EM-2-SUN	0.6 (Sun)	0.02	0.5	
EM-3-CM5	1.8 (CM5) 1260 (Sun)	0.02	0.0	
EM-all-CM5	2.1 (CM5) 120 (Sun)			0.5
AVS Rendering Modules	3.5 (550x580 window)			

Note: The timing data is measured at a typical case: the number of pulse functions = 64; the number of mode functions = 5, and the number of grid points = 101x101.

5 Conclusion and Future Work

The performance limiting factors in this system are the sequential rendering operations on the local machine, and high-latency data transfer over the local area network due to multiple communication protocol layers. We focus here on the feasibility of applying a high-level distributed programming environment to a real application problem which requires both sophisticated 3D data visualization and high performance computing. This work shows that the DVE like AVS can be used not only for data visualization tasks (as primarily with on uniprocessor machines), but also as a general-purpose high level distributed programming tool. We will further examine this approach and compare this data-flow model with those employed by Fortran M[4], CC++ and PVM[19].

Future work in this environment will integrate some low-level message passing mechanisms to allow more flexible and multiple message passing programming paradigms. For example, we could use PVM[19] or FortranD[6] to implement one of the parallel AVS modules on networked workstations. We will also investigate the feasibility and issues concerned with developing a DVE-based programming environment on a MIMD machine. For instance, on a CM5, an extended DVE kernel can take advantages of CM5's high-bandwidth and low-latency internal networks, while many system modules(e.g. 3D rendering) are developed as parallel modules(similar work in CMAVS is being under development at Thinking Machines Corporation[15]). We view this data-flow model as a general, high-level programming environment which integrates data parallelism with control parallelism, and sequential programming with parallel programming.

References

[1] Advanced Visual Systems Inc. *AVS 4.0 Developer's Guide*, May 1992.

[2] Advanced Visual Systems Inc. *AVS 4.0 User's Guide*, May 1992.

[3] G. Cheng, K. Mills and G. Fox, *An Interactive Visualization Environment for Financial Modeling on Heterogeneous Computing Systems*, Proc. of the 6th SIAM Conference on Parallel Processing for Scientific Computing, March 1993, Norfolk, VA.

[4] I. Foster and K. M. Chandy, *Fortran M: A Language for Modular Parallel Programming*, Preprint MCS-P237-0992, Mathematics and Computer Science Division, Argonne National Laboratory, Argonne, Ill., 1992.

[5] G. Fox, *Parallel Computing in Industry: An Initial Survey*, in Proc. of Fifth Australian Supercomputing Conference, World Congress Centre, Melbourne, Australia, December, 1992.

[6] G. Fox, S. Hiranadani, K. Kennedy, C. Koelbel, U. Kremer, C-W Tseng, and M-Y Wu, *Fortran D*

Language Specification, Syracuse Center for Computational Science-42c, Rice COMP TR90-141, 37 pps, 1991.

[7] R. F. Harrington, *Time-Harmonic Electromagnetic Fields*, McGraw-Hill Book Company, New York (1961).

[8] R. F. Harrington, *Field Computation by Moment Methods*, the Macmillan Co., New York (1968). Reprinted by *Krieger Publishing Co.*, Malabar, FL (1982).

[9] R. F. Harrington, *Matrix Methods For Field Problems*, Proc. IEEE, vol. 55, No. 2, pp. 136-149, Feb. 1967.

[10] E. C. Jordon and K. G. Balmain, *Electromagnetic Waves and Radiating Systems*, Second Edition, *Prentice-Hall, Inc.*, Englewood Cliffs, New Jersey (1969).

[11] Y. Lu, A. G. Mohamed, G. Fox and R. F. Harrington, *Implementation of Electromagnetic Scattering from Conductors Containing Loaded Slots on the Connection Machine CM-2*, Proc. of the 6th SIAM Conference on Parallel Processing for Scientific Computing, March 1993, Norfolk, VA.

[12] Y. Lu and R. F. Harrington, *Electromagnetic Scattering from a Plane Conducting Two Slots Terminated by Microwave Network(TE Case)*, Technical Report, TR-91-2, ECE Department, Syracuse University, August 1991.

[13] Y. Lu, A.G. Mohamed, R.F. Harrington, *Implementation of Electromagnetic Scattering From Conductors containing Loaded Slots on the Connection Machine CM-2*, Technical Report, Syracuse Center for Computational Science 270, March, 1992, also CRPC-TR92209.

[14] G. A. Mohmad, G. Fox, G. Laszewski, M. Parashar, T. Haupt, K. Mills, Y. Lu, N. Lin, and N. Yeh, *Applications Benchmarking Set for Fortran-D and High Performance Fortran*, Technical Report, Syracuse Center for Computational Science 327, June, 1992, also CRPC-TR92260.

[15] G. Oberbrunner, *Parallel Networking and Visualization on the Connection Machine CM-5*, the Symposium on High Performance Distributed Computing HPDC-1, September, 1992, pp. 78-84, Syracuse, NY.

[16] G. M. Parulkar, et al, *Remote Visualization: Challenges and Opportunities*, in Proc. of the 2nd IEEE Conference on Visualization, San Diego, CA, October, 1991.

[17] Silicon Graphics Inc. *Iris Explorer User's Guide*, 1992.

[18] L. L. Smarr, *Scientific Visualization from inside the Metacomputer*, keynote speak, in Proc. of the 2nd IEEE Conference on Visualization, San Diego, CA, October, 1991.

[19] V. Sunderam, *PVM: A Framework for Parallel Distributed Computing*, Concurrency: practice and experience, 2(4), Dec. 1990.

[20] Thinking Machines Corporation, *The Connection Machine CM-5 technical summary*, Technical Report, Cambridge, MA, pp. 340-353, October 1991.

[21] J. Van Bladel and C. M. Butler, *Aperture Problems*, (Proc. NATO Adv. Study Inst. on Theoretical Methods for Determining the Interaction of Electromagnetic Waves with Structures,) Ed. by J. Skwirzynski, *Sythoff and Noordhoff international Publishers*, 1979.

Partitioning the Global Space for Distributed Memory Systems

A. Zaafrani and M.R. Ito
Department of Electrical Engineering
University of British Columbia
Vancouver, B.C, V6T 1Z4
email: {zaafrani,mito}@ee.ubc.ca

ABSTRACT

Partitioning the iteration space can significantly affect the execution time of a loop. In this paper, we propose an improvement over previous partitioning methods for single loops with uniform data dependencies. For distributed memory systems, partitioning each loop separately does not guarantee an efficient execution of the code because of across loop data dependence. As a result, a global iteration space is formed so that all loops in a program are considered when partitioning the global space. In addition, a new and general form of expressing data dependence called hyperplane dependence is introduced and used in the partitioning. It is a dependence whose source and destination are subspaces (of any dimension) of the global iteration space.

Keywords: *Partitioning, data dependence, multicomputers, iteration space, parallelizing compilers.*

1 Introduction

Parallel computers can be classified into distributed memory machines (multicomputers) and shared memory machines. Even though multicomputers are more complex to program than shared memory systems, they are more popular because of their scalability, and flexibility (can be inexpensively built from existing resources). Current compiling research for multicomputers is shifting the complexity of programming from the programmer to the compiler. Tasks such as data distribution [1,5], loop partitioning [4,6,8,10,14], communication optimization, and others can be automatically performed by the compiler.

Given that the major sources of parallelism in scientific programs are loops[1], it is essential to extract the right amount of parallelism from these loops especially for multicomputers, where a balance between parallelism and communication ought to be found. As a result, an efficient partitioning of the iteration space of the loops is needed to improve the execution time of the code. In this paper, an improved partitioning called independent tile partitioning is presented. It improves over supernode partitioning [6,10] by decreasing the granularity of computation of the loop without adding any communication overhead.

For multicomputers, improving the execution time of every loopnest in a program separately by finding an efficient partition for that loopnest is not sufficient because of communication overhead across loops. As a result, a global iteration space for the whole program needs to be found so that all dependencies can be considered simultaneously when partitioning the global space. This notion of global iteration space makes across loop dependence analysis as important as the traditional dependence analysis [2,12] usually done for single loops. Because of across loop dependencies, a new and general form of expressing data dependence called hyperplane dependence is introduced in this paper. It is a dependence whose source and destination are subspaces (of any dimension) of the global iteration space.

The remainder of this paper is organized in the following way. Section 2 presents the independent tile partitioning for single loops with uniform dependences. Sec-

---

[1] Loop and loopnest are used interchangeably in this paper to refer to a nested loop.

tion 3 discusses the type of dependences that should be used when partitioning the iteration space. Section 4 addresses four issues related to partitioning multiple loopnests in a program. Section 4.1 finds the global iteration space. Section 4.2 introduces hyperplane dependence which is a new and general form of expressing data dependences. Section 4.3 briefly discusses the mapping of a loopnest iterations into the global iteration space, while section 4.4 applies independent tile partitioning to the global iteration space. Finally, the conclusions can be found in section 5.

2 Iteration space partitioning: single loop case

The iteration space of a nested loop is an n-dimension discrete Cartesian space where every axis in the space corresponds to one loop in the nested loop. Partitioning the iteration space of a loop can be the critical factor that affects its execution time especially for multicomputers where a balance between parallelism and communication needs to be found. In this section, we introduce independent tile partitioning, initially presented in [14]. Only single loopnests with uniform dependence vectors are considered in this section. Multiple loopnests, and non-uniform dependence vectors are considered in section 4. For an n-dimensional loop with m dependence vectors, if $\left(D_1', D_2', \cdots, D_m'\right)$ are the dependence vectors where $D_i' = (d_{i1}, d_{i2}, \cdots, d_{in})$ for $1 \leq i \leq m$, then $D' = \left(D_1', D_2', \cdots, D_m'\right)^T$ is the dependence matrix. The partitioning matrix D, composed of l vectors, is derived from D' as explained later in this section.

The partitioning vectors in D can divide the iteration space into independent sets of iterations (i.e., any two nodes from two different sets are independent), where an iteration $\vec{i} = (i_1 i_2 \cdots i_n)$ is independent of iteration $\vec{j} = (j_1 j_2 \cdots j_n)$ with respect to D if and only if there is no $(\alpha_1, \alpha_2, \cdots, \alpha_l) \in Z^l$ such that $\vec{i} = \vec{j} + (\alpha_1 \alpha_2 \cdots \alpha_l) \times D$. This results in the independent set partitioning presented in [4,8]. The number of independent sets is called I, and set i is called P_i. For each set P_i, where $0 \leq i \leq I-1$, a node a_i from that set is found. Partitioning the iteration space into independent sets and

finding a representative node from each set can be accomplished using the minimum distance algorithm [8]. For every node $p_i \in P_i$, we have $p_i = a_i + (\alpha_1 \alpha_2 \cdots \alpha_l) \times D$, where $(\alpha_1, \alpha_2, \cdots, \alpha_l) \in Z^l$. For each node a_i ($0 \leq i \leq I-1$), a pseudo-node a_i' can be found such that $\forall \; p_i \in P_i$, we have $p_i = a_i' + \left(\alpha_1' \alpha_2' \cdots \alpha_l'\right) \times D$ where $\left(\alpha_1', \alpha_2', \cdots, \alpha_l'\right) \in N^l$ (N is the set of positive integers). These pseudo-nodes are used in the compile time transformation of the loop presented in [14].

Once a_i' is found for $0 \leq i \leq I-1$, each independent set P_i is partitioned into tiles such that tile $tile_{i_1, i_2, \cdots, i_l}^i$ includes all the nodes $a_i' + (\beta_1 \beta_2 \cdots \beta_l) \times D$ where

$$\beta_j \in [i_j \times size_j, (i_j + 1) \times size_j[\text{ where } 1 \leq j \leq l$$
$$size_j = \text{ length of the tiles in the direction of } D_j \tag{1}$$

Figure 1 illustrates independent tile partitioning by showing one independent set divided into subsets of size 3 in the direction of D_1, and of size 2 in the direction of D_2 where $D = \begin{pmatrix} 1 & 1 \\ -1 & 1 \end{pmatrix}$. Note that D divides the iteration space into 2 independent sets. Only one of them is represented in Figure 1 by being subdivided further into tiles. It should also be noted that the wavefront method is used on the subsets so that all subsets in the same front are executed concurrently. Our partitioning method improves on independent set partitioning [4] by dividing the sets into subsets so that the wavefront method can be used on the subsets. It also improves on supernode partitioning [6,10] by dividing a supernode into tiles that include dependent nodes only. This decreases the granularity of computation without adding communication overhead for massively parallel grid machines.

In order to partition the iteration space into tiles of independent iterations as described in the previous paragraphs, we need to find a partitioning matrix D composed of l linearly independent vectors $(D_1, D_2, \cdots, D_l)$ such that every vector in D' can be written as a linear combination of the vectors in D. When D is used as the partitioning matrix, then it has the advantage that every node in an independent set can be expressed as a unique integer

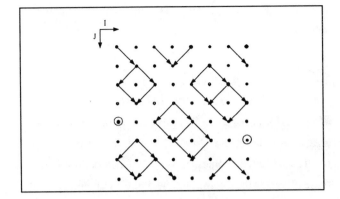

Figure 1. Independent Tile Partitioning for $D = \begin{pmatrix} 1 & 1 \\ -1 & 1 \end{pmatrix}$.

linear combination of the vectors in D (this allows a simple compile time transformation of the loop). In addition, given the assumption that a subset can not start until it gets all the data needed from other subsets, then a sufficient condition for the deadlock-free execution of the loop is that all vectors in D' are positive (or all negative) linear combination of the vectors in D [10]. The last condition is required only if all the dependences in D' are flow dependences. Note that it is essential to include in D as many vectors as possible from D' so that communication between tiles is minimized.

3 Dependence types in partitioning

In the previous section, an efficient partitioning of the iteration space based on the dependence matrix D' is introduced. In this section, we describe the type of data dependence vectors that should be included in D' and consequently be used in partitioning the iteration space. We assume that a dependence should affect the partitioning of the iteration space only if it limits parallelism between iterations or introduces communication overhead between iterations. There are five known types of dependences.

3.1 Flow dependence

A flow dependence from iteration $\vec{i} = (i_1, i_2, \cdots, i_n)$ to iteration $\vec{j} = (j_1, j_2, \cdots, j_n)$ exists in an n-nested loop iff $\vec{i} \leq \vec{j}$ and $\vec{i}$ defines a variable that is used later in $\vec{j}$. As a result,

these two iterations can not be done concurrently. In addition, if the two iterations are executed in two different processors, then a communication statement is needed between these two processors. Therefore, flow dependence should be included in D'.

3.2 Anti-dependence

An anti-dependence from iteration $\vec{i}$ to iteration $\vec{j}$ exists in an n-nested loop iff $\vec{i} \leq \vec{j}$ and $\vec{i}$ uses a variable that is defined later in $\vec{j}$. For multicomputers, anti-dependence does not limit the parallelism between iterations nor does it introduce any communication overhead provided that data is allowed to be replicated. In this case, anti-dependence vectors are only used to enforce data correctness (i.e which processor holds the correct value of a variable after the execution of the loop). For the case when data replication is prohibited, then anti-dependence introduces communication overhead if iteration $\vec{i}$ and $\vec{j}$ are not executed on the same processor. As a result, anti-dependences should be taken into consideration when partitioning the iteration space and be included in D'. However, it should have a lesser weight than flow dependence given that it does not limit parallelism.

In order to compare the use of flow and anti-dependence in the partitioning process, the example in Figure 2.a is considered. The partitioning matrix is $D = \begin{pmatrix} 0 & 1 \\ 1 & 0 \end{pmatrix}$ Note that $D_1 = (0, 1)$ corresponds to the flow dependence in the example while $D_2 = (1, 0)$ corresponds to the anti-dependence. Partitioning the iteration space according to D results in a block partitioning. However, the size of the tiles is yet to be determined and depends considerably on the type of dependencies found in the loopnest. For the example in Figure 2.a, we define the dependence factor df to be equal to $\frac{size_1}{size_2}$ (recall that $size_j$ is the length of the tile in the direction of D_j). This factor expresses the relative importance of flow and anti-dependence. In fact, a df larger than one means that the flow dependence is more important given that more flow dependencies are satisfied in a same tile than anti-dependencies. The execution time of the loopnest in Fig-

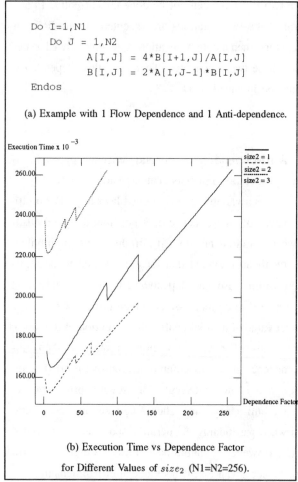

```
Do I=1,N1
    Do J = 1,N2
        A[I,J] = 4*B[I+1,J]/A[I,J]
        B[I,J] = 2*A[I,J-1]*B[I,J]
Endos
```

(a) Example with 1 Flow Dependence and 1 Anti-dependence.

(b) Execution Time vs Dependence Factor

for Different Values of $size_2$ (N1=N2=256).

**Figure 2. Importance of Flow and
Anti-Dependence in Partitioning.**

ure 2.a can be approximated to

$$size_1.C + \left(\left\lceil \frac{N_2}{size_1} \right\rceil - 1 \right).size_2.C + \left(\frac{N_2}{size_1} \right) size_1 . size_2 . E \quad (2)$$

where C is the communication time to send one data element from the source tile to the destination tile while E is the execution time of computing one iteration. Note that the first and second terms represent the communication time of respectively the anti- and flow dependence while the third term represents the computation time. In order to minimize (2), $size_2$ should be set to 1. However, this may require a target machine with a considerably large number of processors. As a result, the optimal dependence factor is given in terms of $size_2$. In this case, minimizing (2) is similar to minimizing the expression

$\left(size_1 + \frac{N_2}{df} - size_2 \right)$ which is equivalent to the expression

$$\left(df.size_2 + \frac{N_2}{df} - size_2 \right) \quad (3)$$

For $N_1 = N_2 = 256$, finding the minimum of (3) results in a $df = 16$ when $size_2 = 1$, $df = 11.3$ for $size_2 = 2$, and $df = 9.2$ for $size_2 = 3$. The plots in Figure 2.b show the execution time on the $MasPar^2$ vs the dependence factor for three different values of $size_2$. It can deduced from these plots that the execution time of the computed optimal dependence factors closely matches the actual optimal execution time (less than 1% difference). We can also conclude from Figure 2.b that ignoring anti-dependence (i.e $size_2 = 1$) when partitioning the iteration space could slow down the execution of the loop. In fact, the optimal execution time of the plot corresponding to $size_2 = 1$ is 10% slower than the optimal execution time of the curve corresponding to $size_2 = 2$. Finally, it can be deduced that the optimal dependence factor for different values of $size_2$ is usually high. As a result, flow dependence should be given more importance than anti-dependence in partitioning the iteration space of the example in Figure 3.a

3.3 Input dependence

An input dependence from iteration $\vec{i}$ to iteration $\vec{j}$ exists in an n-nested loop iff $\vec{i} \leq \vec{j}$ and $\vec{i}$ uses a variable that is also used in $\vec{j}$. If replication of data is allowed, then input dependence should be ignored while partitioning the iteration space because it does not limit parallelism nor does it add any communication overhead. On the other hand, if replication of data is prohibited, then input dependence introduces communication overhead if both iterations $\vec{i}$ and $\vec{j}$ are executed on different processors. In this case, input dependence vectors should be included in D'. Similarly to anti-dependence, input dependence should have a lesser weight than flow dependence when partitioning the iteration space.

---

2   The *MasPar MP-1* system is a massively parallel 2D mesh SIMD machine. The examples presented in this paper use the MPL language (which is an extended dialect for C on the *MasPar*) on a 8192 processing element machine.

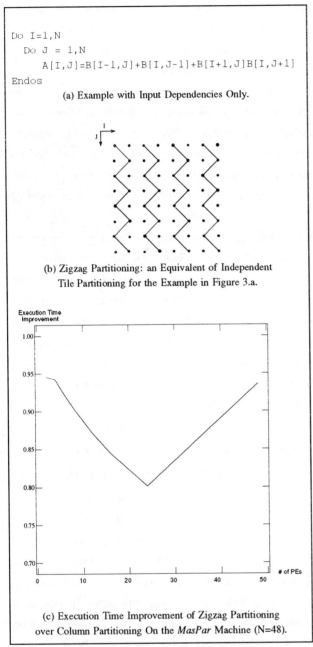

```
Do I=1,N
  Do J = 1,N
     A[I,J]=B[I-1,J]+B[I,J-1]+B[I+1,J]B[I,J+1]
Endos
```

(a) Example with Input Dependencies Only.

(b) Zigzag Partitioning: an Equivalent of Independent
Tile Partitioning for the Example in Figure 3.a.

(c) Execution Time Improvement of Zigzag Partitioning
over Column Partitioning On the *MasPar* Machine (N=48).

**Figure 3. Independent Tiles
Partitioning for Input Dependencies.**

We consider the example in Figure 3.a taken from [5]. There are 6 input dependences in the loopnest. If replication of data is allowed, then the loop can be fully executed in parallel without any communication overhead. If data replication is not permitted, then the partitioning matrix can be chosen to be $D = \begin{pmatrix} 1 & 1 \\ -1 & 1 \end{pmatrix}$. Note that the other four input dependences can be written as linear com-

bination of the vectors in D and therefore are not included in the partitioning matrix. We have $|\det(D)| = 2$. Hence, the iteration space is divided into 2 independent sets [8]. Each independent set is further partitioned into tiles as described in section 2. In [5], the proposed partitions are row, column, and block partitions which are all different from the one proposed here. In order to compare the performance of column partitioning and independent tile partitioning, the independent tile partitioning of the loopnest in Figure 3.a is done according to Figure 3.b (only one of the two independent sets is shown in the figure). This zigzag partitioning is chosen over the one represented in Figure 1 because it allows a more objective comparison between column partitioning and independent tiles partitioning. In fact, every process in both partitions have the same number of iterations (i.e a column is equivalent to a zigzag line).

Figure 3.c shows the execution time improvement of the zigzag partitioning vs the number of processors used. The y-axis represents the zigzag partitioning execution time divided by the column partitioning execution time. The figure shows that the execution time improvement due to zigzag partitioning varies between 6% and 20%. Note that the zigzag partitioning results in only half the communication needed by column partitioning. However, it requires a more complex code generation. It can be deduced from Figure 3.c that, on the *MasPar* machine, the benefits of reducing communication outweigh the disadvantages of complex code generation. We expect an even higher improvement for other distributed memory machines given that firstly the *MasPar* system has a low communication overhead and secondly the penalty of complex code generation is much higher for SIMD machines than it is for *MIMD* machines. Note that when the number of PEs used goes from 24 to 48, the execution time improvement decreases instead of continuing to increase. When $N = 48$, every column is executed on one processor, resulting in a quite simple code generation for column partitioning that cancels most of the execution time improvement of the zigzag partitioning due to reducing communication.

3.4 Output dependence

An output dependence from iteration $\vec{i}$ to iteration $\vec{j}$ exists in an n-nested loop iff $\vec{i} \leq \vec{j}$ and $\vec{i}$ defines a variable that is also defined in $\vec{j}$. We distinguish between two cases of output dependences:

1. Indirect output dependence: The output dependence is due to a combination of flow and/or anti-dependence (ex: $\vec{i} \stackrel{flow}{\rightarrow} \vec{j}$ because of variable a, $\vec{j} \stackrel{anti}{\rightarrow} \vec{k}$ because of the same variable a, then $\vec{i} \stackrel{output}{\rightarrow} \vec{k}$). In this case, the output dependence can be ignored when partitioning the iteration space since the other dependencies that caused it are included in D'.

2. Direct output dependence: A variable in a loop is defined in iteration $\vec{i}$, then defined again in a later iteration $\vec{j}$ without being used in any intermediate iteration between $\vec{i}$ and $\vec{j}$. Uniform dependences of this type are atypical in scientific programming and consequently are ignored.

3.5 Control dependence

A control dependence from iteration $\vec{i}$ to iteration $\vec{j}$ exists in an n-nested loop iff $\vec{i} \leq \vec{j}$ and $\vec{i}$ defines a variable that controls the execution of $\vec{j}$ or some code in $\vec{j}$. For simplicity, control dependence is considered as equivalent to flow dependence.

4 Iteration space partitioning: multiple loop case

In section 2, an efficient partitioning of single loopnests with uniform dependencies is presented. However, partitioning each loopnest in a program separately may not result in an efficient execution of the program, especially for multicomputers, where communication overhead due to across loop data dependence can be costly. In this section, a new method for partitioning the iteration space of a segment is presented, where a segment is defined to be an interval of code from the program with multiple loops (scalar code can be considered as a loop with a single iteration). Partitioning the iteration space of a segment into tiles of iterations and distributing the data

into the subsets is performed only once before the start of the segment execution and can not be redone inside the segment. Dividing a program into segments of code to minimize the overall execution of the program is beyond the scope of this paper and still to be investigated[3]. The notion of segment partitioning results in three issues that are addressed in this section before presenting segment partitioning: 1) forming the global iteration space for the segment, 2) across loops data dependence, and 3) mapping local indexes of each loop into the global iteration space.

4.1 Finding the domain

When every loopnest is considered separately, minimizing the execution time of every loopnest in a segment does not necessarily lead to an efficient execution of the segment because of communication across the loops. Therefore, a global iteration space for the segment called the segment domain needs to be found so that partitioning of iteration space and data distribution is done for the whole segment rather than for each loop separately.

For a segment with k loops, the corresponding domain is the union of the local iteration space of each loop considered separately: $IS = \bigcup_{i=1}^{k} IS_i$, where IS is the domain and IS_i is the iteration space of $loop_i$, the ith loopnest in the segment. The iteration space dimension of $loop_i$ is called dim_i. We define the iteration space dimension of a loop to be the number of indexes used in the subscripts of any array defined inside the loop. As an example, if $A[I, J]$ and $B[I, K]$ are the only arrays defined in a 3–nested loop, then the iteration space dimension of that loop is 3. However, If $A[I, J]$ (or $A[I, J, I]$) is the only array defined in a 3–nested loop, then the dimension of iteration space of that loop is 2.

Once dim_i is found, then IS_i is computed using the parameters (upper and lower limit, and the increment value) of the dim_i loops whose indexes are used in the subscript of any array defined in $loop_i$. In addition, the dimension of the domain Dim can be computed as be-

---

[3] In the meantime, a segment can be considered to include the whole program.

ing equal to $\max\limits_{i=1}^{k}(dim_i)$. Note that every iteration in the local iteration space of a loopnest should be mapped to one iteration in the domain. In order to keep the mapping function from IS_i to IS ($1 \leq i \leq k$) simple, the mapping is done on a dimension level. Initially, the dimensions of a loopnest are mapped lexically to the dimensions in the domain (i.e the jth dimension in IS_i is mapped to the jth dimension of IS). As an example, we consider the code in Figure 5.a. We have $IS_1 = [1..N_1] \times [1..N_2]$, $IS_2 = [3..N_3] \times [1..N_4 - 2]$, and therefore $IS = [1.. \max(N_1, N_3)] \times [1.. \max(N_2, N_4 - 2)]$. Note that the lexical mapping is only temporary since section 4.3 discusses remapping the dimensions of loopnests to decrease the cost of data dependencies in the program.

4.2 Across loop dependence

In the previous subsection, a domain (global iteration space) for the segment is computed. Given that one iteration from IS can include iterations from any IS_i, then across loop data dependence should also be found and be used in partitioning the domain.

Traditional data dependence analysis can be used firstly to investigate the existence of across loop dependencies, and secondly to identify their type by finding the direction vectors or the distance vector [2,12]. However, this is usually achieved for a dependence where both the source and destination are single iterations. In this subsection, a more general form of data dependence called hyperplane dependence is introduced. It is a dependence where the source and destination are subspaces of the iteration space. It should be noticed that data dependencies whose source or destination are subspaces of dimension larger than zero are common mainly across loops (two different loopnests as in Figure 4.a or across loops of a non-perfectly nested loop).

In an n-dimensional global iteration space, a hyperplane dependence is defined as a dependence from $(s(I_1, I_2, \cdots, I_m), s_{dir})$ to $(d(I_1, I_2, \cdots, I_m), d_{dir})$, where $s(I_1, I_2, \cdots, I_m)$ and $d(I_1, I_2, \cdots, I_m)$ are respectively the origins of the subspace source and des-

tination while $s_{dir} = (S_1, S_2, \cdots, S_s)$ and $d_{dir} = (D_1, D_2, \cdots, D_d)$ are the set of direction vectors (basis) that generate the subspace source and destination ($m \leq n$, $s \leq n$ and $d \leq n$). It should be noticed that a traditional uniform dependence corresponds to a hyperplane dependence, where $s_{dir} = d_{dir} = (\vec{0}, \vec{0} \cdots, \vec{0})$ and $d(I_1, I_2, \cdots, I_m) - s(I_1, I_2, \cdots, I_m)$ is a constant. An algorithm that identifies the source and destination of a hyperplane dependence is included in the full version of this paper [13].

4.3 Index mapping

Previously, index mapping was done lexically so that it could be used to compute the domain and find the across loop data dependencies. Given that the cost associated with these dependencies varies considerably depending on the hyperplane source and destination then an improvement over lexical index mapping should be investigated to reduce the overall cost of data dependence in the segment.

In fact, if the cost of a dependence is considered to be the communication cost generated by that dependence, then hyperplane data dependencies can be ranked in ascending order of their cost in the following way: 1) dependence whose hyperplane source is the same as the hyperplane destination 2) dependence with parallel hyperplane source and destination (but not equal) 3) Others. Note that this ranking only considers hyperplane data dependence with the same hyperplane source and destination size. An actual ranking of dependencies and their cost estimation depend on the available architecture, communication mechanism provided by the system, the size of hyperplane source and destination, and the direction vectors of the hyperplane source and destination. Finding the optimal mappings that minimize the overall cost of all dependencies in a program is an *NP-complete* problem. Heuristic approaches that obtain efficient mappings can be found in [7,13].

4.4 Segment partitioning

In previous partitioning methods such as supernode partitioning [6,10] and the independent tile partitioning presented in section 2, only uniform dependence distance vectors are used to partition the iteration space. In addition, iteration space partitioning is usually presented for single loopnests. However, determining an efficient partitioning for each loopnest separately does not guaranty an efficient execution of the segment of code especially for distributed memory machines, where across loop data dependence may result in a considerable communication cost. Other partitioning and data distribution methods that analyze the whole program such as the approaches in [1,5] are not general enough because only a few predetermined partitions (such as column, row, and block partitions) are allowed. With the introduction of hyperplane dependence in section 4.2 as a new form of expressing data dependencies, across loop as well as intra loop data dependence are used to partition the domain of a segment.

A traditional uniform dependence is represented by its distance vector. This vector is used in the partitioning by virtue of being included in the dependence matrix D'. However, a hyperplane dependence from $(s(I_1, I_2, \cdots, I_m), s_{dir})$ to $(d(I_1, I_2, \cdots, I_m), d_{dir})$ is represented by three vectors namely:

i. $O = d(I_1, I_2, \cdots, I_m) - s(I_1, I_2, \cdots, I_m)$, the distance vector between the subspace destination origin and subspace source origin.

ii. $s_{dir} = (S_1, S_2, \cdots, S_s)$, the set of direction vectors of the subspace source.

iii. $d_{dir} = (D_1, D_2, \cdots, D_d)$, the set of direction vectors of the subspace destination.

Among the vectors $(O, S_1, S_2, \cdots, S_s, D_1, D_2, \cdots, D_d)$, only the uniform ones should be used when partitioning the iteration space and are therefore included in the dependence matrix D'. Note that the partitioning vectors due to an across loop dependence should be given less weight than the partitioning vectors of an intra loop dependence because the latter dependence limits parallelism more than the former.

In the remaining of this section, two examples are considered to show the benefits of identifying hyperplane data dependencies on partitioning the global space. The matrix multiplication code of Figure 4.a is investigated first. Without hyperplane dependence analysis, partitioning methods in [6,10,14] may use a column partition, a row partition, or any other partition given that no traditional uniform dependence can be found in both loopnests of the example. However, with hyperplane dependence analysis, two hyperplane dependencies can be recognized. The one from S_1 to S_3 is a dependence from $((I, 0), ((0, 1)))$ to $((I, 0), ((0, 1)))$ while the other, from S_2 to S_3, is a dependence from $((0, J), ((1, 0)))$ to $((0, J), ((1, 0)))$. As a result, the vectors $(0, 1)$ and $(1, 0)$ are used to guide the partitioning process. Note that the O vector for both dependences is the zero vector and hence is ignored. We have $D = D' = \begin{pmatrix} 0 & 1 \\ 1 & 0 \end{pmatrix}$. Partitioning the iteration space according to D using independent tile partitioning (which is equivalent to supernode partitioning [6,10] in this case) leads to a block partitioning.

Figure 4.b shows the execution time on the *MasPar* machine versus the machine size for block partitioning as well as column partitioning for the code in Figure 4.a. The plots clearly indicate that block partitioning is superior to column partitioning especially when a large number of PEs are used (ex. for 48 PEs, the execution time of the code using a block partition is 3 times faster than the one using a column partition). Given the low communication cost on the *MasPar*, we would expect an even better improvement on distributed memory *MIMD* machines, where communication overhead is usually expensive. In fact, for an N^2 iteration space and p PEs available ($\sqrt{p}$ is assumed to be an integer), the execution of the code in Figure 4.a using block partitioning results in every PE receiving data of size N^2/p elements (N^2/p is also assumed to be an integer) from $2(\sqrt{p} - 1)$ different PEs. On the other hand, in column partitioning execution, every PE receives data of size N^2/p from $p - 1$ PEs. Given that $2(\sqrt{p} - 1)$ is much smaller than $p - 1$ (especially for large p), then block partitioning outperforms column partitioning for the code in Figure 4.a.

The second example of this section can be found in Figure 5.a, where two hyperplane dependences exist in the

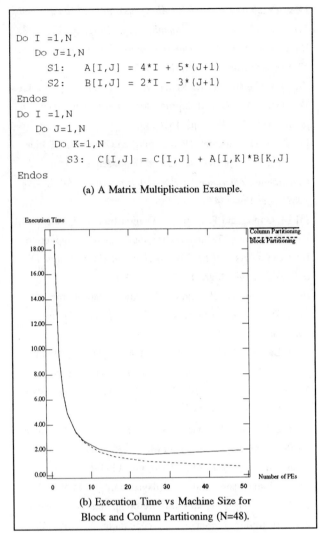

```
Do I =1,N
  Do J=1,N
    S1:   A[I,J] = 4*I + 5*(J+1)
    S2:   B[I,J] = 2*I - 3*(J+1)
Endos
Do I =1,N
  Do J=1,N
    Do K=1,N
      S3:  C[I,J] = C[I,J] + A[I,K]*B[K,J]
Endos
```

(a) A Matrix Multiplication Example.

(b) Execution Time vs Machine Size for
Block and Column Partitioning (N=48).

**Figure 4. Benefits of Using Hyperplane
Dependence information on Partitioning.**

code. The dependence from S_1 to S_4 is a dependence from $((I-2,0),((0,1)))$ to $((I,0),((0,1)))$ while the one from S_2 to S_4 is a dependence from $((I+2,0),((0,1)))$ to $((I,0),((0,1)))$. Hence, the first dependence is represented by the vectors $(2,0)$ and $(0,1)$ while the second dependence is represented by the vectors $(-2,0)$ and $(0,1)$. This results in a partitioning matrix D equal to $\begin{pmatrix} 2 & 0 \\ 0 & 1 \end{pmatrix}$. Figure 5.b shows independent tile partitioning for the above partitioning matrix D when $size_1 = 2$ and $size_2 = 3$. Note that the partitioning of only one of the two independent sets is shown in the figure. Figure 5.c shows the execution time of the segment on the *MasPar*

machine vs the dependence factor, where the dependence factor df is again defined to be equal to $\frac{size_1}{size_2}$. The first two plots in Figure 5.c respectively shows the dependence factor when $size_2 = 1$ and $size_2 = 2$. The latter plot lies entirely above the former one. As a result, the plot with $size_2 = 1$ should be used to determine the size of the optimal partition provided that enough processors are available. For a smaller machine size, another appropriate value of $size_2$ should be used.

The third plot in Figure 5.c shows the block partition (i.e $D = \begin{pmatrix} 1 & 0 \\ 0 & 1 \end{pmatrix}$) execution time when $size_2 = 2$. This partition is selected to compare its performance with independent tiles partitioning given that it is one of the popular predetermined partitions allowed by parallelizing compilers [1,5]. It can be deduced from the second and third plot that independent tile partitioning along with across loop dependence analysis outperforms block partitioning for the example in Figure 5.a. The improvement of our method is between 30% and 40% when a large number of processors are used. Both plots get closer to each other when smaller number of processors are used because, in that case, the execution time is dominated by the computation part which is the same for both methods.

5 Conclusion   In this paper, an efficient multicomputer partitioning of the iteration space of single loops with uniform dependences is presented. Because of across loop data dependences, finding the best partition for each loop separately is not sufficient. In our approach, a global iteration space for a segment of code is formed so that the partitioning is performed for the global space using traditional uniform dependencies as well as hyperplane data dependencies. This has been made possible by the new expression of dependences as hyperplane data dependencies. Current work includes heuristically dividing a program into segments of code so that the overall execution time of the program is minimized.

References

[1] V. Balasundaram, G. Fox, K. Kennedy, and U. Kremer. A Static Performance Estimator to Guide Data Partitioning

```
Do I =1,N1
   Do J=1,N2
      S1:   A[I,J] = ......
      S2:   B[I,J] = ......
      S3:   C[I,J] = ......
Endos
Do I =3,N3
  Do J=1,N4-2
    temp = C[I,J]
    Do K=1,N5
S4 :  C[I,J] = C[I,J]+temp/(A[I-2,K]*B[I+2,K])
Endos
```

(a) Example with Two Hyperplane Dependencies.

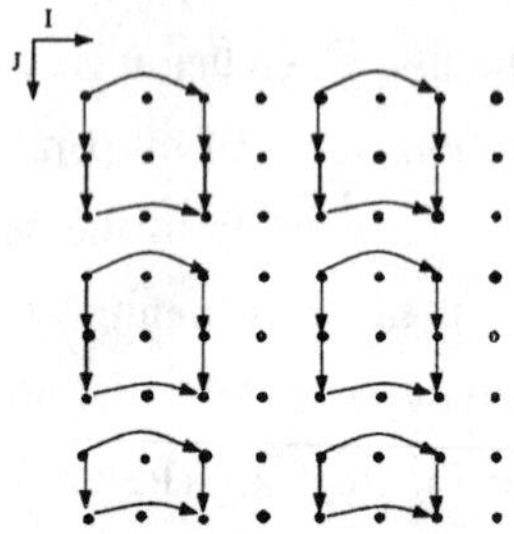

(b) Independent Tile Partitioning for the Segment in (a).

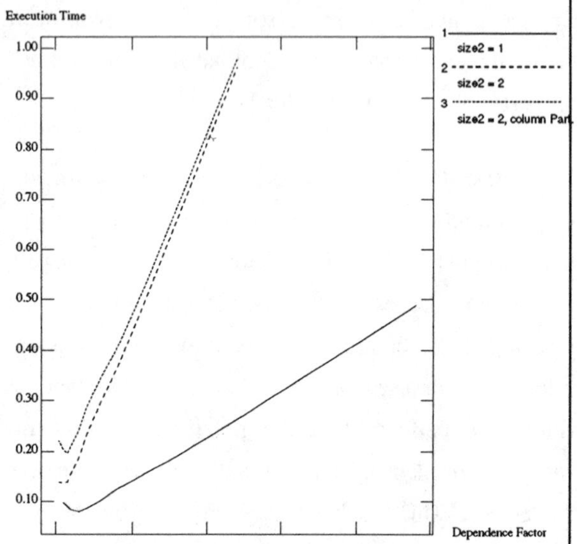

(c) Execution Time vs Dependence Factor for the

Partitioning in Figure 5.b (N1=N2=...=N5=48).

Figure 5. Independent Tile Partitioning
Using Hyperplane Dependence Information.

Decisions. *Third ACM SIGPLAN Symposium on Principle and Practices of Parallel Programming*, Apr. 1991, pp. 213–223.

[2] U. Banerjee. *Dependence Analysis for Supercomputing*, Kluwer Academic, Boston, Mass. 1988.

[3] D. Callahan, and K. Kennedy. Compiling Programs for Distributed Memory Multiprocessors. *Journal of Supercomputing, Vol., 2*, 1989, pp. 151–169.

[4] E. H. D'Hollander. Partitioning and Labeling of Index Sets in Do Loops with Constant Dependence Vectors. *International Conference on Parallel Processing, Vol 2*, Aug. 1989, pp. 139–144.

[5] M. Gupta, and P. Banerjee, Demonstration of Automatic Data Partitioning Techniques for Parallelizing Compilers on Multicomputers. *IEEE Transactions on Parallel and Distributed Systems*, Mar. 1992, pp. 179–193.

[6] F. Irigoin, and R. Triolet. Supernode Partitioning. *15th ACM Symposium on Principles of Programming Languages*, 1988, pp. 319–329.

[7] J. Li, and M. Chen. Index Domain Alignment: Minimizing Cost of Cross-Reference Between Distributed Arrays. *3rd Symposium on Frontiers of Massively Parallel Computation*, Oct. 1991, pp. 424–433.

[8] J.K. Peir, and R. Cytron. Minimum Distance: A Method for Partitioning Recurrences for Multiprocessors. *IEEE Transaction on Computers*, Aug. 1990, pp. 1203–1211.

[9] J. Ramanujam, and P. Sadayappan. A Methodology for Parallelizing Programs for Multiomputers and Complex Memory Multiprocessors. *Supercomputing 89*, Nov. 1989, pp. 637–646.

[10] J. Ramanujam, and P. Sadayappan. Tiling of Iteration Spaces for Multicomputers. *International Conference on Parallel Processing, Vol 2*, Aug. 1990, pp. 179–186.

[11] Z. Shen, Z. Li, and P.C. Yew. An Empirical Study on Array Subscripts and Data Dependencies. *International Conference on Parallel Processing, Vol 2*, Aug. 1989, pp. 145–152.

[12] M.J. Wolfe. *Optimizing Supercompliers for supercomputers*, MIT Press, Cambridge, Mass. 1989.

[13] A. Zaafrani, M.R. Ito. Expressing Across Loop Dependencies through Hyperplane Data Dependence Analysis. *Technical Report*, University of British Columbia, July 1993.

[14] A. Zaafrani, M. R. Ito. Transformation of Doacross Loops on Distributed Memory Systems. *International Parallel Processing Symposium*, Apr. 1993, pp. 824–829.

Session 5:
Data Parallel Compilers
Chair: Ray Cline

Preliminary Experiences with the Fortran D Compiler

Seema Hiranandani
seema@cs.rice.edu

Ken Kennedy
ken@cs.rice.edu

Chau-Wen Tseng
tseng@cs.stanford.edu

Department of Computer Science
Rice University
Houston, TX 77251-1892

Center for Integrated Systems
Stanford University
Stanford, CA 94305

Abstract

Fortran D is a version of Fortran enhanced with data decomposition specifications. Case studies illustrate strengths and weaknesses of the prototype Fortran D compiler when compiling linear algebra codes and whole programs. Statement groups, execution conditions, inter-loop communication optimizations, multi-reductions, and array kills for replicated arrays are identified as new compilation issues. On the Intel iPSC/860, the output of the prototype Fortran D compiler approaches the performance of hand-optimized code for parallel computations, but needs improvement for linear algebra and pipelined codes. The Fortran D compiler outperforms the CM Fortran compiler (2.1 *beta*) by a factor of four or more on the TMC CM-5 when not using vector units. Better analysis, run-time support, and flexibility are required for the prototype compiler to be useful for a wider range of programs.

1 Introduction

Fortran D is an enhanced version of Fortran that allows the user to specify how data may be partitioned onto processors. It was inspired by the observation that modern high-performance architectures demand that careful attention be paid to data placement by both the programmer and compiler. Fortran D is designed to provide a simple yet efficient machine-independent data-parallel programming model, shifting the burden of optimizations to the compiler. It has contributed to the development of High Performance Fortran (HPF), an informal Fortran standard adopted by researchers and vendors for programming massively-parallel processors [15].

The success of HPF hinges on the development of compilers that can provide performance satisfactory to users. The goal of our research is to identify important compilation issues and explore possible solutions. Previous work has described the design and implementation of a prototype Fortran D compiler for regular dense-matrix computations [13, 16, 17]. This paper describes our preliminary experiences with that compiler. Its major contributions include 1) advanced compilation techniques needed for complex loop nests, 2) empirical evaluation of the prototype Fortran D compiler, and 3) identifying necessary improvements for the compiler.

In the remainder of this paper, we briefly introduce the Fortran D language and compiler, then use case studies to illustrate a number of compilation problems and their solutions. We describe experiments comparing the compiler against hand-optimized codes and the CM Fortran compiler. Results are evaluated and used to point out directions for future research. We conclude with a comparison with related work.

2 Background

2.1 Fortran D Language and Compilation

In Fortran D, the DECOMPOSITION statement declares an abstract problem or index domain. The ALIGN statement maps each array element onto the decomposition. The DISTRIBUTE statement groups elements of the decomposition and aligned arrays, mapping them to a parallel machine. Each dimension is distributed in a block, cyclic, or block-cyclic manner; the symbol ":" marks dimensions that are not distributed. Alignment and distribution statements can be executed, permitting dynamic data decomposition. Details of the language are presented elsewhere [10].

Given a data decomposition, the Fortran D compiler automatically translates sequential programs into efficient parallel programs. The two major steps in compiling for MIMD distributed-memory machines are partitioning the data and computation across processors, then introducing communication for nonlocal accesses where needed. The compiler partitions computation across processors using the "owner computes" rule—where each processor only computes values of data it owns [6, 12, 25]. It performs a large number of communication and parallelism optimizations based on data dependence. Details of the compilation process are presented elsewhere [13, 16, 17, 27].

2.2 Prototype Compiler

The prototype Fortran D compiler is implemented as a source-to-source Fortran translator in the context of the ParaScope parallel programming environment [9]. It utilizes existing tools for performing dependence analysis, program transformations, and interprocedural analysis. The current implementation supports:

- inter-dimensional alignments
- 1D BLOCK and CYCLIC distributions
- loop interchange, fusion, distribution, strip-mining
- message vectorization, coalescing, aggregation
- vector message pipelining, unbuffered messages
- broadcasts, collective communications
- SUM, PROD, MIN, MAX, MINLOC, MAXLOC reductions
- fine-grain and coarse-grain pipelining (granularity specified by user via compile-time flag)
- relax "owner computes" rule for reductions, private variables
- nonlocal storage in overlaps & buffers

This research was supported by the Center for Research on Parallel Computation (CRPC), a Science and Technology Center funded by NSF through Cooperative Agreement Number CCR-9120008. This work was also sponsored by DARPA under contract #DABT63-91-K-0005 & DABT63-92-C-0038, the state of Texas under contract #1059, and the Keck Foundation.

338

- loop bounds reduction, guard introduction
- global ↔ local index conversion
- interprocedural reaching decompositions & overlaps
- common blocks
- I/O (performed by processor 0)
- generation of calls to the Intel NX/2 and TMC CMMD message-passing libraries

The prototype compiler accepts a subset of Fortran D. Alignment offsets, multidimensional distributions, and dynamic data decomposition are not yet supported. For simplicity, the prototype compiler requires that all array sizes, loop bounds, and number of processors in the target machine be compile-time constants (though triangular loops are supported). All subscripts must also be of the form c or $i + c$, where c is a compile-time constant and i is a loop index variable. These restrictions are not due to limitations of our compilation techniques, but reflect the immaturity of the prototype compiler and our focus on exploring research directions, especially compile-time optimizations.

3 Compilation Case Studies

Examples in previous work mostly dealt with individual stencil computation kernels from iterative solvers for partial differential equations (PDE). In this section, we illustrate the Fortran D compilation process for linear algebra kernels and larger codes. We point out strengths and weaknesses of the prototype compiler using case studies of four example programs and subroutines: SHALLOW, DISPER, DGEFA, and ERLEBACHER. We find that the Fortran D compiler needs to:

- Provide robust translation of global/local loop bounds and index variables. Reindex accesses into temporary buffers.
- Partition computation in complex non-uniform loop bodies across processors, using statement groups to guide loop bounds & index variable generation. Apply loop distribution and guard generation as needed.
- Compile loop nests containing execution conditions that may affect the iteration space.
- Exploit pipeline parallelism, perform inter-loop communication optimizations.
- Parallelize multidimensional reductions and multi-reductions. Use array kill analysis to eliminate communication for multi-reductions performed by replicated array variables.

3.1 SHALLOW

We begin with SHALLOW, a 200 line benchmark weather prediction program written by Paul Swarztrauber, National Center for Atmospheric Research (NCAR). It is a stencil computation that applies finite-difference methods to solve shallow-water equations. SHALLOW is representative of a large class of existing supercomputer applications. The computation is highly data-parallel and well-suited for MIMD distributed-memory machines.

Figure 1 outlines the version of SHALLOW we used to test the Fortran D compiler; it was modified to eliminate I/O. Data can be partitioned quite simply by aligning all 2D arrays identically, then distributing the second dimension block-wise, resulting in a block of columns being assigned to each processor. The prototype Fortran D compiler was able to generate message-passing code fairly simply. The principal issues encountered during compilation were boundary conditions, loop distribution, and inter-loop communication optimizations.

```
{* Original Fortran D Program *}
PROGRAM SHALLOW
  REAL u(n,n),v(n,n),p(n,n)
  REAL unew(n,n),pnew(n,n),vnew(n,n)
  REAL psi(n,n),pold(n,n),uold(n,n),vold(n,n)
  REAL cu(n,n),cv(n,n),z(n,n),h(n,n)
  DECOMPOSITION d(n,n)
  ALIGN u,v,p,unew,pnew,vnew,psi WITH d
  ALIGN pold,uold,vold,cu,cv,z,h WITH d
  DISTRIBUTE d(:,BLOCK)
  {* initial values of the stream function & velocities *}
  do j = 1,n-1
    do i = 1,n-1
      u(i+1,j) = -(psi(i+1,j+1)-psi(i+1,j))*dy
      v(i,j+1) = (psi(i+1,j+1)-psi(i,j+1))*dx
  do k = 1,Time
    {* periodic continuation *}
    ...
    {* compute capital u, capital v, z, and h *}
    do j = 1,n-1
      do i = 1,n-1
        cu(i+1,j) = 0.5*(p(i+1,j)+p(i,j))*u(i+1,j)
        cv(i,j+1) = 0.5*(p(i,j+1)+p(i,j))*v(i,j+1)
        z(i+1,j+1) = (fsdx*(v(i+1,j+1)-v(i,j+1))-fsdy
          * (u(i+1,j+1)-u(i+1,j))) / (p(i,j)+p(i+1,j)
          + p(i+1,j+1)+p(i,j+1))
        h(i,j) = p(i,j)+.25*(u(i+1,j)*u(i+1,j)+u(i,j)
          * u(i,j)+v(i,j+1)*v(i,j+1)+v(i,j)*v(i,j))
    {* periodic continuation *}
    ...
    {* compute new values u, v, and p *}
    do j = 1,n-1
      do i = 1,n-1
        unew(i+1,j) = uold(i+1,j)+tdts8*(z(i+1,j+1)+z(i+1,j))
          * (cv(i+1,j+1)+cv(i,j+1)+cv(i,j)+cv(i+1,j))
          - tdtsdx*(h(i+1,j)-h(i,j))
        vnew(i,j+1) = vold(i,j+1)-tdts8*(z(i+1,j+1)+z(i,j+1))
          * (cu(i+1,j+1)+cu(i,j+1)+cu(i,j)+cu(i+1,j))
          - tdtsdy*(h(i,j+1)-h(i,j))
        pnew(i,j) = pold(i,j)-tdtsdx*(cu(i+1,j)-cu(i,j))
          - tdtsdy*(cv(i,j+1)-cv(i,j))
end
```

Figure 1: SHALLOW: Weather Prediction Benchmark

3.1.1 Statement Groups

We begin by describing a useful construct called *statement groups*. Realistic programs and linear algebra codes tend to possess large diverse loop nests, with many imperfectly nested statements and triangular/trapezoidal loops. These complex loops increase the difficulty of partitioning the computation and calculating appropriate local and global loop indices and bounds. The Fortran D compiler uses *iteration sets* to represent the set of loop iterations that will be executed by each processor; they are calculated for each statement using the owner computes rule during partitioning analysis. The partition is later instantiated by modifying loop bounds to the union of all iteration sets of statements in a loop, then inserting explicit guards for statements that are executed only on a subset of those iterations.

To aid this process, we found it useful in the Fortran D compiler to partition statements into *statement groups* during partitioning analysis. Statements are put into the same group for a given loop if their iteration sets for that loop and enclosing loops are the same. We mark a loop as *uniform* if all its statements belong to the same statement group. Uniform loop nests are desirable because they may be partitioned by reducing loop bounds; explicit guards do not need to be inserted in the loop. Calculating statement groups can determine whether a loop nest is uniform and guide code generation for non-uniform loops.

One use of statement groups is to guide guard generation. For instance, consider the example in Figure 2. As-

```
      {* Fortran D Program *}    {* Iteration Sets *}
      DISTRIBUTE a(BLOCK)
      do i = 1,n                 [ 1 : n ]
S₁      a(i) = ...               [ 1 : n/P ]
S₂      if (...)                 [ 1 : n/P ]
S₃        a(i) = ...             [ 1 : n/P ]
S₄      a(i-1) = ...             [ 2 : (n/P) + 1 ]
S₅      t = ...                  [ 1 : n ]
      enddo
```

Figure 2: Example: Statement Groups

sume that array a is distributed block-wise across P processors. During partitioning analysis, iteration sets are calculated for each statement. According to the owner computes rule each processor executes the assignment at S_1 only on the $[1 : n/P]$ iterations that assign to local data. The same iteration set is assigned to S_3 and then to S_2 since it encloses only S_3. Because these three statements have the same iteration set, they are placed in the same statement group. S_4 receives a slightly different iteration set, and S_5 is assigned all iterations. The i loop is marked as nonuniform because it encloses statements with different iteration setS, then is assigned the union of the iteration sets for S_1–S_5. During code generation, guards will be generated for the first and second statement groups since they are not executed by all processors on local loop iterations.

3.1.2 Boundary Conditions

SHALLOW contains many code fragments solving boundary conditions for periodic continuations. As a result, the Fortran D compiler needed to insert explicit guards for many statement groups. These boundary conditions also require the creation of several individual point-to-point messages between boundary processors to transfer data required. Putting statements into groups can reduce the number of guards inserted, since all statements in a group share the same guard.

3.1.3 Loop Distribution

Another application of statement groups is to guide *loop distribution*, a program transformation that separates independent statements inside a single loop into multiple loops with identical headers. If the Fortran D compiler detects a non-uniform loop nest, it attempts to distribute the loop around each statement group, producing smaller uniform loop nests. If loop distribution is prevented due to recurrences carried by the loop, the Fortran D compiler must insert explicit guards for each statement group to ensure they are executed only by the appropriate processor(s) on each loop iteration.

Because of the programming style used in writing SHALLOW, almost all loop nests were non-uniform, *i.e.*, contained statements with differing iteration sets. Fortunately, none of the loops carried recurrences, so the Fortran D compiler applies loop distribution to separate statements, creating uniform loop nests. Loop bounds reduction is then sufficient to partition the computation during code generation, except for additional boundary conditions.

3.1.4 Inter-loop Communication Optimizations

While loop distribution enables inexpensive partitioning of the program computation, it has the disadvantage of creating a large number of loop nests. In many cases these loop nests, along with loops representing boundary conditions, required communication with neighboring processors. The prototype Fortran D compiler applies message coalescing

```
{* Original Fortran D Program *}
SUBROUTINE DISPER
   LOGICAL lsat(256)
   DOUBLE PRECISION ddx(256,8,8),ddy(256,8,8)
   DOUBLE PRECISION ddz(256,8,8),pmfr(256,8,8,4,5)
   DOUBLE PRECISION gradx(256),grady(256),gradz(256)
   DECOMPOSITION d(256)
   ALIGN ddx(i,j,k),ddy(i,j,k),ddz(i,j,k) WITH d(i)
   ALIGN lsat(i,j,k,l),pmfr(i,j,k,l,m) WITH d(i)
   ALIGN gradz,grady,gradz WITH d
   DISTRIBUTE d(BLOCK)
   {* compute dispersion terms *}
   do j = 2,4
     do i3 = 1,8
       do i2 = 1,8
         do i1 = 1,256
S₁         if ((i1 .NE. 1) .AND. (i1 .NE. 256)) then
S₂           if (lsat(i1-1,i2,i3,j).AND.lsat(i1+1,i2,i3,j)) then
S₃             grady(i1) = (pmfr(i1+1,i2,i3,j,k)
               - pmfr(i1-1,i2,i3,j,k)) / (0.5*(ddy(i1+1,i2,i3)
               + ddy(i1-1,i2,i3)) + ddy(i1,i2,i3))
               ...
           endif
         endif
         ...
end
```

Figure 3: DISPER: Oil Reservoir Simulation

and aggregation only within a single loop nest. Its output for SHALLOW thus missed many opportunities to combine messages because the nonlocal references were located in loop nests not enclosed by a common loop. By applying message coalescing and aggregation manually across loop nests, we were able to eliminate about half of all calls to communication routines.

3.2 DISPER

DISPER is a 1000 line subroutine for computing dispersion terms. It is taken from UTCOMP, a 33,000 line oil reservoir simulator developed at the University of Texas at Austin. Like SHALLOW, DISPER is a stencil computation that is highly data-parallel and well-suited for the Fortran D compiler. Unfortunately, UTCOMP was originally written for a Cray vector machine. Arrays were linearized to ensure long vector lengths, then addressed through complex subscript expressions and indirection arrays. This style of programming, while efficient for vector machines, does not lend itself to massively-parallel processors.

To explore whether UTCOMP can be written in a machine-independent programming style using Fortran D or HPF, researchers at Rice rewrote DISPER to have regular accesses and simple subscripts in multidimensional arrays [20]. Figure 3 shows a fragment of the rewritten form of DISPER. Its main arrays have differing sizes and dimensionality, but have the same size in the first dimension. Arrays were aligned along the first dimension and distributed block-wise. The resulting code was was for the most part compiled successfully by the prototype Fortran D compiler.

3.2.1 Execution Conditions

The major difficulty encountered by the Fortran D compiler was the existence of execution conditions caused by explicit guards in the input code. There are two types of execution conditions. Data-dependent execution conditions, such as the guard at S_2 in Figure 3, were not a problem. Message vectorization moves communication caused by such guarded statements out of the enclosing loops. Overcommunication may result if the statement is not executed, but the resulting code is still much more efficient than sending individual messages after evaluating each guard.

Execution conditions that reshape the iteration space, on the other hand, pose a different problem. For instance, the guard at S_1 in Figure 3 restricts the execution of statement S_3 on the first and last iteration of loop $i1$. It has in effect changed the iteration set for the assignment S_3, causing it to be executed on a subset of the iterations. These guards are frequently used by programmers to isolate boundary conditions in a modular manner, avoiding the need to peel off loop iterations.

Unlike data-dependent execution conditions, these execution conditions always hold and can be detected at compile-time. If they are not considered, the compiler will generate communication for nonlocal accesses that never occur. Future versions of the Fortran D compiler will need to examine guard expressions. If its effects on the iteration set can be determined at compile-time, the iteration set of the guarded statements must be modified appropriately. Because this functionality is not present in the prototype Fortran D compiler, unnecessary guards and communication in the compiler output were corrected by hand.

3.3 DGEFA

DGEFA, written by Jack Dongarra *et al.* at Argonne National Laboratory, is a key subroutine in LINPACK and the principal computation kernel in the LINPACKD benchmark program. DGEFA performs LU decomposition through Gaussian elimination with partial pivoting. Its memory access patterns are quite different from stencil computations, and is representative of linear algebra computations. As many linear algebra algorithms involve factoring matrices, CYCLIC and BLOCK_CYCLIC data distributions are desirable for maintaining good load balance. These distributions and the prevalence of triangular loop nests pose additional challenges to the Fortran D compiler.

Figure 4 shows the original program, Figure 5 shows the output produced by the prototype Fortran D compiler. For good load balance we choose a column-cyclic distribution, scattering array columns round-robin across processors. The Fortran D compiler then uses this data decomposition to derive the computation partition. Two important steps are generating proper loop bounds & indices and indexing accesses into temporary messages buffers [27]. In addition, we found using statement groups to guide guard generation and identifying MAX/MAXLOC reductions to be necessary.

3.3.1 Guard Generation

DGEFA also demonstrates how statement groups may be used to guide guard generation. During compilation, the Fortran D compiler partitions the statements of the loop body into five statement groups. In Figure 4, the first statement group (S_1–S_4) finds the pivot, and is executed by one processor per iteration of the k loop. The second group is the statement S_5, an assignment to a replicated array that is executed by all processors.

The third statement group (S_6–S_7) calculates multipliers. Analysis shows that like the first group, it is executed by only one processor on each iteration of the k loop. The fourth group (S_8–S_9) calculates the remaining submatrix. Iterations of the inner j loop are partitioned, but all processors execute at least some iterations of j on each k loop iteration (except for boundary conditions). The fifth and final group (S_{10}) is another assignment to a replicated array that is executed by all processors.

Because loop k contains a variety of iteration sets, it is non-uniform. Its iterations are executed by all processors, and explicit guards are introduced for the first and third

statement groups. Note that the third and fourth statement groups contain assignments to t, a replicated scalar. However, the Fortran D compiler determines that t is a private variable with respect to the k loop. With additional analysis, the compiler discovers that it does not need to replicate the assignment on all processors [16].

3.3.2 MINLOC/MAXLOC Reductions

Putting statements S_1 through S_4 in the same statement group requires detecting it as a reduction. The Fortran D compiler recognizes reductions through simple pattern matching. It finds the MAX/MAXLOC reduction in DGEFA by detecting that the *lhs* of an assignment *al* at statement S_3 is being compared against its *rhs* in an enclosing IF statement. The level of the reduction is set to the k loop, since it is the deepest loop enclosing uses of *al*. The reduction is thus carried out by the i loop, which only examines a single column of a. Since array a has been distributed by columns, the reduction may be computed locally by the processor owning the column. The Fortran D compiler inserts a guard to ensure the reduction is performed by the processor owning column k, then broadcasts the result. This example also demonstrates how the compiler relaxes the owner computes rule for reductions and private variables.

For MIN/MAX and MINLOC/MAXLOC reductions, the Fortran D compiler must also search for initialization statements for the *lhs* of assignment statements in the k loop, assigning them the same iteration set as the body of the reduction. Statements S_1 and S_2 are identified as initialization statements for the MAX/MAXLOC reduction at S_3. By putting them in the same statement group as the reduction, the Fortran D compiler avoids inserting an additional broadcast to update the value of *al* at S_2.

3.4 ERLEBACHER

ERLEBACHER is a 13 procedure, 800 line benchmark program written by Thomas Eidson at the Institute for Computer Applications in Science and Engineering (ICASE). It performs 3D tridiagonal solves using Alternating-Direction-Implicit (ADI) integration. Like Jacobi iteration and Successive-Over-Relaxation (SOR), ADI integration is a technique frequently used to solve PDEs. However, it performs vectorized tridiagonal solves in each dimension, resulting in computation wavefronts across all three dimensions of the data array.

Each sweep in ERLEBACHER consists of a computation phase followed by a forward and backward substitution phase. Figures 6 and 7 illustrate the core computation and substitution phases in the Z dimension. We chose to distribute the Z dimension of all 3D arrays blockwise; all 1D and 2D arrays are replicated. Here we relate some issues that arose during compilation of Erlebacher to a machine with four processors, $P_0 \ldots P_3$.

3.4.1 Overlapping Communication

In ERLEBACHER, we discovered unexpected benefits for vector message pipelining, an optimization that separates matching *send* and *recv* statements to create opportunities for overlapping communication with computation [17]. Consider the computation in the Z dimension, shown in Figure 6. The Fortran D compiler first distributes the loops enclosing statements S_1–S_4 because they belong to two distinct statement groups. Message vectorization then extracts all communication outside of each loop nest.

Finally, the Fortran D compiler applies vector message pipelining. It is particularly effective here because it moves

```
{* Original Fortran D Program *}
SUBROUTINE DGEFA(n,a,ipvt)
  INTEGER n,ipvt(n),j,k,l
  DOUBLE PRECISION a(n,n),al,t
  DISTRIBUTE a(:,CYCLIC)
  do k = 1, n-1
    {* Find max element in a(k:n,k) *}
S1    l = k
S2    al = dabs(a(k, k))
      do i = k + 1, n
        if (dabs(a(i, k)) .GT. al) then
S3        al = dabs(a(i, k))
S4        l = i
        endif
      enddo
S5    ipvt(k) = l
      if (al .NE. 0) then
S6      if (l .NE. k) then
          t = a(l, k)
          a(l, k) = a(k, k)
          a(k, k) = t
        endif
        {* Compute multipliers in a(k+1:n,k) *}
        t = -1.0d0 / a(k, k)
        do i = k+1, n
          a(i, k) = a(i, k) * t
S7      enddo
        {* Reduce remaining submatrix *}
S8      do j = k+1, n
          t = a(l, j)
          if (l .NE. k) then
            a(l, j) = a(k, j)
            a(k, j) = t
          endif
          do i = k+1, n
            a(i, j) = a(i, j) + t * a(i, k)
          enddo
S9      enddo
      endif
    enddo
S10 ipvt(n) = n
  end
```

Figure 4: DGEFA: Gaussian Elimination with Pivoting

the *send* C_3 and C_4 before the *recv* in the first two loop nests. If C_3 and C_4 are left in their original positions before S_5, the computation will be idle until two message transfers complete, because the boundary processors P_0 and P_3 will need to first exchange messages before communicating to the interior processors. The prototype thus saved the cost of waiting for an entire message. More advanced analysis could determine that the statements S_1–S_4 are simply incarnations of statement S_5 created to handle periodic boundary conditions. We can perform the reverse of *index set splitting* and merge the loop bodies to simplify the resulting code.

3.4.2 Multi-Reductions

Another problem faced by the Fortran D compiler was handling reductions on replicated variables. A multidimensional reduction performs a reduction on multiple dimensions of an array. Finding the maximum value in a 3D array would be a 3D MAX reduction over an n^3 data set. We examine a special case of multidimensional reduction that we call a *multi-reduction*, where the program performs multiple reductions simultaneously. For instance, finding the maximum value of each column in a 3D array would be a 2D MAX multi-reduction composed of n^2 1D MAX reductions. Unlike normal multidimensional reductions, multi-reductions are directional in that they only transfer data across certain dimensions. This property allows the compiler to determine when communication is necessary. It also allows the problem to be partitioned in other dimensions so that no communication is required.

```
{* Compiler Output for 4 Processors *}
SUBROUTINE DGEFA(n,a,ipvt)
  INTEGER n,ipvt(n),j,k,l
  DOUBLE PRECISION a(n,n/4),al,t,dp$buf1(n)
  do k = 1, n-1
    k$ = ((k - 1) / 4) + 1
    {* Find max element in a(k:n,k$) *}
    if (my$p .EQ. MOD(k - 1, 4)) then
      l = k
      al = dabs(a(k, k$))
      do i = k + 1, n
        if (dabs(a(i, k$)) .GT. al) then
          al = dabs(a(i, k$))
          l = i
        endif
      enddo
      broadcast l, al
    else
      recv l, al
    endif
    ipvt(k) = l
    if (al .NE. 0) then
      if (my$p .EQ. MOD(k - 1, 4)) then
        if (l .NE. k) then
          t = a(l, k$)
          a(l, k$) = a(k, k$)
          a(k, k$) = t
        endif
        {* Compute multipliers in a(k+1:n,k$) *}
        t = -1.0d0 / a(k, k$)
        do i = k+1, n
          a(i, k$) = a(i, k$) * t
        enddo
      endif
      {* Reduce remaining submatrix *}
      if (my$p .EQ. MOD(k - 1, 4)) then
        buffer a(k+1:n, k$) into dp$buf1
        broadcast dp$buf1(1:n-k)
      else
        recv dp$buf1(1:n-k)
      endif
      lb$1 = (k / 4) + 1
      if (my$p .LT. MOD(k, 4)) lb$1 = lb$1+1
      do j = lb$1, n/4
        t = a(l, j)
        if (l .NE. k) then
          a(l, j) = a(k, j)
          a(k, j) = t
        endif
        do i = k+1, n
          a(i, j) = a(i, j) + t * dp$buf1(i-k)
        enddo
      enddo
    endif
  enddo
  ipvt(n) = n
end
```

Figure 5: DGEFA: Compiler Output

The Fortran D compiler handles multi-reductions as follows. If the direction of the multi-reduction crosses a partitioned array dimension, then compilation proceeds as normal. The compiler produces code so that each processor computes part of every reduction in the multi-reduction, then inserts a global collective communication routine to accumulate the results. ERLEBACHER performs 2D SUM multi-reductions along each dimension of a 3D array for each of its three computation wavefronts. Consider statement S_1 in Figure 7, which performs a SUM multi-reduction in the Z dimension. Because this dimension is distributed, the compiler partitions the computation based on f, the distributed *rhs*, and inserts a call to *global-sum* to accumulate the results.

3.4.3 Array Kills

If the multi-reduction does not cross any distributed dimensions, no information is transferred between processors. A processor can then evaluate some of the reductions

```
{* Original Fortran D Program *}
SUBROUTINE DZ3D6P
  REAL uud(n,n,n),uu(n,n,n)
  DECOMPOSITION dd(n,n,n)
  ALIGN uud, uu with dd
  DISTRIBUTE dd(:,:,BLOCK)
  do j = 1,n
    do i = 1,n
S1    uud(i,j,1) = F(uu(i,j,3),uu(i,j,n-1))
S2    uud(i,j,2) = F(uu(i,j,4),uu(i,j,n))
S3    uud(i,j,n-1) = F(uu(i,j,1),uu(i,j,n-3))
S4    uud(i,j,n) = F(uu(i,j,2),uu(i,j,n-2))
    do k = 3,n-2
      do j = 1,n
        do i = 1,n
S5        uud(i,j,k) = F(uu(i,j,k+2),uu(i,j,k-2))
  end


{* Compiler Output for 4 Processors *}
SUBROUTINE DZ3D6P
  REAL uud(n,n,n/4),uu(n,n,-1:(n/4)+2)
  n$ = n/4
C1  if (my$p .EQ. 0) send uu(1:n,1:n,1:2) to P3
C2  if (my$p .EQ. 3) send uu(1:n,1:n,n$-1:n$) to P0
C3  if (my$p .LT. 3) send uu(1:n,1:n,n$-1:n$) to my$p+1
C4  if (my$p .GT. 0) send uu(1:n,1:n,1:2) to my$p-1
  if (my$p .EQ. 0) then
    recv uu(1:n,1:n,n$+1:n$+2) from P3
    do j = 1,n
      do i = 1,n
S1      uud(i,j,1) = F(...)
S2      uud(i,j,2) = F(...)
  endif
  if (my$p .EQ. 3) then
    recv uu(1:n,1:n,-1:0) from P1
    do j = 1,n
      do i = 1,n
S3      uud(i,j,n$-1) = F(...)
S4      uud(i,j,n$) = F(...)
  endif
  if (my$p .GT. 0)
    recv uu(1:n,1:n,n$+1:n$+2) from my$p+1
  if (my$p .LT. 3)
    recv uu(1:n,1:n,-1:0) from my$p-1
  do k = lb$,ub$
    do j = 1,n
      do i = 1,n
S5      uud(i,j,k) = F(...)
  end
```

Figure 6: ERLEBACHER: Computation in Z Dimension

```
{* Original Fortran D Program *}
SUBROUTINE TRIDVPK
  REAL a(n),b(n),c(n),d(n),e(n),tot(n,n),f(n,n,n)
  DISTRIBUTE f(:,:,BLOCK)
  {* perform forward substitution *}
  ...
  {* perform backward substitution *}
  do k = 1,n
    do j = 1,n
      do i = 1,n
S1      tot(i,j) = tot(i,j)+d(k)*f(i,j,k)
    do j = 1,n
      do i = 1,n
S2    f(i,j,n) = (f(i,j,n)-tot(i,j))*b(n)
    do j = 1,n
      do i = 1,n
S3    f(i,j,n-1) = f(i,j,n-1)-e(n-1)*f(i,j,n)
    do k = n-2,1,-1
      do j = 1,n
        do i = 1,n
S4      f(i,j,k) = f(i,j,k)-c(k)*f(i,j,k+1)-e(k)*f(i,j,n)
  end


{* Compiler Output for 4 Processors *}
SUBROUTINE TRIDVPK
  REAL a(n),b(n),c(n),d(n),e(n)
  REAL tot(n,n),f(n,n,0:(n/4)+1),r$buf1(n)
  {* perform forward substitution *}
  ...
  {* perform backward substitution *}
  n$ = n/4
  off$0 = my$p * n$
  do k = 1,n$
    k$ = k + off$0
    do j = 1,n
      do i = 1,n
        tot(i,j) = tot(i,j)+d(k$)*f(i,j,k)
  global-sum tot(1:n,1:n)
  if (my$p .EQ. 3) then
    do j = 1,n
      do i = 1,n
        f(i,j,n$) = (f(i,j,n$)-tot(i,j))*b(n)
    do j = 1,n
      do i = 1,n
        f(i,j,n$-1) = f(i,j,n$-1)-e(n-1)*f(i,j,n$)
    buffer f(1:128, 1:128, n$) into rbuf$1(n*n)
    broadcast rbuf$1(1:n*n)
  else
    recv rbuf$1(1:n*n)
  endif
  do j = 1,n
    do i$ = 1,n,8
      i$up = i$+7
      if (my$p .LT. 3)
        recv f(i$:i$up, j, n$+1) from my$p+1
      do k = ub$,1,-1
        k$ = k + off$0
        do i = i$,i$+8
          f(i,j,k) = f(i,j,k)-c(k$)*f(i,j,k+1)
                     - e(k$)*r$buf1(j*n+i-n)
      if (my$p .GT. 0)
        send f(i$:i$up, j, 1) to my$p-1
  end
```

Figure 7: ERLEBACHER: Solution Phase in Z Dimension

comprising the multi-reduction using local data. Loop bounds reduction is sufficient to partition the reduction; no communication is needed. For instance, a multi-reduction is performed in the Y dimension solution step of ERLEBACHER, shown in Figure 8. Because the Y dimension of f is local, relaxing the owner computes rule allows each processor to compute its reductions locally. Unfortunately the multi-reduction is being computed for tot, a replicated array. The compiler thus inserts a global concatenation routine to collect values of tot from other processors.

This concatenation is the only communication inserted in sweeps in the X and Y dimensions, and turns out to be unnecessary. Array kill analysis would show that the values of tot only reach uses in the next loop nest S_2, where it is accessed only on iterations executed locally. In other words, each processor only uses values of tot that itself computes; values computed by other processors are not needed. This information can be employed to eliminate the unnecessary global concatenation. Array kill analysis has not yet been implemented in the prototype compiler.

3.4.4 Exploiting Pipeline Parallelism

Because the computational wavefront traverses across processors in the Z dimension, the Fortran D compiler must efficiently exploit pipeline parallelism [16]. In Figure 7,

the compiler detects that the k loop enclosing statement S_4 is a cross-processor loop because it carries a true dependence whose endpoints are on different processors. To exploit coarse-grain pipeline parallelism, the compiler interchanges the k loop inwards and strip-mines the enclosing i loop.

This example demonstrates two additional features of the Fortran D compiler. First, note that moving the k loop innermost would convert column-wise array accesses into row-wise accesses, resulting in poor data locality. To avoid these situations the prototype compiler leaves the two innermost loops in the original order when applying coarse-grain pipelining. Second, since the non-

```
{* Original Fortran D Program *}
SUBROUTINE TRIDVPJ
  REAL a(n),b(n),c(n),d(n),e(n)
  REAL tot(n,n),f(n,n,n)
  DISTRIBUTE f(:,:,BLOCK)
  do k = 1,n
   do j = 1,n
    do i = 1,n
S₁   tot(i,k) = tot(i,k) + d(j)*f(i,j,k)
  do k = 1,n
   do i = 1,n
S₂  f(i,n,k) = (f(i,n,k) - tot(i,k))*b(n)
  end
```

```
{* Compiler Output for 4 Processors *}
SUBROUTINE TRIDVPK
  REAL a(n),b(n),c(n),d(n),e(n)
  REAL tot(n,n),f(n,n,0:(n/4)+1)
  n$ = n/4
  off$0 = my$p * n$
  do k = 1,n$
   k$ = k + off$0
   do j = 1,n
    do i = 1,n
     tot(i,k$) = tot(i,k$) + d(j)*f(i,j,k)
  global-concat tot(1:n,1:n)
  do k = 1,n$
   k$ = k + off$0
   do i = 1,n
    f(i,n,k) = (f(i,n,k) - tot(i,k$))*b(n)
  end
```

Figure 8: ERLEBACHER: Solution Phase in Y Dimension

local accesses caused by $f(i, j, n)$ are communicated via a vectorized broadcast, to properly access data in the 1D buffer array the compiler must replace the reference with $r\$buf1(j * n + i - n)$.

4 Empirical Evaluation of Compiler

To evaluate the status of the prototype Fortran D compiler, the output of the Fortran D compiler is compared with hand-optimized programs on the Intel iPSC/860 and the output of the CM Fortran compiler on the TMC CM-5. Our goal is to validate our compilation approach and identify directions for future research. In many cases, problems sizes were too large to be executed sequentially on one processor. In these cases sequential execution times are estimates, computed by projecting execution times for smaller computations to the larger problem sizes. Empirical results are presented in both tabular and graphical form.

4.1 Comparison with Hand-Optimized Code

We begin by comparing the output of the Fortran D compiler against hand-optimized code on the Intel iPSC/860 hypercube. Our iPSC timings were obtained on the 32 node Intel iPSC/860 at Rice University. It has 8 Meg of memory per node and is running under Release 3.3.1 of the Intel software. Each program was compiled under -O4 using Release 3.0 of *if77*, the iPSC/860 compiler. Timings were made using *dclock()*, a microsecond timer.

Speedups for different problem and machine sizes are graphically displayed in Figure 9, with speedups plotted along the Y-axis and number of processors along the X-axis. Solid and dashed lines correspond to speedups for hand-optimized and Fortran D compiler-generated programs, respectively. Each line represents the speedup for a given problem size.

4.1.1 Results for Stencil Kernels

The hand-optimized stencil kernels are taken from a previous study evaluating the effect of different communication & parallelism optimizations on overall performance [17].

We selected a sum reduction (Livermore 3), two parallel kernels (Livermore 18, Jacobi), and two pipelined kernels (Livermore 23, SOR). As before, all arrays are double precision and distributed block-wise in one dimension.

We found that the code generated for the inner product in Livermore 3 was identical to the hand-optimized version, since the compiler recognized the sum reduction and used the appropriate collective communication routine. For parallel kernels, the output of the Fortran D compiler was within 50% of the best hand-optimized codes. The deficit was mainly caused by the Fortran D compiler not exploiting unbuffered messages in order to eliminate buffering and overlap communication overhead with local computation [5, 17].

The compiler-generated code actually outperformed the hand-optimized pipelined codes, even though the two message-passing Fortran 77 versions of the program were nearly identical. We thus assume the differences to be due to complications with the scalar i860 node compiler in the parameterized hand-optimized version. We also observed superlinear speedups for some kernels, probably caused by the increase in total cache size with multiple processors.

4.1.2 Results for SHALLOW

Table 1 contains timings for performing one time step of SHALLOW. It presents speedups as well as the ratio of execution times between hand-optimized and Fortran D versions of the program. We found the program to be ideal for distributed-memory machines. Computation is entirely data-parallel, with nearest-neighbor communication taking place between phases of each time step. The compiler output achieved excellent speedups (21–29), even for smaller problems. To evaluate potential improvements, we performed aggressive inter-loop message coalescing and aggregation by hand, halving the total number of messages. The hand-optimized versions of SHALLOW exhibited only slight improvements (1–10%) over the compiler-generated code, except when small problems were parallelized on many processors (12–26%). Communication costs apparently only contributed to a small percentage of total execution time, reducing the impact and profitability of advanced communication optimizations.

4.1.3 Results for DISPER

Like SHALLOW, DISPER is a completely data-parallel computation that requires only nearest-neighbor communications. Timings for DISPER in Table 2 show near-linear speedups for the output of the Fortran D compiler, once errors introduced by execution conditions were corrected by hand. We also created a hand-optimized version of DISPER by applying aggressive inter-loop message aggregation and unbuffered messages. However, since communication overhead is small, the hand-optimized version only yielded minor improvements (1–3%) for the problem size tested.

4.1.4 Results for DGEFA

Table 3 presents execution times and speedups for DGEFA, Gaussian elimination with partial pivoting. Results indicate that the Fortran D compiler output, shown in Figure 4, provided limited speedups (3–6) on small problems. For larger problems moderate speedups (11–16) were achieved. Due to the large number of global broadcasts required to communicate pivot values and multipliers, performance of DGEFA actually degrades when solving small problems on many processors.

To determine whether improved performance is attainable, we created a hand-optimized version of DGEFA based

Problem Size	Proc	Fortran D time	speedup	Hand-Optimized time	speedup	Hand/FortD
256 × 256	1	*sequential time = 0.728*				
	2	0.354	2.06	0.348	2.09	0.98
	4	0.195	3.73	0.188	3.87	0.96
	8	0.097	7.50	0.091	8.00	0.94
	16	0.056	13.0	0.049	14.86	0.88
	32	0.035	20.8	0.026	28.00	0.74
512 × 512	1	*estimated sequential time = 2.9*				
	2	1.529	1.90	1.521	1.91	0.99
	4	0.707	4.10	0.698	4.15	0.99
	8	0.377	7.69	0.368	7.88	0.98
	16	0.201	14.43	0.191	15.18	0.95
	32	0.107	27.10	0.095	30.53	0.89
1K × 1K	1	*estimated sequential time = 11.6*				
	8	1.620	7.16	1.610	7.20	0.99
	16	0.755	15.36	0.739	15.70	0.98
	32	0.397	29.22	0.380	30.53	0.95

Table 1: iPSC/860 Timings for SHALLOW (in seconds)

Problem Size	Proc	Fortran D time	speedup	Hand-Optimized time	speedup	Hand/FortD
256 × 8 × 8 × 4	1	*estimated sequential time = 39.0*				
	4	9.971	3.91	10.22	3.81	1.03
	8	5.040	7.74	4.979	7.83	0.99
	16	2.440	15.98	2.414	16.16	0.99
	32	1.284	30.37	1.240	31.45	0.97

Table 2: iPSC/860 Timings for DISPER (in seconds)

Problem Size	Proc	Fortran D time	speedup	Hand-Optimized time	speedup	Hand/FortD
256 × 256	1	*sequential time = 2.151*				
	2	1.051	2.05	1.108	1.94	1.05
	4	0.744	2.89	0.683	3.15	0.92
	8	0.670	3.21	0.551	3.90	0.82
	16	0.695	3.09	0.644	3.34	0.93
	32	0.782	2.75	0.758	2.84	0.97
512 × 512	1	*sequential time = 17.53*				
	2	7.988	2.19	7.879	2.22	0.99
	4	4.786	3.66	4.322	4.06	0.90
	8	3.373	5.20	2.601	6.74	0.77
	16	2.908	6.03	2.259	7.76	0.78
	32	2.916	6.01	2.619	6.69	0.90
1K × 1K	1	*estimated sequential time = 140*				
	2	66.74	2.10	68.91	2.03	1.03
	4	36.29	3.86	35.61	3.93	0.98
	8	21.83	6.41	18.93	7.40	0.87
	16	15.32	9.14	10.97	12.76	0.72
	32	12.96	10.80	9.654	14.50	0.74
2K × 2K	1	*estimated sequential time = 1120*				
	8	160.45	6.98	145.8	7.68	0.91
	16	97.22	11.52	76.28	14.68	0.78
	32	68.86	16.26	44.62	25.10	0.65

Table 3: iPSC/860 Timings for DGEFA (in seconds)

Problem Size	Proc	Fortran D time	speedup	Hand-Optimized time	speedup	Hand/FortD
64 × 64 × 64	1	*sequential time = 1.577*				
	2	0.858	1.84	0.805	1.96	0.94
	4	0.721	2.19	0.586	2.69	0.81
	8	0.657	2.40	0.448	3.52	0.68
	16	0.539	2.93	0.311	5.07	0.53
	32	0.613	2.57	0.315	5.00	0.51
96 × 96 × 96	1	*estimated sequential time = 5.3*				
	4	1.517	3.49	1.151	4.60	0.76
	8	1.431	3.70	0.917	5.78	0.64
	16	1.481	3.58	0.813	6.52	0.55
	32	1.334	3.97	0.720	7.36	0.54
128 × 128 × 128	1	*estimated sequential time = 12.6*				
	8	2.738	4.60	1.905	6.61	0.70
	16	2.705	4.65	1.584	7.95	0.58
	32	2.533	4.97	1.347	9.35	0.53

Table 4: iPSC/860 Timings for ERLEBACHER (in seconds)

on optimizations described in the literature [11, 22]. First, we combined the two messages broadcast on each iteration of the outermost k loop. Instead of broadcasting the pivot value immediately, we wait until multipliers are also computed. The values can then be combined in one broadcast. Overcommunication may result when a zero pivot is found, since messages now include multipliers even if they are not used. However, combining broadcasts is still profitable as zero pivots rarely occur.

Second, we restructured the computation so that upon receiving the pivot for the current iteration, the processor P_{k+1} responsible for finding the pivot for the next iteration does so immediately. P_{k+1} performs row elimination on just the first column of the remaining subarray, scans that column to find a pivot and calculates multipliers. P_{k+1} then broadcasts the pivot and multipliers to the other processors before performing row elimination on the remaining subarray. Since row eliminations make up most of the computation in Gaussian elimination, each broadcast in effect takes place one iteration ahead of the matching receive, hiding communication costs by overlapping message latency with local computation.

The hand-optimized version of DGEFA showed little or no improvement for small problems or when few processors were employed. However, it increased performance by over 30% for large problems on many processors, yielding decent speedups (14–25). The Fortran D compiler can thus benefit from more aggressive optimization of linear algebra routines. Experience also indicates that programmers can achieve higher performance for linear algebra codes with block versions of these algorithms. The Fortran D compiler will need to provide BLOCK_CYCLIC data distributions to support these block algorithms.

4.1.5 Results for ERLEBACHER

As we have seen, ERLEBACHER requires global communication and contains computation wavefronts that sequentialize parts of the computation. During compilation the Fortran D compiler performs interprocedural reaching decomposition and overlap analysis, then invokes local code generation for each procedure. The compiler inserts global communication for array SUM reductions, and also applies coarse-grain pipelining. Timings for ERLEBACHER in Table 4 show that the compiler-generated code is rather inefficient, with speedup peaking at 3–5 even for large programs.

To determine how much improvement is attainable, we applied two optimizations by hand. First, we used interprocedural array kill analysis to eliminate unnecessary global concatenation for local multi-reductions in the X and Y sweeps. Second, we hand-tuned the granularity of coarse-grain pipelining, selecting strip sizes of 16 and 24 rather than the default size of 8. These optimizations yielded speedups of 5–9, improving performance by up to 50% over the Fortran D compiler-generated code.

4.1.6 Analysis of Results

By generating output for SHALLOW and DISPER that virtually matched their hand-optimized versions, the Fortran D compiler has demonstrated its effectiveness for parallel stencil computations, despite not producing the most efficient communication. The compiler succeeds because it does a sufficiently good job that communication costs become a minor part of the overall execution time. In particular, scalability is excellent because performance improves as the problem size increases. Implementing additional optimizations is desirable for achieving good speedup for small programs or many processors, but is not crucial.

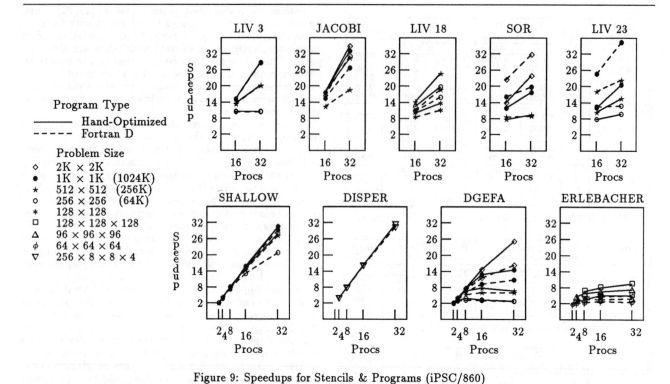

Figure 9: Speedups for Stencils & Programs (iPSC/860)

Instead, the focus should be on improving the flexibility and robustness of the Fortran D compiler, as discussed in Section 5.

In comparison, there is considerable room for improvement when compiling communication-intensive codes such as linear algebra and pipelined computations. Results for DGEFA and ERLEBACHER show that the prototype Fortran D compiler only attains limited speedups. Noticeable performance gains can be achieved through advanced communication optimizations; they are important because communication is performed much more frequently than in parallel stencil computations. The effect of these optimizations on overall execution time increases in importance as the problem size and number of processors increases. In particular, the Fortran D compiler will need to use information from training sets and static performance estimation to select an efficient granularity for coarse-grain pipelining [17].

To summarize, the Fortran D compiler performs extensive analysis for stencil computations and is able to achieve good speedups. More complex linear algebra and pipelined computations require sophisticated optimizations that are not fully incorporated into the prototype compiler, hence we see only modest speedups.

4.2 Comparison with CM Fortran Compiler

We also evaluated the performance of the Fortran D compiler against a commercial compiler. We selected the CM Fortran compiler, the most mature and widely used compiler for MIMD distributed-memory machines, and compared it against the Fortran D compiler on the Thinking Machines CM-5. Our CM-5 timings were obtained on the 32 node CM-5 at Syracuse University. It has Sun Sparc processors running SunOS 4.1.2 and vector units running CMOST 7.2 S2. When combined, the four vector units on

each node can outperform the Sparc by a factor of six or more.

In our experiment, CM Fortran programs were compiled using *cmf* version 2.1 *beta*, with the -O and -vu flags. They were timed using *CM_timer_read_elapsed()*. CM Fortran programs were compared against message-passing Fortran 77 programs using CMMD version 3.0 *final*, the CM message-passing library. Fortran 77 node programs were compiled using the Sun Fortran compiler *f77*, version 1.4, with the -O flag. They were linked with *cmmd* version 3.0 *beta*. Fortran 77 node programs were timed using *CMMD_node_timer_elapsed()*.

4.2.1 Results for Kernels and Programs

The output of the Fortran D compiler was easily ported to the CM-5 by replacing calls to Intel NX/2 message-passing routines with equivalent calls to TMC CMMD message-passing routines. We converted program kernels into CM Fortran by hand for the CM Fortran compiler, inserting the appropriate LAYOUT directives to achieve the same data decomposition [27]. The inner product in Livermore 3 was replaced by DOTPRODUCT, a CM Fortran intrinsic. Jacobi, Livermore 18, and SHALLOW can be transformed directly into CM Fortran. Loop skew and interchange were applied to SOR and Livermore 23 to expose parallelism in the form of FORALL loops. A mask array *indx* is used to implement Gaussian elimination.

The CM Fortran compiler can generate two versions of output. The first uses CM-5 vector units, the second only uses the Sparc node processor. Unfortunately, the current TMC Fortran 77 compiler does not generate code to utilize CM-5 vector units, and the node-level CMF compiler was insufficiently robust to perform experiments. Fortran D message-passing programs are thus forced to rely on the Sparc processor. For the purpose of comparison, we pro-

Program	Problem Size	Sequential Execution Sparc	Fortran D + CMMD Sparc	CM Fortran		CM Fortran / Fortran D	
				Sparc	Vector	Sparc	Vector
Livermore 3	64K	0.005	0.002	0.018	0.005	11.4	3.65
Inner	256K	0.020	0.006	0.032	0.006	5.33	1.07
Product	1024K	0.079	0.024	0.098	0.007	4.08	0.32
Jacobi	512 × 512	0.877	0.024	0.236	0.045	9.83	1.87
Iteration	1K × 1K	3.525	0.093	0.766	0.079	8.24	0.85
	2K × 2K	14.14	0.362	2.834	0.159	7.83	0.44
Livermore 18	128 × 128	0.457	0.019	0.165	0.100	8.68	5.26
Explicit	256 × 256	1.861	0.054	0.332	0.132	6.15	2.44
Hydrodynamics	512 × 512	7.554	0.199	0.994	0.163	4.99	0.82
	256 × 256	1.297	0.029	0.409	0.185	14.1	6.38
SHALLOW	512 × 512	5.210	0.129	1.363	0.256	10.6	1.98
	1K × 1K	20.88	0.520	6.159	0.408	11.8	0.78
Successive	512 × 512	0.376	0.053	17.04	7.559	321	143
Over	1K × 1K	1.519	0.126	116.1	27.39	921	217
Relaxation	2K × 2K	6.134	0.353	209.9	128.6	595	364
Livermore 23	256 × 256	0.389	0.035	2.897	2.516	82.7	71.9
Implicit	512 × 512	1.562	0.118	18.19	8.686	154	73.6
Hydrodynamics	1K × 1K	6.252	0.320	122.7	31.59	383	98.7
	256 × 256	4.791	0.539	10.65	3.604	19.7	6.69
DGEFA	512 × 512	40.61	2.680	104.8	56.50	39.1	21.1
	1K × 1K	337.1	16.82	856.9	162.1	50.9	9.64
	2K × 2K	6809	109.8	8449	1365	76.8	12.4

Table 5: CM-5 Timings for Kernels and Programs (in seconds, using 32 processors)

vide timings for CM Fortran programs using either Sparc or vector units. Table 5 shows the elapsed times we measured on the CM-5 for CM Fortran and Fortran D programs, as well as the ratio of execution times between CM Fortran and Fortran D code. Sequential execution times on a single Sparc 2 workstation are provided for comparison.

We also graphically present the execution times measured on the CM-5. Figure 10 displays measured execution speed. Execution times in seconds are plotted logarithmically along the Y-axis. The problem size is plotted logarithmically along the X-axis. Solid, dotted, and dashed lines represent the CM Fortran using Sparc, CM Fortran using vector units, and Fortran D using Sparc, respectively. All parallel execution times are for 32 processors. Figure 11 displays the ratio of execution times of both versions of CM Fortran code (sparc/vector) to Fortran D (sparc), plotting ratios along the Y-axis.

Results indicate that when utilizing only Sparc processors, the CM Fortran compiler produces code that is significantly slower than the corresponding message-passing programs generated by the Fortran D compiler. The difference is pronounced for small data sizes. The CM Fortran compiler fared best on data-parallel computations such as Jacobi, Livermore 18, and SHALLOW (4–14 times slower). It appears to handle pipelined computations and Gaussian elimination poorly (20+ times slower), even when expressed in a form that contains vector parallelism.

4.2.2   Analysis of Results

Direct comparisons are somewhat misleading, since the CM Fortran compiler (2.1 *beta*) directly generates Sparc code instead of using the Sparc Fortran 77 compiler. Additional factors also affect performance, as evidenced by the fact that for small to medium problems the Fortran D compiler is actually faster than the CM Fortran compiler using vector units. First, the code generated by the CM Fortran compiler uses virtual processes, causing extensive run-time calculation of addresses and much unnecessary data movement even for purely local computation. Second, it utilizes a *host-node* model, where a host processor synchronizes global computation on each node. In comparison,

the Fortran D compiler utilizes a *hostless* model, eliminating global host-to-node synchronization. Finally, few communication optimizations are performed at compile-time.

We note that it is not completely fair to compare a research tool like the Fortran D compiler against a commercial product like the CM Fortran compiler. Because it is a product, the CM Fortran compiler must be able to accept all legal programs and generate correct code. When targeting distributed-memory machines, guaranteeing correctness for complex computations and data decompositions is quite difficult. In comparison, we were able to concentrate on compile-time optimizations by limiting the range of programs accepted by the Fortran D compiler. The CM Fortran compiler is also handicapped because it is designed to generate code that can be executed on any number of processors, whereas the prototype Fortran D compiler targets a fixed number of processors at compile-time.

Nonetheless, our experiments prove that severe performance penalties result if important compile-time decisions are postponed until run-time. Because the CM Fortran compiler for the CM-5 is relatively new (though it is the most mature commercial compiler available), its performance is sure to improve. We hope that our experiences with the prototype Fortran D compiler will aid the development of future CM Fortran and HPF compilers. However, we believe that scientists will need to be patient, since effective HPF compilers will take time.

5   Compiler Improvements

Our preliminary experiences show that the prototype Fortran D compiler has achieved considerable success in generating efficient code for stencil computations, but needs to improve its optimization of linear algebra and pipelined codes. We find, however, that the compiler must become much more flexible before it can become a successful machine-independent programming model.

In the course of conducting our study, we were unable to apply the Fortran D compiler to a large number of standard benchmark programs, despite the fact they contained

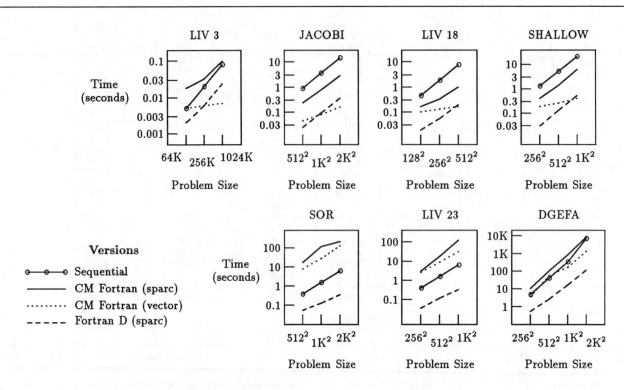

Figure 10: Execution Times (32 Processor Thinking Machines CM-5)

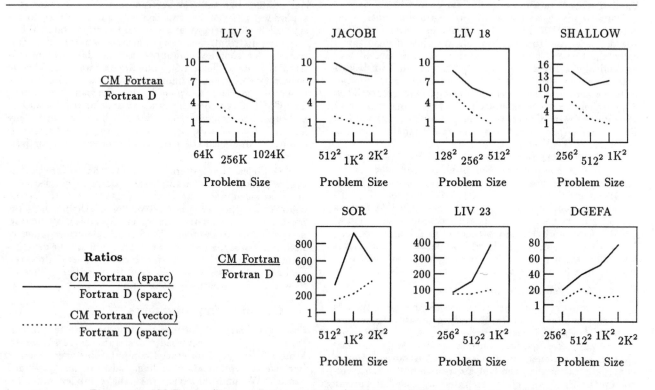

Figure 11: CM Fortran/Fortran D Comparisons (32 Processor Thinking Machines CM-5)

dense-matrix computations that should have been acceptable to the compiler. Even programs that were written in a "clean" data-parallel manner required fairly extensive rewriting to eliminate programming artifacts that the prototype proved unable to handle. The causes for this inflexibility can be categorized as follows.

5.1 Improved Analysis

The lack of symbolic analysis in the prototype Fortran D compiler proved to be a major stumbling block. Unlike parallelizing compilers for shared-memory machines, simply providing precise dependence information was insufficient for the Fortran D compiler. The compiler performs deep analysis that requires knowledge of all subscript expressions and loop bounds in the program. For real programs, constant propagation, forward expression folding, and auxiliary induction variable substitution all need to be performed before the Fortran D compiler can proceed.

The prototype compiler is also inhibited by missing pieces in interprocedural analysis. It does not understand formal parameters that represent subarrays in the calling procedure or multiple entry points. Both symbolic and interprocedural analysis need to be completed and integrated with the prototype compiler before many existing programs can be considered.

5.2 Run-time Support

Another problem with the Fortran D compiler is that it relies almost completely on compile-time analysis. The only run-time support it requires are simple routines for packing and unpacking non-contiguous array elements into contiguous message buffers. The compiler attempts to calculate at compile-time all information, including ownership, partitioning, and communication.

While this approach is necessary for advanced optimizations and generating efficient code, it limits the Fortran D compiler. Real programs, frequently contain components such as indirect references that cannot be easily analyzed at compile-time. In these cases the Fortran D compiler was forced to abort, despite being able to compile the important kernel computations in the program.

What the Fortran D compiler needs are methods of utilizing run-time support, trading performance for greater flexibility in non-critical regions of the program. The compiler can either apply run-time resolution or demand more support from the run-time library to calculate ownership, partitioning, and communication at run-time. Since in most cases the code affected is executed infrequently, the expense of run-time methods should not significantly impact overall execution time.

5.3 Additional Features

A major part of the problem lies with the immaturity of the Fortran D compiler itself. There are a number of dense-matrix computations that it is not able to analyze and compile efficiently. For instance, the prototype compiler does not currently handle non-unit loop steps or subscript coefficients. It is thus unable to compile Red-Black SOR or multigrid computations, both of which possess constant step sizes greater than one.

Computations such as Fast Fourier Transform (FFT), linear recurrences, finite-element, n-body problems, and banded tridiagonal solvers all possess regular but specialized data access patterns that the Fortran D compiler needs to recognize and efficiently support. In addition, run-time support for irregular and sparse computations must also be added. Only when these obstacles are overcome can

the Fortran D compiler serve as a credible general-purpose programming model.

5.4 Rewriting Dusty Decks

Finally, the Fortran D compiler cannot compile a number of "dusty deck" Fortran programs that were originally written for sequential or vector machines. These programs contain programming constructs that the compiler does not understand such as linearized arrays, loops formed by backward GOTO statements, and storing and using constants in arrays. Dusty deck programs have proven to be very challenging for even shared-memory vectorizing and parallelizing compilers. Because of the deep analysis required, they are even more difficult for distributed-memory compilers.

It is not a goal of the Fortran D compiler to be able to automatically parallelize these programs for distributed-memory machines. Requiring users to program in Fortran 90 can help prevent such poor programming practices, and is the approach taken by High Performance Fortran. However, as shown by the performance of the CM Fortran compiler, Fortran 90 syntax does not eliminate the need for advanced compile-time analysis and optimization.

6 Related Work

The Fortran D compiler is a second-generation distributed-memory compiler that incorporates and extends features from previous compilation systems [6, 12, 19, 21, 25]. Compared with other contemporary systems [2, 3, 7, 8, 18, 24], The Fortran D compiler is less flexible but performs deeper compile-time analysis, many more advanced optimizations, requires fewer language extensions, and relies on less run-time support.

Few researchers have published experimental results for large programs. Pingali & Rogers apply message vectorization, message pipelining, and reduction recognition in ID NOUVEAU to parallelize SIMPLE [25]. Koelbel & Mehrotra are able to parallelize ADI integration in KALI by implicitly applying dynamic data decomposition between computation phases [19]. Olander & Schnabel show that DINO programs can be significantly improved through iteration reordering and pipelining [23].

Bromley et al. develop optimizations in CM Fortran compiler for stencils on the CM-2 [4]. By inserting calls to hand-coded microcode routines that apply *unroll-and-jam*, they avoid unnecessary intra-processor data motion, insert communication only for nonlocal data, and improve register usage. The resulting compiler achieves significant improvements in execution speed for a finite-difference seismic model. Hatcher et al. demonstrate that DATAPARALLEL C can achieve speedups for large scientific applications on MIMD architectures [14].

Burns et al. developed techniques for guiding the use of unbuffered messages on the Alliant CAMPUS/800 using data dependence information [5]. They show that unbuffered messages improve overall performance for a collection of hand-parallelized scientific programs. Their studies validate the effectiveness of selected compiler optimizations for complete programs.

Rühl performed studies on a variety of parallel architectures, demonstrating excellent speedups for the OXYGEN compiler [26]. Amarasinghe & Lam use precise data-flow information for arrays from *last-write-trees* in SUIF to avoid over-communication [1]. They report speedups for Gaussian elimination without pivoting.

7 Conclusions

An efficient, portable, data-parallel programming model is required to make large-scale parallel machines useful for scientific programmers. We believe that Fortran D provides such a model for distributed-memory machines.

This paper describes compiler techniques developed in response to problems posed by linear algebra computations, large subroutines, and whole programs. The performance of the prototype Fortran D compiler is evaluated against hand-optimized programs on the Intel iPSC/860. Results show reasonable performance is obtained for stencil computations, though much room for improvement exists for communication-intensive codes such as linear algebra and pipelined computations. The prototype significantly outperforms the CM Fortran compiler on the CM-5.

Our experiences show that the prototype Fortran D compiler requires symbolic analysis, greater flexibility, and improved optimization of pipelined and linear algebra codes. We believe the Fortran D compilation approach will be competitive with hand-optimized programs for many data-parallel computations in the near future. However, additional effort is required before the compiler will be as effective for partially parallel computations requiring large amounts of communication.

8 Acknowledgements

We are grateful to Uli Kremer for providing results for DISPER and our referees for their comments. We wish to thank Geoffrey Fox for use of the TMC CM-5 at Syracuse University. Use of the Intel iPSC/860 was provided by the CRPC under NSF Cooperative Agreement Nos. CCR-8809615 and CDA-8619893 with support from the Keck Foundation.

References

[1] S. Amarasinghe and M. Lam. Communication optimization and code generation for distributed memory machines. In *Proceedings of the SIGPLAN '93 Conference on Program Language Design and Implementation*, Albuquerque, NM, June 1993.

[2] Applied Parallel Research, Placerville, CA. *Forge 90 Distributed Memory Parallelizer: User's Guide*, version 8.0 edition, 1992.

[3] T. Brandes. Efficient data parallel programming without explicit message passing for distributed memory multiprocessors. Internal Report AHR-92-4, High Performance Computing Center, GMD, September 1992.

[4] M. Bromley, S. Heller, T. McNerney, and G. Steele, Jr. Fortran at ten gigaflops: The Connection Machine convolution compiler. In *Proceedings of the SIGPLAN '91 Conference on Program Language Design and Implementation*, Toronto, Canada, June 1991.

[5] C. Burns, R. Kuhn, and E. Werme. Low copy message passing on the Alliant CAMPUS/800. In *Proceedings of Supercomputing '92*, Minneapolis, MN, November 1992.

[6] D. Callahan and K. Kennedy. Compiling programs for distributed-memory multiprocessors. *Journal of Supercomputing*, 2:151–169, October 1988.

[7] B. Chapman, P. Mehrotra, and H. Zima. Programming in Vienna Fortran. *Scientific Programming*, 1(1):31–50, Fall 1992.

[8] C. Chase, A. Cheung, A. Reeves, and M. Smith. Paragon: A parallel programming environment for scientific applications using communication structures. *Journal of Parallel and Distributed Computing*, 16(2):79–91, October 1992.

[9] K. Cooper, M. W. Hall, R. T. Hood, K. Kennedy, K. S. McKinley, J. M. Mellor-Crummey, L. Torczon, and S. K. Warren. The ParaScope parallel programming environ-

ment. *Proceedings of the IEEE*, 81(2):244–263, February 1993.

[10] G. Fox, S. Hiranandani, K. Kennedy, C. Koelbel, U. Kremer, C. Tseng, and M. Wu. Fortran D language specification. Technical Report TR90-141, Dept. of Computer Science, Rice University, December 1990.

[11] G. Geist and C. Romine. LU factorization algorithms on distributed-memory multiprocessor architectures. *SIAM Journal of Scientific Stat. Computing*, 9:639–649, 1988.

[12] M. Gerndt. Updating distributed variables in local computations. *Concurrency: Practice & Experience*, 2(3):171–193, September 1990.

[13] M. W. Hall, S. Hiranandani, K. Kennedy, and C. Tseng. Interprocedural compilation of Fortran D for MIMD distributed-memory machines. In *Proceedings of Supercomputing '92*, Minneapolis, MN, November 1992.

[14] P. Hatcher, M. Quinn, R. Anderson, A. Lapadula, B. Seevers, and A. Bennett. Architecture-independent scientific programming in Dataparallel C: Three case studies. In *Proceedings of Supercomputing '91*, Albuquerque, NM, November 1991.

[15] High Performance Fortran Forum. High Performance Fortran language specification, version 1.0. Technical Report CRPC-TR92225, Center for Research on Parallel Computation, Rice University, Houston, TX, January 1993.

[16] S. Hiranandani, K. Kennedy, and C. Tseng. Compiling Fortran D for MIMD distributed-memory machines. *Communications of the ACM*, 35(8):66–80, August 1992.

[17] S. Hiranandani, K. Kennedy, and C. Tseng. Evaluation of compiler optimizations for Fortran D on MIMD distributed-memory machines. In *Proceedings of the 1992 ACM International Conference on Supercomputing*, Washington, DC, July 1992.

[18] K. Ikudome, G. Fox, A. Kolawa, and J. Flower. An automatic and symbolic parallelization system for distributed memory parallel computers. In *Proceedings of the 5th Distributed Memory Computing Conference*, Charleston, SC, April 1990.

[19] C. Koelbel and P. Mehrotra. Programming data parallel algorithms on distributed memory machines using Kali. In *Proceedings of the 1991 ACM International Conference on Supercomputing*, Cologne, Germany, June 1991.

[20] U. Kremer and Marcelo Ramé. Compositional oil reservoir simulation in Fortran D: A feasibility study on Intel iPSC/860. Technical Report TR93-209, Dept. of Computer Science, Rice University, September 1993.

[21] J. Li and M. Chen. Compiling communication-efficient programs for massively parallel machines. *IEEE Transactions on Parallel and Distributed Systems*, 2(3):361–376, July 1991.

[22] M. Mu and J. Rice. Row oriented Gauss elimination on distributed memory multiprocessors. *International Journal of High Speed Computing*, 4(2):143–168, June 1992.

[23] D. Olander and R. Schnabel. Preliminary experience in developing a parallel thin-layer Navier Stokes code and implications for parallel language design. In *Proceedings of the 1992 Scalable High Performance Computing Conference*, Williamsburg, VA, April 1992.

[24] M. Philippsen and W. Tichy. Compiling for massively parallel machines. In *First International Conference of the Austrian Center for Parallel Computation*, Salzburg, Austria, September 1991.

[25] K. Pingali and A. Rogers. Compiling for locality. In *Proceedings of the 1990 International Conference on Parallel Processing*, St. Charles, IL, June 1990.

[26] R. Rühl. Evaluation of compiler-generated parallel programs on three multicomputers. In *Proceedings of the 1992 ACM International Conference on Supercomputing*, Washington, DC, July 1992.

[27] C. Tseng. *An Optimizing Fortran D Compiler for MIMD Distributed-Memory Machines*. PhD thesis, Dept. of Computer Science, Rice University, January 1993.

Fortran 90D/HPF Compiler for Distributed Memory MIMD Computers: Design, Implementation, and Performance Results*

Zeki Bozkus, Alok Choudhary,† Geoffrey Fox, Tomasz Haupt, and Sanjay Ranka‡
Northeast Parallel Architectures Center, Syracuse University

Abstract

Fortran 90D/HPF is a data parallel language with special directives to enable users to specify data alignment and distributions. This paper describes the design and implementation of a Fortran90D/HPF compiler. Techniques for data and computation partitioning, communication detection and generation, and the run-time support for the compiler are discussed. Finally, initial performance results for the compiler are presented. We believe that the methodology to process data distribution, computation partitioning, communication system design and the overall compiler design can be used by the implementors of HPF compilers.

1 Introduction

Currently, distributed memory machines are programmed using a node language and a message passing library. This process is tedious and error prone because the user must perform the task of data distribution and communication for non-local data access.

There has been significant research in developing parallelizing compilers. In this approach, the compiler takes a sequential Fortran 77 program as input, applies a set of transformation rules, and produces a parallelized code for the target machine. However, a sequential language, such as Fortran 77, obscures the parallelism of a problem in sequential loops and other sequential constructs. This makes the potential parallelism of a program more difficult to detect by a parallelizing compiler. Therefore, compiling a sequential program into a parallel program is not a natural approach. An alternative approach is to use a programming language that can naturally represent an application without losing the application's original parallelism. Fortran 90 [1] (with some extensions) is such a language. The extensions may include the *forall* statement and compiler directives for data partitioning, such as decomposition, alignment, and distribution. Fortran 90 with these extensions is what we call "Fortran 90D", a Fortran 90 version of the Fortran D language [2]. We developed the Fortran D language with our colleagues at Rice University. There is an analogous version of Fortran 77 with compiler directives and other constructs, called Fortran 77D. Fortran D allows the user to advise the compiler on the allocation of data to processor memories. Recently, the High Performance Fortran Forum, an informal group of people from academia, industry and national labs, led by Ken Kennedy, developed a language called HPF (High Performance Fortran) [3] based on a number of languages such as Fortran D, CM Fortran [4] and Vienna Fortran [5]. HPF essentially adds extensions to Fortran 90 similar to the Fortran D directives. Hence, Fortran 90D and HPF are very similar except a few syntactic differences. For this reason, we call our compiler the Fortran 90D/HPF compiler.

From our point of view, Fortran90 is not only a language for SIMD computers [4], but it is also a natural language for specifying parallelism in a class of problems called *loosely synchronous* problems. In Fortran 90D/HPF, parallelism is represented with parallel constructs, such as array operations, *where* statements, *forall* statements, and intrinsic functions. This gives the programmer a powerful tool to express the data parallelism natural to a problem.

This paper presents the design of a prototype compiler for Fortran 90D/HPF. The compiler takes as input a program written in Fortran 90D/HPF. Its output is SPMD (Single Program Multiple Data) program with appropriate data and computation partitioning and communication calls for MIMD machines. Therefore, the user can still program using a data parallel language but is relieved of the responsibility to perform data distribution and communication.

---

*This work was supported in part by NSF under CCR-9110812 (Center for Research on Parallel Computation) and DARPA under contract # DABT63-91-C-0028. The content of the information does not necessarily reflect the position or the policy of the Government and no official endorsement should be inferred. Alok Choudhary is also supported by an NSF Young Investigator Award CCR-9357840.

†Also with ECE Dept.

‡Also with CIS Dept.

The goals of this paper are to present the underlying design philosophy, various design choices and the reasons for making these choices, and to describe our experience with the implementation. That is, in contrast to many other compiler papers which present specific techniques to perform one or more functions, our goal is to describe the overall architecture of our compiler. We believe that the presented design will provide directions to the implementors of HPF compilers.

The rest of this paper is organized as follows. The compiler architecture is described in Section 2. Data partitioning, and computation partitioning are discussed in Sections 3, and 4. Section 5 presents the communication primitives and communication generation for Fortran 90D/HPF programs. In Section 6, we present the runtime support system including the intrinsic functions. Some optimization techniques are given in Section 7. Section 8 summarizes our initial experience using the current version of the compiler. It also presents a comparison of the performance with hand written parallel code. Section 9 presents a summary of related work. Finally, summary and conclusions are presented in Section 10.

2 Compiler System Diagram

Our Fortran 90D/HPF parallel compiler exploits only the parallelism expressed in the data parallel constructs. We do not attempt to *parallelize* other constructs, such as *do* loops and *while* loops, since they are used only as naturally sequential control constructs in this language. The foundation of our design lies in recognizing commonly occurring computation and communication patterns. These patterns are then replaced by calls to the optimized run-time support system routines. The run-time support system includes parallel intrinsic functions, data distribution functions, communication primitives and several other miscellaneous routines. This approach represents a significant departure from traditional approaches where a compiler needs to perform in-depth dependency analyses to recognize parallelism, and embed all the synchronization and low-level communication functions inside the generated code.

Figure 1 shows the components of the basic Fortran 90D/HPF compiler. Given a syntactically correct Fortran90D/HPF program, the first step of the compilation is to generate a parse tree. The front-end to parse Fortran 90 for the compiler was obtained from ParaSoft Corporation. In this module, our compiler also transforms each array assignment statement and

where statement into an equivalent *forall* statement with no loss of information [6]. In this way, the subsequent steps need only deal with *forall* statements.

The partitioning module processes the data distribution directives; namely, decomposition, distribute and align. Using these directives, it partitions data and computation among processors.

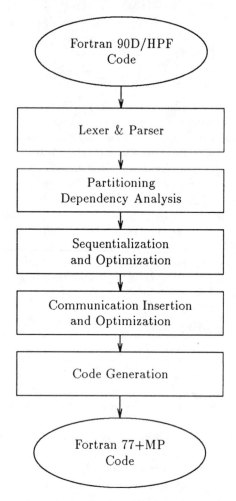

Figure 1: Diagram of the compiler.

After partitioning, the parallel constructs in the node program are sequentialized since they will be executed on a single processor. This is performed by the sequentialization module. Array operations and *forall* statements in the original program are transferred into loops or nested loops. The communication module detects communication requirements and inserts appropriate communication primitives.

Finally, the code generator produces *loosely synchronous* [7] SPMD code. The generated code is structured as alternating phases of local computation and global communication. Local computations consist of operations by each processor on the data in its own memory. Global communication includes any transfer of data among processors, possibly with arithmetic or logical computation on the data as it is transferred (e.g. reduction functions). In such a model, processes do not need to synchronize during local computation. But, if two or more nodes interact, they are implicitly synchronized by global communication.

3 Data Partitioning

The distributed memory system solves the memory bottleneck of vector supercomputers by having separate memory for each processor. However, distributed memory systems demand high locality for good performance. Therefore, the distribution of data across processors is of critical importance to the efficiency of a parallel program in a distributed memory system.

Fortran D provides users with explicit control over data partitioning with both data *alignment* and *distribution* specifications. We briefly overview directives of Fortran D relevant to this paper. The complete language is described elsewhere [2]. The DECOMPOSITION directive is used to declare the name, dimensionality, and the size of each problem domain. We call it "template" (the name "template" has been chosen to describe "DECOMPOSITION" in HPF [3]). The ALIGN directive specifies fine-grain parallelism, mapping each array element onto one or more elements of the template. This provides the minimal requirement for reducing data movement. The DISTRIBUTE directive specifies coarse-grain parallelism, grouping template elements and mapping them to the finite resources of the machine. Each dimension of the template is distributed in either a block or cyclic fashion. The selected distribution can affect the ability of the compiler to minimize communication and load imbalance in the resulting program.

The Fortran 90D/HPF compiler maps arrays to physical processors by using a three stage mapping as shown in Figure 2 which is guided by the user-specified Fortran D directives.

Stage 1 : The alignment of arrays to template is determined by their subscript expressions in the ALIGN directive. The compiler computes f and f^{-1} function from the directive and applies f functions for the corresponding array indices to bring them onto common template index domain. The original indices can be calculated by f^{-1} if they are required. The algorithm to compile align directive can be found in [8].

Stage 2 : Each dimension of the template is mapped onto the logical processor grid, based on the DIS-

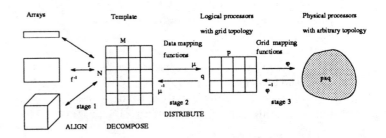

Figure 2: Three stage array mapping

TRIBUTE directive attributes. *Block* divides the template into contiguous chunks. *Cyclic* specifies a round-robin division of the template. The mapping functions μ and μ^{-1} to generate relationship between global and local indices are computed.

Stage 3 : The logical processor grid is mapped onto the physical system. The mapping functions φ and φ^{-1} can change from one system to another but the data mapping onto the logical processor grid does not need to change. This enhances portability across a large number of architectures.

By performing the above three stage mapping, the compiler is decoupled from the specifics of a given machine or configuration. Compilation of distribution directives is discussed in detail in [8].

4 Computation Partitioning

Once the data is distributed, there are several alternatives to assign computations to processing elements (PEs) for each instance of a *forall* statement. One of the most common methods is to use the *owner computes rule*. In the owner computes rule, the computation is assigned to the PE owning the *lhs* data element. This rule is simple to implement and performs well in a large number of cases. Most of the current implementations of parallelizing compilers uses the owner computes rule [5, 9]. However, it may not be possible to apply the owner computes rule for every case without extensive overhead. The following examples describe how our compiler performs computation partitioning.

Example 1 (canonical form) Consider the following statement, taken from the Jacobi relaxation program

```
forall (i=1:N, j=1:N)
  B(i,j) = 0.25*(A(i-1,j)+A(i+1,j)+A(i,j-1)+A(i,j+1))
```

In the above example, as in a large number of scientific computations, the *forall* statement can be written in the canonical form. In this form, the subscript value in the *lhs* is identical to the forall iteration variable. In such cases, the iterations can be easily distributed using the owner computes rule.

Example 2 (non-canonical form) Consider the following statement, taken from an FFT program

```
forall (i=1:incrm, j=1:nx/2)
  x(i+j*incrm*2+incrm) = x(i+j*incrm*2)
                          - term2(i+j*incrm*2+incrm)
```

The *lhs* array index is not in the canonical form. In this case, the compiler equally distributes the iteration space on the number of processors on which the *lhs* array is distributed. Hence, the total number of iterations will still be the same as the number of *lhs* array elements being assigned.

5 Communication

Our Fortran 90D/HPF compiler produces calls to collective communication routines [10] instead of generating individual processor send and receive calls inside the compiled code. There are three main reasons for using collective communication to support interprocessor communication in the Fortran 90D/HPF compiler.

1. *Improved performance estimation of communication costs.* Our compiler takes the data distribution for the source arrays from the user as compiler directives. However, any future compiler will require a capability to perform automatic data distribution and alignments [11]. Such techniques usually require computing trade-offs between exploitable parallelism and the communication costs. The costs of collective communication routines can be determined more precisely, thereby enabling the compiler to generate better distributions automatically.

2. *Improved performance of Fortran 90D/HPF programs.* To achieve good performance, interprocessor communication must be minimized. By developing a separate library of interprocessor communication routines, each routine can be optimized. This is particularly important given that the routines will be used by many programs compiled through the compiler.

3. *Increased portability of the Fortran 90D/HPF compiler.* By separating the communication library from the basic compiler design, portability

is enhanced because to port the compiler, only the machine specific low-level communication calls in the library need to be changed.

5.1 Communication Primitives

In order to perform a collective communication on array elements, the communication primitive needs the following information 1-) send processors list, 2-) receive processors list, 3-) local index list of the source array and, 4-) local index list of the destination array.

There are two ways of determining the above information. 1) Using a preprocessing loop to compute the above values or, 2) based on the type of communication, the above information may be implicitly available, and therefore, not require preprocessing. We classify our communication primitives into *unstructured* and *structured* communication.

Our structured communication primitives are based on a logical grid configuration of the processors. Hence, they use grid-based communications such as shift along dimensions, broadcast along dimensions etc. The following summarizes some of the structured communication primitives implemented in our compiler.

- **transfer:** Single source to single destination message.

- **multicast:** broadcast along a dimension of the logical grid.

- **overlap_shift:** shifting data into overlap areas in one or more grid dimensions. This is particularly useful when the shift amount is known at compile time. This primitive uses that fact to avoid intra processor copying of data and directly stores data in the overlap areas [12].

- **temporary_shift:** This is similar to overlap shift except that the data is shifted into a temporary array. This is useful when the shift amount is not a compile time constant. This shift may require intra-processor copying of data.

- **concatenation:** This primitive concatenates a distributed array and the resultant array ends up in all the processors participating in this primitive.

We have implemented two sets of unstructured communication primitives: 1) where the communicating processors can determine the send and receive lists based only on local information, and hence, only require preprocessing that involves local computations

[13], and 2) where to determine the send and receive lists preprocessing itself requires communication among the processors [14]. The primitives are as follows.

- **precomp_read:** This primitive is used to bring all non-local data to the place it is needed before the computation is performed.

- **postcomp_write:** This primitive is used to store remote data by sending it to the processors that own the data after the computation is performed. Note that these two primitives requires only local computation in the preprocessing loop.

- **gather:** This is similar to *precomp_read* except that preprocessing loop itself may require communication.

- **scatter:** This is similar to *postcomp_write* except that preprocessing loop itself may require communication.

5.2 Communication Detection

The compiler must recognize the presence of collective communication patterns in the computations in order to generate the appropriate communication calls. Specifically, this involves a number of tests on the relationships among the subscripts of various arrays in a forall statement. These tests should also include information about array alignments and distributions. We use pattern matching techniques similar to those proposed by Li and Chen [15]. Further, we extend the above tests to include unstructured communication.

Consider the following forall statement to illustrate the steps involved in communication detection.

FORALL (i1=l1:u1:s1, i2= ..., ...)
LHS($f_1, f_2, ..., f_n$) = RHS1($g_1, g_2, ..., g_m$) + ...

where g_i and f_j, $1 \leq i \leq m$, $1 \leq j \leq n$, are functions of index variables or are indirection arrays.

The algorithm first attempts to detect structured communication if the arrays are aligned to the same template. For each array on the RHS, the following processing is performed. Each subscript of the array is coupled with the corresponding subscript on the LHS array such that both subscripts are aligned with the same dimension of the template. For each such pair, the algorithm attempts to find a structured communication pattern in that dimension according to Table 1. If a structured communication pattern is found then the subscript on the RHS from this pair is tagged with indicating the appropriate communication primitive.

Table 1: Communication primitives based on the relationship between *lhs* and *rhs* array subscript reference patterns for block distribution. (c: compile time constant, s, d: scalar, f: invertible function, V: an indirection array).

Steps	(lhs,rhs)	Comm. primitives
1	(i, s)	multicast
2	$(i, i + c)$	overlap_shift
3	$(i, i - c)$	overlap_shift
4	$(i, i + s)$	temporary_shift
5	$(i, i - s)$	temporary_shift
6	(d, s)	transfer
7	(i, i)	no_communication
8	$(i, f(i))$	precomp_read
9	$(f(i), i)$	postcomp_write
10	$(i, V(i))$	gather
11	$(V(i), i)$	scatter
12	$(i, unknown)$	gather
13	$(unknown, i)$	scatter

If any distributed dimension of an array on the RHS is left untagged then the array is marked with one of the unstructured communication primitives depending on the reference pattern. Note that any pattern that can not be classified according to Tables 1, is marked as *unknown* (such subscripts involving more than one forall index, e.g $I + J$) so that scatter and gather can be used to parallelize any forall statement.

5.3 Communication Generation

Having recognized the type of communication in each dimension of an array for structured communication or each array for unstructured communication in a forall statement, the compiler needs to perform the appropriate program transformations. We now illustrate these transformations with the aid of some examples.

5.3.1 Structured Communication

All the examples discussed below have the following mapping directives.

```
C$ PROCESSORS(P,Q)
C$ DISTRIBUTE TEMPL(BLOCK,BLOCK)
C$ ALIGN A(I,J), B(I,J) WITH TEMPL(I,J)
```

Example 1 (transfer) Consider the statement

FORALL(I=1:N) A(I,8)=B(I,3)

The first subscript of B is marked as *no_communication* because A and B are aligned in the first dimension and have identical indices. The second dimension is marked as *transfer*.

355

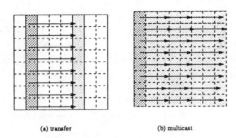

(a) transfer   (b) multicast

Figure 3: Structured communication on logical grid processors.

```
1.    call set_BOUND(lb,ub,st,1,N,1)
2.    call set_DAD(B_DAD,.....)
3.    call transfer(B, B_DAD, TMP,
         source=global_to_proc(3),
         dest=global_to_proc(8))
4.    DO I=lb,ub,st
5.       if(grid(2).EQ.dest)
            A(I,global_to_local(8)) = TMP(I)
6.    END DO
```

In the above code, the *set_BOUND* primitive (line 1) computes the local bounds for computation assignment based on the iteration distribution (Section 4). In line 2, the primitive set_DAD is used to fill the Distributed Array Descriptor (DAD) associated with array B so that it can be passed to the *transfer* communication primitive at run-time. The DAD has sufficient information for the communication primitives to compute all the necessary information including local bounds, distributions, global shape etc. Note that transfer performs one-to-one send-receive communication based on the logical grid. In this example, one column of grid processors communicate with another column of the grid processors as shown in Figure 3 (a).

Example 2 (multicast) Consider the statement

FORALL(I=1:N,J=1:M) A(I,J)=B(I,3)

The second subscript of B marked as *multicast* and the first one as no_communication.

```
1.    call set_BOUND(lb,ub,st,1,N,1)
2.    call set_BOUND(lb1,ub1,st1,1,M,1)
3.    call set_DAD(B_DAD,.....)
4.    call multicast(B, B_DAD, TMP,
         source_proc=global_to_proc(3), dim=2)
5.    DO I=lb,ub,st
6.    DO J=lb1,ub1,st1
7.       A(I,J) = TMP(I)
8.    END DO
```

Line 4 shows a broadcast along dimension 2 of the logical processor grid by the processors owning elements $B(I,3)$ where $1 \leq I \leq N$ (Figure 3 (b).)

5.3.2 Unstructured Communication

In distributed memory MIMD architectures, there is typically a non-trivial communication latency or startup cost. Hence, it is attractive to vectorize messages to reduce the number of startups. For unstructured communication, this optimization can be achieved by performing the entire preprocessing loop before communication so that the schedule routine can combine the messages to the maximum extent. The preprocessing loop is also called the "inspector" loop [16, 13].

Example 1 (precomp_read) Consider the statement

FORALL(I=1:N) A(I)=B(2*I+1)

The array B is marked as *precomp_read* since the distributed dimension subscript is written as $f(i) = 2 * i + 1$ which is invertible as $g(i) = (i-1)/2$.

```
1     count=1
2     call set_BOUND(lb,ub,st,1,N,1)
3     DO I=1, N/P
4        receive_list(count)=global_to_proc(f(i))
5        send_list(count)= global_to_proc(g(i))
6        local_list(count) = global_to_local(g(i))
7        count=count+1
8     END DO
9     isch = schedule1(receive_list,
                 send_list, local_list, count)
10    call precomp_read(isch, tmp,B)
11    count=1
12    DO I=1, N/P
13       if((I.ge.lb).and.(I.le.ub)
                .and.(mod(I,st).eq.0))   ! mask
14          A(I) = tmp(count)
15       count= count+1
16    END DO
```

The pre-processing loop is given in lines 1-9. Note that this pre-processing loop executes concurrently in each processor. The loop covers entire local array bounds since each processor has to calculate the *receive_list* as well as the *send_list* of processors. Each processor also fills the local indices of the array elements which are needed by that processor.

The *schedule1* routine does not need to communicate but only constructs the scheduling data structure *isch*. The schedule *isch* can also be used to carry out identical patterns of data exchanges on several different but identically distributed arrays or array sections. The same schedule can be reused to repeatedly carry out a particular pattern of data exchange on a single distributed array. In these cases, the cost of generating the schedules can be amortized by only executing it once. This analysis can be performed at compile time. Hence, if the compiler recognizes that the same schedule can be reused, it does not generate code for scheduling but it passes a pointer to the already existing schedule.

The *precomp_read* primitive performs the actual communication using the schedule. Once the communication is performed, the data is ordered in a one dimensional array, and the computation (lines 12-15) uses this one dimensional array. The *precomp_read* primitive brings an element into *temp* for each local array element since preprocessing loops coves entire local array. The *if* statement masks the assignment to preserve the semantic of original loop.

Example 2 (gather) Consider the statement

FORALL(I=1:N) A(I)=B(V(I))

The array B is marked as requiring *gather* communication since the subscript is only known at runtime. The receiving processors can know what nonlocal data they need from other processors, but a processor may not know what local data it needs to send to other processors. For simplicity, in this example, we assume that the indirection array V is replicated. If it is not replicated, the indirection array must also be communicated to compute the receive list on each processor.

```
1    count=1
2    call set_BOUND(lb,ub,st,1,N,1)
3    DO I=lb,ub,st
4       receive_list(count)=global_to_proc(V(i))
6       local_list(count) = global_to_local(V(i))
7       count=count+1
8    END DO
9    isch = schedule2(receive_list,
               local_list, count)
10   call gather(isch, tmp,B)
11   count=1
12   DO I=lb,ub,st
13      A(I) = tmp(count)
14      count= count+1
15   END DO
```

Once the scheduling is completed, every processor knows exactly which non-local data elements it needs to send to and receive from other processors. Recall that the task of *scheduler2* is to determine exactly which send and receive communications must be carried out by each processor. The scheduler first figures out how many messages each processor will have to send and receive during the data exchange. Each processor computes the number of elements (*receive_list*) and the local index of each element it needs from all other processors. In *schedule2* routine, processors communicate to combine these lists (a fan-in type of communication). At the end of this processing, each processor contains the send and receive list. After this point, each processor transmits a list of required array elements (*local_list*) to the appropriate processors. Each processor now has the information required to set up the send and receive messages that are needed to carry out the scheduled communication. This is done by the gather primitives.

The gather and scatter operations are powerful enough to provide the ability to read and write distributed arrays with vectorized communication facility. These two primitives are available in PARTI (Parallel Automatic Runtime Toolkit at ICASE) [16] designed to efficiently support irregular patterns of distributed array accesses.

6   Run-time Support System

The Fortran 90D compiler relies on a very powerful run-time support system. The run-time support system consists of functions which can be called from the node programs of a distributed memory machine.

Intrinsic functions support many of the basic data parallel operations in Fortran 90. They not only provide a concise means of expressing operations on arrays, but also identify parallel computation patterns that may be difficult to detect automatically. Fortran 90 provides intrinsic functions for operations such as shift, reduction, transpose, reshape, and matrix multiplication.

Some of the intrinsic functions can be further optimized for the underlying hardware architecture. Our Fortran 90D/HPF compiler has more than 500 parallel run-time support routines and the implementation details can be found in [17].

Arrays may be redistributed across subroutine boundaries. A dummy argument which is distributed differently from its actual argument in the calling routine is automatically redistributed upon entry to the subroutine by the compiler, and is automatically redistributed back to its original distribution at subroutine exit. These operations are performed by the redistribution primitives which transform from *block* to *cyclic* or vice versa.

When a distributed array is passed as an argument to some of the run-time support primitives, it is also necessary to provide information such as its size, distribution among the nodes of the distributed memory machine etc. All this information is stored into a structure which is called *distributed array descriptor* (DAD) [17].

7 Optimizations

Several types of *communication* and *computation* optimizations can be performed to generate a more efficient code. In terms of *computation* optimization, it is expected that the scalar node compiler performs a number of classic scalar optimizations within basic blocks. These optimizations include common subexpression elimination, copy propagation (of constants, variables, and expressions), constant folding, useless assignment elimination, and a number of algebraic identities and strength reduction transformations. However, to use parallelism within the single node (e.g. using attached vector units), our compiler propagates information to the node compiler using node directives. Since there is no data dependency between different loop iteration in the original data parallel constructs such as *forall* statement, vectorization can be performed easily by the node compiler.

Our compiler performs several optimizations to reduce the total cost of communication. Some of *communication* optimizations [15, 18, 14] are as follows.

1. *Vectorized communication.* Vectorization combines messages for the same source and destination into a single message to reduce communication overhead. Since we are only parallelizing array assignments and forall statements in Fortran 90D/HPF, there is no data dependency between different loop iterations. Thus, all the required communication can be performed before or after the execution of the loop on each of the processors involved.

2. *Eliminate unnecessary communications.* In many cases, communication required for two different operands can be replaced by their union. For example, the following code may require two *overlapping_shifts*. However, with a simple analysis, the compiler can eliminate the shift of size 2.

   FORALL(I=1:N) A(I)=B(I+2)+B(I+3)

3. *Reuse of scheduling information.* Unstructured communication primitives are required by computations which require the use of a preprocessor. As discussed in Section 5.3.2, the schedules can be reused with appropriate analysis.

4. *Code movement.* The compiler can utilize the information that the run-time support routines do not have procedural side effects. For example, the preprocessing loop or communication routines can be moved up as much as possible by analyzing

Table 2: Comparison of the execution times of the hand-written code and Fortran 90D compiler generated code for several applications. (Intel iPSC/860, time is in seconds).

Program	Size	\multicolumn{5}{c}{Number of PEs}
		1	2	4	8	16
Gauss Hand	1Kx1K	623.1	446.6	235.3	134.8	79.4
Gauss F90D	1Kx1K	618.7	451.9	261.8	147.2	87.4
Nbody Hand	1Kx1K	6.8	1.7	1.2	0.7	0.4
Nbody F90D	1Kx1K	13.8	5.9	2.4	1.3	0.8
Option Hand	8K	4.2	3.1	1.6	0.8	0.4
Option F90D	8K	4.3	3.1	1.6	0.8	0.4
Pi Hand	64K	0.398	0.200	0.101	0.053	0.030
Pi F90D	64K	0.411	0.207	0.104	0.054	0.032

definition-use chains. This may lead to moving of the scheduling code out of one or more nested loops which may reduce the amount of communication required significantly. We are incrementally incorporating many more optimizations in the compiler.

8 Experimental Results

To illustrate the performance of our compiler, we present benchmark results from four programs and the first 10 Livermore loop kernels. *Gauss* solves a system of linear equations with partial pivoting. *Nbody* program simulates the universe using the algorithm in [10]. *Option* program predicts the stock option pricing using stochastic volatility European model. *Pi* program calculates the value of pi, using numerical integration. The Livermore kernels are 24 loops abstracted from actual production codes that have been widely used to evaluate the performance of various computer systems. Data for all programs were block distributed and were written outside of the compiler group at NPAC by experienced message passing programmers.

Tables 2 and 3 show the performance of compiler generated codes ($F90D/HPF$) and hand-written f77+ MP code. The tables contain data from running these programs with varying number of processors an Intel iPSC/860. The compiler generated codes and hand-written codes use Express as a message passing library. Timings were taken using *extime()* function having an accuracy of one microsecond. The programs were compiled by using Parasoft Express Fortran compiler which calls Portland Group if77 release 4.0 compiler with all optimizations turned on (-O4).

Table 3: Comparison of the execution times of the hand-written code and Fortran 90D compiler generated code for the first 10 Livermore loop kernels. Data size is 16K real. (a 16 node Intel iPSC/860, time is in milliseconds).

Loop #	Type of Application	F90D	Hand	Ratio
1.	Hydrodynamics	2.545	2.550	0.99
2.	Incomplete Cholesky	11.783	10.440	1.12
3.	Inner product	3.253	3.249	1.00
4.	Banded linear equations	5.139	3.212	1.60
5.	Tridiagonal elimination	30928.	30897.	1.00
6.	Linear recurrence relations	1849.1	1886.5	0.98
7.	Equation of state	11.346	3.704	3.06
8.	A.D.I	38.656	20.038	1.92
9.	Numerical Integration	2.255	2.441	0.92
10.	Numerical Differentiation	9.814	4.589	2.13

We observe that the performance of the compiler generated codes are usually within a factor of 2 of the hand-written codes. This is due to the fact that experienced programmer can incorporate more optimization than our compiler currently does. For example, a programmer can combine or eliminate some of the communication or some of intra-processor temporary copying. The compiler uses a more generic packing routine, whereas a programmer can combine communication for the same source and destination for different arrays. Another observation is that our run-time system shift routine is slower than the programmer's shift routines. We are planing to rewrite some part of our run-time shifts using assembly language.

9   Summary of Related Work

Callahan and Kennedy [9] proposed distributed-memory compilation techniques based on data-dependence driven program transformations. These techniques were implemented in a prototype compiler in the ParaScope programming environment. Currently, a Fortran 77D compiler is being developed at Rice [18]. The Fortran 77D compiler introduces and classifies a number of advanced optimizations needed to achieve acceptable performance; they are analyzed and empirically evaluated for stencil computations. SUPERB [5] is a semi-automatic parallelization tool designed for MIMD distributed-memory machines. It supports arbitrary user-specified contiguous rectangular distributions, and performs dependence analysis to guide interactive program transformations. KALI [13] is the first compiler system that supports both regular and irregular computations on MIMD machines.

KALI requires that the programmer explicitly partition loop iterations onto the processor grid. An inspector/executor strategy is used for run-time preprocessing of the communication for irregularly distributed arrays. Dataparallel C [19] is a variant of the original C* programming language, designed by Thinking Machines Corporation for its Connection Machines processor array. Data parallel C extends C to provide the programmer access to a parallel virtual machine. ARF is a compiler for irregular computations [14]. Saltz et al. describe and experimentally characterize ARF compiler and runtime support procedures which embody methods that are capable of handling a wide range of irregular problems in scientific computing. Many techniques especially unstructured communication of Fortran 90D compiler are adapted from ARF compiler. The ADAPT system [20] compiles Fortran 90 for execution on MIMD distributed memory architectures. The ADAPTOR [21] is a tool that transform data parallel programs written in Fortran with array extensions and layout directives to explicit message passing. Li and Chen [22] describe general compiler optimization techniques that reduce communication overhead for Fortran-90 implementation on massivelly parallel machines. Our compiler uses pattern matching techniques to detect communication similar to Li and Chen's. Sabot [23] describes the techniques that are used by the CM compiler to map the fine-grained array parallelism of languages such as Fortran 90 and C* onto the Connection Machine architectures.

10   Conclusions

In this paper, we presented design, implementation and performance results of our Fortran 90D/HPF compiler for distributed memory machines. Specifically, techniques for processing distribution directives, computation partitioning, communication detection and generation were presented. We also showed that our design is portable, yet efficient.

We believe that the methodology presented in this paper to compile Fortran 90D/HPF can be used by the designers and implementors for HPF language.

Acknowledgments

We are grateful to Parasoft for providing the Fortran 90 parser and Express without which the prototype compiler could have been delayed. We would like to thank the other members of our compiler research group R. Bordawekar, R. Ponnusamy, R. Thakur, and J. C. Wang for their contribution in the project including the development of the run-time library functions, testing, and help with programming. We would also like to thank K. Kennedy, C. Koelbel, C. Tseng and S. Hiranandani of Rice University and J. Saltz and his group of Maryland University for many inspiring discussions and inputs that have greatly influenced this work.

References

[1] American National Standards Institue. Fortran 90: X3j3 internal document s8.118. *Summitted as Text for ISO/IEC 1539:1991*, May 1991.

[2] G. C. Fox, S. Hiranadani, K. Kenndy, C. Koelbel, U. Kremer, C. Tseng, and M. Wu. Fortran D Language Specification. Technical report, Rice and Syracuse University, 1992.

[3] High Performance Fortran Forum. High performance fortran language specification version 1.0. *Draft, Also available as technical report CRPC-TR92225 from the Center for Research on Parallel Computation, Rice University.*, Jan. 1993.

[4] The Thinking Machine Corporation. *CM Fortran User's Guide version 0.7-f*, July 1990.

[5] H. Bast H. Zima and M. Gerndt. Superb: A tool for semi Automatic SIMD/MIMD Parallelization. *Parallel Computing*, January 1988.

[6] Z. Bozkus et al. Compiling the FORALL statement on MIMD parallel computers. Technical Report SCCS-389, Northeast Parallel Architectures Center, July 1992.

[7] G. Fox. The architecture of problems and portable parallel software systems. Technical Report SCCS-78b, Syracuse University, 1991.

[8] Z. Bozkus et al. Compiling Distribution Directives in a Fortran 90D Compiler. Technical Report SCCS-388, Northeast Parallel Architectures Center, July 1992.

[9] D. Callahan and K. Kennedy. Compiling programs for Distributed Memory Multiprocessors. *The Journal of Supercomputing*, pages 171–207, 1988.

[10] G. C. Fox, M.A. Johnson, G.A. Lyzenga, S. W. Otto, J.K. Salmon, and D. W. Walker. In *Solving Problems on Concurrent Processors*, volume 1-2. Prentice Hall, May 1988.

[11] R. Schreiber S. Chatterjee, J.R. Gilbert and S.H Tseng. Automatic Array Alignment in Data-Parallel Programs. *Twentieth Annual ACM SIGACT/SIGPLAN Symposium on Principles of Programming Languages*, January 1993.

[12] M. Gerndt. Updating distributed variables in local computations. *Concurrency: Practice and Experience*, September 1990.

[13] C. Koelbel and P. Mehrotra. Supporting Compiling Global Name-Space Parallel Loops for Distributed Execution. *IEEE Transactions on Parallel and Distributed Systems*, October 1991.

[14] H. Berryman J. Saltz, J. Wu and S. Hiranandani. Distributed Memory Compiler Design for Sparse Problems. *Interim Report ICASE, NASA Langley Research Center*, 1991.

[15] J. Li and M. Chen. Compiling Communication -Efficient Programs for Massively Parallel Machines. *IEEE Transactions on Parallel and Distributed Systems*, pages 361–376, July 1991.

[16] J. Saltz R. Das and H. Berryman. A Manual For PARTI Runtime Primitives. *NASA,ICASE Interim Report 17*, May 1991.

[17] I. Ahmad, R. Bordawekar, Z. Bozkus, A. Choudhary, G. Fox, K. Parasuram, R. Ponnusamy, S. Ranka, and R. Thakur. Fortran 90D Intrinsic Functions on Distributed Memory Machines: Implementation and Scalability. Technical Report SCCS-256, Northeast Parallel Architectures Center, March 1992.

[18] S. Hiranandani, K. Kennedy, and C. Tseng. Compiler optimization for Fortran D on MIMD distributed-memory machines. *Proc. Supercomputing'91*, Nov 1991.

[19] Philip Hatcher, Anthony Lapadula, Robert Jones, Michael Quinn, and Ray Anderson. A Production-Quality C* Compiler for Hypercube Multicomputers. *Third ACM SIGPLAN symposium on PPOPP*, 26:73–82, July 1991.

[20] J.H Merlin. Techniques for the Automatic Parallelisation of 'Distributed Fortran 90'. Technical Report SNARC 92-02, Southampton Novel Architecture Research Centre, 1992.

[21] T. Brandes. ADAPTOR Language Reference Manual. Technical Report ADAPTOR-3, German National Research Center for Computer Science, 1992.

[22] M. Chen and J.J Wu. Optimizing FORTRAN-90 Programs for Data Motion on Massivelly Parallel Systems. Technical Report YALEU/DCS/TR-882, Yale University, Dep. of Comp. Sci., 1992.

[23] G. Sabot. A Compiler for a Massively Parallel Distributed Memory MIMD Computer. *The Fourth Symposium on the Frointiers of Massively Parallel Computation*, 1992.

Runtime Compilation Techniques for Data Partitioning and Communication Schedule Reuse*

Ravi Ponnusamy[†‡]   Joel Saltz[†]   Alok Choudhary[‡]

[†]*Computer Science Department*   [‡]*Northeast Parallel Architectures Center*
University of Maryland   *Syracuse University*
College Park, MD 20742   *Syracuse, NY 13244*

Abstract

In this paper, we describe two new ideas by which HPF compiler can deal with irregular computations effectively. The first mechanism invokes a user specified mapping procedure via a set of compiler directives. The directives allow the user to use program arrays to describe graph connectivity, spatial location of array elements and computational load. The second is a simple conservative method that in many cases enables a compiler to recognize that it is possible to reuse previously computed results from inspectors (e.g. communication schedules, loop iteration partitions, information that associates off-processor data copies with on-processor buffer locations). We present performance results for these mechanisms from a Fortran 90D compiler implementation.

1 Introduction

In sparse and unstructured problems the data access pattern is determined by variable values known only at runtime. In these cases, programmers carry out preprocessig to partition work, map data structures and schedule the movement of data between the memories of processors. The code needed to carry out runtime preprocessing can also be generated by a distributed memory compiler in a process we call *runtime compilation* [23]. In this paper, we present methods and a prototype implementation where we demonstrate techniques that make it possible for compilers to efficiently handle irregular problems coded using a set of language extensions closely related to Fortran D [10] or Vienna Fortran [28].

On distributed memory architectures, loops with indirect array accesses can be handled by transforming the original loop into two sequences of code: an *inspector* and an *executor*. The inspector partitions loop iterations, allocates local memory for each unique off-processor distributed array element accessed by a loop, and builds a communication

schedule to prefetch required off-processor data. In the executor phase, the actual communication and computation are carried out [21]. The ARF compiler [26] and KALI compiler [16] used this kind of transformation to handle loops with indirectly referenced arrays (*irregular loops*).

We propose a simple conservative method that often makes it possible to reuse previously computed results from inspectors (e.g. communication schedules, loop iteration partitions, information that associates off-processor data copies with on-processor buffer locations). The compiler generates code that, at runtime, maintains a record of when a Fortran 90D loop or intrinsic may have written to a distributed array that is used to indirectly reference another distributed array. In this scheme, each inspector checks this runtime record to see whether any indirection arrays may have been modified since the last time the inspector was invoked.

In distributed memory machines, large data arrays need to be partitioned between local memories of processors. These partitioned data arrays are called *distributed arrays*. Long term storage of distributed array data is assigned to specific processor and memory locations in the distributed machine. It is frequently advantageous to partition distributed arrays in an irregular manner. For instance, the way in which the nodes of an irregular computational mesh are numbered frequently does not have a useful correspondence to the connectivity pattern of the mesh. When we partition the data structures in such a problem in a way that minimizes interprocessor communication, we may need to assign arbitrary array elements to each processor. In recent years promising heuristics have been developed and tradeoffs associated with the different partitioning methods have been studied [24, 25, 19, 17, 2, 13].

We have implemented the runtime support and compiler transformations needed to allow users to specify the information needed to produce a customized distribution function. In our view, this information can consist of a description of graph connectivity, spatial location of array elements and information that associates array elements with computational load. Based on user directives the compiler produces code that, at runtime, generates a standardized representation of the above information, and then passes this standardized representation to a (user specified) partitioner. The compiler also generates code that, at runtime, produces a data structure that is used to partition loop it-

*This work was sponsored in part by ARPA (NAG-1-1485), NSF (ASC 9213821) and ONR (SC292-1-22913). Author Choudhary was also supported by NSF Young Investigator award (CCR-9357840). The content of the information does not necessarily reflect the position of the policy of the Government and no official endorsement should be inferred

© 1993 ACM 0-8186-4340-4/93/0011 $1.50

```
C  Single statement loop L1
   FORALL i = 1, N
   y(ia(i)) = x(ib(i)) + ... x(ic(i))
   END FORALL
C  Sweep over edges: Loop L2
   FORALL i = 1,N
   REDUCE (ADD, y(end_pt1(i)),
   f(x(end_pt1(i)), x(end_pt2(i))))
   REDUCE (ADD, y(end_pt2(i)),
   g(x(end_pt1(i)), x(end_pt2(i))))
   END FORALL
```

Figure 1: Example Irregular Loops

erations. To our knowledge, the implementation described in this paper is the first distributed memory Fortran compiler to provide this kind of support. We also note that in the Vienna Fortran [28] language definition, a user can also specify a customized distribution function. The runtime support and compiler transformation strategies described here can also be applied to Vienna Fortran.

We will describe the runtime support, compiler transformations and language extensions required to provide the new capabilities described above. We assume that irregular accesses are carried out in the context of a single or multiple statement loop where the only loop carried dependencies allowed are left hand side reductions (e.g. addition, accumulation, max, min, etc). We also assume that irregular array accesses occur as a result of a single level of indirection with a distributed array that is indexed directly by the loop index.

In the example loops shown in Figure 1, we employ Fortran D syntax to depict two loops. The first loop is a single statement loop with indirect array references without dependencies. The second loop is a loop in which we carry out reduction operations. The second loop is similar to those loops found in unstructured computational fluid dynamics codes and molecular dynamics codes. We use this loop to demonstrate our runtime procedures and compiler transformations in the following sections.

We have implemented our methods as part of the Fortran 90D compiler being developed by Syracuse University [9]. Our implementation results on simple templates reveal that the performance of the compiler generated code is within 10% of the hand parallelized version.

This paper is organized as follows. We set the context of the work in Section 2. In Section 3, we describe the runtime technique to save communication schedules. In Section 4 we describe the procedures used to couple data and loop iteration partitioners to compilers. In Section 5 we present an overview of our compiler effort. We describe the transformations which generate the standard data structure and describe the language extensions we use to con-

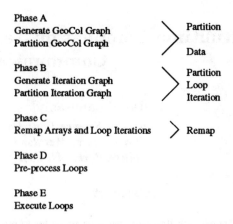

Figure 2: Solving Irregular Problems

trol compiler-linked runtime partitioning. In Section 6 we present performance data to characterize the performance of our methods. We briefly discuss related work in Section 7 and we conclude in Section 8.

2 Overview

2.1 Overview of CHAOS

We have developed efficient runtime support to deal with problems that consist of a sequence of clearly demarcated concurrent computational phases. The project is called CHAOS; the runtime support is called the CHAOS library. The CHAOS library is a superset of the earlier PARTI library [21, 26, 23].

Solving concurrent irregular problems on distributed memory machines using our runtime support, involves five major steps (Figure 2). The first three steps in the figure concern mapping data and computations onto processors. We provide a brief description of these steps here, and will discuss them in detail in later sections.

Initially, the distributed arrays are decomposed in a known regular manner. In Phase A of Figure 2, CHAOS procedures can be called to construct a graph data structure (the GeoCoL data structure) using the data access patterns associated with a particular set of loops. The GeoCoL graph data structure is passed to a partitioner. The partitioner calculates how data arrays should be distributed.

In Phase B, the newly calculated array distributions are used to decide how loop iterations are to be partitioned among processors. This calculation takes into account loop data access patterns. In Phase C we carry out the actual remapping of arrays and loop iterations.

In Phase D, we carry out the preprocessing needed to (1) coordinate interprocessor data movement, (2) manage the storage of, and access to, copies of off-processor data, and (3) support a shared name space. This preprocessing involves generating communication *schedules*, translating array indices to access local copies of off-processor data and allocating local buffer space for copies of off-processor data. It is also necessary to retrieve globally indexed but irregularly distributed data-sets from the numerous local processor memories. Finally, in Phase E we use information from the earlier phases to carry out the necessary computation.

CHAOS and PARTI procedures have been used in a variety of applications, including sparse matrix linear solvers, adaptive computational fluid dynamics codes, molecular dynamics codes and a prototype compiler [23] aimed at distributed memory multiprocessors.

2.2 Overview of Existing Language Support

The data decomposition directives we employ for irregular problems will be presented in the context of Fortran D. While our work will be presented in the context of Fortran D, the same optimizations and analogous language extensions could be used for a wide range of languages and compilers such as Vienna Fortran and HPF. Vienna Fortran, Fortran D and HPF (evolved from Fortran D and Fortran 90) provide a rich set of data decomposition specifications; a definition of such language extensions may be found in [10, 8]. These languages, as currently specified, require that users explicitly define how data is to be distributed.

Fortran D can be used to *explicitly* specify an irregular inter-processor partition of distributed array elements. In Figure 3, we present an example of such a Fortran D declaration. In Fortran D, one declares a template called a *distribution* which is used to characterize the significant attributes of a distributed array. The distribution fixes the size, dimension and way in which the array is to be partitioned between processors. A distribution is produced using two declarations. The first declaration is **DECOMPOSITION**. Decomposition fixes the name, dimensionality and size of the distributed array template. The second declaration is **DISTRIBUTE**. Distribute is an executable statement and specifies how a template is to be mapped onto processors.

Fortran D provides the user with a choice of several regular distributions. In addition, a user can explicitly specify how a distribution is to be mapped onto processors. A specific array is associated with a distribution using the Fortran D statement **ALIGN**. In statement S3, of Figure 3, two of size N each, one dimensional decompositions are defined. In statement S4, decomposition reg is partitioned into equal sized blocks, with one block assigned to each processor. In statement S5, array map is aligned with distribution reg. Array map will be used to specify (in statement S7) how distribution irreg is to be partitioned between processors. An irregular distribution is specified using an integer array; when $map(i)$ is set equal to p, element i of the distribution irreg is assigned to processor p.

```
....
S1  REAL*8 x(N),y(N)
S2  INTEGER map(N)
S3  DECOMPOSITION reg(N),irreg(N)
S4  DISTRIBUTE reg(block)
S5  ALIGN map with reg
S6  ...  set values of map array using some mapping
         method ..
S7  DISTRIBUTE irreg(map)
S8  ALIGN x,y with irreg
....
```

Figure 3: Fortran D Irregular Distribution

The difficulty with the declarations depicted in Figure 3 is that *it is not obvious how to partition the irregularly distributed array*. The map array which gives the distribution pattern of irreg has to be generated separately by running a partitioner. The Fortran-D constructs are not rich enough for the user to couple the generation of the map array to the program compilation process. While there are a wealth of partitioning heuristics available, coding such partitioners from scratch can represent a significant effort. There is no standard interface between the partitioners and the application codes.

3 Communication Schedule Reuse

The cost of carrying out an inspector (phases B, C and D in Figure 2) can be amortized when the information produced by the inspector is computed once and then used repeatedly. Compile time analysis needed to reuse inspector communication schedules is touched upon in [12, 7].

We propose a simple conservative method that in many cases allows us to reuse the results from inspectors. The results from an inspector for loop L can be reused as long as:

- distributions of data arrays referenced in loop L have remained unchanged since the last time the inspector was invoked, and

- there is no possibility that indirection arrays associated with loop L have been modified since the last inspector invocation.

The compiler generates code that at runtime maintains a record of when a Fortran 90D loop's statements or array intrinsic may have written to a distributed array that is used to indirectly reference another distributed array. In this scheme, each inspector checks this runtime record to see whether any indirection arrays may have been modified since the last time the inspector was invoked.

In this presentation, we assume that we are carrying out an inspector for a forall loop. We also assume that all

363

indirect array references to any distributed array **y** are of the form **y**(ia(i)) where **ia** is a distributed array and i is a loop index associated with the forall loop.

A data access descriptor (DAD) for a distributed array contains (among other things) the current distribution type of the array (e.g. block, cyclic, irregular) and the size of the array. In order to generate correct distributed memory code, whenever the compiler generates code that references a distributed array, the compiler must have access to the array's DAD. In our scheme, we will maintain a *global* data structure that contains information on when *any array* with a given DAD may have been modified.

We maintain a global variable **n_mod** which represents the cumulative number of Fortran 90D loops, array intrinsics or statements that have modified any distributed array. Note that we are not counting the number of assignments to the distributed array, instead we are counting the number of times the program will execute any block of code that writes to a distributed array. **n_mod** may be viewed as a global time stamp. Each time we modify an array **a** with a given data access descriptor DAD(**a**), we update a global data structure **last_mod** to associate DAD(**a**) with the current value of the global variable **n_mod** (i.e. the current global timestamp). Thus when a loop, array intrinsic or statement modifies **a** we set **last_mod(DAD(a))** = **n_mod**. If the array **a** is remapped, it means that DAD(**a**) changes. In this case, we increment **n_mod** and then set **last_mod(DAD(a))** = **n_mod**.

The first time an inspector for a forall loop L is carried out, it must perform all the preprocessing. Assume that L has m data arrays x_L^i, $1 \leq i \leq m$, and n indirection arrays, ind_L^j, $1 \leq j \leq n$. Each time an inspector for L is carried out, we store the following information:

DAD(x_L^i) for each unique data array x_L^i, for $1 \leq i \leq m$, and

DAD(ind_L^j) for each unique indirection array ind_L^j, for $1 \leq j \leq n$ and

last_mod(DAD(ind_L^j)), for $1 \leq j \leq n$.

We designate the values of DAD(x_L^i), DAD(ind_L^j) and last_mod(DAD(ind_L^j)) stored by L's inspector as L.DAD(x_L^i), L.DAD(ind_L^j) and L.last_mod(DAD(ind_L^j)).

For a given data array x_L^i and indirection array ind_L^j in a forall loop L, we maintain *two sets of data access descriptors*. For instance, we maintain,

- DAD(x_L^i) the current global data access descriptor associated with x_L^i, and

- L.DAD(x_L^i) is a record of the data access descriptor that was associated with x_L^i when L carried out its last inspector.

For each indirection array ind_L^j, we also maintain two timestamps:

- last_mod(DAD(ind_L^j)) is the global timestamp associated with the current data access descriptor of ind_L^j and,

- L.last_mod(DAD(ind_L^j)) is the global timestamp of data access descriptor DAD(ind_L^j), last recorded by L's inspector.

After the first time L's inspector has been executed, the following checks are performed before the subsequent executions of L. If any of the following conditions is false, the inspector must be repeated for L.

1. DAD(x_L^i) == L.DAD(x_L^i), $1 \leq i \leq m$

2. DAD(ind_L^j) == L.DAD(ind_L^j), $1 \leq j \leq n$

3. last_mod(DAD(ind_L^j)) ==

   L.last_mod(L.DAD(ind_L^j)), $1 \leq j \leq n$.

As the above algorithm tracks possible array modifications at runtime, there is potential for high runtime overhead in some cases. The overhead is likely to be small in most computationally intensive data parallel Fortran 90 codes (see Section 6). Calculations in such codes primarily occur in loops or Fortran 90 array intrinsics, so we need to record modifications to a DAD *once* per loop or array intrinsic call.

We employ the same method to track possible changes to arrays used in the construction of the data structure produced at runtime to link partitioners with programs. We call this data structure a GeoCoL graph, and it will be described in Section 4.1.1. This approach makes it simple for our compiler to avoid generating a new GeoCoL graph and carrying out a potentially expensive repartition when no change has occurred.

We could further optimize our inspector reuse mechanism by noting that there is no need to record modifications to *all* distributed arrays. Instead, we could limit ourselves to recording possible modifications of the sets of arrays that have the same data access descriptor as an indirection array. Such optimization will require interprocedural analysis to identify the sets of arrays that must be tracked at runtime. Future work will include exploration of this optimization.

4 Coupling Partitioners

In irregular problems, it is often desirable to allocate computational work to processors by assigning all computations that involve a given loop iteration to a single processor [3]. Consequently, we partition *both* distributed arrays and loop iterations using a two-phase approach (Figure 2). In the first phase, termed a "data partitioning" phase, distributed arrays are partitioned. In the second phase, called "workload partitioning", loop iterations are partitioned using the information from the first phase. This appears to be a practical approach, as in many cases the same set of distributed arrays are used by many loops. The following two subsections describe the two phases.

4.1 Data Partitioning

When we partition distributed arrays, we have not yet assigned loop iterations to processors. We assume that we will partition loop iterations so as to attempt to minimize non-local distributed array references. Our approach to data partitioning makes an implicit assumption that most (although not necessarily all) computation will be carried out in the processor associated with the variable appearing on the left hand side of each statement - we call this the *almost owner computes rule*.

There are many partitioning heuristics methods available based on physical phenomena and physical proximity [24, 2, 25, 13]. Currently these partitioners must be coupled to user programs in a manual fashion. This manual coupling is particularly troublesome and tedious when we wish to make use of parallelized partitioners. Further, partitioners use different data structures and are very problem dependent, making it extremely difficult to adapt to different (but similar) problems and systems.

4.1.1 Interface Data Structures for Partitioners

We link partitioners to programs by using a data structure that stores information on which data partitioning is to be based. Data structure partitioners can make use of different kinds of program information. Some partitioners operate on data structures that represent undirected graphs [24],[15], [19]. Graph vertices represent array indices, graph edges represent dependencies. Consider the example loops in Figure 1. In both loops, the graph vertices represent the N elements of arrays **x** and **y**. The graph edges in the first loop of Figure 1 are the union of:

edges linking vertices ia(i) and ib(i), i = 1,N

edges linking vertices ia(i) and ic(i), i = 1,N

The graph edges in the second loop of Figure 1 are the union of edges linking vertices end_pt1(i) and end_pt2(i).

In some cases, it is possible to associate geometrical information with a problem. For instance, meshes often arise from finite element or finite difference discretizations. In such cases, each mesh point is associated with a location in space. We can assign each graph vertex a set of coordinates that describe its spatial location. These spatial locations can be used to partition data structures [2, 22].

Vertices may also be assigned weights to represent estimated computational costs. In order to accurately estimate computational costs, we need information on how work will be partitioned. One way of deriving weights is to make the implicit assumption that an owner compute rule will be used to partition work. Under this assumption, computational cost associated with executing a statement will be attributed to the processor owning a left hand side array reference. This results in a graph with unit weights

in the first loop in Figure 1. The weight associated with a vertex in the second loop of Figure 1 would be proportional to the degree of the vertex when functions f and g have identical computational costs. Vertex weights can be used as a sole partitioning criterion in "embarrassingly parallel problems", problems in which computational costs dominate.

A given partitioner can make use of combinations of connectivity, geometrical or weight information. For instance, we find that it is sometimes important to take estimated computational costs into account when carrying out coordinate or inertial bisection for problems where computational costs vary greatly from node to node. Other partitioners make use of both geometrical and connectivity information [5].

Since the data structure that stores information on which data partitioning is to be based can represent **Geometrical**, **Connectivity** and/or **Load** information, we call this the **GeoCoL** data structure.

4.1.2 Generating GeoCoL Data Structure

We propose a directive **CONSTRUCT** that can be employed to direct a compiler to generate a GeoCoL data structure. A user can specify spatial information using the keyword **GEOMETRY**.

The following is an example of a GeoCoL declaration that specifies geometrical information:

C$ **CONSTRUCT** G1 (N, **GEOMETRY**(3, xcord, ycord, zcord))

This statement defines a GeoCoL data structure called **G1** having *N* vertices with spatial coordinate information specified by xcord, ycord, and zcord. The GEOMETRY construct is closely related to the geometrical partitioning or *value based decomposition* directives proposed by von Hanxleden [11].

Similarly, a GeoCoL data structure which specifies only vertex weights can be constructed using the keyword **LOAD** as follows.

C$ **CONSTRUCT** G2 (N, **LOAD**(weight))

Here, a GeoCoL construct called **G2** consists of *N* vertices with vertex *i* having **LOAD** *weight(i)*.

The following example illustrates how connectivity information is specified in a GeoCoL declaration. Integer arrays edge_list1 and edge_list2 list the vertices associated with each of E graph edges.

C$ **CONSTRUCT** G3 (N, **LINK**(E, edge_list1, edge_list2))

The keyword **LINK** is used to specify the edges associated with the GeoCoL graph.

Any combination of spatial, load and connectivity information can be used to generate GeoCoL data structure. For instance, the GeoCoL data structure for a partitioner that uses both geometry and connectivity information can be specified as follows:

C$ **CONSTRUCT** G4 (N, **GEOMETRY**(3, xcord, ycord, zcord), **LINK**(E, edge_list1, edge_list2))

```
      REAL*8 x(nnode),y(nnode)
      INTEGER end_pt1(nedge), end_pt2(nedge)
S1    DYNAMIC, DECOMPOSITION reg(nnode),
      reg2(nedge)
S2    DISTRIBUTE reg(BLOCK), reg2(BLOCK)
S3    ALIGN x,y with reg
S4    ALIGN end_pt1, end_pt2 with reg2
      ....
      call read_data(end_pt1, end_pt2, ...)
S5    CONSTRUCT G (nnode, LINK(nedge,end_pt1,
      end_pt2))
S6    SET distfmt BY PARTITIONING G USING
      RSB
S7    REDISTRIBUTE reg(distfmt)
C     Loop over edges involving x, y
      ....
C     Loop over faces involving x, y
```

Figure 4: Example of Implicit Mapping in Fortran 90D

Once the GeoCoL data structure is constructed, data partitioning is carried out. We assume there are **P** processors:

1. At compile time *dependency coupling code* is generated. This code generates calls to the runtime support that, when the program executes, generates the **GeoCoL** data structures,

2. The **GeoCoL** data structure is passed to a *data partitioning* procedure that partitions the **GeoCoL** into **P** subgraphs.

3. The **GeoCoL** vertices assigned to each subgraph specify an irregular distribution.

The GeoCoL data structure is constructed with the initial default distribution of distributed arrays. Once we have the new distribution given by the partitioner, we redistribute the arrays based on the new distribution. A communication schedule is built and used to redistribute the arrays from the default to the new distribution.

4.2 Linking Data Partitioners

In Figure 4 we illustrate a possible set of partitioner coupling directives for the loop L2 in Figure 1. We use statements S1 to S4 (Figure 4) to produce a default initial distribution of arrays *x* and *y* and the indirection array in loop L1, *end_pt*. The statements S5 and S6 directs the generation of code to construct the GeoCoL graph and call the partitioner. Statement S5 indicates that the GeoCoL graph edges are to be generated based on the relations between distributed arrays **x** and **y** in loop L1 and the relationship is provided by using the keyword **LINK** in the

```
      ....
S'5   CONSTRUCT G (nnode, GEOMETRY(3, xc,
      yc, zc))
S'6   SET distfmt BY PARTITIONING G USING
      RCB
S'7   REDISTRIBUTE reg(distfmt)
C     Loop over edges involving x, y
      ....
C     Loop over faces involving x, y
```

Figure 5: Example of Implicit Mapping using Geometric Information in Fortran 90D

CONSTRUCT statement. The statement S6 in the figure calls the partitioner RSB (recursive spectral bisection) with GeoCoL as input. The user will be provided a library of commonly available partitioners and the user can choose any one one of them. Also, the user can link a customized partitioner as long as the calling sequence matches. Finally, the distributed arrays are remapped in statement S7 using the new distribution returned by the partitioner.

Figure 5 illustrates code similar to that shown in Figure 4 except that here the use of geometric information is shown. Arrays xc, yc, and zc, which carry the spatial coordinates for elements in x and y, are aligned with the same decomposition to which arrays x and y are aligned. Statement S'5 specifies that the GeoCoL data structure is to be constructed using geometric information. S'6 specifies that recursive binary coordinate bisection is used to partition the data.

4.3 Loop Iteration Partitioning

Once we have partitioned data, we must partition computational work. One convention is to compute a program assignment statement S in the processor associated with the distributed array element on S's left hand side. This convention is normally referred to as the "owner-computes" rule. (If the left hand side of **S** references a replicated variable then the work is carried out in all processors). One drawback to the owner-computes rule in sparse codes is that we may need to generate communication within loops even in the absence of loop carried dependencies. For example, consider the following loop:

```
      FORALL I=1,N
S1    x(ib(i)) = ......
S2    y(ia(i)) = x(ib(i))
      END FORALL
```

This loop has a loop independent dependence between S1 and S2 but no loop carried dependencies. Were we to assign work using the owner-computes rule, for iteration i, statement S1 would be computed on the owner of ib(i) (OWNER(ib(i))) while statement S2 would be computed on the owner of ia(i) (OWNER(ia(i)). The value of y(ib(i)) would have to be communicated whenever OWNER(ib(i)) ≠ OWNER(ia(i)).

An alternate convention is to assign all work associated with a loop iteration to a given processor. We have developed data structures and procedures to support iteration partitioning.

Our current default is to employ a scheme that places a loop iteration on the processor that is the home of the largest number of the iteration's distributed array references.

5 Compiler Support

In the previous section we presented directives a programmer can use to implicitly specify how data and loop iterations are to be partitioned between processors. In this section we outline compiler transformations used to carry out this implicitly defined work and data mapping. The compiler transformations generate code which embeds the CHAOS mapper coupler procedures.

We use the example in Figure 4 to show how the compiler procedures are embedded in the code. A (simplified) version of the compiler transformation is shown in Figure 6. We start with BLOCK array distributions. Statements S5 to S7 in Figure 4 are used to generate a data distribution. When the **CONSTRUCT** statement is encountered, the compiler generates code with embedded CHAOS procedure calls, during program execution, the CHAOS procedures generate the GeoCoL data structure. The GeoCoL data structure is then passed to an user specified partitioner. When the **REDISTRIBUTE** statement is encountered, CHAOS data remapping procedure calls are generated to move arrays (x and y) aligned with the initial distribution (reg) to the new distribution (distfmt).

Loop iterations are partitioned at runtime using the method described in Section 4.3 whenever a loop accesses at least one irregularly distributed array.

6 Experimental Results

6.1 Timing Results for Schedule Reuse

In this section, we present performance data for the schedule saving technique proposed in Section 3 for the Fortran 90D compiler implementation. These timings involve a loop over edges of an 3-D unstructured Euler solver [20] for 10K and 53K mesh points and an electrostatic force calculation loop in a molecular dynamics code for 648 atom water simulation [4]; the functionality of these loops is equivalent to the loop L2 in Figure 1. Table 1 depicts the performance results of compiler generated code with and without the schedule reuse technique for

Start with block distribution of arrays x, y and end_pts

Read Mesh (end_pt1, end_pt2, ...)

C$ **CONSTRUCT** G (nnode, **LINK** (nedge, end_pt1, end_pt2))

K1 Call CHAOS procedures to generate GeoCoL data structure

C$ **SET** distfmt BY **PARTITIONING** G **USING RSB**

K2 Pass GeoCoL to RSB graph partitioner

K3 Obtain new distribution format from the partitioner(distfmt)

C$ **REDISTRIBUTE** reg (distfmt)

K4 Remap arrays (x and y) aligned with

  distribution reg to distribution *distfmt*

Figure 6: Compiler Transformations for Implicit Data Mapping

unstructured mesh and molecular dynamics loops, varying the number of processors of Intel iPSC/860 hypercube. The table presents the execution time of the loops for 100 iterations with distributed arrays decomposed irregularly using a recursive binary dissection partitioner. The results shown in the table emphasizes the importance of schedule reuse.

6.2 Timing Results using the Mapper Coupler

In this section, we present data that compares the the costs incurred by the compiler generated mapper coupler procedures with the cost a hand embedded mapper coupler. These timings involve a loop over edges of an 3-D unstructured Euler solver and the electrostatic force calculation loop in a molecular dynamics code. The compiler-linked mapping technique was incorporated in the Fortran 90D compiler being developed at Syracuse University. We present the performance of our runtime techniques on different number of processors on an Intel iPSC/860.

To map arrays we employed two different kinds of parallel partitioners 1) a geometry based partitioner (coordinate bisection [2]) and 2) a connectivity based partitioner (recursive spectral bisection [24]). The performance of the compiler embedded mapper version and hand parallelized version are shown in Table 2.

In Table 2, *Partitioner* depicts the time needed to partition the arrays using the partitioners, *Executor* depicts the time needed to carry out the actual computation and communication, and *inspector* depicts the time taken to build the schedule. In Table 2, *Partition* under Spectral Bisection depicts the time needed to partition the GeoCoL graph data structure using a parallelized version of Simon's eigenvalue partitioner [24]. We partitioned the GeoCoL

Table 1: Performance of Schedule Reuse

(Time in Secs)	10K Mesh Processors			53k Mesh Processors			648 Atoms Processors		
	4	8	16	16	32	64	4	8	16
No Schedule Reuse	400	214	123	668	398	239	707	384	227
Schedule Reuse	17.6	10.8	7.7	30.4	23.0	17.4	15.2	9.7	8.0

Table 2: Unstructured Mesh Template - 53 K Mesh - 32 Processors

(Time in Secs)	Binary Coordinate Bisection			Block Partition	Spectral Bisection	
	Hand Coded	Compiler: No Schedule Reuse	Compiler Schedule Reuse	Hand Coded	Hand Coded	Compiler: Schedule Reuse
Graph Generation	-	-	-	-	2.2	2.2
Partitioner	1.6	1.6	1.6	0.0	258	258
Inspector, remap	4.3	379	4.2	4.7	4.1	4.0
Executor	16.4	17.2	17.2	54.7	13.2	13.9
Total	22.4	398	23.0	59.4	277.5	277.9

graph into a number of subgraphs equal to the number of processors employed. It should be noted that any common parallelized partitioner could be used as a mapper. The *graph generation* time depicts the time required to generate GeoCoL graph. The *Executor* time shown in Table 2 gives the time needed to carry out the executor phase for 100 times. The results shown in the table demonstrate that the performance of the compiler generated code is within 10% of the hand coded version. In table 4, we have included timings for a hand coded block partitioned version of the code in order to quantify the performance effects that arose from the decision to partition the problem. In the blocked version, we assigned each processor contiguous blocks of array elements. We see that the use of either a coordinate bisection partitioner or a spectral bisection partitioner lead to a factor of two to three reduction in the executor time compared to the use of block partitioning. This example also points out the importance of the number of executor iterations on which partitioner should be chosen. When compared to the recursive coordinate bisection partitioner, the recursive spectral bisection partitioner is associated with a faster time per executor iteration but a significantly higher partitioning overhead.

A detailed performance of the compiler-linked coordinate bisection for the unstructured mesh loop and the molecular dynamics loop is shown in Table 3. In Table 4, we present timing results for naive partition of arrays - we assigned each processor contiguous blocks of arrays to processors using BLOCK distribution allowed in HPF. Irregular distribution of arrays performs much better than the existing BLOCK distribution supported by HPF.

7 Related Work

Research has been carried out by von Hanxleden [11] on compiler-linked partitioners which decompose arrays based on distributed array element values, these are called *value*

based decompositions. Our GEOMETRY construct can be viewed as a particular type of value based decomposition. Several researchers have developed programming environments that are targeted towards particular classes of irregular or adaptive problems. Williams [25] describes a programming environment (DIME) for calculations with unstructured triangular meshes using distributed memory machines. Baden [1] has developed a programming environment targeted towards particle computations. This programming environment provides facilities that support dynamic load balancing.

There are a variety of compiler projects targeted at distributed memory multiprocessors [27, 16]. Jade project at Stanford, DINO project at Colorado´ and CODE project at Austin provide parallel programming environments. Runtime compilation methods are employed in four compiler projects; the Fortran D project [14], the Kali project [16], Marina Chen's work at Yale [18] and our PARTI project [21, 26, 23]. The Kali compiler was the first compiler to implement inspector/executor type runtime preprocessing [16] and the ARF compiler was the first compiler to support irregularly distributed arrays [26].

In earlier work, several of the authors of the current paper outlined a strategy (but did not attempt a compiler implementation) that would make it possible for compilers to generate compiler embedded connectivity based partitioners directly from marked loops [6]. The approach described here requires more input from the user and lesser compiler support.

8 Conclusions

In this paper, we have described and and presented timing data for a prototype Fortran 90D compiler implementation. The work described here demonstrates two new

Table 3: Performance of Compiler-linked Coordinate Bisection Partitioner with Schedule Reuse

Tasks (Time in Secs)	10K Mesh Processors			53k Mesh Processors			648 Atoms Processors		
	4	8	16	16	32	64	4	8	16
Partitioner	0.6	0.6	0.4	1.8	1.6	2.5	0.1	0.1	0.1
Inspector	1.2	0.6	0.4	2.0	1.2	0.7	2.2	1.2	0.7
Remap	3.1	1.6	0.9	5.1	3.0	1.9	4.8	2.6	1.5
Executor	12.7	7.0	6.0	21.5	17.2	12.3	8.1	5.8	5.7
Total	17.6	10.8	7.7	30.4	23.0	17.4	15.2	9.7	8.0

Table 4: Performance of Block Partitioning with Schedule Reuse

Tasks (Time in secs)	10K Mesh Processors			53k Mesh Processors			648 Atoms Processors		
	4	8	16	16	32	64	4	8	16
Inspector	1.5	0.9	0.5	3.9	1.9	1.0	2.7	1.5	0.8
Remap	3.1	1.6	0.8	4.9	2.8	1.7	4.5	2.6	1.5
Executor	26.0	20.8	14.7	74.1	54.7	35.3	10.3	7.6	7.3
Total	30.4	23.3	16.0	82.9	59.4	38.0	17.5	11.7	9.6

ideas for dealing effectively with irregular computations. The first mechanism invokes a user specified mapping procedure using a set of directives. The second is a simple conservative method that in many cases makes it possible for a compiler to recognize the potential for reusing previously computed results from inspectors (e.g. communication schedules, loop iteration partitions, information that associates off-processor data copies with on-processor buffer locations).

We view the CHAOS procedures described here as forming a portion of a portable, compiler independent, runtime support library. The CHAOS runtime support library contains procedures that

- support static and dynamic distributed array partitioning,

- partitions loop iterations and indirection arrays,

- remap arrays from one distribution to another and

- carry out index translation, buffer allocation and communication schedule generation,

We consider our work to be a part of the ARPA sponsored integrated effort towards developing powerful compiler independent runtime support for parallel programming languages. The runtime support can be employed in other High Performance Fortran type compilers, and in fact, a subset of the runtime support described here has been incorporated into the Vienna Fortran compiler.

We tested our prototype compiler on computational templates extracted from an unstructured mesh computational fluid dynamics code [20] and from a molecular dynamics code [4]. We embedded our runtime support by hand and compared its performance against the compiler generated code. The compiler's performance on these templates was within about 10% of the hand compiled code.

The CHAOS procedures described in this paper are available for public distribution and can be obtained from netlib or from the anonymous ftp site hyena.cs.umd.edu.

Acknowledgments

The authors would like to thank Alan Sussman and Raja Das for many fruitful discussions and for help in proofreading. The authors would like to thank Geoffrey Fox, Chuck Koelbel and Sanjay Ranka for many enlightening discussions about universally applicable partitioners and how to embed such partitioners into compilers; we would also like to thank Chuck Koelbel, Ken Kennedy and Seema Hiranandani for many useful discussions about integrating into Fortran-D runtime support for irregular problems. Our special thanks go to Reinhard von Hanxleden for his helpful suggestions.

The authors would also like to gratefully acknowledge the help of Zeki Bozkus and Tom Haupt and the time they spent orienting us to internals of the Fortran 90D compiler. We would also like to thank Horst Simon for the use of his unstructured mesh partitioning software.

References

[1] S. Baden. Programming abstractions for dynamically partitioning and coordinating localized scientific calculations running on multiprocessors. *SIAM J. Sci. and Stat. Computation.*, 12(1), January 1991.

[2] M.J. Berger and S. H. Bokhari. A partitioning strategy for nonuniform problems on multiprocessors. *IEEE Trans. on Computers*, C-36(5):570–580, May 1987.

[3] Harry Berryman, Joel Saltz, and Jeffrey Scroggs. Execution time support for adaptive scientific algorithms on distributed memory machines. *Concurrency: Practice and Experience*, 3(3):159–178, June 1991.

[4] B. R. Brooks, R. E. Bruccoleri, B. D. Olafson, D. J. States, S. Swaminathan, and M. Karplus. Charmm: A program for macromolecular energy, minimization, and dynamics calculations. *Journal of Computational Chemistry*, 4:187, 1983.

[5] T. W. Clark, R. v. Hanxleden, J. A. McCammon, and L. R. Scott. Parallelization strategies for a molecular dynamics program. In *Intel Supercomputer University Partners Conference*, Timberline Lodge, Mt. Hood, OR, April 1992.

[6] R. Das, R. Ponnusamy, J. Saltz, and D. Mavriplis. Distributed memory compiler methods for irregular problems - data copy reuse and runtime partitioning. In *Compilers and Runtime Software for Scalable Multiprocessors, J. Saltz and P. Mehrotra Editors*, Amsterdam, The Netherlands, 1992. Elsevier.

[7] R. Das and J. H. Saltz. Program slicing techniques for compiling irregular problems. In *Proceedings of the Sixth Workshop on Languages and Compilers for Parallel Computing*, Portland , OR, August 1993.

[8] D. Loveman (Ed.). Draft High Performance Fortran language specification, version 1.0. Technical Report CRPC-TR92225, Center for Research on Parallel Computation, Rice University, January 1993.

[9] Z. Bozkus et al. Compiling fortran 90d/hpf for distributed memory mimd computers. Report SCCS-444, NPAC, Syracuse University, March 1993.

[10] G. Fox, S. Hiranandani, K. Kennedy, C. Koelbel, U. Kremer, C. Tseng, and M. Wu. Fortran D language specification. Department of Computer Science Rice COMP TR90-141, Rice University, December 1990.

[11] R. v. Hanxleden. Compiler support for machine independent parallelization of irregulr problems. Technical report, Center for Research on Parallel Computation, 1992.

[12] R. v. Hanxleden, K. Kennedy, C. Koelbel, R. Das, and J. Saltz. Compiler analysis for irregular problems in Fortran D. In *Proceedings of the 5th Workshop on Languages and Compilers for Parallel Computing*, New Haven, CT, August 1992.

[13] R. v. Hanxleden and L. R. Scott. Load balancing on message passing architectures. *Journal of Parallel and Distributed Computing*, 13:312–324, 1991.

[14] S. Hiranandani, K. Kennedy, and C. Tseng. Compiler support for machine-independent parallel programming in Fortran D. In *Compilers and Runtime Software for Scalable Multiprocessors, J. Saltz and P. Mehrotra Editors*, Amsterdam, The Netherlands, To appear 1991. Elsevier.

[15] B.W. Kernighan and S. Lin. An efficient heuristic procedure for partitioning graphs. *Bell System Technical Journal*, 49(2):291–307, February 1970.

[16] C. Koelbel, P. Mehrotra, and J. Van Rosendale. Supporting shared data structures on distributed memory architectures. In *2nd ACM SIGPLAN Symposium on Principles and Practice of Parallel Programming*, pages 177–186. ACM, March 1990.

[17] W. E. Leland. Load-balancing heuristics and process behavior. In *Proceedings of Performance 86 and ACM SIGMETRICS 86*, pages 54–69, 1986.

[18] L. C. Lu and M.C. Chen. Parallelizing loops with indirect array references or pointers. In *Proceedings of the Fourth Workshop on Languages and Compilers for Parallel Computing*, Santa Clara, CA, August 1991.

[19] N. Mansour. Physical optimization algorithms for mapping data to distributed-memory multiprocessors. Technical report, Ph.D. Dissertation, School of Computer Science,Syracuse Universit y, 1992.

[20] D. J. Mavriplis. Three dimensional unstructured multigrid for the Euler equations, paper 91-1549cp. In *AIAA 10th Computational Fluid Dynamics Conference*, June 1991.

[21] R. Mirchandaney, J. H. Saltz, R. M. Smith, D. M. Nicol, and Kay Crowley. Principles of runtime support for parallel processors. In *Proceedings of the 1988 ACM International Conference on Supercomputing*, pages 140–152, July 1988.

[22] B. Nour-Omid, A. Raefsky, and G. Lyzenga. Solving finite element equations on concurrent computers. In *Proc. of Symposium on Parallel Computations and theis Impact on Mechanics*, Boston, December 1987.

[23] J. Saltz, H. Berryman, and J. Wu. Runtime compilation for multiprocessors. *Concurrency: Practice and Experience*, 3(6):573–592, 1991.

[24] H. Simon. Partitioning of unstructured mesh problems for parallel processing. In *Proceedings of the Conference on Parallel Methods on Large Scale Structural Analysis and Physics Applications*. Pergamon Press, 1991.

[25] R. Williams. Performance of dynamic load balancing algorithms for unstructured mesh calculations. *Concurrency, Practice and Experience*, 3(5):457–482, February 1991.

[26] J. Wu, J. Saltz, S. Hiranandani, and H. Berryman. Runtime compilation methods for multicomputers. In *Proceedings of the 1991 International Conference on Parallel Processing*, volume 2, pages 26–30, 1991.

[27] H. Zima, H. Bast, and M. Gerndt. Superb: A tool for semi-automatic MIMD/SIMD parallelization. *Parallel Computing*, 6:1–18, 1988.

[28] H. Zima, P. Brezany, B. Chapman, P. Mehrotra, and A. Schwald. Vienna Fortran – a language specification. Report ACPC-TR92-4, Austrian Center for Parallel Computation, University of Vienna, Vienna, Austria, 1992.

Session 5:
Minisymposium
Chair: Carol Hunter

Panel on Smart Access to Large Scientific Datasets

Carol Christian, Panelist
University of California at Berkeley

Robert Cromp, Panelist
NASA Goddard Space Flight Center

Carol Hunter, Panel Moderator
Lawrence Livermore National Laboratory

Lloyd Treinish, Panelist
IBM T.J. Watson Research Center

Abstract:
The enormous technological enhancements in computer chips and processor architectures have provided orders of magnitude improvements to scientific computing in terms of processor(s) performance and network bandwidth. The ultimate result of the technical improvements is multitudes of massive and complex datasets. The analysis of these large scientific datasets is now a problem unto itself. Processor speeds and architectural designs have drastically improved the performance of computer hardware. We also need to focus on functional improvements which optimize the performance of the application scientist working in a distributed computing environment. This panel proposes to discuss methods of providing smart access to scientific data. Among the areas to be discussed:

- required infrastrucure for scientific data stuctures and access
- interactive access of scientific data for generic applications
- widely distributed access of scientific data from data centers across the nation
- the use of metadata as an intermediate level of information
- smart access to data in mass storage

Panelist: Carol Christian
Biographical Sketch

Dr. Carol Christian is currently the Manager of EUVE Guest Observer, Archive, and Berkeley Data Analysis Science Support (DASS) groups at the Center for EUVE Astrophysics (CEA) at UC Berkeley. The Center is responsible for proposal reviews, distribution of mission and science instrument information, and scheduling of targets. In addition, the GO support group designs, implements, tests and distributes the analysis software and documentation associated with the Guest Observer data and assists visiting scientists as well as remote users. Under her management, the EUVE archive and Astrophysics Data System node provide data, documentation, and software are made available to the community through a variety of network services and interfaces. Under Dr. Christian's direction, the DASS group provides data analysis support to EUVE scientists. Dr. Christian directs and coordinates the efforts of the 45 people in the three divisions and acts as co-project manager of the EUVE Project.

Dr. Christian also is the Project Manager for the National Information Infrastructure Testbed / Earth Data System Application. The NIIT applications team comprises representatives from industry, government, and the university community joined in a cooperative organization to study the strategy and problems associated with truly distributed information and computing services. The NIIT team has chosen the Earth Data System as its first reference application in order to study and propose solutions to allow a group of scientists to study the related effects of global weather changes, deforestation, ocean current movements and coastal drainage that until now have not been investigated in an integrated fashion. The project is designed to provide methods for describing and populating databases, linking heterogeneous data stores to the databases, and demonstrating data analysis across a widely distributed computing platform. The EDS provides a distributed computing environment with collaborative tools for utilizing heterogeneous hardware, software and networks.

Panelist: Robert Cromp
Biographical Sketch

Robert F. Cromp is Principal Investigator of the Intelligent Data Management project at NASA, Goddard Space Flight Center at the National Space Science Data Center. He received the B.A. degree in computer science from the State University of New York at Buffalo in 1982, and the M.S. and Ph.D. degrees in computer science from Arizona State University, Tempe, in 1983 and 1988, respectively. He has published in the areas of knowledge acquisition and representation, the theory of strategies, information fusion, automated extraction of metadata from images, machine learning, parallel algorithms, automated expert system development, geographical information systems, natural language processing and discrete mathematics. He also teaches at the University of Maryland/University College and Bowie State University. Dr. Cromp is a member of AAAI, ACM, IEEE, INNS, ASPRS, and MAA.

Panel Moderator: Carol Hunter
Biographical Sketch

Carol Hunter is the Project Manager of the Intelligent Archive effort in Livermore Computing at Lawrence Livermore National Laboratory. The Intelligent Archive's goal is to provide smart access with searching and browsing capabilities to all of the scientists' data at the desktop. It is the intent to provide scientists with smart access to any type of data; stored in any database, system, or archive; and to interface to any application tools. Ms. Hunter was Manager of the Visualization Lab at LLNL and Group Leader of the Computer Graphics Group from 1988 to 1992. As Graphics Coordinator from 1986 to 1988 she was responsible for the long-term planning of graphics hardware and software to support the supercomputer and workstation users at LLNL. Prior to working in Livermore Computing she was graphics workstation project leader, a team leader, and a computer scientist for the Nuclear Software Systems Division at LLNL. Ms. Hunter received her B.S. in Mathematics from California State University in 1972. She is Conference Co-Chair of the IEEE Visualization '93 Conference, Vice President for Conferences of the IEEE Technical Committee on Computer Graphics, and a member of ACM, IEEE, and Bay Area SIGGRAPH.

Panelist: Lloyd Treinish
Biographical Sketch

Lloyd A. Treinish is a research staff member in the Visualization Systems Group of the Computer Science Department at IBM's Thomas J. Watson Research Center in Yorktown Heights, NY. He works on techniques, architectures and applications of data visualization for a wide variety of scientific disciplines within this group, that developed the IBM POWER Visualization System and the IBM Visualization Data Explorer. His research interests range from computer graphics, data storage structures, data representation methodologies, data base management, computer user interfaces, and data analysis algorithms to middle atmosphere electrodynamics, planetary astronomy and climatology. Particularly, Mr. Treinish is interested in generic or discipline-independent techniques for the storage, manipulation, analysis and display of data, and has, for example, applied these ideas to the study of global atmospheric dynamics and ozone depletion. Earlier he did similar work in the development of advanced scientific data systems, including studying space and atmospheric phenomena, for over a decade at the National Space Science Data Center of NASA's Goddard Space Flight Center in Greenbelt, MD. A 1978 graduate of the Massachusetts Institute of Technology with an S.M. and an S.B. in physics, and an S.B. in earth and planetary sciences, Mr. Treinish has been at IBM since April 1990. He is a member of the IEEE Computer Society (IEEE-CS), the IEEE-CS Technical Committee on Computer Graphics, the IEEE-CS Visualization Conference Committee, the Association for Computing Machinery (ACM), ACM SIGGRAPH, the National Computer Graphics Association, the Planetary Society, and the American Geophysical Union.

Session 5:
Panel
Moderator: Henry Shay

National Information Infrastructure (NII) at Supercomputing '93

Henry D. Shay

Lawrence Livermore National Laboratory

We anticipate that NII will actually encompass many different kinds of institutions and enterprises. The kinds of players may be technology providers (hardware or software), carriers (telcos), service providers (libraries, etc.), regulators, or users. The spectrum of possible NII functions includes digital libraries, education, health services, and enterprise integration. The participating institutions comprise federal, state, and local governments, educational systems, GOCO laboratories, commercial enterprises, regulated utilities, and individual citizens. The level of NII technology will be both high and low. Some aspects of NII are actively being implemented today, and other will not commence for several years. The relevant issues span a gamut as broad as any public policy arena: politics, commercial profitability, laws and regulations, national well-being, sociology, and technology.

This panel discussion juxtaposes individuals responsible for driving radically different kinds of NII-like activities. The intent is to explore the many aspects of NII by contrasting their perspectives.

Panelists:

Vint Cerf
President of the Internet Society

Lansing Hatfield
Program Leader - Technology Information Systems
Program, LLNL

Stacey Jenkins
Project manager for MFS Network Technologies on "Iowa's NII"

Ed McCracken
CEO of SGI and member of the board for Smart Valley Project

John Rollwagen
Senior Advisor, St. Paul Venture Capital Inc.

Dale Williams
Vice President for Marketing at Sprint

Session 6:
Parallel I/O I
Chair: Helene Kulsrud

Striping in Large Tape Libraries

Ann L. Drapeau and Randy H. Katz
Computer Science Division
571 Evans Hall
University of California
Berkeley, California 94720

Abstract

Data striping is a technique for increasing the throughput and reducing the response time of large accesses to a storage system. In this paper, we evaluate the effectiveness of applying striping concepts to large tape libraries. Striping in tape libraries is being used with success for applications such as backup and scientific data collection, where data access patterns are strictly sequential. In this paper, we evaluate striped performance for randomly distributed accesses to the tape library. We believe such operations will be characteristic of future tertiary storage databases using large objects, such as on-line libraries and multimedia databases.

Using an event-driven simulator, we show that striped large tape libraries perform poorly for this random workload because striping causes contention for the small number of readers and robot arms in these libraries. Increasing the number of readers results in better striped performance. We also examine how the effectiveness of striping may change as readers and robots improve in performance. We find that striping continues to be an effective technique for increasing the throughput of large accesses if reader and robot performance scale at similar rates.

1 Introduction

Massive tertiary storage systems are commonly composed of large tape libraries that hold hundreds or thousands of tapes in a relatively small footprint. These large libraries generally contain a small number of tape drives or readers, and a small number of robot arms for loading cartridges into readers. This paper uses simulations to evaluate the effectiveness of applying data striping concepts to these libraries.

Data striping is a technique for increasing the throughput and reducing the response time of large accesses to a storage system [11], [6], [7], [4]. In a striped magnetic tape system, a single file is striped or interleaved across several tape cartridges. Because a striped file can be accessed by several readers in parallel, the potential sustained bandwidth to the file is greater than in non-striped systems, where accesses to the file are restricted to a single reader. As a result, large accesses with long periods of data transfer should experience reduced latency, at least under low system load.

Striping, usually without redundancy, is already being used for backups and for capturing large scientific data sets that need to be streamed to or from tape rapidly [2]. Workloads where tape striping has proven beneficial are characterized by large, sequential accesses; usually only a single request is processed at a time, and entire cartridges are written before new cartridges are switched into the readers. The benefits of tape striping seem obvious for such workloads, since the aggregate bandwidth available to an application is multiplied by the number of active readers. This intuition about the usefulness of striping is supported by our results in Section 4.

In this paper, we examine the performance of striped magnetic tape libraries for workloads where the benefits of striping are less obvious. We are interested in requests that are fairly large (hundreds of megabytes or more), but which are randomly distributed through the array rather than strictly sequential. We are also interested in applications that have several requests outstanding at any time. We believe this access pattern will reflect the uses of future tertiary storage databases using large objects, such as on-line libraries and multimedia databases.

Striped large libraries do not perform well for this random workload. A striped system creates more cartridge accesses than a non-striped system, since individual requests span several cartridges in striped library. These extra cartridge switches cause contention for the few readers and robot arms in a large library.

Section 2 of this paper briefly introduces current tape and robot technologies, including measured performance of the Exabyte EXB8500 tape drive and EXB120 tape robot. Section 3 explains our tape and robot models and our event-driven tape array simulator. Section 4 presents two large library simulations, demonstrating that in striped operation on a randomly distributed workload, each library suffers from contention for readers. We show that adding readers alleviates contention. Section 5 focuses on four device and robot characteristics, showing how each affects the performance of striped and non-striped tape operations. Finally, Section 6 shows how the performance of striped and non-striped tape arrays would be affected by different combinations of device and robot improvements.

2 Tape and robot technologies

2.1 Magnetic tape drives

Table 1 shows that the cost and performance of magnetic tape drives vary widely. Inexpensive helical scan drives (Exabyte 8mm and DAT 4mm) have high capacity but low bandwidth and long positioning times. High performance, higher capacity helical scan drives like D1 and DD2 have better bandwidth, but are very expensive and still suffer from long positioning times. Inexpensive serpentine drives (1/4") have somewhat better bandwidth than the inexpensive helical scan drives, but also have long positioning times. Finally, the linear 3490 drives have fast positioning times and moderate bandwidth, but are low capacity. These drives have widely different cost/performance ratios, and there is no clearly superior choice for a tape drive for use in massive storage systems.

To model the performance of magnetic tape drives in our simulator, we measured the operation of several tape drives. Table 2 shows our measurements of the Exabyte EXB8500 8mm helical scan drive. Drive load time is the time from insertion of a cartridge until the drive is ready to transfer data. The eject time is the time for the reader to eject the cartridge after the command to do so has been given. Load and eject times are the means of twenty measurements each; variance was low. Table 2 also shows measurements for rewind and search operations. For the EXB8500 drive, a cartridge must be fully rewound before it can be ejected from a drive. We found that search and rewind behavior can be modeled as linear after a constant startup overhead. Table 2 shows the startup times and linear rewind and search rates for the EXB8500. The table also shows read and write transfer rates achieved for large transfers.

Operation	EXB8500
Mean drive load time (sec)	35.4
Mean drive eject time (sec)	16.5
Constant rewind startup (sec)	23
Rewind rate (MB/sec)	42.0
Constant search startup (sec)	12.5
Search rate (MB/sec)	36.2
Read transfer rate (MB/sec)	0.47
Write transfer rate (MB/sec)	0.48

Table 2: *Measurements of Exabyte EXB8500 8mm helical scan drive.*

2.2 Robots for cartridge handling

Robots for automatically loading cartridges into readers can be loosely classified as either large libraries, smaller libraries, carousels or stackers. Table 3 shows this classification, which is based on cost and the number of cartridges in each system. Table 4 describes an example of each type of robot.

Large libraries contain hundreds or thousands of cartridges, several drives, and one or two robot arms for moving cartridges. These libraries are attractive building blocks for massive storage systems for several reasons. Although they hold many cartridges, they occupy a relatively small footprint, offering a ratio of capacity to square foot of machine room space superior to other robot mechanisms. Also, despite being expensive ($500,000 or more), large libraries offer the best cost per megabyte of storage. The disadvantage of large libraries is that they contain few robot arms and a small number of readers (usually between 4 and 16). Under heavy loads, there is likely to be contention for the readers and robot arms. Since high performance readers are expensive ($100,000 or more), the cost of adding readers to relieve contention may be prohibitive.

There are smaller, less expensive, often slower tape libraries. These hold fewer cartridges than the large libraries and may use inexpensive, lower performance tape drives. Also moderately priced are carousels, which hold approximately 50 cartridges and load one or two tape drives. Finally, the least expensive robotic device ($10,000 or less) is a stacker, which holds approximately 10 cartridges in a magazine and loads one or two readers. Stackers generally have the lowest cost per reader and robot arm, but the highest cost per megabyte of storage and the lowest capacity per square foot compared to other robots. This paper focuses on the performance of large and smaller tape libraries.

Table 5 shows measurements of the robot arm in the Exabyte EXB120 robot. This library has a single robot arm, four Exabyte EXB-8500 readers, and 116 cartridges. We measure the time to remove a cartridge from a drive and place it on a shelf, and the time for a robot arm to grab a cartridge off the shelf and load it into a tape drive. Both values are around 20 seconds, making the EXB120 robot fairly slow compared to other robots. We also measured the time for a robot arm simply to move from one position to another, which varies between 1 and 2 seconds; in our simulations, we use the mean value of 1.4 seconds.

2.3 Cartridge switch penalty

For a workload of randomly distributed accesses to a tape library, cartridge switch operations cause much of the latency of tape accesses. A cartridge switch includes the time to rewind a cartridge in a reader, eject it, return it to the shelf, grab another cartridge, insert it into the reader, and search to the correct position in preparation for data transfer. For the helical scan drives shown in Table 2, cartridge switch times may take several minutes. For example, Table 6 shows that an average cartridge switch for the EXB-120 robot takes over four minutes. Even the expensive, high-bandwidth drives (D1 and DD2) and robots, with faster robot arms and drive mechanics, may take up to a minute for a cartridge switch.

Striped systems generate more cartridge switches than non-striped systems. This is because a striped system divides accesses that, in a non-striped system, would be satisfied by a single cartridge into pieces that require accesses to several cartridges. Because the penalty for switching cartridges is so severe, striped systems must be carefully designed so that the penalties of cartridge switching are offset by the response time gains striping offers. As will be discussed in Sec-

Drive	Capacity Per Cartridge GBytes	Sustained Bandwidth MB/sec	Average Seek sec	Approximate Drive Cost $	Approximate Media Cost $/MByte
Exabyte EXB8500 8mm	5	0.5	40	$3,000	$0.008
DAT 4mm	1.3	0.18	20	$1,000	$0.025
Metrum 1/2"	14.5	2	45	$40,000	
19mm D-1	90	45	N/S	$300,000	$0.0012
19mm DD2	25	15	15	$150,000	
1/2" D-3	20	12	N/S	N/S	N/S
3490 1/2"	.40	6	N/S	$20,000	$0.025
1/4"	2	3	43	$1,000	$0.018

Table 1: *Compares the cartridge capacity, sustained bandwidth, average seek and approximate drive and media cost for different magnetic tape drives. 8mm, 4mm, Metrum, D-1 and DD2 drives are helical scan drives. 1/2" technology uses linear recording. 1/4" drive is serpentine. N/S indicates not specified.*

Type	No. Cartridges	No. Readers	No. Robot Arms	Cost
Large Library	100s to 1000s	several	one or two	high ($100,000+)
Smaller Library	around 100	several	one	moderate
Carousel	around 50	one or two	one per reader	moderate
Stacker	around 10	one	one (magazine or arm)	low (under $10,000)

Table 3: *Classification of storage robots.*

	Metrum RSS-600	Exabyte EXB-120	Spectra Logic 8mm Carousel	Exabyte EXB-10i
Classification	Large Library	Smaller Library	Carousel	Stacker
Number drives	up to 5	4	1 or 2	1
Number cartridges	600	116	45	10
Number robot arms	1	1	1 or 2	1
Cartridge format/capacity	1/2" 14.5 GB	8mm 5 GB	8mm 5 GB	8mm 5 GB
Total capacity (GBytes)	over 6000	580	225	50
Approximate robot cost	$540,000 (2 drives)	$61,965	$27,500 (1 drive)	$8798
Robot cost/MB	$.09	$.10	$.12	$.17
Avg. robot access time (sec)	8	18	10	less than 20

Table 4: *Comparison of four available robotic devices: the Metrum RSS-6000 1/2" system, the Exabyte EXB-120 Library, the Spectra Logic STL-8000H carousel, and the Exabyte EXB-10i Stacker. Prices indicated are list prices.*

Time to pick cartridge from drive	19.2 sec
Time to put cartridge into drive	21.4 sec

Table 5: *Measured times for robot to grab a cartridge from a drive and to push a cartridge into a drive for the EXB-120 robot system.*

Operation	Time (sec)
Rewind time (1/2 tape)	75
Eject time	17
Robot unload	21
Robot load	22
Device load	65
Search (1/2 tape)	84
Total	284

Table 6: *Components of cartridge switch time for Exabyte EXB120 Robot. Total cartridge switch time is over four minutes.*

tion 4, the performance of striped large libraries on workloads of randomly distributed requests is critically dependent on an adequate number of readers in the library.

3 The simulator

We have written an event-driven tape array simulator to study the performance of various tape array configurations. The models for tape device and robot performance used in the simulator are based on the device and robot measurements presented in the previous section. As described in Section 2.1, we model load and eject times, robot arm movement and pick and place times as constant values. We calculate search and rewind times using a model of a constant startup overhead followed by a linear positioning rate. We also make the optimistic assumption in our simulations that the devices operate at streaming rates; this assumption requires adequate buffering in the system and large average requests sizes, which we use in our simulations.

Throughout this paper, we simulate tape arrays as closed systems, keeping the concurrency, or number of outstanding requests, constant. As soon as one request completes, another is initiated. Closed systems have the characteristic that for a constant request size and concurrency, response time and throughput have an inverse relationship; if either decreases, the other increases. The simulator calculates the mean response time and sustained bandwidth of an array based on input files that contain device and robot specifications, striping configuration (interleave unit, redundancy scheme), and request size and position distributions.

In all the simulations to be presented, the request size is kept constant during individual simulation runs, while the starting positions of requests are distributed uniformly over the entire array. The use of these artificial access patterns allows us to control the concurrency and the randomness of the workload. To better reflect the access patterns of real-world applications, some future simulations will be driven by traces of activity in the massive storage system of the National Center for Atmospheric Research [9].

The simulation results in the following sections compare striped and non-striped performance for two tape arrays: a moderately large tape library (the EXB120), and a large, high performance library. The striping configuration for these simulations is small

block interleaving, or RAID3 [10]. The redundancy scheme used is single bit parity. Files are striped over groups of three data cartridges plus one parity cartridge. The workload for these systems is 25% write operations, which require accesses to the parity cartridges, and 75% read operations, which do not require parity accesses. Accesses are uniformly distributed across the entire tape array. These simulations do not include error recovery operations.

4 Large library performance

Because there are only a few readers in most large tape libraries, these libraries are ill-suited to striped operation except for purely sequential workloads or workloads in which only a single request is active at a time. In random workloads with higher concurrencies, contention for the small number of readers makes striped arrays perform poorly compared to non-striped systems. This is because more cartridge switches are performed in the striped system, and these extra switches cause contention for the few readers in the library. In this section, we show two examples of striping in large libraries, and demonstrate that striping can be effective when the system contains enough readers to avoid contention.

Figure 1a shows an example of contention for readers in the Exabyte EXB120 robot. In a series of simulation runs, we vary the request size between 10 MBytes and 1 GByte; the request size stays constant during an individual simulation run. We test randomly distributed workloads with concurrencies of one and four requests. In the graph, striped performance is shown in thin lines, while non-striped is in thicker lines; workloads with concurrency of one (a single outstanding request in the system) are shown in solid lines, while workloads with concurrency of four are shown in dashed lines.

With a single request active in the system, striping improves response time because the data transfer occurs in parallel over several readers. However, at a concurrency of four, striped performance is much worse than non-striped because of contention for the four readers. Some of this contention is alleviated by adding readers to the library. Figure 1b shows simulated performance for the EXB120 system with 16 readers. Striping improves response time compared to non-striped operation at a concurrency of four for requests over 200 MBytes in size. The addition of readers makes it possible for the workload to get the throughput benefits of striping. Thus, an adequate number of readers to handle expected workload concurrency is essential to striped performance. Because the readers in this system are inexpensive, adding readers is feasible.

Figure 2 shows another example of contention for readers, this time for a high performance tape library. The library holds 600 cartridges and four tape drives, with a single robot arm loading the drives. Each cartridge holds 25 GBytes. Table 7 shows simulation parameters for the drive and robot. These parameters are based loosely on product literature for the Ampex DD2 DST600 drive and DST800 robot [1]. (These simulation results do not represent an accurate simulation

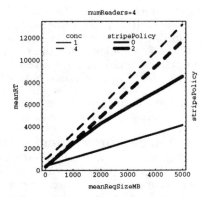

1a: *Response time (seconds) vs. request size for EXB120 with four readers.*

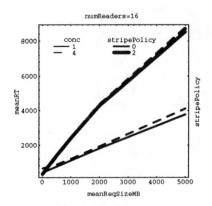

1b: *Response time (seconds) vs. request size for EXB120 with sixteen readers.*

Figure 1: *Performance of EXB120 robots with four and sixteen readers. Indicates striped performance by thin lines (stripe policy = 0), non-striped performance by thick lines (stripe policy = 2). Shows workload with concurrency of one (a single outstanding request) in solid lines, and concurrency of four (four outstanding requests) in dashed lines. (a) At concurrency of one, striping lowers response time compared to non-striped accesses, but at a concurrency of four, the response time of the striped system is worse than the non-striped. This is caused by contention for the four readers. (b) Increasing number of readers to sixteen alleviates contention for four outstanding requests; response time of striped system much lower than non-striped for request sizes greater than 200 MBytes.*

of the DST600 or DST800, which we have not measured.) The simulations in Figure 2 vary request size between 10 MBytes and 10 GBytes, again keeping the request size constant during any one simulation run. The simulations are run at a concurrency of one and four outstanding requests. Figure 2a shows simulated performance of the high performance library with four readers. With one request active, striped response time beats non-striped for requests larger than 500 MBytes. However, at higher concurrencies, striped performance suffers, even for requests over 1 GByte in size. Again, the cause is contention for the small number of readers. When we simulate sixteen drives in the array, shown in Figure 2b, the contention is alleviated. Striped performance is better than non-striped performance at a concurrency of four for requests over 2 GBytes in size.

Note that requests must be very large before striping is advantageous. Because the transfer rate on the reader is so high (15 MBytes/sec), non-striped throughput is high. Only for very large requests do the throughput benefits of striping outweigh the cartridge switch penalties. Another problem with using striping in this high performance library is the large number of readers required to make striping effective, and the high cost of these readers (over $100,000). Adding enough readers to make striping effective may be prohibitively expensive. Thus, striping in such libraries may only be effective for purely sequential workloads or for workloads where request sizes are many gigabytes.

5 Improving individual properties of readers and robots

In this section, we examine the effect on striped and non-striped performance of changing four reader and robot parameters. All these simulations use the EXB8500 reader and the EXB120 robot. We vary a single simulation parameter at a time, keeping the others constant at the measured values described in Section 2. We simulate an EXB120 with sixteen drives, to eliminate the effects of contention for readers. Request size is held constant at 200 MBytes. Concurrency is varied between 1 and 4 outstanding requests.

We simulated drives with improved transfer rates, and found that non-striped systems see greater performance gains than striped ones. Figure 3a shows that striped performance at a concurrency of four (shown

Operation	Time or Rate
Data transfer rate	15 MB/sec
Eject	5 sec
Load	5 sec
Search startup time	5 sec
Search rate after startup	750 MB/sec
Rewind startup time	5 sec
Rewind rate after startup	750 MB/sec
Robot move time	2 sec
Robot pick time	3 sec
Robot place time	3 sec

Table 7: *Simulation parameters for large, high performance library.*

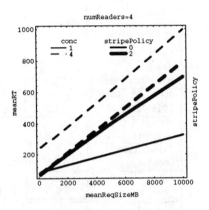
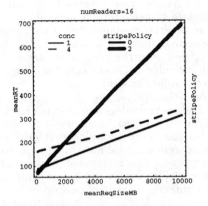

2a: *Response time (seconds) vs. request size for high performance library with four readers.*

2b: *Response time (seconds) vs. request size for high performance library with sixteen readers.*

Figure 2: *High performance library with four and sixteen readers. Indicates striped performance (stripePolicy = 0) by thin lines, non-striped performance (stripePolicy = 2) by thick lines; concurrency of one in solid lines, and concurrency of four in dashed lines. (a) Striped performance is better than non-striped performance at concurrency = 1 for requests over size 500 MBytes; at a concurrency of four, striped performance is worse than non-striped. (b) Increasing the number of readers to sixteen makes striping even at higher concurrencies attractive for large request sizes (over 2 GBytes in size).*

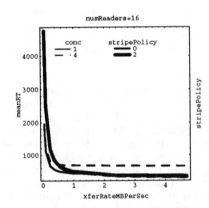
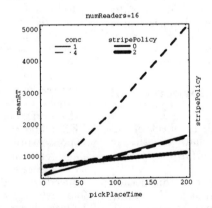
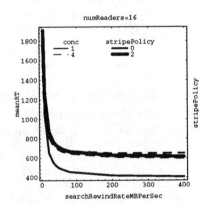

3a: *Response time vs. Reader transfer rate. Increasing only reader transfer rate helps non-striped performance more than striped. The striped system experiences more contention.*

3b: *Response time vs. Robot arm speed. Response time increases as robot arm speed decreases. Striped performance is more dramatically affected, since every access involves several cartridge switches.*

3c: *Response time vs. Search/rewind rate. After search and rewind rates exceed 100 MBytes/sec, performance levels off, indicating that some other parameter limits performance.*

Figure 3: *Comparison of striped and non-striped performance when varying three performance parameters: reader transfer rate, robot arm grab/place time, and search and rewind rates. Striped performance is shown in thin lines, non-striped in thick lines; concurrency of one in solid lines, concurrency of four in dashed lines.*

with the thin dashed lines) experiences contention, while the non-striped system does not. In the non-striped system, the transfer rate eventually becomes high enough that data transfer time is negligible; the response time of an access corresponds to the cartridge switch time (284 seconds for an EXB120 robot). By contrast, in the striped case, the 200 MByte access is split into several cartridge accesses, and the system experiences contention for the readers.

Figure 3b shows that increasing the time for a robot to pick and place cartridges hurts striped performance more dramatically than non-striped performance. This is because more cartridge switches are required in a striped system, since individual requests span multiple cartridges. An increase in pick/place time slows every cartridge switch operation, and is thus particularly damaging to striped performance.

Figure 3c shows that higher search and rewind rates on the readers reduce the penalty for cartridge switches, and thus reduce striped response times more than non-striped, since striped systems perform more cartridge switches. (This is most clearly seen at a concurrency of one.) In these simulations, we use a single value for the search and rewind rates for simplicity, although in reality, the rewind rate is slightly faster. We leave the search/rewind startup overheads at their original values. Most of the benefits of increasing the search/rewind rates are achieved by the time those rates reach 100 MBytes/sec; after this, performance is limited by other parameters.

A final simulation result, not shown in a graph, is that increasing the capacity contained in a single cartridge increases the response time for both striped and non-striped arrays. Since search and rewind rates are unchanged, using higher capacity cartridges results in longer positioning operations. To minimize search and rewind times, shorter tapes with lower capacities are ideal. Unfortunately, this conflicts with the need for high capacity in a massive storage system.

6 Improving overall performance of readers and robots

In the last section, we examined the effect of improving particular reader and robot characteristics; in this section, we look at the effect of improving overall reader and robot performance.

Exabyte Corporation predicts that in this decade both cartridge capacity and throughput for their 8mm helical scan drives will double approximately every two years, reaching 67 GBytes per cartridge and 6 MBytes/sec by the end of the decade, compared to 5 GBytes per cartridge and 0.5 MBytes/sec today [5]. Besides data transfer rate, other components of access time should also improve. Several drive manufacturers are reducing rewind and search times by implementing periodic zones on the tapes where eject and load operations are allowed, rather than requiring that the tape be fully rewound [8]. Robot arms are being made lighter and faster [12]. Other improvements in tape drive mechanics will likely come about as market forces demand higher performance than was required for backup applications.

Speedup:	Original	50%	2X	10X
EXB8500				
Transfer Rate (KB/sec)	470	705	940	4700
Search Rate (MB/sec)	36.2	54.3	72.4	362.0
Search Startup (sec)	12.5	8.3	6.25	1.25
Rewind Rate (MB/sec)	42.0	63.0	84.0	420.0
Rewind Startup (sec)	23.0	15.3	11.5	2.3
Load Time (sec)	65.5	43.3	32.5	6.5
Eject Time (sec)	16.5	11.0	8.25	1.65
EXB120				
Robot Arm Load (sec)	21.4	14.3	10.7	2.1
Robot Arm Unload (sec)	19.5	13.0	9.8	2.0

Table 8: *Simulation parameters for readers and robots at various speedup factors.*

In this section, we focus on potential improvements in the EXB8500 8mm reader and the EXB120 robot, and explore how these speedups affect the performance of both striped and non-striped tape libraries. Table 8 shows the set of parameters used to simulate these improvements. We simulate readers and robots that are 50% faster, twice as fast, and ten times as fast as the original devices. For each simulation, we vary the request size between 10 MBytes and 1 GByte, keeping the request size constant for an individual simulation run.

For the EXB120 robot with four readers, contention for readers continues regardless of whether readers, robots or both are improved. Figure 1a showed the performance of a standard EXB120 robot with EXB8500 readers. Figure 4 shows how the mean response time changes when readers, robots, and both are ten times as fast as currently available devices. In each case, although the mean response time is reduced, striped performance at a concurrency of four is consistently worse than non-striped performance. The contention caused by the small number of readers is not alleviated simply by speeding up the readers and robots. More readers are needed in this system for striping to be effective for loads other than a single outstanding request.

For the rest of this section, we consider only EXB120 robots with 16 readers. When we improve only the reader's performance, leaving the robot unchanged, the performance of the non-striped array improves at a higher rate than the striped system, eventually becoming superior. Figure 1b showed the performance of the standard EXB120 with sixteen readers. Because there are sixteen readers in this system, contention for readers is not a problem, and striped

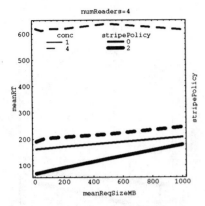
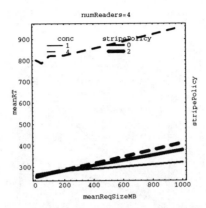
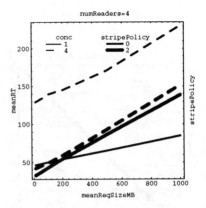

4a: *Response time (sec) for ten times faster reader, unchanged robot.*

4b: *Response time (sec) for unchanged reader, ten times faster robot.*

4c: *Response time (seconds) for ten times faster reader and robot.*

Figure 4: *Improvements in large library performance, with four EXB8500 readers and an EXB120 robot. Part (a) shows performance for improved reader alone; part (b) shows performance for improved robot; part (c) shows performance for faster readers and robots. In each case, mean response time improves, but striped performance remains inferior to non-striped performance at higher concurrencies. The small number of readers generates contention that cannot be resolved by speeding up the readers or robots. Striped performance is shown in thin lines, non-striped in thick lines; concurrency of one in solid lines, concurrency of four in dashed lines.*

performance is superior to non-striped performance for requests over size 200 MBytes. Figure 5 shows the effect of improving the reader performance. The response time of both the striped and non-striped requests decreases, with the non-striped response time decreasing at a faster rate. As a result, the mean request size at which striping is advantageous over nonstriping increases. By the time the reader is ten times as fast as the standard EXB8500, non-striped performance beats striped performance at higher concurrencies, as shown in Figure 5c. This is due in part to contention for the robot arm. At a concurrency of 4, the robot arm utilization for striped operation is around 90% for the largest requests, compared to 30-50% for non-striped. Thus, speeding up only the reader eventually makes striping unattractive in this robot.

Figure 6 shows that when only robot speed is improved, response time is not affected much for either striped or non-striped arrays. In the EXB120, response times are dominated by the long latency of the readers, and improving robot performance alone has little effect.

Finally, Figure 7 shows that when reader and robot speeds are increased at a similar rate, striping continues to be attractive compared to non-striped systems. As response times decrease, the ratio of non-striped to striped response times stays close to 2:1. Eventually, non-striped systems appear to get more advantages from the dual improvements; in Figure 7c, the request size at which striping is advantageous has increased to about 600 MBytes for the workload with a concurrency of four.

7 Summary

In this paper, we have described an event-driven tertiary storage array simulator whose performance models are based on measurements of several tape drive and robot devices. We have used this simulator to compare the performance of striped and non-striped systems, and to predict the performance of large tape libraries with a variety of improvements.

We demonstrated that striped large tape libraries perform poorly on workloads that are not strictly sequential because striping creates contention for a small number of readers. For both mid-range and high performance tape libraries, increasing the number of readers in the system alleviates this contention and makes striping more attractive This strongly suggests that the success of striping in large tape libraries will depend on including an adequate number of readers to handle the expected workload.

We next examined the effects of changing particular tape drive and robot characteristics. Increasing the tape drive's transfer rate doesn't benefit striped performance as much as non-striped because of contention for the readers. Slower robot arms have a more harmful effect on striped than non-striped systems, since the former generate more cartridge switches and utilize the robot arm more heavily. Search and rewind rate improvements reduce the cartridge switch penalty that is so harmful to striped performance. Increasing cartridge capacity causes an increase in average response time because of the extra time required to do search and rewind operations.

Finally, we examined the effect on performance of speeding up readers and robots by certain factors. We discovered that speeding up the drive without speeding up the robot arm eventually hurt striped perfor-

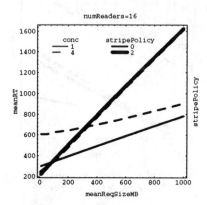
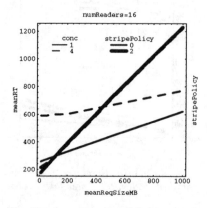
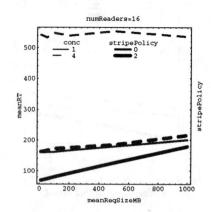

5a: *Response time (sec) for 50% faster reader, unchanged EXB120. EXB120 has 16 readers.*

5b: *Response time (sec) for two times faster reader, unchanged EXB120. EXB120 has 16 readers.*

5c: *Response time (sec) for ten times faster reader, unchanged EXB120. EXB120 has 16 readers.*

Figure 5: *Array performance for EXB120 library with sixteen EXB8500 readers, when readers improve in performance. When reader speedup reaches ten times normal EXB8500 performance, striped performance becomes worse than non-striped performance. For the striped system, performance is limited by the robot arm, which must perform more context switches than the non-striped system. Striped performance is shown in thin lines, non-striped in thick lines; concurrency of one in solid lines, concurrency of four in dashed lines.*

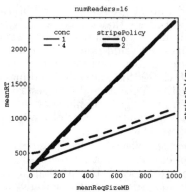
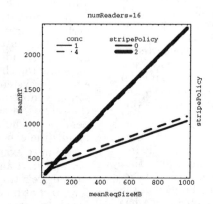
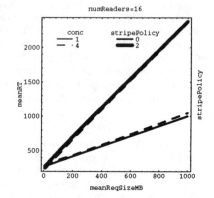

6a: *Response time (sec) for unchanged reader, 50% faster EXB120. EXB120 has 16 readers.*

6b: *Response time (sec) for unchanged reader, two times faster EXB120. EXB120 has 16 readers.*

6c: *Response time (sec) for unchanged reader, ten times faster EXB120. EXB120 has 16 readers.*

Figure 6: *Array performance of EXB120 library with sixteen EXB8500 readers, when robot improves in performance. Improving robot speed has little effect on reducing response time. It does reduce the performance gap between workloads of different concurrencies in a striped system. Striped performance is shown in thin lines, non-striped in thick lines; concurrency of one in solid lines, concurrency of four in dashed lines.*

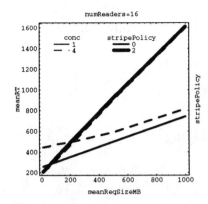 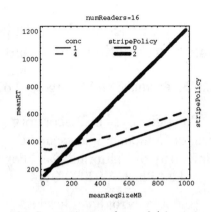 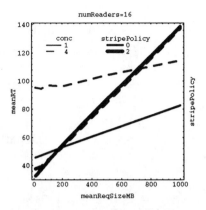

7a: *Response time (seconds) for 50% faster EXB8500 and 50% faster EXB120. EXB120 has 16 readers.*

7b: *Response time (seconds) for twice as fast EXB8500 and twice as fast EXB120. EXB120 has 16 readers.*

7c: *Response time (seconds) for ten times as fast EXB8500 and ten times as fast EXB120. EXB120 has 16 readers.*

Figure 7: *Array performance for EXB120 library with sixteen EXB8500 readers, when both readers and robots improve in performance. Striped performance is consistently better than non-striped performance when drive and robot performance scale at similar rates. Striped performance is shown in thin lines, non-striped in thick lines; concurrency of one in solid lines, concurrency of four in dashed lines.*

mance compared to non-striped performance, since the striped system uses the robot arm more heavily. Speeding up only the robot arm has little effect on response time. Scaling both reader and robot performance at comparable rates keeps striped performance superior even for readers and robots faster than current devices by a factor of ten.

References

[1] Ampex Corporation, Redwood City, California. DST800 and DST600 product literature.

[2] Penelope Constanta-Fanourakis, Ken Kaczar, Gene Oleynik, Don Petravick, Margaret Votava, Vicky White, George Hockney, Steve Bracker, and Jussara M. De Miranda. Exabyte helical scan devices at Fermilab. *IEEE Transactions on Nuclear Science*, 36(5), October 1989.

[3] Ann L. Drapeau and Randy H. Katz. Striped tape arrays. In *Digest of Papers*. Twelfth IEEE Symposium on Mass Storage Systems, April 1993.

[4] Garth Alan Gibson. *Redundant Disk Arrays: Reliable, Parallel Secondary Storage*. PhD thesis, U. C. Berkeley, April 1991. Technical Report No. UCB/CSD 91/613.

[5] Harry C. Hinz. Magnetic tape technology in the 1990s. In *Digest of Papers*. Tenth IEEE Symposium on Mass Storage Systems, May 1990.

[6] M. Y. Kim. Synchronized disk interleaving. *IEEE Transactions on Computers*, C-35:978–988, November 1986.

[7] M. Livny, S. Khoshafian, and H. Boral. Multidisk management algorithms. In *Proceedings SIGMETRICS*, pages 69–77, May 1987.

[8] Metrum Information Storage, Denver, Colorado. RSS-600 Rotary Storage System product literature.

[9] Ethan L. Miller and Randy H. Katz. An analysis of file migration in a Unix supercomputing environment. In *USENIX—Winter 1993*, January 1993.

[10] David A. Patterson, Garth Gibson, and Randy H. Katz. A case for redundant arrays of inexpensive disks (RAID). In *Proceedings ACM SIGMOD*, pages 109–116, June 1988.

[11] K. Salem and H. Garcia-Molina. Disk striping. In *Proceedings IEEE Data Engineering*, pages 336–342, February 1986.

[12] Storage Technology Corporation, Louisville, Colorado. Powderhorn product literatrue.

A Static Analysis of I/O Characteristics of Scientific Applications in a Production Workload

Barbara K. Pasquale and George C. Polyzos

Computer Systems Laboratory
Department of Computer Science and Engineering
University of California, San Diego
La Jolla, CA 92093-0114

{bittel, polyzos}@cs.ucsd.edu

Abstract

Past research on high performance computers for scientific applications has concentrated on CPU speed and exploitation of parallelism, but has, until very recently, neglected I/O considerations. This paper presents a study of the production workload at the San Diego Supercomputer Center from an I/O requirements and characteristics perspective. Results of our analyses support our hypothesis that a significant proportion of I/O intensive, long running, frequently executed scientific applications have predictable I/O requirements.

1.0 Introduction

Past efforts in the development of high performance computer systems have been primarily focused on the computational speeds of processors, often ignoring other important system components, such as the I/O subsystem and the operating system [3, 8, 18, 20]. Resulting progress in the areas of raw processor speed and parallelism, both in hardware and software, has produced GFLOPS machines, but has done little to close the ever widening gap between CPU performance and that of the attached I/O subsystem [1, 8, 9].

Until recently, little concern has been expressed over the growing system imbalance between CPU and I/O performance. Now however, scientific research based on computational approaches has intensified and the number of I/O intensive scientific applications is increasing. For example, applications involving simulation based modeling require and produce massive amounts of data ranging from hundreds of megabytes up to tens of gigabytes per execution. Relying on these large-scale computations and data analysis techniques, progress in many scientific disciplines is limited only by the available capacity of high performance computing [4]. The sheer volume of this data and the need to access, store, distribute and visualize this data intensifies

This work is funded in part by grants from DEC, the U.C. Micro program, and the Sequoia 2000 Project.

I/O demands within the local system and communication requirements across networks [17].

Continuing to increase CPU speeds and to further exploit parallelism without improving the I/O system will create more I/O bound jobs which can become a bottleneck to system performance [1, 8, 9, 11, 12, 19]. In a recent study of the San Diego Supercomputer Center (SDSC), an increase in CPU idle time was directly attributed to I/O blocking [13]. In order to maintain well-balanced systems, we must establish a thorough understanding of the I/O behavior of scientific applications, and from this knowledge, design the mechanisms and implement the policies that are needed to improve the I/O subsystem and provide these I/O intensive applications with their needed resources without degrading overall system performance.

The research presented in this paper describes an I/O workload characterization study of the Cray Y-MP8/864 at SDSC intended to identify I/O intensive applications and to quantify their resource demands. Our goal here is to present some of the observations of that study and to investigate the hypothesis that a high proportion of I/O intensive applications exhibit regular behavior. The I/O metrics considered in this study include the number of total bytes transferred by an application, the *virtual I/O rate*, i.e., the number of bytes transferred per CPU second, and the number and average virtual rate of logical I/O requests. We are interested in identifying a set of I/O intensive applications and in summarizing their I/O resource usage in a way that describes the relationship between the applications, their resource usage, and their contribution to the entire system workload.

The remainder of this paper is organized as follows. In section 2 we discuss the motivation for investigating I/O behavior, and particularly, the roles of static and dynamic characterizations. We also discuss two recent scientific application I/O studies, and present our hypothesis. In section 3 we provide a description of the observed environment at the SDSC. In sections 4 and 5 we progressively present our selection of interesting subsets of the workload and we describe the analyses performed and results obtained. Our conclusions are presented in section 6.

2.0 Motivation

Little attention has been given to the study and analysis of I/O behavior on high performance systems. As a result, our understanding of the effects of current application I/O and projected increases in application I/O is not well established. Scientific applications form an interesting set of programs worthy of study because they absolutely need high performance supercomputers and, therefore, systems should be designed to meet their requirements. Before we can do the latter, we must understand these requirements. We believe that it is necessary to undertake a thorough study of production workloads in order to extract the characteristic behavior of I/O intensive applications.

2.1 Related Research

The analysis of application I/O has been seriously addressed in two recent studies by Miller and Katz [12] and Lim and Condry [10]. By recording detailed information about each I/O request (e.g., type of I/O, request size, number of bytes transferred, file accessed, and file position), they were able to construct run-time profiles depicting an application's I/O behavior over time.

Miller and Katz characterized and modeled the behavior of seven computational fluid dynamics and climate applications to study the effects of proposed software buffer sizes and policies to mitigate the effects of peak I/O bandwidth. Applications analyzed had high I/O rates and used massive data files. The resulting run-time profiles revealed very interesting characteristics about scientific application I/O. Three types of I/O requests were observed: compulsory (I/O accesses to read an initial state and to write interim and final results), checkpointing, and data staging. After the brief initial phase of compulsory I/O, the applications produced bursts of high-volume I/O activity at regular intervals which created a cyclical pattern and ended in a burst of final phase compulsory I/O. They also observed that file accesses were sequential and that request sizes remained constant during the cyclical phase of I/O. They attributed this regularity to the iterative nature of the underlying algorithms.

Lim and Condry analyzed the I/O behavior of four chemistry applications and the Perfect Club benchmark suite to determine how these applications could better exploit gigabit networks. The individual executions of each chemistry application analyzed exhibited a high degree of consistency with respect to the number of read/write accesses, total bytes read or written, disk space usage, data request sizes, and sequential access patterns. Looking at these I/O activities over time, revealed one general pattern of dynamic I/O behavior.

These studies are extremely valuable sources for instrumentation and analysis methodology. They also demonstrate that characterizing application I/O is possible. Their initial results indicate that for the classes of scientific applications considered, I/O activity has, in general, a cyclical pattern, possibly augmented with distinct initial and final phases. However, these studies have dealt with relatively few applications chosen from very specific disciplines, and extrapolating from these results to the I/O behavior problem in general might be questionable. In particular, these studies do not address the question of how prevalent are the selected applications in the system workload, and how intense is their I/O activity in comparison with the remainder of the workload.

2.2 Our Working Hypothesis

The hypothesis we investigate here is that scientific application I/O is predictable. This hypothesis is based on characteristic I/O behaviors discovered in previous studies (described above, but also in our own preliminary investigations of the dynamic behavior of scientific applications), and the following two key observations: (1) scientific applications are highly structured, regular codes, and (2) system configuration and policies influence how resources are used.

Although sophisticated and complex, most scientific applications are based on components that are implementations of well-known algorithms. For example, sparse linear system solvers, FFTs, rapid elliptic problem solvers, multigrid schemes, integral transforms, etc. Given the underlying algorithms of the applications and some specifics of their implementations (e.g., number and type of operations performed, size of data set), an estimate of the required CPU time and memory requirements can usually be obtained.

However, even supercomputer resources are finite, and therefore, the coded application must conform to the physical limitations of the system. The best example of this conformity deals with the use of in-core memory. On a real memory machine like the Cray Y-MP, the entire application and its data set must be resident in memory during execution. Since data sets often eclipse the maximum available memory partition, the technique of data overlaying or data staging is used [12]. At regular intervals in the computation or at each iteration of a looping construct, processing is temporarily suspended while the entire in-core data set is replaced with a new data set. As a result of this data swapping, a cyclic pattern of same size I/O requests is generated by the application. The same is also true when checkpointing is performed [12]. Checkpointing involves writing a portion of the in-core data set to disk to save the state of the computation should the system fail. If failure does occur, the application can then be restarted from the last checkpoint, with minimal recomputation.

Based on the inherent structure of scientific applications and the physical constraints of the system, it is likely that the resource usage of scientific applications, especially I/O, follows a regular and predictable pattern.

2.3 Our Approach

We focus on the characterization of a prominent set of I/O intensive applications rather than overall system behavior because our intent is to investigate current I/O demands as well as future ones, which are not limited to what is observable in current systems. Specifically, we are interested in understanding the issues involved around a potential I/O bottleneck in future supercomputers and to provide tools to prevent it. This scenario is associated with supercomputers that are computationally much more powerful than those of today and also with workloads that are much more I/O intensive. The latter is driven by user expectations about performance of the future machines. Based on current application I/O characterizations one can extrapolate future I/O application requirements, and then through synthesis determine overall I/O workload intensities and patterns.

The first issue that needs to be resolved is how to determine which applications are most worthy of study. The applications selected should span a variety of disciplines and cover the major scientific codes used in these disciplines, as well as represent a frequently executed, I/O intensive component of the workload. In general, this would require a survey of a large number of supercomputer centers, where it would be necessary to analyze the composition of their workloads. Once the major scientific applications of each center are recognized, the results would have to be combined. This is a major undertaking, and outside the scope of our study. However, we conducted such a survey at SDSC, which already supports a diverse workload of many scientific applications. We isolated a set of frequently executed, I/O intensive applications based on measured volumes and rates of I/O activity. The methodology developed for this study can be used to conduct similar studies at other centers.

The second question revolves around how to characterize an application's I/O, in particular, what are the appropriate descriptors. In general, an answer to this question depends on the purpose of the characterization, and characterizations are expected to be objects of study themselves. However, there is one basic dichotomy: static or dynamic characterization. Dynamic characterizations (particularly if they can be made independent of the system and the remainder of the executing workload) are the most powerful, and thus, the most desirable ones. However, they are also expensive to obtain and cumbersome to work with. Therefore, only a limited number of applications can be followed closely in order to provide dynamic profiles of them. On the other hand, static analysis can be applied to a much wider set of scientific applications and should therefore be the first and guiding step for the dynamic analysis.

3.0 The San Diego Supercomputer Center

The system and workload observed for this study was that of the San Diego Supercomputer Center (SDSC) Cray Y-MP8/864. SDSC is one of the five U.S. National Science Foundation sponsored Supercomputer Centers. The SDSC workload spans all major scientific disciplines, including materials science, physics, biochemistry, atmospheric science, chemistry, chemical engineering, astronomy, mechanics, oceanography, and electrical engineering. The user community consists of 2500 researchers from over

150 academic institutions. The amount of data manipulated daily exceeds 1 TB. The broad base of this system's workload and the scientific significance of its applications, makes it an important and appealing environment to study.

Of all the supercomputing resources at SDSC, the Cray Y-MP supports the most diverse I/O workload and contains a wide variety of hardware resources. The Y-MP has a 6 ns clock, 8 CPUs, and 512 MB (or 64M 64-bit words) of memory. For this installation, the Cray Y-MP has been tuned to maximize utilization, with supercomputer idle time only 1% of the available wall clock time. A job mix scheduler attempts to dynamically select an optimal job mix to execute within the real-memory architecture of the Y-MP. Keeping approximately 12 to 15 jobs in memory typically allows a context switch to be made whenever a job is waiting for I/O completion. This tends to maximize the amount of generated I/O in addition to maximizing CPU utilization. The average file system I/O rate of the workload is on the order of 20 MB/s.

To support the I/O requirements of a combined interactive and production workload, the storage system for SDSC's Cray Y-MP is a 5-level buffer and cache hierarchy. Table1 details the levels in this hierarchy and their characteristics [13].

Table 1: SDSC Storage Hierarchy

Caching Level	Size (GB)	Max. Transfer Rate (MB/s)	Daily I/O Volume (GB)	Residency Period
SSD	1	1250	1500	minutes
Local Disks	65	10 /disk	1700	days
Archival Disks	70	2	5	weeks
Tape Robot	1200	--	8	months
Shelf Tape	2000	--	3	years

The critical levels in this hierarchy are the SSD and the local disks. Together these devices must meet the demands of the two major sources of I/O in the system, namely job swapping and application disk I/O. To service the interactive component of the workload, 388 MB of the SSD is allocated as a data cache. This SSD data cache provides for high-speed access to the root file system as well as for interactive swap space for jobs less than 8 MB. The remainder of the SSD is allocated as a data buffer for the temporary file system. Data from this 42 GB file system effectively streams through the SSD with minimal reuse. The local disks serve as a data cache for the temporary and scratch file systems and for swap space for large jobs (i.e., greater than 8 MB).

Large, long running jobs, namely those that require more than 20 minutes of CPU time, 6 MWords of memory, and/or 60 MWords of local disk space, may not be run interactively. Instead, these jobs must be submitted for execution through the NQS (Network Queueing System) Unicos batch facility. Based on the required resources and runtime priority level, users submit their jobs to one of the 27 batch queues.

4.0 I/O Workload Characterization

We first conducted a workload characterization study to isolate the I/O intensive component of the workload. This component represents the set of scientific applications which have extensive demands in terms of I/O volume, i.e., total number of bytes transferred, and average *virtual I/O rate*, i.e., number of bytes transferred per CPU second. By analyzing this component, we can then identify these applications by name and determine their combined resource usage with respect to the entire system workload.

Using the *virtual I/O rate*, rather than real I/O rates, provides us with some basic isolation from the details of the system architecture and the workload executing simultaneously with our target application (and the resource contention it generates). Of course, many other factors cannot be completely controlled, such as idiosyncrasies of the accounting software and the way it charges CPU time to processes. However, the degree of approximation achieved is adequate for the purpose of this stage of the research, where we are more interested in general trends and behavior rather than the details of application dynamics.

4.1 Data Collection

Measurements of application resource usage were obtained from the Cray System Accounting (CSA) utility and collected over a one-month period during February 1992. On a per job-basis, the CSA utility automatically captures an application's resource usage through the use of kernel probes and creates a process account record that summarizes the total resource usage. The recorded resource usage includes: application name, process, user, and job identification numbers, start and end times, total CPU time (including both system and user mode times), total number of bytes transferred, number of logical I/O requests, number of physical I/O requests, the memory high water mark, CPU connect times for multitasked jobs, and I/O wait times.

Although the CSA data only provides aggregate resource usage, it enabled us to analyze the workload at two important levels, the functional level and the physical resource level [3, 5, 7]. Serazzi [16] showed that reliable workload characterizations can capture the functionality of the real system workload while still preserving the underlying physical resource usage. By spanning these two levels, we can describe both the higher level applications and the lower level resource usage simultaneously, so that the relationship between I/O intensive applications and the resources they consume can be understood.

4.2 The Workload

The collected data was separated into two categories: *system utilities* and *user applications*. System utilities represent programs that are available to all users whereas *user*

applications are limited to a single user or a small group of users. Table 2 shows how each component contributes to the overall workload resource usage. As can be noted from the figures of Table 2, the *user* component of the workload has a tremendous impact on total resource usage. Even though it represents an extremely small portion of all executed jobs (5%), it accounts for 92% of total CPU time and 88% of total bytes transferred. The results of this workload characterization study are consistent with an earlier study of the SDSC workload [15] where it was found that *user* applications represented 7% of the workload and consumed 90% of total CPU time and 75% of I/O channel time

Table 2: February 1992 Resource Usage

	Number of Apps. Executed	Number of Distinct Apps.	Cumulative CPU Time (s)	Cumulative Bytes Transferred (MB)
System Utilities	5,651,460 (95%)	445 (12%)	1,566,303 (8%)	5,477,771 (12%)
User Apps.	311,408 (5%)	3,366 (88%)	16,822,314 (92%)	41,552,252 (88%)
Total Workload	5,962,868	3,811	18,388,617	47,030,023

4.3 I/O Intensive Applications

To extract the set of I/O intensive applications from the set of all *user* applications, we produced an average virtual I/O rate ordering of all distinctly named *user* applications and calculated resource statistics with respect to the total workload resource usage. Focusing more on I/O rates rather than total I/O volume is dictated by our desire to investigate applications that might stress the I/O system to the point of affecting their response time or interfere with other applications. Table 3 shows an abbreviated version of this ordering.

Table 3: Average I/O Rate Ordering

Top N Ranked Apps.	% of Distinct User Apps.	% of Total Workload CPU Time	% of Total Workload Bytes Transferred	Min. I/O Rate of Top N Grouping (MB/cpu sec.)
1	0.03	0.001	0.10	230.56
10	0.30	0.300	14.59	107.86
20	0.60	0.600	24.54	80.13
30	0.90	0.600	24.60	71.71
50	1.50	0.660	26.27	49.87
80	2.40	0.690	26.85	35.48
160	4.80	3.160	48.89	18.45
300	8.90	8.230	70.33	6.89
360	10.70	9.930	74.64	4.78
580	17.20	19.900	85.98	1.58

Given that the percentage of CPU time was increasing at the same rate as the number of applications considered, we investigated the average CPU time for these applications. The average CPU times for the top 580 I/O rate ordered applications revealed that 472 of these applications (i.e., 82%) had an average CPU time of approximately 106 seconds or less. These short jobs do not have a significant impact when considering their contribution to total workload bytes transferred. Therefore, to focus attention on those jobs which exert a longer, sustained demand on system resources, we produced a new I/O rate ordering which included only those applications whose average CPU time exceeded 100 seconds. The statistics of this new set are given in Table 4.

Thus, using only 1.5% (i.e., 50) of the *user* applications, we were able to identify a smaller, yet important set of I/O intensive scientific applications, in terms of both volume and rate, whose combined resource usage accounts for 71% of total system bytes transferred and only about 9.5% of total system CPU time (see Appendix A). In addition, this set of applications represents 80.7% of total bytes transferred on behalf of *user* applications. The combined effects of applications like these can exert peaks of I/O load that might considerably stress the I/O subsystem. Therefore, these are the applications that we have selected as candidates for further study.

Table 4: Average I/O Rate Ordering with Average CPU Time > 100 secs.

Top N Ranked Apps.	% of Distinct User Apps.	% of Total Workload CPU Time	% of Total Workload Bytes Transferred	Min. I/O Rate of Top N Grouping (MB/cpu sec.)
1	0.03	0.13	6.73	131.70
10	0.30	1.29	33.63	29.78
20	0.60	3.35	49.26	18.07
30	0.90	4.90	57.63	11.08
50	1.50	9.42	71.08	4.70
80	2.40	12.86	75.97	3.31

5.0 Regularity in I/O Intensive Applications

From the set of 50 I/O intensive applications, 24 were selected for individual analysis (see Appendix A). Our selection criterion was based on the frequency of execution over the month-long observation period. This is important for two reasons. First, in this initial phase of analysis, it is necessary to uncover the I/O intensive applications which are continually present in the workload. Second, several observations are required to make judgements about typical resource usage. For these reasons, we set the execution frequency threshold to 10 executions over the one-month period considered. Although 10 executions might at first seem a low number, one must also consider that many of these scientific applications use hours of Cray CPU time, and therefore, their execution frequency is often limited by the turnaround time of the NQS batch system. Note that

with respect to the entire workload, these 24 applications consumed 6% of the total CPU time and were responsible for 55% of the total number of bytes transferred.

5.1 Cluster Analysis

To find natural partitions or patterns within the resource usage records for a given application, the multidimensional analysis technique of K-means clustering was used [6, 7]. A notable feature of the clustering algorithm is that it uses weighted Euclidean distance as a dissimilarity measure, which allows the size of each cluster to vary in inverse proportion to its variance. The resource usage parameters used in the clustering were: CPU time, memory high water mark, and number of logical I/O requests. An average logical I/O request rate was also calculated for each resulting cluster. Although clustering algorithms are non-trivial because they must recognize "nearness" among the characteristic parameters selected, Calzarossa and Ferrari [2] found that the non-hierarchical K-means algorithm produces reliable results for workload characterization and modeling.

Based on the clusters found for each application, three general patterns of resource usage were observed and are described below.

(1) **Logical I/O Rate and CPU Time**: The logical I/O rate remained fairly stable across marked divisions in CPU time for approximately 1/3 of the applications. For other applications like trans.im, timteb.x, and xm901, the logical I/O rate decreased across increasing divisions in CPU time. In some sense, this behavior can be expected. If an application has intense phases of initial and/or final I/O activity, the average logical I/O rate will naturally decrease for longer-running executions.

(2) **CPU Time**: Several applications showed a small range or fairly constant CPU time across all cluster groupings. However, for more than half of the applications, cluster groupings were separated by marked divisions in CPU time. These applications had both short executions on the order of seconds and long executions on the order of minutes.

(3) **Memory High Water Mark**: The memory high water mark (or memory size), represents the maximum number of main memory words allocated to a program during execution. For virtually all of the applications, this average memory size was consistent across all cluster groups. Looking at the recorded values for all executions of a given application, revealed the reasons for this consistency. Maximum memory sizes for the applications fell into one of three categories: (a) exactly one size, (b) one small range of sizes, or (c) one distinct size (or possibly two) and a small range of sizes. It is also interesting to note that the applications were roughly equally divided among these memory size categories.

Based on the average value for each parameter (e.g., CPU time, number of logical I/O requests, memory space), the individual clusters showed the different resource usage patterns relating to each application. We observed that there were 1 or 2 clusters which described the majority of the individual executions for a given application. Thus, to better understand the relationship between the individual clusters and application resource usage, we calculated the percentage of total application resource usage attributed to each of the individual application clusters. From the percentages obtained, we could determine which individual clusters represent the application as a whole in terms of total resource usage and define its "characteristic" resource usage.

Considering the percentage of individual cluster resource usage, as well as cluster size, it was possible to characterize 15 of the applications by only 1 of its clusters and 6 of the applications by only 2. For the 15 applications with 1 "characteristic" cluster, approximately 95% of CPU time and 97% of logical I/O requests were attributed to the 1 cluster containing 67% of total executions on the average. For the 6 applications with 2 "characteristic" clusters, approximately 95% of CPU time and 95% of logical I/O requests were attributed to the 2 clusters which jointly contained 84% of total executions on the average. The remaining 3 applications (cpmd.x, timteb.x , dir.cpx), however, were each characterized by 3 of their clusters. For these applications, large sized clusters made a small contribution to total resource usage while small sized clusters made a significant contribution. The "characteristic" clusters for each application are described further in Appendix B.

5.2 Regression Analysis

Given that several applications showed consistent logical I/O rates across individual cluster groupings, we decided to investigate statistical correlations between the measured values of CPU time, characters transferred, and logical I/O request count. Clustering algorithms, such as the one we used in the previous section, can detect natural groupings in data based on a specific parameter set, but do not describe statistical relationships between the variables in the selected parameter set. Therefore, we used regression analysis to explore such potential relationships.

As an example of the analysis performed to detect underlying resource usage relationships, we present the data and statistics for application griz.exe. This application has all the characteristics of an application with highly regular resource usage: a consistent logical I/O rate, exactly one memory high water mark, and a range of CPU times. Considering the measured values from the process account records and the calculated logical I/O request rate given in Table 5, it is not difficult to see this regularity. Although data on the number of bytes transferred per logical I/O request was not available, one can expect a high degree of correlation between the logical I/O count and the number of characters transferred in any application. For griz.exe these two measures are near perfectly correlated.

Table 5: CSA Resource Statistics for griz.exe

CPU Time (sec.)	Bytes Transferred	Logical I/O Count	High Water Memory (words)	Logical I/Os per CPU sec.
207.60	4971823104	25415	595968	122.38
177.53	4971823104	25415	595968	143.16
183.73	4885053440	25003	595968	136.09
177.50	4885053440	25003	595968	140.86
174.79	4885053440	25003	595968	143.05
191.64	4884267008	24965	595968	130.27
178.99	4884267008	24965	595968	139.48
177.36	4884267008	24965	595968	140.76
100.70	2694578176	13790	595968	136.91
94.74	2694578176	13790	595968	145.56
93.80	2694578176	13790	595968	147.02
93.69	2694578176	13790	595968	147.19

Next we investigated the relationships between CPU time and both logical I/O count and the total number of bytes transferred. Linear regression analysis showed the major influence CPU time has on the total number of bytes transferred as well as on the number of logical I/O requests. Table 6 provides the actual values from the analysis.

The important result of this analysis is the high value of the coefficient of determination (which describes the goodness of fit of the model), for both models. This strong correlation between CPU time and these I/O measures is compatible with the hypothesis that griz.exe contains a regular, repetitive I/O processing phase, like those observed in [10, 12].

Table 6: Regression Analysis for griz.exe

Dependent Variable	Independent Variable	Coefficient of Determination	t-stat
Bytes Transferred	CPU Time	.964	16.255
Logical I/Os	CPU Time	.963	16.189

Regression results for all selected applications are provided in Appendix C. Table C.1 shows results for the standard linear model:

$$NumBytesTransferred = a \times CPUTime + c$$

We have grouped the 24 applications into three categories based on the regression results. The first group with 8 applications has all regression coefficients positive and relatively high coefficients of determination. This group fits well the hypothesis of regular behavior during the main phase, with I/O volume highly correlated with CPU time, and additional initial and final I/O phases (with positive I/O amounts, independent of the CPU time).

The second group contains only two applications. The coefficients of determination, are very low, suggesting that this model does not fit these applications.

The last group contains 14 applications. Even though R^2 is high (0.866 and above), suggesting a good fit for a linear model, with positive correlation between CPU time and number of bytes transferred, the values of the constant of the regression obtained are negative, which does not fit our hypothesis of I/O during an initial or final phase. The t statistic for the constant is low for 10 of the 14 applications in this group, however, it is typically not advisable to drop the constant of the regression under any circumstances. For some of these applications we can reconcile the negative values of the constant by assuming that the execution incorporates a significant initial or final computational component. The t statistic for the coefficient of the CPU time is always very high, except for the 2 applications of the second group.

In response to the results for this last group and in order to investigate non-linearities in the variables, we attempted to fit the following model,

$$NumBytesTransferred = e^{c} \times CPUTime^{a}$$

which is linear after a logarithmic transformation of the data. Table C.2 in Appendix C shows the results for this model. All applications fit well the above model, except three. The lowest coefficient of determination is obtained for `stone.exe` which also had an unacceptable low value in the case of the first model. (Inspecting the data for this application reveals that there is essentially one run profile for this application, with small, seemingly random, variations in CPU time and number of characters transferred.) The power of CPU time estimated from the regression is roughly between one and two (or close to these values), which is interesting in itself. The estimated constant, c, has values between 8 and 20.

6.0 Conclusions

We studied the production workload of SDSC's Cray Y-MP to identify I/O intensive scientific applications and to examine the regularity in their resource usage. Our workload characterization analysis isolated a set of 50 distinctly named, I/O intensive scientific applications whose aggregate resource usage represented 71% of total system bytes transferred and 9.5% of total system CPU time during a one-month period. Cluster and regression analysis was performed on the most frequently executed applications in this I/O intensive set to determine characterisitc patterns and statistical relationships of individual application resource usage.

Cluster analysis revealed three general patterns in application resource usage: (1) fairly stable logical I/O rates across marked divisions in CPU time, (2) both "short" (i.e., on the order of seconds) and "long" (i.e., on the order of minutes) CPU execution times, and (3) consistent in-core memory usage. Considering the percentage of resource usage attributed to the individual clusters of an application, as well as cluster size, it was possible to use only one or two individual clusters to describe the characteristic resource usage of the entire application. Regression analysis revealed that I/O demands, both in terms of the number of characters transferred and the number of logical requests, show considerable correlation with CPU time consumed. These results support our hypothesis that scientific applications have a high degree of regularity in their functional operation and resource usage.

Speculating on the underlying causes for the observed general patterns of resource usage and the individual application characteristics, we offer the following explanations. The consistency in memory size may be attributed to fixed sized data sets obtained from external data collection devices or to carefully partitioned data sets designed to take advantage of the Y-MP's fixed partition memory scheme. The "short" and "long" divisions in CPU time may be attributed to the size of the data set used or to the degree of resolution required in the computation (i.e., number of repetitions over a single-sized data set). The stability in logical I/O rates across different execution times may represent the dominating effects of a highly regular main processing phase within the application. Through dynamic profiling, Miller and Katz [12] observed a class of scientific applications whose main processing phase consisted of a period of CPU processing followed by a burst of intense I/O activity, which repeated at regular intervals. If one were to assume negligible I/O during the initial and final phases and that the number of I/O requests are constant within each iteration, an application in this class would have a consistent, logical I/O rate across different execution times.

In the end, a regular behavior can only be confirmed through dynamic analysis on a per application basis. To obtain such evidence, it will be necessary to monitor and measure the run-time resource behavior of these applications. We intend to proceed in that direction and the present analysis will guide us in selecting the applications to consider and also to generalize the results obtained by dynamic analysis to classes of applications determined by this study. A first step in this direction is our work described in [14].

7.0 References

[1] Bell, G., "The Future of High Performance Computers in Science and Engineering," Communications of the ACM, Vol. 32, No. 9, pp. 1091-1101, September 1988.

[2] Calzarossa, M., and Ferrari, D., "A Sensitivity Study of the Clustering Approach to Workload Modeling," Performance Evaluation, Vol. 6, pp. 25-33, North-Holland, 1986.

[3] Calzarossa, M., and Serazzi, G., "Workload Characterization for Supercomputers," Performance Evaluation of Supercomputers, Ed. J. L. Martin, pp. 283-315, North-Holland, 1988.

[4] Denning, P. J., and Adams III, G. B., "Research Questions for Performance Analysis of Supercomputers," Performance Evaluation of Supercomputers, Ed. J. L. Martin, pp. 403-419, North-Holland, 1988.

[5] Ferrari, D., "Workload Characterization and Selection in Computer Performance Measurement," Computer, pp. 18-24, July/August 1972.

[6] Hartigan, J. A., Clustering Algorithms, J. Wiley, New York, 1975.

[7] Heidelberger, P., and Lavenberg, S. S., "Computer Performance Evaluation Methodology," IEEE Transactions on Computers, Vol. 33, No. 12, pp. 1195-1220, December 1984.

[8] Hennessy, J. L., and Patterson, D. A., "Computer Architecture: A Quantitative Approach," Morgan Kaufmann Publishers, Inc., 1990.

[9] Katz, R. H., Gibson, G. A., and Patterson, D. A., "Disk System Architectures for High Performance Computing," Proceedings of the IEEE, Vol. 77, No. 12, pp. 1842-1858, December 1989.

[10] Lim, S. B., and Condry, M. W., "Supercomputing Application Access Characteristics," Technical Report No. UIUCDCS-R-91-1708, University of Illinois at Urbana-Champaign, October 1991.

[11] Martin, J. L., "Supercomputer Performance Evaluation: The Comparative Analysis of High-Speed Architectures Against Their Applications," Performance Evaluation of Supercomputers, Ed. J. L. Martin, pp. 3-19, North-Holland, 1988.

[12] Miller, E. L. and Katz, R. H., "Input/Output Behavior of Supercomputing Applications," Proceedings of Supercomputing '91, November 1991.

[13] Moore, R., "File Servers, Supercomputers, and Networking," Proceedings of the NSSDC Conference on Mass Storage Systems and Technologies for Space and Earth Science Applications, 1991.

[14] Pasquale, B. K. and Polyzos, G. C., "I/O Profiles of a Scientific Application on a Workstation and a Supercomputer," Technical Report No. CS93-299, University of California, San Diego, July 1993.

[15] Pasquale, J. C., Bittel, B. K., and Kraiman, D. J., "A Static and Dynamic Workload Characterization Study of the San Diego Supercomputer Center CRAY X-MP," Proceedings of the 1991 ACM SIGMETRICS Conference on Measurement and Modeling of Computer Systems, pp.218-219, May 1991.

[16] Serazzi, G., "A Functional and Resource-Oriented Procedure for Workload Modeling," Performance '81, pp. 345-361, North-Holland, 1981.

[17] Stonebraker, M., and Dozier, J., "Overview of the Sequoia 2000 Project," Proceedings of COMPCON '92, San Francisco, California, February 1992.

[18] Williams, E., "The Effects of Operating Systems on Supercomputer Performance," Performance Evaluation of Supercomputers, Ed. J. L. Martin, pp. 69-81, North-Holland, 1988.

[19] Lazowska, E. D., and Sevcik, K. C., co-chairs, "Report of the Workshop on Scientific Computing Performance Analysis," Division of Advanced Scientific Computing, NSF, Boulder, Colorado, August 29-31, 1989.

[20] Committee on Supercomputer Performance and Development, "An Agenda for Improved Evaluation of Supercomputer Performance," National Research Council, Washington, D.C., 1986.

Appendix A: I/O Intensive Applications

Application and Frequency		Average CPU Time (s)	Average Bytes Transferred (MB)	Average I/O Rate (MB/s)
trans.im*	30	801.03	105499.66	131.70
resm*	13	1527.89	192742.85	126.15
xxpd3	4	2482.97	267818.69	107.86
timteb.x*	60	209.50	20253.62	96.68
fdsol*	18	2344.26	187864.14	80.14
crayfeat*	13	298.41	21298.91	71.38
feat	7	993.00	70061.79	70.56
ocean*	11	8445.38	268202.03	31.76
Analyze*	19	412.04	12697.85	30.82
xm901*	21	832.55	24796.34	29.78
momlw.x*	29	955.85	27333.12	28.60
griz.exe*	12	154.35	4071.45	26.38
d2us5.ms	4	241.75	5715.25	23.64
d2us4.ms	5	294.59	6873.90	23.33
eigen.ss*	20	433.76	8934.10	20.60
xmain	228	724.78	13372.94	18.45
xm824*	32	180.17	3302.58	18.33
d2us4a.m	2	381.26	6759.17	17.73
stress*	140	187.13	3086.23	16.49
tub*	20	3410.72	53334.32	15.64
cgcm*	25	10393.35	158769.12	15.28
forsinc3	1	220.48	3327.23	15.09
invt.x	1	417.31	5882.37	14.10
cxi.x*	11	365.44	4950.74	13.55
cfsconc*	41	2922.90	38710.59	13.24
1913.exe	6	9932.95	119368.62	12.02
rot	8	124.15	1377.96	11.10
ddam	4	1056.82	11708.24	11.08
cas2.exe*	116	1246.07	12582.48	10.10
scf.exe*	34	253.16	2248.77	8.88
stone.exe*	13	102.06	864.65	8.47
dnsavg4.*	13	435.71	3324.99	7.63
cpmd.x*	114	488.62	3542.09	7.25
dir.cpx*	141	662.04	4501.17	6.80
em3dl.x	7	604.58	4087.08	6.76
m927c	2	8647.42	57968.64	6.70
NAST67*	343	228.58	1530.38	6.70
df0008.x	5	765.11	5110.48	6.68
1508.exe	8	2049.28	13522.98	6.60
cadpac41	6	5594.70	36427.14	6.51
df0010.x	5	1191.74	7149.72	6.00
df8000.x	5	1004.62	5796.56	5.77
1311.exe	6	2077.38	11947.11	5.75
1202.exe	21	947.97	4875.57	5.14
df0014.x	5	1430.50	7184.69	5.02
rotm2	4	163.20	766.49	4.70
1705.exe	2	2999.41	13986.94	4.66

* Applications selected for individual analysis.

Appendix B: Cluster Analysis Results

Application	Cluster Size	Cluster % of Total Executions	CPU Time Average (s)	CPU Time % of App. Cumulative CPU	Logical I/O Requests Average (#)	Logical I/O Requests % of App. Cumulative Log. I/Os	Logical I/O Rate Avg. (#/s)	Memory Space Avg. (MWords)
tub	18	90.0	3788.75	99.9	309671.22	99.9	81.73	1.103
cas2.exe	102	87.9	1416.95	99.9	413907.76	99.9	292.11	0.658
cfsconc	15	75.0	7989.04	99.9	12727206.40	99.9	1593.08	0.258
eigen.ss	15	75.0	578.31	99.9	18011.00	99.9	31.14	6.532
ocean	8	72.7	11420.39	98.3	14182056.00	99.9	1241.82	0.451
resm	11	84.6	1802.84	99.8	2133282.91	99.7	1183.29	0.413
momlw.x	19	65.5	1436.79	98.4	599779.37	99.3	417.44	2.910
scf.exe	18	52.9	417.83	87.3	123979.44	98.7	296.72	0.329
Analyze	9	47.3	745.71	85.7	932004.44	98.7	1249.82	0.935
cxi.x	7	63.6	562.92	98.0	39547.57	97.4	70.25	0.776
trans.im	13	43.3	1847.13	99.9	38175.00	96.8	20.67	5.883
stress	65	46.4	381.36	94.6	40587.63	96.3	106.43	5.520
xm824	21	65.6	225.15	82.0	61893.62	96.2	274.90	2.424
fdsol	11	61.1	3356.04	87.4	1248264.73	90.8	371.95	8.074
xm901	17	80.9	947.41	92.1	358000.47	90.4	377.87	2.439
griz.exe	8	66.7	183.65	79.3	25091.75	78.4	136.63	0.595
	4	33.3	95.73	20.7	13790.00	21.6	144.05	0.595
		(100)		(100)		(100)		
crayfeat	6	46.1	504.97	78.1	1152473.33	79.5	2282.25	3.263
	5	38.4	169.85	21.8	354803.20	20.4	2088.92	3.243
		(84.5)		(99.9)		(99.9)		
cgcm	16	64.0	11381.39	70.0	863017.50	21.6	75.83	2.844
	3	12.0	24873.73	28.7	16575317.33	78.0	666.38	2.110
		(76.0)		(98.7)		(99.6)		
dnsavg4	2	15.3	2692.36	95.0	7035.00	72.3	2.61	19.867
	9	69.2	30.95	4.9	568.00	26.2	18.35	19.872
		(84.5)		(99.9)		(98.5)		
NAST67	145	42.2	481.46	89.0	33771.75	87.2	70.14	3.812
	143	41.6	55.61	10.1	4232.97	10.7	76.12	3.809
		(83.8)		(99.1)		(97.9)		
stone.exe	2	15.3	95.18	14.3	35090.00	15.4	368.65	0.284
	8	61.5	97.46	58.7	34837.75	61.4	357.45	0.284
		(76.8)		(73.0)		(76.8)		
cpmd.x	1	0.8	39315.13	70.5	9866752.00	43.7	250.97	3.809
	80	70.1	46.12	6.6	77188.57	27.3	1673.66	0.633
	16	14.0	793.51	22.7	405925.56	28.8	511.56	5.004
		(84.9)		(99.8)		(99.8)		
timteb.x	3	5.0	1161.60	27.7	183205.67	22.3	157.72	5.804
	22	36.6	355.58	62.2	62502.05	55.9	175.78	6.797
	24	40.0	52.36	9.9	22080.29	21.5	421.70	5.797
		(81.6)		(99.8)		(99.7)		
dir.cpx	11	7.8	5246.17	61.8	17395.36	27.7	3.32	7.403
	47	33.3	673.88	33.9	8242.87	56.2	12.23	6.631
	60	42.0	62.89	4.0	1589.13	13.8	25.27	6.945
		(83.1)		(99.7)		(97.7)		

The table is headed "Characteristic Application Clusters".

Appendix C: Regression Analysis Results

Table C.1: Regression Analysis

$$NumBytesTransferred \ = \ a \times CPUTime + c$$

Application and Frequency		c (MB)	t stat	a (MB/s)	t stat	R^2
dnsavg4	13	33.723	0.991	7.736	240.152	1.000
resm	13	5749.900	0.591	125.414	24.571	0.982
trans.im	30	1126.410	0.181	133.459	27.527	0.964
griz.exe	12	435.691	1.829	24.189	16.255	0.964
eigen.ss	20	154.740	0.234	20.734	16.535	0.938
stress	140	179.472	1.543	15.929	41.915	0.927
cpmd.x	113	1769.420	3.080	3.833	24.935	0.849
cxi.x	11	1353.400	1.554	10.169	5.678	0.782
xm824	32	2337.520	4.557	5.796	2.835	0.211
stone.exe	13	876.524	132.063	0.086	1.345	0.141
cgcm	25	-24058.000	-1.279	17.957	12.919	0.879
timteb.x	60	-12064.500	-2.682	156.586	23.197	0.903
fdsol	18	-17945.600	-1.246	89.716	20.051	0.962
crayfeat	13	-564.258	-0.405	74.978	22.711	0.979
ocean	11	-10027.800	-1.348	33.706	57.382	0.997
Analyze	19	-1824.620	-0.755	35.985	11.951	0.894
xm901	21	-1669.81	-0.887	32.504	15.238	0.924
momlw.x	29	1785.100	-1.914	31.149	41.911	0.985
tub	20	-1186.130	-0.189	16.360	10.770	0.866
cfsconc	21	-1672.110	-0.300	13.840	21.371	0.962
cas2.exe	116	-684.313	-5.049	10.889	142.464	0.994
scf.exe	34	-110.348	-0.748	9.532	22.317	0.940
dir.cpx	141	-1249.090	-4.726	8.848	55.377	0.957
NAST67	343	-87.988	-1.739	7.240	52.579	0.890

Table C.2: Regression Analysis -- Logarithmic Transformation

$$NumBytesTransferred \ = \ e^c \times CPUTime^a$$

Application and Frequency		c	t stat	a	t stat	R^2
resm	13	19.202	133.020	0.931	44.018	0.994
eigen.ss	20	9.641	25.604	2.143	30.876	0.981
griz.exe	12	17.572	83.477	0.908	21.616	0.979
cas2.exe	116	12.740	88.369	1.480	66.961	0.975
momlw.x	29	9.402	22.184	2.112	30.376	0.972
cgcm	25	12.457	26.299	1.434	25.935	0.967
trans.im	30	12.315	35.575	1.860	26.530	0.962
crayfeat	13	11.285	13.615	2.205	13.478	0.943
tub	20	8.346	8.889	2.022	16.538	0.938
cfsconc	20	11.402	15.640	1.577	16.229	0.936
scf.exe	34	12.930	28.831	1.542	17.591	0.906
fdsol	18	10.147	9.460	1.941	12.357	0.905
ocean	11	9.936	5.751	1.767	8.408	0.887
cxi.x	11	12.670	12.019	1.650	8.162	0.881
dir.cpx	141	12.257	48.485	1.538	31.419	0.877
timteb.x	60	11.860	27.195	2.074	19.563	0.868
xm901	21	17.556	30.746	0.950	11.071	0.866
cpmd.x	113	12.933	44.882	1.832	24.818	0.847
xm824	32	17.371	51.965	0.880	12.437	0.838
Analyze	19	14.014	18.855	1.464	9.223	0.833
stress	140	12.399	42.245	1.782	26.165	0.832
NAST67	343	14.963	59.944	1.151	21.416	0.574
dnsavg4	13	12.158	6.189	1.759	3.786	0.566
stone.exe	13	20.553	544.015	0.011	1.297	0.133

PIPADS - A Low-Cost Real-Time Visualisation Tool

Andrew Spray, Heiko Schröder, K.T.Lie, Erik Plesner and Peter Bray

Department of Electrical and Computer Engineering,
The University of Newcastle, NSW 2308, Australia.

Abstract

The demand for real-time visualisation of complex data-sets is already well established. However more recently, industrial users wish to make use of tools to aid in the presentation of complex information without making the purchase of an expensive, dedicated visualisation system.

PIPADS - the Parallel Image Processing and Display System is an architecture targetted at supporting real-time image processing tasks at low-cost. The machine uses an inexpensive semi-custom SIMD array which, through supporting scan-line based algorithms can produce mega-pixel perspective views of terrains in real-time.

This paper presents the constraints placed upon the SIMD array, and details the how the architecture and implementation minimise hardware, time and volumetric costs.

1: Introduction

The real-time manipulation and visualisation of massive data-sets is an important capability in many applications ranging from the analysis of fluid dynamics to flight simulation. The ability to visualise process mechanics or physical measurements facilitates analysis and interpretation, therefore there is an increasing demand for this capability from industries not traditionally associated with the supercomputing required for real-time image processing.

It would be desirable to produce an architecture specifically targetted at supporting visualisation tools for industries which do not wish to make large commitments to high performance general-purpose computing engines. The application specific nature of this visualisation machine should ease the optimisation task necessary to produce a high performance architecture at low cost.

The objective of this paper is to present the constraints applied and techniques used to deliver the high performance required for real-time visualisation while using low cost hardware. Specifically, the paper highlights the development of a SIMD (Single Instruction Stream/Multiple Data Stream) array to support scan-line based algorithms for perspective viewing and image processing whilst minimising the hardware and volumetric costs.

The SIMD array developed comprises 1024 16-bit processing elements and can deliver 20 GOPS - sufficient processing power to permit 1 mega-pixel 24-bit pseudo-coloured perspective views to be generated from raw spot-height matrices every 0.05 seconds.

This array forms one component of the Parallel Image Processing and Display System (PIPADS), a complete hardware and software environment for visualisation and massively parallel processing being developed by a consortium of university, governmental and industrial partners (The University of Newcastle and UNSW-Australian Defence Force Academy, CSIRO, and Broken Hill Proprietary respectively). An overview of the PIPADS machine is shown in Figure 1. The effort of the University of Newcastle team discussed in this paper relates to the module marked 'Scan-Line Processor Array'.

The structure of this paper is as follows: Section 2 discusses perspective viewing - an application which contains a range of representative functions suitable to use for developing visualisation hardware. Section 3 overviews a number of existing massively parallel processor products/projects, thereby setting the scene for a detailed discussion in Section 4 of how the SIMD array in the PIPADS machine achieves the 20 GOP performance necessary for megapixel real-time perspective viewing. Section 5 reports on the status of the PIPADS SIMD array development and concludes the paper.

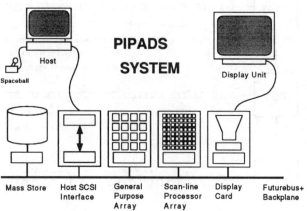

Figure 1: The PIPADS System

2: Application - Perspective Viewing

It is recognised that the breadth of the image processing field is immense, hence a representative subset of visualisation functions had to be identified which could be used to derive suitable hardware constructs for an image processing engine. The application of perspective viewing comprises many such functions and hence is a suitable vehicle for the development of a low-cost image processor.

Within the PIPADS consortium the BHP corporation had an requirement for real-time perspective viewing, for example: it is desirable to be able to assess the mining prospects of an area of land without incurring the costs of actual aerial inspection and detailed photography. This is achievable by extracting computer generated perspective views of landscapes from known land spot heights. The spot heights themselves can be extracted from existing stereographic satellite photographs.

This application from BHP formed the primary objective for the PIPADS machine - an architecture and environment capable of producing 1024×1024 (or greater) pixel perspective views (Figure 2), with 24-bit colour, from raw spot-height data. The views generated are definable from a six-degree of freedom input, thereby permitting fly-throughs, rotations, zooms etc. Additionally,

the frame rate for this real-time visualisation is 20 frames per second, with a maximum latency from input to view of 0.1 seconds.

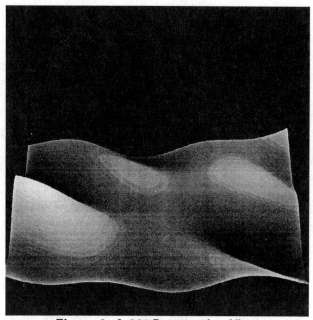

Figure 2: A 30° Perspective View

The performance demands of the perspective viewing application indicate that the use of some form of concurrent architecture is necessary. Additionally, for the low-cost objective to be achieved, it is necessary that the hardware and the software for such a machine should be well matched. This section introduces the algorithmic strategy which appears to be well tailored to the visualisation problem, and outlines the key features of the functions used for perspective viewing which have particular demands on the hardware implementation.

Feasible algorithmic options include the use of vector/polygon based graphics and the use of scan-line processing [1]. Vector based graphics rely on the representation of images as lines and surfaces; perspective generation is evaluated from the orientation and positional inter-relationships of these facets with respect to the observer. Scan-line based algorithms work on images (or multi-dimensional data) one dimension at a time, for example in the same way a 2 dimensional FFT can be carried out as 2 sequential orthogonal FFTs, one calculation on the rows and one on the columns.

The scan-line techniques were adopted for perspective viewing for the following reasons:

- Scan-line processing can straightforwardly be mapped/partitioned into simply constructed SIMD architectures,
- Polygon based algorithms do not scale well with image size and complexity,
- Data flow in polygon based strategies can be highly irregular, possibly leading to problems in data communication rates.
- Data flow in scan-line based algorithms is very uniform, making inter-processor inter-communications straightforward,
- Intrinsically, the scan-line technique works with data at the pixel level, so the facets generated at this level are small (Figure 2), and the effects of boundaries between facets is less noticeable than between the larger facets commonly used with polygon based strategies.

The scan-line based architecture used in the PIPADS machine assigns one processing element to each row of the image (Figure 3), in this project the chief application works with images of 1024×1024 pixel images, hence there are 1024 processing elements making up the array. The precise details of techniques for generating perspective views on such scan-line architectures are shown in Robertson [1], however as an outline, Table 1 below shows the core routines used in the generation of a perspective view.

Preliminary pseudo-coding of the routines above showed that the most time consuming functions were interpolation and transposition, and Table 1 shows that these functions are also the most often used. Thus it is necessary to design an architecture to maximise the efficiency of these functions.

2.1: Transposition

The objective of a scan-line processor array is that a linear array of processors perform operations on a single row or column in an image. The use of a linear array is highly attractive, since it requires only a low I/O bandwidth, it is easy to integrate with local wiring and it intuitively matches the scan-line philosophy. Unfortunately, the fact that a scan-line processor only performs functions on rows (or columns) means that when

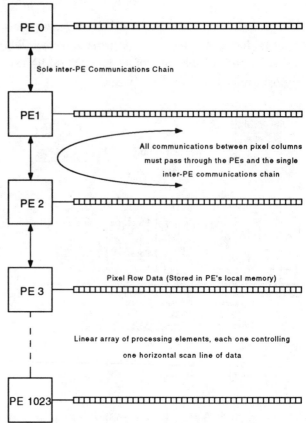

Figure 3: Linear Array of Processors

one wishes to perform operations on columns (or rows) then it is necessary to perform a transposition of the data (the number of transpositions required is dependent upon the final desired rotation of the output view).

The high speed transposition of data in a linear array is not a trivial problem, and indeed Figure 3 shows how the limited bandwidth of a linear array slows this operation. From an algorithmic standpoint it becomes apparent that it is desirable to have a much higher bandwidth. For example if one processing element (PE) were assigned to each pixel P_{ij}, it would be desirable for it to have direct interconnection to the processor at pixel P_{ji}, thus a transpose would take 1 processor cycle (assuming bidirectional communication). Alternatively a full crossbar switch may be desirable to interconnect a 'linear' array - thereby allowing a transposition in O(n) processor cycles (where there are n PEs for an n×n pixel image). Neither of these strategies is feasible for a low-cost architecture, since both require excessive hardware/wiring.

The compromise adopted in the PIPADS scan-line

processor is to interconnect the array in a 2 dimensional toroid, this structure is discussed further in Section 4. In terms of algorithmic effects, the transposition can be undertaken in $O(n\sqrt{n})$ cycles.

Routine	Calls per perspective
Image transpose	4 to 6
Interpolation:	6
Scan-line compression Scan-line uncompression	3
Rotation	3
Perspective projection	2
Masking	1
Image downloading	1
Image uploading	Average → 0

Table 1: Key Perspective View Routines

2.2: Interpolation

Interpolation/extrapolation is undertaken each time a rotation or compression/uncompression (Figure 4) is required.

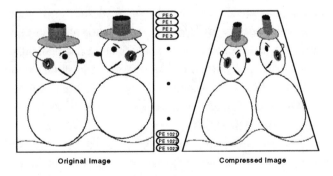

Original Image   Compressed Image

Figure 4: Image Compression

As has already been mentioned, in PIPADS each row is assigned to a processing element, this means in the case of a 1024×1024 image each PE must manage the data for 1024 pixels and indeed each PE has a local memory for storing all these data. During interpolation or extrapolation, each row performs a function involving a multiplication and division between data which are held in local memories. It is not straightforward to perform interpolations between data in the same column by shuffling information around the array, so interpolation is undertaken along rows.

Thus to produce a new datum half way between two existing pixels, one would find the average of the data in columns i and j. This requires that both data must be resident in the PE for the computation to proceed - meaning that at every interpolate stage at least one new datum must be read in from memory. The architectural issue this raises is that even on a simple processing element it would be desirable to pre-fetch data from memory while other computation is being carried out. Secondly, it is desirable that the addressing scheme allows quick calculation of 'next addresses'. This topic is also dealt with in Section 4.

2.3: Overview

For the perspective viewing application as a whole, pseudo-coded versions of the complete algorithm were generated, simulated, verified and modified allowing for different hardware constructs. In the analyses, for a 1024 processing element SIMD array, the initial brute force approach with no optimisations for communications or memory addressing led to a total of 400 million instructions needing to be broadcast to an array every second (20 perspective views per second). Clearly the naïve approach was insufficient.

The architecture now developed requires only 18 million instructions to be broadcast to the array every second (and each instruction is now also quicker), the chief causes for this reduction have been the optimisations outlined in Section 4.

3: Architectural Background

Traditionally, massively parallel architectures such as the Connection Machine [2], CLIP4 [3], DAP [4], MPP

[5] have been constructed from simple bit-serial processing elements (PEs). More recently, increasing flexibility has been introduced into the PEs, for example, in the implementation of associative arrays such as ALAP [6] and SCAPE [7], or through the capability to modify the instruction words within the individual PEs - as in GAPP [8].

The above architectures maintain fine granularity of processing elements in order to utilise the advantages of high clock speeds, straightforward Very Large Scale Integration (VLSI) applicability, and the capability to extract fine grained parallelism efficiently.

There are however, problems which are not particularly well matched to the fine grained processing element approach, hence some architectures have developed with heterogeneity of processing elements such as Connection Machine [9], or coarser grained elements (MASPAR [10]), or both (CLIP7 [11]).

The perspective viewing application is suited coarser grained elements (capable of handling data bandwidths of greater than 1-bit), since input and output data are often in the 8, 16 or 24-bit range. Additionally, since it is most common that the same operations are performed on the entire data-set, the design simplicity of a homogenous array appears favourable. Thus it would seem that an architecture similar to the Maspar (though more dedicated to visualisation) would be desirable.

The PIPADS approach can be likened to the Maspar, SLAP [12] and Princeton Engine [13] architectures. In particular, PIPADS is similar to the Princeton Engine and SLAP in that it uses 16-bit processing elements to undertake scan-line processing, however a number of architectural differences exist between the strategies.

The Maspar is a general purpose massively parallel processor (with up to 16384 processing elements), and inherently it is less optimised for visualisation than PIPADS. At the processing element level, the two architectures are similar in terms of their functionality, however the data bandwidth within the Maspar is 4 bits, and this is smaller than would commonly be used for visualisation. In terms of communications capabilities one important difference exists - PIPADS does not support a global router: it has been possible to re-cast the visualisation algorithms used to avoid the need for such a

resource (and hence expenditure).

The Princeton Engine has an array of up to 2048 processing elements, its PEs are more complex than those of PIPADS - for example the Princeton Engine incorporates multiple datapaths for concurrent multiplication/shifting/addition/memory accesses. In terms of communications capabilities there is a considerable difference between the two architectures: the Princeton Engine's network has the topology of a linear array which it augments by making use of the 'reconfigurable bus' concept [14], while the PIPADS machine uses a simple toroid. In overview, the PIPADS approach is targetted at employing less expensive hardware than that used in machines such as the Princeton Engine (and IBM's Power Visualization System - a shared memory machine with 32 i860s). However, it is to be noted that the Princeton Engine has also been used to support scan-line processing for perspective viewing [15] - indeed the Sarnoff Team based these visualisation demonstrations on the same algorithms produced by Robertson [1].

The SLAP (Scan Line Array Processor) architecture is an array of 512 processing elements targetted at supporting scan-line image processing flexibly. The PIPADS and SLAP processing elements support similar functionality - logical, arithmetic and shift operations, however for general PE data the intercommunications network is richer in PIPADS - the SLAP architecture is a linear/ring based array (though it supports a second linear datapath which is dedicated to the video stream). In the SLAP machine the array controller block has a more active rôle in the processing than with PIPADS, for example, the controller block contains buffers which can feed the array with normal images or transposed images automatically. The PIPADS architecture stores all data relevant to a particular row locally to a processing element, and does not have to wait for data to be systolically fed out of a centralised buffer. Both architectures have been designed with image processing applications in mind, though at the implementation level, SLAP is targetted at 512×512 images (at 30 frames per second) whereas PIPADS works with 1024×1024 images (at 20 frames per second). In both cases, there are plans to update and improve the architectures.

4: Design Optimisations

As a preliminary, this section will describe the structure of the PIPADS scan-line processor array, then design decisions which achieved the speedups mentioned in Section 2 will be explained.

4.1: Overview - Hardware

The scan-line array processor (shown schematically in Figure 5) is an architecture spread across five printed circuit boards, these boards are:

- The motherboard containing the array controller, the I/O interface to the Futurebus[+] backplane, the frame buffer and the routine library memory
- Four daughter cards supporting the processor array and the local memories for the PEs.

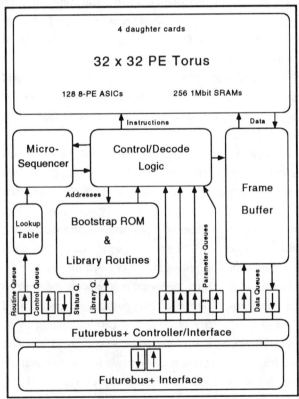

Figure 5: The Scan-Line Array System

The scan-line array is activated by calls from a host being passed to the motherboard. These calls are decoded and they initiate library routines which drive the array controller (an AMD microsequencer). The motherboard also handles the passing of parameters to the sequencer and array, and manages the up- and downloading of images via the frame buffer to the array. All operations within the array and the motherboard are controlled by the microsequencer (except a nominal amount of bootstrapping logic).

Image data flows to and from the array through a wide (512 bit) bus, this bus is multiplexed onto the interprocessor communications lines at one side of the array.

The array itself is a SIMD structure of 1024 identical processing elements each with local memory space. Physically, the array comprises 128 semi-custom (gate array) ASICs, and 256 1Mbit RAMs.

Each ASIC contains 8 16-bit processing elements, and a memory management unit. The processing elements contain 16 general purpose registers, and can perform integer arithmetic, logical functions, conditional evaluations and arbitrary distance shifts. Each processing element can address up to 16,384 16-bit words of local memory. Local memory is accessed through shared data and address lines, where the memory management unit prevents clashes for the memory resource, and allows memory accesses to be performed while other computation is being carried out within the processing elements.

The design of the ASICs, the array and the motherboard has been very conservative, since from the project conception it has been deemed more important to have a working system than a fast system. This has led to the design being heavily buffered (indeed in the ASIC, to conform with design rules over half the logic utilisation is buffering). Other features of the system are that it uses a 2 phase non-overlapping clocking strategy and signals are deeply pipelined so that they have only to travel short distances before being re-synchronised.

4.2: Overview - Software

It has already been mentioned that the execution of the perspective viewing algorithms is initiated by routine calls from the host to the library routines on the motherboard. However where do the perspective view routines come from, and what form do they take?

The 'Bootstrap ROM and Library Routines' module shown in Figure 5 includes a ROM containing a toolbox of functions to start up the motherboard and the array, and to undertake commonly required tasks. The rest of the block comprises SRAM which is loaded with perspective view routines or any other function which the user desires the array to undertake.

The format of the ROM and RAM is 1Mega-word long and 64-bits wide (including padding). Each memory word is broken down into several fields including: the instruction word for the array to obey, the next address for the microsequencer, fields for data to be sent to the array and/or the microsequencer, control signals to permit parameters from the host to be downloaded into the sequencer and/or the array (and to notify where the parameters are located), and control signals to co-ordinate data transfer between the array and the frame buffer, and between the frame buffer and the host.

The generation of such data is a long and tedious task, and an assembler is used to convert PIPADS assembler code into the 16-bit array instructions and control/microsequencer data for the library routines. The motherboard housekeeping functions (microsequencer control, parameter control and frame buffer control) are hidden from the user, since these routines have already been coded as core functions for the architecture. The assembler allows access to the board level control, though this is not a necessary task for the user.

The PIPADS assembler accepts free-form files of assembler code and interprets the usual constructs such as macros, loops, and conditionals. It can automatically optimise code for maximum concurrency between array and motherboard functions or for minimum library memory usage. The assembler produces binary output data which can be loaded directly into the library memory (or loaded into the PIPADS scan-line array simulator).

The perspective view routines themselves have been handcoded into PIPADS assembly language, and have verified to be functional with the simulator (which produced the image in Figure 2).

At a higher level still, there is the processing performed within the host and other cards in the PIPADS machine, this relates to work undertaken at CSIRO - Division of Information Technology, and at UNSW-ADFA and is not within the scope of this paper.

4.3: Transposition

The PIPADS scan-line processor is not a sole product in its own right, but complements the system shown in Figure 1; as such not only must the array meet the requirements placed on it by the application, but it must also conform with the requirements of the rest of the system.

All the hardware for the PIPADS system intercommunicates through a Futurebus[+] backplane, this resource is a very high bandwidth bus, and a very valuable asset [16]. The most difficult constraint applied to the scan-line array processor is that it must occupy no more than 3 Futurebus[+] slots. This means that the interfacing to the Futurebus[+], the array controller with visualisation library memory, the frame buffering and the array itself must not occupy a volume greater than 7 litres.

The volumetric constraint has had significant impact on the design of the array, not least because it bounds the size and number of chips for processing elements. In order to make greatest use of board area, surface mount chips were selected, and this in turn limited the pin-out (pin grid arrays can offer a greater number of I/O connections per unit area, however they make use of both sides of a printed circuit board).

In Section 2 it was pointed that in order to have fast transposition it is desirable to have a high communications bandwidth, this is in direct contradiction to the volumetric requirement. The compromise achieved was a two dimensional toroidal array. This array is arranged in the manner shown in Figure 6 such that the local interconnections do not extend over large distances.

In normal operation the toroid still appears the same as in a linear array - the data in a particular register in all PEs will be the data specific to a certain column of an image. However, when inter-processing element transfers are effected, correction must be made for the fact that the processor to the north of PE 32 is PE 63 and not PE 31. This feature is inconvenient for simple movements of data but for the case of transposition it is very useful, since data now can 'jump' blocks of 32 PEs by moving East or West.

The fact that a 2 phase non-overlapping clocking strategy is used enables some saving in the I/O requirement for the ICs, while still offering a high communications bandwidth. This is effected by splitting the 16-bit communication data words into 2 8-bit halves and transmitting one half each clock phase.

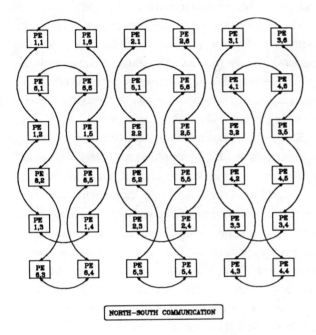

NORTH—SOUTH COMMUNICATION

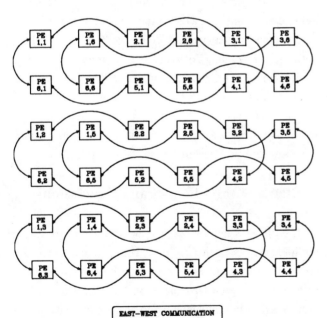

EAST—WEST COMMUNICATION

Figure 6: Communication Network on a 6 × 6 Torus

The communications bandwidth is only half the problem for transposition - it is necessary to manage which memory locations are read and which locations written for each processing element. The fastest transpose technique that has been identified by Newcastle team is to move all the data along diagonals parallel to the leading diagonal at once.

Consider Figure 7 remembering that each processing element manages the memory for a whole pixel row. Firstly the data along diagonal m is translated leftwards then downwards and stored in diagonal m'.

This results in a datum at (i,j) moving to (j,i) and a datum moving from (x, i) to (i, x)

In the next stage, data along diagonal n is moved to diagonal n'.

This results in a datum at (i, j-1) moving to (j-1, i) and a datum (x+1, i) to (i, x+1)

Observing the effects of memory accesses in row i while progressing from step 1 to step 2, it is possible to see that, for reading data each step the memory location is incremented, and for writing the memory location is decremented (the reverse is the case when data flows in the opposite direction - diagonal m' to diagonal m).

By generating hardware to automatically handle the pointer movement considerable savings can be made in the calculation of sources and destinations of memory accesses.

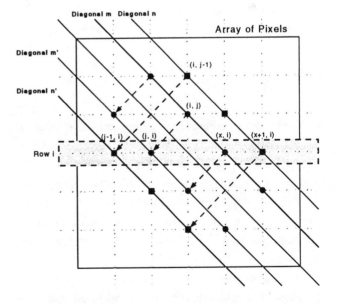

Figure 7: Transposition of an Image

Since the array is a toroidally connected network, it is often more efficient to move data 8 positions left than 24 positions right, likewise this scrolling of end-around data movement can be accommodated in the memory accessing:

Assuming that an image has 1024 (0...1023) pixel columns,

- when a pointer to a memory location reaches count 1023, and the count is to be incremented, the end-around feature can be incorporated by resetting the count to 0
- likewise when the pointer reaches 0 and is to be decremented the count is set to 1023

In the PIPADS machine this automatic wrapping facility also considerably simplifies the transpose algorithm and enhances its speed. The wrap capability is hard-wired into each PE but the wrap 'size' is programmable so that images do not have to be constrained to 1024 columns.

It is also noted that the hardware ensures that only the current image 'page' is accessed during wrapping:

If *Image_1* occupies memory locations 0...511,

and *Image_2* occupies memory locations 512...1023 If the situation exists that the wrapping size is specified to be 512 locations, and *Image_2* is being accessed then the pointers will always remain in the range 512...1023 even when a wrap occurs (from 1023 to 512 or 512 to 1023).

The complete transposition algorithm can be implemented in just over 34,000 instructions for 1 megapixel image on a 32×32 toroidal array with memory pointers and wrapping.

4.4: Interpolation

The implementation of interpolation requires on average one datum to be read from memory for each interpolation to be carried out. As has been mention in Section 4.1, all processing elements on a single chip share access to a local memory, this means they must take turns to read the data they require. Hence, with 8 processing elements per IC this constitutes a considerable stall in the calculation rate achievable during interpolation.

It would be desirable if the memory accesses could be overlapped in time with other computation, this is indeed possible, however if a multiply and/or divide are single cycle operations, then the processing still becomes significantly stalled. Alternatively, a study of the algorithms used in perspective viewing, and in fact many other image processing applications shows that the number of memory accesses necessary is evenly balanced with the numbers of multiplications needed.

This observation led to the implementation of multi-cycle multiplication and division within the processing elements. The simpler multiply (shift and conditional add) and divide (restoring shift-subtract) enabled the processing element clocking rate to be increased beyond that required for fully parallel multiplication and division.

The multiplication now requires 16 instruction cycles to be completed and the divide requires 17 (16 for modulus). The number of cycles to guarantee all processing elements have extracted/written their data from/to memory is 8, hence it is now possible to read one operand and write one result while multiplication and division are being carried out. For interpolation, the I/O and the computation is much better balanced, with 18 fast instruction cycles (RDB: 1, MUL: 7, WRB: 1, MUL: 9) to perform two memory accesses and a multiply rather than 17 very slow cycles (RDB: 8, MUL: 1, WRB: 8).

The above strategy assumes that a memory prefetch is being carried out, i.e. while a multiplication is active the *next* operand is being read in (and the *last* result written out). This prefetching does require extra registers to buffer the incoming data (so it won't interfere with current computation).

This section of the paper has presented two techniques which have caused a considerable increase in performance for a low-cost architecture for visualisation.

5: Status of the PIPADS and Conclusion

The PIPADS machine is now entering the phase where preliminary assessments are being undertaken by commercialising parties. For the scan-line array processor architecture, a prototype has still to be assembled, this prototype is a full implementation of the motherboard, but only supporting an array of 64 processing elements.

Currently, the PE ASICs are in fabrication, the daughter cards have been laid out, and the motherboard is entering the layout stage, having been successfully verified to a low level in VHDL.

For a fully populated array of 1024 processing elements, the scan-line processor can deliver 20×10^9 16-bit operations per second, 300M floating point operations per second (customised format - 14-bit exponent 16-bit mantissa), 5GBytes/sec memory bandwidth, 40GBytes/sec inter-processor bandwidth, and 640Mbytes/sec off board communications (Futurebus$^+$ limited). This architecture is sufficient to be able to generate 1024×1024 24-bit pixel perspective views at a rate of 20 frames per second.

The paper as a whole has introduced the PIPADS scanline array processor and has shown a number of techniques for enhancing the performance of low cost hardware to meet the demands of a real-time visualisation engine.

6: Acknowledgments

The authors wish to acknowledge the support, help and encouragement of Phil Robertson, David Keightley and Neale Fulton from the Centre for Spatial Information Systems (CSIRO - Division of Information Technology, Canberra, ACT), Trevor Hobbs, Brendan Boesen and Ickseon Kim from UNSW-ADFA (Canberra, ACT), Mike Moore and Lawrence Leung from BHP Research Labs (Newcastle, NSW), and Meiyun Zheng, Will McGovern and Gavin Turner from The University of Newcastle.

7: References

[1] Robertson P.K.: "Spatial Transformations for Rapid Scan-Line Surface Shadowing", IEEE Computer Graphics & Applications, pp 30-38, March 1989.

[2] Hillis W.D.: "The Connection Machine", The MIT Press, Cambridge, Massachusetts, ISBN 0-262-08157-1, 1985.

[3] Preston K., Duff M.J.B.: "Modern Cellular Automata, Theory and Applications" Plenum Press, New York & London, ISBN 0-306-41737-5, 1984.

[4] Reddaway S.F.: "DAP A Distributed Array Processor" IEEE Symposium on Computer Architecture, pp 61-65, 1973.

[5] Batcher K.E.: "Design of a Massively Parallel Processor" IEEE Transactions on Computers, Vol C-29, No 9, pp 836-840, September 1980.

[6] Finnila C.A., Love H.H.: "The Associative Linear Array Processor" IEEE Transactions on Computers, Vol C-26, No 2, pp 112-125, February 1977.

[7] Lea R.M.: "SCAPE : A Single-Chip Array Processing Element for Signal and Image Processing" IEE Proceedings, Vol 133, Pt E, No 3, pp 145-151, May 1986.

[8] NCR: "Geometric Arithmetic Parallel Processor Manual" NCR, Drayton, Ohio, USA, 1984.

[9] Lin M., Tsang R., Du D.H.C., Klietz A.E., Saroff S.: "Performance Evaluation of the CM-5 Interconnection Network", Preprint 92-111, Army High Performance Computing Research Center, University of Minnesota, Minneapolis, October 1992.

[10] Maresca M., Fountain T.J.: "Scanning the Issue", Proceedings of the IEEE, Special Issue on Massively Parallel Computing, Vol 79, No 4, pp 395-401, April 1991.

[11] Fountain T.J., Matthews K.N., Duff M.J.B.: "The CLIP7A Image Processor" IEEE Transactions on Pattern Analysis and Machine Intelligence, Vol 10, No 3, pp 310-319, May 1988.

[12] Fisher A.L., Highnam P.T.: "The SLAP Image Computer", in 'Parallel Architectures and Algorithms for Image Understanding', V.K. Prasanna Kumar (ed.), Academic Press, Boston, ISBN 0-12-564040-4, 1991.

[13] Chin D., Passe J., Bernard F., Taylor H., Knight S.: "The Princeton Engine: A Real-Time Video System Simulator", IEEE Transactions on Consumer Electronics, Vol 34, No 2, May 1988.

[14] Li H., Maresca M.: "Polymorphic-Torus Network" IEEE Transactions on Computers, Vol C-38, No 9, pp 1345-1351, September 1989.

[15] Kaba J., Matey J., Stoll G., Taylor H. Hanrahan P.: "Interactive Terrain Rendering and Volume Visualization on the Princeton Engine" National Information Display Laboratory, David Sarnoff Research Center, Princeton, New Jersey.

[16] Robertson P.K. et al: "PIPADS: A Vertically Integrated Parallel Image Processing and Display System" 9 pp, Fifth Australian Supercomputing Conference, Melbourne, Australia, December 1992.

Session 6:
Optimizations for
High-Performance Compilers
Chair: Doug Pase

To Copy or Not to Copy:
A Compile-Time Technique for Assessing When Data Copying Should be Used to Eliminate Cache Conflicts*

Olivier Temam[†], Elana D. Granston[†],   William Jalby[‡]

University of Leiden,   University of Versailles

Abstract

In recent years, loop tiling has become an increasingly popular technique for increasing cache effectiveness. This is accomplished by transforming a loop nest so that the temporal and spatial locality can be better exploited for a given cache size. However, this optimization only targets the reduction of capacity misses. As recently demonstrated by several groups of researchers, conflict misses can still preclude effective cache utilization. Moreover, the severity of cache conflicts can vary greatly with slight variations in problem size and starting addresses, making performance difficult to even predict, let alone optimize. To reduce conflict misses, data copying has been proposed. With this technique, data layout in cache is adjusted by copying array tiles into temporary arrays that exhibit better cache behavior. Although copying has been proposed as the panacea to the problem of cache conflicts, this solution experiences a cost proportional to the amount of data being copied. To date, there has been no discussion regarding either this tradeoff or the problem of determining *what* and *when* to copy. In this paper, we present a compile-time technique for making this determination, and present a selective copying strategy based on this methodology. Preliminary experimental results demonstrate that, because of the sensitivity of cache conflicts to small changes in problem size and base addresses, selective copying can lead to better overall performance than either no copying, complete copying, or copying based on manually applied heuristics.

Key words: selective copying, cost–benefit analysis, data copying strategies, loop tiling, data reuse, cache conflicts, compiler-directed cache management, program optimization.

1   Introduction

In recent years, loop tiling [1, 6, 11, 12, 13] has become an increasingly popular technique for increasing cache effectiveness. Accomplished via a combination of strip-mining, interchanging, and occasionally skewing, loop tiling can be used to transform a loop nest so that the temporal and spatial locality can be better exploited for a given cache size. A simple example of loop tiling is presented in Figure 2, where a tiled version of the loop nest from Figure 1 is presented.

```
DO j1 = 0, N3-1
  DO j2 = j1, N1-1
    DO j3 = j2, N2-1
      C(j1,j3) += A(j1,j2) * B(j2,j3)
    ENDDO
  ENDDO
ENDDO
```

Figure 1: *Original loop nest.*

```
DO jj2 = 0, N2-1, B2
  DO jj3 = 0, N3-1, B3
    DO j1 = 0, N1-1
      DO j2 = jj2, min(jj2+B2-2,N2-1)
        DO j3 = jj3, min(jj3+B3-1,N3-1)
          C(j1,j3) += A(j1,j2) * B(j2,j3)
        ENDDO
      ENDDO
    ENDDO
  ENDDO
ENDDO
```

Figure 2: *Tiled loop nest.*

Unfortunately, loop tiling only targets the reduction of *capacity misses*, namely misses that are due to using a cache whose size is too small to hold the working set of cache lines. Typically, however, caches have a very low degree of associativity. Often, they are direct-mapped. Therefore, as demonstrated in [3, 7, 10], they can still suffer from a high degree of *conflict misses*, thereby precluding effective cache utilization. Moreover, the severity of performance degradation can vary greatly with slight variations in problem size and starting addresses, making performance difficult to even predict, let alone optimize.

To illustrate this, consider the reference to B in the loop nest in Figure 2. During any given execution of the j_1 loop (i.e., execution of all N_1 iterations of the j_1 loop), the same tile of array B is accessed. Therefore, if this tile of $B_2 B_3$ elements can be brought into cache on the first iteration of the j_1 loop and remain there until the last iteration, $(N_1 - 1)B_2 B_3$ of the $N_1 B_2 B_3$

*Support was provided by the Esprit Agency DGXIII under Grant No. APPARC 6634 BRA III.

[†]High Performance Computing Division, Department of Computer Science, Leiden University, Niels Bohrweg 1, 2333 CA Leiden, The Netherlands

[‡]Universite de Versailles, 78000 Versailles, France

410

accesses to elements in this tile can be eliminated.

Can this tile be kept in cache during this period? Note that this tile consists of B_2 intervals of B_3 elements. Assume row major order and suppose that a direct-mapped cache is used. The virtual address corresponding to reference $B(j_2, j_3)$ is ADDR $B + j_3 + N_2 j_2$, where N_2 is the leading dimension of array B and ADDR B is the base address of array B. Assuming that the cache can hold C_S array elements, the cache distance between the starting locations of two consecutive intervals is $N_2 \bmod C_S$. As can be seen in Figure 3, if $N_2 \bmod C_S < B_3$, the elements of the different intervals associated with the tile will *interfere* with each other in cache, causing elements to be flushed prematurely.

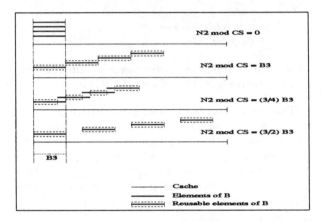

Figure 3: *Four possible cache mappings for the tile associated with the reference to array B in the tiled loop nest (Figure 2).*

To reduce conflict misses, [7] have proposed *data copying*. With this technique, data layout in cache is adjusted by copying array tiles to temporary arrays that exhibit better cache behavior. For example, as shown in Figure 4, to eliminate the aforementioned interferences between elements within a tile of array B, the tile can be copied so that intervals are stored consecutively in a temporary $COPY$ array. The copying is performed before executing the loop where the array is reused. When the loop is executed, the copy is accessed instead of the original array. Because the copy has a better *footprint* in cache, reuse preventing interferences among the elements of the tile are avoided.

The effects of cache conflicts and data copying on the example loop nest can be seen graphically in Figure 5, where hit ratios for three versions of tiled matrix-matrix multiply are depicted, as the problem size N is varied, where $N = N_1 = N_2 = N_3$, and all matrices are of size $N \times N$.

Architectural parameters are based on those of Digital's Alpha chip [8]. We assume a direct-mapped

```
DO jj2 = 0, N2-1, B2
  DO jj3 = 0, N3-1, B3

C   Copy tile for array B into array COPY

    DO k2 = jj2, min(jj2+B2-2,N2-1)
      DO k3 = jj3, min(jj3+B3-1,N3-1)
        COPY(k3+B3*k2) = B(k2,k3)
      ENDDO
    ENDDO

    DO j1 = 0, N1-1
      DO j2 = jj2, min(jj2+B2-2,N2-1)
        DO j3 = jj3, min(jj3+B3-1,N3-1)
          C(j1,j3) += A(j1,j2) * COPY(j3+B3*j2)
        ENDDO
      ENDDO
    ENDDO
  ENDDO
ENDDO
```

Figure 4: *Tiled loop nest from Figure 2 after copying array B.*

cache of $C_S = 1024$ elements (8K bytes) partitioned into lines of $L_S = 4$ elements (32 bytes) each. Based on these cache parameters, a block size of $B_2 = B_3 = 24$ has been selected, which is in the range recommended in [7] when no copying is used.

The three versions correspond to the following cases:
(1) no copying as shown in Figure 2,
(2) copying only array B as shown in Figure 4, and
(3) complete copying, where all arrays (A, B, and C) are copied.
Note the instability in the hit ratio for the no copying case, which varies greatly with small changes in problem size. In contrast, the hit ratio is fairly stable when copying is used. This trend can also be observed with other benchmarks [10]. In the case of matrix multiply, most of the benefit can be derived from just copying array B, indicating that most of the conflict misses are due to this array. However, slightly more benefit can be derived from copying other arrays as well.

If we were to judge solely by hit ratios, clearly, we would always want to copy everything possible. However, *copying is not free*. Furthermore, hit ratios alone do not tell the whole story. First, there is loop overhead in creating a copy. Second, whenever a temporary $COPY$ array is loaded with data from an original array, the elements from the original array are loaded into cache. Because a copy is being made, these elements will not be reused. Hence, they pollute the cache.

The overall performance of these same three cases has also been simulated, accounting for delays due to misses and instruction overhead for copying. A memory access latency of 20 cycles is assumed on a cache miss. Copying is assumed to require 5 cycles per array element. Figure 6 shows the overhead for copying

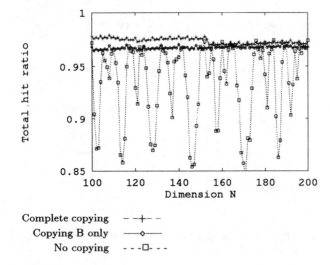

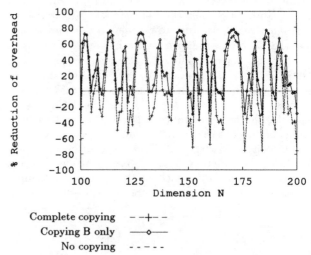

Complete copying	– –+– –
Copying B only	—⊙—
No copying	– – –□– – –

Figure 5: *Hit ratio of tiled matrix-matrix multiply with and without copying.*

Complete copying	– –+– –
Copying B only	—⊙—
No copying	– – – – –

Figure 6: *Simulated performance of tiled matrix-matrix multiply, with and without copying.*

relative to the case of no copying, where

$$\begin{aligned} overhead = \ &\#\_of\_cache\_misses \times memory\_latency\_in\_cycles \\ &+ \#\_of\_array\_elements\_copied) \times \#\_of\_cycles\_for\_one\_copy. \end{aligned}$$

For this choice of parameters, when *both* costs and benefits of copying are considered, it is not worthwhile to copy everything: the cost outweighs the benefits.

As shown in this example, the costs and benefits of copying must be carefully analyzed. Most research on optimizing for data locality optimizing barely addresses this issue. Of the few that do discuss data copying [1, 7, 11], none present general, automatable guidelines for determining *when* and *what* to copy. Without such guidelines, copying cannot be *effectively* incorporated into production compilers. Without copying, the behavior of loop tiling algorithms can vary greatly with small changes in problem size and starting address, thereby forcing the selection of smaller tile sizes that permit only a small fraction of the available cache space to be utilized [7].

To address this problem, we present a compile-time method for identifying the arrays that are victims of interferences, and for estimating the amount of interferences. [1] We also propose a selective copying strategy based on this methodology, and present preliminary experimental results.

---

[1] In this paper, we give simpler approximate formulas where sufficient. This entails leaving out ceilings, floors, and significantly small constants, where approximate formulas will do. The reason for this is two-fold: first, this increases readability. Second, the added precision is not necessary for our purposes. Therefore, one would want to use the approximate formulas in a compiler. Experiments have been conducted demonstrating that the approximate formulas are generally sufficiently precise for their purpose, namely computing costs and benefits, and making performance estimates [4].

The remainder of this paper is organized as follows. Section 2 provides an overview of data copying. Section 3 presents a formal framework that is needed for the presentation of our selective copying algorithm. Section 4 describes our selective copying algorithm, and addresses coherence issues. Section 5 summarizes this work and discusses future research directions.

2 Data Copying
2.1 Problems

Although copying is a conceptually simple idea, it can be difficult to implement, due to coherence problems and those of assessing costs and benefits.

Coherence When a second copy of a tile of data is made above which the hardware is ignorant, hardware coherence maintenance mechanisms cannot be relied upon to maintain coherence between the two copies. If the tile is read within the loop nest, the tile must be copied to the temporary array variable beforehand. If the temporary array is modified during the loop nest, it must be copied back to the original array afterwards.

With one reference, this is fairly straightforward. Suppose, however, that there are multiple references to the same data. If all the references are read references, there will not be any coherence problems, but there may be data duplication. However, if one of these is a write reference, then either copying should not be applied to any references whose associated tiles overlap with that of the write reference, or all references accessing the data to be modified must access the same copy. In the latter case, a *dominant* tile [2] of data must be copied that encompasses the tiles of all references that overlap with the write reference.

Assessment of Costs and Benefits The ability to effectively apply data copying is *critical* for efficient utilization of loop tiling. [4, 7] demonstrate experimentally that on average without copying only a small fraction of the cache can be efficiently utilized, or equivalently, that the best tile size can be far smaller than the theoretical optimum. This significant difference arises because cache interferences are ignored in the computation of the theoretically optimum tile size. However, when copying is used, most significant interferences can be removed. Therefore, the best tile size approaches the theoretical optimum and more of the cache space is effectively utilized.

The benefits achieved from data copying are directly proportional to the impact of cache interferences. For example, suppose that in a loop nest of index j_1 two references $Y(j_1)$ and $Z(j_1)$ overlap in cache, but only by one or two cache lines. Then, the cost of copying probably outweighs potential gains.

The cost is proportional to both cost of making the copy and the cost of useful data that is flushed from cache in the process. However, copying has a cost. Consider Figure 4 where array B is copied into array $COPY$. Because all elements of B must still be brought into cache once, they can flush elements from other arrays, including array $COPY$, that could otherwise have been reused. Similar pollution occurs when a temporary array is copied back to an original array. This pollution increases the cost of copying.

2.2 Strategies

On what basis should copying decisions be made? In the literature, complete copying and copying based on manual insights have been used. We describe these two approaches. We also introduce the notion of *selective copying* based on a cost–benefit analysis of the worthwhileness of copying.

Complete Copying If complete copying is used, as proposed by Bodin et al. [1], all copyable arrays are blindly copied. The term *copyable* excludes those that cannot be copied, due to complicated subscript expressions, or because coherency problems might arise. For example, such problems might arise when indirect addressing is used.

With respect to the copyable references, the cache is managed like a local memory, so no interferences can arise among copied arrays. However, as shown in Figure 6, complete copying can entail significant overhead that can easily outweigh the benefits.

Heuristic Copying Alternatively, we can copy only some of the tiles. Although no automatic selection method is discussed in the literature, several heuristics have been manually applied to sample codes based on researchers' insights. The first of these heuristics is based on detecting when the intervals associated with a tile might overlap and copying to avoid self-interferences. For example, [7] present a case study of matrix-matrix multiply (Figure 2), where the authors detect that the most significant source of interference is due to self interference on array B. Using this insight, they successfully eliminate a major source of interferences by copying this array. Another insight that can be used is to note that regular and severe interference can occur when two references have the same linearized stride, and have base addresses that map close together in cache.

Selective Copying The above and other heuristic approaches can detect some cases where copying *might* be useful. However, these heuristics are not easily automatable. Moreover, as demonstrated in Section 1, the benefits of copying can vary drastically with small changes in problem size and starting address. To overcome these limitations, we propose *selective copying*, whereby the benefits and costs of copying are estimated on a case-by-case basis, and copying applied only where profitable.

As an example of the benefits of using selective copying, recall the performance graph in Figure 6. For some problems sizes, only array B should be copied and for some problem sizes, copying should not be used all at. Because of the instability demonstrated by the example presented here and by other experimental studies [10], only an automatable analysis technique can consistently select the best option.

3 Definitions

We now present formal definitions of concepts that are needed for the development of our selective copying algorithm that is described in Section 4.

3.1 Reuse Sets and Interference Sets

Consider a tiled loop nest in which there are n loops $j_1, \ldots, j_n$, n being the loop level of the innermost loop.

```
DO j1 = 0 , N1-1
   DO j2 = 0 , N2-1
      ...
         DO jn = 0 , Nn-1
            Loop Body
         ENDDO
      ...
   ENDDO
ENDDO
```

There are m controlling loops and $n - m$ tiled loops. For example, in Figure 2, the controlling loops are $jj_2, \ldots, jj_m, j_1$, and the tiled loops are $j_2, j_3 \cdots j_{n-m+1}$.)

Definition 3.1 A **reference** $R(c_1 j_{q_1} + d_1, c_2 j_{q_2} + d_2, \ldots, c_n j_{q_n} + d_n)$, $1 \leq q_i \leq n$, is a memory access to virtual address $r = r_0 + \sum_{i=1}^{n} r_i j_i$. (Note: q_i's need not be distinct.)

Note that we limit subscript expressions to a subset of those that can be expressed as linear combinations of the loop indices. This restriction should not be very limiting in practice, since such subscript expressions encompass a very large number of array references commonly found in numerical codes [14]. These restrictions make it easy to identify the reuse for a given reference R.

Definition 3.2 *If $r_l = 0$, $m \leq l \leq n$, then reference R has **reuse** on level l of the loop nest (i.e., the level of loop j_l).*

Intuitively, a reference has reuse at the level of loop j_l, if at least one element referenced at R is referenced multiple times within a single execution of this loop. The tiling optimization attempts to restructure loops to exploit reuse within the innermost $n - m + 1$ loops. Hence, we only consider reuse within these loops.

Definition 3.3 *Let l be the level of the innermost loop on which reuse occurs for a reference R. Let $f(j_1, \ldots, j_n)$ be the subscript expression corresponding to R. For a given iteration of loop j_l, the **theoretical reuse set** of reference R is the set of array elements that could be reused assuming an infinite cache:*

$$\text{TRS}(R) = \{R(f(j_1, j_2, \ldots, j_n) \mid 0 \leq j_i \leq B_k, l < i \leq n)\}.$$

Its size, denoted $\mid \text{TRS}(R) \mid$, is measured as the number of array elements in the reuse set.

Definition 3.4 *The **dimension** of the theoretical reuse set of R is $\text{DIM}(\text{TRS}(R)) = n - l$, where l is the innermost loop at which reuse occurs.*

In tiled loop nests, the dimension of a reuse set is rarely larger than 2. Therefore, in the remainder of this paper, only reuse sets of dimensions 1 and 2 are considered.

Definition 3.5 *The **actual reuse set** of R, denoted $\text{ARS}(R)$, is the set of cache locations to which map the subset of the theoretical reuse set that is free from self interferences.*

A cache location is the fraction of a cache line that contains a single array element. The size of an actual reuse set is measured in cache locations or cache lines. Unless obvious from context, units (e.g., cache locations or cache lines) will be stated.

The contents of an actual reuse set, as opposed to a theoretical one, are dependent on cache parameters.

Definition 3.6 *The **position** of actual reuse set of R is the address in cache of the first element in the set with the smallest address in memory:*

$$r(\text{TRS}(R)) = (r_0 + \sum_{i=1}^{l} r_i j_i) \mod C_S.$$

Definition 3.7 *The cache space occupied by a set, potentially wrapping around cache, and ignoring holes is the **envelope** of the set, denoted $\text{ENV}(< \text{set} >)$.*

Definition 3.8 *The **density** of a set, denoted $\text{DEN}(< \text{set} >)$, is the ratio of the number of elements in a set over the size of its envelope.*

Examples To illustrate these concepts, consider the reference R_B to array B in the tiled matrix-matrix multiply example (Figure 2). R_B has reuse at loop j_1 which is at loop level 3. Therefore, its dimension is $\text{DIM}(\text{TRS}(R_B)) = 2$. In figure 3, four different cases are shown. For each case, the sizes of R_B's theoretical reuse set, actual reuse set, envelope and density are shown in Table 3.1. The size of the theoretical reuse set is independent of the mapping to cache, so it is the same in all four cases, $B_2 B_3$. When $N \mod C_S = 0$, B_3 cache locations are used. However, self interferences cause every element to be flushed out before it can be reused. When $N \mod C_S = B_3$, there is no self interference, so the size of the actual reuse set is the same as that of the theoretical reuse set. When $N \mod C_S = 3B_3/4$, approximately half the of the elements in the tile suffer from self interference. Therefore, at any given time, only 2/3 of the cache locations occupied by these data are productively used. In each of these three cases, the elements are contiguous in cache, and hence the envelope of the set has a density of 1. In the final case, elements are not contiguous, and therefore the density is less than 1.

Suppose the reuse set for a reference R suffers interferences due to reference R'.

Definition 3.9 *The set of array elements accessed by reference R' is the **theoretical interference set** computed at loop level j_l, where l is the level of the innermost loop at which the reuse of R occurs.*

$$\text{TIS}(R')_l = \{R'(f(j_1, j_2, \ldots, j_n) \mid 0 \leq j_i \leq B_i, n \leq i < l)\}.$$

The level may be omitted if obvious from context.

Note that the computation of a theoretical interference set is identical to that of a theoretical reuse set, except for the determination of the loop level at which the sets are computed.

Definition 3.10 *The **actual interference set** of R', denoted $\text{AIS}(R')_l$, is the set of cache locations to which map the theoretical interference set $\text{TIS}(R')_l$.*

The actual interference set is exactly equal to the cache footprint of the theoretical reuse set.

3.2 Translation Groups and Spatial Reuse Groups

Definition 3.11 *References R and R' are **in translation** if the $r(\text{TRS}(R)) - r(\text{TRS}(R'))$ is constant.*

$N_2 \bmod C_S$	theoretical reuse set size $\mid \mathrm{TRS}(R_B) \mid$	actual reuse set size $\mid \mathrm{ARS}(R_B) \mid$	size of envelope $\mid \mathrm{ENV}(\mathrm{FT}(R_B)) \mid$	density of envelope $\mathrm{DEN}(\mathrm{FT}(R_B))$
0	$B_2 B_3$	0	B_3	1
B_3	$B_2 B_3$	$B_2 B_3$	$B_2 B_3$	1
$\frac{3}{4} B_3$	$B_2 B_3$	$\frac{1}{2}(B_2+1)B_3$	$\frac{1}{4}(3B_2+1)B_3$	1
$\frac{3}{2} B_3$	$B_2 B_3$	$B_2 B_3$	$\frac{3}{2}(B_2-1)B_3$	$\frac{2B_2}{3(B_2-1)}$

Table 1: *Characteristics of the reuse set for the reference R_B to array B in Figure 2 for each of the four mappings shown in Figure 3.*

If references R and R' are in translation, the two arrays are moving through cache at the same speed.

Definition 3.12 *A* **translation group** τ *includes all references that are mutually in translation.* [2]

Observation 3.1 *The translation groups $\tau_1, \ldots, \tau_{n_r}$ partition the array references of a loop into equivalence classes.*

Each translation group τ_i can be further subdivided into into *array groups*.

Definition 3.13 *If there exist two references $R, R' \in \tau_i$ such that their reuse sets intersect when measured in cache lines, then R and R' belong to the same* **array group** α^i.

For this determination, only intersections between references in the same translation group are considered. We ignore those between references of distinct translation groups.

Observation 3.2 *The array groups $\alpha_1^i, \ldots, \alpha_{n_\alpha}^i$ of a translation group τ_i partition the references of a translation group into equivalence classes.*

Examples To illustrate the concepts of translation groups and array groups through examples, consider a normalized loop nest where loop indices j_2 and j_3 correspond to the tiled loops. Assume that these two loops have upper bounds N_2 and N_3, respectively. Assume that reuse groups are measured in units of cache lines. Suppose the loop nest contains the pair of references $U(j_3)$ and $U(j_3+5)$ (with $N_3 > 5$). Because this pair has a non-zero intersection between their reuse sets, they would belong to both the same translation group and the same array group.

Consider instead the pair of references $U(j_3)$ and $U(j_3 + N_3 + 5)$. In this case, the pair would belong to the same translation group. However, there is no intersection between their actual reuse sets. Therefore, the two would belong to distinct array groups.

Suppose that the loop nest contained the two references $V(j_3)$ and $W(j_3)$. This pair would belong to the same translation group but, trivially, to distinct array groups. Suppose we consider a pair of 2 dimensional references: $A(j_2, j_3)$ and $B(j_2, j_3)$. If A and B have the same leading dimension, then their positions are constant and they belong to the same translation set. In either case, they belong to different array groups.

Meanwhile, the pair $V(j_3)$ and $V(j_2)$ would correspond to distinct translation groups, and therefore, even though they reference the same array, to distinct array groups. If line size is greater than one, the pair $V(2 * j_3)$ and $V(2 * j_3 + 1)$ belong to the same array group, even though they never reference the same array elements.

The notions of *reuse set, interference set, dimension, envelope* and *density* defined earlier in terms of a single reference can be applied to a group of references as well. Because the definitions are the natural extensions of these terms, formal definitions are omitted in the interest of brevity.

3.3 Interferences

As suggested in [7], interferences can be partitioned into self and cross interferences. We further partition the latter category into internal and external cross interferences.

Definition 3.14 *Interference between references R and R' is termed* **internal cross interference** *if R and R' belong to the same translation group.*

Definition 3.15 *Interference between references R and R' is termed* **external cross interference** *if R and R' belong to distinct translation groups.*

4 Selective Copying
4.1 Overview

Selective copying can be used to evaluate the costs and benefits of eliminating each of the three categories of interferences. This is done in three steps.

---

[2] The notion of an translation group is based on an intuition similar to the notion of uniformly generated dependences [5]. Specifically, both are based on the notion of references whose relative difference in memory addresses is constant over time. However, the use of this information is quite different. We are interested in collecting groups of references with similar motion with respect to their footprints in cache, while uniformly generated dependences capture those references that access the same data. Therefore, a translation group can include references that access differing arrays, while a group of uniformly generated dependences, by definition of dependence, clearly does not.

- **Step 1:** Each array group is evaluated separately. Where benefits outweigh costs, references that suffer from self interference are copied.

- **Step 2:** Each translation group is processed separately. Where benefits outweigh costs, references that exhibit internal cross interference are copied.

- **Step 3:** Interferences between translation group are evaluated. Where benefits outweigh costs, references that exhibit external cross interference are copied.

Let t_{lat} be the number of cycles required to access a line from memory, and t_{copy} be the instruction overhead (in cycles) for copying a single element. Given, a memory reference R, its benefit from copying is the expected decrease in the number of memory accesses multiplied by the memory latency.

$$\text{benefit}(R) = \#\_of\_misses\_removed \times t_{lat},$$

where $\#\_of\_misses\_removed$ is the total number of interference-related cache misses eliminated during the entire execution of the loop. Meanwhile, the *cost* of copying R is the overhead for copying, that includes both the additional memory accesses and the instruction overhead for performing the copying.

$$\text{cost}(R) = (\#\_of\_cache\_lines\_to\_be\_copied) \times t_{lat} + (\#\_of\_elements\_to\_copy) \times t_{copy}.$$

Intuitively, a reference is copied if the benefit outweighs the cost. All the cost/benefit computations presented in this paper can be done symbolically, with final decisions delayed until run time when necessary.

At any given step, only interferences due to the type of interference being targeted are evaluated. Note that deciding to copy an array during one step can alter the translation set to which it belongs. This must be taken into account during later steps.

By eliminating *damaging* self interferences first (i.e., all those for which the benefit outweighs the cost), those that remain after Step 1 can generally be considered to be insignificant. Therefore, they can be ignored during Step 2.

Similarly, after Step 2, damaging self and internal cross interferences have been eliminated. Therefore, when evaluating interferences between translation groups in Step 3, we can assume that there are no significant interference within translation groups.

Note that state of the art algorithms for optimizing data locality [1, 6, 11] compute the optimal block size assuming the sum of the tile sizes is smaller than the cache. Therefore, there should be sufficient cache space for all tiles (equivalently, reuse sets) to be copied. In opposition to the technique described in [1], however, all tiles are not necessarily copied.

Section 4.2 discusses coherence and pollution issues. Sections 4.3–4.5 expand on each of these steps, respectively. Additional details and examples can be found in [9, 10].

4.2 Maintaining Coherence and Minimizing Data Duplication

Consider two references R and R' with non-empty reuse sets. Suppose there is a dependence between the two reuse sets that is carried by a tiled loop. In general, the degree of overlap between their respective reuse sets depends on the array group to which these references belong. If R and R' belong to different array groups, then the overlap is likely to be relatively minor. If R and R' belong to the same array group, then overlap is likely to be very significant.

Therefore, we use the simple heuristic: *array groups are copied together*. A dominant tile is computed for the array group, and the cost of copying the group is computed as the cost of copying the dominant tile. Based on this assumption, it is straightforward to detect and mark uncopyable references as a preprocessing step. The following rule is used: *if there is a dependence between two references R and R' such that* (1) *one of R and R' is a write, and* (2) *either R and R' belong to distinct array groups, or one of R and R' has been previously marked uncopyable,* *then both R and R' are marked uncopyable.*

4.3 Step 1: Removing Self Interferences

Proposition 4.1 *If reuse occurs on loop level l, the total number of additional memory requests due to self interferences for one reference is*

$$N_1 \times \ldots \times N_l \times (\mid TRS(R) \mid - \mid ARS(R) \mid).$$

Therefore, the benefit of copying (in cycles) corresponds to the number of self-interference misses avoided:

$$\text{benefit}(R) = N_1 \times \ldots \times N_1 \times (\mid TRS(R) \mid - \mid ARS(R) \mid) \times t_{lat}.$$

If copying is used, the reuse set must be copied $N_1 \times \ldots \times N_{l-1}$ times (since the reuse set changes on loop $l-1$). The cost corresponds to the number of memory requests needed to load the elements of the reuse set of R ($\mid TRS(R) \mid$ requests, where $\mid TRS(R) \mid$ is expressed in cache lines) and to the instructions necessary to make the $N_{l+1} \times \ldots \times N_n$ copies. Furthermore, each time the reuse set is copied, it flushes $\mid ARS(R) \mid$ cache lines from cache, and therefore brings the same amount of cache misses [3]. Consequently, the total cost of copying in cycles is

$$\text{cost}(R) = N_1 \times \ldots \times N_{l-1} \times ((\mid ARS(R) \mid + \mid TRS(R) \mid) \times t_{lat} + (N_1 \times \ldots \times N_{l-1} \times N_{l+1} \times \ldots \times N_n) \times t_{copy})$$

If one reference is the victim of self interferences, other references within the same translation group are

---

[3]this is a conservative estimate of the cost

416

also victims of self interferences. Consequently, it is often possible to evaluate the cost and benefit for one array group (or reference, if there is a single reference in an array group), and extend the result to all other array groups (or references) within the translation group [10].

The main steps of the algorithm for removing self interferences via copying are the following:

```
/* Step 1: Remove self interferences */
For each translation group τ
    Define an array COPY_τ.
    /* COPY_pos is the index of COPY_τ
       where the next tile will be copied. */
    Initialize copy position COPY_pos to 0
    For each array group α in τ
        Compute cost and benefit of copying α
            to remove self interferences
        If benefit(α) > cost(α)
            Copy α into consecutive locations of
                COPY_τ starting at index COPY_pos.
        Endif
    Endfor
Endfor
```

Note that copying to remove self interferences can also remove internal cross interferences. Suppose there were internal cross interferences between two references prior to Step 1. If both these references are copied, the cross internal interferences between them are also eliminated at the end of this step. Further note however, that copying increases the size of the actual reuse set to that of the theoretical reuse set. Because of this, copying can potentially increase external cross interferences.

Example Let us consider the example of Figure 2, i.e., tiled matrix-matrix multiply. Let us pick two cases that induce none and many interferences respectively according to graph 5, i.e., $N = 176$ and $N = 128$. Let us also choose $B_2 = B_3 = 24$. Because $N < C_S$ in both cases ($C_S = 1024$), $N \mod C_S = N$. Therefore, the cache distance between two consecutive intervals is N.

Let us consider $N = 176$, and assume that the cache position of the beginning of the first interval is cache location 0 (the initial position does not influence the amount of sel-interferences). The number of possible cache positions for the beginning of the intervals of array B is $\frac{C_S}{\gcd(N,C_S)} = 64$. Because 64 is larger than the number of intervals, i.e., 24, it is not certain overlapping, i.e., self interference, occurs. Because $24 \times 176 > 1024$, the 24 intervals to be loaded are going to wrap around cache. $\lfloor \frac{1024}{176} \rfloor = 5$, so wrap around occurs on the 6th interval. Similarly every 5 or 6 intervals wrap around occurs. Let us now check the distribution of intervals in cache. After wrap around, the cache position of the 6th interval is 32 (Figure 7). This means the interval falls in between the first and second interval of the previous series of intervals. The distance between the end of the first interval and the

beginning of this interval is $32 - 24 = 8$. Similarly, when the second wrap around occurs, the beginning of the first interval of the third series is located 8 cache locations after the end of the first interval of the second series. Therefore, after 6 such series (approximately 36 intervals) overlapping occurs between the first interval of the sixth series and the second interval of the first series (Figure 7). Because $B_2 = 24$, there are approximately 4 series, so no overlapping actually occurs in our case. There are no additional memory requests due to self interferences. If B_2 were equal to or greater than 36, then self interferences would have occurred.

Therefore, in this case, the layout of elements of B in cache is optimal with respect to self interferences, so it is not necessary to copy to avoid them. In fact, copying would actually *degrade* performance, because of the overhead entailed (Figure 6).

Next consider the case where $N = 128$. There are $\frac{C_s}{\gcd(N,C_s)} = 8$ possible cache positions for the beginning of the intervals of array B (Figure 7). Therefore, self interference begins when the 9th interval is brought in cache. Whenever 16 or more intervals of array B are brought into cache, total overlapping occurs and no element can be reused.

Because $B_2 = 24$, all elements of array B are victims of self interferences. No reuse is possible. There are approximately $B_2 \times \frac{B_3}{L_S}$ additional memory requests due to self interferences, per iteration of loop j_1. In total, there are $\frac{N_1 N_2 N_3}{B_2 B_3} \times (B_2 \frac{B_3}{L_S})$ additional memory requests due to self interferences. Because $N_2 \times N_3$ copy operations are needed to copy array B, the total cost of copying is equal to $\frac{N_2 N_3}{L_S} \times t_{lat} + N_2 N_3 \times t_{copy}$ cycles, whereas the benefit is equal to $\frac{N_1 N_2 N_3}{L_S} \times t_{lat}$ cycles.

Consequently, in this case, copying is extremely useful. It allows reutilization of *all* elements of B, whereas, in the version of the loop nest without copying, *no* element of B can be reused. Thus, the overhead due to copying is far smaller than the benefit.

In this case, $24 \times 8 = 192$ cache locations are flushed when elements to be copied are brought into cache. In contrast, in the previous case where no overlapping occurred, using copying would cause $24 \times 24 = 576$ cache locations to be flushed. Note that the less useful copying is, the more costly it is.

4.4 Step 2: Removing Internal Cross Interferences

Proposition 4.2 *The total number of additional memory requests due to internal cross interferences between two references of the same translation group is*

$$N_1 \times \ldots \times N_l \times DEN(ARS(R^1)) \times DEN(AIS(R^2)) \times CL(R^1, R^2).$$

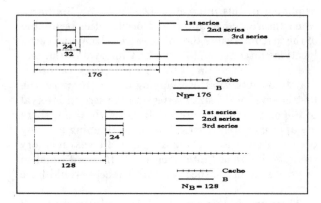

Figure 7: *Effect of the leading dimension of array B from tiled matrix-matrix multiply (Figure 2) on the occurrence of self interferences involving elements of B.*

where $CL(R^1, R^2)$ is the number of cache lines where the envelopes of the actual reuse set of R^1 and actual interference set of R^2 overlap.

Therefore, the benefit of copying corresponds to the number of external cross-interference misses avoided:

benefit=$N_1 \times \ldots \times N_l \times$DEN(ARS($R^1$))$\times$DEN(AIS($R^2$))$\times$CL($R^1, R^2$).

Based on the above, the benefit of copying can be computed for an entire array group [10].

The cost of copying in Step 2 is generally the same as in Step 1, except when the array group has already been selected for copying in Step 1, in which case the array can be copied for free. The algorithm for removing internal cross interferences via copying is shown below:

```
/* Step 2: Remove internal cross interferences */
For each translation group τ
    Define COPYτ (if not defined in Step 1)
    For each array group α in τ
        Compute total potential benefit from removing
            internal cross interferences within α
        If benefit(α) > cost(α)
            /* Copy α if possible */
            Compute the relative cache distances (or
                "holes") between all actual interference
                sets of all array groups in τ
            If ∃ hole ≥ size of theoretical reuse set of α
                Set COPYpos to start of hole
                Copy reuse set of α into COPYτ
                    starting at COPYpos
            Endif
        Endif
    Endfor
Endfor
```

It is necessary to find a sufficiently large hole between all actual interference sets of the other array groups of the translation group τ, so that no more internal cross interference occur between α and other array groups. The size of the hole needs to be greater or equal than the size of the theoretical reuse set of α since the entire reuse set is copied in consecutive locations of array $COPY_\tau$.

4.5 Step 3: Removing External Cross Interferences

The relative cache positions of the actual reuse set and the actual interference set of two array groups belonging to different translation groups repeat periodically, with a period of P iterations of loop l) [10]. Let I_λ correspond to an interval of possible relative cache positions over a period, and $CL(R^1, R^2; \lambda)$ to the overlapping of the two sets (expressed in cache lines) for a given value of $\lambda \in I_\lambda$.

Proposition 4.3 *The total number of additional memory requests due to external cross interferences between two references belonging to distinct translation groups is*

$$\frac{N_1 \times \ldots \times N_l}{P} \sum_{\lambda \in I_\lambda} \text{DEN(ARS}(R^1)) \times \text{DEN(AIS}(R^2)) \times \text{CL}(R^1, R^2; \lambda).$$

The benefit of copying corresponds to the number of external cross-interference misses avoided:

benefit=$N_1 \times \ldots \times N_l \times$
$\sum_{\lambda \in I_\lambda}$ DEN(ARS(R^1)) $\times$ DEN(AIS(R^2)) $\times CL(R^1, R^2; \lambda)$.

The benefit can also be computed for an entire array group. The cost for copying an array group is the same as in Step 1, unless the array was selected for copying in Step 1 or Step 2, in which case the cost is nothing. The algorithm for removing external cross interferences is outlined below:

```
/* Step 3: Remove external cross interferences */
For each translation group τ
    For each array group α in τ
        For each translation group τ' ≠ τ
            For each array group in τ'
                Evaluate amount of external cross
                    interferences with α
            Endfor
            Deduce benefit of copying α with respect to τ'
        Endfor
        If ∃ τ' such that benefit(α, τ') > (α, τ')
            Pick τ' for which benefit is maximal
            Copy reuse set of α into COPYτ' (or into
                any other COPY array that would not
                conflict with COPYτ')
        Endif
    Endfor
Endfor
```

It may be possible to copy α into a $COPY$ array other than the one associated with τ', because sometimes the mapping of a translation group is such that this will not interfere with other translation groups, or array groups within other translation groups [10]. Array groups already tagged for copying during Steps 1 or 2 are ignored because copying them again could introduce internal cross interferences, which are usually more significant than external cross interferences.

There are two types of external cross interferences: cross interferences between two references that exhibit temporal reuse, and cross interferences between one reference which exhibits temporal reuse and another reference that does not. In general, copying to remove the first type of external cross interferences brings little benefit as illustrated in Figure 6. The second type of interferences is more damaging, but it is usually considered to be difficult to remove such interferences. Precise analysis of external cross interferences sometimes allows partial if not total removal of such interferences [10].

5 Summary

Interferences can prevent reuse from being exploited, even in loops that were optimized *specifically* to exploit this reuse. To address this problem, several researchers have proposed the use of data copying. Yet, no guidelines have been presented in the literature for determining what and when to copy.

In this paper, we have demonstrated that, with blind copying, the cost can outweigh the benefit. We have also shown that hit ratio alone cannot be used to determine the optimal set of references to copy. Furthermore, this optimal set can be difficult to assess without analyzing the costs and benefits on a case-by-case basis. Additionally, care must be taken because copying can introduce both coherence problems and pollution via duplication of data. To address these problems, we proposed *selective copying*, a compile-time strategy for determining what and when to copy based primarily on an analysis of cache conflicts. Our strategy uses a simple heuristic approach to preserve coherence and minimize data duplication.

In the development of our strategy, a new framework has evolved for categorizing references and the three types of interferences that can occur. We showed that all three are necessary, as substantially different techniques are needed to asses the impact of each type.

There are three steps in our compile time strategy. During each step, we target the elimination of a particular interference type. Within each step we evaluate the cost and benefit of eliminating interferences of that type on a case-by-case basis. By attacking the interference categories in the specified order, computation is substantially simplified. Computations can be done symbolically at compile time when necessary, with final decisions postponed until runtime.

Acknowledgements

The authors would like to thank Christine Fricker for her thought-provoking insights on the subject of cache interferences.

References

[1] F. Bodin, C. Eisenbeis, W. Jalby, and D. Windheiser. A Quantitative Algorithm for Data Locality Optimization. In *Code Generation-Concepts, Tools, Techniques*. Springer-Verlag, 1992.

[2] C. Eisenbeis, W. Jalby, D. Windheiser, and F. Bodin. A Strategy for Array Management in Local Memory. In *Proceedings of the Third Workshop on Programming Languages and Compilers for Parallel Computing*, 1990.

[3] J. Ferrante, V. Sarkar, and W. Thrash. On Estimating and Enhancing Cache Effectiveness (Extended Abstract). In *Proceedings of the Fourth Workshop on Languages and Compilers for Parallel Computing*, 1991.

[4] C. Fricker, O. Temam, and W. Jalby. Accurate Evaluation of Blocked Algorithms Cache Interferences. Technical report, Leiden University, Mar. 1993.

[5] K. Gallivan, W. Jalby, and D. Gannon. On the Problem of Optimizing Data Transfers for Complex Memory Systems. In *Proceedings of the International Conference on Supercomputing*, pages 238–253, July 1988.

[6] K. Kennedy and K. S. McKinley. Optimizing for Parallelism and Data Locality. In *Proceedings of the International Conference on Supercomputing*, pages 323–334, July 1992.

[7] M. Lam, E. E. Rothberg, and M. E. Wolf. The Cache Performance of Blocked Algorithms. In *Fourth International Conference on Architectural Support for Programming Languages and Operating Systems*, Apr. 1991.

[8] R. L. Sites, editor. *Alpha Architecture Reference Manual*. Digital Press, 1992.

[9] O. Temam. *Study and Optimization of Numerical Codes Cache Behavior*. PhD thesis, University of Rennes, France, May 1993.

[10] O. Temam, E. Granston, and W. Jalby. To Copy or Not to Copy: A Compile-Time Technique for Assessing When Data Copying Should be Used to Eliminate Cache Conflicts. Technical Report 93-11, University of Leiden, 1993.

[11] M. Wolf and M. Lam. A Data Locality Optimizing Algorithm. In *Proceedings of the ACM SIGPLAN '91 Conference on Programming Language Design and Implementation*, volume 26(6), pages 30–44, June 1991.

[12] M. J. Wolfe. Iteration Space Tiling for Memory Hierarchies. In *Proceedings of the 3rd SIAM Conference on Parallel Processing for Scientific Computing*, pages 357–361, 1987.

[13] M. J. Wolfe. More Iteration Space Tiling. In *Supercomputing '89*, 1989.

[14] S. Zhiyu, Z. Li, and P.-C. Yew. An Empirical Study on Array Subscripts and and Data Dependencies. Technical Report 840, Center for Supercomputing Research and Development, University of Illinois at Urbana-Champaign, Aug. 1989.

Mobile and Replicated Alignment of Arrays in Data-Parallel Programs

Siddhartha Chatterjee *   John R. Gilbert †   Robert Schreiber *

Abstract

When a data-parallel language like Fortran 90 is compiled for a distributed-memory machine, aggregate data objects (such as arrays) are distributed across the processor memories. The mapping determines the amount of *residual communication* needed to bring operands of parallel operations into alignment with each other. A common approach is to break the mapping into two stages: first, an *alignment* that maps all the objects to an abstract template, and then a *distribution* that maps the template to the processors.

We solve two facets of the problem of finding alignments that reduce residual communication: we determine alignments that vary in loops, and objects that should have replicated alignments. We show that loop-dependent mobile alignment is sometimes necessary for optimum performance, and we provide algorithms with which a compiler can determine good mobile alignments for objects within do loops. We also identify situations in which replicated alignment is either required by the program itself (via spread operations) or can be used to improve performance. We propose an algorithm based on network flow that determines which objects to replicate so as to minimize the total amount of broadcast communication in replication. This work on mobile and replicated alignment extends our earlier work on determining static alignment.

1 Introduction

Parallelism is expressed in data-parallel array languages like Fortran 90 [1] in the form of operations on arrays and array sections. Compiling such a program for a distributed-memory parallel machine requires a model for the mapping of the data to the machine. We view the mapping as an *alignment* to a Cartesian index space called a *template*,

followed by a *distribution* of the template to the processors. The alignment phase positions all array objects in the program with respect to each other so as to reduce realignment communication cost. In the distribution phase that follows, the template is distributed to the processors. This two-phase approach separates the language issues from the machine issues, and is used in Fortran D [7], High Performance Fortran [10], and CM-Fortran [16].

The goal of compilation is to produce data and work mappings that reduce completion time. Much of this goal can be achieved by judicious alignment of the arrays. We consider only alignment here.

Completion time has two components: computation and communication. Communication can be separated into *intrinsic* and *residual* communication. Intrinsic communication arises from computational operations such as reductions that require data motion as an integral part of the operation. Residual communication arises from nonlocal data references required in a computation whose operands are not mapped to the same processors. As we only consider alignment in this paper, we take the view that objects are mapped identically to processors if and only if they are aligned. We use the term *realignment* to refer to residual communication due to misalignment; we seek to determine array alignments that minimize realignment cost. Communication for transpose, spread, and vector-valued subscript operations can in some cases be removed by suitable alignment choices. Our theory makes these forms of communication residual rather than intrinsic, and thus encompasses such optimizations [5].

A suitable alignment for the code fragment of Figure 1(a) is shown in Figure 1(b). Note that *V* moves at each iteration of the loop; it has a mobile alignment.

In this paper, we present algorithms to automatically determine good mobile alignments. We develop a detailed and realistic model of realignment cost that accounts for control flow in loops, and we formulate the alignment problem as a constrained optimization of the realignment cost. We present approximate solutions for mobile stride and offset alignment for array objects occurring within loops, where we allow the offset alignment to be a compiler-determined affine function of loop induction variables. We also show that replication may be viewed as an extension of offset alignment, and show that the problem of determining

*Research Institute for Advanced Computer Science, Mail Stop T045-1, NASA Ames Research Center, Moffett Field, CA 94035-1000 (sc@riacs.edu, schreibr@riacs.edu). The work of these authors was supported by the NAS Systems Division via Cooperative Agreement NCC 2-387 and Contract NAS 2-13721 between NASA and the Universities Space Research Association (USRA).

†Xerox Palo Alto Research Center, 3333 Coyote Hill Road, Palo Alto, CA 94304-1314 (gilbert@parc.xerox.com). Copyright ©1993 by Xerox Corporation. All rights reserved.

```
real A(100,100), V(200)



do k = 1, 100

   A(k,1:100) = A(k,1:100) + V(k:k+99)
enddo
```

(a)

```
real A(100,100), V(200)
template T
align A(i,j) with T(i,j)

do k = 1, 100
   realign V(i) with T(k,i-k+1)
   A(k,1:100) = A(k,1:100) + V(k:k+99)
enddo
```

(b)

Figure 1: (a) A Fortran 90 program fragment requiring mobile alignment. (b) A mobile alignment for the program fragment.

the optimal replication strategy can be reduced to a network flow problem.

Several other authors have considered static alignment [2, 9, 12, 13, 17]. Our earlier research [4, 5, 8] dealt with static alignment. We extend that work to handle mobile alignment here. Knobe, Lukas, and Steele [12] and Knobe, Lukas, and Dally [11] address the issue of dynamic alignment. Their notion of dynamic alignment is alignment depending on quantities whose values are known only at runtime, which may include loop induction variables as well as other arbitrary runtime values. This paper focuses on mobile alignment in the context of loops, where the alignment of an object is an affine function of the loop induction variables.

The paper is organized as follows. Section 2 formalizes the notion of alignment and defines mobile alignment. It also introduces our graph model for the alignment problem. Section 3 poses and solves the problem of mobile stride alignment. Section 4 poses and solves the problem of mobile offset alignment, covering fixed- and variable-sized objects and loop nests. Section 5 describes an algorithm for determining replicated offset alignments. Finally, Section 6 presents conclusions, open problems, and future work.

2   The alignment problem

An alignment is a mapping that takes each element of an array to a cell of a *template*. The template is a conceptually infinite Cartesian grid, with as many dimensions as necessary; it is a piece of "graph paper" on which all the array objects in a program are positioned relative to each other. The *alignment phase* of compilation aligns all array objects of the program to the template. The *distribution phase* then assigns template cells to actual processors. This paper discusses only the alignment phase.

If A is a d-dimensional array, and g_1 through g_t are integer-valued functions, we write

$$A(i_1, \ldots, i_d) \boxplus T[g_1(i_1, \ldots, i_d), \ldots, g_t(i_1, \ldots, i_d)]$$

to mean that the specified element of A is aligned to the specified element of the t-dimensional template T. Multiple templates may be useful in some cases, but this paper only considers alignment to a single template. Thus we omit the template name and just write $A(i) \boxplus [g(i)]$, where i is a d-vector and g is a function from d-vectors to t-vectors.

We restrict our attention to alignments in which each axis of the array maps to a different axis of the template, and array elements are evenly spaced along template axes. Such an alignment has three components: *axis* (the mapping of array axes to template axes), *stride* (the spacing of array elements along each template axis), and *offset* (the position of the array origin along each template axis). Each g_k is thus either a constant f_k or a function of a single array index of the form $s_k i_{a_k} + f_k$. The array is aligned one-to-one into the template. (In Section 5, we extend this to one-to-many alignments in which an array can be replicated across some template axes.)

An *array-valued object* (object for short) is created by every array operation and by every assignment to a section of an array. The compiler determines an alignment for each object of the program rather than to each program variable. The alignment of an object in a loop may be a function of the loop induction variable; such an alignment is *mobile*.

2.1   Examples

We now give examples of the various kinds of alignment.

Example 1 (Offset alignment) Consider the statement

```
A(1:N-1) = A(1:N-1) + B(2:N).
```

If the alignments are $A(i)\boxplus[i]$ and $B(i)\boxplus[i]$, then a one-unit nearest-neighbor shift is necessary. However, the statement can be executed without communication if $A(i) \boxplus [i]$ and $B(i) \boxplus [i-1]$.

Example 2 (Stride alignment) Consider the statement

```
A(1:N) = A(1:N) + B(2:2*N:2).
```

421

If $A(i) \boxplus [i]$ and $B(i) \boxplus [i]$, then general communication is needed to bring A and the section of B together. The alignments $A(i) \boxplus [2i]$ and $B(i) \boxplus [i]$ avoid communication.

Example 3 (Axis alignment) Consider the statement

```
B = B + transpose(C),
```

where B and C are two-dimensional arrays. If $B(i_1, i_2) \boxplus [i_1, i_2]$ and $C(i_1, i_2) \boxplus [i_1, i_2]$, then general communication is needed to transpose C. However, if $B(i_1, i_2) \boxplus [i_1, i_2]$ and $C(i_1, i_2) \boxplus [i_2, i_1]$, then the operands are aligned, and no communication is necessary.

Example 4 (Mobile offset alignment) Consider the code fragment in Figure 1. This can be executed optimally if $A(i_1, i_2) \boxplus_k [i_1, i_2]$, and $V(i_1) \boxplus_k [k, i_1 - k + 1]$. We use the symbol $\boxplus_k$ to emphasize the dependence of the alignment on the loop induction variable k.

Example 5 (Mobile stride alignment) Consider the code fragment

```
real A(1000), B(1000), V(20)

do k = 1, 50
   V = V + A(1:20*k:k)
   B(1:20*k:k) = V
enddo
```

Suppose $A(i) \boxplus_k [i]$ and $B(i) \boxplus_k [i]$. If the stride alignment of V is static, then any alignment of V is equally good, with a cost of two general communications per iteration. The cost drops to one general communication per iteration with the mobile stride alignment $V(i) \boxplus_k [ki]$.

2.2 Alignment-distribution graphs

Our main tool in this paper is a modified and annotated data flow graph that we call the *alignment-distribution graph*, or ADG for short. In this section we briefly describe the ADG and formulate the alignment problem as an optimization problem on the ADG. A companion paper [3] presents a more formal and complete treatment of the ADG. The ADG is closely related to the static single-assignment form of programs developed by Cytron *et al.* [6]. Figure 2 shows the ADG for the program fragment in Figure 1.

Nodes in the ADG represent computation; edges represent flow of data. Alignments are associated with endpoints of edges, which we call *ports*. A node constrains the relative alignments of the ports representing its operands and its results. An edge carries residual communication cost if its ports have different alignments. The goal is to provide alignments for the ports that satisfy the node constraints and minimize the total edge cost.

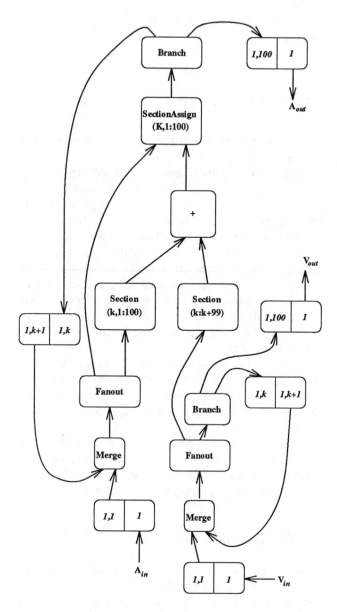

Figure 2: The ADG corresponding to the program fragment of Figure 1.

2.2.1 Edges

The ADG has a port for each (static) definition or use of an object. An edge joins the definition of an object with its use. Multiple definitions or uses are handled with merge, fanout, and branch nodes as described below. Thus every edge has exactly two ports. The purpose of the alignment phase is to label each port with an alignment. All communication necessary for realignment is associated with edges; if the two ports of an edge have different alignments, then the edge incurs a cost that depends on the alignments and the total amount of data that flows along the edge during program execution.

2.2.2 Nodes

Every array operation is a node of the ADG, with one port for each operand and one port for the result. Figure 2 contains examples of a "+" node representing elementwise addition, a *Section* node whose input is an array and whose output is a section of the array, and a *SectionAssign* node whose inputs are an array and a new object to replace a section of the array, and whose output is the modified array. (*SectionAssign* is called *Update* by Cytron *et al.* [6].)

When a single use of a value can be reached by multiple definitions, the ADG contains a *merge node* with one port for each definition and one port for the use. (This node corresponds to the ϕ-function of Cytron *et al.* [6].) When a single definition reaches multiple uses within the same basic block, the ADG contains a *fanout node*. When a single definition can reach multiple alternate uses (*e.g.*, due to conditional constructs), the ADG contains a *branch node*. Figure 2 contains examples of merge, fanout, and branch nodes. Fanout nodes represent opportunities for so-called *Steiner optimization*, as discussed in Section 6. Finally, the ADG for a program with loops contains *transformer nodes* that delimit iteration spaces as described below.

Nodes constrain the alignments of their ports. An elementwise operation like "+" constrains all its ports to have the same alignment. A merge or fanout node enforces the same constraint. If A is a two-dimensional array in a two-dimensional template, a node `transpose(A)` constrains its output to have the opposite axis alignment from its input; thus any communication necessary to transpose the array is assigned to the input or output edges rather than to the node itself. *Section* and *SectionAssign* nodes enforce constraints that describe the position of a section relative to the position of the whole array; for example, the node for the section `A(10:50:2)` constrains its output object to have the same axis as its input, twice the stride of its input, and an offset equal to 10 times the stride of A plus the offset of A.

2.2.3 Iteration spaces

The ADG represents data flow, not control flow. To model communication cost accurately, we must account for the fact that data can flow over a particular edge many times during the program's execution, and each time the data object may have a different size. Section 6 discusses how to model arbitrary control flow. Here we deal with the important special case in which the only control flow is in the form of do loops.

An edge inside a nest of k loops is labeled with a k-dimensional *iteration space*, whose elements are the vectors of values taken by the loop induction variables (LIVs). Both the size of the data object on an edge and the alignment of the data object at a port are functions of the LIVs, so they may vary over the iteration space.

For every edge that carries data into, out of, or around a loop, we insert a *transformer node* to describe the relationship between the iteration spaces at the two ports. Figure 2 contains examples. A loop-back transformer node, in a loop do k = l:h:s, constrains the alignment of its input as a function of $k + s$ to equal the alignment of its output as a function of k. Consider a $(1, k/1, k+1)$ transformer node as in Figure 2. An offset alignment of $2k + 3$ on the input ("k") port and of $2k + 1$ on the output ("$k+1$") port satisfies the node's constraints. The $(1/1, 1)$ transformer node on entry to this loop constrains its input position (which does not depend on k) to equal its output position for $k = 1$.

2.3 Cost model

Finally, we describe the communication cost of the program in terms of the ADG. A *position* is an encoding of a legal alignment. The *distance* $d(p, q)$ between two positions p and q is a nonnegative number giving the cost per element to change the position of an array from p to q. The set of all positions is a metric space under the distance function d [4].

In this paper we will use two metrics: the *discrete metric*, in which $d(p, q) = 0$ if $p = q$ and $d(p, q) = 1$ otherwise, and the *grid metric*, in which p and q are grid points and $d(p, q)$ is the L_1 (or Manhattan) distance between them. We use the discrete metric to model axis and stride alignment, since any change of axis or stride requires general communication. The discrete metric is a simple model of general communication that abstracts away from such machine-specific details as routing, congestion, and software overhead. We use the grid metric to model offset alignment. The grid metric is *separable*, meaning that the distance between two points in a multidimensional grid is equal to the sum of the distances between their corresponding coordinates in one-dimensional grids. This property allows allows us to solve the offset alignment problem independently for each axis [4].

We model the communication cost of the program as follows. Let E be the set of edges of the ADG, and let $\mathcal{I}_{xy}$ be the iteration space for edge (x, y). For a vector i in $\mathcal{I}_{xy}$, let $w_{xy}(i)$ be the data weight, which is the size of the data object on edge (x, y) at iteration i. Finally, let π be a feasible mobile alignment for the program—that is, for each port x let $\pi_x(i)$ be an alignment for x at iteration i that satisfies all the node constraints. Then the realignment cost of edge (x, y) at iteration i is $w_{xy}(i) \cdot d(\pi_x(i), \pi_y(i))$, and the total realignment cost of the program is

$$C(\pi) = \sum_{(x,y) \in E} \sum_{i \in \mathcal{I}_{xy}} w_{xy}(i) \cdot d(\pi_x(i), \pi_y(i)). \quad (1)$$

Our goal is to choose π to minimize this cost, subject to the node constraints.

2.4 Restrictions on mobile alignment functions

So far we have not constrained the form that mobile alignments may take. In principle, we could allow them to be arbitrary functions of the LIVs. For reasons of tractability, we consider only the (important) case in which mobile alignments of objects to be affine functions of the LIVs. Thus, the mobile offset or stride alignment function for an object within a k-deep loop nest with LIVs $i_1, \ldots, i_k$ is of the form $\alpha_0 + \alpha_1 i_1 + \cdots + \alpha_k i_k$, where the coefficient vector $\alpha = (\alpha_0, \ldots, \alpha_k)$ is what we must determine. We write this alignment succinctly in vector notation as αi^T, where $i = (1, i_1, \ldots, i_k)$. Both α and i are $(k+1)$-vectors. This reduces to the constant term α_0 for an object outside any loops.

Likewise, we restrict the extents of objects to be affine in the LIVs, so that the size of an object is polynomial in the LIVs.

3 Mobile stride alignment

We use the discrete metric to model communication costs arising from stride changes. Let the strides at the ports of an edge be αi^T and $\alpha' i^T$. If $\alpha = \alpha'$, then the ports will be aligned at every iteration; if the constant terms α_0 and α'_0 differ but all other components are equal, then they are always misaligned; otherwise, they are almost always misaligned. We approximate this situation by considering the objects to be misaligned in all iterations unless $\alpha = \alpha'$.

As the distance function in equation (1) is independent of the LIV, we can move it outside the summation over the iteration space, and write the communication cost of edge (x, y) as the product of a weight and a distance. The distance is the discrete metric on $(k+1)$-vectors; the weight

is the sum over all iterations of the size of the object at each iteration, $W = \sum_{i \in \mathcal{I}_{xy}} w_{xy}(i)$. Since the weight is polynomial in the LIVs, the sum can be evaluated in closed form. We can now use compact dynamic programming, a technique we have previously developed for static axis and stride alignment [5], to solve this problem.

4 Mobile offset alignment

Consider an object with offset alignment αi^T. Since the problem is separable, we can determine offsets with respect to one template axis at a time. If there are no loops in the code, the solution reduces to our earlier solution for static offset alignment [5].

The contribution of edge (x, y) to the residual communication is

$$C_{xy} = \sum_{i \in \mathcal{I}_{xy}} w_{xy}(i) |(\alpha - \alpha') i^T|, \quad (2)$$

where $\pi_x(i) = \alpha i^T$, $\pi_y(i) = \alpha' i^T$, and $\mathcal{I}_{xy}$ is the iteration space associated with the edge. Even if $w_{xy}(i)$ is constant, the absolute value in equation (2) makes its closed form complicated. Rather than seek an algorithm to minimize this cost function, we choose instead to approximate it by one for which the solution is straightforward. After reviewing the solution for static offset alignment, we show the solution for fixed-size objects in singly-nested loops ($k = 1$), and then generalize to variable-size objects and to loop nests.

4.1 Offset alignment by linear programming

We review how the static offset alignment problem for the grid metric can be reduced to linear programming [5]. Let the integer π_x be the offset alignment of port x. Then the residual communication cost (which is the function we want to minimize) is $C(\pi) = \sum_{(x,y) \in E} C_{xy}(\pi)$; so

$$C(\pi) = \sum_{(x,y) \in E} w_{xy} |\pi_x - \pi_y|.$$

Nodes introduce linear constraints relating the offsets of their ports. See [3] for more details. To remove the absolute value from the objective function, we introduce a variable θ_{xy} for every edge (x, y) of the ADG, and add two inequality constraints,

$$\begin{aligned} \theta_{xy} + \pi_x - \pi_y &\geq 0 \\ \theta_{xy} - \pi_x + \pi_y &\geq 0, \end{aligned}$$

that guarantee that $\theta_{xy} \geq |\pi_x - \pi_y|$. The new objective function is then

$$\sum_{(x,y) \in E} w_{xy} \theta_{xy}.$$

The transformed problem is equivalent to the original one, because $\theta_{xy} = |\pi_x - \pi_y|$ at optimality. This transformation introduces $|E|$ new variables and $2|E|$ new constraints.

If the offsets that result from the linear program are fractional, we round them to integers. The rounded solutions are not necessarily optimal integer solutions; in general, rounding an LP solution may not even preserve feasibility. However, in the case of offset alignment with the grid metric, we argue that rounding is a reasonable approach. It is straightforward to round the offsets so as to satisfy all the node constraints. The template can be thought of as a discrete approximation to a continuous L_1 metric space in which the edge costs are continuous functions of real-valued offsets. The unrounded LP optimizes this problem exactly, so we expect that the discrete optimum is not very sensitive to rounding. We will refer to this algorithm as rounded linear programming, or RLP. (We have also experimented with using mixed integer linear programming.)

4.2 Fixed-size objects and singly-nested loops

Assume for this section that the data weight of edge (x, y) is constant and equal to 1, and that $\mathcal{I}_{xy} = \ell : h : s$. Call $(\alpha - \alpha')i^T$ the *span* of edge (x, y) at iteration i. If the span does not change sign in the interval $[\ell, h]$ (as shown in Figure 3(a)), the summation and the absolute value in equation (2) can be interchanged. Then $C_{xy} = |\sum_{i \in \ell : h : s}(\alpha - \alpha')i^T|$, the closed form for which is

$$C_{xy} = \frac{h - \ell + s}{s}|(\alpha_0 - \alpha_0') + \frac{\ell + h}{2}(\alpha_1 - \alpha_1')|. \quad (3)$$

Note that the term inside the absolute value is the average distance spanned by edge (x, y). We can reduce this to RLP with one new variable per edge.

In general, however, the span may change sign in the iteration space, and interchanging the summation and the absolute value is incorrect, as shown in Figure 3(b). In this case, we partition the iteration space into m equal subranges $\mathcal{I}_1, \ldots, \mathcal{I}_m$, each subrange corresponding to a set of consecutive iterations, and decompose the communication cost as follows:

$$C_{xy} = \sum_{j=1}^{m} \sum_{i \in \mathcal{I}_j} |(\alpha - \alpha')i^T|. \quad (4)$$

We then pretend that the span does not change sign within any subrange, which leads to the approximate cost model

$$C_{xy} \approx \widehat{C}_{xy} = \sum_{j=1}^{m} |\sum_{i \in \mathcal{I}_j}(\alpha - \alpha')i^T|. \quad (5)$$

Now we fix m, expand the outer sum explicitly, and evaluate each inner sum using equation (3), as shown in Figure 3(c). Clearly, the span can change sign in at most one

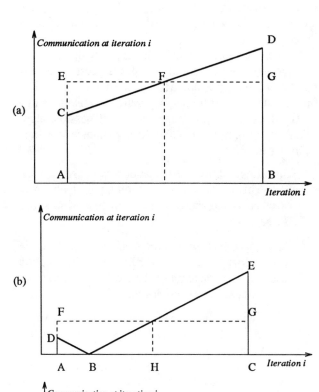

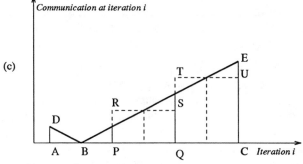

Figure 3: Approximating the cost of communication in loops. The actual communication cost is equal to the area under the heavy curve. (a) If the communication function does not have a zero crossing, then $ABDC \equiv ABGE$, and our approximation is exact. (b) If the communication function has a zero crossing, then $ABD + BCE \not\equiv ACGF$. The maximum relative error in approximation occurs when B coincides with H, and is proportional to AC. (c) To reduce the maximum relative error, we partition the iteration space AC into subranges AP, PQ, and QC. As there are no zero crossings in subranges PQ and QC, the approximations there are exact. The approximation in subrange AP is incorrect, but the maximum relative error is reduced. In general, at most one of the subranges can have a zero crossing.

subrange; therefore, at least $(m - 1)$ of the subrange sums are correct. We then reduce to RLP with m new variables per edge.

We now bound the error. We can show that the cost C at the approximate solution exceeds the cost at the best possible solution by at most a factor of $(1 + 2/m^2)$. (We can further reduce the error bound by using unequal intervals.)

The discussion above suggests several possible algorithms for solving the mobile offset alignment problem, which we now list.

1. **Unrolling:** Make every iteration a subrange, and use RLP. This is equivalent to unrolling the loop. It is exact, but is impractical unless the number of iterations is small.

2. **State space search:** Approximate the iteration space as a single subrange, and use RLP. Using this solution as an initial guess, optimize the exact cost equation (4) by, for example, steepest descent.

3. **Tracking zero crossings:** Split the iteration space into two equal subranges, and use RLP. If the span has a zero crossing in the range, locate it, and move the subrange boundaries to coincide with this point. Now solve the new RLP and iterate until convergence. This solves a sequence of fixed-size problems, each with $2|E|$ new variables. Convergence of this method is not guaranteed.

4. **Recursive refinement:** Approximate the iteration space as a single subrange, and use RLP. Now examine the solution to determine subranges (at most one per edge) in which the span has a zero crossing. Break each subrange in two at the zero crossing, and formulate and solve a new RLP. Continue the refinement until some stopping criterion is satisfied (*e.g.*, there are no more subranges to be refined, the objective function shows no further improvement, we run out of time). This requires solving a sequence of progressively larger problems.

5. **Fixed partitioning:** Partition the iteration space into three subranges, and use RLP. The solution is guaranteed to be within 22% of optimal. This requires solving a single problem with $3|E|$ new variables. (A five-way partition would reduce the error bound to 8%.)

We advocate the fixed partitioning method as a good compromise between speed, reliability, and quality.

4.3 Variable-size objects in singly-nested loops

Now suppose that $\mathcal{I}_{xy} = \ell : h : s$ and that the data weight of edge (x, y) at iteration i is $\beta_0 + \beta_1 i$, where β_0 and β_1 are integer constants. Then the communication cost of the edge is

$$C_{xy} = \sum_{i \in \ell : h : s} (\beta_0 + \beta_1 i) |(\alpha - \alpha') i^T|.$$

Assuming the span does not change sign in $[\ell, h]$, we can write the communication cost of edge (x, y) as

$$C_{xy} = |(\beta_1 \sigma_1 + \beta_0 \sigma_0)(\alpha_0 - \alpha'_0) + (\beta_1 \sigma_2 + \beta_0 \sigma_1)(\alpha_1 - \alpha'_1)|,$$

where $\sigma_0 = \sum_{i \in \ell : h : s} 1$, $\sigma_1 = \sum_{i \in \ell : h : s} i$, and $\sigma_2 = \sum_{i \in \ell : h : s} i^2$ can be evaluated in closed form:

$$\sigma_0 = (h - \ell + s)/s.$$
$$\sigma_1 = (s\sigma_0^2 + (2\ell - s)\sigma_0)/2.$$
$$\sigma_2 = (2s^2\sigma_0^3 + (6s\ell - 3s^2)\sigma_0^2 + (6\ell^2 - 6s\ell + s^2)\sigma_0)/6.$$

We then determine the alignment coefficients as in Section 4.2.

4.4 Loop nests

The method generalizes to loop nests as follows. Divide the index range for each LIV into three subranges. The Cartesian product of this decomposition divides the iteration space into 3^k subranges, over each of which we assume that there is no sign change in the span; we sum the cost over each subrange, yielding one term in the approximate cost. We then solve for the minimizer of the approximate cost as in Section 4.2. It is also possible to use other quadrature rules to approximate the cost over each subrange.

For a k-deep loop nest, the problem has $3^k |E|$ variables. This technique will therefore not scale well for deep loop nests. We do not expect this to be a problem for Fortran 90, where array operations and `forall` loops are used to express in parallel what would be loop code in a sequential language.

The Cartesian product formulation handles imperfect and trapezoidal loop nests quite naturally. The key to this is the transformer nodes that bridge the different levels of the loop nest.

5 Replication

Until now we have considered alignment as a one-to-one mapping from an object to the template. We now relax our definition and make it a one-to-many mapping, introducing the notion of *replication*. We define replication as an offset alignment that is a set of positions rather than a single position. We restrict the possible sets of positions to be triplets `l:h:s`.

A d-dimensional object aligned to a t-dimensional template has d *body axes* (which require axis, stride, and offset alignments) and $(t-d)$ *space axes* (which require only offset alignments). Our notion of replication allows the offset alignment along a space axis of an object to be a regular section of the corresponding template axis. We use the symbol $*$ to indicate replication across an entire template axis. For example, $A(i) \boxplus [i, 10]$ aligns A with one position along the second template axis; $A(i) \boxplus [i, 10:20:2]$ aligns A with a subset of the second template axis; and $A(i) \boxplus [i, *]$ replicates A across all of the second template axis. A broadcast communication occurs on an edge along which data flows from a fixed offset to a replicated offset.

5.1 Replication labeling

Offset alignment begins with a phase called *replication labeling*, whose purpose is to decide which ports of the ADG should have replicated positions. In this section, we propose an algorithm for replication labeling. Our algorithm labels ports as being replicated or non-replicated, but does not determine the extent of replication. Instead, we plan to generate the extents of replicated alignments in a storage optimization phase that follows replication.

There are three sources of replication:

- A `spread` operation causes replication.

- The use of lookup tables indexed by vector-valued subscripts is more efficient if the lookup table is replicated across the processors; we will replicate them with the programmer's permission.

- A read-only object with mobile offset alignment in a space axis can be realized through replication.

Subject to these sources, we want to determine which other objects should be replicated, in order to minimize broadcast communication during program execution. We model the problem as a graph labeling problem with two possible labels (replicated, non-replicated) and show that it can be solved efficiently as a min-cut problem.

Figure 4 shows why replication labeling is useful. In the example, a broadcast will occur in every iteration if A is not replicated, while a single broadcast will occur (at loop entry) if it is replicated. This is the solution found by our method.

After replication labeling, we discard from the ADG every edge with a replicated endpoint and proceed to find offsets for the non-replicated ports as described in Section 4. The justification for this is that an edge whose tail is replicated requires no communication, while an edge whose head is replicated requires the same amount of communication regardless of the offset of the (non-replicated) tail.

```
real A(100), B(100,200)

do K = 1,200
   A = cos(A)
   B = B + spread(A, dim=2, ncopies=200)
enddo
```

Figure 4: Replication of the array A.

5.2 Labeling by network flow

Recall that we determine offsets independently for each template axis. We call the axis we are currently labeling the *current axis*. We must label every port of the ADG either "replicated" (**R**) or "non-replicated" (**N**). The constraints on this labeling are as follows:

1. A port for which the current axis is a body axis has label **N**.

2. The node for a `spread` along the current axis has its input port labeled **R** and its output port labeled **N**.[1]

3. A port for a read-only object with a mobile alignment in the current axis, and for which the current axis is a space axis, has label **R**.

4. Some other ports have specified labels, such as ports at subroutine boundaries, and ports representing replicated lookup tables.

5. At every other node, all ports must have the same label.

Subject to these constraints, we want to complete the labeling to minimize replication communication. We associate with each ADG edge a weight that is the expected total communication cost (over time) of having the tail non-replicated and the head replicated; the weight is therefore the sum over all iterations of the size of the object communicated.

The object is to complete the labeling, satisfying the constraints, and minimizing the sum of the weights of the edges directed from **N** to **R** ports. We now show that this is a min-cut problem and can be solved by standard network flow techniques.

Theorem 1 *An optimal replication labeling can be found by network flow.*

---

[1]This sounds strange, but it correctly assigns any necessary communication to the input edge rather than to the node. Thus a `spread` node performs neither computation nor communication, but just converts a replicated object to a higher-dimensional non-replicated one.

Proof: We define a weighted, directed graph G, which is a slightly modified version of the ADG. The vertices of G are as follows: Each node of the ADG except current-axis spreads is a vertex of G. If the node has a port labeled **N** or **R**, the vertex of G has the same label. (No node except a current-axis spread can have two ports with different labels.) Each current-axis spread corresponds to two vertices of G, one for each port, with the input-port vertex labeled **R** and the output-port vertex labeled **N**. Finally, G has a new source vertex s labeled **N** and a new sink vertex t labeled **R**. The edges of G are as follows: Each directed edge of the ADG corresponds to an edge of G with the same weight. Also, there is a directed edge of infinite weight from the source s to every vertex with label **N**, and a directed edge of infinite weight from every vertex with label **R** to the sink t.

A *cut* in G is a partition of its vertices into two sets X and $\overline{X}$, with $s \in X$ and $t \in \overline{X}$. The *cost* of a cut is the total weight of the edges that cross it in the forward direction, that is, the total weight of directed edges (x, y) with $x \in X$ and $y \in \overline{X}$.

Every replication labeling is a cut, and the cost of the labeling is the same as the cost of the cut. Every cut of finite cost is a replication labeling (since no infinite-cost edge can cross it in the forward direction), and hence a minimum-cost cut is an optimum replication labeling. The max flow/min cut theorem [14, Theorem 6.2] says that the cost of a minimum cut is the same as the value of a maximum flow from the source to the sink. □

Both the max flow and the min cut can be found in low-order polynomial time by any of several algorithms [14, 15]. In particular, it can be solved using linear programming. This is ideal for us, since we already require a linear programming package for determining mobile offset alignments. This is less efficient asymptotically than other methods, but should be adequate for our purposes.

6 Remarks and Conclusions

We have presented compiler optimizations for determining replication and mobile offsets within loops. We have proved that an optimal replication labeling can be found by network flow. For mobile alignment, we have presented an approximate reduction to rounded linear programming, with error bounds on the solution quality.

We now describe several extensions we are currently pursuing.

The framework for determining mobile offset alignment can be extended to handle user-defined runtime functions. The idea is to incorporate such functions in the offset alignment, and treat a mismatch in positions as a shift of unknown distance. This allows us to use techniques similar to those used in Section 4 to solve the problem.

While we have concentrated on loop programs, our framework can in fact deal with arbitrary control flow. Static single-assignment form can be constructed for programs with arbitrary control flow graphs. In the presence of arbitrary control flow, we can use the control dependence graph [6] to associate a control weight c_e of execution with every edge e of the ADG, and minimize the *expected realignment cost*

$$\sum_{(x,y) \in E} \sum_{i \in \mathcal{I}_{xy}} c_{xy}(i) \cdot w_{xy}(i) \cdot d(\pi_x(i), \pi_y(i)).$$

Fanout nodes in an ADG represent the possibility of Steiner optimization, in which we determine an optimum fanout tree for communicating an object from the position in which it is defined to the positions in which it is used [5]. The fanout node is an approximation to a Steiner tree, which should be constructed in a pass after alignments have been determined.

Our replication algorithm does not determine the extent of replication for an object. This could be handled after replication labeling by propagating lower bounds on such extents. The algorithm also does not deal with storage allocation issues for replicated objects. In particular, it does not deal with the possibility of storing just one copy per physical processor rather than a copy per template cell. We feel that this decision fits with other storage optimization decisions in a separate phase of the compiler.

A chicken-and-egg situation exists between replication labeling and determining mobile offset alignment, as replication can be motivated by a mobile alignment for a read-only object. Our current proposal is to iterate the replication labeling and mobile alignment phases until quiescence.

The only reason for restricting replication to space axes is that we do not yet completely understand the ramifications with regard to storage and communication of allowing replication in body axes. Extending the notion of replication to body axes would provide a more elegant theory.

We do not, however, foresee extending the definition of alignment to make it a many-to-one mapping (collapsing). This complicates the alignment phase, and we feel that it is best handled in the distribution phase by mapping some template axes to memory. Clearly, there are interactions between alignment and distribution, as decisions taken in the distribution phase (such as mapping certain template axes to memory) can radically alter the assumptions made in the alignment phase. We propose handling such interactions by iterating the two phases until quiescence.

We now have a comprehensive theory of alignment analysis within a single procedure. Our next major efforts are to validate our approach by implementing these techniques, to develop a theory of distribution, and to understand the interprocedural aspects of alignment and distribution analysis.

References

[1] American National Standards Institute. *Fortran 90: X3J3 internal document S8.118 Submitted as Text for ANSI X3.198-1991, and ISO/IEC JTC1/SC22/WG5 internal document N692 Submitted as Text for ISO/IEC 1539:1991*, May 1991.

[2] J. M. Anderson and M. S. Lam. Global optimizations for parallelism and locality on scalable parallel machines. In *Proceedings of the ACM SIGPLAN'93 Conference on Programming Language Design and Implementation*, pages 112–125, Albuquerque, NM, June 1993.

[3] S. Chatterjee, J. R. Gilbert, and R. Schreiber. The alignment-distribution graph. In *Proceedings of the Sixth Annual Workshop on Languages and Compilers for Parallelism*, Portland, OR, Aug. 1993. To appear.

[4] S. Chatterjee, J. R. Gilbert, R. Schreiber, and S.-H. Teng. Optimal evaluation of array expressions on massively parallel machines. In *Proceedings of the Second Workshop on Languages, Compilers, and Runtime Environments for Distributed Memory Multiprocessors*, Boulder, CO, Oct. 1992. Published in SIGPLAN Notices, 28(1), January 1993, pages 68–71. An expanded version is available as RIACS Technical Report TR 92.17 and Xerox PARC Technical Report CSL-92-11.

[5] S. Chatterjee, J. R. Gilbert, R. Schreiber, and S.-H. Teng. Automatic array alignment in data-parallel programs. In *Proceedings of the Twentieth Annual ACM SIGACT/SIGPLAN Symposium on Principles of Programming Languages*, pages 16–28, Charleston, SC, Jan. 1993. Also available as RIACS Technical Report 92.18 and Xerox PARC Technical Report CSL-92-13.

[6] R. Cytron, J. Ferrante, B. K. Rosen, M. N. Wegman, and F. K. Zadeck. Efficiently computing static single assignment form and the control dependence graph. *ACM Trans. Prog. Lang. Syst.*, 13(4):451–490, Oct. 1991.

[7] G. C. Fox, S. Hiranandani, K. Kennedy, C. Koelbel, U. Kremer, C.-W. Tseng, and M.-Y. Wu. Fortran D language specification. Technical Report Rice COMP TR90-141, Department of Computer Science, Rice University, Houston, TX, Dec. 1990.

[8] J. R. Gilbert and R. Schreiber. Optimal expression evaluation for data parallel architectures. *Journal of Parallel and Distributed Computing*, 13(1):58–64, Sept. 1991.

[9] M. Gupta. *Automatic Data Partitioning on Distributed Memory Multicomputers*. PhD thesis, University of Illinois at Urbana-Champaign, Urbana, IL, Sept. 1992. Available as technical reports UILU-ENG-92-2237 and CRHC-92-19.

[10] High Performance Fortran Forum. High Performance Fortran language specification version 1.0. Draft, Jan. 1993. Also available as technical report CRPC-TR 92225, Center for Research on Parallel Computation, Rice University.

[11] K. Knobe, J. D. Lukas, and W. J. Dally. Dynamic alignment on distributed memory systems. In *Proceedings of the Third Workshop on Compilers for Parallel Computers*, pages 394–404, Vienna, Austria, July 1992. Austrian Center for Parallel Computation.

[12] K. Knobe, J. D. Lukas, and G. L. Steele Jr. Data optimization: Allocation of arrays to reduce communication on SIMD machines. *Journal of Parallel and Distributed Computing*, 8(2):102–118, Feb. 1990.

[13] J. Li and M. Chen. The data alignment phase in compiling programs for distributed-memory machines. *Journal of Parallel and Distributed Computing*, 13(2):213–221, Oct. 1991.

[14] C. H. Papadimitriou and K. Steiglitz. *Combinatorial Optimization: Algorithms and Complexity*. Prentice-Hall, Inc., 1982.

[15] R. E. Tarjan. *Data Structures and Network Algorithms*. Society for Industrial and Applied Mathematics, Philadelphia, PA, 1983.

[16] Thinking Machines Corporation, Cambridge, MA. *CM Fortran Reference Manual Versions 1.0 and 1.1*, July 1991.

[17] S. Wholey. *Automatic Data Mapping for Distributed-Memory Parallel Computers*. PhD thesis, School of Computer Science, Carnegie Mellon University, Pittsburgh, PA, May 1991. Available as Technical Report CMU-CS-91-121.

Advanced Compiler Optimizations for Sparse Computations*

Aart J.C. Bik and Harry A.G. Wijshoff

High Performance Computing Division, Department of Computer Science, Leiden University
P.O. Box 9512, 2300 RA Leiden, the Netherlands
ajcbik@cs.leidenuniv.nl and harryw@cs.leidenuniv.nl

Abstract

Regular data dependence checking on sparse codes usually results in very conservative estimates of actual dependences that will occur at run-time. Clearly, this is caused by the usage of compact data structures that are necessary to exploit sparsity in order to reduce storage requirements and computational time. However, if the compiler is presented with dense code and automatically converts it into code that operates on sparse data structures, then the dependence information obtained by analysis on the original code can be used to exploit potential concurrency in the generated code. In this paper we present synchronization generating and manipulating techniques that are based on this concept.

1 Introduction

Nowadays compiler support usually fails to optimize sparse codes because compact storage formats are used for sparse matrices in order to exploit sparsity with respect to *storage requirements* and *computational time*. This exploitation results in complicated code in which, for example, subscripted subscripts are used.

Restructuring compilers were formerly used to detect parallelism in serial software and to generate code that exploits certain characteristics of the target machine. The advantages of this approach are that not only investments made in existing serial programs are saved, but also the complexity of coding and maintaining new parallel programs is reduced. Consequently, the question arises whether it is also possible to let the restructuring compiler convert code that operates on simple data structures into a format that exploits certain characteristics of these data structures. In case of sparse matrices this would imply that the computation is defined on the enveloping data structures (i.e. dense matrices) and that the compiler transforms these data structures into sparse data structures. This does not only simplify the task of the programmer and enables the compiler to select a suited sparse data structure, but also has the advantage that the compiler is initially presented with clear code on which regular data dependence checking and standard optimizations can be performed. Elaboration of this idea has resulted in a data structure selection and transformation method, initially proposed in [5] and presented in more detail in [6]. This bottom-up method automatically identifies statements in the dense code that can exploit sparsity to save *computational time*, and selects a *compact* data structure for every sparse matrix, based on the access patterns through these matrices. Data structure transformations are applied afterwards, i.e. code is generated that operates on the selected data structures.

In this paper we discuss how information about data dependences, obtained by analysis on the original dense code, can be used to determine which dependences will actually hold after this code has been converted into sparse code. In section 2, we present some background, and discuss the impact of conversion into sparse code on actual dependences. In section 3, the elimination of dependences is used to reduce generated synchronization in candidate concurrent loops. Although more parallelism is expressed afterwards, the resulting code usually contains too much overhead to be practical. Therefore, in section 4 overhead reducing manipulations are presented, that possibly decrease potential concurrency. A summary and topics for further research are given in section 5.

2 Preliminaries

In this section we summarize data dependence theory, and discuss the elimination of dependences by automatic conversion into sparse code.

---

*Support was provided by the Foundation for Computer Science (SION) of the Netherlands Organization for the Advancement of Pure Research (NWO) and the EC Esprit Agency DG XIII under Grant No. APPARC 6634 BRA III. This paper is an extended abstract of technical report 92-24 [4].

2.1 Data dependences

Statements that appear in a loop body at nesting depth d are called **indexed statements** of degree d, denoted by $S(\vec{\mathtt{I}})$, where $\vec{\mathtt{I}} = (\mathtt{I}_1, \ldots, \mathtt{I}_d)$. Such statements have different **instances**, where each instance is obtained by substitution of a corresponding value for every surrounding loop index. Statements of degree 0 only have one instance. The **execution order** '$<_O$' holds on statement instances and reflects the order of execution. Clearly, $S_l(\vec{\imath}) <_O S_m(\vec{\jmath})$ holds if $\vec{\imath} \prec \vec{\jmath}$ [2], or $\vec{\imath} = \vec{\jmath}$ and S_l lexically precedes S_m in the program, if only indices of loops that surround *both* statements are considered and these loops have positive stride. Information about **data dependences** [1, 12, 17, 19, 25, 27] is essential for a restructuring compiler to determine which transformations are valid, i.e. do not change the semantics of the original program. We use the following definition of data dependences between instances $S_l(\vec{\imath}) <_O S_m(\vec{\jmath})$: a **flow dependence** holds if $\mathrm{OUT}(S_l(\vec{\imath})) \cap \mathrm{IN}(S_m(\vec{\jmath})) \neq \emptyset$, an **anti dependence** if $\mathrm{IN}(S_l(\vec{\imath})) \cap \mathrm{OUT}(S_m(\vec{\jmath})) \neq \emptyset$, and an **output dependence** holds if $\mathrm{OUT}(S_l(\vec{\imath})) \cap \mathrm{OUT}(S_m(\vec{\jmath})) \neq \emptyset$, where sets IN and OUT contain all variable instances that are respectively read or written by a statement instance. An intermediate write to a variable instance does not 'hide' dependences (cf. memory-based dependences [20]), so that dependences cannot emerge as certain statement instances are not executed.

A **static** flow, anti or output dependence between **source statement** S_l and **sink statement** S_m, denoted by $S_l \delta_{\vec{v}} S_m$, $S_l \overline{\delta}_{\vec{v}} S_m$, or $S_l \delta_{\vec{v}}^o S_m$, holds if there is such a dependence between *at least* one pair of their instances. For an arbitrary static dependence, notation $S_l \delta_{\vec{v}}^* S_m$ is used. The **direction vector** $\vec{v}$, for $v_i \in \{=, <, >, \leq, \geq, \neq, *\}$, indicates the direction of the dependence in the iteration space, where '$*$' is used for an unknown direction. Cross-iteration (or loop-carried) dependences hold between instances that are executed in different iterations of the same loop. Self-dependences hold between instances of the same indexed statement.

2.2 Conversion into sparse code

Storage requirements are reduced if only nonzero elements in a sparse matrix A are stored. The indices of explicitly stored elements, referred to as **entries**, are indicated by set $E_A \supseteq \{(i,j) \in I_A \times J_A \,|\, a_{ij} \neq 0\}$, where $I_A \times J_A$ is the **index set** of the enveloping dense matrix. Central to the reduction of computational time is the observation that statement instances where a zero is assigned to a non-entry or where the left-hand side equals the right-hand side do not have to be executed.

Therefore, for each occurrence $\mathtt{A}(F_A(\vec{\mathtt{I}}))$ of a matrix A that is in fact sparse, where $F_A : \mathbf{Z}^d \to \mathbf{Z}^2$ represents both subscript functions, a **guard** '$F_A(\vec{\mathtt{I}}) \in E_A$' is used in a multiway IF-statement to differentiate between operations on entries and zero elements. An **abstract data structure** $\mathtt{A}'$ is used as representation for an actual data structure that will be selected. A function $\sigma_A : E_A \to AD_A$ maps indices of entries to corresponding addresses in $\mathtt{A}'$. For example, a reference to an element results in the following code:

$$\mathtt{X = A}(F_A(\vec{\mathtt{I}})) \;\rightarrow\;
\begin{array}{l}
\texttt{IF } F_A(\vec{\mathtt{I}}) \in E_A \texttt{ THEN} \\
\quad \texttt{X = A}'[\sigma_A(F_A(\vec{\mathtt{I}}))] \\
\texttt{ELSEIF } F_A(\vec{\mathtt{I}}) \notin E_A \texttt{ THEN} \\
\quad \texttt{X = 0.0} \\
\texttt{ENDIF}
\end{array}$$

Branches in which sparsity can be exploited are eliminated, as illustrated below:

$$\mathtt{X = X + A}(F_A(\vec{\mathtt{I}})) \;\rightarrow\;
\begin{array}{l}
\texttt{IF } F_A(\vec{\mathtt{I}}) \in E_A \texttt{ THEN} \\
\quad \texttt{X = X + A}'[\sigma_A(F_A(\vec{\mathtt{I}}))] \\
\texttt{ENDIF}
\end{array}$$

Guards and σ_A-lookups reflect the overhead that is inherent to compact data structures. Since usually reduction in execution time is outweighted by test overhead [10, 18], techniques to eliminate overhead are applied. A basic technique is **encapsulation** of a dominating guard (which determines the iterations that must be executed) in the execution set of the surrounding loop. This is feasible, if the addresses of all *entries* along the access patterns in that loop can be easily generated, since these are the elements for which the guard holds. A semantically equivalent loop with fewer iterations and overhead results. For example, encapsulation of guard '$(\mathtt{I}, \mathtt{J}) \in E_A$' in the execution set of the J-loop is shown below:

```
DO I = 1, N                           DO I = 1, N
  DO J = 1, N                           DO AD ∈ PAD_A^I
    IF (I,J) ∈ E_A THEN                    J = π_2 · σ_A^{-1}(AD)
      X = X + A'[σ_A(I,J)] * J   →         X = X + A'[AD] * J
    ENDIF                                ENDDO
  ENDDO                               ENDDO
ENDDO
```

Set $PAD_A^{\mathtt{I}}$ contains the addresses of all entries along **access pattern** $\{(\mathtt{I}, \mathtt{J}) \,|\, 1 \leq \mathtt{J} \leq \mathtt{N}\}$, while column indices (i.e. $\pi_2 \cdot \sigma_A^{-1}(\mathtt{AD})$, where $\pi_i \cdot \vec{x} = x_i$) must be available per entry to restore the value of the loop index. Subsequently, a compact data structure is selected that enables the encapsulation of guards throughout the program, possibly after access patterns have been reshaped. A suitable storage scheme, for instance, stores entries and $\pi_i \cdot \sigma_A^{-1}$ values along each access pattern consecutively in two parallel arrays $\mathtt{AVAL}$ and $\mathtt{AIND}$. Elements in arrays $\mathtt{ALOW}$ and $\mathtt{AHIGH}$ are used to indicate the address interval for each access pattern.

Finally, code is generated. Guards and σ_A-lookups are combined and converted into appropriate tests and subroutine calls. References to A', $\pi_i \cdot \sigma_A^{-1}$ and PAD_A^I are replaced by corresponding data structures, as illustrated below for the previous example:

```
DO I = 1, N
   DO AD = ALOW(I), AHIGH(I)
      J = AIND(AD)
      X = X + AVAL(AD) * J
   ENDDO
ENDDO
```

A further discussion on the automatic conversion into sparse code can be found in [5, 6].

2.3 Data dependence elimination

After conversion into sparse code, many statement instances will not be executed at run-time. Naturally this affects the actual existing data dependences, since *a data dependence with a sink or source statement instance that is not executed does not hold.* For instance, in the following fragment, data dependences $S_1\delta S_2$ and $S_2\delta S_3$ hold, reflecting the fact that these statement instances must be executed serially:

```
S₁: B(3) = EXPR
S₂: ACC = ACC + A(1,3) * B(3)
S₃: C(1) = 6.0 * ACC
```

In the resulting sparse code, only the branch that corresponds to guard '$(1,3) \in E_A$' remains for S_2. Consequently, if a_{13} is not an entry, S_2 is not executed and the dependence chain $S_1 \rightarrow S_2 \rightarrow S_3$ is broken. Because S_1 and S_3 are independent, which can be tested directly if memory-based dependences are computed, concurrent execution of these statements becomes valid. Therefore, a possible transformation is to move S_1 and S_3 into the IF-statement of S_2, with a COBEGIN/COEND-construct [9, 21, 27] in the ELSE-branch to indicate concurrency at statement level. This effectively places implicit indirect synchronization between S_1 and S_3 under control of the guard:

```
    IF (1,3) ∈ E_A THEN
S₁:   B(3) = EXPR
S₂:   ACC = ACC + A'[σ_A(1,3)] * B(3)
S₃:   C(1) = 6.0 * ACC
    ELSEIF (1,3) ∉ E_A THEN
       COBEGIN
S₁:      B(3) = EXPR
S₃:      C(1) = 6.0 * ACC
       COEND
    ENDIF
```

If the nonzero structure of A is known at compile-time, only the branch that will be taken at run-time is generated. This transformation, which can be easily generalized to collapse independent COBEGIN-constructs

that are separated by a single dependence chain, is only valid if S_1 cannot change the value of the guard, i.e. a_{13} cannot be inserted or deleted. The former case clearly prohibits correct concurrent execution.

Since not much gain in execution time can be expected from this kind of fine grain parallelism alone, a similar technique on cross-iteration dependences is presented in the following section.

3 Loop concurrentization

Since numerical programs spend most execution time inside loops, executing different iterations on different processors of a multiprocessor can reduce execution time substantially. A DOALL-loop is used if all iterations are independent and can be executed concurrently, while a DOACROSS-loop is used if a partial execution order on some parts of the iterations must be imposed. In the latter construct, synchronization between the execution of different iterations is required to constrain this ordering. In [7, 8] this is modeled with an initial delay, while synchronization primitives **testset/test** and **post/wait** are presented in [14, 15, 16, 17, 25, 27]. The latter, referred to as random synchronization, is used in this paper. In a busy-waiting [21] implementation, each **post** sets a unique bit on which completion of a corresponding **wait** depends. Several **wait** instances can test the same bit. Automatic concurrent loop detection consists of generation of synchronization statements to assure that cross-iteration dependences, implied by the original serial execution, are not violated during program execution. Methods for automatic generation of synchronization and elimination of redundant synchronization are presented in [13, 14, 15, 16, 26].

We assume that enough information is available to determine per static cross-iteration dependence all statement instances on which underlying dependences hold, e.g. by means of dependence distances vectors. A **post** is placed directly *after* every source statement, while a corresponding **wait** is placed *before* every sink statement. If the following serial loop, for example, is converted into a concurrent loop, all underlying dependences of static dependence $S_1\delta_< S_2$, which have distance 4, are enforced by instances of the induced **wait** and **post** statements (**wait** does not block on out-of-bounds iterations):

```
        DO I = 1, N - 4
S₁:     A(I+4) = ...
S₂:     ... = A(I)         →
        ENDDO
```

```
DOACROSS I = 1, N - 4
   A(I+4) = ...
   post(ASYNC,I)
   wait(ASYNC,I-4)
   ... = A(I)
ENDDOACROSS
```

432

The **synchronization variable ASYNC** has one parameter, so it can be implemented as bit vector with one bit per iteration. In general, however, there is one parameter per loop that surrounds the source in order to distinguish between its different instances. Similarly, parameters are used for all loops that cause several sink instances per source instance.[1] If $I_{p_1}..I_{p_n}$ and $I_{w_1}..I_{w_{n'}}$ denote respectively the (possibly overlapping) indices of these loops, then $n + n'$ parameters are required, while **post**(SYNC, $I_{p_1}..I_{p_n}, \ldots$) and **wait**(SYNC, $\ldots, I_{w_1}..I_{w_{n'}}$) are generated to enforce this dependence. The remaining parameters depend on the relation between indices of every source and sink pair. All synchronization variables can be implemented as bit-arrays of appropriate dimension.

3.1 Static nonzero structures

In many loops, synchronization statements of lexically backward dependences enforce (nearly) serial execution of the loop. Consider, for example, concurrentization of the following loop in which static dependences $S_1 \delta_= S_2$ and $S_2 \delta_< S_1$ hold:

```
                              DOACROSS I = 2, N
DO I = 2, N                     wait(BSYNC,I-1)
S1:C(I)=B(I-1)          →       C(I)=B(I-1)
S2:B(I)=B(I)+A(I,2)*C(I)        B(I)=B(I)+A(I,2)*C(I)
ENDDO                           post(BSYNC,I)
                              ENDDOACROSS
```

Dependence $S_1 \delta_= S_2$ is enforced by serial execution of every iteration. However, $S_2 \delta_< S_1$ must be *explicitly* enforced by synchronization, which effectively serializes the loop. If matrix A is sparse, conversion into sparse code yields guard '$(I,2) \in E_A$' for S_2. Therefore, if a_{32} is not an entry, for example, instance $S_2(3)$ is not executed and a similar situation as in section 2.3 occurs: dependence chain $S_1(3) \to_= S_2(3) \to_< S_1(4)$ is broken. Iterations 3 and 4 become independent (otherwise more synchronization statements would have been generated).

Similar arguments hold if the arcs of this chain are labeled as '<' and '=', or '<' and '<' (in case of two '='-labels, the transformation of section 2.3 can be used to increase concurrency within an iteration). Consequently, if the sink or source statement instance of a cross-iteration dependence is under control of a guard, corresponding **post** and **wait** instances can be brought under control of that guard. Because for each cross-iteration dependence, the generated guard of either the **wait** or the **post** is equal to the guard of *another* iteration, the value of that guard must be invariant, i.e. the

---

[1] This unconventional approach is initially taken to maintain a unique **post-wait** correspondence. In section 4, the redundancy of some parameters is exploited.

nonzero structure of the matrix must be static during execution of the loop. Since no assignments to elements of matrix A are performed in the previous example, the following code is generated:

```
        DOACROSS I = 2, N
          IF (I > 2) THEN
            IF (I-1,2) ∈ E_A wait(BSYNC,I-1)
          ENDIF
S1:       C(I) = B(I-1)
S2:       IF (I,2) ∈ E_A THEN
            B(I) = B(I) + A'[σ_A(I,2)] * C(I)
            post(BSYNC,I)
          ENDIF
        ENDDOACROSS
```

The generated guards provide that each instance of **post** and **wait** is under control of the guard of the corresponding instance of S_2. Because the guard of the **wait** is identical to the guard of the previous iteration, an out-of-bounds test is required. The following diagram shows the resulting serial execution order if all elements are entries, and possible overlap if a_{32} is not stored, for N=4:

I	2	3	4	2	3	4
t	$S_1(2)$	wB2	wB3	$S_1(2)$	wB2	$S_1(4)$
i	$S_2(2)$	·	·	$S_2(2)$	·	$S_2(4)$
m	pB2	·	·	pB2	·	pB4
e		$S_1(3)$	·		$S_1(3)$	
		$S_2(3)$	·			
↓		pB3	·			
			$S_1(4)$			
			$S_2(4)$			
			pB4			

Consider, as another example, concurrentization of the outermost loop in the inner product form of forward substitution for a linear system $L\vec{x} = \vec{b}$, where L is the lower triangular part of a matrix A. Straightforward generation of synchronization statements for $S_2 \delta_< S_1$ results in the given code:

```
DO I = 1, N              DOACROSS I = 1, N
  DO J = 1, I - 1          DO J = 1, I - 1
S1: X(I) = X(I) -             wait(XSYNC,J,I)
+       A(I,J) * X(J)   →     X(I)=X(I)-A(I,J)*X(J)
  ENDDO                     ENDDO
S2: X(I) = X(I)/A(I,I)      X(I) = X(I) / A(I,I)
ENDDO                       post(XSYNC,I,{I < i ≤ N})
                          ENDDOACROSS
```

Underlying dependences of $S_2 \delta_< S_1$ hold between a single source statement instance, and sink statement instances in *all* following iterations. Therefore, a second parameter is used to differentiate between dependences to different sink instances in iterations of the I-loop. Because the dependence is caused by variables X(I) and X(J), the J-index value in all sink instances is equal to the iteration in which the source instance is executed, which is used to derive the form of remaining parameters. Sets are used as parameters if convenient, which

433

has as additional advantage that boundary conditions are implicitly expressed, if operations on empty sets are not performed.

After conversion into sparse code, every instance of S_1 is only executed if '$(\text{I}, \text{J}) \in E_A$' and, consequently, synchronization is guarded accordingly. This is implicitly done for **wait** instances if this statement is kept inside the AD-loop after encapsulation, while the guard explicitly appears in the second parameter of **post**:

```
DOACROSS I = 1, N
    DO AD ∈ PAD_A^I
        J = π₂ · σ_A⁻¹(AD)
        wait(XSYNC,J,I)
S₁:     X(I) = X(I) - A'[AD] * X(J)
    ENDDO
S₂: IF (I,I) ∈ E_A THEN
        X(I) = X(I) / A'[σ_A(I,I)]
    ELSEIF (I,I) ∉ E_A THEN
        X(I) = X(I) / 0.0    (error)
    ENDIF
    post(XSYNC,I,{I < i ≤ N|(i,I) ∈ E_A})
ENDDOACROSS
```

The execution order in case a_{43} is not stored, is shown in the following diagram for N=4 (for a dense matrix, $S_2(4)$ appears on the 10th step):[2]

I	1	2	3	4
t	$S_2(1)$	wX1,2	wX1,3	wX1,4
i	pX1,2-4	.		
m		$S_1(2,1)$	$S_1(3,1)$	$S_1(4,1)$
e		$S_2(2)$	wX2,3	wX2,4
		pX2,3-4	.	
↓			$S_1(3,2)$	$S_1(4,2)$
			$S_2(3)$	$S_2(4)$

Note that we have ignored $S_1\delta_{<<}S_1$, because this dependence is covered by synchronization of $S_2\delta_< S_1$ (see section 4.1). However, if L is lower *unit*-triangular, statement S_2 is not required and only $S_1\delta_{<<}S_1$ remains, formed by dependences between guarded source *and* guarded sink statement instances. Consequently, synchronization is brought under control of the guards of all corresponding statement instances. Synchronization requires three parameters: the first and second indicate the specific instance of the source, while the third is used to differentiate between dependences to different sink instances of the I-loop:

```
DOACROSS I = 1, N
    DO AD ∈ PAD_A^I
        J = π₂ · σ_A⁻¹(AD)
        wait(XSYNC,J,{1 ≤ j < J|(J,j) ∈ E_A},I)
S₁:     X(I) = X(I) - A'[AD] * X(J)
        post(XSYNC,I,J,{I < i ≤ N|(i,I) ∈ E_A})
    ENDDO
ENDDOACROSS
```

---

[2]More concurrency can sometimes be achieved by reordering iterations of the J-loop (e.g. interchanging iterations 2 and 3 during I=4 saves one time step if $(3,1) \notin E_A$ and $(3,2) \notin E_A$).

The guard of every source statement instance is implicitly present in the **post** instances after encapsulation and explicitly present in the corresponding **wait** instances. The opposite holds for the guard of every sink instance. Consequently, dependences on empty iterations are also eliminated.

Another way to express forward substitution is the outer product form presented below. Synchronization of $S_2\delta_{<=}^* S_2$, caused by X(J) in the source and sink, and $S_2\delta_<^* S_1$, caused by X(J) and X(I), requires three and two parameters for XUPD and XDIV respectively:

```
DOACROSS I = 1, N
    wait(XDIV,{1 ≤ i < I},I)
S₁: X(I) = X(I) / A(I,I)
    DO J = I + 1, N
        wait(XUPD,{1 ≤ i < I},J,I)
S₂:     X(J) = X(J) - A(J,I) * X(I)
        post(XUPD,I,J,{I < i < J})
        post(XDIV,I,J)
    ENDDO
ENDDOACROSS
```

Because I < J holds for instances of S_2, underlying dependences of $S_2\delta_{<=}^* S_2$ do not reach all following iterations, i.e. constraint $i <$ J appears in the **post** on XUPD because J indices of the source and sink are equal. The remaining cross-iteration dependence $S_2\delta_{<<}S_2$, caused by X(J) and X(I), is covered (see section 4.1). Conversion into sparse code results in the following fragment:

```
DOACROSS I = 1, N
    wait(XDIAG,{1 ≤ i < I|(I,i) ∈ E_A},I)
S₁: IF (I,I) ∈ E_A THEN
        X(I) = X(I) / A'[σ_A(I,I)]
    ELSEIF (I,I) ∉ E_A THEN
        X(I) = X(I) / 0.0    (error)
    ENDIF
    DO AD ∈ PAD_A^I
        J = π₁ · σ_A⁻¹(AD)   (row index)
        wait(XUPD,{1 ≤ i < I|(J,i) ∈ E_A},J,I)
S₂:     X(J) = X(J) - A'[AD] * X(I)
        post(XUPD,I,J,{I < i < J|(J,i) ∈ E_A})
        post(XDIAG,I,J)
    ENDDO
ENDDOACROSS
```

Clearly, the AD-loop can also be executed concurrently. The updating sequence of S_2 cannot be reordered in this case because it is explicitly synchronized. An execution order for N=4 is shown in the following diagram in case a_{43} is not stored. Synchronization can be done with a single synchronization variable, as explained in sections 4.2 and 4.3:

I	1	2	3	4
	$S_1(1)$	wX1,2	wX1-2,3	wX1-2,4
t	$S_2(1,2-4)$	.	.	.
i	pX1,2-4	.		.
m		$S_1(2)$		
e		wX1,3-4		
		$S_2(2,3-4)$		
↓		pX2,3-4		
			$S_1(3)$	$S_1(4)$

434

3.2 Dynamic nonzero structures

So far, values of guards used in synchronization were *invariant* in one execution of the concurrentized loop. This is true if no assignments to elements of the corresponding matrix occur (as in e.g. triangular solve), or if all assignments are performed within a static nonzero structure (as in e.g. *LU*-decomposition after symbolic factorization [10, 28]). In general, however, the nonzero structure might change during execution of the loop due to insertions and deletions of entries (referred to as **creation** and **cancellation** respectively). Generation of an identical guard in two different iterations is only valid if changes in value between both evaluations are correctly accounted for. Although this complicates synchronization generation, concurrency can still be found.

Consider, for example, conversion into sparse code with concurrent I-loop of the following fragment, if the technique of the previous section for static dependences $S_1 \delta_< S_3$ and $S_3 \delta_< S_2$ is used, i.e. under the assumption that values of the guards are invariant. Function new_A returns a new address in A' and adapts σ_A, E_A and AD_A accordingly as side-effect to account for creation:

```
        DO I = 2, N - 2
S₁:     A(I+2,2) = X
S₂:     C(I) = B(I-1)
S₃:     B(I) = B(I) + A(I,2) * C(I)
        ENDDO
                  ↓
        DOACROSS I = 2, N - 2
S₁:     IF (I+2,2) ∈ E_A THEN
            A'[σ_A(I + 2,2)] = X
        ELSEIF (I+2,2) ∉ E_A THEN
            A'[new_A(I + 2,2)] = X
        ENDIF
        IF (I < N - 4) THEN
            IF (I+2,2) ∈ E_A post(ASYNC,I)
        ENDIF
        IF (I > 2) THEN
            IF (I-1,2) ∈ E_A wait(BSYNC,I-1)
        ENDIF
S₂:     C(I) = B(I-1)
S₃:     IF (I,2) ∈ E_A THEN
            wait(ASYNC,I-2)
            B(I) = B(I) + A'[σ_A(I,2)] * C(I)
            post(BSYNC,I)
        ENDIF
        ENDDOACROSS
```

Incorrect executions are possible. For example, if iteration 2 is delayed and $(3,2) \notin E_A$ holds, so that **wait(BSYNC,3)** is not executed, premature evaluation of the guard of **wait(ASYNC,2)** and $S_3(4)$ occurs:

I	2	3	4
t			$S_1(4)$
i		$(6,2) \in E_A$:pA4	
m			$S_2(4)$
e			$(4,2) \in E_A$:wA2
			$(4,2) \in E_A$:$S_3(4)$
↓	$S_1(2)$		
	$(4,2) \in E_A$:pA2		

If a_{42} is inserted by $S_1(2)$, $S_3(4)$ is not executed and **B(4)** contains an incorrect value afterwards. On the other hand, if cancellation was possible in S_1, deadlock could result for a conditionally executed **post**. A similar problem arises for creation, if an instance of the *sink* can alter the value of a guard on which execution of the source instance depends. These problems are solved by application of the following rule: *disable generation of a guard in synchronization statements, if the value of this guard can be affected by the corresponding source or sink statement instance* (note that other guards may still be generated).

However, evaluation of guards that belong to other iterations must also be correctly synchronized. The following diagram shows that an incorrect execution can still result if synchronization on **ASYNC** is performed unconditionally, because iteration 5 evaluates guard '$(4,2) \in E_A$' before $S_1(2)$ has been executed. If a_{42} is inserted in iteration 2, a premature value of **B(4)** is stored in **C(5)** by $S_2(5)$:

I	2	3	4	5
t			$S_1(4)$	$S_1(5)$
i			pA4	pA5
m			$S_2(4)$	$(4,2) \in E_A$:wB4
e			wA2	$S_2(5)$
	$S_1(2)$		.	
	pA2			
↓	$S_2(2)$		$(4,2) \in E_A$:$S_3(4)$	
	$(2,2) \in E_A$:$S_3(2)$		$(4,2) \in E_A$:pB4	

In general, the problem occurs for a *particular* guard whenever a statement instance (A) might alter the value of this guard on which a preceding or following execution of (D) depends, while synchronization between (D) and another statement instance (I) is only required if (D) is executed. The possible basic situations, which can be detected at compile-time, are presented schematically in the following picture:

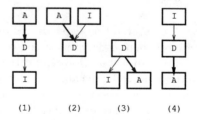

Synchronization between (A) and (D) (boldfaced arc) is independent of the guard under consideration by application of the previous rule. An incorrect execution is prevented if the following rules are applied for the generation of that guard for synchronization between (D) and (I) or vice versa. If there are several (A) instances that can affect the value of the guard under consideration, a combination of appropriate rules is applied:

Case 1 Since evaluation of the guard of **wait** in (I) must be performed after execution of (A), synchronization between (A) and (I) is required.

Case 2 Irrespective of the relative execution order between (A) and (I), the **post** of (I) can be executed independently, while the guard is still generated for the **wait** of (D).[3]

Case 3 If (A) will be executed after (I), synchronization between (I) and (A) is required, while generation of the guard for synchronization between (D) and (I) is disabled otherwise.

Case 4 Synchronization between (I) and (A) is required to assure that the value of the guard is evaluated before redefined.

A conservative decision in all cases is to disable generation of the current guard for synchronization between (D) and (I). In some cases, newly generated synchronization between (A) and (I) can be brought under control of guards of (A) or (I) and one of the previous cases might apply again. At any stage, this process can be terminated by the conservative decision stated above. For example, since case 1 is applicable in the previous problem, a test on the same bit, i.e. '**wait(ASYNC,I - 3)**', before evaluation of '$(I - 1, 2) \in E_A$' ensures correct execution, which is, however, also achieved by unconditional synchronization on **BSYNC**.

Another example where the nonzero structure of the matrix changes during execution, is LU-factorization without pivoting:

```
     DO I = 1, N - 1
        DO J = I + 1, N
S₁:        A(J,I) = A(J,I) / A(I,I)
           DO K = I + 1, N
S₂:           A(J,K) = A(J,K) - A(J,I) * A(I,K)
           ENDDO
        ENDDO
     ENDDO
```

Since all cross-iteration dependences are carried by the outermost loop, concurrentization of the J-loop is a common optimization. However, if the code is converted into sparse code, the amount of concurrency can drastically decrease because many iterations of the J-loop get disabled, since only so-called target rows are considered [28]. Therefore, concurrentization of an outermost loop might be useful, which also introduce less startup overhead [17, 25, 27].

Loop interchanging yields the JIK-version, in which $S_2\delta_{<<}S_1$ and $S_2\delta_{<<=}S_2$ hold. The first dependence is caused by **A(J,K)** and **A(I,I)**. Consequently, the value of **I** in a sink statement instance of this dependence

is equal to the values of **J** and **K** in the corresponding source of a previous iteration. Therefore, in terms of the sink, all instances $S_2(I, i, I)$ where $1 \le i < I$ are sources. Synchronization of this dependence requires three parameters to indicate source instances, and one parameter to identify the different sink instances per source. Synchronization of the second dependence, caused by **A(J,K)** and **A(I,K)**, has a similar structure. Values of **I** and **K** in a sink are equal to the values of **J** and **K** in the corresponding preceding source. Because **I** < **K** holds in the sink, instances of S_2 are only a source if **J** < **K** holds for this instance. If variables **ADIAG** and **AROW** are used for synchronization, the following code results:

```
     DOACROSS J = 2, N
        DO I = 1, J - 1
           wait(ADIAG,I,{1 ≤ i < I},I,J)
S₁:        A(J,I) = A(J,I) / A(I,I)
           DO K = I + 1, N
              wait(AROW,I,{1 ≤ i < I},K,J)
S₂:           A(J,K) = A(J,K) - A(J,I) * A(I,K)
              IF (J = K) post(ADIAG,J,I,K,{J < j ≤ N})
              IF (J < K) post(AROW,J,I,K,{J < j ≤ N})
           ENDDO
        ENDDO
     ENDDOACROSS
```

Consider conversion into sparse code if the need for new synchronization is prevented, i.e. a guard is only generated in case 2. Clearly, guard '$(J,I) \in E_A$' and '$(J,I) \in E_A \wedge (I,K) \in E_A$' result for S_1 and S_2 respectively. Since for $S_2\delta_{<<}S_1$, the guard '$(J,I) \in E_A$' of the sink can only be altered by preceding statement instances in the same iteration of J ($S_2\delta_{=<}S_1$, caused by **A(J,K)** and **A(J,I)** hols, while no anti or output dependences caused by **A(J,I)** have S_1 as source) case 2 applies and the guard is generated for the **wait**. Because case 1 applies for the guards of the source ('$(I,K) \in E_A$' with $S_2\delta_{<<=}S_2$, caused by **A(I,K)** in the sink, and guard '$(J,I) \in E_A$' with $S_2\delta_{=<<}S_2$, caused by **A(J,I)**)), generation of these guards is disabled. Note that $S_1\delta_{==}S_2$ is harmless, because S_1 cannot cause creation. Dependence $S_2\delta_{<<=}S_2$ self disables generation of guard '$(I,K) \in E_A$' belonging to its sink, while generation of guards belonging to the source is again disabled. Because case 2 applies for '$(J,I) \in E_A$' of the sink, this guard appears in the **wait**.

The resulting code is shown below. Guard '$(J,I) \in E_A$' has been hoisted out the innermost loop, is collapsed with the identical guard of S_1, and is encapsulated in the I-loop (insertions in the corresponding row complicates code generation [6]). Encapsulation of '$(I,K) \in E_A$' in the K-loop is prohibited by the presence of unguarded synchronization:

---

[3]Note that in the bit-array implementation it is allowed that certain **post**-signals are not consumed.

```
DOACROSS J = 2, N
   DO AD ∈ PAD_A^J
      I = π_2 · σ_A^{-I}(AD)
      wait(ADIAG,I,{1 ≤ i < I},I,J)
S_1:  IF (I,I) ∈ E_A THEN
         A'[AD] = A'[AD] / A'[σ_A(I,I)]
      ELSEIF (I,I) ∉ E_A THEN
         A'[AD] = A'[AD] / 0.0      (error)
      ENDIF
      DO K = I + 1, N
         wait(AROW,I,{1 ≤ i < I},K,J)
S_2:     IF (J,K) ∈ E_A ∧ (I,K) ∈ E_A THEN
            A'[σ_A(J,K)] = A'[σ_A(J,K)] - A'[AD] * A'[σ_A(I,K)]
         ELSEIF (J,K) ∉ E_A ∧ (I,K) ∈ E_A THEN
            A'[new_A(J,K)] = - A'[AD] * A'[σ_A(I,K)]
         ENDIF
         IF (J = K) post(ADIAG,J,I,K,{J < j ≤ N})
         IF (J < K) post(AROW,J,I,K,{J < j ≤ N})
      ENDDO
   ENDDO
ENDDOACROSS
```

4 Implementation issues

Although, the methods considered so far may reveal all potential parallelism if concurrency at statement instance level is expressed in a complete data-flow like manner, it suffers from many disadvantages. The generated guards, for instance, introduce substantial runtime overhead. Synchronization also might increase run-time overhead and the demand for memory or special hardware resources, depending on the implementation of the **wait**- and **post**-primitives. A complete data-flow like execution is only achieved if sufficient processors are available and scheduling is done without intrusive overhead. Since usually the number of iterations exceeds the number of processors, concurrency might be lost because the scheduling of iterations of DOACROSS-loops [19] must account for all possible forward dependences, so that the execution set cannot be reordered arbitrarily. In this section, methods to make the derived code more feasible are discussed.

4.1 Synchronization elimination

Redundant synchronization elimination [13, 14] consists of the detection and elimination of so-called covered dependences, which are dependences that are implicitly enforced by synchronization of other dependences or by execution order constraints that are imposed by the architecture, such as serial execution within every iteration. These techniques can also be used for synchronization of guarded statements, with the additional constraint that a dependence can only be covered by synchronization of another dependence if '$guard_{covered} \Rightarrow guard_{covering}$' holds. For example, $S_1 \delta_{<<} S_1$ in the sparse version of inner product forward

substitution is covered by synchronization of $S_2 \delta_< S_1$, because identical subscripts are used, the source and sink of the latter follows and precedes respectively the source and the sink of the former [13], and '$(i_1, j_1) \in E_A \wedge (i_2, i_1) \in E_A \Rightarrow (i_2, i_1) \in E_A$' holds.

4.2 Memory requirements reduction

Reduction in memory demands is achieved if the distinction between dependences that emerge from a single source instance to several sink instances is eliminated, by dropping the corresponding parameters, so that the same bit is tested in all corresponding **wait** instances.

The following lemma can be used to move synchronization statement instances (cf. [27]), which can assist in reducing memory requirements:

Lemma Execution of synchronization statement instances can be arbitrarily interchanged with the execution of following or preceding statement instances in one iteration of the concurrentized loop, for instances of **post** and **wait** respectively, without affecting the original semantics (proof in [4]).

Consider the following example, where synchronization of $S_1 \delta_< S_2$ initially requires three parameters:

```
                          DOACROSS I = 3, L
 DO I = 3, L                 DO J = 1, M
    DO J = 1, M                 A(I) = ...
S_1:   A(I) = ...               post(ASYNC,I,J,{1 ≤ k ≤ N})
    ENDDO                    ENDDO
    DO K = 1, M     →       DO K = 1, N
S_2:   ... = A(I-2)            wait(ASYNC,I-2,{1 ≤ j ≤ M},K)
    ENDDO                       ... = A(I-2)
 ENDDO                       ENDDO
                          ENDDOACROSS
```

As stated above, the third parameter can be dropped. By application of the lemma on the unrolled K-loop, all **wait** instances can be hoisted before this loop. Since this yields N identical consecutive **wait** statements, these statements are replaced by one statement. Similarly, all **post** instances can be hoisted after the J-loop. However, replacing the resulting statements by one **post** statement requires collection of all different used parameter values, referred to as **aggregation**, which yields '**post(ASYNC,I,{1 ≤ j ≤ M})**'. Clearly, parameters of which the whole range is used in all statements can also be dropped. Consequently, '**post(ASYNC,I)**' and '**wait(ASYNC,I-2)**' between the two loops suffices. Effectively, the **post** of a source is placed after the *last* read or write, while the **wait** of a sink is placed before the *first* read or write (cf. [13]).

Guards that were present in sets that are dropped by application of the previous two optimizations appear as disjunctions in the resulting code, as shown below for forward substitution for unit-triangular L. The resulting conditions reflect the fact that synchronization is required if at least one source instance *and* at least one sink instance is executed:

```
DOACROSS I = 1, N
  DO AD ∈ PAD_A^I
    J = π₂ · σ_A⁻¹(AD)
    IF ⋁_{j=1}^{J-1} (J,j) ∈ E_A  wait(XSYNC,J)
    X(I) = X(I) - A'[AD] * X(J)
  ENDDO
  IF (⋁_{i=I+1}^{N} (i,I) ∈ E_A) ∧ (⋁_{j=1}^{I-1} (I,j) ∈ E_A) post(XSYNC,I)
ENDDOACROSS
```

Finally, consecutive identical **post** statements on different synchronization variables, can be replaced by one **post** statement, if the remaining variable is used in all corresponding **wait** statements, which reduces the number of synchronization variables required.

4.3 Guard elimination

In all cases, the guards of both the **post** and **wait** can be eliminated, at the potential loss of concurrency. Characteristics of the nonzero structure might help to determine which conditions are very likely to hold. It is also possible to eliminate the guard of the **post** only. For example, in the outer product code, dropping one parameter yields '$⋁_{i=I+1}^{J-1}(J,i) ∈ E_A$' as condition of the **post** on XUPD. If this disjunction is ignored, all synchronization can be done on XDIAG, since the **post** statements become identical.

4.4 Application of aggregation

No potential concurrency was lost in the previous example of aggregation, because all instances were involved in the dependence. In general however, overlap might decrease by synchronization movement, because the granularity of concurrency becomes more coarse. The advantage are that in some cases fewer parameters are required as shown above, or operations on subsets can be replaced by barriers [25, 27] as explained below.

Consider, for example, the inner product forward substitution where the second parameter of XSYNC is dropped. Hoisting all instances of **wait(XSYNC,J)** before the AD-loop followed by aggregation results in the following code, where $W^I = \{1 ≤ j < I | (I,j) ∈ E_A\}$ and all guards of the **post** are eliminated:

```
DOACROSS I = 1, N
  wait(XSYNC,W^I)
  ...
  post(XSYNC,I)
ENDDOACROSS
```

Clearly, since **wait(XSYNC,∅)** is non-blocking, iterations in $I^1 = \{1 ≤ i ≤ N | (W^i = ∅)\}$ are independent of other iterations. Consequently, these iterations can be moved into a DOALL-construct, after which all associated **post** instances are aggregated. Repetitive application results in the following code, where aggregated synchronization operations are replaced by implicit barriers at the end of each DOALL-loop, for $I^L = \{i ∈ \{1 \dots N\} \setminus \bigcup_{k=1}^{L-1} I^k | W^i ⊆ \bigcup_{k=1}^{L-1} I^k\}$

```
DO L = 1, min{l ∈ N|(I^l = ∅)} - 1
  DOALL I ∈ I^L
  ...
  ENDDOALL
ENDDO
```

Pre–evaluation code that determines I^L by levelization of the iteration dependence graph can be generated by the compiler. The gain of pre–evaluation is more substantial if the results can be used several times or if compile-time evaluation is possible.

Similar manipulations can be performed on loops in which the nonzero structure changes, although guarded synchronization instances cannot be interchanged with instances that might alter the values of any guard involved. For example, the following version of the concurrentized JIK-version of LU-factorization can be derived. The **wait** instance cannot be hoisted before the AD-loop, since the value of the (implicit) guard '$(J,I) ∈ E_A$', and thus the dependence pattern, might be altered by preceding statement instances:

```
DOACROSS J = 2, N
  DO AD ∈ PAD_A^J
    I = π₂ · σ_A⁻¹(AD)
    wait(ASYNC,I)
    ...
  ENDDO
  post(ASYNC,J)
ENDDO
```

Other work has addressed the possibility to deal with dependence patterns determined by *loop invariant* values of arrays used in subscripts by **run-time dependence checking**, based on the *conservative* results of dependence analysis. In subscript blocking [19], pre-evaluation determines maximum subsets of successive independent iterations, without reordering of the execution set. In [14, 16, 26] maximum subsets of arbitrary independent iterations are determined. Overhead is introduced because iterations are masked at run-time with a mask that is re-computed between the execution of successive subsets. Finally, in [22, 23] the iterations of a particular loop-structure are partitioned and reordered by pre–evaluation code, and executed in a DOACROSS-like construct or as a sequence of

DOALL-loops on so-called wavefronts, corresponding to the sequence of DOALL-loops found in this section. Repeated startup overhead is eliminated, if each processor fetches iterations of I^L if available, and executes a barrier statement before shifting to I^{L+1}.

5 Summary

In this paper, we have explored the automatic exploitation of concurrency in sparse codes. The techniques described rely on the explicit introduction of random synchronization in the original dense code. Thereupon, this code in converted into sparse code, while sparsity is used to reduce synchronization. At this moment, the techniques in this paper are being implemented into the MT1 compiler [3]. Research needs to be done into the exploitation of specific nonzero structures, as well as a more effective implementation of these ideas. Other issues, such as data structure interference in dynamic data structures (cf. [28]), that complicate concurrentization must also be dealt with.

References

[1] U. Banerjee. *Dependence Analysis for Supercomputing*. Kluwer Academic Publishers, Boston, 1988.

[2] U. Banerjee. *Loop Transformations for Restructuring Compilers: The Foundations*. Kluwer Academic Publishers, Boston, 1993.

[3] Aart J.C. Bik. A prototype restructuring compiler. Master's thesis, Utrecht University, 1992. INF/SCR-92-11.

[4] Aart J.C. Bik and Harry A.G. Wijshoff. Advanced compiler optimizations for sparse computations. Technical Report no. 92-24, Dept. of Computer Science, Leiden University, 1992.

[5] Aart J.C. Bik and Harry A.G. Wijshoff. Compilation techniques for sparse matrix computations. In *Proceedings of the International Conference on Supercomputing*, pages 416–424, 1993.

[6] Aart J.C. Bik and Harry A.G. Wijshoff. On automatic data structure selection and code generation for sparse computations. In *Proceedings of the Sixth Annual on Languages and Compilers for Parallelism Workshop*, 1993.

[7] Ron G. Cytron. Doacross, beyond vectorization for multiprocessors. In *Proceedings of the 1986 International Conference on Parallel Processing*, pages 836–844, 1986.

[8] Ron G. Cytron. Limited processor scheduling of doacross loops. In *Proceedings of the 1987 International Conference on Parallel Processing*, pages 226–234, 1987.

[9] E.W. Dijkstra. Cooperating sequential processes. In F. Genuys, editor, *Programming Languages*. Academic Press, New York, 1968.

[10] I.S. Duff, A.M. Erisman, and J.K. Reid. *Direct Methods for Sparse Matrices*. Oxford Science Publications, 1990.

[11] Alan George and Joseph W. Liu. *Computer Solution of Large Sparse Positive Definite Systems*. Prentice-Hall Inc., 1981.

[12] David J. Kuck. *The Structure of Computers and Computations*. John Wiley and Sons, New York, 1978. Volume 1.

[13] Zhiyuan Li and Walid Abu-Sufah. On reducing data synchronization in multiprocessed loops. *IEEE Transactions on Computers*, pages 105–109, 1987.

[14] Samuel P. Midkiff. *The Dependence Analysis and Synchronization of Parallel Programs*. PhD thesis, C.S.R.D., 1993.

[15] Samuel P. Midkiff and David A. Padua. Compiler generated synchronization for do loops. In *Proceedings of the 1986 International Conference on Parallel Processing*, pages 544–551, 1986.

[16] Samuel P. Midkiff and David A. Padua. Compiler algorithms for synchronization. *IEEE Transactions on Computers*, pages 1485–1495, 1987.

[17] David A. Padua and Michael J. Wolfe. Advanced compiler optimizations for supercomputers. *Communications of the ACM*, pages 1184–1201, 1986.

[18] Sergio Pissanetsky. *Sparse Matrix Technology*. Academic Press, London, 1984.

[19] C.D. Polychronoupolos. *Parallel Programming and Compilers*. Kluwer Academic Publishers, Boston, 1988.

[20] William Pugh and David Wonnacott. An evaluation of exact methods for analysis of value-based array data dependences. In *Proceedings of the Sixth Annual Workshop on Languages and Compilers for Parallel Computing*, 1993.

[21] Michael J. Quinn. *Designing Efficient Algorithms for Parallel Computers*. McGraw-Hill, 1987.

[22] Joel H. Saltz, Ravi Mirchandaney, and Kathleen Crowley. The doconsider loop. In *ACM Conference Proceedings, 3th International Conference of Supercomputing*, pages 29–40, 1989.

[23] Joel H. Saltz, Ravi Mirchandaney, and Kathleen Crowley. Run-time parallelization and scheduling of loops. *IEEE Transactions on Computers*, pages 603–612, 1991.

[24] Gerard Tel. Introduction to distributed algorithms, volume 1. Course Notes INF/DOC-92-05, Utrecht University, 1992.

[25] Michael J. Wolfe. *Optimizing Supercompilers for Supercomputers*. Pitman, London, 1989.

[26] Chuan-Qi Zhu and Pen-Chung Yew. A scheme to enforce data dependence on large multiprocessor systems. *IEEE Transactions on Software Engineering*, Volume SE-13:726–739, 1987.

[27] H. Zima. *Supercompilers for Parallel and Vector Computers*. ACM Press, New York, 1990.

[28] Zahari Zlatev. *Computational Methods for General Sparse Matrices*. Kluwer Academic Publishers, 1991.

Session 6:
Workshop
Debuggers for High
Performance Computers

Debuggers for High Performance Computers

Jeffrey S. Brown

Los Alamos National Laboratory

Abstract

What direction should production debugger development be taking? What are the top user priorities? How can the development of heterogeneous/distributed debuggers be facilitated? Should there be a standard debugging language? This workshop promotes an open exchange of information among debugger developers and users from the academic, research, and commercial communities. The goal is to advance the state of applied debugging technology by indicating what new techniques should be integrated into the production debuggers used by the high-performance community. Discussions will encompass the debugging requirements of traditional vector supercomputing and high-end workstation users, as well as parallel programmers.

Abstracts of the Talks

IVD: An Interactive Visualization Debugger for Parallel Applications

Ming C Hao, Vineet Singh, Alan Karp,
Milon Mackey Jane Chien
Hewlett-Packard Laboratory
Palo Alto, CA.

IVD is an interactive visualization debugging tool which integrates data and performance visualization with the debugging functions. It is an on-going experimental project in Hewlett-Packard. Debugging can be triggered not only by the status of a program's execution (such as an infinite loop) but also by global performance conditions of the parallel application and the underlying parallel processing system (such as poor processor utilization).

IVD is built on a multi-user client-server model. Key features include the ability to use existing sequential visualization and debugging tools to make them like a single debugger to perform standard debugging operations. (e.g., single -step). Users do not need to install a special tool on each workstation. This approach allows users to concentrate on their work without learning new software, providing wide usability to all users in all available system environments.

IVD explores automatic error notification. Based on the specified performance thresholds, IVD alerts users with beeps or flashing lights when an error condition is detected during a run. At that time, the user can stop the program, display the contents of variables or source code, set new values, and resume execution.

IVD uses deterministic replay to preserve message processing order to aid cyclic debugging. Most internal computations in the parallel programs can be different during separate runs on the same input data. This non-deterministic internal behavior is caused by race conditions. It is very difficult or impossible for the user to reproduce the error without deterministic replay.

For ease of use, IVD offers an easy-to-use graphical user interface. Users can simply manage the program during a visualization debugging session by simply pressing buttons.

This talk will present the motivation, design, and a description of the current prototype working with PVM. Examples of its use will be shown.

MulTVision: A Tool for Visualizing Parallel Program Executions

Robert H. Halstead, Jr.
DEC Cambridge Research Lab

MulTVision is a visualization tool that supports both performance measurement and debugging by helping a programmer see what happens during a specific, traced execution of a program. MulTVision has two components: a debug monitor and a replay engine. A traced execution yields a log as a by-product; both the debug monitor and

442

the replay engine use this log as input.

The debug monitor produces a graphical display showing the relationships between tasks in the traced execution. Using this display, a programmer can see bottlenecks or other causes of poor performance. Each task is shown in the debug monitor's display as a horizontal band colored to indicate the changes in the task's state (running, queued, or blocked) over time. Arrows between tasks indicate synchronization and other intertask relationships. Zooming and panning functions allow the user to focus on the task set and time interval of interest. Information of special importance about a task can be noted by laying down a "signpost" on that task at the time of interest, showing information such as the expression whose value the task is computing and the processor on which it is currently running. Signposts are useful for making annotations on the trace, noting significant facts about the trace so they can all be viewed together. Finally, the replay engine can be commanded to perform a replay to the time corresponding to the current cursor position on the debug-monitor display; this capability connects the functions of the debug monitor and the replay engine.

The replay engine can be used to reproduce internal program states that existed during the traced execution. The replay engine uses a novel log protocol -- the "side-effect touch protocol" -- oriented toward programs that are mostly functional (have few side effects). Measurements show that the tracing overhead added to mostly functional programs is generally less than the overhead already incurred for task management and synchronization operations.

The visual complexity of large task displays currently limits MulTVision's effective use to program executions that create at most thousands to tens of thousands of tasks. While there are many interesting programs that can be investigated without exceeding this limit, current work focuses on improving the debug monitor's display to permit working with even larger program executions, as well as increasing the flexibility and range of display styles offered.

On-line Determination of the Safety of Message-Passing Parallel Programs

Robert Cypher Eric Leu
IBM Research Division
Almaden Research Center
650 Harry Road
San Jose, CA 95120, U.S.A.
e-mail: {cypher,leu}@almaden.ibm.com

One of the main reasons that parallel computers are not more widely used is the lack of tools that help the programmer to develop correct, reliable, and portable software. These two last issues are much more crucial in the context of parallel programming than in sequential programming, mainly because parallel programs often exhibit non-deterministic behavior: two executions of the same program with the same input data may lead to different results, or worse, may execute correctly during a first run, and deadlock during another run.

Addressing both reliability and portability, our study aimed at determining the conditions that parallel programs have to satisfy and the properties that the communication subsystem has to provide in order to guarantee deterministic behavior of the programs, regardless of timing variations and properties of the underlying hardware. Focusing on message-passing communication, we have proven that only the following four factors can create non-deterministic program behavior:

o Racing messages. Due to communication delays and message latencies, messages may be received by a process in an order that may change from one execution to another. A message is said to race if there exists two or more receive operations, any one of which could have received the message.

o System buffer dependency. Most existing message-passing protocols use system buffers to improve the performance of the communication subsystem. A program execution is said to be dependent on system buffers if the given execution of the program is impossible on top of a communication subsystem that does not use system buffers.

o Non-deterministic system calls. Interactions with the external environment of the program (e.g. reading the clock, the value of a captor, asking the system for a random number) may result in a non-deterministic behavior of the program.

o Interference between sends. Different send operations issued from multiple source processes to a single destination process are interfering if messages that the receiver does not wish to select can prevent the reception of a message that the receiver does wish to receive.

By defining a safe program execution to be one that is race-free, system buffer independent, and free of non-deterministic system calls, we formally proved that safe executions will behave deterministically on any machine (independent of the system buffers present) if interference between sends is prevented by the communication subsystem. Moreover, we have shown that the safety of an execution can be determined efficiently on-line.

The goal of this talk is to give an overview of our study and its main results. We will present a new program execution model that enables both blocking and non-blocking message-passing communication primitives to be considered, and show how race-free executions and independence from system buffers may be expressed formally in terms of the model. The main results will be discussed, and an efficient algorithm for the on-line determination of the safety of a program execution will be given.

Proposal of a Standard Debugger Server Protocol

Doreen Y. Cheng
Robert T. Hood
NASA Ames Research Center
MS/258-6
Moffett Field, CA 94035
dcheng@nas.nasa.gov
rhood@nas.nasa.gov

Productivity of developing programs on massively parallel computers and a network of workstations can be greatly improved if a common debugging user interface (UI) is provided for the machines. Experience of building a common UI on top of vendor-provided debuggers has revealed the deficiencies of this simple approach. It was found that response time was slow because of unnecessary data transformations performed. In a distributed environment, this problem could be crippling.

A better way of providing a common UI is to split a debugger into two main layers; an application service layer (ASL) and a machine service layer (MSL). The ASL provides a common UI and supports the programming models chosen by an organization which may or may not be supported by a vendor (e.g. message-passing using MPI). An ASL can be developed by a vendor or a user organization. However, the MSL, which should be provided by a vendor, encapsulates the services that depend on machine architecture, operating systems, and compilers. The two layers communicate using a standard protocol.

This approach allows user sites to design common UI that can efficiently carry out debugging tasks on sequential machines, massively parallel machines, and a network of heterogeneous computers. The UI can be designed to suit the specific needs of an organization, freeing vendors from customizing UIs for different users. Furthermore, the modular design of a debugger can greatly reduce the effort by vendors to port it from product to product.

This presentation will describe the scope of the standard, the user operations supported by the protocol, an architecture of a parallel/distributed debugger, the high-level functions of ASL and MSL, and the partitioning of the knowledge between ASL and MSL. A draft of the proposed protocol will be distributed to the interested parties, and discussions will be called for in the following Bird-of-Feather sessions during SC '93.

Semantic Debugging of Programs with Black-Boxes

Zvika Berkovich and Dror Zernik
Technion Israel

Large systems are usually developed using ready-made software modules that are only known by their interface and functionality, while their internal implementation is hidden or even inaccessible. This development strategy is the foundation of software engineering, but it introduces a difficulty in debugging programs which use these "Black-Boxes". To overcome this difficulty, a new debugging strategy is proposed: knowing the predefined functionality of a Black-Box, semantics may be used for describing its run-time behavior. Based on this description high level abstractions that the user understands, can be formed. We extended known semantics into "script language". In this language, the run-time behavior is defined by a combination of basic operations performed by certain program entities (actors or objects), at certain program states.

A prototype was built, based on GDB, which supports this language. In addition, we demonstrate the strength of our approach in debugging X11 programs. The results of our work is a new approach to system debugging, and its implications on the debuggability requirements of software modules.

A Unified Approach to Source Level Debugging of Optimized Code

Orit Edelstein, Yael Gafni, Ron Y. Pinter
Vladimir Rainish, Dror Zernik

The ability to debug highly optimized programs at the source code level is sometimes a requirement and often a desired capability. Meeting this challenge is difficult both when dealing with traditional, mostly machine independent optimizations, such as common subexpression elimination, as well as when introducing transformations such as instruction reordering which are common place with today's superscalar machine architectures. These difficulties manifest themselves both in the areas of control and data, and they touch upon many interesting issues in language processing.

We present a unified framework that allows accurate modelling and effective handling of optimized code so as to support a kernel of debugging primitives. Our main results are:

* A model for statement boundaries which is a natural extension to current computational models that are in use for debugging.

* A method for mapping and tracking of values, includ-

ing algorithms to support it

* An extensive compiler-debugger interface

Part of this approach is an intentional deviation from the traditional computational model as it is reflected by the semantics of debugging operations so as to allow optimizations to take place. Our work is independent of any specific compiler architecture or design, although its details must be tailored to any such system individually. The results are foundational in nature and require further investigation and experimentation.

Toward a Non-Intrusive Approach to Debugging Distributed Memory Programs through Perturbation Analysis

Madalene Spezialetti
EECS Department, 19 Memorial Drive West
Lehigh University, Bethlehem, PA 18015
mspezial@porthos.eecs.lehigh.edu

Rajiv Gupta
Dept. of Computer Science, 211 Mineral Ind. Bldg.
University of Pittsburgh, Pittsburgh, PA 15260
gupta@cs.pitt.edu

The introduction of instrumentation into a program to collect and analyze data for debugging purposes will generally result in some increase in the execution time of the instrumented program. Consequently, the occurrence of some actions of the original program could be delayed. Programs representing distributed memory computations are often non-deterministic in nature and hence the execution of such programs is not only dependent upon the program input, but also on the timing of the execution. Thus, an attempt to monitor the run-time behavior of a distributed program through code instrumentation, such as during debugging, can potentially alter the program's behavior.

In general, any form of execution delay can be considered to be intrusive since it affects the timing behavior of the program. However, if we are interested only in certain aspects of a program's behavior it is usually possible to tolerate some limited form of intrusion. For example, for a non-real time application we may want to observe the execution of the program; however, we may not be interested in the precise timing of various activities. A weaker form of intrusion may be acceptable in this situation. In particular, a perturbation that does not alter the execution of the distributed computation is acceptable. Thus, this work presents an approach to viewing intrusion from the perspective of the potential effects of the instrumentation on the behavior of certain aspects of the program. More precisely, we consider a perturbation to be intrusive if it can delay some of the participants of a non-deterministic computa-

tion in such a way that the outcome of the non-deterministic event can be altered [1]. If none of the participants is delayed or all of the participants are delayed identically, we consider the delay to be non-intrusive.

This talk will present perturbation analysis techniques which were developed to identify the situations in which the run-time monitoring activities can be performed non-intrusively, that is, the techniques determine whether the perturbation of a process at a given point can influence the outcome of a non-deterministic event. The techniques determine the affects of a perturbation under all executions, thus enabling points in a program where monitoring activities can be performed non-intrusively to be identified. The perturbation analysis consists of two phases. First, we determine, for each point in a process, the set of processes with which the process must have directly or indirectly communicated, using deterministic synchronous communication, prior to reaching that point. The second phase analyzes the behavior with respect to a given perturbation. The analysis performed in the second phase adapts the results from the analysis of the first phase and uses the changes in the results to determine whether the perturbation is intrusive. The second phase allows a delay to be analyzed at a small incremental cost following No hardware support is needed to carry out non-intrusive monitoring activities at the identified points.

Knowing those portions of code into which instrumentation can be non-intrusively introduced can be utilized for a variety of purposes. A number of these uses will be discussed, such as debugging programs for performance anomalies, real time behavior, and reducing the interference of debugging by the movement or accumulation of monitoring instrumentation.

Panels

Industrial Research and Development

Ming Hao, Hewlett-Packard Laboratory
Robert Halstead, Jr., DEC Cambridge Research Lab
Eric Leu, IBM Almaden Research Center
Rich Title, Thinking Machines Corporation
Dennis Parker, Cray Research, Incorporated
Don Breazeal, Intel Supercomputer Systems Division

User Needs

Cherri Pancake, Oregon State University
Hugh M. Caffey, BioNumerik Pharmaceticals, Inc.
Dennis Cottel, NCCOSC, RDT&E Division

Session 6:
Panel
Moderator: Linda Stanberry

Parallel C/C++: Convergence or Divergence?

Linda Stanberry, Moderator

Lawrence Livermore National Laboratory

Abstract

C has been noted for its wide portability. C++ is touted as the next generation C. Both languages, however, have multiple proposals for parallel extensions. For C, this includes two different ANSI- sponsored efforts, X3H5 and X3J11.1. Since C++ is itself in the throes of standardization, parallel C++ proposals are finding their audience among MPP vendors and C++ users in an ARPA-sponsored HPC++ consortium. The number of proposals is large and still growing, and questions arise of whether and how these proposals can converge in order to extend/preserve/protect the investment of the user community.

In this panel we will bring together representatives from the ANSI committees, MPP vendors, and from independent research efforts to discuss the motivation for their respective proposals, to determine the interoperability of the proposals, and to argue for or against merging of proposals for a standard.

Topics and viewpoints

This panel will address the on-going exploration of extensions to C and C++ for parallel programming models. There are parallel C dialects for shared memory models, and for data parallel models. There are model-independent dialects. There are language-independent models that are supposed to guide the design of parallel dialects. There are single-threaded models and multi-threaded models. And then there are the parallel C++ dialects that have elements of all the above, but with an object-oriented flavor.

Are all these dialects really necessary, or is this proliferation just the necessary prelude to standardization? Are there clear and sufficient similarities among the dialects to define a standard now, or is it too soon in the evolutionary process to attempt a standard? Will there be multiple standards for multiple models?

Assuming that there will be a parallel C standard and a parallel C++ standard in the not-too-distant future, will they allow or promote language interoperability? Will C++ users be able to utilize C and Fortran libraries? Will users be able to easily port a program written in one dialect to another MPP?

This panel hopes to present the current status of standardization in the parallel C and C++ areas by answering questions such as these. It is expected that many other related questions will be raised in the process.

David Culler will represent an engineering view of parallel programming, as reflected in Split-C. Split-C is a modest parallel extension to C which allows the programmer to minimize the remote access frequency in operations on regular and irregular data structures and to perform the remaining remote accesses efficiently, by overlapping communication and computation. Like C, it adopts the view that the language system should assist, rather than get in the way of performance tuning at the algorithmic level. Its goal is to provide a generic, little language with few surprises.

James Frankel will represent the data parallel approach of Thinking Machine Corporation's C* Language. The C* Language is a superset of Standard C which includes constructs to allow the description, allocation, and layout of parallel data; the manipulation of such parallel data through simple C syntax; additional syntax to deal with which positions of parallel data participate in data operations, performing communication, and operating on aggregate data. It provides an environment in which efficient, debuggable, and maintainable parallel programs may be created. The future direction of C* and how it may be changed by C++ activities will also be presented.

Dennis Gannon will describe several experimental extensions to C++ designed to aid in the construction of parallel programs. pC++ adds a concurrent aggregate class type that provides compatibility with HPFF Fortran and simple generalization of data parallelism for object oriented programs.

Phil Hatcher will represent the proposal being formulated by the Data Parallel C Extensions subgroup of ANSI X3J11.1 (Numerical C Extensions Group). The key goal of this proposal is to extend C to effectively support the data parallel paradigm across a broad spectrum of parallel architectures. A second goal is to maintain the transparency of C: high-cost operations should be explicit in the source code. The current proposal borrows heavily from Thinking Machines Corporation's C*, with numerous extensions, including elemental functions, parallel pointers, nodal functions, and data distribution directives.

448

© 1993 ACM 0-8186-4340-4/93/0011 $1.50

Carl Kesselman will discuss how C++ can be extended to make a general pupose parallel processing language. He will describe Compositional C++ (CC++) developed in conjunction with Mani Chandy. CC++ provides a few simple extensions to the C++ type system and two simple control constructs that together provide an elegant mechanism for thread based concurrency that extends from MPP systems to heterogeneous networks of servers.

James Larus will represent the data parallel research on C** at University of Wisconsin. C** is a slight extension to C++ that introduces aggregates of elements, which can be manipulated by large-grain data parallel functions.

Walter Rudd will represent the C language binding to the language-independent model for parallel programming that is being developed by the ANSI Technical Committee X3H5, Parallel Processing Constructs for High Level Programming Languages. The language-independent model is a shared-memory model that emphasizes procedural decomposition of programs into blocks that can be executed by more than one process. These blocks are further decomposed into regions in which parallel execution can improve performance. The C language binding to the model is an extension to ANSI Standard C that implements the features required by the model.

Panelists

David Culler is an Assistant Professor in the Computer Science Division at UC Berkeley and a Presidential Faculty Fellow. He received an AB (1980) in Mathematics from UC Berkeley, and an MS (1985) and PhD (1989) in Computer Science from M.I.T. His research interests include parallel architectures, programming languages, run-time systems, and models for portable algorithmic design.

James Frankel is a Senior Scientist at Thinking Machines Corporation, Cambridge, MA. He received a BS (1977) from the University of Rochester, and an SM (1979) and PhD (1983) from Harvard University. His research interests include the future direction of parallel programming languages and compilers, and general issues of systems software for massively-parallel distributed memory computers.

Dennis Gannon is an Associate Professor in the Department of Computer Science at Indiana University. He received a PhD (1976) in Mathematics from UC Davis, and a PhD (1980) in Computer Science from University of Illinois, Urbana-Champaign. He is also Research Director at the Center for Innovative Computer Applications at Indiana University.

Phil Hatcher is an Associate Professor of Computer Science at the University of New Hampshire. He received a BS (1978) and MS (1979) from Purdue University, and a PhD (1985) from the Illinois Institute of Technology (1985). He is co-author (with Michael J. Quinn) of the book *Data-Parallel Programming on MIMD Computers* and is Associate Editor of *IEEE Parallel and Distributed*

Technology.

Carl Kesselman is a Senior Research Fellow in the Computer Science Department at California Institute of Technology. He received a PhD in Computer Science from UCLA in 1991. His research interests include parallel programming environments, parallel programming languages and computational biology. He also worked with Dennis Gannon and Mani Chandy to organize the ARPA-sponsored Parallel C++ Workshop in May 1993.

James Larus is an Assistant Professor in the Computer Sciences Department at the University of Wisconsin--Madison. He received an AB (1980) in Applied Mathematics from Harvard University, and an MS (1982) and PhD (1989) in Computer Science from the UC Berkeley. His research interests include parallel programming, programming languages, and compilers.

Walter G. Rudd is Tektronix Professor and Head in the Department of Computer Science at Oregon State University. He received a BA (1966) in Physics and Mathematics from Rice University, and a PhD (1969) in Physical Chemistry from Rice University. He is also Director of the Oregon Advanced Computing Institute and vice-Chair of ANSI X3H5 (Parallel Processing Constructs for High-Level Programming Languages).

Linda Stanberry is a Computer Scientist in the Computation Department at Lawrence Livermore National Laboratory. She received a BA (1976) and MS (1981) from California State University, Northridge. She is also LLNL's representative to X3J11 (C), X3J11.1 (NCEG), and X3J16 (C++), and Numerical Editor for *The Journal of C Language Translation*.

Session 7:
Parallel I/O II
Chair: Helene Kulsrud

Design and Evaluation of Primitives for Parallel I/O *

Rajesh Bordawekar   Juan Miguel del Rosario   Alok Choudhary[†]

Northeast Parallel Architectures Center, 3-201 CST, Syracuse Univ., Syracuse, NY 13244

Abstract

In this paper, we show that the performance of parallel file systems can vary greatly as a function of the selected data distributions, and that some data distributions can not be supported.

We have devised an alternative scheme for conducting parallel I/O - the Two-Phase Access Strategy - which guarantees higher and more consistent performance over a wider spectrum of data distributions. We have designed and implemented runtime primitives that make use of the two-phase access strategy to conduct parallel I/O, and facilitate the programming of parallel I/O operations. We describe these primitives in detail and provide performance results which show that I/O access rates are improved by up to several orders of magnitude. Further, we show that the variation in performance over various data distributions is restricted to within a factor of 2 of the best access rate.

1 Introduction

Parallel computers have become the preferred computational instrument of the scientific community due to their immense processing capacities. Some of the commercially available parallel computers include Intel Paragon [10], nCUBE [13], CM-5 [15].

As scientists expand their models to describe physical phenomena of increasingly large extent, the memory capacity of parallel machines, although immense, become insufficient to contain all the required computational data, and I/O becomes important [1]. Thus, a system with limited I/O capacity can severely limit

the performance of the entire program - this is known as the I/O bottleneck problem. This problem has become critical, and the need for high I/O bandwidth has become significant enough that most parallel computers such as the Intel iPSC/2 [8], Intel iPSC/860 [14], Intel Touchstone Delta [9, 4], and the nCUBE [11] now provide some measure of support for parallel I/O.

The goal of parallel I/O is to provide a bottleneck free communication pathway between the processors and I/O devices. This is made possible in hardware by the scalability of the hardware architecture design. For example, as shown in figure 1, the I/O connections between the processor array and the I/O devices, which are a scalable collection of multiple physical paths of fixed bandwidth, are viewed as a single channel of higher bandwidth. In software, a parallel file system provides increased performance by declustering data across the disk array (a technique called striping) thereby distributing the access workload over multiple servers.

Parallel file systems vary in their level of support for data distribution mappings; some provide no support whatsoever. The inconvenience of having to explicitly specify and control file access for a given data distribution has prompted recent proposals for the inclusion of parallel I/O support primitives into parallel programming languages such us HPF Fortran [7] and Vienna Fortran [2]. These primitives could then be implemented as library routines which accept a description of the desired data distribution from the user, and manage data access based upon the correspondence between the user mapping, and the mapping defined by the parallel file system (i.e., the distribution of data across the disks).

1.1 Contributions of the paper

For experiments presented in this paper we limit overselves to the Intel Touchstone Delta file system called Concurrent File System (CFS). We show that the performance of the CFS can vary greatly as a function of the data distribution. Further, that parallel I/O for certain common data decompositions can

---

*This work was sponsored by ARPA under contract # DABT63-91-C-0028. Alok Choudhary's research is also supported by an NSF Young Investigator Award CCR-9357840. The content of the information does not necessarily reflect the position or the policy of the Government and no official endorsement should be inferred. This research was performed in part using the Intel Touchstone Delta System operated by Caltech on behalf of the Concurrent Supercomputing Consortium. Access to this facility was provided by the Center for Research on Parallel Computation (CRPC).

[†]Also with ECE Dept.

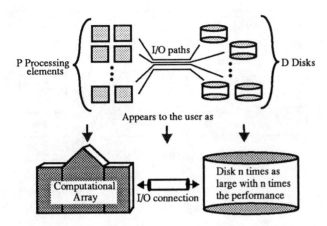

Figure 1: Scalability in computation and I/O

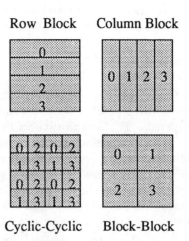

Figure 2: Data Distributions in Fortran 90D/ HPF

not be supported by CFS (i.e., access for these is sequentialized). Based upon these observations, we have devised an alternative scheme for conducting parallel I/O - the two-phase access strategy - which guarantees more consistent performance over a wider spectrum of data distributions [11].

In order to facilitate the programming of parallel I/O operations, we have designed a set of primitives which we have implemented in a runtime library that makes use of the two-phase access strategy. This runtime system supports a number of parallel file systems, thus providing a common I/O interface for parallel programs.

1.2 Organization

The purpose of this paper is to describe the I/O primitives interface design and to present some performance results. The paper has the following organization. In section 2, we overview current parallel language support for data distribution. In section 3, we consider several data decomposition strategies, present performance results for the CFS based upon direct access (i.e., the access strategy used by a typical parallel program on the basis of programmer specified data distribution), and analyze the costs associated with this type of access. Performance results were obtained on the Intel Touchstone Delta [9, 3]. In section 4, we describe the design and implementation of the runtime system employing the two-phase strategy. In section 5, we present experimental performance results for the runtime primitives. Finally, we summarize in section 6.

2 Languages Supporting Data Distribution

We concentrate on parallel programs which use the Single Program Multiple Data (SPMD) programming paradigm for MIMD machines. This is the most widely used model for large-scale scientific and engineering applications. In such applications, parallelism is exploited by a decomposition of the data domain. To achieve load-balance, express locality of access, reduce communication, and other optimizations, several decompositions and data alignment strategies are often used (e.g., block, cyclic, along rows, columns, etc.) (figure 2). To enable such decompositions to be expressed in a parallel program, several parallel programming languages or language extensions have emerged. These languages provide intrinsics that permit the expression of mappings from the problem domain to the processing domain, allow a user to decompose, distribute and align arrays in the most appropriate fashion for the underlying computation. An example of parallel languages which support data distribution includes Vienna Fortran [2], Fortran D [5] and High Performance Fortran or (HPF) [7, 6].

In order to address the I/O bottleneck problem, these languages propose to provide some support for parallel I/O operations. Important examples include Vienna Fortran [2] and High Performance Fortran [7, 6].

3 Analysis of Data Distributions for Parallel I/O

In this section, we will analyze the data mapping from the disks (distributed files) to the compute nodes.

We discuss the I/O costs associated with various data distributions and present experimental results.

3.1 Mapping Problem

In order to perform a mapping from distributed file to processor array, we note that two mappings have to be considered. The organization of the file data over the set of disks represents the first mapping, M1. The second mapping, M2, involves the (more familiar) mapping of data over the set of processing elements. For parallel I/O to take place efficiently, both these mappings must be resolved into a data transfer strategy. Current parallel file systems on the nCUBE/2 [11] and the Intel Touchstone Delta resolve these mappings into a single data transfer mapping which is used to compute proper source and destination addresses during file data access - we call this *direct access*. Problems arise from this approach in cases where the first and second mappings resolve into a data transfer mapping (representing an access strategy) that performs poorly. In succeeding sections, we will show that such problematic mapping pairs are quite common.

The enormous costs associated with such a direct access strategy mapping is illustrated in figure 3. In section 3.3, using the experimental results, we show that this type of access strategy gives very poor performance.

To illustrate a mapping that can not be supported by existing systems, consider a program that has to read data into a distributed array in a Block-Block decomposition (see Figure 2). Suppose that the data is stored over the distributed disks in column-major order. The current Intel CFS (Concurrent File System) could not support this requirement because it does not allow any processor to read data while others idle, this is illustrated in figure 4. The exception to this is mode 0 (independent file pointers to a shared file); this mode would require the programmer to manage file pointer adjustment throughout the program.

3.2 Direct Access Cost Analysis

Since the cost of data access is dominated by per message startup latency, and seek time, the cost of data movement can be evaluated on the basis of the total number of requests needed to complete a transaction (e.g., process of reading in a 4Kx4K matrix into the computational array). Figure 3 illustrates the dependence of the number of requests on data distribution; we see that a Row-Cyclic distribution generates many more requests than a Row-Block distribution.

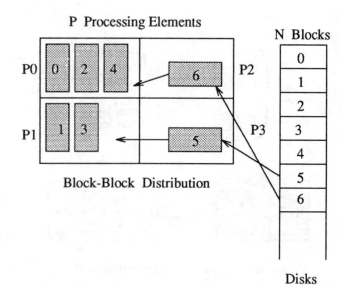

Figure 4: CFS Access for Block-Block Distribution with Column-major Disk Storage Pattern

Table 1: Number of I/O Requests as a Function of Data Distributions for 2-D Arrays.(R_{dist})

Distr. Type	R_{dist}	S_{dist}
Block-Block	$N * \sqrt{P}$	$\frac{N}{\sqrt{P}}$
Block-Cyclic	$N * \sqrt{P}$	$\frac{N}{\sqrt{P}}$
Cyclic-Block	N^2	1
Cyclic-Cyclic	N^2	1

Table 1 shows R_{dist} and S_{dist} for an N*N array distributed over P processors, where R_{dist} is the number of requests per transaction when considering only the data distribution and ignoring contributions from the stripe size; and S_{dist} is the size of the largest contiguous block of data that can be transferred between a processor and an I/O device per request(i.e., request size). In generating the table, it is assumed that the data is stored in a column-major one-dimensional map over the disks.

Thus, the total number of requests for a given transaction, R_{trans}, as a function of both data distribution and stripe size S_{stripe}, can be expressed as

$$R_{trans} = R_{dist} \times \frac{S_{dist}}{min(S_{dist}, S_{stripe})} \qquad (1)$$

Note that the assumption that S_{stripe} equals S_{dist} is equivalent to ignoring stripe size contributions (i.e., assumption in table 1) and that we do obtain the

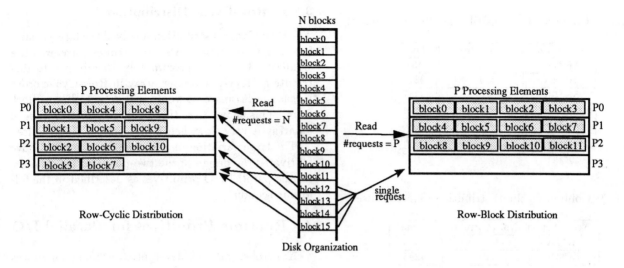

Figure 3: Effects of Distribution upon Number of Requests (M2 Map)

results in the table.

For the following discussion, it is assumed for simplicity that the either S_{stripe} divides S_{dist} or vice versa (i.e., $GCD(S_{stripe}, S_{dist}) = MIN(S_{stripe}, S_{dist})$).

3.3 Direct Access Performance

In this section we present performance results for direct access using various data distributions. The experiments were conducted on an Intel Touchstone Delta. The Delta is a 16x32 mesh structured, 512 processor multicomputer with two disks connected on either side of each row; thus, it has 64 disks.

In these experiments, the mesh size was varied from 4 processors to 512 processors and all 64 disks were used. For each mesh size the data array size was varied; a square two-dimensional array was distributed across the processors. The smallest array used was 1Kx1K (1MByte), and the largest was 20Kx20K (400 MBytes). For each mesh size, the array was distributed in four ways: Row-Block, Row-Cyclic, Column-Block, Column-Cyclic. The larger arrays were distributed over larger mesh sizes such as 256 and 512.

An input file was distributed over 64 disks in a round-robin fashion (32 I/O nodes, 2 disks per I/O node) with a stripe size of 4 Kbytes in column major fashion.

The Concurrent File System (CFS) on the Delta supports several modes of operation, each one determining a degree of synchronization and sharing of file pointers.

For our experiments, we restrict ourselves exclusively to mode 3 (shared file pointer, synchronized ac-

cess) since this gives the best performance for direct access [4].

3.3.1 Column-Block Distribution

This distribution conforms with the column-major data distribution over the disks. It requires a single application level I/O request per processor and each processor node can read the entire distributed data in one I/O access.

Table 2 shows the performance for the Column-Block array distribution. The table shows the size of the array (file on disks), the number of processors participating in the read, the transaction completion time, and the observed bandwidth. For small arrays and number of nodes, the bandwidth of the I/O system is under-utilized. As the data size and number of processors increase, the I/O bandwidth is more effectively utilized. However, beyond a certain point, the I/O system becomes a bottleneck due to the large number of processors performing I/O.

The read rate increased quickly in proportion to the processor grid size, but plateaued at about 64 processors. Degradation in the performance was observed after 256 processors due to a large synchronization overhead.

3.3.2 Column-Cyclic Distribution

Table 3 shows the read access times for the same parameters but with a Column-Cyclic data distribution. Even though the degree of parallelism in the data access remains the same, the number of I/O requests increases because each processor must make an indi-

Table 2: Column Block Distribution (Time in msec)

Array Size	No. of Procs.	Time
1K*1K	4	431
4K*4K	4	2277
5K*5K	16	3357
5K*5K	64	3324
10K*10K	256	13707
20K*20K	512	70953

Table 3: Column Cyclic Distribution (Time in msec)

Array Size	No. of Procs.	Time
1K*1K	4	4353
4K*4K	16	5233
5K*5K	64	11407
10K*10K	256	116763
20K*20K	512	252980

vidual request for each column. This increases the access time as illustrated in table 3. The drop in performance versus the Column-Block distribution is consistent for all configurations and it ranges between a factor of 2 to 10.

3.3.3 Row-Block Distributions

Table 4 shows the performance for a Row-Block distribution. This read operation essentially involves a transposition of the data as it is being read from the disks. Table 1 shows that the number of logical requests is NxP for this decomposition. We observe from table 4 that the performance degradation due to the decomposition is almost two orders of magnitude when compared to that of the Column-Block distribution.

We do not present performance figures for larger configurations (i.e., large array and system sizes) since the time to complete these experiments exceeded practical limits.

Table 4: Row Block Distribution (Time in msec)

Array Size	No. of Procs.	Time
1K*1K	4	17051
2K*2K	4	25966
4K*4K	16	71205
5K*5K	16	91536
5K*5K	64	38018

3.3.4 Row-Cyclic Distribution

The Row-Cyclic distribution involved the largest number of I/O requests. Also the request size was the smallest. It took approximately 15 minutes to distribute a 1Kx1K character array in Row-Cyclic order versus the 467 msec. it would require in Column-Block form. This shows that the direct row distribution of an array is very slow, hence, not possible in practice.

The large variation in performance observed above motivated the design of the two-phase access strategy for the parallel I/O primitives as described in the following section.

4 Runtime Primitives for Parallel I/O

A number of high level programming languages have recently introduced intrinsics that support parallel I/O through a runtime library. By using these primitives, I/O operation instructions within applications become portable across various parallel file systems. Further, the primitives are convenient to use; the instructions for carrying out parallel I/O operations don't involve much more than a declaration of the data decomposition mapping and the use of open, close, read, and write routines

Yet, these language supported I/O primitives suffer from a serious drawback. Because they use a direct access mechanism to perform the I/O, the user data distribution mapping remains tightly linked to the file mapping to disks. Thus, they are susceptible to the same performance fluctuations and limitations (e.g., unsupported data distributions) that are observed of the parallel file systems.

Motivated by these facts we have implemented a runtime system for parallel I/O. This system will provide the portability and convenience of language supported I/O primitives. In addition, because it makes use of the two-phase access strategy (discussed below) to carry out I/O, it effectively decouples user mappings from the file mappings of the parallel file system, and provides consistently high performance independent of the data decompositions used.

Advantages of Runtime I/O Primitives:

1. The runtime system can be easily ported on various machines which provide parallel file systems.

2. Complex data distributions (Block-Block or Block-Cyclic) are made available to the user.

3. Primitives allow the user to control the data mapping over the disks. This is a significant advantage since the user can vary the

number of disks to optimize the data access time.

4. The primitives allow the programmer can change the data distribution on the processors dynamically.

5. The data access time is significantly improved and is made more consistent since the primitives use two-phase access strategy.

4.1 Approach

Our I/O strategy involves a division of the parallel I/O task into two separate phases. In the first phase, we perform the parallel data access using a data distribution, stripe size, and set of reading nodes (possibly a subset of the computational array) which conforms with the distribution of data over the disks (i.e, we introduce an intermediate mapping $M2'$, and access data with $M2' = M1$). On Touchstone Delta, the column-block distribution is the conformal mapping. Hence we access (read/write) the data from the disks using this mapping. Subsequently, in phase two, we redistribute the data at run-time to match the application's desired data distribution (i.e., from $M2'$ to M2).

By employing the two-phase redistribution strategy, the costs inherent in many of the I/O configurations are avoided. The redistribution phase improves performance because it can exploit the higher bandwidths made available by the higher degree of connectivity present within the interconnection network of the computational array.

In the subsection that follows, we discuss the run-time I/O primitives. A brief description of the purpose of each primitive, its functional flow, and syntax is provided followed by some performance results.

4.2 General Description

The runtime primitives library provides a set of simple I/O routines. These include **popen, pclose, array_map, proc_map, pread** and **pwrite**. Though the exact syntax of these routines varies from C to Fortran, the basic data structures remain the same. This section presents a brief overview of each primitives. Syntax description and implementation details are presented in [3].

4.2.1 popen

The **popen** primitive concurrently opens a file using a specified number of processors P' ($P' \in P$, where P

Table 5: The File Descriptor Array (FDA): Fortran Version

Unit	Access	Form	Status	No. of disks	No. of procs
3	0	0	1	64	4

is the number of processors on which the program is executing). The choice of P' is important in the systems like Intel Paragon [10] which provide I/O dedicated compute nodes. That is, often the number of processors involved in generating I/O requests must be smaller than the number of processors requiring the data to achieve better performance [4].

The user passes file information to the **popen** primitive which is then stored in a two dimensional array called File Descriptor Array(FDA) using the file unit number as a key. The file information includes file name, file status, file form, access pattern and the number of disks on which the file will be distributed. For a statement

call **popen**(3,'TEST','SEQUENTIAL, 'UNFORMATTED','NEW',-1,4)

opens a file called TEST over 4 processors. The corresponding FDA is shown in table 5. The file will be distributed over all the disks (number_of_disks = -1). If the number_of_processors is -1, the file will be opened by default number of processors (P).

4.2.2 pclose

The **pclose** primitive performs concurrent closing of the parallel files. The **pclose** primitive gets the unit number of the file as an input. Using this as a key, the primitive obtains the number of processors (P'). Using the file unit number, these processors close the file.

4.2.3 array_map

This primitive is semantically similar to the compiler directives in HPF or VF. A Fortran D or HPF compiler would directly extract this information from the distribution directives.

The **array_map** primitive returns an integer called **array descriptor** which will be used by **pread** and **pwrite** routines for acquiring the necessary array information. A table called the Array Description Table or (ADT) is used to store the array information. The user provides the global size of the array, the distribution type, the processor distribution along each

Table 6: The Array Description Table (ADT)

Info	1	2	3	4	5	6	7
Global Size	64	64	-1	-1	-1	-1	-1
Distr. Code	1	1	-1	-1	-1	-1	-1
Block Size	-1	-1	-1	-1	-1	-1	-1
nprocs	2	2	-1	-1	-1	-1	-1

dimension and the block size (for CYCLIC distributions).

For example, consider array A(64,64) distributed in BLOCK-BLOCK form over 4 processor arranged in 2*2 mesh. The corresponding Array Description Table is shown in table 6. The value -1 is used to denote don't-care entries.

4.2.4 proc_map

The **proc_map** primitive is used for mapping the processors from the physical to the logical domain. The proc_map initializes the logical processor grid according to the user specifications. The dimension of the logical processor grid can vary from 1 to 7. The *proc_map* routine allows two kinds of mappings, one is the system-defined mapping and the second is the user-defined mapping. The user has to pass the number of processors in each dimension, the mapping mode and (or) processor mapping information. **proc_map** initializes a global data structure called P_INFO array, which is used by **pread** and **pwrite** routines. Using the **proc_map** primitive the programmer can change the logical processor configuration during the execution of the program.

4.2.5 pread

The **pread** primitive reads a distributed array from the corresponding file. The **pread** primitive reads the data from the file using P' processors and distributes the data over P processors ($P' \in P$). The **pread** primitive uses the unit number as a key to access the file information from the FDA. The global array information is obtained using the array_descriptor. In general, the runtime system would use a distribution for intermediate access which performs the best, given a specific file distribution. For our experiments, we use column-block distribution for I/O access because we assume that the files are stored in the column-major fashion on the disk arrays. The two-phase access is used by **pread** to read the data from the file using P' processors. Then the data is redistributed over the

1. Read the input parameters.
2. Get the global array information using ADT.
3. Obtain the logical mapping of the processors (P) participating in array distribution from proc_map.
4. Use the unit number to acquire information on the file such as the number of disks, number of processors (P').
5. If the target data distribution is same as the conformal access distribution and $P' = P$ then read the data using the same distribution, go to 10.
6. If the two-phase data access is used, then read the data using the conforming distribution. The reading is performed by P' processors.
7. From the global array distribution, calculate the data that needs to be communicated.
8. Compute the communication schedule for data redistribution.
9. Distribute the data over P processors to obtain the target data distribution.
10. Stop.

Figure 5: pread Algorithm

P processors to obtain the target data distribution. Figure 5 shows the **pread** algorithm.

4.2.6 pwrite

The **pwrite** primitive is used to write a distributed array using P' processors to the file that was opened (created) by popen. The **pwrite** uses the array_descriptor to get the array information, the unit number to get the file information and **proc_map** to obtain the logical grid information. The runtime primitive will choose a distribution for intermediate access which performs the best for a specific file distribution. If the processor distribution and the conformal distribution don't match, data is first distributed from P to P' processors. After the distribution, data is written by P' processors using the conforming distribution. Figure 6 shows the **pwrite** algorithm.

4.3 A Sample Program

This section provides a sample Touchstone Delta Fortran program using the I/O primitives (Figure 7). The programmer wants to read and write an array in the column-cyclic fashion. The two dimensional array A(64,64) is distributed over 4 processors. Thus the size of the local array is A(64,16). The ADT and the FDA are initiated as the arrays A_INFO and F_INFO respectively. The file TEST is opened by 4 processors

1. Read the input parameters.
2. Get the global array information using ADT.
3. Obtain proc_map to obtain the logical mapping of the processors (P) participating in array distribution.
4. Use the unit number to acquire information on the file such as number of disks, number of processors (P').
5. If the target data distribution is same as the conformal access distribution and $P' = P$ then write the data using the same access distribution, go to 11.
6. If the two-phase data access is used, then redistribute the data over P' processors using 7,8,9.
7. From the global array information, calculate the data that needs to be communicated.
8. Compute the communication schedule for data distribution.
9. Distribute the data over P' processors in conforming access fashion.
10. Write the data on the disks using the conforming access distribution.
11. Stop.

Figure 6: pwrite Algorithm

```
PROGRAM EXAMPLE
size_info(7),distr_info(7),block_size(7),proc_info(7)
A(64,16),ad,array_map,mybuffer
TEMP(1024),mymap(1536)
COMMON /INFO/ F_INFO,P_INFO,A_INFO
size_info(1)=64 size_info(2)=64
distr_info(1)=0 distr_info(2)=2
block_size(1)=-1 block_size(2)=-1
proc_info(1)=1 proc_info(2)=4
call proc_map(proc_info,0,mymap)
call popen(3,'TEST',0,0,0,-1,-1) !Old File
ad = array_map('A',size_info,distr_info,
block_size,proc_info)
call pread(A,64,16,ad,3,TEMP,iobuffer)
Use a temporary buffer called TEMP of size iobuffer.
Computation Starts here
................
call pwrite(A,64,16,ad,3,TEMP,iobuffer)
call pclose(3)
END
```

Figure 7: A Sample Program For Performing Parallel I/O

using the **popen** primitive. The file TEST will be distributed over the default number of disks (number of disks = -1). The programmer then initializes the processor grid using the **proc_map** primitive. The user passes 0 as the map-mode, thus initiating the system mapping. In this case, the user supplied map (using the mymap array) will be ignored. The **array_map** primitive will be used to obtain the global array information. The array_map returns the array-descriptor "ad" which is used in the **pread** and **pwrite** primitives. The **pread** primitive will read the array A from the file associated with the unit 3 using the conformal access distribution. (e.g. for Touchstone Delta column-block distribution). Since the resultant distribution is column-cyclic, the data will be redistributed over 4 processors to obtain the resultant column-cyclic distribution. Note the convenience offered to the programmer by the primitive because the user no longer needs to worry about pointer manipulations, file distribution, buffering etc. After computation, the array A will be written into the file associated with the unit 3 using **pwrite**. Since the processor distribution is not same as the conformal distribution, **pwrite** will redistribute the data from column-cyclic to corresponding conformal distribution (column-block) and then write the array to the file using the column-block distribution (conformal distribution for Touchstone Delta).

5 Experimental Results

In this section we present performance results for the runtime primitives when used in conjunction with a variety of data distributions. The tables below contain Best Read, Redistribute, Total Read, and Direct Read times for the four 1-dimensional distributions considered in this paper.

For a given array size, the Best Read time represents the minimum of the read times of the four distributions; the Best Read time is derived from the distribution that most closely conforms to the disk storage distribution for the given file. The Redistribution time is the time it takes to redistribute data from the conforming distribution to the one desired by the application. The Total Read time is the sum of the Best Read and Redistribution times; it denotes the time it takes for the data to be read using the optimal Read access and then be redistributed (two-phase access). The Direct Read time is the time it takes to read the data with the selected distribution using direct access. The last row of each table shows the speedup obtained from using the two-phase access strategy over the direct access strategy. Note that the Block-Block distribution is not supported by CFS, hence tables 11 and 12 do not present any performance numbers for direct access. (1 denotes Column Block access, 2 column

Table 7: Comparing Direct Access with Two-phase Access (16 Processors, 5K*5K Array, time in msec)

Distr Mode	Best Read	Re Distr.	Total Read	Direct Read	Speedup
1	3357	-	**3357**	3357	**1**
2	3357	1805	**5162**	9890	**1.92**
3	3357	673	**4030**	69939	**17.36**
4	3357	2603	**5960**	*	**> 604**

Table 8: Comparing Direct Access with Two-phase Access (16 Processors, 10K*10K Array, time in msec)

Distr. Mode	Best Read	Re Distr.	Total Read	Direct Read	Speedup
1	10376	-	**10376**	10376	**1**
2	10376	7105	**17481**	19271	**1.10**
3	10376	2772	**13148**	84683	**6.44**
4	10376	10320	**20696**	*	**> 173**

Table 9: Comparing Direct Access with Two-phase Access (64 Processors, 5K*5K Array, time in msec)

Distr. Mode	Best Read	Re Distr.	Total Read	Direct Read	Speedup
1	3324	-	**3324**	3357	**1**
2	3324	703	**4027**	11407	**2.83**
3	3324	246	**3570**	38018	**10.65**
4	3324	768	**4092**	*	**> 879**

Table 10: Comparing Direct Access with Two-phase Access (64 Processors, 10K*10K Array, time in msec)

Distr. Mode	Best Read	Re Distr.	Total Read	Direct Read	Speedup
1	11395	-	**11395**	11395	**1**
2	11395	2478	**13873**	63400	**4.57**
3	11395	1028	**11623**	78767	**6.78**
4	11395	3092	**14487**	*	**> 248**

cyclic access, 3 denotes Row Block and 4 represents Row cyclic access.)

Tables 7 and 8 show access times for 5Kx5K and 10Kx10K arrays, read and distributed over 16 processors respectively. The Best Read time occurs for the Column-Block distribution. For all cases below, the '*' symbol denotes a read time on the order of hours. The following observations are made by comparing the direct access read times with run-time data redistributions. For all cases, the performance improvement range from a factor of 2 up to several orders of magnitude. For example, in table 7 the amount of overhead avoided by using the redistribution strategy (i.e., the difference between the Total Read Time and Direct Read Time) ranges from 1.7 secs, to well over 60 minutes for the 5K Row-Cyclic case. More importantly, the deviation in Total Read time is at most a factor of 1.9 as opposed to the widely varying results produced by the direct access approach.

Tables 9 and 10 shows access times for 5Kx5K and 10Kx10K arrays, read and distributed over 64 processors. The reduction in cost ranged from 7.4 secs, to over 60 minutes for the 5Kx5K Row-Cyclic case. Note that the variation in Total Read time is again very small (at most a factor of 1.27). However, for all the four types of distribution, the total read time is nearly consistent (of the same order). Thus using the two-phase access we are able to get the data distribution performance which is independent of both the disk distribution and the processor distribution.

Tables 11 and 12 show access times for arrays distributed in the Block-Block fashion over 16 and 64 processors respectively. Again, note that the read time is consistent with the times obtained for other distributions.

5.1 Discussion

The results above show that for every case, regardless of the desired data distribution, performance is improved to within a factor of 2 of the Best Read Time performance for all distributions. Further, the cost of redistribution is small compared with the Total Read Times. This indicates an effective exploitation of the additional degree of connectivity available within the interconnection network of the computational array. Further, the results also show that by using the run-time primitives, the data can be distributed in Block-Block fashion effectively.

Table 11: Block-Block Distribution over 16 Processors using the Runtime Primitives (time in msec)

Size	Best Read	Redistr.	Total Read
1K*1K	467	112	579
2K*2K	717	416	1133
4K*4K	2328	1253	3181

Table 12: Block-Block Distribution over 64 Processors using the Runtime Primitives(time in msec)

Size	Best Read	Redistr.	Total Read
1K*1K	350	82	432
2K*2K	1100	186	1286
4K*4K	2462	577	3039

6 Conclusions

The need for high performance parallel I/O has become critical enough that most manufacturer's have provided some support for parallel I/O within their file systems. Recently, several high performance languages have proposed the inclusion of primitives to support parallel I/O.

We have shown that, using the direct access approach made available by production file systems, performance of existing file systems are inconsistent and depends upon both the data distribution and the file mapping to disk. We provide an example of how support for some of the more complex data distributions may not be provided. Also, we describe how programming language extensions, although simplifying the programming, do not alleviate the problems that exist within the file system.

We presented a set of runtime primitives which make use of the two-phase access strategy, and showed that the runtime primitives achieve consistent performance across a variety of data distributions, and allows the user to avail of complex data distributions such as Block-Block and Block-Cyclic. Further, the primitives allow the user to choose a subset of processors for performing I/O in order to optimize access on the basis of the selected data distribution.

References

[1] Alok Choudhary, Parallel I/O Systems, *Journal of Parallel and Distributed Computing*, January/February 1993.

[2] P. Brezany, M. Gerndt, P. Mehrotra, and H. Zima. Concurrent File Operations in a High Performance Fortran. *Supercomputing'92*, pages 230-238, November 1992.

[3] Rajesh Bordawekar. Issues in Software Support for Parallel I/O. Master's Thesis, ECE. Dept., Syracuse University, May 1993.

[4] Rajesh Bordawekar, Juan Miguel del Rosario, and Alok Choudhary. An Experimental Performance Evaluation of Touchstone Delta Concurrent File System. *ICS'93*, pages 367-377, July 1993.

[5] Geoffrey Fox, Seema Hiranandani, Ken Kennedy, Uli Kremer, and Chau-Wen Tseng. Fortran D Language Specification. Technical Report Rice COMP TR90-141. Rice University, December 1990.

[6] Zeki Bozkus, Alok Choudhary, Geoffrey Fox, Tomasz Haupt, and Sanjay Ranka. Fortran 90D/HPF Compiler for Distributed Memory MIMD Computers: Design, Implementation, and Performance Results. *Supercomputing'93* (to appear), November 1993.

[7] High Performance Fortran Forum. High Performance Fortran Language Specification Version 1.0. Technical Report CRPC-TR92225. CRPC, Rice University, January 1993.

[8] James C. French, Terrence W. Pratt, and Mriganka Das. Performance Measurement of the Concurrent File System of the Intel iPSC/2 Hypercube. *Journal of Parallel and Distributed Computing*, January/February 1993.

[9] Intel. Touchstone Delta System Description. Intel Advanced Information, Intel Corporation, 1991.

[10] Intel. Paragon XP/S System Description. Intel Advanced Information, Intel Corporation, 1992.

[11] Juan Miguel del Rosario. High Performance Parallel I/O System. *Institute of Electronics, Information and Communication Engineers Transactions*, Japan, August 1992.

[12] Juan Miguel del Rosario, Rajesh Bordawekar, and Alok Choudhary. A Two-Phase Strategy for Achieving High-Performance Parallel I/O. Technical Report, SCCS-408, NPAC, December 1992.

[13] nCUBE. nCUBE-2 Systems: Technical Overview. Technical Report, nCUBE Corporation, 1992.

[14] Paul Pierce. A Concurrent File System for a Highly Parallel Mass Storage System. *Fourth Conference on Hypercube Concurrent Computers and Applications*, pages 155-160, 1989.

[15] Thinking Machines Corp. CM-5 System Description. Technical Report, Thinking Machines Corporation, 1991.

Applications-Driven Parallel I/O *

N. Galbreath[†]   W. Gropp   D. Levine

Mathematics and Computer Science Division
Argonne National Laboratory
Argonne, IL 60439-4801

Abstract

We investigate the needs of some massively parallel applications running on distributed-memory parallel computers at Argonne National Laboratory and identify some common parallel I/O operations. For these operations, routines were developed that hide the details of the actual implementation (such as the number of parallel disks) from the application, while providing good performance. An important feature is the ability for the application programmer to specify that a file be accessed either as a high-performance parallel file or as a conventional Unix file, simply by changing the value of a parameter on the file open call. These routines are examples of a parallel I/O abstraction that can enhance development, portability, and performance of I/O operations in applications. Some of the specific issues in their design and implementation in a distributed-memory toolset are discussed.

1 Introduction

In order to run Grand Challenge computational science applications on massively parallel processor (MPP) systems in a production mode, both high-performance parallel I/O systems and programmer-friendly software will be required. Unfortunately, I/O systems and software have been largely neglected by both high-performance computing researchers and vendors. Issues such as I/O as a bottleneck, the scalability of I/O architectures, and ease of use of I/O software remain largely unexplored. There has been little experimental study of I/O access patterns and types of usage, particularly in the context of scientific computing. We believe the first step in developing

appropriate parallel I/O (PIO) software is an analysis of the I/O requirements of a few key application domains. An equally important second step is the evaluation of different implementation strategies. In this paper we report on the results of a study of parallel I/O requirements at Argonne National Laboratory (ANL) and a distributed-memory system we have developed to support these requirements. In order to meet the requirements, this system has been designed to provide high-level I/O operations, such as "write array to parallel file," rather than the more elemental I/O operations, such as "write byte stream to parallel file." This approach has the advantage that, to the applications programmer, parallel I/O does not appear very different from sequential I/O. This simplifies the process of developing and debugging a program, as well as investigating various algorithms for implementing the high-level parallel I/O operation. Del Rosario and Choudhary [3] provide a recent overview of many issues in high-performance parallel I/O.

This paper is laid out as follows. In Section 2 we discuss the types of I/O being done in some computational science applications at ANL and the methods we use to abstract out the main ideas. In Section 3 we describe the `PETSc/Chameleon` package used in our implementation and the parallel I/O routines we have developed. Finally, in Section 4 we make some concluding remarks and discuss our future plans.

2 I/O Requirements of Computational Science Applications

2.1 Types of I/O Usage

To decide what types of parallel I/O functionality we wanted in our system, we began by examining the I/O requirements of various Grand Challenge computational science applications at ANL that were running on distributed-memory computers. We chose to

---

*This work was supported by the Office of Scientific Computing, U.S. Department of Energy, under Contract W-31-109-Eng-38.

[†]Current address: Boston University.

focus on the I/O needs of the applications rather than the expression of those needs in current code so as to avoid being biased by code written for existing I/O interfaces.

Applications perform I/O for various reasons. The most obvious is to output the results the program computes. Some other reasons are to initialize the program, to hold in temporary scratch files data structures that do not otherwise fit in main memory, and to save the state of a job so that it can be restarted later. While each of these requirements is routinely handled in a sequential program, MPP systems raise a number of questions. Among these are the following: What programming model is being used? Should all processors write to the same file, or each to its own file? In what format should the data be stored (e.g., different formats may be needed depending on whether the program is being debugged or run in production mode)? Below we provide more detail about the I/O requirements of computational science applications at ANL.

2.1.1 Input

Most programs need to read some data to initialize a computation. The input data varies in size from small files containing a few important parameters to large data files that initialize key arrays and databases. Also, some applications require periodic input, such as boundary information or other datasets that occur at some interval for the duration of a run, *not* just initially.

Key questions include whether a replicated or distributed data structure is being read, and if a distributed data structure is being read, which data to map to which processors, and whether each processor executes the read or whether only one processor executes the read (and broadcasts to all others, in the case of a distributed-memory programming model).

One application at Argonne is mesoscale climate modeling. Future work with this model will investigate four-dimensional data assimilation. This involves input of data from observations and potentially also weather radar. This data may be obtained in real time or from tape. It is quite likely that the speed and frequency of this data acquisition will become the limiting step in the calculations unless the I/O capabilities of the MPP machines being used can keep pace with CPU performance.

2.1.2 Debugging

A common need for performing I/O arises when debugging a parallel program. We note in particular the somewhat complicated case where the parallel calculation of a distributed data structure is being compared with the same calculation done by the original sequential program. Questions arise as to how to write the parallel data structure so that it may "easily" be compared with the sequential calculations and so that the differences may be "easily" isolated.

As one example, an electromagnetics code in use at ANL solves a nonlinear problem by repeatedly solving a system of linear equations. In the parallel program the matrix is distributed by rows. At each nonlinear iteration, an iterative parallel linear solver is called to solve the current system of equations. From the solution a new matrix is generated and solved, and this process continues until convergence. Debugging the parallel code required comparing of the sequential and parallel versions of the matrix to see whether they were the same. In a second example, subtle boundary condition errors were occurring on the faces of a cube in a three-dimensional superconductivity code. Again, to isolate the parallel bug required comparisons of the sequential and parallel values of those faces, which changed each time step.

It is typical in debugging a sequential program to compare results before and after a "fix". On Unix systems a common way to do this is using the diff command to test for differences. An aim of our system is to provide the user the capability when debugging to have a parallel file written in a conventional Unix format so that traditional debugging methods may be used.

2.1.3 Scratch Files

Scratch files are often used to hold data structures containing intermediate calculations that do not fit into main memory or that a user does not wish to recompute. Speed of access and file size are usually the important considerations for these files.

For example, at the heart of a computational chemistry program is an iterative algorithm to compute the lowest eigenvector and eigenvalue of a large, sparse symmetric matrix. The algorithm requires the computation of matrix-vector products of the matrix with various trial vectors. The matrix is not stored, but rather the matrix-vector products are computed using knowledge of the underlying structure of the matrix. However, the trial vectors and corresponding matrix-vector products must be stored during the iterative procedure. These vectors are stored by distributing them across the memories of the processors. In order to study larger molecular systems, an efficient means to handle larger vectors must be developed. This will require paging of the distributed vectors to secondary storage, and caching in main memory only a small fraction of these vectors at each node. For such a scheme to work, the algorithms, software, and hardware involved must be efficient and robust so that the I/O activity involved at each iteration does not become an overwhelming bottleneck.

A similar storage requirement arises in the n-body portion of a computational biology application. A portion of the calculation requires the determination of forces on the atoms resulting from quantum mechanical effects. The calculation of the quantum mechanical effects can require the evaluation of tens of millions of integrals. Since the value of these integrals remains constant for a particular configuration of atoms, a tradeoff is to either store the integrals to disk or recalculate them in order to avoid expensive I/O accesses. The number of integrals required increases as the cube of the number of electrons. The ability to access these integrals from main memory can make a difference in calculation speed by at least one to two orders of magnitude. Hence, the type of calculations that are feasible is partly limited by the I/O access speed.

2.1.4   Checkpoint/Restart

For long-running production codes, it is desirable to have the ability to save the state of the computation in order to continue computing from that point at a later date. Most operating systems on traditional, sequential high-performance computers provide such a capability at the operating system level. Sometimes an application may have such a facility built into the logic of the program.

In a distributed-memory context, a checkpoint requires saving one or more distributed arrays as well as (usually replicated) scalars. A key question is whether to save to one file or many and, if so, in what order. Another consideration is, whether the restart can be done *independently* of the number of processors the checkpoint was taken on. This is the most general case. However, it requires that only one checkpoint file be written. This in turn requires that the distributed data structures be written to a single file in their natural sequential format. Most users implementing their own parallel checkpoint/restart capabilities have tried to avoid this single file approach because of the code complexity involved in having each processor calcu-

late the global location(s) for its data values. As a result, most current checkpoint/restart efforts *are* dependent upon the number of processors used. Finally, an additional complication arises if checkpoint/restart capabilities are already designed and deeply incorporated within an existing sequential code. Here, the parallel programmer is faced with the prospect of ripping out all the old sequential code and designing a new parallel version.

2.1.5   Output

Output from a program takes many forms; it can be a small file with a few results or a large file containing all the values from several arrays. Sometimes the output is postprocessed and only a small subset of the data actually used. Often time-dependent data is involved, and large files are generated periodically.

As examples, two codes used to model high-temperature superconductivity and global climate change, respectively, at ANL are time-dependent and three-dimensional. In both codes, the algorithmic kernel is the numerical solution of a time-dependent partial differential equation. The main computational data structure is a grid, and users are interested in the value of one or more parameters defined at each grid point.

These codes produce several types of output: (1) "small" result files containing the values of a few "interesting" parameters every k time steps; (2) files containing those "interesting" parameters sampled more frequently and output in a form for use in a postprocessing tool that plots the value of the parameter as a function of the time step; and (3) files that hold results for each grid point for several different parameters of interest. An individual file is created for each discrete time step, and the results are analyzed with the aid of a postprocessing graphics package.

2.2   I/O Abstractions

Abstraction is a key idea in contemporary computer science. The idea is to use a series of layers so that the higher layers mask the inconvenience of working directly with the lower layers. A common example is the translation of high-level languages to assembly language and then to machine code. Abstractions are also commonly used in I/O where, for the high-level language programmer, they can hide details such as buffering, actual layout of a file on a device, or even the type of storage media being used.

We believe abstractions to be even more important for parallel I/O because of the additional complications. First, there are hardware considerations. Modern parallel systems have a wide variety of storage devices intended to provide both high-performance and large capacity. Currently, there are as many approaches to parallel I/O on MPP systems as there are MPP vendors. Second are the software considerations. Parallel computing introduces a number of new concepts such as distributed and replicated data structures. This situation is further complicated by the wide variety of parallel programming models in current use.

One decision that must be made early in the design of a parallel file system is how the bytes are mapped from the application to the file. For example, a simple striping system to eight disks may say that the jth byte of the file is placed on disk ($j/blocksize$) mod 8. This mapping is determined at the time a file is opened; some proposals for parallel file systems provide ways for the user to control the mapping on a file basis. We have observed that often it is more convenient if the mapping is based on the object rather than a file. For example, two arrays written to the same file may have different "natural" mappings. An example of such a case includes adaptive computations where the size of the data may vary during the computation. Crockett [2] classifies a number of parallel file organizations.

Our aim is to analyze many computational science applications at ANL and abstract out of them common hardware and software requirements. In the case of hardware, our approach is to give the user a common set of calls that will work across all or most commercial MPP machines and workstation clusters. The user need not be concerned whether the underlying implementation stripes a file across parallel disks or uses high-speed tape. Also, since the calls are portable across systems, a particular vendor's hardware is hidden from the user.

In the case of software, analysis of the types of I/O usage in computational science applications identified several common themes, including reading and writing a replicated value (scalar or array), and reading and writing a partitioned and distributed array. Accordingly, it is this functionality that we seek in our system by providing subroutine calls that allow the user not to have to be concerned with issues such as deciding which processor will write a replicated value, calculating the location in a file for each distributed array element, and handling processor synchronization. We also wish to provide the user the ability to open a parallel file as if it were a regular sequential file. Finally, by providing a portable set of calls, we free the user from having to learn each parallel computer vendor's parallel I/O interface.

3 Parallel I/O Programming Interface

3.1 Distributed Data Structures

Our initial implementation of this work has been done in the context of the distributed-memory programming model. In this model a global data structure is decomposed among the memories of the individual processors. The individual parts of this distributed data structure are then operated on in parallel. A common instance of this in many scientific and engineering applications is the single program, multiple data (SPMD) model. In the SPMD model each processor executes a copy of the same program on the data in its memory.

We assume there are several kinds of data of interest. For example, there is replicated data, such as scalar values or small arrays that exist in duplicate in each processor's memory. Also, there are arrays that have been partitioned and distributed across the processor memories. Another type of data is where each processor has a large block of contiguous data. Additional kinds of data include arrays on a subset of the processors, more general data layouts (such as data from an irregular mesh), and more complicated data elements (such as structures rather than individual reals or integers). Rather than try to predict all possible data arrangements, we have chosen to support, at a high level, those operations needed in our applications. Our implementations of the low-level I/O operations are intended to be more general, but as a result are significantly more difficult to use.

3.2 The PETSc/Chameleon Package

Our parallel I/O system has been implemented in the context of the PETSc/Chameleon package. The PETSc/Chameleon [4] package is a collection of routines that provide a hierarchy of models for parallel programming on distributed-memory parallel computers. These routines are intended to provide a consistent, easy-to-use model of message-passing that enables access to all of the power of a distributed-memory computer. This package supports both native (vendor) communications libraries and several popular "portable" communications packages. The "portable" packages supported include p4, PICL, and PVM; The PETSc/Chameleon package runs on any system that these packages support. Of these, p4 [1] supports the widest variety of systems, including workstations and massively parallel computers.

The PETSc/Chameleon package currently comprises hundreds of routines, mostly in C. It provides support for a variety of common message-passing primitives and provides routines that support collective operations that involve a collection of processors including all processors and subsets of all processors.

3.3   Overview of Parallel I/O Routines

All of the parallel I/O routines are organized as follows. First, a parallel file is opened with PIFopen; this specifies the kind of parallel file (see below) and returns a file descriptor (or context) that is used in all of the other parallel I/O routines. This corresponds to an fopen in C or, more approximately, an OPEN in Fortran. At this point, the action of the parallel routines may be modified in much the same way that C permits a FILE to be modified with routines such as setbuf. Next, actual input and output are performed by using routines for specific operations such as "output a distributed array" or "read in a scalar." Finally, the parallel file is closed with PIFclose.

3.3.1   Function Calls

The PIFopen call opens a parallel file for future use. It must be called before any parallel I/O commands are issued. It returns a file pointer to be used in all subsequent PIO calls. Two important parameters are processors, which allows the specification of which set of processors will be involved in any subsequent PIO calls (typically, but not always, this will be all processors), and ftype, which (like low-level C open commands) allows specification of what mode the file should be open in. Our goal with the ftype parameter is to provide a "parallel" mode where the parallel file will be opened for access in whatever way provides the highest possible I/O performance. The actual implementation will be highly vendor-specific. In the "as-sequential" mode the parallel file will be a conventional Unix file. The PIFclose call closes a file and frees any buffers allocated to it.

The PIFWriteCommon call writes a nondistributed (i.e., a global or single) variable once to a file. The implementation is responsible for deciding which processor will actually write the variable to the file. The PIFReadCommon call reads a data value and scatters that value to all of the processors. The implementation is responsible for deciding which processor will read the value. The parameter fmat is a string that specifies the format the data will be read or written in.

(It is similar to the C printf command specifiers with some restrictions.) The data is written unformatted if fmat is not specified. Other parameters describe the data itself (location, data type, and size).

The two functions PIFWriteDistributedArray and PIFReadDistributedArray are used for reading and writing a partitioned and distributed array. PIFWriteDistributedArray writes a distributed array to a *single* file. PIFReadDistributedArray reads an array from a single file into a distributed-memory environment and partitions the data among the processors according to the descriptor array sz of type PIFArrayPart. Array sz contains the total number of elements in the entire array, the starting indices in each dimension for the process, the ending indices in each dimension for the process, and the index of the *first* global array element. The th dimension of a distributed array is defined by the ith element sz[i] of sz. Besides sz, the other unique parameter is nd, which specifies the number of dimensions in the array. The other parameters are the same as those used in PIFWriteCommon and PIFReadCommon.

The two functions PIFread and PIFwrite are used by each processor to read/write a block of data to a file. Important parameters are the length of the block of data and the data type. In the "as-sequential" mode, the blocks are read/written in processor rank order. In the "parallel" mode, many tasks *may* write simultaneously. PIFwrite and PIFread are optimized for the case where each processor may have a single large *contiguous* block of data that it wishes to read/write.

3.3.2   Implementation Details

The implementation is very important for performance. In this section we briefly describe some of the issues and two different implementations. Our abstraction-oriented approach has allowed us to experiment with a number of ideas without changing the source code of the applications, with the result that we have been able to speed up some applications by simply relinking them.

Some issues. Any parallel I/O system provides one or more disk systems attached in some way to one or more parallel nodes. For example, a disk may be placed at every parallel node. In another case, all the parallel nodes may be connected to a set of "service" nodes that manage the actual I/O traffic between the parallel nodes and the disk(s). Still others may connect the disk system to an external network. This wide range of options makes it nearly impossible to specify a single low-level approach that is both portable and efficient.

Figure 1 is a diagram of how the PIO system is implemented on a "generic" parallel I/O system. Above the dotted line are the parts visible to the user: the parallel nodes and their memories. The darkened areas in the memories represent blocks of data that are to be written by each processor.

Beneath the dotted line are the parts managed by the PIO system or provided by the underlying hardware. The "aggregated data" is managed by the PIO routines. The PIO routines receive the data from the user and may pack or shuffle it before passing it on to the exchange network. The exchange network is an abstraction which *may* have a direct hardware realization. It is used to pass the aggregated data to the nodes that interface directly with the I/O system. For example, in the Intel DELTA the exchange network is the mesh that connects the parallel compute nodes to the I/O service nodes. In the IBM SP-1, where each compute node is directly attached to its own local disk, the exchange network is a no-op, since the "aggregated data" is written directly to the processor's local disk. The output of the exchange network is passed to the nodes that interface directly to the physical I/O network. For example, in a Sun workstation network these "nodes" might be a single workstation (in the "as-sequential" case). The IBM SP-1 at ANL is unique in that there exists a second tier in the I/O system. Here, the I/O nodes are every fourth parallel node in the system which has a fiber channel connection to a RAID disk.

Two issues that need to be considered in writing a parallel file are how many processors request the operating system to write to the disks and what buffer sizes are used. The first of these issues is fairly obvious; we would like to use exactly as many processors as are directly connected to the disks so that the operating system does not try to rearrange the data that we wish to write, generating a communications bottleneck in moving the data between processors. The second is more subtle. If the library or application chooses buffer sizes that do not match those of the disks, the impact on performance can be much greater than a simple factor of two or three (caused by a read-modify-write cycle where a single write would have sufficed). Depending on how the operating system is managing the parallel file system, a write of data that spans two disk buffers may actually span two disks, causing additional communication traffic and loss of performance.

Two implementations. For writing a file in the "as-sequential" mode, we experimented with two different implementations. Both of these use a single process to write to the file; this simplifies the interface with the operating system at some cost in performance (though on workstations the cost is slight since, eventually, a single process is writing the file). The first implementation is unbuffered: each processor generates the data that it wants written and sends it to the master process, along with information on where to write it. The second implementation divides the output into buffers; each processor contributes to the buffer, and then the buffers are gathered up and written out by the master processor. The first approach minimizes the amount of data that is sent between processors; the second uses fewer communications and disk operations. In our experiments, the second approach was significantly faster. Note that both approaches were used with the same application program without changing the application code.

For the parallel implementation for systems with a disk per node, each processor opens a file on the local node (the name of this file system is provided by the implementation, allowing the user to use the same relative file name independent of the system). On systems with vendor-supplied parallel file systems, a parallel file is opened. In this case, the implementation can use the local network to move data around so that reads/writes from the parallel file system are as fast as possible (by mapping bytes from the application's natural format to the file system's natural format).

We plan to try additional implementations. For example, we can relax the requirement that the "as-sequential" file be written in that form until the `PIFclose` is called. This will allow us to write the file in a parallel format, taking advantage of the parallelism in the disk system, followed by a single merge of that parallel file into a single file. Other implementations could exercise more care in matching the buffers used by the `PIF` routines to the operating system.

3.4 Programming Examples

The program fragment in Figure 2 is taken from a superconductivity code. It writes the distributed, three-dimensional array `ps` and the scalars `nx`, `ny`, `nz` (number of grid points) and `hlx`, `hly`, `hlz` (grid spacing) to a file for postprocessing graphics. The `sz` descriptor array defines the six fields `mdim`, `ndim`, `start`, `end`, `gstart`, and `gend` for each dimension of `ps`. For each dimension these fields contain the global array size, the local array size, the starting and ending indices for the local part of the array, and the global

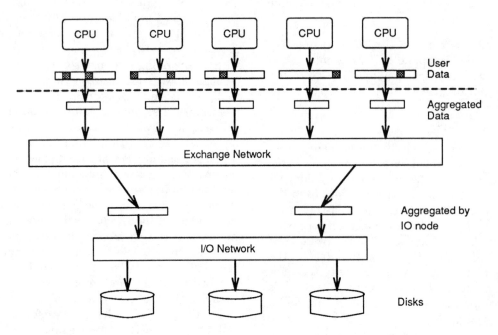

Figure 1: A generic parallel I/O system

indices for the local part of the array.

First, the sz descriptor is defined. Second, the parallel file "outfile" is opened. Third, all processors make the PIFWriteCommon call to write the scalars nx, ny, nz, hlx, hly, and hlz. Fourth, all processors call PIFWriteDistributedArray to write their piece of the ps array. Finally, all processors flush and close the parallel file. An important point is that the "ghost points" (the extra memory allocated by each processor to hold neighboring values of its distributed array) are *not* written to the parallel file.

3.5 Performance

Our primary intent in this section is to show that improved performance may be achieved using the "parallel" file format when compared to the "as sequential" file format. We caution that the results presented here were not run on a standalone system and the read and write speeds can reflect disk cache access time, and so should *not* be considered benchmark data. They are presented strictly to demonstrate the flexibility of the PIO system and the different levels of performance that may be achieved.

The experiments were performed as follows. To measure the input (read) rate of a parallel file access, a parallel file was opened, read from using PIFread, and closed. Only the latter two steps were timed. To measure the output (write) rate of a parallel file access, a parallel file was opened, written to using PIFwrite,

and closed. Again, only the latter two steps were timed. Since the timing includes closing the file(s), the writes are flushed out of the application (though not necessarily out of the OS onto the disks). Our experiments were performed on two Sun Sparc workstations connected over an Ethernet network, and on a 32-node IBM SP-1. All reads and writes were done using PIFread and PIFwrite in an unformatted mode. p4 was used for the underlying message-passing system.

Table 1 contains results from the Sun Sparc workstation experiments. In the "parallel" implementation each workstation writes to a local disk. In the "as-sequential" implementation one processor manages all the I/O, with the other processor sending or receiving data to and from the managing processor via messages. Here, the file resides on a single disk that is accessed over an Ethernet network. In all examples the file size used was 64k.

The main point we wish to make in Table 1 is the performance difference achieved using the "parallel" file format as opposed to the "as sequential" case. For the application programmer this performance difference is achieved simply by switching the choice of file format in the PIFopen call.

Table 2 contains results from the IBM SP-1 experiments. In all cases the "parallel" implementation was used and the file size was fixed at 16 MB. In the IBM SP-1 "parallel" implementation, each processor

```
void write_graphics (ps, nx, ny, nz, hlx, hly, hlz,
                     sx,ex,sxgp,exgp,sy,ey,sygp,eygp,sz,ez,szgp,ezgp)
{
    int    *nx, *ny, *nz;
    int    *sx, *sy, *sz, *ex, *ey, *ez;
    int    *sxgp, *sygp, *szgp, *exgp, *eygp, *ezgp;
    double *hlx, *hly, *hlz, *ps;

    PIFILE *fp;
    PIFArrayPart sz[3];

    sz[0].mdim   = nx;
    sz[0].ndim   = ex + exgp - sx + sxgp + 1;
    sz[0].start  = sxgp;
    sz[0].end    = sxgp + ex - sx ;
    sz[0].gstart = sx - sxgp;
    sz[0].gend   = ex + exgp;

    sz[1].mdim   = ny;
    sz[1].ndim   = ey + eygp - sy + sygp + 1;
    sz[1].start  = sygp;
    sz[1].end    = sygp + ey - sy;
    sz[1].gstart = sy - sygp;
    sz[1].gend   = ey + eygp;

    sz[2].mdim   = nz;
    sz[2].ndim   = ez + ezgp - sz + szgp + 1;
    sz[2].start  = szgp;
    sz[2].end    = szgp + ez - sz;
    sz[2].gstart = sz - szgp;
    sz[2].gend   = ez + ezgp;

    fp = PIFopen("outfile", ALLPROCS, O_WRONLY | O_CREAT, 0);

    PIFWriteCommon(fp, NULL, sizeof(int),    nx, 1, MSG_INT);
    PIFWriteCommon(fp, NULL, sizeof(int),    ny, 1, MSG_INT);
    PIFWriteCommon(fp, NULL, sizeof(int),    nz, 1, MSG_INT);
    PIFWriteCommon(fp, NULL, sizeof(double), hlx, 1, MSG_DBL);
    PIFWriteCommon(fp, NULL, sizeof(double), hlz, 1, MSG_DBL);
    PIFWriteCommon(fp, NULL, sizeof(double), hlz, 1, MSG_DBL);
    PIFWriteDistributedArray(fp, NULL, sizeof(double), sz, 4, ps, MSG_DBL);

    PIFflush(fp);
    PIFclose(fp);
}
```

Figure 2: Example program fragment

Table 1: Sun Sparc Workstation Results

File Format	No. Proc.	Read MB/s	Write MB/s
"parallel"	2	6.8	3.7
"as-sequential"	2	.8	.1

Table 2: IBM SP-1 Results for a 16 MB File

No. Proc.	Blocksize	Read MB/s	Write MB/s
4	4MB/8k	6	26
8	2MB/64k	12	40
16	1MB/16k	26	30

wrote directly to its own local disk. The parameters that were varied were the number of processors used and the "blocksize"—the amount of data read/written with a single call to `PIFread`/`PIFwrite`. The first column is the number of processors used; the second column is the blocksize at which the read or write rate was a minimum. The third and fourth columns contain the *minimum* read or write rates achieved over all blocksizes tested.

We emphasize that disk cache effects should not be discounted. Increasing numbers of processors lead to smaller subdivisions of the parallel file and possibly better chances of disk cache hits. The drop in write rate for sixteen processors is anomalous and may simply reflect a load imbalance caused by other tasks.

Again, the real point we wish to stress in this section is that our system provides an interface design that hides the underlying implementation from the user. It permits *both* high-performance, non-synchronous parallel I/O using the "parallel" file format and the ability to write a parallel file in a sequential format for debugging—with only a single change by the user: a different value for the file format parameter on the `PIFopen` call.

4 Conclusions and Future Work

In this paper we have described the I/O requirements of some computational science applications at Argonne National Laboratory and discussed a distributed-memory system we have developed to support these requirements on MPP systems. Two key points in our work are the use of high-level abstractions and portability among MPP systems.

We believe the ability to use abstractions is very important. An applications developer goes through a number of steps such as development, debugging, and production to get a (parallel) code working. Each of these phase has certain unique requirements associated with it. With our approach, the abstraction of file type allows a parallel programmer to easily switch between the requirements of different phases. For example, in the debugging phases a programmer may desire output in the form of contiguous ASCII files on his "home" file system, while unformatted and stripped files may be desirable for production computing. With the file type option to the `PIFOpen`, our system supports all of these without requiring any code changes by the user.

Portability is also a key aspect of our work. By integrating our system in the context of the `PETSc/Chameleon` package we achieve portability among the large number of systems this package runs on. Somewhat optimized implementations of our system currently exist for the IBM SP-1, Intel MPP systems, and Sun workstation networks.

We remark in passing that the operations described here are natural ones to support in languages such as High Performance Fortran. We fully expect that, as more real applications are run on parallel computers, there will be enhanced support for parallel I/O. We hope that our work will (a) allow applications to use parallel I/O in the short term and (b) provide a testbed for implementations and program annotations (guides to the runtime system about the parallel I/O). In addition, we expect to add additional abstractions, such as those for unstructured data, that are beyond the scope of current language standards.

Availability and Documentation

The `PETSc/Chameleon` system is in the public domain. The complete distribution can be obtained by anonymous ftp from info.mcs.anl.gov. Take the file chameleon.tar.Z from the directory pub/pdetools. If you wish to use the `PETSc/Chameleon` with `p4`, take the file pub/p4/p4-1.3.tar.Z The `PETSc/Chameleon` distribution contains all source code, installation instructions, a users guide in both ASCII text and latexinfo format, and a collection of examples in both C and Fortran.

Acknowledgments

We thank Paul Bash, John Michalakes, and Ron Shepard for helpful discussions about their applications.

References

[1] Ralph Butler and Ewing Lusk. Monitors, messages, and clusters: The p4 parallel programming system. *Journal of Parallel Computing*. to appear (Also Argonne National Laboratory Mathematics and Computer Science Division preprint P362-0493).

[2] T. Crockett. File concepts for parallel I/O. In *Proceedings of Supercomputing'89*, pages 574–579, 1989.

[3] J. M. del Rosario and A. Choudhary. High performance I/O for parallel computers: Problems and prospects. Preprint, 1993.

[4] W. Gropp and B. Smith. Users manual for the Chameleon parallel programming tools. Technical Report ANL-93/23, Argonne National Laboratory, 1993.

Parallel Access to Files in the Vesta File System

Peter F. Corbett   Dror G. Feitelson   Jean-Pierre Prost   Sandra Johnson Baylor

IBM T. J. Watson Research Center

P. O. Box 218, Yorktown Heights, NY 10598

Abstract

The Vesta parallel file system is intended to solve the I/O problems of massively parallel multicomputers executing numerically intensive scientific applications. It provides parallel access from the applications to files distributed across multiple storage nodes in the multicomputer, thereby exposing an opportunity for high-bandwidth data transfer across the multicomputer's low-latency network. The Vesta interface provides a user-defined parallel view of file data, which gives users some control over the layout of data. This is useful for tailoring data layout to match common access patterns. The interface also allows user-defined partitioning and repartitioning of files without moving data among storage nodes. Libraries with higher-level interfaces that hide the layout details, while exploiting the power of parallel access, may be implemented above the basic interface. We show how collective I/O operations can be implemented, and define six parallel access modes to Vesta files. Each mode has unique characteristics in terms of how the processes share the file and how their accesses are interleaved. The combination of user-defined file partitioning and the six access modes gives users very versatile parallel file access.

1   Introduction

Massively parallel computers have the potential to exploit the improved cost-performance of microprocessors and the increased memory capacities available today. Unfortunately, the performance of the I/O subsystems of massively parallel computers has not been keeping pace with their processing and communications capabilities. This phenomenon has its roots in two major technical problems, one in the I/O subsystem hardware, the other in its software. This paper describes the Vesta parallel file system, which is a software solution to the problem of I/O in massively parallel computers. While Vesta does not directly solve the hardware aspect of the problem, it provides a means of using parallelism to overcome the hardware limitations of single storage devices.

Computation, communication, memory, and I/O have to be balanced to obtain the maximum performance available from any computer. Massively parallel computers are targeted at numerically intensive supercomputing applications, which often require high bandwidth and low latency access to large amounts of data (sometimes as much as hundreds of Gigabytes). Such applications have typically been run on uniprocessor computers with very high performance I/O subsystems. To maintain the balance between computation and I/O when the applications are run on massively parallel computers, parallel I/O subsystems must be considered. This conclusion is further strengthened by the observation that while magnetic disk latency, bandwidth and capacity have all been improving, the rate of improvement has been significantly less than that for microprocessors [8]. Indeed, parallel I/O subsystems are already being used even for uniprocessors.

Another aspect of the problem has been the lack of software to support I/O in large parallel jobs running on massively parallel computers. While much effort has been focused on compilers and message passing libraries for parallel computers, relatively little research or development has been focused on providing I/O in these computers. Most of the recent research on file systems has concentrated on distributed file systems, such as NFS [16], Coda [17], or the Sprite file system [11]. This is not very relevant to massively parallel computers, because the requirements are very different. Distributed file systems are designed to cope with high-latency unreliable communications across LANs, and try to guarantee high availability for multiprogramming workloads. Massively parallel computers employ low-latency reliable networks, and are used for highly parallel applications. Such applications often require large amount of concurrent I/O from the parallel processes to one or a few large files.

One promising way to provide the large I/O bandwidth required in massively parallel computers is to use multiple disks in parallel. Two ways of doing so have emerged in recent years: disk striping and file declustering. In disk striping, the data is distributed at a small granularity, so that every block is distributed across all the disks [14]. This approach is used, for example, in the Connection Machine's Data Vault, where striping is at the bit level [19]. This approach does not require fundamental changes in the system software, because the apparent interface is that of a single disk that just happens to be much larger and faster than

472

regular disks. But this advantage is also an Achilles heel, because the aggregate bandwidth of all the disks must pass through a single channel on its way to memory. Ultimately, this limits the number of disks that can be used. It also requires that the aggregate of all I/O accesses made by the parallel compute nodes be multiplexed onto this channel. Thus, this approach limits the scalability of both the I/O server and client.

The alternative is to use declustering, where different blocks are stored on distinct disks [10]. This is used in the Bridge file system [7], in Intel's Concurrent File System (CFS) [13], and in various RAID schemes [12]. The declustered disks often are distributed across multiple file storage nodes. Using this scheme, accesses to different parts of the file can proceed independently, and therefore can be serviced in parallel. If the buffers used for the I/O operation reside on the storage nodes, there are no inherent bottlenecks.

Concurrent file systems that use declustering, such as CFS, nevertheless hide this feature from their users. The user interface uses the traditional notion of a file being a linear sequence of records (or bytes), and the mapping to multiple disks is done beneath the covers. Thus users are prevented from tailoring their I/O patterns to match the available disks. Small accesses might require data residing on two different disks. To get around this problem, the Bridge design includes special tools that know about the internal parallel structure of files and exploit it to improve performance.

In contrast, the Vesta file system exposes its parallel structure at the user interface. While users do not have full control over the mapping of data to disks, they are able to create files that are partitioned so as to match the parallelism in their applications. The partitions are mapped to different storage nodes. Each process can then perform most of its accesses to its own partition, with minimal interference from other processes. Additionally, Vesta allows parallel file access using different decompositions of the file data, without requiring any movement of the data.

The rest of this paper is organized as follows. The next section outlines Vesta's design principles, and explains how it is meant to be used. Section 3 details the user interface, and explains how users can control and exploit the layout of files. Section 4 describes two high-level interfaces implemented above the Vesta interface: one using a canonical view of declustered Vesta files, and the other using collective I/O operations to synchronize the participating processes. As part of these interfaces, we define six parallel access modes to Vesta files. Finally, Section 5 presents the conclusions.

2 The Vesta Parallel File System

The overriding goal of the Vesta file system is to provide high performance for scientific applications on massively parallel multicomputers. This workload is characterized by very large files which are mostly read. In many cases, the file data is distributed among the application processes, such that each reads a certain part, and all together read the whole file. This is different enough from I/O on traditional supercomputers that storing the whole file sequentially on one device, even a very fast device, is not an efficient solution. The following design principles were identified based on this workload, and guided the design of Vesta.

- *Parallelism.* The first and foremost vehicle for achieving high performance is parallelism. The Vesta design conserves the parallelism from the application interface down to the disks. This is done by providing a parallel interface which eliminates any points where access is serialized. In particular, it is easy to create situations in which multiple compute nodes access multiple storage nodes at the same time, independently of each other, and over separate communication channels. Such access patterns result in low latency and high bandwidth, owing to the tightly-coupled architecture of multicomputers.

- *Scalability.* The design point for Vesta was a system of 32K nodes, a large fraction of which were to be dedicated storage nodes. This precluded any serial bottlenecks or centralized lookups in file accesses. Each access is addressed directly to the storage node where the required data resides, with no node-to-node indirection. This is achieved by a combination of means. First, file metadata is distributed on all the storage nodes, and is found by hashing the file name. The metadata is only accessed once when the file is first attached to the application. Thereafter, compute nodes can identify the storage nodes which contain accessed data using a combination of the metadata they obtained, parameters of the parallel view of the file that they are using, and the offset. Block lists for the file are maintained on each storage node independently, for the local partition of the file. Data is not cached on compute nodes. This is possible due to the relatively low latency of the network. It is quite likely that some higher level I/O libraries built on top of Vesta may cache data locally at the compute nodes.

  Scalability does not only mean support for large systems; it also means support for many large files. Vesta files can reach a defined maximum size of 2^{64} bytes, with up to 2^{48} bytes per storage node (practically limited by physical storage capacity). The system is capable of handling a defined maximum of 2^{56} objects (practically limited by system table sizes).

- *MIMD style*. The Vesta interface is designed in a MIMD style, meaning that different functions can be called on different compute nodes, independently of each other. However, it does not preclude a SPMD loosely synchronous style interface, including collective I/O operations, from being implemented in an I/O library above Vesta. Support for such higher-level interfaces is built into the Vesta interface.

- *Reliability*. Reliability is an important concern in large parallel systems, and especially in the I/O subsystem, which is responsible for persistent storage of data. Vesta guards against data loss by using RAID devices in each storage node independently of other nodes [8], thus saving network traffic. It also provides efficient and coherent checkpointing of files under application control, even during continued access to the file. In addition, Vesta provides a flexible interface to external archival storage systems, allowing files to be exported for safekeeping elsewhere.

In addition to the design principles listed above, the design is also influenced by the architecture of the target machines. Vesta was designed to run on the Vulcan multicomputer at the IBM T. J. Watson Research Center. This is a distributed memory, message-passing machine, with nodes connected by a multistage packet-switching network. The nodes include both compute nodes, used to execute application processes, and storage nodes, used by the parallel file system. The network provides high bandwidth communication with low latency, independent of which nodes are involved in the communication. Therefore the software does not have to take locality considerations into account.

Ideally, the storage nodes should be designated for use exclusively as Vesta file system servers, as is the case in Vulcan. Dedicated storage nodes also exist in practically all commercial multicomputers, e.g. the CM-5 [9], the Intel iPSC/2 [13] and Paragon, the nCUBE, and the Tera architecture [1]. This reduces the overhead due to I/O activity experienced on compute nodes, and prevents large asynchronous interruptions of the computation. It is not expected that the storage nodes will be able to contain all the files owned by all the potential users of the computer. Therefore Vesta is intended to be used as a staging area, where files are stored while they are actually in use. Once a file is not needed online, it can be offloaded to an archival mass storage system that provides reliable and cost-effective long term storage outside the multicomputer.

By virtue of being an internal system, Vesta gains important advantages in terms of being able to support the requirements of parallel applications. Communication between the application's processes and the storage nodes has low latency, on the order of tens to hundreds of microseconds. Accesses as small as 1–10KB are supported efficiently by Vesta, using memory buffers in the storage nodes. Applications that access a whole file can expect good performance even if each process only accesses a discontiguous subset of the file.

The external, network-connected mass storage systems used for scientific data archival do not provide such a good match. Access across a LAN suffers from high latency, and high efficiency can be achieved only by sequential access to very large data blocks, on the order of 1–10MB. By serving as a staging area, Vesta bridges the mismatch between the requirements of parallel applications and the characteristics of external archival storage systems. The parallel application sees a parallel file system with low latency response, and high aggregate parallel bandwidth. Vesta imports and exports files from external servers in large sequential blocks, over one or a few high-latency high-bandwidth channels. This approach is particularly advantageous if the application requires much data reuse.

3 Parallel Access at the Vesta Interface

The Vesta user interface defines the parallel structure of files at two levels: the physical layout of the data, and the logical view of the data. The physical layout determines how many storage nodes are used, and the minimal unit of data for interleaving. Given a certain physical layout, applications may open the file in many different logical views. In particular, it is possible to create disjoint logical partitions of the file, such that each processor can access only its own partition and has no knowledge of other partitions.

3.1 Physical partitioning

Traditional file systems promote the notion that a file is a linear sequence of records. Vesta promotes a 2-D structure: a file is composed of a certain number of physical partitions, each of which is a linear sequence of records. The number of physical partitions and the record size are set when a file is created, and do not change throughout the lifetime of the file.

Physical partitions are actually an abstraction of storage nodes. By specifying the number of physical partitions in the file, the user is setting the ideal number of storage nodes that should be used. This ideal depends on the data in the file. For example, if the file contains input parameters for a weather prediction code based on a finite differences model, the number of physical partitions can reflect a partitioning of the space at a certain granularity. If the system has more storage nodes than the file has physical partitions, each physical partition will be mapped to a distinct storage node. If there are less storage nodes than physical partitions, the physical partitions will be distributed evenly on all the storage nodes. This is functionally transparent to the application.

It is important to note that when files have multiple physical partitions, there is no single natural order of the records in the file. For example, should all the records in the first physical partition come before those in the second physical partition, and so on? In Vesta, the canonical ordering is single-record stripes across all the physical partitions: the first record in each partition, taken in the order of partition number, followed by the second record in each partition, and so on.

3.2 Logical partitioning

The canonical record ordering is not imposed on users, and is only used by external interfaces that are oblivious of the internal structure of Vesta files. Applications that use the parallel Vesta interface are required to define their own ordering by setting several parameters. These parameters define a division of the file records into disjoint subsets, called logical partitions, and ordering within these subsets. Each setting of the parameters results in a different logical partitioning (or more simply, "view") of the file. Hence the apparent sequencing of records in the file can be changed by changing the view of the file. Different views of the file can be used without actually moving the data. Each compute node sets its own view locally, independently from all other compute nodes.

The view is set when the file is opened. Opening is a local operation that follows attaching. An attached file can be opened any number of times, with different views. To understand how the view is defined, recall that a Vesta file is a 2-D structure. The view definition is based on a rectangular 2-D template, that is repeated one or more times to create a rectangular pattern. Records falling under each template belong to a distinct logical partition of the file. This pattern is then repeated to tile the 2-D structure of the file. Those parts of the file that fall under the same template in different tiles constitute a logical partition of the file.

An example is given in Fig. 1. The template has a width (called the horizontal group size, or Hgs) of 2, and a height (called the vertical group size, or Vgs) of 3. The records within the template are numbered from 0 in column major order. This template is repeated six times to create the tiling pattern: 3 times in the horizontal dimension (this is called the horizontal interleave, Hi), and twice in the vertical dimension (called the vertical interleave, Vi). These repetitions represent six logical partitions, which are each identified by an ordered pair that specifies their location in the pattern.

The bottom of the figure shows the logical partitioning that is obtained when this pattern is used to tile a file with 12 physical partitions and 12 records in each. The pattern is repeated four times to complete the tiling. Six logical partitions are formed, as indicated by different shades of gray. Each partition contains 24 records, which are sequenced first along the horizontal repetitions and then along the vertical ones.

To our knowledge, Vesta is the first system to offer this type of subsetting and parallel views of a file. A somewhat similar concept has been suggested for the management of memory-mapped segments in the Chagori system on the K2 multicomputer, but it seems that it was never implemented [18]. The parallel I/O software for the nCUBE also provides different partitionings of the data [4, 5]. The methodology used there is to permute the bits of the offset into the file and divide them into two groups, one indicating the partition and the other indicating the offset in that partition. By changing the permutation it is possible to obtain different interleaving patterns. However, due to the use of bit positions, the block sizes must always be powers of two. Vesta is more flexible in this respect. Moreover, users of nCUBE have no control over the mapping of the logical partitions to storage nodes, which is done by the system.

3.3 Accessing Vesta Files

In all aspects of its design, Vesta is intended to be used by parallel applications running on multiple compute nodes, and accessing data stored in files that are distributed over multiple storage nodes. This model of an I/O subsystem differs in many ways from uniprocessor and distributed computing environments. These differences are manifest in the operations required to gain access to a file, and in the data access operations themselves.

Gaining access to a file in a Unix file system requires making an `open` system call. The `open` call allows a process to optionally create a file, if the named file does not already exist. It also validates the requested access to the file, checking if the owner of the accessing process has the permissions to access the file in the requested mode, and it sets up an entry in the file table maintained by the file system that allows one or more processes to access the file data. It also records the fact that a process has opened the file in the file inode. Finally, it creates an entry in the process's file descriptor table that maps the file descriptor returned to the user into an index into the system file table. The Unix `close` operation undoes most of the work done by the `open` system call, with the exception of deleting the file, which is done by the `unlink` system call [3].

In Vesta, the equivalent operations to those performed by Unix `open` are performed by three separate functions: `Vesta_create`, `Vesta_attach`, and `Vesta_open`. Vesta is based on a client server model, with the client running as part of each application process on the compute nodes, and the server running on the storage nodes. The reason for separating these functions is to minimize the communication required between the client and the server. This allows libraries built on top of Vesta to be implemented efficiently.

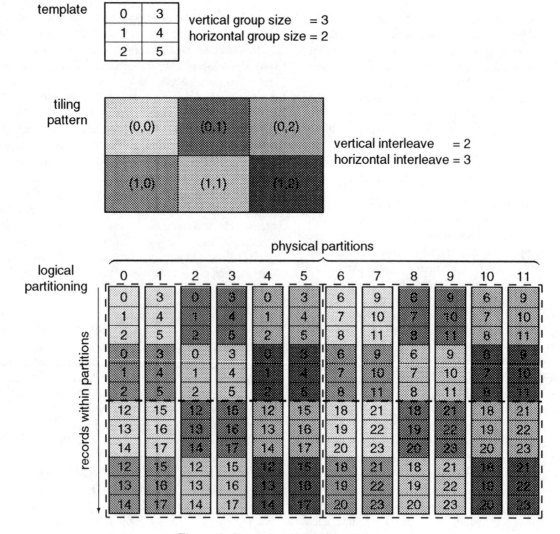

Figure 1: *Example of logical partitioning.*

Vesta_create creates new parallel files. Along with the file name and access permissions, parameters are provided to Vesta_create to specify how many physical partitions the file will have, and what its basic unit of striping (its record size) is. Creating files in Vesta is a serial, single-process operation on the client side, but may require the participation of several or all nodes at the Vesta server side. Vesta_attach is used to inform the server that a parallel program is going to access the file. Each process in the parallel program must attach the file before it can access it. Attaching the file provides a process with data about the file, including the number of physical partitions, the record size, and where the partitions are located. Therefore, attach is inherently parallel, and requires direct or indirect communication between the Vesta client associated with each user process and the Vesta server. To support attaching files to large jobs, Vesta_attach_share and

Vesta_attach_accept functions are provided to share the file metadata — returned by an initial Vesta_attach call — among processes.

Once a file is attached, opening it is done locally, with no interaction with the Vesta server. All data associated with and required by Vesta_open are stored locally at each compute node. Each call to Vesta_open returns a file descriptor which provides access to one logical partition of a file. The logical view taken of the file, as well as the specific logical partition opened, are defined by five parameters provided in the Vesta_open call (Vgs, Vi, Hgs, Hi, and the partition number). The same Vesta file can be opened several times by a process, with the same or different opening parameters supplied to each call. Each call to Vesta_open creates a new offset into the specified logical partition. Vesta also allows more than one process to share an offset using the Vesta_open_share and `Vesta_open_accept` function calls. Shared offsets are read and updated atomically when any sharing process accesses the file through the shared file descriptor.

Data access operations (read and write) in Vesta are directed against logical partitions of a file. Data can be accessed relative to the current offset, or relative to the beginning of a logical partition. In addition to normal, synchronous `Vesta_read` and `Vesta_write` operations, there are three ways to improve performance. First, any Vesta data access function can be issued with a flag set to CAUTIOUS or RECKLESS. If an access is CAUTIOUS, it is guaranteed to be performed atomically, and in a sequentially consistent and linear ordering with other CAUTIOUS accesses. Accesses labelled RECKLESS may be performed nonatomically if they access data on multiple storage nodes. The concurrency control mechanism used in CAUTIOUS accesses has some performance cost, so it is advisable to use RECKLESS in cases where accesses are sure to be non-conflicting (e.g. when each process has opened a different logical partition in the same file view, when accesses are all reads, or when such nondeterminism is allowable).

The second mechanism to improve performance is to use asynchronous reads and writes, `Vesta_read_q` and `Vesta_write_q`. These functions can be called to start an access. At some later point, when the data is actually needed in the case of reads, or when a buffer is to be reused in the case of writes, the operation can be polled for completion. This allows the latency of reads and writes to be overlapped with local computation in the application processes. The third mechanism is prefetching data in advance. This hides the latency by telling the Vesta server to prefetch the data from the disks to the storage nodes' buffers. Later, when the actual `Vesta_read` is issued, the data will already be buffered.

3.4 The Power of Logical Partitioning

There are many possible applications of logical partioning of files. One interesting application which demonstrates the power of providing application programmers and I/O library writers with the ability to dynamically partition files is matrix multiplication (Fig. 2).

It is well known that higher efficiency is achieved by blocking matrix operations [20]. Assume matrices are stored in Vesta files such that each column of the matrix corresponds to one physical partition. Using Vesta logical partitioning, it is easy to open a band across the rows of matrix A, another along the columns of matrix B, and a third for the block where they intersect in matrix C. The bands from A and B are read into memory, and the multiplication is performed. The result is then written into C. No index calculations need be performed.

Note that the format of all three files is the same. Each is partitioned according to its role in this instance of ma-

```
pdim = sqrt( PROC_NUM );
blk_size = MAT_SIZE / pdim;
float A[MAT_SIZE][blk_size],
      B[blk_size][MAT_SIZE],
      C[blk_size][blk_size];
Vgs = blk_size; Vi = pdim;
Hgs = MAT_SIZE; Hi = 1;
fda=Vesta_Open("A",Vgs,Vi,Hgs,Hi,me/pdim);
Vgs = MAT_SIZE; Vi = 1;
Hgs = blk_size; Hi = pdim;
fdb=Vesta_Open("B",Vgs,Vi,Hgs,Hi,me%pdim);
Vgs = blk_size; Vi = pdim;
Hgs = blk_size; Hi = pdim;
fdc=Vesta_Open("C",Vgs,Vi,Hgs,Hi,me);
Vesta_Read(fda,A,MAT_SIZE*blk_size);
Vesta_Read(fdb,B,MAT_SIZE*blk_size);
for (i=0 ; i<blk_size ; i++)
  for (j=0 ; j<blk_size ; j++) {
    C[i][j] = 0;
    for (k=0 ; k<MAT_SIZE ; k++)
      C[i][j] += A[k][j] * B[i][k];
  }
Vesta_Write(fdc,C,blk_size*blk_size);
```

Figure 2: *Implementation of blocked matrix multiplication using logical partitioning.*

trix multiplication, but this partitioning is not recorded in the file itself. The product of one multiplication can be used as a factor in a subsequent multiplication, by simply repartitioning the file differently.

4 High Level Interfaces

Vesta is intended to support user level I/O libraries that provide a variety of parallel file I/O services, as well as high performance sequential I/O services. At present, we are designing a loosely synchronous SPMD parallel I/O library, with collective I/O operations. Eventually, it is intended that Vesta will be accessible through C, Fortran, and HPF (High Performance Fortran) interfaces, as well as through its basic function call interface from C programs. It is also expected that Vesta will be usable by HPF compilers as a scratch space for temporary data for programs with large data sets. In this case, a user may be able to write a program without specifying whether files or memory are used for temporary storage space. Additionally, we plan to do further research in the area of providing parallel pipelines between programs using Vesta files as intermediate storage space. In this section, we present the features of Vesta that support parallel and sequential file I/O services, and describe what some of these services might be.

4.1 Implementation of Traditional Sequential Interfaces

Vesta provides a MIMD interface. With very little effort, language specific I/O libraries (e.g. C and Fortran) can be built on top of a subset of Vesta functions. To emulate traditional program I/O services, such libraries require only a predefined, sequential, canonical view of files. In Vesta, the canonical view of files is one record wide striping across all physical partitions of the file. This corresponds to a logical view of the file that has only one logical partition, opened with parameters $Vgs = 1$, $Vi = 1$, $Hgs = 1$, and $Hi = 1$. Using Vesta in this manner amounts to using Vesta as a concurrent file system, and does not take advantage of the flexibility provided by its parallel interface. However, Vesta should still perform well when used this way.

In a concurrent I/O library that presents a single canonical view of files to application programs, there are several possible modes of file access. In all of these modes, the option of using Vesta logical file partitions is not available at the user interface. However, certain concurrent file access modes may give some rudimentary partitioning of the file among the parallel processes. There is no guarantee of any correspondence between this level of partitioning and the physical layout of the file, so there is no assurance that data access patterns will be matched in any way to the physical distribution of the data. In the following section, several file access modes are discussed in the context of logically partitioned files accessed through a parallel I/O library. Each of these modes may also be provided by a concurrent I/O library to access files that are seen by the canonical sequential view. These modes correspond in most cases to modes of file access available through either the Express I/O or the Intel CFS I/O user libraries.

In addition to the libraries using the canonical view to provide applications with sequential files, it is possible to create a library that provides common 2-D structures. Such a library has been implemented for the nCUBE parallel I/O system [6]. In Vesta, such a library will be able to take advantage of the underlying 2-D Vesta files. For example, if the user interface to the library includes access modes corresponding to rows and columns of a 2-D matrix, these can be mapped directly to Vesta physical partitions. This approach guarantees a certain level of correspondence between access patterns and file layout.

4.2 An SPMD Library with Collective I/O Operations

SPMD computing is emerging as a convenient and useful model for the development and compilation of large parallel programs. The essential feature of SPMD programs is that all processes in a job run the same code. This is typically done in a loosely synchronous manner, meaning that the processes are coordinated by occasional barrier synchronizations. This ensures predictable and consistent program behavior. In many cases the barriers are part of a collective operation, which might include data communications among the processes.

A parallel I/O library for SPMD programs should provide coordinated access to parallel files from all processes in a parallel program. In particular, it should define what happens when all the processes issue the same library call at approximately the same time. One option is to treat the library calls as collective operations that actually require all the processes to synchronize. Another is to let each process perform its call independently from all the others, thus reducing the synchronization requirements and the ensuing overhead. In the low-level Vesta interface, described in Section 3, function calls are local and do not enforce any coordination among processes. But Vesta is designed to support SPMD libraries with collective operations, implemented above the low-level interface. In particular, some Vesta functions are designed primarily for such libraries. A major goal was to allow libraries that decouple concurrent read and write operations, while maintaining reasonable parallel semantics. This is done at the expense of making attach and open calls synchronous. In this section we discuss a proposal for the design of an SPMD library, and show how Vesta supports it. Note that this library actually does not require all the processes to run the same single program. Multiple programs are possible, as long as they include the same sequence of calls to collective operations.

Before a Vesta file can be accessed, it has to be attached and opened. As all the processes must do so, it makes sense to define these operations as collective operations. If the processes are asynchronous and independent, each must call Vesta_attach separately to get the file metadata, which could cause a bottleneck at the storage node that stores this metadata. The implementation of the SPMD attach function uses a tree structure imposed on the processes to streamline the procedure and prevent any bottlenecks. In such an implementation, only one or a few processes call Vesta_attach to get the metadata. They then use Vesta_attach_share and Vesta_attach_accept to propagate the metadata through the tree. When all the processes receive the metadata, the collective attach operation terminates, and the processes can proceed with their individual executions.

The Vesta_open function call is a local operation that

does not require any coordination with other processes. However, in an SPMD library, open should also be a collective operation. The reason is that it provides an opportunity to check that all the processes are going to access the file in a consistent way. Specifically, we propose that when a file is opened an access mode be associated with it. This access mode is then used to interpret the meaning of subsequent read and write operations on the file. In certain access modes, these read and write operations are independent of each other, and therefore can be done without synchronization among compute nodes. In other modes, these operations require inter-process synchronization.

A classification of the access modes proposed for the Vesta SPMD library is given in Fig. 3. Similar access modes are used in the Express system Cubix model of computation [15] and in Intel's CFS [2]. In fact, Vesta provides a very good base on which to build either the Express or the Intel parallel I/O library. Current Express implementations emulate parallel I/O by serializing the I/O requests, and performing them on a standard Unix file interface. Thus, no true parallelism is achieved. The Intel CFS I/O library is much closer to what Vesta can provide in terms of potential performance, as it is implemented on top of a file system that declusters data across multiple storage nodes. However, the CFS I/O library has very little notion of parallelism, essentially providing a few mechanisms for indexing into a sequential file that has no underlying parallel structure visible to the user. Vesta improves upon previous systems by providing the means to partition files into disjoint logical partitions, that can be accessed independently with no synchronization or concurrency control.

The most important mode of parallel file access in Vesta occurs when each application process opens a different logical partition of a file, but using the same view (mode A). Given that the open call is a collective operation, the library can check that indeed this is the case. Now, all accesses to the file made by the different processes are guaranteed to be nonconflicting, and concurrency control can be turned off. The accesses made by different processes can proceed independently of each other; read and write are *not* collective operations in this mode.

The ability to have multiple logical partitions opened at the same time can be exploited by an SPMD library to allow switching between various views of the file, coordinated by a global synchronization of the processes. For example, access to a two-dimensional matrix mapped onto a Vesta file can be toggled between row and column access very quickly, and in each view all the accesses can be performed asynchronously, with no further coordination among the processes. The act of toggling the view is a collective operation. First, a check is made that all the processes indeed intend to switch over to the same view. Then the Vesta_set_view function is called locally in each process. This function call

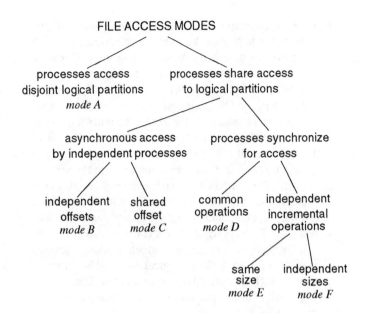

Figure 3: *Classification of access modes to parallel files.*

forces subsequent read and write operations to use the new file view.

Mode A is the recommended and preferred mode of access for highest performance. Other modes are provided to ease the use of shared logical partitions and to provide an easy migration path from Express and CFS to Vesta. Logical partitions are shared when they are opened by more than one process. For example, this can happen when the view has fewer logical partitions than processes (perhaps just one logical partition covering the whole file). In mode B, these processes may each have their own offsets into the logical partition, and make uncoordinated accesses to the file. This is equivalent to "async" mode in Express, and mode 0 in CFS. This mode also offers high performance, but may give unpredictable results if one or more processes are writing data. Therefore mode B is most appropriate when processes are read-sharing data.

In contrast with mode B, mode C provides all the processes with a shared offset into the logical partition. This is equivalent to mode 1 in CFS. It is not recommended that many processes share the same offset, as a performance bottleneck will result where the offset is stored. However, this mode is useful in a number of cases. For example, it is convenient to share an offset into a file used to collect trace records. Whenever a process wishes to record a trace, it just writes it to the file. Because the same offset is shared by all the processes, the trace records will become interleaved in the order in which they were generated. There is no requirement that all processes produce the same numbers of trace records, or that they do so at the same time.

In modes A, B, and C, read and write operations by different processes are independent. In modes D, E, and

F, they are collective operations that synchronize all the processes. Mode *D* provides common operations, in which all the processes do exactly the same thing: they all read or write the same data at the same offset. It is largely equivalent to "single" mode in Express. In the case of `read`, this mode is best implemented by having one process actually read the data, and then broadcasting the data to the other processes. In the case of `write`, there are two options. One is to first check that all the processes are indeed attempting to write exactly the same data, and then to write the verified data once. This suffers from high overhead for checking the data. An alternative is to arbitrarily write the data from one of the processes, and discard the data of the others. The semantics of Express require that a check be made.

Finally, there are two access modes that allow processes to read or write to a shared logical partition in an order specified by the cardinality of their process IDs. If all accesses are of the same size, then the library can easily compute the offsets at which each process will be making its accesses, and it can make these accesses independently of each other in whatever order they occur. This is our mode *E*, which is equivalent to CFS mode 2. However, in most cases, it would seem that mode *A* would provide a simpler and faster mechanism for partitioning and accessing the file than can be provided by mode *E*, with similar functionality provided to the user. If all the ordered accesses to the file are of different sizes, then they must be explicitly ordered by the library before being issued to the file system. This is a more complex mode to implement than the others, and requires some mechanism — such as a parallel prefix computation or token passing — for correctly setting the offset for each access. This is our mode *F*; it is equivalent to "multi" mode in Express and mode 3 in CFS.

4.3 Parallel Pipelines between Programs

It is quite feasible in Vesta to logically partition a large file among several processes, with each process running on a separate compute node, and small groups of processes sharing access to each logical partition. Within each group, each process could perform a different operation on the data. Using mode *B* for example, one process in each group could read the data from a logical partition, perform some operation on it, and send its results to another process, which in turn would perform another operation on the data before writing it back to the same logical partition.

This opens the possibility of generalizing the parallel interfaces between parallel programs. Building from the model provided by Unix, individual parallel programs could be pipelined, with the output of one parallel program being piped in parallel to the input of the next program in the pipeline. In Unix, pipelines are actually temporary files, invisible to the user, that are created when the programs in the pipeline begin executing and are deleted when the programs terminate.

Vesta files can also be used as the temporary files that buffer data between pipelined parallel programs. Parallel utilities could be written and executed to read their input either from a regular Vesta file, or from a temporary parallel pipeline file. The output could also be either a regular Vesta file or another parallel pipeline file. Utilities would have to accept input from files with different numbers of physical partitions. They would also have to write output to files with different numbers of physical partitions, with the number of output partitions possibly being some function of the number of input partitions. The parallel pipeline files would each have one writer and one reader. It is possible that fairly complex data transformations can be performed between parallel utilities by the pipeline operator, simply by writing data into the file in one logical view, and reading it out using a different logical view. As an example, a permuting parallel pipeline could be set to perform row-column, or block-shuffled permutations on the output data of one program before reading it into the next program. The permuting parallel pipeline capability would also allow parallel utilities with different numbers of processes to be pipelined together.

It is our goal to design and implement the permuting parallel pipeline operators, and to provide a parallel I/O library that allows programs to write to and read from parallel pipelines. In Unix, the basic pipelining mechanism has been used to implement a large number of generally useful utilities that are available on all Unix systems. We expect that if we provide a reasonably efficient and easy-to-use implementation of permuting parallel pipelines, users will find many uses for them, and will write many generally useful parallel utilities. We also expect that some users will find the parallel pipelining function useful for constructing complex programs out of parallel program building blocks.

5 Conclusions

The Vesta file system provides a new interface that allows users to exploit parallel I/O. The interface provides parallel views of file data, and supports dynamic file decomposition. The parallel view of the data is preserved from the application down to the disks. The system is scalable to massively parallel computers with many storage nodes, and promises high performance for I/O on tightly-coupled multicomputers. Vesta also provides an interface that will support high level concurrent and parallel I/O libraries. Building on the Vesta file system, we plan to develop permuting parallel pipelines as a mechanism for pipelining parallel programs.

At the time of writing, the implementation of Vesta has just been completed. This implementation includes all the functions needed to manipulate files and Xrefs (Vesta's counterpart to Unix directories), and to access data using the full power of logical partitioning. The current implementation of the storage node's device drivers is built on top of the AIX Journaled File System, rather than writing new device drivers. The measured performance penalty for disk access using AIX file accesses, as opposed to using device drivers directly, is relatively small ($< 20\%$). We are currently testing and measuring the performance of Vesta on clusters of IBM RS/6000 workstations.

A major unanswered question is how useful Vesta's notions of parallel files and dynamic file decomposition are to users. We have had different reactions from many different potential users, some of whom are quite enthusiastic, and others who are very reluctant to consider anything other than standard sequential Fortran I/O in their parallel programs. We intend to start experimentation with real parallel applications, in order to evaluate the performance benefits of file partitioning and to obtain user feedback.

Vesta offers a significantly richer interface than concurrent and sequential file systems. Vesta also incorporates many architectural and implementation features that should provide good scalable performance in massively parallel computers. A key to performance is the mapping of the application parallelism directly to the physical distribution of file data. We expect this to be beneficial in many applications. For users who only require concurrent I/O services, Vesta will function very well as a concurrent file system. However, we hope that once we provide good parallel I/O libraries, and once users become familiar with Vesta, they will prefer to use the parallel file interfaces.

Acknowledgements

We wish to thank Brian Herr for evaluating the performance impact of a Vesta implementation above the Journaled File System, Blake Fitch, Mark Giampapa, and Peter Hochschild who implemented the message-passing kernels which Vesta uses, and Yarsun Hsu for his managerial support of the whole project.

References

[1] R. Alverson, D. Callahan, D. Cummings, B. Koblenz, A. Porterfield, and B. Smith, "The Tera computer system". In *Intl. Conf. Supercomputing*, pp. 1–6, Jun 1990.

[2] R. K. Asbury and D. S. Scott, "Fortran I/O on the iPSC/2: is there read after write?". In 4th *Conf. Hypercubes, Concurrent Comput., & Appl.*, vol. I, pp. 129–132, Mar 1989.

[3] M. J. Bach, *The Design of the UNIX Operating System*. Prentice-Hall, 1986.

[4] E. DeBenedictis and J. M. del Rosario, "nCUBE parallel I/O software". In 11th *Intl. Phoenix Conf. Computers & Communications*, pp. 117–124, Apr 1992.

[5] E. P. DeBenedictis and J. M. del Rosario, "Modular scalable I/O". *J. Parallel & Distributed Comput.* **17(1&2)**, pp. 122–128, Jan/Feb 1993.

[6] J. M. del Rosario, "High performance parallel I/O on the nCUBE 2". *IEICE Trans.* **J75-D-I(8)**, pp. 626–636, Aug 1992. (Abstract in *IEICE Trans.* **E75-D(5)**, p. 737, Sep 1992).

[7] P. C. Dibble, M. L. Scott, and C. S. Ellis, "Bridge: a high-performance file system for parallel processors". In 8th *Intl. Conf. Distributed Comput. Syst.*, pp. 154–161, 1988.

[8] R. H. Katz, G. A. Gibson, and D. A. Patterson, "Disk system architectures for high performance computing". *Proc. IEEE* **77(12)**, pp. 1842–1858, Dec 1989.

[9] C. E. Leiserson, Z. S. Abuhamdeh, D. C. Douglas, C. R. Feynman, M. N. Ganmukhi, J. V. Hill, W. D. Hillis, B. C. Kuszmaul, M. A. St. Pierre, D. S. Wells, M. C. Wong, S-W. Yang, and R. Zak, "The network architecture of the Connection Machine CM-5". In 4th *Symp. Parallel Algorithms & Architectures*, pp. 272–285, Jun 1992.

[10] M. Livny, S. Khoshafian, and H. Boral, "Multi-disk management algorithms". In *SIGMETRICS Conf. Measurement & Modeling of Comput. Syst.*, pp. 69–77, 1987.

[11] M. N. Nelson, B. B. Welch, and J. K. Ousterhout, "Caching in the Sprite network file system". *ACM Trans. Comput. Syst.* **6(1)**, pp. 134–154, Feb 1988.

[12] D. A. Patterson, G. Gibson, and R. H. Katz, "A case for redundant arrays of inexpensive disks (RAID)". In *SIGMOD Intl. Conf. Management of Data*, pp. 109–116, Jun 1988.

[13] P. Pierce, "A concurrent file system for a highly parallel mass storage subsystem". In 4th *Conf. Hypercubes, Concurrent Comput., & Appl.*, vol. I, pp. 155–160, Mar 1989.

[14] K. Salem and H. Garcia-Molina, "Disk striping". In *Proc. Intl. Conf. Data Engineering*, pp. 336–342, 1986.

[15] J. Salmon, "CUBIX: programming hypercubes without programming hosts". In *Hypercube Multiprocessors 1987*, M. T. Heath (ed.), SIAM, 1987.

[16] R. Sandberg, D. Goldberg, S. Kleiman, D. Walsh, and B. Lyon, "Design and implementation of the Sun network filesystem". In *Proc. Summer USENIX Technical Conf.*, pp. 119–130, Jun 1985.

[17] M. Satyanarayanan, J. J. Kistler, P. Kumar, M. E. Okasaki, E. H. Siegel, and D. C. Steere, "Coda: a highly available file system for a distributed workstation environment". *IEEE Trans. Comput.* **39(4)**, pp. 447–459, Apr 1990.

[18] P. Steiner, "Extending multiprogramming to a DMPP". *Future Generation Comput. Syst.* **8(1-3)**, pp. 93–109, Jul 1992.

[19] L. W. Tucker and G. G. Robertson, "Architecture and applications of the Connection Machine". *Computer* **21(8)**, pp. 26–38, Aug 1988.

[20] J. S. Vitter and E. A. M. Shriver, "Optimal disk I/O with parallel block transfer". In 22nd *Ann. Symp. Theory of Computing*, pp. 159–169, May 1990.

Session 7:
Sparse Matrices
Chair: Bob Ward

Distributed Memory Matrix-Vector Multiplication and Conjugate Gradient Algorithms

John G. Lewis

Mathematics and Engineering Analysis
Boeing Computer Services
M/S 7L-22
P.O. Box 24346
Seattle, WA 98124-0346

Robert A. van de Geijn

Department of Computer Sciences
University of Texas
Austin TX 78712

Abstract

The critical bottlenecks in the implementation of the conjugate gradient algorithm on distributed memory computers are the communication requirements of the sparse matrix-vector multiply and of the vector recurrences. We describe the data distribution and communication patterns of five general implementations, whose realizations demonstrate that the cost of communication can be overcome to a much larger extent than is often assumed. Our results also apply to more general settings for matrix-vector products, both sparse and dense.

1 Introduction

Exploiting sparsity in solving sparse linear algebraic equations is crucial in minimizing the complexity requirements for both arithmetic and storage. However, maintaining sparsity has often flown in the face of obtaining high performance from high performance machines. Introducing parallelism into sparse algorithms is not usually viewed as a move likely to result in observed high "efficiency" vis a vis peak rates.

It is common folk wisdom that the primary bottleneck on distributed memory multicomputers is the communications network. We do not dispute this assumption. However, our conclusions from this study lead us to argue against a common approach to such problems, in which communications is avoided at whatever cost required. We try to meet the communications issue head on, and find that with the appropriate formulations we are successful enough in doing so.

Our results are obtained from a single problem, solving sparse symmetric linear systems with the conjugate gradient algorithm. This is of sufficient generality and importance that it is one of the eight benchmark applications developed by the NAS project at NASA Ames Research Center. It was chosen as an important problem that is difficult for multiprocessors. This paper describes implementation issues for the NAS Conjugate Gradient Benchmark, as implemented on the Intel iPSC/860 hypercube. The difficulty of this benchmark for distributed memory machines may be measured by the performance numbers originally obtained by NAS: in megaflops, 70 for a 128 processor iPSC/860, 105 for a 32,768 processor CM-2, and 127 for one Cray Y-MP processor.

2 Notation

Our parallel computer consists of p processing nodes. These are viewed as a logical 2D mesh of dimension $r \times c$, where $p = rc$ and p, c, r are all integer powers of two. The processing nodes are labeled $\mathcal{P}_{ij}$, $i = 0, \ldots, r-1$ and $j = 0, \ldots, c-1$. Physically, these nodes may form a hypercube or mesh. In either case, wormhole routing and low hardware latency ensures that in the absence of network conflicts the communication of a message of length n items can be modeled by $\alpha + n\beta$, where α equals the (mostly software) latency. Performing an arithmetic operation like floating point addition or multiplication is assumed to require time γ.

3 The NAS Parallel CG Benchmark

The NAS Parallel CG Benchmark is formally an application of the inverse iteration algorithm for finding eigenvalues. However, the essential part of the benchmark is the solution of unstructured sparse positive definite linear equations. The problem is deliberately unstructured to test the computer's communication features and to simulate the behavior of models on very irregular domains. The test matrices are created with a reproducible, but random, sparsity pattern. For benchmark purposes, a system of 14,000 equations is used. The coefficient matrix has 1,853,104 nonzeros, averaging 132 nonzeros per row.

Variants of the Conjugate Gradient method have been developed that require only one innerproduct per iteration, reducing both the communications and synchronization overhead. However, this is a secondary effect in comparison to the communication required for the sparse matrix-vector product and the vector recurrence. For simplicity, we use the standard Conjugate Gradient algorithm, the main iteration of which is given in Figure 1.

Figure 1: Conjugate Gradient Iteration

```
do until convergence
      y = Ax            sparse matrix-
                        vector multiply
      α = ρ/(xᵀy)       ddot
      z = z + αx        daxpy
      ρ₀ = ρ
      r = r − αy        daxpy
      ρ = rᵀr           ddot
      β = ρ/ρ₀
      x = r + βx        daypx
enddo
```

In any parallel implementation, the work of this recurrence must be distributed among the processors. In our implementations, the boxed operations require sharing of data or communication. Our data distributions are such that all of the other operations will be performed only on local data.

4 Useful Global Communication Patterns

In this section, we describe a number of basic communications patterns used in the various implementations. We concentrate on the basic approaches that are appropriate for hypercubes and meshes, and their theoretical performance. We will describe the algorithms as if all nodes are involved in the operation and the nodes are arranged in a 1D mesh. In our codes, we also use them for communications within groups that form 1D submeshes of a 2D mesh or independent subcubes of the full hypercube.

4.1 Broadcast

Starting with a vector $\mathbf{x}$ of length n on node $\mathcal{P}_i$, the operation completes with $\mathbf{x}$ reproduced on all nodes. For the vector lengths encountered in the NAS CG Benchmark, it suffices to consider the commonly used minimum spanning tree broadcast. In [2] it is shown that this can be done both on hypercubes, like the iPSC/860, and on meshes with worm-hole routing, like the Touchstone Delta, in time

$$\log_2(p)(\alpha + n\beta). \tag{1}$$

4.2 Global Collect

Assume vectors $\mathbf{x}_i$ initially reside on $\mathcal{P}_i$, $i = 0, \ldots, p - 1$. Then the global collect is used to concatenate these vectors, leaving the result $[\mathbf{x}_0|\mathbf{x}_1|\ldots|\mathbf{x}_{p-1}]$ duplicated on all nodes. This operation is often called a simultaneous broadcast or all-to-all communication. We use different algorithms for hypercubes and meshes. On a hypercube a recursive doubling algorithm can be used [8, 11], yielding time

$$\log_2(p)\alpha + \frac{(p-1)}{p}n\beta. \tag{2}$$

On meshes a "bucket" algorithm can used [3], yielding time

$$(p-1)\alpha + \frac{(p-1)}{p}n\beta. \tag{3}$$

4.3 Global Summation

Given that each processor, $\mathcal{P}_i$, owns a vector, $\mathbf{x}_i$, of length n, we wish to form $\mathbf{y} = \sum_{i=0}^{p-1} \mathbf{x}_i$. We will describe several approaches, which differ both in complexity and in how the result is to be left distributed among the nodes.

Fan-in A very simple approach to global summation uses a minimum spanning tree in the tree or mesh to combine to the root. This leaves the answer only at the root. If all nodes require the answer, this can be accomplished by a broadcast (fan-out) using the (same) minimum spanning tree. On meshes, network conflicts can be avoided, yielding a time for the fan-in on both hypercubes and meshes of

$$\log_2(p)(\alpha + n\beta + n\gamma).$$

The fan-out time is given by (1).

Recursive Halving This is a more sophisticated global summation algorithm for hypercubes. Essentially, communication identical to the recursive doubling collect is performed, except in reverse, with a summation of the incoming and local vector portions. The time required is

$$\log_2(p)\alpha + \frac{p-1}{p}n\beta + \frac{p-1}{p}n\gamma.$$

This operation leaves a portion of the result of length approximately n/p on each node. If the result is to be left duplicated among the nodes, it must be followed by a collect, adding the time given in (2). On meshes, this operation inherently incurs network conflicts. See [4, 11] for details of implementation on hypercubes and meshes.

Bucket This is a more sophisticated global summation algorithm for rings of nodes. The communication is identical to the bucket collect, except in reverse, with a summation of the incoming and local vector portions. On rings, the time required is

$$(p-1)\alpha + \frac{p-1}{p}n\beta + \frac{p-1}{p}n\gamma.$$

This operation leaves a portion of the result of length approximately n/p on each node. If the result is to be left duplicated among the nodes, it must be followed by a collect, adding the time given in (3). This implementation avoids network conflicts on ring architectures. See [4] for details of mesh implementation that reduces the communication startup requirements.

4.4   Two Dimensional Matrix Transpose

Let us assume for simplicity that the nodes form a logical *square* two dimensional array, $\mathcal{P}_{ij}$. The two dimensional matrix transpose simultaneously exchanges vectors between all pairs $\mathcal{P}_{ij}$ and $\mathcal{P}_{ji}$. In [7] it is observed that when the nodes of the hypercubes are labeled in the usual natural ordering, this operation requires $\sqrt{p}$ messages to pass through each diagonal node $\mathcal{P}_{ii}$, creating severe contention in the network. They show, however, that if the bit representations

of the row and column indices are interleaved to form the index of the processor, no network conflicts occur. Similar network conflicts occur on meshes, but cannot be so easily avoided.

5   Sparse Matrix-Vector Multiplication Kernels

There are three standard representations for unstructured sparse matrices, to which correspond three numeric kernels. The most general format is a list of triples $\{< i, j, \mathbf{a}_{ij} >\}$, one triple for each of the nz nonzeros in the matrix. The corresponding numeric kernel for the matrix-vector product $\mathbf{y} = \mathbf{A}\mathbf{x}$ is

> **for** $k = 1$ **to** nz **do**
> $\quad \mathbf{y}_{i_k} = \mathbf{y}_{i_k} + \mathbf{A}_{i_k, j_k} \mathbf{x}_{j_k}$.

This simple kernel does not take advantage of vector hardware, even if the triples are sorted according to either the row or column indices.

Two representations that simultaneously reduce storage overhead and have the potential to use vector hardware are storage by rows or by columns. If by rows, each row of the matrix is represented by a list of pairs $\{< j, \mathbf{a}_{ij} >\}$, listing the rnz_i nonzeros in the i-th row. Similarly, each column can be represented by the pairs $\{< i, \mathbf{a}_{ij} >\}$, giving the cnz_j nonzeros in the j-th column. The corresponding kernels are

row storage
> **for** $i = 1$ **to** n **do**
> $\quad$ **for** $k = 1$ **to** rnz_i **do**
> $\quad\quad \mathbf{y}_i = \mathbf{y}_i + \mathbf{A}_{i, j_{i,k}} \mathbf{x}_{j_{i,k}}$.

The inner loop is an indirectly addressed variant of a dot product, known as `ddoti` [5].

column storage
> **for** $j = 1$ **to** n **do**
> $\quad$ **for** $k = 1$ **to** cnz_j **do**
> $\quad\quad \mathbf{y}_{i_{j,k}} = \mathbf{y}_{i_{j,k}} + \mathbf{A}_{i_{j,k}, j} \mathbf{x}_j$.

This inner loop is an indirectly addressed elementary row operation `daxpyi`.

The kernels `ddoti` and `daxpyi` attain vector performance on machines with hardware gather-scatter. On superscalar machines they do not achieve true vector speed; they do outperform the first kernel, unless rnz_i (cnz_j) is very small, by reducing the number of address calculations. Predicting asymptotic performance on the Intel i860 is complicated by the cache structure.

For reasonable combinations of n and rnz_i (cnz_j), approximations at performance are given in Table 1 below. Memory bottlenecks on the Intel i860 generally make `ddoti` the fastest of these three kernels. There are two sets of performance figures given for a single Intel i860 processor. The first is for a very sparse problem with very low cache reuse; the second is an approximation of the NAS test problem, but with the effect of simultaneous communication removed. These results reflect the best use of assembly code or inline Fortran coding of the kernels. Actual performance lies between these figures. It is clear from these performance figures that the overall performance of the iPSC/860 on the conjugate gradient benchmark is limited by the i860's performance on indirectly addressed loops.

Table 1: Sparse Vector Kernels on Intel i860 in Megaflops

	daxpyi	ddoti	triples
very sparse	2.2	3.3	2.0
moderately sparse	3.1	3.8	2.5

6 Five Implementations of Matrix-Vector Multiplication

We will describe five different implementations of distributed memory matrix vector multiplication. The key decision is data distribution, where we note that each processor will perform the numeric operations corresponding to some submatrix of $\mathbf{A}$. Our fundamental rule is "owner computes" – each processor will compute $\mathbf{A}_{ij}\mathbf{x}_j$ for each value $\mathbf{A}_{ij}$ in its submatrix. Each processor will need access to the datum $\mathbf{x}_j$ for every column j in which it holds a nonzero $\mathbf{A}_{ij}$, and it will modify each corresponding value $\mathbf{y}_i$. We use only rectangular submatrices; this is generally sufficient for such randomly sparse problems.

We add to the usual data distribution rules the requirement that the output vector $\mathbf{y}$ be distributed exactly as is the input vector $\mathbf{x}$. This suits an algorithm in which a sequence of matrix-vector products is computed, such as the conjugate-gradient algorithm, in which the output vector $\mathbf{y}$ is used to compute the input vector for the next iteration. The implementations for matrix-vector multiply given below become implementations of the conjugate gradient algorithm simply by having each processor perform the unboxed operations in Figure 1 on the entries in $\mathbf{x}, \mathbf{y}$ and $\mathbf{r}$ that it owns.

For simplicity, the algorithms are presented only for even powers of 2 processors, which give rise to square 2D mesh partitioning. All of these algorithms generalize to rectangular mesh partitionings. Our theoretical results are presented for the general case, but even there we assume perfect load balance in the sense of assuming even distribution of entries of A. This is not far from true in this randomly sparse example, but it is not precisely correct. In all estimates, n denotes the matrix dimension, while nz equals the number of nonzeros in the matrix.

6.1 1D-Version (Method 1)

Let
$$\mathbf{A} = \begin{pmatrix} \mathbf{A}_0 \\ \vdots \\ \mathbf{A}_{p-1} \end{pmatrix}, \quad \mathbf{y} = \begin{pmatrix} \mathbf{y}_0 \\ \vdots \\ \mathbf{y}_{p-1} \end{pmatrix}.$$
Then
$$\mathbf{y}_i = \mathbf{A}_i \mathbf{x}.$$
The following algorithm will form $\mathbf{y}$ and leave it distributed like $\mathbf{x}$:

1. Assign $\mathbf{A}_i$ and $\mathbf{x}$ to $\mathcal{P}_i$.
2. Form $\mathbf{y}_i = \mathbf{A}_i x$.
3. Collect $\mathbf{y}_i$ to form $\mathbf{y}$ duplicated on all nodes.

For hypercubes, we estimate the total time as
$$2\left(\frac{nz}{p}\right)\gamma + \log_2(p)\alpha + \frac{p-1}{p}n\beta.$$

On rings, $\log_2(p)$ must be replaced by $(p-1)$. On square physical meshes, the bucket collect can be adjusted to require only $2(\sqrt{(p)}-1)$ startups.

6.2 Row-Fan-In, Column-Fan-Out (Method 2)

We now consider several algorithms that use two-dimensional matrix decompositions. First, partition
$$\mathbf{A} = \begin{pmatrix} \mathbf{A}_{00} & \cdots & \mathbf{A}_{0(c-1)} \\ \vdots & & \vdots \\ \mathbf{A}_{(r-1)0} & \cdots & \mathbf{A}_{(r-1)(c-1)} \end{pmatrix}, \mathbf{x} = \begin{pmatrix} \mathbf{x}_0 \\ \vdots \\ \mathbf{x}_{c-1} \end{pmatrix}.$$
Then
$$\mathbf{y} = \mathbf{A}\mathbf{x} = \begin{pmatrix} \mathbf{A}_{00}\mathbf{x}_0 + \cdots + \mathbf{A}_{0(p-1)}\mathbf{x}_{(c-1)} \\ \vdots \\ \mathbf{A}_{(r-1)0}\mathbf{x}_0 + \cdots + \mathbf{A}_{(r-1)(c-1)}\mathbf{x}_{(c-1)} \end{pmatrix}.$$

The following algorithm will form $\mathbf{y}$, leaving it distributed like $\mathbf{x}$:

1. Assign $\mathbf{A}_{ij}$ and $\mathbf{x}_j$ to $\mathcal{P}_{ij}$.

2. Form $\mathbf{A}_{ij}\mathbf{x}_j$.

3. Perform a fan-in from the processors in each row i to the diagonal processor $\mathcal{P}_{ii}$ in that row, leaving $\mathbf{y}_i = \sum \mathbf{A}_{ij}\mathbf{x}_j$ on $\mathcal{P}_{ii}$.

4. Broadcast $\mathbf{y}_i$ from $\mathcal{P}_{ii}$ to all nodes within column i.

The estimated total time for both hypercubes and meshes is

$$\left[2\left(\frac{nz}{p}\right) + \log_2(c)\frac{n}{r}\right]\gamma +$$
$$\log_2(p)\alpha + \left[\log_2(c)\frac{n}{r} + log_2(r)\frac{n}{c}\right]\beta.$$

Notice that the communication requirements have decreased considerably: Total traffic has been reduced from $\mathcal{O}(n)$ to $\mathcal{O}(log_2(p)n/\sqrt{p})$. However, the data distribution results in only the $r = \sqrt{p}$ diagonal processors $\mathcal{P}_{ii}$ owning portions of recurrence vectors $\mathbf{x}$, $\mathbf{y}$ and $\mathbf{r}$. Thus, the remaining steps of the CG algorithm are computed only on a subset of the machine. The next two decompositions attempt to fully parallelize the entire CG algorithm.

6.3 Overdecomposition (Method 3)

Our next method attempts to parallelize all of the CG algorithm, while also reducing the perceived overhead of communication. This scheme uses an overdecomposition of the matrix. The matrix is partitioned into $p \times p$ blocks. The processor assignment is such that each processor owns p blocks or submatrices, $\sqrt{p}$ of which lie in each of $\sqrt{p}$ block rows and $\sqrt{p}$ block columns. In addition, each node is the root of a row fan-in and a column fan out. The message volume remains the same as in method 2, but the number of messages increases from $\log_2(p)$ to $2\sqrt{p}\log_2(\sqrt{p})$. The increased startup costs are more than offset in this implementation by overlapping computation and communication. Overlapping is achieved by allowing each processor to compute the submatrix products on partial data it has already received, when it would otherwise be waiting for data from other processors. Similarly each processor participates in row summations for which it has computed the entirety of its block row of submatrix products, while still computing remaining submatrix products. The running time of this algorithm is extremely difficult to estimate accurately, because each node may be computing and

have as many as $\sqrt{p}$ messages in transit at any time. Assuming the maximum overlap of computation and communication, we estimate the total running time on hypercubes as:

$$\max\left\{2\left(\frac{nz}{p}\right)\gamma, \left[\log_2(p)\frac{n}{p}\right]\beta\right\} +$$
$$[c\log_2(c) + r\log_2(r)]\alpha + \log_2(c)\frac{n}{r}\gamma.$$

This is a very optimistic estimate for the effect of overlapping. However, the more crucial issue is the rapidly increasing number of messages, which prevents this formulation from scaling to very large numbers of nodes.

On the current generation of hypercubes, this approach successfully increases the number of messages to reduce total time, as shown in §7. However, the code for this method is quite complex. In effect it requires multiprocessing on each node, which on the iPSC/860 was implemented with Intel specific handler driven communication. Details go beyond the scope of this paper. Furthermore, the number of nonzeros per block is very small. This elevates to a significant role the additional $\mathcal{O}(n/\sqrt{p})$ overhead associated with two loops in `ddoti` and `daxpyi`. In fact, this method requires use of the slower "triple" storage approach because the decomposition is too fine for the sparse vector kernels. (This would not be an issue for a dense version of the code.)

6.4 Doubling/Halving (Method 4)

Our fourth algorithm also has the property of parallelizing all of the CG iteration, but without overdecomposing $\mathbf{A}$. This scheme uses the same decomposition of $\mathbf{A}$ as Method 2. The vector $\mathbf{x}$ is refined beyond Method 2; as in Method 3, additional messages are used to achieve higher speed. However, a more refined use of additional communication allows this method to scale.

Let $\mathbf{A}$ and $\mathbf{x}$ be partitioned as in Method 2, that is,

$$\mathbf{A} = \begin{pmatrix} \mathbf{A}_{00} & \cdots & \mathbf{A}_{0(c-1)} \\ \vdots & & \vdots \\ \mathbf{A}_{(r-1)0} & \cdots & \mathbf{A}_{(r-1)(c-1)} \end{pmatrix}, \mathbf{x} = \begin{pmatrix} \mathbf{x}_0 \\ \vdots \\ \mathbf{x}_{c-1} \end{pmatrix}.$$

Furthermore, decompose the subvector

$$\mathbf{x}_j = \begin{pmatrix} \mathbf{x}_{0j} \\ \vdots \\ \mathbf{x}_{(c-1)j} \end{pmatrix}$$

We subdivide $\mathbf{x}$ into p pieces $\mathbf{x}_{ij}$ of length approximately n/p, so that the collected subvectors $\mathbf{x}_{*j}$ are conformal with the partitioning of $\mathbf{A}$. To each node, $\mathcal{P}_{ij}$, we assign the subvector $\mathbf{x}_{ij}$. Distribute $\mathbf{y}$ (and $\mathbf{r}$) in the same manner. The following algorithm will form $\mathbf{y}$, leaving it properly distributed:

1. Assign $\mathbf{A}_{ij}$ and $\mathbf{x}_{ij}$ to $\mathcal{P}_{ij}$.

2. Form $\mathbf{x}_j$ by performing a collect within each column of nodes, leaving the result on each of those nodes. (Use recursive doubling on hypercubes or buckets on meshes).

3. Form $\mathbf{A}_{ij}\mathbf{x}_j$.

4. Perform a summation within rows by recursive halving for hypercubes or bucket for meshes. This leaves $\mathbf{y}_{ji}$ on $\mathcal{P}_{ij}$.

5. Send $\mathbf{y}_{ji}$ from $\mathcal{P}_{ij}$ to $\mathcal{P}_{ji}$.

We estimate the total time for hypercubes as

$$\left[2\left(\frac{nz}{p}\right) + \left(\frac{c-1}{c}\right)\left(\frac{n}{r}\right) \right]\gamma +$$
$$(\log_2(p) + 1)\alpha +$$
$$\left[\left(\frac{c-1}{c}\right)\left(\frac{n}{r}\right) + \left(\frac{r-1}{r}\right)\left(\frac{n}{c}\right) + \frac{n}{p} \right]\beta.$$

This estimate assumes that the processor mapping described in §4.4 is used for hypercubes. For meshes, $\log_2(p)$ must be replaced by $(c + r - 2)$, and network conflict will occur, which is ignored in this formula.

It should be noted that this is essentially a sparse version of the dense matrix–vector multiplication algorithm in Fox, et.al. [6], with the additional observation that only a transpose is needed to complete the data movement for the iteration. This method was independently discovered by Hendrickson, Leland and Plimpton [7], who observed the need to avoid network conflicts in the mapping of the mesh of processors to a hypercube.

6.5 Transpose Free Doubling/Halving (Method 5)

Our final algorithm is very similar to Method 4, except that the transpose operation is avoided by using a different data decomposition, a partial overdecomposition, for the matrix $\mathbf{A}$. Methods 2 and 4 assign a processor a single, contiguous, block of $\mathbf{A}$. Our alternative data decomposition is motivated by the distribution of vector $\mathbf{x}$ and the fact that the result vector $\mathbf{y}$ must be distributed like $\mathbf{x}$.

Let $\mathbf{x}$ be partitioned as in Method 2, with the subvectors decomposed as in Method 4, so that

$$\mathbf{x} = \begin{pmatrix} \mathbf{x}_0 \\ \vdots \\ \mathbf{x}_{c-1} \end{pmatrix} \text{ and } \mathbf{x}_j = \begin{pmatrix} \mathbf{x}_{0j} \\ \vdots \\ \mathbf{x}_{(c-1)j} \end{pmatrix}.$$

We partition $\mathbf{A}$ into $p \times c = rc \times c$ blocks so that the column partitioning is conformal with the coarse partitioning of $\mathbf{x}$ and the row partitioning is conformally with the fine partitioning of $\mathbf{y}$, that is,

$$\mathbf{A} = \begin{pmatrix} \mathbf{A}_{00} & \cdots & \mathbf{A}_{0(c-1)} \\ \vdots & & \vdots \\ \mathbf{A}_{(r-1)0} & \cdots & \mathbf{A}_{(r-1)(c-1)} \\ \mathbf{A}_{(r)0} & \cdots & \mathbf{A}_{(r)(c-1)} \\ \vdots & & \vdots \\ \mathbf{A}_{(2r)0} & \cdots & \mathbf{A}_{(2r)(c-1)} \\ \vdots & & \vdots \\ \mathbf{A}_{(cr-1)0} & \cdots & \mathbf{A}_{(cr-1)(c-1)} \end{pmatrix}.$$

Begin by assigning $\mathbf{x}_{ij}$ and $\mathbf{y}_{ij}$ to processor $\mathcal{P}_{ij}$. We want to assign blocks in the partitioning of $\mathbf{A}$ to $\mathcal{P}_{ij}$ in such a way that no transposition is needed. Note that collecting the pieces within column j results in vector $\mathbf{x}_j$. This indicates that node $\mathcal{P}_{ij}$ should be assigned submatrices of $\mathbf{A}$ taken from the j-th column of submatrices, as these submatrices occur in products with $\mathbf{x}_j$.

Next, consider the recursive halving sum within rows of processors. We would like the subvector $\mathbf{y}_{ij}$ to be left on $\mathcal{P}_{ij}$. Without specifying which submatrices $\mathbf{A}_{kj}$ are assigned to each processor $\mathcal{P}_{ij}$, let $\mathbf{y}^{(i)}$ be the vector obtained by concatenating all vectors $\mathbf{y}_{kj} = \mathbf{A}_{kj}\mathbf{x}_j$ computed by the i-th row of processors. With $\mathbf{A}$ decomposed as in Method 4, $\mathbf{y}^{(i)}$ is the concatenation of $\{\mathbf{y}_{ji}, j = 0, \ldots, c\}$. What we want instead is the concatenation of $\{\mathbf{y}_{ij}, j = 0, \ldots, c\}$. We can obtain this by noting that the block rows of $\mathbf{A}$ that should be assigned to the i-th row of processors are exactly those block rows that appear in the concatenation of $\{\mathbf{y}_{ij}, j = 0, \ldots, c\}$. That is, processor $\mathcal{P}_{ij}$ should be assigned blocks from block rows $i, i + r, i + 2r, \ldots, i + (c - 1)r$ of $\mathbf{A}$ and from block column j. This assigns to $\mathcal{P}_{ij}$ the matrix

$$\mathbf{B}_{ij} = \begin{pmatrix} \mathbf{A}_{ij} \\ \mathbf{A}_{(i+r)j} \\ \vdots \\ \mathbf{A}_{(i+(c-1)r)j} \end{pmatrix}.$$

The following algorithm will form $\mathbf{y}$, leaving it properly distributed:

1. Assign $\mathbf{B}_{ij}$ and $\mathbf{x}_{ij}$ to $\mathcal{P}_{ij}$.

2. Form $\mathbf{x}_j$ by performing a collect within each column of nodes, leaving the result on each of those nodes. (Use recursive doubling on hypercubes or buckets on meshes).

3. Form $\mathbf{B}_{ij}\mathbf{x}_j$.

4. Perform a summation within rows by recursive halving for hypercubes or bucket for meshes. This leaves $\mathbf{y}_{ij}$ on $\mathcal{P}_{ij}$.

We estimate the total time for hypercubes as

$$\left[2\left(\frac{nz}{p}\right) + \left(\frac{c-1}{c}\right)\left(\frac{n}{r}\right)\right]\gamma +$$
$$\log_2(p)\alpha + \left[\left(\frac{c-1}{c}\right)\left(\frac{n}{r}\right) + \left(\frac{r-1}{r}\right)\left(\frac{n}{c}\right)\right]\beta.$$

No transpose is required. For meshes, $\log_2(p)$ must be replaced by $(c + r - 2)$.

This data decomposition can be described in standard terms. We partition the original matrix A into $p \times c$ subblocks and assign these subblocks in a blocked fashion to columns, and a wrapped fashion to rows. Assuming that $\mathbf{B}_{ij}$ is treated as a single block, the granularity of this algorithm is identical to Method 4; the partial overdecomposition does not cause performance problems as it does in Method 3.

6.6 Performance Prediction and Scalability

To illustrate the expected performance of the different implementations, let us use some representative machine constants for the iPSC/860: $\alpha = 350\mu sec, \beta = 3\mu sec, \gamma = .2\mu sec$. These parameters should not be taken too literally, since there is a considerable dependence on details of implementation. However, fixing these parameters allows us to exhibit trends.

In Figure 2 we use our simple complexity model to estimate performance of the different approaches as a function of the number of nodes. In this graph, 1D represents Method 1, 2D fan Method 2, 2D over Method 3, 2D hyp d/h Methods 4 and 5 on a hypercube, and 2D mesh d/h Methods 4 and 5 on a mesh. *In these predictions, network conflicts are ignored, making the curves for Methods 4 and 5 essentially identical.* Notice that quickly computation becomes insignificant, as indicated by the curve comp. only.

Clearly Method 1 does not scale because the message volume per processor does not decrease. In all of

Figure 2: Estimated execution time of the sparse matrix-vector multiply.

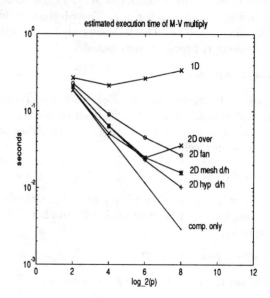

the other methods the message volume decreases, but not linearly, as the number of processors increases. In addition, all have an increasing term, the startup cost for messages, which grows (mostly) logarithmically. The startup term accounts for the difference between the estimate for a mesh and a hypercube for Methods 4 and 5. The estimate for the effect of the rapid growth in number of messages for Method 3 shows that it will not scale beyond the current number of nodes on the iPSC/860. For very large numbers of nodes, communication severely dominates computation. However, it should be noted that for future architectures, like the Intel Paragon, both α and β can be expected to decrease considerably more than γ, as is already the case for the Touchstone Delta.

Including the additional vector operations of the conjugate gradient algorithm increases the complexity by

$$2\log_2(p)(\alpha + \beta) + 10\frac{n}{q}\gamma,$$

where q is the number of processors participating in the vector operations. The visual effect of each term on the graph is negligible. The logarithmic growth of the α term is less important than the departure from linearity of the β term. The effect of the vector computations is an increase of less than 5% in the computation cost for all but Method 2. In this latter case $q = \sqrt{p}$, so the recurrence work at $p = 256$ is 160%

of the matrix-vector multiply. However, the computation cost has become so small that even tripling it will make only a small change in the **2D fan** curve.

7 Experiments on the Intel iPSC/860

The five algorithms described in §6 were all implemented in Fortran on the Intel iPSC/860 hypercube system. This was part of a larger study in which we considered a number of other factors, such as forced versus unforced and asynchronous versus synchronous messages, assembly language versus fortran for the matrix-vector product kernels, sorted versus unsorted index lists for the sparse matrix, rectangular mesh configurations, and single and double innerproduct versions of the conjugate gradient algorithm. More details on this study will be reported in [9], which will also include further performance results to be obtained from the Intel Delta system.

The results presented herein are the best results we obtained with each of our five algorithms. All of these implementations using forced messages and all but method 3 use asynchronous (isend/irecv) message paradigms. Method 3 requires the use of handler (hrecv) routines for message receipt.

The numeric kernels are all in-line Fortran. The results for the *triples* kernel are given for nonzeros stored in sparse column-major storage, that is, so that the indices appear sorted by columns, and by rows within each column. This ordering appears to make better use of the i860 cache than does row-major or random orderings.

The timings are all obtained in the form required by the NAS benchmarks; the table gives the elapsed time in seconds for the entire inverse iteration algorithm that constitutes the "conjugate gradient" benchmark.

In our experiments, three factors provided the greatest increases in performance. Table 2 demonstrates the dramatic effect of data partitioning. The proper choice of numeric kernel is also important, as demonstrated by the performance on method 3. Note however that the triples choice is only effective in this overdecomposition case; everywhere the `ddoti` approach is much superior. The third factor is the use of *forced* messages, which requires additional storage planning and care in synchronization.

Table 3 provides some preliminary results from the Intel Touchstone Delta mesh computer. These provide an indication of the scalability of these re-

---

[1]standard mapping, with collisions in transpose
[2]interleaved mapping, no collisions in transpose

Table 2: Conjugate Gradient Benchmark Performance on Intel iPSC/860 hypercubes

method	numeric kernel	128 processors		
		grid	time	megaflops
Original NAS				70
1	ddoti	128×1	20.6	73
2	ddoti	16×8	11.9	126
2	ddoti	32×4	10.3	146
3	ddoti	16×8	13.6	111
3	triples	16×8	8.6	174
4^1	ddoti	8×16	9.4	160
4^2	ddoti	8×16	8.5	176
5	ddoti	8×16	8.3	**181**

Table 3: Conjugate Gradient Benchmark Performance on Intel Delta mesh multiprocessor

method	numeric kernel	physical grid	time	megaflops
4	ddoti	4×8	17.2	87
4	ddoti	8×4	17.2	87
4	ddoti	8×8	9.6	156
4	ddoti	8×16	6.1	246
4	ddoti	16×8	5.8	257
4	ddoti	16×16	3.9	382
4	ddoti	16×32	3.3	449

sults, especially inasmuch as these are results from Method 4, rather than the better scaling, transpose free Method 5.

8 Conclusion

The five variants on the matrix vector multiplication represent a classic case study of the incremental development of the parallel implementation of a numerical algorithm. The 1D implementation can be regarded as a "least effort" implementation, which actually requires no explicit communication. The communications primitives for the global summation (dot product) and global collect are usually provided by the vendor. In fact, the results given here, which use a refined global collect created by the second author, exceed the performance of the original NAS parallel implementation.

The fan-in/fan-out 2D implementation is a second effort that attempts to reduce communication requirements. This is similar to NAS's implementation. The most important difference between it and the NAS version is the use of asynchronous and forced messages. This illustrates, unfortunately, the need to observe details in the native communications operations. Both of these techniques require care in memory management, complicating the programming effort.

The final three versions illustrate the potential improvements that can come from using more robust communications primitives, even when they increase the number of messages, and perhaps even the volume of traffic. However, both represent difficulties in coding, particularly for Method 3, where the overlapping of communication and computation is achieved only with a complex code. Further, this approach does not scale well for fixed problem sizes. The last two implementations retain portability and modularity, while yielding good performance across a range of machine sizes, even when the problem size is fixed. The final implementation places lower requirements on the communication network.

All except the initial code demonstrate a gap in the communications libraries of most MPP vendors. The communications patterns in §4 are natural fits for both problem and architecture. Reductions and broadcasts across natural groupings of processors, not full machines, occur in many other applications, but these operations are not commonly supported by vendors.

We should observe that all of these implementations ignore special sparsity structure in **A**. Randomization is a reasonable approach to obtaining load balancing [10], but if load balance can be obtained otherwise, the sparsity structure of **A** may permit special purpose communication patterns. Our implementations, especially Method 5, should be regarded as "best general purpose", or perhaps "best worst case", approaches.

Acknowledgments

We would like to acknowledge the input of a number of people into this effort, including, in alphabetical order, Bruce Hendrickson, Robert Leland, Shaoze Ouyang, James C. Patterson, David Payne, and Yun Shen. This research was performed in part using the Intel Touchstone Delta System operated by the California Institute of Technology on behalf of the Concurrent Supercomputing Consortium. Access to this facility was provided by Intel Supercomputing Systems Division

References

[1] D. Bailey, J. Barton, T. Lasinski and H. Simon (editors). The NAS Parallel Benchmarks. Report RNR-91-022, NASA Ames Research Center, Moffett Field, CA, Jan. 1991.

[2] M. Barnett, D. Payne, and R. van de Geijn. Optimal broadcasting in mesh-connected architectures. Technical Report TR-91-38, Department of Computer Sciences, The University of Texas at Austin, Dec. 1991.

[3] M. Barnett, R. Littlefield, D.G. Payne, and R. van de Geijn. Efficient Communication Primitives on Mesh Architectures with Hardware Routing, Sixth SIAM Conf. on Par. Proc. for Sci. Comp., Norfolk, Virginia, March 22-24, 1993.

[4] M. Barnett, R. Littlefield, D.G. Payne, and R. van de Geijn, Global Combine on Mesh Architectures with Wormhole Routing, in the proceedings of the *7th International Parallel Processing Symposium*, Newport Beach, CA, April 13-16, 1993.

[5] D.S. Dodson and J.G. Lewis, Sparse Extensions to the FORTRAN Basic Linear Algebra Subprograms, ACM Trans. Math. Softw 17 (1991), pages 253–263.

[6] G. Fox, et.al., *Solving Problems on Concurrent Processors: Volume 1*, Prentice Hall, Englewood Cliffs, NJ, 1988.

[7] B. Hendrickson, R. Leland, and S. Plimpton, A Parallel Algorithm for Matrix-Vector Multiplication, Tech. Rep. SAND 92-2765, Sandia National Laboratories, Albuquerque, NM, March 1993.

[8] C.-T. Ho and S.L. Johnsson, Distributed Routing Algorithms for Broadcasting and Personalized Communication in Hypercubes, In *Proceedings of the 1986 International Conference on Parallel Processing*, pages 640–648, IEEE, 1986.

[9] J.G. Lewis, S. Ouyang, J. Patterson, D. Payne, Y. Shen and R.A. van de Geijn, Sparse Matrix Vector Multiply and Conjugate Gradient Algorithms on Distributed Memory Computers, in preparation.

[10] A.T. Ogielski and W. Aiello, Sparse Matrix Computations on Parallel Processor Arrays, SIAM J. Sci. Comp 14 (1993), pages 519–530.

[11] R.A. van de Geijn. On global combine operations. LAPACK Working Note 29, Technical Report CS-91-129, University of Tennessee, 1991. Modified version to appear in JPDC.

A Spectral Algorithm for Envelope Reduction of Sparse Matrices

Stephen T. Barnard

Cray Research Inc.
NASA Ames Research Center
Moffett Field, CA 94035

Alex Pothen

Computer Science Dept.
University of Waterloo
Waterloo, Ontario N2L 3G1
Canada

Horst D. Simon

Computer Sciences Corp.
NASA Ames Research Center
Moffett Field, CA 94035

Abstract

A new algorithm for reducing the envelope of a sparse matrix is presented. This algorithm is based on the computation of eigenvectors of the Laplacian matrix associated with the graph of the sparse matrix. A reordering of the sparse matrix is determined based on the numerical values of the entries of an eigenvector of the Laplacian matrix. Numerical results show that the new reordering algorithm can in some cases reduce the envelope by more than a factor of two over the current standard algorithms such as Gibbs-Poole-Stockmeyer (GPS) or SPARSPAK's reverse Cuthill-McKee (RCM).

1 Introduction

Methods for the numerical solution of symmetric positive definite sparse linear systems of equations usually start out with reordering the coefficient matrix in order to reduce the fill-in during Gaussian elimination. An important class of reordering algorithms attempts to reduce the envelope or profile of the underlying sparse matrix. Algorithms for the reduction of the envelope or profile, or the related frontal methods, are still the method of choice for many structural engineering applications, for example in the computational structural mechanics testbed (CSM) at NASA Langley [17]. Implementations of these methods are also widely distributed in most of the finite element software packages such as MSC/NASTRAN or ANSYS. Parallel algorithms for the actual numerical factorization of a matrix in envelope format have been investigated [22, 28].

Here a new algorithm for reordering problems in sparse matrix computations is presented. It is related to the pseudoperipheral node algorithm described by Grimes et al. [15]. This heuristic algorithm for reducing the envelope of a sparse matrix has several features which set it apart from traditional reordering algorithms such as the Gibbs-Poole-Stockmeyer (GPS), Gibbs-King (GK), or SPARSPAK's reverse Cuthill-McKee algorithm (RCM) [6, 12, 13, 18]. The traditional algorithms are all graph algorithms, which operate on integer arrays representing the graph. A typical operation is the search for all neighbors of a node in the graph. These types of algorithms generally do not vectorize, and there is no obvious way to implement them in parallel. In contrast the new algorithm proposed here is based on the computation of an eigenvector of a special matrix, and hence involves standard floating point operations, such as matrix vector multiplications, dot products etc. Algorithms for these operations not only vectorize easily, but also can be implemented in parallel with little effort.[1] The algorithm is also iterative in nature, in the same sense that SOR or the Lanczos methods are iterative. It allows a user to terminate the reordering process depending on a stopping criterion, thus permitting the user to make trade-offs in ordering time versus storage efficiency. Since the new algorithm is based on spectral properties of the graph it will be called the *spectral algorithm*.

The algorithm is motivated by some theoretical results by Fiedler, and Juvan and Mohar. Let A be the adjacency matrix of the graph, and D the diagonal degree matrix; then the Laplacian matrix L is defined by $L = D - A$. The matrix L is a singular M-matrix, and its applications to graphs have been investigated by Fiedler [9, 10, 11]. By its construction, the smallest eigenvalue of L is zero; if the graph is connected, the corresponding eigenvector is $(1, 1, ...1)^T$. An eigen-

---

[1] Parallel implementation of the basic spectral method, which uses the Lanczos algorithm to find eigenvectors, is straightforward. Parallel implementation of the "multilevel" enhancements described in Section 3 is more difficult, but possible in principle.

vector corresponding to the first nonzero eigenvalue will be called a Fiedler vector. The new algorithm will use a Fiedler vector for the construction of an envelope-reducing matrix reordering. Juvan and Mohar [16] have advocated the use of the Fiedler vector for 'p-sum' and bandwidth reducing orderings. In recent years spectral algorithms have found a number of applications in solving discrete optimization problems. Most notably, spectral algorithms provide an excellent heuristic for partitioning unstructured meshes for parallel computation on distributed-memory machines. The spectral algorithm for partitioning is discussed in [23] and [26]. A spectral algorithm has been used for the general sparse matrix reordering problem in [24]. Here we take advantage of a recent very fast multilevel implementation of the recursive spectral bisection algorithm described in [5].

Efficient implementations of sparse matrix algorithms [1, 2, 8, 19, 27] on supercomputers demonstrate that very high levels of performance are attainable with general sparse algorithms. Hence there there are no good reasons to use envelope schemes for sparse matrix factorizations for the sake of performance alone. Furthermore, it has long been known that general sparse methods are considerably more efficient with respect to storage [12]. The authors of [2] presented numerical evidence that general sparse methods outperform envelope methods in both respects. However, envelope methods and related methods such as frontal or skyline methods continue to be the standard solution option in many commercial structural analysis packages. Thus, demonstrating the efficiency of the new spectral algorithm offers the potential of great performance improvements in these packages without making substantial changes to the underlying data structures.

Although initially envelope-reducing orderings were developed for use in envelope schemes for sparse matrix factorization, these orderings have been used in the past few years in several other applications. The RCM ordering has been found to be an effective preordering in computing incomplete factorization preconditioners for preconditioned conjugate gradient methods. Such orderings have also been used in parallel matrix-vector multiplication and tridiagonalization of sparse symmetric matrices.

Spectra of graphs have been investigated in detail by a large number of researchers in graph theory [7]. The results summarized in [7, 20] are primarily of theoretical interest. The idea of using spectral properties of the graph for solving computational problems has been proposed in [3] for graph coloring and in [15] for

the computation of a pseudo-peripheral node. The concepts and algorithms developed here are applied to the graph bisection problem in [23] (for some more theoretical results see also [25]). The results of the current study and of [23] are very encouraging. They indicate that spectral algorithms are a promising approach for solving computational problems in discrete mathematics. It is indeed remarkable that an algebraic quantity such as an eigenvector can be used in the solution of a discrete graph or sparse matrix problem.

In Section 2 the theoretical results of Fiedler will be summarized. Some additional evidence will be presented to justify the proposed new algorithm. In Section 3 we will present the spectral algorithm and discuss its numerical implementation. In particular the multilevel algorithm will be introduced, which uses coarsening of the underlying graph combined with Rayleigh Quotient Iteration (RQI). This multilevel algorithm allows the efficient computation of the Fiedler vector. Numerical results and comparisons with GPS, GK, and RCM will be presented in Section 4. These results indicate that the new algorithm is often considerably more efficient in reducing the storage requirements, while requiring a comparable amount of execution time. A journal version of this paper containing a more complete discussion of these results will be published elsewhere [4].

2 Theory

We consider an undirected, connected graph $G = (X, E)$, where X is the set of nodes (or vertices), and E is the set of edges. Let $X = \{x_i | i = 1, ... n\}$, and denote the edges $e \in E$ by $e = (x_i, x_j)$. The elements a_{ij} of the *adjacency matrix* $A(G)$ of G are defined by

$$a_{ij} = \begin{cases} 1 & \text{if nodes } i \text{ and } j \text{ are adjacent} \\ 0 & \text{otherwise.} \end{cases} \quad (1)$$

If G is the ordered graph of a symmetric positive definite matrix M, this definition proves to be useful for our purposes. In this case the a_{ij} could be defined directly by

$$a_{ij} = \begin{cases} 1 & \text{if} & m_{ij} \neq 0 \text{ and } i \neq j \\ 0 & \text{if} & m_{ij} = 0 \text{ or } i = j \end{cases}. \quad (2)$$

Let $d(x)$ denote the degree of a node $x \in X$, and let $D(G)$ denote the diagonal matrix with diagonal entries $d(x_i)$. The matrix $L = L(G) = D(G) - A(G)$ is called the *Laplacian matrix* of G.

494

In the context of this paper the spectral properties of L are of most interest. Consider the eigenvalue problem

$$Lu = \lambda u. \qquad (3)$$

The n eigenpairs $(\lambda_i, u_i), i = 1, \ldots n$ are called the *Laplacian spectrum* of G, or the spectrum of G.

Proposition 1 *The Laplacian spectrum has the following properties:*

1. *All eigenvalues are real and non-negative.*

2. *The smallest eigenvalue is $\lambda_1 = 0$; the multiplicity of 0 as an eigenvalue of L is equal to the number of connected components of G.*

3. *Let k be the number of connected components of G. Then the vectors $u_1, u_2, \ldots u_k$, where the entries of u_j corresponding to vertices in the j-th component of G are set to 1, and all other entries are equal to 0, are k linearly independent eigenvectors corresponding to the zero eigenvalue. Hence for a connected graph G, the eigenvector corresponding to the zero eigenvalue is $(1, 1, \ldots 1)^T$.*

For the remainder of this section the discussion will be restricted to the case of a connected G. The extension to the more general situation is straightforward. The eigenvalue of particular interest here is λ_2, the smallest positive eigenvalue of L. An eigenvector of L corresponding to λ_2 has been called by Fiedler the *characteristic valuation of G* [11]. Here we will call λ_2 for short the *Fiedler value*, and any corresponding eigenvector a *Fiedler vector*. If the Fiedler value is a multiple eigenvalue (for example, if G has symmetries), the Fiedler vector is not unique.

The Fiedler value has a number of properties related to the connectivity of the graph G. The smaller the Fiedler value, the more "disconnected" is the graph, with the limiting case of a zero Fiedler value corresponding to a graph with two disconnected components. For more details, see Mohar [20]. The Fiedler value and the Fiedler vector have been used in a companion study [23] for a new algorithm for the graph bisection problem.

A result concerning the Fiedler vector which is the key to the envelope-reduction method is the following theorem due to Fiedler [11]:

Theorem 1 *Let G be a connected graph, and $u = (u_1, u_2, \ldots u_n)$ be a Fiedler vector of G. For $\rho \leq 0$ define*

$$S(\rho) = \{x_i \in X | u_i \geq \rho\}. \qquad (4)$$

Then the subgraph induced on $S(\rho)$ is connected. Similarly, if $\rho \geq 0$, then $S'(\rho) = \{x_i | u_i \leq \rho\}$ induces a connected subgraph.

Let us now consider the envelope of a graph, or of the corresponding sparse matrix. For a set of vertices $X = \{x_i | i = 1, \ldots n\}$ we define the local bandwidth β_i to be

$$\beta_i = \max_{j < i, (x_i, x_j) \in E} i - j.$$

Then the envelope is defined by the set of indices $\{i, j\}$ which lie within the local band; i. e.,

$$Env(G) = \{\{i, j\} | i - \beta_i \leq j < i, i = 1, \ldots n\}.$$

We are interested in the size of the envelope; i.e. in $\eta = |Env(G)|$. In other applications the bandwidth $\beta = \max_i \beta_i$ is of interest.

In order to relate Theorem 1 to an algorithm for envelope reduction, we describe the concept of an *adjacency ordering* of a graph G. Let G_i denote the subgraph induced by the set of nodes $X_i = \{x_j | j = 1, 2, \ldots, i\}$. Furthermore, for a subset Y of the nodes, $Y \subseteq X$, the adjacency set of Y, denoted by $Adj(Y)$, is defined

$$Adj(Y) = \{x_i \, \epsilon \, X - Y \, | \, \{x_i, x_j\} \, \epsilon \, E \text{ for some } x_j \epsilon Y\}. \qquad (5)$$

Then the nodes of a graph are ordered according to an adjacency ordering if $x_{i+1} \in Adj(X_i)$, for $i = 1, 2, \ldots, n-1$. By its construction, the Cuthill-McKee ordering (but not the reverse Cuthill-McKee ordering (RCM) from SPARSPAK [12]) is an adjacency ordering.

Theorem 1 permits us to show that the Fiedler vector implies an ordering that is almost an adjacency ordering. Let $u = (u_1, u_2, \ldots u_n)^T$ be a Fiedler vector of the graph $G = (X, E)$. Let the nodes $x_i \in X$ be ordered such that $i \leq j$ if $u_i \leq u_j$. Let us consider the two sets of vertices corresponding to positive and to negative entries in the Fiedler vector; i.e., define $X_P = \{x_i | u_i > 0\}$ and $X_N = \{x_i | u_i < 0\}$. Let the vertices in X_N be numbered by $i = 1, \ldots k$, and the vertices in X_P by $i = p, \ldots n$. We have $k \leq p$. It is possible that $k < p$, since entries in the Fiedler vector can be zero. Then Theorem 1 implies that for $i = k+1, \ldots n$, $x_{i+1} \in Adj(X_i)$. A similar statement holds if we add vertices with negative entries in the Fiedler vector in decreasing order to the set X_P. This means that the order implied by the Fiedler vector has the property of an adjacency ordering if vertices with positive Fiedler vector entries are added in increasing order to X_N, or if vertices with negative Fiedler vector entries are added in decreasing order to X_P. However, there exist examples for which the spectral ordering is not an adjacency ordering.

This argument suggests that ordering the nodes of the graph (or the corresponding matrix) according to the entries of a Fiedler vector in increasing order will result in an ordering which reduces the envelope. Juvan and Mohar [16] arrive at a similar conclusion for the 'p-sum' and bandwidth problems, based on a different analysis not as closely related to the sparse matrix case.

A second argument in favor of the spectral ordering uses the minimizing property of eigenvectors to show that the spectral ordering minimizes a continuous quantity which is closely related to the size of the envelope. First note that the size of the envelope can be written as

$$\eta = |Env(G)| = \sum_{i=1}^{n} \beta_i = \sum_{i=1}^{n} \max_{j < i, (x_i, x_j) \in E} (i - j),$$

and an upper bound on the work in an envelope factorization is

$$\omega = |Work(G)| = \sum_{i=1}^{n} \beta_i^2 = \sum_{i=1}^{n} \max_{j < i, (x_i, x_j) \in E} (i - j)^2.$$

We consider the quantity σ, which is closely related to ω, defined as

$$\sigma = \sum_{i=1}^{n} \sum_{j < i, (x_i, x_j) \in E} (i - j)^2. \tag{6}$$

If we consider norms then η is related to the inf norm, whereas σ is related to the 2-norm. We will show that using a Fiedler vector is closely related to to minimizing σ over all possible permutations of the vertices. Thus the spectral ordering does not attempt to minimize the envelope size *per se*, but a closely related quantity, which can be considered the "Euclidean norm" of the envelope.

Equation (6) can be rewritten as

$$\sigma = \sum_{(x_i, x_j) \in E} (i - j)^2,$$

and note that for any vector $u \in R^n$, we have

$$u^T L u = \sum_{(x_i, x_j) \in E} (u_i - u_j)^2$$

by using the properties of the Laplacian matrix L. We now consider a special set of vectors $\mathcal{P}$, which we will call permutation vectors. If n is even then the components of $p \in \mathcal{P}$ are a permutation of the integers

$$-n/2, -n/2 + 1, ..., -1, +1, ..., n/2 - 1, n/2 ;$$

if n is odd then let $\mathcal{P}$ consist of the vectors, which have permutations of

$$-(n - 1)/2, ..., -1, 0, 1, ..., (n - 1)/2$$

as components. Note that by construction all vectors $p \in \mathcal{P}$ are orthogonal to e, the vector with all components equal to 1. We consider the permutation vectors as vectors in R^n, even though their components are integers. Clearly a choice of a permutation vector p implies a permutation of the vertices of the graph.

We are trying to determine the permutation which minimizes $\sigma(p)$, i.e.

$$\min_{p \in \mathcal{P}} \sigma(p) = \min_{p \in \mathcal{P}} \sum_{(x_i, x_j) \in E} (p_i - p_j)^2.$$

This is equivalent to minimizing σ above, since we have only shifted all integers by a constant amount. If we relax the condition $p \in \mathcal{P}$ to $p \in R^n, p^T e = 0$, then we can apply the minimizing property of the eigenvectors (Rayleigh-Ritz) to find that $p = u$, where u is the Fiedler vector of L, minimizes $\sigma(p)$ over all such vectors $p \in R^n$. Now u is an arbitrary real vector, and we need to find the closest permutation vector. But this vector is obtained by considering the permutation derived from the sorted Fiedler vector. (This result will be stated and proved more formally in the complete paper.)

Hence we have shown that the Fiedler vector minimizes a continuous version of a problem closely related to the envelope minimization problem. There are three possible sources of loss of optimality: when going from the envelope minimization problem to the quadratic envelope problem (i.e. considering σ instead of η), when we replace the discrete problem by continuous problem (i.e. considering $\sigma(p)$ with $p \in R^n$), and when we construct the permutation from the best continuous approximation (i.e. sort the Fiedler vector and derive a permutation). In spite of these possible sources of deviations from the optimum, our numerical results show that the Fiedler vector is a highly effective tool for computing orderings with small envelopes.

3 The Spectral Algorithm for Envelope Reduction

Based on the theorems in Section 2 the following new algorithm for reducing the envelope of a sparse matrix can be formulated. Since the algorithm is based on properties of the spectrum of the Laplacian matrix L, it will be called the *spectral algorithm*.

Algorithm 1 *Spectral Algorithm*

1. *Given the sparsity structure of a matrix M, form the Laplacian matrix L.*

2. *Compute a Fiedler vector u of L.*

3. *Sort the components of the Fiedler vector in non-decreasing order, and reorder the matrix M using the corresponding permutation vector.*

The implementation of steps 1 and 3 are relatively straightforward. The formation of the Laplacian matrix requires the computation of the degree of the nodes x_i. Step 3 is a simple sort of the entries of u, and recording the resulting permutation of indices. This can be done quickly by any efficient sorting algorithm such as quicksort. Computationally the difficult part is step 2.

The standard algorithm for computing a few eigenvalues and eigenvectors of large sparse symmetric matrices is the Lanczos algorithm. Since the Lanczos algorithm is discussed extensively in the textbook literature [14, 21], there is no need to include a detailed description of the standard algorithm here. Recently, we have developed a much more efficient multilevel method for finding the Fiedler vector [5]. The multilevel method requires three elements in addition to the Lanczos algorithm:

- **Contraction:** Construct a series of smaller graphs that in some sense retain the global structure of the original large graph.

- **Interpolation:** Given a Fiedler vector of a contracted graph, interpolate this vector to the next larger graph in a way that provides a good approximation to next Fiedler vector.

- **Refinement:** Given an approximate Fiedler vector for a graph, compute a more accurate vector efficiently.

Graph contraction is accomplished by first finding a maximal independent set of vertices, which are to be the vertices of the contracted graph. The edges of the contracted graph are determined by growing domains from the selected vertices in a breadth-first manner, adding an edge to the contracted graph when two domains intersect. A series of ever smaller contracted graphs is constructed until the size of the vertex set is less than some number (typically 100). The Lanczos algorithm can then be used to find the Fiedler vector of the smallest graph very quickly. This Fiedler vector is then interpolated to a vector corresponding to the next larger graph. This interpolated vector yields a very good approximation to the Fiedler vector of the larger graph. The approximation is then refined using the Rayleigh Quotient Iteration algorithm, which, because of its cubic convergence, usually requires only one or perhaps two iterations to obtain an acceptable result. This process of interpolation and refinement is continued until the Fiedler vector of the original graph is determined.

4 Numerical Results

This section shows some numerical results for three sets of matrices. The first set, shown in Table 1, are some matrices for structural analysis applications from the Boeing-Harwell dataset. The next set, shown in Table 2, are some miscellaneous matrices from the Boeing-Harwell dataset. Finally, the third set, shown in Table 3, is a selection of matrices used at NASA.

The spectral algorithm outperforms the other algorithms (i.e., finds the reordering with the smallest envelope) in 14 out of 18 cases (as shown in the "Rank" column of the tables). In those cases in which the result of the spectral algorithm is inferior (i.e., BCSSTK13, BKSSTK33, SHUTTLE, and CAN1072), it is still fairly close to the best result. In several cases, however, the spectral algorithm finds a reordering with an envelope substantially smaller than any of the other algorithms, sometimes by a factor of more than two. The run time of the spectral algorithm is usually, but not always, substantially greater than that of the other algorithms. [2]

The GPS, GK, and RCM algorithms, which are all closely related, attempt to decrease the envelope size, and in the process, seem to reduce the bandwidth as well. These algorithms use a local search technique (breadth-first search) from a pseudo-peripheral vertex to generate a long, skinny level structure. The spectral algorithm, by contrast, relies on the global information in the Fiedler vector components. The results show that the bandwidths of the spectral reorderings are often much greater than those of the other reorderings, even when the spectral envelopes are much smaller. This can be seen in Figures 1 through 3, which show the sparse matrix structure of the original BARTH4 matrix and of the SPECTRAL and GPS reorderings. A black dot indicates a nonzero element. (The GK and RCM reorderings look very similar to the GPS reordering.) An attractive possibility is to make limited

---

[2]The computations were performed on a Silicon Graphics workstation with a 33 MHZ IP7 processor.

Table 1: **Results (Boeing-Harwell — Structural Analysis)**

Title (equations) (nonzeros)	Envelope	Bandwidth	Run time (sec.)	Algorithm	Rank
BCSSTK13	64,486	455	3.92	SPECTRAL	4
(2,003)	58,542	223	.64	GPS	3
(11,973)	57,501	145	.57	GK	2
	56,299	198	.08	RCM	1
BCSSTK29	3,067,004	882	31.33	SPECTRAL	1
(13,992)	6,948,091	1,505	9.53	GPS	2
(316,740)	7,040,998	869	5.29	GK	3
	7,374,140	914	2.37	RCM	4
BCSSTK30	9,135,742	4,769	76.11	SPECTRAL	1
(28,924)	15,686,968	16,947	78.10	GPS	2
(1,036,208)	23,242,990	2,515	61.65	GK	3
	23,242,990	2,512	6.32	RCM	4
BCSSTK31	19,622,179	4,761	53.33	SPECTRAL	1
(35,588)	22,330,987	1,880	22.05	GPS	2
(608,502)	23,416,579	1,104	9.12	GK	3
	23,641,124	1,176	4.69	RCM	4
BCSSTK32	27,614,531	13,792	87.02	SPECTRAL	1
(44,609)	49,457,764	3,761	102.44	GPS	2
(1,029,655)	50,067,390	2,339	79.48	GK	3
	52,170,122	2,390	7.83	RCM	4
BCSSTK33	3,788,702	1,199	29.36	SPECTRAL	3
(8,738)	3,571,395	932	5.20	GPS	1
(300,321)	3,717,032	519	3.22	GK	2
	3,799,285	749	1.82	RCM	4

Table 2: **Results (Boeing-Harwell — Miscellaneous)**

Title (equations) (nonzeros)	Envelope	Bandwidth	Run time (sec.)	Algorithm	Rank
SSTMODEL	89,401	228	1.95	SPECTRAL	1
(3,345)	104,562	125	.28	GPS	2
(13,047)	110,936	83	.17	GK	4
	105,421	88	.10	RCM	3
BLKHOLE	121,044	426	.57	SPECTRAL	1
(2,132)	169,219	134	.17	GPS	2
(8,502)	173,243	106	.12	GK	4
	171,437	105	.07	RCM	3
CAN1072	53,689	354	1.35	SPECTRAL	2
(1,072)	48,538	234	.20	GPS	1
(6,758)	74,067	159	.13	GK	4
	56,361	175	.05	RCM	3
DWT2680	94,630	142	.73	SPECTRAL	1
(2,680)	96,591	92	.28	GPS	2
(13,853)	101,769	65	.19	GK	3
	102,983	69	.11	RCM	4
POW9	30,857	264	.43	SPECTRAL	1
(1,723)	64,788	201	.14	GPS	2
(4,117)	69,446	116	.10	GK	3
	79,260	133	.05	RCM	4

use of a local reordering strategy to improve the envelope parameters obtained from the spectral method. It is not clear if such a scheme might reduce the bandwidth as well.

5   Summary

The numerical results are very encouraging for the following reasons:

1. The spectral algorithm is a new type of algorithm for reordering sparse matrices. The spectral algorithm can find reorderings which are sometimes substantially better than the reorderings computed with conventional algorithms.

2. Since this is an iterative algorithm, it allows the user to make tradeoffs between fast ordering times and higher storage requirements, and slower ordering time combined with less storage requirements. These trade-offs are not easily possible with the conventional algorithms.

3. Since the ordering involves mainly floating point computation the algorithm becomes very competitive on very large problems on machines like the

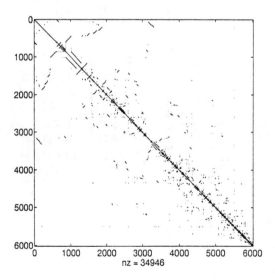

Figure 1: Sparse matrix structure of original BARTH4 matrix.

Table 3: **Results (NASA)**

Title (equations) (nonzeros)	Envelope	Bandwidth	Run time (sec)	Algorithm	Rank
BARTH4	349,016	593	5.81	SPECTRAL	1
(6,019)	658,181	280	.54	GPS	2
(23,492)	669,239	213	.33	GK	3
	725,950	215	.21	RCM	4
FLAP	10,522,995	1,784	42.05	SPECTRAL	1
(51,537)	12,367,171	1,019	24.96	GPS	3
(531,157)	12,339,642	743	19.08	GK	2
	12,598,705	874	4.19	RCM	4
SHUTTLE	566,496	631	2.30	SPECTRAL	3
(9,205)	531,420	92	1.12	GPS	1
(45,966)	531,422	92	.93	GK	2
	567,887	150	.32	RCM	4
SKIRT	698,644	1,021	14.60	SPECTRAL	1
(12,598)	1,013,423	425	3.20	GPS	2
(104,559)	1,039,544	309	2.46	GK	3
	1,068,993	314	.82	RCM	4
PWT	5,133,567	1,629	12.40	SPECTRAL	1
(36,519)	5,520,603	450	29.65	GPS	2
(181,313)	5,638,855	340	28.27	GK	4
	5,652,184	340	1.67	RCM	3
IN3C	425,433,734	9,492	109.97	SPECTRAL	1
(262,620)	519,316,395	3,780	56.97	GPS	2
(1,026,888)	526,302,263	2,473	26.28	GK	3
	581,700,745	2,746	12.88	RCM	4
BODY	6,706,747	2,496	25.03	SPECTRAL	1
(45,087)	10,526,446	1,081	13.60	GPS	2
(208,821)	10,658,164	667	8.42	GK	3
	11,470,411	756	2.23	RCM	4

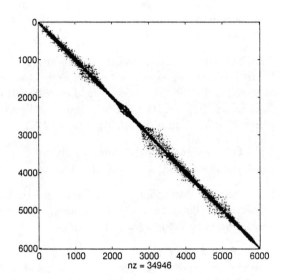

Figure 2: Sparse matrix structure of the Spectral reordering.

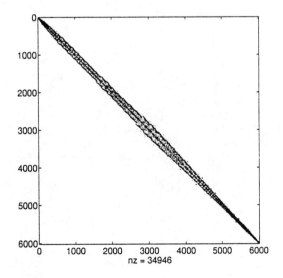

Figure 3: Sparse matrix structure of the Gibbs-Poole-Stockmeyer (GPS) reordering.

Cray Y-MP, where floating point arithmetic is considerably faster than integer arithmetic.

4. The ordering is insensitive to the initial ordering of the matrix.

Acknowledgement

This work was supported through NASA Contract NAS 2-12961; and by NSF grant CCR-9024954, DOE grant DE-FG02-91ER25095, and NSERC grant OGP0008111.

References

[1] P. Amestoy and I. S. Duff. Vectorization of a multiprocessor multifrontal code. *Int. J. Supercomputer Applications*, 3(3):41 – 59, 1989.

[2] C. C. Ashcraft, R. G. Grimes, J. G. Lewis, B. W. Peyton, and H. D. Simon. Recent progress in sparse matrix methods for large linear systems. *International Journal on Supercomputer Applications*, 1(4):10 – 30, 1987.

[3] B. Aspvall and J. R. Gilbert. Graph coloring using eigenvalue decomposition. *SIAM J. Alg. Disc. Meth.*, 5(4):526 – 538, 1984.

[4] S. T. Barnard, A. Pothen, and H. D. Simon. A spectral algorithm for envelope reduction of sparse matrices. In preparation, 1993.

[5] S. T. Barnard and H. D. Simon. A fast multilevel implementation of recursive spectral bisection for partitioning unstructured problems. Technical Report RNR-092-033, NASA Ames Research Center, Moffett Field, CA 94035, November 1992.

[6] E. Cuthill and J. McKee. Reducing the bandwidth of sparse symmetric matrices. In *Proceed. 24th Nat. Conf. Assoc. Comp. Mach.*, page P69. ACM Publications, 1969.

[7] D. Cvetkovic, M. Doob, and H. Sachs. *Spectra of Graphs*. Academic Press, New York, 1980.

[8] A. Dave and I. S. Duff. Sparse matrix calculations on the CRAY-2. *Parallel Computing*, 5:55 – 64, 1987.

[9] M. Fiedler. Algebraic connectivity of graphs. *Czechoslovak Math. J.*, 23(98):298 – 305, 1973.

[10] M. Fiedler. Eigenvectors of acyclic matrices. *Czechoslovak Math. J.*, 25(100):607 – 618, 1975.

[11] M. Fiedler. A property of eigenvectors of nonnegative symmetric matrices and its application to graph theory. *Czechoslovak Math. J.*, 25(100):619 – 633, 1975.

[12] J. A. George and J. W. H. Liu. *Computer Solution of Large Sparse Positive Definite Systems.* Prentice Hall, Englewood Cliffs, 1981.

[13] N. Gibbs, W. Poole, and P. Stockmeyer. An algorithm for reducing the bandwidth and profile of a sparse matrix. *SIAM J. Num. Anal.*, 13:236 – 249, 1976.

[14] G. H. Golub and C. F. Van Loan. *Matrix Computations.* Johns Hopkins University Press, 1989.

[15] R. G. Grimes, D. J. Pierce, and H. D. Simon. A new algorithm for finding a pseudoperipheral node in a graph. *SIAM J. Matrix Anal. Appl.*, 11(2):323 – 334, 1990.

[16] M. Juvan and B. Mohar, Optimal linear labelings and eigenvalues of graphs, *Discr. Appl. Math.*, 36, 153–168, 1992.

[17] N. Knight, R. Gillian, S. McCleary, C. Lotts, E. Poole, A. Overman, and S. Macy. CSM testbed development and large-scale structural applications. In E. J. Pitcher, editor, *Science and Engineering on Cray Supercomputers*, pages 359 – 387, Minneapolis, MN, 1988. Cray Research.

[18] J. G. Lewis. Implementations of the Gibbs-Poole-Stockmeyer and Gibbs-King algorithms. *ACM Trans. on Math. Soft.*, 8:180 – 189, 1982.

[19] J. G. Lewis and H. D. Simon. The impact of hardware gather/scatter on sparse Gaussian elimination. *SIAM J. Sci. Stat. Comp.*, 9(2):304 – 311, 1988.

[20] B. Mohar. The Laplacian spectrum of graphs. Technical report, Dept. of Mathematics, Univ. of Ljubljana, 61111 Ljubljana, Yugoslavia, 1988.

[21] B. N. Parlett. *The Symmetric Eigenvalue Problem.* Prentice Hall, Englewood Cliffs, New Jersey, 1980.

[22] E. L. Poole and A. L. Overman. The solution of linear systems of equations with a structural analysis code on the NAS CRAY-2. Technical Report Contractor Report 4159, NASA Langley Research Center, Hampton, Virginia, December 1988.

[23] A. Pothen, H. D. Simon, and K. P. Liou. Partitioning sparse matrices with eigenvectors of graphs. *SIAM J. Mat. Anal. Appl.*, 11(3):430 – 452, 1990.

[24] A. Pothen, H. D. Simon, L. Wang, and S. T. Barnard. Towards a fast implementation of spectral nested dissection. In *Proceedings of Supercomputing '92*, IEEE Computer Soc. Press, pages 42 – 51, Minneapolis, Minnesota, 1992.

[25] D. L. Powers. Graph partitioning by eigenvectors. *Lin. Alg. Appl.*, 101:121 – 133, 1988.

[26] H. D. Simon. Partitioning of unstructured problems for parallel processing. *Computing Systems in Engineering*, 2(2/3):135 – 148, 1991.

[27] H. D. Simon, P. Vu, and C. W. Yang. Performance of a supernodal general sparse solver on the CRAY Y-MP: 1.68 GFLOPS with autotasking. Technical Report RNR-89/04, NASA Ames Research Center, Moffett Field, CA 94035, 1989.

[28] O. Storaasli, D. Nguyen, and T. Agarwal. Parallel-vector solution of large-scale structural analysis problems on supercomputers. In *Proceedings of the AIAA/ASME/ASCE/AHS/ASC 30th Structures, Structural Dynamics and Materials Conference, Vol. II*, pages 859 – 867, Mobile, Alabama, 1989.

An Efficient Block-Oriented Approach To Parallel Sparse Cholesky Factorization

Edward Rothberg

Intel Supercomputer Systems Division
14924 N.W. Greenbrier Parkway
Beaverton, OR 97006

Anoop Gupta

Computer Systems Laboratory
Stanford University
Stanford, CA 94305

Abstract

This paper explores the use of a sub-block decomposition strategy for parallel sparse Cholesky factorization, in which the sparse matrix is decomposed into rectangular blocks. Such a strategy has enormous theoretical scalability advantages over more traditional column-oriented and panel-oriented decompositions. However, little progress has been made in producing a practical sub-block method. This paper proposes and evaluates an approach that is simple to implement, provides slightly higher performance than column (and panel) methods on small parallel machines, and has the potential to provide much higher performance on large parallel machines.

1 Introduction

The Cholesky factorization of sparse symmetric positive definite matrices is an extremely important computation, arising in a variety of scientific and engineering applications. Sparse Cholesky factorization is unfortunately also extremely time-consuming, and is frequently the computational bottleneck in these applications. Consequently, there is significant interest in performing the computation on large parallel machines. Several different approaches to parallel sparse Cholesky factorization have been proposed. While great success has been achieved for small parallel machines, success has unfortunately been quite limited for larger machines.

Virtually all parallel approaches to sparse Cholesky factorization [3, 9, 16] perform a 1-dimensional decomposition of the sparse matrix. That is, they distribute either rows or columns of the matrix among processors. Such a decomposition has two major limitations. The first is that it produces enormous volumes of interprocessor communication. Communication grows linearly in the number of processors [11], resulting in communication volumes that are difficult to sustain on all but the smallest parallel machines. The second limitation is that a 1-D decomposition produces extremely long critical paths. Since the critical path represents a lower bound on parallel runtime, parallel speedups are severely limited.

Both of these limitations can be overcome (in theory) by moving to a sub-block, or 2-D decomposition. Such a decomposition has been shown to be extremely effective for parallel dense factorization [22]. It is not clear, however, whether a similar decomposition would be practical for sparse problems. A few investigations [1, 21, 23] have been performed, but these contained little or no exploration of practical algorithms. This paper provides a detailed analysis of a new block-oriented algorithm, including performance results from an efficient implementation.

This paper focuses on two practical and important issues related to a 2-D decomposition approach. The first is implementation complexity. The fact that most sparse factorization methods use a 1-D decomposition indicates that this decomposition is more natural. A block approach might significantly complicate the implementation. The second issue is the efficiency of a parallel block-oriented method for practical machine sizes. While parallel scalability arguments can be used to show that a block approach would give better performance than a column approach for extremely large parallel machines, these arguments have little to say about how well a block approach performs on smaller machines.

Regarding complexity, we find that a block approach need not be much more complicated than a column approach. We describe a simple strategy for performing a block decomposition and a simple parallel algorithm for performing the sparse Cholesky computation in terms of these blocks. The approach retains the theoretical scalability advantages of block methods. We term this block algorithm the *block fan-out method*, since it bears a great deal of similarity to the parallel column fan-out method [9].

Regarding efficiency, we explore this issue in two parts. We first consider a sequential block factorization code and compare its performance to that of a true sequential program to determine how much efficiency is lost in moving to a block representation. The losses turn out to be quite minor, with the block approach producing roughly 80% of the performance of an efficient sequential method. We then consider parallel block factorization, looking at the issues that potentially limit its performance. The parallel block method is found to give high performance on a range of parallel machine sizes. For larger machines, performance is good but not excellent, primarily due to load balance problems. We quantify the load imbalances and investigate the causes.

This paper is organized as follows. We begin in Section 2 with some background on sparse Cholesky factorization. Section 3 then discusses our experimental environment, including

503

a description of the sparse matrices we use as benchmarks and the machines we use to study the parallel block factorization approach. Section 4 describes our strategy for decomposing a sparse matrix into rectangular blocks. Section 5 describes a parallel method that performs the factorization in terms of these blocks. Section 6 then evaluates the parallel method, both in terms of communication volume and achieved parallel performance. Conclusions are presented in Section 7.

2 Sparse Cholesky Factorization

The goal of the sparse Cholesky computation is to factor a sparse symmetric positive definite $n \times n$ matrix A into the form $A = LL^T$, where L is lower triangular. The computation is typically performed as a series of three steps. The first step, *heuristic reordering*, reorders the rows and columns of A to reduce *fill* in the factor matrix L. The second step, *symbolic factorization*, performs the factorization symbolically to determine the non-zero structure of L given a particular reordering. Storage is allocated for L in this step. The third step is the *numerical factorization*, where the actual non-zero values in L are computed. This step is by far the most time-consuming, and it is the focus of this paper. We refer the reader to [10] for more information on these steps.

The following pseudo-code performs the numerical factorization step:

```
1.  for k = 1 to n do
2.      for i = k to n do
3.          L_ik := L_ik/√L_kk
4.      for j = k + 1 to n do
5.          for i = j to n do
6.              L_ij := L_ij − L_ik L_jk
```

Only the non-zero entries in the sparse matrix are stored, and the computation performs operations only on non-zeroes. The factorization is most often expressed in terms of columns of the sparse matrix. Within a column-oriented framework, steps 2 and 3 are typically thought of as a single operation, often called a column division or $cdiv(k)$ operation. Similarly, steps 5 and 6 form a column modification, or $cmod(j, k)$, operation.

This column-oriented formulation of the sparse factorization has formed the basis of several parallel sparse factorization algorithms, including the fan-out method [9], the fan-in method [3], and the distributed multifrontal method [16]. The details of these various methods are not relevant to our discussion, so we refer the reader to the relevant papers for more information. We simply note that for each of these methods, communication volumes grow linearly in the number of processors [3, 11]. Since available communication bandwidth in a multiprocessor typically grows much more slowly, this communication growth represents a severe scalability limitation.

Recent research in parallel sparse Cholesky factorization [2] has shown that the communication needs of column-oriented sparse factorization can be greatly reduced. Through limited replication of data and careful assignment of tasks to processors, communication can be made to grow as the square root of the number of processors, thus improving scalability. Communication volume is not the only thing that limits scalability

in column-oriented approaches, however. A column formulation also leads to very long critical paths, thus placing a large lower bound on parallel runtime. For a dense $n \times n$ matrix, the sequential computation requires $O(n^3)$ operations while the length of the critical path and thus the best case parallel runtime is $O(n^2)$ operations. Similar bounds apply for sparse problems.

An alternative formulation of the factorization problem divides the matrix into rectangular sub-blocks. This formulation leads to greatly reduced communication volumes and exposes significantly more concurrency. Specifically, communication volumes grow as the square root of the number of processors, and the critical path grows as $O(n)$ [22]. It is an open question whether this formulation can be efficiently applied to parallel sparse factorization, and this is the question we address here.

Before we begin our discussion of a block decomposition of the sparse matrix, we first discuss two important concepts in sparse factorization that will be relevant to our presentation. The first is the concept of a *supernode* [5]. A supernode is a set of adjacent columns in the factor matrix L whose non-zero structure consists of a dense lower-triangular block on the diagonal, and an identical set of non-zeroes for each column below the diagonal. Supernodes arise in any sparse factor, and they are typically quite large. By formulating the sparse factorization computation as a series of supernode-supernode modifications, rather than column-column modifications as described before, the computation can make substantial use of dense matrix operations. The result is substantially higher performance on vector supercomputers and on machines with hierarchical memory systems. For more details on supernodal factorization, see [5, 17, 18]. The regularity in the sparse matrix captured by this supernodal structure will prove useful in this paper for producing an effective decomposition of the sparse matrix into rectangular blocks. We will return to this issue shortly.

One thing we should note is that it is possible to improve the performance of parallel sparse column-oriented methods by grouping sets of adjacent columns from within the same supernode into *panels*, and distributing these panels among the processors [17, 18]. We use the term *column-oriented* in this paper to refer to methods that treat columns as indivisible entities. Thus, panel methods fit this description. When we compare the performance of our parallel block-oriented method to that of a parallel column-oriented method, we will actually compare against the higher-performance parallel panel method.

Another important notion in sparse factorization is that of the *elimination tree* of the sparse matrix [15, 20]. This structure concisely captures important dependency information. If each column of the sparse matrix is thought of as a node in a graph, then the elimination tree is defined by the following parent relationship:

$$parent(j) = \min\{i | l_{ij} \neq 0, i > j\}.$$

It can be shown that a column is modified only by descendent columns in the elimination tree, and equivalently that a column modifies only ancestors [15]. The most important property captured in this tree for parallel factorization is the property that disjoint subtrees are independent, and consequently can be processed in parallel. This fact will be relevant later in this paper.

504

Table 1: Benchmark matrices.

Name	Equations	NZ in A	NZ in L	FP ops to factor
GRID100	10,000	39,600	250,835	15.7M
GRID200	40,000	159,200	1,280,743	137M
BCSSTK15	3,948	113,868	647,274	165M
BCSSTK16	4,884	285,494	736,294	149M
BCSSTK17	10,974	417,676	994.885	144M
BCSSTK18	11,948	137,142	650,777	141M
BCSSTK29	13,992	605,496	1,680,804	393M

3 Experimental Environment

Since our interest in this paper is to consider practical performance issues for block methods, we will present performance numbers for realistic sparse matrices factored on real machines. This section briefly describes both the matrices we use as benchmarks and the machines on which we perform the factorizations.

3.1 Benchmark Matrices

The benchmark matrices we consider in this paper are drawn from the Boeing/Harwell sparse matrix test set [6]. Since our interest is in factorization on large machines, we have chosen some of the largest sparse matrices in the collection. We also include two regular 2-D, 5-pt grid problems. Table 1 gives brief descriptions of the matrices. For each matrix, the table shows the number of rows and columns in the matrix, the number of non-zeroes in the matrix, the number of non-zeroes in the factor, and the number of floating-point operations (in millions) required for the factorization. All matrices except the two grid problems are preordered using the multiple minimum degree ordering heuristic [14] before being factored. A simple nested dissection ordering is used for the grid problems.

3.2 Target Machines

This paper will present performance numbers from several parallel machines. We now briefly describe the parallel machines that are considered.

Performance numbers for sequential and small-scale parallel machines are obtained from a Silicon Graphics 4D/380 multiprocessor. The 4D/380 contains eight high-performance RISC processors, each consisting of a MIPS R3000 integer unit and an R3010 floating-point co-processor. The processors execute at 33 MHz, and are rated at 27 MIPS and 4.9 double-precision LINPACK MFLOPS. The machine has a hierarchical memory organization; memory references serviced from the processor cache are significantly less expensive than references that must be serviced from main memory.

We also provide performance numbers from the Stanford DASH machine, a 48-processor distributed-shared-memory machine [13]. The DASH machine is built out of a network of 12 4-processor SGI 4D/340 nodes. Each 4D/340 node contains some portion of the global shared memory. A processor can cache any location in the global memory. A processor memory reference that is serviced from its cache requires a single cycle. A reference to a location held in the memory local to

a processor requires roughly 30 cycles. A reference to a location held in a non-local memory requires roughly 100 cycles. Our factorization implementation for the Stanford DASH machine explicitly places matrix data in the memory local to the processor that owns that part of the matrix.

In order to provide a more detailed understanding of the performance of parallel machines on this computation, this paper also makes use of multiprocessor simulation. To keep simulation costs manageable, we perform this simulation in terms of high-level factorization tasks. A single task might represent a matrix block modification operation or the transmission of a large message from one processor to another. We model the costs of these high-level operations in terms of what we believe are the three most important determinants of performance on a parallel machine: the number of floating-point operations performed, the number of data items fetched from memory, and the amount of data moved between processor memories. The parallel simulation is performed as a discrete-event simulation of these tasks. We do not have space in this paper to describe the exact details of our simulation; details can be found in [17]. We simply note that the costs we use for floating-point operations, memory fetches, and interprocessor communication roughly match those of the DASH machine, and they are quite comparable to those of several other distributed-memory parallel machines.

4 Block Formulation

Having described our evaluation environment, we now move on to the question of how to structure the sparse Cholesky computation in terms of blocks. Our first step in describing a block-oriented approach is to propose a strategy for decomposing the sparse matrix into blocks. Our goal in this decomposition is to retain as much of the efficiency of the sequential factorization computation as possible.

4.1 Block Decomposition

When dividing a matrix into blocks, we believe the three most important issues are: (1) producing blocks with simple internal non-zero structures, so that block operations can be performed efficiently; (2) producing blocks that interact with other blocks in simple ways, so that bookkeeping overheads are minimized; and (3) producing blocks that are as dense as possible, so that per-block computation and storage overheads are minimized. With these goals in mind, the approach we take to decomposing the sparse matrix into blocks is to perform a global partitioning on the matrix, guided by the supernodal structure. More precisely, we divide the columns of the matrix $(1 \ldots n)$ into contiguous sets $(\{1 \ldots p_2 - 1\}, \{p_2 \ldots p_3 - 1\}, \ldots, \{p_N \ldots n\}$, where N is the number of partitions and p_i is the first column in partition i). All columns within a particular partition must be members of the same supernode (although a partition will frequently be a subset of a supernode). An identical partitioning is performed on the rows. A simple example is shown in Figure 1. A block L_{IJ} (we refer to partitions using capital letters) is then the set of non-zeroes that fall simultaneously in rows $\{p_I \ldots p_{I+1} - 1\}$ and columns $\{p_J \ldots p_{J+1} - 1\}$.

This global partitioning approach addresses the above-mentioned issues quite well. Each block has a very simple

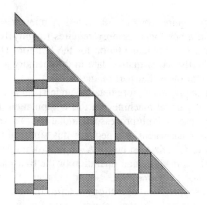

Figure 1: Example of globally partitioned matrix.

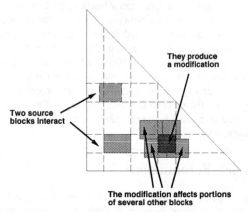

Figure 2: Example of irregular block interaction. Dashed lines indicate boundaries of affected areas.

non-zero structure. Since the block is a portion of a supernode, all rows in the block are dense. The blocks also share common boundaries. As a result, block interactions are extremely regular. As we will soon demonstrate, this decomposition leads to a computation structure where a block interacts with a block above it to produce a modification to a block to its right. Without these common boundaries, block modifications would be quite complicated, with portions of blocks modifying portions of other blocks (see Figure 2).

One issue that this distribution scheme does not address is the block density issue. The global nature of the partitions does not allow the blocks to be tailored to match the local sparsity structure of the matrix. We will see in the next section that this is not actually a significant problem. While blocks will often not be completely dense, this sparsity has little effect on the efficiency of the overall computation.

Before proceeding, we note that Ashcraft [1] proposed a similar decomposition strategy independently.

4.2 Structure of the Block Factorization Computation

One important goal we had in choosing this block decomposition was to retain as much efficiency as possible in the block factorization computation. We now describe a sequential algorithm for performing the factorization in terms of these blocks and evaluate that algorithm's efficiency. The parallelization of

the sequential approach that we derive here will be described later.

At one level, the factorization algorithm expressed in terms of blocks is quite obvious. The following pseudo-code, a simple analogue of dense block Cholesky factorization, performs the factorization. Note that I, J, and K iterate over the partitions in the sparse matrix.

```
1.  for K = 1 to N do
2.      L_KK := Factor(L_KK)
3.      for I = K + 1 to N with L_IK ≠ 0 do
4.          L_IK := L_IK L_KK^{-1}
5.          for J = K + 1 to N with L_JK ≠ 0 do
6.              for I = J to N with L_IK ≠ 0 do
7.                  L_IJ := L_IJ - L_IK L_JK^T
```

The above pseudo-code works with a column of blocks at a time. Steps 2 through 4 divide block column K by the Cholesky factor of the diagonal block. Steps 5 through 7 compute block modifications from all pairs of blocks in column K. We store the blocks by columns, so that all blocks in a column can be easily located. We also keep a hash table of all blocks (hashing on the row and column index), so that destination block L_{IJ} in step 7 can be located quickly.

Now consider the implementation of the individual operations in the pseudo-code. The block factorization in step 2 is quite straightforward to implement. Diagonal blocks are guaranteed to be dense, so this step is simply a dense Cholesky factorization. The multiplication by the inverse of the diagonal block in step 4 is also quite straightforward. This step does not actually compute the inverse of L_{KK}. Instead, it solves a series of triangular systems. While the block L_{IK} is not necessarily dense, the computation can be performed without consulting the non-zero structure of the block.

The remaining step in the above pseudo-code, step 7, is both the most important and the most difficult to implement. It is the most important because it sits within a doubly-nested loop and thus performs the vast majority of the actual computation. It is the most difficult because it works with blocks with potentially different non-zero structures and it must somehow reconcile these structures. More precisely, recall that a single block in L consists of some set of dense rows from among the rows that the block spans (see the example in Figure 1). When a modification is performed in step 7 above, the structure of L_{IK} determines the set of rows in L_{IJ} that are affected. Similarly, the structure of L_{JK} determines the set of columns in L_{IJ} that are affected.

Block modification is most conveniently viewed as a two stage process. A set of modification values is computed in the first stage, and these values are subtracted from the appropriate entries in the destination block in the second, or scatter stage. The first stage can be performed as a dense matrix-matrix multiplication. The non-zero structures of the source blocks L_{IK} and L_{JK} are ignored temporarily; the two blocks are simply multiplied to produce a modification.

During the second stage, the resulting modification must be subtracted from the destination. If the modification has the same non-zero structure as the destination block, then the subtraction is trivial. Otherwise, we must first determine the relationship between the non-zero structures of the modification

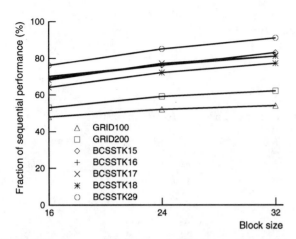

Figure 3: Performance of a sequential block approach, relative to a sequential left-looking supernode-supernode approach.

and of the destination. This information can then be used to scatter the modification into the destination. While this scatter is much more expensive than direct addition of the modification into the destination, it is also much less common.

4.3 Performance of Block Factorization

We now look at the performance obtained with a sequential program that uses a block decomposition and block implementation. Since our goal is to create an efficient *parallel* approach, performance is studied for the case where the matrix is divided into relatively small blocks. The blocks should not be too small, however, because of the overheads that will be associated with block operations. We consider 16 by 16, 24 by 24, and 32 by 32 block sizes. To produce blocks of the desired size B, we form partitions that contain as close to B rows/columns as possible. For example, with a block size of $B = 16$, a supernode of width 51 would be split into three partitions of size 17. Since partitions represent subsets of supernodes, some partitions will naturally be much smaller than B.

We found that the block approach as described above actually produces quite low performance for several of the matrices. The reason was the presence of many small supernodes, which led to many small blocks and significant overheads. We were able to improve performance dramatically by performing *supernode amalgamation* [4] before executing the block factorization. Amalgamation is a process of selectively adding non-zeroes to the factor matrix in order to combine small supernodes with nearly-identical non-zero structures into larger supernodes.

The performance obtained with the sequential block approach on a single processor of the SGI 4D/380 after amalgamation is shown in Figure 3. This performance is expressed as a fraction of the performance obtained with an efficient sequential code (a supernode-supernode left-looking method; among the most efficient sequential approaches [17]). Performance numbers for the sequential method are given in Table 2. The results indicate that the block approach is quite efficient. With only two exceptions, block method performance for $B = 32$ is roughly 80% of that of a true sequential method. Performance falls off somewhat when $B = 24$, and it decreases further when

Table 2: Sequential performance on SGI 4D/380 (supernode-supernode left-looking method).

Name	Performance (MFLOPS)
GRID100	5.6
GRID200	6.7
BCSSTK15	7.9
BCSSTK16	7.8
BCSSTK17	7.5
BCSSTK18	7.2
BCSSTK29	7.8

$B = 16$, but the resulting efficiencies are still roughly 70%.

5 Parallel Block Method

We now turn to the question of how to parallelize the sequential block computation. This question can be divided into two different questions. First, how will processors cooperate to perform the work assigned to them? And second, what method will be used to assign this work to processors? This section will address these two questions in turn.

5.1 Parallel Factorization Organization

We begin our description of the parallel computation by assuming that each block will have some specific owner processor. In our approach, the owner of a block L_{IK} performs all block modification operations with L_{IK} as their destination. With this choice in mind, we present the parallel block fan-out algorithm in Figure 4. The rest of this section will be devoted to an explanation of the algorithm.

The most important notion for the block fan-out method is that once a block L_{IK} is *complete*, meaning that it has received all block modifications and has been multiplied by the inverse of the diagonal block, then L_{IK} is sent to all processors that could own blocks modified by it. Blocks that could be modified by L_{IK} fall in block-row I or block-column I of L. When a block L_{IK} is received by a processor p (step 2 in Figure 4), processor p performs all related modifications to blocks it owns. The block L_{IK} produces block modifications only when it is paired with blocks in the same column K. Thus, processor p considers all pairings of the received block L_{IK} with completed blocks it has already received in column K (these blocks are held in set $Rec_{K,p}$) to determine whether the corresponding destination block is owned by p (steps 10 and 11). If the destination L_{IJ} is owned by p ($map[L_{IJ}] = p$), then the corresponding modification is performed (steps 12 and 13). Each processor maintains a hash table of all blocks assigned to it, and the destination block is located through this hash table.

A count is kept with each block ($nmod[L_{IJ}]$), indicating the number of block modifications that still must be done to that block. When the count reaches zero, then block L_{IJ} is ready to be multiplied by the inverse of L_{JJ} (step 20 if L_{JJ} has already arrived at p; step 6 otherwise). A diagonal block L_{JJ} is kept in $Diag_{J,p}$, and any blocks waiting to be modified by

```
1.  while some L_IJ with map[L_IJ] = MyID is not complete do
2.      receive some L_IK
3.      if I = K /* diagonal block */
4.          Diag_{K,MyID} := L_KK
5.          foreach L_JK ∈ Wait_{K,MyID} do
6.              L_JK := L_JK L_KK^{-1}
7.              send L_JK to all P that could own blocks in row J or column J
8.      else
9.          Rec_{K,MyID} := Rec_{K,MyID} ∪ {L_IK}
10.         foreach L_JK ∈ Rec_{K,MyID} do
11.             if map[L_IJ] = MyID then
12.                 Find L_IJ
13.                 L_IJ := L_IJ - L_IK L_JK^T
14.                 nmod[L_IJ] := nmod[L_IJ] - 1
15.                 if (nmod[L_IJ] = 0) then
16.                     if I = J then /* diagonal block */
17.                         L_JJ := Factor(L_JJ)
18.                         send L_JJ to all P that could own blocks in column J
19.                     else if (Diag_{J,MyID} ≠ ∅) then
20.                         L_IJ := L_IJ L_JJ^{-1}
21.                         send L_IJ to all P that could own blocks in
                               row I or column I
22.                     else
23.                         Wait_{J,MyID} := Wait_{J,MyID} ∪ {L_IJ}
```

Figure 4: Parallel block fan-out algorithm.

the diagonal block are kept in $Wait_{J,p}$. The sets $Diag$, $Wait$, and Rec can be kept as simple linked lists of blocks.

One issue that is not addressed in the above pseudo-code is that of block disposal. As described above, the parallel algorithm would retain a received block for the duration of the factorization. To determine when a block can be thrown out, we keep a count $ToRec_{K,p}$ of the number of blocks in a column K that will be received by a processor p. Once $|Rec_{K,p}| = ToRec_{K,p}$, then the storage associated with blocks in column K is reclaimed.

We note that a small simplification has been made in steps 11 through 14 above. For all blocks L_{IJ}, I must be greater than J, a condition that is not necessarily true in the pseudo-code. The reader should assume that I is actually the larger of I and J, and similarly that J is the smaller of the two.

5.2 Block Mapping for Reduced Communication

We now consider the issue of mapping blocks to processors. Our general approach is to restrict the set of processors that can own blocks modified by a particular block L_{IK} and thus decrease the number of processors to which the block must be sent. The actual restriction is done by performing a *scatter decomposition* [7] (sometimes referred to as a *torus-mapping*) of the blocks in the sparse matrix.

More precisely, assume that P processors are used for the factorization, and assume for the sake of simplicity that P is a perfect square ($P = s \times s$). Furthermore, assume that the processors are arranged in a 2-D grid configuration, with the bottom left processor labeled $p_{0,0}$, and the upper right pro-

cessor labeled $p_{s-1,s-1}$. To limit communication, a row of blocks is mapped to a row of processors. Similarly, a column of blocks is mapped to a column of processors. We choose round-robin distributions for both the rows and columns, where $map[L_{IJ}] = p_{I\bmod s, J\bmod s}$. Other distributions could be used. By performing the block mapping in this way, a block L_{IK} in the sparse factorization need only be sent to the row of processors that could own blocks in row I and the column of processors that could own blocks in column I. Every block in the matrix would thus be sent to a total of $2s = 2\sqrt{P}$ processors. Note that communication volume is independent of the block size with this mapping; every block in the matrix is simply sent to $2\sqrt{P}$ processors.

The scatter decomposition is appealing not only because it reduces communication volume, but also because it produces an extremely simple and regular communication pattern. All communication is done through multicasts along rows and columns of processors.

5.3 Enhancement: Domains

Before presenting performance results for the block fan-out approach, we first note that the method as described above actually produces more interprocessor communication than competing column approaches for small parallel machines. To understand the reason, consider a simple 2-D $k \times k$ grid problem. The corresponding factor matrix contains $O(k^2 \log k)$ non-zeroes, and the parallel factorization of this matrix using a column approach generates $O(k^2 P)$ communication volume [11]. In the block approach, every non-zero in the matrix is sent to

$O(\sqrt{P})$ processors, so the total communication volume grows as $O(\sqrt{P}k^2 \log k)$. The communication in the block approach grows less quickly in P, but it grows more quickly in k. The k term is more important for small P.

An important technique for reducing communication in column methods involves the use of *domains* [1, 3]. Domains are large sets of columns in the sparse matrix that are assigned en masse to a single processor. They are perhaps most easily understood in terms of the elimination tree of L. Recall that disjoint subtrees in the elimination tree are computationally independent, and consequently can be processed concurrently. By assigning the columns of an entire subtree (a domain) to a single processor, the communication that would have resulted had these columns been distributed among processors is avoided.

More precisely, by localizing all columns in a domain to a single processor, all modifications to these columns can be performed without the need for interprocessor communication. Furthermore, the modifications from all columns within a domain to all other entries in the matrix can be computed and aggregated within the owner processor, again with no communication. That processor can then send the aggregate modifications to the appropriate destinations. In a column approach, the aggregate modification is sent out on a column-wise basis. We refer the reader to [3] for more details.

Ashcraft suggested [1] that domains can be incorporated into a block approach as well. The basic approach is as follows. The non-zeroes within a domain are stored as they would be in a column-oriented method. The domain factorization is then performed using a column method. The aggregate domain modification is computed column-wise as well. We use an extremely efficient left-looking supernode-supernode method for both. Once the aggregate modification has been computed, it is sent out in a block-wise fashion to the appropriate destination blocks.

Of course, the domains must be carefully assigned to processors so that processors do not sit idle, waiting for other processors to complete local domain computations. Geist and Ng [8] described an algorithm for assigning a small set of domains to each processor so that the amount of domain work assigned to the processors is evenly balanced. All results from this point on use the algorithm of Geist and Ng to produce domains.

With the introduction of domains, the parallel computation becomes a three phase process. In the first phase, the processors factor the domains assigned to them and compute the modifications from these domains to blocks outside the domains. In the second phase, the modifications are sent to the processors that own the corresponding destination blocks and are added into their destinations. Finally, the third phase performs the block factorization, where blocks are exchanged between processors. Note that these are only logical phases; no global synchronizations is necessary between the phases.

Consider the effect of domains on communication volume in a block method for a 2-D grid problem. We first note that the number of non-zeroes not belonging to domains in the sparse matrix can be shown to grow as $O(k^2 \log P)$, versus $O(k^2 \log k)$ without domains [12]. Total communication volume for these non-zeroes using a block approach is thus $O(\sqrt{P}k^2 \log P)$. The other component of communication volume when using domains is the cost of sending domain mod-

ifications to their destinations. The total size of all such modifications is $O(k^2)$, independent of P, so domain modification communication represents a lower-order term. Total communication for a 2-D grid problem is thus $O(\sqrt{P}k^2 \log P)$.

6 Evaluation

This section evaluates the parallel block fan-out approach proposed in the previous section. We first look at performance on a small-scale multiprocessor. Then, we consider performance on moderately-parallel machines (up to 64 processors), using our multiprocessor simulation model and using the DASH machine.

6.1 Small Parallel Machines

The first performance numbers we present come from the Silicon Graphics SGI 4D/380 multiprocessor. Parallel speedups are shown in Figure 5 for 1 through 8 processors. All speedups are computed relative to a left-looking supernode-supernode sequential code. The figure shows that the block fan-out method

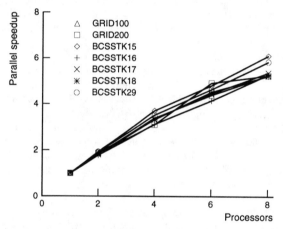

Figure 5: Parallel speedups for block fan-out method on SGI 4D-380, $B = 24$.

is indeed quite efficient for small machines. In fact, performance is slightly higher than that of our highly efficient panel-based parallel code [19]. Speedups on 8 processors are roughly 5.5-fold, corresponding to absolute performance levels of 40 to 50 double-precision MFLOPS. Speedups are less than linear in the number of processors for two simple reasons. First, the block method is slightly less efficient than a column method. We believe this accounts for a roughly 15% performance reduction. Second, the load is unevenly distributed among the processors. A simple calculation reveals that processors spend roughly 15% of the computation on average sitting idle. These two factors combine to give a relatively accurate performance prediction.

6.2 Moderately Parallel Machines

We now consider performance on larger machines.

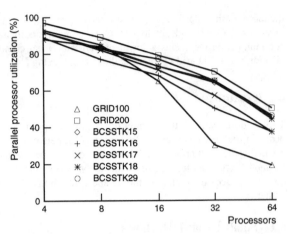

Figure 6: Simulated parallel efficiencies for block fan-out method, $B = 24$.

6.2.1 Simulated Performance

Figure 6 shows simulated processor utilization levels for between 4 and 64 simulated processors, using a block size of 24. It is clear from the figure that the block approach exhibits less than ideal behavior as the machine size is increased. On 64 processors, for example, utilization levels drop to roughly 40%. Further investigation reveals that the primary cause of the drop in performance is a progressive decline in the quality of the load balance.

The quality of the load distribution clearly depends on the method used to map blocks to processors. Recall that we use a very rigid mapping strategy, where block L_{IJ} is assigned to processor $p_{I \bmod s, J \bmod s}$. One possible explanation for the poor behavior of this strategy is that it does not adapt to the structure of the sparse matrix; it tries to impose a very regular structure on a matrix that is potentially comprised of a very irregular arrangement of non-zero blocks.

While the mismatch between the regular mapping and the irregular matrix structure certainly contributes to the poor load balance, it is our belief that a more important factor is the wide variability in task sizes. In particular, since a block is modified by some set of blocks to its left, blocks to the far right in the matrix generally require much more work than blocks to the left (more accurately, blocks near the top of the elimination tree require more work than blocks near the leafs). Furthermore, since the matrix is lower-triangular, the number of blocks in a column decreases towards the right. The result is a small number of very important blocks in the bottom-right corner of the matrix.

To support our contention that the sparse structure of the matrix is less important than the more general task distribution problem, Figure 7 compares the quality of the load balance obtained for matrix BCSSTK15 to the load balance obtained using the same mapping strategy for a dense matrix. The curves show the maximum obtainable processor utilization levels with the block mappings. The dense problem is chosen so as to perform roughly the same number of floating-point operations as the sparse problem.

Note that the load balance can be improved by moving to a smaller block size, thus creating more distributable blocks

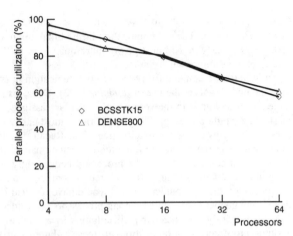

Figure 7: Parallel utilization upper bounds due to load balance for BCSSTK15, compared with load balance upper bounds for a dense problem ($B = 24$). The two problems require roughly the same number of floating-point operations.

and making the block distribution problem easier. However, smaller blocks also increase block overheads. For the larger benchmark sparse matrices, decreasing the block size from $B = 24$ to $B = 16$ increases simulated parallel efficiencies for $P = 64$ from 40%-45% for $B = 24$ to 50%-55% for $B = 16$. A block size of less than 16 further improves the load balance, but achieves lower performance due to overhead issues.

The general conclusion to be drawn from these simulation results is simply that large machines require relatively large problems to achieve high processor utilization levels. In particular, the sparse matrices that we study here are too small to make good use of a 64 processor machine. Of course, it may be possible to significantly improve parallel load balance with a better mapping strategy. A more general function could be used to map columns of blocks to columns of processors, and to map rows of blocks to rows of processors. This matter will require further investigation.

6.2.2 Communication Volume

An important determinant of parallel performance that we have not considered so far is interprocessor communication volume. Figure 8 shows the volume of communication that a block fan-out method generates. The figure shows relative communication, as compared with a parallel column multifrontal method. Interestingly, the block approach does not always produce less communication than the column approach on 64 or fewer processors. While the growth rates, $O(P)$ for columns and $O(\sqrt{P} \log P)$ for blocks, favor the block approach, constants make these rates less relevant for small P. However, the trends clearly favor the block approach.

An interesting thing to note here is that relative communication is quite a bit higher for the two grid problems than for the other matrices. The reason is that the column multifrontal approach does very well communication-wise for sparse matrices whose elimination trees have few nodes towards the root and instead quickly branch out into several independent subtrees. The two grid problems have this property. The block approach derives no benefit from this property.

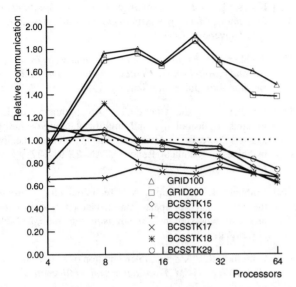

Figure 8: Communication volume of block approach, relative to a column-oriented parallel multifrontal approach.

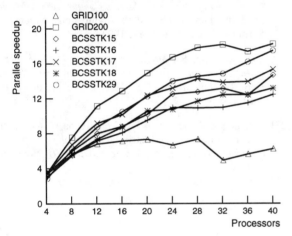

Figure 9: Parallel speedups for block fan-out method on the Stanford DASH machine, $B = 24$.

6.2.3 DASH Performance

We now provide performance numbers from a block fan-out implementation on the Stanford DASH machine. Figure 9 shows achieved parallel speedups on 1 to 40 processors, again compared with a sequential left-looking supernode-supernode method. Recall that the sequential method obtains between 7 and 8 MFLOPS on these problems. The figure shows that speedups are relatively low, ranging from 12 to 18 on 40 processors. These speedups are somewhat lower than those predicted by the simulation. We believe the main cause of this difference is an assumption we made in the simulation. We assumed that the processor could perform computation simultaneous with communication. The DASH machine has limited ability to hide communication latencies.

While these speedups are relatively low, we should note two important items about the results. First, the absolute parallel performance levels of the DASH machine are still quite re-

spectable. The 40 processor machine achieves roughly 100 double-precision MFLOPS. Second, we note that these performance numbers are roughly 10% to 40% higher than corresponding numbers from our panel-oriented parallel multifrontal implementation [17].

6.2.4 Summary

To summarize this section, we note that our block fan-out approach provides good performance for moderately-parallel machines, although parallel speedups are well below linear in the number of processors for the matrices we have considered. An important limiting factor is the relatively small size of the matrices and the relatively poor load balance that results from our rigid block distribution scheme. Regarding communication volumes, we find that the block approach produces comparable amounts of traffic to a column approach on 64 or fewer processors. Even so, we found that the block approach produces higher performance that a competing panel-oriented approach on the 8 processor SGI 4D/380 and the 40 processor Stanford DASH machine.

At this point, we wish to reiterate that communication and concurrency growth rates greatly favor the block method on large parallel machines. The fact that a block approach produces slightly better performance than column approaches for relatively small machines leads us to conclude that the block approach will provide significant benefits for practical parallel machine sizes.

7 Conclusions

It is becoming increasingly clear that column approaches are inappropriate for sparse Cholesky factorization on large parallel machines. One thing that has been much less clear is whether the alternative, a 2-D matrix decomposition, is truly practical. This paper has proposed a parallel block algorithm that is quite practical. The primary virtues of our approach are: (1) it uses an extremely simple decomposition strategy, in which the matrix is divided using global horizontal and vertical partitions; (2) it is straightforward to implement; (3) it provides good per-processor performance, since it performs the vast majority of its work within dense matrix-matrix multiplication operations; (4) it is efficient on moderately parallel machines, providing performance that is comparable to that of efficient column (and panel) methods; and (5) it shows good promise for large parallel machines.

Acknowledgments

We would like to thank Rob Schreiber and Sid Chatterjee for their discussions on block-oriented factorization. This research is supported under DARPA contract N00039-91-C-0138. Anoop Gupta is also supported by an NSF Presidential Young Investigator Award.

References

[1] Ashcraft, C.C., *The domain/segment partition for the factorization of sparse symmetric positive definite matrices,*

Boeing Computer Services Technical Report ECA-TR-148, November, 1990.

[2] Ashcraft, C.C., "The fan-both family of column-based distributed Cholesky factorization algorithms", in *Graph Theory and Sparse Matrix Computation*, IMA Volumes in Mathematics and its Applications, Volume 56, Springer-Verlag, New York, 1993.

[3] Ashcraft, C.C., Eisenstat, S.C.., Liu, J.L., and Sherman, A.H, "A comparison of three column-based distributed sparse factorization schemes", Research Report YALEU/DCS/RR-810, Computer Science Department, Yale University, 1990.

[4] Ashcraft, C.C., and Grimes, R.G., "The influence of relaxed supernode partitions on the multifrontal method", *ACM Transactions on Mathematical Software*, 15(4): 291-309, 1989.

[5] Ashcraft, C.C., Grimes, R.G., Lewis, J.G., Peyton, B.W., and Simon, H.D., "Recent progress in sparse matrix methods for large linear systems", *International Journal of Supercomputer Applications*, 1(4): 10-30, 1987.

[6] Duff, I.S., Grimes, R.G., and Lewis, J.G., "Sparse Matrix Test Problems", *ACM Transactions on Mathematical Software*, 15(1): 1-14, 1989.

[7] Fox, G., et al, *Solving Problems on Concurrent Processors: Volume 1 - General Techniques and Regular Problems*, Prentice Hall, 1988.

[8] Geist, G.A., and Ng, E., "Task scheduling for parallel sparse Cholesky factorization", *Internation Journal of Parallel Programming*, 18(4): 291-314, 1989.

[9] George, A., Heath, M., Liu, J., and Ng, E., "Solution of sparse positive definite systems on a hypercube", *Journal of Computational and Applied Mathematics*, 27(1): 129-156, 1989.

[10] George, A., and Liu, J., *Computer Solution of Large Sparse Positive Definite Systems*, Prentice-Hall, 1981.

[11] George, A., Liu, J. and Ng, E., "Communication results for parallel sparse Cholesky factorization on a hypercube", *Parallel Computing*, 10: 287-298, 1989.

[12] Hurlbert, L, and Zmijewski, E., "Limiting communication in parallel sparse Cholesky factorization", *SIAM Journal on Scientific and Statistical Computing*, 12: 1184-1197, 1991.

[13] Lenoski, D., Laudon, J., Gharachorloo, K., Weber, W.D., Gupta, A., Hennessy, J., Horowitz, M., and Lam, M., "The Stanford DASH multiprocessor", *IEEE Computer*, 23(3):63-79, March, 1992.

[14] Liu, J., "Modification of the minimum degree algorithm by multiple elimination", *ACM Transactions on Mathematical Software*, 12(2): 127-148, 1986.

[15] Liu, J., "The role of elimination trees in sparse factorization", *SIAM Journal on Matrix Analysis and Applications*, 11:134-172, 1990.

[16] Lucas, R. *Solving Planar Systems of Equations on Distributed-Memory Multiprocessors*, PhD thesis, Stanford University, 1988.

[17] Rothberg, E., *Exploiting the memory hierarchy in sequential and parallel sparse Cholesky factorization*, Ph.D. thesis, Stanford University, January, 1993.

[18] Rothberg, E., and Gupta, A., "An evaluation of left-looking, right-looking, and multifrontal approaches to sparse Cholesky factorization on hierarchical-memory machines", Technical Report STAN-CS-91-1377, Stanford University, 1991.

[19] Rothberg, E., and Gupta, A., "Techniques for improving the performance of sparse matrix factorization on multiprocessor workstations", *Supercomputing '90*, p. 232-243, November, 1990.

[20] Schreiber, R., "A new implementation of sparse Gaussian elimination", *ACM Transactions on Mathematical Software*, 8:256-276, 1982.

[21] Schreiber, R., "Scalability of sparse direct solvers", in *Graph Theory and Sparse Matrix Computation*, IMA Volumes in Mathematics and its Applications, Volume 56, Springer-Verlag, New York, 1993.

[22] Van De Geijn, R., *Massively parallel LINPACK benchmark on the Intel Touchstone Delta and iPSC/860 systems*, Technical Report CS-91-28, University of Texas at Austin, August, 1991.

[23] Venugopal, S., and Naik, V.K., "Effects of partitioning and scheduling sparse matrix factorization on communication and load balance", *Supercomputing '91*, November, 1991.

Session 7:
Minisymposium
Chair: Don Heller

Gordon Bell Prize Lectures 1993

D. E. Heller
CRPC
Rice University
P.O. Box 1892
Houston, TX 77251

A. Karp
HP Labs 3U-7
Hewlett-Packard
1501 Page Mill Road
Palo Alto, CA 94304

H. D. Simon
Mail Stop T045-1
Comp. Sciences Corp.
NASA Ames Res. Center
Moffett Field, CA 94035

Abstract

The Gordon Bell Prize recognizes significant achievements in the application of supercomputers to scientific and engineering problems. In a special session at Supercomputing '93 the finalists of the 1993 prize competition will give presentations about their winning entries. In this note we summarize the rules for the Gordon Bell Prize, and give a brief review of the history of this Prize, which reflects some of the developments in high performance computing in the last five years.

1 Introduction

The Gordon Bell Prize recognizes significant achievements in the application of supercomputers to scientific and engineering problems. In contrast to serial processing, typically used in personal computers as well as in many larger machines, parallel processing allows a task to be broken down into many subtasks that are performed simultaneously on multiple processors sometimes numbering in the hundreds or even the thousands. Writing programs for these powerful systems is a major challenge for software and computer engineers. Gordon Bell, a former National Science Foundation division director, now an independent consultant, offers the prizes to spur the transition of parallel processing from computer science research to useful applications.

In 1993 prizes were offered in three categories: performance, price/performance, and compiler parallelization. The performance prize recognizes those who solved a real problem in less elapsed time than anyone else. The price/performance prize encourages the development of cost-effective supercomputing. The compiler prize encourages the development of smart, parallelizing compilers. Entries are coordinated by Computer magazine, a publication of the

IEEE Computer Society. This will be the sixth of ten awardings of the Gordon Bell Prize, and the third award ceremony to be held at a Supercomputing '9X conference. Winners and honorable mentions for the 1993 competition will be announced following the presentations.

2 Rules for the 1993 Competition

The 1993 prizes will be given in two of three categories:

1. *Performance:* The entrant will be expected to convince the judges that the submitted program is running faster than any other comparable engineering or scientific application. Suitable evidence will be the megaflop rate based on actual operation counts or the solution of the same problem with a properly tuned code on a machine of known performance, such as a Cray Y-MP. If neither of these measurements can be made, the submitter should document the performance claims as well as possible.

2. *Price/performance:* The entrant must show that the performance of the application divided by the list price of the smallest system needed to achieve the reported performance is better than that of any other entry. Performance measurements will be evaluated as for the performance prize. Only the cost of the CPUs, memory, and any peripherals critical to the application need be included in the price. For example, if the job can be run on diskless compute servers, the cost of disks, keyboards, and displays need not be included.

3. *Compiler parallelization:* The combination of compiler and application that generates the most speed-up will be the winner. Speed-up will be measured by dividing the wall clock time of the

parallel run by that of a good serial implementation of the same job. These may be the same program if the entrant can convince the judges that the serial code is a good choice for a uniprocessor. Compiler directives and new languages are permitted. However, anyone submitting an entry in other than a standard, sequential language will have to convince the judges that the parallelism was detected by the compiler, not by the programmer.

There are some general conditions:

1. The submitted program must have utility; it must solve a problem that is considered a routine production run, such as making daily weather predictions or solving an important engineering or scientific problem. It should not be a contrived or experimental problem that is intended just to show high speed-up.

2. Entrants in the price/performance category must demonstrate that the machine they used has real utility. Only list prices of components should be used. If the machine is not on the market, the entry is probably not eligible although the judges will consider any reasonable estimate of the price.

3. One criterion the judges will use for all categories is how much the entry advances the state of the art of some field. For example, an entry running at 15 Gflops but solving a problem in a day that previously took a year might win over an entry running at 20 Gflops solving a more mundane problem. Entrants who believe their submission meets this criterion are advised to document their claims carefully.

4. In all cases the burden of proof is on the contestants. The judges will make an honest effort to compare the results of different programs solving different problems running on different machines, but they will depend primarily on the submitted material.

3   The 1993 Competition

The finalists shattered records in 1993 Gordon Bell Prize competition. Increased participation, record-breaking performance, and high overall quality were indicative of rapid progress in the application of parallel processing to scientific and engineering problems.

With 23 entries in this year's competition, participation was nearly double that of any previous year, and results improved markedly in several areas. The performance reported by the top entry was over eight times the previous best, and two entries exceeded 60 billion floating-point operations per second (Gf/s). More significantly, 12 entries achieved sustained rates exceeding 25 percent of the theoretical peak performance of the machines they ran on. Price/performance improved by almost 600 percent, to 7.5 Gf/s/million dollars.

The 1993 finalists are

- Peter Lomdahl, Pablo Tamayo, Niels Gronbech-Jensen, and David M. Beazley, of Los Alamos National Laboratory for "50 Gflops Molecular Dynamics on the Connection Machine 5."

- Lyle N. Long and Matt Kamon of Pennsylvania State University, and Denny Dahl, Mark Bromley, Robert Lordi, Jacek Myczkowski, and Richard Shapiro of Thinking Machines Corp., for "A Deterministic Parallel Algorithm to Solve a Model Boltzmann Equation (BGK)."

- Robert W. Means, Bret Wallach, and David Busby of HNC Inc., and Robert C. Lengel Jr. of Tracor Applied Sciences Inc. for "Bispectrum Signal Processing on HNC's SIMD Numerical Array Processor (SNAP)."

- Gary Sabot, Skef Wholey, Jonas Berlin, and Paul Oppenheimer of Thinking Machines Corp. for "Parallel Execution of a Fortran 77 Weather Prediction Model."

- Many of the entries reported very high performance on Cray Research C90 processors. The fifth finalist is thus Cray Research itself – the first time a company has been so honored in Gordon Bell Prize competition. Sara Graffunder will represent Cray, under the title "Barrier-breaking Performance for Industrial Problems on the CRAY C916."

Since the winners will be only announced during the conference, we will make no further comments on their work here.

Acknowledgements

Horst D. Simon acknowledges support for his work through contract NAS 2-12961 with the National Aeronautics and Space Administration.

Barrier-Breaking Performance for Industrial Problems on the CRAY C916

Sara K. Graffunder

Cray Research, Inc.

Abstract

Nine applications, including third-party codes, were submitted to the Gordon Bell Prize committee showing the CRAY C916 supercomputer providing record-breaking time to solution for industrial problems in several disciplines. Performance was obtained by balancing raw hardware speed; effective use of large, real, shared memory; compiler vectorization and autotasking; hand optimization; asynchronous I/O techniques; and new algorithms. The highest GFLOPS performance for the submissions was 11.1 GFLOPS out of a peak advertised performance of 16 GFLOPS for the CRAY C916 system. One program achieved a 15.45 speedup from the compiler with just two hand-inserted directives to scope variables properly for the mathematical library. New I/O techniques hide tens of gigabytes of I/O behind parallel computations. Finally, new iterative solver algorithms have demonstrated times to solution on 1 CPU as high as 70 times faster than the best direct solvers.

1. Introduction

The performance of computer systems is often described using terms like giga-floating-point operations per second (GFLOPS), MIPS or I/O bandwidth and capacity, and the value of such systems is often expressed in dollars-per-Mflop and cost performance or equivalence to some earlier supercomputer standard. However, the ability to meet application-driven resource demands defines the real measure of the performance and value of true supercomputers. Determining the possibility of solving a new grand challenge problem based on benchmarks using smaller problems or measuring performance on only part of the analysis is meaningless if the true measure of performance is time to solution. In addition, measuring performance strictly in terms of GFLOPS may overlook a new algorithm which has eliminated a majority of the floating-point operations to achieve a milestone performance in time to solution. The barrier-breaking performance for the nine applications reported in this paper demonstrates the real power of a balanced approach to meeting the application-driven

resource demands of the real users of supercomputers today.

All of the applications described in this paper were run on the CRAY C916 supercomputer and demonstrate superior performance as measured by total time to solution. The problems are taken, in several cases, from applications which are used daily in production environments where the analysis results often make a financial difference to the organizations which run them. The superior performance is not obtained automatically by running on fast hardware. It is rather the result of a balanced effort that is driven by the resource demands of the problems to be solved. Several applications used in this paper are third-party codes: ANSYS, GEOSYS, MNDO91, and SUPERMOLECULE. Some are a subset of some 20 applications which have achieved 6 GFLOPS or better (out of a peak advertised capacity of 16 GFLOPS) on the CRAY C916 system. All times reported are actual elapsed wall-clock times or, where noted, total CPU time for complete job runs.

The nine applications are discussed by discipline. For each application the major work accomplished to obtain the CRAY C916 performance is described briefly. The high GFLOPS performance is obtained through the optimization of computationally intensive regions of the various codes. However, the time-to-solution performance is obtained by improving I/O performance and introducing new algorithms. The factors which effectively exploit the CRAY C916 supercomputer resources include the following:
- autotasking and automatic vectorization
- hand-inserted parallelization directives
- effective use of the large, real, shared memory
- asynchronous I/O software
- new mathematical algorithms.

2. Computational fluid dynamics

Three CFD applications were submitted: DRAG4D [1], which models unsteady, three-dimensional viscous incompressible flow for Nissan Motor Co., Ltd.; LANS3DUP [2], a three-dimensional steady/unsteady compressible Navier-Stokes/Euler code used by the

Institute of Space and Astronautical Science in Japan, and MHD3D, a magnetohydrodynamics spectral code from NASA Goddard Space Flight Center which is used for studying the evolution of the heliospheric plasma.

The DRAG4D example achieved 6.87 GFLOPS on a CRAY C916 system using 60 megawords of memory. The solver is more than 99 percent vectorized and 98 percent parallelized by the Cray CF77 compiling system. Nissan saves $400,000 per year on wind tunnel tests by using this CFD analysis.

LANS3DUP combines an LU-ADI implicit time integration algorithm with high-resolution upwinding to compute the right-hand-side steady-state part. On 15 CPUs of a CRAY C916, LANS3DUP achieved 6.7 GFLOPS, which also represents a 12.27/15 speedup over the single-CPU run.

For MHD3D [3], a grid of 128^3 lattice points was solved. This corresponds to a flow Reynolds number of 1000, which is the largest computation that can conveniently be done today but is still substantially smaller than the Reynolds number for the actual heliosphere. This 128^3 grid required 97 Mwords of memory and 34 hours of CPU time on the CRAY C916 and is not feasible on a workstation. For the 100-step submitted run, the Cray Research CF77 compiling system was used to vectorize and autotask the code. Aggressive inlining of subroutines was used. The single CPU elapsed time was 3833 seconds and the MFLOPS were 520. On 16 CPUs the elapsed time was 248 seconds (15.45/16 speedup) and the MFLOPS were 8025 (8.02 GFLOPS). With the exception of one subroutine, the parallelization was obtained entirely by compile-line directives. In the subroutine containing the three-dimensional Fast Fourier Transform driver, just two microtasking directives were inserted to scope properly the arguments to the Cray mathematical library routines.

3. Computational Chemistry

In computational chemistry, two third-party applications have demonstrated outstanding GFLOPS performance. MNDO91 [4], a semi-emprical code is used to determine thermodynamic information such as heat of formation, which can be used to predict the relative stability of different molecules, and to identify transition states and reaction intermediates. SUPERMOLECULE [5], formerly the chemistry DISCO program, is an *ab initio* quantum chemistry electronic-structure program. Such programs are widely used in both industry and academia.

MNDO91 was run on a large molecule, c960, a member of the fullerene family. We are unaware of any studies of comparable sized molecules using MNDO91 or related methods. The problem used 150 Mwords of memory, ran in 39.5 minutes of elapsed time on the CRAY C916, and required 9.75 hours of CPU time. The GFLOPS performance, based on elapsed time, was 11.16. This is the best GFLOPS performance we have seen on a complete application on the CRAY C916 system. The computations in this application were dominated by dense matrix multiplications but, additionally, over 96 million slower integrals were computed only once and stored in the large main memory. While the c960 molecule is primarily of academic interest at this point, a large chemical company has recently used MNDO91 to study the effect of molecular structure on the flexibility of polymers.

The SUPERMOLECULE program is notable because it has been designed to take advantage of multiple processors, has exploited methods to reduce I/O to avoid MPP bottlenecks, and has been used to benchmark a number of workstations and MPP systems. The benchmark problems are therefore sized to run on smaller machines as well as larger, which sometimes is a disadvantage for the larger machines. Nonetheless, the CRAY C916 results, obtained with minimal effort using Cray autotasking directives and libraries, were consistently the fastest. The largest benchmark case ran on the CRAY C916 system at 7.19 GFLOPS on 16 processors.

4. Seismic analysis

Two seismic codes have demonstrated very high levels of performance on the CRAY C916. The one-pass 3-D poststack depth-migration is part of Geco-Prakla's production code GEOSYS [6]. The 3-D prestack Kirchhoff time or depth migration code [7] written at Cray Research explores the Cray C916 system's ability to handle this relatively new application of a well-known theory.

The GEOSYS migration code's one-pass algorithm is implemented in FORTRAN, with the code being fully vectorized and autotasked for multiple CPUs. The algorithm is a time-consuming finite-difference approach working in the frequency space domain. Fewer than 20 compiler directives are added to achieve the multitasking. The migration is done in a cascade, with every CPU computing the result of one depth layer looping over all the frequencies. Since the CPU's do independent computations with the frequencies delayed by one for each successive CPU, more memory is required for every concurrently computed depth layer. Intermediate results cannot be held in memory, and so asynchronous disk I/O on four channels runs parallel to the computation.

For a test survey of 630x315 common depth points, a processing length of 5 seconds (or 1250 layers) and migration depth of 3.4Km, the performance of 10.1 GFLOPS was obtained on the CRAY C916 system in an elapsed time of 661 seconds while doing 12 gigabytes of I/O (or 18.5 MB/s). This represents a speedup of 15.15 over the single-CPU performance. Since 1985, when Geco-Prakla (then called Prakla-Seismos AG) ran similar jobs on a Cyber 205 in 100 CPU hours (which might have taken weeks to run), the turnaround for this work has improved 500 times. The 10.1 GFLOPS performance is, of course, impressive, because it allows the work to be done in interactive time.

The full 3-D Kirchhoff migration scheme was designed at Cray Research to study the feasibility of structural imaging of the earth on a general-purpose supercomputer. The method has received extensive coverage on MPP systems, and Cray is also involved in investigating its application for MPP. However, the shared memory of the CRAY C916 system and its random-access SSD for fast I/O seemed ideally suited for this work. The algorithm has been optimized, vectorized, and microtasked. In fact, the autotasking compiler achieves nearly 100% parallelization. Performance reached almost 9 GFLOPS for one test problem, with all problems running in the 8 GFLOPS range. This means that a prestack migration can be completed in 30 hours for 10,000 shot gathers of prestack data for a 2Km by 2Km region on the surface and 500 grids in depth.

5. Structural analysis

Large-scale structural analysis simulations place ever-increasing demands on computer resources as the problems grow from single-step static analyses to multi-step nonlinear analyses used to accurately predict the response of real physical systems. The 250,000 degree-of-freedom model of a proposed new design for the Space Shuttle Liquid Oxygen Pump Housing is an example of such a problem. This problem was modeled using the ANSYS [8] code, a general-purpose, commercial, finite-element-analysis tool used in virtually every engineering discipline. Initially the analysis was carried out using 14 smaller subassembly models requiring a total of 29 separate runs on a CRAY X-MP system over about one week of elapsed time. On the CRAY C916 system, a single run of just over 3 hours was required to solve one large global model at a sustained rate of nearly 6 GFLOPS. During the analyses over 27 Gwords (216 Gbytes) of data were transferred to disk in parallel with the computations while parallel processing in the equation solver effectively used multiple CPUs. Even greater throughput performance was obtained by running two separate analyses simultaneously, each using 8 CPUs. A total of 45 Gwords (360 Gbytes) of data was transferred to and from disk storage and both jobs completed in 4.5 hours, sustaining a combined rate of over 7 GFLOPS.

The CPU performance of ANSYS was improved by adding an assembly language kernel to the equation solvers. This kernel achieves near peak vector performance for large-scale problems and with the addition of a single autotasking directive this kernel was used within a parallel algorithm for direct solution of linear systems. The I/O performance of ANSYS for large problems was improved

dramatically without any modification to the source code. A new Flexible File I/O (FFIO) library, developed at Cray Research, was used to exploit parallel processing of I/O. This new FFIO library includes layers which give users flexible control of disk striping of files, an intelligent read-ahead, write-behind cache, and an event layer to capture detailed information about each I/O request. The key features of the new FFIO library are controlled by users by setting up one or two environment variables.

6. Algorithmic breakthroughs for acoustics, CFD, and electromagnetics

For many industrial applications using boundary integral techniques, the principal computational requirement is the solution of large, dense linear systems of equations. Traditionally these systems are solved using some form of LU decomposition and can be well-suited for massively parallel computers. However, for the very large problems of interest in these disciplines the numerical stability of LU decomposition may make them unreliable and the complexity of operations is too high to obtain a solution in a reasonable time, even at sustained teraflops (TFLOPS) rates. For example, a 2 million degree-of-freedom complex dense linear system would still require more than 8 months on a supercomputer at an assumed rate of 1 TFLOPS. The new preconditioned iterative methods offer an alternative approach which is mathematically stable and has a much lower arithmetic complexity when compared to LU decomposition. The new methods developed by scientists from Elegant Mathematics, Inc., and Cray Research are based on the ILU preconditioned GMRES(k) iterative method [9]. These new methods perform at rates which exceed 2 GFLOPS on the CRAY C90 architecture and, more importantly, offer solution times which are far below methods which use the traditional LU solvers.

An acoustic radiation model of a car engine was solved using the new iterative solver. The estimated LU decomposition time for the 10,586 degree-of-freedom linear system is 3515 seconds, assuming a 900 MFLOP single processor performance on a CRAY C90 system. The iterative solver required just 44.5 seconds to solve this problem to 10 orders of magnitude reduction in the error residual using only 12 iterations. On 4 processors this time was further reduced to 23.6 seconds using an early implementation in which all parts were not yet parallelized. Compared to the idealized LU performance of 900 MFLOPS per CPU with perfect linear speedup, the new method is almost 80 times faster on one CPU and still over 30 times faster on 4 CPUs.

To obtain the same time to solution for the acoustic radiation problem using the LU decomposition algorithm would require a computer capable of sustaining over 125 GFLOPS. If price/performance is defined by time-to-solution using the best algorithm, this new iterative algorithm on the CRAY C94 ($10 M list price) gives an equivalent price/performance of 12.5 GFLOPS/$M, assuming that the LU decomposition is the basis of comparison on other MPP systems.

A CFD application from a flow simulation demonstrated the algorithmic advantage of the new iterative solvers by comparing the nearly 8-fold increase in the time for LU factorization, from 2500 seconds for a 10,472 equation dense linear system to almost 20,000 seconds for a 20,682 equation dense linear system to the 4-fold increase in iterative solution time, from 55 seconds to 210 seconds.

Finally, from computational electromagnetics, a 10,000 equation problem with over 700 right-hand-sides demonstrates up to 2.7 GFLOPS performance on a 4 processor CRAY C90 for the iterative method. These examples demonstrate that the most challenging large problems of the future require not only hardware speed and I/O capacity but fundamental algorithmic changes as well in order to really reduce time to solution while improving price/performance.

7. Conclusion

The performance of the CRAY C916 supercomputer on a variety of real, customer applications demonstrates that a high percentage of the theoretical peak performance of this machine can be obtained for many types of analysis. The highest GLOPS performance obtained 11.1 GFLOPS, while parallel speedup of over 15 were obtained in more than one application. The largest commercial application code among the submissions, ANSYS, achieved over 7 GFLOPS throughput performance running 2 simultaneous jobs while transferring 45 Gwords of data to disk. The most important aspect of these performance milestones of several GFLOPS is the reduced time to solution. The high sustained rates are possible because of a balanced approach designed to satisfy application-driven resource demands which include machine resources such as compilers, new I/O libraries, performance tools, and hardware technology but, just as importantly, human resources supplying new state-of-the-art algorithms and directing optimization where automatic tools cannot detect parallelism adequately. The examples presented reflect the essence of the Gordon Bell Prize competition which has challenged hardware vendors and researchers alike to focus on the use of supercomputer technology rather than the technology itself.

Acknowledgements

Sara Graffunder wishes to acknowledge that all of the work done to obtain and measure performance for the nine entries was done by the authors listed in references 1-9. Her only role was to summarize the nine entries here, often using the exact words of the entries submitted to the Gordon Bell Prize committee. In addition, Trudy Sprague provided invaluable help in obtaining information about these applications and she and Eugene Poole gave critical help with the final paper. Any errors should be attributed to Sara, of course. She also has copies of the original submissions and will help interested people get in touch with the submitters.

References

[1] R. Himeno and K. Fujitani, *DRAG4D*, (Gordon Bell Prize Submission), 1993.

[2] F. Kozo, *The LANS3DUP Code, Features, and Benchmark Results*, (Gordon Bell Prize Submission), 1993.

[3] W. T. Stribling and J.Abeles, *MHD3D a Magnetohydrodynamics Spectral Code*, (Gordon Bell Prize Submission), 1993.

[4] B. Elkin and W. Thiel, *MND091*, (Gordon Bell Prize Submission), 1993.

[5] M. Feyereisen, *ab initio chemistry program (DISCO) SUPERMOLECULE*, (Gordon Bell Prize Submission), 1993.

[6] K. Ketelsen, *3-D Poststack Migration at 10 Gigaflops Speed*, (Gordon Bell Prize Submission), 1993.

[7] J. Kao, *Multitasked Computation of the 3-D Prestack Kirchhoff Time or Depth Migration on the Cray Y-MP/C90 System*, (Gordon Bell Prize Submission), 1993.

[8] E. Poole, J. Bauer, J. Swanson and G. Helmick, *Achieving Gigaflop Performance in a Commercial Finite Element Structural Applications Code on a CRAY C916 Supercomputer*, (Gordon Bell Prize Submission), 1993.

[9] S. Kharchenko, P. Kolensnikov, E. Tyrtyshnikov, A. Yeremin, M. Heroux, and Q. Sheikh, *A Class of Iterative Solvers for Dense Linear Systems*, (Gordon Bell Prize Submission), 1993.

50 GFlops Molecular Dynamics
on the Connection Machine 5

Peter S. Lomdahl, Pablo Tamayo, Niels Grønbech-Jensen, and David M. Beazley

Theoretical Division and Advanced Computing Laboratory

Los Alamos National Laboratory, Los Alamos, NM 87545

Abstract

We present timings and performance numbers for a new short range three dimensional (3D) molecular dynamics (MD) code, SPaSM, on the Connection Machine-5 (CM-5). We demonstrate that runs with more than 10^8 particles are now possible on massively parallel MIMD computers. To the best of our knowledge this is at least an order of magnitude more particles than what has previously been reported. Typical production runs show sustained performance (including communication) in the range of 47-50 GFlops on a 1024 node CM-5 with vector units (VUs). The speed of the code scales linearly with the number of processors and with the number of particles and shows 95% parallel efficiency in the speedup.

1 Introduction

The use of molecular dynamics (MD)[1] to study dynamical properties of solids and liquids has been known for decades, but it is only the recent proliferation of powerful massively parallel computers that begins to makes detailed studies of realistically sized systems possible. A cube of material 1000 atoms on the side measures roughly $0.5\mu m \times 0.5\mu m \times 0.5\mu m$ - while this may seem like a very small piece of material - it contains 10^9 atoms. Solving Newton's equations for a billion interacting atoms still represents a formidable problem for MD. However, realistic calculations in materials science require system sizes in this range if the dynamics of defects like dislocations and grain-boundaries is to be studied. An additional problem is presented by the short time scale that is accessible by the MD method, which is typically tens or maybe hundred of *nano*-sec. at best. Ideally one would like to use the MD method for second long simulations with at least 10^9 atoms. While this goal is still very far away, there is substantial current interest in the development of fast MD algorithms[2, 3, 4, 5, 6, 7]

which allow for the simulation of at least million atom systems.

We have developed an new scalable MD algorithm based on a message-passing multi-cell approach which allows for simulating at least 10^8 particles interacting via a relative short range potential. We have implemented the algorithm in a code, SPaSM (Scalable Parallel Short-range Molecular dynamics), on the Connection Machine 5 (CM-5) and demonstrated that simulations with tens of millions of atoms can now be performed routinely. In addition, it is clear that simulations with 10^8 particles are now possible at a sustained rate of 50 GFlops. To our knowledge the performance numbers are the best reported to date for any MD simulation and may well be the highest for any 3D production code implementing a substantial amount of unstructured communication. In preliminary 2D studies, we simulated the fracture dynamics of a piece of material with 2 million atoms that is being pulled apart in a tensile experiment. We are currently using SPaSM to study dynamic fracture physics with millions of atoms in 3D.

2 MD Simulations

The MD method concerns the solution of Newton's equation of motion for N interacting particles. This general N-body problem involves the calculation of $N(N-1)/2$ pair interactions in order to compute the total force on any given particle:

$$m_i \frac{d^2 \mathbf{r}_i}{dt^2} = -\sum_{j \neq i} \frac{\partial V_{ij}(|\mathbf{r}_j - \mathbf{r}_i|)}{\partial \mathbf{r}_i}, \qquad (1)$$

here $\mathbf{r}_i$ indicates the instantaneous position and m_i the mass of particle i. The complexity of the force calculation is simplified considerably if the potential $V_{ij}(r)$ has a finite range of interaction. This is a reasonable approximation of the atomistic interactions in many solids and fluids. In our timings here we have used the Lennard-Jones 6-12 (LJ) potential

$$V(r) = \begin{cases} 4\epsilon\left(\left(\frac{\sigma}{r}\right)^{12} - \left(\frac{\sigma}{r}\right)^{6}\right) & 0 < r \leq r_{max} \\ 0 & r_{max} < r \end{cases} \quad (2)$$

Here σ and ϵ are the usual LJ parameters. The potential is cut-off at r_{max}, i. e. no particles interact beyond this range. We include here timings and performance numbers for two values of r_{max}. We stress that while more complicated and accurate potentials which include many-body effects are available, the amount of work needed in the force calculation is represented well by the LJ potential especially when the cut-off is $r_{max} = 5\sigma$. The number of interacting neighbors for each particle depends on the value of the cut-off distance r_{max} and the particle density ρ.

Our code is written in ANSI C with explicit calls to the CMMD message-passing library. The kernel of the force calculation is coded in the CM-5 vector unit (VU) assembler language, CDPEAC, and consists of approximately 60 lines of code. All our calculations were performed in *double precision*.

3 Multi-cell algorithm

Our algorithm has been described in detail in[7]. Here we briefly outline its main features, illustrating the algorithm in 2D, but it extends naturally to 3D. Space is considered to be a rectangular region with periodic boundary conditions.

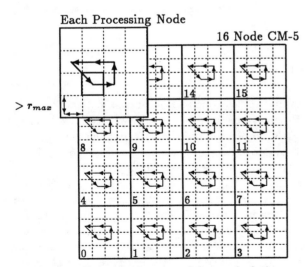

Figure 1. *Processor layout and force calculation.*

This region is subdivided into large cells that are assigned to the processing nodes (PNs) on the CM-5. The region assigned to each PN is further subdivided

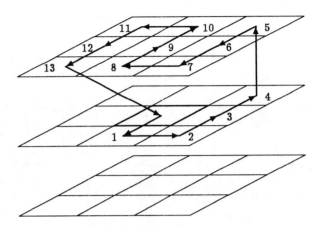

Figure 2. *3D interaction path*

into small cells with dimensions slightly larger than the cutoff distance. Particles are assigned to a particular cell geometrically according to the particle's coordinates. In Fig. 1, solid lines represent processor boundaries while dashed lines represent the cells created on each PN. For large simulations, many thousands of cells per PN may be created (this does not explicitly depend on the number of PNs being used). Associated with each cell is a small block of memory for storing a sequential list of particles. To compute the forces for particles in a cell, we first compute all of the interactions between particles in that cell. Afterwards, forces between particles in neighboring cells are calculated by following an interaction path that visits neighboring cells. The path in 2D is shown in Fig. 1 and in 3D in Fig. 2. As we follow the path, accelerations are accumulated by the original cell and any visited cells (using Newton's third law). To calculate all of the forces, this procedure is carried out on all cells on all of the PNs. Cells will accumulate accelerations from their lower neighbors when they calculate their interactions. Whenever the interaction path crosses a processor boundary, message passing is used to communicate particle data. After all forces have been calculated, the particle positions are updated. Since our algorithm is geometrically based, all of the data structures must be updated to account for positional changes. The particle coordinates are checked and if a particle is in the wrong cell it is moved to the proper cell. If the new cell is on a different PN, asynchronous message passing is used to send the particle to its new PN. Each PN checks for incoming particles and places them in the proper cell when received. Since a large number of cells may be created on each PN (even for moderately sized systems) hundreds or even thousands of message-passing calls may be re-

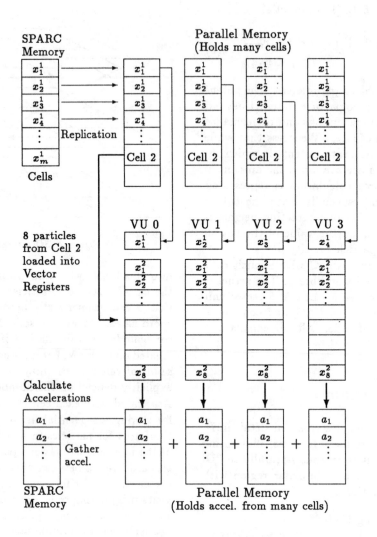

Figure 3. Calculating forces on the VUs.

quired for each time step. The amount of communication and calculation for 3D is substantial due to an increased number of neighboring cells and a more complicated interaction path.

4 Using The Vector Units and Parallel Memory

On each processing node, the CM-5 has four vector units (VUs) that perform fast vector arithmetic in a SIMD mode. Each VU has a peak speed of 32 Mflops for a combined speed of 128 Mflops per node. In addition to performing arithmetic operations, the VUs also act as memory controllers with each VU con-

trolling an 8 Mbyte bank of memory. The 32 Mbytes of memory on each PN can be accessed by both the SPARC processor and the VUs, but the memory is divided into two separate areas for this purpose. SPARC memory is memory that has been allocated for use by the SPARC processor. All usual SPARC operations perform normally in this area. Parallel memory is a special memory allocation that allows the four VUs to perform simultaneous load/store operations. Each VU allocates an identically structured memory region in the 8 Mbyte memory bank that they control. When loads or stores are performed, each VU accesses its particular bank. This allows the VUs to operate on four different data sets in a SIMD mode. The SPARC processor can access any particular bank of parallel memory, but the VUs can not directly access SPARC memory. Transferring data between the two memory regions can be done using special instructions, but accessing SPARC memory from the VUs is slow and should be avoided as much as possible. As a general rule, any operations involving the VUs must use parallel memory for optimal performance.

To access the VUs, we have implemented the force calculation in CDPEAC (the assembler language for controlling the CM-5 vector units). The kernel of the force calculation takes two cells of particles and calculates the resulting accelerations between the particles. This calculation is described in detail in Fig. 3. First, the particle coordinates from the two cells are copied from SPARC memory and replicated across all four VUs in parallel memory. Eight particles from cell 2 are then loaded onto all four VUs. We then loop over all of the particles in cell 1 and calculate the accelerations between these particles and the eight particles loaded from cell 2. At each step, four different particles from cell 1 are loaded (a different particle on each VU). This allows the VUs to calculate 32 interactions simultaneously. Once all particles in cell 1 have been processed, the next set of eight particles from cell 2 is loaded and the process is repeated. The calculation continues, calculating 32 interactions per step, until all accelerations have been calculated. Afterwards, the resulting accelerations are gathered from parallel memory and saved back to SPARC memory.

All internal data structures in our code are stored in SPARC memory. This allows the data to be easily accessible to functions that do not require the VUs. Whenever particles are used in the force calculation, they are copied to parallel memory. For simulations with a cutoff of $r_{max} = 5\sigma$, each cell may contain several hundred particles and most of the time is spent calculating interactions in the force kernel. The extra overhead associated with copying the particles from SPARC memory to parallel memory is small so we pay a minimal penalty for using SPARC memory in this case. For simulations with a smaller cutoff such as $r_{max} = 2.5\sigma$, the number of cells per processor increases dramatically while the number of particles per cell decreases. In this case, it is more difficult to keep the VUs busy and our use of parallel memory becomes more critical.

To obtain better performance with a smaller interaction cutoff r_{max}, several modifications have been made. The main performance problem is that of loading the particles into parallel memory from SPARC memory. If we use the same scheme developed for large cutoff distances, each cell is loaded into par-

allel memory whenever needed in the force calculation. This results in each cell being loaded to parallel memory as many as 14 times (once when calculating self-interactions and 13 times when neighboring cells calculate their interactions). To reduce the amount of loading, a parallel memory caching scheme has been implemented. A buffer for holding a collection of cells is allocated in parallel memory. Each time a cell is encountered in the force calculation, this buffer is checked to see if that cell has already been loaded. If not, it is loaded to parallel memory and the previous contents (if any) saved back to SPARC memory (including accelerations). The loading process operates according to a FIFO scheme and eventually new cells will begin to replace previously loaded cells in the cache. As the force calculation proceeds, previously loaded cells will no longer be necessary in the calculation (after they have remained in the cache sufficiently long) and can be saved back to SPARC memory without having to be reloaded. This property is due to the fact that the interaction path has a finite range and will not see cells that were loaded much earlier in the calculation. By making the cache sufficiently large, each cell will be loaded to parallel memory only once and a substantial improvement in performance is obtained.

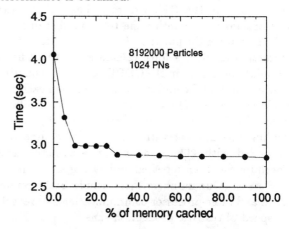

Figure 4 : Effect of caching on iteration time

In our code, the amount of memory available for caching can be adjusted. This gives us increased flexibility since our code can be optimized for memory (by using a small cache) or for speed (by using a larger cache). This allows us to run small simulations at increased speed or large simulations with more than 10^8 particles by simply adjusting our memory usage. Caching has significantly improved our code performance for simulations with a cutoff of $r_{max} = 2.5\sigma$. The speedup obtained by caching for a particular simulation is shown in Fig. 4. As more memory is added to the cache, the iteration time drops rapidly. In the figure we also see that little speedup is gained by caching more than 30% of the cells. For very large simulations, we have found that even adding a small cache of 1-2% of the cells can dramatically improve performance.

5 Timings and performance

In Table 1 ($r_{max} = 5\sigma$) we summarize the timings for runs on a variety of CM-5 processor partitions with different number of particles, N, in the range from 1 million to 131 million. The particles, in each case, were arranged in a uniform 3D cubic lattice at constant density $\rho = N/\sigma^3 = 1$. With this density and interaction cutoff, each particle has approximately 520 interacting neighbors. This configuration is unstable and will undergo a phase change where the particles rearrange in an face-center-cubic (fcc) configuration. This choice of initial conditions thus guarantees that the particles are moving between processors and realistic inter-processor communication is involved.

In the table, the update time per time step and the corresponding GFlop rates are given (the numbers in parenthesis are the GFlop rates.) The GFlop rates were obtained by counting the total number of interactions between the particles during a time step. Each interaction involves a force calculation with 42 floating point operations in the CDPEAC kernel (counting multiply, add, and compare as one operation each and divide as five)[8]. The GFlop numbers are calculated by multiplying the total interaction count by 42 and dividing this number with the time for a time step (measured with `CMMD_node_timer_elapsed`). This procedure was then repeated and averaged over many time steps. Our numbers thus include both computation and inter-processor communication and reflects the speed of realistic production runs.[1]

In Table 2 we summarize our recent timings for runs with a cutoff of $r_{max} = 2.5\sigma$. The update time per time step and the GFlop rates are given. All runs were performed using parallel memory caching. In each case, 25% of the cells were cached except for the run with 131 million particles that used a 3% cache. With a cutoff of $r_{max} = 2.5\sigma$, each particle has approximately 65 interacting neighbors. Since each particle has fewer neighbors, it is more difficult to keep the VUs busy during the force calculation. Consequently, the GFlop rates are lower. However, our best timing

---

[1] The bare kernel of the force calculation (with no communication or SPARC memory operations) runs at 68.5 GFlops.

for $r_{max} = 2.5\sigma$ is our run with 65 million particles on 1024 PNs. In this case, the update time is 16.55 seconds which corresponds to 250 *nano*-sec. per particle update. To the best of our knowledge, this is the best reported time to date [6]. Using minimal parallel memory caching, we were also able to simulate 180 million particles with an update time of 55.6 seconds.

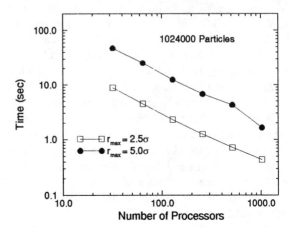

Figure 5 : MD update time vs. number of processors

In Fig. 5 we illustrate the scaling properties of our code. The data are for runs with 1 million particles and two different values of the cut-off $r_{max} = 5\sigma$ and $r_{max} = 2.5\sigma$. A near linear dependence is found for both values of the cut-off. This is of course also evident from the numbers in Tables 1 and 2. It should also be noted that our algorithm scales linearly with the number of particles for a fixed number of processors.

Particles	$r_{max} = 5\sigma$		$r_{max} = 2.5\sigma$	
	Comp.	Comm.	Comp.	Comm.
1024000	82.5%	17.5%	78.0%	22.0%
4096000	88.5%	11.5%	77.2%	23.8%
16384000	91.9%	8.1%	84.8%	15.2%
65536000	93.2%	6.8%	89.5%	10.5%
131072000	94.4%	5.6%	90.8%	9.2%

Table 3: Timing breakdown for 1024 PNs

In Table 3 the breakdown of computation and communication time is given. For the larger simulations, each processor may have many thousands of cells. As a result, calculating the accelerations may require several thousand message passing calls. Depending on the value of r_{max}, each message passing call may involve a transfer of 800-10000 bytes. Despite the large amount of communication, our algorithm is dominated by the calculation of forces for both values of r_{max}. In

Particles	Processors					
	32	64	128	256	512	1024
1024000	47.94 (1.5)	25.41 (2.9)	12.56 (5.8)	6.79 (10.7)	4.30 (16.9)	1.66 (43.7)
2048000	94.39 (1.5)	48.39 (3.0)	24.43 (5.9)	12.75 (11.4)	6.92 (21.0)	3.16 (47.0)
4096000	186.83 (1.6)	95.28 (3.1)	47.98 (6.0)	25.57 (11.4)	14.00 (20.7)	6.17 (47.0)
8192000	-	188.00 (3.1)	95.11 (6.1)	50.63 (11.5)	28.12 (20.6)	12.13 (47.8)
16384000	-	-	185.77 (6.2)	95.52 (12.2)	52.60 (22.1)	23.68 (49.0)
32768000	-	-	-	190.81 (12.2)	101.55 (22.9)	46.71 (49.7)
65536000	-	-	-	-	204.91 (22.6)	92.91 (50.0)
131072000	-	-	-	-	-	183.01 (50.7)

Table 1: Update times per time step in sec. (GFlops in parenthesis). Cut-off: $r_{max} = 5\sigma$

Particles	Processors					
	32	64	128	256	512	1024
1024000	8.90 (0.81)	4.51 (1.61)	2.32 (3.12)	1.26 (5.74)	0.72 (10.07)	0.44 (16.55)
2048000	-	8.96 (1.62)	4.44 (3.26)	2.46 (5.90)	1.36 (10.65)	0.74 (19.54)
4096000	-	-	8.79 (3.29)	4.81 (6.03)	2.67 (10.84)	1.36 (21.27)
8192000	-	-	16.83 (3.44)	8.81 (6.58)	4.80 (12.07)	2.47 (23.50)
16384000	-	-	-	16.95 (6.84)	8.74 (13.26)	4.49 (25.82)
32768000	-	-	-	-	16.90 (13.72)	8.54 (27.14)
65536000	-	-	-	-	-	16.55 (28.01)
131072000	-	-	-	-	-	34.26 (27.06)

Table 2: Update times per time step in sec. (GFlops in parenthesis). Cut-off: $r_{max} = 2.5\sigma$.

the table, computation time includes the calculation of forces and the numerical integration. The communication time includes all message passing during the interaction calculation and the time to redistribute the particles after each time step.

With a cutoff of $r_{max} = 5\sigma$, the speedup from a run with 4 million particles on a 32 node CM-5 to the same run on a 1024 node CM-5 is over a factor 30 and corresponds to 95% parallel efficiency. We were also recently able to run SPaSM on a 4 PN CM-5 with 1 million particles. The update time here was 367 sec. The speedup achieved with same run on 1024 PNs is a factor 221, representing 86% parallel efficiency. Our best performance number, 50.7 GFlops, represents 40% of the theoretical peak performance of 128 GFlops on a 1024 node CM-5. The 50.7 GFlops also represents a cost/performance number of 1.95 GFlops/$Million.

6 Conclusion

We have demonstrated that three-dimensional multi-million particle MD simulations can now be performed routinely on massively parallel MIMD computer systems. To demonstrate the practicality of the algorithm, we present a few time frames from a million particle impact simulation. The simulated particles have an interaction cut-off of $r_{max} = 2.5\sigma$ and the time step of the integration is $\Delta t = 0.01$ time units. The system is initiated with one block of particles in a fcc lattice with $200 \times 200 \times 25$ (10^6) atoms, and a projectile in a fcc lattice with the dimensions $20\sigma \times 20\sigma \times 40$ layers (14000) atoms. The projectile has a velocity of 10 towards the block (~ 1.3 times the sound velocity in the lattice). This initial condition is shown in Fig. 6a. In Fig. 6b we show the system at $t = 2.5$. The projectile has made contact with the block and has partially penetrated. The hexagonal nature of the lattice is seen to dominate the phonons emitted on the surface of the block, even though the projectile makes contact with a square (20×20) shape. Finally, in Fig. 6c, we show the particles at $t = 5$, where part of the projectile has been absorbed in the block. Other parts of the projectile have disintegrated into almost free particles. We are currently using SPaSM to perform other multi-million atom simulations.

The impact simulation shows the inherently unstructured nature of MD simulations. In principle, every particle is free to move to any location within the system. This may require a substantial amount of communications and data management. However, we have been able to achieve high performance by carefully analyzing the problem and mapping it to the architecture of the CM-5. Our algorithm is dominated by computation with communication requiring only 5-20% of the overall time. Our algorithm scales linearly with the number of processors and the number of particles. With an interaction cutoff of $r_{max} = 5\sigma$, runs with a sustained calculation rate of 50 Gflops can be performed on a 1024 PN CM-5. With a smaller cutoff of $r_{max} = 2.5\sigma$, we can achieve an update time of 250 *nano*-seconds per particle. This fast update time allows us to run large MD simulations that have been impossible to perform in the past. Using all of the memory of the CM-5, we have also been able to simulate more than 180 million particles in 3D. While we may not be able to model 1 billion particles on current machines, this goal now seems within reach as next generation machines become available.

Acknowledgments

We thank the Advanced Computing Laboratory for generous support, in particular M. Krogh and D. Rich provided major assistance. We also express our appreciation to D. Dahl, A. Greenberg, C. Lobron, A. Mainwaring, and L. Tucker from TMC for valuable suggestions regarding CDPEAC and CMMD.

References

[1] *Computer Simulations of Liquids*, M. P. Allen and D. J. Tildesley. Clarendon Press, Oxford (1987).

[2] A. I. Mel'čuk, R. C. Giles, and H. Gould, *Computers in Physics*, May/June 1991, p. 311.

[3] P. Tamayo, J. P. Mesirov, and B. M. Boghosian, *Proc. of Supercomputing 91*, IEEE Computer Society (1991), p. 462.

[4] B. L. Holian et al. Phys. Rev. A **43**, 2655 (1991).

[5] R. C. Giles and P. Tamayo, *Proc. of SHPCC'92*, IEEE Computer Society (1992), p. 240.

[6] S. Plimpton and G. Heffelfinger, *Proc. of SHPCC'92*, IEEE Computer Society (1992), p. 246.

[7] D. M. Beazley and P. S. Lomdahl, *Message-Passing Multi-Cell Molecular Dynamics on the Connection Machine 5*, Parall. Comp. (1993) (in press).

[8] *DPEAC Reference Manual*, Thinking Machines Corporation (1992), Cambridge, Massachusetts.

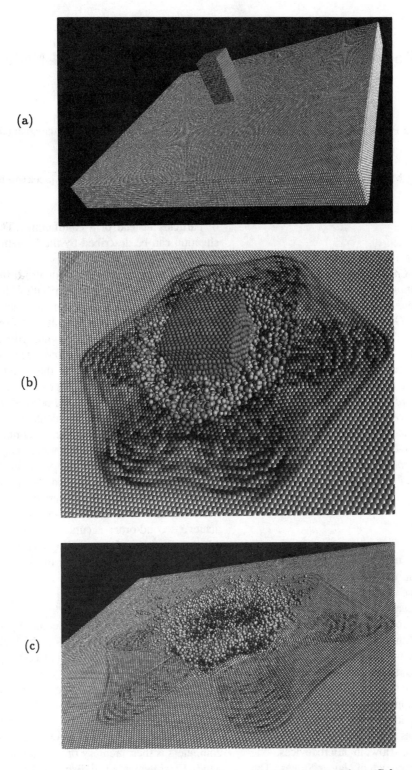

(a)

(b)

(c)

Figure 6. An impact simulation with 1014000 particles. Colors indicate kinetic energy with bright colors indicating high energy.

[For color plate see page 929]

Solving the Boltzmann Equation at 61 gigaflops on a 1024-Node CM-5

L. N. Long

The Pennsylvania State University, University Park, PA 16802   lnl@cac.psu.edu

J. Myczkowski

Thinking Machines Corporation, 245 First Street, Cambridge, MA 02142   jacek@think.com

Abstract

This paper documents the use of a massively parallel computer, specifically the Connection Machine CM-5, to solve the Boltzmann equation to model one-dimensional shock wave structure, a boundary layer, and general 3-D flow fields. The Bhatnagar-Gross-Krook (BGK) model for the collision term combined with a finite difference scheme was used to model the flow. This collision term requires accurate knowledge of the density, temperature, and mean velocity. Great care must be taken in their calculation to insure conservation, which proved to be the most difficult part. The algorithm, however, is well suited to the Connection Machine, and accurate results were obtained with great efficiency. The 1-D version of the code (which actually models a 5-D problem in phase space) was optimized for the CM-5 and sustained 61 gigaflops on a 1024-node CM-5.

Introduction

The theory of gas dynamics may be approached from two directions: the macroscopic or the microscopic. In the macroscopic approach, one considers the gas to be a continuum and employs equations such as Navier-Stokes using aggregate quantities, for example density, velocity, and temperature. This approach works well for a relatively high density, however for low density, or rarefied, problems, where the mean free path is of considerable length compared to some dimension of the system, this continuum approach breaks down. For instance, in order to model flows in the low density of the upper atmosphere, such as the flow over the Space Shuttle upon reentry or the flow in microdevices, one cannot use the continuum approach of Navier-Stokes. The Navier-Stokes equations are only valid when the mean free path is much smaller than the characteristic lengths in the flow. For these cases, one must treat the gas microscopically, that is, consider it to be a conglomeration of particles instead of a continuum. This more general situation can be described by the Boltzmann equation.

The Boltzmann equation is an integro-differential equation in terms of the particle distribution function, $f(x,v,t)$. Unfortunately, the Boltzmann equation, even for the simplest cases, is quite difficult to solve analytically or numerically. In some cases, numerical schemes have involved various simplifications specific to the given problem in order to reduce the computing resources needed. The only general approach has been the direct simulation Monte Carlo method (DSMC) [1], which involves random sampling to calculate various parameters. This method requires significant computing resources. The DSMC method is very communication intensive [2] and may never fully utilize the power of vector or parallel computers. The other major drawback to DSMC is that it is essentially a first-order accurate, explicit method [3]. More traditional numerical schemes may be able to achieve second-order accuracy with an implicit scheme, which may offer dramatic improvements in efficiency. This will be especially true if the newer algorithms can more effectively use massively parallel computers, which is true of the present algorithm.

The algorithm used here was specifically designed for data parallel computers. Drawing on the authors experience with DSMC [2,3] and continuum codes [4,5] on parallel computers, a new algorithm was developed [6,7] that exploits the power of massively parallel computers for rarefied gas dynamics.

A key difference between parallel and serial/vector computers is their memory organizations. Most massively parallel architectures use distributed memory. Serial and vector computers rely on shared memory. The distributed nature of parallel computer memory introduces additional constraints into the programming model by requiring a careful data layout and an understanding of the costs of interprocessor communications. Since most algorithms designed to solve scientific problems will require communication, it is crucial to understand the additional complexity introduced by distributed memory. An effective algorithm for a massively parallel computer must satisfy a number of conditions. Some of the more important are locality and regularity of the communication pattern. On conventional architectures the number of flops (floating point operations per second) is a good indicator of algorithm efficiency. This not the case on parallel computers, where interprocessor communications do not contribute to useful flops but do contribute to the total execution time.

It should always be remembered that a code that achieves a high flop rate on a parallel computer is not necessarily the *best* algorithm. Another algorithm that uses more communications at the expense of the floating point hardware may converge faster and prove to be a better algorithm. The ultimate measure of performance is how long it takes to solve a problem. Codes that do achieve very high peak speeds though are useful as guidelines for optimization and for illustrating peak obtainable performance levels.

The Boltzmann equation

The Boltzmann equation governs the seven-dimensional particle distribution function, $f(x,v,t)$, and from f, one can calculate the macroscopic flow quantities. This distribution function governs the number density of molecules in physical (x) and velocity (v) space. It may also be a function of time. The general form of the Boltzmann equation for a monatomic gas and no external forces can be written

$$\frac{\partial f}{\partial t} + v \cdot \nabla f =$$

$$\iiint_{-\infty}^{\infty} \int_{0}^{4\pi} \left[f(v^*) f(w^*) - f(v) f(w) \right] g \, I \, d\Omega \, Dw$$

where g is the relative velocity between two particles having velocity v and w before collision and v^* and w^* after collision, I is the differential collision cross-section for scattering into the elementary scattering angle $d\Omega$, and Dw is the differential element of volume in w-space. The right hand side is known as the collision term and accounts for changes in the distribution function due to particle collisions. Calculating the collision term is the main difficulty in solving the Boltzmann equation. Simplifications of this term have been developed for various cases. Any model for this term must: (i) conserve mass, momentum and energy, (ii) yield a Maxwellian distribution at equilibrium conditions, and (iii) tend to drive a nonequilibrium distribution towards the Maxwellian distribution.

For some flows, the Bhatnagar, Gross, and Krook (BGK) model [8,9] of the collision term can be used. The basic idea of the BGK equation is that a detailed description of the collision process may not be necessary and that a larger scale approximation may be appropriate. Fairly simple collision models have been used in DSMC with some success (e.g. the variable hard sphere model).

The BGK equation was used in this study,

$$\frac{\partial f}{\partial t} + v \cdot \nabla f = \alpha \left(f_0 - f \right)$$

where α = collision frequency and f_0 is the local Maxwellian

$$f_0 = \frac{n \beta^3}{\pi^{3/2}} e^{-\beta^2 (v - u_0)^2}$$

where n, u_0, and $T = 1 / (2R\beta^2)$ are the local density, mean velocity and temperature, respectively, and R is the gas constant. One can find n, u_0, and T from the following moments of f,

$$n = \iiint_{-\infty}^{\infty} f \, Dv$$

$$n \, u_0 = \iiint_{-\infty}^{\infty} v \, f \, Dv$$

$$2 \, R \, T = \frac{1}{\beta^2} = \frac{2}{3n} \iiint_{-\infty}^{\infty} (v - u_0)^2 f \, Dv$$

In the limits of zero and infinite Knudsen numbers, this equation duplicates the Boltzmann equation exactly. For finite Knudsen numbers it is an approximation to the Boltzmann equation and yields a Prandtl number, Pr, of unity. One can approximate the viscosity-temperature relation using, for example, the Sutherland viscosity law. If this is done, however, the thermal conductivity will be slightly in error since Pr = 1.

Algorithm

To find a solution, f, of the BGK equation, an algorithm was designed specifically for data-parallel computers.

This algorithm [6,7] has the following features :

1. Upwind finite differences for the spatial derivatives.
2. Runge-Kutta time-stepping scheme for the time derivative.
3. Gaussian quadrature for the integrals over velocity space.
4. Least squares method for conservation.

Thus one must discretize the independent variables x, v, t of $f(x,v,t)$.

Mapping to the CM-5

To solve the finite difference equation on the CM, one must first decide how to distribute the physical and velocity mesh over the processors for optimal utilization of the CM. This requires a close look at the operations performed at each step in the iteration process.

An explicit scheme will calculate $f(x_i, v, t_{i+1})$ from terms such as
$f(x_{i-1}, v, t_i)$, $f(x_i, v, t_i)$, $f(x_{i+1}, v, t_i)$, and $f_0(x_i, v, t_i)$,
where f_0 is the local Maxwellian distribution. The scheme used here distributes the spatial dimension across the processors. Calculating f at the next time step then involves iterating over the velocity space points. Some interprocessor communication is necessary since the difference approximation to $\partial f/\partial x$ requires f at adjacent mesh points, but this is minimal and only involves nearest neighbor communication. Also, since the integration to calculate n, T, and u_0 is done over all the velocity space for each physical space point, each processor's memory contains all the necessary data to calculate these moments and no interprocessor communication is necessary. This is a tremendous advantage and results in nearly optimal use of the CM.

Quadrature and conservation

For each point in physical space, one needs to keep track of a full 3-D mesh of points in velocity space to represent the distribution function at that point. This distribution is then used to approximate the integrals for calculating n, u_0, and T. The macroscopic quantities n, u_0, and T are given by the three moments of f shown earlier. Over the discretized space, any number of integration schemes can be used. The algorithm implemented was Gaussian quadrature. Seven points were used in each direction for a total of 343 points in velocity space, which is equivalent to using a 13th order polynomial in each velocity direction. It is important to find n, u_0, and T such that

calculation of the moments of f_0 by quadrature gives exactly the same result as that for f by quadrature. Thus conservation of mass, momentum, and energy is accomplished, i.e. the zeroth, first, and second moments of $f-f_0$ must be zero.

This is accomplished by requiring that :

(1) The moments of f_0 and the moments of f are exactly equal.
(2) The "equilibrium" distribution is close (in a least squares sense) to a Maxwellian.

That is, n, u_0, and T are computed from the moments of f (by quadrature). These macroscopic quantities then define a Maxwellian f_M. This Maxwellian is then corrected so that the above two requirements are satisfied. This is accomplished using the following algorithm [10,11] :

$$f_{0_k} = f_{M_k} + A^T [A A^T]^{-1} A (f_k - f_{M_k})$$

For a 1-D flow, A is a 3 x 343 matrix representing the quadrature weights (in 3 velocity dimensions) for the three moments and the subscripts k on the distribution functions denote points in velocity space. For 3-D flow A would be a 5 x 343 matrix, so the problem is not changed significantly when going to 3-D problems.

Now, the BGK collision term can be written

$$\alpha (f_{0_k} - f_k) = \alpha (A^T M - I) (f_k - f_{M_k})$$

where

$$M = [A A^T]^{-1} A$$

and I is a 343x343 identity matrix. Note that A is a constant matrix and the product of A^T and M could be computed and stored as a front-end array, but this yields an inefficient scheme. The inefficiency results due to the numerous broadcasts required from the front-end to the CM and the large number of operations required, $O(343^2)$. Doing the operations this way would also continually break the computation pipeline, so the ALUs would not be able to achieve peak speed.

By leaving the scheme in the form shown above, one can store copies of the matrices A^T and M on each processor (2058 numbers). Storing the square matrix $A^T M$ would not be practical since it would amount to 343^2 numbers per processor. Keeping A^T and M separate also reduces the number of operations required, $O(343)$. The performance advantages of storing these matrices on the CM are enormous. It allows one to compute the collision terms without performing <u>any</u> communication. And these terms represent the most compute intensive portions of the algorithm.

Code optimization

The CM-5 node design [12] is centered around a standard bus. To this bus are attached a RISC microprocessor, a CM-5 Network Interface, and floating point hardware. All logical connections to the rest of the system pass through the Network Interface (NI). The node memory consists of standard DRAM. The arithmetic hardware consists of four vector units (VU), one for each memory bank, connected separately to the node bus. Each VU is a memory controller and computational engine controlled by a memory-mapped control-register interface.

There are two places in the FORTRAN 90 (CMF - Connection Machine Fortran) code that have been optimized. The first optimization can be described as a "stencil" operation. This is illustrated with the code fragment below.

```
     real, array ( pnodes, xnodes)    :: f, fold
cmf$ layout f(:serial, :news), fold(:serial, :news)
     do np = 1, pnodes
             coef  = rkc(irkc) * up(np) / dx * dt
             if ( up(np) .gt. 0.0 ) then
                  f(np,2:xnodes) = fold(np,2:xnodes) - coef *
( f(np,2:xnodes) - f(np,1:xnodes-1) )
             else
                f(np,1:xnodes-1) = fold(np,1:xnodes-1) - coef
                    *( f(np,2:xnodes ) - f(np,1:xnodes-1))
             endif
          enddo
```

where irkc, dx, and dt are assumed to be constant in this do loop. In this code fragment the first dimension of the arrays is completely contained within a processor (serial axis). The second dimension is spread across the processors (news axis). When written in CMF this code fragment is not executed optimally. The major problem is that communications operations involve data motion on-chip as well as off-chip (only off-chip data is necessary) and the fact that contextualization is expensive. We have rewritten this code fragment using assembler language (CDPEAC). In this code we have optimized communications in two ways. The physical (on-chip) part of the communication is vectorized across the serial dimension. For example if for vector unit (VU) p, first(p) and last(p) are the first and last indices along the news

axis holding data stored on that VU then each VU first does:

$$t1 = f(:,first(p)-1)$$
$$t2 = f(:,last(p)+1)$$

This is implemented with calls to an optimized communication primitive. The on VU motion is incorporated into the computation (and thus entirely eliminated). The up array is broadcast to all the VU's.

The on VU kernel has the same basic structure as the fortran loop above (i.e. outer loop on the serial dimension, inner loop on the news dimension). There are two versions of the inner loop, one for the up(np) > 0.0 case and one for the other. Consider the up(np) > 0.0 case. Effectively we do:

$$trow(1) = t1(i)$$
$$trow(2:n) = f(i, first(p):last(p)-1)$$

$$f(i, first(p):last(p)) = fold(i, first(p):last(p) - coef *$$
$$(f(i, first(p):last(p)) - trow)$$

However we don't explicitly build the temporary, trow. In the vector code we have a vector register, Vf, which holds the direct access to f. If we explicitly constructed trow, the last 15 elements of the vector register holding it would be the same as the first 15 elements of Vf. Rather than duplicating them we simply put the one different element of trow in Vf[-1] and use Vf[-1] as the vector register for trow. Before starting the inner loop we put t1(i) into Vf[-1]. Each time we load a new piece of f into Vf we first copy Vf[15] to Vf[-1]. The vector loop takes 3 cycles per vector element, a subtraction (t = f - trow) with overlapped load from f, a sub-multiply (fold - coef * t) with an overlapped load from fold and a store with movement from Vf[15] to Vf[-1] overlapped. A similar approach is used for the up(i) <= 0.0 case.

To handle the boundary conditions (i.e. not overwriting f(i, 1) when up(i) > 0.0 and not overwriting f(i,xnodes) when up(i) <= 0.0) we take advantage of fact that f is the same as fold in those positions. Figuring this out required information from other parts of the code than what we have above. Given that, on the first node we overwrite t1 with f(:,1) and on the last node we overwrite t2 with f(:,xnodes). So in such a boundary position the statement is eg:

$$f(i,1) = fold (i,1) - coef * (f(i,1) - t1(i))$$

and since t1(i) is the same as f(i,1) this reduces to

f(i,1) = fold(i,1)

which is fine since fold and f are the same at this position.

The second optimization is the rewrite in assembler (CDPEAC) of a matrix vector multiply operator. The code fragment is shown below :.

```
      DOUBLE PRECISION, ARRAY(xnodes) ::
           alt1, alt2, alt3
      DOUBLE  PRECISION,  ARRAY(pnodes, xnodes)  ::
           aatia1, aatia2, aatia3, ftmp

CMF$  LAYOUT aatia1  (:SERIAL,:NEWS)
CMF$  LAYOUT aatia2  (:SERIAL,:NEWS)
CMF$  LAYOUT aatia3  (:SERIAL,:NEWS)
CMF$  LAYOUT ftmp    (:SERIAL,:NEWS)

      DO p=1,pnodes
        alt1(:) = alt1(:) + aatia1(p,:) * ftmp(p,:)
        alt2(:) = alt2(:) + aatia2(p,:) * ftmp(p,:)
        alt3(:) = alt3(:) + aatia3(p,:) * ftmp(p,:)
      END DO
```

The major consideration in this optimization is to reduce the number of memory references made by the code emitted by the CMF compiler. The CMF compiler was executing 6 flops per 10 memory references. The optimized version of that code achieves an asymptotic rate of 24 flops per 16 memory references.

Results

Reference 6 presented a one-dimensional version of the BGK algorithm and some shock wave structure calculations. Figure 1 shows an example simulation result, the velocity profile through a Mach=1.5 shock wave for a monatomic gas. These results were obtained in 2000-3500 time steps using 1024 spatial nodes. Also shown are the BGK results of Liepmann et al [13] for velocity and temperature. This version of the code was highly optimized to achieve the high gigaflop rates.

The new three-dimensional BGK code was used to simulate the Rayleigh problem (impulsively started boundary layer), in order to verify the formulation. Diffuse reflection solid surface boundary conditions were implemented. Figure 2 shows the profile of the velocity component perpendicular to the wall for the same conditions (supersonic, hot wall) that were used in Refs. 1 and 2. These results correspond to a non-dimensional time of five.

Qualitative results for two three-dimensional flows are presented in Figures 3 and 4. Figure 3 shows Mach number contours around a cubical body moving at Mach = 1.5 with a Reynolds number (based on body length) equal to 50. The bow shock and wake are clearly visible. The far-field boundary conditions also work well, since no reflection of the shock is apparent. Figure 4 shows Mach = 0.5 flow through a square duct, with a Reynolds number (based on duct length) of 1000. The very thick boundary layer is apparent. Both of these flows were computed using the same code, with minor changes to the boundary conditions.

Code performance

The 1-D version of the code was run on the Los Alamos National Labs 1024-node CM-5 and a 32-node CM-5 at Thinking Machines Corporation. The results are shown in Table 1 for 10 time steps. The program achieved roughly half of the peak speed of the CM-5 and demonstrated scalability.

It should also be pointed out that the unoptimized CMF code ran quite well, achieving roughly 40 gigaflops (31 % of peak speed) on a 1024-node CM-5. On a 32K CM-2, 2.9 GFlops were measured (32-bit precision). An 8K CM-200 achieved 1.0 (32-bit precision) and 0.7 (64-bit) precision) gigaflops. Scaling these results to a 10 MHz 64K processor CM-200, would yield approximately 8 gigaflops.

The 3-D version of the code has essentially the same collision term as the 1-D code (except A is 5x343 for 3-D). The only difference between the two codes is that the 3-D code has the full gradient term

$$\mathbf{v} \bullet \nabla f$$

instead of the simple 1-D term $\partial f / \partial x$. The majority of the computations are in the collision term. So, while we have not completely optimzed the 3-D code, it is expected to sustain very high computational speeds.

Conclusions

The Connection Machine has proved itself a valuable tool for solving the BGK equation. The algorithm developed had a good balance of computation and communication, which made the solution on the CM very efficient. When enforcing the conservation laws, the CM proved very effective since all the processor computations turned out to be independent of one another and required no communication.

Knowledge of experimental trends and also a comparison

to results of past work gives confidence that the algorithm is properly modeling the physics of the gases. With the physics properly in place, this algorithm can now be developed further to model more complex problems.

Acknowledgment

This work was supported by the National Science Foundation (ASC-9009998) and The Pennsylvania State University. The authors would also like to acknowledge the significant contributions of M. Bromley, D. Dahl, R. Lordi, and R. Shapiro of Thinking Machines Corporation and M. Kamon [14] currently a graduate student at MIT.

References

1. G. A. Bird, *Molecular Gas Dynamics*, Oxford Univ. Press, Glasgow, 1976.

2. B. C. Wong and L. N. Long, "The DSMC Method on the Connection Machine," Computing Systems in Engineering, Vol.. 3 , No. 4, Dec., 1992.

3. L. N. Long, "Navier-Stokes and Monte Carlo Results for Hypersonic Flow," AIAA Journal, Vol. 29, No. 2, Feb., 1991.

4. L. N. Long, M. N. S. Khan and H. T. Sharp, "Massively Parallel Three-Dimensional Euler/Navier-Stokes Method," AIAA Journal, Vol. 29, No. 5, May, 1991.

5. L. N. Long, "Gas Dynamics on the Connection Machine," Proceedings of Parallel CFD '92, Rutgers, NJ, May, 1992.

6. L. N. Long, M. Kamon, J. Myczkowski, "A Massively Parallel Algorithm to Solve the Boltzmann (BGK) Equation", Computing Systems in Engineering, Vol. 3, , No. 4, Dec., 1992.

7. L.N. Long, B.C. Wong, and J. Myczkowski, "Deterministic and Non-Deterministic Algorithms for Rarefied Gas Dynamics," Proceedings of the 18th International Symposium on Rarefied Gas Dynamics, to appear in AIAA Progress in Astronautics and Aeronautics, 1993.

8. W. G. Vincenti and C. H. Kruger, *Introduction to Physical Gas Dynamics*, Krieger, Malabar, 1986.

9. C. K. Chu, "The High Mach Number Rayleigh Problem According to the Krook Model," *Rarefied Gas Dynamics*, ed. C.L. Brundin, pp. 589-605, 1967.

10. R. M. Freund, Private Communication, Boston, MA, Aug., 1991.

11. G. Strang *Introduction to Applied Mathematics*, Wellesley-Cambridge Press, Wellesley, 1986.

12. CM-5 Technical Summary, Thinking Machines Corporation, Cambridge, Massachusetts, Oct., 1991.

13. H. W. Liepmann, R. Narasimha and M. T. Chahine, "Structure of a Plane Shock Layer," The Physics of Fluids, Vol. 5, No. 11, November 1962.

14. M. Kamon, "A Massively Parallel Algorithm to Solve the BGK Equation for Shock Wave Structure," Penn. State Univ. Honor's Thesis, Engineering Science Department, May, 1991.

Table 1.   64-bit Performance results for 10 time steps of the 1-D BGK code on a 1024-node CM-5.

Processor Nodes	Number of Grid Points in X	Total Number of Unknowns	Floating Point Operations	CPU Seconds	Gigaflops	Percent of Peak Speed
32	16,384	5,619,712	$1.49 * 10^{10}$	7.57	1.97	48 %
1024	524,288	179,830,784	$4.76 * 10^{11}$	7.84	60.71	46 %

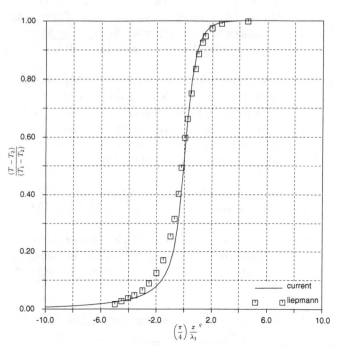

Figure 1. BGK Temperature predictions through a Mach=1.5 shock compared to Liepmann et al results.

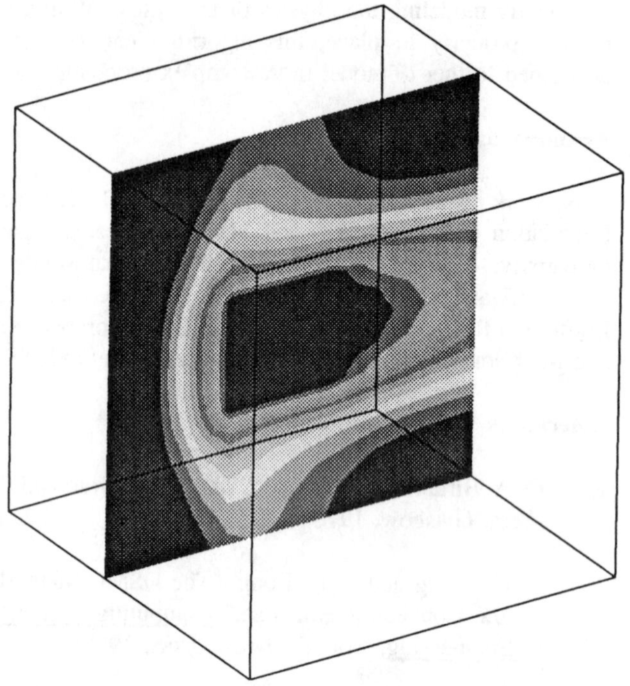

Figure 3. Mach number contours around a supersonically moving body predicted by the 3-D BGK code.

[For color plate see page 930]

T = 5

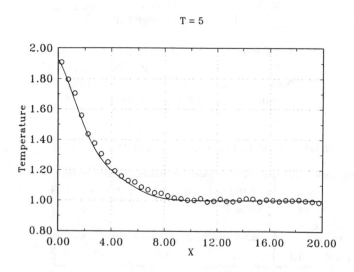

Figure 2. BGK temperature predictions near a hot, supersonic wall compared to DSMC predictions.

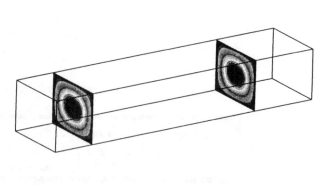

Figure 4. Velocity contours in a square duct predicted by the 3-D BGK code.

Bispectrum Signal Processing on HNC's SIMD Numerical Array Processor (SNAP)

Robert W. Means, Bret Wallach, David Busby

HNC, Inc., San Diego, CA 92121

Robert C. Lengel Jr.

Tracor Applied Sciences, Inc., Austin, TX 78725

Abstract

Supercomputers and parallel processors are increasingly being applied to problems traditionally described as signal and image processing problems. The primary activities occurring in either processing area are detection, enhancement, and classification of signals embedded in additive noise. The bispectrum is a processing technique that can be used for improving the detection of signals in noise. It is an order N^2 operation performed over a two dimensional frequency plane and, because of computational demands, has not been used much in practice.

HNC has developed a commercially available SIMD Numerical Array Processor (SNAP) and implemented Tracor's computationally demanding bispectrum signal processing code as a submission for the Gordon Bell prize. The SNAP is a SIMD array of parallel processors connected in a linear ring. A SNAP system with 32 processors (SNAP-32) demonstrated a performance of over 7.5 GIGAFLOP per million dollars.

Processing and Detection Algorithm

The frequency domain implementation of the detection process is usually performed using the power spectrum. Each realization of N discrete time series points are transformed to the frequency domain using the Discrete Fourier Transform (DFT)

$$(1) \qquad \mathbf{X}[k] = \sum_{n=0}^{N-1} \mathbf{x}[n] e^{i2\pi nk/N} \qquad k = 0,1,2,...,N-1$$

where n and k are variables representing the index of time and frequency, respectively. Implementing the DFT using a Fast Fourier Transform (FFT) algorithm reduces this computational requirement to the order of N*logN operations. The power spectrum is estimated by multiplying each Fourier coefficient X[k] by its complex conjugate. The variance in the power spectrum estimate may be improved by ensemble averaging M spectra.

After computing an ensemble average of power spectra, each frequency component is compared against a threshold level that represents the expected variance of a noise-only input. A frequency component higher than the threshold implies detection.

The power spectrum is referred to as a second-order spectrum. Higher-order spectra (HOS) are products of more than the two frequency coefficients that are used in the power spectra. The HOS offer a unique feature not present in the power spectrum that can be used to detect signals in additive noise. Specifically, the theoretical estimate of zero-mean, symmetrically distributed additive noise is zero for the third-order spectrum (commonly referred to as the bispectrum) and other higher-order spectra. By contrast, signals of interest produce a non-zero bispectrum. Detection of those signals within additive noise can be accomplished more readily with HOS since the comparator threshold can be set near zero ensuring a high detection probability and a low probability of false alarm.

Each component of the bispectrum is estimated by a triple product of Fourier coefficients as

$$(2) \qquad \mathbf{S}_{XXX}[j,k] = \mathbf{X}[j]\mathbf{X}[k]\mathbf{X}^*[j+k]$$

where j and k represent frequency domain indices for the two dimensional bispectrum plane. As in the case of a power spectrum, a comparator examines the output levels of each component in the (j,k) plane and determines if a threshold was exceeded. The number of operations required to compute the bispectrum is significantly increased relative to the power spectrum. There are $N^2/8$ independent components of the bispectrum while there are only N/2 independent components of the power spectrum.

Signal requirements to produce a bispectrum containing one or more detectable signals can be inferred from equation 2. The signal must contain a component whose

535

frequency is the sum of the frequencies of the other two components. Ensemble averaging adds the requirement that the phase of these three components be coupled. A familiar physical process that produces signals that meet these criteria is the quadratic (x^2) nonlinearity. Signals that pass through limiting amplifiers such as Frequency Modulated radio meet this requirement. Human speech and vocalizations of marine mammals produce non-linear features such as harmonics and overtones. Bearing vibration where failure is imminent exhibits harmonics of the bearing rotation frequency separated by the race rotation frequency. These are but a few of the natural and man-made signals that satisfy the bispectrum frequency selection and phase coupling requirements.

Program Description

The computer program accumulated statistics from 10,000 ensemble averages of bispectrums of a noisy time sampled signal. Each ensemble average was over a set of 64 bispectra. The major portions of the algorithm that computed the ensemble average are the following:

1. Zero the ensemble accumulation arrays: Three arrays of size 256 x 512.
2. Create a signal that consists of a sine wave at f_1 with random phase, a sine wave at f_2 with random phase, and a sine wave at $f_1 + f_2$ with phase coherency. The sine wave at $f_1 + f_2$ is assumed to be produced by a nonlinearity that preserves phase coherency in the mixing process. The time signal is of length 1024.
3. Create a random noise signal with a Gaussian distribution and add it to the signal of length 1024 created in step 2.
4. Compute the FFT and the power spectrum of the signal created in step 3.
5. Zero the bispectrum arrays: Three arrays of size 256 x 512.
6. Calculate the bispectrum   This step is the largest time consumer. It consists of calculating and storing 256 x 512 products of three complex numbers.
7. Accumulate the bispectrum and power spectrum into the ensemble averages and normalize.
8. Repeat steps 2 through 7 sixty four times.

Steps 1-8 took 0.7 seconds on the Cray Y-MP/8 and took 0.4 seconds on the SNAP-32. The whole program took two hours of Cray Y-MP/8 CPU time and took over 8 hours of wall clock time. Only one of the Y-MP/8's processors was used. Included in the 0.4 seconds that the

SNAP-32 took is a display of the bispectrum as a gray scale image on a Sun SPARCstation monitor. The display operation is pipelined and runs in parallel with the execution of the algorithm on the SNAP linear array. It contributed a small amount to the total measured SNAP execution time of 0.37 seconds (measured with no display performed).

Hardware System Description

The SNAP-32 system is composed of three parts: the linear array of HNC100 chips, the SNAP Controller, and the Balboa host interface processor. A front end host computer such as a Sun SPARCstation is also required. The configuration for a system with two Linear Array boards (32 parallel processing elements) is illustrated in Figure 1. The Balboa 860, the SNAP Controller and the Linear Array boards are all 6U VME boards. The Balboa 860 is a general purpose coprocessor board with an Intel i860 processor and 16-64 MBytes of memory. The Linear Array board has four HNC100 chips with each chip containing four processing elements. The SNAP Controller board has a microsequencer for executing program microcode, global memory accessible by all the processing elements and two bit-slice microprocessors for generating addresses for local and global memory accesses. The system architecture is extensible such that up to four Linear Array boards can be connected together and controlled by a single SNAP Controller. A system with two Linear Array boards, a SNAP-32, operates at 1.28 gigaflops peak performance.

Each HNC100 chip in the Linear Array board contains four processing elements with each one connected to its neighbor in a linear array. Figure 2 is a block diagram of a Linear Array board. The last chip in the last board is connected to the first chip in the first board so that a ring systolic architecture is created. The global memory is connected to all the processing elements in the array by means of a broadcast bus that allows data in the global memory to be broadcast to all processing elements at the same time. Alternatively, data in any single processing element can be broadcast to either all other processing elements or to a single processing element The unique combination of the global data bus and the systolic data bus provides the SNAP SIMD architecture with efficient alternative methods of passing data between processing elements. All the processing elements are controlled by a single instruction from the external controller. Local and global memory addresses are generated by the Controller board.

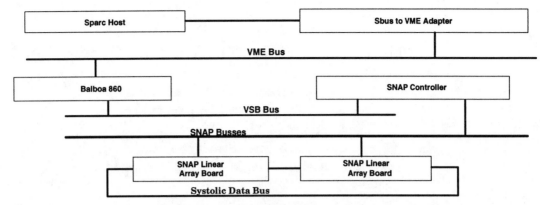

Figure 1. SNAP System Configuration

Three separate parallel arithmetic units exist in each processing element: a 32-bit floating point multiplier, a 32-bit floating point arithmetic logic unit, and a 32-bit integer arithmetic logic unit. The floating point units support the ANSI/IEEE Standard P754-1985.

Price/Performance

In counting performance, we count add, subtract, multiply, divide and initialize to zero as one flop each. The operations of all transcendentals are counted as ten flops each. For an ensemble average of 64 bispectrums, the total number of flops is approximately 151.3 million. With a 0.7 second execution time, the Cray Y-MP/8 is performing at 216 megaflops. With a 0.37 second execution time, the SNAP-32 is performing at a rate of 409 megaflops.

The price of a Cray Y-MP/8 is approximately $15,000,000.00 and has a peak megaflop rating of 2,664 megaflops. The price of a SNAP-32, is $49,950.00 and has a peak megaflop rating of 1,280 megaflops. A host SPARCstation is also necessary to run the SNAP. The price for a Sun SPARCstation Classic is now $4,295.00. Dividing the SNAP-32 execution time by the price of $54,145.00 gives:

7.55 GIGAFLOPS PER MILLION $

Since only one of the Cray's 8 processors was used, its price is cut proportionally and dividing the Cray Y/MP-8 execution time by the equivalent price of $1,875,000 gives:

115 MEGAFLOPS PER MILLION $

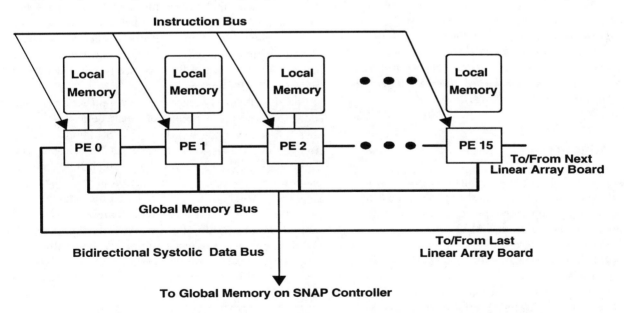

Figure 2. SNAP Linear Array Board Block Diagram

Parallel Execution of a Fortran 77 Weather Prediction Model

Gary Sabot, Skef Wholey,
Jonas Berlin, and Paul Oppenheimer
Thinking Machines Corporation
245 First Street
Cambridge, MA 02142

Abstract

This work presents the first MPP execution of the ARPS storm prediction code, and it is a significant step beyond the best previous runs on the fastest machines available. ARPS, a real third-party application developed in Fortran 77 by scientists for their own use, was greatly sped up though execution on a massively parallel machine. There are three notable features to our entry. First, the execution was made possible because of new automatic parallelizing compiler technology, a new tool called CMAX. The entire 65,000 line program was translated, compiled, and then executed on a CM-5; our results were achieved with the help of CMAX rather than brute force rewriting. Second, we achieved good speedups as we increased the number of processors. Finally, performance on large CM-5's is significantly better than performance on any previous ARPS platform.

We obtained the following results. First, a speedup of 907 on a 1024 processor CM-5. The best previous speedup of ARPS on a parallel platform was 8.2. Second, that run was 57 times faster than the fastest previously available ARPS platform with published timings, a Cray Y-MP. Finally, we achieved at least 2 times the price/performance of a Cray Y-MP.

1 Introduction

We took a real third-party application that was developed in Fortran 77 by scientists for their own use and achieved significant speedups on a massively parallel machine. We believe that CMAX, ARPS, and our entry advances the state of the art in both storm prediction and in automatic parallelization of scalable Fortran 77 applications.

This paper is structured as follows: Section 2 contains a description of ARPS. Section 3 contains a description of CMAX. Section 4 describes the changes we made to the Fortran 77 ARPS code as we tuned it. The remaining sections describe our timings, calculations, and final results.

2 ARPS

2.1 Application Overview

We have taken an atmospheric modeling code, ARPS 3.1 (Advanced Regional Prediction System), and ported the entire application to a massively parallel computer, the Connection Machine® system (CM). ARPS 3.1 contains over 65,000 lines of modern, well written Fortran 77 [1]. It was implemented by scientists who had a mental model of a parallel machine and avoided making assumptions about the underlying memory model. Since ARPS 1.0 was made available in October, 1990, ARPS has been executed by scientists on workstations, workstation clusters, and vector machines[1]. The code has evolved as new features were added and as dictated by user experience and tuning. Kernels taken from ARPS have been timed on various parallel platforms, but we believe that this is the first massively parallel port of the entire ARPS application.

Speed is obviously critical to any weather prediction code; to be useful, a prediction must be available well ahead of the evolving weather. CAPS (The Center for Analysis and Prediction of Storms, an NSF Science and Technology Center) believes that a 1000x1000x20 kilometer domain with a uniform horizontal grid spacing of 1 kilometer will nominally be required for regional-scale prediction. For ARPS 3.0, CAPS found that the code would have to execute at 1 Teraflop (based on Cray Y-MP measurements) in order to predict the weather 100 times faster than it was occurring. Thus, a Teraflop machine would be able to produce a 4 hour forecast in about 2.5 minutes.

---

[1] Including Cray Y-MP, C90, DEC VAX, DEC Alpha, IBM RS6000 workstations and clusters, Alliant, Convex, Stardent, IRIS 4D, IBM 3090, Apollo, Sun.

The largest problem size we executed, 1024x1024x32, corresponds to that of the grand challenge problem of regional weather prediction, but ran about one fifth as fast as real time.

2.2 ARPS details

The description of the computational core of ARPS below is paraphrased from the ARPS 3.0 manual[1].

ARPS is a generalized non-hydrostatic, compressible atmospheric model designed for storm- and mesoscale phenomena with an emphasis on severe convection. It can accommodate a variety of strategies for assimilating observed data, particularly from Doppler radars, and uses adaptive gridding to represent multiple spatial scales from several kilometers down to a few tens of meters. The ARPS is now being field tested as the operational prototype for regional numerical prediction centers across the U.S. ARPS is extensively documented and professionally-written, and is designed for easy modification. ARPS is currently being used by some 80 groups worldwide, both in meteorology as well as CS and applied math.

The governing equations of ARPS include the prognostic equations for momentum, heat (potential temperature), mass (pressure) and water substances, and the equations of state. These equations are represented in a curvilinear coordinate system. The curvilinear coordinates can be defined numerically as well as analytically, making it more flexible than conventional terrain-following coordinates. The governing equations are the result of direct transformation from the Cartesian system, and are expressed in a fully conservative form.

The ARPS code that solves for momentum, pressure, mixing, smoothing, and thermodynamic energy equations is structured so that separate Fortran subroutines perform high level, discrete operations such as differencing, averaging, and so on. ARPS's authors chose this methodology to make the code maintainable (operators can be modified individually) and scalable (each operator is vectorizable). The cost is that additional temporaries are needed to pass entire arrays between operators. All calculations are single precision.

ARPS defines a base state which is assumed to be horizontally homogeneous, hydrostatic and time invariant. The thermal energy equation and pressure equation are written as the prognostic equations for potential temperature and pressure. Six water/ice quantities (water vapor, cloud water, rainwater, cloud ice, snow and hail) are predicted using the equations. The interactions between the water substances and their feedback on the thermal field are described by the microphysics parameterization (incorporating the physics of the underlying problem into the numerical technique leads to performance that is superior to conventional discrete methods). The subgrid scale turbulence is represented by the Smagorinsky/Lilly first order closure scheme. Other mixing processes of a computational nature are also included. Five different lateral boundary conditions are supported, including symmetric, periodic, zero-normal gradient, open radiation, and user specified. Initial mass and wind conditions can be set based on data from WSR-88D scanning Doppler radars.

In Figure 1 is an image from ARPS which captures the 3-D rotational structure of an incipient tornado within a numerically simulated storm. It is a 3-D perspective view of two parallel planes with the 3-D vortex tube going directly from top to bottom. The simulation and image shown were produced by CAPS senior scientist Dr. Ming Xue using ARPS.

3 The CMAX Translator

Our entry made use of CMAX, an application translator that vectorizes and transforms Fortran 77 into CM Fortran [8, 11]. The CM Fortran is then compiled for execution on a Connection Machine system (a CM-2, CM-200, or CM-5). That compilation process is described elsewhere [6, 7, 5]. Figure 2 illustrates this two-step compilation process. We used the Prism software development environment to profile and optimize the input Fortran 77 code [9]. We changed the Fortran 77 in order to improve the execution of the translated output code. As is noted in Section 4 below, most of our changes are applicable to many target architectures.

The CMAX translator converts applications written in scalable Fortran 77 to parallel Connection Machine Fortran. The most obvious part of the translation problem, and one addressed by a number of previous translators as well as CMAX, is loop vectorization: the substitution of array syntax and intrinsics for Fortran 77 DO loops. A less obvious (but equally important) part of the translation problem is the conversion of constructs arising from Fortran 77's linear memory model into code which does not rely on storage or sequence association. Most such constructs can only be detected and repaired through interprocedural analysis and transformation; CMAX is the first translator to perform such repairs.

One simple interprocedural transform involves the propagation of data distribution directives between subroutines. A more interesting example is *axis elision*. Fortran 77 users often pass n-minus-k-dimensional slices of n-dimensional arrays to subprograms in a way that assumes sequence association. For example, they might

Figure 1: Incipient tornado within a storm numerically simulated by ARPS.

4 Tuning the Application

This section is a kind of diary describing the changes we made to ARPS to improve performance. The timings here are meant to give a feel for the relative importance of each optimization and are based on numbers that we happened to jot down while tuning. Different timings below were made by different people under different load conditions, for different problem sizes, and for different subsets of the program (i.e., don't draw any but the most obvious conclusions; most pairings of these timings are like apples and oranges.) Refer to Section 6 for complete, accurate, consistent timings of our end result. Our timings in this section are CPU busy times for the kernel of the program; our timings in Section 6 are wallclock times for the entire application.

The following modifications were made to ARPS during the initial stages of porting:

- ARPS passed through CMAX version 0.8. Fifty-nine CMF$LAYOUT array data distribution directives were inserted. Separate one, two, three, and four dimensional versions were made of a routine that had previously been called with arguments of varying ranks in order to zero them. The same change was made to an array copy routine. ARPS then ran on the CM.

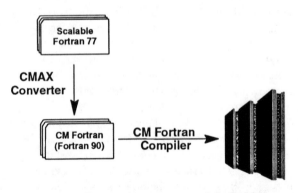

Figure 2: Conversion process using CMAX.

pass a two-dimensional slice of a three-dimensional array A as A(1,1,n). CMAX recognizes when caller and callee are cooperating in this manner and produces CM Fortran that does not depend on sequence association. In this case, the call would pass A(:,:,n). Often, interprocedural transforms change the interface to a subroutine. CMAX generates copies of subprograms before modifying them in cases where multiple callers need to call a subprogram with different interfaces.

- A bug in CMAX was detected preventing vectorization of certain reduction loops. Temporaries were inserted to allow vectorization of these loops, and the bug has been fixed in CMAX 1.0.

- 6 CMAX$NODEPENDENCE directives were inserted to allow vectorization of 6 dependence-free loops that CMAX thought contained dependences. CMAX 1.0 vectorizes the loops without the directives

At this point, when we executed ARPS on a problem of size 35x35x35 on a 32 processor CM-5, the code took 9.9 seconds per iteration of a simulated 6 second time step. The data distribution was to parallelize along the three spatial dimensions, but not along the time dimension. This distribution was determined by directives in the input program, as described above. CMAX obeys user directives, but in other cases it is not sophisticated enough to generate anything more complicated than a simple block layout (that is, it does not attempt to optimize data layout [10]).

The serial time dimension of length 3 (past, present, future) was the rightmost dimension. Unfortunately, the current version of CM Fortran, CMF 2.1b1, is more efficient when non-parallelized dimensions are gathered at the left [12]. We modified our makefile to call a CMAX utility tool to automatically permute the arrays in ARPS, moving the time dimension to be leftmost. This reduced the per iteration time to 4.9 second per iteration.

ARPS had been performing a nearest neighbor computation in one part of the code, which CMAX translated into an expression containing a number of EOSHIFTs (End Off Shift). The boundary was later set and its shifted value was never used. Unfortunately, the latest version of CSHIFT (Circular Shift) in the CM Fortran run time library is currently more optimized than EOSHIFT. We modified the Fortran 77 code to perform a circular shift, but made this code conditionally compile only for the CM, since it could slow down execution on other platforms. We switched to the latest version of the CM Fortran run time library (which contained the fast CSHIFT) and the iteration execution time dropped to 4.0 seconds per iteration.

Next, we switched to the latest version of the CM Fortran compiler itself, to try out the improvements made to its optimizer. We gained about 5% from this change. We were surprised that the impact of the new compiler's improved optimizer was so small. We investigated and discovered an explanation: As mentioned earlier, high level array operations in ARPS (such as differencing) are performed by separate subroutines, each of which loops over entire arrays. CMAX is able to vectorize the loops in each subroutine, and CM Fortran then implements the vectorized loops. However, CM Fortran is unable to fuse the loops between different subroutines, since it does not operate interprocedurally.

To overcome this problem, we implemented a simple tool that looked for directives of the form "C$INLINE function from file" and performed the requested subroutine inlining. We added 15 INLINE directives to the program (placing them based on our profiling results) and recompiled. This improved execution speed by 12%. Next, we investigated a problem that profiling had highlighted: the treatment of boundary conditions.

A large amount of time was spent computing various equations along borders. The border computations made use of a number of 2 dimensional arrays to hold coefficients. The coefficients were applied to the 2D faces of a 3 dimensional array. In order to bring the 2D data to the 3D array, CM Fortran was forced to use expensive, general-purpose communication. We decided to trade space for time: we modified the Fortran 77 to store the coefficients in the outer faces of a new 3D array rather than in multiple 2D arrays. This change wastes the interior of the new array, but by itself improves execution on the CM by about 15%. When combined with inlining, the improvement is 26%.

Our next change again involved boundary conditions. There were 6 expensive calculations (x,y,z momentum, pressure, potential temperature) which took place along 4 2D faces and 4 1D corners of a 3D array. Thus, each subroutine contained 8 (4+4) loop nests, and there were 6 subroutines like this. We again traded space for time by introducing a 3D bitmask array that indicated for each element whether it was a member of the interior, corner, or a face. We then fused the 8 loop nests, and the 8 single line loop bodies turned into a single line in the fused loops; the line made use of the bitmask array. It also exposed multiply-adds to the CM Fortran scheduler that had previously been obscured. This improved execution time by about 12%.

The final change we made was to perform all computations in double precision rather than single precision. Double precision uses twice as much memory, and thus reduces the largest solvable problem (and the vector length) for a fixed size memory by a factor of two, but switching to double precision still sped the run up by 15%. The reason is that the CM-5 memory system is optimized for 64-bit operands, which are the standard in the scientific computing community.

	CPU time	User Time	Elapsed time
32x32x31	68	158	228
64x64x32	237	877	1459

Table 1: Times in seconds for simulating ten minutes (100 time steps of 6 seconds) of weather on a Cray Y-MP.

Machine	Relative CPU time
Cray Y-MP	1.0
Convex C3	2.50
Alliant FX/80	11.00
VAX VMS 6520 w/Vector	13.78
IBM RS6000 Model 530H	16.44

Table 2: CPU time for ARPS on various platforms, relative to Cray Y-MP.

5   Timings for Other Platforms

All ARPS timings that are discussed in this entry are for the same set of initial conditions, which include a temperature perturbation that, over the course of a model run, develops into a long-lasting storm. The base state of the atmosphere was initialized using a sounding profile observed on May 20, 1977 in Ft. Sill, Oklahoma.

As our base, we use timings for ARPS 3.1 on a single processor of a Cray Y-MP (peak speed of 667 Mflops) which were given to us by Ken Johnson of the Supercomputer Computations Research Institute (SCRI) at Florida State University. The information is presented in Table 1.

For our own CM timings below, we will use wallclock time exclusively (as with the Cray, busy time is significantly smaller.) Our CM runs were on dedicated machines free from other users, while the Cray runs took place on loaded machines. Therefore, for comparison purposes, we will use the Cray run's User Time and not its wallclock time.

The ARPS 3.1 timings on the Cray Y-MP are all preliminary timings; although ARPS 3.0 has been tuned for the Y-MP, it is certainly possible that changes have been introduced that may permit further tuning (rough measurements of performance indicate that ARPS 3.1 is getting a 15% lower megaflop rate on the Y-MP than ARPS 3.0). [2] contains timing information for ARPS 3.0 on a variety of platforms. For ARPS 3.0, CPU time relative to the Cray Y-MP is shown in Table 2.

ARPS 3.0 has also been executed on a network of sixteen RS6000 workstations, model 320H, using PVM [2, 3]. The PVM host was an RS6000 workstation model 530. This is the only other parallel execution of the entire ARPS application that we are aware of. The execution achieved a speedup of 4.11 when using 16 processors to execute a 32x31x32 problem. In fact, the same speedup was achieved using 8 processors; communication overhead was largely responsible for the slowdown when adding processors. A 128x62x32 problem was also executed on 16 processors and achieved a predicted speedup over one processor of 8.20.

6   CM-5 Timings

All timings below are wallclock times for a complete execution of 600 time steps of 6 seconds each (1 hour of simulated weather), and include I/O and initialization time. Initialization took several minutes on the larger problems. We used the latest beta releases of all Thinking Machines software. The philosophy of beta software is "functionality first, performance second." Therefore, we expect that CM-5 ARPS performance will improve with future releases of CM-5 software.

In-house at Thinking Machines, we only have access to small, 64 processor machines. For timings on larger machines, we had to beg and borrow (but not steal) time on customer machines. Due to this limited access, we were not able to completely fill in our chart of run times. The 1024 processor machine at LANL was the most difficult to schedule time on. We therefore ran one problem to completion on it, and ran two other partial runs which we then extrapolated into full run timings[2]. These two partial runs are italicized in the tables below.

The 1 processor timings used the Sun f77 compiler and executed on 1 processor of a CM-5, in single precision. All other timings used CMAX to translate Fortran 77 to CM Fortran, followed by the CM Fortran compiler, and are double precision. The difference favors the 1 processor run time, reducing our speedup numbers.

Table 3 shows wallclock time for simulating 1 hour of weather on the CM-5 with various numbers of processors, for different volumes of space. Figure 3 presents a graph of the same data.

In addition to overall run time, another interesting way to view this data is as the rate at which grid points are processed though a time step, as shown in Table 4.

---

[2]The estimated time for a 600 time step run was derived by taking the portion of the 10 time step run time that was not due to initialization, multiplying it by 60, and then adding the initialization back in.

Problem Size	Processors							
	1	4	32	64	128	256	512	1024
32x32x32	16783	4186	950	573				
64x64x32	62220	16156	2882	1431	696	706	702	
128x128x32		70337	9137	5183			1098	
256x256x32								2066
512x512x32							12512	*5077*
1024x1024x32								*17559*

Table 3: Times in seconds for simulating one hour (600 time steps of 6 seconds) of weather. Italicized numbers are estimates extrapolated from runs of 10 time steps due to limited resource availability; all others are measured wallclock times for full runs including all initialization and I/O time.

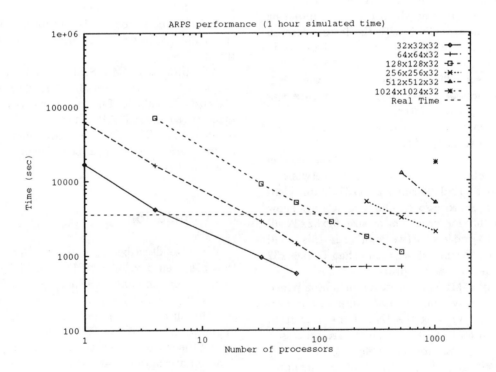

Figure 3: Measured wallclock times for simulating one hour of weather on various size CM-5 computers. Each connected line represents a single problem size. Points below the horizontal dashed line represent runs that predict weather faster than the weather actually occurs.

Problem Size	Processors							
	1	4	32	64	128	256	512	1024
32x32x32	1171	4697	20696	34312				
64x64x32	1264	4868	27288	54957	112993	111393	112027	
128x128x32		4472	34428	60693			286496	
256x256x32								609047
512x512x32							402267	*991378*
1024x1024x32								*1146542*

Table 4: Rate of processing in terms of simulated gridpoint timesteps per second. Italicized numbers are estimates extrapolated from short runs; others are based on measured wallclock time for full runs.

7 Calculations

Here we perform calculations on our the timings to qualify for three of the four categories of the Gordon Bell Prize.

7.1 Compiler Parallelization and Speedup

We believe the calculations for both of these categories are related, so we combine them here.

We calculate compiler parallelization by comparing the fastest rate on any CM-5 with the fastest rate on a single CM-5 processor. The relevant numbers are in Table 4.

For a 1 processor CM-5 run, the best rate was 1264.

For a 512 processor CM-5 run, the best rate was 402267, giving a speedup of 318.

For a 1024 processor CM-5 run, the best rate was 1146542, giving a speedup of 907.

Our speedups far exceed the previous best parallel speedup of 8.2 which was achieved on the network of RS6000s. In those RS6000 runs, a 32x31x32 problem bottomed out at 8 processors. Our CM timings show consistent speedup for problems of size 32x32x32 all the way up to 64 processors (we didn't run this small problem on larger machines); we found that a 64x64x32 problem bottomed out at 128 processors.

Since the Cray Y-MP is the fastest machine on which ARPS was previously run, we now compare our performance to that. Viewing the User Time data from Table 1 as the rate at which grid points are processed through a time step, we produce Table 5.

Taking the best Cray rate, we find that the 1024 processor CM-5 run is 57 times faster.

7.2 Price/Performance

The measured rate for a 32 processor CM-5 is 20696, which is close to the Cray's best rate, and for the same

Problem Size	Rate
32x32x31	20091
64x64x32	14945

Table 5: Rate of processing in terms of simulated gridpoint timesteps per second for the Cray Y-MP.

problem size. We can confidently state that a 32 processor CM-5 Scale 3 has identical performance to a Cray Y-MP for this problem. For problem 16 times larger, this same CM improves its price/performance by a factor of 1.7.

A 32 processor CM-5 Scale 3, ready to run, with 512 Mbytes of memory, costs about $1,000,000. A Cray Y-MP costs $2,000,000[3] for 1 processor with 128 Mbytes of memory (a 64x64x32 ARPS problem takes up 64 Mbytes of memory). Therefore, we have improved the price performance for running a fixed size problem by at least a factor of two.

8 Conclusion

We have described a real, third-party application that has been developed in Fortran 77 by scientists for their own use and has been sped up though execution on a massively parallel machine. The execution was possible because of new parallelizing compiler technology in the form of CMAX. We believe that our entry advances the state of the art in both storm prediction and in automatic parallelization of scalable Fortran 77 applications. The speed of parallel execution opens up new possibilities for the operational testing of ARPS, both in the size of the simulated area and in the level of detail possible. The CMAX-based method used for the port

---

[3]This figure is taken from the February 1993 Datapro (volume 3, number 2).

will allow future versions of the ARPS to be ported to the CM with virtually no additional investment of time.

We obtained the following results:

- On a 1024 processor CM-5 run, a speedup of 907 over a 1 processor run, with the help of CMAX. These numbers exceed the best previous speedup on a parallel platform of 8.2.

- We achieved consistent speedups over a wide range of machines sizes, up to 128 processors, for a modest, fixed sized problem. This is an improvement on previous parallel work which bottomed out at 8 processors.

- A 1024 processor CM-5 is 57 times faster than the fastest previously available ARPS platform.

- We achieved at least 2 times the price/performance of a Cray Y-MP.

9 Acknowledgments

We would like to thank CAPS and all those who have worked on the various versions of ARPS, in particular Kelvin Droegemeier and Ken Johnson. We would also like to thank the customers whose CM-5s we used to take our timings, LANL, and NCSA, Kapil Mathur for help in performing the LANL runs, and Jim Hutchinson for help with timing calculations. Our entry would not have been possible without CMAX. The CMAX project was initiated by Robert Millstein and Clifford Lasser; Skef Wholey and Gary Sabot drove the project at Thinking Machines while coordinating with developers at Applied Parallel Research Inc., in particular Shaul Sweed, Dennis Goodrow, and Gene Wagenbreth. Proofreading wuz don by David Loshin. Finally, a number of other Thinking Machines employees helped make CMAX a better product, including Rob Jones, Kirk Jordan, Rich Loft, Janet Marantz, Niraj Srivastava, Rich Title, and Yasunari Tosa.

References

[1] Center for Analysis and Prediction of Storms, University of Oaklahoma. *ARPS Version 3.0 User's Guide*, 1992.

[2] Kelvin Droegemeier, Ming Xue, Ken Johnson, Kim Mills, and Matthew O'Keefe. Experiences with the scalable-parallel ARPS cloud/mesoscale prediction model on massively parallel and workstation cluster architectures. In *Proceedings, 5th Workshop on the Use of Parallel Processors in Meteorology*. European Center for Medium Range Weather Forecasts, November 1992.

[3] Kenneth W. Johnson, Jeff Bauer, Gregory A. Riccardi, Kelvin K. Droegemeier, and Ming Xue. Distributed processing of a regional prediction model. Submitted to Montly Weather Review. Also available as a tech report from Florida State University, FSU-SCRI-93-85., 1993.

[4] John Levesque and Richard Friedman. The state of the art in automatic parallelization. In *Proceedings of Supercomputing Europe*, February 1993.

[5] Gary Sabot, Lisa Tennies, Alex Vasilevsky, and Richard Shapiro. Compiler parallelization of an elliptic grid generator for 1990 Gordon Bell Prize. In H. D. Simon, editor, *Scientific Applications of the Connection Machine, 2nd edition*, pages 364–378. World Scientific, 1992.

[6] Gary W. Sabot. A compiler for a massively parallel distributed memory MIMD computer. In H. J. Siegel, editor, *Frontiers of Massively Parallel Computation*, pages 12–20. IEEE Computer Society, October 1992.

[7] Gary W. Sabot. Optimized CM Fortran Compiler for the Connection Machine Computer. In *Proceedings of Hawaii International Conference on System Sciences 25*, pages 161–172. IEEE Computer Society, 1992.

[8] Gary W. Sabot and Skef Wholey. CMAX: A Fortran translator for the Connection Machine system. In *Proceedings of 7th International Conference on Supercomputing*, pages 147–156, 1993.

[9] Thinking Machines Corporation. *Prism User's Guide*, version 1.2 edition, March 1993.

[10] Skef Wholey. *Automatic Data Mapping for Distributed-Memory Parallel Computers*. PhD thesis, Carnegie Mellon University, May 1991. CMU-CS-91-121.

[11] Skef Wholey, Cliff Lasser, and Gyan Bhanot. Flo67: A case study in scalable programming. *International Journal of Supercomputer Applications*, 6(4), Winter 1992. To appear.

[12] Gary W. Sabot (with David Gingold and Janet Marantz). CM Fortran optimization notes: Slicewise model. Technical Report TMC-184, Thinking Machines Corporation, Cambridge, Massachusetts 02142, March 1991.

Session 7:
Minisymposium
EDS/NIIT

Session 8:
Visualization Environments
Chair: Allan Tuchman

A Visualization Environment for Supercomputing-based Applications in Computational Mechanics

Constantine J. Pavlakos, Larry A. Schoof and John F. Mareda

Sandia National Laboratories
Applied Visualization Group
Dept. 1425
P. O. Box 5800
Albuquerque, NM 87185

Abstract

In this paper, we characterize a visualization environment that has been designed and prototyped for a large community of scientists and engineers, with an emphasis in supercomputing-based computational mechanics. The proposed environment makes use of a visualization server concept to provide effective, interactive visualization to the user's desktop. Benefits of using the visualization server approach are discussed. Some thoughts regarding desirable features for visualization server hardware architectures are also addressed. A brief discussion of the software environment is included. The paper concludes by summarizing certain observations which we have made regarding the implementation of such visualization environments.

1.0 Background

As a multiprogram engineering laboratory, Sandia National Laboratories (SNL) has major research and development responsibilities for nuclear weapons, arms control, energy, environment, and other areas of strategic importance to national security. To accomplish this diversified mission, analysts employ computational mechanics methods to support the entire laboratory in solving problems in fluid dynamics (steady state and transient, compressible and incompressible), thermodynamics (heat transfer), hydrodynamics (impact physics, penetration mechanics), solid mechanics (structural/thermal analysis, fracture mechanics, ground subsidence, impact modeling) and structural dynamics. To assist these analysts in performing these analyses most efficiently, the Applied Visualization Group was formed and tasked to develop a next-generation scientific visualization environment.

For the creation and implementation of this environment, an extensive list of functional specifications was developed in response to users' requests. Included in these specifications were the following requirements/constraints:

- Service 150 scientists / engineers.

- Support 20 simultaneous visualization users.

- Allow efficient visualization of large databases. Analyses currently executed on our supercomputer routinely generate results files between 100MB and 1GB in size. Results files in the 10GB-100GB range are anticipated.

- Allow for visualization at the desktop. Analysts desire to visualize results in their offices where the information used to perform the analysis (e.g. material properties, input loads, model constraints, etc.) is readily available.

- Utilize existing desktop hardware. All users had a display device (workstation or X-terminal) on their desks but the only commonality was that they were X11 windows devices. A related constraint was to be able to replace desktop displays in the future without requiring the replacement of the entire visualization environment.

A few motivating factors which drove the users to request the development of a new environment are worthy of note. First, computing resources (i.e., cpu speeds, internal memory sizes, disk sizes, etc.) have matured in the past few years to the point that 3D analyses are now run routinely, although visualization of the results is still quite painstaking. Secondly, users are demanding to interact with their data sets rather than post-process their results using batch-oriented procedures. Previously, "batch graphics" on a supercomputer was the only practical option for some problems due to the size of individual data fields (e.g. a scalar field of temperature at each grid point for one instant in time) as well as the size of the entire results file (10-40 scalar values at each grid point for all time steps) which was unwieldy to download. A third factor, related to the previous two, is the expectation of a *consistent* response time in visualizing analysis results. Users want to see an image generated at their desk within a certain time threshold, regardless of the complexity of the problem. Although an acceptable response time has been difficult to quantify, the general consensus of our users is that a few seconds (<10) is satisfactory for generating a complex image.

In order to transform user requirements into a proposed hardware / software solution, it was necessary to understand the application environment.

2.0   Application Environment

The analysis environment employed by our engineers / scientists can be divided into three primary phases: problem definition, typically performed on a local server; simulation, executed on a central supercomputer; and visualization, currently done on either a local server or a central supercomputer, depending on the size of the problem. It is critical to understand each of these phases in order to design an environment that allows efficient use of resources. In examining these processes, particularly the visualization process, we determined that database accessibility was a major issue. Indeed, from a high-level perspective, the database is the central hub of the environment and each process is simply an application accessing the hub (see Figure 1). Database issues will be discussed further in Section 6.0, Software Environment.

A required function incorporated into this model is simulation tracking: that is, monitoring the results of an analysis as it is executing. A future evolution of this functionality will be simulation steering, in which parameters within the simulation are modified when there is evidence that the results are going awry. An example of this is adaptive meshing, in which the simulation geometry is discretized more finely in regions where the gradient of a calculated variable is very high.

Within this model, the visualization process can be divided into the following four steps, as Upson, et al [1] described: (1) input; (2) filtering into another form that is more informative and perhaps less voluminous; (3) mapping data into geometry; (4) rendering geometry into images. It is important to note that this process involves

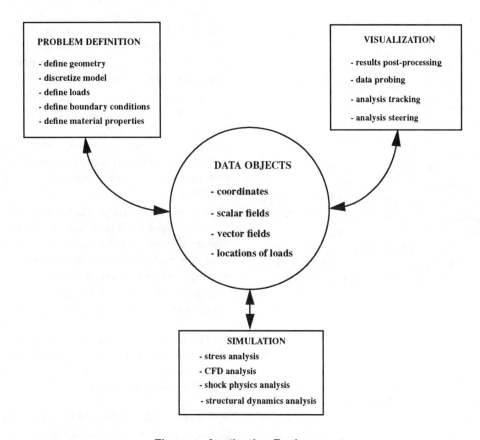

Figure 1: Application Environment

551

much more than just rendering objects. Although geometric transformations of an object (the most used function of the rendering step) are important to analysts, the other steps often dominate the entire process, especially when processing large data sets. We have experienced this during our prototyping. In one specific case, a low cost workstation with a fast cpu and no graphics acceleration processed data to produce an image an order of magnitude more quickly than a high end workstation with graphics acceleration, but a slower cpu.

This phenomenon is particularly true with time dependent data sets, in which the analyst is concerned about changes in the time domain, not just the space domain (see Section 6.0, Software Environment). Yet, most special purpose hardware accelerates only the rendering step, leaving the other steps to be performed by a general purpose cpu. What is needed is a balanced approach: maximum processing power available to each of the stages as required. We must be cautious that the complete visualization process is not obscured by the polygons/sec wars being waged among workstation vendors.

3.0 Proposed Network / Hardware Configuration

In order to do highly interactive visualization of supercomputing results, a very tight, high-speed integration is required between the supercomputer(s), large storage facilities, and the visualization components. The goal is to implement the equivalent of a super graphics workstation.

Consider the architecture of a standalone high performance graphics workstation. Such a system typically includes one or more general purpose cpus for computation, a large high-speed disk farm, and extra processing power for pseudo real-time graphics, all bundled together in a tightly integrated system. This architecture is analogous to the proposed network architecture for supercomputing-based applications depicted in Figure 2, which uses a "supernet" to integrate the supercomputing, storage, and visualization components. Based on current technology, alternatives for such a "supernet", such as HiPPI and Ultra-Net, provide transfer rates on the order of 100MB/sec (peak).

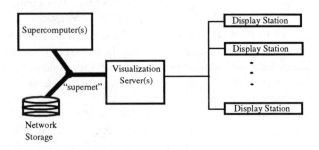

Figure 2: Proposed Network Architecture

There are a number of alternatives for what kinds of visualization systems to implement and where to put them. Certainly, one alternative is to purchase a high-performance graphics workstation for each user. This, unfortunately, would be prohibitively expensive, since our visualization requirements mandate high-end workstation configurations and we have many users to support.

A second alternative is to provide some smaller number of high-performance graphics workstations at appropriately distributed locations which could be shared. This approach has been attempted several times at Sandia, generally failing due to users' unwillingness to go down the hall to use a special system -- users prefer to use the system at their desk, even at significantly reduced performance. This approach also has the problem of contention for a physical resource (i.e. the limited number of high-end graphics workstations).

An additional problem with both of the above alternatives is the implementation of the tight communications interface (i.e. "supernet") with the supercomputer(s) and file store. The number of visualization systems together with their distributed locations would make high-speed communications very expensive as well as technically challenging.

This course of reasoning led us to conclude that what we need is a "visualization server" which would provide the aggregate equivalent of some number of high-end graphics workstations, together with the ability to deliver images to desktop displays at acceptable rates.

Conceptually, the capabilities desired for such a visualization server are characterized as follows:

- The server should have the aggregate power of multiple (in our case, preferably 10-20) high performance graphics systems bundled into a single system, accessible by multiple simultaneous users.

- The server should be able to compute images at the same rate as a standalone, high performance graphics system. All that remains is to get the images to the desktop. The difference in graphics performance between using a central visualization server and sitting directly in front of a high-performance graphics workstation should be only the time to transmit the image (not the time to compute it).

- The server should be able to drive conventional desktop displays, via conventional communications media, as fast as possible.

The concept of a shared, centralized visualization server is not entirely a novel idea. Alliant Computer Systems tried to sell the idea for a long time [2], and others have promoted the concept as well [3]. A number of vendors are currently promoting systems as visualization servers, including Convex and IBM (Power Visualization System). However, no vendor that we are aware of currently meets all of the desired features as we have characterized them.

Some ideas and/or emerging technologies which have the potential to make visualization servers more viable include:

- The concept of generating images, at high performance graphics rates, not just to a local console, but into more general purpose memory, from where the image can be redirected to an arbitrary display (Stellar's Virtual Pixel Map architecture was a step in this direction [4]).

- Higher speed networking technology, resulting in higher speed transmission of images to the desktop.

- Various image transmission techniques, including image compression schemes and digital video.

- PEX [5] as a mechanism for distributing the rendering process between the server and the desktop.

Benefits of a centralized visualization server include:

- Cost-effectiveness. Consider the case of serving 100 users, of which 10-20 need to do visualization simultaneously. The cost of purchasing 100 medium-level graphics workstations at $50,000 each would be $5,000,000. The cost of 100 high-end graphics workstations at $100,000 each would be $10,000,000. Even if a server were to cost $2,000,000, the cost of the server plus 100 low-cost, desktop stations at $10,000 each would be $3,000,000. While this cost-analysis may be over-simplified and may not be applicable to all environments, the potential for cost savings is clear.

- Pseudo-high-performance graphics to the desktop for a large community of users.

- The ability to run problems of a magnitude over and above that possible on a standalone workstation (since the equivalent of multiple cpu/memory/graphics resources is bundled together).

- Simplification of the super-high-speed communication problem between the supercomputer(s), storage, and visualization system(s) (only a few connections, and the machines can be in close proximity).

3.1 Our Prototype Environment

A prototype configuration which adopts the aforementioned model has been implemented at Sandia, as an adaptation to our production supercomputing environment. This configuration is depicted in Figure 3. The configuration includes a CRAY YMP, a terabyte network storage system, and a Convex C220 which is currently acting as a visualization server. These systems are interconnected by an UltraNet, which uses an HSX interface into the CRAY, a VME interface into the network storage system, and a HiPPI into the visualization server. The visualization server has 2 cpus and 512 MB of memory, which has allowed us to experiment with some large problems. The visualization server is connected to remote desktop displays via Ethernet and FDDI. FDDI connectivity is extended from Sandia, New Mexico to Sandia's branch site in California via a long-haul FDDI/ATM interface.

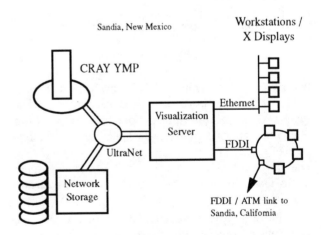

Figure 3: Prototype Network Configuration

We have measured memory-to-memory data transfer rates (tcp/ip) between the CRAY and the visualization server at rates up to 5 MB/s. Since this is on the order of disk access rates, we can hope to access CRAY disk data from the visualization server without noticing any significant network overhead. On the other hand, NFS data rates have been slow, similar to Ethernet. It is clear that, in order to maximize record-level network-file-access data through-put, we will have to overcome the protocol limitations of NFS. FTP rates for file transfers between the CRAY, network storage, and the visualization server have been measured at about 2-3 MB/s. It is important to note that measurements were taken during normal working hours, with a normally loaded CRAY (typically saturated) and network storage system. Also, communications with the network storage system are currently bandwidth-limited by the VME interface.

The prototype visualization server is expected to be replaced in the latter part of 1993 with a new production machine, which is currently being procured.

4.0 Visualization Server Architectures

A proposed conceptual architecture for a visualization server is shown in Figure 4.

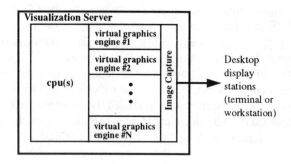

Figure 4: Conceptual Visualization Server

The server includes one or more processors for computation, a number of "virtual graphics engines" which support high speed rendering, and the ability to capture images produced by these virtual graphics engines and transmit the images to the desktop (for example, using X Windows). The virtual graphics engines, which may be realized in the form of special-purpose graphics hardware or as more general-purpose computational resources used to do graphics, are dynamically allocatable to one or more visualization processes.

A more detailed characterization of the idealized requirements for a visualization server would include:

- Well-balanced computation and graphics power which can support multiple users. The architecture should be scalable to support differing requirements based on number of simultaneous users and visualization problem complexity.

- Configurable with lots of memory (greater than 1 GB), preferably shared memory (or at least having the

appearance of shared memory) which is accessible by whatever processors the system uses, at very high speed internal data rates (e.g. on the order of 100MB/sec - 1 GB/sec).

- The ability to take advantage of high-speed rendering capabilities, while delivering the resulting image into more general purpose memory, rather than to a console frame buffer.

- State-of-the-art external connectivity for the highest-speed possible communications between supercomputer(s), large storage, and the visualization server.

- Mechanisms for making best use of up-to-date, conventional communications wiring for transmission of graphical data between the visualization server and the desktop.

- A multi-user, virtual resource environment which allows complete, dynamically-allocatable access to all internal resources, on a demand basis. It should be possible for a large visualization task to allocate more resources (up to the whole machine, depending on availability), in order to maintain adequate response.

- Minimized contention for any physical resources which are used to realize the virtual resource environment, such as frame buffer memory and graphics pipelines.

Massively parallel (MP) processors are well suited to certain aspects of visualization, including rendering. It would seem that such processors could be used as effective components within a visualization system. However, the need to support multiple simultaneous users executing a variety of visualization processes suggests that a MIMD (Multiple Instruction Multiple Data) architecture is needed, or at least multiple SIMD (Single Instruction Multiple Data) engines which could be allocated dynamically.

A hybrid architecture which includes some combination of MP, vector, and scalar processor components, integrated with a shared memory and high-bandwidth internal communications is intriguing (see Figure 5). This architecture would allow distribution of visualization sub-processes across the various components based on which parts run best on which components. It would be particularly important for a hybrid architecture of this nature to be well-balanced in order to make effective use of each of the major processing components.

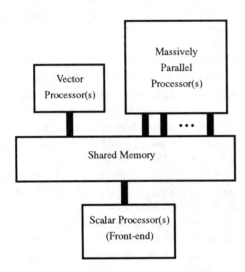

Figure 5: A Hybrid Architecture

In order to understand what features make a good visualization server, it is useful to examine various existing architectures and identify strengths and weaknesses.

- Case 1. A multi-cpu, high-end graphics workstation -- While this kind of system may offer adequate computational power for a modest number of users, its specialized high-speed graphics capabilities are typically only accessible from a local graphics console.

- Case 2. A traditional mini-supercomputer with a small number of processors (<10)-- This system offers strong computational performance, but lacks any specialized graphics components. All rendering is performed in software, on the general purpose cpus.

- Case 3. A traditional workstation host connected to a SIMD MP accelerator -- The MP accelerator can be used for graphics acceleration, as well as for other visualization tasks. However, the SIMD accelerator can only operate on a single user's job at any one time, resulting in contention for this resource. Multiple, perhaps smaller, MP accelerators could be used to alleviate this problem. The front end would need to be powerful enough to support multiple users, and the communications between the front end and the accelerators must be at very high speeds (on the order of 100 MB/sec or greater).

- Case 4. A MIMD parallel machine, based on vector or superscalar cpus, with high-speed access to a pool of shared memory -- The processors can be dynamically allocated for graphics tasks and computational tasks,

across multiple users. Certain processors, such as the i860, offer proven graphics performance. This architecture is attractive; however, it must be shown that such a machine can effectively deliver aggregate computational and graphics performance over its distributed architecture.

5.0 Getting the Picture to the Desktop

A key to maximizing the effectiveness of a centralized visualization server is transmitting images between the visualization server and the desktop at effective rates. Nominally, we have been using conventional X Windows and Ethernet to transmit images, generally requiring about 2-4 seconds to transmit a 500x500, 8-bit image. While this performance is less than desirable, it has been acceptable in our environment -- it does not provide real-time animation, but it does provide interactive response.

More recently, we have been very encouraged by experiments with FDDI. Using a relatively unloaded FDDI, we have been able to update images (500x500 8-bit) between the visualization server and a networked display at up to 3 frames per second (AVS running on the visualization server, rendering a simple geometry -- see Section 6.0, Software Environment). We have also been very pleased with the recently installed long-haul FDDI/ATM link between Sandia, New Mexico, and Sandia, California [6]. In preliminary testing, usage of the visualization environment from California was virtually indistinguishable from usage of the same environment from a local networked display. When pushing images to California, we get up to about 2.5 frames per second (same test as above).

Data compression techniques may be used to further reduce the time necessary to update an image, particularly for viewing animation. In the not-too-distant future, hardware compression / decompression schemes such as JPEG and MPEG [7] should reduce the image transmission time such that reasonable quality animation (30 frames / second) will be possible over the network.

While we have focused on transmission of raster images between the visualization server and the desktop, 3-dimensional graphics protocols such as PEX provide an alternative, at least for some applications. Instead of transmitting an image, the visualization server can transmit 3D graphical data, such as polygons, to the desktop where local rendering takes place. If the local display system has sufficient power to accommodate the application's needs, this can be a very pleasing mode to work in. However, effective use in this mode requires a terminal or workstation which supports effective 3-dimensional rendering, potentially adding significant expense to the cost of a local display system.

Our preliminary experiences with PEX as a mechanism for distributing our visualization applications have not been encouraging. When using low-cost PEX systems, the performance has been inadequate for our class of problems. When using a more substantial PEX system ($25,000 retail price, 32 MB memory), performance was acceptable for smaller problems. However, for certain larger problems, we were unable to download the resulting 3-dimensional geometries due to insufficient memory in the local system. Finally, while PEX may be useful for generating transformed views of static graphical models, it is not particularly useful for viewing time-dependent animation sequences, where the graphics data changes from frame to frame, requiring downloading of new data to produce each frame.

6.0 Software Environment

The use of software standards, such as X11 and PEX, have and will continue to play a critical role in the success of our project. Our experience has shown that a software environment should not be dependent on any specific computer architecture due to the transient nature of hardware. Because significant effort is required to customize software for a given application, an ideal environment would allow the replacement of the system hardware with minimal software modification.

This criteria was used in our selection of the Application Visualization System (AVS) [1] as the core of our prototype software environment. AVS satisfied our requirements because of the following features:

- Modular -- small, functional modules can be developed which can be used and reused to construct a variety of applications.

- Extensible -- functionality can be easily extended by writing application specific modules or by integrating other software tools, including commercial or public domain software.

- Distributable -- AVS applications can span across a network computing environment.

- Ubiquitous -- AVS has been ported to most workstation platforms and is not reliant on proprietary hardware.

Because AVS is a general purpose visualization toolkit, not a production system to be released to an end user, developers should anticipate spending time customizing it for their specific application. An area in which we have devoted significant effort has been database design.

At the root of our database issues is the size of results files generated on our supercomputers. Because the problems we solve are highly dynamic (nonlinear, large deformation), time-dependent solution schemes are necessary. A couple of examples which are representative of the large data sets we need to visualize are worth noting.

Figure 6 represents material boundaries from an analysis of a debris cloud consisting of 297 steel particles (red) with an average size of .76mm impacting a 12.7mm aluminum target at an impact velocity of 4300 m/s. The grid size for this data was 250 x 250 x 100 (6.25 million cells). Since the problem involves two materials (two fields), a total of 12.5 million data values (4 bytes each, 50MB total) were used to do the visualization. This, in turn, is only a fraction of the total memory used by the entire visualization process to produce the resulting image. This data was visualized on the Convex visualization machine in our prototype environment, which has 512MB of memory -- we were unable to visualize this data on smaller conventional workstations because of insufficient memory. We were also unable to download the resulting isosurface polygons onto a PEX terminal with 32MB of memory, due to the number of polygons (3 million triangles) generated. Generating pictures of this data requires on the order of 3-5 minutes a frame on the Convex.

As an example of a large finite element data set, Figure 7 shows equivalent plastic strain on a model of a prototype joint (used to connect mechanical components) under design. The displayed model consisted of 489,000 finite elements. The analysis model was one-quarter of the displayed model (the entire model was not necessary due to symmetry) and was composed of 122,000 elements and 165,000 nodes. The results database (about 1.4 GB in size) contained over 60 time slices, with 11 variables per time slice for each element and 12 variables per time slice for each node. On our prototype visualization server, processing of a single time slice of data (including input, filtering, mapping and rendering) takes about 30 minutes. A simple geometric transformation of the object requires about 1.5 minutes (rendering only). Note that the rendering time is a small fraction of the total visualization.

Although the processing of large problems is still painful on our prototype visualization server, visualization of nominal size problems is at acceptable response levels. We expect performance to be significantly improved with the imminent purchase of a new visualization server.

Due to the criticality of the database, tasks were spawned to design or modify databases for two analysis categories: those whose geometries are structured grids and those whose geometries are unstructured grids (typically finite element analyses). After accumulating extensive input from analysts and analysis code developers, we sum-

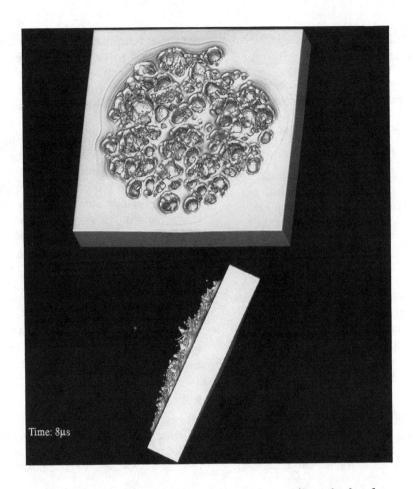

Figure 6: Visualization from a 6.25 million cell analysis of a debris cloud of steel particles impacting an aluminum plate.

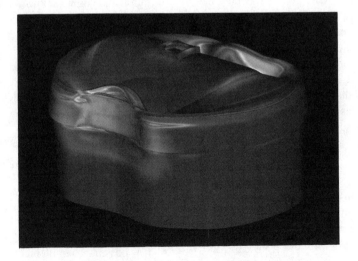

Figure 7: Visualization of equivalent plastic strain on a finite element model of a prototype joint (489,000 elements).

[For color plate see page 928]

marized the requirements for both databases into the following functional specifications:

- C and FORTRAN library interfaces -- application codes should access the database through library routines.

- random access of data -- access any variable at any time slice.

- extensible, object-based structure -- allow the database definition to be extended for new features or data objects without necessitating the modification of all application codes that use the database.

- portable -- the database should be machine independent.

- simultaneous write/read access -- allow one application (i.e., an analysis code) to write data while another application (i.e., a visualization code) reads data; necessary for simulation tracking.

Also, the users of codes utilizing structured grids desired the following additional features.

- support for data encodings -- implement data compression techniques to reduce the size of results files.

- allow rectilinear, cylindrical, and spherical coordinates.

Two approaches were used to address the database issues. For analyses using structured meshes, an in-house developed data file format has been defined which allows random access as well as implementation of special compression techniques [8]. For problems solved with unstructured meshes, an application-specific interface to the netCDF [9] library, which supports random access, was created [10]. Although both of these solutions took a significant amount of time and effort to define and implement, it has become evident to us that proper data management (i.e. prudent access as well as data flow) is critical to an effective visualization process.

7.0 Future Work

Ultimately, we expect to install a production visualization environment for our engineering science community before the end of 1993. In the meantime, we expect to continue development and testing within our prototype environment.

A key task is to complete the acquisition of a new visualization server machine. In order to do so, we expect to benchmark a variety of potential visualization server systems. The benchmarks will be based on our specific applications, and will attempt to assess the impact of large problems as well as multiple simultaneous users. This effort should provide us with additional, concrete data regarding the effectiveness of various visualization server architectures.

Software efforts will continue to emphasize efficient processing of large, centrally-deposited visualization databases in this distributed environment. Additionally, once the high-speed integrated environment is in place, we expect to begin examining the potential use of more direct interactive visualization (versus post-processing), such as for steering our supercomputer applications.

While this work has been based in our traditional, production supercomputing environment, we are already beginning to address the integration of massively parallel machines. The impact, if any, of such machines on our distributed architecture will be assessed. The capacity of such machines to generate even greater quantities of data will further intensify our efforts to develop methods for effective processing of large problems.

8.0 Conclusion

In designing and prototyping an environment for highly interactive scientific visualization of large, supercomputer-generated databases, we have made the following observations:

- The visualization process involves more than just graphics. Indeed, while well-balanced general computation and graphics power are required to insure optimal throughput, we have judged computation power to be the more critical resource. That is, given the choice of a visualization system that does superior graphics with modest computational power and another which has superior computational power with modest graphics power, the system with superior computational power would be preferred.

- A tight, high-speed integration is required between our supercomputer, large data storage facilities, and visualization components in order to allow effective processing of our large databases. Additionally, software must be implemented intelligently in order to do efficient data management.

- It is possible to implement a centralized visualization server which provides pseudo-high-performance graphics to the desktop for multiple users. The benefits of a centralized visualization server include: cost-effectiveness for a large user community; the ability to apply aggregate resources to very large problems; and simplified implementation of high-speed networking.

Acknowledgments

This work performed at Sandia National Laboratories supported by the U. S. Department of Energy under contract DE-AC04-76DP00789.

Marlin Kipp and Debra Campbell for the calculations and visualization associated with Figure 6.

Gregory Sjaardema for the calculations associated with Figure 7.

References

[1] C. Upson, et al., "The Application Visualization System: A Computational Environment for Scientific Visualization," IEEE Computer Graphics and Applications, Vol. 9, No. 4, Jul. 1989.

[2] "Hardware Strategies for Scientific Visualization," Panels Proceedings SIGGRAPH '88.

[3] D. Salzman and J. Grimes, "Graphics Superworkstations and the Last Hurrah," IEEE Computer Graphics and Applications, Vol. 9, No. 4, Jul. 1989.

[4] B. Apgar, B. Bersack, and A. Mammen, "A Display System for the Stellar Graphics Supercomputer Model GS1000," Computer Graphics, ACM SIGGRAPH, Vol. 22, No. 4, Aug. 1988.

[5] R. J. Rost, J. D. Friedberg and P. L. Nishimoto, "PEX: A Network-Transparent 3D Graphics System," IEEE Computer Graphics and Applications, Jul. 1989.

[6] J. N. Naegle, N. Testi, C. Pavlakos and H. Chen, "Using a Private SMDS/ATM Network to Provide Long-Haul Supercomputing Visualization Services," Cray User Group Conference, Spring 1993.

[7] Communications of the ACM, Vol. 34, No. 4, Apr. 1991.

[8] C. J. Pavlakos and D. L. Campbell, "Visualization for Applications in Shock Physics," SAND 93-0916C, Sandia National Laboratories conference submittal, Mar. 1993.

[9] R. K. Rew and G. P. Davis, "NetCDF: An Interface for Scientific Data Access," IEEE Computer Graphics and Applications, Jul. 1990.

[10] L. A. Schoof, "EXODUS II: A Finite Element Data Model," SAND 92-2137, Sandia National Laboratories, in process.

VASE: The Visualization and Application Steering Environment

David J. Jablonowski
University of Illinois
465 CSRL
1308 W. Main St.
Urbana, IL 61801

John D. Bruner
University of Illinois
465 CSRL
1308 W. Main St.
Urbana, IL 61801

Brian Bliss
Convex Computer Corporation
3000 Waterview Parkway
P.O. Box 833851
Richardson, TX 75083

Robert B. Haber
University of Illinois
111J Talbot Lab.
104 S. Wright St.
Urbana, IL 61801

Abstract

The visualization and application steering environment (VASE) provides interactive visual computing and steering for scientific and engineering programs. VASE defines an abstraction for a steerable program structure and provides tools that create and manage collections of these steerable codes. It is designed to work with existing codes written in Fortran. Based upon simple annotations in the source code, VASE tools construct a high-level model of each application and enable the user to work with this model rather than at the detailed source-code level. Collections of steerable codes execute in a distributed environment.

This paper describes the design objectives for VASE, its architecture, and its implementation, and illustrates its use with an example application.

1 Introduction

Visualization is widely recognized as an effective tool for understanding the large data sets produced by large-scale scientific and engineering applications. The results generated by today's scientific and engineering codes are often complex and interdependent, perhaps comprising several different arrays of values that must be interpreted together in order to be understood. Visualization allows the user of such a code to apply his or her innate visual pattern recognition skills to comprehend its data.

Visualization is also a valuable tool for application development. When the programmer or end user of a code can visually examine its data, he or she may be able to identify areas in which the code can be improved. Perhaps the programmer originally chose algorithms that do not faithfully reflect the underlying physical process, or perhaps the visual presentation of data suggests alternative algorithms with better convergence properties. Perhaps some valid, but unexpected, result has occurred and the underlying cause must be uncovered.

Scientific visualization is typically performed as a post-processing step. Output statements are inserted into the application source code, and during execution the program writes programmer-selected data into output files. After execution has completed, a visualization package reads the data files and displays them.

However, computational scientists can derive much greater benefit from a visualization system that permits them to observe how their data evolves during the execution of their applications. As described in [1], this need is addressed by two complementary capabilities: *interactive visual computing* and *steering*.

An interactive visual computing system displays data from an application while the application is running. This approach allows the user to monitor its progress. In many cases, particularly for long-running codes, the user can employ this capability to terminate execution when the visual display reveals errors in data, algorithms, programming, or modelling; such early termination can help prevent considerable unnecessary computation.

Ideally, an interactive visualization interface provides the user with the ability to select datasets and their display methods interactively. This requires a suite of powerful display methods, coupled with a mechanism for constructing datasets at run-time.

Steering extends this model by providing the user with an interactive means to modify the state of the program at run-time. In the simplest case, the user can steer a computation by altering the values of key parameters. More generally, steering should allow the user to experiment with new or modified algorithms by interactively adding new code at key places in the application.

Steering can be used to explore the solution space computed by an application, to experiment with new algorithms, or to hasten the solution of a problem through user interaction. For example, in the past, optimization of complex design problems often leads to infeasible designs. The problem stems from the inability of designers to include all of the relevant design goals and constraints in the initial formulation of the optimization program. Using interactive visualization and steering, the designer can detect problems in the early iterations of the optimization and use steering to modify interactively the objective and constraint functions to achieve a more desirable result.

VASE, the Visualization and Application Steering Environment, is a collection of programming tools and system software that add interactive visualization and steering capabilities to application codes. VASE defines an abstraction for a steerable program structure and provides tools that create and manage collections of these steerable codes. The tools construct a high-level model of the application and allow the user to work with this model; the user need not be concerned with the low-level details of the source code. VASE coordinates the execution of these collections of codes in a heterogeneous distributed environment.

VASE is *not* a set of new built-from-scratch display methods. It is not intended to replace existing visualization packages. Instead, VASE enhances the value of these packages by providing them with run-time visualization and application steering capabilities.

The remainder of this paper is divided into four sections. Section 2 discusses the design requirements for VASE. Section 3 describes the architecture and implementation of VASE, and section 4 presents an example based on a toplogy optimization application. Finally, section 5 summarizes the current state of VASE and our future plans.

2 Design requirements

An interactive visualization system should be easy to use, both by the author (or maintainer) of the application code and by its eventual end users. These people will likely not be computer scientists; rather, they will be scientists or engineers in other disciplines who use computational methods to advance their own field. "Ease of use" of an interactive visualization system for these users can be difficult to quantify, but some attributes that characterize such a system can be identified.

First, such a system should not require a significant shift in the way that applications are written and maintained.

Existing applications should not require significant recoding. The discipline scientists who develop (and use) these applications should be able to concentrate on the high-level aspects of the science or engineering problem to be solved, not upon the details of the visualization system. This design objective was fundamental to the direction of our work. A corollary to this requirement is that the visualization system must support the language most commonly chosen for science and engineering codes: Fortran.

Interactive visualization and steering can be implemented directly in a program by a sufficiently capable programmer. However, in general this approach requires a substantial effort. The structure of the source code may need to be altered to accommodate the needs of the visualization system, and the presence of the extra source code will obscure its original application-oriented structure. Users will resist adding interactive visualization and steering capabilities unless changes to the source code are kept to a minimum.

An alternative approach is to design a new scientific visualization environment from scratch. An example of such a system is SCENE[2], which uses Smalltalk's object-oriented architecture and interactive nature to provide a powerful framework for visualization and steering. Visual programming languages such as VPL[3] and Khoros[4] carry this technique even further, allowing their users to define their computation and visualization by constructing data-flow graphs. (Khoros does allow the programmer to convert C or Fortran source code into nodes in its data-flow graph.) However, all of these approaches require a considerable shift in the programming language and practices of the application developer. While perhaps appropriate for new codes written "from scratch," they do not mesh well with existing scientific and engineering codes.

Second, an interactive visualization and steering system should present a high-level model of the application program to its users. The person who uses the application may not always be the same one who wrote it, and the end user should not be required to understand all of the coding details. Instead, he or she should be able to work with an abstracted model of the code that hides unnecessary details of coding. This model will serve both to document the structure of the code and to focus the attention of the end user upon the places where it is safe and appropriate to perform visualization and steering operations.

Data-flow models have shown great success in describing data transformations within visualization packages and describing the flow of data between application codes and the visualization packages. Examples of this approach are AVS[5], ApE[6], SGI's Iris Explorer, and IBM's Data Explorer.

However, data-flow models are not well suited to modelling the internal structure of the large (Fortran) scientific and engineering codes that are in widespread use today. A control-flow model, which can visually depict Fortran codes in a form similar to the familiar flowchart, seems a better match. Therefore, our design objective was to present a hybrid model to users: control-flow to describe the internal structure of applications, and data-flow to describe the communications between a set of applications — most typically, between a scientific or engineering code and a visualization package.

Third, although a high-level model of an application should express the code's overall structure, its key datasets, and its important parameters for steering, the model should not unnecessarily constrain the way in which datasets are extracted and steering is accomplished. In some cases, steering may require that some additional code be executed at key places within the application. Such a capability requires some form of run-time command interpretation.

Fourth, an interactive visualization system should take advantage of the considerable wealth of academic and commercial visualization products available. Dataset selection and steering should be implemented in a way that leverages this technology base.

Finally, it should be possible to employ a heterogeneous collection of processors for interactive visualization and steering. Large-scale scientific and engineering codes may execute on a vector supercomputer, while the mapping and rendering of the graphic images may be better suited to a dedicated graphics engine. It should be easy for a user to assign these different processes to hosts, to set up connections between them, and potentially even to reconfigure the setup while the application is running. Support for a heterogeneous environment implies that the interactive visualization system will hide from the user details such as data format conversion (e.g., differences in word lengths, "big endian" versus "little endian" byte ordering, or IEEE versus non-IEEE floating-point formats).

3 VASE architecture and implementation

3.1 Overview

The design of VASE is based upon the authors' previous experience in high-performance distributed visualization systems, including the RIVERS[7] project at the National Center for Supercomputing Applications and the Vista[8] project at the Center for Supercomputing Research and Development. A previous paper[9] describes VASE at an earlier phase in its development.

In the expected case, a user of VASE has at least one non-trivial application to be adapted for interactive visualization and steering. This application is often quite large,

and its logic is often correspondingly complex. VASE defines an abstract model for the application that expresses its basic structure while hiding implementation details. VASE divides the activities associated with creating and using this model into two phases: the *pre-compilation* and *post-compilation* phases.

During the pre-compilation phase, a person or persons familiar with the internal structure of the application uses VASE tools to define the structure of the program and to specify *VASE breakpoints* — points within the program where visualization and steering may be performed. Other VASE tools automatically generate instrumented source code that includes the original application source code plus the breakpoints. The instrumented source code produced in the pre-compilation phase is compiled and linked with a run-time library to create a VASE application.

In the post-compilation phase, end users work with an abstracted structure of programs (rather than the full source code). During this phase, the users employ VASE tools to *configure* and *execute* a set of applications. Typically this set will include a scientific or engineering code and one or more visualization tools. Configuration information includes the hosts upon which the programs will execute, inter-process communication channels between the programs, and management of the flow of data between programs (e.g., from the scientific code to a display tool).

VASE is implemented as a collection of programming tools and system software. The tools include program analysis and synthesis tools as well as graphical user interfaces for breakpoint insertion and distributed application configuration and execution. The system software includes an interactive controller and a set of servers that coordinate and monitor the communications of distributed applications.

3.2 The steerable program structure

Interactive visualization and steering require access to some application data structures at specific points in an application. To select the appropriate datasets, both VASE and the end user must work with a model that describes its essential algorithms and data without a glut of unnecessary low-level details. VASE defines a *steerable program structure* into which all applications are converted. The steerable structure serves both as a framework for steering and as an abstraction of the program's logic. This structure is defined during the pre-compilation phase of the application.

The steerable program structure of an application is based upon the control-flow graph of its subroutines. The graph comprises a set of *logical blocks* and corresponding *control flow arcs*. Each logical block represents a group of contiguous source code lines. The application developer chooses the grouping based upon his or her understanding of the code. Arcs represent the control flow between blocks. Blocks may be nested: an outer block may contain a set of inner blocks. The granularity of blocks depends on how much of the program's structure must be conveyed in order for the end user to steer the application effectively during its post-compilation phase.

The steerable program abstraction also defines the extent to which program variables will be available for visualization and steering during the post-compilation phase. At run-time it is generally not necessary or desirable to provide unrestricted access to an application's variables at all points within the program. Variables may not always hold meaningful values (e.g., a loop index variable may have no meaning outside of the loop). Arrays and other groups of related variables will only be self-consistent at certain times during execution. Reading these variables at other points would produce potentially confusing results, and modifying them (e.g., to perform steering) could be unsafe.

The VASE program abstraction restricts access to variables according to the control-flow graph of the application. Logical blocks are "black boxes" whose variables and internal implementation details are hidden from the end user. Data access for visualization and steering is only permitted between blocks, on the arcs of the graph, and typically only a few of these arcs represent places where such access is actually meaningful. The application developer or maintainer identifies these points by annotating some arcs with VASE breakpoints and identifying the appropriate variables at each point. In the post-compilation phase, the user will only have access to the application at these breakpoints.

3.3 Execution-time model

The ultimate goal of VASE is to orchestrate the execution of VASE applications. It provides mechanisms for interactive steering and data transfer between a set of network-distributed VASE applications. The organization and interaction of VASE processes that support its run-time environment are discussed here.

Figure 1 illustrates the (TCP/IP) network communications that are used to control the distributed set of processes that constitute a VASE session. Each session contains exactly one instance of the *Configuration and Execution Tool*, which is part of the VASE run-time user interface. The Configuration and Execution Tool sends control messages and data to applications and graphically displays feedback from these applications. It starts a *VASE Server* for each machine on which a VASE application is to execute. When each VASE application process first begins execution, it spawns its own copy of a *VASE Application Server*. The per-machine VASE Server and per-application VASE Application Servers pass control messages between the Configuration and Execution Tool and the individual VASE applications.

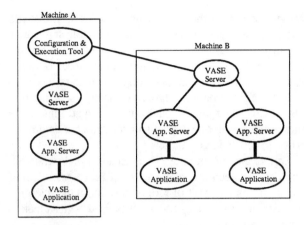

Figure 1: Structure of VASE server processes

3.4 Breakpoint scripts, ports, and data channels

Interactive visualization and steering are performed at breakpoints. During the pre-compilation phase, the application developer creates breakpoints on some control-flow arcs and selects variables in the program that are to be made accessible at these breakpoints. During the post-compilation phase, these variables are accessed at breakpoints under the control of scripts. Each breakpoint may have a script that is executed each time the breakpoint is encountered. Scripts are written in an extended subset of the C programming language.

A breakpoint script can be written before the application process begins execution. The script can also be modified while the application is running. Scripts can define new script-local variables. They can also reference symbols and routines outside the scope of the script, including compiled routines in the application, routines from the standard C library, C intrinsics and built-in functions, and the application variables that were selected during the pre-compilation phase.

Scripts can read and write variables in the application, can control the flow of data between processes (e.g., they can send data to a visualization process), and can call subroutines defined in the application program. Because they can be changed while the application is running, scripts provide a flexible basis for steering. Simple steering can be accomplished by pausing the application and interactively assigning a new value to a parameter. More sophisticated alternatives are also available, for example, a new algorithm can be added to the program by implementing it in a VASE breakpoint script.

Each VASE application process contains a *VASE interpreter* to process *VASE breakpoint scripts*. The VASE interpreter is based upon the Application Executive[10] developed as part of the Vista project at CSRD. The VASE interpreter is linked directly into the executable application and therefore has direct access to the application process address space. Direct access to this address space is important for the efficient manipulation of large data sets from scripts. The alternative approach of using a separate process for the interpreter would, on some platforms, incur substantial context-switching and interprocess communication to access large data sets.

Scripts implement interactive visualization by transferring data between a configured set of processes. This is accomplished by a pair of scripts: a script in the scientific application writes data, and a script in the visualization application reads it.

VASE ports are the endpoints for data communication between VASE application processes. They can be added to or removed from applications at any time. Ports are named, and breakpoint scripts can reference them by name using special VASE read and write primitives. A script may read data from or write data to a port; I/O may be either blocking or non-blocking.

VASE users create *data channels* between application processes by specifying connections between pairs of ports. Connected data channels between VASE ports give the user a dynamic data-flow model for asynchronous distributed applications that complements the static control-flow model reflected in the VASE steerable program structures. These data channels can be specified or removed, either before the application processes begin execution, or dynamically, as the processes are executing.

The VASE script interpreter provides functions that read and write typed data with automatic format conversion (e.g., word size, byte order, floating-point format) when necessary; however, the data channels themselves are untyped. VASE uses DTM (Data Transfer Mechanism)[11] to transfer data between application processes. DTM is built on top of TCP/IP and supports automatic data conversions between several platforms including Sun SPARCstations, the Silicon Graphics IRIS, and the Cray YMP.

3.5   Creating VASE applications

Figure 2 summarizes the procedure for creating a VASE application. The first step is to create steerable program structures for selected routines of the applications. In the pre-compilation phase the application source code is annotated with VASE program abstraction directives. These directives are non-executable START and END statements that delimit block boundaries. Blocks delimited by these directives may be nested. Each block is given a name that describes its function. These annotations are the *only* changes that must be made to the application source code. They do not require any functional changes to the exist-

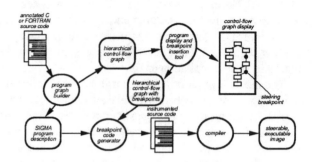

Figure 2: Creating a VASE application

```
C#START  "block name"  "optional description"
C#END  "block name"
```

Figure 3: VASE program abstraction directives

ing code. Because they are implemented as comments, the source code can still be compiled directly and executed independently of VASE, if desired. Figure 3 shows the syntax of these directives.

A utility based upon SIGMA[12], a syntactic and semantic analysis toolkit, reads the annotated source code and generates a control flow graph describing its steerable program structure as well as an internal parsed representation of the source code.

Next, the application developer or maintainer uses the VASE *Breakpoint Insertion Tool* to insert breakpoints. This tool graphically displays steerable program structures as directed graphs. Using the mouse, the developer inserts breakpoints on control flow arcs at all places where he or she anticipates that access to data for visualization or steering may be desirable. The developer also selects, on a per-breakpoint basis, the application variables that should be accessible in the breakpoint script.

After breakpoints have been inserted, another SIGMA-based utility generates instrumented source code for the application. This instrumented source code includes all of the original application source code, control variable definitions for VASE, and VASE breakpoints in the form of conditional calls to library routines. This source code is compiled and linked with the VASE libraries to form a VASE executable.

Notice that our approach requires the application developer or maintainer to specify breakpoint locations *before* the application is compiled. This design decision was selected for three reasons. First, this approach is portable, because it does not depend upon system-specific mechanisms for runtime breakpoint insertion. Second, because the breakpoint locations are visible to the object-code compiler, the compiler will ensure that the program state is consistent at the breakpoint call. By contrast, if the breakpoints were inserted at run-time, compiler optimizations might rearrange or eliminate some computations, making it difficult to identify points at which the state would be consistent. This problem is well known to users of source-level debuggers and optimizing compilers.

Finally, requiring the developer to specify breakpoints in the pre-compilation phase provides a clean mechanism for that person to restrict access to application variables during the post-compilation stage. The end user's attention can be focused upon the important data sets without the clutter of unnecessary variables, a non-trivial concern when a relatively large application might have hundreds of application variables.

Nonetheless, sometimes the end user needs or wants more access to the application. This is particularly true during application development, when the "developer" and "user" are the same person. The ideal location of breakpoints and the necessary variables may not be obvious at this time. Therefore, VASE provides a convenient interface to enable read and write access to all variables at a breakpoint. Later, when the application is more mature, the developer can reduce the number of breakpoints and accessible variables to a more focused set.

3.6 Configuration and execution tool

In VASE, configuration and execution of individual applications and sets of applications are unlikely to be strictly sequential events. Rather, it is likely that the applications will be re-configured during execution. For this reason, configuration and execution are both performed by the VASE *Configuration and Execution Tool*.

An initial configuration is created before the applications are executed, but it can be changed later (either while the applications are running or between runs). Configuration includes:

- adding or deleting applications from the set;
- specifying the host on which each application runs;
- adding, removing, or modifying data ports;
- adding or removing data channels between applications;
- altering breakpoint scripts; and
- changing the *mode* of breakpoints.

The *mode* of a breakpoint indicates what occurs when execution of an application process encounters the breakpoint. The possible modes and their significance are:

disabled: the breakpoint is ignored;

execute: any associated script is executed, after which execution of the application resumes;

pause: the application pauses at the breakpoint to allow user interaction; and

execute and pause: any associated script is executed, after which the application pauses.

Disabled breakpoints incur very little run-time overhead. VASE breakpoints are implemented by conditional calls to a library function. If the breakpoint is disabled, the library routine is not called.

The Configuration and Execution Tool manages the execution of all applications within a configured set. It can spawn and kill applications individually or as a group. Applications can be spawned automatically with a pre-configured set of command-line arguments, or manually, in which case VASE sets up an environment for its execution but the user is responsible for starting it. This latter mode gives the user complete control over the context in which an application process runs.

3.7 Recompilation and Debugging

The source code for scientific and engineering applications is unlikely to be completely static. Established codes will still undergo occasional maintenance in the form of "bug fixes" and new features. Codes that are being actively developed may change considerably more. When the original application source code is changed, a new control flow graph must be constructed and a new VASE application must be built. However, VASE minimizes the work that the application developer must perform to create a new version of a VASE application. In many cases, the basic structure of the new code will be very similar to the structure of the old code. When building a new steerable application, VASE reuses, as much as possible, the previously-defined control flow graph, breakpoint and variable information, and breakpoint scripts. In the simplest case, VASE can build a new steerable application with no manual input. In other cases, for example, when the structure of a code block has changed considerably, the developer may need to use the interactive VASE tools to identify the new location and variables of VASE breakpoints in the modified region.

It is possible to use a source-level debugger to debug a VASE application. As noted in the previous section, VASE applications can be started manually by the user, e.g., under control of a debugger. The user can then use the debugger in the usual way to examine variables, set debugging breakpoints, and step through the source code. This activity is invisible to the VASE environment. At present, the debugger uses the VASE-instrumented source code rather

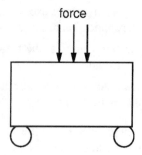

Figure 4: Toplogy optimization problem

than the original source code; however, the additional instrumentation does not greatly perturb the original structure of the code.

4 Using VASE: a computational mechanics example

To illustrate the process of interactive visualization and steering with VASE, we use an example from computational mechanics. The application *optilin* is concerned with finding the optimal shape of a structure constructed from a fixed amount of elastic material to be distributed within a given candidate domain. No restriction is placed on the topology of the structure's configuration, that is, as many holes can be introduced as desired. In the present example, the candidate domain is a rectangular region with roller supports at the lower corners; see Figure 4. A vertical distributed load is applied at the center top of the domain. The specific problem is to find the stiffest structure for the given loading and support conditions, using a total volume of material that does not exceed 20% of the candidate domain.

Optilin employs an optimality criterion method to update the shape of the structure. A new candidate shape is calculated at each iteration as a function of the shape from the previous iteration, the current strain state, and a parameter η (eta):

$$\widehat{\rho}_{k+1} = \min\left\{ \left(\frac{\int_{\Omega_\rho} \frac{\partial}{\partial \rho} W''(\rho, u) N_\rho d\Omega}{\lambda \int_{\Omega_\rho} N_\rho d\Omega} \right)^{\eta} \widehat{\rho}_k, 1.0 \right\}$$

Details of the problem can be found in [13].

In order to observe and potentially steer optilin, we need some feedback as its algorithm iterates. This feedback is provided by the IRIS Explorer data visualization system[14]. The Explorer was *not* converted to a VASE application, because we did not have access to its source code. Instead, a simple front-end to Explorer was constructed

```
c#START"Read input"
c      =========================
c      Input of noninteractive data
c      =========================
c
       call inputb
c#END "Read input"
c
c      =========================
c      Echo of the input data
c      =========================
c
       if (outsel(1).eq.1) call esindat
c#START "Compute initial volume"
c      =========================
c      Compute the element volumes
c      =========================
c
       call elvol
c#END "Compute initial volume"
c
c#START "Initialize design"
c      =========================
c      Set the initial densities and modes for the elements
c      =========================
c
       call optminit
c#END "Initialize design"
```

Figure 5: Annotated source code for optilin

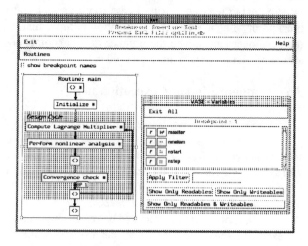

Figure 6: Defining breakpoint 1 with the breakpoint insertion tool

which is composed of two parts: a very small VASE application, *dtmTransfer*, repeatedly reads data from a VASE port and writes it into the Explorer system, and a small custom Explorer module reads data in the format written by dtmTransfer.

Figure 5 shows a portion of optilin's source code instrumented with VASE directives to denote logical blocks. A VASE utility is then run on the annotated source code to generate the control flow arcs.

Figure 6 shows the VASE Breakpoint Insertion Tool as the breakpoint is being inserted into optilin. A steering

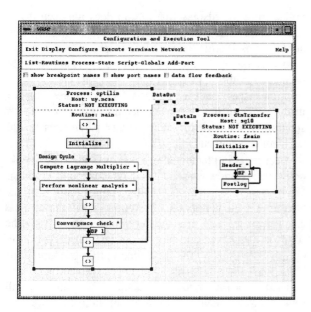

Figure 7: VASE configuration and execution tool

Figure 8: Breakpoint script creation

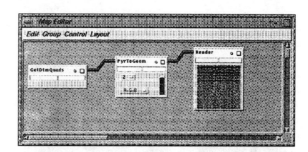

Figure 9: IRIS Explorer visualization map

breakpoint is inserted within the iterative part of the algorithm immediately after the point where the structure's shape is calculated. The window in the foreground allows the developer to select those variables that are to be accessible to scripts. By clicking on the "r" and "w" buttons, the developer can make variables readable and writable, read-only, or inaccessible.

After the breakpoint is inserted, another VASE utility generates the instrumented source file. This instrumented source file is then compiled and linked with the VASE libraries to create a VASE application.

Similar steps convert the dtmTransfer program into a VASE application.

Next, the VASE Configuration and Execution Tool is used to assign hosts, create VASE ports, define connections between ports, and create breakpoint scripts. Figure 7 shows an instance of this tool with some configurations already performed. An output port called *DataOut* has been added to optilin, and an input port called *DataIn* has been added to dtmTransfer. A data channel has been specified connecting *DataOut* to *DataIn* to allow data to flow from optilin to dtmTransfer. The data channel is indicated by a dashed line. This line will become solid when both applications begin executing and the channel is physically established.

Figure 8 shows another Configuration and Execution Tool window that displays the detailed state of optilin's breakpoint. The breakpoint script writes optilin's data to the output port *DataOut*.

Finally, the configured set can be executed. First, the Explorer system is started. Figure 9 shows the Explorer user interface with the data-flow map of modules used to achieve the desired data visualization. *GetDtmQuads* reads data from the dtmTransfer application.[1] The other modules are standard Explorer modules. *PyrToGeom* converts the format of data produced by *GetDtmQuads* and passes it to *Render*, which displays it.

The VASE applications are started. Optilin executes on a Cray YMP and dtmTransfer on the same Silicon Graphics IRIS workstation on which the Explorer system is running. Figure 10 shows the appearance of the Configuration and Execution Tool as the applications are executing. Notice the data channel line is now solid, which indicates that the data connection has been established. This line will change color as data is being transferred. Other feedback features include breakpoint symbols changing color and shape when they are active, and port symbols changing color when they

---

[1] dtmTransfer and GetDtmQuads communicate by means of a pre-arranged TCP/IP port.

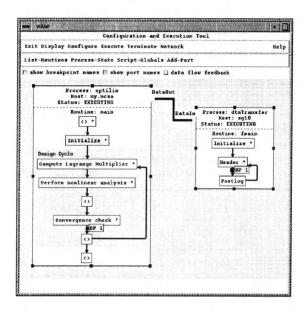

Figure 10: Execution of the set of applications

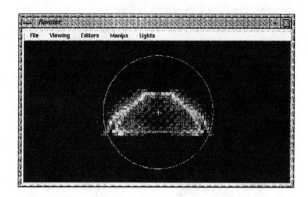

Figure 11: Rendered topology image from IRIS Explorer

[For color plate see page 932]

are being written to or read from. These features can be disabled if desired, usually for performance reasons.

The dtmTransfer breakpoint is configured in the *Execute Script* state, as is the breakpoint in optilin. In this mode, the script will execute when the breakpoint is encountered, after which the application will continue execution.

Optilin will run with no user intervention until either the user changes the state of the breakpoint or optilin's algorithm converges on a solution. Figure 11 shows one set of optilin's data being output by the Explorer Render module.

As optilin iterates, the data displayed by Explorer's Render module changes slightly as the algorithm attempts to converge on a solution. After several iterations we may

notice from the display that optilin does not seem to be converging. Rather, the display may suggest that the iterations are oscillating between two shapes. The desire then is to *steer* the application by making an adjustment to the optimality criterion method used to generate the candidate solution shapes. Such a condition does not represent a bug in the program but rather an incomplete *a priori* understanding of the necessary convergence parameters for the problem being considered.

Steering is implemented in two steps. First, the breakpoint state window is opened, and the breakpoint's mode is changed to *pause*. This causes the application to stop the next time it encounters the breakpoint. Then, the script is changed to set eta to a smaller value, such as 0.8. The script is then saved and sent to optilin, and execution of optilin is resumed. The next time optilin encounters its breakpoint, the new script, with its new value of eta will be used. For this particular example, the value 0.8 will cause the subsequent iterations of optilin to converge to a solution.

Modifying a parameter such as eta is the simplest form of steering. Based upon the application, considerably more complex steering is possible. For example, as optilin is used repeatedly to study various problems, our experience with it may lead us to a heuristic algorithm for modifying the convergence parameter eta dynamically. We can experiment with this algorithm by writing it as a breakpoint script that reads several program variables and computes a new value of eta each time the breakpoint is encountered.

5 Conclusions and future work

VASE is a powerful tool that provides interactive visualization and steering for scientific and engineering applications running in a distributed environment. Its capabilities complement those of commercial visualization packages.

VASE defines and constructs high-level abstract models for individual application codes and interconnected sets of codes. The internal structure of applications is described as a control-flow graph, whereas a data-flow model describes their interaction. Because VASE uses powerful syntactic and semantic analysis tools to construct its models, it does not require significant source code changes. Existing programs can be converted into VASE applications quickly and easily.

VASE version 1.0 is available by anonymous FTP from the host sp2.csrd.uiuc.edu in the directory CSRD_Software/Vase.

Our future plans for VASE include both some evolutionary changes that will enhance its capability to work with applications and some more-substantial restructuring. Two significant goals are an improved run-time user interface and the ability to use VASE on a broader range of parallel machines.

The existing scripting capability provides considerable flexibility for data selection and steering. However, it requires VASE users to write scripts in C, although their applications are written in Fortran. Although we intend to develop a Fortran-like interface, our long-term goal is to supplement the script interface with more powerful, higher-level facilities. For instance, to assist the user in the definition of complex data sets, we are considering the use of object-oriented data models[15]. Similarly, steering is currently accomplished by editing breakpoint scripts, but in many cases a direct-manipulation interface (e.g., using the mouse to manipulate controls such as sliders, or to graphically interact with elements of a visualization display to modify geometry or boundary data) would be considerably more convenient.

VASE is based upon the SPMD model of parallel execution. Steering breakpoints are inserted in serial sections of the program, where there is only one thread of control. This maps well to uniprocessors, vector processors, and shared-memory parallel processors that exploit parallelism at the loop level. However, the current VASE model of execution does not map well to more general MIMD systems.

Although VASE can coordinate the activities of a distributed set of processes, this approach becomes cumbersome for more than a small number of processors. In order to support larger systems, and those with message-passing rather than shared-memory architectures, the steerable program abstraction must be redefined. Often these architectures require applications to be recoded or restructured for good performance. In light of this need for the codes to be rewritten, it may be appropriate to revisit our decision to use a control-flow abstraction to model applications. Perhaps a dataflow model or hybrid model for individual applications would be more suitable for programs that use explicit message-passing to exchange data between processors. Corresponding changes in the interface provided by the Configuration and Execution Tool will be required so that the user is not overwhelmed with information about the code's structure.

Acknowledgement

This work was supported in part by the Air Force Office of Scientific Research under grant 90-0044.

References

[1] "Visualization in Scientific Computing," *Computer Graphics*, vol. 21, November 1987.

[2] R. L. Peskin, S. S. Walther, A. M. Froncioni, and T. I. Boubez, "Interactive Quantitative Visualization," *IBM Journal of Research and Development*, vol. 35, pp. 205–226, January/March 1991.

[3] D. Lau-Kee, A. Billyard, R. Faichney, Y. Kozato, P. Otto, M. Smith, and I. WIlkinson, "VPL: An Active, Declarative Visual Programming System," in *1991 IEEE Workshop on Visual Languages*, pp. 40–46, August 1991.

[4] J. Rasure and C. Williams, "An Integrated Data Flow Visual Language and Software Development Environment," *Journal of Visual Languages and Computing*, vol. 2, pp. 217–246, September 1991.

[5] C. Upson *et al.*, "The Application Visualization System: A Computational Environment for Scientific Visualization," *IEEE Computer Graphics and Applications*, vol. 9, pp. 30–42, July 1989.

[6] D. S. Dyer, "A Dataflow Toolkit for Visualization," *IEEE Computer Graphics and Applications*, vol. 10, pp. 60–69, July 1990.

[7] R. Haber, "Scientific Visualization and the RIVERS Project at the National Center for Supercomputing Applications," in *Scientific Visualization*, pp. 231–236, IEEE Computer Society Press, 1990.

[8] A. Tuchman, D. Jablonowski, and G. Cybenko, "Run-Time Visualization of Program Data," in *Proceedings of Visualization '91*, October 25 1991.

[9] R. Haber, B. Bliss, D. Jablonowski, and C. Jog, "A Distributed Environment for Run-Time Visualization and Application Steering in Computational Mechanics," *Computing Systems in Engineering*, vol. 3, pp. 501–515, December 1992.

[10] B. Bliss, "Interactive Steering Using the Application Executive," in *Proceedings of Supercomputing Debugging Workshop*, November 14–16, 1991.

[11] J. Terstriep, "DTM: Data Transfer Mechanism." User documentation, National Center for Supercomputing Applications, University of Illinois at Urbana-Champaign, December 1990.

[12] D. Gannon, J. K. Lee, B. Shei, S. Sarukkai, S. Narayana, N. Sundaresan, D. Attapatu, and F. Bodin, "Sigma II: A Tool Kit for Building Parallelizing Compilers and Performance Analysis Systems," in *Proceedings 1992, IFIP Edinburgh Workshop on Parallel Programming Environments*, April 1992. Also in *Programming Environments for Parallel Computing*, IFIP Transactions A-11, N. Topham, R. Ibbet, and T. Bemmerl, eds., North-Holland Press, pp. 17–36.

[13] C. S. Jog, R. B. Haber, and M. P. Bendsøe, "A Displacement-Based Formulation for Topology Design with Self-Adaptive Layered Materials," in *Topology Design of Structures* (M. P. Bendsøe and C. A. Mota Soares, eds.), Kluwer Academic Publishers, 1992.

[14] "Getting Started with IRIS Explorer™." Document No. 007-1372-010, Silicon Graphics, Inc. Mountain View, CA, December 1991.

[15] R. B. Haber, B. Lucas, and N. Collins, "A Data Model for Scientific Visualization with Provisions for Regular and Irregular Grids," in *Proceedings of Visualization '91*, pp. 298–305, 1991.

Volume Rendering of 3D Scalar and Vector Fields at LLNL

Roger Crawfis, Nelson Max, Barry Becker, Brian Cabral

Lawrence Livermore National Laboratory
P.O. Box 808
Livermore, CA 94551

Abstract

Simulation of complex 3-dimensional phenomena generate data sets which are hard to comprehend using conventional 2-dimensionally oriented visualization tools. One way to overcome this limitation is to employ various volume visualization techniques. While early volume visualization techniques worked well on simple scalar volumes they failed to exploit frame buffer hardware capabilities and handle higher order data such as vector fields. Work at Lawrence Livermore National Laboratory has centered on developing new techniques and extending existing techniques. This paper describes the various algorithms developed for volume rendering, and presents new methods of examining vector fields in a volumetric fashion.

Introduction

Computer simulations dealing with the atmosphere, the ocean, hydrodynamics, electro-magnetics, structural response, and environmental clean up, generate very large and complex data sets consisting of not only several scalar variables, but also vector and tensor quantities. Understanding an individual scalar field from a three-dimensional simulation is often difficult with current visualization tools. Understanding 3D vector fields and complex relationships is even more arduous. In order to understand the tens of gigabytes of data being generated from today's supercomputers, better visualization techniques and tools are needed. Better visualization tools are even more urgent as we progress to massively parallel architectures and larger more complex problems.

Volume rendering allows us to examine a substantial amount of a single 3D scalar field at a single time step. Research into visualizing 3D scalar fields has progressed over the past few years from iso-contour surfaces, to direct volume rendering of regularly gridded data, and then irregularly structured data, but all methods operate on a single scalar field. A minor amount of effort has been placed on understanding the interactions between several scalar fields. Even less effort has been directed towards understanding vector or tensor fields. Correcting these deficiencies has been the thrust of our research. This paper describes the various algorithms developed for volume rendering, and presents new methods of examining vector fields in a volumetric fashion.

Volume Rendering

The rendering of three-dimensional scalar fields has received much attention over the past several years. There are three common ways to visualize a scalar function in a volume (1) interactively move a color coded 2D slice through the volume [Nielson90], (2) draw contour surfaces [Lorensen87], or (3) integrate a continuos volume density along viewing rays [Max90]. The second method is a generalization of plotting contour lines in 2D. The other methods generalize the color coding of a 2D scalar field, although the 3D color field can only be viewed in either 2D slices or projections. The first two methods are generally termed *indirect* volume rendering, while the third method is termed *direct* volume rendering, or simply volume rendering. These terms imply the basic architecture of the techniques: indirect volume rendering converts the 3D field into geometric surface primitives which are then rendered to form an image, while direct volume rendering converts the field directly into the image. Henceforth, we will use the term volume rendering to refer strictly to direct volume rendering.

There has been much research on volume rendering algorithms over the past few years, leading to several competing algorithms. Four common approaches to volume rendering are (1) ray tracing, (2) analytical scan conversion, (3) hardware compositing, and (4) splatting. Various advantages/disadvantages exist with each of these algorithms. Many flavors of each of these algorithms also exist. We have implemented a version of each of these and extended them to

570

examine vector fields rather than or in addition to a single scalar field.

Before describing each of these algorithms and our extensions to them, some background information is useful. The basic premise of volume rendering is to simulate the absorption and scattering of light passing through a volume. There have been several computer graphics papers on the scattering, transmission, and shadowing of light propagating through clouds of particles. Kajiya and Von Herzen [Kajiya84], Rushmeier and Torrence [Rushmeier87], Blinn [Blinn82], and Max [Max86a] [Max86b] all suggest methods of correctly accounting for the shadowing, but the computation required is prohibitive. Instead, we chose to ignore the shadowing entirely, and only occlude the light on the way to the viewer, after a single scattering event. This leads to the following very simple illumination calculation. We model light as ambient illumination shining equally from all directions, and not shadowed along its path to any scattering particle. Under these assumptions, the result is the same as modeling glowing particles, as in the *density emitter* model of Sabella [Sabella88]. Sabella assumes that the volume density r(x,y,z) glows with an energy Cr per unit length, and absorbs with an optical density of tr per unit length, where C and t are constants for any fixed material.

Consider a ray, R(t) = (x(t),y(t),z(t)), leaving the eye and passing through the volume. Then the total optical density of the cloud along the ray from the eye to a point R(t) is $\int_0^t \tau\rho(u)du$, so light starting from P(t) is attenuated by the transparency factor $\exp(-\int_0^t \tau\rho(u)du)$ [Blinn82]. The length dt of the ray glows with energy Cr(t)dt, so the total glow energy reaching the eye is

$$I = \int_0^t C\rho(t)e^{-\int_0^t \tau\rho(u)du} \, dt. \tag{1}$$

These integrals can be calculated analytically when C, t, and r are constant or linearly interpolated within a volume cell [Max90], [Williams92].

Current graphics hardware does not offer assistance in calculate this integral directly. It does however offer assistance in compositing or *alpha-blending* two colors together and offers support for texture mapping (placing a decal or picture on an object). We strive to take full advantage of these capabilities where appropriate.

Ray Tracing Volume Densities

Ray tracing is one method for solving the single scattering illumination integral given above. This technique requires casting rays from a viewpoint through a volume for each pixel in the output image. Various sampling and illumination techniques are employed to approximate and extend equation (1) (see [Upson88], [Levoy89], or [Danskin92]). In our implementation we use two types of sampling along a ray: one in which the samples are evenly spaced and one where the samples occur only on the faces of the rectilinear data cells. In this latter cases the samples are unevenly spaced. This approach to volume rendering makes it easy to use very sophisticated lighting or shading models at an increased computational cost.

One approach to visualizing volumetric vector fields is to map the vector field onto a scalar field and then volume render the result. We [Cabral93] have developed an algorithm, known as Line Integral Convolution (LIC), which performs this mapping. The technique can be thought of as a data operator which filters a 3-dimensional input image as a function of a 3-dimensional vector field, producing an output 3-dimensional voxel image.

For each each cell centered voxel containing a vector, or *vectel,* a local parametrically defined streamline is computed using a variable step Euler's method. (Other streamline computation techniques could be used, such as Runge-Kutta. We chose the technique described in [Cabral93] for reasons of efficiency and simplicity). This parametric curve, *p(x,y,z,s),* is used to cut a 1-dimensional slice out of the input image, *F(x,y,z)*. The 1-dimensional slice can be thought of as a signal in the curve's parameter, *s*. This signal then filtered using a standard 1-dimensional convolution. The general form of this operator is given by the following integral equation:

$$F'(x,y,z) = \frac{\int\limits_{-L}^{L} F(p(x,y,z,s))k(s)ds}{\int\limits_{-L}^{L} k(s)ds} \qquad (2)$$

where $k(s)$ is the convolution kernel and $2*L$ is the length of the streamline. The denominator is a normalization term designed to keep the brightness of the output voxels in the range of the input voxels. The LIC integral, eq. (2), is performed once for every vectel, producing a scalar value for the corresponding output voxel.

If an isotropic, uncorrelated input image is used, such as white noise, the LIC operator can be thought of as correlating this noise image along local vector streamlines. This produces an image which on average is fairly homogeneous. Volume rendering this image without first weighting either the input or output image with another scalar field would result in only visualizing the outer surface of the volume. Figure 1 is a volumetric rendering of an electrostatic vector field consisting of two attractive charges. Here the input image is white noise weighted by the magnitude of the vector field. LIC is run on this input image and the resulting scalar volume is then rendered using the ray tracing approach described above.

Coherent Scan Conversion of Volume Densities

Max, Hanrahan and Crawfis [Max90] describe a technique for scan converting the back and front faces of an individual volume cell, and integrating the density of the rays passing through the front and back faces. The algorithm is exact for density fields which vary linearly. They also describe a general sorting algorithm for Delaunay triangulation, and discuss the intermixing of contour surfaces and the density clouds.

We have made several extensions to this algorithm, not documented in [Max90]. The contour surface can be color coded using a different scalar field than that used for the contouring. A list of data fields is processed for each vertex. One data field can specify the contouring, another the color of the density volume, and still another the opacity of the density volume. More general mappings can be used that take into account several data fields, the vertex positions, and information indicating which side of any contouring surfaces the vertex lies on.

We have extended this algorithm to allow for the contour surfaces to be covered with a three-dimensional texture. In particular, we applied a three-dimensional cloud texture to the contour surfaces of the percent cloudiness field resulting from a global climate simulation. We used the wind velocities to advect the texture coordinates given to this 3D texture, allowing the clouds to move with the wind where appropriate, and providing a sense of the wind blowing over the clouds in other areas. Figure 2 is a still from an HDTV animation done using this technique. The volumetric rendering was turned off for this image and an analytically computed atmospheric haze was added.

Hardware Projection and Compositing of Volume Densities

Shirley and Tuchman [Shirley90] describe an algorithm for dividing tetrahedral volume cells into up to four simpler tetrahedra. Each simple tetrahedron projects to a screen triangle with two vertices projecting to the same screen point A, and two faces perpendicular to the screen. Thus the thickness varies linearly from a maximum at A to zero at the opposite edges. Shirley and Tuchman compute the color and transparency at each vertex, and use the shading hardware inside the graphics rendering pipeline to interpolate these values at each pixel. Then they use the "alpha compositing" hardware to hide the background image behind the tetrahedron, according to the computed transparency, before adding in the new color.

Since these computations can all be done by the high speed hardware pipelines on modern workstations, they are quite fast. However, as we saw above, the correct transparency is an exponential function of the optical density, which is not linear. Thus, the density should be interpolated linearly across the triangle and then the exponential should be taken at every pixel. If instead, the transparency is computed only at the vertices, and then linearly interpolated across the triangles, visible artifacts will result.

It is not possible to compute an exponential per pixel inside current rendering pipelines, but an equivalent result can be achieved using texture mapping hardware. A 1D texture table is used, which is addressed by the optical density, and returns the transparency. The texture coordinate is then specified as the optical density at each vertex, and will be interpolated across the triangle by the shading hardware, before being used as a texture address. This gives an accurate transparency for every pixel, and eliminates the artifacts.

We use this algorithm for a new vector visualization technique which we call flow volumes [Max93b]. We have extended the concept of stream lines or flow ribbons to their volume equivalent. A seed polygon is placed into the flow field under user control. This polygon acts as a smoke generator. As the vector field passes through the polygon, smoke is propagated forward, sweeping out a volume (Figure 5) which is subdivided into tetrahedra. Compression and expansion of the volume due to the flow can be taken into account by adjusting the opacity based on the tetrahedron's volume. As the flow volume expands, we employ an adaptive mesh refinement technique to ensure the curvature of the resulting volume is accurate. The complex topology of the flow volume would require a general sorting method to yield a valid back-to-front sort. However, for this application, we can require that the smoke or dye be a constant color throughout the volume. It can then be shown [Max93b] that the resulting integration of the volume density is independent of the order the volume cells are processed. Thus, no sorting is required. Since we are only rendering the smoke, and not an entire volume, and using the hardware for the rendering, we have achieved real-time interaction. We have also added additional features that allow the user to watch moving puffs of smoke, control the time propagation of the smoke, and combine opaque geometry with the smoke. Figure 4 shows an aerogel simulation, where the tiny cubes are the zones containing the aerogel, and the blue smoke represents a flow through the aerogel.

Hardware Splatting of Volume Densities

Westover [Westover89] used an idea called splatting, where each voxel is treated as a single sampling point and a continuos 3D signal is reconstructed. The contribution of each voxel point to the volume density is then determined by its reconstruction kernel, and these are composited into the image independently in back-to-front order. Westover [Westover90] later used an accumulation buffer to reconstruct an entire sheet's contribution before it is composited into the image. Since the individual splats overlap, this avoids problems in the sorting, however, a much more noticeable change in the volume density occurs when the arrangement into sheets must change.

Laur and Hanrahan [Laur91] extended the splatting technique to handle hierarchical representations of the sampled data field. They also approximated the gaussian used in the reconstruction by a small polygonal mesh and utilized the graphics hardware to render the splat. This allowed for a quick coarse representation of the data that evolved into a more accurate representation adaptively. The Explorer product from SGI uses a variant of this technique without the adaptive refinement.

In reconstructing the 3D signal, a gaussian function is usually used. An unattractive property of this is its infinite extent. Every splat theoretically contributes to the entire volume density. Some finite extent is usually chosen and the splat is either abruptly cut-off or forced to zero. Max [Max92] uses an optimal quadratic function with a limited extent for the reconstruction of 2D signals. We [Crawfis93] have extended this for a cubic function for the reconstruction of 3D signals, which is optimal for all viewing angles. Using this function as a hardware texture map on a simple square splat gives a more accurate rendering of the volume density, and for large problems consisting of many small splats is actually faster than using the polygonal mesh of [Laur91]. We have added this to the Explorer system.

We [Crawfis92] developed a methodology for integrating a vector representation into the scalar splat. This algorithm however uses a sampling and reconstruction approach (which we called a filter) and does not make use of the graphics hardware. Figure 3. illustrates this technique for the wind field of a global climate simulation. We [Crawfis93] have now merged this concept with volume rendering via splatting by extending the texture splats above to include an anisotropic representation of the vector field. The splat is not only oriented perpendicular to the viewing direction, but also rotated to align the texture with the projected vector direction. A table of textures with different vector lengths is used to foreshorten the vector as its direction becomes parallel to the viewing direction. By using the appropriate controls of the texture mapping hardware, the volume density can be represented using one color scheme, and the vector field represented using another. Figure 6 shows the percent cloudiness field and the wind velocities for the global climate simulation. By cycling through a sequence of textures with changing displacements, we can make the textures move in the flow specified by the vector field.

Sorting

The scan conversion, hardware projection, and splatting methods of volume rendering all require a back to front sort of the volume cells. For rectangular lattices, the location of the viewpoint within the data volume (or of its projection onto a face or edge of the data volume) can easily be used to specify a sorting order. This sorting method extends recursively to octree or other rectilinear adaptive mesh refinements. For a more general mesh of convex data without holes, sorting can be done using a topological sort [Knuth73] [Max90] on a directed graph representing cell adjacency (with the direction of an edge specifying which of the two adjunct cells is in front). This sort may detect cycles, but it can be proved that cycles do not occur for Delaunay triangulations. [Edelsbrunner89], [Max90], or for the particular geometries which occur in our climate simulations [Max93a]. We are also working on a version of the Newell, Newell, and Sancha sort [Newell72] applied to volume cells instead of to polygons. This algorithm will split offending cells when cycles are detected. It also does not require the adjacency information, which may not be available in certain situations (for example, finite element simulations with sliding interfaces), and can deal with non convex volumes with holes. Williams [Williams91] also generalizes the directed graph method to non-convex data volumes, but his method is not guaranteed to be correct.

Conclusions

We have explored the use of volume rendering for scientific visualization and extended the algorithms for representing vector field data as well as scalar field data. The algorithms cover a wide gamut of techniques, from the very interactive flow volume generator for studying specific areas, to the ray-traced vector volumes and vector splatting techniques for representing global views of the vector field. These algorithms are a necessary step towards better visualization techniques for large data sets produced from complex three-dimensional simulations on supercomputers and massively parallel machines.

This paper has given a broad overview of our work. More details can be found in the references: [Max90], [Crawfis91], [Crawfis92], [Max92], [Cabral93], [Crawfis93], [Max93a], and [Max93b]. These papers also give other new material on the usage of volume rendering and our extensions to vector field rendering.

Future Work

Most of the extensions mentioned here are in their early development. Much work is still needed in applying them to various application data and making refinements. In particular, the proper choice of textures for the textured isocontour and the vector splatting techniques is an open area of research. Better subdivision and splitting algorithms are needed for the flow volume algorithm. We have also developed the basic framework for multivariate representations, but have only tried it out for very simple mappings. More complex mappings (presumably application specific) need to be studied, and a more efficient and flexible framework put into place.

Acknowledgments

The authors are indebted to the many people who provided the data used in the visualization in this paper. Tony Ladd and Elaine Chandler provided the aerogel data. The climate data is courtesy of Jerry Potter, the Program for Climate Model Diagnosis and Intercomparison at Livermore, and the European Centre for Medium-range Weather Forecasts. The authors would like to thank Chuck Grant for many helpful comments. This work was performed under the auspices of the US Department of Energy by Lawrence Livermore National Laboratory under contract number W-7405-ENG-48, with specific support from an internal (LDRD) research grant.

References

[Blinn82] Blinn, James, Light Reflection Functions for Simulation of Clouds and Dusty Surfaces. Computer Graphics Vol. 16 No. 3 (Siggraph '82) pp. 21-29.

[Cabral93] Cabral, Brian and Casey Leedom, *Imaging Vector Fields Using Line Integral Convolution,*

[Crawfis91] Crawfis, Roger and Michael Allison. *A Scientific Visualization Synthesizer.* In *Proceedings Visualization '91.* Gregory Nielson and Larry Rosenblum eds., IEEE Los Alamitos, CA, pp. 262–267.

[Crawfis92] Crawfis, Roger and Nelson Max, *Direct Volume Visualization of Three-Dimensional Vector Fields.* Proceedings of the 1992 Workshop on Volume Visualization (October 1992), ACM SIGGRAPH New York. pp. 55-60.

[Crawfis93] Crawfis, Roger and Nelson Max, *Texture Splats for 3D Vector and Scalar Field Visualization.* In Proceedings Visualization '93 (October 1993), IEEE Los Alamitos, CA, pp. 261-266

[Danskin92] Danskin, John and Pat Hanrahan, *Fast Algorithms for Volume Ray Tracing.* Proceedings of the 1992 Workshop on Volume Visualization (October 1992), ACM SIGGRAPH New York. pp. 91-98.

[Edelsbrunner89] Edelsbrunner, Herbert *An Acyclicity Theorem in Cell Complexes in d Dimensions.* Proceedings of the ACM Symposium on Computational Geometry (1989) pp. 145-151.

[Kajiya84] Kajiya, James T. and Brain P. Von Herzen,. *Ray Tracing Volume Densities..* Computer Graphics Vol. 18 No. 3 (SIGGRAPH '84) pp. 165174.

[Knuth73] Knuth, Donald E. *The Art of Computer Programming Volume 1: Fundamental Algorithms.* 2nd Edition. Addison-Wesley Reading, MA (1973).

[Laur91] Laur, David and Pat Hanrahan, *Hierarchical Splatting: A Progressive Refinement Algorithm for Volume Rendering.* Computer Graphics Vol. 25 No. 4 (July 1991, SIGGRAPH '91) pp. 285–288.

[Levoy89] Levoy, Marc. *Design for a Real-Time High-Quality Volume Rendering Workstation.* In *Proceedings of the Chapel Hill Workshop on Volume Visualization,* pp. 85-92.

[Loreensen87] Lorensen, William E. and Harvey E. Cline, A High Resolution 3D Surface Construction Algorithm. Computer Graphics Vol. 21 No. 4 (SIGGRAPH '87) pp. 163-169.

[Max86a] Max, Nelson, *Light Diffusion through Clouds and Haze.* Computer Vision, Graphics, and Image Processing Vol. 33 (March 1986) pp. 280-292.

[Max86b] Max, Nelson, *Atmospheric Illumination and Shadows.* Computer Graphics Vol. 20 No. 4 (Siggraph '86) pp. 117-124.

[Max90] Max, Nelson, Pat Hanrahan, and Roger Crawfis, *Area and Volume Coherence for Efficient Visualization of 3D Scalar Functions.* Computer Graphics Vol. 24 No. 5 (November 1990, Special issue on San Diego Workshop on Volume Visualization) pp. 27–33.

[Max92] Max, Nelson, Roger Crawfis, and Dean Williams, *Visualizing Wind Velocities by Advecting Cloud Textures.* Proceedings Visualization '92, IEEE Los Alamitos, CA. pp. 179-184.

[Max93a] Max, Nelson, Barry Becker, and Roger Crawfis, *Volume and Vector Field Visualization for Climate Modelling.* IEEE Computer Graphics and Applications, (July 1993) pp. 34-40.

[Max93b] Max, Nelson, Barry Becker, and Roger Crawfis, *Flow Volumes for Interactive Vector Field Visualization.* In Proceedings Visualization '93 (October 1993), IEEE Los Alamitos, CA, pp. 19-24.

[Newell72] Newell, M. E., R. G. Newell, and T. L. Sancha, *A solution to the Hidden Surface Problem.* Proceedings of the ACM National Conference 1972, pp. 443-450.

[Nielson90] Nielson, G. and B. Hamann, *Techniques for the Interactive Visualization of Volumetric Data.* In *Proceedings Visualization '90,* IEEE Los ALamitos, CA pp. 45-60.

[Rushmeier87] Rushmeier, Holly E. and Kenneth E. Torrance *The Zonal Method for Calculating Light Intensities in the Presence of a Participating Medium* Computer Graphics Vol. 21 No. 4 (SIGGRAPH '87) pp. 293302.

[Sabella88] Sabella, Paolo. *A Rendering Algorithm for Visualizing 3D Scalar Fields.* Computer Graphics Vol. 22 No. 4 (SIGGRAPH '88) pp. 51–58.

[Shirley90] Shirley, Peter, and Allan Tuchman, *A Polygonal Approximation to Direct Scalar Volume Rendering.* Computer Graphics Vol. 24 No. 5 (November 1990, Special issue on San Diego Workshop on Volume Visualization) pp. 63–70.

[Upson88] Upson, Craig and Michael Keeler, *VBUFFER: Visibile Volume Rendering,* Computer Graphics Vol. 22 No. 4 (July 1988, SIGGRAPH '88) pp. 59-64.

[Westover89] Westover, Lee. *Interactive Volume Rendering.* In Proceedings of the Chapel Hill Workshop on Volume Visualization, May 1989, pp. 9–16.

[Westover90] Westover, Lee. *Footprint Evaluation for Volume Rendering.* Computer Graphics Vol. 24 No. 4 (SIGGRAPH '90) pp. 367–376.

[Williams91] Williams, Peter L., *Visibility Ordering Meshed Polyhedra* ACM Transactions on Graphics Vol. 11 No. 2 (April 1992) pp. 103-126.

[Williams92] Williams, Peter, and Nelson Max, *A Volume Density Optical Model.* Proceedings of the 1992 Workshop on Volume Visualization, ACM, New York, pp. 61-68.

[For color plate see page 931]

Figure 1: Electrostatic field consisting of two charges, volumetrically ray traced using the vector to scalar converter.

Figure 2: The percent cloudiness field rendered using wind velocities to advect the texture coordinates given to this 3D texture.

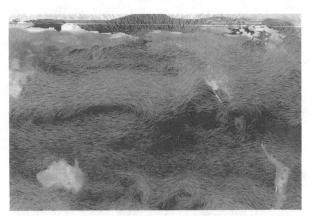

Figure 3: The vector filter algorithm applied to the wind field. Upper winds are in red, surface winds are in cyan.

Figure 4: A flow volume weaving through an aerogel substance.

Figure 5: The flow volume algorithm applied to the global climate data set.

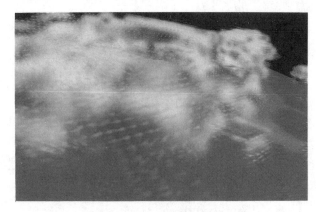

Figure 6: The clouds and wind fields rendered using the textured splats algorithm.

Session 8:
Run-Time Support for Parallelism
Chair: Doreen Cheng

Compiler and Runtime Support for Structured and Block Structured Applications [1]

Gagan Agrawal   Alan Sussman   Joel Saltz

Dept. of Computer Science
University of Maryland
College Park, MD 20742
{gagan, als, saltz}@cs.umd.edu

Abstract

Scientific and engineering applications often involve structured meshes. These meshes may be nested (for multigrid or adaptive codes) and/or irregularly coupled (called Irregularly Coupled Regular Meshes). We have designed and implemented a runtime library for parallelizing this general class of applications on distributed memory parallel machines in an efficient and machine independent manner. In this paper we present how this runtime library can be integrated with compilers for High Performance Fortran (HPF) style parallel programming languages. We discuss how we have integrated this runtime library with the Fortran 90D compiler being developed at Syracuse University and provide experimental data on a block structured Navier-Stokes solver template and a small multigrid example parallelized using this compiler and run on an Intel iPSC/860. We show that the compiler parallelized code performs within 20% of the code parallelized by inserting calls to the runtime library manually.

1 Introduction

In recent years, distributed memory parallel machines have been widely recognized as the most likely means of achieving scalable high performance computing. However, there are two major reasons for their lack of popularity among the developers of scientific and engineering applications. First, it is very difficult to parallelize application programs on these machines. Second, it is not easy to get good speed-ups and efficiency on communication intensive applications. Current distributed memory machines have good communication bandwidths, but they also have high startup latencies that often result in high communication overheads.

Recently there have been major efforts in developing programming language and compiler support for distributed memory machines. Based on the initial work of projects like Fortran D [9, 13] and Vienna Fortran [5], the High Performance Fortran Forum has recently proposed the first version of High Performance Fortran (HPF) [8]. HPF allows programmer to specify the layout of distributed data and specify parallelism through operations on array sections and through parallel loops. Proposed HPF compilers are being designed to produce Single Program Multiple Data (SPMD) Fortran 77 (F77) code with message passing and/or runtime communication primitives. HPF offers the promise of significantly easing the task of programming

distributed memory machines and making programs independent of a single machine architecture.

It is recognized that reducing communication costs is crucial in achieving good performance on applications [12]. While current systems like the Fortran D project [13] and the Vienna Fortran Compilation system [5] have implemented a number of optimizations for reducing communication costs (like message blocking, collective communication, message coalescing and aggregation), these optimizations have been developed only in the context of regular problems (i.e. in code having only regular data access patterns). Special effort is required in developing compiler and runtime support for applications that do not necessarily have regular data access patterns. Our group has already developed compiler embedded runtime support for completely irregular computations [10].

One class of scientific and engineering applications involves structured meshes. These meshes may be nested (as in multigrid or adaptive codes) or may be irregularly coupled (called Irregularly Coupled Regular Meshes) [6, 7]. Multigrid codes typically have a number of meshes at different levels of resolution, so may require array section moves with non-unit strides. Multigrid codes are often used in computational fluid dynamics applications. Examples of Irregularly Coupled Regular Mesh (ICRM) problems include multiblock Navier-Stokes solvers and structured adaptive multigrid problems. These problems have the following characteristics:

- The data is divided into several interacting regions (called blocks or subdomains).

- There exists a computational phase during which computation in each block can be carried out independently.

- Data access patterns within each block are regular.

- Communication between subdomains is restricted to regular array sections (possibly including non-unit strides).

Block structured grids are frequently used in computational fluid dynamics to model geometrically complex objects that cannot be easily modeled using a single regular mesh. In Figure 1, we show how the area around a wing has been modeled with a block structured grid. Block structured grids are used in applications such as turbulence, combustion, global climate modeling and device simulation [2, 3, 14, 16, 17].

We have developed a set of runtime primitives for parallelizing these applications on distributed memory machines

[1]This work was supported by ARPA under contract No. NAG-1-1485, by NSF under grant No. ASC 9213821 and by ONR under contract No. SC 292-1-22913. The authors assume all responsibility for the contents of the paper.

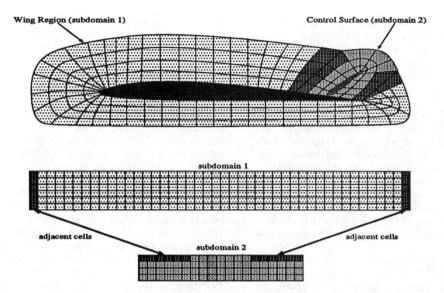

Figure 1: Block structured grid around a wing, showing an interface between blocks

in an efficient, convenient and machine independent manner. These routines are collectively called the multiblock Parti library [6]. These primitives allow a user to

- Lay out distributed data in a flexible way, to enable good load balancing and minimize interprocessor communication,

- Give high level directions for performing data movement, and

- Distribute the computation across the processors using the owner computes rule.

The primitives have been designed so that communication overheads are significantly reduced (by using message aggregation). These primitives provide a machine-independent interface to the compiler writer and applications programmer. We view these primitives as forming a portion of a portable, compiler independent, runtime support library.

In this paper we address the problem of integrating this runtime support into compilers for HPF style parallel programming languages. We discuss the additional functionality required in the current version of HPF to facilitate proper data layout for these applications. We discuss how the compiler can identify the data access patterns that can be efficiently handled using the runtime support for block structured problems. We also discuss the compiler transformations required for automatically generating the calls to these primitives.

We have implemented these compiler transformations in the Fortran 90D (F90D) compiler being developed at Syracuse University [4]. We have parallelized a representative part, which we call a *template*, of a three dimensional Navier-Stokes solver using this compiler. We present experimental data for this compiler parallelized application run on an Intel iPSC/860 and compare it with that of a hand parallelized (i.e. parallelized by inserting calls to the runtime library by hand) version. We have also experimented with a multigrid template that involves regular section moves with strides. We find that the compiler

parallelized code always performs within about 20% of the hand parallelized code. We discuss the optimizations that we have used to achieve this performance. We also discuss other possible optimizations and their impact on the performance of the compiler parallelized code.

Several other researchers have also developed runtime libraries or programming environments for block structured applications. Baden [14] has developed a Lattice Programming Model (LPAR). This system, however, achieves only coarse grained parallelism since a single block can only be assigned to one processor. Quinlan [15] has developed P++, a set of C++ libraries for grid applications. While these provide a convenient interface, the libraries do not optimize communication overheads.

The rest of this paper is organized as follows. In Section 2, we introduce the runtime library that we have developed. In Section 3, we discuss how the compiler recognizes the data access patterns that can be handled using the runtime primitives that we have developed. In this section we also discuss the compiler transformations for automatically inserting the calls to the runtime library routines. In Section 4, we present experimental results on the performance of a compiler parallelized multiblock Navier-Stokes solver template and a multigrid template run on an Intel iPSC/860. We conclude in Section 5.

2 Multiblock Parti Primitives

In this section we describe the details of the runtime support library that we have designed for parallelizing block structured codes on distributed memory machines. We first discuss the nature of computation and communication in block structured applications and then describe the primitives to facilitate parallelization of these applications.

In typical block structured problems there are at most a few dozen blocks of varying sizes. We therefore assume that we will have to assign at least some of the blocks to multiple processors, so that there are two levels of parallelism available. Coarse-grain parallelism is available for processing the blocks concurrently. Associated with each block is a self-contained computation that can, except for boundary conditions, be operated upon independently of the other blocks. In addition, the computation for individual blocks has fine-grain parallelism available. Applying coarse-grain parallelism will help to keep communication overhead to a manageable fraction of the computation time.

For a typical block structured application, the main body of the program consists of an outer sequential (time step) loop, and an inner parallel loop. The inner loop iterates over the blocks of the problem, after applying boundary conditions to all the blocks (including updating interfaces between blocks). Applying the boundary conditions involves interaction (communication) between the blocks. In the inner loop over the blocks, the computation in each block involves only intra-block regular communication. Partitioning of the parallel loop is the source of the coarse-grained parallelism for the application. Furthermore, within each iteration of the inner loop there is fine-grained parallelism available in the form of (large) parallel loops.

Several forms of run-time support are required for block structured applications. First, there must be a means for expressing data layout and organization on the processors of the distributed memory parallel machine. Second, there must be methods for specifying the movement of data required both because of partitioning of individual meshes (intra-block parallelism) and because of interactions between different meshes (inter-block parallelism). Third, there must be some way of transforming distributed array indexes specified in global coordinates (as in sequential code) into local indexes on a given processor in the distributed memory parallel machine.

The binding of blocks to processors has important performance implications, both in terms of reducing communication overheads and achieving load balance. In irregularly coupled regular mesh applications, there are computational phases that involve interactions only within each block. Therefore, communication overheads are reduced if each block is not divided across a large number of processors. Since the amount of computation associated with each block is directly proportional to the number of elements in the block, good load balancing is achieved by binding processors to blocks in a ratio proportional to their sizes. Therefore, the blocks are distributed onto disjoint subsets of processor space. The relative sizes of these processor spaces are determined by the relative number of grid points in each block.

Since, in a typical block structured application, the number of blocks and their respective sizes is not known until runtime, the distribution of blocks onto processors is done at runtime. The distributed array descriptors (DAD) [4] for the arrays representing these blocks are, therefore, generated at the runtime. Distributed array descriptors contain information about the portions of the arrays residing on each processor, and are used at runtime for performing communication and distributing loops iterations. We will not discuss the details of the primitives that allow the user to specify data distribution. For more details, see [18].

Two types of communication are required in block structured applications: intra-block communication because a single block may be partitioned across the processors of the distributed memory parallel machine, and inter-block communication because of boundary conditions between blocks, caused by the assignment of blocks to different processors to obtain coarse-grained parallelism. The data access pattern in the computation within a block is regular. This im-

plies that the interaction between grid points is restricted to nearby neighbors. Such communication is handled by allocation of extra space at the beginning and end of each array dimension on each processor. These extra elements are called *overlap*, or *ghost*, cells [5]. Depending upon the data access pattern in a loop, the necessary data is copied from other processors and is stored in the overlap cells.

The communication is performed in two phases. First, a subroutine is called to build a communication *schedule* that describes the required data motion, and then another subroutine is called to perform the data motion (sends and receives on a distributed memory parallel machine) using a previously built schedule. Such an arrangement allows a schedule to be be used multiple times in an iterative algorithm. This amortizes the cost of building schedules, so that the preprocessing time should not be a significant part of the execution time of this type of program.

The communication primitives include a procedure *Overlap_Cell_Fill_Sched*, which computes a schedule that is used to direct the filling of overlap cells along a given dimension of a distributed array. *Overlap_Cell_Fill_Sched* executes on each processor that contains a part of the distributed array, and, for a given processor i, determines both which other processors require data that is stored on processor i and which other processors store data that processor i requires.

The primitive *Regular_Section_Copy_Sched* carries out the preprocessing required to copy the contents of a regular section [11], *source*, in one block into a regular section, *destination*, in another (or the same) block. The interactions between blocks for block structured applications are limited to the exchange of regular sections. The *Regular_Section_Copy_Sched* primitive supports data moves between arbitrary rectangular sections of two blocks, and can transpose the data along any dimension. For a given processor, *Regular_Section_Copy_Sched* produces a schedule that specifies a a set of send and receive calls for interprocessor communication along with a pattern of intra-processor data transfers (for the parts of the source and destination subsections that reside on the same processor).

The schedules produced by *Overlap_Cell_Fill_Sched* and *Regular_Section_Copy_Sched* are employed by a primitive called *Data_Move* that carries out both interprocessor communication (sends and receives) and intra-processor data copying.

The final form of support provided by the multiblock Parti library is to transform all indexes into distributed arrays from the global value (an index into the whole distributed array) to a local index on the processor executing a distributed array reference. Two primitives, *Local_Lower_Bnd* and *Local_Upper_Bound*, are provided for transforming loop bounds (returning, respectively, the lower and upper indexes of a given dimension of the referenced distributed array). In general, however, each distributed array reference (read or write) must have the array index transformed from a global to a local reference for correct parallel execution.

3 Compiler Support

In this section we first discuss the additional functionality required in the current version of HPF to support block structured applications. We describe how a compiler can analyze the data access patterns associated with a loop, to recognize communication patterns that can be handled using the runtime primitives for block structured problems.

We then describe the compiler transformations for generating the calls to these runtime primitives. We also briefly discuss how loop iterations are distributed to achieve parallelism.

We have implemented the transformations in the Fortran 90D compiler being developed at Syracuse University. In the current version of this compiler, parallelism can be expressed through single statement *forall* loops and Fortran 90 array expressions. The current version of HPF also allows multiple statement *forall* loops and do loops with no loop carried dependencies (via the independent statement) to express parallelism. Although we are restricted to single statement *forall* loops in the Fortran source code, there is still sufficient expressiveness to exploit parallelism in application codes.

3.1 Language Support

The current version of HPF does not support all the functionality required for block structured applications. In block structured problems, the problem geometry is divided into a number of blocks of different sizes. As we have discussed in the previous section, each of these blocks needs to be distributed onto a portion of the processor space. The current version of the HPF does not provide any convenient mechanism for distributing arrays (or templates) onto a part of the processor space. We allow the programmers to create *subspaces* of the processor space. Arrays or templates can then be mapped onto any processor subspace. We will not discuss the details of the syntax that our experimental compiler uses for declaring processor subspaces.

With the block distributions supported in the current version of HPF, the entire array gets distributed uniformly across the processors of the distributed memory parallel machine. This may not be ideal for load balancing for many applications. While the programmer may declare a large array, not all the elements of the array may be actual mesh points participating in computation. Some of the array elements at both ends of each dimension may be used for participating in exchanges between blocks. We refer to such array elements as *external ghost cells*. For example, the actual declared arrays for a given block may be $52 \times 12 \times 12$, with two external ghost cells at the beginning and end of each dimension. This means that the actual mesh representing the computation is of size $48 \times 8 \times 8$. It is these mesh points that must be distributed evenly across the processors onto which the block is distributed, so that the computation load will be evenly balanced. The external ghost cells at both ends of each dimension are then stored at the first and last processor along that dimension in the processor space. For example, if an array with 8 elements, plus two external ghost cells on each end (for a total of 12 elements), is distributed on 4 processors, we would like to store 2 mesh points on each processor along that dimension. The first and last processors can then store the external ghost cells at the beginning and end, respectively. This results in a much better load balance than simply distributing 3 array elements onto each processor (which will result in the first and last processors having only 1 real mesh point and the intermediate processors having 3 real mesh points each).

The current version of HPF does not provide any mechanism for specifying external ghost cells. We need additional functionality in the align statement to express them. We do this by explicitly specifying the number of external ghost cells at the beginning and end of each dimension:

!HPF\$ DIMENSION A(105,105)
!HPF\$ ALIGN A(i,j) WITH T(i:2:3,j:2:3)

This example says that an array of size 105x105 is aligned with a template of size 100x100, with 2 external ghost cells at the beginning of each dimension and 3 external ghost cells at the end of each dimension. If the template T is distributed by blocks onto a two dimensional processor space, A(3:102,3:102) also gets distributed in the same fashion. Our purpose here is not to introduce new syntax but to achieve the additional functionality that we need. We believe that this functionality will be added, in some form, in a future version of HPF.

3.2 Identifying Communication Patterns

In this subsection we discuss how the compiler identifies the communication patterns that can be handled using the runtime support for block structured problems. While we have designed the runtime support with block structured applications in mind, the runtime primitives can also be used to efficiently handle communication for many other types of applications. Our purpose is not to provide a general framework for compiling *forall* statements; we are only interested in recognizing the patterns that can be handled efficiently using the primitives we have developed.

We do not consider applications in which indirection arrays may need to be analyzed to identify communication patterns. The irregular communication arising from use of indirection arrays can be handled using the Parti primitives for irregular problems, which have also been integrated with compilers for HPF-style languages (including the Rice University Fortran 77D compiler [10] and the Syracuse University Fortran 90D compiler [4]). F90D and HPF also provide a number of intrinsic functions (such as reduction, spread, etc.). We assume that if a computation can be done using these intrinsics, it is either written this way by the programmer or is recognized by the compiler in an early phase of the compilation.

We restrict our discussion to the problem of analyzing a single statement *forall* loop for communication patterns. F90D also provides array expressions for expressing parallelism, but these array expressions can always be translated into equivalent *forall* loops.

We classify the data access patterns associated with a *forall* loop as being one of three kinds:

- Completely regular ones (not involving any communication).

- Ones that can be handled by filling in overlap cells.

- Ones that require regular section moves.

Consider any *forall* statement with array expressions involving an array A on the left hand side and an array B as one of the arrays on the right hand side. The form of the *forall* statement is assumed to be as follows:

$$\text{forall } (i_1 = lo_1 : hi_1 : st_1, \ldots, i_m = lo_m : hi_m : st_m)$$
$$A(f_1, \ldots, f_j) = \cdots B(g_1, \ldots, g_n) \cdots$$

The i_k, $(k = 1..m)$ are the loop variables associated with the *forall* statement. lo_k, hi_k and st_k are respectively the lower bound, upper bound and the stride for each loop variable. For the left hand side array A, $f_1, f_2, .., f_j$ are the subscripts. Similarly, for the right hand side array B, $g_1, g_2, .., g_n$ are the subscripts. The array subscripts f and g are either loop invariant scalars or a a linear function of some loop variable. The form of the subscript is:

$$f_k = c1_k i1_k + d1_k$$

$$g_k = c2_k i2_k + d2_k$$

Here, $i1_k$ and $i2_k$ are loop variables. If a subscript is a loop invariant scalar, then we say that the loop variable $i1_k$ (or, $i2_k$), is ϕ and $c1_k$ (or, $c2_k$) is 0. $c1_k$, $c2_k$, $d1_k$ and $d2_k$ may be expressions, but they must not involve any loop variable. Our primitives are not applicable for cases in which multiple loop variables are associated with a particular array subscript or when the same loop variable appears in more than one subscript for a particular array or when a subscript is a higher order function of a loop variable. Such cases are handled by the current Fortran 90D compiler using the Parti primitives for irregular problems. Also, the HPF specification allows the lower bound, upper bound and stride expressions for each loop variable to be evaluated in any order. Consequently, the lower bound, upper bound and stride for any loop variable are not allowed to be a function of any other loop variable. It is possible, in general, that a loop variable may appear only on the right hand side array or only in the left hand side array. If a particular loop variable appears only in the right hand side, this represents successive overwrites on the same memory location of the left hand side array. Such code is not likely to appear in practice and therefore, we do not consider this case. If a particular loop variable appears only in the left hand side array, this represents a spread operation. We assume that it is written using the intrinsic spread operation, and is not a part of the *forall*.

Depending upon how the arrays A and B are distributed and aligned with respect to each other, we consider three different cases. These are:

Case I: Arrays A and B are aligned to different templates.

Case II: Arrays A and B are identically aligned to the same template. This case also requires that A and B are arrays of identical shape and size, i.e. having the same number of dimensions and the same size in each dimension.

Case III: Arrays A and B are aligned to the same template, but with a different stride, offset and/or index permutation. This means that the the arrays A and B are mapped to the same processor subspace, but each in a different manner.

In this paper, we restrict to discussing the details of cases I and II only. Case III is a generalization of case II; details of the analysis for this case are presented in [1].

3.2.1 Case I

Since the arrays are aligned to distinct templates, the communication is always handled using the regular section move primitive from the runtime library. We expect that if

a user has declared distinct templates then they are either distributed over different processor subspaces, or have a different number of distributed dimensions. Therefore, there is no regularity in the communication associated with a *forall* statement containing references to such arrays.

It is possible that a programmer may create more than one template with the same number of distributed dimensions, distributed over the same processor subspace. We can extend our analysis to consider the processor subspace over which distinct templates are distributed in determining any regularity in the communication required. However, we do not discuss this possibility here.

3.2.2 Case II

The data access patterns associated with this case may be completely regular, or may require overlap cells to filled in, or may require a regular section move.

Let $DD(A)$ denote the set of dimensions of the array A that are distributed. Under the assumptions for Case II, $DD(B) = DD(A)$. In terms of the form of the *forall* statement and the array subscripts that presented in Section 3.2, the condition for the associated communication to require a regular section move is :
$$\exists j \in DD(A) \text{ s.t.}$$

1. $i1_j \neq i2_j$, or,

2. $c1_j \neq c2_j$, or,

3. $d1_j \neq d2_j$ and either $d1_j$ or $d2_j$ is not a compile time constant, **or,**

4. $i1_j = \phi$, $i2_j = \phi$ and $d1_j \neq d2_j$.

The first condition states that there is index permutation. In that case, a regular section move will be required. The second condition states that, along the jth dimension, the elements of the arrays A and B are being accessed with different strides. Again, this case will require a regular section move. The third condition corresponds to the fact that there are non-constant offsets. If there are constant offsets, then only the overlap cells need to be filled in. For overlap cells, space needs to be allocated at compile time, so the number of overlap cells must be known at compile time. If the offsets are not compile time constants, then we use a regular section move to handle communication. This situation can also be handled by shifts into a temporary array [4]. The fourth condition says that along dimension j a loop variable does not appear in either the left hand side or the right hand side index and the loop invariant scalars are different. This represents a copy from one location to another, but because of the loop variables associated with other dimensions, will typically require a regular section of data to be moved. Since the distributed array descriptor is not available at compile-time, it cannot be determined at compile time whether this data move will require any interprocessor communication. So we handle this kind of data move using the regular section move primitives we have already discussed.

The data access pattern requires filling in overlap cells, if the following condition holds:

1. A regular section move is not required **and**

2. $\exists j \in DD(A)$ s.t. $d1_j \neq d2_j$.

Arrays A and B are aligned identically

L.H.S. Expr.	R.H.S. Expr.	Reg. Sec. Move Req.	Overlap Fill Req.
A(i,j)	B(j+2,i+1)	YES	NO
A(i,j)	B(2*i,j)	YES	NO
A(i,j)	B(i+n1,j+2)	YES	NO
A(i,j)	B(i+1,j+2)	NO	YES
A(i,j)	B(i,j)	NO	NO

Figure 2: Analyzing communication for Case II

The first condition just states that we have not already determined that a regular section move is required. The second condition states that there is a difference in the offsets along some (distributed) dimension. Overlap cells must be filled along each dimension in which there is a difference in the offsets. In Figure 2 we show examples for the different possibilities within case II, for identically aligned two dimensional arrays A and B.

3.3 Generating calls to the runtime library

Once the nature of the communication required has been identified, the compiler must insert the appropriate calls to the runtime primitives. We identify each distributed dimension j of the array B for which $d1_j \neq d2_j$. One call to the schedule building primitive $Overlap\_Cell\_Fill\_Sched$ and one to the data moving primitive $Data\_Move$ is inserted for each such dimension. Since all computations are distributed using the owner computes rule, overlap cells are filled in for the right hand side array B.

If there is more than one array on the right hand side, then the analysis described in Section 3.2 is done for each such array. For each of the right hand side arrays that requires a regular section move, a temporary array is declared and a regular section move is done from the right hand side array into the temporary array. If there is only one array on the right side (i.e. the forall loop represents only a copy and does not have any computation), then the regular section move is performed directly from the right hand side array to the left hand side array.

3.4 Distributing loop iterations

Once the calls have been inserted for communicating the required array elements, the loop iterations must be distributed among the processors (i.e. the loop bounds need to adjusted to compute on data local to a processor). As we stated earlier, this is done by using the owner computes rule. Since the distributed array descriptors are built at runtime, it is not possible to compute the local loop bounds on each processor at compile time.

We partition the loop based upon the portion of the distributed arrays that are owned by a given processor. This is done by inserting runtime calls to the the library primitives $Local\_Lower\_Bound$ and $Local\_Upper\_Bound$. For arrays that are not in canonical form, we can still partition the loop based upon the owners compute rule. Consequently, we never need to scatter any data after the loop has been executed.

```
C      ORIGINAL F90D CODE
C      Arrays A, B and C are distributed identically
          FORALL (i = 1:100,j = 1:100)
        .  A(i,j) = B(i+1,j) + C(i,j)

C      TRANSFORMED CODE
       Dim   =    1
       No_Of_Cells = 1
       sched =      Overlap_Cell_Fill_Sched(DAD,
                    Dim,No_Of_Cells)
C      DAD is dist. array desc. for A, B and C
C      i is dimension 1, j is dimension 2
       Call    Data_Move(B,sched,B)
       L1    =    Local_Lower_Bound(DAD,1)
       L2    =    Local_Lower_Bound(DAD,2)
       H1    =    Local_Upper_Bound(DAD,1)
       H2    =    Local_Upper_Bound(DAD,2)
       do 10 i = L1,H1
       do 10 j = L2, H2
10     A(i,j) =      B(i+1,j) + C(i,j)
```

Figure 3: Overlap cell fill and loop bounds adjustment

In Figure 3 we show an example of how the calls to primitives for filling in overlap cells are inserted by the compiler. In Figure 4, we show how the compiler inserts calls to the primitives for moving regular sections. In both examples, the transformed code containing the calls to the runtime library will run as SPMD code on each processor of the distributed memory parallel machine. In the compiler generated code schedule building primitives will be called every time any forall loop requiring communication is executed. The hand coded version can build a schedule once and reuse it in subsequent iterations. Similarly, in the compiler generated code, runtime calls to the loop bound adjustment primitives will be made each time a loop is executed. The hand coded version can reuse the adjusted bounds over the multiple time steps, and also for multiple loops that have the same loop bounds. These two factors may cause the compiler generated code to perform worse than the hand parallelized code.

4 Experimental Results

In this section we present the experimental results we have obtained on the performance of a compiler parallelized an irregularly coupled regular mesh template and a multigrid template.

We have parallelized a template from a multiblock computation fluid dynamics application that solves the thin-layer Navier-Stokes equations over a 3D surface (multiblock TLNS3D), using the prototype Fortran 90D compiler described in Section 3. The version of the multiblock TLNS3D code we are working with was developed by Vatsa et al. [19] at NASA Langley Research Center, and consists of nearly 18,000 lines of Fortran 77 code. The template, which was designed to include portions of the entire code that are representative of the major computation and communication patterns of the original code, consists of nearly 2,000 lines of F77 code. We have hand parallelized this template by manually inserting calls to the multiblock Parti routines.

```
C    ORIGINAL F90D CODE
C    Arrays A, B are distributed identically
         forall (i = 1:100:2,j = 1:50) A(i,j) = B(2*j,i)

C    TRANSFORMED CODE
     NumSrcDim =   2        NumDestDim  =   2
     SrcDim(1)  =  2        DestDim(1)   =   1
     SrcDim(2)  =  1        DestDim(2)   =   2
     SrcLos(1)  =  2        DestLos(1)   =   1
     SrcLos(2)  =  1        DestLos(2)   =   1
     SrcHis(1)  =  100      DestHis(1)   =   100
     SrcHis(2)  =  100      DestHis(2)   =   50
     SrcStr(1)  =  2        DestStr(1)   =   2
     SrcStr(2)  =  2        DestStr(2)   =   1
     Sched      =  Regular_Section_Move_Sched
                   (DAD,DAD,NumSrcDim,
                   NumDestDim, SrcDim, SrcLos,
                   SrcHis, SrcStr, DestDim,
                   DestLos, DestHis, DestStr)
     Call Data_Move(B,Sched,A)
```

Figure 4: Regular section move

ONE BLOCK: 49 X 9 X 9 Mesh (50 Iterations)

No. of Proc	Compiler	Hand F90	Hand F77
4	6.99	6.88	6.20
8	4.17	4.06	4.00
16	2.47	2.35	2.28
32	1.55	1.45	1.41

Figure 5: Performance comparison for small mesh, one block (sec.)

We converted the F77 code to F90D manually, by rewriting the the major computational parts of the code using single statement *forall* loops and F90 array expressions, also adding the required data distribution directives. We then parallelized the code by running it through the F90D compiler. We also created a hand parallelized F90 version of the template in which all computations are done with single statement *forall* loops, but the calls to the runtime primitives are inserted manually.

We now compare the relative performances of compiler parallelized F90 code, hand parallelized F90 code and hand parallelized F77 code, varying the mesh size and number of blocks for the application, and also varying the number of processors used on an Intel iPSC/860. In Figure 5, we present the performance results on a $49 \times 9 \times 9$ mesh (with one block), comparing the performance of the three versions from 4 to 32 processors. In Figure 6, we present the performance results on a $49 \times 17 \times 9$ mesh (split into two blocks), comparing the performance of the three versions from 8 to 32 processors. The compiler parallelized F90 code performs within around 20% of the hand paral-

TWO BLOCKS: 49 X 17 X 9 Mesh (50 Iterations)

No. of Proc	Compiler	Hand F90	Hand F77
8	7.49	6.69	6.17
16	4.64	4.07	4.03
32	2.88	2.32	2.30

Figure 6: Performance comparison for larger mesh, two blocks (sec.)

lelized F77 code. The hand parallelized F90 code performs worse than the hand parallelized F77 code. This is because, in the F90 version, all computation is done through single statement *forall* loops that result in the creation of (large) temporary arrays. Such use of temporary storage, and the fact that no loop fusion between parallel loops is done by the compiler, increases the number of cache misses on each processor. However, the difference in performance between the F90 and F77 hand parallelized versions decreases as the number of processors increases. This is because as the number of processor increases, less memory is required on each processor, so the effect on cache utilization is less significant. The difference in performance of the hand parallelized F90 and the compiler parallelized code comes from two major factors. First, in the compiler generated version, the runtime calls for computing new loop bounds are made in each loop iteration, as compared to only once for the hand parallelized version. Second, as the template is run over a large number of time steps, the compiler generated version makes repeated calls to the runtime library to build communication schedules, whereas in the hand parallelized version the calls are lifted out of the time step loop. To reduce the additional cost due to this second factor, our runtime library saves schedules. When a call is made for generating the schedule, the library searches a hash table to check if any schedule with exactly the same parameters is present. If so, the saved schedule is returned. This technique still has the overhead of searching through the hash table, as compared to a hand parallelized version. To study the exact costs of each of these factors, we present a more detailed experiment.

In Figure 7, we study the effect of the optimization in the library of saving schedules. Version I is a compiler parallelized version in which the library does not save any schedules. This version performs badly because of the high cost of rebuilding the schedules for every iteration. Version II is the compiler parallelized version in which the library saves schedules. This results in a major gain in performance. Version III represents the case where the compiler performs sophisticated interprocedural analysis to reuse the schedules during successive time steps. While our current compiler technology does not perform such optimization, we can study the effect of this optimization by generating the code to reuse the schedules by hand. Version III performs better than version II, in which the schedules are reused within the library, but the difference is not large.

In the compiler parallelized version, runtime calls are made to the functions for adjusting loop bounds for each *forall* loop on each time step. The hand parallelized version can store the loop bounds computed during the first time

TWO BLOCKS : 49 X 9 X 9 Mesh (50 Iterations)

No. of Proc.	Compiler Version I	Compiler Version II	Compiler Version III	Compiler Version IV	Compiler Version V	Hand F90
4	13.45	7.63	7.41	7.39	7.33	6.79
8	15.51	4.78	4.58	4.65	4.54	4.19
16	11.72	2.85	2.71	2.70	2.62	2.39
32	8.01	1.85	1.79	1.73	1.66	1.47

Version I   : Runtime Library does not save schedules
Version II   : Runtime Library saves schedules
Version III   : Schedule reuse implemented by hand
Version IV   : Multiple Statement *forall* loops
Version V   : Loop bounds reused within a procedure

Figure 7: Effects of various optimizations (in sec.)

$$\text{Forall}(i=1:N,j=1:N)$$
$$\text{FINE}(2{*}i,2{*}j) \quad = \quad \text{COARSE}(i,j)$$

$$\text{Forall}(i=1:N,j=1:2N)$$
$$\text{FINE}(2{*}i-1,j) \quad = \quad (\text{FINE}(2{*}i,j) + \text{FINE}(2{*}i-1,j+1) + \text{FINE}(2{*}i-2,j) + \text{FINE}(2{*}i-1,j-1))/4$$

$$\text{Forall}(i=1:2N,j=1:N)$$
$$\text{FINE}(i,2{*}j-1) \quad = \quad (\text{FINE}(i,2{*}j) + \text{FINE}(i+1,2{*}j-1) + \text{FINE}(i,2{*}j-2) + \text{FINE}(i-1,2{*}j-1))/4$$

Figure 8: Multigrid mesh refinement code

step, for subsequent reuse. Additionally, a procedure may contain several loops involving the same array on the left hand side that have the same loop bounds. Our compiler generates separate runtime calls for adjusting loop bounds for each such loop. Such optimizations will be implemented in a future version of the compiler.

In Figure 7, the difference between version III and the hand parallelized F90 version shows the extra cost of generating loop bounds at runtime for each forall loop during each time step. The results show that generating loop bounds at runtime is the major factor in the performance difference between the compiler parallelized version and the hand parallelized versions.

If the source language allows multiple statement *foralls*, then the number of runtime calls to the loop bound adjustment routines will be substantially reduced. Version IV, created by hand, has the loop bound adjustment calls inserted as if the language supports multiple statement forall loops. This version performs slightly better than version III. In version V, we show the results of an unimplemented optimization in which the compiler is able to identify the loops with the same left hand side array and same loop bounds within a subroutine. Then the compiler needs to generate calls to the loop bound adjustment functions only once for each such set of loops. This optimization also provides an improvement over version IV.

We have also used the compiler to parallelize a multigrid style mesh refinement in which there are regular section moves with strides. The code, part of which is shown in Figure 8, involves copying from a coarse grid into a finer grid, followed by interpolation on the finer grid. Again we compare the performance of the compiler generated code and the hand parallelized F90 code. The results are shown in Figure 9. For the first iteration, the time taken by the compiler generated version and the hand parallelized version are identical. For subsequent iterations, the time taken by the compiler generated version is greater, but it is within 10% of the hand parallelized version. The compiler parallelized code performs worse because of the additional costs of adjusting loop bounds at runtime and the lookups into hash tables required to reuse schedules.

5 Conclusions

To reliably and portably program distributed memory parallel machines, it is important to have both a machine independent language and runtime support for optimizing communication. High Performance Fortran and its variants have emerged as the most likely candidates for machine independent parallel programming on distributed memory machines.

Scientific and engineering applications frequently involve structured grids or meshes. These meshes may be nested (as in adaptive or multigrid solvers) or irregularly coupled (ICRMs). Block structured grid applications are a significant part of scientific and engineering applications. We have designed and implemented a set of (compiler embed-

No. of Proc.	Compiler: 1st iteration	Compiler: Per Subsequent Iteration	By hand: 1st iteration	By hand: Per Subsequent Iteration
4	.36	.226	.36	.207
8	.33	.125	.33	.119
16	.22	.098	.22	.095
32	.17	.060	.17	.056

Figure 9: Multigrid mesh refinement performance (sec.)

dable) runtime primitives for parallelizing these applications in an efficient, convenient and machine independent manner.

In this paper we have addressed the problem of integrating the runtime support for block structured applications with a compiler for an HPF-like parallel programming language. We have presented the method the compiler uses to analyze the data access patterns associated with parallel loops. These methods are used to identify communication patterns that can be efficiently handled using the communication primitives that the multiblock Parti library supports. We have also presented a set of simple loop transformations that the compiler performs for automatically generating calls to the runtime primitives.

We have implemented the compiler analysis method in the Fortran 90D compiler being developed at Syracuse University. We consider this work to be a part of an integrated effort toward developing a powerful runtime support system for HPF compilers. To measure the performance overheads of the compiler parallelized code, we performed experiments with a template from a 3D multiblock Navier-Stokes solver and a multigrid template. We compared the performance of compiler parallelized code with the performance of hand parallelized F90 and F77 codes, and have shown that the compiler parallelized code performs within 20% of hand parallelized F77 code. The optimization of having the runtime library save and reuse communication schedules allows the compiler parallelized code to perform almost as well as hand parallelized code. We have also experimented with other optimizations. The optimization of reusing computed loop bounds within a subroutine improves the performance of the compiler parallelized code and brings it within 10% of the hand parallelized version.

We plan to integrate our runtime support with other compilers, including the Fortran 77D compiler being developed at Rice University [13] and the Vienna Fortran Compilation System [5]. We also plan to work on applying both our runtime support and compiler techniques to other block structured applications.

Acknowledgements

We gratefully acknowledge our collaborators, Geoffrey Fox, Alok Choudhary, Sanjay Ranka, Tomasz Haupt, and Zeki Bozkus for many enlightening discussions and for allowing us to integrate our runtime support into their emerging Fortran 90D compiler. The detailed discussions we had with Sanjay Ranka, Alok Choudhary and Zeki Bozkus during their visits to Maryland were extremely productive. We are also grateful to V. Vatsa and M. Senetrik at NASA Langley for giving us access to the multiblock TLNS3D application code.

References

[1] Gagan Agrawal, Alan Sussman, and Joel Saltz. Compiler and runtime support for structured and block structured applications. Technical Report CS-TR-3080 and UMIACS-TR-93-45, University of Maryland, Department of Computer Science and UMIACS, April 1993.

[2] M.J. Berger and P. Colella. Local adaptive mesh refinement for shock hydrodynamics. *Journal of Computational Physics*, 82:67–84, 1989.

[3] M.J. Berger and J. Oliger. Adaptive mesh refinement for hyperbolic partial differential equations. *Journal of Computational Physics*, 53:484–512, 1984.

[4] Zeki Bozkus, Alok Choudhary, Geoffrey Fox, Tomasz Haupt, Sanjay Ranka, and Min-You Wu. Compiling Fortran 90D/HPF for distributed memory MIMD computers. Submitted to the Journal of Parallel and Distributed Computing, March 1993.

[5] B. Chapman, P. Mehrotra, and H. Zima. Programming in Vienna Fortran. *Scientific Programming*, 1(1):31–50, Fall 1992.

[6] C. Chase, K. Crowley, J. Saltz, and A. Reeves. Parallelization of irregularly coupled regular meshes. In *Proceedings of the Sixth International Conference on Supercomputing*. ACM Press, June 1992.

[7] A. Choudhary, G. Fox, S. Hiranandani, K. Kennedy, C. Koelbel, S. Ranka, and J. Saltz. Software support for irregular and loosely synchronous problems. *Computing Systems in Engineering*, 3(1-4):43–52, 1992. Papers presented at the Symposium on High-Performance Computing for Flight Vehicles, December 1992.

[8] D. Loveman (Ed.). Draft High Performance Fortran language specification, version 1.0. Technical Report CRPC-TR92225, Center for Research on Parallel Computation, Rice University, January 1993.

[9] Geoffrey Fox, Seema Hiranandani, Ken Kennedy, Charles Koelbel, Uli Kremer, Chau-Wen Tseng, and Min-You Wu. Fortran D language specification. Technical Report CRPC-TR90079, Center for Research

on Parallel Computation, Rice University, December 1990.

[10] R. v. Hanxleden, K. Kennedy, C. Koelbel, R. Das, and J. Saltz. Compiler analysis for irregular problems in Fortran D. In *Proceedings of the 5th Workshop on Languages and Compilers for Parallel Computing*, New Haven, CT, August 1992.

[11] P. Havlak and K. Kennedy. An implementation of interprocedural bounded regular section analysis. *IEEE Transactions on Parallel and Distributed Systems*, 2(3):350–360, July 1991.

[12] S. Hiranandani, K. Kennedy, and C. Tseng. Evaluation of compiler optimizations for Fortran D on MIMD distributed-memory machines. In *Proceedings of the Sixth International Conference on Supercomputing*. ACM Press, July 1992.

[13] Seema Hiranandani, Ken Kennedy, and Chau-Wen Tseng. Compiling Fortran D for MIMD distributed-memory machines. *Communications of the ACM*, 35(8):66–80, August 1992.

[14] Scott R. Kohn and Scott B. Baden. An implementation of the LPAR parallel programming model for scientific computations. In *Proceedings of the Sixth SIAM Conference on Parallel Processing for Scientific Computing*, pages 759–766. SIAM, March 1993.

[15] Max Lemke and Daniel Quinlan. P++, a C++ virtual shared grids based programming environment for architecture-independent development of structured grid applications. Technical Report 611, GMD, February 1992.

[16] S. McCormick. *Multilevel Adaptive Methods for Partial Differential Equations*. SIAM, 1989.

[17] J.J. Quirk. *An Adaptive Grid Algorithm for Computational Shock Hydrodynamics*. PhD thesis, Cranfield Institute of Technology, January 1991.

[18] Alan Sussman and Joel Saltz. A manual for the multiblock PARTI runtime primitives. Technical Report CS-TR-3070 and UMIACS-TR-93-36, University of Maryland, Department of Computer Science and UMIACS, May 1993.

[19] V.N. Vatsa, M.D. Sanetrik, and E.B. Parlette. Development of a flexible and efficient multigrid-based multiblock flow solver; AIAA-93-0677. In *Proceedings of the 31st Aerospace Sciences Meeting and Exhibit*, January 1993.

Implementing a Parallel C++ Runtime System for Scalable Parallel Systems[1]

F. Bodin
Irisa
University of Rennes
Rennes, France
Francois.Bodin@cs.irisa.fr

P. Beckman, D. Gannon, S. Yang
Dept. of Comp. Sci.
Indiana University
Bloomington, Indiana 47405
{beckman,gannon,yang}@cs.indiana.edu

S. Kesavan, A. Malony, B. Mohr
Dept. of Comp. and Info. Sci.
University of Oregon
Eugene, Oregon 97403
{kesavans,malony,mohr}@cs.uoregon.edu

Abstract

pC++ is a language extension to C++ designed to allow programmers to compose "concurrent aggregate" collection classes which can be aligned and distributed over the memory hierarchy of a parallel machine in a manner modeled on the High Performance Fortran Forum (HPFF) directives for Fortran 90. pC++ allows the user to write portable and efficient code which will run on a wide range of scalable parallel computer systems. The first version of the compiler is a preprocessor which generates Single Program Multiple Data (SPMD) C++ code. Currently, it runs on the Thinking Machines CM-5, the Intel Paragon, the BBN TC2000, the Kendall Square Research KSR-1, and the Sequent Symmetry. In this paper we describe the implementation of the runtime system, which provides the concurrency and communication primitives between objects in a distributed collection. To illustrate the behavior of the runtime system we include a description and performance results on four benchmark programs.

1   Introduction

pC++ permits programmers to build distributed data structures with parallel execution semantics. For "distributed memory" machines, with a non-shared address space, the runtime system implements a shared name space for the objects in a distributed collection. This shared name space is supported by the underlying message passing system of the target machine. In the case of "shared memory" architectures, the runtime system uses the global addressing mechanism to support the name space. A thread system

on the target machine is used to support the parallel tasks.

After a short introduction to pC++ we give a detailed description of each runtime system. To illustrate the behavior of the runtime system we include performance results for four benchmark programs.

2   A Brief Introduction to pC++

The basic concept behind pC++ is the notion of a distributed collection, which is a type of concurrent aggregate "container class" [7, 9]. More specifically, a *collection* is a structured set of objects distributed across the processing elements of the computer. In a manner designed to be completely consistent with HPF Fortran, the programmer must define a distribution of the objects in a collection over the processors and memory hierarchy of the target machine. As HPF becomes more available, future versions of the pC++ compiler will allow object level linking between distributed collections and HPF distributed arrays.

A collection can be an *Array*, a *Grid*, a *Tree*, or any other partitionable data structure. Collections have the following components:

- A collection class describing the basic topology of the set of elements.

- A size or shape for each instance of the collection class; e.g., array dimension or tree height.

- A base type for collection elements. This can be any C++ type or class. For example, one can define an Array of *Float*s, a Grid of *FiniteElement*s, a Matrix of *Complex*, or a Tree of *X*s, where *X* is the class of each node in the tree.

- A *Distribution* object. The distribution describes an abstract coordinate system that will be distributed over the available "processor objects" of the target by the runtime system. (In HPF [8],

[1] This research is supported by ARPA under Rome Labs contract AF 30602-92-C-0135, the National Science Foundation Office of Advanced Scientific Computing under grant ASC-9111616, and Esprit under the BRA APPARC grant.

the term *template* is used to refer to the coordinate system. We will avoid this so that there will be no confusion with the C++ keyword *template*.)

- A function object called the *Alignment*. This function maps collection elements to the abstract coordinate system of the *Distribution* object.

The pC++ language has a library of standard collection classes that may be used (or subclassed) by the programmer [10, 11, 12, 13]. This includes collection classes such as *DistributedArray*, *DistributedMatrix*, *DistributedVector*, and *DistributedGrid*. To illustrate the points above, consider the problem of creating a distributed 5 by 5 matrix of floating point numbers. We begin by building a *Distribution*. A distribution is defined by its number of dimensions, the size in each dimension and how the elements are mapped to the processors. Current distribution mappings include *BLOCK*, *CYCLIC* and *WHOLE* , but more general forms will be added later. For our example, let us assume that the distribution coordinate system is distributed over the processor's memories by mapping *WHOLE* rows of the distribution index space to individual processors using a *CYCLIC* pattern where the ith row is mapped to processor memory i mod P, on a P processor machine.

pC++ uses a special implementation dependent library class called *Processors*. In the current implementation, it represents the set of all processors available to the program at run time. To build a distribution of some size, say 7 by 7, with this mapping, one would write

```
Processors P;
Distribution myDist(7,7,&P,CYCLIC,WHOLE);
```

Next, we create an alignment object called `myAlign` that defines a domain and function for mapping the matrix to the distribution. The matrix `A` can be defined using the library collection class *DistributedMatrix* with a base type of *Float*.

```
Align myAlign(5,5,"[ALIGN(domain[i][j],
                      myMap[i][j])]");
DistributedMatrix<Float> A(myDist,myAlign);
```

The collection constructor uses the alignment object, `myAlign`, to define the size and dimension of the collection. The mapping function is described by a text string corresponding to the HPF alignment directives. It defines a mapping from a domain structure to a distribution structure using dummy index variables.

The intent of this two stage mapping, as it was originally conceived for HPF, is to allow the distribution coordinates to be a frame of reference so that different arrays could be aligned with each other in a manner that promotes memory locality.

2.1 Processors, Threads, and Parallelism

The processor objects used to build distributions for collections represent a set of threads. Given the declaration

```
Processors P;
```

one thread of execution is created on each processor of the system that the user controls. These new *processor object* (PO) threads exist independent of the main program control thread. (In the future, pC++ will allow processor sets of different sizes and dimensions.) Each new PO thread may read but not modify the "global" variables; i.e., program static data or data allocated on the heap by the main control thread. Each PO thread has a private heap and stack.

Collections are built on top of a more primitive extension of C++ called a *Thread Environment Class*, or `TEClass`, which is the mechanism used by pC++ to ask the processor object threads to do something in parallel. A `TEClass` is declared the same as any other class with the following exceptions:

- There must be a special constructor with a *Processors* object argument. Upon invocation of this constructor, one copy of the member field object is allocated to each PO thread described by the argument. The lifetime of these objects is determined by their lifetime in the control thread.

- A `TEClass` object may not be allocated by a PO thread.

- The () operator is used to refer to a single thread environment object by the control thread.

- A call to a `TEClass` member function by the main program control thread represents a transfer of control to a parallel action on each of the threads associated with the object. (Consequently, member functions of the `TEClass` can read but cannot modify global variables.) The main control thread is suspended until all the processor threads complete the execution of the function. If the member function returns a value to the main control thread, it must return the same value from each PO thread or the result is undefined.

- If a `TEClass` member function is invoked by one of the processor object threads, it is a sequential action by that thread. (Hence, there is no way to generate nested parallelism with this mechanism.)

These issues are best illustrated by an example.

```
int x;          // c++ global
float y[1000];  // c++ global

TEClass MyThreads{
   int id;              // private thread data
 public:
   float d[200];        // public thread data
   void f(){id++;}      // parallel functions
   int getX(int j){return x;}
};

main() {
 Processors P;    // the set of processors
 MyThreads T(P);  // implicit constructor
                  // one thread object/proc.
 // a serial loop
 for(int i=0; i<P.numProcs(); i++)
   T(i).id=i; // main control thread can
              // modify i-th thread env.
 T.f(); // parallel execution on each thread
 // an implicit barrier after parallel call
}
```

In this example, the processor set P is used as the parameter to the thread environment constructor. One copy of the object with member field id is allocated to each PO thread defined by P. The lifetime of T is defined by the main control thread in which it was created. (However, in the current implementation the storage is not automatically reclaimed.) Figure 1 illustrates the thread and memory model that the language provides.

The main control thread can access and modify the public member fields of the TEClass object. To accomplish this, one uses the () operator, which is implicitly overloaded. The reference T(i).id refers to the id field in the ith TEClass object. Note that the value of the expression T.id within the main control thread may not be well defined because each thread may have a different value for id. However the assignment T.id = 1 is valid and denotes an update to all members named id.

An individual PO thread cannot modify the local fields of another PO thread, but it can access them by means of the () operator. The only other way for PO threads to communicate is by means of native system message passing, but this is not encouraged until a C++ binding for the standard message passing interface is defined.

The call T.f() indicates a branch to a parallel operation on each PO thread. After the parallel execution

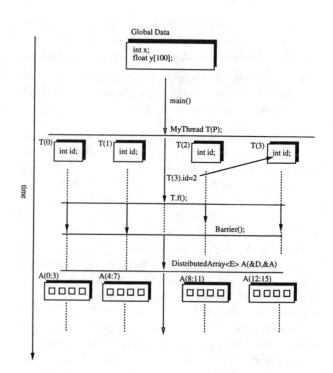

Figure 1: TEClass Objects, Collections and Processor Threads

of the method, there is a barrier synchronization before returning to the main control thread. In the case of invoking an object such as T.getX(), which has a non-void return value, it is essential that the function returns an identical value for each main PO thread for a given main thread invocation.

Note that the TEClass mechanisms provide a simple and direct way to "wrap" message passing SPMD style C++ routines inside a standard sequential main program. In this way, many of the special libraries of parallel C++ code already designed can be easily integrated into this model [16, 17].

2.2 Collections and Templates

The C++ language provides the *templates* mechanism to build parameterized classes. Collections are very similar to templates defined over TEClasses. In fact, it is *almost* sufficient to describe a collection class as

```
template <class ElementType>
TEClass MyCollection: Kernel<ElementType> {
   MyCollection(Distribution &D,Align &A)::
     Kernel(D,A) { ...}

   ...

};
```

590

where `Kernel` is a super-template class that defines the concurrent aggregate structure of the collection. Indeed, as will be shown in the following sections of this paper, it is the structure of `Kernel` and its basic constructors and member functions that is at the core of the runtime system for pC++.

While the construction above is nearly sufficient to define collections, it does not give us everything we want. In particular, collections define a generalization of data parallelism as follows. Let `C` be a collection type and `E` an element type. Assume `E` has the form

```
class E {
    int a;
    void f();
    E & operator +(E&);
};
```

and let `x` and `y` be declared to be of type `C<E>`. Because + is defined on the elements, one can write `x+y` and this means the "pointwise" addition of the elements and the result is a new collection of type `C<E>`. In a similar manner the expression `x.a + y.a` is a new collection of type `C<int>`. In addition, the expression `x.f()` means the parallel application of the element member function `f` to each member of the collection. These operations, together with collection specific reductions form the main parallel control in pC++.

To accomplish this we provide a special form of the C++ template construct with a distinguished class parameter, called `ElementType`, which defines the type of the element in the collection. The exact syntax is shown below:

```
Collection<class ElementType>
TEClass CollName: ParentCollection {
  public:
   CollName(Distribution &D, Align &A);
  private:
  protected:
   // TEClass member functions and fields.
   // Methods declared here are executed in
   // parallel by the associated PO thread.
  MethodOfElement:
   // Fields declared here are added to each
   // element, Methods to the element class.
}
```

Data fields defined in the public, private and protected areas are components of the underlying `TEClass` object. The size and shape of the collection and the way in which the elements of the collection are distributed to the processor object threads is defined by the `Distribution` and `Alignment` objects supplied to the constructor for the collection. The set of elements that are mapped to a single PO thread object is called the "local collection" for that thread. The data structure that contains and manages these elements is part of the `Kernel` class which is a required ancestor of any collection.

2.3 Communication Between Elements in a Collection

One of the key ideas behind collection classes is to enable the programmer to build a distributed data structure where data movement operators can be closely linked to the semantics of the data type. For example, elements of a *DistributedGrid* need to access their neighbors. A *Tree* node will often reference its children or parent. Each application has a topology of communication and global operators that must be supported efficiently by the collection structure.

If `c` is a collection of type `C<E>`, then any processor thread may access the ith element of `c` by the `Kernel` functions

```
c->Get_Element(i);
c->Get_ElementPart(i, offset, size);
```

The first function accesses the ith element and places a copy in a local system buffer and returns a pointer of type (`ElementType *`). The second function accesses part of an element at a given offset and size and make a copy in the buffer. In other collections, such as distributed arrays, matrices and grids, the operator (`...`) has been overloaded. For example, if `c` is a two dimension collection, then expressions like

```
x = c(i,j) + c(i+1,j)
```

work by calling the `Get_Element` function if a reference is not to a local element.

3 The pC++ Runtime System

`Get_Element` and `Get_ElementPart` are the only communication primitives in pC++ that allow processor threads to access the shared name space and remote elements. Notice that this differs significantly from the "message passing" style that is common in SPMD programming. In the latter model, all synchronization is accomplished by matching a send operation with a corresponding receive. In pC++, any processor object thread may read any element of any collection, but only the owner object thread may modify the element; this is equivalent to the "owner computes" semantics found in HPF. All synchronization is in terms

591

of barrier operations that terminate each collection operation.

The runtime system for pC++ must manage three distinct tasks.

1. *The allocation of collection classes.* This involves the interpretation of the alignment and distribution directives to build the local collection for each processor object.

More specifically, each processor object must have a mechanism whereby any element of the collection can be identified. In a shared address space environment, this may be a table of pointers or a function that computes the address of an element. In the non-shared address space model, this may be the name of a processor that either has the object or knows where to find it. Depending upon the execution model of the target, this task may also involve the initialization of threads associated with each processor object.

2. *The management of element accesses.* In particular, access management requires an effective, efficient implementation of `Get_Element` and `Get_ElementPart` functions.

This activity can be seen as a compiler-assisted "local caching" of a remote element to the local processor thread's address space. In a shared address space environment, alternative memory management schemes may be used to improve memory locality. If there is no shared address space, these functions require a "one-sided" communication protocol – if processor X needs an element from processor Y, processor X must wake up an agent that has access to the address space of Y which can fetch the data and return it to X.

3. *Termination of parallel collection operations.* All parallel collection operations are barrier synchronized before returning to the main thread.

Note that only the processor objects involved in the computation of the collection operation must be synchronized and not every processor in the system need be involved. However, as we shall see, this may be required for some implementations.

Some restrictions are imposed by the current pC++ compiler that are important to note for the runtime system implementation. The current version of the pC++ compiler generates SPMD code in which the set of processor objects for each collection is the same as the set of processors in the user's execution partition. There is one execution thread per processor and, on one processor, all local collection objects share this

thread. In true SPMD style, the main thread is duplicated and is run with the single local thread on each processor.

This model of execution is consistent with all current HPF implementations, but imposes some limitations on the programmer. For example, it is not possible to have two different collection operations going on in different subsets of processors concurrently. Furthermore, this limits the system from having nested concurrency by building collections of collections. Even with these limitations this is still a powerful programming model. These limitations will be removed in future versions of the compiler.

In the paragraphs that follow, we will look at the shared address and distributed address space implementations of the current pC++ execution model.

3.1 Distributed Memory Systems

Distributed memory parallel systems consist of a set of processing nodes interconnected by a high-speed network. Each node consists of a processor and local memory. In the case of a non-shared, distributed memory system, each processor only has access to its local memory and a message system is used to move data across the network between processors.

One common approach to building a shared memory system on top of a non-shared, distributed memory computer is called *shared virtual memory* (SVM). In SVM, the message passing system is used to move pages from one processor to another in the same way a standard VM system moves pages from memory to disk. Though these systems are still experimental [14, 15], they show great promise for providing a support environment for shared memory parallel programming models. Because pC++ is based on a shared name space of collection elements, we use SVM techniques to build the runtime system for the Intel Paragon and the Thinking Machines CM-5.

More specifically, our model is based on ideas from Koan[15]. The basic idea is that each collection element has a *manager* and a *owner*. The owner of the element is the processor object that contains the element in its local collection. As with pages in an SVM, we assume that an element may be moved from one local collection to another at run time, for load balancing reasons, or, in the case of dynamic collections, may be created and destroyed at run time. In other words, we assume that the distribution map may be dynamic. Although this dynamic feature of the system is not being used by the current compiler,[2] it is a design

---

[2]It will be supported in future releases.

requirement for the runtime system implementation. The purpose of the element manager is to keep track of which processor object owns the element. The manager is static and every processor thread knows how to find the manager. Elements are assigned managers by a simple cyclic distribution. The algorithm for implementing the function `Get_Element(i)` is given as follows:

1. Let p be the processor thread that is executing `Get_Element(i)` for an element i of some collection. Let P be the number of processors. The index m of the manager processor thread is given by `m = i mod P`. Thread p sends a message to m requesting the identity of the owner.

2. The manager q is "interrupted" and looks in a table for the owner o of element i and sends this value to p.

3. The requester p then sends a message to o asking for element i.

4. The owner o is "interrupted" and sends a copy of element i to the requester p.

Hence, the primary implementation issues for a given machine reduce to:

- How is a processor interrupted when a request for an element or owner is received?

- How is the table of owner identifiers stored in the manager?

- How is the barrier operation implemented?

The current pC++ compiler assumes no mechanism exists for interrupting a processor thread. Instead, the compiler generates calls to a function called `Poll()` in the element and collection methods. By calling `Poll()`, a thread can check a queue of incoming messages and reply to requests in a reasonably timely manner. Unfortunately, calling `Poll()` periodically is not sufficient to prevent starvation. If no interruption mechanism exists on the target, it is necessary to make sure that the `Barrier()` function also calls `Poll()` while waiting for the barrier to complete.

The final issue to consider in the runtime environment is that of allocating the collection elements. In the current version a large table is created in each processor object that stores pointers to the local collection. A second table in each processor object stores the index of the owner of each element that is managed by that processor. Because all of the elements and both tables can be allocated and created based on the distribution and alignment data, it is straightforward

to parallelize this task in the distributed memory environment. (This is in contrast to the shared memory situation where synchronization is necessary to ensure that each processor has access to pointers to all the elements.)

3.1.1 The Thinking Machines CM-5

The CM-5 is a distributed memory machine based on a fat tree network. Each processor is a Sparc CPU together with four vector units. (In the experiments described here the vector units are not used.) The basic communication library is CMMD 3.0 Beta which is based on a re-implementation of the Berkeley CMAM Active Message layer [5, 6]. The active message layer provides very good support for short messages that consist of a pointer to a local function to execute and three words of argument. In addition, the system can be made to interrupt a processor upon the receipt of a message, or it can be done by polling. One can switch between these two modes at run time. Our experience indicates that using a combination of polling and interrupts works the best. During barrier synchronization, the interrupt mechanism is used. The CMMD barrier operation is very fast (4 microseconds).

3.1.2 The Intel Paragon

The Intel Paragon is a distributed memory machine based on a grid network. Each processor contains two i860s. One i860 is used to run the user code and one handles the message traffic and talks to the special mesh router. (Unfortunately, our testbed Paragon system is running "pre-release" software which only uses one of the i860s.) The basic communication library is the NX system that has been used for many years on the Intel machines. NX only provides a very primitive interrupt driven message handler mechanism; consequently, only the polling strategy can be used. Furthermore, NX is not well optimized for very short messages, such as locating the owner of an element. In addition, implementing a barrier function that must also poll for messages is non-trivial and results in slow operation. Barrier execution takes approximately 3 milliseconds. However, the native NX barrier which does not do polling is not much faster (about 2 milliseconds). Combined with the effect of pre-release software, the performance of the pC++ runtime system on the Intel Paragon is non-optimal.

3.2 Shared Memory Systems

There are three main implementation differences in the pC++ runtime system on a shared memory versus a distributed memory machine. The most obvious difference is that message communication is not required for accessing remote collection elements. All collection elements can be accessed using address pointers into the shared memory space. A related difference is that collection element tables need only be allocated once, since all processors can directly reference tables using their base address. However, it may be beneficial to have multiple copies of the tables to improve memory locality during Get_Element operations. In contrast, it is necessary to have a separate collection element table on each processor node in a distributed memory machine. The third difference is in how collections are allocated. In a distributed memory machine, the owner of elements of a collection allocates the space for those elements in the memory of the processor where it (the owner process) will execute. In a shared memory machine, the space for an entire collection is allocated out of shared memory space. Care must be taken in memory allocation to minimize the contention between local processor data (i.e., the data "owned" by a processor) and remote data. Achieving good memory locality in a shared memory system, using processor cache or local memory, will be important for good performance.

3.2.1 General Strategy

The current pC++ runtime system that we have implemented for shared memory machines has the following general, default properties:

- Collection element tables: Each processor has its own copy of the element table for each collection.

- Collection allocation: Each processor object allocates all the space for its local elements. The processor objects then exchange local element addresses to build the full collection element table.

- Barrier synchronization: The barrier implementation is chosen from optimized hardware/software mechanisms on the target system.

3.2.2 The BBN TC2000

The BBN TC2000 [1] is a scalable multiprocessor architecture which can support up to 512 computational nodes. The nodes are interconnected by a variant of a multistage cube network referred to as the *butterfly switch*. Each node contains a 20 MHz Motorola 88100 microprocessor and memory which can be configured for local and shared access. The contribution of each node to the interleaved shared memory pool is set at boot time.

The parallel processes are forked one at a time via the nX system routine fork_and_bind. This routine creates a child process via a UNIX fork mechanism and attaches the child to the specified processor node. The collection element tables and local collection elements are allocated in the local memory space on each node of the TC2000. There are several choices under nX for allocating collection elements in shared memory: across node memories (e.g., interleaved or random) or on a particular node's memory with different caching policies (e.g., uncached or cached with copyback or write-through cache coherency). Currently, the TC2000 pC++ runtime system allocates collection elements in the "owner's" node memory with a write-through caching strategy. The TC2000 does not have special barrier synchronization hardware. Instead, we implemented the logarithmic barrier algorithm described in [2]. Our implementation requires approximately 70 microseconds to synchronize 32 nodes. This time scales as the log of the number of processors.

3.2.3 The Sequent Symmetry

The Sequent Symmetry [3] is a bus-based, shared memory multiprocessor that can be configured with up to 30 processors. The Symmetry architecture provides hardware cache consistency through a copy-back policy and user-accessible hardware locking mechanisms for synchronization. For our prototype implementation, we used a Symmetry S81 machine with 24 processors (16 MHz Intel 80386 with a Weitek 1167 floating point coprocessor) and 256 MBytes of memory across four memory modules interleaved in 32 byte blocks.

Using Sequent's parallel programming library, the implementation of the pC++ runtime system was straightforward. Because all memory in the Sequent machine is physically shared in the hardware, the local allocation of the collection element tables on each processor is only meaningful relative to the virtual memory space of the process. All collection element tables are allocated in the local data segment of each process, making them readable only by the process that created them. In contrast, collection elements must be allocated in a shared segment of the virtual address space of each process; a shared memory allocation routine is used for this purpose. Unfortunately, there is no way to control the caching policy in software; copy-back is the hardware default. Barrier synchronization is implemented using a system-supplied barrier routine which takes advantage of the hardware locking facilities of the Sequent machine. It is very efficient – the barrier performance on 8, 12, 16, and 20 processors is 34, 47, 58, and 70 microseconds, respectively.

3.2.4 The Kendall Square Research KSR-1

The KSR-1 is a shared virtual memory, massively-parallel computer. The memory is physically distributed on the nodes and organized as a hardware-coherent distributed cache [4]. The machine can scale to 1088 nodes, in clusters of 32. Nodes in a cluster are interconnected with a pipelined slotted ring. Clusters are connected by a higher-level ring. Each node has a superscalar 64-bit custom processor, a 0.5 Mbyte local sub-cache, and 32 Mbyte local cache memory.

For the pC++ runtime system implementation, we used the POSIX thread package with a KSR-supplied extension for barrier synchronization. The collection allocation strategy is exactly the same as for the Sequent except that no special shared memory allocation is required; data is automatically shared between threads. However, the hierarchical memory system in the KSR is more complex than in the Sequent machine. Latencies for accessing data in the local sub-cache and the local cache memory are 2 and 18 cycles, respectively. Latencies between node caches are significantly larger: 150 cycles in the same ring and 500 cycles across rings. Although our current implementation simply calls the standard memory allocation routine, we suspect that more sophisticated memory allocation and management strategies will be important in optimizing the KSR performance.

4 Performance Measurements

To exercise different parallel collection data structures and to evaluate the pC++ runtime system implementation, four benchmark programs covering a range of problem areas were used. These benchmarks are briefly described below. The results for the benchmarks on each port of pC++ follow.

BM1: Block Grid CG. This computation consists of solving the Poisson equation on a 2-dimensional grid using finite difference operators and a simple conjugate gradient method without preconditioning. It represents one type of PDE algorithm.

BM2: A Fast Poisson Solver. This benchmark uses FFTs and cyclic reductions along the rows and columns of a two dimensional array to solve PDE problems. It is typical of a class of CFD applications.

BM3: The NAS Embarrassingly Parallel Benchmark. Four NAS benchmark codes have been trans-lated to pC++; we report on two. The BM3 program generates 2^{24} complex pairs of uniform $(0, 1)$ random numbers and gathers a small number of statistics.

BM4: The NAS Sparse CG Benchmark. A far more interesting benchmark in the NAS suite is the random sparse conjugate gradient computation. This benchmark requires the repeated solution to $A * X = F$, where A is a random sparse matrix.

4.1 Distributed Memory Systems

The principal runtime system factors for performance on non-shared, distributed memory ports of pC++ are message communication latencies and barrier synchronization. These factors influence performance quite differently on the TMC CM-5 and Intel Paragon. For the CM-5, experiments for 64, 128, and 256 processors were performed. Because of the large size of this machine relative to the others in the paper, we ran several of the benchmarks on larger size problems. For the BM1 code running on a 16 by 16 grid with 64 by 64 sub-blocks, near linear speedup was observed, indicating good data distribution and low communication overhead relative to sub-block computation time. Execution time for BM2 is the sum of the time for FFT transforms and cyclic reduction. Because the transforms require no communication, performance scales perfectly here. In contrast, the cyclic reduction requires a communication complexity that is nearly equal to the computational complexity. Although the communication latency is very low for the CM-5, no speedup was observed in this section even for Poisson grid sizes of 2,048. For the benchmark as a whole, a 25 percent speedup was observed from 64 to 256 processors. As expected, the BM3 performance showed near linear speedup. More importantly, the execution time was within 10 percent of the published manually optimized Fortran results for this machine. For the BM4 benchmark, we used the full problem size for the CM-5. While the megaflop rate is low, it matches the performance of the Cray Y/MP un-tuned Fortran code.

Results for the Paragon show a disturbing lack of performance in the messaging system, attributed primarily to the pre-release nature of this software. Experiments were performed for 4, 16, and 32 processors. The BM1 benchmark required a different block size choice, 128 instead of 64, before acceptable speedup performance could be achieved, indicative of the effects of increased communication overhead. At first glance, the speedup improvement from BM2 contradicts what was observed for the CM-5. However, using a smaller number of processors, as in the Paragon case, has the effect of altering the communications / computation ratio. Collection elements mapped to the same processor can share data without communication, while if the collection is spread out over a large number of processors almost all references from one element to another involves network traffic. Speedup behavior similar to the Paragon was observed on the CM-5 for equivalent numbers of processors. For the BM3 benchmark, a 32 node Paragon achieved a fraction of 0.71 of the Cray uniprocessor Fortran version; speedup was 19.6. However, the most significant results are for the BM4 benchmark. Here, the time increased as processors were added. This is because of the intense communication required in the sparse matrix vector multiply. We cannot expect improvements in these numbers until Intel finishes their "performance release" of the system.

4.2 Shared Memory Systems

The shared memory ports of the pC++ uncover different performance issues from the distributed memory ports regarding the language and runtime system implementation performance. Here, the ability to achieve good memory locality is the key to good performance. Clearly, the choice of collection distribution is important, but the memory allocation schemes in the runtime system will play a big part. To better isolate the performance of runtime system components and to determine the relative influence of different phases of the entire benchmark execution where the runtime system was involved, we used a prototype tracing facility for pC++ for shared memory performance measurement. In addition to producing the same performance results reported above for the distributed memory systems, a more detailed execution time and speedup profile was obtained from the trace measurements. Although space limitations prevent detailed discussion of these results, they will be forthcoming in a technical report.

In general, we were pleased with the speedup results on the Sequent Symmetry, given that it is a bus-based multiprocessor. For all benchmarks, speedup results for 16 processors were good: BM1 (14.84), BM2 (14.15), BM3 (15.94), and BM4 (12.33). Beyond 16 processors, contention on the bus and in the memory system stalls speedup improvement. Although the Sequent implementation serves as an excellent pC++ testbed, the machine architecture and processor speed limits large scalability studies. The Symmetry pC++ runtime system implementation is, however, representative of ports to shared memory parallel machines with equivalent numbers of processors; e.g., the shared

memory Cray YM/P or C90 machines. Using the four processor Sequent speedup results (3.7 to 3.99) as an indication, one might expect similar speedup performance on these systems. (Note, we are currently porting pC++ to a Cray YM/P and C90.)

The performance results for the BBN TC2000 reflect interesting architectural properties of the machine. Like the Sequent, benchmark speedups for 16 processor were encouraging: BM1 (14.72), BM2 (14.99), BM3 (15.92), and BM4 (11.59). BM1 speedup falls off to 23.89 and 32.36 at 32 and 64 processors, respectively, but these results are for a small 8 by 8 grid of subgrids, reflecting the small problem size performance encountered in the CM-5. BM2 speedup continues at a fairly even clip, indicating a better amortization of remote collection access costs that resulted in high communication overhead in the distributed memory versions. BM3 speedup was almost linear, achieving 31.48 for 32 processors and 58.14 for 64 processors. Unlike the Sequent, the BM4 speedup beyond 16 processors did not show any significant architectural limitations on performance.

The pC++ port to the KSR-1 was done most recently and should still be regarded as a prototype. Nevertheless, the performance results demonstrate the important architectural parameters of the machine. Up to 32 processors (1 cluster), speedup numbers steadily increase. BM1 to BM3 speedup results are very close to the TC2000 numbers; BM3 speedup for 64 processors was slightly less (52.71). However, BM4's speedup at 32 processors (9.13) is significantly less than the TC2000's result (17.29), highlighting the performance interactions of the choice of collection distribution and the hierarchical, cache-based KSR-1 memory system. Beyond 32 processors, two or more processor clusters are involved in the benchmark computations; we performed experiments up to 64 processors (2 clusters). As a result, a portion of the remote collection references must cross cluster rings; these references encounter latencies 3.5 times as slow as references made within a cluster. All benchmark speedup results reflect this overhead, falling to less than their 32 processor values.

5 Conclusion

Our experience implementing a runtime system for pC++ on five different parallel machines indicates that it is possible to achieve language portability and performance scalability goals simultaneously using a well-defined language/runtime system interface. The key, we believe, is to keep the number of runtime system requirements small and to concentrate on efficient implementations of required runtime system functions.

The three main pC++ runtime system tasks are collection class allocation, collection element access, and barrier synchronization. The implementation approach for these tasks is different for distributed memory than for shared memory architecture.

In the case of the distributed memory machines, the critical factor for performance is the availability of low latency, high bandwidth communication primitives. (Note that we have not made use of the CM-5 vector units or of highly optimized i860 code in the benchmarks.) While we expect the performance of these communication layers to improve dramatically over the next few months, we also expect to make changes in our compiler and runtime system. One important optimization will be to use barriers as infrequently as possible. In addition, it will be important to overlap more communication with computation.

In the case of shared memory machines, the performance focus shifts to the memory system. Although the BBN TC2000 architecture was classified as a shared memory architecture for this study, the non-uniform times for accessing collection elements in this machine result in runtime system performance characteristics similar to the distributed memory system. The more classic shared memory architecture of the Sequent Symmetry will require a closer study of memory locality trade-offs. Clearly, the choice of where to allocate collections in the shared memory can have important performance implications. In a hierarchical shared memory system, such as the KSR-1, the goal should be to allocate collection elements in a way that maximizes the chance of using the faster memory closer to the processors and that minimizes the possible contention and overhead in accessing remote memory. The problem for the runtime system becomes what memory allocation attributes to chose. The default choice is not guaranteed to always be optimal. Future versions of shared memory runtime systems may use properties of the collection classes to determine the appropriate element layout.

References

[1] BBN Advanced Computer Inc., Cambridge, MA. *Inside the TC2000*, 1989.

[2] D. Hensgen, R. Finkel, and U. Manber. Two Algorithms for Barrier Synchronization. *Int'l. Journal of Parallel Programming*, 17(1):1–17, 1988.

[3] Sequent Computer Systems, Inc. *Symmetry Multiprocessor Architecture Overview*, 1992.

[4] S. Frank, H. Burkhardt III, J. Rothnie, *The KSR1: Bridging the Gap Between Shared Memory and MPPs*, Proc. Compcon'93, San Francisco, 1993, pp. 285–294.

[5] T. von Eiken, D. Culler, S. Goldstein, K. Schauser, *Active Messages: a Mechanism for Integrated Communication and Computation*, Proc. 19th Int'l Symp. on Computer Architecture, Australia, May 1992.

[6] D. Culler, T. von Eiken, *CMAM - Introduction to CM-5 Active Message communication layer*, man page, CMAM distribution.

[7] A. Chien and W. Dally. *Concurrent Aggregates (CA)*, Proceedings of the Second ACM Sigplan Symposium on Principles & Practice of Parallel Programming, Seattle, Washington, March, 1990.

[8] High Performance Fortran Forum, *Draft High Performance Fortran Language Specification*, Version 1.0, 1993. Available from titan.cs.rice.edu by ftp.

[9] J. K. Lee, *Object Oriented Parallel Programming Paradigms and Environments For Supercomputers*, Ph.D. Thesis, Indiana University, Bloomington, Indiana, June 1992.

[10] J. K. Lee and D. Gannon, *Object Oriented Parallel Programming: Experiments and Results* Proc. Supercomputing 91, IEEE Computer Society and ACM SIGARCH, 1991, pp. 273–282.

[11] D. Gannon and J. K. Lee, *Object Oriented Parallelism: pC++ Ideas and Experiments* Proc. 1991 Japan Society for Parallel Processing, pp. 13-23.

[12] D. Gannon, J. K. Lee, On Using Object Oriented Parallel Programming to Build Distributed Algebraic Abstractions, *Proc. CONPAR/VAPP*, Lyon, Sept. 1992.

[13] D. Gannon, *Libraries and Tools for Object Parallel Programming*, Proc. CNRS-NSF Workshop on Environments and Tools For Parallel Scientific Computing, 1992, St. Hilaire du Touvet, France. Elsevier, Advances in Parallel Computing, Vol.6.

[14] K. Li, *Shared Virtual Memory on Loosely Coupled Multiprocessors*, Ph.D. Thesis, Yale University, 1986.

[15] Z. Lahjomri and T. Priol, KOAN: a Shared Virtual Memory for the iPSC/2 Hypercube, *Proc. CONPAR/VAPP*, Lyon, Sept. 1992.

[16] M. Lemke and D. Quinlan, a Parallel C++ Array Class Library for Architecture-Independent Development of Numerical Software, *Proc. OON-SKI Object Oriented Numerics Conf.*, pp. 268–269, Sun River, Oregon, April 1993.

[17] J. Dongarra, R. Pozo, D. Walker, An Object Oriented Design for High Performance Linear Algebra on Distributed Memory Architectures, *Proc. OON-SKI Object Oriented Numerics Conf.*, pp. 257–264, Sun River, Oregon, April 1993.

Concert — Efficient Runtime Support for Concurrent Object-Oriented Programming Languages on Stock Hardware

Vijay Karamcheti and Andrew Chien
University of Illinois at Urbana-Champaign
1304 West Springfield Ave., Urbana, IL 61801
{*vijayk,achien*}*@cs.uiuc.edu*

Abstract

Inefficient implementations of global namespaces, message passing, and thread scheduling on stock multicomputers have prevented concurrent object-oriented programming (COOP) languages from gaining widespread acceptance. Recognizing that the architectures of stock multicomputers impose a hierarchy of costs for these operations, we have described a runtime system which provides different versions of each primitive, exposing performance distinctions for optimization. We confirm the advantages of a cost-hierarchy based runtime system organization by showing a variation of two orders of magnitude in version costs for a CM5 implementation. Frequency measurements based on COOP application programs demonstrate that a 39% invocation cost reduction is feasible by simply selecting cheaper versions of runtime operations.

1 Introduction

Concurrent object-oriented programming (COOP) languages are an attractive approach for programming massively-parallel computers. Object encapsulation can be used to hide details of concurrency control and implementation, providing much needed modularity in concurrent programs. Fine-grained COOP languages are particularly promising since they expose a great deal of concurrency by allowing its expression at the object level. Numerous researchers have been exploring fine-grained object-oriented approaches [1, 2, 3, 4, 5].

Implementations of COOP languages face not only the challenges of object-oriented languages, but also several additional challenges related to concurrency and distribution.[1] In particular, COOP language implementations must provide a global object namespace, implement the communication necessary for remote method invocation, and schedule method invocations on objects. One reason why COOP languages have not gained widespread

acceptance is the perception that these features cannot be implemented efficiently on multicomputers built from conventional processors (stock hardware). This claim is reinforced by the use of custom hardware in the highest performance implementations of COOP languages. Implementations of CST on the J-machine [6] and ABCL on the EM-4 [7] exploit hardware support for message passing, method dispatch, global name translation, and thread scheduling to achieve high performance.

Such custom hardware efforts focus on minimizing the cost of all runtime operations by supporting a few general-purpose primitives efficiently. This reduces the cost difference between situations; e.g., making the cost of accessing a remote object comparable to that of accessing a local object. This design philosophy works well for custom hardware where fundamental cost distinctions between different cases are small[2]. On the other hand, in stock hardware where cost distinctions are more pronounced, general-purpose implementations cannot be fast. Thus, this approach implies slowing down the common cases.

Our approach focuses on a runtime design which distinguishes between the expensive and inexpensive cases, thereby complementing efforts to improve overall execution efficiency of COOP languages on stock hardware. The rationale for this approach is the recognition that some cost differences (such as the local/remote dichotomy) are fundamental to parallel machines, particularly those based on stock hardware. These cost distinctions must be recognized and effectively managed to achieve efficient execution of fine-grained COOP languages. In this paper, we present the design of the Concert runtime which embodies this design philosophy. Our design provides several versions of each runtime operation with varying cost and functionality, allowing the compiler or programmer to choose the most efficient version. The Concert runtime also increases opportunities to use low-cost versions by supporting spec-

---

[1] For the purposes of this paper, we only consider implementations on distributed memory parallel machines.

[2] inter-node operations are faster because of closely coupled processor-network interfaces, while intra-node operations are slower because of slower clock rates, shorter pipelines, and fewer registers.

ulative compilation and runtime mechanisms such as group scheduling of computations.

An example Figure 1 illustrates the benefits of static selection of the cheapest appropriate version of method invocation. In the general case, an invocation from **A** to **B** requires several steps, due to concurrency and distribution concerns (see Figure 1(a)): *translation* to obtain the target object location from a global name, message *creation* to marshal arguments for remote delivery, *transfer* to send them to the target, and *scheduling* to enforce concurrency constraints and support blocking invocations. In a general implementation, the overhead of these steps are required even if **B** is on the same node as **A**.

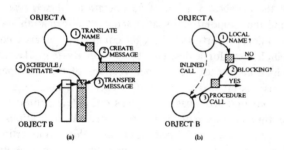

Figure 1: Invocations: (a) general-purpose, (b) with runtime checks and static selection.

The sequence shown with solid lines in Figure 1(b) uses runtime checks to reduce invocation cost. A check to ensure that **B** is located on the same node, followed by a check to ensure that the invocation is non-blocking allows the method to be invoked with a procedure call. A considerably cheaper invocation (dashed line in Figure 1(b)) is possible if the compiler knows about the location of **B** and the non-blocking nature of the handler. It could eliminate the runtime checks (which may have cost comparable to the actual invocation), and make use of global information not available at runtime (e.g., **B** will *always* remain on the same node) to statically inline the method code. Such static selection is particularly important for object-oriented languages which have high procedure call frequencies because it enables interprocedural optimizations.

The Concert runtime is part of the Concert project [8] whose goal is to achieve efficient and portable execution of concurrent object-oriented languages on a variety of hardware platforms. The Concert system focuses on execution grain size tuning relying on aggressive program analysis and careful information management at every stage from the compiler to the runtime system.

Overview The rest of the paper is organized as follows. Section 2 briefly describes a computational model for COOP languages and then describes the key compo-

nents of the runtime interface. In Section 3, we use an example, method invocation, to illustrate the range of cost and functionality choices that are available to a compiler or programmer. Costs of runtime versions (based on a CM5 implementation) and analyses of optimization opportunities in application programs are presented in Section 4. Finally, Section 5 discusses the related work, and Section 6 summarizes the paper and the current status of the project.

2 The Concert runtime

This section surveys the design of the Concert runtime system. First, we briefly describe an abstract computation model which embodies characteristics common to many COOP languages proposed so far [2, 3, 4, 9, 5]. We then present the Concert runtime interface which provides the runtime operations required by the abstract model.

2.1 Computation model of COOP languages

COOP languages express computation as a set of autonomous communicating entities (objects). Generally, these objects reside in a globally shared object namespace and send method invocations to each other. Each invocation request involves the sending of a message containing the method-selector and invocation arguments to the target object. An invocation request is accepted and scheduled according to a language-specific policy which may depend upon local object state. Invocations accepted by the object result in method executions which may in turn send other invocation requests, create additional objects, and modify object state. Invocation requests can behave like remote procedure calls, requiring reply messages which are processed as invocations on the activation frame. A theoretical basis for reasoning about COOP languages can be found in [1]. A wide variety of COOP languages [2, 3, 4, 9, 5] can be modeled by specializing the message acceptance and scheduling policies of this abstract computation model.

2.2 Components of the Concert runtime interface

The dynamic nature of the abstract computation model and a distributed implementation make runtime support for the following operations essential.

- *name translation* to map the object global name to a physical memory location.
- *message delivery* to deliver the invocation requests,
- *type-dependent dispatch* to execute messages based on the object type and state,
- *storage management* to efficiently allocate and free storage for objects and messages, and
- *activation scheduling* to schedule the user computation for increased data locality.

Name translation is necessary for supporting object location and migration. Message delivery is essential for communicating method invocations between objects on different nodes. Type dependent dispatch is a staple of object-oriented languages, and storage management supports dynamic object creation. Activation scheduling can have a significant impact on locality and reuse of data in upper levels of the memory hierarchy.

The Concert runtime provides multiple versions of each runtime operation, exposing the fundamental performance distinctions for static selection of the version with the needed functionality. The runtime system modules and their usage interactions are shown in Figure 2. The overall structure has three levels: Level 1 provides a global namespace, communication mechanisms and local storage management; Level 2 provides resource management mechanisms and frameworks for speculative compilation; and Level 3 uses a combination of first level operations to provide a distributed object space, and support method invocation, object creation, and object migration.

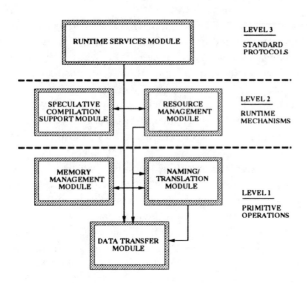

Figure 2: Components of the Runtime Interface.

The first level is composed of three modules:

- **Data Transfer Module** which delivers invocations,
- **Naming and Translation Module** which maps public names of objects to physical memory addresses, and
- **Memory Management Module** which allocates and frees local storage chunks.

The runtime provides several versions of each operation, each appropriate for a different situation. For example, the runtime provides two versions of translation, one for node-private names, the other involving public names which

may require remote access. The versions expose the cost difference, allowing it to be managed intelligently.

Level 2 provides mechanisms whose goal is to utilize system resources more efficiently, and consists of

- **Resource Management Module** which provides mechanisms for load balancing and efficient utilization of local processor resources, and
- **Speculative Compilation Support Module** which provides runtime support for speculative compilation.

The speculative compilation support module provides three kinds of runtime primitives to facilitate speculative optimization. *Runtime checks* determine actual object properties at runtime, enabling the runtime selection of the cheapest version of an operation. *Assertions* extend the temporal and spatial scope of information about an object property and allow the compiler to generate code which tests for a desired object property (e.g., locality, which allows use of cheaper versions of runtime operations), assert that property, then execute a long sequence of code optimized based on the assertion (e.g., eliminating runtime checks, replacing general method invocations by procedure calls or inlined functions). Without assertions, to generate safe code, the compiler would have to assume that object properties could change at arbitrary times, limiting optimization. The runtime ensures that the assertion either remains true or if it becomes false, a special callback function is invoked to restore the code sequence to the general (and more costly) version. Our measurements show that assertions can payoff even for single method invocations. However, the cost of invalidating an assertion can be very high; thus, optimizations using assertions must be applied with discretion. *Hints* extend both checks and assertions by allowing the compiler to influence malleable object properties such as locality. Hints enable a compiler to communicate optimization assumptions to the runtime system by indicating that it would be beneficial if a particular property were true. Hints given to the runtime are non-binding; they typically guide runtime policies.

Level 3 implements a set of basic protocols for operations such as method invocation, object creation, and object migration. The **Runtime Services Module** provides several versions of these protocols by combining different versions of the Level 1 runtime operations.

The design of Concert runtime components described in this section is driven by cost hierarchies prevalent in stock multicomputers. The next section uses an example to illustrate this cost-hierarchy based design in more detail.

3 Cost and functionality choices for method invocation

In this section, we focus on a key example, *method invocation*, to illustrate the utility of providing several versions of runtime operators. Method invocation is the central operation in the execution of any object-oriented language. The basic steps *translate* the object public name to a physical memory address, *transfer* the method-selector and invocation arguments to the destination object, and *schedule and initiate* the computation by finding and invoking the appropriate handler. The overall cost depends upon several factors such as type and location of the target object, number of arguments, and the scheduling policy. In this section, we describe the key factors influencing cost of each step; each significant cost distinction is reflected in a new version of the operation.

3.1 Name translation

Name translation associates an object name with a ⟨*node,address*⟩ tuple giving location of the corresponding storage segment. The cost of translation depends on

- whether the object has a *public* or *private* name, and
- whether or not the object is *relocatable*.

Public names belong to a global namespace and can be used by other objects to send messages without knowing the actual object location, while *private* names are entries in a local namespace and must be qualified with node addressing information. Relocatable elements require translation which involves querying an associative structure; non-relocatable elements do not. Different translation versions (Figure 3) are available for each described situation.

Name translation is cheapest when no translation is required, intermediate cost when the translation is found locally, and maximum cost when a public name is looked up in a global associative table using one or more remote operations. Thus, the different versions correspond to the basic performance distinction between *local* and *remote* operations. This cost distinction is fundamental and arises from the difference in local and remote access times for multicomputer architectures which will persist and perhaps increase in the future.

The performance difference among the versions implies that an efficient implementation must exploit the cost hierarchy, using the cheapest appropriate names. For example, consider objects and activation frames (contexts). Typically, objects are globally accessible and relatively long-lived, requiring relocatability. On the other hand, activation frames are accessible to a small set of continuations and are relatively short-lived. Consequently, public names are

Situation	Version	Description
non-relocatable	`xlate_null`	–
relocatable, private name	`xlate_pvt`	private name → *address*
relocatable, public name	`xlate_pub`	public name → ⟨*node,address*⟩

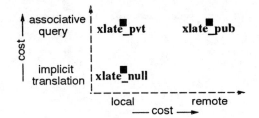

Figure 3: Versions of name translation.

appropriate for objects, while private names suffice for activation frames. As we will show in Section 4, such simple optimizations can give significant performance gains.

3.2 Data transfer

The data transfer operation delivers invocation arguments and reply values to target elements. The cost of data transfer depends on

- whether the transfer target is *local* or *remote*, and
- the *memory hierarchy level* containing the data at the source and destination.

If the data resides in different memory hierarchy levels at source and destination (e.g., the source data might be in registers but needs to reside in memory at the destination), additional work is required to move data up/down the memory hierarchy. Remote transfers cross processor boundaries and involve additional cost for marshalling local references in the outgoing data. Hardware communication primitives[3] may cause additional data movement up/down the memory hierarchy. Data transfer versions are listed in Figure 4.

Since most data transfers are accompanied by a handler invocation, all versions *integrate handler invocation with actual data transfer*. This integration reduces the overhead from data reception to dynamic method dispatching [12] and has been used in the J-machine [13] and the *active message* facility [14].

The different data transfer versions reflect two basic performance distinctions: *local* versus *remote* transfers, and *register* versus *memory* access costs. Remote transfers cost more than corresponding local transfers due to routing and network interface delays. Local memory transfers are more

---

[3]The CM5 [10] provides a register-to-register primitive, while the Paragon [11] provides a memory-to-memory transfer operation.

601

Situation	Version	Description
local	lsend	register → register
destination	lsend_mem	memory → memory
remote	rsend	register → register
destination	rsend_mem	memory → memory

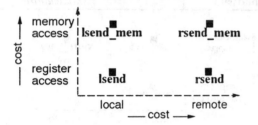

Figure 4: Versions of data transfer operation.

expensive than register movements because memory data must be moved to and from registers in load/store architectures. The cost difference between remote versions of register-to-register and memory-to-memory transfers depends on both access-cost differences and the hardware communication primitives. Based on technology trends, the above distinctions will be more pronounced in future systems: network latency will increase (in units of processor cycles) and memory hierarchies will get deeper with a larger cost to go from top to bottom.

The cost distinctions amongst different versions make it critical to choose an appropriate version for performance. For example, non-blocking invocations with few arguments should use lsend or rsend, since the small messages need not be buffered. On the other hand, blocking invocations should use memory-to-memory versions because the message must be buffered and integrating it with data transmission avoids having to copy arguments into a frame at the destination. Other examples include always preferring local versions over remote ones, and integrating handler invocation with data transfer to allow execution of a portion of the user method in the invoked handler. In Section 4, we show that the costs of different versions range over two orders of magnitude; thus, the above optimizations can yield sizeable performance gains.

3.3 Scheduling and initiation

The scheduling and initiation operations include all steps between data reception and execution of the user handler: *dispatch* binds selector to user code, *frame allocation* obtains an activation frame, and *scheduling* initiates the computation. The cost of these operations depends on

- the time of *binding* the selector to user code,
- whether or not the handler *blocks*, and

- the policy used for *scheduling* the computation.

Selectors can be bound to procedures at compile time or at runtime using a dispatch table based on type and object state information. A handler is potentially blocking if it may suspend awaiting the reply to an outstanding invocation. Non-blocking handler invocations can avoid the cost of frame allocation, using the system stack to execute immediately. Execution can be deferred and scheduled later later with a group of related computations, improving data locality but requiring argument storage and activation enqueuing. The different scheduling and initiation operations (shown in Figure 5) each capture a distinct situation.

Operation	Version	Description
dispatch	s_bind	static binding
	d_bind	delayed binding via dispatch table
frame allocation	alloc_stack	non-blocking method: stack allocation
	alloc_frame	blocking method: heap allocation
scheduling	sched_now	immediate execution
	sched_ind	delayed execution, indiv. scheduled
	sched_grp	delayed execution, group scheduled

Figure 5: Versions of scheduling and initiation.

The different runtime operations correspond to three basic performance distinctions: *compile-time* versus *runtime* binding, *stack* versus *heap* allocation, and *immediate* versus *delayed* execution. Moving work to compile time, as in static binding, reduces runtime cost. Stack allocating activation frames can reduce storage allocation costs. And, immediate execution avoids allocating storage to hold data until it can be processed. The cost of delayed execution points out a clear tradeoff between scheduling overhead and the efficient use of processor resources. As we will show in Section 4, the performance differences amongst the versions suggest that specialization is essential for high efficiency. Making the optimizations expressible in the runtime interface is a critical step in that direction.

Summary Method invocation in a distributed COOP implementation involves the composition of several runtime operations. In this section, we have described a range of invocation choices arising from fundamental cost distinctions, such as *local* and *remote* operations, *register* and *memory* accesses, *stack* and *heap* allocation, and *immediate* and *delayed* execution. In the next section, our measurements show the cost implications of different choices, and the performance advantages of making them explicit.

Operation	Version	Implementation		Cost	
				_µs_	_cyc._
Name Translation	`xlate_null`	translation implicit in name.		0.03	1
	`xlate_pvt`	hashtable of associations.		0.91	30
	`xlate_pub`	distributed hashtable (with local caching).	_min_	3.59	120
			max	16.07	536
			obs	11.70	390
Data Transfer (Local)	`lsend` reg→reg	register arguments of integrated invocation.		0.15	5
	`lsend_mem` mem→mem	argument copying into preallocated buffer.		2.88	96
Data Transfer (Remote)	`rsend` reg→reg	built with CMAM_4() from [15].		7.05	235
	`rsend_mem` mem→mem	built with CMAM() from [15].		15.65	520
Scheduling & Initiation	`s_bind`	known at compile time.		0.00	0
	`d_bind`	C++-like dispatch table.		0.09	3
	`alloc_stack`	modify stack pointer.		0.03	1
	`alloc_frame`	binned memory allocator.		3.72	124
	`sched_now`	frame setup and procedure call.		0.14	5
	`sched_ind`	computation stored in central scheduler queue.		3.27	108
	`sched_grp`	scheduling queue associated with object: all waiting computations scheduled together.		4.06	134

Table 1: Cost of different versions of runtime operations.

4 Implementation and performance results

The Concert runtime is currently being used as an execution environment for Concurrent Aggregates (CA) [3] programs on both the Thinking Machines CM5 [10] and a thread-based uniprocessor simulator. We use these implementations to measure runtime operation costs, and CA program statistics to conservatively estimate opportunities for using low cost versions of runtime operations. Performance measurements validate the existence of a cost hierarchy for each operation, justifying its reflection in the runtime interface. Dynamic statistics show that less expensive versions can be used in many cases, dramatically reducing effective cost of runtime operations. We are constructing a compiler which will automatically optimize execution by selecting cheaper versions of runtime operations [8].

4.1 Costs of primitive runtime operations

The costs of various runtime operations are given in Table 1. Operation latency in $µ$seconds and CM5 processor cycles was measured using a synthetic program which repeatedly performed the runtime operation of interest. Accuracy was ensured by measuring over an interval 10^5 times larger than the 1$µ$second timer resolution. The actual CM5 hardware used was a 33 Mhz clock, 32 Mbytes per node,

128 PN partition with the node network interface supporting five 32-bit word messages. Note that the cost of operations involving remote access is dominated by software overhead (the hardware network latency is small in all cases).

Based on the data in Table 1, we observe a clear cost hierarchy amongst versions for each operation. In the following sections, we make more specific observations.

Name translation `xlate_pub` is implemented using a globally distributed hash table with local caching. The three timings for `xlate_pub` correspond to the minimum cost of finding the translation in the local cache, the maximum cost when translation requires a remote access, and the observed cost based on CA application programs. Our performance data shows that translation cost spans several orders of magnitude from essentially free for non-relocatable private names to tens of $µ$seconds for an access to the globally distributed hash table. Thus, using low cost versions for translation yields significant performance gains.

Data transfer All measurements for data transfer versions use a transfer size of four 32-bit words. Table 1 shows that for local invocations, register-to-register transfer is an order of magnitude cheaper than the memory-to-memory alternative; most of the difference is attributable to buffer management. For remote invocations, register-to-register transfer is two times cheaper than the memory-to-memory

Implementation	Clock rate	Send/Reply		Dispatch		Translation	
	MHz	μs	cyc.	μs	cyc.	μs	cyc.
CST(on J-m/c)	28.3	6.36/7.8	180/220	0.6/1.6	18/46	0.9/2.6	26/74
ABCL(on EM-4)	12.5	9	112	0.24	3	–	–

Table 2: Min/Max costs of runtime operations on custom-hardware implementations.

alternative. Clearly, register-to-register versions give significant benefits for small transfers; however memory-to-memory transfers are required for large amounts of data which cannot be buffered in registers. In many machines, transfer cost increases with message size, and both the CM5 [10] and AP1000 [16] incorporate special mechanisms for sending small messages.

Scheduling and initiation   Dynamic binding using C++ like dispatch tables [17] costs only a few instructions more than static binding. However, the cost of frame allocation for blocking invocations is significant implying that non-blocking invocations are worth dealing with specially. Both sophisticated forms of scheduling, individual and group, are much more expensive than the simple sched_now approach, suggesting that such approaches must give significant locality benefits to be worthwhile.

Our measurements of runtime operation costs present a different profile from that of COOP language implementations on custom hardware (see Table 2). The numbers show that such implementations provide relatively flat cost hierarchies, with no more than a factor of three difference in cost; thus, choosing the most general mechanism incurs only a modest performance penalty. In contrast, operation costs in the stock-hardware based Concert runtime span two orders of magnitude, making the choice of the cheapest appropriate mechanism essential for good performance.

4.2   Method invocation cost

To demonstrate the performance impact of choosing cheaper versions of runtime operations, we consider a range of implementations for the method invocation operation. Table 3 presents costs of some typical method invocation sequences. In all cases, the method invocation takes two arguments, a selector, and a continuation.[4] As in Section 4.1, for operations involving xlate_pub, three numbers corresponding to the minimum, maximum, and observed timings are presented. The table shows that the *cheapest invocation sequence (4 cycles) is as inexpensive as a procedure call* in an imperative language. The most expensive sequence (**1275** cycles) is three orders of magnitudes more expensive, and corresponds to a naive implementation of

---

[4]While this number of arguments is small, it allows us to contrast invocation sequences with and without hardware supported communication. The new CM5 network interface supports larger messages.

a fine-grained COOP language. The different situations presented in Table 3 bring out the cost-functionality trade-offs associated with providing features like heap-allocated activation frames (increases cost by **150** cycles), sophisticated scheduling (incurs cost of **120** cycles), and relocatable namespaces (cost ranges from **140** to **450** cycles).

Table 3 also shows the costs of corresponding operations in the ABCL/onAP1000 implementation [18] which focuses on improving the worst-case efficiency of runtime primitives. The numbers show the Concert runtime to be as fast as the ABCL/onAP1000 implementation for comparable invocation sequences, implying that the observed cost-hierarchy is not merely an artifact of poor implementation of the worst-case version. The order of magnitude cost difference for the cheapest invocation sequence (**4** cycles versus **58** cycles) validates our claim about traditional runtime designs charging for unnecessary functionality. Some Concert operations are more expensive only because they provide additional functionality such as relocatable namespaces, larger message sizes, and flexible scheduling.

4.3   Opportunities for optimization

Higher performance by capitalizing on low-cost versions of runtime operations is possible only if there are opportunities to use the cheaper versions. To demonstrate the extent to which the cost distinctions are exploitable, we present frequency measurements of optimization opportunities for a set of CA applications [3], and characterize the effective reduction in costs of runtime operations. The applications include **pcbroute** which uses concurrent A^* search to route nets around obstacles on a board, **logicsim** which is an event-driven logic simulation, and **multigrid** which implements the multigrid relaxation technique.

In the following discussion, effective reduction in an operation's cost is computed by weighting it with the fraction of times an optimizable event occurs. Percentage reductions in the effective cost of an operation are presented relative to the most general (expensive) version of the operation in Tables 1 and 3. For operations involving xlate_pub, the baseline used is the observed cost.

Low-cost versions of name translation   Global names and remote translation are unnecessary in many cases. To estimate opportunities for using cheaper versions, Table 4 presents the message target statistics for each application.

Description of Sequence	Versions Used	Cost			
		Concert		ABCL/AP1000	
		μs	*cyc.*	*μs*	*cyc.*
non-susp. local invoke, reg→reg transfer, static binding, scheduled immed.	`xlate_null, lsend, s_bind, alloc_stack, sched_now`	0.1	4	2.3	58
susp. local invoke, reg→reg transfer, dynamic binding, scheduled later	`xlate_null, lsend, d_bind, alloc_frame, sched_ind`	8.4	277	9.6	240
non-susp. remote invoke, reg→reg transfer, dynamic binding, scheduled immed.	`xlate_null, rsend, d_bind, alloc_stack, sched_now`	7.7	252	8.9	223
		min–max (obs)	*min–max (obs)*		
remote translation, non-susp. remote invoke, reg→reg transfer, dynamic binding, scheduled immed.	`xlate_pub, rsend, d_bind, alloc_stack, sched_now`	11.9–27.1 (21.4)	397–904 (713)		
remote translation, susp. remote invoke, reg→reg transfer, dynamic binding, scheduled immed.	`xlate_pub, rsend, d_bind, alloc_frame, sched_now`	16.3–31.8 (25.9)	543–1053 (865)		
remote translation, susp. remote invoke, mem→mem transfer, dynamic binding, scheduled later	`xlate_pub, rsend_mem, d_bind, alloc_frame, sched_ind`	28.6–44.2 (38.3)	941–1456 (1275)		

Table 3: A wide range of method invocation costs.

Two kinds of optimizations reduce the cost of translation. The first optimization associates private names with activation frames (see Section 3.1) allowing `xlate_pvt` to be used for all reply messages. Replies constitute over **40%** of all messages; consequently, this reduction from the baseline `xlate_pub` (11.7μs) to `xlate_pvt` (0.91μs) will reduce translation cost by **37%**.

program name	total msgs	reply msgs	invoke msgs to i^{th} neighbor		
			1	*2*	*3*
`pcbroute`	116,883	47%	14%	5%	3%
`logicsim`	219,788	43%	24%	15%	7%
`multigrid`	582,913	41%	19%	11%	6%

Table 4: Message target statistics in CA programs.

The second optimization reduces the cost seen by invocation messages. From Table 4, we observe that applications demonstrate significant invocation locality (i.e., objects tend to communicate with a small set of preferred objects) with **35%** of *all* messages being invocations from an object to one of its three most preferred neighbors. Translation costs can be reduced by exploiting this locality to cache translations to preferred neighbors. Since invocations are separate from replies, reducing the cost for `xlate_pub` from 11.70μs to its minimum possible (3.59μs) yields an additional translation cost reduction of **24%**.

Low-cost versions of data transfer   On machines such as the CM5 which supports hardware transfer mechanisms for small messages, data transfer cost can be significantly

reduced by using appropriate versions for such transfers. To evaluate the impact of this optimization, Table 5 presents the distribution of message sizes in each application. Approximately **50%** of the messages are four words or less, so they can benefit from the cheaper register-to-register versions. Even with the conservative assumption that all message destinations are remote (else `lsend` can be used), this optimization reduces the cost of data transfer by **28%**.

program name	total msgs	msgs of size (words)			
		1–4	*5–9*	*10–14*	*15+*
`pcbroute`	116,883	58%	27%	11%	4%
`logicsim`	219,788	47%	28%	13%	12%
`multigrid`	582,913	44%	41%	14%	1%

Table 5: Message size distribution in CA programs.

program name	invocations		
	total	*# non-blocking*	*% non-blocking*
`pcbroute`	61525	36289	59%
`logicsim`	18764	9756	52%
`multigrid`	34440	14012	41%

Table 6: Invocation statistics in CA programs.

Low-cost scheduling and initiation versions   Table 6 presents the fraction of invocations which are non-blocking. Such invocations comprise **50%** of the total and can be implemented using (*i*) stack allocation (using `alloc_stack` instead of `alloc_frame`), and (*ii*) by executing a portion of the user computation in the integrated handler (using

Optimization	Version Enabled	optimiz. cases	cost redn. (primitive)	cost redn. (invocation)
reply msgs to activation frames	`xlate_pvt`	40%	37%	11.5%
invoke msgs to preferred objects	`xlate_pub(min)`	35%	24%	7.5%
short (1–5 words) msg transfers	`rsend`	50%	28%	11.6%
non-suspending invocations	`alloc_stack`	50%	29%	5.0%
	`sched_now`	50%	19%	3.3%
Total reduction in cost of method invocation				38.9%

Table 7: Reductions in invocation cost by using lower-cost versions.

`sched_now`). Using the program stack for the activation frame reduces the scheduling and initiation cost by **29%**. A further reduction of **19%** is possible by starting user-handler execution immediately.

Table 7 summarizes the cost reductions described in this section by applying them to a composite method invocation operation. An overall improvement of at least **39%** is possible from optimizations which choose appropriately specialized versions of runtime operations. It is interesting to note that all the basic runtime operations contribute to the overall reduction, suggesting that hierarchical interfaces are necessary for all of them. Further performance gains are possible by exploiting resource-management mechanisms and support for speculative compilation to proactively structure the computation, increasing optimization opportunities. As an example, consider group scheduling of computations to benefit from state reuse. Table 8 presents a conservative estimate of the number of activations that can be deferred and group scheduled. This number has been obtained by processing application traces and counting the unordered activations on an object. This number is remarkably high, **40% – 70%** of all invocations can be group scheduled, indicating the potential for large performance gains.

program name	Scheduling Quanta		
	# indiv. scheduled	# group scheduled	% redn.
`pcbroute`	119262	66692	44%
`logicsim`	36877	15460	58%
`multigrid`	53972	13816	74%

Table 8: Scheduling statistics in CA programs.

5 Related work

Our work is related to many efforts focusing on runtime support for efficiently executing irregular computations on stock hardware [19, 20]. It differs from runtime systems for coarse-grained object-oriented languages such as COOL [21] and Mentat [22], by focusing on fine-grained object-level concurrency.

The ABCL/onAP1000 implementation [18] is most similar with our work but adopts a traditional design, emphasizing techniques for reducing access latency and object-creation costs. The general versions in Concert are as efficient as in the ABCL system, while the cheaper versions cost significantly less. Our work complements the ABCL work by distinguishing low-cost operations from expensive ones, exposing the distinctions for optimization.

Our work is also similar to the Threaded Abstract Machine(TAM) [23]. Although TAM supports a different language model (extended hybrid dataflow), both systems enable optimization by providing the compiler with a range of mechanisms for managing synchronization, scheduling and storage and an associated cost hierarchy. The speculative compilation module in the Concert runtime reflects additional support not present in TAM, required because of the dynamic nature of object-oriented languages which limits the applicability of static analysis and optimization.

6 Conclusion

We have described a novel approach for efficiently executing COOP languages on stock multicomputers. The key is a runtime interface which exposes the essential performance distinctions between different versions of a runtime operation, allowing their use to be optimized. Since these cost distinctions driving the runtime design arise from basic architectural structures such as the local/remote dichotomy, and deep memory hierarchies, we believe them to be fundamental; consequently, the only path to higher efficiency is to choose cheap versions, decreasing the frequency of expensive ones.

Timing measurements on a CM5 based runtime implementation bear out our claim of cost distinctions between different versions of primitive operations in a method invocation. Expensive versions have cost comparable to previously published results, while inexpensive ones cost significantly less. The runtime differs from special-hardware implementations in providing versions with costs spanning two orders of magnitude; clearly, the ability to choose the cheapest version is essential for good performance. Frequency measurements on CA applications reveal ample opportunity for efficient exploitation of cheaper versions of runtime operations. Based on a few simple optimizations, effective invocation cost reductions of at least **39%** has been shown possible.

Current efforts focus on continued tuning of the implementation. We are integrating this runtime interface into the Concert system along with compilation techniques to exploit the available hierarchy of runtime operators.

Acknowledgements

The authors would like to thank John Plevyak for participating in several discussions and assisting with the runtime system implementation, and the anonymous reviewers for their helpful comments.

The Concert project and the authors of this paper are supported in part by NSF grant CCR-9209336, ONR grant N00014-92-J-1961, NASA grant NAG 1-613, and a special-purpose grant from the AT&T Foundation. Some of the work reported in this paper was done on a CM5 at the National Center for Supercomputing Applications.

References

[1] G. Agha, *Actors: A Model of Concurrent Computation in Distributed Systems.* Cambridge, MA: MIT Press, 1986.

[2] P. America, "POOL-T: A parallel object-oriented language," in *Object-Oriented Concurrent Programming* (A. Yonezawa and M. Tokoro, eds.), pp. 199–220, MIT Press, 1987.

[3] A. A. Chien, *Concurrent Aggregates: Supporting Modularity in Massively-Parallel Programs.* Cambridge, MA: MIT Press, 1993.

[4] W. Dally and A. Chien, "Object oriented concurrent programming in cst," in *Proceedings of the Third Conference on Hypercube Computers*, (Pasadena, California), pp. 434–9, SIAM, 1988.

[5] A. Yonezawa, ed., *ABCL: An Object-Oriented Concurrent System.* MIT Press, 1990. ISBN 0-262-24029-7.

[6] W. Horwat, "Concurrent smalltalk on the message-driven processor," Master's thesis, Massachusetts Institute of Technology, Cambridge, Massachusetts, June 1989.

[7] M. Yasugi, S. Matsuoka, and A. Yonezawa, "ABCL/onEM-4: A new software/hardware architecture for object-oriented concurrent computing on an extended dataflow supercomputer," in *Proceedings of the ACM Conference on Supercomputing '92*, 1992.

[8] A. Chien, V. Karamcheti, and J. Plevyak, "The concert system – compiler and runtime support for efficient fine-grained concurrent object-oriented programs," Tech. Rep. UIUCDCS-R-93-1815, Department of Computer Science, University of Illinois, Urbana, Illinois, June 1993.

[9] C. Houck and G. Agha, "HAL: A high-level actor language and its distributed implementation," in *Proceedings of the 21st International Conference on Parallel Processing*, (St. Charles, IL), pp. 158–165, August 1992.

[10] Thinking Machines Corporation, Cambridge, Massachusetts, *Connection Machine CM-5, Technical Summary*, November 1992.

[11] Intel Corporation, *Paragon XP/S Product Overview*, 1991.

[12] T. Baba, et al., "A parallel object-oriented total architecture: A-NET," in *Proceedings of IEEE Supercomputing '90*, pp. 276–285, IEEE Computer Society, 1990.

[13] W. J. Dally, A. Chien, S. Fiske, W. Horwat, J. Keen, M. Larivee, R. Lethin, P. Nuth, S. Wills, P. Carrick, and G. Fyler, "The J-Machine: A fine-grain concurrent computer," in *Information Processing 89, Proceedings of the IFIP Congress*, pp. 1147–1153, Aug. 1989.

[14] T. von Eicken, D. Culler, S. Goldstein, and K. Schauser, "Active Messages: a mechanism for integrated communication and computation," in *Proceedings of the International Symposium on Computer Architecture*, 1992.

[15] T. von Eicken and D. E. Culler, *Building Communication Paradigms with the CM-5 Active Message layer (CMAM).* University of California, Berkeley, 2.4 ed., September 1992.

[16] T. Shimizu, T. Horie, and H. Ishihata, "Low-latency message communication support for the AP1000," in *International Symposium on Computer Architecture*, pp. 288–297, 1992.

[17] B. Stroustrup, *The C++ Programming Language.* Addison Wesley, second ed., 1991.

[18] K. Taura, S. Matsuoka, and A. Yonezawa, "An efficient implementation scheme of concurrent object-oriented languages on stock multicomputers," in *Proceedings of the Fifth ACM SIGPLAN Symposium on the Principles and Practice of Parallel Programming*, 1993.

[19] M. C. Carlisle, A. Rogers, J. H. Reppy, and L. J. Hendren, "Early experiences with olden," in *Proceedings of the Sixth Workshop on Languages and Compilers for Parallel Machines*, 1993.

[20] W. C. Hsieh, P. Wang, and W. E. Weihl, "Computation migration: Enhancing locality for distributed-memory parallel systems," in *Proceedings of the Fifth ACM SIGPLAN Symposium on the Principles and Practice of Parallel Programming*, pp. 239–248, 1993.

[21] R. Chandra, A. Gupta, and J. L. Hennessy, "Data locality and load balancing in COOL," in *Proceedings of the Fourth ACM SIGPLAN Symposium on Principles and Practice of Parallel Programming*, 1993.

[22] A. Grimshaw, "Easy-to-use object-oriented parallel processing with Mentat," *IEEE Computer*, May 1993.

[23] D. Culler, A. Sah, K. Schauser, T. von Eicken, and J. Wawrzynek, "Fine-grain parallelism with minimal hardware support: A compiler-controlled threaded abstract machine," in *Proceedings of the Fourth International Conference on Architectural Support for Programming Languages an Operating Systems*, pp. 164–75, 1991.

Session 8:
Workshop
High Performance Fortran

High Performance Fortran: Implementor and Users Workshop

Alok Choudhary *

Charles Koelbel

Mary Zosel

Syracuse University
Syracuse, NY

Rice University
Houston, TX,

Lawrence Livermore
National Lab

Abstract

High Performance Fortran (HPF) is anticipated to be an industry-wide standard language portable from workstations to massively parallel supercomputers, implemented by many vendors. Functions needed on the highest-performance parallel machines are particularly well-supported in HPF. The definition of HPF, (version 1, completed May 1993) incorporated feedback from a large number of users during the language design phase.

The purpose of this workshop is to continue the interaction among developers of compilers and software tools for HPF, potential users of HPF and hardware developers. Specifically, this workshop focuses on the feedback from the implementors of HPF as well as from users of the initial implementations. The reports will be followed by a discussion for the purpose of gathering user and implementor input about how the HPF specification might be changed to strengthen the language and make it useful for a broader class of applications.

1 Background

The annual SuperComputing conferences have played an important part in the development of High Performance Fortran, starting with SC91 when Ken Kennedy and Geoffrey Fox described the initial motivation behind the development of Fortran- D in a panel discussing problems related to portability for parallel computing. There was a wide response to this work, and by the time that SC91 was here, there was already pressure to standardize the language associated with this research project. This was discussed in a birds-of-a-feather session at SC91, and resulted in the creation of the High Performance Computing Forum (HPFF). A specific goal of HPFF was to have a draft language specification ready in time for workshop presentation calling for public feedback at SC92. It is now appropriate that a workshop at SC93 explore the initial experiences with the first version of HPF.

Version 1.0 of HPF language specification was released in May 93 after incorporation of changes suggested during the 3 month comment period [HPF-Spec92].

2 Motivation for HPF

Since its introduction in the 1950s, Fortran has been the language of choice for scientific and engineering programming. Support for Fortran is available on virtually all computers ranging from personal computers and workstations to servers, mainframes, and supercomputers. Fortran itself has evolved over this period, most recent version being Fortran 90 which incorporates many new features including Array Constructs, Elemental Intrinsic Functions, Reduction Intrinsic Functions, Dynamic Storage Allocation, enhanced support for Modular Programming etc.

Exploiting the full capability of modern parallel architectures, however, increasingly requires more information than that can be expressed even in Fortran 90. Such information includes indicating

- opportunities for parallel execution,

- types of available parallelism,

- data mapping among processors,

- placement of data within a single processor, and

- specification of control parallelism.

Over the last year, High-Performance Fortran Forum, an informal coalition of industrial, academic, and government groups defined extensions to Fortran 90. These extensions in conjunction with the base Fortran

---

*Supported by ARPA contract # DABT63-91-C-0028 and NSF Young investigator award CCR-9357840.

90 language are termed as "High-Performance Fortran (HPF)".

The basic goal of the HPFF was to define a language which will serve as a platform for portable parallel programming. It is believed that most vendors of parallel computers and third party compiler and system software developers for parallel computers will adopt HPF.

3 An Overview of HPF

HPF is designed to provide a portable extension to Fortran 90 for writing data parallel applications. It includes features for mapping data to parallel processors, specifying data parallel operations, and methods for interfacing HPF programs to other programming paradigms. HPF uses compiler directives where ever the extensions do not cause a potential change to the meaning of the program and explicit language extensions where the semantic meaning is changed.

The parallelism in a program, expressed by constructs like array assignment, FORALL statements, DO INDEPENDENT loops, intrinsic and standard library procedures, and EXTRINSIC procedures, determines how many operations a computer can possibly do at one time. It is then the compiler's responsibility to schedule those operations on the physical machine so that the program runs as fast as possible.

Communication in a program is an overhead that opposes parallelism. HPF puts much of the burden of communication on the compiler; the user supplies a very high-level data mapping strategy and the system generates the details of the communication it implies.

The data mapping directives are probably the most publicized features in HPF. They describe how data is to be divided up among the processors in a parallel machine. The presumption is that the processor responsible for some data (also called the processor that owns the data) can read or write it much faster than another processor. HPF describes the data-to-processor mapping in two stages using the DISTRIBUTE and ALIGN operations. DISTRIBUTE is an HPF directive that describes how an array is divided into even-sized pieces and distributed to processors in a regular way. ALIGN is an HPF directive that describes how two arrays "line up" together. A group of arrays that are usually used together in a predicable manner may be aligned together to some base array, or to some abstract TEMPLATE and then distributed with a single DISTRIBUTE directive.

Additional data mapping directives allow redistribution (REDISTRIBUTE) and realignment (RE-ALIGN) of data arrays and allow specification of abstract processor arrangements (PROCESSORS) for the purpose of load balance and memory balance across the physical processors of a machine.

The interface between subprograms requires special features for conveying the expectations about the distribution and alignment of the subprogram arguments. Three basic forms are supported: a prescriptive specification, where the programmer gives a specific mapping and the compiler coerces the argument appropriately; a descriptive specification, where the programmer alleges that the argument already has certain mapping properties, and a transcriptive specification where the compiler is instructed to adapt to whatever mapping the incoming argument may have. When an explicit Fortran 90 interface is specified for a subprogram, the compiler will assure conformance for all arguments in the subprogram invocation.

Traditional FORTRAN features for storage association (COMMON and EQUIVALENCE) have a strong interaction with data mapping directives. Some uses of storage association make data mapping either highly inefficient or even impossible, e.g. two different distributions for arrays associated by EQUIVALENCE. HPF gives a set of rules for use of COMMON and EQUIVALENCE and supplies a SEQUENCE directive to allow the programmer to specify that storage association is required. A similar set of restrictions is applied to passing subprogram arguments when the shape of the argument is not the same on both sides of the call.

The new HPF features for parallelism are primarily syntax extensions, along with one additional directive. The FORALL construct extends Fortran 90 array operations by supplying a multi-dimensional set of index values that are used to evaluate the results of each statement in the construct. HPF introduces PURE functions . These are functions that have no side-effects and thus may be used inside a FORALL statement and still provide deterministic results. The HPF INDEPENDENT directive may be applied to either the FORALL construct or to the Fortran DO loop. A programmer can use it to promise the compiler that the FORALL or DO does not make any "bad" data accesses that force the loop to be run sequentially. With this information, a compiler knows it is safe to produce parallel code.

Additional HPF language extensions introduce a few new intrinsic procedures and an extensive library. These allow for interrogation of the machine and mapping characteristics and also define many data parallel operations such as combining-scatter operations.

These data parallel operations allow these common operations to be optimized by the HPF vendor for maximum efficiency on a given machine, while still maintaining the portability of the user's code.

The last new feature of HPF is a recognition that many programs need to use more than a single programming paradigm. The EXTRINSIC program interface definition allows a programmer to give explicit notice to the compiler that the program is entering a different model of execution. For machines that support MIMD type operations, HPF defines one additional programming paradigm called HPF_LOCAL where data references are specifically local to a processing node rather than global to the entire processor set.

Finally, HPF recognizes that efficient implementation of all of the HPF features in addition to full Fortran 90 is potentially incompatible with timely productions of compilers that allow the programmer portable data parallel programs. As a result, a subset of the language is defined for the purpose of encouraging early access to basic features.

4 Vendor Endorsement of HPF

Many vendors have already announced efforts to develop software tools to support HPF. These vendors include TMC, MasPar, DEC, Intel, APR, KAI and PGI. Other active participants from the industry who have shown considerable interest in supporting HPF (but have not made any formal announcements yet) include IBM, Cray Research, Convex, HP, Ncube, Meiko, Fujitsu and Archipel.

5 Goals of the Workshop

The main goal of this workshop is to continue the interaction among developers of compilers, potential users of HPF and hardware developers. Specifically, the goals are to

- stimulate discussion among implementors of HPF so that they can share their experiences,

- to provide feedback to the implementors from the users and other workshop attendees, and

- identify potential problem areas, limitations of the language and identify features that may be desirable in the newer versions of HPF.

6 WHat next for HPF?

In the interest of getting a specification completed so that implementations could begin, HPFF knowingly limited discussion in some important areas. The current plan for HPFF is to reconvene with a meeting in early 94 calling for proposals of features that should be included, clarified, (or even eliminated) in a second version of HPF. This would be followed by a set of meetings similar to the first set of HPFF meetings. Important features for discussion include support for unstructured arrays and parallel I/O, in addition to areas of the language that have been identified as needing clarification.

Acknowledgements

We would like to thank Ken Kennedy and Geoffrey Fox who initiated the HPF effort. Special thanks to all our colleages in the HPFF for their strong commitment to the entire process without which HPF would not have been defined in time. Finally, on behalf of HPFF, we would like to express our gratitude to hundres of people from all over the world who provided constant input and feedback during and after the language definition process.

Bibliography

[ABMSW92] J. C. Adams, W. S. Brainerd, J. T. Martin, B. T. Smith , J. L. Wagener , Fortran 90 Handbook, Intertext-McGraw Hill, New York, NY, 1992

[ALS91] E. Albert, J. Lukas and G. Steele, Jr. Data Parallel Computers and the FORALL Statement , Journal of Parallel and Distributed Computing, October 1991.

[BCFH93] Z. Bozkus, Alok Choudhary, Geoffrey C. Fox, T. Haupt, and S. Ranka, *Fortran 90D/HPF Compiler for Distributed Memory MIMD Computers: Design, Implementation, and Performance Results*, Supercomputing '93, November 1993 (to appear), Portland, OR. (R)

[CMZ92] B. Chapman, P. Mehrotra and H. Zima , Programming in Vienna Fortran , Scientific Programming 1,1, August 1992.

[CMZ93] B. Chapman, P. Mehrotra and H. Zima , High Performance Fortran Without Templates: An Alternative Model for Distribution and Alignment , In Proceedings of the Fourth ACM SIGPLAN Symposium on Principles and Practice of Parallel Programming (PPoPP) , San Diego, CA, May, 1993.

[CW92] M. Chen and J. Cowie , Prototyping Fortran-90 Compilers for Massively Parallel Machines , Proceedings of the SIGPLAN '92 Conference on Program Language Design and Implementation, San Francisco, CA., June, 1992.

[Fox86] G. Fox, M. Johnson, G. Lyzenga, S. Otto, J. Salmon and D. Walker, Solving Problems on Concurrent Processors,, Prentice-Hall, Englewood Cliffs, NJ, 1988

[FHKKKTW91] G. Fox, S. Hiranandani, K. Kennedy, C. Koelbel, U. Kremer, C. Tseng and M. Wu , Fortran D Language Specification , report COMP TR90-141 (Rice) and SSCS-42c (Syracuse), Department of Computer Science, Rice University, Houston, Texas, and Syracuse Center for Computational Science, Syracuse University, Syracuse, New Your, April 1991.

[F9091] International Organization for Standardization and International Electrotechnical Commission , Fortran 90 [ISO /EC 1539: 1991 (E)], May 1991. Also ANSI X3.198-1992.

[HPFSpec92] High Performance Fortran Forum , High Performance Fortran Language Specification, version 1.0, Center for Research on Parallel Computation, Rice University, Technical Report CRPC-TR92225, Revised May 1993. To appear in Scientific Programming , vol. 2, no. 1.

[HPFJoD92] High Performance Fortran Forum , High Performance Fortran Journal of Development, Center for Research on Parallel Computation, Rice University, Technical Report CRPC-TR933300, May 3, 1993. To appear in Scientific Programming , vol. 2, no. 1.

[HKK:Overview] S. Hiranandani, K. Kennedy, C. Koelbel and U. Kremer and C. Tseng , An Overview of the Fortran D Programming System , In Languages and Compilers for Parallel Computing, Fourth International Workshop, ed. U. Banerjee, D. Gelernter, A. Nicolau and D. Padua , Springer-Verlag, Santa Clara CA., Aug. 91.

[KLS90] K. Knobe, J. Lukas and G. Steele, Jr. , Data Optimization: Allocation of arrays to Reduce Communication on SIMD Machines,, Journal of Parallel and Distributed Computing, Vol 8 No. 2, Pages 102-118, Feb. 1990.

[KLSSZ93] C. Koelbel, D. Loveman, R. Schreiber, G. Steele, Jr., and M. Zosel, The High Performance Fortran Handbook, MIT-Press, Cambridge, MA., To appear 1993.

[KM92] C. Koelbel , An Overview of High Performance Fortran , Fortran Forum , Vol. 11 No. 4, Dec. 1992.

[DBL93] D. B. Loveman , High Performance Fortran, IEEE Parallel and Distributed Technology, Vol. 1, No. 1, Feb. 1993.

[DBL92] D. B. Loveman , Elemental Array Assignment – the FORALL Statement , Proceedings of the Third Workshop on Compilers for Parallel Computers, Vienna, Austria, July 1992.

[MR90] M. Metcalf and J. Reid, Fortran 90 Explained, Oxford Science Publications, 1990.

[GLS93] G. L. Steele Jr., High Performance Fortran : Status Report , ACM SIGPlan Notices ,Vol. 28 No. 1, Jan. 1993.

[TMC91] Thinking Machines Corporation , CM Fortran Reference Manual , Cambridge, Massachusetts , July 1991.

[MilSt1753] US Department of Defense , Military Standard, MIL-STD-1753: FORTRAN, DoD Supplement to American National Standard X3.9- 1978 , November 9 , 1978.

[ZBCM92] H. Zima, P. Brezany, B. Chapman, P. Mehrotra and A. Schwald, Vienna Fortran — A Language Specification, Version 1.1, ICASE Interim Report No. 21, Hampton VA., Mar. 1992.

[ZC91] H. Zima and B. Chapman , Supercompilers for Parallel and Vector Computers , Addison-Wesley, New York, NY, 1991.

Session 8:
Minisymposium
Chairs: Fran Berman and
Tom Kitchens

MINISYMPOSIUM:
THE HETEROGENEOUS COMPUTING CHALLENGE

Moderators:

Francine Berman
Department of Computer Science and Engineering
University of California at San Diego

Tom Kitchens
Office of Scientific Computing
U. S. Department of Energy

The goal of the Heterogeneous Computing Challenge is to demonstrate state-of-the-art heterogeneous processing utilizing SCInet, the network infrastructure on the exhibition floor of Supercomputing '93, through a friendly competition. The participants developed significant applications accessing the various computing systems on the exhibition floor and elsewhere over the several SCInet networks. They also participated in the LeMans FunRun, a heterogeneous "race".

The projects were judged with respect to the following categories:

1. *The most elegant: The application uses the unique strengths of each of the various computing platforms and includes an appropriate graphical user interface.*
2. *The most heterogeneous: The application must be sensible and use the most multiple distinct platforms on the floor.*
3. *The best speedup: The application must demonstrate the most improved performance using a heterogeneous collection of platforms in comparison to the same application running on any of the individual platforms in the collection.*
4. *The best LeMans FunRun: The first to finish the LeMans FunRun or the one which is most complete at the end of 20 minutes.*

The LeMans FunRun was introduced at SC '93 to graphically illustrate the fun and frustration of heterogeneous computing. The contest uses SCInet and many of the platforms on SCInet and was held during the SC '93 welcoming reception. The LeMans FunRun 'course' was to complete a graphical puzzle where the data dependences that govern most of heterogeneous computing are simulated by requiring that a part of the puzzle can only be added if a contiguous part has been previously obtained. The exception is that the first part which has no dependencies and can be choosen at will. The LeMans FunRun was implemented by Jason Secosky and Allan Snavely."

The friendly judges are:

Margaret Simmons, Los Alamos National Laboratory
Dona Crawford, Sandia National Laboratory
Bob Voigt, National Science Foundation
Ben Peek, Advanced Digital Communications Consortium
Joan Francioni, University of Southwestern Louisiana

John Gustafson, Iowa State University
Vaidy Sunderam, Emory University
Dennis Duke, Florida State University
Bart Miller, University of Wisconsin
Gary Montry, Southwest Software

The purpose of this minisymposium is to allow the participants to describe their projects and their strategies for utilizing the heterogeneous systems involved. The following is a list of the projects submitted.

1993 ACM 0-8186-4340-4/93/0011

SmartNet - A PVM based Management System for Near Optimal Scheduling of Very Heterogeneous HPC Resources (Machines and Networks)

Richard F. Freund,
NRaD Code 423

Mark Campbell, SAIC	Mitch Gregory, SAIC	John Myles, NRaD
David Fogel, Orincon	Mike Halderman, SAIC	Mary Nguyen, Paramax
Larry Fogel	Matt Kussow, SAIC	David Schwarze, SAIC
Mike Gherrity, NRaD	John Lima, SAIC	Bruce Sonnenfeld, NRaD

SmartNet is a management scheme for near-optimal allocation of very heterogeneous HPC resources, including both machines and networks. Currently it is PVM-based, but it could be based on any or on multiple Distributed Computing Environments. SmartNet is specifically designed for very heterogeneous configurations, i.e., for those in which opportunistic load-balancing is insufficient as a primary allocation paradigm. SmartNet makes automatic allocation decisions based on theoretical and experiential information about relative affinities of various tasks to different machines.

It also includes effects of predicted network latencies. The heart of the SmartNet procedures consists of:

a. An expected Time to Compute (ETC) function which predicts performance of various tasks on different machines and networks.
b. A Look Ahead/Look Back (LALB) strategizer function which near-optimally fits the new submitted tasks to the existing queue of currently executing and already allocated jobs.

Heterogeneous Computing for Genetic Sequence Analysis (*)

Alexander Ropelewski and Hugh Nicholas
Pittsburgh Supercomputing Center

Gordon Springer and Tim Patrick
University of Missouri

A genetic sequence represents DNA, RNA, and protein molecules as an unbroken sequence of letters, a character string. Analysis of sequences may help to identify the molecular basis of genetic diseases such as cystic fibrosis and sickle cell anemia. We propose to demonstrate an application that will assist biomedical researchers analyzing unknown DNA or protein sequences. This system will allow a user sitting at a workstation to access local and remote computing facilities to fully analyze an experimental sequence. The analysis is steered by the researcher and could include performing database searches on multiple heterogeneous supercomputers, analyzing and retrieving literature citations for appropriate sequences, and analyzing a set of sequences that are homologous with the experimental sequence. This process will save the researcher valuable time by automating many steps in the analysis process.

(*) Supported in part by NIH/NLM HPCC grant R01 LM05513 to the Univ. of Missouri & the Pittsburgh Supercomputing Center and NIH/NLM 5 T15 LM07089-02. Computer time by the generosity of the Pittsburgh Supercomputing Center, the National Center for Supercomputing Applications, the San Diego Supercomputer Center, Cornell Theory Center, the North Carolina Supercomputing Center, and Supercomputing '93 vendors.

PVM Takes Over the World

Al Geist
Oak Ridge National Lab (ORNL)

Jack Dongarra
ORNL and the University of Tennessee

Bob Manchek
University of Tennessee

Adam Beguelin
Carnegie Mellon University

Weicheng Jiang
University of Tennessee

Three Computational Grand Challenges will be run across as many different machines on the SC93 floor. The demonstrations have been designed to show the exploitation of heterogeneity at the application level as well as the network level. The applications are:

First Principles Electronic Structure Code
Climate modeling code
Groundwater transport code

At least one of the Grand Challenges will be run on a virtual machine composed of a Paragon, CM-5, and C90 by using PVM (Parallel Virtual Machine.) The range of machines on the SCInet provides a unique opportunity to link together a virtual machine with unparalleled heterogeneity. The goal of this entry is to illustrate heterogeneity, portability, and robustness in large scale applications while only requiring a Unix Operating System and PVM.

Seismic Ray Tracing

Diane Gomez and Juan Meza
Sandia National Laboratories

Other co-conspiritors at
Weidlinger Associates

Seismic methods are one of the main tools used in modern oil exploration, reservoir delineation, and mapping. Due to computational constraints in the past, a two-dimensional approach was used, but in recent years, with increasing and more readily available computational power, truly three-dimensional surveys have become more common. These three-dimensional surveys not only provide increased resolution and reliability, especially in areas of complex geology, but they are also cost effective on vector supercomputers.

With the advent of more powerful workstations another approach based on network computing is becoming more attractive. This idea is based on using a local area network of workstations as a parallel computer with individual workstations representing nodes. This entry will demonstrate the use of distributed computing parallel methods for a seismic ray tracing problem and their use in the seismic inverse problem. Our ray tracing module is organized in such a way that independent tasks are apparent, and only a moderate amount of development is required to create a parallel version. Since each task can vary in computational complexity and workstations in a network can vary in their computational power issues of load balancing must also be addressed.

High Speed Distributed Computing

David Forslund
Los Alamos National Laboratory (LANL)

David Rich, LANL   Michael Krogh, LANL   Bob Tomlinson, LANL
Stephen Pope, LANL   Stephen Poole, Forefronts, Inc.   John Reynders, LANL
Chuck Hansen, LANL   Jim Brewton, LANL

Several applications using Gigabit networking were run illustrating the usability of HIPPI circuit-switching technology. These demonstrate the usefulness of heterogeneous supercomputing, code portability (same code runs on a CM-5 and on a cluster of workstations), and high bandwidth communications. The applications are:

Coupled global ocean/atmosphere models
Oil and Gas data analysis
Distributed visualization
Portable Numerical Tokamak application

The entry demonstrates the "real" applications using distributed computing with maximum heterogeneity to obtain high performance gigflop rates with large speedups using HIPPI connected machines on the SCInet.

An Object-Oriented Distributed Ray Casting Volume Renderer

Joel Welling, Jamshid Mahdavi, Gwendolyn Huntoon
Pittsburgh Supercomputing Center

The project is a distributed volume renderer. Interprocessor communication is mediated by PVM; a Motif user interface running on a simple workstation provides control. Rendering is done by dividing the volume dataset into subvolumes and ray casting each subvolume. The system is completely object oriented, including a C++ base class which allows the creation of objects which reside simultaneously on two nodes of the network. PVM does its work by providing communication between the two halves of these objects. Speed-up is the primary goal of this project. The benefit is a tool that will do the compute-intensive task of volume rendering either on a remote server or on a network of workstations. Or maybe on a remote server which is a network of workstations. The approach is unique and works for all platforms for which PVM is supported.

Distributed Analysis of Plasma Data

William Meyer, Richard Frobose, Richard Mark
Lawrence Livermore National Laboratory

Jonathan Brown
National Energy Research Supercomputer Center (NERSC)

This project demonstrates the feasibility of using distributed resources to analyze time critical data from a magneticly confined fusion plasma experiment. It uses the combined processing power of a CRI C90 and a collection of high end workstations from IBM, DEC, and HP to generate a sequence of false color images of the plasma's soft x-ray emission intensity. The application uses Open Software Foundation's Distributed Computing Environment (DCE) software to provide a standards-based, flexible method of distributing the application across the available processors. This allows the scientists to marshal a vast array of processing resources to solve a problem that could not otherwise be solved within the time constraints imposed by the experiment.

Terrain Visualization on the MAGIC Gigabit Testbed

Timothy J. Salo et al.
Minnesota Supercomputer Center, Inc.

An interactive, real-time, terrain visualization application on the MAGIC Gigabit Testbed will be demonstrated. MAGIC (Multidimensional Applications and Gigabit Internetwork Consortium) was established to develop a very high-speed, wide-area networking testbed that will address these challenges and demonstrate real-time, interactive exchange of data at gigabit-per-second (Gbps) rates among multiple distributed servers and clients. The terrain visualization will run on a high-end graphics workstation (Silicon Graphics, Inc. Reality Engine) located at SC '93. The application uses terrain data stored on a distributed image server system located at EROS Data Center in Sioux Falls, South Dakota. The graphics workstation and the image server system in South Dakota will be connected by a high-speed, wide-area ATM network.

The MAGIC terrain visualization allows a user to view and navigate through a representation of a landscape created from aerial images of the area of interest. The application consists of a digital representations of terrain; and the visualization system. The digital description of the shape and appearance of the subject terrain is a two-dimensional grid of elevation values known as a digital elevation model (DEM). The appearance of the terrain is represented by a set of aerial images, known as orthographic projection images (ortho-images), that have been specially processed to eliminate the effects of perspective distortion and that are in precise registration with the DEM. The visualization system uses the digital description and allows the user to control the viewpoint, viewpath, and other aspects of the visualization in real time using a suitable input device.

The MAGIC image server system (ISS) stores, organizes, and retrieves both the terrain models and the raw images and supporting information used to compute these models. The ISS consists of multiple, coordinated data servers that are designed to be distributed around a wide-area network. This approach to system architecture will permit location-independent access to databases, and allow for system scalability.

The AHPCRC Heterogeneous Computing Challenge

Thomas M. Ruwart, Ken Chin-Purcell, and Jim MacDonald
Army High Performance Computing Research Center (AHPCRC)

The AHPCRC (University of Minnesota) ran a highly parallelized interactive CFD (Computational Fluid Dynamics) simulation code distributed across four different types of supercomputers interconnected with HiPPI. The simulation was displayed on a Silicon Graphics ONYX system that allows the user to manipulate the position and shape of an object inside the flow field. These parameters are fed back into the simulation in a closed-loop feedback fashion to produce real-time, interactive CFD. The code is dynamically load balanced according to the processing resources available on each of the supercomputers used to run the simulation. Four supercomputers planned for this demonstration: the Thinking Machines CM-5, a Cray C90, an Intel Paragon, and a MassPar MP2. The Silicon Graphics will be used to display the results of the simulation and provide simulation processing control. The simulation will be simultaneously displayed on the Gigapixel-per-second video wall currently under development at the AHPCRC.

Heterogeneous Computing at Sandia National Laboratories

Heterogeneous computing has been exploited in several areas at Sandia National Laboratories (SNL). Demonstrations of some of these SNL applications presented at HCC/SC '93 are listed below.

ATM heterogeneous networking with desktop video conference applications: Connections from SC '93 to SNL/Ca and SNL/NM. Helen Chen and Bob Mines

Parallel Distributive Computing with Heterogeneous workstations over ATM using the Heterogeneous Environment and Testbed (HEAT). Helen Chen, Rob Armstrong

Display a modeling code that shows the impact of a projectile on a material using distributive, interactive AVS over an ATM connection. The code is capable of varying the characteristics of the material and the speed of the projectile. Dino Pavlakos

Demonstrate ATM over a OC3 connection to SNL/Ca. Steve Gossage

LeMans FunRun. Richard Gay et al.

Earth Sciences application using HEAT. Spencer Nelson et al.

Fluid Dynamics modeling program. Greg Evans

Session 9:
Super Micros
Chair: David Culler

*T: Integrated Building Blocks for Parallel Computing

G. M. Papadopoulos, G. A. Boughton
Lab for Comp. Sci.
MIT
545 Technology Square
Cambridge, MA 02139
greg@think.com, gab@abp.lcs.mit.edu

R. Greiner
Motorola
Motorola, Inc, DW220
2900 South Diablo Way
Tempe, AZ 85282
bobg@phx.mcd.mot.com

M. J. Beckerle
Motorola
Motorola Cambridge Research Center
One Kendall Square, Bld 200
Cambridge, MA 02139
mikeb@mcrc.mot.com

Abstract

In this paper we present two hardware components for high performance parallel computing: a superscalar RISC microprocessor with an integrated 400 megabytes/sec user-level network interface (the 88110MP), and a companion 8×8 low-latency packet router chip (ARCTIC). The design point combines very low message overhead and high delivered communications bandwidth with a commercially competitive sequential processor core. The network interface is directly programmed in user mode as an instruction set extension to the Motorola 88110. Importantly, naming and protection mechanisms are provided to support robust multi-user space and time sharing. Thus, fine-grain messaging and synchronization can be supported efficiently, without compromising per-processor performance or system integrity. Preliminary performance modeling results are presented.

1 Introduction

There seems to be little debate that the future of high performance computing, and perhaps all computing, is MIMD parallelism [4, 16]. But there is also little debate that, at least in the near-term, the technology and marketing factors that drive the design of the individual processors will be their suitability as components as *single* processors in workstations, PC's, and *small* shared memory multiprocessor servers, not as components in large scale parallel machines or even workstation clusters. Unfortunately, this also means that these hot microprocessors are often less than ideal processing elements for large scale MIMD parallelism; the principal and most obvious shortcoming is a lack of mechanisms that are tailored for scalable interprocessor communication and synchronization. The result: individual nodes will offer highly competitive performance on sequential streams that exhibit good locality, but communication and synchronization among nodes will have substantial execution overhead.

The goal of the *T project (pronounced 'Start') is to bring very low cost, fine grain communications to high performance sequential processors. We have accomplished this by extending an existing superscalar microprocessor, the Motorola 88110, with an integrated network messaging unit. The design approach is very simple. We have added two new sets of register files, a transmit and a receive register file, and provided new instructions for moving data between these and existing floating point and integer registers, for launching messages into the network and for consuming incoming messages. We have also added extensive support for a variant of active messages and fine grain multithreading we call *microthreading*.

While this degree of explicit register-level coupling of a network within a processor datapath is not new (*cf* the J-machine MDP [7], iWarp [3], Monsoon [19, 20, 21], Epsilon [10] and the EM-4 [22]), we believe we have made significant contributions in accomplishing the integration in a way which is consistent with superscalar execution and, most importantly, which supports UNIX-style protection and naming. In fact, most of our architectural effort has been invested in supporting a user mode network interface, essential for our performance goals, that works within a protected multitasking, multi-user environment, and in dealing with the vagaries of speculative, multiple issue instruction execution.

A companion hardware component is an 8×8 packet routing chip that emphasizes high sustained network throughput while minimizing per-hop latency. The ARCTIC chip builds upon our previous experience with the very successful PaRC router [12] used in Monsoon and similarly provides sophisticated input packet buffer management, virtual cut-through routing, and robust error detection. In addition, ARCTIC provides specialized support for randomized routing on fat-tree networks, the network topology used in *T systems. Each ARCTIC link is a 16-bit wide, 100 Mbaud GTL (a low voltage swing CMOS technology), yielding a raw data rate of 200 Megabytes/sec/link. Our modified processor, the 88110MP, also directly drives two 200 Megabytes/sec GTL links, for an aggregate peak per processor performance of 400 Megabytes/sec — equivalent to the existing local bus bandwidth of an unmodified 88110.

---

*This report describes research done at the Laboratory for Computer Science of the Massachusetts Institute of Technology. Funding for the Laboratory is provided in part by the Advanced Research Projects Agency of the Department of Defense under the Office of Naval Research contract N00014-89-J-1988. Portions of the research were funded by the National Science Foundation's Young Investigator Awards (NSF 91-112).

2　The High Cost of Communicating

The unavoidably high transport latency of interprocessor communications is often identified as a fundamental issue in any form of multiprocessing [2]. While this ultimately may be true, the fact is that in commercial parallel and distributed systems, the *overhead* of interprocessor communication dominates communication latency. That is, a processor will typically expend many more cycles on network protocol and in driving the network interface hardware than is incurred by the actual transport of a packet from one processor to another.

For existing commercial machines the overhead for communication completely dominates the transport latency. Most of this overhead is either due to user-kernel interactions for kernel-mode networks (Paragon, Meiko[1]), unoptimized message library software (CM5), or a basic mismatch between the built-in communications mechanisms and message-passing (KSR1). We note that active messages [25] can substantially reduce the software overhead for those machines that provide a user mode network interface — for example the message overhead on the CM5 has been reduced to three microseconds using active messages. Still, we consider this well over an order of magnitude too high for fine grain message passing.

In contrast, the research machines have obtained much better levels of communications performance by employing novel processor architectures with deeply integrated network interfaces. But as interesting as these processor architectures might be in their own right, they clearly do not represent the overwhelming trend towards parallel machines built from commodity superscalar RISC microprocessors.

Even so, there are many lessons to learn in the way that the network is integrated into the processor pipelines of these research architectures. An appropriate view of one of the primary contributions of the *T effort is the assimilation of the network interface ideas — especially those from Monsoon (and the other multithreaded dataflow architectures), the J-machine, Alewife [1] and iWarp — into mainstream processor architecture. We have also been influenced by the network interface study of Henry and Joerg [11].

3　Processor-Integrated Networking

If frequent, fine grain interprocessor communication is to be at all practical, then messaging overheads need to be *orders of magnitude* smaller than what is experienced on contemporary commercial multiprocessors — overheads should be measured in a small number of instruction times, not hundreds or thousands. For example on Monsoon, a research multithreaded dataflow processor [19, 20, 21], a sender can format and launch

a message in exactly one cycle, and a receiver can process an incoming message (storing its value and performing an n-ary join) in one or two cycles. In terms of throughput, the processor-network interface can sustain a rate of one message in and one message out every three cycles. The network interface is literally part of the processor pipeline and a visible aspect of the user instruction set architecture.

The primary architectural objective of *T was to assimilate Monsoon-like communications performance into high-end sequential processor design. To do so, we had to reconcile the often competing demands of lightweight and asynchronous fine grain messages with "stateful" and speculative superscalar processing. We call our approach *processor-integrated networking* to denote what we believe is a simple yet highly effective way of integrating low overhead communications directly into a RISC processor instruction set. We believe that this has been accomplished in a way that is completely consistent with single stream speculative and multi-issue execution and, most importantly, supports user-mode programming within a fully protected multiuser environment.

In this section, we develop the instruction set architecture of the integrated message unit (the MSU) on our modified superscalar processor, the 88110MP. This is done in three layers. First, we show the basic user-mode operations for transmitting and receiving messages. Second, we describe how active messages are directly implemented on top of the first layer with either polling or interrupts. Finally, we illustrate how the processor supports a fine grain multithreading and synchronization model called *microthreads*.

3.1　Layer 0: Register-level Transmit and Receive

The integration of basic message formatting and reception into the processor instruction set is very simple. As shown in Figure 1, two new user mode register sets, a transmit file (`tx`) and a receive file (`rx`), have been added to the baseline 88110, a commercial dual-issue superscalar microprocessor [15, 9]. Each register file looks to user code like a conventional 24 word (32-bit) set of registers whose contents can be read and written by transferring data to and from these files and the existing general purpose integer and floating point files. There are three basic instructions provided in layer 0:

`sttx`	Store into Transmit Registers (and optionally send current message)
`ldrx`	Load from Receive Registers
`rxpoll`	Poll Receive Status (and optionally get next message)

Transmitting a Message

To transmit a message, the destination node is written into transmit register zero (`tx0`), the message length (in words) is written into `tx1`, and the message payload is written into registers `tx2`–`tx23`, as appropriate

[1]The Meiko CS-2 supports direct user mode interaction with a network interface processor, but a substantial fraction of the overhead (about ten microseconds) is attributable to memory protection mechanisms enforced by the network interface.

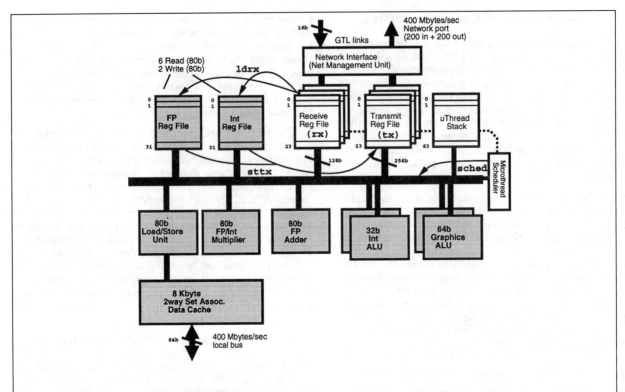

Figure 1: The top-level 88110MP datapaths. The shaded boxes indicate the datapath elements of the base 88110. The other boxes show the datapath elements that form the on-chip network extension.

for the message length. Then, the message is submitted into the network using a `go` operation. Finally, the transmit code must check that the message was actually accepted by the network (network flow control being the common reason for rejection), and then retry transmission when necessary.

While these are the basic operations, the user code path length for message transmission has been heavily optimized by eliding several operations into a single instruction. The principal transmit instruction is `sttx` (store into transmit register) and comprises four operands:

```
sttx[.go]  r-status, r-src1, r-src2, tx-dest
```

where,

- `.go` is an option that, when present, causes the current message in the `tx` file to be transmitted (*after* the transfers indicated by the current instruction are effected).

- `r-status` is a register in the integer register file that is written with the current transmitter status.

- `r-src1, r-src2` are two (single or double word) registers from either the integer or floating point files whose contents are to be deposited into `tx` registers.

- `tx-dest` is the (first) destination register in the `tx` file that is to receive the contents of the two source registers. Up to three subsequent `tx` registers will be written (in the same cycle) when `r-src1` and `r-src2` denote double word source registers.

The setting of the message length register `tx1` is also optimized — if `tx1` has not been written, it is automatically set when a `sttx.go` is executed. After an `sttx.go` is executed and the returned status `r-status` indicates that the message was accepted by the network interface, then the user is given a fresh transmit register file in which a new message may be composed on the very next clock.[2] The code fragment below shows how `sttx` can be used to create and send a short message comprising three double words (24 bytes) of payload:

```
send_msg:
    sttx.sd    r0, r2, dr4, tx0   ; clock 1
    sttx.dd.go r1, dr6, dr8, tx4  ; clock 1
    bb1        30, r1, msg_sent    ; clock 2
msg_not_sent:
    bsr        _retry_tx
msg_sent:
    ...                            ; clock 3
```

The first `sttx` instruction deposits the destination node (from integer register `r2`) into `tx0` and copies the first double word of data from integer registers `r4` and `r5` (denoted by `dr4`) into `tx2-3`. Note that the message length register `tx1` is *not* set by this first `sttx`.

---

[2]In fact, both the transmit and receive files are only the visible part of *queues* of outgoing and incoming messages. The management of these queues also interacts with the protection mechanisms, as we shall see in a moment.

The second `sttx` stores two more double words into `tx4-7` and sends the completed message, as indicated by the `.go` extension. This second `sttx` implicitly sets the message length in `tx1`.

Every `sttx` returns a transmit status value in register `r-status`. The first `sttx` discards this value (by writing into `r0`), but second `sttx.go` records the status into `r1`. The status reflects the disposition of this message; that is, was the message accepted by the transmitter and sent? There are several reasons why a `sttx.go` might not succeed. The most common would be that the transmitter is in flow control and all outgoing transmit buffers are full. In this case, the software could wait and then retry the transmission, or queue the message for later transmission.

Importantly, if a message is not transmitted then *it is still retained in the transmit register set*. The 88110MP also provides instruction set extensions for reading the transmit registers (`ldtx`) and writing the receive registers (`strx`). This means that message retry and queueing software can be written as generic user mode handlers — we do not require the user code to be able to reconstruct every message that could possibly fail transmission. In this regard, we consider the register model of a network interface to be superior to the FIFO models of the J-machine and iWarp.

Finally, note that the `sttx` instructions are dual-issued by the 88110MP. This is discussed in more detail below, but observe that a message with 24 bytes of payload can be sent in two cycles, *including* the time required to check the transmit status.[3] Larger messages can be constructed for transmission at the rate of thirty-two bytes per cycle.

Receiving a Message

The receive register set is analogous to the transmit register set. An application code can directly poll for messages, and handle them entirely in user mode with no transfers of control into the operating system. As in transmission, this mechanism is highly optimized. There are two primary instructions used for receiving messages: `rxpoll` and `ldrx`. The `rxpoll` instruction is used to determine if a new message is ready to be received:

```
rxpoll[.next]  r-status
```

where `.next` is an option that, when present, causes the next incoming message to be copied into the `rx` file. Any of the fields of the new message are available to subsequent instructions, including those immediately following the `rxpoll.next`. R-status is a register in the integer register file that is written with the current receiver status.

---

[3]The code could be optimized further with a `bb1.n` that exposes the extra instruction slot that occurs when the branch is issued. The branch should predict along the `msg_sent` path, so there is no delay slot after the branch in this case.

The `ldrx` instruction is the dual of the `sttx` and is used for copying fields from the `rx` file into the integer or floating point registers:

```
ldrx  r-dest, rx-source
```

R-dest is a single or double word register from either the integer or floating point files which is written with the contents of the indicated `rx-source` register from the `rx` file.

A receive code fragment is given below which performs the receive action for a 24-byte message sent by the transmit example code. In the code below we test for a message in the receiver using an `rxpoll.next` instruction. If a message is present, then this instruction (as indicated by the `.next` option) moves the message into the receive registers:

```
;;;
;;; message in rx registers:
;;; Word 0 = node, Word 1 = length.
;;; Words 2 to 7 contain the message data itself.
;;;
    ...
    rxpoll.next r1
    bcnd   NO_MSG,r1, out      ; leave if no msg
    ldrx   dr2, rx2            ; clock 1
    ldrx   dr4 ,rx4            ; clock 1
    ldrx   dr6, rx6            ; clock 2
    ldrx   dr8, rx8            ; clock 2
    ;; message now in general purpose regs dr2 to dr9
    ...
    ...
```

The incoming message can be consumed at sixteen bytes per cycle — half of the rate that messages can be constructed because the general purpose integer and floating register files have fewer write ports than read ports.

Multiple Instruction Issue

A principal advantage of processor-integrated networking is that the performance of the network interface can track processor performance. In the 88110MP implementation, we are able to devote almost all of the general purpose register file read and write bandwidth to message processing. Our ultimate goal is to establish a reasonably standardized instruction set extension that could be brought forward by new processors in an ISA family, and thereby enjoy a communications/computation balance that scales with higher instruction issue rates. In this way we hope that code generation and scheduling techniques that are developed for other function units will apply directly for the network instruction extension. Contrast this approach with bus-connected, or cache-connected schemes where the read latencies (as measured in instruction times) continue to grow as processors get faster, further decoupling the computation for communication and creating new challenges in code generation for each new processor.

In the 88110MP implementation, frequent network instruction combinations are permitted to dual-issue. In particular, it is possible to issue two `sttx` instructions (or two `ldrx` instructions) in the same cycle as long as the `tx` (or `rx`) registers refer to different "banks" of the transmit (receive) register files. Specifically, these register files are two-way interleaved on four-word boundaries for the transmitter and two-word boundaries for the receiver.[4] When the dual-issue constraints are met, the 88110MP delivers very high bandwidth message transmission (thirty-two bytes per cycle) and reception (sixteen bytes per cycle). Instruction issue hardware is dedicated to checking constraints, so that instruction ordering only affects performance, not correctness.

Speculative Execution

While it is straightforward to design a network unit for multiple issue, speculative execution (branch prediction) introduces a set of subtle problems. The most obvious is that the transmit and receive register files are visible processor state, and the `sttx` and `strx` instructions modify that state. Thus, the effects of these instructions have to be undone if they are issued speculatively after a mispredicted branch. Actually, the challenge here is no harder than for the integer and floating point register files and the same set of techniques apply (*e.g.,* history buffers). But because we did not want to introduce the design complexity for our first version of the 88110MP, we have instead placed a single-assignment constraint on register updates: a given `tx` or `rx` register is written at most once along any program path between any two side-effecting message operations (*e.g.,* `sttx.go`).

The more interesting interactions with speculative execution happen with respect to `sttx.go` instructions to launch messages in the network and `.next` operations to advance the receive register set. Consider the speculative execution of a `sttx.go` which later turns out to be the result of a mispredicted branch. How do you *recall* a message from the network(!)? Our approach is to permit one outstanding `sttx.go` that is remembered by the message interface until the instruction retires, and only then is the message actually sent. Even more subtle is the status returned (in `r-status`) by an `sttx.go`: it must represent the status of the message *as if it were actually sent*. This problem is made easier by the fact that the `sttx.go` atomically returns a status that is associated with the transmit state on the clock that the instruction is issued. Contrast this with a separate instruction to check the transmit status — if the status checking instruction is issued on a clock after the `.go`, there is the possibility that the flow control state of the transmitter has changed in the intervening cycles.

In summary, incorporating the message interface as an instruction set extension can yield very high

performance by riding the trends in speculative and multi-issue execution. The downside to this is that the implementation must deal with thorny issues of instructions that cause a number of interesting side effects.

3.2 Layer 1: Support for Active Messages

The layer 0 operations for transmitting and receiving messages offer a base transport-like layer for communicating messages. The underlying contract of the network is:

> If the network accepts a packet (indicated through `r-status` after a `sttx.go`), then it promises to ultimately deliver that packet error-free to the indicated destination node as long as all nodes in the network promise to consume incoming packets.

The network contract makes no guarantees about packet ordering and only promises to deliver packets if every node promises to receive them. This means that if the network *does not* accept a packet then the transmitting code has to be prepared to receive packets until the blocking condition no longer exists, else the contract is violated and network deadlock may occur. It also means that we have to have a place to put the contents of the packets we are receiving in the meantime *and* that the processing of the receive packets can't themselves require a response to be transmitted.

The traditional way of abstracting the network contract to the application is through a message-based communications library which provides scheduling and internal buffering for received messages. Various end-to-end flow control protocols overlay the packet transport and provide some immunity from network deadlock. Unfortunately, these kinds of message libraries invariably introduce an unacceptably high communications overhead.

In contrast, Berkeley's *active messages* [25] rationalizes the network contract and exposes it directly to the application. Under the active messages model, every message carries an instruction pointer (IP) which points to the handler for that message on the destination node. Each handler is specialized to the particular message and is responsible for directly operating on the message contents, including copying any message data into local data structures and performing synchronization operations. Handlers are divided into two types: *reply handlers* that can execute to completion without creating network messages, and *request handlers*, such as a remote load server, that need to send response messages.

One can view message handlers as very lightweight threads that "interrupt" a background thread — the main computational thread on a node. The message handlers communicate to the background thread through shared data structures (*e.g.,* a stack frame) and synchronization variables (*e.g.,* decrementing a counting semaphore).

---

[4]That is, tx0–3, tx8–11, tx16–19 are in Bank 0 and tx4–7, tx12–15, tx20–23 are in Bank 1. A similar pattern holds for the receiver, except the boundaries are every two words.

IP:FP Active Messages

88110MP supports a variant of active messages wherein the second double word of a message encodes a pair of pointers, an instruction pointer (IP) and a frame pointer (FP). The FP should be considered a pointer to a context, such as a procedure activation frame, an object, or a heap location. The latter would be typical of request handlers for remote read and write operations. Refer to Figure 2.

Of course, no extra hardware support is required to implement active messages — it is possible to make an efficient implementation directly on top layer 0 message primitives. For example, a background thread could poll for an incoming message, extract the IP from rx2 and then jump to the message handler.

Microscheduling Support

The 88110MP implementation provides *microscheduling* support to make the polling of active messages more efficient. The basic primitive is the sched instruction, which returns a double word value comprising an IP:FP pair:

```
sched     r-ip:fp
```

If there is a message ready at the receiver, the sched instruction advances the receive register set (*i.e.,* it implicitly performs a .next operation) and then extracts words two and three from the message (the assumed IP:FP) and returns them in r-ip:fp. If no message is ready at the receiver, then the sched instruction will return a default IP:FP pair that can be set by the user code. One way that the default pair can be set is through the rxsched instruction:

```
rxsched   r-ip:fp, r-default-ip:fp
```

Rxsched is just like sched except that the default IP:FP pair is supplied — if there is no message then this value is returned. Also, the message unit remembers the default pair and will return it as appropriate for any subsequent sched operation. To perform polling in the background thread requires only a two instruction sequence:

```
;;;   Assume that r_continue already set up with IP:FP
;;;   pointing to label 'continue'
;;;
   rxsched   r2_3, r_continue
   jmp       r2

continue:
```

Each active message handler ends with the idiom sched r2_3; jmp r2, and control is thereby threaded through all of the incoming messages and finally returned to the background thread once all messages are handled.

Interrupt Support

For a variety of reasons relating to polling overhead and network congestion control, it may be desirable to have incoming messages interrupt the background thread. Although we have not modified the 88110 to vector these interrupts directly to user mode — something highly desirable but beyond our engineering resources for this version — we have made the incoming message interrupt maskable under user mode control. Thus, when the user code enabled interrupts, an incoming message causes a lightweight kernel interrupt which immediately reflects the interrupt back to user mode, *i.e.,* the kernel handler does not save and restore user registers. The user mode access of the enable/disable bit permits inexpensive critical sections to be established without invoking the kernel. Importantly, the enable/disable operation is *serializing*: no subsequent instructions will be issued until the operation retires. This way, the user code can be assured that instructions which immediately follow an interrupt disable are part of the critical section.[5]

Some system implementations may desire that every incoming message interrupt the kernel. For this case, we note that the kernel mode has its own interrupt enable bit which takes priority over the user bit. Also, the kernel has a watchdog timer feature that cannot be disabled in user mode — if the receiver flow controls the network for more than a specified number of cycles, then an interrupt is generated. See the discussion on protection in section 4.

3.3   Layer 2: Microthreading

Under active messages there is conceptually a single background thread that periodically yields to active message handlers. Synchronization between the incoming active messages and the background thread is *ad hoc,* typically involving shared semaphores that are queried by the background thread. In contrast, the 88110MP supports the message-driven *T *microthreading* model [18] wherein the execution of message handlers can cause *data threads,* short non-blocking instruction sequences, to be queued for execution. At a high level, the *T microthreading model is a direct descendant of Berkeley's Threaded Abstract Machine (TAM) [23].

Under TAM, incoming messages are processed by *inlets* that correspond to the message handlers under active messages. In general, an inlet will deposit the data-part of the message into an offset in an activation frame whose base is given by the FP field on the message. Then, the inlet will decrement a counting semaphore (also found in the activation frame) and, if the semaphore is zero, will queue a continuation for a data thread described by the pair IP_{DT}:FP,

---

[5]Again, contrast this with an off-chip based network unit. Even if the interrupt enable bit is mapped into the user mode address space, guarantees that following instructions are indeed part of a critical section requires synchronization of the processor with external bus cycles (for example, by performing a non-cacheable read and then touching the result).

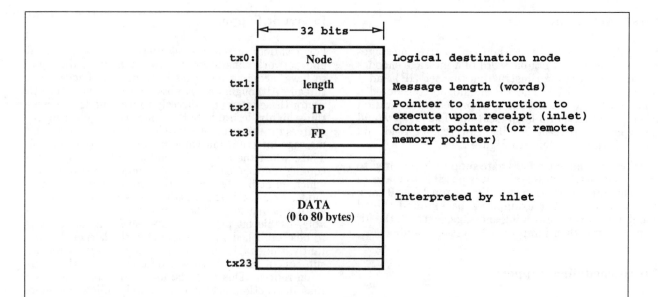

Figure 2: Format of *T messages for active messages and microthreads. The first double word of the message encodes the logical destination node and the total message length. The second double word encodes an IP:FP pair, with the IP pointing to the entry instruction in the message handler and FP pointing to a context — typically an activation frame, an object, or a heap location.

where IP_{DT} points to the first instruction in the data thread code. Data threads are executed as background threads: inlets will be executed as long as there are incoming messages, but then data thread continuations are dequeued and executed to completion.

Microthread Stack

The 88110MP provides an on-chip, 32-entry cache for a microthread stack that stores descriptors for data threads awaiting execution. The microthread stack is part of the user's process state and is manipulated in user mode. Entries on the stack are 64-bit IP:FP pairs. The IP points to the entry instruction for a data thread and FP points to the thread's environment, typically an activation frame. Pushing a new entry onto the stack can be performed several ways. The fork instruction unconditionally pushes an IP:FP pair onto the stack:

```
fork   r-status, r-ip:fp
```

where r-ip:fp is a double register containing the data thread microthread descriptor to push, and r-status is a destination register that is written with current stack status. The status indicates how many words are remaining in the stack cache and user software is responsible for not overflowing the cache. Even more useful for the counting semaphore model of TAM is the conditional cfork:

```
cfork  r-status, r-ip:fp, r-semaphore
```

which conditionally pushes the contents of r-ip:fp if the contents of r-semaphore is zero.

Although microthread descriptors can be explicitly popped from the stack using the poput instruction, the primary way of popping descriptors is *implicitly* with sched (see section 3.2). Specifically, the IP:FP pair returned by a sched or rxsched instruction will be, in priority order, from either (1) the header of an incoming message, (2) the poll return IP:FP, (3) the top of the microthread stack, or (4) the "idle" microthread. These priorities can be adjusted[6], but the high level idea is that the hardware is providing a very simple scheduling veneer that collapses many tests — *e.g.,* incoming message present, in polling mode, microthread stack empty — into a single jump that dispatches directly to a message handler, data thread, idle handler, or returns to a polling thread. Put another way, a sched instruction is like asking "give me the next thing to do", where the answer is given as a pointer to a piece of code to execute (the IP) and a context in which to perform the execution (the FP).

A common case in message handlers is the execution of a conditional fork (cfork) of a data thread followed by a sched and jmp in order to dispatch to the next thing to do. As a further pathlength reduction, the cfork and sched instruction can be elided into a single cpost instruction:

---

[6]There are in fact eleven priority levels that can be selectively enabled by user code. For example, it is possible to reverse the "normal" priority of selecting incoming messages over the microthread stack. There are also hooks for *dynamically* escaping from the priority structure, but this is beyond the scope of this paper.

```
cpost r-next-ip:fp, r-fork-ip:fp, r-semaphore
```

where the contents of `r-fork-ip:fp` are pushed onto the microthread stack if the contents of `r-semaphore` are zero. The register `r-next-ip:fp` is written with the descriptor for the next thing to do. Note that if popping a descriptor from the microthread stack is the highest priority activity when the instruction is issued, then `r-next-ip:fp` is given the value of `r-fork-ip:fp` and the stack is not affected.

4 Naming and Protection

Giving direct user mode network access can be very efficient, but is of little value if it comes at the expense of security and system integrity. One of the fundamental challenges of providing an efficient user mode network interface is do so in a way that is compatible with the naming and protection mechanisms expected by modern operating systems.

Interference among separate processes sharing a network can occur in many ways. A malicious process might try to intercept messages destined to another process, forge new messages and inject them into another process, or congest the network in such a way as to interfere with communications and induce deadlock in another process. These, of course, are in addition to the usual requirements of memory protection on each node. Our *T implementation provides naming and protection mechanisms to support user mode network access within a complete multiuser environment.

4.1 Naming mechanisms

A *T *global virtual address* comprises a node-part and an offset-part, `node:offset`. `Node` is a logical node number that is translated by the transmitter hardware into a network route to a physical node (see section 5). The `offset` of a global virtual address is a local address that is valid on the target physical node. Thus, the IP:FP pairs on message are *local virtual addresses* that are translated into physical addresses at the physical node by using the pre-existing MMU mechanisms during load and store operations. More simply, name translation happens in two phases: a logical-to-physical translation of the node happens at transmit time on the sending node, while a virtual-to-physical translation of a memory offset happens on the receiving node and uses the existing virtual memory translation mechanisms.

The first phase of the translation happens in the *network management unit (NMU)* (see Figure 1) which employs a small content addressable map from logical nodes to network routes. The mapping is prioritized and allows the translation of variable-sized blocks of logical nodes into routes, similar to modern TLBs. The route table is accessible only by privileged instructions (*i.e.*, it is not loadable by user code). If the user code creates a message with a node that is not mapped by the table, then the message is not sent and is inserted into the transmit miss queue.

4.2 Protection Mechanisms

Along with the physical route, the network management unit also inserts a parallel process Id called a *partition Id (PID)*[7] into the header of each outgoing message. Refer to Figure 3. Whenever a message is received, this PID is examined and compared (by hardware) with the PID for the user process currently executing on the destination node. The incoming message is thereby sorted into one of four on-chip receive queues: the active user queue, high and low priority kernel queues, and the "others" queue called the *miss* queue.[8]

User mode messages received by a processor that is currently executing a parallel process corresponding to the message's PID, will be queued for that process without any other software intervention — in particular, the kernel is not invoked unless the user code has sensitized interrupts on incoming user mode messages. When a user mode message is received whose PID *does not* match the currently registered user process, the message is placed in the miss queue and an interrupt is posted to the kernel. Also, any packets that have been corrupted in transmission as determined by a CRC error are inserted in the miss queue. Kernel mode packets (PID $\equiv$ 0) are inserted in either a high or low priority kernel queue depending on the header of the packet (this interacts with network priorities — see below) and an interrupt is posted to the kernel, unless the processor is already in kernel mode.

Optionally, the kernel can elect to be interrupted whenever a message arrives for the currently executing user process — even if there is a PID match. Alternatively, the kernel can elect to be interrupted only after the user mode message queue is full and has placed the network in flow control for specifiable number of cycles. This can be used to mitigate the effects of user-user network interference, as described below.

Because the head of the message queues actually form the `tx` and `rx` register sets, the kernel automatically gets its own set of these registers whenever the 88110MP changes mode. Thus, O/S does not need to save and restore the user's version of the `tx` and `rx` sets until it wants to swap user processes. Note that the microscheduling stack state is *not* replicated, however. If the kernel desires microscheduling support it must save and restore the stack state.

4.3 Network Interference and Virtual Channels

The protection mechanisms described above are sufficient to prevent a malicious or errant user mode

---

[7]We distinguish partition Id from process Id because, depending on the operating system, user mode processes on separate processors that correspond to the same parallel process may be assigned different process Ids. If these processes are given the same partition Id for communication, then messages can be exchanged without any operating system intervention.

[8]In the 88110MPthere is a common pool of eight receive buffers (register sets) which are dynamically allocated to the four queues.

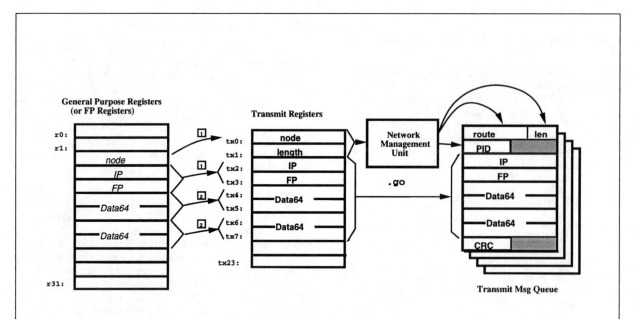

Figure 3: Naming and protection mechanisms are provided by the network management unit (NMU). This illustration shows how the short message from the example in section 3.1 is formatted for transmission. The NMU translates the destination node to a physical route using a small CAM, and inserts the currently active user PID in the message header. The PID is compared by the receiver hardware on the destination node in order to sort the message into one of four queues.

process from aliasing or stealing packets for other user mode processes or the kernel. Further, they permit a processor to run its own scheduler and memory manager without synchronizing with other processors.[9] However, it is possible for a user process to interfere with other processes by deadlocking the network and thereby not allowing competing processes to make progress. This can happen whenever the physical buffering resources in the network are shared by two processes and when one process jams the network with messages and places links into flow control (this condition occurs frequently, even in correctly executing programs).

There are several different approaches to avoiding networking interference. One is to provide a *virtual channel* [8, 3] for each process. In effect, a virtual channel is created by dedicating message buffers that cannot be consumed by other virtual channels. This way, a message in a virtual channel can always make progress independent of the state of the other channels. Another way to mitigate the effects of interference in a user mode network is to *space partition* the network where user processes are space and time scheduled such that two processes never share the same set of network links at the same time. Space partitioning is implemented on the CM5 by isolating users in separate subtrees of a fat-tree [6]. Kernel messaging (including I/O) can traverse through the root. Unfortunately, a pure reliance on space parti-

tioning restricts system organization, and in particular the way in which I/O devices can be distributed throughout the machine.[10]

The *T system architecture takes a mixed strategy. The network is virtualized into low and high priorities. User messages are always sent in low priority whereas the kernel can label a message for high priority. High priority messages are guaranteed to make progress even if the low priority channel is deadlocked. Beyond this, multiple user processes are given separate space partitions (*T uses a fat-tree network topology). We note that the packet timeout mechanism and PID tagging *does* permit users to physically share space partitions, but with a potential degradation of performance.

5 ARCTIC: A Companion Message Routing Chip

ARCTIC[11] is a high performance 8 × 8 packet routing chip based upon the highly successful PaRC [12], a 4 × 4 100 Mbytes/sec/link packet router used in Monsoon. Like PaRC, ARCTIC routers can store and forward packets during times of high network utilization,

---

[9]Such synchronization (*e.g.,* gang scheduling) is not required to provide protection guarantees, but might be highly desirable for performance reasons.

[10]Kernel mode-only fabrics (Intel Paragon[5]) avoid the deadlock aspect of network interference. Of course, this is at the expense of the overhead of the user-kernel interaction required to send and receive messages. One view of this overhead, then, is from the buffer management and flow control algorithms employed by the kernel to avoid network interference.

[11]A Routing Chip That Is Cool

but use virtual cut-through routing to avoid the latency of buffering when there is no contention for a desired output link. While an ARCTIC router might be used in a wide variety of networks, we have added special routing support for use in a fat-tree topology [13], the network topology used in *T systems.

The link signalling conventions are directly compatible with the links on the 88110MP. Each link is unidirectional and capable of sustaining a raw transfer rate of 200 Mbytes/sec. Flow control and buffer management algorithms provide a high and low priority virtual channel for each link. The 88110MP uses the high priority channel for kernel packets, and the low priority channel for user and non-critical O/S services.

A key design goal was to make ARCTIC a *modeless router*. Aside from configuration registers to establish the physical routing addresses algorithm, an ARCTIC chip has no knowledge of user versus kernel packets, space partitioning or context switching. All ARCTIC routing decisions are deterministic with respect to the physical routing address on each packet. Space partitioning, route randomization and faulty link avoidance are all properties of the route generation algorithm at the source 88110MP. While this design position gives up some potential performance under highly loaded conditions[12], it permits deterministic management of network resources by the nodes and avoids dynamic configuration and context switching issues in the router. The route generation CAM in the NMU is sophisticated enough to provide random up-route generation in a fat tree while being able to suppress paths that traverse known-bad links.

Input links are configured to either be an *up-link* or a *down-link,* depending on whether the link is a member of the up-part of the fat-tree or the down-part. For up-links, routing is determined by each input section by comparing the *down-route* part of the physical route in message header with the contents of a configuration register that establishes the position (height) of the router in the fat-tree. A decision is made to forward the message further up the tree according to the *up-route,* or to send the packet down the tree as indicated by the *down-route.* Down-links route according to the *down-route* field in the message header. We emphasize that all routing decisions are deterministic. Pseudo-randomization of up paths can be performed at the source by suitably programming the route generation CAM in the 88110MP NMU.

The data link uses a 16 bit wide data path and each bit is transmitted using a single ended GTL driver. Data is sent at 100Mbits/sec on each signal line synchronous with a 50MHz differential clock that is transmitted with the data. The ARCTIC clocking convention is *plesiochronous* [14]: each router runs on its own independent 50MHz clock. A router transmits its clock along with the data on each output link. The input sections use the incoming clock clock to safely latch

---

[12]Permitting a router to make a local routing decision on the basis of instantaneous link load can improve throughput in some circumstances.

link data, and to clock the link data into a free input buffer. There are thus nine clock domains, one for each of the eight input sections and one for the ARCTIC core and all output sections. This technique proved to be highly reliable on PaRC, which to date has yet to record a single packet delivery failure in fielded systems.

Also as in PaRC, flow control is performed on packet boundaries. The ARCTIC protocol differs, however, in that the output section of the transmitter keeps track of the number of available buffers in the input section of the receiver to which it is connected. The input section has a single back link on which it modulates a Manchester encoded buffer free signal every time one of its input buffers becomes available.

This flow control strategy has two advantages compared with a traditional "back pressure" flow control line. First, it cuts the effects of the link latency in half — a back pressure line needs to assert early enough to account for two link delays worth of *in situ* data. Second, the link delay itself is not part of the flow control algorithm, so the link delay does not have to be parameterized in the flow control logic. The flow control self-adapts to link length.

6   Preliminary Performance Modeling

Although both the 88110MPand ARCTIC chips are still under development,[13] we have used a variety of techniques to model expected system performance. Here, we briefly report on an extension of performance modeling technique used to compare the J-machine and the CM5 under fine grain parallelism [24]. This approach develops a comprehensive file of "machine costs" that detail the expected number of cycles it takes a processor, including its network interface, to perform the abstract operations under TL0, Berkeley's intermediate language for fine grain multithreading. These costs are then factored into instruction frequency statistics gathered from instrumenting the threaded execution of a variety of benchmark codes written in Id [17]. The average execution time in terms of cycles per TL0 instructions are reported.

Figure 4 reproduces the data from the original J-machine and CM5 study and adds our data for *T . Overall, the 88110MPimplementation yields an average of 3.5 cycles/TL0 instruction, in contrast to about 12 cycles for the J-machine (modified to include a floating point unit and a data cache) and 14 cycles for the CM5 (modified to include an improved network interface). Of course, the *T implementation also benefits from the dual-issue nature of the 88110MP. In our model, however, we have conservatively rated the 88110MPat 1.3 instructions per clock. We believe that these preliminary data attest to the broad scale yet balanced attack on network overhead without compromising sequential code performance.

---

[13]First silicon for both parts is expected in 4Q93.

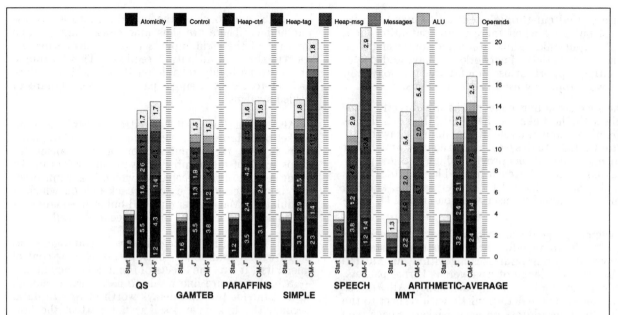

Figure 4: A cycle per TL0 instruction comparison of the J-machine (modified to include floating point hardware and a cache) and the CM5 (modified to include a better network interface). The x-axis is in units of cycles per TL0 instruction. The benchmark codes were written in Id and compiled into TL0. QS is a quicksort, GAMTEB is a neutral particle transport problem, PARAFFINS enumerates paraffin isomers, SIMPLE is a fluid dynamics problem with heat conduction, and MMT is a blocked matrix multiply.

7   Conclusion

We believe that we have struck a good balance in combining the demands of competitive sequential performance with the tightly coupled network interface of experimental machines such as Monsoon, the J-machine and iWarp. While the mapping of the network into user mode registers is not difficult by itself, we have done so in a way that is consistent with speculative superscalar execution and, importantly, supports a naming and protection model consistent with modern operating systems. Our preliminary modeling shows that the payoff may be overall cycle efficiencies of better than a factor of three when compared with the latest commercial and research machines. We hope that this design helps the pave the way to network interfaces that are as closely coupled to processors in the future as load/store units are today.

References

[1] A. Agarwal, D. Chaiken, G. D'Souze, K. Johnson, D. Kranz, J. Kubiatowica, K. Kurihara, B.-H. Lim, G. Maa D. Nussbaum, M. Parkin, and D. Yeung. *The MIT Alewife Machine: A Large-Scale Disributed-Memory Multiprocessor*. Technical Report MIT LCS TM-454, MIT Laboratory for Computer Sciences, Cambridge,MA, 1991.

[2] Arvind and R. A. Iannucci. *Two Fundamental Issues in Multiprocessing*. In Proceedings of DFVLR - Conference 1987 on Parallel Processing in Science and Engineering, Bonn-Bad Goes-dberg, W. Germany, Springer-Verlag LNCS 295, June 25-29 1987.

[3] S. Borkar, R. Cohn, G. Cox, T. Gross, H Kung, M. Lam, M. Levine, B. Moore, W. Moore, C. Peterson, J. Susman, J. Sutton, J. Urbanski, J. Webb. *Supporting Systolic and Memory Communication in iWarp*. In Proceedings of the 17th ISCA, June 1990.

[4] E. Brooks. *The Attack of the Killer Micros*. Supercomputing '89, Reno, Nevada, 1989.

[5] I. Corporation. *Paragon XP/S Product Overview*. 15201 N.W. Greenbrier Parkway, Beaverton, OR 94006, 1991.

[6] T.M. Corporation. *The Connection Machine CM-5 Technical Summary*. Technical report, Thinking Machines Corporation, 245 First Street, Cambridge, MA, Jan 1992.

[7] W. Dally, L. Chao, A. Chien, S. Hassoun, W. Horwat, J. Kaplan, P. Song, B. Totty, S Wills. *Architecture of a Message-Driven Processor* In Proceedings 14th Annual International Symposium on Computer Architecture, Pittsburgh, PA, pages 189-196, June 1987.

[8] W.J. Dally, R. Davison, J.A.S. Fiske, G. Fyler, J.S. Keen, R.A. Lethin, M. Noakes, and P.R. Nuth. *The Message-Driven Processor: A Multicomputer Processing Node with Efficient Mechanisms*. IEEE Micro, April 1992.

[9] K. Diefendorff and M. Allen. *Organization of the Motorola 88110 Superscalar RISC Microprocessor.* IEEE Micro, April 1992.

[10] V. Grafe, G. Davidson, J. Hoch, and V. Holmes. *The Epsilon Dataflow Processor.* In Proceedings of the 16th Annual International Symposium on Computer Architecture, Jerusalem, Israel, pages 36-45, May 29-31 1989.

[11] D. Henry and C. Joerg. *A Tightly Coupled Processor-Network Interface.* In Proceedings 5th International Conference on Architectural Support for Programming Languages and Systems (ASPLOS), Boston, MA, pages 111-122, October 12-15 1992.

[12] C.F. Joerg. *Design and Implementation of a Packet Switched Routing Chip* Technical Report MIT/LCS/TR-482, Dec 1990.

[13] C.E. Leiserson. *Fat Trees: Universal Networks for Hardware-Efficient Supercomputing.* C-34(10), Oct 1985.

[14] D.G. Messerschmitt. *Synchronization in Digital System Design.* IEEE Journal on Selected Areas in Communications, October 1990.

[15] Motorola, Inc. *MC88110 Second Generation RISC Microprocessor User's Manual, 1991.* Part number MC88110UM/AD.

[16] D.E. Nielsen. *General Purpose Parallel Supercomputing.* Technical Report UCRL-ID-108228, Lawrence Livermore National Laboratory, 1991.

[17] R.S. Nikhil. *Id (Version 90.1) Reference Manual.* Technical Report CSG Memo 284-2, MIT Laboratory for Computer Science, July 15 1991.

[18] R.S. Nikhil, G.M. Papadopoulos, Arvind. **T: A Multithreaded Massively Parallel Architecture* In Proceedings of the 19th ISCA, May 1992.

[19] G.M. Papadopoulos. *Implementation of a General Purpose Dataflow Multiprocessor.* MIT Press, 1991.

[20] G.M. Papadopoulos, D.E. Culler. *Monsoon: An Explicit Token Store Architecture.* In Proceedings 17th International Symposium on Computer Architecture, Seattle, WA, May 1990.

[21] G.M. Papadopoulos, K.R. Traub. *Multithreading: A Revisionist View of Dataflow Architectures* In Proceedings 18th International Symposium on Computer Architecture, Toronto, Canada, March 1991.

[22] S. Sakai, Y. Yamaguchi, K. Hiraki, T. Yuba. *An Architecture of a Dataflow Single Chip Processor.* In Proceedings 16th Annual International Symposium on Computer Architecture, Jerusalem, Israel, pages 46-53, May 28-June 1, 1989.

[23] K.E. Schauser, D.E. Buller, T. von Eicken. *Compiler-Controlled Multithreading for Lenient Parallel Languages* In Proceedings 5th ACM Conference on Functional Programming Languages and Computer Architecture, Cambridge, MA, pages 50-72, August 1991, Springer-Verlag LNCS 523.

[24] E.Spertus, W.J. Dally, S. Goldstein, K. Schauser, T. von Eicken, D.E. Culler. *Evaluation of Mechanisms for Fine-Grained Parallel Programs in the J-Machine and the CM-5.* In Proceedings of the 20th Annual International Symposium on Computer Architecture, San Diego, CA, May 17-19 1993.

[25] T. von Eicken, D.W. Culler, S.C. Goldstein, K.E. Schauser. *Active Messages: a Mechanism for Integrated Communication and Computation.* In Proceedings of the 19th ISCA, May 1992.

The *T project represents the collaborative effort of many people from our two institutions, particularly Professor Arvind and Al Vezza of MIT, and Tony Dahbura and Jim Richey of Motorola, Inc., and also S. Aditya, B.S. Ang, S. Asari, L. Avirett-Mackenzie, R. Barua, T. Bousman, S. Brobst, M. Carlon, A. Carnevali, A. Caro, P. Carr, S. Chamberlin, Y. Chery, D. Chiou, K. Cho, S. Coorg, J. Costanza, R. Davis, T. Deng, M. Duh, T. Durgavich, G. Edirisooriya, S. Edirisooriya, E. Ewy, D. Faust, C. Flood, D. Fumia, E. Greenwood, M. Halbherr, E. Heit, D. Henry, J. Hicks, J. Hoe, C. Joerg, R.P. Johnson, T. Kish, T. Klemas, J. Kulik, B. Kuszmaul, J. Kwon, P. Jones, W.C. Leung, V. Liggett, T. Lindsay, M. Nadworny, V. Natarajan, M. Naumann, R. Nikhil, M. Nodine, E. Ogston, R. Olson, R. Radhakrishnan, G. Rao, C. Seed, M. Sharma, A. Shaw, J. Stoy, H. Thompson, R. Tiberio, R. Wilson, H. Wong, and Y. Zhou.

Enhanced Superscalar Hardware: The Schedule Table

James K. Pickett, David G. Meyer, PhD

Advanced Micro Devices, Purdue University

Abstract

In the push for ever increasing performance out of processor architectures, there is a need to expand beyond the limitations of existing scalar approaches. Superscalar architectures provide one such means. By dynamically executing more than one instruction per clock cycle, superscalar architectures can improve performance without relying solely on technology improvements for these gains. This paper examines a new technique for superscalar control implementation, called the schedule table. The schedule table facilitates dependency checking, out of order instruction issue, out of order execution, branch prediction, speculative execution, precise interrupts, and fast and efficient misprediction recovery.

1 Introduction

Superscalar microprocessors are characterized as architectures that issue multiple instructions per cycle from the same instruction stream. Superscalar architectures utilize multiple functional units to improve the performance. The functional units may be of various types such as an integer ALU, a floating point ALU, a load pipe, etc. Functional units of the same type may also be replicated, e.g., contain multiple integer ALUs. A superscalar architecture of degree two issues two instructions per clock cycle. The superscalar design decreases the execution time by decreasing the CPI.

Superscalar architectures have the advantage of binary compatibility with industry standard processors. Recompilation for different issue rates is not necessary since the hardware handles all of the dependencies and scheduling. The disadvantage of superscalar designs is the extra hardware associated with multiple functional units, resolving dependencies, and scheduling multiple instructions concurrently. If there is not enough parallelism within the program, these additional resources set idle and can potentially even slow the execution due to

the additional overhead required for scheduling instructions. One final point is that the parallelism of the superscalar approach can be increased as much as required in order to match the parallelism inherent within the instruction stream.

For a superscalar architecture, a RISC, CISC, or hybrid of the two could be chosen to design an instruction set. To decode and analyze the dependencies of multiple instructions in the same cycle is a requirement. Given this requirement, the simple decode format, register based operations, and simple addressing modes of RISC style architectures make them easier to implement. The superscalar model used in this research is based on the instruction set of the MIPS R2000.

Both hardware and software solutions have been suggested to implement superscalar approaches. The earliest works on hardware dependency checking were done by Tomasulo[17] and Keller[7]. Since those early papers, there has been work done by numerous authors. The dispatch stack[1], checkpoint repair[5], the reorder buffer[12], history buffer[12], future file[12], and the register update unit[15,16] have all been suggested as ways to implement precise interrupts. In addition, the SIMP[10] and Metaflow DRIS[8,11] have been proposed directly as superscalar architectures.

In addition to the hardware based approaches, there have been several articles on software based approaches to multiple instruction issue. There have been superscalar optimizing compilers such as the IMPACT[3] project, the SF/960 Scheduler[4], basic block enlargement[9], boosting[14], and others[19].

Finally, there is the debate on whether there exists sufficient instruction parallelism for superscalar architectures to exploit. There have been papers for[18,2], and papers against[6,13]. This is still an open issue, one which this paper will not address.

2 The Simulation Model

The pipeline timing diagram for the MIPS R2000 and the superscalar model developed as part of this research are shown in Figure 1. The execution of an R2000 instruction consists of five pipe stages: Instruction Fetch (IF), Read (RD), Arithmetic/Logic Unit operation (ALU), Memory Access (MEM), Register Write back (WB). Each cycle is further divided into two phases, designated phase one ($\Phi 1$) and phase two ($\Phi 2$). During the first half of the IF stage, an instruction address is selected by the branching logic and pretranslated to a physical address. In the second half of the IF stage and the first half of the RD stage, the instruction is retrieved from the instruction cache. During the second half of the RD stage, three blocks operate simultaneously to decode the instruction, fetch operands from the register file, and compute a new instruction address.

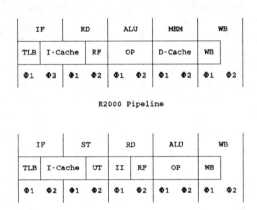

Figure 1. Pipeline Timing Comparison.

The execution of an instruction on the superscalar model consists of five stages: Instruction Fetch (IF), Schedule Table access (ST), Read (RD), Arithmetic/Logic Unit operation (ALU), Register Write back (WB). As in the R2000, each cycle is divided into two phases. During the first half of the IF stage, an instruction address is selected by the branching logic and pretranslated to a physical address. In the second half of the IF stage and the first half of the ST stage, the instruction is retrieved from the instruction cache. During the second half of the ST stage, four blocks operate simultaneously to decode the instruction, perform dependency checking on the operands already present within the schedule table, write the instruction into the schedule table, and compute a new instruction address. In the first half of the RD stage, the source operand tags for the instruction are written into the schedule table and the instructions are scheduled for execution. The second half of the RD stage fetches the operands from the schedule table or the register file.

An important point to note here is that the superscalar approach has an additional cycle before the ALU

operation. In the case of a taken branch instruction, this adds an extra delay cycle to the branch penalty. Where the R2000 has a one cycle branch penalty, the superscalar model has a two cycle branch penalty.

The block diagram for the superscalar approach that is being modeled is given in Figure 2.

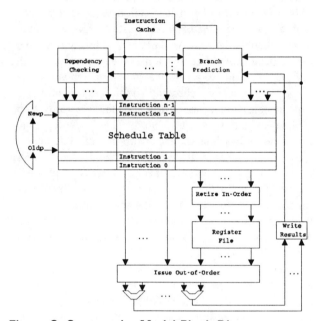

Figure 2. Superscalar Model Block Diagram.

Register renaming through destination tags is performed automatically with the schedule table. As each instruction is decoded, it is assigned a sequential entry in the schedule table. The address of this entry is the destination tag for the result of that instruction. Since these tags are assigned sequentially and in order at instruction decode, the order is preserved when these instructions are retired, regardless of the issue and execution completion order. This approach does not require any associative logic to implement.

The head (oldp) pointer is the address of the bottom of the schedule table where the next instruction to be retired to the register file is located. The tail (newp) pointer is the address of the top of the schedule table where the next instruction should be inserted. The normal checks for a full or empty queue must be performed for the schedule table also.

The source dependencies for instructions that have been decoded need to be determined before they can be written to the schedule table from the decoder. This requires concurrently determining the latest tag value for each of the source registers, or determining if the latest value is in the register file instead. The schedule table uses associative logic to compare the destination register number in the schedule table to each of the source register numbers from the decoder in parallel. The search is done from the newest pointer entry to the oldest pointer entry, i.e., backwards through the table relative to the original instruction ordering for all of the current entries. The first comparison entry that matches will disable all of the entries below it in the schedule table from responding. This way only the latest destination value that matches will respond. If none of the destination register numbers match, then the latest bit will not be set; this will serve as the indicator of whether to use the tag value or the register file value to access the source operands.

The dependency checking logic determines the dependencies among the instructions that are ready to be written to the schedule table. The issue logic for instruction #0 assigns the tags from the schedule table to the src id to be written to the schedule table. The instruction #1 issue logic checks to see if the source register for instruction #1 matches the destination register for instruction #0. If it does, the source id to be written to the schedule table is the destination id for instruction #0. Otherwise, it is the source tag for instruction #1 from the schedule table. This procedure is done individually for each source register in the instruction. The same type of operation is performed for each of the subsequent instructions, with the number of previous dependencies to check also increasing with each new instruction. This obviously requires an associative search with a carry chain between instructions.

To find which instructions are ready to execute, the schedule table must be searched associatively. An instruction is ready to execute if its sources are both unlocked, its valid bit is set, and there is a functional unit available for that instruction based on its instruction class number. A read port is required for each instruction that is submitted in parallel to a functional unit. Once the instruction is submitted to the functional unit, the valid bit is cleared for that instruction to prevent it from being resubmitted.

Speculative execution increases the performance attainable by allowing instructions that follow a conditional branch that has not yet been resolved to be executed. Branch prediction determines which path to follow in the instruction stream when the outcome of a conditional branch has not been determined. Once the conditional branch instruction is executed, the outcome of the instruction is compared to the predicted branch direction. If the outcome matches, the speculative execution was correct and no further action is required. If the prediction was incorrect, a branch repair mechanism is needed to recover the correct state and continue the proper execution.

Quick and efficient recovery from a mispredicted branch is paramount to achieving a performance gain from speculative execution. As part of this research a simple yet very efficient mechanism for mispredicted branch recovery has been devised! When a mispredicted branch is detected in the branch unit, the ID for that instruction is used to reset the newest pointer in the schedule table. This action automatically invalidates any incorrect results and prevents them from being written to the register file. Incorrect results cannot have been written yet since they occur after the branch instruction and instructions are retired in order. The final task that occurs in parallel is to invalidate any instructions currently in progress within a functional unit. All of this can be accomplished in one clock cycle without any additional overhead required in hardware or software.

With multiple functional units operating in parallel, it is necessary to be able to read multiple source operands in parallel. Each instruction potentially has two source operand values to read, thus requiring two ports per instruction from both the schedule table and the register file. With the schedule table described here, it is possible to access these values by using the tags as an address field to the buffer. No associative logic is needed for this operation.

Each functional unit produces one result that must be written back to the schedule table. This requires one port per functional unit to be able to write all of the results back in parallel. The result carries the destination tag with it so the schedule table location where the value should be stored may be addressed directly. Therefore no associative logic is required for this operation in the schedule table.

The results that are ready to be retired from the schedule table are those that have completed, for which no exceptions have occurred, and for which all previous instructions have completed and are retired or ready to be retired. The results are written from the schedule table directly to the register file. The results are written in parallel and in the original instruction order to the register file, up to the maximum number of ports shared between the schedule table and the register file. The schedule table is responsible for determining which instructions are ready to retire and if any instructions write to the same address. If two or more instructions are ready to retire and have the same destination address, then only the newest instruction among these should be written to the register file.

The arithmetic units for superscalar design should not be any different than in normal high performance sequential designs. The difference will be in having multiple functional units and in the number of each type to have.

This will require a tradeoff based upon the parallelism available in the code used for analysis.

3 Schedule Table Hardware Overhead

An important consideration in the design and analysis of superscalar architectures is the impact that the additional hardware overhead has on the clock cycle time due to the associative searching that is required to implement this type of approach. This section will address these issues and show that associative searching can be accomplished in the same amount of time as the execution operations of the functional units. This will show that the superscalar approach presented in this research can be implemented without impacting the cycle time of the machine. There is the impact of the additional pipeline stage, which was addressed previously in the discussion of the pipeline stages shown in Figure 1.

The first point to be examined is the dependency checking hardware within the schedule table. A sample portion of the dependency checking hardware is shown in Figure 3. The Addr0 - Addr3 lines represent the address of the instruction within the schedule table, which is also its destination tag value. Oldest and Newest are the pointer values to the oldest and newest instruction within the schedule table. The Src1 and Src2 buses are the source fields from the instruction being read out of the instruction cache. The Lat1, Tag1, Lat2, and Tag2 values are the latest and tag values for the source one and two operands, respectively.

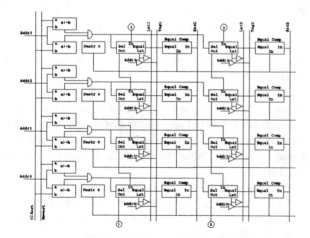

Figure 3 Dependency Checking Hardware for the Schedule Table

As shown in Figure 3, each instruction entry in the schedule table requires two comparators to test its destination register value against the source register values

of each instruction that is prefetched. Each instruction entry also requires two additional comparators for testing against the newest and oldest pointer values. The last additional piece of logic required is the carry chain that determines which instruction entry should respond. This carry chain is a circular chain that wraps around the schedule table, as indicated by the connection circles numbered 1 and 2. It is this carry chain that is the determining factor in the speed of dependency checking. Assuming a schedule table size of 32, which is a reasonable size based upon results that are to be presented in a later paper, then the carry chain is 32 bits long. This is the same length as a carry chain for a 32 bit ALU. From this, the conclusion can be drawn that the dependency checking would not increase the cycle time of the machine.

The second point to be examined is the instruction issue hardware within the schedule table. An illustration of the instruction issue hardware is shown in Figure 4. The Addr0-Addr3 lines represent the address of the instruction within the schedule table, which is also its destination tag value. Oldest and Newest are the pointer values to the oldest and newest instruction within the schedule table. The Tag1 and Tag2 buses are the tag values for instructions that have been selected to be issued. The Ready1 and Ready2 signals indicate that the corresponding tag values are valid instructions for issue.

As shown in Figure 4, a requirement for being issued is that the instruction occurs after the oldest pointer and up to and including the newest pointer location. In addition, the lock bits must both be clear, the valid bit set, and the instruction has to be of the proper instruction class. Once again it is a carry chain that determines the latency of instruction issue. The carry chain that determines the instruction issue must run the full length of the schedule table. As was the case for dependency checking, with a schedule table of 32 entries, the instruction issue cycle time should match that of a 32 bit ALU. So for instruction issue there should be no impact on the cycle time due to the associative searching for instructions ready to issue.

The third point to consider is writing the results back into the schedule table. Since the destination tag value is the address of the instruction in the schedule table, no associative searching is required to write the results back into the schedule table. Therefore, no overhead in writing results from the functional units is incurred.

The fourth and final point to be considered is retiring instructions from the schedule table to the register file. For a parallelism of n, where n is generally the instruction fetch rate, only the n oldest instructions in the schedule table need to be examined to see if their update bit is set, and that no outstanding exception conditions exist for those instructions. This is a very short carry chain which will be quicker than the ALU cycle time. Retiring instructions therefore does not incur any additional cycle time overhead.

As a result of this examination, it is apparent that the schedule table can be implemented without extending the cycle time beyond that normally required for a functional unit carry chain. Although an extra pipeline structure is required, there should be no impact on the minimum clock cycle attainable.

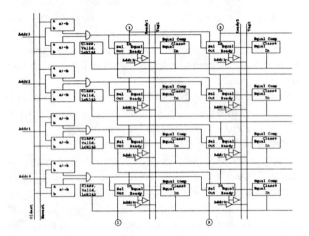

Figure 4 Instruction Issue Hardware for the Schedule Table

4 Schedule Table Comparison to Previous Approaches

In this section, the schedule table is compared with alternative approaches previously described in the literature. Specifically, the register update unit[15] and the Metaflow DRIS[11] (Deferred-scheduling, Register-renaming Instruction Shelf) approaches are considered.

4.1 Determining Available Instruction Entries

Writing instructions from the instruction cache into a buffer requires determining which entries are available within the buffer. The register update unit[15], the Metaflow DRIS[11], and the schedule table are all managed as a circular queue with a head and a tail pointer. Determining if there is an entry available is simply a matter of checking the pointers and using the tail pointer as the position of the next available entry. Subsequent instructions are written to sequential locations following the tail pointer.

4.2 Register Renaming

The register update unit[15] includes two n-bit counters with each register in the register file to provide multiple instances of a destination register. The counters represent the number of instances (NI) and the latest instance (LI). The counters are both incremented when an instruction with a destination register Ri is issued. NI is incremented up to 2^n-1, while LI is incremented modulo n. The counter based approach limits assigning tags since a group of instructions fetched in the same cycle could share the same destination register. If this is the case, the counter has to be incremented multiple times in the same cycle, but sequentially, so each instruction that has the same destination register can get its counter value.

The Metaflow DRIS[11] and the schedule table both use the address of the instruction entry as the renamed register value. This allows any number of instances of a register, and automatically assigns tags in parallel without any hardware overhead required.

4.3 Dependency Checking

To perform dependency checking requires that instructions read from the instruction cache have their source registers compared to the destination registers of instructions that have been previously buffered.

For the register update unit[15], if an operand is not immediately available and NI is not equal to zero, the tag subfield monitors the result bus for a matching tag. If a match occurs, the data is written into the reservation station. No associative search is needed by the RUU to generate its tags for dependency checking. Associative logic is needed in the reservation stations so the value of the source operands can be stored when they become available on the result bus.

The Metaflow[11] approach searches the DRIS for each operand of each instruction that is fetched. The source registers are compared against the destination registers for instructions that have their latest bit set. If a match is found in the DRIS, then the tag of the destination register is returned.

When an instruction is written into the DRIS, it has its latest bit set, and any previous instruction which had that same destination register has its latest bit cleared. This simplifies finding the most recent instruction to write a register when multiple stored instructions all write the same destination register, but it creates difficulties when doing speculative execution. Either way, an associative search of the DRIS is still required to find the tag values.

For this research, the schedule table is searched for each operand of each instruction that is fetched. The source registers are compared against the destination registers for instructions that are present within the table and lie between the two pointers. If a match is found in the schedule table, then the tag of the most recent destination register is returned. This approach always searches all the instructions from the newest pointer to the instruction after (one newer than) the oldest pointer, and allows the first instruction that matches, and only that instruction, to respond with its destination tag value (its address).

4.4 Instruction Issue

The register update unit[15] checks the ready bits of its source operands to determine when an instruction can be issued to the functional units. Highest priority is given to load/store instructions, and next highest priority to the instructions which have been in the register update unit the longest. An associative search of the register update unit is needed to determine the next instruction to issue. The source operands reside with the instruction in the register update unit, so no additional overhead is required to determine if the values reside in the register file or the buffer. There is overhead in storing both source operands, however.

The scheduler for the Metaflow DRIS[11] examines all of the instructions in the DRIS whose operands are unlocked and issues the oldest of those instructions to be executed. The DRIS also examines the functional unit class of the instruction and can skip over instructions if no resources for that particular class are available that cycle. It is not clear how it is determined if a source operand still resides in the DRIS or whether it has been retired to the register file, since the instruction referencing it was placed in the DRIS. Most likely the tag used by the source operand is compared against the pointer values to determine if the destination operand still exists within the DRIS. If the operand does not, the value is read from the register file. (Note that a different approach may be actually used by Metaflow; few details concerning this appear in the literature.)

The instruction issue logic for the schedule table examines all of the instructions from the instruction after the oldest pointer to the newest pointer instruction. Any instruction whose valid bit is set and whose locked bits are cleared is a candidate for issue. Instructions are issued based upon their functional class availability. When an instruction is issued, its valid bit is cleared so that it cannot be reissued. The latest bit in the schedule table was set for a source operand if there was a match during dependency checking. This latest bit now allows the schedule table to easily determine if the operand still resides in the schedule table, or if it is in the register file. Instructions that are retired to the register file clear the latest bit for matching source operands that are dependent

on them, so the latest bit is a dynamic indicator of the location of the source operands.

4.5 Writing Results to the Buffer

Each instruction in the register update unit[15] monitors the result bus to determine when its result becomes available. By matching its counter value and register against those that an instruction carries with it, it writes the proper result when that value becomes available. This requires comparison logic in the register update unit, to check its destination tag against the tags that are on the result buses each cycle.

For the Metaflow DRIS[11], the destination tag is the address of that instruction in the DRIS, so writing the results is a simple task that does not require any associative logic to implement. At the same time that the instruction results are written, the executed bit is set. The DRIS also uses the destination tag to search for and unlock any source operands that were locked on that tag value. This portion does require comparators to match against the tag and clear the lock bits.

The schedule table makes it simple to write a destination result since the destination tag is the address of the instruction in the schedule table. No associative searching is required since direct addressing can be used. The destination tag is used to clear the lock bits on instructions that have source operands dependent on this instruction. Finding and clearing the lock bits does require associative searching to accomplish.

4.6 Retiring Results to the Register File

To retire results to the register file, the executed bit within the register update unit[15] is monitored. When the executed bit is set for the instruction that is at the head of the queue, the results of its destination register are sent to the register file and its associated NI counter within the register file is decremented. It is difficult for the register update unit to write multiple destination values to the register file. If two or more destinations reference the same register value, the NI counter must be decremented two or more times in the same cycle, or a stalling must occur. This is a limiting factor of having the counters determine the tags.

The DRIS[11] evaluates the oldest instructions each cycle. If the executed bit is set, all older instructions have retired or are being retired this cycle, there are no exception conditions on this instruction, and a write port to the register file is available, then the instruction is retired to the register file and the pointer is updated.

The schedule table in this research follows the same general flow as the DRIS, but checks the update bit instead of the executed bit to determine if an instruction is ready to retire.

4.7 Branch Repair

To allow speculative execution of instructions requires a repair mechanism to recover from mispredictions.

Extending the register update unit[15] to support branch prediction and conditional execution is currently under investigation by Sohi[15]. However, the counter based scheme does not appear to support branch prediction and conditional execution, since recovering from a misprediction would require changing the counter values to their previous values before the misprediction occurred, which is impossible since the count values at that point are no longer known. The register update unit therefore does not appear to be capable of supporting recovery from speculative execution.

The ID of an instruction in the Metaflow DRIS[11] identifies the location of an instruction that needs to be deleted from the DRIS. This ID also becomes the next register instance number to use. Unfortunately, the latest bit values are no longer correct, since they have been changed by subsequent instructions entering the DRIS. Those instructions were then deleted when a misprediction occurred. The latest bits need to be reconfigured before any subsequent instructions may be entered into the DRIS. Delay due to decoupled scheduling and branch repair is large. This critical limit is a consequence of how the latest bits are implemented.

Branch repair is where the schedule table is truly unique in its approach, and where a critical solution is necessary in order to make speculative execution an effective approach to improving performance. Upon a misprediction, the schedule table resets the newest pointer to point to the location where misprediction occurred. Subsequent instructions that enter the schedule table are written after the pointer. Since new instructions search for dependencies on all existing instructions between the pointers, no information that is needed to proceed with fetching, issuing, or executing instructions is lost or needs to be recreated. This is the only approach currently described in the literature that does not have to go through some extensive procedure or incur excessive overhead, in order to do branch repair and speculative execution repair in a superscalar environment.

4.8 Memory Reference Instruction Handling

No details are provided on how the register update unit[15] handles load and store instructions, so this section will concentrate solely on the Metaflow DRIS and the schedule table.

The Metaflow DRIS[11] processes loads and stores in two phases. The first phase determines the memory address once the operands for the memory calculation are unlocked. When the calculated address is written back into the DRIS, the address of a load instruction is compared against the addresses of any older store instructions, and the address of a store instruction is compared against any newer load instructions. If there is an address match, the load instruction is locked upon the store. For a store instruction, its second phase is the retire phase, where it is written to memory. For the load instruction, its second phase consists of scheduling the load after all older store instructions target addresses are known, and the load instruction's target address is not locked. The load instruction is then executed to retrieve its value from memory. There is no load bypassing performed.

The schedule table can implement load and store instruction execution in one of two ways. In the first way, loads must wait until all previous store instructions have had their target address computed. Then the load instruction may execute and retrieve its operand either from memory or from the matching store instruction in the schedule table, if the target addresses match. This is commonly referred to as load bypassing. The second method is the unique approach implemented in this research that has been dubbed speculative loads. This allows a load instruction to execute before preceding store instructions, even if the store instruction has not calculated its target address, if the load and the store instructions do not reference the same register location for their target address calculation. A recovery mechanism is also implemented for the case of misprediction due to the speculative load.

5 Initial Performance Results

This section presents initial results for the performance of the schedule table. Figure 5 is the chart of in order issue for the schedule table model on three of the integer SPEC89 benchmarks. Eqntott shows the highest performance at 1.89 instructions per cycle, followed by Xlisp at 1.84 instructions per cycle, and Espresso at 1.68 instructions per cycle. The schedule table model shows good improvement as the fetch rate increases from one through four. By eight instructions, the performance curve is beginning to level out.

Figure 6 demonstrates the schedule table model for out of order issue. The performance increase is much more pronounced, with the number of instructions per cycle still increasing significantly even at the eight instruction per cycle fetch rate. The performance increases for sixteen instructions per cycle, but the performance curve has flattened out by thirty two instructions per cycle. At a fetch rate of eight, Eqntott executes 2.79 instructions per cycle, while Espresso and Xlisp execute 3.94 and 3.60 instructions per cycle respectively.

the overall performance more significantly with out of order issue than with in order issue.

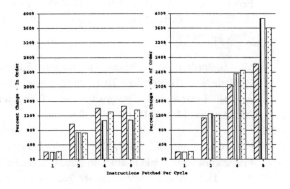

Figure 7. Complete Model Percentage Comparison.

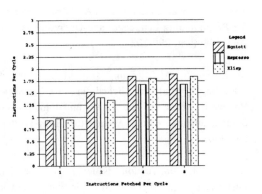

Figure 5. Complete Model, In Order.

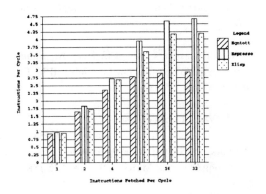

Figure 6. Complete Model, Out of Order.

Figure 7 is the chart showing the percentage performance improvement for in order issue (left half of chart) and out of order issue (right half of chart) for the schedule table model. At the fetch rate of eight, and with in order issue, espresso has a 110% performance increase. Eqntott and xlisp have 140% and 130% improvements in performance respectively. At the same fetch rate, but with out of order issue, eqntott has a performance gain of 260%, xlisp gains 360%, and Espresso has a performance gain of over 380%. All of these represent tremendous gains over the in order issue. This exhibits the fact that the improvements made increase

6 Summary and Conclusions

In this paper, a unique approach to superscalar architectures, the schedule table, was presented. The simulation model of the schedule table with its associated pipeline timing was presented in section 2. The timing was compared to that of the MIPS R2000, and the additional pipeline stage for the superscalar architecture was shown. An overview of the operation of the schedule table was then presented. Section 3 presented the hardware overhead that is required for the schedule table. This section covered the points of the architecture implementation that could degrade the cycle time due to the associative processing that is required. It was shown that the schedule table is capable of achieving superscalar operation without increasing the cycle time of a basic 32 bit processor. Section 4 gave a comparison of the schedule table to two previously published approaches, the register update unit[15] and the Metaflow DRIS[11]. Register renaming, dependency checking, instruction issue, writing results to the buffer, writing results to the register file, branch repair and memory reference instruction handling were all analyzed for the three approaches. The unique branch repair technique of the schedule table was highlighted as a way to achieve single cycle recovery from branch misprediction. Section 5 presented initial results for the schedule table model.

In summary, the schedule table is a promising technique to improve performance in superscalar architectures. Results showing the performance improvement will be available in a future paper.

LIST OF REFERENCES

1. R.D. Acosta, J. Kjelstrup, and H.C. Torng, "An Instruction Issuing Approach to Enhancing Performance in Multiple Functional Unit Processors," IEEE Trans. Computers, Vol. C-35, No. 9, Sep. 1986, pp. 815-828.

2. M. Butler et al., "Single Instruction Stream Parallelism is Greater than Two," Proc. of the 18th Annual International Symposium on Computer Architecture, May 1991, pp. 276-286.

3. P.P. Chang et al., "IMPACT: An Architectural Framework for Multiple-Instruction-Issue Processors," Proc. 18th Annual International Symposium on Computer Architecture, May 1991, pp. 266-275.

4. D.N. Glass, "Compile-time Instruction Scheduling for Superscalar Processors," Compcon, Spring 1990, pp. 630-633.

5. W.W. Hwu and Y.N. Patt, "Checkpoint Repair for High Performance Out of Order Execution Machines," IEEE Trans. Computers, Vol. 36, No. 12, Dec. 1987, pp. 1496-1514.

6. N.P. Jouppi and D.W. Wall, "Available Instruction-Level Parallelism for Superscalar and Superpipelined Machines," Proc. of the 3rd International Conference on Architectural Support for Programming Languages and Operating Systems, Apr. 1989, pp. 272-282.

7. R.M. Keller, "Look-Ahead Processors," Computing Surveys, Vol. 7, No. 4, Dec. 1975, pp. 177-195.

8. B.D. Lightner and G. Hill, "The Metaflow Lightning Chipset," Compcon, Spring 1991, pp. 13-18.

9. S. Melvin and Y. Patt, "Exploiting Fine-Grained Parallelism Through a Combination of Hardware and Software Techniques," Proc. of the 18th Annual International Symposium on Computer Architecture, May 1991, pp. 287-296.

10. K. Murakami et al., "SIMP (Single Instruction stream/Multiple instruction Pipelining): A Novel High Speed Single Processor Architecture," Proc. of the 16th Annual International Symposium on Computer Architecture, May 1989, pp. 78-85.

11. V. Popescu et al., "The Metaflow Architecture," IEEE Micro, June 1991, pp. 10-13, 63-73.

12. J.E. Smith and A.R. Pleszkun, "Implementing Precise Interrupts in Pipelined Processors," IEEE Trans. Computers, Vol. 37, No. 5, May 1988, pp. 562-573.

13. M.D. Smith, M. Johnson, and M.A. Horowitz, "Limits on Multiple Instruction Issue," Proc. of the 3rd International Conference on Architectural Support for Programming Languages and Operating Systems, Apr. 1989, pp. 290-302.

14. M.D. Smith, M.S. Lam, and M.A. Horowitz, "Boosting Beyond Static Scheduling in a Superscalar Processor," Proc. of the 17th Annual International Symposium on Computer Architecture, May 1990, pp. 344-354.

15. G.S. Sohi, "Instruction Issue Logic for High Performance, Interruptable, Multiple Functional Unit, Pipelined Computers," IEEE Trans. Computers, Vol. 39, No. 3, March 1990, pp. 349-359.

16. G.S. Sohi and S. Vajapeyam, "Instruction Issue Logic for High Performance, Interruptable Pipelined Processors," Proc. of the 14th Annual International Symposium on Computer Architecture, May 1987, pp. 27-34.

17. R.M. Tomasulo, "An Efficient Algorithm for Exploiting Multiple Arithmetic Units," IBM Journal, Jan. 1967, pp. 25-33.

18. D.W. Wall, "Limits of Instruction-Level Parallelism," Proc. of the 4th International Conference on Architectural Support for Programming Languages and Operating Systems, March 1991, pp. 176-188.

19. H.S. Warren Jr., "Instruction Scheduling for the IBM RISC System/6000 Processor," IBM J. Res. Develop., Vol. 34, No. 1, Jan. 1990, pp. 85-97.

RISC Microprocessors and Scientific Computing

David H. Bailey
NASA Ames Research Center
Mail Stop T045-1
Moffett Field, CA 94035

Abstract

This paper discusses design features in currently available RISC microprocessors that sometimes result in less-than-optimal sustained performance on large-scale scientific calculations. Recommendations for future designs are suggested.

1. Introduction

Scientists accustomed to running large-scale, computationally intensive applications have traditionally utilized conventional vector supercomputers, such as those manufactured by Cray Research, Inc., Fujitsu or NEC. However, many scientists are now using RISC workstations, not just to edit their source codes and display their results, but to perform their computations as well. Further, RISC processors are now being incorporated into highly parallel supercomputers, and some observers predict that such systems will ultimately dominate high-end computing.

The reason for this interest is of course the recent sharp rise in the peak performance of RISC processors, and the expectation of continued increases in the future. Indeed, on many scientific applications, particularly those that enjoy high levels of data locality, RISC-based computers already feature superior sustained performance per dollar, when compared with conventional vector computers. However, not all applications run equally well on the RISC systems. This phenomenon is analogous to the situation in vector computing, where some scientific applications run quite well, but others do not. Given the important role that RISC processors are likely to play in the future of scientific computing, it is clear that users and designers of these systems need to better understand the factors that affect delivered performance.

RISC is an acronym for "reduced instructed set computer," a concept popularized a few years ago by researchers at Stanford, Berkeley and IBM. In this paper, however, "RISC processor" will be used more loosely to designate any of the recently developed high-performance floating-point microprocessors. Indeed, the issues raised herein have very little, if anything, to do with the basic concept of reduced instruction set computing. Rather we will deal with other features common to many of these processors.

In the following, 64-bit data is assumed in all discussion of performance rates. Thus, for instance, Mflop/s denotes millions of 64-bit floating point operations per second, and Mword/s denotes millions of 64-bit words per second.

2. Division

Several features common to many current RISC processors result in less-than-optimal performance when systems incorporating these processors are used for large-scale scientific computations. One example of such a feature is the design of the divide operation.

The IBM RS6000 processor has an IEEE-compliant floating point divide operation, which employs a Newton iteration scheme and requires 20 clock periods. The Hewlett-Packard PA-RISC floating point divide also requires 20 clock periods. The MIPS R4400, which is used in the new Challenge series workstations from Silicon Graphics, Inc., requires 36 clock periods. Of currently popular RISC processors, it appears that only the Sun SuperSPARC can perform a floating point divide in under ten clock periods (see Table 1).

On the Intel i860, divisions are performed in software by means of a Newton iteration scheme. This sequence requires 38 clock periods. If a true IEEE-compliant quotient is required, an additional sequence of operations is required that increases this cost by a factor of five, to approximately 190 clock periods. The IEEE-compliant divide operation on the DEC Alpha processor requires 63 clock periods.

On most RISC processors, including the PA-RISC and the Alpha, the divide operation cannot be pipelined like add and multiplies, or at least the time required for subsequent divides is only two or three clock periods shorter than for the first. There is some potential for compilers to optionally perform divides using software Newton iterations with pipelined add and multiply operations. But none of the vendors has yet pursued this avenue, and it is not clear that acceptably accurate results can be obtained in this manner with a significant time savings.

By contrast, the Cray-2, Cray Y-MP and C-90 processors can perform vectorized divisions at a rate of one result every four clock periods (although scalar divides are not nearly as fast — the divide latency on the C-90 is 28 clock periods). One important disadvantage of the current Cray systems is that they do not perform IEEE arithmetic, and quotients are not guaranteed fully accurate. This fact results in some rather annoying anomalies (such as $7.0/7.0 \neq 1.0$). Most users of Cray systems have found these "features" acceptable, although there are some situations where Cray's arithmetic is problematic.

A processor of the NEC SX-3 can perform one division every two clock periods, in vector mode, and the results are fully accurate — they are not merely the product of the numerator with an approximation to the reciprocal of the denominator. On the other hand, one SX-3 CPU can perform eight floating point adds and eight floating point multiplies per clock period, so that its peak divide performance is 1/16 that of its peak add or peak multiply performance.

How important is the performance of the divide operation in scientific computation? It is true that many important inner computational loops have no divide operations whatsoever. In most other cases, divisions can be moved out of inner loops, either by the programmer or by optimizing compilers. But there are loops where the divisors are not constant, and thus cannot be moved out of the loop. And even in those cases where divide operations can be moved out of inner loops, unless the inner loop length is fairly large the cost of the single divide operation can still dominate the cost of the loop if the processor requires scores of clock periods to complete it.

An example of an important divide-intensive numerical algorithm is the tridiagonal solver of ADI schemes, which are used for certain partial differential equation problems. Of $9n$ floating point operations in the inner loop, n of these are floating-point divisions. Such considerations are not entirely academic. Colleagues of the author at NASA Ames Research Center, who developed and implemented the NAS Parallel Benchmarks [6, 7], have found that the slow performance of the divide operation on the Intel i860 processor significantly reduces the sustained performance of the iPSC/860 system on the block tridiagonal and scalar pentadiagonal benchmarks.

The lack of fast hardware for integer division may also become a serious issue when RISC processors are used in distributed memory parallel computers, a path now taken by Intel, Thinking Machines, Cray and others. Consider a one-dimensional array of length $716,800 = 700 \times 1024$ mapped to a 1024 processor machine. Element A_j is located at offset $j \bmod 700$ on processor $[j/700]$. Hence the need for a fast integer divide operation. Partly for this reason, Cray has proposed a programming model for an upcoming highly parallel system that places somewhat artificial limits on array distributions [12].

3. Main Memory Bandwidth

All of the current selection of high-performance RISC microprocessors employ a cache memory system and some scheme for virtual memory management. The objective is to provide the illusion of a very large memory, possibly extending to disk, all of which is readily accessible by the processor for high throughput performance. Bandwidth between this cache memory and the processing units is generally quite high. Bandwidth between main memory and the processing units typically is significantly lower.

The Intel i860, for example, has an eight Kbyte internal data cache. It can, in a single clock period, transfer 16 bytes, or two operands, between the internal cache and two adjacent registers. Concurrently with this operation it can perform floating point operations on data in other registers. With a clock rate of 40 Mhertz, the theoretical peak performance is 60 Mflop/s, and its cache memory bandwidth is 80 Mword/s. This ratio of roughly one operand per operation has been found to be acceptable for scientific computing. This is the ratio for the MasPar MP-2 and the vector processors of the TMC CM-5. Cray systems can fetch two operands and store one operand every clock period, during which time two floating point operations can be performed. Thus its ratio is 1.5.

The performance of the i860 on data in main memory is not so good. From main memory it can only load one 64-bit word every two clocks, or store one word every three clocks. These figures assume a long vector operation using a particular machine instruction. Conventional loads and stores from main memory require even more time. Thus there is a ratio of at least six between achievable cache and main memory bandwidth figures. This is a limitation of the processor and cannot be corrected with a secondary cache.

This limited main memory bandwidth is reflected in the performance of the i860 on real scientific codes. Figure 1 (solid line) gives performance rates

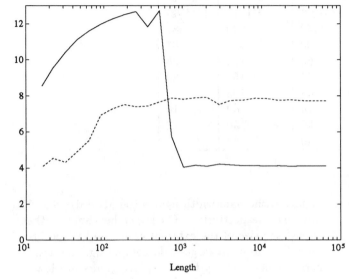

Figure 1: i860 Performance on a Fortran DAXPY Loop (Mflop/s). Solid: O4 compiler option. Dashed: Mvect option.

of Fortran-coded DAXPY loops of different lengths (assuming the start of the data vectors are in cache). This code was compiled with a recent version of the Intel-supported Portland Group compiler, using O4 optimization. The performance is roughly 12 Mflop/s until the vector length is sufficiently large that the two vectors cannot be held entirely in cache, at which time it drops sharply to only about four Mflop/s. The dashed line in Figure 1 give performance rates with the Mvect option, which utilizes an instruction that bypasses cache. As can be seen, this results in improved long vector performance, but poorer short vector performance. Even with this option, long vector performance is only about 60% of the short vector, cached data performance.

For other types of Fortran loops typical of scientific application codes, the results are similar. For instance, on the NAS Parallel Benchmarks [7], the 128-node Intel iPSC/860 system typically achieves only about five percent of its peak multiprocessor performance. This is partly due to contention in the network, but the other principal factor is low single node performance, typically only four to six Mflop/s from Fortran or C. While further improvements in the compiler can be expected to marginally improve these rates, there seems little hope that sustained rates of more than eight to ten Mflop/s will ever be achieved on the main body of real scientific codes [11].

The latest edition of the i860, known as the i860XP, improves the main memory bandwidth by means of burst load and store operations. It remains to be seen how much actual improvement will be realized by the user, since the i860XP Fortran and C compilers are still not able to exploit these special instructions in most loops.

The situation is somewhat better with other RISC processors. The IBM RS6000 series features a larger cache (64 Kbytes on the model 370). Here the ratio between internal cache bandwidth and main memory is unity (one operand per clock period), and both of these figures are one-half the floating point computation. Partly as a result of this excellent main memory bandwidth, its resulting Linpack 100×100 performance rate is a respectable 26 Mflop/s.

However, the four-way associative design of the IBM RS6000 cache produces some rather odd behavior with respect to strides. Programmers of cache-based systems are prepared for slowdown anytime the strides of memory accesses are not unity, since these result in poor cache utilization. But few programmers are aware that additional slowdowns result for certain strides such as 73 or 102. It turns out that such strides result in poor performance because they are very nearly simple fractions of 512 [5].

The Hewlett-Packard PA-RISC processor runs at 99 Mhertz. It has a large cache, typically one Mbyte, and it can fetch or store one operand every clock period (after the first). However, data in main memory data can be fetched or stored at a rate of only one word every three clock periods. As with several of the other processors, the PA-RISC can perform up to two floating point operations every clock period.

The R4400 processor, which is used in some new Silicon Graphics workstations, runs at 100 Mhertz. It can fetch or store a operand from the internal cache every clock period. It has an external cache, typically one Mbyte, from which it can access a word every other clock period, which is the same rate for data in main memory. It can perform a floating point operation every other clock period, for a peak rate of 50 Mflop/s.

The 40 Mhertz Sun SuperSPARC processor has a 16 Kbyte internal primary data cache (four-way set-associative). The transfer rate from the primary cache is one word per clock cycle. Since three instructions may be issued simultaneously (floating point, integer, load/store), the theoretical peak performance is 40 Mflop/s, and the bandwidth between the cache and the CPU is 40 Mword/s. To improve memory performance, a direct mapped secondary cache of one Mbyte

Processor	Clock (Mhz)	Divide (CP)	Cache BW (MW/s)	Memory BW (MW/s)	Peak Perf. (MF/s)	Linpack (MF/s)
Cray C-90/1	240	4		1440	960	387
Cray Y-MP/1	166	4		500	333	161
IBM RS/6000	62	20	62	62	125	26
DEC Alpha	150	63	150	37	150	30
HP PA-RISC	99	20	99	33	198	41
Intel i860	40	190	80	16	60	10
SGI (R4400)	100	36	100	50	50	17
SuperSPARC	40	7	40	40	40	

Table 1: Performance Characteristics

has been added.

The DEC "Alpha" RISC processor features a full 64-bit design and a 150 to 200 Mhertz clock, depending on model. Since it can perform a floating point operation in every clock period, its theoretical peak performance is cited as 150 to 200 Mflop/s. However, in spite of its much faster peak speed, the size of the Alpha's primary cache is the same as that of the i860: only eight Kbytes.

Like other recently announced RISC processors, the bandwidth (and latency) to and from main memory for the DEC Alpha is significantly lower than that of the cache. The Alpha can load or store a word from main memory only about every four clock periods (peak rates). Thus the ratio between achievable internal cache and main memory bandwidths is at least four. The latency for main memory accesses on the Alpha is about 20 clock periods, which is more than six times that of cache accesses (three clock periods). In an attempt to deal with this disparity, the DEC Alpha, like some others, features support for a second-level external cache, typically consisting of about one Mbyte of SRAM. The peak rate for loads and stores from second-level cache is one word every two to three clock periods, and the latency is roughly eight clock periods.

This information is summarized in Table 1. It is interesting to note that the Linpack 100 × 100 performance of an individual system appears to be well estimated as one-half of the minimum of the memory bandwidth and peak performance figures. The only systems that achieve significantly greater rates than this estimate are the DEC Alpha and HP PA-RISC processors. But these systems benefit from an external cache, which is sufficient to completely contain the Linpack 100 × 100 benchmark. Indeed, their Linpack performance figures are roughly half of the sec-

ondary cache bandwidth figures (60 Mword/s and 99 Mword/s, respectively). On larger benchmarks that exceed the size of the external cache, and which better reflect modern large-scale computing, the actual performance rates of these two processors are lower. For example, the performance of the Alpha on the PERFECT suite is 18 Mflop/s. Note that this figure is much closer to half of its main memory bandwidth figure (37.5 Mword/s). No Linpack 100 × 100 figure was available for the SuperSPARC; however, its Linpack 1000 × 1000 figure of 22 Mflop/s is in general agreement with this rule.

4. Performance per Dollar

One advantage of RISC processors over vector processors is that they obtain respectable performance on loops with apparent or real recursions, or with short loop lengths. On the other hand, with some tuning the vector systems generally achieve rather high performance. On the NAS Parallel Benchmarks, for example, a Cray Y-MP processor achieves (with minor tuning) over 65 Mflop/s on all eight tests, and it exceeds 175 Mflop/s on all but two tests [7]. 175 Mflop/s is 53 percent of the theoretical peak rate of a Y-MP processor.

The principal reason that the Cray Y-MP generally sustains such a high percentage of its peak performance is that its main memory bandwidth is well matched to its peak computation rate. The total main memory bandwidth of the eight-processor Y-MP is 4 Gword/s, which is actually a greater figure than its peak computing rate, which is 2.6 Gflop/s. By comparison, the main memory bandwidth of the 128-processor Intel iPSC/860 system is 2 Gword/s, which figure is only about one fourth of its peak computation rate (7.6 Gflop/s). When the Intel main memory bandwidth figure is reduced by roughly half to account for interprocessor communication, the resulting ratio of four is roughly what is observed in overall system performance between these systems on the NAS Parallel Benchmarks [7].

Nonetheless, when prices of systems are considered, the RISC systems do reasonably well, even when comparing main memory (i.e. not cache resident) performance statistics. The Intel iPSC/860 system, for instance, costs only about one-sixth that of an eight-processor Y-MP system. Thus the total main memory bandwidth per dollar of the Intel iPSC/860 is three times that of the Cray Y-MP. On the NAS Parallel Benchmarks, the sustained performance per dollar of the Intel is on a par with the Y-MP. Were it not for for other factors, such as the relatively immature state of compilers for the Intel system, and its limited inter-processor network bandwidth, it is likely that the Intel would surpass the Cray in this measure also. NAS Parallel Benchmark figures are not yet available for parallel systems based on the DEC Alpha. But if we consider a workstation system, and take 18 Mflop/s as typical of sustained performance, it is clear that the Alpha workstation, which can be purchased for as little as $25,000, is considerably less than a tenth as costly as a Y-MP processor that sustains 180 Mflop/s.

In short, it appears that even with the shortcomings addressed in this paper, RISC processor systems still deliver sustained performance per dollar that is now competitive with the vector systems on most applications, and much better on some. Nonetheless, one can ask whether their sustained performance rates (as well as their sustained performance per dollar figures) might have been even better had greater emphasis been placed on main memory bandwidth, as opposed to increasing the performance on data in the primary cache.

5. Large-Scale Scientific Computing

Some large-scale scientific programs can be expected to run quite well on the current RISC systems. Clearly those that have been written from scratch on a cache-based workstation by expert programmers can be expected to run at somewhat higher performance rates than those ported from other systems without significant alteration. Another class of applications that will perform well on RISC-based systems, relative to vector systems, are those with loops that are not readily vectorizable, or those with short inner loops. Others that can be expected to do well are codes that utilize libraries, such as LAPACK [2], which have been highly tuned for cache-based systems, among others.

One example of an application that performs very well on RISC systems relative to vector systems is a vortex roll-up simulation code developed by the author [8]. It behaves very well in cache memories, be-cause the computations involve high precision arithmetic operations that are naturally very well localized. By comparison, this code does not run efficiently on a Cray Y-MP, due principally to unavoidably short inner loop lengths. For these reasons, a multiprocessor implementation of this program on the Intel iPSC/860 system out-performs one processor of a Cray Y-MP when only eight i860 nodes are utilized. Thus on this application the Intel system achieves much higher performance per dollar than the Cray.

Another fortunate class of applications are those based on dense matrix computations, which can be structured to run efficiently in cache systems [13, 14, 15]. Indeed, the impressive performance achieved by the LAPACK library on a variety of systems is due in large part to the utilization of these blocking techniques.

Other important scientific applications are not so fortunate. The most common reasons for less-than-optimal performance are: (1) the application was previously implemented on another system (such as a vector system) where data locality was not a performance issue; (2) the code employs numerical algorithms that do not feature high levels of data locality.

We have already discussed the impact of the divide operation on large-scale scientific applications. Now let us investigate the impact of the cache design on these codes. To that end, four types of numerical algorithms will be examined to see whether they can be expected to run well on cache-based RISC processor systems (1) as is, (2) after processing by intelligent software tools that may be available in the future, (3) after significant revision by expert programmers, and (4) after the wholesale substitution of advanced, cache-efficient algorithms in important compute-intensive routines. In the following, by an "expert programmer", we will mean a programmer who is highly skilled in tuning scientific codes on cache-based computers and is generally knowledgeable in numeric techniques, but who does not necessarily have specialized expertise in state-of-the-art numerical algorithms.

6. Loop Ordering

The order in which loops are ordered can significantly affect the sustained performance of this code on a cache-based system. Consider, for example, the following code fragment:

```
      DIMENSION A(15,1000), C(15)
 . . .
      DO 120 I = 1, 15
         S = 0.D0
C
```

```
         DO 110 J = 1, 1000
            S = S + J * A(I,J)
 110     CONTINUE
C
            C(I) = S
 120     CONTINUE
```

This code design makes good sense on a vector system, since the inner loop vector length is large and the stride of accesses in the inner loop is an odd number.

However, on a cache system this might not be the best approach, because of the nonunit stride accesses in the A array. It might be better to write this code as follows:

```
         DIMENSION A(15,1000), C(15)
  . . .
         DO 100 I = 1, 15
           C(I) = 0.D0
 100     CONTINUE
C
         DO 120 J = 1, 1000
           DO 110 I = 1, 15
             C(I) = C(I) + J * A(I,J)
 110       CONTINUE
 120     CONTINUE
```

This code design features unit stride inner loops, which are definitely better for cache systems. The fact that the inner loop vector length is only 15 has no adverse consequence on a RISC system. On the contrary, this limited vector length is an advantage on the RISC system — the C vector is cache-resident and has a very high level of data re-use. Indeed, while the first variant runs nearly twice as fast than the second on a Cray Y-MP, the opposite is true on a node of the Intel iPSC/860.

In this case, "smart" compilers are now available that can automatically perform this loop interchange. But other cases require changes over multiple subroutine boundaries, rather than merely within the context of a single nested loop as above (consider the case where the loop lengths are not constants as above but instead are subroutine arguments).

An even more effective transformation of this type is to "block" nested loops to enhance cache utilization. Software tools, such as those now being developed at Rice University [9] and Stanford [16], may soon be able to assist in this effort. However, the current state of the art in this area is indicated by the fact that these software tools are not yet able to successfully optimize Gaussian elimination with partial pivoting (GEPP). This operation can, however, be manually

blocked for improved cache performance. In fact, a hand-tuned, cache-efficient implementation of GEPP has been included in the LAPACK library [2]. Thus it appears it will be a while before highly effective, fully automatic software tools of this sort are available.

7. Transpose Operations

At the heart of many two and three-dimensional scientific applications, similar operations must be performed in each dimension. On vector computers these are often implemented as a sequence of calls to subroutines that are virtually identical, except for the dimension in which multidimensional arrays are accessed.

It is clear that a Fortran routine which accesses arrays by other than the first dimension will not perform well on a cache-based system, since such accesses have nonunit stride. One solution is to revise the design of such programs to perform array transpositions between the computational steps, so that computations can always be done with unit stride data accesses. The resulting code may even be simpler than before, since often the same unit stride computational routine can be employed in each dimension. It should be pointed out, however, that in some cases the performance of the resulting code is not much better than the original, since there is insufficient computation to offset the cost of the transpose operation. But in other cases it is profitable to make such a change.

Even if an application is recoded with a design that interleaves computation and array transposition steps, there remains the problem of performing array transpositions efficiently on a cache-based system. Straightforward Fortran loops to transpose a large matrix are not effective since they involve typically involve large memory strides.

It is possible to perform transpositions in a cache-efficient manner by "blocking" the transpose: one fetches two opposing blocks from main memory to cache (note that each column of these blocks can be fetched with unit stride), transposes each block in cache, and then returns each of the transposed blocks to the opposite location. This is best described as follows, where A_{ij} and B_{ij} denote blocks small enough that both can simultaneously fit in cache:

$$\begin{bmatrix} A_{11} & A_{12} & A_{13} & A_{14} \\ A_{21} & A_{22} & A_{23} & A_{24} \\ A_{31} & A_{32} & A_{33} & A_{34} \\ A_{41} & A_{42} & A_{43} & A_{44} \end{bmatrix}^t = \begin{bmatrix} A_{11}^t & A_{21}^t & A_{31}^t & A_{41}^t \\ A_{12}^t & A_{22}^t & A_{32}^t & A_{42}^t \\ A_{13}^t & A_{23}^t & A_{33}^t & A_{43}^t \\ A_{14}^t & A_{24}^t & A_{34}^t & A_{44}^t \end{bmatrix}$$

Another efficient scheme for transposing arrays in a hierarchical memory system is based on Fraser's algorithm. This scheme is described in [3].

It is certainly possible now for expert programmers to make these transformations, although it is laborious to do so for a very large program. It is probable that future compilers and other software tools will be able to automatically transform such code into more cache-efficient designs. But as before, it seems unlikely that highly effective tools of sort will be available for two or three more years.

8. Fast Fourier Transforms

The next example to be examined is the computation of the one-dimensional fast Fourier transform (FFT). Unfortunately, many FFT algorithms in the literature, if implemented in a straightforward manner, include such undesirable features as large, power-of-two memory strides. These strides also hamper vector computer performance. Fortunately, there are variant FFT algorithms that do not involve power-of-two memory strides, and which in fact can be implemented with exclusively stride one memory accesses [4]. These algorithms have been used on vector computers for some while.

However, even these algorithms typically have one feature that is undesirable for cache systems: the principal main memory arrays are both accessed roughly t times to perform a 2^t-point FFT. Is it possible to reduce the number of times these data arrays are accessed? Yes, as it turns out. However, no amount of loop restructuring or other superficial manipulation of the code will accomplish this. Instead, a completely different technique for performing the FFT must be employed. One such algorithm can be sketched as follows, where the size of the input complex vector is $n = n_1 n_2$ words, and where the cache is assumed to hold at least $4b \max(n_1, n_2)$ words. See [3] for details.

1. Consider the data in main memory as a $n_1 \times n_2$ complex matrix in column-major (Fortran) order. Fetch the data b rows at a time into the cache. For each batch of b rows, perform b individual n_2-point FFTs on the $b \times n_2$ complex array in cache.

2. Multiply the resulting data in each batch by certain roots of unity: the element fetched from location (j, k) in the original complex matrix is multiplied by $e^{-2\pi ijk/n}$.

3. Transpose each of the resulting $b \times n_2$ complex matrices into a $n_2 \times b$ matrix, using the cache, and store the resulting data in main memory. Store successive batches of data in successive contiguous sections of main memory.

4. Consider the resulting data in main memory as a $n_2 \times n_1$ complex matrix. Fetch the data b rows at a time into the cache. For each batch of b rows, perform b individual n_1-point FFTs on the $b \times n_1$ complex array in cache, and return the resulting b rows to the same locations in main memory from which they were fetched. The result is a correctly ordered discrete Fourier transform.

With this algorithm, the principal main memory data arrays need only be accessed two times, no matter what the size of the FFT. Note that all of the individual n_1-point and n_2-point FFTs are performed entirely in the cache.

It is true that the FFT is an operation that is often available in vendor-supplied libraries, and thus one could argue that individual scientists do not need to be concerned these issues — they can merely use library routines. However, many scientists regrettably have incorporated their own "home-grown" FFT routines into their program files, in order to make their codes more easily portable between systems. Also, it is important to note that vendor-supplied FFT routines in many cases do not employ an advanced algorithm. For instance, the FFT routine supplied by Intel on the iPSC/860 employs a conventional algorithm that is efficient only for transforms small enough to fit into cache (see Figure 2). Of the major RISC vendors, only IBM appears to have implemented an advanced FFT algorithm [1] similar to the one described above.

9. Iterative Methods

Iterative methods are increasingly important in solving large, sparse systems of linear equations. They are typically found at the center of economically important, large-scale computations. The most important methods in use today include the multigrid and Krylov subspace methods, of which the conjugate gradient method is the prototype. The book of Golub and Van Loan [10] is a good reference for these methods. Unfortunately, these methods cannot be restructured to work well with memory hierarchies.

The problem is to solve the equation $Ax = b$ where A is a given sparse nonsingular matrix and b a given vector. The set of nonzero elements of A is generally much too large for cache, since it typically requires many Mbytes of storage. The conjugate gradient and related methods compute a sequence $\{x_k\}$ of vector iterates that converges to the solution x.

The nature of these algorithms is that all of A must be accessed from memory, once per iteration, before any of it is accessed again, so the computation proceeds at main memory rather than cache speeds. In

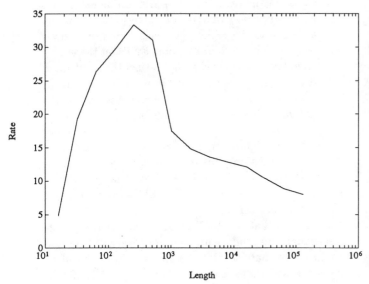

Figure 2: i860 Performance on a Library FFT (Mflop/s)

the case of the Krylov subspace methods, a dot product involving the vector Ax_k has to be computed before x_{k+1} can be. Thus, the matrix-vector product at one iteration cannot be pipelined in any way with the matrix-vector product at the preceding or following iteration.

With the multigrid methods, data on fine grids is accessed only one or two times before computation passes to coarser grids. These grids thus represent a bottleneck analogous to the dot products in Krylov subspace methods.

At the present time, there is a significant amount of research activity in this field, and there is some hope for improved algorithms in the future. Improved preconditioners, for example, may reduce the number of iterations required for the conjugate gradient method to converge. Domain decomposition methods, which work by solving a sequence of smaller systems of equations for subsets of the unknowns, use much smaller sparse matrices that may fit in cache. There is also some hope for "block iterative methods," which may provide the power of the iterative schemes in a more cache-efficient design. Some other iterative methods, such as the Jacobi, Gauss-Seidel, and successive over-relaxation methods, may be organized to work well with memory hierarchies. In general, however, these latter methods are much slower and less reliable than multigrid and Krylov subspace methods. In any event, none of these alternate schemes can be automatically

derived from the codes for other iterative methods.

10. Future Outlook

The problem of quantifying data locality in various types of scientific applications is a very important and timely one. This problem is closely related to the question of whether an application can be efficiently implemented on a distributed memory multiprocessor. Clearly this problem deserves a great deal of study by the research community, and the answers will only be evident after many scientists have studied many different applications.

We have seen that in each of the four cases studied above, there are either known algorithms and implementation techniques that are better suited to cache memories, or else there is some hope that advanced algorithms and tools now being developed will provide scientists with a cache-efficient alternative in the future. It might turn out that it is always possible to find algorithms and implementation techniques that are reasonably cache-efficient, in the sense that data once fetched into the cache can be profitably accessed numerous times before being returned to main memory. In that case the RISC vendors' assumption that caches are broadly effective in sustaining high performance will be upheld.

On the other hand, it might be that there remain a significant number of important scientific applications which feature an unavoidably low degree of cache-level data locality. For these problems, RISC systems with large ratios in performance between data in cache and main memory will have much less of an edge in sustained performance per dollar, compared with other architectures, and may even be surpassed in this statistic by other designs.

While there is some uncertainty on the long-term outcome on this question, in the near term (within the next two or three years), the answer seems considerably clearer: a significant segment of important scientific applications will not perform at optimal rates on current cache-based RISC systems. Thus even at this point in time, it seems essential that designers of cache systems be reasonably modest in their designs.

An analogy with the history of vector computing is instructive in this regard. One of the early vector systems, the CDC 205, featured superior performance on codes with long, unit stride loops. Other vector systems, notably the Cray-1 and Cray X-MP, featured a more flexible design, allowing nonunit strides and making more modest assumptions about typical vector lengths. These latter systems, while they could not compete with the CDC 205 on specially selected, highly-tuned codes, exhibited respectable performance across a much wider spectrum of real-world applications. This was a principal reason that they ultimately prevailed.

11. Conclusions and Recommendations

Many in the scientific computing community have observed that both the workstation market and the high-end supercomputer market have the same design goal: a high level of sustained performance on real scientific and engineering applications. These same persons have further argued that the massive investment being made in RISC microprocessors will force supercomputer vendors to employ these "commodity" processors in their systems.

However, this may not necessarily happen — it may turn out that the workstation market has sufficiently distinct requirements from high-end supercomputing that each will pursue its own path in processor development. Indeed, it is interesting to note that of the principal contenders in the latest generation of highly parallel supercomputers, only Intel and Cray are relying on commodity RISC processors for high-performance floating-point computation. Others, including Thinking Machines, nCUBE, Kendall Square Research, Fujitsu and Meiko, are relying on custom processors for this purpose.

If this divergence does occur, then much of this discussion may prove moot. On the other hand, if it becomes clear that the requirements of these two markets are converging, then it is essential that both designers and the users of RISC systems consider these issues. Otherwise both the high-end supercomputing market and even the workstation market itself may suffer from less-than-optimal sustained performance on many important applications.

Two features of current RISC processors have been discussed in length above: (1) the large cost of divide operations, relative to the cost of adds and multiplies, and (2) the limited bandwidth between processors and main memory, relative to the bandwidth between processors and cache, or in other words overly optimistic ratios between cache and main memory performance. Both are problems of degree rather than fundamental concept.

What does the author recommend? First of all, I suggest that the cost of an integer divide operation be no more than about ten times the cost of an integer add or multiply, and that the cost of a floating point divide operation be no more than about ten times the cost of a floating point add or multiply (based on a series of divides with non-constant divisors). This ratio is higher than the ratio on Cray systems (four), but it seems acceptable even for applications that make heavy use of divisions.

With respect to main memory bandwidth, I certainly urge designers of future systems to make this as large as possible, recognizing that there will always be design costs and trade-offs that will limit this. What about the balance between bandwidth and latency to main memory, as compared with bandwidth and latency to cache? A factor of two appears tolerable, and a factor of four is not fatal. But I believe that ratios beyond this level will not add significant value for many large scientific codes, and whatever resources were devoted to such caches could more profitably be employed in seeking ways to obtain higher bandwidth and lower latency to main memory.

One additional useful design point can be deduced as follows. Just as programmers of vector systems can be expected to tune their codes so that inner loops are reasonably long and so that strides are not powers of two, it is reasonable to ask some tuning effort by programmers of cache-based RISC systems. For example, it is reasonable to assume that with some effort many scientific application can be revised to feature mainly unit stride accesses (for instance by employing computational steps interleaved with array transpositions). In return, it seems reasonable to ask that future RISC-based systems be able to process contiguous data without significant slowdown. For instance, it seems reasonable to insist that a unit stride DAXPY loop run equally fast for data in cache as for long vectors that cannot be held in cache.

It may be that changes can be made to the design of the cache systems in RISC processors to make them more broadly effective for large-scale scientific computation. Some have suggested special instructions that load data from main memory, at a stride, directly into the registers (the Intel i860 has an instruction along these lines). Another possibility is to make changes to the basic cache organization, such as the number associativity classes. Parallel computing using RISC processors would receive a boost if processors included support for high speed, low latency interprocessor communication (such as "virtual shared memory"). At the present time, manufacturers of parallel systems that employ RISC processors must utilize separate custom-designed devices to provide this functionality, and the cost of this custom circuitry is emerging as a dominant factor in the total cost of the system. Even in a workstation system, such features could prove valuable as a basis for implementing multiworkstation, networked parallel computing.

In any event, it is a pity that there is not a greater degree of mutual communication between the RISC processor community and the scientific computing community. Clearly both communities have much to gain from such interaction. This article is written with the hope of fostering this dialogue.

Acknowledgments

The author wishes to acknowledge a significant contribution by Robert S. Schreiber of the RIACS organization at NASA Ames Research Center. Others who have made valuable suggestions to this manuscript include E. Barszcz of NASA Ames; R. Fatoohi, H. Simon, V. Venkatakrishnan and S. Weeratunga of Computer Sciences Corp.; P. Bjorstad, currently visiting RIACS; A. Gupta of Stanford University; A. Karp of Hewlett-Packard; S. Oberlin of Cray Research, Inc.; B. Parady of Sun Microsystems, Inc.; M. Humphrey of Silicon Graphics, Inc., D. Scott of Intel Scientific Computers; and D. Smitley of the Supercomputing Research Center.

References

[1] R. C. Agarwal, and J. W. Cooley, "Fourier Transform and Convolution Subroutines for the IBM 3090 Vector Facility", *IBM Journal of Research and Development*, vol. 30 (1986), p. 145 - 162.

[2] E. Anderson, Z. Bai, C. Bischof, J. Demmel, J. Dongarra, J. DuCroz, A. Greenbaum, S. Hammarling, A. McKenney, S. Ostrouchov and D. Sorenson, *The LAPACK Users' Guide*, SIAM, Philadelphia, 1992.

[3] D. H. Bailey, "FFTs in External or Hierarchical Memory", *Journal of Supercomputing*, vol. 4 (1990), p. 23 - 35.

[4] D. H. Bailey, "A High-Performance FFT Algorithm for Vector Supercomputers", *International Journal of Supercomputer Applications* vol. 2 (1988), p. 82 - 87.

[5] D. H. Bailey, "Unfavorable Strides in Cache Memory Systems", RNR Technical Report RNR-92-015, NASA Ames Research Center, 1992.

[6] D. H. Bailey, E. Barszcz, J. T. Barton, D. S. Browning, R. L. Carter, L. Dagum, R. A. Fatoohi, P. O. Frederickson, T. A. Lasinski, R. S. Schreiber, H. D. Simon, V. Venkatakrishnan, and S. K. Weeratunga, "The NAS Parallel Benchmarks", *Intl. Journal of Supercomputer Applications*, v. 5, no. 3 (Fall 1991), pp. 63 - 73.

[7] D. H. Bailey, E. Barszcz, L. Dagum and H. D. Simon, "NAS Parallel Benchmark Results", *Proceedings of Supercomputing '92*, IEEE, p. 386 - 393.

[8] D. H. Bailey, R. Krasny and R. Pelz, "Multiple Precision, Multiple Processor Vortex Sheet Roll-Up Computation," Technical Report RNR-90-028, NAS Applied Research Branch, NASA Ames Research Center, October 1992.

[9] S. Carr and K. Kennedy, "Compiler Blockability of Numerical Algorithms", *Proceedings of Supercomputing '92*, IEEE, p. 114-124.

[10] G. H. Golub and C. F. Van Loan, *Matrix Computations*, Johns Hopkins, Baltimore, 1989.

[11] K. Lee, "On the Floating Point Performance of the i860 Microprocessor", Technical Report RNR-90-019, NAS Applied Research Branch, NASA Ames Research Center, October 1990. Also in the *Intl. Journal of High Speed Computing*, to appear.

[12] D. Pase, "MPP Programming Model", Cray Research, Inc. 1992.

[13] R. S. Schreiber, "Block algorithms for Parallel Machines," in Martin Schultz, editor, *Numerical Algorithms for Modern Parallel Computer Architectures*, IMA Volumes in Mathematics and Its Applications, vol. 13, Springer-Verlag, New York, 1988, p. 197 - 207.

[14] R. S. Schreiber and G. Shroff, "On the Convergence of the Cyclic Jacobi Method for Parallel Block Orderings," *SIAM Journal on Matrix Analysis and Applications*, vol. 10 (1989), p. 326 - 346.

[15] R. S. Schreiber and C. Van Loan, "A Storage Efficient WY Representation for Products of Householder Transformations," *SIAM Journal on Scientific and Statistical Computing*, vol. 10 (1989), p. 53 - 57.

[16] M. E. Wolf and M. S. Lam, "A Data Locality Optimizing Algorithm", *Proceedings of the 1991 SIGPLAN Conference on Programming Language Design and Implementation*, ACM, June 1991.

Session 9:
Communication
Intensive Algorithms
Chair: Vineet Singh

Efficient Transposition Algorithms for Large Matrices[*]

S. D.Kaushik[1], C.-H. Huang[1], J. R. Johnson[2], R. W. Johnson[3], and P. Sadayappan[1]

Abstract

We present transposition algorithms for matrices that do not fit in main memory. Transposition is interpreted as a permutation of the vector obtained by mapping a matrix to linear memory. Algorithms are derived from factorizations of this permutation, using a class of permutations related to the tensor product. Using this formulation of transposition, we first obtain several known algorithms and then we derive a new algorithm which reduces the number of disk accesses required. The new algorithm was compared to existing algorithms using an implementation on the Intel iPSC/860. This comparison shows the benefits of the new algorithm.

Keywords: Tensor product, Stride permutation, Matrix transposition, Parallel algorithm, External memory.

1 Introduction

Many applications require efficient transposition algorithms for matrices that are too large to fit into main memory. For example, two-dimensional Fourier transforms [2, 4, 17] can be implemented using two passes – one-dimensional Fourier transforms of the rows followed by one-dimensional Fourier transforms of the columns. If a matrix is too large to fit in main memory and is stored in the row-major order, accessing the columns of the matrix is very expensive because the access to each matrix element requires a separate disk access. Therefore, an efficient two-dimensional Fourier transform will perform matrix transposition between the two passes.

Efficient transposition of large matrices stored in external storage is a non-trivial problem and has been widely studied in the literature. Performing in-place transposition using a naive element-wise approach requires $O(N^2)$ disk accesses. The first algorithm requiring $O(N \log N)$ disk accesses for performing the in-place transposition of matrices stored on disk was proposed by Eklundh [6]. The algorithm required that at least two rows of the matrix fit into main memory. Extensions to this approach for the transposition of arbitrary square and rectangular matrices were presented in [1, 3, 5, 8, 13, 14, 16]. In this paper, we address the efficient disk-based transposition of large matrices. We present an algorithm that requires fewer disk accesses than Eklundh's algorithm.

The paper is organized as follows. Section 2 provides a brief overview of tensor products and the various conventions used in the paper. Section 3 first presents the basic tensor product formulation of matrix transposition and then develops the tensor product formulas for some existing matrix transposition algorithms. In Section 4, implementation and performance issues of the various matrix transposition algorithms are discussed. A new algorithm is derived that requires a significantly smaller number of disk accesses than existing algorithms. Extensions of the algorithm to deal with rectangular matrices are also derived. Analysis for the number of disk accesses and volume of data transferred is provided for all the algorithms. In Section 5 performance results are presented. Conclusions and future directions are given in Section 6.

2 An overview of tensor products

In this section, we give an overview of the tensor product notation and the properties which are used in the derivation of the matrix transposition algorithms (see [9] for a detailed exposition).

Definition 2.1 (Tensor Product) *Let A and B be two matrices of size $m \times n$ and $p \times q$, respectively. The tensor product of A and B is the block matrix*

---

[*]This work was supported in part by DARPA, order number 7898, monitored by NIST under grant number 60NANB1D1151, DARPA, order number 7899, monitored by NIST under grant number 60NANB1D1150, and NSF grant CCR-9211016.

[1]Department of Computer and Information Science, The Ohio State University, Columbus, OH 43210.

[2]Department of Mathematics & Computer Science, Drexel University, , Philadelphia, PA 19176.

[3]Department of Computer Science, St. Cloud State University, St. Cloud, MN 56301.

obtained by replacing each element $a_{i,j}$ by $a_{i,j}B$. That is, $A \otimes B$ is an $mp \times nq$ matrix defined as

$$A \otimes B = \begin{bmatrix} a_{0,0}B & \cdots & a_{0,n-1}B \\ \vdots & \ddots & \vdots \\ a_{m-1,0}B & \cdots & a_{m-1,n-1}B \end{bmatrix}$$

The tensor product satisfies the following basic properties, where α is a scalar, I_n denotes the $n \times n$ identity matrix, and the products and inverses are defined.

1. $(\alpha A) \otimes B = A \otimes (\alpha B) = \alpha(A \otimes B)$.

2. $(A + B) \otimes C = (A \otimes C) + (B \otimes C)$.

3. $A \otimes (B + C) = (A \otimes B) + (A \otimes C)$.

4. $1 \otimes A = A \otimes 1 = A$.

5. $A \otimes (B \otimes C) = (A \otimes B) \otimes C$.

6. $^t(A \otimes B) = {}^tA \otimes {}^tB$.

7. $(A \otimes B)(C \otimes D) = AC \otimes BD$.

8. $A \otimes B = (I_{m_1} \otimes B)(A \otimes I_{n_2}) = (A \otimes I_{m_2})(I_{n_1} \otimes B)$.

9. $(A_1 \otimes \cdots \otimes A_t)(B_1 \otimes \cdots \otimes B_t) = (A_1 B_1 \otimes \cdots \otimes A_t B_t)$.

10. $(A_1 \otimes B_1) \cdots (A_t \otimes B_t) = (A_1 \cdots A_t \otimes B_1 \cdots B_t)$.

11. $(A \otimes B)^{-1} = A^{-1} \otimes B^{-1}$.

12. $I_m \otimes I_n = I_{mn}$.

13. $(A \oplus B) \otimes C = (A \otimes C) \oplus (B \otimes C)$, where $\oplus$ denotes the direct sum.

14. $I_m \otimes B = \bigoplus_{i=1}^{m} B$, the direct sum of m B's.

All of these identities follow from the definition or simple applications of preceding properties (see [9]).

Let $\mathbf{F}^n$ be the vector space of n-tuples of elements from the field $\mathbf{F}$ and let $\mathbf{F}^{m \times n}$ be the vector space of $m \times n$ matrices. The collection of elements $\{e_i^m | 0 \leq i < m\}$, where e_i^m is the vector with a one in the i-th position and zeros elsewhere, form the standard basis for $\mathbf{F}^m$. The collection of matrices $\{E_{i,j}^{m,n} | 0 \leq i < m$ and $0 \leq j < n\}$, where $E_{i,j}^{m,n}$ is the $m \times n$ matrix with a one in the (i, j)-th position and zeros elsewhere, form the standard basis for $\mathbf{F}^{m \times n}$.

The following relationship between the basis elements will be used throughout the paper.

1. $e_i^m \otimes e_j^n = e_{in+j}^{mn}$.

2. $e_i^m \, {}^t e_j^n = e_i^m \otimes {}^t e_j^n = E_{i,j}^{m,n}$.

3. $e_{i_1}^{n_1} \otimes \cdots \otimes e_{i_t}^{n_t} = e_{i_1 n_2 \cdots n_t + \cdots + i_{t-1} n_t + i_t}^{n_1 \cdots n_t}$.

Definition 2.2 (Tensor Basis) *Let $\mathbf{F}^N$ be the vector space of N-tuples over the field $\mathbf{F}$. Assume that $N = n_1 \cdots n_t$. The collection of elements $\{e_{i_1}^{n_1} \otimes \cdots \otimes e_{i_t}^{n_t} | 0 \leq i_1 < n_1, \ldots, 0 \leq i_t < n_t\}$ is a basis for $\mathbf{F}^N$ and will be called the* tensor basis.

This basis makes explicit the index calculations that are required to access the elements of a multidimensional array that are stored row-wise in linear memory.

3 Tensor product formulation for matrix transposition

In this section we show how to derive a variety of matrix transposition algorithms by factoring a permutation related to matrix transposition. The factorization will be obtained using a special class of permutations related to the tensor product, called tensor permutations. Tensor permutations are sometimes called array index permutations [7] and explored in more detail in [12] and [11]. The material in this section summarizes material in [11] and [10].

If an $m \times n$ matrix, A, is stored by rows in linear memory and ^tA, the transpose of A is also stored by rows in linear memory, then the permutation which maps A to ^tA is a stride permutation.

Definition 3.1 (Stride Permutation)

$$L_n^{mn}(e_i^m \otimes e_j^n) = e_j^n \otimes e_i^m$$

The notation indicates that elements of a vector of length mn are loaded into m segments each at stride n.

This permutation induces a linear transformation mapping e_{in+j}^{mn} to e_{jm+i}^{mn}. For example

$$L_2^6 \begin{pmatrix} x_0 \\ x_1 \\ x_2 \end{pmatrix} \otimes \begin{pmatrix} y_0 \\ y_1 \end{pmatrix} = L_2^6 \begin{pmatrix} x_0 y_0 \\ x_0 y_1 \\ x_1 y_0 \\ x_1 y_1 \\ x_2 y_0 \\ x_2 y_1 \end{pmatrix} =$$

$$\begin{pmatrix} y_0 \\ y_1 \end{pmatrix} \otimes \begin{pmatrix} x_0 \\ x_1 \\ x_2 \end{pmatrix} = \begin{pmatrix} x_0 y_0 \\ x_1 y_0 \\ x_2 y_0 \\ x_0 y_1 \\ x_1 y_1 \\ x_2 y_1 \end{pmatrix}.$$

As a permutation,

$$L_2^6(x_0 e_0^6 + x_1 e_1^6 + x_2 e_2^6 + x_3 e_3^6 + x_4 e_4^6 + x_5 e_5^6) =$$
$$x_0 e_0^6 + x_1 e_3^6 + x_2 e_1^6 + x_3 e_4^6 + x_4 e_2^6 + x_5 e_5^6,$$

which permutes the coordinates into two segments of length 3 each at stride 2.

$$\begin{pmatrix} x_0 \\ x_2 \\ x_4 \\ x_1 \\ x_3 \\ x_5 \end{pmatrix} = \begin{pmatrix} 1 & 0 & 0 & 0 & 0 & 0 \\ 0 & 0 & 1 & 0 & 0 & 0 \\ 0 & 0 & 0 & 0 & 1 & 0 \\ 0 & 1 & 0 & 0 & 0 & 0 \\ 0 & 0 & 0 & 1 & 0 & 0 \\ 0 & 0 & 0 & 0 & 0 & 1 \end{pmatrix} \begin{pmatrix} x_0 \\ x_1 \\ x_2 \\ x_3 \\ x_4 \\ x_5 \end{pmatrix}.$$

Stride permutations are a special case of the following class of permutations.

Definition 3.2 (Tensor Permutation) *Let σ be a permutation of $\{0, 1, \ldots, t-1\}$. Then σ acts on $F^{n_1} \otimes \cdots \otimes F^{n_t}$ by permuting the tensor basis.*

$$\sigma(e_{i_1}^{n_1} \otimes \cdots \otimes e_{i_t}^{n_t}) = e_{i_{\sigma(1)}}^{n_{\sigma(1)}} \otimes \cdots \otimes e_{i_{\sigma(t)}}^{n_{\sigma(t)}},$$

which induces a linear transformation

$$T_\sigma^{(n_1,\ldots,n_t)} e_{i_1 n_2 \cdots n_t + \cdots + i_{t-1} n_t + i_t}^{n_1 \cdots n_t} =$$
$$e_{i_{\sigma(1)} n_{\sigma(2)} \cdots n_{\sigma(t)} + \cdots + i_{\sigma(t-1)} n_{\sigma(t)} + i_{\sigma(t)}}^{n_{\sigma(1)} \cdots n_{\sigma(t)}}.$$

Tensor permutations can be implemented with nested loops. The following loop gives an example for the stride permutation L_n^{mn}.

$$y \leftarrow L_n^{mn} x \equiv \quad \text{for } i = 0, \ldots, m-1$$
$$\text{for } j = 0, \ldots, n-1$$
$$y_{jm+i} \leftarrow x_{in+j}$$

To formally show the relationship between stride permutations and matrix transposition we introduce an operator that stores a matrix in linear memory.

Definition 3.3 (Row-Major Storage Operator) *Let $\rho^{(m,n)}$ be the linear transformation from $F^{m \times n}$ onto F^{mn} defined by $\rho^{(m,n)} E_{i,j}^{m,n} = e_i^m \otimes e_j^n = e_{in+j}^{mn}$. ρ is the transformation that stores an $m \times n$ matrix in linear memory using row major ordering.*

The relationship between transposition and stride permutation is given in the following diagram.

$$\begin{array}{ccc} A & \longrightarrow & {}^t A \\ \downarrow & & \downarrow \\ \rho^{(m,n)}(A) & \xrightarrow{L_n^{mn}} & \rho^{(n,m)}({}^t A) \end{array}$$

For example, The validity of this diagram can be proven by applying the various operators to a basis for $F^{m \times n}$.

$$\begin{aligned} L_n^{mn}(\rho^{(m,n)}(E_{i,j}^{m,n})) &= L_n^{mn}(e_i^m \otimes e_j^n) \\ &= e_j^n \otimes e_i^m \\ &= \rho^{(n,m)}(E_{j,i}^{n,m}) \\ &= \rho^{(n,m)}({}^t E_{i,j}^{m,n}) \end{aligned}$$

Therefore algorithms for matrix transposition can be obtained by factoring the permutation L_n^{mn}. The following properties of stride permutations, which easily follow from the definition, can be used to obtain useful factorizations.

Lemma 3.1

$$\begin{aligned} L_r^{rs} L_s^{rs} &= I_{rs} \\ L_{st}^{rst} &= L_s^{rst} L_t^{rst} = L_t^{rst} L_s^{rst} \\ L_t^{rst} &= (L_t^{rt} \otimes I_s)(I_r \otimes L_t^{st}) \end{aligned}$$

The last factorization in this Lemma can be used to decompose a permutation into two permutations, one which operates locally and can be performed in main memory and the other which permutes segments of consecutive elements and can be performed during block disk reads and writes. The permutation $I_r \otimes L_t^{rt}$ is equal to the direct sum of r copies of the stride permutation L_t^{rt}. If the input vector is partitioned into r segments each of length st, then $I_r \otimes L_t^{st}$ permutes each of the segments using the stride permutation L_t^{st}. Clearly each permutation is local to its segment. The permutation $L^{rt} \otimes I_s$ permutes segments of length s. This permutation can be implemented during a block read or a block write, where a segment of the vector is loaded or stored to main memory or disk.

One way of obtaining natural factorizations is to regard A as a block matrix and then to permute within the blocks and amongst the blocks. This approach is beneficial for hierarchical memory where the entire matrix does not fit into fast memory: blocks can be loaded into memory, permuted, and when the blocks are transferred back the blocks themselves can be permuted.

Let A be an $m_1m_2 \times n_1n_2$ matrix. We can view A as an $m_1 \times n_1$ matrix whose elements are $m_2 \times n_2$ matrices. If

$$A = \begin{pmatrix} A_{1,1} & A_{1,2} \\ A_{2,1} & A_{2,2} \end{pmatrix},$$

then

$$^tA = \begin{pmatrix} ^tA_{1,1} & ^tA_{2,1} \\ ^tA_{1,2} & ^tA_{2,2} \end{pmatrix}.$$

This leads to the following factorization.

$$\begin{aligned} L_{n_1n_2}^{m_1m_2n_1n_2} \\ = (I_{n_1} \otimes L_{n_2}^{m_1n_2} \otimes I_{m_1})(L_{n_1}^{m_1n_1} \otimes I_{m_2n_2}) \\ (I_{m_1n_1} \otimes L_{n_2}^{m_2n_2})(I_{m_1} \otimes L_{n_1}^{m_2n_1} \otimes I_{n_2}) \\ = (I_{n_1} \otimes L_{n_2}^{m_1n_2} \otimes I_{m_1})(L_{n_1}^{m_1n_1} \otimes L_{n_2}^{m_2n_2}) \\ (I_{m_1} \otimes L_{n_1}^{m_2n_1} \otimes I_{n_2}). \end{aligned}$$

This can be verified by applying this equation to the basis $e_{i_1}^{m_1} \otimes e_{i_2}^{m_2} \otimes e_{j_1}^{n_1} \otimes e_{j_2}^{n_1}$: $(I_{m_1} \otimes L_{m_2}^{m_2n_1} \otimes I_{n_2})(L_{n_1}^{m_1n_1} \otimes L_{n_2}^{m_2n_2})(I_{m_1} \otimes L_{n_1}^{m_2n_1} \otimes I_{n_2})(e_{i_1}^{m_1} \otimes e_{i_2}^{m_2} \otimes e_{j_1}^{n_1} \otimes e_{j_2}^{n_1})$ is equal to $L_{n_1n_2}^{m_1m_2n_1n_2}(e_{i_1}^{m_1} \otimes e_{i_2}^{m_2} \otimes e_{j_1}^{n_1} \otimes e_{j_2}^{n_1})$.

The permutation $I_{m_1} \otimes L_{n_1}^{m_2n_1} \otimes I_{n_2}$ converts converts the row major representation of the matrix A into a block representation, where the elements of each block are stored in row-major order and the blocks themselves are stored in row major order. The permutation $I_{m_1n_1} \otimes L_{n_2}^{m_2n_2}$ corresponds to transposing the elements of each $m_2 \times n_2$ block. The permutation $L_{n_1}^{m_1n_1} \otimes I_{m_2n_2}$ corresponds to a block transpose on the matrix whose elements are $m_2 \times n_2$ matrices. Finally the permutation $I_{n_1} \otimes L_{n_2}^{m_1n_2} \otimes I_{m_2}$ converts back to row-major ordering.

In the remainder of this section, we list the factorizations of the stride permutations corresponding to three transposition algorithms. The first algorithm is due to Ecklundh [6], the second algorithm is due to Stone [15], and the third algorithm is a new algorithm which is obtained by modifying Stone's algorithm. All three algorithms are presented in a mixed radix form for rectangular matrices. In the remainder of the paper these algorithms will be further explored and analyzed.

Theorem 3.1 (Ecklundh's Algorithm) *Let A be an $M \times N$ matrix where $M = m_1 \cdots m_t$ and $N = n_1 \cdots n_t$. Let $T_{(i,j)}$ be the tensor permutation that exchanges the basis elements in the i and j positions.*

$$L_N^{MN} = \prod_{i=1}^{t} T_{(i,i+t)}$$

For example, Let A be a 16×16 matrix. $L_4^{16} = T_{(1,3)}T_{(2,4)}$, where $T_{(1,3)}(e_{i_1}^2 \otimes e_{i_2}^2 \otimes e_{j_1}^2 \otimes e_{j_2}^2) = (e_{j_1}^2 \otimes e_{i_2}^2 \otimes e_{i_1}^2 \otimes e_{j_2}^2)$, and $T_{(2,4)}(e_{i_1}^2 \otimes e_{i_2}^2 \otimes e_{j_1}^2 \otimes e_{j_2}^2) = (e_{i_1}^2 \otimes e_{j_2}^2 \otimes e_{i_2}^2 \otimes e_{i_2}^2)$. If we apply these two permutations one after the other to this tensor basis, it is clear that $L_4^{16} = T_{(1,3)}T_{(2,4)} = T_{(2,4)}T_{(1,3)}$. This computation generalizes to give a proof of the Theorem.

Theorem 3.2 (Stone's Algorithm) *Let A be an $M \times N$ matrix where $M = m_1 \cdots m_t$ and $N = n_1 \cdots n_t$. Then*

$$L_N^{MN} = \prod_{i=1}^{t} L_{n_i}^{MN}$$

Proof : This factorization follows from Lemma 3.1.

Theorem 3.3 (Modified Stone's Algorithm) *Let A be an $M \times N$ matrix where $M = m_1 \cdots m_t$ and $N = n_1 \cdots n_t$. Then*

$$\begin{aligned} L_N^{MN} &= \prod_{i=1}^{t}(L_{n_i}^{Mn_i} \otimes I_{N/n_i})(I_M \otimes L_{n_i}^N) \\ L_N^{MN} &= \prod_{i=1}^{t}(L_{n_i}^N \otimes I_M)(I_{N/n_i} \otimes L_{n_i}^{Mn_i}) \end{aligned}$$

Proof : This factorization follows from Stone's algorithm and an application of Lemma 3.1.

4 Matrix Transposition Algorithms

In this section, we present programs for various factorizations presented in Section 3 and analyze their performance. We first describe the memory hierarchy and the model used for measuring performance of the algorithms.

Consider an $n_1 \times n_2$ matrix $X(0 : n_1 - 1, 0 : n_2 - 1)$ to be transposed. X resides in external memory and is stored in row-major order. The transposed matrix is stored as $Y(0 : n_2 - 1, 0 : n_1 - 1)$ in external memory. If the transposition method used is "in-place" then Y occupies the same external memory locations as X. If a "dual-place" method is used then X and Y occupy different locations in the external memory. The external storage unit is assumed to have sufficient storage for both X and Y simultaneously.

The external memory is composed of blocks of data, each of size b bytes. The blocks can be accessed

659

using *direct access*, i.e., the beginning of a block can be accessed in a random fashion. However, access to a byte of data within a block requires sequential access of all preceding bytes in that block. An access to external memory specifies the block address and the number of elements following this address to be read into main memory. The external memory access time t_a is composed of two components - access setup time t_s, and the total element access time. If n elements are to be accessed then $t_a = t_s + n * t_e$, where t_e is the time required per element transfer after data transfer has been initiated. The setup time is often the dominating component of external memory access time as $t_s >> t_e$. For instance, the typical setup time is 30 ms. The element transfer rate is approximately 1 Mb/s which yields an element transfer time of 1 μs. The main memory size is M bytes and we assume that $b|M$, i.e., the main memory can store an integer number of external memory blocks. The matrix is stored in external memory such that each row begins at a block boundary, i.e., $b|n_2$.

The total number of passes, i.e., the number of times the entire matrix is read from and stored back to the disk, has been previously used as a measure of goodness. While the number of passes reflects the volume of data movement, it does not accurately reflect the total time required for the transposition. With the increase in the element transfer rates the number of disk accesses forms a significant fraction of the total disk time. The time for transposition on external storage is dominated by the time spent in data transfer between main memory and external memory. We use a combination of the number of passes and disk accesses to model the disk performance of transposition algorithms. For an $m \times n$ matrix, requiring k passes and l disk accesses per pass the time required for transposition can be characterized by $k \cdot l \cdot t_s + m \cdot n \cdot k \cdot t_e$.

We now estimate the number of passes and accesses required for the transposition algorithms presented in Section 3.

4.1 Block transposition algorithm

Consider an $N \times N$ matrix, where $N = nb$. Block matrix transposition corresponds to the following factorization of $L_{nb}^{(nb)^2}$.

Lemma 4.1 $L_{nb}^{(nb)^2} = (I_n \otimes L_b^{nb} \otimes I_b)(L_n^{n^2} \otimes I_{b^2})(I_{n^2} \otimes L_b^{b^2})(I_n \otimes L_n^{nb} \otimes I_b)$

The block transposition algorithm involves two steps and requires the that block size be smaller

than the memory size, i.e., $b^2 < M$. The matrix $X(0 : nb - 1, 0 : nb - 1)$ is viewed as an $n \times n$ block matrix composed of $b \times b$ blocks. In the first step, which corresponds to the factor $I_{n^2} \otimes L_b^{b^2}$, each of the $b \times b$ blocks is transposed. In the second step, which corresponds to the factor $L_n^{n^2} \otimes I_{b^2}$, the $n \times n$ block matrix is transposed by exchanging the appropriate blocks. The matrix is stored in external memory in a linearized fashion. Accessing the blocks of the matrix will require several non-contiguous accesses. The factor $I_n \otimes L_n^{nb} \otimes I_b$ corresponds to reading in from and writing to external memory the appropriate blocks. If the algorithm were performed as a sequence of four linear transformations, it would require 4 passes over the matrix. However, the four operations can be performed in a single pass if the algorithm operates on one block at a time. The resulting algorithm reads a block into main memory, performs the block transposition and stores it back to external memory at its appropriate position in the transposed matrix. The code is shown below:

```
do i₁ = 0, n - 1
  do j₁ = 0, n - 1
    /*Read block (i₁, j₁) into A(0 : b² - 1)*/
    do k = 0, b - 1
      S₁ :   A(bk : b(k + 1) - 1)
              ← X(i₁b + k, bj₁ : b(j₁ + 1) - 1)
    enddo
    /*Transpose A(0 : b² - 1)*/
    A(0 : b² - 1) ← L_b^{b²}(A(0 : b² - 1))
    /*Store A(0 : b² - 1) into block (j₁, i₁)*/
    do k = 0, b - 1
      S₂ :   Y(j₁b + k, bi₁ : b(i₁ + 1) - 1)
              ← A(bk : b(k + 1) - 1)
    enddo
  enddo
enddo
```

The transposition is illustrated as a sequence of linear transformations in Fig. 1(a) for $n = 2, b = 2$. Fig. 1(b) illustrates the two intermediate steps. Fig. 1(c) shows how the transposition can be performed in a block-by-block fashion. The algorithm is efficient in the number of passes. Since each $b \times b$ block is read into main memory only once, the transposition requires a single pass over the matrix. However, the algorithm requires a large number of disk accesses. Each execution of S_1 requires a disk read and each execution of S_2 requires a disk write. The algorithm requires a single pass and a total of $n^2 b$ disk reads and $n^2 b$ disk writes.

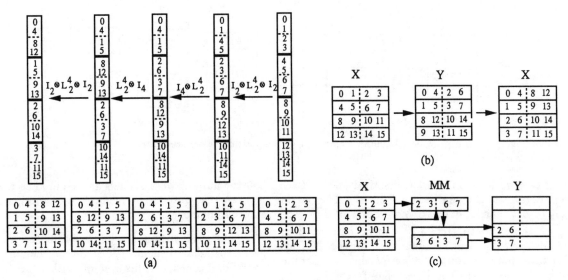

Figure 1: Block matrix transposition of square matrix $n = b = 2$

4.2 Eklundh's algorithm

Eklundh's algorithm deals with transposition of matrices with sizes which are perfect powers of two. Consider an $N \times N$ matrix X, where $N = 2^n$. The following factorization yields Eklundh's algorithm.

Lemma 4.2

$$L_{2^n}^{2^{2n}} = \prod_{k=0}^{n-1} \left(I_{2^{n-k-1}} \otimes (I_2 \otimes L_{2^{n-1}}^{2^n}) L_2^{2^{n+1}} \otimes I_{2^k}\right)$$

The code is shown below:

```
do j = 0, n − 1
  do l = 0, 2^{n-j-1}
    S : Perform (I_2 ⊗ L_{2^{n-1}}^{2^n}) L_2^{2^{n+1}} ⊗ I_{2^j}
       on X(l * 2^{j+1} : (l + 1)2^{j+1} − 1).
  enddo
enddo
```

The statement S can be performed by reading in the appropriate pair of rows and exchanging element pairs. The code as presented in [6] is shown below. The algorithm for $N = 4$ is illustrated in Fig. 2(a). The first pass corresponds to $\left(I_4 \otimes L_2^4\right)\left(I_2 \otimes L_2^8\right)$ while the second pass corresponds to $\left(I_2 \otimes L_2^4 \otimes I_2\right)\left(L_2^8 \otimes I_2\right)$. Fig. 2(b) illustrates one step of the first pass.

```
do k = 0, n − 1
  Read rows i = i_{n-1} ⋯ i_0 and j = j_{n-1} ⋯ j_0
  s.t. i_k ≠ j_k and i_p = j_p ∀ p ≠ k
  Exchange elements X(i, j') and X(j, j'')
    s.t. j'_k ≠ j''_k, j'_k ≠ i_k and j'_p = j''_p, ∀ p ≠ k
  Write back rows i and j.
enddo
```

The algorithm consists of n steps. In each step, the matrix is read into main memory, two rows at a time. Appropriate elements of these two rows are exchanged and the rows written back to external memory. With the exception of the first step, the two rows are not contiguous in external memory. Thus each step requires one pass over the matrix, N read accesses and N write accesses. Totally $2n * N$ disk accesses and n passes are performed.

The algorithm can be extended to matrices with sizes which are not powers of two, by embedding into a matrix with size which is a power of two. The smallest such matrix is used for the embedding. A similar embedding is used for transposing rectangular matrices.

4.3 Single-radix transposition algorithm

Consider an $N \times N$ matrix such that $N = 2^n$. The following factorization of $L_N^{N^2}$ gives the single radix algorithm.

Lemma 4.3 $L_N^{N^2} = \prod_{i=0}^{n-1} (L_2^N \otimes I_N)(I_{N/2} \otimes L_2^{2N})$

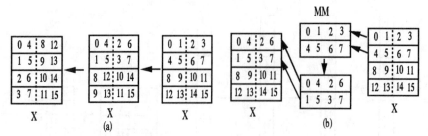

Figure 2: Eklundh's algorithm - transposition of square matrix ($N = 4$)

The algorithm involves n identical steps. Each step permutes the matrix as follows. The factor $I_{N/2} \otimes L_2^{2N}$ corresponds to $N/2$ copies of L_2^{2N} acting on the entire matrix. L_2^{2N} can be performed by loading two consecutive rows each of size N from disk into main memory and performing the permutation L_2^{2N} on these two rows. The factor $L_2^N \otimes I_N$ corresponds to performing the permutation L_2^N on the rows of the matrix. A straightforward implementation of the above factorization would require two passes over the matrix in every step. The first pass performs $I_{N/2} \otimes L_2^{2N}$ and the second pass performs $L_2^N \otimes I_N$. However, one pass can be eliminated by combining the two operations. The algorithm corresponds to loading in two consecutive rows of the matrix into main memory, performing L_2^{2N} on the rows and then storing each row into disk as determined by the permutation L_2^N. Each step then requires a single pass over the matrix. The code for this algorithm is shown below:

```
do i = 0, n − 1
  do j = 0, N/2 − 1
    /*Read j-th pair of rows into A(0 : 2N − 1)*/
    S₁ :  A(0 : 2N − 1) ← X(2j : 2j + 1, 0 : N − 1)
    /* Perform L₂²ᴺ on the two rows*/
    A(0 : 2N − 1) ← L₂²ᴺ(A(0 : 2N − 1))
    /*Store the rows*/
    j₁ ← L₂ᴺ(2j) ;  j₂ ← L₂ᴺ(2j + 1);
    S₂ :  Y(j₁, 0 : N − 1) ← A(0 : N − 1);
    S₃ :  Y(j₂, 0 : N − 1) ← A(N : 2N − 1);
  enddo
enddo
```

An application of the method for $N = 4$ is illustrated in Fig. 3. Fig. 3(a) presents the transposition as a sequence of linear transformations. Fig. 3(b) illustrates one step in the first pass.

The algorithm requires n passes over the matrix. The term $I_{N/2} \otimes L_2^{2N}$ corresponds to $N/2$ disk reads. The term $L_2^N \otimes I_N$ corresponds to N disk writes. Thus the algorithm requires a total of $\frac{3Nn}{2}$ disk accesses. Comparing with Eklundh's algorithm, we note that

half the number of disk reads are required as the pair of rows read into main memory are contiguous on external memory.

The transposition can be performed on a multiprocessor (shared memory/distributed memory with access to a concurrent file system) with P processors. Since N is large, we assume that $P < \frac{N}{2}$ and $P | \frac{N}{2}$. We have the following factorization.

$$L_N^{N^2} = \prod_{i=0}^{n-1} (L_2^N \otimes I_N)(I_P \otimes I_{\frac{N}{2P}} \otimes L_2^{2N})$$

Each processor performs $I_{\frac{N}{2P}} \otimes L_2^{2N}$ and writes the associated rows to the appropriate locations in disk. The code is shown below:

```
do i = 0, n − 1
  doall p = 0, P − 1
    do j = N/2P p, N/2P (p + 1) − 1
      /*Read j-th pair of rows*/
      S₁ :  A(0 : 2N − 1) ←
            X(2j : 2j + 1, 0 : N − 1)
      /* Perform L₂²ᴺ on the two rows*/
      A(0 : 2N − 1) ← L₂²ᴺ(A(0 : 2N − 1))
      /*Store the rows*/
      j₁ ← L₂ᴺ(2j) ;  j₂ ← L₂ᴺ(2j + 1);
      S₂ :  Y(j₁, 0 : N − 1) ← A(0 : N − 1)
      S₃ :  Y(j₂, 0 : N − 1) ← A(N : 2N − 1)
    enddo
  enddoall
enddo
```

Parallel code can be generated for all the remaining algorithms in a similar manner.

4.4 Mixed-radix transposition algorithm

We now present a mixed-radix transposition algorithm. The resulting algorithm is useful when the matrix to be transposed has dimensions which are not powers of single integer.

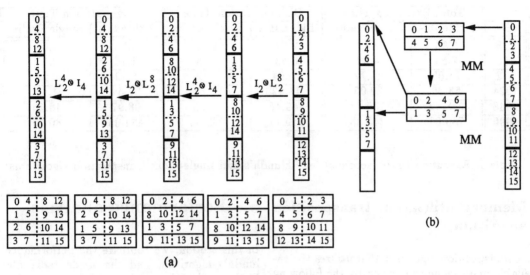

Figure 3: Transposition of square matrix $N = 4$ (single radix factorization)

Consider an $N \times N$ matrix where $N = r_0 \times \cdots \times r_{t-1}$, $r_i \in Z$, $0 \leq i < t$. Let $r_{max} = max(r_i)$, $0 \leq i < t$. We require that $r_{max} N \leq M$, i.e., at least r_{max} rows of the matrix should fit into the main memory. We have

Lemma 4.4 $L_N^{N^2} = \prod_{i=0}^{t-1}(L_{r_i}^N \otimes I_N)(I_{N/r_i} \otimes L_{r_i}^{r_i N})$

The algorithm involves t steps. Step i permutes the matrix according to the permutation sequence $(L_{r_i}^N \otimes I_N)(I_{N/r_i} \otimes L_{r_i}^{r_i N})$. The two permutations can be combined and performed in a single pass as follows. At step i, r_i consecutive rows at a time are loaded into main memory, the permutation $L_{r_i}^{r_i N}$ performed on the rows, and then each row stored into disk in a position determined by $L_{r_i}^N$. The code is shown below:

```
/* Allocate space for A(0 : r_max N - 1) */
do i = 0, t - 1
  do j = 0, N/r_i - 1
    /*Read the j-th set of r_i consecutive rows*/
S_1 :  A(0 : r_i N - 1) ←
         X(r_i j : r_i(j + 1) - 1, 0 : N - 1)
    /* Perform L_{r_i}^{r_i N} on the two rows*/
    A(0 : r_i N - 1) ← L_{r_i}^{r_i N}(A(0 : r_i N - 1))
    /* Store the rows*/
    do k = 0, r_i - 1
      k_1 ← L_{r_i}^{r_i N}(j r_i + k);
S_2 :    Y(k_1, 0 : N - 1) ←
           A(kN : (k + 1)N - 1)
    enddo
  enddo
enddo
```

The number of passes over the matrix is t, the number of factors. The number of disk reads is $N * \sum_{i=0}^{t-1} \frac{1}{r_i}$ and the number of disk writes is Nt. Thus, the total number of disk accesses is $N * (t + \sum_{i=0}^{t-1} \frac{1}{r_i})$.

The mixed-radix factorization can be generalized to rectangular matrices of size $kN \times N$ matrix, where $N = r_0 \times \cdots \times r_{t-1}$, $r_i \in Z$, $0 \leq i < t$, $k \in Q$, $kN \in Z$.

Lemma 4.5 $L_N^{kN^2} = \prod_{i=0}^{t-1}(L_{r_i}^{kN} \otimes I_N)(I_{kN/r_i} \otimes L_{r_i}^{r_i N})$

The mixed-radix transpostion algorithm for rectangular matrices requires that $kN/r_i \in Z$. However, if $k \in Q$, $r_i | kN$, $0 \leq i \leq t - 1$ need not be true. This places some restrictions on the possible factorizations of N. Also all the previously presented algorithms require that at least two rows of the matrix can be stored in main memory at a time. The following factorization removes this restrictions.

Lemma 4.6 $L_N^{kN^2} = \prod_{i=0}^{t-1}(L_{r_i}^{kN r_i} \otimes I_{N/r_i})(I_{kN} \otimes L_{r_i}^N)$

The two permutations in each of the t steps can be performed in a single pass. The transposition algorithm requires that only a single row of the matrix be stored in the main memory and the total number of passes is t. The number of reads is kNt and the number of writes is $kN * \sum_{i=0}^{t-1} r_i$. The total number of disk accesses is $kN * (t + \sum_{i=0}^{t-1} r_i)$. A restriction placed on the selection of the r_i's is that $b | \frac{N}{r_i}$. This restriction arises as disk reads or writes should begin at a block boundary.

	Total Execution Time		Disk Operation Time		Computation Time	
N	Eklundh's	Single Radix	Eklundh's	Single Radix	Eklundh's	Single Radix
128	3.13	1.77	2.87	1.73	0.26	0.06
256	7.58	4.30	6.43	4.05	1.16	0.25
512	21.05	10.77	15.94	9.82	5.12	0.96
1024	63.96	32.05	41.42	27.87	22.54	4.18
2048	248.42	106.78	149.46	88.63	98.97	18.16
4096	750.81	342.85	319.77	262.80	431.05	80.05

Table 1: Execution times (seconds) for Eklundh's and single-radix transposition algorithms

4.5 Memory utilization transposition algorithm

A matrix transposition algorithm that utilizes the entire available main memory is given by the following factorization. Since $N|M$, if $N = r_0 \times \cdots \times r_{t-1}$ then $r_i | M$, $0 \leq i < t$.

Lemma 4.7 $L_N^{kN^2} = \prod_{i=0}^{t-1} (L_{r_i}^{\frac{kN^2 r_i}{M}} \otimes I_{\frac{M}{r_i}})(I_{\frac{kN^2}{M}} \otimes L_{r_i}^M)$

The algorithm involves t steps. Step i reads in $\frac{M}{N}$ rows into main memory at a time, performs the stride permutation $L_{r_i}^M$ on these rows and stores blocks of size $\frac{M}{r_i}$ back to disk as determined by $L_{r_i}^{\frac{kN^2 r_i}{M}}$. The code is shown below.

```
do i = 0, t - 1
   do j = 0, kN²/M - 1
      /*Read the j-th set of rᵢ consecutive rows*/
      S₁ :  A(0 : M - 1) ←
            X(M/N j : M/N (j + 1) - 1, 0 : N - 1)
      /* Perform L^M_{rᵢ} on the two rows*/
      A(0 : rᵢN - 1) ← L^{rᵢN}_{rᵢ}(A(0 : rᵢN - 1))
      /* Store the rows*/
      do k = 0, rᵢ - 1
         k₁ ← L^{kN²rᵢ/M}_{rᵢ}(jrᵢ + k);
         S₂ :  Y(k₁, 0 : M/rᵢ - 1) ←
               A(k M/rᵢ : (k + 1) M/rᵢ - 1)
      enddo
   enddo
enddo
```

The number of passes is t. The number of disk read accesses is $\frac{tkN^2}{M}$ and the number of disk write accesses is $\frac{kN^2}{M} * \sum_{i=0}^{t-1} r_i$. The total number of accesses is $\frac{kN^2}{M}(t + \sum_{i=0}^{t-1} r_i)$.

5 Performance analysis

In this section, we compare the performance of Eklundh's algorithm and the single radix algorithm. Both require that at least two rows of the matrix fit in the main memory.

The algorithms were implemented on the Intel iPSC/860^{TM} using the Concurrent File System^{TM}. The Concurrent File System gives node programs high-speed access to a large amount of disk storage. Timings were taken using the millisecond wallclock `mclock`.

Table 1 presents the execution times required by Eklundh's algorithm and the single radix algorithm for various matrix sizes. The table shows the total execution time, the time spent in disk operations (disk operation time) and the time spent in main memory operations (computation time). The disk time includes the time spent in disk seeks and accesses. Table 1 shows that the single radix algorithm always outperforms Eklundh's algorithm in the disk time, computation time and thus total time required.

Eklundh's algorithm and the single radix algorithm require the same number of passes over the input matrix. However, the single radix algorithm reads pairs of contiguous rows from external memory while Eklundh's algorithms reads pairs of non-contiguous rows from external memory. Thus Eklundh's algorithm requires a greater number of disk accesses. This difference in disk accesses is reflected in the difference in the total disk time of each algorithm.

Comparing the computation times, we note that the computation time for Eklundh's algorithm exceeds that for the single radix algorithm. This difference can be attributed to locality effects and the additional cost of identifying elements to be exchanged in Eklundh's algorithm. The single radix algorithm performs the stride permutation on elements in main memory. This involves accessing elements in main memory at stride two and leads to good cache usage. Eklundh's algorithm makes a single pass over the elements in main memory. For each element it determines if the element needs to be exchanged and the corresponding element it needs to be exchanged with. This additional cost is incurred for every element. Also the elements to be exchanged are separated by a large power-of-two stride. For $N = 4096$, the computation time exceeds the disk time for Eklundh's algorithm. We believe this effect is due to the additional computation cost and poor cache performance.

6 Conclusion

In this paper, we have presented the framework of tensor products to generate efficient programs for the disk-based transposition of large matrices. We have demonstrated that several existing algorithms correspond to algebraic factorizations of the tensor product formulation of matrix transposition. We present a new mixed radix factorization which provides an algorithm which significantly reduces the number of disk accesses required. Similar to previously presented algorithms this algorithm requires that at least two rows of the matrix fit into main memory. Extensions of this algorithm for varying matrix sizes are also presented. The algorithms have been implemented on the Intel iPSC/860 using the Concurrent File System.

References

[1] W. O. Alltop. A computer algorithm for transposing nonsquare matrices. *IEEE Trans. Computers*, C-24(10):1038–1040, 1975.

[2] G. L. Anderson. A stepwise approach to computing the multidimensional fast Fourier transform of large arrays. *IEEE Trans. Acoustics and Speech Signal Processing*, ASSP-28(3):280–284, 1980.

[3] M. B. Ari. On transposing large $2^n \times 2^n$ matrices. *IEEE Trans. Computers*, C-27(1):72–75, 1979.

[4] D. H. Bailey. FFTs in external or hierarchical memory. *J. Supercomputing*, 4:23–35, 1990.

[5] L. G. Delcaro and G. L. Sicuranza. A method on transposing externally stored matrices. *IEEE Trans. Computers*, C-23(9):801–803, 1974.

[6] J. O. Eklundh. A fast computer method for matrix transposing. *IEEE Trans. Computers*, 20(7):801–803, 1972.

[7] D. Fraser. Array permutation by index-digit permutation. *J. ACM*, 23(2):298–309, 1976.

[8] G. C. Goldbogen. Prim : A fast matrix transpose method. *IEEE Trans. Software Engineering*, SE-7(2):255–257, 1981.

[9] R. A. Horn and C. R. Johnson. *Topics in Matrix Analysis*. Cambridge University Press, Cambridge, 1991.

[10] J. R. Johnson. A tensor product formulation of matrix transposition. *Appl. Math Letters*, 1993.

[11] J. R. Johnson, C.-H. Huang, and R. W. Johnson. Tensor permutations and block matrix allocation. In *Second International Workshop on Array Structures (ATABLE-92)*, 1992. Ed. G. Hains and L. Mullin, Publication No. 841, Dept. of Information and Operation Research, University of Montreal, 1992.

[12] J. R. Johnson, R. W. Johnson, D. Rodriguez, and R. Tolimieri. A methodology for designing, modifying and implementing fourier transform algorithms on various architectures. *Circuits Systems Signal Process*, 9(4):449–500, 1990.

[13] H. K. Ramapriyan. A generalization of Eklundhs's algorithm for transposing large matrices. *IEEE Trans. Computers*, C-24(12):1221–1226, 1975.

[14] U. Schumann. Comment on 'a fast computer method for matrix transposing'. *IEEE Trans. Computers*, C-22(5):542–543, 1973.

[15] H. S. Stone. Parallel processing with the perfect shuffle. *IEEE Trans. Computers*, C-20(2):153–161, 1971.

[16] R. E. Twogood and M. P. Ekstrom. An extension of Eklundh's matrix transposition algorithm and its application to digital signal processing. *IEEE Trans. Computers*, C-25(12):950–952, 1976.

[17] C. Van Loan. *Computational framework for the Fast Fourier Transform*. SIAM, 1992.

A Practical External Sort for Shared Disk MPPs

Xiqing Li, Gordon Linoff, Stephen J. Smith,
Craig Stanfill, Kurt Thearling

Thinking Machines Corporation
245 First Street, Cambridge MA, 02142
smith@think.com

Abstract

An external sort has been implemented and analyzed for a shared disk MPP computer system. In this implementation, we have considered many real world constraints. Decision support functionality in database systems, for instance, often requires that external sorting be done in place on disk, support variable length records, and be restartable from any point of interruption with no loss of data. These three constraints, along with the more standard requirements of speed and stability, affect the choice and implementation of the external sorting algorithm. The implementation of the sample sort algorithm described here meets these requirements. Although written using high level file processing directives, the implementation sorts a 10 GB file in 1.5 hours on a 64 processor Connection Machine CM-5 with a DataVault disk system.

1: Introduction

Our intention in building an external sort (where the size of the data to be sorted is larger than main memory) was to produce a system that met the requirements of real world problems and could be implemented in a reasonably short period of time with a high level programming model. Given these goals we pursued an external version of the sample sort algorithm, at times sacrificing performance in favor of simplicity and portability by using existing high level file access routines (close, open, read, write, seek, append, delete and truncate). Applying this strategy, a sorting system capable of sorting 10GB of data in under 1.5 hours was designed and developed in about 6 staff-months. Because the code is written in C using a MIMD (Multiple Instruction Multiple Data) message passing library and high level file access routines, the algorithm and our results should map well to other parallel computers with single-input single-output disk access.

1.1: Practical requirements

In designing and implementing a practical external sort useful for scientific and commercial databases, we determined that the following features in addition to speed and stability were important:

- *Variable Length Records.* The sort should support records of variable length with the length encoded in the data (in our case the records varied between 600 and 4,000 bytes).
- *In-Place.* The sort should use a constant amount of extra disk space regardless of the amount of data being sorted.
- *Restartable.* The sort should be completely restartable from any point of interruption to avoid loss of data.

We assumed that records would consist of two parts: a fixed-length header containing the length of the record followed by a variable number of fixed-length fields. The start of a record could be determined only by extracting the position and length of the preceding record. Such a format is common for data files produced by serial machines but it proves to be a bit of a nuisance when trying to find record starts on a parallel machine. However, the fact that record location in this case is an inherently serial process did not significantly affect total system performance when implemented on a massively parallel computer.

The requirements that the sort be in-place and restartable are complementary. To be in-place, sorted data must overwrite the original data. Since it is critical that the original data not be lost, the sort must be able to be restarted from any point in the algorithm. The algorithm itself is divided into various steps. Between steps, important data is stored in a checkpoint file which allows the sort to resume from the checkpoint.

Though our intent was to provide a real world sort we did assume some simplifications for the construction of keys. Specifically:

- *Fixed Length*. Keys are of known but arbitrary length and are in a consistent position relative to the beginning of each record.
- *Canonical Ordering*. Keys are considered to be of unsigned integer type (either they started off this way or were converted to this form in a pre-processing step).

These two assumptions about the keys were made so that we could focus on the algorithmic details of the sort. Internally, we chose a local quicksort and an internal sample sort instead of a radix sort in order to allow the sort to be comparison based and eventually support complex composite keys [5]. Such composite keys might consist of data from anywhere within the record and with a variety of data types (floating point, integer, ASCII, EBCDIC) and sorting direction (ascending or descending).

2: The external sample sort algorithm

External sorting algorithms have recently been placed into two classes: those that perform a full, in memory, internal sort before redistributing the records and those that perform a redistribution of the keys followed by an internal sort [2][14]. Mergesort and external hyperquicksort fall into the first class [23], and sample sort [6] falls into the second class. In either case the response time of the system is often determined by the permutation of the data on disk and not by the in memory sort itself. This is especially true in many real world applications where the keys make up only a small portion of the total record length. In these cases, all the keys can often fit in the main memory of the computer at one time and can be sorted there in a single pass. This seeming advantage provides little or no benefit in reality since a randomized permutation on disk is no faster than a sort except for unrealistically small memory sizes [1]. Thus in terms of overall speed for the disk permutation there are two dominant factors - the number of times the data is moved between disk and memory and the number of random disk accesses required for these moves.

The goals of our external sort further limited the choice of algorithm. In particular, the requirements of being in-place and restartable strongly suggested a sample sort algorithm. To reach the performance goals, we had to minimize the amount of I/O even on very large data sets. For these reasons we chose a sample sort algorithm that required three reads and two writes of the data but is $O(D^2)$ in the number of disk accesses (D = data size in bytes).

For the largest data file actually sorted for this paper (10GB), the quadratic cost of disk accesses was not the dominant factor but did approach 25% of the total time. For significantly more data or smaller memory the time spent in random disk access would become the dominant cost. The sample sort algorithm can be extended to reduce this cost of disk access by performing multiple passes of the algorithm, effectively trading the cost of more data movement for fewer disk accesses. Another advantage of sample sort is that it well fit our file system primitives and provided a simple, high-level implementation.

2.1: The algorithm

The sample sort algorithm proceeds by first partitioning the records to be sorted into several bucket files, each smaller than main memory. The records in one bucket file are ordered with respect to the records in the next (ordered for example by "less than"). These bucket files are then loaded into main memory, sorted and appended to a growing sorted file of all the data.

In order to perform the partitioning of the data into ordered buckets, *splitting values* must be determined that define the boundaries between each bucket. For example, consider three buckets defined by the two splitters 362 and 1098. All records whose keys < 362 go into bucket 0; records where 362 <= key < 1098 go into bucket 1; and all other records go into bucket 2. To obtain the splitters that perfectly partition the records between buckets would require a sort in and of itself and thus defeat the purpose of finding the splitters. To circumvent this, a sampling of the keys is performed to estimate the splitters. To further refine this estimate, keys are often sampled at a much higher rate than actually required (oversampling). These candidate splitters are then sorted and only every *j*th candidate splitter is chosen as a splitter of the actual bucket files (where *j* equals the oversampling ratio). Oversampling provides a better estimate of the perfect splitters and bounds can be placed on the variance of the splitters [6].

The sample sort algorithm, and its variants, has been implemented and improved on several times for internal (in memory) sorting on MPP systems [6][12][13][15][16] though it has not been often used for external sorting. A recent article has, however, shown an implementation for a shared-nothing disk architecture (a local disk per processing node) [11].

The shared-nothing architecture was shown to be useful for sample sort like algorithms using probabilistic splitting [11]. In their paper DeWitt et al. use a variant of the sample sort algorithm for a "multiple-input multiple-output" sorting problem where the data file is initially distributed across the disks. The final sorted file is required to end up partitioned into nearly equal sized sorted runs on each disk with all keys on one disk ordered with respect to all keys on the next disk. Their algorithm proceeds by gathering splitting candidates randomly from each disk and determining the splitters via a central coordinator. The splitters are then broadcast to each node and a distribution stage is entered where each record is directed via the splitters to the correct processing node. Each node collects the incoming records in a buffer and when the buffer is full, sorts it and then writes it out to disk. These sorted runs are later merged at each node.

Several modifications of the internal sample sort algorithm also needed to be made for the shared disk implementation presented in this paper. Specifically, the requirements of keeping the sort in place and restartable affected the overall design. There are three main stages of the external sample sort algorithm (see figure 1):

1. The data file is read to sample the keys for splitters and to set *posts*. Posts fall only on record boundaries and mark the starts and ends of *chunks* which break up the original file into pieces that can fit in main memory. Defining the posts in this stage is necessary as the data file will be read backwards in stage 2, which is not possible for variable length records unless the posts have previously been marked.

2. The chunks are read into memory in reverse order and their records are distributed to the bucket files based on the splitters obtained in stage 1. As each bucket file grows the original data file is truncated, keeping the sort in place.

3. Each bucket file is read into memory in sequence, sorted and then appended to the final sorted file. The bucket files are deleted as they are used up.

This algorithm will perform an in-place sort (free disk space equal in size to the memory is required as a buffer) and can be made restartable by writing out checkpoint information during each stage. In stage 2, we truncate the original data file after each memory load because the records in that chunk have already been added to the bucket files (since we can only truncate from the end of the file this necessitates reading the file backwards). In stage 3, we delete each successive bucket file as the final sorted file grows because each record in the bucket file has already been added to the final sorted file. Because all of the original data is always resident somewhere on disk (though at some points there may be up to one memory load of duplicate data), we do not have to worry about specifically backing up or checkpointing the data, which could otherwise become expensive and complicated.

This algorithm also has the advantage over mergesort in that it flushes memory of all data on each step within each stage. In mergesort, data loaded into memory from several sorted runs usually cannot all be written directly to the sorted file. This remaining data in memory must then be elaborately checkpointed to determine exactly how much has been written to the sorted file and how much must still be retained in the original data file. A possible solution to this problem, though we have not seen it implemented, would be to sample the sorted runs as in [2] and to only load into memory data from each run that would fit in the current partition. This would, however, also require searching the sorted runs for splitter break points, and since it could only be based on partitions defined by sampling, there would always be the possibility that the partition would overflow usable memory.

For the sample sort algorithm described here the checkpoint data needed to restart and continue the sort at each stage is:

1. All the posts and samples (as they are collected) and a pointer to the progress made in the original file.

2. The sizes of the bucket files and the chunks that have been deleted.

3. The length of the sorted output file and the list of deleted bucket files.

In addition to the constraints of restartability and keeping the sort in place, there is always the danger that the key sampling will be poor and a bucket file will be too large to fit in main memory. Internal sample sorts often solve this problem by resampling the original data and resplitting the data into buckets. In the case of an in-place external sort, restarting in this way is not possible since the original data has already been overwritten. The solution is to recursively call stages 1 and 2 of the external sorting algorithm on the overflowing buckets in order to divide them into smaller buckets that do fit into main memory.

2.2: The Internal Sort

The internal sort used in stage 3 is also a sample sort. We will here quickly review this internal sample sort algorithm and the differences between it and a similar implementation on a parallel computer slightly different from the one described in [6] (see [10][21] for MPP implementations of other algorithms).

For large data sets with large keys (> 8 bytes) previous work has shown that sample sort can be a superior algorithm to radix, bitonic, quicksort, and others [6]. Since these constraints closely follow those of our current problem, sample sort was used for the internal sort in stage 3 of the external sort. Note that a fast radix sort capable of sorting 1 billion 32-bit keys in under 18 seconds has been implemented on the CM-5 [22]. Because of the linear dependence of the radix algorithm on key length and the eventual need for a comparison-based sort for general keys, we abandoned radix and implemented the sample sort algorithm instead.

The main idea of the internal sample sort is the same as for the external version - redistribute the original data to buckets where every key in each bucket is ordered with respect to every key in the next bucket, and then sort the buckets. In this case the buckets are not stored in files but in the memory of each individual processor. The splitters

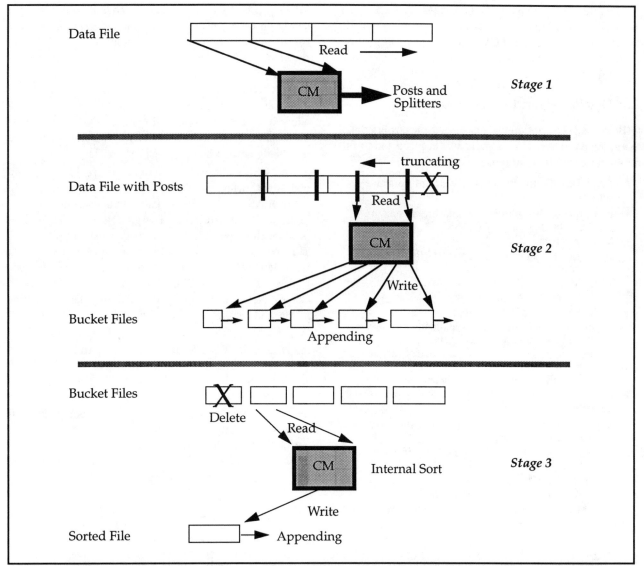

Figure 1. The three stages of the in-place, external sample sort. In stage 1 the unsorted data file is read to collect candidate splitters and to mark boundaries between variable length records (posts). In the second stage the original file is read backwards and truncated as the data is distributed to the buckets as determined by the splitting values. In the third stage each bucket file (which will fit entirely into memory) is sorted in turn and deleted as the final sorted file grows.

between the buckets are again determined by oversampling. There are four main stages in the internal sample sort:

1. Determine bucket splitters.
2. Distribute keys and location information to the correct bucket.
3. Locally sort and enumerate the keys in each bucket.
4. Use the enumeration information to send the records to the correct final location.

The main differences between the current internal sample sort and that described in [6] are:

- Since the records are so much larger than the keys, only the key, the record length and a pointer back to the original record are sent to the buckets.

- The value returned from the local sort to the original record reflects the byte position for the record rather than its rank since the records are variable length (this is accomplished with a plus scan, also known as a parallel prefix operation, over the record lengths in the sorted buckets).

- The local sort is a quicksort not a radix sort. On a MIMD machine such as the CM-5, the option for a local quicksort was more attractive. It requires less memory space and uses a comparison sort (which allows for eventual expansion to composite keys of multiple fields and types).

The internal sort requires a bit more than twice as much memory as the original data and was timed at about 64MB/sec on a 64 processor node CM-5. The majority of the time for the sort was spent in performing the interprocessor permutation of the records after the keys had been ranked.

2.3: Detailed algorithm description

Below is a description that provides the necessary detail to implement the external sample sort in-place and to fulfill the restartability requirement.

1. Read data file to extract candidate splitters and set posts
   a. Initialize file pointer for data file at start or from checkpoint
   b. Do over data of data file
      i. Read data from data file starting at file pointer
      ii. Mark record boundaries
      iii. Set post
      iv. Select candidate splitters
      v. Write current posts, candidate splitters and file pointer to checkpoint
   c. Sort candidate splitters and select actual splitters
   d. Write splitters and posts to checkpoint data
2. Read data from between posts and write to bucket files
   a. Initialize file pointer for data file from checkpoint or to end of file
   b. Open bucket files (truncating them if necessary to sizes stored in checkpoint data)
   c. Do backwards over data file
      i. Set file pointer to next post from end
      ii. Read data from file pointer to end of file
      iii. Locally sort data to determine bucket files
      iv. Write data to bucket files with append
      v. Write file-pointer and bucket file sizes to checkpoint data
      vi. Truncate data file to file-pointer
3. Read bucket files, sort, then write to sorted file
   a. Truncate sorted file to length in checkpoint data
   b. Do for bucket files
      i. Read in first available bucket file or next bucket file in checkpoint data
      ii. Sort bucket
      iii. Write data to output file in append mode
      iv. Write sorted file length and next bucket file to checkpoint data
      v. Delete current bucket file

3: Implementation and performance

This external sort was written in C running on each parallel node, with a MIMD message passing library and file system primitives provided by the CM-5 CMMD package

[4][17][8]. Users write standard C code that runs independently on each processing node, interspersing interprocessor communication and synchronization calls where required. All disk data transfers were accomplished with a file system model of the disk (e.g. the buckets for the sample sort are files rather than locations within files or specifically mapped sections of the disk). This high level model allowed simpler implementation of the system although it hid some important issues such as fragmentation which eventually need to be addressed for very large files.

The CM-5 consists of from 16 to 16,384 processing nodes, each using the SPARC chip set with accompanying optional ASIC vector units. The external sort does not currently use the vector units. The processing nodes are independent and have their own local memory of up to 32MB. They communicate with each other via two networks: the Data Network and the Control Network. The Data Network is used for point-to-point processor communication. The Control Network is used for broadcasting data, synchronization, and parallel prefix operations (scans).

The CM-5 disk system used for these experiments was the DataVault. It is a RAID (Redundant Array of Inexpensive Disks) level 2 disk system (32 data disks, 7 ECC disks, and 3 spares) capable of 20 MB/sec for data transfer [20]. The DataVault transfers data to the processing nodes over the data network and thus is physically and computationally distinct from the processing nodes (see Figure 2). A higher performance, scalable, RAID level 3 disk system is now available on the CM-5, though the results presented in this paper were obtained by running on a DataVault.

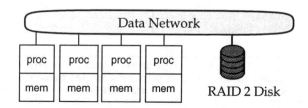

Processing Nodes

Figure 2. Shared disk MPP with RAID 2 disk system. Performance figures presented in this paper were obtained on a Connection Machine CM-5 with a DataVault disk system.

Multiple DataVaults can be added to a CM-5 for increased bandwidth; they attach at available addresses on the data network similar to the way a processing node does. For this research our CM-5 consisted of 64 processor nodes, each with 16 MB of local memory (1 GB total), no vector units, and a single DataVault shared among the 64 processing nodes. Because only a single DataVault was used and its disks were not accessed independently this algorithm would be classified as a single-input, single-output shared disk system (as opposed to the multiple input, multiple output, "shared-nothing" architectures reported by others [11][18]).

The average length of the records for the performance benchmarks reported was 2,300 bytes and varied uniformly between 600 and 4,000 bytes. Each key was an unsigned integer of 4 bytes. The system was tested on 6 different sized files of 1, 2, 3, 5, 7, and 10GB and the results are shown in Table 1.

TABLE 1. External Sorting Performance

Data (GB)	Stage 1 (secs)	Stage 2 (secs)	Stage 3 (secs)	Total (hours)
1	71	156	218	0.12
2	136	310	418	0.24
3	201	529	607	0.37
5	316	921	1042	0.63
7	479	1507	1559	0.99
10	671	2457	2266	1.49

Table 1 shows that as the database size increases the time spent in stage 1 increases nearly linearly but the time spent in stage 2 and 3 increases much more quickly. We expect that this is due to the quadratic growth in the number of disk accesses with respect to database size that occurs in stage 2. We might also expect to see a similar effect in stage 3 due to disk fragmentation as the larger files took up most of the available space on disk. (There was approximately 12GB of total available disk space leaving only 2GB of free space for the 10 GB file; fragmentation likely occurred).

4: Analysis

4.1: I/O model

Moving data between disk and memory has two primary components that determine the time spent: the overhead for accessing the disk (including movement of the disk head and rotational latency) and the data transfer time. Previous analyses of sorting algorithms have combined these two costs into a single measure describing the transfer of an I/O or disk block [1][9][19]. The assumption has been that I/O can be divided into fixed-sized blocks, each of which is large enough so that the data transfer time dominates the overhead. This is an appealing model since it allows an algorithm's performance to be modelled solely on the number of block I/Os instead of having to consider the amount of data transferred and the number of accesses separately. There are, however, several disadvantage to

using a fixed block size for analyzing the algorithm presented in this paper.

In our case the data transfer rate from disk is approximately 20 MB/sec and though there are no preset restrictions on the block size the latency of the DataVault is relatively high, roughly 200 ms for reads. If a preselected block size were used such that latency were only 10% of the total transfer time, the block size would have to be 36 MB (2 seconds total access time consisting of 0.2 seconds for latency and 1.8 seconds for data transfer). This is too large for most applications of the sample sort algorithm. There will in fact be cases where we will want to allow the fraction of time spent in disk access to grow or shrink in order to optimize the performance over the entire algorithm. For example, the most I/O intensive part of the algorithm is stage 2 where chunks are read into memory and split into buckets. We will call the amount written to each bucket from a single chunk a *bucket-chunk*. It represents the maximum amount of data that can be written out at one time during this stage of the algorithm. If the size of a bucket-chunk is ever smaller than the preset block size, bandwidth will be used inefficiently. This can happen for large data sets.

For the results shown in this paper the chunk size was 300 MB and the average bucket size was 240 MB (smaller than the chunk size to allow for variations caused by sampling). The bucket-chunk size, though, varies depending on the number of buckets and hence on the size of the input. For a 1 GB file, each chunk of 300 Mbytes is written to 5 buckets, so the average size of a bucket-chunk is 60MB. For a 5 GB file, there are 22 buckets and the average bucket-chunk size is 14 Mbytes. For a 10 GB file, the average is only 7 Mbytes. When there is much more than 1 Gbyte of data, the average size is considerably smaller than the 36 MB chosen to minimize latency. Using a fixed block size in such cases wastes bandwidth.

Fortunately, the shared-disk system allows arbitrary and dynamic block sizes for I/O. We have chosen to model our algorithms by separating the access latency and data transfer costs. This more detailed analysis shows that latency becomes a significant factor as the data grows. At certain ratios of data to memory size, the splitting phase of the sample sort should be performed in multiple passes, paying the expense of moving the data more often in order to dramatically reduce the cost of random disk access.

4.2: Data storage/transfer hierarchy

The transfer of data between disk and memory coupled with disk access latencies are the dominant costs of this and most other parallel external sorting algorithms. The remaining costs usually decrease dramatically (often by more than a factor of 10) as the data become more and more localized to the individual processing unit. A useful model of an external sort could thus be made by modelling all "computation" as data movement.

We would like to explore such a simplified model to analyze the external sample sort algorithm. For a typical serial machine, these levels of data storage for memory access consist of the disk, the memory, cache memory, and registers. For the CM-5, a similar hierarchy exists with some additional levels of distinction representing other important differences in the rates at which the data can be moved. The important data storage and transfer levels for the CM-5 are shown in the table below.

TABLE 2. Data Storage Hierarchy for a 64 PN CM-5 with Datavault

Storage Access Level	Transfer Rate (Gbyte/sec)	Access Latency (secs)
Disk	0.020	0.2
Interprocessor	0.256	0.000004
Intraprocessor	1.024	negligible
Intraprocessor (vector units)	16.384	negligible

To model the performance of a system, as we have above, requires simplifying many of its complex behaviors that take advantage of data locality such as caching, and DRAM paging. For our purposes, the simplified level of abstraction should model the system adequately. The important aspects of the system to note are:

- 10+ times performance increase between disk and interprocessor bandwidth;
- 50 times performance improvement from disk to intraprocessor data movement; and
- the high cost of disk access compared to other forms of data movement.

Given this we can see, for instance, that if disk I/O is used as frequently as other operations, then the I/O is the dominating cost and that improving the processing performance (by adding vector units, for instance) would have little impact on overall system performance.

4.3: The model

We would now like to build a model to predict where the time will be spent for different amounts of data. The following are important parameters for our model:

P Number of processors

D Total data (GB)

K Key length + record number (GB)

K' Key length + record number + auxiliary location information (GB)

R Record length (GB)

M_d Usable memory for sampling and distribution (stages 1,2) (GB)

M_s Usable memory for internal sort (stage 3) (GB)

B_d Disk data bandwidth (GB/sec)

B_i Interprocessor data bandwidth (GB/sec)

B_m Intraprocessor data bandwidth (GB/sec)

L_r Total disk access latency for reads (secs)

L_w Total disk access latency for writes (secs)

Note that the interprocessor (between processor) and intraprocessor (in memory) bandwidth refers to the bandwidth for the entire computer, not for individual processors. Note also that not all of the system memory can be used to store the data during the internal sort and the distribution to buckets. Consequently we have broken up the memory into two different parameters (M_s and M_d). This is because the portions of the algorithm used in these sections are not completely in place. For instance the internal sort requires a buffer slightly larger than the size of the data to be sorted.

We can now model the external sort based on the assumptions already made about the performance of the CM-5. The model of the time for each stage of sample sort is as follows:

$$T_{\text{stage1}} = \frac{D}{B_d} + \frac{D}{B_i} + L_r \left\lceil \frac{D}{M_d} \right\rceil \qquad \text{1.1 (read)}$$

$$T_{\text{stage2}} = \frac{D}{B_d} + \frac{D}{B_i} + L_r \left\lceil \frac{D}{M_d} \right\rceil \qquad \text{2.1 (read)}$$

$$+ \frac{D}{B_m} + \frac{D}{B_m} (\frac{K}{R}) \log \frac{M_d}{PR} \qquad \text{2.2 (split)}$$

$$+ \frac{D}{B_d} + \frac{D}{B_i} + L_w \left\lceil \frac{D}{M_d} \right\rceil \left\lceil \frac{D}{M_s} \right\rceil \qquad \text{2.3 (write)}$$

$$T_{\text{stage3}} = \frac{D}{B_d} + \frac{D}{B_i} + L_r \left\lceil \frac{D}{M_s} \right\rceil \qquad \text{3.1 (read)}$$

$$+ \frac{D}{B_i} (1 + 2\frac{K'}{R}) + \frac{D}{B_m} (\frac{K'}{R}) \log \frac{M_s}{PR} \qquad \text{3.2 (sort)}$$

$$+ \frac{D}{B_d} + \frac{D}{B_i} + L_w \left\lceil \frac{D}{M_s} \right\rceil \qquad \text{3.3 (write)}$$

The time of the first stage (line 1.1 above) is modelled by the costs of reading all of the data from disk (D/B_d) and the cost of rearranging it across the processors (D/B_i). This rearrangement of the data is necessary to accommodate load balancing between the processors and to allow for the disk data structure to be independent of the number of processors on the CM-5. The final term on line 1.1 reflects the costs of disk access per chunk where the total number of chunks in the file is $\left\lceil \dfrac{D}{M_d} \right\rceil$.

In stage two there are three main sections: line 2.1 where the data is read in by chunks (as in stage 1), line 2.2 where the data is locally ordered by a quicksort and then split into buckets, and line 2.3 where the local buckets on each processor are written to the buckets resident on disk. It is important to note that line 2.3 contains a term that is quadratic with respect to the size of the database. This term arises because for every chunk that is read into memory the data must be distributed to every bucket and there are $\left\lceil \dfrac{D}{M_s} \right\rceil$ buckets and $\left\lceil \dfrac{D}{M_d} \right\rceil$ total chunks. When the access cost of a write and/or the ratio of the database size to usable memory size is high, this will be an important term in the total cost of the algorithm.

The equation for the cost of the local quicksort on line 2.2 can be derived in the following way. The sort of the records is accomplished by sorting pointers to the records based on the keys and then locally reordering the records based on this rank. Locally reordering the records contributes the D/B_m term. The ranking of the records is derived by observing that there will be D/M_d parallel quicksorts in all and for each of these there will be M_d/PR records per processor. Each quicksort will then make (M_d/PR) $log(M_d/PR)$ comparisons of K gigabytes of data (where $log = log_2$). Since the data bandwidth of the local memory of each processor is B_m/P the equation would be:

$$\frac{D}{M_d}\left(\frac{KP}{B_m}\right)\frac{M_d}{PR}\log\frac{M_d}{PR}$$

which simplifies to the second term on line 2.2.

We model the key comparisons within the quicksort as simple data movement even though they will be somewhat more expensive and there should be some multiplicative constant for this term. This abstraction does not seriously compromise the model, however, as the cost of the intraprocessor data movement is minimal in comparison to the costs of interprocessor and disk data movement. The dominating terms of this model will, in fact, be the reads and writes of all the records that occur in each stage and the quadratic number of disk seeks that occur in stage 2.

Stage three is modelled by a read (line 3.1), an internal sort (line 3.2), and a write (line 3.3). The read and the write are similar to those in stages 1 and 2, except that the cost of disk access is dependent on the number of buckets, not on the number of chunks (lines 1.1 and 2.1) or on the product of the number of chunks and buckets (line 2.3)

The internal sample sort of stage 3 (line 3.2) is modelled by an intraprocessor quicksort (similar to line 2.2), two

sends of the keys and auxiliary location information, and a single interprocessor permutation of the full record data to sorted order.

4.4: Comparing the model to experimental results

It is often important and instructive to compare any theoretical results with an actual implementation as was done in [3][7]. This model of the sample sort is compared to the actual performance data in figure 3. The model proves to be a good match for the first stage of the algorithm, but the costs in the second and third stages grow at a faster rate than predicted by the model. Since the only non-linear term in the model is the latency of disk access, we may consider that the actual cost of random disk access may be higher than the 200ms that was directly measured. We further expect that some of the mismatch between the model and the actual timings in stage 3 is due to file fragmentation, which would also contribute a quadratic disk access term not explicitly included in the model. A multipass version of the external sample sort can, however, decrease this quadratic number of disk accesses and the degree of file fragmentation.

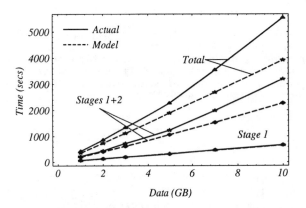

Figure 3. Comparison of the performance model and actual performance. The model of the sample sort algorithm fits the actual data well for the first stage. For the second and third stages the actual time to sort is growing faster than the model. Since the only non-linear term in the model is latency of disk accesses, it is hypothesized that the model underestimates this time or should have another non-linear term, perhaps to account for disk fragmentation.

Since the model is a relatively good match to the actual performance, we can use it to see how much time is being spent in moving the data at each level of the memory hierarchy. Figure 4 shows the percentage of time spent in moving the data at each of these levels. It also includes the latency of disk access which, though not a dominant term for these size runs, is growing at a greater rate than the other factors.

Figure 5 shows the model when the database sizes are allowed to grow up to a terabyte while the memory is held constant. Here the quadratic number of disk accesses becomes the dominating term for large databases and methods to minimize the number of accesses will be critical. It may be, however, that the memory of the computer will be increased proportionally to the growth of the database and thus the cost of disk access could be held nearly constant. In this case, as in the cases we ran experimentally, the data transfer between disk and memory would need to be minimized; speeding up other sections of the algorithm would have little effect on the overall performance of the system.

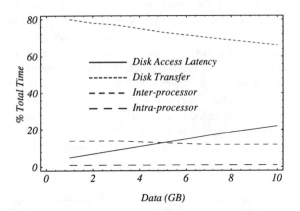

Figure 4.   Costs of data movement from model. This figure shows that data transfer between disk and memory is the dominating cost for the external sort over the region studied. Data movement between processors contributed some 15% and local data movement approximately 1% of the total time.

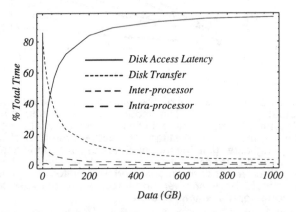

Figure 5. Differing costs of data movement with database size. The model was run for databases from 0.001 GB to 1000 GB and the amount of time spent at each level of the memory hierarchy was recorded. This graph shows that if memory size is held constant as the database continues to grow, that eventually the disk access latency becomes the dominating cost. Large databases pay heavily for disk access because the number of buckets is so large and very small databases also pay heavily for latency because of the very small data transfers used in reading and writing the files.

5: Conclusion

The research presented in this paper reflects the effort to produce a practical external sort on existing shared disk MPP computer systems. We have shown that several of the real world constraints of both scientific and commercial users, such as keeping the sort in place, can have dramatic effects on the performance. Specifically, we have shown that, though it is relatively easy to perform an external sort in three full reads and two full writes, the cost of random disk access can quickly become the dominant factor as the number of accesses grows quadratically with the database size. There may be ways to reduce this cost and the cost of file fragmentation by perhaps trading off multiple reads and writes for a reduced number of disk accesses, but there may be even better ways to control file fragmentation on disk. Unfortunately, they require low level control of the disk system which, though of interest, would have limited the portability of our algorithm and the usefulness of our results to other shared disk MPP systems.

There are still several open questions that would be of benefit to answer. We would like to know, for instance, what effect a multiple pass version of the external sample sort algorithm would have on the number of disk accesses and on file fragmentation. If we could then incorporate this modification into our model it would be possible to optimize the number of passes in the multiple pass sample sort algorithm. We would also like to extend the sort to include complex keys, which is an important real world constraint that we considered but did not implement. Despite these important further improvements, this research has nonetheless already contributed a simple high level algorithm for external sorting that is relatively easy to implement and should map well to many shared disk MPP architectures. The parametric models, in fact, should allow for high level performance evaluations and optimizations of this algorithm even before it is implemented.

Acknowledgments

We would like to thank Michael Berry and Paul Barth for their help in determining the constraints of the sorting problem and Michael Best for his work in providing the high level file system interface. We would also like to thank Dave Waltz, Marco Zagha and Tom Cormen for their review and criticisms of early drafts of this paper.

References

[1] A. Aggarwal, J. S. Vitter. "The Input Output Complexity of Sorting and Related Problems", *CACM*, vol. 31, no. 9, pp. 1116-1127, Sept. 1988.

[2] B. A. Baugsto, J. F. Greipsland. "Parallel Sorting Methods for Large Data Volumes on a Hypercube Database Com-

puter", *Proc. of the Sixth Intl. Workshop on Database Machines*, Springer-Verlag, pp. 127-141, 1989.

[3] M. Beck, D. Bitton, W. K. Wilkinson. "Sorting Large Files on a Backend Multiprocessor", *IEEE Transactions on Computers*, vol. 37, no. 7, pp. 769-778, July 1988.

[4] M. Best, A. Greenberg, C. Stanfill, L. Tucker. "CMMD I/O: a Parallel Unix I/O", Submitted to: *IEEE 7th International Parallel Processing Symposium, 1993.*

[5] G. E. Blelloch, L. Dagum, S. J. Smith, K. Thearling, M. Zagha. "An Evaluation of Sorting as a Supercomputer Benchmark" Submitted to: *International Journal of High Speed Computing, 1993.*

[6] G.E. Blelloch, C.E. Leiserson, B.M. Maggs, C.G. Plaxton, S.J. Smith, M. Zagha. "A Comparison of Sorting Algorithms for the Connection Machine CM-2". *3rd Annual ACM Symposium on Parallel Algorithms and Architectures,* July 1991, Hilton Head, SC, pp. 3-16.

[7] P. Carnevali "Timing Results of Some Internal Sorting Algorithms on the IBM 3090". *Parallel Computing,* 6, North-Holland, 1988, pp. 115-117.

[8] Thinking Machines Corporation. *CM-5 Technical Summary.* January 1992. Cambridge, MA.

[9] T. Cormen. "Fast Permuting on Disk Arrays", *Journal of Parallel and Distributed Computing (to appear)*1992.

[10] L. Dagum. "Parallel Integer Sorting With Medium and Fine-Scale Parallelism". *International Journal of High Speed Computing (to appear),* 1993.

[11] D. Dewitt, J. F. Naughton, D. A. Schneider, "Parallel Sorting on a Shared-Nothing Architecture using Probabilistic Splitting". *Proceedings of the International Conference on Parallel and Distributed Information Systems.* Miami Beach, Florida. IEEE Computer Society Press. 1991.

[12] W. Dobosiewicz. "Sorting by Distributive Partitioning". *Information Processing Letters.* v. 7, no. 1. January, 1978.

[13] W. D. Frazer, A. C. McKellar. "Samplesort: A Sampling Approach to Minimal Storage Tree Sorting". *Journal of the Association for Computing Machinery,* v. 17, no. 3, July, 1970, pp. 496-507.

[14] G. Graefe. "Parallel External Sorting in Volcano", *University of Colorado Technical Report*, CU-CS-459-90, Boulder, Colorado, 1989.

[15] W. Hightower, J. F. Prins, J. H. Reif. "Implementations of Randomized Sorting on Large Parallel Machines". *Proceedings of the 4th ACM Symposium on Parallel Algorithms and Architectures*, July, 1992.

[16] J. S. Huang, Y.C. Chow. "Parallel Sorting and Data Partitioning by Sampling". *Proceedings of the IEEE Computer Society's Seventh International Computer Software and Applications Conference.* pp. 627-631, November 1983.

[17] C. Leiserson, et.al. "The Network Architecture of the Connection Machine CM-5", *4th Annual ACM Symposium on Parallel Algorithms and Architectures,* July 1992, .

[18] R. A. Lorie, H. C. Young. "A Low Communication Sort Algorithm for a Parallel Database Machine". *Proceedings of the Fifteenth Conference on Very Large Data Bases*, pp. 125-134, Amsterdam, 1989.

[19] M. Nodine. "Greed Sort: An Optimal External Sorting Algorithm for Multiple Disks", Brown University Technical Report No. CS-90-04, 1990.

[20] D. Patterson, G. Gibson, R. Katz. "A Case for Redundant Arrays of Inexpensive Disks (RAID)". Proceedings of ACM SIGMOD, Chicago, pp. 109-116, 1988.

[21] J.F. Prins, J.A. Smith. "Parallel Sorting of Large Arrays on the MasPar MP-1." *Proc. of 3rd Symposium on Frontiers of Massively Parallel Computation*, College Park, MD IEEE, October, pp. 158-167, 1990.

[22] K. Thearling, S. J. Smith. "An Improved Supercomputer Sorting Benchmark." *Proceedings of Supercomputing '92.* 1992.

[23] B.A. Wagar. "Hyperquicksort: A Fast Sorting Algorithm for Hypercubes". In M.T. Heath, editor, *Hypercube Multiprocessors 1987 (Proceedings of the Second Conrference on Hypercube Multiprocessors),* pp. 292-299, Philadelphia, PA, 1987. SIAM.

Compute Intensity and the FFT

Douglas Miles

Cray Research Superservers, Inc.
3601 SW Murray Blvd. Beaverton, Oregon 97005
miles@cray.com

Abstract

The fast Fourier transform (FFT) is a challenging algorithm to implement efficiently on a parallel computer. Recent algorithm advances have led to greatly improved FFT performance on parallel vector computers such as the CRAY-2 and CRAY Y-MP. Variations on these techniques can be used to extend this improved performance to other parallel architectures. A simple evaluation reveals that the FFT inherently has a relatively high degree of computation per data word, or compute intensity. This high compute intensity is lost when the FFT computation is reduced to simple vector operations. Viewing the algorithm from a high level and exploiting compute intensity is the key to achieving high performance on parallel computers such as the CRAY APP.

This paper describes how high compute intensity programming techniques combined with algorithms in the literature can result in efficient single- and multi-dimensional FFTs on large numbers of processors on the CRAY APP. The CRAY APP is a shared-memory parallel computer based on the Intel i860 microprocessor. It incorporates up to 84 i860s in an architecture which allows for very efficient gang scheduling and barrier synchronization. FFT performance figures for various data set sizes and processor configurations are included.

1.0 INTRODUCTION

Algorithm advances in recent years by Bailey [1][2] and others [3][4][5] have resulted in improved power-of-two FFT performance on vector and parallel-vector computers. The difficulties presented by power-of-two memory strides and the potential pitfalls of computing out of a hierarchical memory system have largely been overcome. An extension of these concepts can be used to achieve high FFT performance on the emerging class of microprocessor-based parallel computers. These systems typically have lower main memory bandwidth than traditional parallel-vector supercomputers, and rely heavily on effective use of code and data caches for high performance. Effective management of the memory hierarchy and utilization of unit strides remain important considerations in obtaining optimal performance on these systems.

In [2], Bailey reports that the performance of a radix-4 implementation of his vector FFT algorithm on the CRAY-2 is significantly faster than the corresponding radix-2 implementation. This is due to the fact that radix-4 iterations require only half the number of data accesses to main memory. This observation points to the fact that compute intensity [6], the number of computations performed on each data word accessed from main memory, increases with the radix of the FFT butterfly computations. An extrapolation and slight variation of this simple observation results in an FFT algorithm which can deliver significantly high performance on computer systems with only a fraction of the main-memory bandwidth found in traditional parallel-vector supercomputers.

Sections 2 and 3 outline the concept of *Compute Intensity* and describe the implications of this concept for FFT algorithms. Section 4 describes an algorithm for multiple 1D complex FFTs which exploits the concept of compute intensity. For reference, section 5 gives a brief outline of the CRAY APP. The sections which follow provide performance data for FFT algorithms implemented on the CRAY APP. Performance in excess of 2 Gflops is achieved on multiple 1D FFTs in 32-bit precision. Performance approaching 1 Gflop is achieved performing multi-dimensional FFTs and very large 1D FFTs in 32-bit precision. The algorithm described here represents a slight variation on algorithms previously described in the literature. It is unique primarily in its application of these techniques to optimize the performance of the FFT algorithm on bandwidth-limited parallel systems incorporating cache-based microprocessors.

2.0 Compute Intensity

The term *Compute Intensity* [6] is defined as follows:

$$Compute \ Intensity = \frac{Total \ Number \ of \ Operations}{Number \ of \ Input \ \& \ Output \ Points}$$

For numerical computations such as the FFT, the operation count used in calculating Compute Intensity is based on floating-point computations. Since a radix-2 complex FFT calculation of length N requires

$$5Nlog_2N$$

floating-point operations on N complex words, it has an intensity of:

$$I = \frac{5Nlog_2N}{4N} = \frac{5}{4}log_2N$$

The FFT, like many algorithms commonly used in technical computing, has a compute intensity that grows with problem size [10]. The intensity of an algorithm can be used as a metric to determine the performance potential of the memory system on a given computer.

$$Performance \ Potential \ = \ Intensity \times Memory \ Bandwidth$$

or

$$\frac{Operations}{Second} = \frac{Operations}{Word} \times \frac{Words}{Second}$$

This definition is independent of the floating-point processing capabilities of a given machine. It is an architectural parameter that determines the maximum performance a memory system can sustain for a given algorithm assuming that memory bandwidth is used efficiently and is saturated. Many architectures have higher performance potential based on memory bandwidth than based on the more traditional metric of peak Mflops. For example, a radix-2 complex FFT of length 256 has an intensity of

$$I = \frac{5}{4}log_2256 = \frac{5}{4} \times 8 = 10$$

Thus, a relatively modest 250 megawords/sec of memory bandwidth can support

$$10 \ \frac{Flops}{Word} \ \times \ 250 \ \frac{Megawords}{Second} \ = \ 2500 \ MFLOPS$$

performing multiple complex FFTs of length 256. In the following sections, it will be shown that an appropriate FFT algorithm implemented on the CRAY APP can approach this performance level.

3.0 Compute Intensity of the FFT

As noted in the introduction, the intensity of the FFT algorithm [7] increases with the radix of the implementation. To see this, disregard for a moment the issue of whether roots of unity are accessed in the inner loop. The basic component of any radix-2 FFT calculation (here we assume a decimation-in-frequency implementation) is the *butterfly* operation between 2 complex elements A and B:

$$C = \quad (A + B)$$
$$D = \Omega \times (A - B)$$

where Ω is the appropriate complex root of unity. These complex operations are performed using 6 real additions and 4 real multiplications. Since the complex words A and B must be fetched and the complex words C and D must be stored, the intensity of a radix-2 butterfly calculation is:

$$\frac{10 \ Floating \ Point \ Operations}{8 \ Memory \ Word \ Accesses} = 1.25$$

One alternative to the radix-2 algorithm is a radix-4 algorithm which is based on the following butterfly operation between 4 complex elements:

$$E = \quad (A + B + C + D)$$
$$F = \Omega_1 \times (A + Bi - C - Di)$$
$$G = \Omega_2 \times (A - B + C - D)$$
$$H = \Omega_3 \times (A - Bi - C + Di)$$

where i is equal to $\sqrt{-1}$. Radix-4 butterfly calculations require 22 real additions, 12 real multiplications, and 16 memory word accesses. Thus radix-4 butterflies have the following compute intensity:

$$\frac{34 \ Floating\text{-}Point \ Operations}{16 \ Memory \ Word \ Accesses} = 2.125$$

The graph in figure 1 shows the increasing intensity of radix-2^m FFT butterfly calculations as m increases. The figures are extrapolated for radices larger than 8. For comparison, the intensity of radix-2 FFTs of length 2^m is included as well.

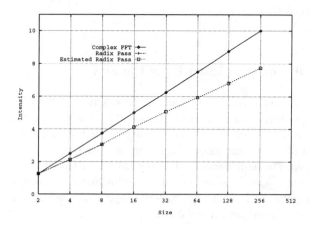

Figure 1: The compute intensity of FFT butterflies

As noted in section 2 the potential performance of an algorithm on a given main memory system increases linearly with its intensity. Thus the higher the radix factors for the FFT computation can be pushed, the higher the potential performance. The goal is to run as close to peak arithmetic speed as possible. However, the task of coding implementations beyond radix-4 or radix-8 quickly becomes untenable. By using a scheme that groups radix-2 butterfly computations together, a compromise can be made which exploits the intensity of high radix factors while not requiring undue programming effort.

4.0 High Intensity Multi-1D FFT Algorithm

4.1 The Algorithm

The power-of-two complex FFT algorithm can be viewed as consisting of arbitrarily large power-of-two radix passes. Assume we wish to perform an FFT on a vector X of length N, where

$$N = 2^n = 2^{n-k} 2^k$$

A standard radix-2 implementation performs n radix-2 passes, with $N/2$ radix-2 butterflies in each pass. A high radix implementation might perform only 2 passes, one of radix-2^{n-k}, and one of radix-2^k. While the radix-2 implementation requires $2n$ memory accesses for each complex element, the high radix implementation requires only 4 accesses to each element of X. This results in a several-fold increase in intensity even for FFTs of only a few thousand elements in length, and a corresponding decrease in the amount of main memory bandwidth required to per-

form the FFT algorithm at full processor speed. Figure 2 illustrates how the intensity of an FFT algorithm increases as the maximum radix factor increases.

The intensity values in figure 2 are calculated presuming that any power-of-two radix up to the maximum can be used in the calculation of the FFT of a given length. Thus if the maximum radix is 16, any FFT of size up to 16 can be done with a single pass. An FFT of size 32 would require one radix-16 pass and one radix-2 pass, and thus the intensity for an FFT of length 32 is less than that for an FFT of length 16. In general, as the maximum radix is increased, the intensity over a given range of FFT sizes increases.

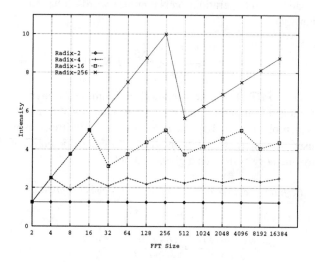

Figure 2: Increasing FFT intensity through high radix factors

There is a variation on a pure high radix implementation which provides the same intensity benefits but requires much less programming effort. To see this, view X as a 2^k by 2^{n-k} matrix as illustrated in figure 3.

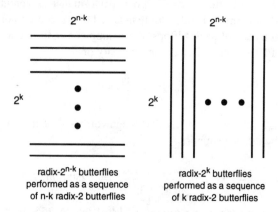

Figure 3: A 1D vector viewed as a 2D structure

Each row of the matrix represents a set of elements which would be grouped together to perform a radix-2^{n-k} butterfly. In this algorithm, each radix-2^{n-k} butterfly is actually performed using a sequence of radix-2 butterflies. This equates to performing a radix-2^{n-k} butterfly on each row without going to the trouble of eliminating redundant operations. The necessary roots of unity for performing each of the radix-2 butterflies can either be gathered from a standard radix-2 table, or can be pre-generated in a table that ensures stride one accesses will always be used. Once the row butterflies are complete, each column is processed using similar radix-2^k butterflies. The results must then be transposed to restore natural order to the output vector.

Given that this algorithm is intended for use on multiple relatively short vectors, one or more of the rows and columns can easily be contained in a microprocessor data cache. The intensity of a high radix butterfly implemented in this manner is slightly higher than that found in a true high radix butterfly (figure 1), resulting in a slight sacrifice of efficiency. However, the number of operations required remains identical to a radix-2 implementation. In what follows, the term *overpass* is used to distinguish high radix passes implemented in this manner from true radix-2^k passes, since the goal of this technique is to minimize the number of passes over data stored in main memory. The discussion which follows assumes a maximum of two overpasses are required to perform the full FFT calculation. A generalization to more than two overpasses is straightforward [5], but results in optimization issues that can largely be avoided when only two overpasses are required.

This algorithm is identical to that outlined in [1], with the exception that true 2^{n-k}-length or 2^k-length FFTs are not performed on the rows and columns of the matrix. Using roots of unity generated for a true 2^n-length FFT eliminates the need to perform the element-wise twiddle factor multiplication required in Bailey's 4-step FFT. Eliminating this step reduces the required number of operations and minimizes the number of roots of unity that must be maintained in the data cache. Maintaining unit stride accesses to the table elements requires the generation of a table that is up to twice as large as usual. However, since the algorithm is intended for use on multiple relatively short vectors, the requirement for twice the usual number of roots of unity is not particularly burdensome.

On systems such as the CRAY APP, which can perform power-of-2 memory strides at high bandwidth, the transpose can be performed on-the-fly during the vector store operations following the column FFTs. This results in only 2 passes through the data stored in main memory. If the transpose operation must be performed explicitly at the end of the algorithm, then two more accesses per word are required, resulting in a total of 3 passes through the data in main memory.

4.2 Data Access Patterns

The advantages of this algorithm become immediately apparent in systems which incorporate multiple cache-based microprocessors. The higher the intensity of an algorithm, the fewer transfers required between main memory and the on-chip data cache. As mentioned in the introduction, maintaining unit strides throughout the course of an algorithm is as important on cache-based microprocessors as it is on vector processors. Many microprocessors are designed for use with cache-line-based memory systems, and can maintain high external bus bandwidths only on unit stride accesses. Other processors, such as the Intel i860XR, provide full bus bandwidth for arbitrarily strided vector accesses, but have a limited Translation Lookaside Buffer reach (256K bytes on the i860XR) [9]. As a result, striding across the rows of a large matrix can degrade memory performance by an order of magnitude.

To perform an ordered FFT overpass internal to the processor data cache requires space for input data, output data, and roots of unity. If $D = 2^d$ is the number of real words available in the data cache, the largest power-of-two radix overpass that can be processed completely internal to the data cache is of size $D/8$. In the discussion which follows,

$$K = 2^k = 2^{d-3}$$

is referred to as the maximum *kernel size* for a given processor. For purposes of load-balancing in parallel systems, if more than one overpass is required it is optimal to set the kernel size as close as possible to the square root of the FFT size. This ensures that the number of processors required to saturate the available memory bandwidth will be minimized. It also increases the number of sections of data that can be processed in parallel.

The blocking that occurs naturally in a high radix FFT implementation results in a highly parallel algorithm. By grouping the blocks appropriately, efficiency of the memory access patterns can be optimized. Recall figure 3, which presented a vector X of length $N = 2^n$ as a 2^k by 2^{n-k} matrix. Assume for simplicity that $k = d - 3$ as outlined above. The memory access patterns for the two overpasses can be organized as in figure 4. In order to minimize self-interference in a set-associative data cache, it is advantageous to copy the vectors of data so they can be processed in contiguous regions of memory. On a vector-capable microprocessor such as the i860, these vectors can be explicitly moved in and out of the data cache using one- and two-dimensional vector load and store operations [11].

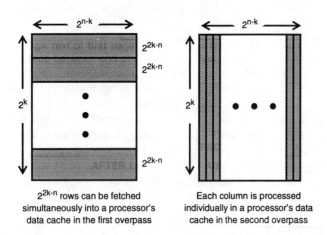

Figure 4: Organizing memory access patterns for vectorization

In this case, each column of the matrix is equal to the maximum kernel size. Since the rows are of length 2^{n-k}, it is possible to process

$$\frac{2^k}{2^{n-k}} = 2^{2k-n} = \frac{K^2}{N}$$

radix-2^{n-k} butterflies in the cache of a single processor. This suggests that for the first overpass the matrix should be divided into N/K sub-blocks, each consisting of K^2/N rows. The two-dimensional vector accesses required to fetch one of these sub-blocks into the data cache are as efficient as unit stride accesses as long as the main memory interleave does not exceed K^2/N. On cache-based processors which are not vector-capable (do not provide strided vector access at the word level), full bandwidth can be sustained as long as the cache line size does not exceed K^2/N words. Systems which rely on pre-fetch mechanisms to sustain full bandwidth are likely to incur some penalty in this step by fetching too far down each of the columns of the matrix.

The CRAY APP implementation of this algorithm is based on the Stockham FFT [2][3]. As a result, the first overpass can be performed in-place and the required vector store operations in the first overpass will also be as efficient as unit stride accesses. This will not be true for all choices [3] of the underlying FFT algorithm.

In the second overpass, the 2^{n-k} columns of the matrix match the maximum kernel size because k has been set equal to d - 3. Thus each column can be viewed as an independent parallel section, and accessed using unit stride vector fetches of length 2^k. However, the second overpass cannot be done in-place. For example, the radix-2^k butterfly on the first column of the matrix operates on elements $0,1,2,...,K-1$ of X, and produces output elements $0,N/K,2N/K,...,(K-1)N/K$. Thus the vector stores in this case must either be performed using power-of-two strides, or the vector must be explicitly transposed after the radix-2^k pass is completed. In either case, the second overpass will be much more efficient on processors which provide full speed word-level vector accesses.

4.3 Parallelization Issues

The algorithm described in section 4.1 is intended for use on multiple relatively small 1D vectors; on the columns of a matrix for example. Thus the roots of unity required for a given set of radix-2^{n-k} butterflies, or for a given radix-2^k butterfly, can be pre-generated and fetched into the data cache using unit stride accesses. These roots of unity can then be re-used by processing the same butterflies on several of the 1D vectors. It is for this reason that the fetching of roots of unity is not included in the compute intensity calculations given previously.

Figure 4 outlines the data access patterns for a single 1D vector. Figure 5 is similar but illustrates the data parallelization that occurs when the algorithm is applied to multiple 1D vectors.

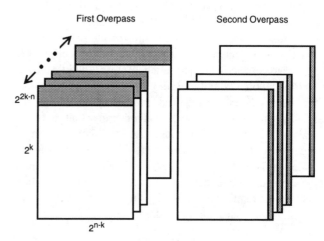

Each plane represents one vector. Each shaded sub-block uses the same roots of unity.

Figure 5: Blocking over multiple 1D vectors

Each processor can amortize the cost of fetching a given set of roots of unity over several of the input vectors by operating on the same sub-block in each of the vectors. By mapping appropriate groups of blocks to each processor, the cost of fetching roots of unity will be incurred only once in each overpass by most of the processors. Certain processors fetch two sets of roots of unity if their group of blocks spills over the last column of the input matrix.

Computation on each of the blocks can be performed completely independently. Thus in a matrix with L columns, there are $2^{n-k}L$ sections which can all be processed in parallel. For example, if 240 FFTs of length $2^{10} = 1024$ are to be processed using a kernel of size $2^8 = 256$, there are a total of $2^{n-k}*240 = 960$ parallel sections on which to operate in each overpass. Note that there is a requirement for a system-wide barrier synchronization between overpasses. Given appropriately low parallel processing overheads, there is enough work to allow several hundred processors to be used effectively.

5.0 The CRAY APP

5.1 CRAY APP Hardware

The CRAY APP is a multiple-bus, programmable parallel processor designed to accelerate a variety of applications [8,10]. Its architecture (Patent Pending) is illustrated in figure 6.

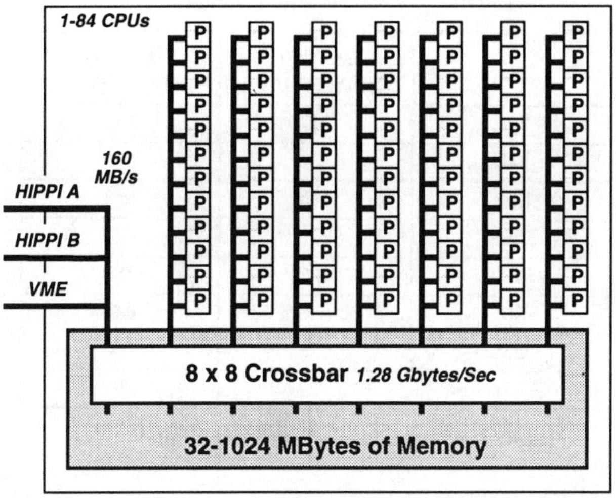

CRAY APP (Patent Pending)

Figure 6: The CRAY APP

The CRAY APP consists of 4 to 84 processing elements and 7 buses. Each bus supports up to 12 processing elements. The CRAY APP buses incorporate specialized hardware which allows all of the processors to work together efficiently on a single application [10]. The buses are connected to a low latency shared memory by a crossbar.

The CRAY APP can be configured with 1, 3, 5, or 7 buses and 4, 8, or 12 processing elements on each bus. A minimum configuration consists of 4 processing elements and a single bus while the maximum configuration consists of 84 processors and 7 buses. Any of these processor configurations can incorporate up to 1 Gbyte of main memory. The processing elements are based on the 40MHz Intel i860XR 64-bit microprocessor [8]. Each processor is rated at 80 Mflops for single-precision operations, 60 Mflops for double-precision operations, and 40 peak Mflops performing an equal number of double-precision multiplications and additions. Each bus provides a peak bandwidth of 160 megabytes per second. At a given time, only one processing element on each bus can access memory. In a seven-bus CRAY APP, up to seven processing elements can simultaneously access memory, which translates to a 1.12 Gbytes/second total transfer rate between processors and memory.

All of the buses connect to memory via a crossbar. The crossbar is an eight by eight circuit switched network that connects eight sources (address and data) to eight destinations (address and data). Seven of the crossbar sources are buses, while the eighth connects to a pair of bi-directional HiPPI interfaces. All eight crossbar destinations connect to the eight ports of memory, allowing up to eight simultaneous accesses to eight different areas in memory. These can be re-arbitrated every cycle without penalty. Conflicts on a memory port are queued until all requests are satisfied. The crossbar can provide a distinct 64-bit data word to each of the seven processor buses and one of the HiPPI interfaces every 20MHz cycle. The maximum memory latency is 150 ns (for comparison, CRAY Y-MP maximum latency is 100 ns).

A standard SPARC system is incorporated as a front-end to provide various system and network services. The CRAY APP itself runs under the control of a microkernel which is responsible for managing the execution of CRAY APP programs. The microkernel is responsible for functions such as initializing the processors, creating and deleting program processes and process threads, managing process stacks, handling exceptions, managing HiPPI data transfers, and switching contexts between users.

6.0 Performance

The high intensity multiple 1D FFT algorithm outlined in section 4 has been implemented on the CRAY APP. It provides a basis for multi-dimensional FFT algorithms as well as an algorithm for performing long 1D FFTs [1]. The following tables indicate the performance achieved by the CRAY APP on these algorithms. All calculations are performed in 32-bit precision, provide ordered (unscrambled) results, and use a fixed kernel size of 256. Standard radix-2 operation counts are used to compute Mflops, though some of the algorithms actually perform a larger number of operations. Table 1 illustrates the performance of the CRAY APP on the multiple 1D complex FFT algorithm.

FFT Length	Number of FFTs	MFLOPs CRAY APP/728	MFLOPs CRAY APP/756
16	65536	512	560
32	32768	792	982
64	16384	1049	1432
128	8192	1230	1892
256	4096	1350	2300
512	2048	936	1089
1024	1024	1025	1164
2048	512	1106	1272
4096	256	1157	1292
8192	128	1189	1264

Table 1: Multi-1D 32-bit Complex FFT Performance

The data sets used in the timings for table 1 were chosen to be of uniform size to eliminate performance effects caused by increased efficiency due to an increased data set size. Performance increases as the FFT size (and therefore the intensity) increases, then drops off when the FFT size increases from 256 to 512 points. This is the point at which the algorithm moves from requiring only 1 overpass to requiring 2 overpasses. Performance begins to ramp up again as the FFT size is further increased, but not as rapidly as would be expected based on increasing intensity. The reasons for this are not fully understood, but are believed to be attributable to TLB misses incurred during the two-dimensional vector fetches required in the first of the two overpasses.

The main memory bandwidth of the CRAY APP is saturated at 8 processors per bus using this algorithm and a 256 point kernel. Thus configurations larger than 56 processors see no added performance benefits unless a higher intensity algorithm can be used. Performance of the length

512 and 1024 cases is improved by performing an in-place (with bit-reversal) algorithm that dynamically generates the required table elements, thus requiring only one pass over the data in main memory (the i860XR data cache size is 8K bytes, so a maximum of 1024 32-bit complex words can be stored in the cache). This results in greatly increased compute intensity for these cases, and hence requires more processors to saturate the available memory bandwidth. These cases perform as shown in table 2 when this technique is used (note the larger processor configurations).

FFT Length	Number of FFTs	MFLOPs CRAY APP/756	MFLOPs CRAY APP/784
512	2048	1289	1880
1024	1024	1353	1910

Table 2: Alternate high intensity algorithm for sizes 512 and 1024

Using the multiple 1D FFT algorithm as a building block, Bailey's 4-step FFT algorithm is used to perform large 1D Complex FFTs. Timings for this algorithm on vectors up to 2^{22} points in length are reported in table 3. All timings were performed on a single complex vector. The twiddle factor multiplication required between the row and column FFT passes of Bailey's algorithm can actually be performed at the same time as the transpose by using several processors per bus on the CRAY APP. However, since the limited TLB reach of the i860XR results in severe performance degradation when striding across the rows of a large matrix, transposes are performed before the first step to get the rows in contiguous memory and after the last step to properly order the outputs. Thus the algorithm actually proceeds in 5 steps.

FFT Size	MFLOPs CRAY APP/728	MFLOPs CRAY APP/784
32K	247	292
64K	336	449
128K	415	588
256K	465	724
512K	422	780
1M	445	847
2M	508	762
4M	529	792

Table 3: Long 1D 32-bit Complex FFT Performance

Two-dimensional complex FFTs have been implemented as well. As in the 4-step FFT, large two-dimensional transforms require a matrix transposition in between the row and column FFTs in order to minimize the effects of TLB missing. However, only two transposes are required as opposed to the three required in the 4-step FFT. The performance results are shown in table 4. Note that for the smaller sizes a 28 processor system actually runs faster than an 84 processor system. This is believed to be due to the fact that the larger number of parallel sections per processor results in a reduced aggregate number of TLB misses. In essence, re-use of the TLB entries outweighs the benefits of using a larger number of processors in these cases. In practice the number of processors used can be artificially constrained to maximize performance on any configuration.

FFT Size	MFLOPs CRAY APP/728	MFLOPs CRAY APP/784
64^2	180	155
128^2	485	393
256^2	631	690
512^2	489	919
1024^2	542	1061
2048^2	762	830

Table 4: 2D 32-bit Complex FFT Performance

In order to accommodate a broader range of three-dimensional FFTs, radix-3 capability has been added for those cases in which only one overpass is required. Radix-5 capability is being added as well, but timings were not available at the time of this writing. In the case of 3D FFTs, three matrix transposes are required to leave the data in its original order. Table 5 lists the performance results for 3D FFTs on the CRAY APP using the multiple 1D algorithm described above.

FFT Size	MFLOPs CRAY APP/728	MFLOPs CRAY APP/784
32^3	280	260
48^3	375	427
64^3	424	542
81^3	558	730
108^3	548	799
128^3	497	758
144^3	548	848
162^3	613	943
243^3	672	1063

Table 5: 3D 32-bit Complex FFT Performance

7.0 Conclusion

A high intensity FFT algorithm results in the effective use of a large number of microprocessors on a shared-memory interconnect. By implementing simplified high radix passes, the speed of today's cache-based microprocessors can be fully exploited on FFT calculations. As on current vector supercomputers, maintaining stride one accesses is an important factor in achieving high performance on these microprocessors. This is particularly true on microprocessors which rely on cache-line-based memory accesses to maintain full off-chip bandwidth.

There are several important aspects of the FFT algorithm in general which have not been addressed in this paper. Real-to-complex FFTs, commonly encountered in seismic, signal, and image processing applications, have been implemented on the CRAY APP using the same basic algorithm (real FFTs of length N are performed via complex FFTs of length N/2) with comparable performance. Mixed radix capability has only been extended to the cases in which one overpass is required. Given the increased floating-point requirements of non-power-of-two radix passes, extending this technique to multiple overpasses should be well-suited for mixed-radix FFTs.

8.0 References

[1] Bailey, D. H., *FFTs in External or Hierarchical Memory*, Journal of Supercomputing, vol. 2 (1990), p. 23-35.

[2] Bailey, D. H., *A High-Performance FFT Algorithm for Vector Supercomputers*, International Journal of Supercomputer Applications, vol. 2 (1988), p. 82-87.

[3] Swarztrauber, P. N., *Vectorizing the FFTs*, Parallel Computations, 1982, p. 51-83.

[4] Swarztrauber, P. N., *FFT Algorithms for Vector Computers*, Parallel Computing, 1984, p. 45-63.

[5] Averbuch, A., et al, *A Parallel FFT on an MIMD Machine*, Parallel Computing 15 (1990), p. 61-74.

[6] Hockney, R. W., and Jesshope, C. R., *Parallel Computers Second Edition*, Johns Hopkins Press, 1986.

[7] Brigham, E. O., *The Fast Fourier Transform and its Applications*, Prentice Hall, 1988.

[8] *APP Programmers Guide*, Cray Research Superservers, Inc. April 1992.

[9] *i860 Microprocessor Family Programmer's Reference Manual*, Intel Corporation, 1991.

[10] Carlile, B. R., *Algorithms and Design: The CRAY APP Shared-Memory System*, COMPCON Spring '93 Digest of Papers.

[11] Miles, D., *Beyond Vector Processing: Parallel Programming on the CRAY APP*, COMPCON Spring '93 Digest of Papers.

Session 9:
Invited Presentations
Dave Dixon
Dennis Gannon

Session 9:
Minisymposium
Mass Storage
Chair: Dick Watson

Session 10:
Parallel Rendering
Chair: John Hart

A Novel Memory Access Mechanism for Arbitrary-View-Projection Volume Rendering

Tzi-cker Chiueh
Computer Science Department
State University of New York at Stony Brook
Stony Brook, NY 11794

chiueh@cs.sunysb.edu

Abstract

Direct rendering of volume data is both conceptually simpler and more capable of producing visually superior results than other rendering methods. Speical hardware architecture for direct volume rendering enables interactive exploration of volume data from arbitrary projection angles, which would otherwise take significantly longer due to its enormous computation and memory requirements. This paper proposes a new architecture called **FAVOR**, *which features a novel memory access scheme that eliminates the most critical bottleneck in hardware rendering machines, And provides conflict-free parallel accesses to volume data. A preliminary performance analysis shows that the extra overhead incurred by this scheme is rather marginal, within 20% of the target performance for a 16 frames/sec volume rendering rate at the 512x512x512 resolution.*

1. Introduction

Volume rendering is a rendering paradigm for volume data based on three-dimensional voxels, rather than polygons or other two-dimensional graphics primitives. Just as computer graphics has evolved from vector to raster rendering, it is generally believed [KAJI91] [KAUF91] that volume rendering will eventually replace raster rendering and become the dominant rendering technique. Compared to raster graphics, volume graphics enjoys many advantages [KAUF93]. Most notable among them are decoupling of scan conversion from rendering, the ability to render the inner structures as well as surfaces, the capability to integrate geometric and volumetric representations, and the performance advantage of precomputing and storing view-independent information [KAUF93].

Perhaps the biggest disadvantage of volume rendering, compared to polygonal rendering, is its computation and storage overhead. Consider a 512x512x512 cube, each voxel of which is assumed to be represented by 2 bytes. This requires 256 MBytes for a single cube. For real-time dynamic volume rendering (i.e., 30 frames per second), the total amount of data that needs to be touched within one second is 7.68 GBytes. As for computation requirement, it is estimated to be on the order of 10 GIPS for real-time dynamic volume visualization at 512^3 resolution. Based on the computation and storage requirements estimated above, it is clear that only supercomputers or special-purpose machines are capable of delivering the targeted level of performance. Unfortunately, after a closer examination even conventional supercomputers are hard pressed to perform this task. This is because volume rendering requires very little repeated computation on each voxel, it is moving the data around actually that accounts for a significant portion of the overall performance overhead. Conventional supercomputer memory systems simply don't have adequate latency and bandwidth capabilities for efficiently transferring such a large amount of data.

There are two kinds of real-time volume rendering: *dynamic* and *static*. The former refers to rendering volume data sequences at 30 frames per second. The latter refers to interactively exploring the same set of volume data from different projection angles. Dynamic volume rendering in general demands more computation and storage performance than static volume rendering. In fact, it is not even clear what kinds of peripheral devices (I/O or networks) are capable of supplying a data rate of 7.68 GBytes/sec, even when there is such a machine that can provide the targeted rendering performance. In this work, we aim at supporting real-time dynamic volume rendering. As a corollary, the proposed system should also be able to support interactive static volume rendering.

This paper proposes a volume rendering machine architecture called *FAVOR* (for **F**ast **A**rbitrary-**P**rojection-**A**ngle **VO**lume **R**endering), which features a novel data memory access mechanism that can provide parallel conflict-free memory access for *arbitrary-angle* projections on a cube of volume data. As a result, the entire machine architecture is greatly simplified compared to previous proposals to build similar machines. This mechanism is based on a tight coupling of hardware and algorithmic techniques, which collectively eliminate the critical memory access bottleneck in volume rendering.

The rest of this paper will be organized as follows. In Section Two, we will briefly describe the volume rendering algorithm to be implemented in hardware, to motivate the FAVOR architecture. In Section Three, the general system architecture and its memory system are described in detail. Section Four presents a preliminary evaluation of the performance of FAVOR. Related works in this area are described in Section Five for comparison and to set the contribution of this work in perspective. Section Six concludes this paper with a summary of main results and future plans.

2. Direct volume visualization algorithm

Visualizing volume data directly based on a voxel representation is a relatively young idea. Prior to its introduction, people use either interactive methods such as *wireframe contours*, or surface fitting methods such as *marching cubes*. These methods tend to put certain constraints on the kind of volume data that can be visualized (e.g., amorphous data does have "thin surfaces") or limits the way rendering is performed (e.g., surface fitting can't handle branching). Direct volume rendering presents a most general model for visualizing volume data, at the price of more expensive hardware requirements. There are basically two kinds of direct volume rendering methods: *projection algorithms* and *ray casting* algorithms. Projection algorithms such as *splatting* calculate the pixels in the image plane that are affected by each shaded voxel, and performs a front-to-back traversal of the volume data to blend the affected image quads associated with each voxel to form a complete image plane. Essentially the computation is

initiated from the object space to the image space.

Ray-casting is just the opposite in that the computation is from the image space to the object space. Because this allows a significant reduction in data manipulation, FAVOR chooses to implement ray casting directly in hardware. The basic algorithm of ray casting is as follows:

Given a projection angle;
Foreach pixel in the image plane
    Form a projection ray R into the volume data
    Obtain sample voxel values on R through interpolation
    Foreach sample v(i, j, k) on R, from front to back
        Check v(i, j, k) in the data classification table
        Find its corresponding normal, color, and opacity
        Weigh voxel color with opacity
        Form accumulated color and opacity values
    Endfor
    Pixel is assigned the final accumulated color
Endfor

The algorithm for color and opacity values accumulation depends on the applications, e.g., first opaque, last opaque, or α compositing. Because α compositing is the most general one, we will illustrate the architecture of FAVOR assuming the α compositing formulation. Let A_i and C_i denote the accumulated α and color values after the i-th sample on a projected ray, and α_i and c_i the opacity and color values associated with the i-th sample. The color and opacity value accumulation formulas are as follows

$$A_i = A_{i-1} + \left[1 - A_{i-1} \right] * \alpha_i \qquad (1)$$

$$C_i = C_{i-1} + \left[1 - A_{i-1} \right] * \alpha_i * c_i \qquad (2)$$

Because the rays projected from the image plane can be processed in parallel, ray casting provides abundant opportunities for parallelization. In addition, because rendering is based on rays emitted from the image plane, the computation complexity is affected more by the resolution of the image plane than that of the volume data. In particular, the computation complexity is $O(M^2)$ rather than $O(N^3)$, where M and N are the linear dimensions of the image plane and volume data cube, respectively. From a hardware standpoint, ray casting allows exploitation of concurrency in the form of both parallelism and pipelining, which collectively improves both latency and throughput, an important architectural consideration for real-time dynamic volume visualization. In contrast, projection methods require traversal of the volume data cube, regardless of the image plane resolution. Moreover, projection algorithms only offer voxel-level parallelism. Exploitation of higher levels of parallelism structures so far remain elusive. Therefore FAVOR chooses ray casting as the underlying algorithm for direct volume rendering.

3. Fast arbitrary-projection-angle volume rendering

FAVOR is designed to meet the following performance requirement: Volume rendering of a volume data cube sequence from arbitrary projection angles, with each cube at a 512x512x512 resolution, 16 cubes per second, and each voxel is 8-bit wide. Suppose the viewing image plane is also 512x512, then FAVOR needs to complete the processing of a ray cast from the image plane within $2^{-9} * 2^{-9} * 2^{-4}$ second, or roughly 256 nanoseconds. Recall that each ray potentially involves 512 voxels. This imposes a very high computation demand on the hardware architecture. Parallelism is a feasible solution but in itself doesn't solve the whole problem. The reason is that to support arbitrary projections of a volume data cube, the memory system must be able to provide the same data bandwidth independent of the data access pattern. Just as interleaved memory systems in conventional vector machines may suffer from bandwidth degradation due to bank conflicts, it is a challenging task to build a conflict-free volume data memory system that supports arbitrary projection views. FAVOR successfully solves this problem by carefully integrating hardware structures and software algorithms, as explained in Sections 3.2 and 3.3.

3.1. The system architecture

The basic system architecture of FAVOR is very similar to a generic multiprocessor, as shown in Figure 1. Volume data sets residing in the Volume Data Memory Subsystem, are accessed in parallel from the Compositing Processing Subsystem through a 64x512 programmable interconnection network. The memory subsystem consists of sixty-four banks, each of which internally assumes an interleaved memory structure. Details are in the next subsection. The network is implemented through a cascading series of multiplexers, demultiplexers, and buses, and

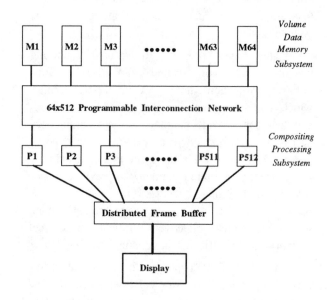

Figure 1   System Architecture of FAVOR

is capable of transporting sixty-four data elements from the memory subsystem to any 64-module subset of the processing subsystem. Each data element contains an 8-bit color and an 8-bit α value, and therefore is 16-bit wide. Interconnection networks are also internally pipelined to exploit various levels of concurrency. Each module in the compositing processing subsystem takes a pair of color and α values and implement the operations specified in Equations (1) and (2). Because multiplication and addition require only 8-bit-wide data paths, each processing module can be implemented in a single chip. Since data elements are retrieved from the memory subsystem sixty-four at a time, the compositing processing subsystem is decomposed into groups of sixty-four processors. Computation in one processor group could be overlapped with data movement in other processor groups. The results of the processing subsystem are sent to a distributed 2D frame buffer with multiple access ports for final display.

FAVOR exploits the parallelism in the ray casting algorithm in a very different way than conventional approaches. Instead of processing individual rays from the image plane independently, FAVOR manipulates a group of rays (called a *ray group*) one at a time. Consequently, instead of completing one ray every 256 nanoseconds, FAVOR attempts to complete 512 rays in 128 microseconds. As an example (see Figure 2), conventional architectures pipeline the

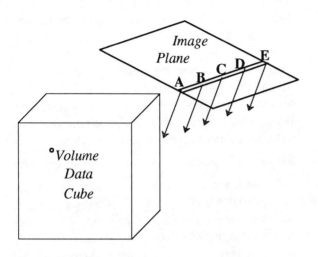

Figure 2   Ray-by-Ray vs Ray-Group Parallelism

processing of projection rays by completing the operations associated with ray A before starting the processing of ray B, and so on. FAVOR, on the other hand, processes the first voxels of rays A, B, C, D, and E, then the second voxels, the third voxels, and so on. This approach not only avoids the problem of processing ordering among the voxels within a projection ray, but also provides a framework for conflict-free parallel access to voxel data, as explained next.

3.2. Memory hardware

Given the system architecture described above, it should be clear that the key to the success of the entire system is whether the memory subsystem is capable of timely supplying the data needed for real-time rendering of *arbitrary projections* of a volume data sequence. If the volume rendering algorithm exploits ray-by-ray parallelism, it is impossible to build a memory system that can guarantee parallel conflict-free accesses for arbitrary projections. To see why this is the case, suppose the memory subsystem is organized as an interleaved memory with a linear bank selection function as follows:

$$Bank \ \ Number = \Big[a*X + b*Y + c*Z \Big] \ mod \ N \ \ (3)$$

where X, Y, and Z are the 3D coordinates of a voxel, N is the number of modules in the memory subsystem, and a, b, and c are integer coefficients. Given a voxel's 3D coordinate, one can determine the number of the memory bank in which it physically resides according to Equation (3). Using non-linear functions

of 3D coordinates is possible but is computationally infeasible for high-performance systems and therefore is excluded from further consideration. If rendering proceeds on a ray-by-ray basis, the memory subsystem needs to transfer one ray of data simultaneously to the compositing processors. In other words, each voxel on an arbitrary ray must be on a different bank to avoid contention on the memory ports. Mathematically, it means that given a ray, any two voxels on that ray (X_1, Y_1, Z_1) and (X_2, Y_2, Z_2) must satisfy the following condition:

$$\Big[a*\Big[X_1 - X_2 \Big] + b*\Big[Y_1 - Y_2 \Big] + c*\Big[Z_1 - Z_2 \Big] \Big] \ mod \ N \neq 0$$

$$(4)$$

However, if the projection ray happens to be perpendicular to the vector (a, b, c), then there is no way such a condition can be satisfied. Therefore a parallel memory system that provides conflict-free access to any arbitrary ray on a cube is theoretically impossible.

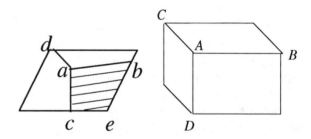

Image   Plane   Data   Cube

Figure 3   Ray Group Retrieval of Volume Data

To solve this problem, we abandon the ray-by-ray rendering approach. Instead, a group of rays are processed simultaneously. By retrieving corresponding voxels on a ray group concurrently, it becomes possible to access these voxels without causing bank conflicts. Let's call the voxel of a ray that is i voxels away from the root of the ray (in the image plane) the i-th voxel. We will call the set of i-th voxels of a ray group the i-th *voxel front* of a ray group. The key idea of this approach is to decompose the pixels on the image plane into subsets and the projection rays associated with each subset of pixels form a ray group. Instead of decomposing the pixels based on a row-major or column-major ordering, the decomposition depends on how the three major axes of the data cube are projected on the image plane. For example, in Figure 3, the closest three major axes of the data cube, **AB, AC,** and **AD,** are projected onto the image plane as **ab, ac,** and **ad** respectively.

The projections of the axes decompose the image plane into at most three regions (could be fewer, depending on the rendering projection angle). Each such region is further decomposed into a set of pixel lines that are in parallel with either of the region's associated projections of the major axes. The projection rays of a pixel line form a ray group. The advantage of this organization is that each voxel front of such a ray group is guaranteed to form a voxel line that is in parallel with the corresponding major axis in the data cube. Therefore, as long as the memory subsystem guarantees conflict-free parallel accesses to voxel lines that are in parallel with three major axes, this access scheme allows each voxel front of such a ray group to be retrieved without contention. For example in Figure 3, the **aceb** region of the image plane is decomposed into a set of pixel lines, each of which is in parallel with **ab,** the projection of **AB.** Each pixel line corresponds to a ray group. Consequently the voxel fronts of each ray group form a voxel line that parallels with **AB.** Essentially the traversing order of the pixels on the image plane are arranged according to the user-specified rendering projection angle so that parallel accesses to the voxel fronts of a ray group never cause conflicts.

Ray-group-based parallel rendering, together with projection-angle-specific image plane traversal order, significantly reduces the bandwidth requirements of the volume data memory subsystem. Specifically the memory subsystem now only needs to support conflict-free parallel accesses to voxel lines in parallel with three major axes (these voxel lines will be referred as *beams.*), *regardless of the rendering projection angle.* Assuming a bank number formulation in the form of Equation (3), to provide conflict-free parallel accesses to beams, (a, b, c) must not be perpendicular to (1, 0, 0), (0, 1, 0), and (0, 0, 1). A simple qualified choice of (a, b, c) is (1, 1, 1). Therefore the bank number computation becomes

$$Bank\ Number = \left\lceil X + Y + Z \right\rceil \ mod\ N \qquad (5)$$

For data to move from the memory system to the processors smoothly, both the memory subsystem and the interconnection network need to be conflict-free. The current interconnection network design is only capable of transferring sixty-four data items at a time. The reasons for this design decision are twofold. First, a 512x512 interconnect costs significantly more than a 64x512 network. Second, the system simply cannot exploit the bandwidth provided by a 512x512 network anyway, because it is very difficult for the memory subsystem to match that bandwidth. Because the targeted ray access cycle time is 256 ns, and each memory access is decomposed into 8 subtransactions (because $\frac{512}{64} = 8$), each memory bank in Figure 1 needs to supply a data item every 32 ns. Currently DRAM chips have at best 40 ns access time and 70 ns cycle time. One can choose to use SRAMs or high-end DRAMs, but this seems excessively expensive considering the amount of memory needed for a data cube.

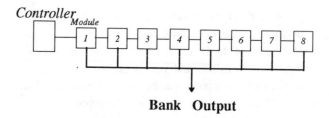

Bank Output

Figure 4   Module Interleaving Inside a Memory Bank

We decide to apply the idea of interleaving inside each memory bank shown in Figure 1. As shown in Figure 4, a memory bank consists of 8 memory modules managed by a controller. The data in a memory bank are sequentially interleaved on eight memory modules. Interleaving overlaps data transfers with data accesses, and therefore mask the relative long latency of slower DRAMs. From a memory bank's standpoint, one data item is output every 32 ns. But from a memory module's standpoint, one data item is output every 256 ns, which is within the capability of commodity DRAM chips. In summary, the memory subsystem design exploits intra-bank interleaving and inter-bank parallelism to achieve the 256 ns targeted ray access cycle time for dynamic real-time volume rendering.

3.3. Access algorithms

Given the position of the image plane and its normal vector, the access algorithm locates the closet vertex of the data cube to the image plane, calculates the projections of the three major axes spanning from this vertex, and determines a set of pixel lines whose corresponding ray groups will be the basic unit for parallel rendering. We will illustrate the access algorithm by considering four cases, from simple to complicated. Without loss of generality, let's assume that the data cube is characterized by (0, 0, 0) and (511, 511, 511), and the image plane is characterized by (0, 0, 0) and (511, 0, 511), as shown in Figure 5(a). Further assume that the closet vertex is (0, 0, 0), and its three spanning axes are (511, 0, 0), (0, 511, 0), and (0, 0, 511). We will also assume that the center of the image plane is always aligned with the center of the data cube.

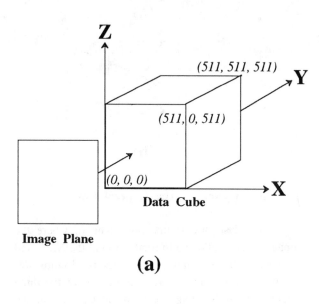

(a)

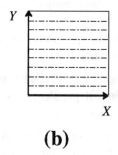

(b)

Figure 5   The First Case

In the first case, the normal vector of the image plane is (0, 1, 0) as shown in Figure 5(a). This case corresponds to orthographic projection. Since the normal vector is in parallel with one of the axes, the Y axis, only the X and Z axes can be projected to the

image plane. The resultant projections and pixel lines are shown as arrows and dashed lines respectively in Figure 5(b). Because the projections of the X and Y axes are perpendicular with each other, there will only be a single partition of the image plane. All the pixel lines are in parallel with the projections of either the X axis or Y axis.

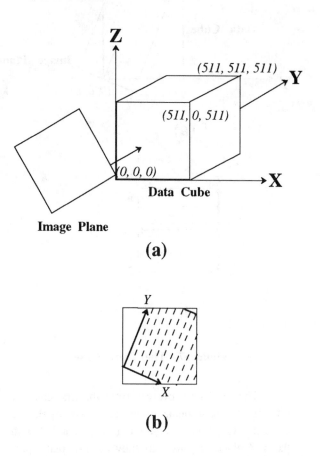

Figure 6   The Second Case

In the second case (shown in Figure 6(a)), the image plane is rotated around the Y axis by θ, and the normal vector remains the same as the first case. Again only the X and Z axes will have projections on the image plane, and they are perpendicular with each other. The resultant pixels lines, shown in Figure 6(b), are chosen to be in parallel with the Y axis' projection because this generates fewer pixel lines than the other possibility where pixels lines are in parallel with the X axis' projection. Note that some of the pixel lines are no longer 512-pixel wide. This could make a performance difference because the hardware at most handles 64 rays at a time. Fewer rays in a ray group could reduce the number of iterations to process a ray group.

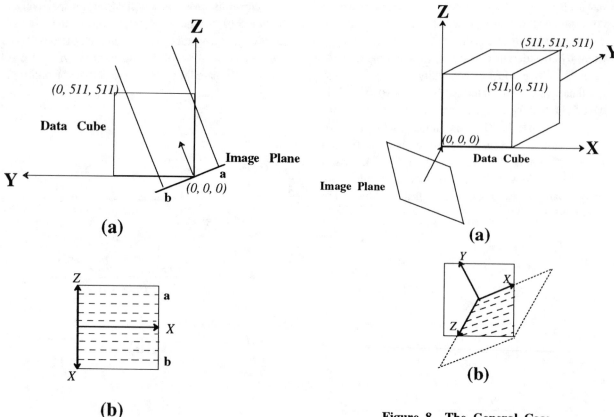

(a)

(b)

Figure 7   The Third Case

Figure 8   The General Case

The third case evolves from the first case by rotating the image plane around the X axis by θ. The corresponding normal vector is now in parallel with the Y-Z plane. Figure 7(a) shows a Y-Z plane perspective of the situation. Figure 7(b) shows the projections of the X, Y, and Z axes on the image plane. Although the image plane are partitioned into two regions, the pixel lines in each region are all in parallel with the projection of the X axis. Although the width of each pixel line in this case is 512-pixel wide, the depth of the projection ray groups of the pixel lines varies depending on the locations of the pixel lines. For example, shown in Figure 7(a) the projection rays from the pixels on the pixel line denoted by **a** intersect with the data cube significantly less than those associated with the pixel line denoted by **b**, and the extent of intersection determines the ray's depth, i.e., the number of voxel fronts to be processed in a ray group.

The last case is the most general, where the image plane is allowed to rotate around the X, Y, and Z axes by θ_x, θ_y, and θ_z respectively. Figure 8(a) shows such a scenario. The projections of the three main axes on the image plane in this case are shown in Figure 8(b). These projections decompose the image plane into three regions. For each region, the following algorithm is used to determine the corresponding pixel lines:

[1]   Use the region's associated two projections to form a minimal parallelogram that can cover the entire region.

[2]   Choose the orientation of the pixel lines in the region so that the number of pixel lines is minimized.

This algorithm applies to regions that contain multiple vertices of the image plane. As an example, Figure 8 (b) shows how the region bounded by the projections of the X and Z axes are covered by a parallelogram formed by these projections, and the final pixel lines are chosen to minimize the number of pixel lines in the region. Again the pixel lines are represented by dashed lines. In this case, neither the width nor the depth of the pixel lines is 512-pixel long.

4. Performance evaluation

Although the memory access scheme described above guarantees conflict-free parallel accesses to the volume data memory regardless of the projection angle of volume rendering, there is an implicit performance overhead associated with this approach. This scheme may need to process more ray groups than the conventional approach, where the number of ray groups is always 512 for a 512x512x512 cube. This can be seen from Figure 8(b). Since the average width of the pixel lines is less than 512, and there are totally 512x512 pixels on the image plane, it follows that more than 512 pixel lines are needed to render the entire image plane. In the worst case, this scheme may need to process three times as many pixel lines as the conventional approach.

However, there are two reasons why these "extra" pixel lines won't have as significant a performance impact as they seemingly suggest. First, because the memory hardware handles 64 rays at a time, additional pixel lines don't necessarily imply more processing overhead. For example, a 512-pixel pixel line takes as much processing as two 252-pixel lines. Second, the pixel lines near the boundary of the image plane typically correspond to projection rays that have significant less depth than those at the center of the plane. Because the processing time of a projection ray in FAVOR depends on its depth, some of the extra pixel lines don't cost as much processing overhead as others.

To evaluate the performance of this scheme, we will use the number of memory cycles as the metric. In a memory cycle, at most 64 data elements can be transferred from the memory system to the processors. A group of N rays, each of which is M-voxel deep, costs

$$\lceil \frac{N}{64} \rceil * M \tag{6}$$

Table I shows the number of memory cycles needed by the proposed scheme for rendering a volume data set under different projection angles. Projection angles are specified as combinations of θ_x, θ_x, and θ_x, which denote the rotation angles in degrees around the X, Y, and Z axes. The order of rotation is X first, then Y, and Z. Again assume Figure 5(a) as

the initial condition. Performance is expressed as a percentage of the targeted latency, which is $512x512x\frac{512}{64}=2,097,152$ memory cycles.

θ_x	θ_y	θ_x	Percentage of Targeted Latency
0	0	0	100%
0	30	0	85%
30	0	0	90%
30	30	30	117%
30	45	60	105%
45	30	45	98%
60	60	30	95%

Table I Performance Estimate of FAVOR's Memory Access Scheme

We simulate the operation of the memory access algorithm, down to the level of individual projection rays, and calculate the number of memory cycles needed to completely render a 512x512x512 cube on a 512x512 image plane according to Equation (6). The first three entries correspond to the first three cases considered above. The second case is faster than the target latency because the rays associated with some pixels on the image plane don't intersect with the cube and therefore incur no processing overhead. The third case is faster because the depth of some of the projection rays is smaller than 512. The last four entries correspond to the fourth case. Surprisingly there are cases that actually incur less delay than the target latency. Most importantly, the gap between the target latency and the slower cases is within 20%, as opposed to a factor of three. Of course, these are just preliminary performance results. More extensive simulation or theoretical analysis should give a better estimate of the bounds of this gap.

5. Related works

There are several machines that have been or being built currently specifically for accelerating computer graphics. University of North Carolina at Chapel Hill have built a *Pixelplane* [FUCH89] machine that uses of-the-shelf i860 processors connected through a ring-like network. This machine is designed mainly for 2D geometry processing, although relatively fast volume rendering performance results have also been reported from *Pixelplane*. The follow-on project of *Pixelplane* is *Pixelflow*, which takes a network compositing approach to provide scalability across large-scale cinema-realism rendering. The basic graphics primitives used by *Pixelflow* are still 2D objects rather than voxels.

The group in State University of New York at Stony Brook pioneered the hardware architecture for direct volume rendering. *Cube-I* [KAUF88] is based on a cubic frame buffer and a voxel multiple write (VMWB) bus, and is capable of supporting 16x16x16 resolution real-time rendering. *Cube-II* is basically a single-chip implementation of *Cube-I*. *Cube-III* aims at supporting roughly the same resolution as FAVOR but is based on a ray-by-ray approach for parallel rendering. This machine consists of a 3D memory system, a 2D memory system, and a cone processor tree that perform composition and shading.

The ray casting machine [KEDE89] from Duke University is a system that is specifically designed for Curve Solid Classification, a computational utility central to many applications of geometric modeling. The ray-casting machine classifies a regular lattice of parallel lines, and is a parallel, pipelined, bit-serial machine made out of two bit-serial building blocks: Classification Combine processor and incremental primitive classifier. This machine doesn't directly support voxel manipulation, either.

6. Conclusion

Volume rendering to raster rendering is what raster graphics to vector graphics. Because of its uniformity, voxel representation is emerging as the dominant data structure for 3D objects. Direct volume rendering is conceptually simpler and capable of producing visually better results than any other approaches. Despite its numerous advantages, the enormous demands of direct volume rendering on memory and computation could seriously limit its wide-spread use. Although memory and processors are getting cheaper and faster, designing a hardware architecture to exploit the inherent parallelism in volume rendering is still a technical challenge. The most critical bottleneck of such machines may well be the memory subsystem, especially for dynamic real-time rendering of volume data from arbitrary projection angles.

This paper proposes a architecture called *FAVOR*, which features a novel memory access scheme that carefully integrates software algorithms and hardware structures to provide conflict-free parallel memory access. The key idea of this scheme is to process a group of rays simultaneously rather than one ray at a time. By carefully choosing a right rendering order for the pixels on the image plane, the system guarantees that the voxel front of each ray group will form a voxel line (called a *beam*) that is in parallel with one of the main axes. Because the memory hardware can provide conflict-free parallel access to voxels on a beam, the integration of software algorithms and hardware structures collectively ensures that parallel memory accesses to volume data never cause contentions.

We have carried out a preliminary performance analysis of the proposed memory access scheme. The results show that the performance overhead is significantly lower than suggested by the number of pixel lines. In this performance study, we ignore the complex address generation issues related to discrete geometry, and assumes a smooth pipeline between pixel lines and image regions. To fully validate the proposed scheme, more detailed and extensive simulations are needed and will be performed in the future.

Reference

[FUCH89]   H. Fuchs, et al., "Pixel-Planes 5: A Heterogeneous Multiprocessor Graphics System," Computer Graphics (July 1989) vol.23, no.3, p. 79-88. SIGGRAPH '89 Conference Proceedings. Boston, MA, USA. July 1989.

[KAJI91]   J. Kajiya, Keynote Address at SIGGRAPH '91.

[KAUF88]   A. Kaufman, R. Bakalash, "Memory and Processing Architecture for 3D Voxel-Based Imagery," IEEE Computer Graphics and Applications (Nov. 1988) vol.8, no.6, p. 10-23.

[KAUF91]   A. Kaufman, *Volume Visualization*, IEEE Computer Society Press, 1991.

[KAUF93]   A. Kaufman, D. Cohen, R. Yagel, "Volume Graphics". To appear in IEEE Computer Magazine.

[KEDE89]   G. Kedem, J. Ellis, "The Ray-Casting Machine," *Parallel Processing for Computer Vision and Display*, Leeds, UK, 12-15 Jan. 1988, p. 378-401.

Efficient Feed-Forward Volume Rendering Techniques
for Vector and Parallel Processors

Raghu K. Machiraju and Roni Yagel

Department of Computer and Information Science
The Ohio State University

Abstract

Rendering volumes represented as a 3D grid of voxels requires an overwhelming amount of processing power. In this paper we investigate efficient techniques for rendering semi-transparent volumes on vector and parallel processors. Parallelism inherent in a regular grid is obtained by decomposing the volume into geometric primitives called beams, slices and slabs of voxels. By using the adjacency properties of voxels in beams and slices, efficient incremental transformation schemes are developed. The slab decomposition of the volume allows the implementation of an efficient parallel feed-forward renderer which includes the splatting technique for image reconstruction and a back-to-front method for creating images. We report the implementation of this feed-forward volume renderer on a hierarchical shared memory machine with individual pipelined processors.

1: Introduction

Representation by *spatial-occupancy enumeration* methods allows a simple yet versatile method for the generation and display of three-dimensional objects. The most common spatial enumeration is obtained when a solid is decomposed into identical cells called *voxels* which are arranged in a fixed, regular, rectilinear grid. To ascribe visual properties, spatial occupancy functions and colors are assigned to voxels. *Binary* voxel [9] and *variable-density* voxel techniques ([2], [11],[12]) arise from the use of binary and continuous spatial occupancy functions, respectively.

Several methods exist for the rendering of volumes. One class of these methods converts the voxel representation into surface and line primitives [13]. However, methods of this class suffer from various disadvantages that mainly arise from the ambiguity of determining the exact position of the surface. As an alternative, **direct methods** have been developed to render volumes. These methods can be classified as *object order* or *image order*. Object order methods require the enumeration of all voxels of a volume and the determination of the affected pixels on a screen. Image order techniques, on the other hand, deter-

mine all the voxels of a volume which affect a given pixel on the screen. Hybrid methods exist in which the volume is traversed in both object and image order. Westover [24] employs the synonymous terms *feed-forward* and *backward-feed* for object and image order methods, respectively. We shall also use these terms to classify volume rendering methods.

Feed-forward methods are also called *projective* or *element tossing* methods. The viewing transformation matrix is applied to all voxels enumerated in some order, thus providing an intermediate volume which is then projected onto a two dimensional screen. Feed-forward methods are easy to implement. However, such a direct application of the transformation matrix causes the appearance of holes (absence of voxels) or doublings (presence of multiple voxels) in pixels of the image. **Reconstruction** in three-dimensions can be performed to annul the effect of these artifacts. Hanrahan proposed a method of decomposing the transformation matrix into a series of lower dimensional shears [8]. Such a decomposition would allow for the easier supersampling operation along a single dimension [19]. Splatting [24] is another reconstruction technique employed to reduce the impact of holing and doubling artifacts. **Hidden volume elimination** is used to determine the visibility order of the voxels. Several standard methods used for hidden surface elimination can be employed fruitfully. Z-buffer and front-to-back [18] and back-to-front [5] methods have been commonly employed, while the A-buffer [3] method has been used for rendering gaseous volumes.

Backward-feed methods, which include ray-casting, have been specifically developed for rendering volumes. In ray-casting, rays are cast from the observer's eye location through the pixels of the image. The color assigned to the pixel is that of the background or the accumulated color obtained by traversing the object. Holes are not created in images rendered by backward-feed methods. However, some reconstruction is still needed to remove the effects of aliasing and is usually achieved through supersampling techniques. Backward-feed methods, although simple to describe, require sophisticated techniques for efficient implementation [26].

© 1993 ACM 0-8186-4340-4/93/0011 $1.50

Hybrid methods have been investigated and reported ([22], [25]). These methods can combine the advantages of both the forward and backward methods. Unlike the backward-feed methods, these are simple to implement and they do not suffer from the holing and doubling problems of the feed-forward methods.

In this paper we consider only the feed-forward method of volume rendering. Our selection of this class stems from our desire to develop real-time, fast methods which could be used for the display of images of intermediate quality. Our feed-forward renderer consists of four components or stages, namely transformation, shading, reconstruction and display. These stages are arranged in the form of a pipeline with the input volume being first provided to the transformation stage. By using different permissible permutations of the stages in the pipeline or by using different techniques within a stage, different implementations can be obtained.

We describe the various stages of our feed-forward rendering method in section 2. Also, the rationale for a parallel implementation is discussed therein. In section 3 we describe various decompositions of a volume into different regular geometrical primitives. These primitives allow the development of efficient techniques for transforming and rendering volumes on vector and parallel processors. Section 4 first describes efficient techniques to transform volumes on vector and pipelined processors, and then a parallel implementation of our feed-forward method. Experimental results are presented in section 5 and section 6 contains some concluding remarks.

2: Feed Forward Volume Rendering

2.1: The Rendering Pipeline

The feed forward volume rendering pipeline takes its input from object space. The input volume is in the form of a mesh of size n^3, where n is the resolution along each of the three axes. In this work we assume that the input is composed of semi-transparent voxels each having an opacity value. Both orthographic and perspective projections are employed by the pipeline for viewing.

The volume is transformed first. Voxels are enumerated in an ordered fashion and are individually transformed. The order of enumeration is usually determined by visibility considerations and is described in a following paragraph. **Transformation** of a voxel is effected by multiplying its coordinate vector with the transformation matrix. The transformation matrix is constructed from viewing parameters such as the position of the eye and the direction of the view vector.

To get realistic images, **shading** is necessary. Shading requires the determination of the normal in either space. The normal can either be computed analytically for geomet-

rical objects (spheres, cones, etc.) or estimated by using gray-level gradient schemes [16]. **Reconstruction** is achieved by splatting each voxel onto a two-dimensional image plane. Splatting requires the projection of a voxel onto a two-dimensional image plane of size m^2, where m is the screen dimension. The effect of a splat is often compared to throwing a snow-ball onto a glass window. All pixels lying in the *footprint* or extent of influence of a voxel are affected by its splat through a change in color and opacity. This dissipative operation causes existing holes to fill up and reduce the effect of doubling, since less of a voxel resides at each pixel site after splatting. The footprint controls the efficacy of the splatting operation. In practice, the footprint is a two-dimensional table and usually implements discrete box or Gaussian filters. Correct reconstruction requires that the voxels be splatted in the back-to-front or front-to-back visibility order. For a given volume orientation it is possible to determine this order *a priori* [5]. This visibility order is used to enumerate the voxels in object space for transformation.

Compositing is performed using the *over* operator [17]: when compositing back-to-front a new pixel of opacity a_n and color c_n onto another pixel existing on the image having color C_{in} and opacity A_{in}, the resulting color C_{out} and opacity A_{out} are given by the equations listed below. Initially, C_{in} is set to the background color and A_{in} to zero.

$$A_{out} = a_n + A_{in} \cdot (1 - a_n)$$
$$C_{out} = c_n \cdot a_n + C_{in} \cdot (1 - a_n)$$

The sheer amount of data that arises even from a coarse resolution volume is enormous. A volume of 256x256x256 resolution requires that sixteen million voxels be processed. Real-time generation of intermediate quality images for most volumes severely taxes the capabilities of most sequential computers. It is therefore obvious that achieving real-time interaction with volumes calls for parallel processing. One option, which lacks generality, is based on special-purpose architectures [10]. Alternatively, increasingly available general-purpose parallel processors could be employed to reduce the total volume rendering time.

In this paper we report the implementation of a parallel feed-forward renderer, which has been incorporated in the Denga system of renderers [21]. The faster feed-forward method is used for previewing and scene composition while a ray-tracer is used only for final image production. Our renderer uses methods which can be implemented on any sequential or parallel computer. However, these methods find an especially efficient realization on some popular classes of parallel machines. Variations of these methods have been implemented on Silicon Graphics, CRAY-Y/MP, CM-2, and the PVM distributed system. In this paper we only report on our IBM Power Visualization System (PVS) implementation.

2.2: Volume Rendering on Parallel Machines

Some implementations of direct volume rendering have recently been reported for a variety of parallel architectures. A few of them exist on experimental parallel processors, such as the Princeton Engine [20] or the DASH parallel system [15]. Other implementations have been conducted on commercially available parallel machines such as the AMT DAP [1], Connection Machine CM-2 ([19], [20]), MasPar MP-1 ([25], [27]), Intel iPSC-2 [14], nCube [4], Silicon Graphics multiprocessor workstation [6] and network of Suns [24].

The viewing algorithms adopted in the afore-mentioned implementations are many and varied. Several are based on backward-fed methods. In [14] and [15] ray-casting is used, while in [19] our template-based ray-casting [26] was implemented. Others, including [1], [19], and [27] adopted a feed-forward method, wherein the multiple shear decomposition was implemented. Elvins's feed-forward method, on the other hand, included splatting as the reconstruction method of choice [4].

Efficient implementations of volume rendering methods on parallel machines are dependent on the class of the architecture, namely SIMD (Single-Instruction-Multiple-Data) or MIMD (Multiple-Instruction-Multiple-Data), the architecture of each processor of the machine ensemble (pipeline or vector architectures), memory organization (completely shared, hierarchical, or only local) and the interconnection network (mesh, hypercube, omega, or a bus). Also essential are the supported parallel programming paradigms and tools.

One measure of efficient implementation is the equity of computational load among all processors of the ensemble, or the *load balance* achieved. Another metric is the amount of synchronization (on pure shared memory machines) or communication (on ensembles with local memories) that arises. An even better metric is the ratio of the total communication to computation for each processor. Small ratios are desirable, since communication costs which are high on parallel processors should be kept small relative to the amount of computation. One way to achieve a small value of this ratio is to use large or coarse grains. A *grain* is the amount of work assigned to each processor. For machines with local memory, large grain sizes are a necessity for efficient implementation.

Although the earlier reported work provides invaluable insights for volume rendering, many of the efforts were not directed at efficient and general implementations. There was no attempt to exploit parallelism inherent in the volumes. Our feed-forward method reported herein exploits parallelism present in the geometry of a rectilinear volume. The resulting implementation on a hierarchical shared memory machine is general, load balanced, requires little communication and scales well with the size of the volume. The parallel machine used for our implementation was the IBM Power Visualization System (PVS). The Power Visualization System is a MIMD class of machine. The machine ensemble comprises of Intel i860 RISC (Reduced-Instruction-Set-Computer) processors. These processors are inter connected by a common bus. The memory organization is hierarchical. Each i860 processor can access sixteen (16) Megabytes of local memory and a maximum of five-hundred-and-twelve (512) Megabytes of global shared memory. The global memory is connected to the processors by the same common interconnection bus. The architecture of PVS provides parallelism at two levels. Besides exploiting the parallelism among the different processors, extra parallelism can be obtained by taking advantage of the pipelined execution (RISC-style) on the i860 processor. Both levels of parallelism have been exploited in our parallel implementation.

3: Geometrical Decomposition of Volumes

A volume represented by a rectilinear grid can be embedded in the three-dimensional Euclidean space. If the grid lines are regularly spaced in all dimensions then the voxels form cubes. We denote a object space grid point P by a four-tuple $[P_x, P_y, P_z, 1]$ in the homogenous four-dimensional space XYZ1 of resolution n. The image space is denoted by UVW1 and the coordinates for the same voxel in image space is represented by the four-tuple $[P_u, P_v, P_w, 1]$. We now define some geometrical primitives which can be used as the units of computation on vector and parallel processors.

A *beam* is the set of grid points with two of the three coordinates being fixed. Thus a *yz-beam at (j, k)* is the set $B_{yz:(j,k)} = \{(x,y,z) \mid y \equiv j, z \equiv k, 0 \le j, k < n, 0 \le x < n \}$.

In a similar way we define xy-beams and xz-beams. A *slice* is the set of grid points having one fixed coordinate. A *z-slice at k*, is therefore the set $S_{z:k} = \{(x,y,z) \mid z \equiv k, 0 \le k < n, 0 \le x, y < n \}$.

Thus, all voxel planes perpendicular to the z-axis are z-slices. Similarly, we can define x-slices and y-slices. A z-slice at k would therefore have yz-beams parallel to the x-axis and xz-beams parallel to the y-axis. Finally, we define a *slab* to be a set of consecutive slices along one of the principal axis. A volume can then be considered to be collection of consecutive slabs. Figure 1 shows the decomposition of a volume into beams, slices and slabs. There exist two properties of these primitives which are of interest. The first one is spatial coherency, while the second one is spatial order.

Spatial coherency exists between voxels in a beam, between beams in a slice, and between slices in a slab. This coherency stems from the adjacency of grid points in object space. Knowing the coordinates of a voxel in a beam, the coordinates of the adjacent voxel can be determined. This allows the efficient transformation of volumes through the

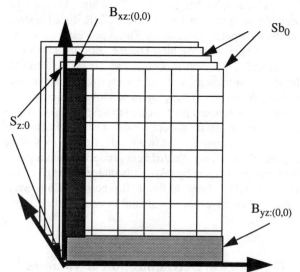

Figure 1: Decomposition of volumes into slices and beams. $S_{z:0}$ is the first slice of the volume, $B_{yz:(0,0)}$ and $B_{xz:(0,0)}$ are the first x and y beams of slice $S_{z:0}$. Slab Sb_0 consists of the first three slices.

use of constant incremental updates which is discussed in the next section.

There exists an inherent *spatial ordering* between slabs in a volume and between slices in a slab along the viewing direction, thus providing a visibility order among slabs and slices. Spatial ordering can also be enforced between beams in a slice along one of the two axes of the slice and between voxels along the axis of a beam. The inherent order of these different primitives lends itself well to efficient hidden volume elimination such as the back-to-front and front-to-back algorithms. These methods require that the visibility order of the voxels be maintained while forming the image though composition.

4: Efficient Methods for Feed-forward Volume Rendering

In the earlier section we mentioned how slice and beam primitives provide an inherent spatial coherency between voxels. This coherency lends itself well to incremental transformation of volumes. In this section we first show how a volume can be transformed incrementally. In the following subsection we show how incremental transformations can be efficiently implemented on vector and pipelined processors. Then, in the subsequent subsection a simple and efficient parallel implementation of our feed-forward pipeline is described. This parallel implementation employs the inherent spatial ordering of slices and slabs to display semi-transparent volumes. Finally, in the last two subsections we make some observations about the tech-

niques proposed in this section and then compare our method with previously reported methods.

The term transformation here includes all viewing transforms and shape/position changing transformations. Once again, the transformation of a volume consists of several matrix vector multiplies and is expressed by the matrix equation:

$$[P_u, P_v, P_w, 1] = [P_x, P_y, P_z, 1] \cdot T$$

,where P is a grid point. The four-tuple on the right hand side contains the coordinates of P in the source object space XYZ1, while the coordinates P in the target image space UVW1 are given by the tuple on the left hand side of the equation. T is the transformation matrix of order 4 as shown below. Application of the above multiplication to a data set

$$\begin{bmatrix} t_{00} & t_{10} & t_{20} & t_{30} \\ t_{01} & t_{11} & t_{21} & t_{31} \\ t_{02} & t_{12} & t_{22} & t_{32} \\ t_{03} & t_{13} & t_{23} & t_{33} \end{bmatrix}$$

of n^3 voxels requires a total of $16n^3$ floating point multiplications and $12n^3$ floating point additions. However, by using spatial coherency the number of operations and hence the time to transform a volume can be greatly reduced. It will be shown in the next subsection that a volume of resolution n^3 can be transformed with a little more than $3n^3$ additions.

4.1: Incremental Transformations

Suppose P and Q are two adjacent grid points along the x-beam $B_{yz:(j,k)}$ with Q being enumerated after P that is:

$$Q_x = P_x + 1, Q_y = P_y = j, Q_z = P_z = k$$

The transformed coordinates of point Q is first expressed in terms of the coordinates of P. It is true that

$$[Q_u, Q_v, Q_w, 1] = [P_x + 1, P_y, P_z, 1] \cdot T$$

Through simple algebra we can express the above product as the sum of two vectors. The right most vector T_1 is the first row of the transformation matrix.

$$[Q_u, Q_v, Q_w, 1] = [P_x, P_y, P_z, 1] \cdot T + T_1$$

$$T_1 = [t_{00}, t_{10}, t_{20}, t_{30}]$$

Finally,

$$[Q_u, Q_v, Q_w, 1] = [P_u, P_v, P_w, 1] + T_1$$

Thus the coordinates of Q in the image space can be directly determined from those of P. Each incremental update requires three additions. To begin the incremental process we need one matrix vector multiplication to compute the updated position of the first grid point. For the remaining n^3-1 grid points we need at most $3n^3$ additions. An immediate advantage of incremental computation is that it reduces the number of floating point multiplications, which are more expensive than floating point additions. We now show how incremental transformation lends itself well to processors with vector and pipelined facilities.

4.2: Incremental Transformation on Vector and Pipelined Processors

Vector and pipelined processors achieve fast execution by performing similar operations on a continuous stream of data. Vector processors have instruction sets which operate on data sets called vectors while pipelined RISC processors rely on mostly software techniques which can fill the pipelined stages of the functional units. Incremental transformation steps can be *vectorized* or *pipelined* and thus reduce the total time spent in this stage of the pipeline. This involves the identification of certain operations as vectorizable, wherein the basic unit of computation is a vector.

It is not necessary that the same incremental scheme be used to transform the entire volume. The incremental computation can be organized into several phases. Each phase consists of updates in a particular direction. Figure 2 shows a particular scheme of incremental computation. The order of enumeration of the voxels shown here is front-to-back along the viewing axis. A similar scheme can be employed for back-to-front. The incremental scheme can be divided into four phases:

· **Seed Phase** - In this phase, a single grid point (usually the lowest point of the grid in the first slice) is transformed through the use of a matrix-vector multiply. This grid point forms the seed for consequent updates.

· **Voxel Phase** - Incremental computation is used to transform an entire beam. The first vertical beam, $B_{xz:(0, k)}$ is updated using the seed. As shown in the previous section, the second row of the transformation matrix T is added to a previously enumerated grid point. The updates here are of a sequential nature.

· **Beam Phase** - In the third phase beams $B_{xz:(j,k)}$, $0 < j < n$ are updated. Beam $B_{xz:(j, k)}$ is used to update beam $B_{xz:(j+1, k)}$. The first row of matrix T is used for incremental updates, since the enumeration is along the x-axis. If each beam is considered to be a vector of length n, then the updates in this phase are essentially vector additions. At the end of this phase, the first slice, $S_{z:0}$, is completely transformed.

· **Slice Phase** - Updated slice $S_{z:k}$ is used to incrementally update the next slice $S_{z:k+1}$. The third row of T is used for updates in this phase (since the enumeration is along the z-

direction). Once again the updates are essentially vector additions, except that the length of the vectors is n^2.

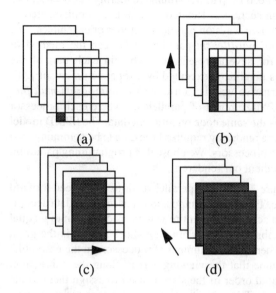

Figure 2: The four phases of incremental updates: (a) seed phase (b) voxel phase (c) beam phase (d) slice phase. The beam and slice phases can be expressed as vector operations. The arrow indicates the direction of incremental computation

If the order of enumeration is back-to-front along the z-axis (the enumeration orders along x and y remain the same), the seed phase is initiated on the last slice and the third row is *subtracted* instead of being added to the previous slice coordinates. The same scheme can be implemented for any other order of the axes.

In summary, we have reduced the transformation process from a set of matrix-vector multiplication into a sequence of vector additions. Each beam or slice is considered to be a vector of length n or n^2 respectively. On processors with vector or pipelining facilities the beam and slice phases are amenable to very fast execution. The description above used a slice as a basic unit of processing. Beams of voxels can be treated in the same way, except the maximum possible vector length is limited to n and not n^2. This discussion is pertinent for all kinds of transformations of regular grids between any two spaces.

In section 5 we provide transformation times for volumes on the IBM PVS machine. The usefulness of incremental computations would be evident then. In the next section we present our parallel implementation of the feedforward pipeline which includes incremental transformations in the first stage.

4.3: Parallel Volume Rendering

The need for parallel volume rendering has been shown earlier in section 2. Renderers have been implemented in basically two ways on parallel machines or ensembles. The *functional parallelism* paradigm has been the method of choice for several researchers wherein each part of the graphics pipeline is executed by a separate processor [24]. An alternative way is to use the *single-program-multiple-data* (SPMD) model of parallelism, where each processor executes the same code on different data. The SPMD model of volume rendering requires little data to be communicated between processors. We chose this programming paradigm to implement our renderers.

Figure 3 shows the parallel versions of the feed forward pipeline. The slab decomposition is used as the data decomposition scheme. The entire volume is divided into p equal sized slabs, each containing n/p slices (which is the grain size), where p is the number of processors in the ensemble. We assume that the viewing axis is along the z-direction. The spatial order of the slabs is used to assign them to the processors. Thus, the ith slab is assigned to the ith processor. It is important that this order be maintained for a correct implementation of the back-to-front method. All processors execute the first three stages of the pipeline on the slab assigned to it. Every slice of the assigned slab is transformed

and reconstructed on every processor and a local image is then created in the processor's local memory. The transformation is performed by using, whenever possible, the pipelined or vectorized incremental schemes of the previous subsection. Reconstruction is done on each slice of the assigned slab. Local images are created by employing the back-to-front compositing on each slab. These local images are then combined to form the final image. The combining phase is the only part of the parallel pipeline which requires communication between processors.

Combining can be done in at least two different ways. The central strategy requires that all processors send their images to one processor which then composites all of them in a strict image order, which is same as the slab order. Although, simple to implement, this strategy is inefficient in the presence of a large number of processors. The reason lies in the network congestion that arises when all processors attempt to send their images to the single distinguished processor. The hierarchical strategy exploits more parallelism and should be the method of choice for large ensembles. In the latter strategy, cognizance is given to the fact that combining is essentially a reduction operation and can be implemented in a tree-like fashion on parallel processors. Our parallel renderers implement both strategies. Communication between processors on the PVS is achieved

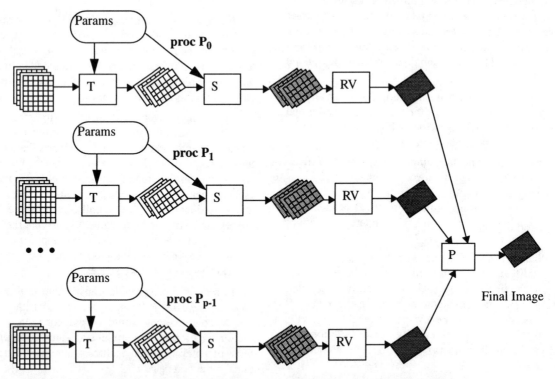

Figure 3: Parallel Feed Forward rendering. The slabs are assigned to processors P$_0$-P$_{p-1}$ in their spatial order. Local images are created on each of the processors which are later combined to obtain the final image. The stages are denoted by T = Transformation, S =Shading, RV= Reconstruction & Visibility and P = Parallel Combining.

through the use of the global shared memory. Multiple image buffers equal in number to the size of the ensemble are created. Each processor, after generating its own local image, deposits it into a pre-allocated buffer. This image is then combined through one of the combining schemes. This method avoids costly synchronization overheads that are required to support concurrent memory accesses.

The pseudo-code for the feed-forward rendering pipeline is presented in Figure 4. We assume that the viewing matrix T is a matrix of order 4 and that slice S is two dimensional array of n^2 triples. The subscripts for S describe the type and location of the slice, the first being the axis and second the number of the slice. This code is executed on all processors of a parallel ensemble. Each processor P_j, $0 \leq j < p$, reads in its slab of volume. Then it creates the viewing matrix and initializes the local image. The last slice on each processor is transformed first. The transformation is done incrementally. The seed, voxel and beam phases are first completed. At the end of these three phases the last slice of each processor is completely processed. This slice is projected onto a image plane I_s and then splatted therein. Afterwards, this image plane is composited with the local image I_j. Consecutive slices are transformed by the slice phase of the incremental transformation. As with the last slice, each slice is consecutively splatted and composited. After all slices are processed, the local images are all combined through a central strategy. The final image is displayed by one of the processors, designated as the display processor. The hierarchical combining strategy is similarly implemented. In the following subsection some observations on our implementation are presented.

4.4: Salient Features of the Parallel Implementation

• Incremental transformations even on sequential processors can reduce the transformation time, since the operation count is substantially reduced and the more expensive multiplication operations are replaced by cheaper additions.

• The efficiency of beam and slice transformations is higher for volumes of larger resolution. Large resolutions yield longer vectors which lead to more efficient pipelined execution.

• All voxels are transformed without being checked for occupancy. This strategy allows efficient implementation of this stage on most pipelined/vector processors. The presence of occupancy checks can slow down the pipeline unless the processor is equipped with a mask register. On the PVS no mask register exists and hence no occupancy checks are performed. For dense volumes, wherein the most of the grid points are occupied, the *no-questions-asked* strategy of the transformation stage would be beneficial.

```
On each processor P_j with slices S_{z:k0},...,S_{z:kl}
    Construct a viewing matrix T
    Initialize the image I_j
                                    /* Seed Phase */
    S_{z:k0}[0,0] := [0, 0, k_0] . T
                                    /* Voxel Phase (sequential) */
    for i := 1 to n-1 do
        S_{z:k0}[0,i] := S_{z:k0}[0,i-1] + [t_{01}, t_{11}, t_{21}]
    endfor
                                    /* Beam Phase (n-vector) */
    for i := 1 to n-1 do
        for j := 1 to n-1 do
            S_{z:k0}[i,j] := S_{z:k0}[i-1,j] + [t_{00}, t_{10}, t_{20}]
        endfor
    endfor
                                    /* First slice */
    Project S_{z:k0} to image plane I_s
    Splat voxels of S_{z:k0} on I_s
    Composite I_s with local image I_j
                                    /* Slice Phase (n^2-vector) */
    for k := k_0+1 to k_l do
        for i := 1 to n-1 do
            for j := 1 to n-1 do
                S_{z:k0+1}[i,j] := S_{z:k0}[i,j] + [t_{02}, t_{12}, t_{22}]
            endfor
        endfor
                                    /* Slice k */
        Project S_{z:k} to image plane I_s
        Splat voxels of S_{z:k} on I_s
        Composite I_s with local image I_j
    endfor

    if (P_j is the display processor)then
        Combine all images to produce I_f
        Display I_f
    else
        Deposit image I_j in global memory
    endif
```

Figure 4: The pseudo code for a parallel version of the feed-forward pipeline with incremental slice coherent transformations, splatting and front-to-back compositing. This code is executed for each view. Combing is done across the interconnection network and the image is displayed by a designated processor.

• The implementation is load balanced for dense volumes, since each processor is given the same number of slices.

• All pixels of the image planes are composited even if their opacities are zero. The composition of two images is a highly vectorizable operation and can be very efficiently implemented on all pipelined and some vector processors if no checks are instituted for zero opacities.

• The amount of data transferred between any two processors is m^2. Communication is required only in the combining phase. The ratio of communication to computation, per processor, is pm^2/n^3 which is inversely proportional to the slab size, since m is proportional to n. Thus a large slab size is preferable.

• The implementation is general and not limited to only certain viewing angles and transformations. Perspective views can also be rendered.

• Volume data is evenly distributed only once to all processors, without any data duplication. I /O on existing parallel processors is slow and should be avoided.

• Changes in viewing parameters do not cause any movement of data between processors. It is customary for the users of an interactive rendering system to view the three-dimensional object from a variety of positions and even perform further transformations to it. Such changes to the computational parameters (the transformation matrix for instance) are broadcast to all processors, and no further costly exchange of data is needed.

4.5: Comparisons with other Implementations

Westover implemented a feed-forward method with splatting on a network of Suns [4]. Westover's parallel implementation was not motivated by the geometry of the volume. Although, he did use incremental transformation of volumes there was no mention about the benefits of conducting incremental computations on vector and parallel processors. Also, he did not resort to the more convenient slice abstraction to determine the slice ordering. Finally, no timings were provided. We feel that the implementation may not have provided small rendering times given the high latency of the ethernet-based network used.

Elvins has also implemented a similar feed-forward renderer with splatting on a nCube [4]. However this implementation suffers from several drawbacks and is very slow. Elvins's parallel implementation was also not motivated by the geometry of the volume and did not employ any incremental methods. His implementation gave rise to a large amount of communication and was not scalable. No cognizance was also given to the interconnection network of the parallel processor and thus the rich connectivity of the hypercube was not utilized. The task structure employed also did not map well to a distributed memory machine like the nCube. In the next section we present the results of some experiments. We first attempt to show the efficacy of the incremental transformation scheme and then report rendering times of our parallel feed-forward pipeline.

5: Experimental Results

We report three sets of experimental results. The first set of experiments shows the efficacy of plain incremental computations, the second set shows the utility of pipelined execution, while the third exhibits the performance of a parallel implementation of the feed-forward pipeline which includes incremental transformations. All experiments reported herein were conducted on a 32-processor Power Visualization System with five-hundred-and-twelve (512) Megabytes of global memory. For sets one and two only the transformation code was included. Although the experiments for set two reported here were conducted on pipelined processors, similar results were obtained when conducted on a CRAY-Y/MP, a machine with individual vector processors. For the third experiment the pseudo-code of section 4.3 was implemented with the addition of hierarchical compositing.

5.1: Unoptimized Incremental Transformations

Volumes of different sizes were transformed without and with incremental transformations. Coherency schemes which used either beams or slices as the basic unit of processing were used. Compiler options were used to switch off all optimizations which resulted in pipelined code. Table 1 shows the transformation times in seconds. Thus even plain incremental transformations are useful, although incremental computations with beams yield faster transformations than when used with slices. We suspect that larger memory access times for two dimensional arrays may be playing a role here.

Table 1: Transformation times (in seconds) for brute-force, beam, and slice based incremental schemes on a single processor of IBM Power Visualization System.

N	Plain	Beams	Slices
64	.369	0.161	0.380
128	2.92	1.273	3.014
256	31.962	10.132	24.396
512	232.973	153.981	195.422

5.2: Slice and Beam Coherent Transformations

Table 2 provides performance figures for implementations using the beam and slice based incremental transformations. The algorithms scale almost linearly with the number of processors, especially for larger volumes. For smaller volumes the advantage of slice coherency is not evident. Once again we suspect that the larger memory access times makes the use of slice primitive more expensive. However, for larger volumes the longer pipelines arising from the use of slices provides faster execution and the transformation times are smaller by a factor of three.

5.3: Parallel Feed Forward Rendering

We report the rendering time for a volume of size 100x100x100 on 1, 2, 5 and 10 processors. The component-

Table 2: Transformation times in seconds) for beam and slice based coherent schemes on eight processor IBM Power Visualization System. The top number is the time for a beam coherent implementation, while the bottom one is for the slice coherent implementation.

n	p=1	p=2	p=4	p=8
64	0.196	0.131	0.092	0.086
	0.060	0.097	0.089	0.103
128	1.408	0.731	0.396	0.243
	0.440	0.360	0.270	0.250
256	10.156	5.657	1.734	0.958
	3.443	1.921	1.080	0.489
512	81.892	40.968	20.489	10.211
	27.219	13.873	7.120	3.773

wise break up of the times is provided. The reconstruction filter used was of size 5x5 and a screen of size 73x173 was used for display. The objects rendered were voxelized spheres, whose normals were computed on-the-fly for shading computations. The centralized method of combining was used in the last stage of the pipeline. Table 3 includes the time spent in each stage of the parallel pipeline. From the table we can notice that the time for transforming the volume is relatively small. The use of slice coherency makes this component of the rendering time insignificant. The splatting time includes the time required to shade the voxels. It decreases with larger number of processors. This time component depends on the grain size and the denseness of the volume. Thus as the number of processors increases, the grain size falls and hence the trend. Compositing time decreases with number of processors, since there are less number of slices to composite. Finally, the impact of the centralized combining scheme is evident in the presence of larger number of processors. The total rendering time of this implementation is quite scalable with the number of processors. Also, a transformation scheme was implemented in which all voxels were checked for occupancy before they were transformed. The time incurred for a volume of 100x100x100 on ten processors is 2.54 seconds. This proves the usefulness of the no-questions-asked strategy.

6: Conclusions

In this paper we investigated efficient methods of feedforward rendering of regular grids on vector and parallel processors. Parallelism was derived from the geometry of the volume by decomposing the volume into beam, slice and slab geometrical primitives. The spatial coherency properties of slices and beams were then used to incrementally transformation of volumes. Such a transformation it was shown required less arithmetic operations than the usual method of transforming volumes. On pipelined and vector processors, it was then shown how incremental transformation can be implemented as a vector operation and thus yielding smaller transformation times. The inherent spatial order of the slices and slabs allows the implementation of a load balanced volume renderer which can display transparent volumes. This renderer was described in a good amount of detail and compared against previous implementations. Experiments were then conducted on the IBM Power Visualization System to show that incremental transformation indeed reduces the time expended in the transformation stage of the pipeline and that the renderer is scalable to the point allowed by the architecture of the machine.

Table 3: Component-wise breakup of the total rendering time. The various time symbols are T_t = transformation, T_s=splatting, T_c=compositing, T_p=combining, and T=total rendering time.

Stage	p=1	p=2	p=5	p=10
T_t	0.220	0.114	0.050	0.027
T_s	6.815	3.372	1.381	0.721
T_c	2.911	1.469	0.649	0.339
T_p	0.055	0.068	0.522	0.584
T	10.001	5.023	2.602	1.672

7: Acknowledgments

We would like to thank the Advanced Computer Center for Arts and Design at The Ohio State University and specifically Wayne Carlson and Don Stredney for their support of this project. We thank the Ohio Supercomputer Center for allowing the use of the CRAY-Y/MP and the PVS. We thank the NASA Lewis Research Center and specifically Mourine Cain and Jay Horowitz for their support and for providing the opportunity to test our methods on the SGI, Hypercube and the IBM Cluster (LACE). We appreciate the help and support of Jeff Hamilton and Lloyd Treinish of IBM Watson Labs, who allowed us to use the thirty node PVS machine. Finally, we thank Kim Ciula for her efforts in proof reading the draft copy of this paper.

This project was supported by the National Science Foundation under grant CCR-9211288.

8: References

[1] Cameron, G.G, and Underill, P.E.,"Rendering Volumetric Medical Image Data on a SIMD Architecture Computer", SPIE, Visualization in Biomedical Computing 1992, Vol. 1808, pp. 137- 142.

[2] Drebin, R. A, Carpenter, L., Hanrahan, P.,"Volume Rendering", Computer Graphics, Vol. 22, No. 4, August 1988, pp. 65-74.

[3] Ebert, D. S., Parent, R. E.,"Rendering and Animation of Gaseous Phenomena by Combining Fast Volume and Scanline A-buffer Techniques", Computer Graphics, Vol.24, No. 4, August 1990, pp. 357-366.

[4] Elvins, T. T.,"Volume Rendering on a Distributed Memory Parallel Computer", Proceedings of Visualization'92, Boston MA, October 1992, pp. 93-98.

[5] Frieder, G., Gordon, D., and Reynolds R.,"Back to Front Display of Voxel-Based Objects", Computer Graphics and Applications, Vol. 5, No. 1, January 1985, pp. 52-60.

[6] Fruhauf, M.,"Volume Rendering on a Multiprocessor Architecture with Shared Memory: A Concurrent Volume Rendering Algorithm", Proceedings of Second Eurographics Workshop on Visualization in Scientific Computing, 1992.

[7] Goldwasser, S. M., Reynolds, R. A., Talton, D. A., Walsh, E. S.,"High Performance Graphics Processors for Medical Imaging Applications", Parallel Processing for Computer Vision and Display, Dew, P. M., Earnshaw, R. A., and Heywood, T. R., (eds.), Addison-Wesley, 1989, pp. 461-470.

[8] Hanrahan, P.,"Three-Pass Affine Transforms for Volume Rendering", Computer Graphics, Volume 24, No. 5, November 1990, pp. 71-77.

[9] Herman, G. T., Liu H. K., "Three-Dimensional Display of Human Organs From Computer Tomograms," *Computer Graphics and Image Processing*, Vol. 9, No. 1, January 1979, pp. 1-21.

[10] Kaufman, A., Bakalash, R., Cohen, D., Yagel, R., "A Survey of Architectures for Volume Rendering", IEEE Engineering in Medicine and Biology, Vol. 9, No. 4, December 1990, pp.18-23.

[11] Levoy, M., "Display of Surfaces from Volume Data", IEEE Computer Graphics and Applications, Vol. 8, No. 5, May 1988, pp. 29-37.

[12] Levoy, M., "A Hybrid Ray Tracer for Rendering Polygon and Volume Data", IEEE Computer Graphics and Applica-tions, Vol. 10, No. 3, March 1990, pp. 33-40.

[13] Lorenson, W. E., Cline, H. E., "Marching Cubes: A High Resolution 3D Surface Construction Algorithm", Computer Graphics, Vol. 21, No. 4, July 1987, pp. 163 - 169.

[14] Montani, C., Perego, R., Scopigno R., "Parallel Volume Visualization on a Hypercube Architecture", Proceedings of 1992 Workshop on Volume Visualization, October 1992, Boston, MA, pp. 9-15.

[15] Nieh, J., Levoy, M.,"Volume Rendering on Scalable Shared-Memory MIMD Architecture", Proceedings of 1992 Workshop on Volume Visualization, Boston, MA, pp. 17-24.

[16] K. H. Hoehne and A R. Bernstein, "Shading 3D-Images from CT Using Gray-Level Gradients", IEEE Transactions on Medical Imaging, Vol. MI-5, No. 1, March 1986, pp. 45-47.

[17] Porter, T., Duff, T.,"Compositing Digital Images", Computer Graphics, Vol. 18, No.3, July 1984, pp. 253-259.

[18] Reynolds, R., Gordon, G., Chen, L., "A Dynamic Screen Technique for Shaded Graphic Display of Slice-Represented Objects", Computer Vision, Graphics, Image Processing, Vol. 38, No. 3, June 1987, pp. 275-298.

[19] Schroder, P., Salem, J. B., "Fast Rotation of Volume Data on Data Parallel Architecture", Proceedings of Visualization'91, San Diego, CA, pp. 50-57.

[20] Schroder, P., Stoll, G.,"Data Parallel Volume Rendering as Line Drawing", Proceedings of 1992 Workshop on Volume Visualization, October 1992, Boston, MA, pp. 25-32.

[21] Stredney, D., Yagel, R., May, S. F., Torello, M., "Supercomputer Assisted Brain Visualization with an Extended Ray Tracer",1992 Workshop on Volume Visualization, Boston, MA, pp. 33-38.

[22] Upson, V., Keeler, M., "V-Buffer: Visible Volume Rendering," Computer Graphics, Vol. 22, No. 4, August 1988, pp. 59-64.

[23] Westover, L.,"Footprint Evaluation for Volume Rendering," Computer Graphics, Vol. 24, No. 4, August 1990, pp. 367-376.

[24] Westover, L., "Splatting: A Parallel, Feed-Forward Volume Rendering Algorithm", Ph.D Thesis, Department of Computer Science, University of North Carolina at Chapel Hill, July 1991.

[25] Wittenbrink, C., Somani, A., "2D and 3D Optimal Parallel Image Warping Techniques", private communication, 1992.

[26] Yagel, R., Kaufman, A., "Efficient Methods for Volume Rendering", Computers and Graphics, Proceedings of Eurographics'92, September 1992, Cambridge, England, pp. 153-157.

[27] Veznia, G., Fletcher, P. A., Robertson, P. K., "Volume Rendering on the MasPar MP-1", Proceedings of 1992 Workshop on Volume Visualization, October 1992, Boston, MA, pp. 3-8.

Fast Data Parallel Polygon Rendering

Frank A. Ortega

X-Division Numerical Laboratory
Los Alamos National Laboratory
Los Alamos, New Mexico 87545

Charles D. Hansen   James P. Ahrens*

Advanced Computing Laboratory
Los Alamos National Laboratory
Los Alamos, New Mexico 87545

Abstract

This paper describes a data parallel method for polygon rendering on a massively parallel machine. This method, based on a simple shading model, is targeted for applications which require very fast rendering for extremely large sets of polygons. Such sets are found in many scientific visualization applications. The renderer can handle arbitrarily complex polygons which need not be meshed. Issues involving load balancing are addressed and a data parallel load balancing algorithm is presented. The rendering and load balancing algorithms are implemented on both the CM-200 and the CM-5. Experimental results are presented. This rendering toolkit enables a scientist to display 3D shaded polygons directly from a parallel machine avoiding the transmission of huge amounts of data to a post-processing rendering system.

1   Introduction

In recent years, massively parallel processors (MPPs) have proven to be a valuable tool for performing scientific computation. The memory systems on this type of computer are far greater than those found on traditional vector supercomputers. As a result, scientists who utilize these MPPs can execute their three dimensional simulation models with a much finer grid resolution than previously possible. These extremely large grid sizes prove to be both a blessing and a curse. The finer grids allow for better simulation of the underlying physics. However, the finer grids also cause a data explosion when visualization and analysis are applied to them. A fully populated 64K CM-200 has 8 gigabytes of physical memory. A 1024 node CM-5 contains 32 gigabytes of physical memory. While it is true that time-steps in current simulations don't utilize the entire memory systems of these machines, it is not uncommon for a data set from a single time-step in a dynamic simulation to be in excess of several gigabytes.

Geometry provides an excellent representation of simulations in the visualization process. Some scientific simulations contain explicit geometry. For example, material interface boundaries may be explicitly represented. For simulations which do not contain explicit geometry, there are a plethora of visualization techniques which generate geometry as an intermediate representation: isosurfaces, particles, spheres, vectors, icons, etc. In some cases, such as sparse data sets, geometry extraction proves to be a compression technique without information loss. However, it is more typical for geometric extraction techniques to generate larger amounts of data than is present in the original data set[13].

One proven analytical technique for scientific visualization is the generation of isosurfaces. Two common methods for visualizing isosurfaces are volumetric rendering with a specific opacity map and the extraction of 3D contours[17, 18]. Volumetric techniques directly render the data set into an image. The rendering process, especially for large non-uniform data sets, can be quite time consuming[7]. This poses a problem if the viewing angle is not known *a priori* and needs to be determined interactively. Contouring techniques, on the other hand, extract a geometric representation of the specified contour(s). Typically, these are in the form of polygons. An advantage of this class of techniques is that the view direction can be changed interactively by rendering the polygons at high frame rates.

Recent research results have shown that 3D contours can be efficiently extracted at interactive rates from large dynamic data sets on massively parallel processors[13]. These techniques can generate over 1.24 million polygons for each time-step of a dynamic simulation with a grid size of only 256^3.[1] These large polygon sets impede interactive visualization on machines with dedicated graphics hardware in two ways: the amount of local-area network traffic and the total number of polygons throughput for the dedicated graphics hardware. In the simplest case (disregarding color information), each vertex of each polygon consists of 3 floating point locations and 3 floating point normal positions or 24 bytes/vertex. With 250,000 polygons (assuming triangles), this is 18Mbytes per time-step. To transfer this size of data on an ethernet, the best-case transfer time is 14.4 seconds and the average-case transfer time is much worse. Obviously, the amount of data overloads the network capacity. Additionally, 250,000 polygons is at the limit of dis-

---

*Author's current address is Department of Computer Science, University of Washington, Seattle, WA 98195

[1]Currently, this is not considered a large data set. Typically simulations on an MPP machine use grid resolution upwards of 512^3.

joint polygons/second which state of the art graphics engines can render.

One solution would be to move the entire data set over to the workstation and generate the isosurfaces locally utilizing optimization techniques such as spatial decomposition. Another similar solution would be to analyze the raw data set with a commercially available visualization tool such as AVS, Explorer, etc. In addition to network transport issues, the problem with both of these solutions is that the size of the data set overwhelms the workstation. The size of the raw data can be over 128Mbytes per time step. In addition to the network problems previously mentioned, our experience is that data sets of this magnitude cause the workstation to page excessively with memory page faults when generating the isosurface. While it is true that environments such as AVS are being ported to MPPs, it has been our experience that the geometry component of these environments is not supported on the MPP but is still utilized on the workstation. The necessitates the transport of data, albeit filtered data, to the workstation.

A more appropriate solution would be to render the geometry on the MPP where the data already exists. This is completely compatible with the previously described MPP isosurfacing techniques and utilizes the power of the massively parallel computer to generate an image. The goal of this research is to develop a rendering algorithm which is efficient for large numbers of polygons.[2] For such large polygon sets, we make the assumption that most of the polygons will cover a relatively small number of pixels since scientific data sets tend to produce such polygons. As we will show, image generation time is much less than direct volume rendering and network traffic is limited to the image size rather than the data size. Additionally, this model extends the usefulness of visualization environments such as AVS or Explorer since images are transferred to a workstation rather than full, or reduced, data sets which still require further processing. Another benefit of this approach is the capability of directly calling rendering functions from the running computational model. This allows not only for simulation monitoring/steering but also has proven to be an extremely useful tool in the debugging process.

In the next section, previous work in this field will be reviewed followed by a description of the data parallel rendering algorithm. Load balancing is a critical issue which will be addressed. Results from experiments on both a CM-200 and a CM-5 will be presented.

2 Related Work

An increasing number of parallel polygonal rendering algorithms have been developed. The main strategy has been to perform parallelization in two stages: scan conversion and rasterization. This strategy follows the gross functionality which is implemented in most hardware graphics pipelines. The standard graphics pipeline is shown in Figure 1. Polygons are

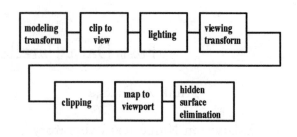

Figure 1: Standard Graphics Pipeline

transformed from world space to screen space, clipping to the screen is performed, polygons are scan converted, and hidden surface elimination is performed. Lighting can be applied either to the vertices before scan conversion (Gouraud shading) or at each pixel (Phong shading).

Scott Whitman investigated the problem of polygonal rendering on a shared memory massively parallel processor, the BBN TC-2000[20]. He split the standard graphics pipeline into three stages: front-end, rasterization, and back-end. In the front-end stage, the polygons are read into the system, transformed, back-face culled, clipped to the screen, and stored in shared memory. When the polygons are stored in shared memory, a bucketization is performed to determine in which image tiles the polygon lies. The bounding box is used as the determinant. The rasterization phase is similar to the standard graphics pipeline. Polygons are scan converted, shaded, Z-buffered, and finished scan lines are stored in a virtual frame buffer. The back-end writes the virtual frame buffer to the actual frame buffer. Whitman explores many different tiling schemes but the basic parallel rendering follows the steps outlined.

Thomas Crockett and Tobias Orloff implemented a standard scan-line conversion algorithm on a distributed memory system message passing, the INTEL iPSC/860[6]. They approached the problem by combining the first three stages of the standard graphics pipeline and splitting the rendering process into two distinct steps: splitting polygons into trapezoids and rasterizing the transformed trapezoids. They evenly distributed the polygons to all processors and also divided the image space into equally sized horizontal strips. Thus, their algorithm achieves both object space and image space parallelism. The algorithm alternates between splitting triangles into trapezoids and rasterization.

Fiume, Fournier, and Rudolph presented a spanning scan line algorithm which ran on a simulator for an ultracomputer[8]. They proposed language extensions to implement a Z-buffer. The algorithm assigned each PE a span consisting of a trapezoidal or triangular regions. The PEs synchronized at the end of processing for each scan line. This led to a load balancing problem. The authors suggest splitting the scan line

[2]We consider 250K and upwards a large polygon set.

if it is greater than some M number of pixels.

Crow, Demos, Hardy, McLaughin, and Sims utilized a Connection Machine, CM-2, to develop and implement a photorealistic renderer[9]. Their goal was to provide very high quality rendering for one of the film production houses in Hollywood. Since they were working on a SIMD machine, they chose to program their algorithm in a data parallel manner. They split the traditional polygonal rendering pipeline into four stages: transforms, clipping, scan conversion and shading. Rather than following earlier approaches on the CM-2, they assigned each of the vertices to a processor for transformation. The transformation matrices were passed one after the other and applied to the vertices. Clipping was done by assigning one polygon to each processor. Scan conversion was handled similarly. Shading was handled by assigning a processor to each pixel. Their algorithm was effective for hundreds of thousands of polygons with complex photo realistic rendering features although no timings were presented.

Schroder and Drucker describe a data parallel ray-tracing algorithm for heterogeneous databases[19]. Although ray-tracing is a different problem than polygon rendering by scan coversion, we include this related work since it provides an alternative to rendering on a massively parallel processor. Their algorithm addresses the load balancing problem by continually remapping available resources. They start by allocating one processor per ray. Each ray processor allocates the number of processors required to test insections with objects. As rays travel down through the ray-tree, processors sets are continually allocated. The time to render scenes containing small number of objects (7381 spheres and one polygon), varied from 98.3 to 118.7 sec on a 32K CM-2. Although the algorithm produces ray-traced images, the time is much slower than required. As pointed out, we are interested in rendering upwards from 250K polygons.

3 Parallel Progamming Models

Architecturally, MPPs fall into two classes of machine: MIMD and SIMD/SPMD. Similarly, there are two programming models for parallelism which are exploited in massively parallel systems: control parallelism and data parallelism.

The control parallel model divides a task up into a number of subtasks that can run concurrently. For example, one could assign each stage of the rendering pipeline to a processor. Each of these tasks can execute concurrently and independently. It is not necessary for the tasks to execute in lockstep. Typically, there is some synchronization barrier which synchronizes these independent tasks for the next step in the process. Since each of the tasks execute independently, this model maps well onto MIMD architectures such as the CM-5 from Thinking Machines, Inc. [5] and the Paragon XP/S from the Scientific Supercomputer Division of Intel, Inc. [1].

In the data parallel model the same operation is performed on all the selected data elements. For example, given an array of numbers, a constant could be added to each number. In the data parallel model

this operation would logically occur simultaneously on each element of the array. Actual hardware may or may not perform this operation simultaneously on all selected data elements. This would depend on whether or not enough physical processors exist for each data element. In the case where there is more data than processors, each physical processor is given a number of data elements upon which it operates. Each of these data elements is considered a virtual processor. The concept of a virtual processor allows one to treat the program as if there were a physical processor per data item. This model maps well onto SIMD/SPMD architectures such as the CM-200 and CM-5 [3] from Thinking Machines, Inc.[4], the MP1 from MasPar Computer Corp. [2], and the Pixar Image Computer [16].

It has been recognized that for some problems the data parallel model is somewhat easier to program than the control parallel model. Modern scientific compilers, such as Fortran 90 and C*, take advantage of the data parallel model in their language constructs. Furthermore, it has been shown that data parallel programs can achieve good speedup on MIMD architectures [10].

4 A Data Parallel Renderer

The choice to employ the data parallel programming model for the polygonal rendering algorithm was made for several reasons. Our computing facilities include several Connection Machines from Thinking Machines Corporation. While the CM-5 at our site is a MIMD MPP, the CM-200s are strictly SIMD MPPs. It was our desire to develop an algorithm which would be portable to both machines. Secondly, the scientific applications which run on these MPPs utilize CMFortran as their primary language. Ease of use was a high priority so we wanted to develop an algorithm suite which would integrate well with existing applications. Lastly, we wanted a rendering environment which would take advantage of the CM/AVS visualization software on the CM-5 yet perform rendering in near real-time. Since the current version of CM/AVS relies on the workstation (the AVS kernel) to perform rendering, performance suffers for large data sets due to the poor response time seen with network traffic. Additionally, CM/AVS currently is restricted to the data parallel programming model on the CM-5.

The basic idea behind the data parallel renderer is to maximize the number of operations occurring in parallel while minimizing communication. While this trait is desirable in both data parallel and task parallel programming models, the SIMD/SPMD nature of data parallel programs imposes additional constraints. In data parallel programs, there is only one thread of control. For efficient programs, it is necessary to maximize the set of active processors at any given step in an algorithm. This is accomplished by judicious assignment of data to the processors, sometimes referred to as *layout*. To determine the optimal layout for the rendering process, let us examine the previously described

---

[3] The CM-5 can actually be programmed with either model. The Run Time System has support which causes the machine to run as a SPMD MPP.

standard graphics pipeline with respect to data operations. The basic steps are as follows:

1. transform the polygons according to interactive controls (rotations, translation and scaling)

2. transform the polygons from world space to screen space and clip polygons which are outside the viewport

3. shade the vertices

4. scan convert the polygons

5. clip the line segments against the viewport

6. perform hidden surface elimination

The first step is to transform the polygons by applying desired rotations, translations and scalings. This is accomplished by building a 4 x 4 homogeneous affine transformation matrix constructed from the individual transformations. This transformation matrix is applied to each vertex resulting in transformed polygons as desired. The key point is that all operations are performed on the vertices.

The next step transforms the polygons from world space to screen space by applying a perspective or orthogonal transformation to each of the vertices. This step can be combined with the previous step by correctly concatenating the perspective (or orthogonal) transformation matrix with the transformation matrix representing the desired rotations, translations and scalings. All operations are performed on the vertices.

We could perform back-face culling at this point. However, this introduces a conditional into the data parallel execution stream and as long as there are many more polygons than processors, it is no less efficient to render the back-facing polygons even though they'll most likely be occluded by some other object. The implementation of the renderer includes back-facing culling.

Next, shading is performed for each polygon. In this implementation, we are optimizing for speed. Therefore, we perform simple Gouraud shading. In Gouraud shading, the shading is computed at each vertex and then linearly interpolated across an edge when forming a scan line segment and linearly interpolated across the scan line segment during rasterization, resulting in a smoothly shaded object. More advanced shading techniques would be easy to implement. Like the first two steps, all the operations are performed on the vertices.

The fourth step scan converts the polygons by determining which polygon edges intersect a particular scanline and interpolating the X, Z and shaded color information along the polygon edge to determine the value for a particular Y scan-line. We start the scan-conversion process by finding, for each polygon, any intersections that a scan line makes with each of the polygon sides. Since polygons completely outside the viewport are ignored, there must be at least two intersections but, depending on the polygon shape, there

may be many intersections. In order to process a general polygonal shape, the polygon scan line intersections are sorted in ascending X order and grouped into line end pairs. The even-odd rule is then used to select the segments that are inside the polygon[15]. This operation is performed on polygon edges.

Next, the line segments which are completely outside the viewing window are discarded. This operation is performed on all line segments generated from the scan conversion step.

Hidden surface elimination is accomplished by employing a parallel Z-buffer algorithm[11]. This is done by rasterizing the line segments produced from the scan conversion process, clipping the resulting pixels against the viewport and then Z-buffering the non-clipped pixels. This operation is performed on pixels.

The first three steps operate on vertices while the fourth step operates on polygons. The fifth step operates on line segments and the final step operates on pixels. This analysis by data operations provides an excellent method for data layout.

If we strictly followed this, we would remap the virtual processors from vertices to polygons to line segments to pixels. The remapping of virtual processors involves general communication which is costly. If we map each polygon to a virtual processor and then iterate over the vertices within each polygon, we can eliminate one of the costly communications. The trade off is that this might result in a load balancing problem. When the polygon set contains polygons with varying numbers of vertices, iterating over the vertices within a polygon will result in idle virtual processors. The occurs when the iteration reachs the last vertex for some polygons while the polygons with more vertices still have remaining vertices to be processed. This can be mitigated by re-triangulating the polygons resulting in equal number of vertices for each polygon[14]. When this is the case, there is no load balancing problem since the steps involving vertices are perfectly balanced.

The data layout starts by assigning each polygon to a virtual processor. This layout is utilized by steps one through four. The scan conversion step generates line segments. These are each assigned a virtual processor. The fifth step marks as inactive, the virtual processors whose line segments fall outside the viewport. The last step uses the remaining line segments to generate pixels which are assigned to virtual processors used in the Z-buffering. Thus, there are only two remappings. The first four steps operate on objects thereby performing object space parallelism where as the last two steps operate on line segments and pixels thereby performing image space parallelism.

The most interesting parts of the algorithm are the scan conversion and Z-buffering. Let us look more closely at those steps.

To save time and maximize the parallelism across polygons, a modified scan line conversion algorithm was used [12]. This algorithm is not restricted to convex polygons and scan converts arbitrarily complex polygons including those with holes. For this algorithm, we make the assumption that the polygonal set consists of large numbers of small polygons. We have found this is a valid assumption since the target application of this renderer is scientific data, particularly data derived from very large computational models. Typical polygonal set sizes can range from 100,000 to millions of polygons [13]. This algorithm takes advantage of the fact that each polygon has relatively few scan lines passing through it compared with the number of scan lines in the image.

The scan conversion process iterates over the maximum number of scan lines through any polygon. Since scan conversion is concurrently executed for all polygons in parallel, it is bounded by the maximum number of scan lines within any polygon. The number of iterations necessary to process the entire set of polygons is the maximum number of scan lines spanning any polygon. This is, of course, the polygon with the maximum image-space height in Y. At the initiation of this step, the first scan line within every polygon is processed simultaneously. As the number of scan lines processed approaches the maximum, fewer polygons will be processed, since some polygons, the ones with a smaller number of scan lines passing through them, will have completed the scan conversion process. We address this load balancing issue in the next section.

The line segments are sorted into ascending X order as previously described. At this stage, the end points and color data for the segments are gathered into a data structure such that the start and end points are assigned to virtual processors in a data parallel manner. This utilizes generalized router communication to map the line segments to virtual processors.

In the Z-buffering step, line segments from the previous steps are converted to pixels. Processing the lines to pixels in parallel requires iterating over the number of pixels in the X direction of the longest line. The first pixels from all the lines are processed, then the second, etc. For the shorter line segments, the virtual processors are marked as inactive when the segment completes this pixelization process. The Z and color values for the pixels are interpolated from the line end points. Any pixels that lie outside the viewport are clipped.

Since the polygon scan lines are processed in parallel, there is a good possibility that many of the segments will generate pixels with the same image location. The Connection Machine can not handle these "collisions" correctly with standard inter-processor communications. The generalized data router must be used in conjunction with a sendmax combiner [3]. This utility uses the router for fast communications but it presents another problem: the utility can only work with one sending array at a time, and the color value for the pixel needs to be stored in the image array for the pixel which has the maximum z value. This problem was solved by combining the z values and the color value into a double precision array before the Z-buffer compare. These are the values saved into the Z-buffer. When displaying the image, the image data is extracted from the Z-buffer.

5 Loading Balancing the Renderer

In the renderer, there are two key loops, one for scan converting polygons into line segments and one for Z-buffering the line segments. The bulk of the renderer's computation time is spent processing these loops. Both of these loops have the following general form:

```
max_iteration = MAXIMUM_VALUE(iter)
do i=1,max_iteration
    WHERE (i .le. iter)
        ...loop code...
    ENDWHERE
enddo
```

The parallel array *iter* contains the number of loop iterations for each data element processed in the loop. The number of loop iterations is data-dependent. In the scan conversion code, *iter* contains the number of scan lines in each polygon. During each iteration, a different scan line from each polygon is processed in parallel.

In the data parallel programming model, the loop executes for the maximum number of iterations. In the best case, the iteration values are the same. Such a loop is said to be balanced. If the iteration values vary over a wide range the loop is said to be unbalanced. Unbalanced loops are inefficient. As the loop progresses, processors become idle because they have finished their iterations. A second source of inefficiency results from any serial code in the loop being repeated for the maximum number of iterations.

A load balancing algorithm was developed which balances this type of data parallel loop. The algorithm works only for data parallel loops with independent loop iterations. That is, each iteration does not depend on any values computed in previous iterations. The algorithm has the following properties:

- Speeds up the computation of unbalanced data sets

- Has a low added cost to the computation of balanced data sets

- Utilizes the existing memory space

- Utilizes the existing code with simple modifications

Clearly, the algorithm should speed up the computation of unbalanced data sets. Any extra work to balance the data adds a cost to the computation of balanced data sets. If it is unknown whether the input data sets are balanced or unbalanced, a tradeoff can be made: non-optimal speed up of the unbalanced computations for a lower added cost to balanced ones. The renderer's input data sets will be balanced or unbalanced depending on the algorithm and the data used to generate them. For example, an isosurface algorithm will generate a fairly balanced data set if the input data is dense and on a uniform grid since the polygon sizes will be bounded by the cell size of the grid. An isosurface algorithm which performs a coplanar merge on its resulting polygons, however, can create unbalanced data sets since some polygons might be substantially larger than others. Unbalanced data sets can also result from the application of viewing transforms in the renderer. For example, applying a wide-angle perspective view transform to a balanced data set can result in an unbalanced data set, since, in the transformed data set, polygons closer to the viewer are much larger than polygons far from the viewer.

The load balancing algorithm utilizes existing memory space so that the full memory of the machine can be devoted to rendering the data sets. This is especially important for the massive data set sizes the renderer must handle. Since developers can utilize their existing code, the algorithm can easily be used as a mechanism for load balancing other loops of this form.

The load balancing algorithm is implemented in the data parallel programming model. In this model, virtual processors provide the abstraction of having one processor per data element of each parallel array. The data elements from each parallel array are stored in each virtual processor's data space. For example, in the scan conversion loop, each virtual processor stores information about one polygon: the x,y,z coordinates of each vertex, color and normal information. Each virtual processor's data space also contains the number of loop iterations needed to process the loop data.

A virtual processor is *freed* if it will stay idle during all remaining loop iterations. Virtual processors are freed before and during the execution of the loop. Virtual processors are freed before loop execution if they are not assigned work initially. In the scan conversion loop, virtual processors are not assigned work initially if the polygons in their data space are clipped or backface culled. Polygons are clipped when they lie outside the user's viewport window. Zooming in on the objects being viewed can cause polygons to be clipped. Polygons are back-face culled when their surface normals point away from the viewing direction. Virtual processors are freed during loop execution when they complete their specified number of iterations.

Any free virtual processors can take on new work. A virtual processor takes on new work by copying the relevant data from an active heavily loaded virtual processor's data space into its own. The remaining iterations of the active virtual processor are then split between all processors which share the data. For example, if the work is split between two virtual processors, one processor will compute the lower half of the iterations and the other the upper half. By splitting the iterations between virtual processors, the loop iterations are balanced across the virtual processors and the maximum number of iterations needed to complete the loop is reduced.

A distribution function is used to compute how free virtual processors are assigned new work. The inputs to the function are the number of free virtual processors and the iteration array. The output of the function is a distribution. A distribution is a parallel array which contains the number of free virtual processors assigned to each active data space.

Computing an optimal sequence of distributions is np-complete. So, the load balancing algorithm uses a heuristic function to calculate a distribution. A new distribution is computed at the beginning of each loop iteration using the current number of free virtual processors and iteration array values.

The distribution function is computed as follows: first, the average of the current number of iterations is computed. The average is computed by summing the current active iteration array values and dividing this sum by the number of data elements in the iteration array. The average is used to decide how free virtual processors are assigned to active data spaces. If there are more free virtual processors than active virtual processors, the free processors are distributed equally to all active processor's data spaces whose iterations are greater than the average. The remainder of the free processors are left idle. If there are less free virtual processors than active processors then the previous distribution is returned, resulting in no new load balancing.

The average is used because it is a lower bound on the new maximum number of iterations that can be achieved by any distribution of free processors. Since the average is the lower bound, there is no reason to assign free processors to data spaces with iterations less than or equal to the average.

To distribute active data spaces to free virtual processors, a sequence of communication steps is executed. These steps should only be executed when the iterations saved outweigh the communication costs. In order to assess when it is beneficial to distribute free processors, information about the new distribution is computed and timing statistics are taken.

The new maximum number of loop iterations with the current distribution is computed to decide whether the communication steps should occur. This value is computed by adding one to all distribution array elements where their corresponding iteration array elements are active. This addition incorporates all the currently active processors in the iteration array into the distribution array. The iteration array is then divided by the distribution array. This result calculates what the value of the iterations will be after has splitting occurs. The maximum of this result is the new maximum number of iterations.

Timing statistics are also computed to assess whether the communication steps should occur. Each time the communication steps are executed, they are timed and an average of the execution times is updated. The body of the loop is also timed, and an average of the execution times is updated each iteration. The ratio of the average communication step time and the average loop body time gives a measure of the time for the communication steps in terms of loop iterations. An initial estimate of this ratio is supplied by the developer.

Using the new maximum iteration and ratio value, a test is computed: if the new maximum number of iterations plus the ratio is less than the current maximum iteration than it is profitable to distribute the free virtual processors.

At the beginning each loop iteration, the free virtual processors are counted and the distribution function is called. The test is executed. If the test is successful, active data spaces are distributed to the free virtual processors. The following pseudo-code provides an overview of the load balancing algorithm:

```
max_iteration = MAXIMUM_VALUE(iter)

loop until max_iteration

    compute the distribution and the
    new maximum number of iterations
    based on current number of free
    virtual processors

    ratio = INT(average communication
    time / average loop time)

    if (new_max_iteration + ratio .lt.
    max_iteration) then
        do load balancing communication
        steps

        max_iteration = new_max_iteration
    endif

    ...loop code...
endloop
```

6 Experiments

Several experiments were run on both the CM-200 and the CM-5. All timings were for an image size of 512×512. A smaller image size would speed up the rendering and a larger size would slow down the rendering. Table 1 shows the times for rendering a data set consisting of 228,288 small polygons on the CM-200 with partition sizes of 16K, 32K and 64K. Table 3 shows the times for rendering the same data set on the CM-5 with partition sizes of 32, 64, 128, 256, and 512 nodes. Table 2 shows the times for rendering a data set with large polygons while Table 4 shows the times for rendering the same data set on the CM-5. The rows of each table contain data for three different viewing angles. The first row is the data for a viewing angle of (0,0), the second row is the data for a viewing angle of (45,45), and the third row is the data for a viewing angle of (90,90). The columns are partition sizes for each of the MPPs. All times are reported in seconds. The data set with small polygons fits our assumption that geometry generated from scientific data on massively parallel computers will typically be composed of many small polygons (polygons which have few scanlines passing through them). The data set with large polygons violates this assumption and the times are given to show the effect. Figure 2 shows the results of rendering a data set generated from a hydro-dynamics code running on the CM-200 and the CM-5[4].

As can be seen, the times shown for the data set containing large polygons are an order of magnitude slower on both the CM-200 and the CM-5. This is

---

[4] See the color plates for a better picture of Figure 2.

Times (sec)			Polygons/second		
16K	32K	64K	16K	32K	64K
1.894	1.04	0.571	120,532	219,507	399,803
1.637	0.848	0.482	139,455	269,207	473,626
1.162	0.625	0.335	196,461	365,260	681,456

Table 1: Rendering of Small Polygons on CM-200

Times (sec)			Polygons/second		
16K	32K	64K	16K	32K	64K
22.094	15.005	8.574	9,866	14,527	25,423
18.015	11.855	6.834	12,100	18,387	31,896
10.548	6.789	4.039	20,665	32,108	53,969

Table 2: Rendering of Large Polygons on CM-200

Times (sec)				
32	64	128	256	512
5.756	4.754	1.482	0.796	0.463
3.402	2.877	0.966	0.498	0.302
2.476	1.048	0.550	0.401	0.236

Polygons/second				
32	64	128	256	512
39,660	48,020	154,040	286,794	493,062
67,104	79,349	236,322	458,409	755,920
92,200	217,832	415,069	569,296	967,322

Table 3: Rendering of Small Polygons on CM-5

Times (sec)				
32	64	128	256	512
37.326	20.169	12.488	8.466	6.220
30.684	16.034	9.758	6.393	4.717
17.261	9.353	5.543	3.594	2.590

Polygons/second				
32	64	128	256	512
5,939	10,807	17,455	25,746	35,045
7,104	13,595	22,338	34,097	46,212
12,628	23,306	39,325	60,651	84,163

Table 4: Rendering of Large Polygons on CM-5

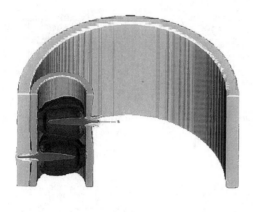

Figure 2: Image of Oil Well Perforator with 355,948 Small Polygons

[For color plate see page 932]

because some polygons covered over 3/4 of the image. Recall that as the size of the polygons increases, the polygon rasterizing speed decreases due to the iterative loops over the maximum polygon height and the maximum scan line size. The addition of the load balancing algorithm to the renderer helps alleviate this problem.

On a 64K CM-200 partition, rendering speeds of over 600,000 polygons per second were achieved on the small polygon data set. These are disjoint polygons and we have found this to be three times the speed of our SGI 380/VGX, whose published rendering times are over one million meshed polygons per second. However, the workstation rendering speed is dramatically reduced when the polygons to be rendered are not in cache and the polygons are disjoint rather than meshed. On a 512 node partition of the CM-5, rendering speeds of close to one million non-meshed polygons per second were recorded. This exceeds the speed of current state of the art dedicated graphics hardware.

Figure 3 shows the speedup of the algorithm run on the CM-200 while Figure 4 shows the speedup of the algorithm run on the CM-5. The speedup curves are relative to the implementation on the smallest partition available for each of the MPPs. While the demonstrated speedup is not linear, the graphs show that near linear speedup for the data set with small polygons was achieved. Rendering the data set with large polygons exhibited worse speedup due to the large number of iterations being performed.

The renderer's scan conversion loop has been modified to use the load balancing algorithm. Load balancing the scan conversion loop improves the renderer's performance on unbalanced data sets. These improvements are detailed in Tables 5 and 6. On balanced

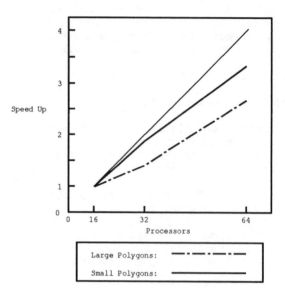

Figure 3: CM-200 speed up

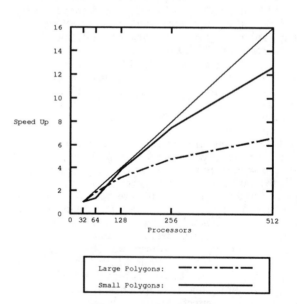

Figure 4: CM-5 speed up

Times (sec)				
32	64	128	256	512
29.387	17.580	11.029	7.544	5.712
22.585	13.288	8.235	5.624	4.201
16.034	8.985	5.465	3.650	2.832

Table 5: Rendering of Unbalanced Polygons without Load Balancing on CM-5

Times (sec)				
32	64	128	256	512
11.482	7.047	4.180	2.368	1.502
12.381	7.284	4.128	2.481	1.556
13.191	7.194	4.371	2.561	1.765

Table 6: Rendering of Unbalanced Polygons with Load Balancing on CM-5

Times (sec)				
32	64	128	256	512
63.456	37.178	23.169	16.062	12.291
55.330	31.446	19.351	13.250	10.493
13.462	7.453	4.385	2.856	2.150

Table 7: Rendering of Zoomed and Clipped Unbalanced Polygons without Load Balancing on CM-5

Times (sec)				
32	64	128	256	512
18.244	10.063	5.666	3.205	2.023
36.318	19.679	10.778	5.882	3.733
13.811	7.711	4.453	1.767	1.234

Table 8: Rendering of Zoomed and Clipped Unbalanced Polygons with Load Balancing on CM-5

data sets, performance is slightly degraded, by 2 to 7 percent of the render's performance without the load balancing modifications. Performance is especially improved on data sets which have been zoomed and clipped because of the many free virtual processors available before the loop executes. These improvements are shown in Tables 7 and 8. The times were obtained by appling a scale factor of 3 to the unbalanced data set. With a viewing angle of (0,0) on this zoomed and clipped unbalanced data set, performance of the render with load balancing is 3 to 6 times faster than the performance of the render without the load balancing modifications.

The unbalanced data set was generated by merging the output polygons of an isosurface algorithm. This was done to reduce the number of polygons in the data set. The original isosurface polygons are shown in Figure 5[5]. The merged isosurface polygons are shown in Figure 6. Note the difference between the data sets, the polygons in the original data set are approximately the same size whereas the polygons in the merged data set have many different sizes, varying from extremely large polygons to extremely small polygons.

Load balancing the Z-buffering loop does not currently improve the renderer's performance. A small portion of the degradation results from the overhead of doing the load balancing (i.e. the initialization, distribution function calculation and testing). The larger portion results from timing fluctuations. The body of the Z-buffering loop is a single communication call. The execution time of this single communication call varies greatly. The communication ratio used to decide when to load balance is inaccurate because the average execution time of the single communication call varies so much over time. Unprofitable communication steps take place and the overall performance

[5]See the color plates for a better picture of Figure 5 and Figure 6.

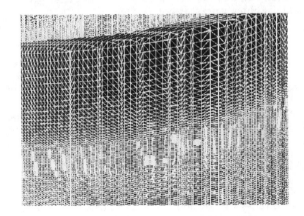

Figure 5: Closeup Image of Original Polygon Edges

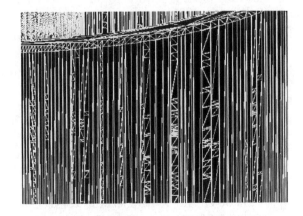

Figure 6: Closeup Image of Merged Polygon Edges

[For color plate see page 932]

of the renderer degrades. This is a limitation of the load balancing algorithm: if the communication ratio is inaccurate, performance can be degraded.

7 Conclusions

This paper described a data parallel method of polygon scan conversion allowing the visualization of large 3D simulations directly from a massively parallel processor. This allows scientists to evaluate the simulation as it is running or shortly thereafter without the need to transfer huge amounts of data from a massively parallel processor to a graphics workstation. Issues involving load balancing were addressed and a data parallel load balancing algorithm was presented. The load balancing algorithm achieves the desired speed tradeoff between the computation of unbalanced data sets and balanced data sets by using a simple heuristic function to calculate the distribution of free virtual processors. The algorithm improves performance and only utilizes existing memory space. It does this by making use of virtual processors which are freed before and during loop execution. Performance data was provided that showed the rendering method can out-perform high-end commercially available graphics workstations.

8 Acknowledgements

We wish to thank John Fowler of Los Alamos National Laboratory for encouragement and assistance with this paper. We would also like to thank Harold Trease of Los Alamos National Laboratory for help with some CMFortran issues. The Advanced Computing Laboratory (ACL) at Los Alamos National Laboratory generously provided computing iron and tremendous assistance with timing runs. David Rich of the ACL was particularly stellar with the generosity of his time.

References

[1] Intel Corporation. Paragon XP/S product overview, 1991.

[2] MasPar Computer Corporation. MP-1 family data-parallel computers, 1990.

[3] Thinking Machines Corporation. CM Fortran user's guide, 1991.

[4] Thinking Machines Corporation. Connection machine CM-200 series technical summary, 1991.

[5] Thinking Machines Corporation. The connection machine CM-5 technical summary, 1991.

[6] T. Crockett and T. Orloff. A parallel rendering algorithm for MIMD architectures. Technical Report 91-3, NASA Langley Research Center, 1991.

[7] Todd Elvins. A survey of algorithms for volume visualization. *Computer Graphics Quarterly*, 26(3), August 1992.

[8] E. Fiume et. al. A parallel scan conversion algorithm with anti-aliasing for a general purpose ultracomputer. *Computer Graphics*, 17(3), July 1983.

[9] F. Crow et al. 3D image synthesis on the connection machine. In *SIGGRAPH Course Notes: Parallel Processing and Advanced Architectures in Computer Graphics*, pages 107–128, 1989.

[10] P. Hatcher et al. Architecture independent scientific programming in data parallel C: Three case studies. In *Proceedings of Supercomputing '91*, pages 208–217, 1991.

[11] Foley, van Dam, Feiner, and Hughes. *Computer Graphics: Principles and Practice*. Addison Wesley, 1990.

[12] John D. Fowler. A reduced set scan line algorithm. Internal Document, Los Alamos National Laboratory.

[13] C. Hansen and P. Hinker. Massively parallel isosurface extraction. In *Proceedings of Visualization '92*, pages 77–83, 1992.

[14] P. Hinker and C. Hansen. Geometric optimization. In *Proceedings of Visualization '93*, 1993.

[15] Oliver Jones. *Introduction to the X Window System*. Prentis Hall, Englewood Cliffs, New Jersey, 1989.

[16] A. Levinthal and T. Porter. Chap - a SIMD graphics processor. *Computer Graphics*, 18(3), July 1984.

[17] Mark Levoy. Efficient ray tracing of volume data. *ACM Transactions of Computer Graphics*, 9(3), July 1990.

[18] W. Lorensen and H Cline. A high resolution 3D surface construction algorithm. In *Computer Graphics*, volume 21, pages 163–169, 1987.

[19] Peter Schroder and Steven Drucker. A data parallel algorithm for raytracing of heterogeneous databases. In *Proceedings of Computer Graphics Interface*, 1992.

[20] Scott Whitman. *Multiprocessor Methods for Computer Graphics Rendering*. Jones and Bartlett, Boston, 1992.

Session 10:
Cache Coherence
Chair: Jim Barton

Cache Coherence Using Local Knowledge *

Ervan Darnell [†]   Ken Kennedy

Computer Science Department, Rice University, Houston, TX   77251-1892

Abstract

Typically, commercially available shared memory machines have addressed the cache coherence problem with hardware strategies based on global inter-cache communication. However, global communication limits scalability and efficiency.

"Local knowledge" coherence strategies, which avoid global communication at run-time, offer better scalability, at the cost of some additional cache misses. The most effective local knowledge strategies described in the literature are those based on generation timestamps (TS).

We propose a new strategy, TS1, that requires less extra storage than TS, only one extra bit per cache line, and can produce more cache hits by exploiting sophisticated compiler analysis. TS1 handles common synchronization paradigms including DOALL, DOACROSS, and critical sections.

Early results show TS1 is, worst case, slightly slower than TS. Best case, TS1's flexibility allows for significant improvements.

1   Introduction

Data race free programs executing on a shared memory multiprocessor are expected to have the same semantics as if they were executing on a sequential processor. For this to be the case, memory must appear sequentially consistent [10]. Caches on shared memory multiprocessors must have some global knowledge about executing programs otherwise they could fail to preserve sequential consistency by retaining stale values.

Most approaches to the cache coherence problem have focused on hardware mechanisms to maintain coherence. Unfortunately, the overhead of maintaining coherence in hardware can be high; scaling systems based on hardware coherence is a difficult problem [15]. Snoopy cache strategies, which monitor some common bus, are now in common use for small

scale systems [16, 18]; however, snoopy strategies are problematic for large-scale machines because such machines cannot be based on a single, central broadcast medium for lack of sufficient bandwidth. Directory strategies [2, 8, 11, 19], in which a directory entry associated with each memory location (or cache line) indicates which processors have cached values for that location, seem more promising for large-scale systems. However, directories can require large amounts of additional storage and directory maintenance operations may substantially increase network traffic.

As an alternative to using a hardware mechanism that supports global communication between caches, a compiler could perform global analysis and augment the code with cache control directives to maintain coherence. This approach does not hinder the scalability of the machine. However, since compiler analysis must be conservative, some valid values will be unnecessarily removed from cache with this approach, thus reducing hit rates.

In this paper, we propose a local knowledge only coherence strategy, TS1 (Time Stamping with 1 bit), that, for a particular granularity of compiler analysis, achieves the best hit rate that any such strategy can at a cost of one additional bit per cache line, sufficient logic to set, reset, or copy this bit to the *valid* bit, and a fast invalidate. We compare TS1 to previous local knowledge only coherence strategies. We show that time-stamping and TS1 achieve the same effect with naive compiler support but that TS1 can more readily utilize improved compiler analysis.

Section 2 provides an overview of some of the terminology we use. Section 3 discusses some of the better previous local strategies. Section 3.5 shows that time stamping strategies provide optimal hit ratios for a given granularity of compiler analysis. Section 4 describes our new strategy for achieving the same effect as time-stamping at lower hardware cost. It also discusses the impact of the accuracy of compiler analysis. Section 5 gives some preliminary results comparing TS and TS1. Section 6 discusses extensions to other types of synchronization. Section 7 concludes and discusses possible future directions.

---

*This work was supported in part by the National Science Foundation under Cooperative Agreement CCR-9120008 through its research contracts with the Center for Research on Parallel Computation at Rice University.

[†]corresponding author: ervan@cs.rice.edu

```
DOALL I
    A(I)=...         A(2) write allocated on processor 2
ENDDO

DOALL I
    A(I+1)=...       A(2) write allocated on processor 1
ENDDO

DOALL I
    B(I)=A(I)+1      Access stale A(2) on processor 2
ENDDO
```

Figure 1: Example of stale access in the absence of coherence control

2 Definitions and framework

Fork-join programs are composed of a series of *epochs*[4]. Each *epoch* consists of one or more *instances* which run in parallel. Each epoch is either a (fork-join) parallel loop with no internal synchronization, e.g. a Fortran DOALL, or a serial region between parallel loops. Serial regions can be nested serial loops and/or those parts of serial loops enclosing parallel loops. A serial region is an *epoch* with one *instance*.

The instances (iterations) of a parallel loop are scheduled on processors at run time. The compiler must assume that a given instance could be executed on any processor. All coherence strategies known to us make this assumption. If scheduling is known at compile time, a different set issues arises and different techniques are applicable.

We regard non-unit cache line size aliasing as an orthogonal problem. Our discussion assumes that the cache line size is one word.

Staleness occurs when a location is accessed on processor p_i, written subsequently on processor $p_j, j \neq i$, and read again still later on processor p_i (without its cache being updated to reflect the new value). For example, in figure 1, if processor p_i gets iteration i, the reference to A(2) in the last epoch would be stale (without coherence). Any additional references that happen between the first and second epochs will not change the situation. If A(2) were written on p_i between the second and third epochs (not shown in the figure) it would again be valid (on p_i) without coherence control.

Numerous previous authors have tried to capture this notion in various analytical ways [4, 6, 9]. Here we simply note the dynamic behavior that causes staleness without addressing its detection at compile time.

Coherence is maintained by making sure that values are communicated between caches when necessary. Values are updated from cache to main memory either by using write-thru cache or write-back cache triggered by synchronization events. Values are moved from main memory to cache on demand when they are not found in the cache. Stale values are removed from caches at the correct time so that subsequent reads will load the new values. This removal may be done by anything from explicit operating system calls that the compiler inserts to the hardware failing to register a hit because of some combination of bits.

2.1 Semantics of fork-join

The semantics of fork-join, e.g. DOALL, parallelism is that the fork-join loop be data race free; there can be no carried dependence, i.e. a value cannot be written in one instance (iteration) and read on another within the same epoch (DOALL).

A value can be read on several processors in the same epoch so long as none write it. The lack of carried dependence might be proven by the compiler or asserted by the programmer. In either case, it has the following important implication: If a value, x, is accessed in epoch e on p_i it will be coherent in epoch $e + 1$ on p_i without any coherence control or communication with main memory. This is true because x being accessed on p_i during e means that it could not have been written on p_j during e. By the definition of staleness, x is still coherent in epoch $e + 1$ on p_i.

The same value being read on different processors during epoch e does not present a problem because it cannot be written on any processor during epoch e. These properties are trivially preserved by serial regions.

2.2 Local versus global knowledge

To avoid staleness, each cache must account for what is written by every processor, including those to which it is not directly connected. This set of writes can be exactly the locations written or any approximating superset. If this global knowledge of what is written is shared at run time, we would characterize it as a *global strategy*. Global strategies are usually thought of as hardware strategies, e.g. snoopy caches [16, 18] and directory based caches [2, 11, 19]. Other global strategies, e.g. OS level page strategies [17], are software strategies.

Cache misses have four causes: initial loading, cache size, cache organization (e.g. associativity), and invalidation to preserve coherence between processors (sharing induced). Coherence strategies are concerned only with the last category, sharing induced misses. No currently existing global strategy causes a logically unnecessary sharing miss. They are in that sense optimal. The drawback of global strategies is the that scalability is impaired by the cost of maintaining global knowledge at run time.

If no global knowledge is shared at run time, then coherence must rely on locally collected knowledge plus whatever global knowledge was collected at compile time. Previous local knowledge strategies have been referred to in the literature as software [4, 6] or hardware [14] strategies depending on whether *most* of the work was done in software or hardware. We consider all of these strategies to be similar and refer to them collectively as *local strategies*.

A local strategy will likely never result in a globally optimal hit ratio for a processor because some useful runtime knowledge will be unavailable. The effectiveness of local strategies can vary widely depending on the program being run and the strategy being used. The principal advantage of local strategies is that they are scalable because no global knowledge need be com-

```
DOALL I=1,N
   A(I)=...
ENDDO

DOALL I=1,N
   IF (c1) A(I+1)=...
ENDDO

DOALL I=1,N
   B(I)=A(I)+1
ENDDO
```

Figure 2: Global versus Local coherence

```
DOALL I=1,N
   A(I)=...
ENDDO

DOALL I=1,N
   A(I)=A(I)+...
ENDDO

DOALL I=1,N
   B(I)=A(I)+1
ENDDO
```

Figure 3: Dynamic versus static coherence

municated at run time to maintain coherence. They rely on what *could* happen not what *does*. We use *could* happen to mean that the compiler cannot disprove it.

The fundamental limitation of local strategies is that if an *instance* (task) could write a value (and it cannot be determined for certain at compile time), other *instances* must assume that it has. A task need make no assumptions about what it itself does because sufficient marking bits can be used locally to make whatever determinations are useful regardless of the incompleteness of compiler analysis.

Figure 2 gives an example of where a local strategy would fail to achieve the same hit ratio as a global strategy. If condition c1 is always false (for a given execution) but is not analyzable by the compiler, all potential reuse of cached values of A between the first and third epochs will be lost using a local strategy but preserved using a global strategy.

2.3 Dynamic versus static coherence

Local strategies are either static or dynamic. Static local strategies decide which cache lines to invalidate and when that invalidation should occur, using only compile time knowledge. In contrast, dynamic strategies can use run time information as well; which data actually gets invalidated depends on the actual execution path of the program. This comes in two forms, knowing (part of) the processor schedule and intrainstance control flow. Dynamic strategies take advantage of reuse that exists only because of a particular run time schedule. Static strategies must assume worst case scheduling (though they can still exploit some inter epoch reuse).

Dynamic strategies strictly improve on static strategies. Any static strategy can be changed to a dynamic strategy that will not cause any more sharing misses and will usually do much better. The tradeoff is that dynamic strategies require some additional hardware support to handle marking bits. Static strategies require no hardware support other than the ability to invalidate cache lines under software control. Static strategies can be used on some existing machines, such as the BBN TC2000[6, 7].

Figure 3 shows an example for which static strategies are inherently inefficient. The value of A written

in the first epoch cannot be allowed to reach the third epoch. Since the second epoch (with the write) *might* have a different schedule than the first, an invalidate must remove the value from cache that was loaded in the first epoch. This will cause either the read in the second epoch or the third epoch to miss (depending on where the invalidate occurs). But if the schedules for all epochs are actually the same at run time this would be unnecessary. A dynamic strategy could recognize this and preserve reuse in both the second and third epochs.

3 Previous approaches

We briefly survey some previous local strategies in order to give credit to previous authors in this area and to show what improvement TS1 makes. Knowing the different approaches helps for understanding the core issues of local strategies and not being distracted by often disparate implementation approaches. Those aspects of previous strategies not directly concerned with coherence are covered in section 6.3.

3.1 Fast Selective Invalidation

One of the first strategies was Fast Selective Invalidate (FSI) [4]. FSI determines at compile time which references access shared variables that might have been previously written. These are designated *memory reads*. For *memory reads* to be cache hits they must be found in the cache and have a special *epoch* bit set (originally called a change bit). Accesses to shared variables set the *epoch* bit. All of the *epoch* bits are reset at every epoch boundary. With this strategy, no shared value crosses an epoch boundary in cache, ensuring that caches are coherent. The penalty is that no inter-epoch reuse is preserved for shared variables. FSI is a static strategy.

3.2 Life Span Strategy

Life Span Strategy (LSS) [3] is an improvement over FSI. Instead of resetting the *epoch* bit after every epoch, the *epoch* bit for a given cache line is reset after the end of the next epoch. This is implemented with an extra bit in each line, the stale bit, that marks the passage of one epoch boundary. Thus any referenced value is preserved into next epoch. This is valid by DOALL semantics as previously noted (section 2.1). LSS is a dynamic strategy.

The LSS paper describes an extension to preserve a value in cache for any fixed number of epochs. The number of epochs it survives must be determined at compile time. Its maximum value is the shortest path (in number of epochs) that could be taken before another write. The actual path between writes at run time could be much longer. The count is stored in unary so that updating the count can be done with a shift and checking for validity can be done by examining the last bit. Values which are not referenced will eventually be removed from cache. If, in practice, values stay in cache for only a few epochs due to cache size limitations, a small number of bits can be used for the extended LSS at no great cost. Additional bits would not help because the values would already be evicted before the count runs out.

3.3 Parallel Explicit Invalidation

Parallel Explicit Invalidation (PEI) [12] works by combining an invalidate with each write instruction. Writing an element in an array invalidates everything in the array except for the element itself. This achieves coherence because anything written on a different processor will be removed from the cache of this processor before the next epoch (sufficient dummy writes are added to make sure this invariant is maintained in the presence of uncertain control flow and serial epochs). The PEI strategy preserves inter-epoch reuse by leaving the value written on this processor in cache. PEI is a dynamic strategy.

The implementation uses a bit mask to control the region invalidated. This requires that write instructions have enough additional bits to contain the mask. It does, however, allow for essentially constant time invalidation. It also allows for many special cases to be handled with more precision (assuming the compiler analysis is sufficient). In some instances, it can improve on the hit ratio time-stamping would achieve. However, in general, it fails to preserve intra-epoch reuse when there are multiple references to the same array in one instance. Those values that are lost to intra-epoch reuse are also lost to inter-epoch reuse. The use of an *epoch* bit alone would not suffice to prevent this. For PEI to achieve good results, arrays, or in the worst case, each dimension of an array, must occupy an amount of memory equal to a power of two.

3.4 Time Stamping

Time stamping (TS) strategies [4, 14] are more effective at preserving reuse than any of the previously mentioned strategies. For a given quality of compiler analysis, it is impossible to achieve a better hit ratio with any other local strategy. The trade-off is that they require several extra bits per cache line, extra bits per memory access instruction, several extra counters per processor, and extra logic in the cache controller. Time stamping is a dynamic strategy.

In time stamping, there is a counter (referred to as a clock) for each array which tracks the number of epochs in which the array was possibly written. Each processor has a copy of all of the clocks. At the *end* of an epoch, each processor increments its clocks for each array that might have been written during that epoch on *any* processor. This requires no global communication. The clock value for an array represents the last epoch where the array could have been written.

Each cache line has a time stamp. When a value is accessed, its time stamp is set to what the current clock value for its array will be in the next epoch. Example, if the current clock value for array A is 5, a write to A(1) is loaded into cache with a time stamp of 6 because the clock will be incremented at the end of this epoch. A read of A(1) in a loop with no write would set the time stamp to 5 because the clock will not be incremented at the end of the epoch.

A value becomes stale when its time stamp is less than the corresponding clock. If the time stamp equals the clock value, there has been no write since the last access to the cache line. By DOALL semantics (section 2.1) this also holds for the epoch where the value is written. For an epoch after a write, the cache line will contain its prior time stamp value, but the clock will have been incremented. The cache hardware will find that time stamp < clock, conclude the value is stale, and issue a miss.

Both previous time stamping strategies operate on the whole array level. This is not necessary. It would be possible for time stamping to operate on the section level. However, it would require a separate clock for each section of each array. This would not only require extra clocks but extra bits in the instruction word to specify which clock was relevant.

There is a peculiar limitation to TS. The clocks can overflow. When that happens all cache lines which depend on that clock must be invalidated. This is the same problem extended LSS suffers. Time stamping uses binary counters and the impact is much less. Time stamping ages its cache lines by incrementing clocks on the processor while leaving the cache lines unchanged. Extended LSS ages its cache lines by decrementing counters in the cache line. This distinction will prove useful as explained in section 4.

3.5 A unified view of previous approaches

Despite very different implementations, all of these approaches are variants of the same essential strategy. During epoch e_w location x (some array element) is written on processor p_j; at the end of epoch e_w, processor $p_i, j \neq i$, invalidates location x in its cache. Processor p_i might not know exactly what location x is. It approximates with the smallest set of locations sure to contain x.

FSI and LSS make the pessimistic assumption that x could be anywhere. TS assumes all of the array which x is in could have been written. PEI uses the best available compiler analysis, which is at least as good as the same array analysis of TS. Extended

LSS also uses the best available analysis to determine where x could be, but it unions the results over all paths causing it to invalidate more. TS and PEI are concerned only with the run time (inter epoch) path and are in this respect superior to extended LSS.

Dynamic and static strategies both must make the same estimate about how large the set is that encompasses x. Static schemes must also estimate the processor schedule, which means they must assume the worst case. Dynamic schemes, however, know part of the schedule, the part that occurs on the local processor. If x is accessed on p_i in epoch e_w, a dynamic scheme knows that p_j never actually wrote x (section 2.1) regardless of the compile time analysis. It can then avoid the invalidation of x. LSS, TS, and PEI all take advantage of this.

After the end of epoch e_w, if x was not referenced on p_i during e_w, p_i has no run time information about x and it must rely entirely on the compiler's analysis for whether or not p_j might write x in e_w. If the compiler then indicates that p_j appears to write x, a local strategy must invalidate x on p_i before the next read of x on p_i (if the next reference to x on p_i is a write, then it does not matter whether or not x was invalidated). If a strategy invalidates *only* when these two conditions are met (x not referenced on p_i and apparently written on p_j), it is optimal in the sense that no local strategy, with the same granularity of compiler analysis, could have a better hit rate. This is how time-stamping behaves. It is an optimal local strategy. PEI is not optimal because it invalidates before it knows that x is not referenced on p_i. LSS is optimal only in the trivial sense that it uses a know-nothing compiler.

In practice, this utilization of DOALL semantics can make a dramatic difference because it captures reuse when subsequent loops have the same schedule and same reference pattern, for instance a DOALL inside of a serial loop will likely meet this condition. Deliberate attempts to increase loop affinity [13] will further improve the benefit of dynamic strategies.

4 One-Bit Time Stamping

Even though both proposed time-stamping strategies [4, 14] are hit-rate optimal local strategies, they require substantial additional hardware. TS1 achieves the same optimal hit ratio with fewer special bits per cache line and no special bits per instruction word. It also avoids the need for special hardware to load and compare the proper time stamp in a cache line. But, it does require a more sophisticated invalidate.

4.1 Hardware support

TS1 requires a *valid* bit per cache line and an additional bit, the *epoch* bit. In TS1, caches set the *epoch* bit on any reference to that line (read, write, hit, or miss). At the end of a given epoch, e, a special instruction resets the *epoch* bit for every line in the cache. We assume that the cache implementation can do this in $O(1)$ time by having every cache line respond in parallel. Since all of the *epoch* bits were reset on entry to epoch e from the end of epoch $e - 1$, the *epoch* bit reflects which cache lines have been accessed during epoch e.

By the assumed semantics of DOALL loops (section 2.1), any cache line with its *epoch* bit set in epoch e can be left in cache for epoch $e + 1$ without causing a stale access. We use this observation in defining a special *invalidate* that operates optimistically. When a particular cache line is the object of an invalidate, it is actually invalidated only if the *epoch* bit is reset, otherwise it remains valid and in cache, i.e. the invalidate copies the *epoch* bit to the *valid* bit.

4.2 Implementation of the invalidate

There are several choices for the actual implementation of the invalidate that trade-off hardware cost for run time efficiency.

A slow but inexpensive implementation would be to have a low level invalidate instruction which could invalidate either a particular line or a particular page. The high level invalidate would then loop over the proper range of pages and lines. Even though this would take $O(|section|)$, acceptable performance could still be achieved. Previously, we examined the efficiency of this kind of invalidate for a static strategy [7].

A faster, but more complex, invalidate could work by using a bit mask to determine which addresses to invalidate. With only '=' comparators and no extra storage, a section could be invalidated in $O(\log(|section|))$ time. Special layouts and strides could reduce this further. This is similar to what PEI does.

Other authors have proposed $O(1)$ time invalidation implementations which work by accessing cache row and column addresses [1].

4.3 Software support

To determine what to invalidate, TS1 uses compile time analysis to determine what is written for each epoch. The compiler makes its best estimate that is sure to include every address actually written. The main task of this analysis is to determine which parts of shared arrays are written. A naive analysis could simply note which arrays appear on the left hand side of an assignment and then conclude that every element of any such array is modified. More sophisticated analysis could try to determine which sections of arrays are actually modified. For every section (or whole array) that is modified, the compiler inserts an invalidate for that range of addresses at the end of the epoch being analyzed. Since schedules are not known, the same set of invalidates is used for every processor.

At run time, for each epoch, some accesses occur, setting the *epoch* bits, then the invalidates are executed as the next to last instruction, removing soon to be stale values, and finally all of the *epoch* bits are reset in preparation for the next epoch.

For a value, x, to be stale for epoch e_r on processor

Operation	Applies to	Bit Assignments	
		Valid Bit	*Epoch* Bit
Read	word	1	1
Write	word	1	1
Invalidate	section	*Epoch* Bit	-
end of epoch	all of cache	-	0

Table 1: Effect of operations on TS1 control bits

State	TS Time Stamp	TS1 Epoch Bit	TS1 Valid Bit
just accessed	= clock[+1]	= 1	= 1
not yet stale	= clock	= 0	= 1
stale	< clock	= 0	= 0

Table 2: Possible 'ages' of a cache line

p_i, it must have been written during epoch e_w, $e_w < e_r$ on p_j, $j \neq i$ and have been in p_i's cache on epoch $e_w - 1$. TS1 prevents staleness because x would appear in an invalidate on p_i at the end of epoch e_w. The value in cache in epoch $e_w - 1$ would be removed since p_i did not access x on epoch e_w and left its epoch reset from the end of epoch $e_w - 1$.

If compile time analysis were perfect, TS1 would have the same hit rate as a global scheme. The conservative assumptions that must be made at compile time cause some reuse to be missed. This is the loss that any local scheme must suffer.

4.4 Contrast between TS1 and previous strategies

The best way to understand why TS1 and TS have the same behavior is to return to TS and see it from a different point of view. There are only three states that a cache line can be in with respect to its clock, *just referenced*, *not yet stale*, and *stale* (Table 2). Taking these in reverse order, the *stale* state indicates that for a value x in epoch $e_w + 1$ a new value might have been written in epoch, e_w, after x was loaded in the cache in an earlier epoch, e_a. The *not yet stale* state persists from *after* epoch e_a when x was last accessed *through* epoch e_w which actually makes the line stale (DOALL semantics, section 2.1). The *just accessed* state sets the time stamp so that it will be in the *not yet stale* state in the next epoch. The *just accessed* state persists only for epoch e_a. The time stamp will be either clock+1 or clock depending on whether or not there is a write in epoch e_a.

TS1 implements these same three states by using the *epoch* bit in addition to the *valid* bit. This economy is possible because TS1 invalidates only those locations which could have been written. TS1 ages cache lines explicitly by updating bits in the cache line. TS ages cache lines implicitly by updating a processor clock for later comparison. TS is a lazy strategy.

TS as proposed enforces coherence on the whole array level. TS1 can be used to enforce coherence at the finest available resolution of compiler analysis. This is no worse than the whole array level and often better. TS could in principle do this well too by having a distinct clock for every section of an array which can be recognized at compile time. The cost of that could grow large.

LSS could utilize the same high level of analysis but it makes the pessimistic assumption that all paths are taken. Also, its counters quickly overrun regardless of the path taken. TS1 achieves at least the same hit rate as PEI because both can use the best available compiler analysis.

Another way to view this distinction of different strategies is the manner in which global information is passed. In FSI and LSS, global knowledge is never passed. In TS, global knowledge is passed implicitly by each processor incrementing an array clock for those arrays which might have been modified. In TS1 and PEI, global knowledge is passed implicitly by invalidating a section of memory that could have been written on a different processor. For local strategies, there is no way to avoid the invalidate because it is responsible for conveying the global information. The invalidate can be implicit, explicit, pessimistic, or reasonably precise, but it still has the same function. Table 3 summarizes the costs and capabilities of the different strategies.

4.5 Example

In figure 4, DOALLs are expanded into the worksharing part (PDO) where each processor gets some number of iterations, the common part that all processors execute, and the BARRIER, which is the end of the DOALL. Applying the TS1 compile time phase inserts the INVALIDATE's. For each of the three DOALL epochs, there is an invalidate to cover what was written in that epoch. Table 4 shows the effect on TS1 control bits for the simple schedule, processor 1 gets iteration 1 on each epoch. At line 11, A(1) and B(1,*) have been referenced on p_1 in this epoch. So all cache lines holding these values are valid and have the *epoch* bit set. At line 12, the invalidate removes everything written on p_2 from p_1's cache. If B(2,1) were present on p_1 it would be removed at this point. B(1,1) however has its *epoch* bit set and stays in the cache on p_1. All *epoch* bits are reset at the barrier. At line 21 only B(1,1) has its *epoch* bit set on p_1 since it was the only reference. The invalidate does not reference A or columns of B other than the first. So, all of those stay in cache. The invalidate of B(1,1) finds the *epoch* bit set and leaves it in cache. At line 30, all references are then hits.

Using the same example for TS, the write to B in the second epoch would cause all columns of B to be invalidated. Thus, in the third epoch, all but one element of B would be a miss on p_1.

For LSS, A would suffer the same as the other columns of B and would miss in the third epoch.

For PEI, the second epoch would be handled perfectly by only invalidating the first column of B. How-

725

	FSI	LSS	PEI	TS	TS1
Inter Epoch Reuse	No	Yes	Yes	Yes	Yes
Granularity of analysis	N/A	whole program	array section	array	array section
bits/cache line	2	3	0	$2 + n_{clock}$	1
bits/instruction	1	2	n	$5 + r_{clock}$ (for reads) $2 + r_{clock}$ (for writes)	0
special bits/processor	0	0	0	$s * n_{clock}$	0
cost of invalidate	O(1)	O(1)	O(1)	O(S)	$O(\sum_{i=1}^{S} \log(s_i))$
handles DOACROSS	No	No	No	Yes	Yes

Notation

n	number of address bits
n_{clock}	number of bits needed to hold clock value
r_{clock}	number of bits to designate a clock
S	number of distinct sections (or arrays) which are written in an epoch
s_i	size of the ith section out of S total sections

Table 3: Comparison of methods

```
    PDO I=1,N
       DO J=1,N
          B(I,J)=A(I)+1
       ENDDO
    ENDDO
11
    CALL INVALIDATE (B(1,1),B(N,N))
    BARRIER
12
    PDO I=1,N
       B(I,1)=0
    ENDDO
21
    CALL INVALIDATE (B(1,1),B(N,1))
    BARRIER
22
    PDO I=1,N
       DO J=1,N
30        C(I,J)=B(I,J)+A(I)
       ENDDO
    ENDDO
    CALL INVALIDATE (C(1,1),C(N,N))
```

Figure 4: Example compiler output for TS1

	Array Element on Processor 1		
Statement	A(1)	B(1,1)	B(1,2)
11	1 , 1	1 , 1	1 , 1
12	1 , 0	1 , 0	1 , 0
21	1 , 0	1 , 1	1 , 0
22	1 , 0	1 , 0	1 , 0
30	hit	hit	hit

Table 4: Example of bit handling in TS1, Entries: *valid* bit, *epoch* bit

ever, the first epoch would leave only the last column in cache. In the third epoch, the first and last column of B plus all of A would hit. The rest of B would miss.

5 Performance

The execution time of TS versus TS1 depends on two factors, the hit rate and the additional cycles used by a more sophisticated invalidate. We present experimental data on the former. We analyze the latter using reference traces from a real program combined with a hypothetical implementation of an invalidate

We compared TS and TS1 on a small test suite of scientific Fortran programs. These were chosen because they were available, familiar to the authors, and easily convertible to use with simulator. Our methodology was to apply the TS and TS1 algorithms by hand to parallel Fortran programs. For TS1, the same invalidate calls were added at the end of each epoch as the compiler would have produced. We assumed the compiler could recognize only affine subscript expressions. For TS, invalidate calls were applied to whole arrays in an epoch for which the array appeared on the left hand side of an assignment. This has the same effect on hit rate as the suggested TS implementation. These modified programs were then run through the the RPPT [5] simulator. This simulator operates by modifying the assembly code to trap at every global memory reference which is then passed off to a particular architecture simulator.

For identical runs of the test programs, we compared TS, TS1, and hardware coherence. For hardware coherence, we simulated write back caches with an invalidate protocol (WB).

Cyclic work distributions were used. Statistics reflect only shared data and not local data or instruction caching. Caches of sufficient size were simulated

	Procs	Size	TS	TS1	WB
LU	10	100	88.7	89.8	90.8
Heat Flow	20	60	62.6	63.5	63.5
Direct	4	4	97.1	97.1	97.7
Erlebacher	10	20	96.0	97.2	97.6

Table 5: Hit Ratios (%) for different strategies

so that no evictions occurred due to cache size or organization limitations.

Our test programs were:

LU decomposition - a blocked right looking LU decomposition with a blocking factor of 5.

Heat Flow - a simple 2-D heat flow relaxation

Direct - a simplex solver

Erlebacher - a tridiagonal solver for finding derivatives

5.1 Hit rates

Table 5 shows the hit rates for our test suite. Similar relative hit ratios resulted from different combinations of processor and block sizes, except for extreme cases. For larger problem sizes with evictions, the gap narrows.

In both LU and Heat Flow, TS1 managed to find extra hits by not invalidating the whole array in loops that set border elements of the (sub-)arrays. Direct made heavy use of indirection arrays which defeat all attempts at analysis. TS1 could do no better than TS in this case. For Erlebacher, TS1 was able to find substantial benefit because the main computation was distributed through several loops, many of which only modified a small section of a given array.

5.2 Invalidate overhead

Erlebacher is more than a computational kernel (so is Direct, but it showed no improvement). So, we focus on Erlebacher.

To better analyze this case, we looked more carefully at the *miss margin*, the number of extra misses per processor that TS suffers compared to TS1. For a fixed problem size, TS1 does worse as the number of processors increase because the total hit rate is only slightly affected causing the number of misses per processor to drop almost linearly. For a fixed number of processors, TS1 is favored by the same reasoning (for all but the simplest of invalidate implementations). Most importantly, as main memory latency increases TS1 is favored. For an invalidate cost model(section 4.2), we assumed that a contiguous section can be invalidated in $1 + \lfloor \log_2(|section|) \rfloor$ "invalidate cycles" (by "invalidate cycle" we mean the time it takes to invalidate a single, aligned, power-of-2-sized block) We applied this cost model to a series of Erlebacher runs where the problem size was varied from 2 to 30 as the number of processors varied from 1 to 15. We

Procs	Size	Refs	Miss Margin	Cost	Penalty
		1,000's / processor			
1	2	7.8	0.1	0.8	0.2
2	4	16.2	0.1	1.9	0.3
3	6	31.9	0.3	3.6	0.4
4	8	52.8	0.6	5.6	0.5
5	10	79.2	0.9	8.2	0.5
6	12	110.8	1.3	11.6	0.5
7	14	147.9	1.7	15.0	0.6
8	16	190.3	2.2	19.0	0.7
9	18	238.1	2.8	24.1	0.7
10	20	291.2	3.4	29.1	0.7
11	22	349.7	3.7	34.5	0.8
12	24	413.6	4.8	40.3	0.8
13	26	482.8	5.1	49.0	0.8
14	28	557.45	6.4	56.2	0.9
15	30	637.33	7.4	63.9	0.9

Cost: Invalidate cycles for $\log_2(s_i)$ metric
Penalty: Invalidate cycles for whole array invalidates

Table 6: Erlebacher Profitability

chose this as a natural scalability condition because the hit rate for TS stayed fairly constant with this condition. The raw data is summarized in table 6. For each run, it lists the total shared data references, the miss margin, the invalidate cost (for invalidating precise sections), and worst case TS1 penalty (in invalidate cycles). All of these are normalized to be per processor. Profitability depends on the relative cost of a miss versus the cost of an invalidate cycle. Figure 5 shows the profitability region for some hypothetical miss costs. The profitability is expressed as the percent speed up for a completely memory bound program (compute time is completely overlapped) with the assumption that cache hits take 1 processor cycle and an invalidate cycle takes 2 processor cycles. For different invalidate cycle costs, figure 5 would look essentially the same by scaling the miss cost the same amount. For real machines, we expect the cost of a miss to be 10's of cycles. We expect an implementation of invalidate to be possible where one invalidate cycle takes only 2 processor cycles.

For this test case, if the cost of a miss is almost negligible (1 invalidate cycle) then careful invalidation gains nothing and loses in overhead. If the cost of a miss is 20 cycles, it is a break even proposition. For higher miss costs, TS1 improves performance by paying for the invalidate overhead with time saved from more cache hits.

For miss costs less than 20 cycles, it is possible to switch from a precise invalidate to one which invalidates the whole array. This has the same hit rate as TS, but greatly reduces overhead. For instance, in the 15 processor case the overhead of invalidating whole arrays is about 0.3% (0.9/637*(2 processor cycles/ invalidate cycle)), even if every reference were a hit. The "loss lower bound" line in figure 5 represents this.

TS1 can often perform better than TS. Where it does worse, there is a fall back option, whole array invalidates, to cushion the loss to a tolerable amount.

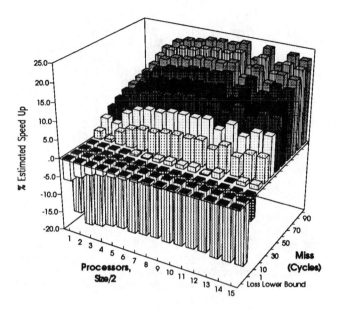

Figure 5: Erlebacher Speed Up

6 Other issues

6.1 DOACROSS

The assumed model for DOACROSS is that later iterations (instances) can wait on earlier iterations. There can be multiple waits on the same previous iterations or several different previous iterations. The compiler cannot necessarily determine anything about the nature of the synchronization. The only guarantee is that no dependences go from later to earlier iterations. A legal schedule for any DOACROSS would be to do the first p iterations with proper posting and waiting, then synchronize all p processors, and do the next p iterations, etc. Unlike DOALL, there can be carried dependence between iterations of a DOACROSS. So, each instance of a DOACROSS epoch must conceptually be treated like a different mini-epoch.

The leverage that local strategies get from the semantics of DOALL (section 2.1) must be abandoned here. For DOACROSS, the *epoch* bit in TS1 indicates that values can be reused on subsequent instances (not epochs). Since two subsequent iterations are almost certain to be scheduled to different processors, the *epoch* bit is useless.

Of the previous strategies surveyed, only Min and Baer's TS [14] handles DOACROSS. It increments the version number for an array at the end of a DOACROSS epoch. To preserve the semantics inside of the DOACROSS, any reference which could be overwritten in a later instance of the same DOACROSS epoch, is marked so that it will be removed at the end of the instance. Conversely, any read which could have been preceded by a write in a previous instance is invalidated on entry to this instance (intra-instance locality is still preserved).

Min and Baer's TS still preserves inter-epoch reuse if it can be proven (via the best available compiler analysis) that a given access will not be over-written on a later instance in the same epoch. Likewise, a read need not be forced to miss if it can be proven that no write on a previous instance of this epoch could reach it. Min and Baer's TS handles this situation with extra bits in the instruction word to specifically mark this condition. This is no longer optimal, even in the restricted sense of local strategies being optimal. Certain kinds of inter-instance intra-epoch reuse could be recognized by a local strategy, but are lost here.

TS1 could work in essentially the same way as TS for DOACROSS by adding the same extra bits. These extra bits could be avoided by changing the invalidation strategy. Instead of invalidating at the end of each epoch, the invalidate could be moved to the start of each instance. The invalidate would then handle those values written since this processor was last scheduled. For instance, if processors are assigned to iterations in strictly cyclic order and there are 5 processors. Then, processor 5, when it gets assigned iteration 11, would invalidate everything written on iterations 7 through 10. Iteration 6 writes were previously performed on processor 5 and do not need to be invalidated. Iterations before 6 were handled when processor 5 was assigned iteration 6. At the end of the DOACROSS, every processor must invalidate writes that occurred since it was last scheduled. This preserves the same inter-epoch reuse as Min and Baer's TS strategy.

In some cases involving DOACROSS, a *live* value is guaranteed to be invalidated before its next reference. In this case, there is no need to allocate a cache line. Read-thru and write-thru could selectively be used to advantage. Min and Baer [14] discuss this at length. This can be done with the bits already present in their strategy. TS1 could accommodate this with extra instruction bits performing the same function as in the Min and Baer strategy.

6.2 Critical sections

For critical section semantics that require inter-instance dependences to be entirely within critical sections, it is a simple matter to maintain coherence. Whatever is written in the critical section must be updated before the end of the section. Whatever is read in the critical section that could be written in another critical section must be invalidated on entry to the critical section.

6.3 Cache line size

Cache lines larger than one word cause aliasing problems. Values are read when they do not appear to be (as seen by the compiler). These values must also be kept coherent. There are several ad hoc methods of dealing with the aliasing problem, e.g. padding of array dimensions, changing layout order, and stripping loops. In truly desperate cases, it may be necessary to always use write-thru or not use caching at all. We assume that such objects are allocated on special cache pages in order to indicate different handling.

7 Conclusions

We believe the proper way to consider coherence strategies is in a framework of local knowledge versus global knowledge, and not as software versus hardware. This paper contributes to that framework.

As local strategies continue to improve their hit rates and decrease their implementation costs, it becomes feasible, at least for scientific codes, to build shared memory multiprocessors which rely on local strategies instead of global strategies for cache coherence. These machines have fewer obstacles to scalability. They may also be less hardware intensive than the sophisticated global strategies which have been proposed for medium and large scale parallelism.

In this paper, we propose a new local strategy, TS1 that improves on the best previously existing local strategy, time-stamping, by achieving better hit ratios, requiring fewer bits per cache line, and no extra bits per instruction. For a given granularity of compiler analysis, no local scheme could ever achieve a higher hit ratio. TS1 requires an *epoch* bit per cache line, a mechanism to invalidate an address range of cache lines, and a compiler that can recognize which array sections are written in a given epoch. If the compiler can only recognize arrays, and not sections, TS1 will have the same hit rate as time-stamping.

Simulation studies show that TS1 almost always has better hit ratios than TS and never worse. TS1 occasionally has slightly worse performance, but often appreciably better performance. An open question is to determine how efficiently a range based invalidate can be implemented. If only inefficient or hardware intensive implementations can be found, TS1 will not be as effective as our data suggest.

Acknowledgments

We would like to thank U. Rajagopalan and S. Dwarkadas for their assistance in modifying the RPPT simulator to handle the specific needs of a local strategy. We would also like to especially thank John Mellor-Crummey for his many useful suggestions on improving this paper.

References

[1] D. A. Abramson, K. Ramamohanarao, and M. Ross. A scalable cache coherence mechanism using a selectively clearable cache memory. *The Australian Computer Journal*, 21(1), Feb. 1989.

[2] L. M. Censier and P. Feautrier. A new solution to coherence problems in multicache systems. *IEEE Transactions on Computers*, C-27(12):1112–1118, Dec. 1978.

[3] H. Cheong. Life-span strategy - a compiler-based approach to cache coherence. In *Proceedings of 1992 International Conference on Supercomputing*, July 1992.

[4] H. Cheong and A. Veidenbaum. Compiler-directed cache management for multiprocessors. *Computer*, 23(6):39–47, June 1990.

[5] R. Covington, S. Dwarkadas, J. Jump, J. Sinclair, and S. Madala. Efficient simulation of paralle computer systems. *International Journal in Comuter Simulation*, 1:31–58, 1991. overview of RPPT.

[6] R. Cytron, S. Karlovsky, and K. McAuliffe. Automatic management of programmable caches. In *Proc. of the 1988 International Conference on Parallel Processing*, pages 229–238, Aug. 1988.

[7] E. Darnell, J. Mellor-Crummey, and K. Kennedy. Automatic software cache coherence through vectorization. In *Proceedings of 1992 International Conference on Supercomputing*, July 1992. Also available as expanded Technical Report CRPC-TR92197, Center for Research on Parallel Computation, January 1992.

[8] D. James, A. Laundrie, S. Gjessing, and G. Sohi. Scalable coherent interface. *Computer*, 23(6), June 1990.

[9] S. Karlovsky. Automatic management of programmable caches: Algorithms and experience. Technical Report 89-8010, Center for Supercomputing Research and Development, University of Illinois, Urbana, IL, July 1989.

[10] L. Lamport. How to make a multiprocessor that correctly executes multiprocess programs. *IEEE Transactions on Computers*, C-28(9), Sept. 1979.

[11] D. Lenoski, J. Laudon, K. Gharachorloo, W. Weber, A. Gupta, J. Hennessy, M. Horowitz, and M. Lam. The Standford DASH multiprocessor. *Computer*, 25(3):63–79, Mar. 1992.

[12] A. Louri and H. Sung. A compiler directed cache coherence scheme with fast and parallel explicit invalidation. In *Proc. of the 1992 International Conference on Parallel Processing*, pages 2–9, Aug. 1992.

[13] E. P. Markatos and T. J. LeBlanc. Using processor affinity in loop scheduling on shared-memory multiprocessors. in *Proceedings of 1992 International Conference on Supercomputing*, pages 104–113, Nov. 1992.

[14] S. Min and J. Baer. Design and analysis of a scalable cache coherence scheme based on clocks and timestamps. *IEEE Transactions on Parallel and Distributed Systems*, 3(1):25–44, Jan. 1992.

[15] S. Min, J. Baer, and H. Kim. An efficient caching support for critical sections in large-scale shared-memory multiprocessors. In *Proc. of the 1990 International Conference on Supercomputing/Computer Architecture News*, pages 4–47, June 1990. Special issue of Computer Architecture News, 18(3), Sept. 1990.

[16] A. Osterhaug, editor. *Guide to Parallel Programming on Sequent Computer Systems*. Sequent Technical Publications, San Diego, CA, 1989.

[17] K. Peterson and K. Li. Cache coherence for shared memory multiprocessors based on virtual memory support. In *Proceedings of the 7th International Parallel Processing Symposium*, Apr. 1993.

[18] D. Schanin. The design and development of a very high speed system bus - the encore multimax nanobus. In *Proceedings of the Fall Joint Computer Conference*, pages 410–418, Nov. 1986.

[19] J. Willis, A. Sanderson, and C. Hill. Cache coherence in systems with parallel communication channels & many processors. In *Supercomputing '90*, pages 554–563, 1990.

A Cache Coherence Scheme
Suitable for Massively Parallel Processors

Reid Baldwin
Department of Computer Science
Michigan State University

Abstract

A new approach to cache coherent networks is proposed and analyzed. This approach is highly scalable, so it is appropriate for massively parallel multiprocessors. The network switches of a MIN are enhanced such that they are capable of handling the majority of the cache coherence burden. The latency for both reads and writes is $O(\log N)$ independent of the number of copies. The memory overhead of this approach is $O(C \log^2 N)$.

1 Introduction

1.1 Motivation

Caches have been used very successfully in uniprocessors to dramatically increase performance by reducing accesses to the slow main memory. Large multiprocessors generally have much longer main memory access times than uniprocessors, and the access times increase with system size. The potential for performance improvement by using caches in multiprocessors is even greater than for uniprocessors [3]. The use of private caches is crucial to the advancement of very large multiprocessors.

However, when caches are used in shared memory multiprocessors, some scheme must be used to ensure consistency between caches. When the same cache line is stored in two or more caches and one processor updates the line, all processors must get the new value on subsequent reads. This problem is referred to as the cache coherence problem and has been the focus of a great deal of research[7]. However, existing solutions to this problem exhibit poor scalability which has hindered the development of very large multiprocessors.

1.2 Existing approaches

The distinguishing feature of a cache coherence scheme is the method employed to find all of the cached copies when necessary. A variety of schemes for finding copies have been proposed.

One approach, called snoopy schemes, is to let each cache controller monitor the bus to determine what all other processors are doing[2, 7]. The limitation of snoopy caches is that memory accesses of all processors must be visible to all other processors. This severely limits the number of processors.

Directory based schemes avoid the need for a broadcast medium by maintaining directories of which processors have copies of which lines. Maintaining these directories requires a substantial amount of additional memory. I will discuss several of the many variants briefly. For a more complete discussion, please refer to [1].

In a traditional full-map directory scheme, the memory module stores a directory entry with each cache line. The directory entry has one bit for each processor, indicating the presence or absence of that cache line in that processor's cache. Stenstrom[7] proposed an alternate full directory scheme in which the directory is kept with a cached copy, reducing the memory overhead.

One variant, called chained directories, reduces the memory overhead by storing pointers to each copy in a linked list. The memory only needs to store a pointer to the front of the list. The caches each store a pointer to the next processor in the list.

Partial directory schemes reduce the overhead by storing a small constant number, i, of pointers to copies instead of using a bit for each processor. When more than i processors wish to cache the line, a directory overflow occurs. There are two ways of handling directory overflows. In a partial directory with broadcast, designated $Dir_i B$, future coherence messages are broadcast to all processors. In a partial directory without broadcast, designated $Dir_i NB$, one of the existing copies is invalidated to make room for a pointer to the new copy.

In cache coherent networks, the network switches maintain sufficient state information to route messages to appropriate processors. Generally, each switch contains a cache indicating which of the subnetworks corresponding to its ports have copies. Some schemes require a multilevel inclusion property that for every entry in a processor cache, there must be a corresponding entry in every switch cache between the processor and the memory module. When conflicts occur in a switch cache, some line in a processor cache must be invalidated to maintain the inclusion property. Some cache coherent networks avoid the inclusion requirement by handling switch cache misses with a broadcast [6].

1.3 Outline

In this paper, I propose an alternative approach to cache coherence reduces memory overhead while providing superior performance when many cached copies exist. The proposed system offers significant advantages for the very large systems that are likely in the future. I describe the proposed approach in section 2.

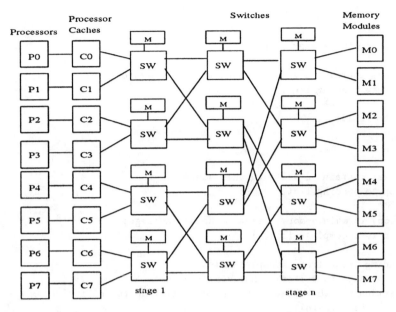

Figure 1: System Layout for a System with 8 Nodes

Section 3 contains a proof of correctness of the scheme and the proposed protocol. In section 4, I illustrate that the memory overhead is substantially less than for other schemes. The performance is examined in section 5, and found to be competitive with, and in some situations superior to, existing schemes. Finally, I suggest some possible enhancements in section 6.

2 Description

To keep the description as clear as possible, I will present the essential elements of the scheme first. Then, I will present a detailed protocol and illustrate with an example. Discussion of enhancements will be delayed until a later section.

2.1 Assumptions

I will assume that memory is connected to processors using a multistage interconnection network (MIN) with n stages of k x k switches (see figure 1). It will also work for any k-ary n-cube, such as a mesh or hypercube, by mapping the network to a MIN. There are $N = k^n$ processors and memory modules. Each processor has a private cache. An additional cache is associated with each switch.

The switches are crossbar networks with the ports toward the processors called processor ports and the ports toward the memory called memory ports (see figure 2). Each switch has k^2 bi-directional channels, so that any processor port can be connected to any memory port. Each switch also has a small buffer to store at least one message while waiting for access to the next switch. Messages are forwarded to the next stage as soon as possible instead of setting up the entire path first as in circuit switching.

2.2 Finding copies

The state is recorded in the caches associated with each switch. For each address in these caches, the

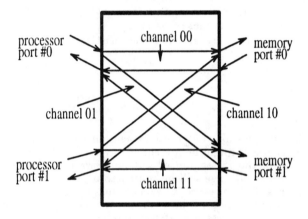

Figure 2: A 2x2 Switch

switch stores a count of the number of data lines "matching" the address that have been passed via each channel. Unlike other cache coherent networks, the tag for each line is not stored. The switch caches are addressed with a subset of the bits of the memory address. As will be discussed in section 5.1, this subset should be different for each stage.

A multicast message from main memory (such as an invalidate or update message) is routed to all caches with a copy by utilizing the counters described above. When a multicast message arrives at a memory port of a switch, the switch looks up the counters for all channels which use that memory port. If the count of lines passed on a channel is one or more, then that line might be present in a cache and the message must be forwarded along that channel. The message may be forwarded along zero, one, or several processor ports. It is possible that the lines counted do not include the

```
Repeat forever {
get message; switch based on message type {
  subscribe request:
    if (incomplete list contains a write to address in requested line)
      add transaction to pending list;
    else
      send a subscribe reply;
  unsubscribe:
    ignore it;
  write request:
    if (incomplete list contains a write to that address)
      add transaction to pending list;
    else
      { update the copy in main memory; issue an update message;
      add transaction to incomplete list; }
  acknowledge:
    remove corresponding write from incomplete list;
    send write reply message to writer; issue verify message;
    for (each transaction for that line in the pending list up to and including the first write)
      { if (the message is a write)
        { update the copy in main memory; issue an update message;
        add transaction to incomplete list; }
      else /* message is a read */
        send a subscribe reply;
      remove transaction from pending list; }
} }
```

Figure 3: Psuedocode for Memory Modules

line in question, but the message must be forwarded whenever it might be present. Conversely, if the count is zero, the message need not be forwarded. In this way, the message will be routed to a superset of the caches that have a copy. When a message is routed to a cache that doesn't have a copy, the recipient simply ignores the message. If the number of unnecessary messages is small, they will not reduce performance considerably. In section 5.1, I show that the frequency of unnecessary messages can easily be made small.

2.3 Consistency models

Before discussing the protocol, I must define precisely what is meant by cache consistency, and what primitives must be provided. There are several different models of memory consistency. Sequential consistency, the most stringent consistency model, insist that all memory accesses appear as if they are atomically performed as some interleaving of the memory accesses performed by each of the processors. The weak consistency and release consistency models are less restrictive [4, 5].

Any of these consistency models can be implemented by placing *fence* operations at the correct points in the code[5]. Fence operations delay the initiating of the next access until all previous accesses are completed. By definition, a write transaction is completed as soon as all copies have been updated and a read transaction is completed as soon as the write that

supplied the data has completed. For example, to implement sequential consistency, a fence must be placed before every memory transaction. Weak consistency and release consistency require fewer fences. The key to implementing the fence operation is that each cache controller must receive a verify message when a write has been propagated to all copies.

2.4 Protocol

Two categories of protocol have been proposed: write-invalidate and write-update. Write-invalidate protocols, which are more common, invalidate all remote copies prior to each write. Write-update protocols propagate the new value to all copies. Which category is superior depends on application characteristics. Write-update protocols result in a lower miss rate because lines are not invalidated. However, by granting exclusive access to a processor following a write, write-invalidate protocols perform better when successive accesses to a line are usually by the same processor.

Both categories of protocol have been implemented in simulation for the proposed method of finding copies. A write-update protocol is presented here. The psuedocode for the protocol is presented in Figures 3 through 5. The details of the protocol are more complicated than a snoopy protocol because the transactions are not atomic. For example, memory modules must treat a write request somewhat differently if the

```
Repeat forever {
get message; switch based on message type {
  subscribe request from processor port:
    forward subscribe request to appropriate memory port;
  subscribe reply from memory port:
    forward subscribe reply to appropriate processor port;
    increment appropriate counter in switch cache;
  unsubscribe request from processor port:
    forward unsubscribe request to appropriate memory port;
    decrement appropriate counter in switch cache;
  write request from processor port:
    forward write request to appropriate memory port;
  update message from memory port:
    check counters in switch cahe for the channels involving that memory port;
    if (at least one counter is non-zero)
      forward update message along corresponding processor ports;
    else
      send acknowledgement along appropriate memory port;
    add transaction to incomplete list, recording which processor ports received messages;
  acknowledge message from processor:
    update transaction in incomplete list, noting that acknowledgement was received;
    if (acknowledgements received along all processor ports which received update messages)
      send acknowledge message along appropriate memory port;
  verify message from memory port:
    forward verify message to each processor port that received the update messages;
    remove transaction from incomplete list;
} }
```

Figure 4: Psuedocode for Switches

previous write request for that address has not completed.

In addition to the counters, the following state information is maintained. Each word in a cache line can be in one of 3 states:

MISSING No data is stored for that line

COMPLETE The write that stored the data has completed

INCOMPLETE The write that stored the data might not have completed.

Each cache maintains a list of pending transactions and incomplete transactions and a status bit called **fenced** which indicates whether the processor is waiting on a fence operation. Memory modules must also keep lists of pending and incomplete transactions. Each switch keeps a list of incomplete updates indicating on which processor ports the update messages were sent and whether they have been acknowledged.

When a processor issues a read, the cache controller checks the status of the requested word and the tag for the appropriate cache line. If the tag matches and the status is not MISSING, then it is a read hit and the data can be returned immediately. If the status is INCOMPLETE, the transaction must be added to the list of incomplete transactions.

If the status was MISSING or the tag did not match, then it is a read miss and the data must be requested from main memory. Instead of simply reading a cache line following a read miss, a cache *subscribes* to the line. It receives the current value and also receives updates whenever the line is subsequently modified. To subscribe, the cache issues a subscribe request and places the transaction in the pending list. Upon receiving the subscribe request, the memory module waits until the most recent write to that line has completed, and then sends the data back to the switch in a subscribe reply. As the switches route the subscribe reply to the cache, they increment the appropriate counters. When the cache controller receives the subscribe reply, it removes the read transaction from the pending list and returns the data to the processor.

When a cache line must be replaced to make room for the new data, an unsubscribe request is sent to cancel the subscription. As the switches route the unsubscribe request to the memory modules, they decrement the appropriate counter.

When a processor issues a write, the cache controller immediately sends a write request to the memory module and places the transaction into the incomplete list. The cache is not updated yet. If a previous write to that address is still incomplete, the memory module places the request in a pending list. Once all

733

```
Repeat forever {
get message; switch based on message type {
  read request from processor:
     if (tag does not match) or (status is MISSING) /* read miss */
        { send a subscribe request to adjacent switch; add transaction to pending list; }
     else /* read hit */
        { send data to processor; if (status is INCOMPLETE) add transaction to incomplete list; }
  write request from processor:
     send write request to adjacent switch; add transaction to incomplete list;
  fence request from processor:
     if (both incomplete and pending lists are empty)
        send fence clearance message to processor;
     else
        set fenced = TRUE;
  subscribe reply from switch:
     if (status of line is not MISSING) send unsubscribe message for replaced line;
     place new data into cache line; set cache line status to COMPLETE;
     if (pending list contains read request for address)
        { send data to processor; remove the read request from pending list; }
     if (fenced) and (both pending and incomplete list now empty)
        { send fence clearance to processor; set fenced = FALSE; }
  update message from switch:
     if (tag matches) and (status is not MISSING)
        { update data in cache; set status of cache line to INCOMPLETE; }
     send acknowledge message to switch;
  verify message from switch:
     if (tag matches) and (status is not MISSING)
        set status of cache line to COMPLETE;
     remove any read transactions for that line from incomplete list;
     if (fenced) and (both pending and incomplete list now empty)
        { send fence clearance to processor; set fenced = FALSE; }
  write reply from switch:
     remove any write transactions for that line from incomplete list;
     if (fenced) and (both pending and incomplete list now empty)
        { send fence clearance to processor; set fenced = FALSE; }
} }
```

Figure 5: Psuedocode for Cache Controllers

previous writes have completed, the memory module updates main memory and issues an update message into the network. As switches receive the update message, they consult their memories and forward the update message whenever a counter is non-zero, adding the transaction to their incomplete list. The update message reaches all caches that have a copy and perhaps some others. When the cache receives an update message, it checks to see if it has the data and updates it if it is present, changing the status to INCOMPLETE. It then sends back an acknowledgement. As soon as a switch has received an acknowledgement from every port on which it sent the update, it sends an acknowledgement on its memory port. When the single acknowledgement is returned to the memory module, the write has completed and the memory module issues a verify message. The switches locate the transaction

in the list of incomplete updates and route the verify messages to exactly the same caches that received the update message. The switch can then remove the transaction from the list. When a cache receives a verify message it sets the status to COMPLETE and removes any incomplete read transactions from the incomplete list. To make sure the writer is informed of the completion of the transaction, a write reply is sent by the memory module to the writer. Upon receiving the write reply, the cache controller can remove the write transaction from its incomplete list.

When a processor issues a fence message, the cache controller checks the incomplete and pending lists. If they are empty, a fence clearance message is returned immediately. Otherwise, the fenced bit is set and the processor is not allowed to issue any more request. After any message that can remove transactions from

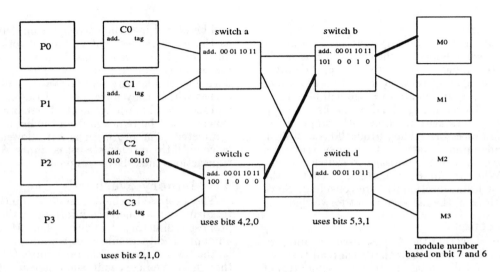

Figure 6: State of system after P2 subscribes to 00110010

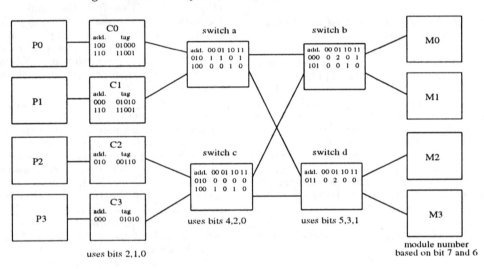

Figure 7: State of system after several more subscribe requests

the incomplete or pending lists (subscribe replies, verify messages, and write replies), the cache controller must check whether the processor should be allowed to clear the fence.

2.5 Example

In the following example, I will use a system with only four processors, four memory modules, and eight bit addresses. In this system, each processor cache and each switch cache have eight entries. The processor caches are direct mapped based on the 3 lowest order bits of the address. The memory module is determined by the 2 highest order bits. The switch caches in the first and second stages use bits 4,2,0 and 5,3,1 respectively (an arbitrary choice). Figure 6 illustrates the state of the system after processor 2 subscribes to address 00110010. Bits 5, 3, and 1 of the address are 1, 0, and 1 and the data is passed to processor port 1 from memory port 0 of switch b. Therefore, switch b increments the 10 entry at location 101 of its memory as it

forwards the data. Similarly, switch c increments the 00 entry at location 100 in its memory. Figure 7 shows the state of the system after 01010000 has been subscribed by P1 and P3, 11001110 has been subscribed by P0 and P1, and 01000100 has been subscribed by P0.

To illustrate how updates are routed, observe what happens when 11001110 is updated. Memory module 3 will send an update message to switch d. Since the update message arrived at memory port 1, the switch will consult the 01 and 11 entries at the appropriate switch address (011). The 01 entry is non-zero, so switch d forwards the message to switch a (processor port 0). The 11 entry is zero, so switch d can be sure that no processor which uses its processor port 1 has a copy. When switch a receives the message, it consults the 01 and 11 entries at location 010. Since they are both non-zero, the update is sent to both P0 and P1. The update has been forwarded to exactly the correct processors.

To illustrate how unnecessary messages are generated, observe what happens when 01010000 is modified. When the update arrives at switch c, the switch will consult the 00 and 10 entries at location 100. Since both are non-zero, an update message will be sent to both P2 and P3, even though P2 does not have a copy.

Unnecessary messages are frequently stopped before reaching processors. When 01000100 is modified, switch b sends update messages to both switch a and switch c, even though the message to switch c is unnecessary. When the message arrives at switch c, the 00 and 10 entries at location 010 are consulted. Since they are both zero, the message is not forwarded.

3 Correctness

In order to show that the proposed scheme and protocol are correct, I must show that each read transaction will return valid data and that the semantics of fence operations are observed.

Lemma 1 *Update messages will be sent to all cached copies of a modified cache line.*

For any cached copy, there must have been a subscribe reply which supplied the data. That subscribe reply would have traveled through a series of channels leading from the main memory module to the cache. The counter for each of those channels would have been incremented at that time. For each time the counter was decremented by an unsubscribe, it would have been incremented by a previous subscribe. Therefore, the counters for each of those channels would be at least one. Any update message for the modified line would be forwarded on those channels, eventually reaching the copy. □

Theorem 1 *All read request will be answered with valid data.*

The memory controllers enforce a strict ordering on the writes to a particular address by only allowing one write to progress at a time. To be considered valid, the returned data must have been supplied either by the most recently completed write to that address or a subsequent (incomplete) write. If the address was in the cache at the time the most recently completed write was performed by the main memory, then the data was either updated or unsubscribed before the update arrived. There is no way that the address could remain in the cache with the old data. If the address is not in the cache when the read request arrives, a subscribe request will be issued and the subscribe reply will contain valid data. □

Theorem 2 *Processors will not be allowed to clear a fence until all transactions issued before the fence have completed.*

For a read hit, if the write that supplied the data has not yet completed, the status of that cache line would be incomplete, and the transaction would be placed into the incomplete list. All write transactions will be placed into the cache's incomplete list as soon as the write request enters the network. Therefore, all incomplete transactions from a processor will be placed in the incomplete list. The memory module does not send a write reply or verify message until all caches with a copy have received the update message and sent an acknowledgement. Therefore, the transactions will not be removed from the list until they have completed. The processor is not allowed to clear the fence until the incomplete list is empty, so all previous transactions must have completed. □

4 Memory overhead

The proposed scheme uses substantially less total memory for coherence information than previously proposed directory schemes. Let M be the total amount of data memory in a multiprocessor and C be the total amount of cache memory ($C << M$). Although the average count is not dependent on N, there will be some lines which are subscribed to by most or all processors. Therefore, the number of bits allocated for each counter must be $O(\log N)$. The number of lines in each switch cache is approximately the same as the number of lines in each processor cache. There are $O(C/N)$ counters per switch and $O(N \log N)$ switches. Therefore, the memory overhead of this approach is $O(C \log^2 N)$.

The memory overhead is summarized in Table 1. For a traditional full directory, N bits are needed for each line in main memory. In Stenstrom's full directory [7] N bits are required for each cache line and $M \log N$ bits for pointers from each line in memory to the directory. Chained directories require $M \log N$ bits for pointers to the beginnings of the linked lists and $C \log N$ bits for the linked lists. A partial directory with i pointers requires $iM \log N$ bits of overhead. In other cache coherent networks, each switch cache line required k bits for the map and $\log N$ bits for the tag. However, to reduce the frequency of extra invalidations or switch cache misses, the switch caches must have considerably more lines than the processor caches.

Scheme	Storage Overhead
Proposed Scheme	$O(C \log^2 N)$
Full Directory	$O(MN)$
Stenstrom	$O(CN + M \log N)$
$Dir_i B$	$O(M \log N)$
$Dir_i NB$	$O(M \log N)$
Chained Directory	$O(C \log N + M \log N)$
Coherent Network	$O(C \log^2 N)$

Table 1: Summary of Memory Overhead

5 Performance analysis

In order to determine if this scheme is practical, we must evaluate the bandwidth (throughput) requirements on the interconnection network and the latency of main memory accesses. The bandwidth is the number of messages the network can transmit per unit time. Latency is the elapsed time between a processor issuing a request and receiving the response. Latency will usually degrade performance for read request because the processor cannot proceed until it gets the new value. The processor can proceed after a write request, but it may be blocked by a *fence* operation. Substantial delays may occur if many *fence* operations are required to enforce the consistency model, as described in section 2.4.

The performance of the proposed scheme will be compared to alternate methods of finding copies by assuming that all schemes use similar write-update protocols. The results are similar if write-invalidate protocols are assumed. I will begin by analyzing the frequency of unnecessary messages. Then, I will analyze the latency of read and write transactions disregarding contention. Finally, I analyze the number of messages which must be exchanged for each transactions. More messages implies higher utilization of bandwidth and longer delays due to contention.

The actual performance depends heavily on application characteristics. In general, the proposed scheme is superior to others when the number of copies of each line is high, as might be expected in a very large system.

5.1 Analysis of unnecessary messages

As mentioned before, some unnecessary messages will reach processors. In this section, I show that the fraction of messages which are unnecessary can easily be limited by using large enough switch caches.

Let the average count in switch caches be λ, the cache size be h_{proc} lines and the switch cache size be h_{switch}. Each of the Nh_{proc} cache lines that is occupied will be counted in exactly one counter in each stage. Each stage contains N/k switches with h_{switch} addresses and k^2 counters per address (one for each channel). Therefore,

$$\lambda = \frac{Nh_{proc}}{\frac{N}{k}k^2h_{switch}} = \frac{h_{proc}}{kh_{switch}}. \qquad (1)$$

If the access pattern is uniform, the distribution of counts is binomial, but it can be accurately approximated by a poisson distribution. From the poisson distribution function, the probability that the count will be 0 is $e^{-\lambda}$. This implies that when the line in question has not been passed, the probability of sending an unnecessary message, will be

$$P = 1 - e^{-\lambda}. \qquad (2)$$

Lemma 2 *If an update message arrives at a switch in stage i, and there are no copies of the memory line accessible through that switch, then the expected number of update messages reaching processors is $(kP)^i$.*

The proof will be by induction. Since there are k possible channels on which a message might be forwarded, the expected number of messages at stage $i-1$ is (kP). For $i = 1$, the expected number of messages reaching processors is kP, providing an induction basis. Since a different subset of the address bits is used

at each stage, the probability of passing the message is independent of other stages. For $i > 1$, the expected number of messages reaching processors is the expected number of messages reaching stage $i-1$ times the expected number of messages reaching processors as a result of each of those messages, which is $(kP)^{i-1}$ by the induction hypothesis.

$$E[\#messages] = kP(kP)^{i-1} = (kP)^i \square$$

The independence between stages is important. If the same subset of bits were used in each stage, any unnecessary message would reach at least one cache. The cache line that caused the counter to be non-zero would also cause the counters to be non-zero for the remaining path to the cache containing that line. However, by using a different (not necessarily disjoint) subset of the memory address, the cache line that causes the unnecessary message will probably be included in a different counter in the remaining stages.

Theorem 3 *If there is exactly 1 copy of a memory line, then the expected number of unnecessary messages reaching processors is $z = (k-1)P\frac{1-(kP)^n}{1-kP}$*

At each stage along the path from memory to the copy, the switch will send a necessary message on one channel and will send an unnecessary message on each of the $k-1$ others with probability P. By the previous Lemma, an unnecessary message generated in stage i (sent to stage $i-1$) will result in an expected number of unnecessary messages of $(kP)^{i-1}$. The expected total number of unnecessary messages is therefore

$$z = \sum_{i=1}^{n}(k-1)P(kP)^{i-1} = (k-1)P\frac{1-(kP)^n}{1-kP}\square$$

Theorem 4 *If there are b copies of a memory line ($b > 1$), then the expected number of unnecessary messages reaching processors is less than zb*

When only one copy exist, the expected number of unnecessary messages is z. If a second copy exist, the necessary message to the first copy will branch at some stage i, $1 \le i \le n$. The second copy will generate unnecessary messages only in stages 1 through $i-1$. Thus, the expected number of unnecessary messages attributable to the second copy is $(k-1)P\frac{1-(kP)^{i-1}}{1-kP}$ which is less than z. Each additional copy will generate unnecessary messages only for that part of its route that differs from previous copies. $\square$

Theorem 5 *If $P < 1/k$, then the expected ratio of unnecessary messages to necessary messages is bounded by $\frac{(k-1)P}{1-kP}$, independent of network size.*

$$\frac{E[\#unnec.]}{\#nec.} \le \frac{zb}{b} < \lim_{n \to \infty} z = \frac{(k-1)P}{1-kP}\square$$

To illustrate, if the processor caches and switch caches each have the same number of entries and $k = 2$, then $\lambda = .5$, $P = .393$, and $z < 1.85$. As λ decreases, z decreases rapidly. If $\lambda = .25$, $P = .221$ and $z < 0.397$. In $Dir_i B$ and cache coherent networks without inclusion, the expected ratio of unnecessary messages to necessary messages increases rapidly as network size increases.

5.2 Latency analysis

Disregarding contention, the latencies for read and write transactions are determined by the latencies of point to point and multicast messages. For all of the schemes, read misses can be handled by point to point messages in $O(\log N)$ time. The average read latency will depend on both the miss latency and the miss rate. The miss rate will be slightly higher for $Dir_i NB$ due to invalidations following directory overflows. Writes require an acknowledged multicast message to all copies of the written line.

Latencies for multicast messages, such as update messages and verification messages, differ significantly depending on the scheme used. For most directory schemes, the sender must either send multiple point to point messages or a single message with a list of addresses. For b destinations, it takes the source $O(b)$ time to send the message in either case. Therefore, the last message will arrive $O(b + \log N)$ after sending commences. Multicast are performed the same way for partial directories, but b is always less than or equal to the small constant i, so the latencies are $O(\log N)$. For a chained directory scheme, a message to destination j is sent only after a message is received at destination $j - 1$. The total latency is therefore $O(b \log N)$. In the proposed scheme, as well as other cache coherent networks, multicast require $O(\log N)$ time. Unlike a point to point message, however, each switch must consult the counters before forwarding the message. Therefore, the latency is a constant factor larger than for a point to point message.

Scheme	Read-Miss Latency	Write Latency
Proposed	$O(\log N)$	$O(\log N)$
Full Dir.	$O(\log N)$	$O(b + \log N)$
$Dir_i B$	$O(\log N)$	$O(\log N)$
$Dir_i NB$	$O(\log N)$	$O(\log N)$
Chained Dir.	$O(\log N)$	$O(b \log N)$
Coh. Networks	$O(\log N)$	$O(\log N)$

Table 2: Summary of Latencies without Contention

The contention free latencies of the various schemes are shown in table 2. The latencies of the proposed scheme are at least within a constant factor of the corresponding latencies for any other scheme. If there are many copies of a line, the proposed scheme will outperform most other schemes either in terms of write latency or hit rate.

5.3 Bandwidth analysis

The channel utilization is determined by the number of messages required to complete each transaction, and by the miss rate. As the number of messages required for each transaction increases, the channel utilization increases and performance decreases. The miss rate influences the number of subscribe transactions. The bandwidth requirements are summarized in table 3. Schemes with sub-optimal hit rates are marked with an asterisk.

For a full or partial directory, each read-miss results in two messages, a subscribe request and subscribe reply. For $Dir_i NB$, an additional two messages are required when a directory overflow occurs. For a full directory or $Dir_i NB$, each write request results in $2 + 3b$ messages. For $Dir_i B$, there are $2 + 3b$ messages when the directory is big enough and $2 + 3N$ messages when the directory overflows.

For a chained directory, read-misses generate three messages, a subscribe request, a subscribe reply, and a message to add the new copy to the chain. A write generates $2 + 2b$ messages. The write request goes to the memory module. The update goes to the head of the chain and then to the remaining $b - 1$ processors in the chain. The end processor in the chain sends the verify message to the writer and to the head of the chain. The verify message must then traverse the remaining $b - 1$ processors in the chain.

For the proposed scheme, each read-miss generates two messages. Following a write, the update message will reach b processors with a copy and an average of at most bz additional processors. Each write will result in an average of at most $2 + 3b + 3bz$ total messages in stage 1. Fewer messages will be generated in other stages due to the natural combining of the scheme. As discussed in section 5.1, z can be made small for any N.

Other cache coherent networks behave similarly, except that no upper bound on unnecessary messages can be established without an inclusion property. A miss in a switch cache will usually result in a message to almost all processors in the subnetwork [6]. Very high hit rates in the switch caches are needed in order to achieve acceptable performance.

Scheme	Expected No. of Messages	
	Read-Miss	Write
Proposed	2	$< 2 + 3b + 3bz$
Full Dir.	2	$2 + 3b$
$Dir_i B$	2	$2 + 3b$ $(b \leq i)$ $2 + 3N$ $(b > i)$
$Dir_i NB$*	$2 (b \leq i)$ $4 (b > i)$	$2 + 3b$
Chained Dir.	3	$2 + 2b$
Coh. Network /wo Inclusion	2	$> 2 + 3b$
Coh. Network /w Inclusion*	2	$2 + 3b$

Table 3: Summary of Bandwidth Requirements

6 Enhancements

There are several improvements which can be made to the protocol described in section 2.4 which are noteworthy. I describe them separately because they are not critical to the basic idea of the approach and would obfuscate the description and analysis.

6.1 Excluding non-shared data

As illustrated in section 5, reducing this average count would improve performance. One simple way that the count can be reduced is by not counting private and static data (including instructions). There would need to be separate message types for these types of data. The update, acknowledge, and verify messages could be avoided following writes to private data, virtually eliminating write latencies for those transactions. The required changes to the protocol are straight forward and substantial performance improvement results.

6.2 Hybrid schemes

An attractive alternative would be to combine this approach with the Dir_iB approach. In the hybrid scheme (call it Dir_iMC for multicast), the proposed approach would be used instead of broadcast when the directory size is exceeded. Cached lines that do not overflow their directories could be excluded from the counters, which would allow very low average counts with smaller switch memories. The hybrid scheme would retain the advantages of Dir_iB when the number of copies is low and the advantages of the proposed scheme when the number of copies is high.

7 Conclusion

A new cache coherence approach has been described which is very scalable. The memory overhead of this approach is only $O(C \log^2 N)$. The latencies, both for reads and writes, remain $O(\log N)$ independent of the number of copies. Although some unnecessary messages are generated, the ratio of unnecessary message to necessary messages can easily be made small, independent of N. The proposed scheme outperforms others when the number of cached copies is large. This is significant since most applications have at least some data that is widely shared. A hybrid scheme, Dir_iMC, would blend the benefits of partial directories when the number of copies is low with the benefits of the proposed scheme when the directories overflow.

References

[1] David Chaiken, Craig Fields, Kiyoshi Kurihara, and Anant Agarwal. Directory-based cache coherence in large scale multiprocessors. *IEEE Computer*, pages 49–58, May 1990.

[2] Angel L. DeCegama. *The Technology of Parallel Processing*, volume 1. Prentice-Hall, 1989.

[3] Michel Dubios and Shreekant Thakkar. Cache architectures in tightly coupled multiprocessors. *IEEE Computer*, pages 9–11, May 1990.

[4] Kourosh Gharachorloo, Daniel Lenoski, James Laudon, Phillip Gibbons, Anoop Gupta, and John Hennessy. Memory consistency and event ordering in scalable shared-memory multiprocessors. In *The 17th Annual International Symposium on Computer Architecture*, pages 15–25, 1990.

[5] Christoph Scheurich and Michel Dubois. Correct memory operations of cache-based multiprocessors. In *The 14th Annual International Symposium on Computer Architecture*, pages 234–243, 1987.

[6] Steven L. Scott and James R. Goodman. Performance of pruning cache directories for large-scale multiprocessors. *IEEE Transactions on Parallel and Distributed Systems*, 4(5):520–534, 1993.

[7] Per Stenstrom. A survey of cache coherence schemes for multiprocessors. *IEEE Computer*, pages 12–24, May 1990.

A Distributed Shared Memory Multiprocessor: ASURA
— Memory and Cache Architectures —

Shin-ichiro MORI[†], Hideki SAITO[†], Masahiro GOSHIMA[†],
Mamoru YANAGIHARA[‡], Takashi TANAKA[‡], David FRASER[‡],
Kazuki JOE[‡], Hiroyuki NITTA[‡] and Shinji TOMITA[†]

† Dep. of Information Science
Faculty of Engineering, Kyoto University
Sakyo-ku, Kyoto, 606-01 Japan

‡ KUBOTA Corporation
2-47, Shikitsuhigashi 1-chome
Naniwa-ku, Osaka, 556-91 Japan

Abstract

ASURA is a large scale, cluster-based, distributed, shared memory, multiprocessor being developed at Kyoto University and Kubota Corporation. Up to 128 clusters are interconnected to form an ASURA system of up to 1024 processors. The basic concept of the ASURA design is to take advantage of the hierarchical structure of the system. Implementing this concept, a large shared cache is placed between each cluster and the inter-cluster network. The shared cache and the shared memories distributed among the clusters form part of ASURA's hierarchical memory architecture, providing various unique features to ASURA.

In this paper, the hierarchical memory architecture of ASURA and its unique cache coherence scheme, including a proposal of a new hierarchical directory scheme, are described with some simulation results.

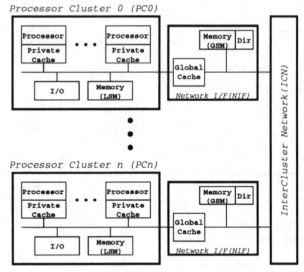

Dir:Directory, LSM:Locally Shared Memory,
GSM:Globally Shared Memory

Figure 1: Overview of ASURA

1 Introduction

Many multiprocessor systems have been developed and have now become widely available as commercial and research machines. However, there is still a strong demand for Massively Parallel Processing since there exist numerous applications (such as QCD, fluid dynamics, and many-body systems) which contain inherent parallelism that is too vast to solve on available machines.

Working towards the goal of massively parallel processing, the cluster based multiprocessor is one of the promising approaches and many recent large scale systems, such as Cedar [21], DASH [22], Paradigm [11], Willow [4], and the Intel Paragon XP/S [31], have followed this approach. Another machine of this class, ASURA, is proposed in this paper.

The ASURA cluster is configured as a bus-based, shared memory multiprocessor with up to 8 processors. The clusters, interconnected through the Inter-Cluster Network (ICN), form a distributed shared memory multiprocessor. Figure 1 and table 1 show, respectively, an overview of ASURA and the specifications of a prototype.

E-mail: moris@kuis.kyoto-u.ac.jp

In order for ASURA to scale from 2 to 128 clusters, the ICN must also be scalable over a certain configuration range according to the customer's requirements. Several candidate topologies for the ICN will be provided from which various configurations for the network can be chosen. In all cases, optical fiber is used as the medium of data transfer and, as a result, we can obtain a transfer rate of 400 megabytes per second for each communication link.

For ease of programming and of porting existing programs to the new architecture, ASURA provides a shared memory environment though the memory modules are physically distributed among the clusters. In order to implement a large scale, distributed, shared memory (DSM) machine efficiently, ASURA adopts a hierarchical cache architecture. This allows it to alleviate memory contention and decrease the latency of memory accesses simultaneously.

The key feature of ASURA is its shared cache and the design of its system-wide cache-coherence mechanism which takes into account the line sizes at the various levels of the hierarchy. Although several researchers [4][11][30] have discussed the issue of hierarchical cache design for large scale shared memory machines, little has been discussed about how to deal

Table 1: Specification of ASURA prototype

CPU	R4000MC (50MHz)		15MFLOPS(DP LINPAC)
Number of CPUs per cluster			2, 4, or 8
Number of clusters			2~128
Private Cache	Associativity		1 (direct-map)
	Size		1MB~4MB (SRAM)
	Line size		32B
	Write policy		Write-back
LSM	Size	each cluster	256MB
		full system	32GB
Global Cache	Associativity		4
	Size		8MB~32MB (DRAM)
	Line size		1024B
	Write policy		Write-back
GSM	Size	each cluster	16MB~4GB
		full system	2GB~512GB

with the line size difference between different levels of the cache hierarchy. Furthermore most of the previous research has been done on centralized shared memory machines instead of DSM machines.

By adopting this hierarchical cache architecture, the intra-cluster architecture can be designed for fine grain parallel processing while the inter-cluster architecture can be targeted towards coarse grain parallel processing. Consequently, the ASURA architecture provides an effective parallel processing environment over a wide range of shared memory applications.

The next section explains ASURA's memory and cache architectures. Section 3 discusses how cache coherence is enforced in ASURA and a new directory based coherence mechanism is proposed for the hierarchical cache system. Some simulation results are shown in section 4. Section 5 contains a conclusion to this paper.

2 Memory Architecture

2.1 Memory Organization

As shown in figure 1, an ASURA cluster is basically a tightly coupled multiprocessor with centralized shared memory. Considering the system as a whole, ASURA has another level of shared memory which is distributed among clusters. Figure 2 shows the memory architecture of ASURA.

In ASURA, the first type of the shared memory mentioned above is shared only among the processors in the cluster and is called Locally Shared Memory or LSM. The other type of shared memory is accessible from any processor in the system and is called Globally Shared Memory or GSM. Thus ASURA's address space is partitioned into two spaces, private space and common space, corresponding to LSM and GSM respectively as indicated in figure 3.

Although this kind of memory organization has been examined also in Paradigm [11], and Willow [4], the distributed style of GSM in ASURA is different

from the centralized style of GSM in those machines. According to the notation of Willow, this kind of memory organization is referred to as *layered memory organization*. As long as the hardware cost is acceptable, the layered memory organization in ASURA has advantages over the flat, or non-layered, memory organization like DASH [22]. These advantages are listed below.

1. Hierarchical data sharing: Data which is local to a cluster, such as processor local variables, stack, code, and part of the system data, can be stored in the LSM. Moreover, one may allocate a copy of read only data, shared among many clusters, to the LSM of each cluster. For instance, image data for computer graphics applications, like surface data for ray-tracing and volume data for volume-rendering, can be allocated to the LSM. In addition, such data may be excluded from inclusion in the shared cache to maintain *the Multi Level Inclusion (MLI) property*[1]. In this way, hierarchical data sharing allows the efficient use of GSM and thus increases the hit ratio of the shared cache.

2. Concurrency of memory accesses: By separating GSM and LSM, GSM in different clusters can be accessed without involving the intra-cluster bus on the GSM side. In other words, GSM accesses and LSM accesses can be performed concurrently at the same cluster.

3. Flexibility of LSM management: In ASURA, LSM management in one cluster is independent of LSM management in the other clusters. Thus, a cluster is not restricted in its LSM management policy. However, if the shared memory of each cluster is provided only as GSM, as in DASH, then when a cluster would like to enforce a memory management scheme for local data located in its shared memory, it must first negotiate with the other clusters.

4. Scalability in memory size: The private address space for each cluster is independent of the other clusters as shown in figure 3 so the total LSM size over the whole system scales with the number of clusters, though the size is 32GB currently. However the maximum GSM size is fixed at 512 GB independently of the number of clusters.

Table 2 summarizes the memory architectures of various cluster based systems for comparison.

2.2 Cache Architecture

In order to offer a shared memory environment on a large scale multiprocessor like ASURA, it is necessary to simultaneously alleviate memory contention and decrease memory access latency. To satisfy these requirements, cache memory plays an important role.

For this purpose, ASURA introduces a hierarchical cache architecture reflecting the hierarchy of the sys-

---

[1]Following the literature [3], "A MultiLevel cache hierarchy has the inclusion property if the contents of a cache at level $i+1$, L^{i+1}, is a superset of the contents of all its children caches, L^i, at level i."

Table 2: The Summary of Memory Architectures of Typical Cluster Based System

	GSM	LSM	GSM Access	Cache Coherence Control	
				w.r.t. GSM	w.r.t. LSM
Paragon XP/S	No	Yes	–	–	?
Cedar	Yes	Yes	UMA	Cacheability control	
DASH	Yes	No	NUMA	Snoop-based(Intra-cluster) Directory-base(Inter-cluster)	–
Paradigm(node)	Yes	Yes	UMA	Directory	Directory?
ASURA	Yes	Yes	NUMA	Snoop-based(Intra-cluster) Directory-base(Inter-cluster)	Snoop-based

GSM: Globally Shared Memory   NUMA: Non-Uniform Memory Access
LSM: Locally Shared Memory   UMA: Uniform Memory Access

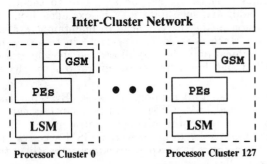

GSM:Globally Shared Memory, LSM:Locally Shared Memory
PEs:Processing Elements(max.#=8)

Figure 2: Memory architecture of ASURA

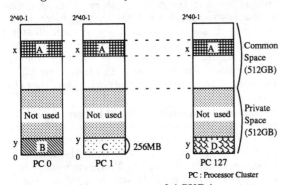

Figure 3: Memory map of ASURA prototype

tem structure, as shown in figure 4. In this figure, and also in the following discussion, the on-chip primary cache together with the secondary cache is treated as a private cache for simplicity. Thus, in ASURA, not only is each processor configured with a private cache but also, each cluster contains a shared cache.

Each processor has a dedicated private cache, or PCache and it allows the caching of data from both the LSM and the GSM. The shared cache placed in the NIF (Network InterFace) of each cluster is shared by at most 8 processors and contains data cached from only the GSM. This shared cache is referred to as the global cache or GCache. In particular, the existence of the GCache distinguishes ASURA from DASH.

The major advantage of the GCache is that it divides the cluster from the network. This enables the

GSM to be isolated from the cluster-bus of the cluster. Then the cluster-bus can be optimized to access the LSM for fine grain parallel processing. On the other hand, for GSM accesses, the GCache provides an interface between the intra-cluster bus and Inter-Cluster Network(ICN). This isolates the differences in the communication protocol, transfer rate, cache line size between the two levels. This fact make it possible to optimize the cluster level architecture independent of the system level.

Several researchers [4][11][30] have discussed the issues of hierarchical cache design, however, little has been reported concerning the line size. In a hierarchical cache architecture, the line sizes at each level of the hierarchy need not be equal and, on the contrary, they should be selected according to the architectural issues present at each level. Hence the GCache line size has been enlarged, taking into account the other cluster level design factors. Note that the effect of enlarging the line size of the GCache is hidden from the PCache and the effect has no influence on the optimization of the intra-cluster architecture. This is because the *MLI (Multi Level Inclusion) directory*, which is provided as a part of the coherence enforcement mechanism in the GCache, absorbs this effect. This is the most important feature of ASURA's hierarchical cache architecture.

The characteristics of the GCache are summarized below.

1. Up to 8 cache misses are serviced concurrently.
   ASURA adopts a split protocol for the cluster-bus. The memory access request and its reply are treated as separate bus transactions, therefore any processor can issue a memory access request before the previous requests from the other processors are

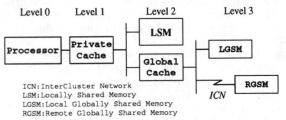

ICN:InterCluster Network
LSM:Locally Shared Memory
LGSM:Local Globally Shared Memory
RGSM:Remote Globally Shared Memory

Figure 4: Memory hierarchy of ASURA

completed. These access requests are served in pipelined manner, and in order not to block the pipeline even after a cache miss occurs an eight-way bypass mechanism had been prepared in the GCache. Consequently, the GCache continues to serve consecutive requests while doing line-fetches for the previously missed lines.

2. Large cache size.
   Since the access speed of the global cache need only be as fast as LSM, DRAM can be used to implement the data array. Thus, it becomes cheaper to include a large cache, which may be up to 32 MB in ASURA.

3. Long line size.
   ASURA adopts an unusually long line size of 1024 bytes for the GCache, while the line size of the PCache is 32 bytes. Hereafter, for clarity, the PCache line will be referred to as the *sub-line* and the GCache line as the *line* to distinguish between them.
   The merits of a long line size for the GCache are shown below.

   - Compensation for relatively long ICN latency: ASURA uses optical fiber as an ICN communication medium which provides a maximum transfer rate of 400 MB/s for each link. However, the long latency of the ICN, which is at least 1μs, prevents the effective transfer speed from achieving the maximum transfer speed of the link. The long line size of the GCache compensates for the latency and improves the effective transfer speed.

   - Reduction of directory overhead: As discussed in the next section, to realize directory based cache coherence control for a large scale shared memory system like ASURA, the directory size should be less than a few percent of the total memory size. Since directory size is inversely proportional to the line size, or coherence block size, the long line size for the GCache helps to decrease the directory overhead in hardware cost.

   - Prefetching effect: Under data-parallel, for example `do-all`, type program executions, if a miss occurs in the private cache of one of the processors in a cluster, the other processors are also likely to miss on the same or nearby data. If the GCache line size is several times longer than the PCache line size then these misses can effectively be merged into one GCache line fetch. In this way, the long line size of the GCache provides a prefetching effect for the PCache, while providing the effects of memory access combining for the ICN and GSM.

   - Explicit cache management in terms of software: Explicit software cache management has been proposed in order to improve cache performance [4][11]. However, the overhead of such software schemes makes it hard to apply them to caches with ordinary line sizes. The gain in effective transfer rate with the long line size of

the GCache overcomes this overhead. Explicit cache management in ASURA is discussed in the next section.

Of course, there are some arguments against the long line size, one of which is the problem of false sharing. Some research has been done on this problem using both compile time static analysis approaches [15][29][18] and run time detection approaches [9][14][20]. Hopefully, the results of this research can be applied to ASURA to alleviate the false sharing problems.

3 Cache Coherence

3.1 Coherence Enforcement Strategy

In each of ASURA's clusters because writable, shared data may be cached into both the GCache and each of the processors' PCaches, cache coherence problems will occur and must be solved. There are basically two approaches, the hardware based approach [2][28] and the software based approach [5][10].

Software based approaches become promising as the system size goes up because, in order to preserve cache coherence, they rely on self-invalidation of stale data at each processor and don't require any inter-processor communication for stale data invalidation. They are however still in the research stage, and are not yet sophisticated enough for practical use.

Therefore, a hardware based approach has been adopted in ASURA while leaving it possible for the software to assist with the hardware based cache coherence enforcement. Hence if we have a compiler which has the ability to manage the cache satisfactorily, or if the programmer offers information about data sharing, ASURA can use this information for coherence enforcement as will be discussed later in section 3.2.

In the development of ASURA's cache coherence enforcement strategy, the matters of intra-cluster and inter-cluster cache coherence enforcement are considered first, independent of each other. This is possible because the cluster level and the system level architectures have been separated by the global cache. Then, they are united in a hierarchical fashion to enforce the coherence between PCaches and GSMs. In ASURA, this coherence is enforced by maintaining the Multi Level Inclusion (MLI) property. This is referred to as cache coherence *hierarchical cache coherence*, in contrast with intra- and inter-cluster cache coherence.

Consequently, system wide memory coherence is maintained through these three kinds of coherence control in a hierarchical manner reflecting the system's structure.

The following two sections describe the intra- and inter-cluster cache coherence controls in more detail and section 3.1.3 describes how hierarchical cache coherence is preserved.

3.1.1 Intra-cluster Cache Coherence

Like ordinary bus based systems, ASURA adopts the snooping scheme. To enforce coherence between PCaches and either LSM or the GCache, the write-back write policy has been chosen.

The GCache appears as normal memory from the view point of intra-cluster cache coherence. Therefore, GCache and LSM can be treated as a single unit for implementing the intra-cluster coherence control, except that the GCache has to snoop the cluster bus in order to reflect modifications on PCache lines to the state of corresponding GCache lines.

In order to enforce intra-cluster cache coherence, one of the following states: INVALID, CLEAN (unmodified, possibly shared), and DIRTY (modified, no other copy), is assigned to each PCache line and the state is represented by the V and M bits of the PCache tag array (figure 5(a)). Intra-cluster cache coherence is maintained in the following way (see figure 6).

1. Read miss : The PCache which causes the miss puts a read request on the cluster bus. If any other PCache in the same cluster has a copy of the PCache line in state DIRTY, this PCache 1) responds the request by writing back the line to LSM or GCache, 2) releases the ownership of the line, and 3) sets its state to CLEAN. Otherwise, LSM or GCache responds to the request by putting corresponding data on the cluster bus. The requesting PCache picks up the corresponding data from the bus, puts it into its data array, and set its state to CLEAN.

2. Write miss : The PCache which caused the miss puts a write request on the cluster bus. If any other PCache in the same cluster has a copy of the PCache line in the DIRTY state then this PCache 1) responds to the request by writing back the line to the LSM or the GCache, 2) transfers the ownership of the line to the requesting PCache, and 3) sets the state of the line to INVALID. Otherwise, the LSM or the GCache responds to the request by putting the corresponding data on the cluster bus. All PCaches other than the requesting one set the state of their copy of the line to INVALID. The requesting PCache reads the corresponding data from the bus, stores it into its data array in the DIRTY state. In any case, if the write miss is caused by a processor's write on a CLEAN line, no data transfer is made on the bus. By observing the ownership transfer on the cluster bus, the GCache knows the state of any of the sub-lines cached in a PCache.

3. Replacement : When the PCache needs to replace a line on a read or write miss, the PCache set the states of the corresponding sub-line to INVALID, and it is written back if the sub-line had been in the DIRTY state.

4. Read hit / Write hit : No coherence enforcement transaction is made.

3.1.2 Inter-cluster Cache Coherence

In this section, the coherence control between the GCaches and the GSM, and between the GCaches is considered. Directory based inter-cluster cache coherence is discussed here.

The directory schemes [8] can be classified as either full-map directory, limited directory, or chained directory.

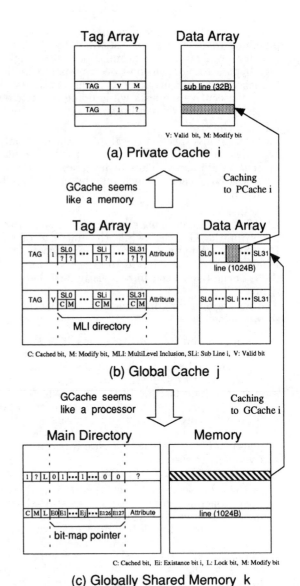

Figure 5: The Hierarchical Cache Coherence Enforcement Mechanism

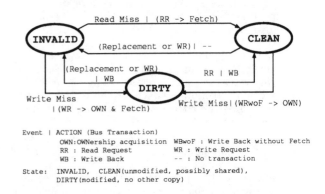

Figure 6: State Transition Diagram

For simplicity of control, ASURA uses a full-map directory. The drawback of using a full-map directory is directory overhead. In our case, this overhead is proportional to the number of GCaches and inversely proportional to the GCache line size.

However, the GCache line size of 1024 bytes, which is 32 times the PCache line size, makes it possible to reduce the directory overhead of ASURA to a fraction of what it would have been if the line size were the same size as the PCache line. At the same time, the width of the directory is kept narrow because the directory is managed in units of clusters, or GCaches, instead of processors, or PCaches.

So far, several interesting techniques have been proposed to reduce the directory overhead without enlarging the line size [6][19][23]. However, most of these techniques aren't adopted because they increase the complexity of the directory itself and this complexity may prevent high speed coherence control and increase time required to develop the machine.

The organization of the full-map directory is shown in figure 5(c). This directory is referred to as the *main directory* in contrast with the *MLI directory* which is provided for the purposes of ensuring the MLI property and absorbing the effect of enlarging the GCache line size. Each *main directory* entry associated with a line is composed of three parts: 1) 3-bit status, 2) a bit map pointer of 128 bits, and 3) a field to specify the line attributes which are mentioned in section 3.2. The 3-bit status indicates 1) whether the line is cached, with the C bit, 2) whether the line is modified, with the M bit, and 3) whether the line is locked, with the L bit. The L bit is used as part of the synchronization mechanism for Locking. Each bit of the bit map pointer indicates if the corresponding GCache has a cached copy of the line or not. The attribute field contains the information not only on the characteristics of the line but also on how the line is manipulated. Such information is stored into this field by software, the operating system perhaps, when the associated page is allocated to a GSM.

3.1.3 Assurance of the Multi Level Inclusion property

To guarantee the MLI property [3] in ASURA, all lines residing in PCaches in a cluster must be contained in either their parent LSM or their parent GCache, where the word "parent" means being closer to the memory in the memory hierarchy. At the same time, all lines residing in the GCaches must be included in the set of all lines in the GSMs.

The inclusion relation 1) between GCaches and GSMs, and 2) between PCaches and their parent LSM with respect to the PCache lines which come from the LSM, are always maintained naturally. Consequently, the inclusion relation that must be considered is that 3) between PCaches and their parent GCache with respect to the PCache lines which come from the GCache. Then only the third inclusion relation will be discussed hereafter.

Assurance of the MLI property requires a slightly stronger restriction than necessary for hierarchical cache coherence enforcement. For instance, from the

view point of the hierarchical cache coherence enforcement, a PCache may contain data which does not exist in its parent GCache as long as the hierarchical coherence is maintained, though this situation is not allowed if the MLI property is to be assured. However, the advantages of the MLI property, like the filtering of inter-cluster coherence enforcement traffic, overcomes the disadvantage of this stronger restriction.

As a result, the coherence enforcement to keep the MLI property is initiated when a GCache receives 1) an invalidation or 2) a write-back request from GSM, and when a replacement of 3) clean or 4) dirty line occurs in the GCache.

In the first and third cases, where the data is not modified in this cluster, all of the sub-lines corresponding to the line are invalidated first, and then the GCache line is invalidated.

In the second case, all of the dirty sub-lines corresponding to the line are written back to the GCache first, and then the GCache line is written back to memory. The last case is slightly different from the second case in that it requires invalidations of the GCache line and its corresponding sub-lines after the line is written back.

For simplicity, in the above discussion of coherence enforcement, the difference between the line sizes of the GCaches and the PCaches has not been mentioned. Although the difference is not an essential part of assuring the MLI property, in practice, not only for the efficiency of the coherence enforcement but also for concealing the system level architecture from that of the cluster level, this difference must be taken into account.

As discussed in section 2.2, the line sizes of the GCache and PCache are 1024 bytes and 32 bytes respectively. 32 sub-lines with consecutive addresses belong to the same GCache line. Therefore at most 32 sub-lines with different addresses have to be invalidated or written back when a GCache line is invalidated or written back. The sub-line invalidation requests, which are treated as *Write Request without Fetch*, can be issued in a pipelined manner and they theoretically don't need any acknowledgment. At most 32 invalidation requests need to be issued for an invalidation of a GCache line since all 8 PCaches snoop on the cluster bus. The sub-line write-back requests, which are treated as *Read Request*, can be issued in a pipelined manner as well, but each of them needs an acknowledgment or a write-back corresponding to each sub-line. This causes two more problems to arise.

To explain the first problem, it is assumed that the situation where a sub-line which belongs to a dirty GCache line is cached into PCaches (in state CLEAN) or is not cached into any PCache (in state INVALID). In this situation, there is no PCache which replies to the write-back request for the sub-line because there is no dirty sub-line corresponding to this request, so the GCache which issued this request will wait until a timeout occurs for an acknowledgment.

The second problem is not as serious as the first and is an efficiency problem. If all 32 invalidation requests are issued whenever a GCache line is invalidated or replaced then it may cause unnecessary traffic on the intra-cluster bus because some of the sub-lines are not cached at all.

These problems have originated due to the the lack of information about each sub-line. It would be possible to solve these problems if some history information for each sub-line were to be kept. For this purpose, a directory, which we refer to as the MLI directory, has been created and placed in the tag array of the GCache as shown in figure 5(b). Each directory entry is created dynamically when the tag entry for the associated line is allocated. In order to track the status of each sub-line, the C bit and the M bit are provided for each sub-line.

The meanings of the C bit and the M bit are the same as the meanings of those in the main directory with the exception that they represent the status of a sub-line instead of a line. These two bits are updated whenever a PCache accesses a corresponding sub-line. When a GCache line is invalidated or written back, whether due to replacement or inter cluster coherence enforcement, by examining the corresponding MLI directory entry only the necessary coherence work need be done.

As well as a C bit and a M bit for each sub-line, each MLI directory entry has some bits to store the attributes associated with the line. These attributes are used for coherence enforcement in the GCache.

Here, we should mention that the GCache is not required to be as fast as the PCache, and hence the overhead of the MLI directory itself and that of the directory management are not significant.

The organization of the MLI directory itself is quite similar to the sectored directory [6] except that the MLI directory does not need either a bit vector to track the PCaches which have a copy of the sub-line nor the pointers to the PCaches which have ownership (write privileges) of the sub-line. The reason why we don't need them is simply that the cluster is a bus-based architecture with a snooping based coherence scheme. However there are great differences between them. 1) In the MLI directory, the unit of data caching to the PCache is a sub-line, while it would be a line in the sectored directory. This characteristic makes it possible to offer transparency of the system level architecture, such as the line size of the GCache, to the cluster level architecture. 2) Each entry of the MLI directory is dynamically allocated in the tag array of the GCache when the corresponding GCache line is allocated, so that the directory overhead is proportional to the total cache size instead of the total memory size which may be a few tens, or rather hundreds, times larger than the total cache size.

3.2 Software assist for cache coherence

As has been shown in the previous two sections, ASURA implements a hierarchical cache coherence scheme in hardware. However, with this scheme, inter-cluster communication is required to enforce cache coherence on the fly. In order to reduce this run time overhead, software can assist with the hardware coherence enforcement.

The advantages of software based coherence enforcement are derived primarily from the use of 1) knowledge about the characteristics of the data, and 2) knowledge of how the data is manipulated during the program execution, or the semantics of the data.

Firstly the typical case where software assistance can greatly reduce the run time overhead [27] is shown. Counter based barrier synchronization is examined, where the counter is decreased by one each time the process participating in the barrier reaches the synchronization point in its program. If hardware based cache coherence is enforced without software assistance, then network traffic to invalidate or update the line arises at each counter modification. For the processes which are awaiting the completion of the synchronization, however, the intermediate value of the counter toward the completion is irrelevant. They only need to know when the value of the barrier counter reaches zero. Therefore all this network traffic except the last message, which signifies the completion of the synchronization, is unnecessary. If the hardware were informed of the semantics of the data in some way by software, this unnecessary traffic could be avoided. This is what the software is asked to do.

Hereafter, the manner in which software assist is implemented in ASURA is described. The basis of our software assist is the attribute marking scheme [4][5] where the attributes corresponding to the line guide the hardware coherence enforcement.

Other than the basic attributes like *cacheable*:allows caching of data, *non-coherent*: disables hardware coherence control, and *exclusive*: allows only a single PCache (or GCache) to hold a cached copy of data, the following attributes are presently being considered and implemented in ASURA by the addition of some additional hardware. A line may be assigned several of these attributes simultaneously.

1. *Update on write-back* : When a line marked with this attribute is written back from a GCache, the main directory updates the other cached copies of the line, and thus the corresponding PCache sub-lines too. For data with one writer and many readers this avoids extra cache misses. A broadcast option is also available for this attribute. Note that this is not like a *reflective memory system* [24] where the update is enforced whenever a processor modifies data; ASURA enforces the update only when a GCache line is written back to memory.

2. *Resident* : is used to force a specific line to reside in the GCache. Once a line marked with this attribute is fetched into the GCache, this line will never be replaced unless it is forcibly invalidated with the GCache I/O command mentioned later.

3. *Store Allocate No Fetch* : When a write access to a line marked with this attribute causes a miss in a GCache, the GCache allocates an entry for this line and requests the GSM to acquire the ownership of the line, but does not require the GSM to supply the data. In order to reduce unnecessary data transfer through the IPN, this attribute can be added to a line which a cluster completely overwrites without any previous reference to the line.

4. *Out-of-MLI* : allows a PCache to hold copies of GSM data regardless of the existence of corre-

sponding GCache lines in its parent GCache. All coherence enforcement requests related to lines with this attribute have to be forwarded to cluster buses even if the GCache does not have an entry for the corresponding line.

5. *Barrier Synchronization variable* : can be thought of as a variety of the *update on write-back* attribute. The difference is that, instead of updating the GCache lines and the corresponding PCache sublines at every occurrence of write-back, it updates them when the GSM storing the line has received the specified number of writes to the line.

These attributes are stored into corresponding attribute fields of the main directory (figure 5(c)) first and are copied into attribute fields of the GCache tag array (figure 5(b)) when the line is fetched. Then these attributes are used as a guideline both by the GCaches and by the main directory whenever coherence enforcement actions are required.

In addition to the attribute marking scheme mentioned above, ASURA provides the software (or the programmer) the means to manage both GCaches and GSMs explicitly in the form of I/O commands to the GCache. Currently, the following I/O commands for data transfer [7], cache coherence [10], and synchronization [22] are provided.

- *MOVE* command: forces a pre-fetch or a write-back on the specified line depending on the argument of the command. This command can be used to hide memory access latency.

- *Line-transfer* command: performs data transfer from a specified source address to a specified destination address through the GCache where this command is initiated. The length of data to be transferred is fixed as the GCache line size. The data transfer is performed as follows: 1) Invalidate the GCache line associated with the destination address if it exists in the GCache. Note that the write back is not needed even if the line is in the DIRTY state. 2) Fetch the source line into the GCache if the GCache does not contain the line. 3) Change the tag address of the line associated with the source address with the destination address, and inform the main directory of the change if needed. If the source line was in the DIRTY state it must be written back before changing the tag address. 4) Write back the destination line if needed. It is recommended that the *store allocate no fetch* attribute is assigned to the destination line. Since the line-transfer uses a tricky technique of operating on the GCache tag array, data transfer can be performed without moving the data at all if the GCache contains the source line in CLEAN state. This command is well suited for the copy-on-write operation.

- *Invalidation* command: invalidates the specified line by invalidating or if needed, forcing a write-back before the invalidation, and makes the associated GCache entry empty.

- *Lock/Unlock* command: provides GCache line based synchronization primitives. ASURA supports a *queue based lock* mechanism, as well as

DASH, where the existence bits of the main directory are used to trace clusters waiting the acquirement of the lock. *Lock/Unlock* commands combined with *MOVE* command could support a rather complex command which forces a pre-fetch of a line when the Lock associated with the line is acquired or forces a write-back of a line when the Lock associated with the line is released.

4 Performance Simulation

4.1 Simulation Environment

ASURA's performance has been investigated by the use of trace-driven simulation. As the trace data, transaction sequences on each cluster bus were used, which are composed of the time, address, and the access type for each transaction, instead of the address traces for each processor.

Although various simulations have been done [16][26], here the scalability of ASURA and the effect of the long GCache line size is focused upon.

Matrix multiplication ($C = A \times B$) and LU decomposition ($A = L \times U$), where A,B,C,L and U are matrices of size 1024×1024, have been chosen as sample programs.

All matrices are initially distributed among the GSMs so that their sub-matrices, of form $MATRIX[nI + i, *]$ {n | 0,1,...,1024/I} where I: Number of Clusters, are allocated to the GSM of cluster i.

In order to extract cluster level parallelism, the *data owner compute rule* is applied to the code. To extract fine grain parallelism inside each cluster, the code was further optimized so that it could fit within the subline size of a PCache.

Among the various available ASURA configurations, the configuration shown in figure 7 was used throughout these simulations, where the number of processors in a cluster is fixed at 8. A cache size of 8 KB for the primary on chip cache, 2 MB for the secondary cache, and 16 MB for the GCache and the memory access latencies shown in table 3 were assumed. The memory access latencies were derived from a hardware logic simulator.

4.2 Simulation Results

Figure 8 shows the simulation results both for matrix multiplication(**MATMUL**) and for LU decomposition(**LU**), where (a) and (c) show performance versus the number of clusters, and (b) and (d) show performance versus the GCache line size.

Table 3: Memory Access Latencies

Memory		Latency [ns]
Private Cache	Primary	10
	Secondary	200
Global Cache		1500
GSM	Local Cluster	2000 (+ 2.5 × n)
	Local Ring	2500 (+ 2.5 × n)
	Remote Ring	3000 (+ 2.5 × n)

n: GCache line size [Byte]

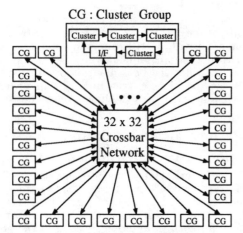

CG : Cluster Group

Note 1 : Number of Clusters in a Cluster Group is in the range from 1 to 4.
Clustes inside a CG are interconnected by a ring network.
Note 2 : In case of 16 clusters organization, a 16x16 crossbar network which is
a quarter of the 32x32 crossbar network is used.

Figure 7: A ring-crossbar configuration of ASURA

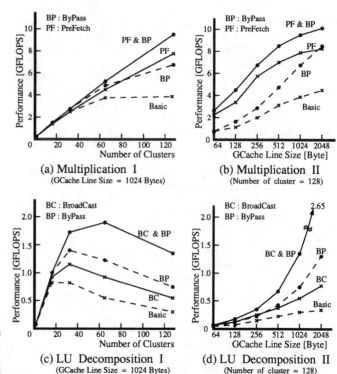

(a) Multiplication I
(GCache Line Size = 1024 Bytes)

(b) Multiplication II
(Number of cluster = 128)

(c) LU Decomposition I
(GCache Line Size = 1024 Bytes)

(d) LU Decomposition II
(Number of cluster = 128)

Figure 8: Simulation Results

In the case of **MATMUL**, the effect of the software prefetching(**PF**) and of the GCache bypass buffer(**BP**) were examined. When the GCache bypass buffer is used the requested data passes through the GCache without waiting the completion of GCache line refill. As shown in figure 8(a), the basic performance scales well up to 64 clusters. Using **BP**, scalability was confirmed up to 128 clusters. The beneficial effect of **PF** was also confirmed. By using **BP** together with **PF**, ASURA could achieve a performance of 9.6 GFLOPS with 128 clusters. This is about 100 times the performance of 93 MFLOPS which is achieved by a single cluster.

For **LU**, the effect of broadcasting(**BC**) was examined. This was simulated by setting the *Update on Write-Back* attribute and explicitly executing the *MOVE* command. The effect of **BP** was also examined. In these simulations (see figure 8(c)), performance increases with the number of cluster until about 32 or 64 clusters. It then starts decreasing with any further increases in the number of clusters. It is assumed that this is because the amount of computation becomes too small compared to the amount of communication required.

For both applications, as shown in figure 8(b) and (c), the performance scales up with the increase of GCache line size. We also confirm that, the larger the line size becomes, the more the effect of **BP** becomes significant because the time spent to transfer a line becomes dominant factor of memory access latency.

From these results, it is concluded that the ASURA architecture and its uniquely long GCache line size are justified as long as the applications have enough parallelism to exploit both system-level coarse grain parallelism and cluster-level fine grain parallelism.

5   Conclusion

An overview of ASURA, a cluster based multiprocessor system has been given. ASURA offers a shared memory environment though Globally Shared Memories (GSMs) are distributed among the clusters. For the efficient use of distributed shared memory, ASURA is configured with a shared cache, the Global Cache (GCache), on each cluster as an interface between the cluster and the InterCluster Network (ICN). Along with the Locally Shared Memory (LSM), provided independently of the GSM, the GSM and the GCache form a layered memory architecture.

As a result of providing a GCache on each cluster, it becomes possible to consider the inter-cluster and intra-cluster architectures independent of each other. This is also true for cache coherence enforcement. In order to enforce intra-cluster cache coherence, a snooping mechanism is provided for each processor. To enforce inter-cluster cache coherence, assuring the MLI property, a new hierarchical directory scheme has been developed where the directory is composed of two separate directories corresponding to the memory hierarchy: the main directory for the GSM and the MLI directory for the GCache.

In addition, ASURA provides software the means to improve the efficiency of cache coherence enforcement. The property labeling scheme allows the software to set cache line attribute which are used for coherence enforcement, while several I/O commands are available for software to manage the GCache directly.

Finally, simulation results have been presented that

confirm that the ASURA architecture could offer a wide range of scalability and it could achieve a performance level of 9.6 GFLOPS in a 128 cluster configuration. It was also confirmed that the long GCache line size of 1024 bytes is justified for some large scale numerical computation.

Acknowledgment

We would like to acknowledge the considerable contributions from M. Yamaguchi and K.Yamada both with KUBOTA Corp. We would like to thank Prof. S. Agusa of Nagoya Univ., Prof. H.Nakashima of Kyoto Univ. and the referees of this paper for the useful comments. We would also like to thank students in the Tomita Laboratory of Kyoto University and also the staff of the office of computer business in KUBOTA Corporation for their collaboration.

References

[1] Adve, S.V. and Hill, M.D., "WEAK ORDERING - A NEW DEFINITION AND SOME IMPLICATIONS," *Comuter Sciences Technical Report*, #902, Computer Sciences Department, University of Wisconsin-Madison, December 1989.

[2] Archibald, J. and Bear, J.-L., "An Economical Solution to the Cache Coherency Problem," *Proc. 11th Ann. Int'l. Symp. Comput. Architect.*, pp.355–362, June 1984.

[3] Baer, J.-L. and Wang, W.-H., "Architectural Choices for Multilevel Cache Hierachies," *Proc. 1987 Int'l. Conf. on Parallel Processing*, pp.258–261, 1987.

[4] Bennet, J.K., et al., "Toword Large-Scale Shared Memory Multiprocessing," *SCALABLE SHARED MEMORY MULTIPROCESSORS*, ed. by Michel Dubois and Shreekant Thakkar, pp.281–300, Kluwer Academic Publisheers, 1991.

[5] Brantley, W.C., et al., "RP3 Processor-Memory Element," *Proc. 1985 Int'l. Conf. on Parallel Processing*, pp.782–789, Aug. 1985.

[6] O'Krafka, B.W. and Newton, A.R., "An Empirical Evaluation of Two Memory-Efficient Directory Methods," *Proc. 17th Ann. Int'l. Symp. Comput. Architect.*, pp.138–140, May 1990.

[7] Callahan, D., et al., "Software Prefetching," *ASPLOS IV*, pp.40 – 52, 1991.

[8] Censier, M. L. and Feutrier, P., "A New Solution to Cache Coherence Problems in Multicache System," *IEEE Trans. on Computers*, Vol. C-27, No. 12, pp.1112 – 1118, Dec. 1978.

[9] Chen, Y.-C. and Veidenbaum, A.V., "A Software Coherence Scheme with the Assistance of Directories," *CSRD Report No. 1106*, pp.1–22, June 1991.

[10] Cheong, H. and Veidenbaum, A.V., "Compiler-Directed Cache Management in Multiprocessors," *IEEE Computer*, vol.23, no.6, pp. 39-47, June 1990.

[11] Cheriton, D.R., et al., "Pradigm:A Highly Scalable Shared-Memory Multicomputer Architecture," *IEEE computer*, pp.33–46, February 1991.

[12] Dubois, M., et al., "Memory Access Buffering in Multiprocessors," *Proc. 13th Ann. Int'l. Symp. Comput. Architect.*, pp.434–442, 1986.

[13] Dubois, M., et al., "Synchronization, Coherence, and Event Ordering in Multiprocessors," *IEEE computer*, pp.8–21, February 1988.

[14] Dubois, M., "Delayed Consistency," *SCALABLE SHARED MEMORY MULTIPROCESSORS*, ed. by Michel Dubois and Shreekant Thakkar, pp.207–218, Kluwer Academic Publisheers, 1991.

[15] Eggers, S.J. and Jeremiassen, T.E., "Eliminating False Sharing," *Proc. 1991 Int'l. Conf. on Parallel Processing*, pp.I-377 – I-381, Aug. 1991.

[16] Fraser, D. and Tanaka, T., "An overview of ASURA's Network with Simulation Results," *IPSJ technical report of SIG. Arc.*, Vol.93, No.20, pp.133–140, March 1993.

[17] Gharachorloo, K., et al., "Memory Consistency and Event Ordering in Scalable Shared-Memory Multiprocessors," *Proc. 17th Ann. Int'l. Symp. Comput. Architect.*, pp.15–26, May 1990.

[18] Guarna, Jr., V.A., "A Technique for Analyzing Pointer and Structure References in Parallel Restructuring Compilers," *Proc. 1988 Int'l. Conf. on Parallel Processing*, pp.212–220, 1988.

[19] Gupta A., et al., "Reducing Memory and Traffic Requirements for Scalable Directory-Based Cache Coherence Schemes," *Proc. 1991 Int'l. Conf. on Parallel Processing*, pp.I-312 – I-321, 1990.

[20] Hosomi, T., et al. "A Hardware Cache Coherence Scheme with the assistance of software," *IPSJ technical report of SIG. Arc.*, Vol.93, No.20, pp.117–124, Mar. 1993 (in Japanease).

[21] Konicek, J., et al., "The Organization of the Cedar System," *Proc. 1991 Int'l. Conf. on Parallel Processing*, pp.149–156, Aug. 1991.

[22] Lenoski, D., et al. "The Directory-based Cache Coherece Protocol for the DASH Multiprocessor," *Proc. 17th Ann. Int'l. Symp. Comput. Architect.*, pp.148–159, May 1990.

[23] Maa, Y.-C., et al., "Two Economical Directory Schemes for Large-Scale Cache Coherent Multiprocessors," *ACM SIGARCH Comput. Architect. News*, vol.19, no.5, pp.10–18, Sept. 1991.

[24] Maples, Creve., "A High-Performance Memory-Based Interconnection System for Multicomputer Environments," *Proc. of Supercomputing'90*, pp.295-304, 1990.

[25] Mori, S., et al., "The Kyushu University Reconfigurable Parallel Processor – Cache Architecture and Cache Coherence Schemes –," *Proc. Int'l Symp. on Shared Memory Multiprocessing*, pp.218–229, April 1991.

[26] Naito, J., et al., "Performance Evaluation of the ASURA Cluster," *IPSJ technical report of SIG. Arc.*, Vol.92, No.97, pp.73–80, December 1992 (in Japanese).

[27] Saito, H., et al, "The Event Correspondent Cache Coherency Scheme and Its Application to Barrier Synchronization," *IPSJ technical report of SIG. Arc.*, Vol.92, No.95, pp.9-16, Aug. 1992 (in Japanese).

[28] Stenström, P., "A Survey of Cache Coherence Schemes for Multiprocessor," *IEEE Computer*, vol.23, no.6, pp. 12-24, June 1990.

[29] Torrellas, J., et al., "Shared Date Placement Optimization to Reduce Muliprocessor Cache Miss Rates," *Proc. 1991 Int'l. Conf. on Parallel Processing*, pp.II-266 – II-270, 1990.

[30] Wilson Jr., A.W., "Hierarchical Cache/Bus Architecture for Shared Memory Multiprocessors," *Proc. 14th Ann. Int'l. Symp. Comput. Architect.*, pp.244–252, 1987.

[31] "Paragon XP/S Product Overview," *Intel Corporation*, 1991.

Session 10:
Workshop
Runtime Support for
Parallel Compilers

Common Runtime Support for High-Performance Parallel Languages

Parallel Compiler Runtime Consortium *

Geoffrey C. Fox, Sanjay Ranka, Michael Scott, Allen D. Malony,
Jim Browne, Marina C. Chen, Alok Choudhary, Thomas Cheatham,
Jan Cuny, Rudolf Eigenmann, Amr Fahmy, Ian Foster,
Dennis Gannon, Tom Haupt, Mike Karr, Carl Kesselman,
Chuck Koelbel, Wei Li, Monica Lam, Thomas LeBlanc,
Jim Openshaw, David Padua, Constantine Polychronopoulos, Joel Saltz,
Alan Sussman, Gil Weigand, Kathy Yelick

1 Introduction

Parallel Computers have recently become powerful enough to outperform conventional vector based supercomputers. Several parallel languages are currently under development for exploiting the data and/or task parallelism available in the applications. In this report, we propose the development of a basic public domain infrastructure to provide runtime support for high level parallel languages. This would support several projects developing different compilers for a given language such as C++, ADA, or Fortran but also give a unified support for compilers of different languages. There are two particularly important motivations for this common runtime support system.

Firstly, it will accelerate the development of new compiler projects investigating particular modules or concepts by providing a public domain infrastructure which can be built on and not replicated.

Secondly there is currently no universally "best" language; each excels in different aspects of the performance, expressivity, reliability, user familiarity and other metrics. This fact is corroborated by the findings of the recent multiagency workshop on HPCC and grand challenge applications at Pittsburgh. A typical example of software development involved using C++ as a high level language to achieve modularity, Fortran as a high performance assembly language for coding the computationally intensive fragments, and

using AVS for visualization and some coarse grain software integration. Thus integrated support of different languages appears an essential pragmatic feature of high performance computing environments.

The above issues were discussed by several researchers which led to a workshop at Syracuse University on common runtime support for compilers and formation of the Parallel Compiler Runtime Support Consortium. Three central and relatively orthogonal topics were identified for common runtime support:

1. Common Runtime Support for Data parallelism

2. Common Runtime Support for Task parallelism

3. Performance and Debugging Infrastructure for Compiler Runtime Systems

Data parallelism and Task parallelism are two important kinds of exploitable parallelism available in most applications. The need for debuggers and performance estimation is of utmost importance for any software environment.

The parallel runtime compiler consortium was originally put together on the initiative of Gil Weigand. The current members of the consortium represent many of the major compiler groups supported by ARPA. The purpose of this report is to present important issues in providing a common framework for runtime support of compilers. The report is organized into three general parts, corresponding to the above three topics. Each part represents the discussions of a working group and provides a detailed analysis of the issues, implications and organization required for a common runtime support. The working groups were

---

*The workshop at Syracuse was sponsored by DARPA under contract # DABT63-91-C-0028. The content of the information does not necessarily reflect the position or the policy of the Government and no official endorsement should be inferred.

coordinated by Sanjay Ranka, Michael Scott and Alan Malony respectively.

Details and background of this report can be accessed via anonymous ftp from minerva.npac.syr.edu

2 Data Parallelism

Recently there have been major efforts in developing programming language and compiler support for parallel machines. For example, High Performance Fortran has been standardized. A similar effort is currently in progress for HPC++. We use the term High Performance Language (HPL), to refer to HPF, HPC++, an extended (data parallel) form of ADA, or some other relevant language.

A system that would allow different components, perhaps written in various HPLs, to operate with each other and execute in an integrated fashion is sorely needed for the following reasons: (1) different pieces of an application program in one HPL may be best handled by different runtime components (e.g. program segments with regular data access patterns versus irregular access patterns); (2) different components may be best written in one or more HPLs due to the nature of the components and the particular types of language support (e.g. Ada/HPF combination); (3) building components that are reusable across different applications, perhaps written in different HPLs; (4) sharing of infrastructure (data structures, intermediate forms, etc.) across systems.

We believe that there is a great deal of commonality in the support for parallelism in these languages, since parallelism is inherent in the problem and not in the problem's representation in a particular HPL. We should develop a unified framework for integrating and accommodating different program transformation and runtime components for supporting data parallelism. The runtime components developed will be available in the public domain. This will allow groups to build and test compiler subsystems and will accelerate research and development in this area.

The following is a summary of important research issues and innovations that would result from designing such a unified framework:

- *Portable and Scalable Multi-platform Runtime Support*

  Runtime support must efficiently support the address translations and data movements that occur when one embeds a globally indexed program onto a multiple processor architecture. Compilers and runtime support for HPLs can be built in a way that assumes the availability of multiple independent processors and an interface to a message passing system (such as PVM, Express, proprietary vendor message passing systems, MPI, etc.). Alternately compilers and runtime support can assume the existence of hardware supported address translation and data migration mechanisms, such as those found on Kendall Square KSR-1 machines. The issue there will be purely figuring out how data should be migrated.

  We expect that all HPL compilers will make use of at least some optimizations for reducing communication costs such as message blocking, collective communication, message coalescing, aggregation and latency hiding. Prototype runtime support has been developed to carry out these optimizations in the contexts of structured, adaptive, block structured and tree structured problems [1, 2, 3, 4, 5, 6, 7]. We will develop an integrated runtime support system that carries out address translation and communication optimizations, this runtime support will be built on top of a message passing interface.

  We will also develop versions of common runtime support to take advantage of hardware supported distributed shared memory mechanisms. HPL data structure decompositions and processor mappings will make it necessary to carry out rather complex mappings between logical program addresses and locations in the machine's distributed memory. Given these complex mappings, we do not expect hardware supported distributed shared memory alone to be able to efficiently handle data migration and address translation. Instead, we will develop runtime support capable of leveraging the capabilities of hardware supported distributed shared memory.

- *Methodology for Integrated Multilanguage Support*

  We would design and develop common code and data descriptors, and libraries and routines which operate on them for supporting data parallelism in HPLs. This would allow different programming languages to share data structures that are distributed across the memory hierarchy of scalable parallel systems and operate upon them.

  We would design a common compiler data movement interface specification that will provide a set of communication standards that compilers can link into the runtime system for applications. Unlike the user level message passing interface standard, the compiler interface can be more extensive in its capabilities, ranging from very low level primitives that exploit special hardware properties to very high level primitives directly coupled to the common array and data structure formats. The interface standard will make it possible to write compilers that achieve a much greater efficiency on a wider variety of machines than we can with current user level message passing mechanisms. In addition, a common runtime interface will allow a compiler to be easily adapted to a new machine, and still allow customization in the library implementation to improve performance.

- *Methodology for structuring code and data representations to support extensibility*

  We will develop a methodology for the engineering aspect of the described runtime support to allow ease of use, modification, specialization, and extension. The kind of extension we consider includes support for new distributed data structures, new language features, new runtime system mechanisms and algorithms, and new message passing or distributed shared memory interfaces.

3 Task Parallelism

We define *task* parallelism as parallelism not dictated by the distribution of data structures. It includes the execution of different functions in parallel, as well as the parallelization of loops via mechanisms other than (or in addition to) the "owner computes" rule commonly found in HPF, pC++, etc. Task parallelism is common in many existing systems. It is particularly useful for irregular applications. Recent research also suggests that there are important classes of applications that require both task and data parallelism in order to obtain good performance [8, 9, 10].

The requirements of a runtime system for task-level parallelism are different from those for data parallelism. First, there is a need for dynamic creation of tasks or processes. Dynamic load balance is necessary since these tasks generally have very different execution times. Second, the interactions between different tasks can be very complex and need the support of sophisticated synchronization primitives. Finally, to take advantage of locality of reference, it is important to cache and replicate data dynamically. The runtime system must provide support for processes to locate data in the distributed address space and to manage the local memory.

We recommend that research efforts in task-parallel runtime systems be combined to build common runtime infrastructure. The common infrastructure would be built in layers, and all layers would be accessible to top-level clients. The infrastructure should run on a variety of high performance parallel machines, including cache-coherent multiprocessors like DASH or the KSR-1, NUMA machines like the Cray T3D, and distributed-memory multicomputers like the Intel Paragon or the Thinking Machines CM-5. It should support high level parallel languages such as CC++ [11], Jade [12], Natasha [20], and Fortran M [13], as well as parallelizing compilers that generate multithreaded or task parallel code [14, 15, 16, 17, 18, 19]. Prototypes of many of the layers we envision already exist (often as part of working runtime systems for specific languages and machines), so the implementation effort should be manageable.

A common runtime infrastructure for task parallelism would have the following benefits:

- Provide a machine-independent layer for portability across machines. This will leverage the lower level system construction currently being done by individual groups.

- Enable shared efforts, both within the group of developers and for external groups that currently lack the resources to build portable runtime systems.

- Encourage better software design through the definition of interfaces between pieces of software.

- Provide validation of results by facilitating comparisons between different approaches on a common software architecture.

- Allow for inter-operability between different runtime systems. With an open layered architecture, compiler writers would be able to access whichever level provides appropriate functionality.

- Enable the comparative study of multiple programming paradigms and multiple machine architectures. Because top-level clients will run on a common substrate, which in turn runs on many machines, "apples and apples" comparisons between languages and compilers will be considerably easier, as will comparisons between machines.

- Provide a framework for identifying commonality in runtime systems built for ostensibly different environments (e.g. on different hardware, or for different languages). Beyond the common facilities described in this report, it is likely that additional opportunities for standardization will be found as research progresses, e.g. in the area of scheduling policies.

There are currently a number of efforts to develop task-parallel runtime systems for a variety of high-level programming languages, such as CC++ [11], Jade [12], Natasha [20], and Fortran M [13]. In addition, several groups are developing parallelizing compilers that recognize implicit task parallelism in sequential programs [14, 15, 16, 17, 18, 19]. These efforts have resulted in runtime software for a large set of machines, but because the systems were developed independently, each typically runs on only one or two machines. A common runtime system for task-level parallelism would support multiple machines, and multiple high-level programming languages and compilers.

To manage the complexity of such a system, we recommend development of a runtime system architecture consisting of well-defined layers of abstraction. Each layer will be exposed to the user—some compilers may be built only on lower layers whereas others may use a mixture of all layers. In addition, multiple instances of a single layer may exist to permit efficient implementations on different architectures, or to provide a different set of abstractions to higher layers. For example, locality may be achieved by a shared object system, a virtual shared memory layer, or hardware shared memory.

In describing our system architecture, we separate functions into control and data hierarchies. The control hierarchy provides threads, scheduling, synchronization, and load balancing facilities, while the data hierarchy contains names (addresses), data objects, and object relocation facilities. In practice, of course, control and data management facilities are seldom independent; a single software module is likely to provide a combination of both. Interactions between them include reduction operations, aligning data and control (i.e. scheduling for locality), associating synchronization objects with data objects (to facilitate relaxed consistency) and waiting for prefetch/poststore operations to complete.

We expect there to be substantial commonality in both the control and data hierarchies across the spectrum of architectures and programming paradigms. At the same time, alternative module implementations, and even alternative interfaces, will be needed in certain layers in order to accommodate major architectural differences, or to provide the performance

and functionality required by dissimilar programming paradigms. Protocol hierarchies for communication networks provide an instructive analogy. The ISO hierarchy [21] provides a conceptual framework for layered protocols, and Arizona's x-kernel project [22] provides an excellent example of the identification and exploitation of commonality in different protocol stacks.

4 Performance and Debugging Infrastructure

The rapidly evolving state of system, run-time, and application software demands performance evaluation and debugging technology that is portable across diverse implementation platforms, and that can be readily extended to include the results of emerging research. Creating a common performance evaluation and debugging infrastructure that meets these requirements for current application and run-time software implies a research effort with two specific foci:

1. integration of application and run-time software with both extant and proposed performance and debugging analysis systems through the specification and development of software interfaces that isolate the implementation of specific instrumentation and analysis techniques behind software "firewalls," ensuring that instrumented software can be ported to systems with different instrumentation implementations; and

2. application of performance evaluation and debugging techniques during run-time software execution through new, dynamic performance and debugging instrumentation, query, and presentation techniques, enabling the development of adaptive application and run-time software.

No single performance analysis or debugging tool provides all the functionality needed to debug and optimize all software, nor should it; experience has shown that a collection of simpler tools is preferable to a single, complex tool. However, software developers should be able to easily integrate, combine, and analyze data from multiple instrumentation and data analysis tools. At present, this is not possible. The goal of the software integration focus is to provide run-time system software developers a set of standard, high-level interfaces to performance and debugging tools. Without these standard interfaces, individual run-time system projects would likely design and develop performance and debugging software specific to their problem area, rather than deal with the nuances of each tool's use. Not only would these systems be incompatible, they would be unable to exploit cross-domain information (e.g., run-time library and compiler information) in a uniform way. A common platform can be achieved only through the standardization of software interfaces that isolate the implementation of specific performance/debugging instrumentation and analysis techniques behind software boundaries. These interfaces provide an integration veneer which ensures that application and run-time software can be ported to systems with differing performance and debugging implementations. For tool developers, the standard interfaces will provide broad access to performance and debugging software that is compliant with the interface definitions.

Although standard software interfaces support a portable, reusable performance evaluation and debugging infrastructure, the requirements posed by emerging software systems challenge existing performance and debugging technology. Run-time systems for high-level languages (e.g., for HPF and HPC++); environments for creating and accessing parallel, distributed data structures; and software for adaptive application execution and run-time decision analysis will all require new performance and debugging techniques, particularly for dynamic instrumentation, run-time queries, dynamic guidance, and execution state access. The present opportunity to develop new performance and debugging techniques in concert with run-time software is unique. Exploiting this opportunity will maximize the likelihood that the resulting software will be well-targeted, quickly applied, and reused by future run-time system development efforts.

The Performance Evaluation and DebuggInG softwaRE infrastructurE (PEDIGREE)[1] research project will create a portable, extensible performance evaluation and debugging infrastructure, based on the research foci above, that is broadly applicable to both run-time libraries and application software. In particular, the PEDIGREE infrastructure will include the following key components:

- standard software interfaces for performance and debugging tools;

- dynamically activated performance instrumentation, application-initiated performance queries, performance-directed decision procedures, and data presentation techniques that allow software developers to guide computations; and

---

[1] The PEDIGREE acronym is intended to imply a common basis for performance and debugging support that will be applicable to all run-time system software.

- run-time debugging infrastructure that utilizes techniques for dynamic breakpointing to uniformly support run-time breakpoint management, state and event-based query, and dynamic visualization.

Standard interfaces will allow both instrumented run-time systems and applications to be moved to different parallel systems without porting a particular performance or debugging implementation. In addition, standard interfaces will encourage the development of "meta-tools" that combine data from multiple performance and debugging systems. The primary focus of existing tools is user-level performance analysis and debugging; the new infrastructure will enable run-time systems to access performance and debugging data during their execution and to use this data as input to dynamic decision procedures.

We believe that by delivering these three PEDIGREE components, current and future runtime system and application software developments will more likely utilize common performance evaluation and debugging tools rather than develop specialized software, leading to a sorely needed integration and uniformity of technology in the two areas.

References

[1] Harry Berryman, Joel Saltz, and Jeffrey Scroggs. Execution time support for adaptive scientific algorithms on distributed memory machines. *Concurrency: Practice and Experience*, 3(3):pp. 159–178, June 1991.

[2] Sandeep Bhatt, Marina Chen, James Cowie, Cheng-Yee Lin, and Pangfeng Liu. Object-Oriented Support for Adaptive Methods on Parallel Machines. *OONSKI'93 Object Oriented Numerics Conference*, Sunriver, Oregon, April 25-27, 1993.

[3] S. Bhatt, M. Chen, C.Y. Lin, and P. Liu. Abstractions for Parallel N-body Simulations. *Proceedings of Scalable High Performance Computing Conference (SHPCC '92)*, Williamsburg, Virginia, April 1992.

[4] Zeki Bozkus, Alok Choudhary, Geoffrey Fox, Tomasz Haupt, Sanjay Ranka, and Jhy-Chun Wang. Message Passing Environment Requirements for the Fortran 90D Compiler. Technical Report SCCS-FEB-93, Northeast Parallel Architectures Center at Syracuse University, February 1993.

[5] R. Das, R. Ponnusamy, J. Saltz, and D. Mavriplis. Distributed memory compiler methods for irregular problems - data copy reuse and runtime partitioning. J. Saltz and P. Mehrotra, editors, *Languages, Compilers and Runtime Environments*

for Distributed Memory Machines, pp. 185–220. Elsevier, 1992.

[6] S. Ranka, J.C. Wang, and M. Kumar. Personalized Communication Avoiding Node Contention on Distributed Memory Systems. *Proceedings of the 1993 International Conference on Parallel Processing*, St. Charles, IL, August 1993.

[7] A. Sussman, J. Saltz, R. Das, S. Gupta, D. Mavriplis, R. Ponnusamy, and K. Crowley. PARTI primitives for unstructured and block structured problems. *Computing Systems in Engineering*, 3(1-4):pp. 73–86, 1992. Papers presented at *the Symposium on High-Performance Computing for Flight Vehicles*, December 1992.

[8] L. A. Crowl, M. Crovella, T. J. LeBlanc, and M. L. Scott. Beyond Data Parallelism: The Advantages of Multiple Parallelizations in Combinatorial Search. TR 451, Computer Science Department, University of Rochester, April 1993.

[9] T. Pratt. Kernel-Control Parallel Versus Data Parallel: A Technical Comparison. In *Proceedings of the Second Workshop on Languages, Compilers, and Run-Time Environments for Distributed Memory Multiprocessors*, pages 5-8, Boulder, CO, 30 September – 2 October 1992. In *ACM SIGPLAN Notices 28*:1 (January 1993).

[10] J. Subhlok, J. M. Stichnoth, D. R. O'Hallaron, and T. Gross. Programming Task and Data Parallelism on a Multicomputer. In *Proceedings of the Fourth ACM Symposium on Principles and Practice of Parallel Programming*, San Diego, CA, 20-22 May 1993.

[11] K. M. Chandy and C. Kesselman. Compositional C++: Compositional Parallel Programming. California Institute of Technology, 1992.

[12] M. C. Rinard, D. J. Scales, and M. S. Lam. Jade: A High-Level Machine-Independent Language for Parallel Programming. *Computer*, 26(6):28-38, June 1993.

[13] I. T. Foster and K. M. Chandy. Fortran M: A Language for Modular Parallel Programming. Preprint MCS-P327-0992, Argonne National Laboratory, June 1992.

[14] R. Eigenmann, J. Hoeflinger, G. Jaxon, Z. Li, and D. Padua. Restructuring Fortran Programs for Cedar. *Proceedings of the 1991 International Conference on Parallel Processing*, I, Architecture:57-66, August 1991.

[15] C. D. Polychronopoulos and others. Parafrase-2: A Multilingual Compiler for Optimizing, Partitioning, and Scheduling Ordinary Programs. In *Proceedings of the 1989 International Conference on Parallel Processing*, St. Charles, IL, August 1989.

[16] W. Li and K. Pingali. Access Normalization: Loop Restructuring for NUMA Compilers. In *Proceedings of the Fifth International Conference on Architectural Support for Programming Languages and Operating Systems*, pages 285-295, Boston, MA, 12-15 October 1992.

[17] S. P. Amarasinghe and M. S. Lam. Communication Optimization and Code Generation for Distributed Memory Machines. In *Proceedings of the SIGPLAN '93 Conference on Programming Language Design and Implementation*, Albuquerque, NM, 21-25 June 1993.

[18] J. M. Anderson and M. S. Lam. Global Optimizations for Parallelism and Locality on Scalable Parallel Machines. In *Proceedings of the SIGPLAN '93 Conference on Programming Language Design and Implementation*, Albuquerque, NM, 21-25 June 1993.

[19] D. Padua and R. Eigenmann. Polaris: A New Generation Parallelizing Compiler for MPPs. Technical Report 1306, Center for Supercomputing Research and Development, University of Illinois at Urbana-Champaign, 1993.

[20] L. A. Crowl and T. J. LeBlanc. Control Abstraction in Parallel Programming Languages. In *Proceedings of the International Conference on Computer Languages*, pages 44-53, Oakland, CA, April 1992.

[21] A. S. Tanenbaum. Network Protocols. *ACM Computing Surveys*, 13(4):453-489, December 1981.

[22] L. Peterson, N. Hutchinson, S. O'Malley, and H. Rao. The x-Kernel: A Platform for Accessing Internet Resources. *Computer*, 23(5):23-33, May 1990.

[23] W. J. Bolosky, R. P. Fitzgerald, and M. L. Scott. Simple But Effective Techniques for NUMA Memory Management. In *Proceedings of the Twelfth ACM Symposium on Operating Systems Principles*, pages 19-31, Litchfield Park, AZ, 3-6 December 1989.

Session 10:
Invited Presentations
Dennis Muren
Margaret Simmons

Session 10:
Minisymposium
Chair: Doreen Cheng

Heterogeneous Distributed Computing
— Summary of A Minisymposium

Doreen Y. Cheng
CSC/NASA Ames Research Center
MS 258-6
Moffett Field, CA 94035
dcheng@nas.nasa.gov

As workstations become more powerful and speed and bandwidth of networks increase, parallel computing on a network of heterogeneous systems becomes more attractive. However, heterogeneity makes effective use of resources more difficult. Four presentations in the minisymposium discussed the software assistance required to alleviate these difficulties. The first speaker described overall requirements and issues in heterogeneous distributed computing. The second speaker presented an approach to extending a message-passing interface and providing a full set of tools necessary for heterogeneous distributed computing. The third speaker emphasized the necessity of providing a safer message-passing interface, and the last speaker described the status of tools that manage resources in a heterogeneous environment.

Ranka and colleagues first described four important factors in achieving high utilization of heterogeneous resources: (1) inter-machine communication latency and bandwidth, (2) increasing communication cost accompanied by increasing number of machines used, (3) varying capacity of machines and networks, (4) different data representations. Analysis of the characteristics of parallel scientific applications led to the conclusion that data/task decomposition and distribution is crucial to efficient use of varying capacity of resources. However it is difficult to achieve efficient decomposition and distribution in general cases. After surveying existing parallel languages and libraries, they pointed out that no single language is sufficient for parallel scientific applications.

Hiding the complexity of using network communication primitives (e.g. UNIX sockets) within a library is helpful but insufficient. Beguelin and colleagues revealed that future PVM will use the open-*system* approach to integrate tool modules provided in other environments. In this way, PVM will provide capabilities for debugging, profiling, performance visualization, dynamic process migration, and fault tolerance. In addition, it will support communication of multimedia and computation on MPPs.

Many message-passing interfaces (e.g. PVM, P4, PICL, PARMACS, EXPRESS) were developed to increase application portability. However, for such an approach to be successful, communication domains of subprograms must be ensured against interference with each other. Skjellum and Grant emphasized the importance of providing safety and correctness in addition to high performance in a message-passing interface. Based on this requirement, they compared PVM with the *Message Passing Interface* (MPI).

Managing heterogeneous resources in a multi-user, multi-owner environment is important for distributed computing. Requirements for load balance, fault tolerance, non-intrusiveness, and checkpoint/restart have introduced technical as well as political difficulties. In the last presentation, Freund described a new approach used in SmartNet after he compared the existing resource management tools. SmartNet uses relative affinities between tasks and machines for automatic task allocation.

In summary, we need programming languages sufficient for expressing parallel scientific algorithms and data/task partitioning and distribution. We need safe and efficient low-level programming interfaces (e.g. message passing) and tools for debugging and performance optimization. We also need an environment that automatically migrates processes to balance load and tolerates failures.

Heterogeneous Computing on Heterogeneous Systems: Software and Application Issues *

Sanjay Ranka, Maher Kaddoura, Albert Wang, Geoffrey Fox **

Most applications like Image Undertanding, Multidisciplinary Analysis and Design, and Command and Control require integrating algorithms from diverse areas such as image processing, numerical analysis, graph theory, artificial intelligence and databases. These problems are difficult to solve on one parallel machine because they consist of several parts, each of which requires differing types and amounts of parallelization. In this paper we study software and application issues related to using heterogeneous systems for high-performance computing. A typical environment would consist of a suite of high-performance SIMD and MIMD parallel machines and workstations connected by a high speed interconnection network.

1 Important Issues

Parallel processing on a network has much in common with the loosely-coupled distributed model of computation. Four important considerations for achieving high utilization of resources are as follows:

1. *Network latency and bandwidth*: The scalability of applications which can be parallelized depends on the network latency. Lowering latency is much more difficult than increasing the bandwidth. The latter can be achieved by using wide data paths and large bandwidth media.

2. *Processor selection*: The number and identities of a subset of processors must be selected for a task. Using a large number of machines for computation may have a tradeoff of increasing communication cost. Furthermore, in multiuser environments, the available resources may change dynamically.

3. *Mapping*: The heterogeneous environment may involve processors with different capabilities. In some cases, the interconnection network is also heterogeneous and provides different latency and bandwidth between processor pairs. The work assigned to each machine should be matched to its capabilities, and interprocessor communication should be matched to network capabilities.

4. *Data conversion*: Data items may be represented differently on various types of machines due to differences in machine architectures, the programming languages used, and the way the compilers generate code for them.

2 Problem Classification and Mapping

It is convenient to classify problems into synchronous, loosely synchronous, asynchronous, embarrassingly parallel and heteroproblems [1]. In regular and synchronous problems, there is data parallelism with identical algorithms applied to each point in the data domain and identical data dependency patterns between data domain points. Loosely synchronous problems are data parallel, but different data points evolve differently. Points are also often connected in an irregular, data-dependent manner. The class of heteroproblems have two or more subtasks, with each subtask belonging to one of the above categories. Each subtask in such an application can be parallelized individually. The class of embarrassingly parallel problems requires little communication and synchronization and can be easily parallelized, while the class of asynchronous problems requires tailored parallelizations. For the rest of this section, we will concentrate on the requirements for synchronous, loosely synchronous, and heteroproblems. We will assume that the resources available to the user are fixed throughout the completion of tasks or reasonably large periods of time (in which case a remapping and repartitioning can be performed).

Mapping of regular and synchronous problems on homogeneous machines is relatively well understood. However, the mapping of such problems reduces in most cases to mapping on non-uniform computational environments. Multi-dimensional arrays need to be decomposed into subarrays such that the size of each subarray is proportional to the computational power of the corresponding node, and internode communication is minimized [2].

*This work was supported by DARPA under contract # DABT63-91-C-0028. The content of the information does not necessarily reflect the position or the policy of the Government and no official endorsement should be inferred. Sanjay Ranka was also supported in part by NSF under CCR-9110812.
** 4-116 Center for Science and Technology, School of Computer Science, Syracuse University,

The handling of most irregular and loosely synchronous problems requires the use of runtime information to partition the computation in such a fashion that each processor receives an amount of computation proportional to their computational power and total communication is minimized. The computational structure for many irregular and loosely synchronous problems can be described in terms of a computational graph. Several algorithms are available in the literature for partitioning and mapping this computational graph onto uniform parallel machines. Further research is required for performing the mapping onto nonuniform machines.

The mapping of heteroproblems requires mapping of different tasks on to different machines. Tasks of different types should be sent to the most appropriate machine(s) for execution. These tasks may run concurrently or have some dependence graph. Thus, scheduling and synchronization is required to to guarantee that tasks the required ordering. The mapping problem for this class of problems for a general heterogeneous platform is very complicated, because the computation time for different tasks on different machines needs to be estimated, and the total resources need to be subdivided among tasks such that total time is minimized. Total time includes the cost of communication and/or I/O required.

3 Languages and Tools

Achieving good performance on a parallel machine requires a close coupling between the application requirements and the software environment. At a recent multiagency workshop on HPCC and grand challenge applications at Pittsburgh, the application scientists concluded that no one particular language was sufficient for the parallelization of their applications. A typical example of software development involved using C++ as a high-level language to achieve modularity, Fortran as a high-performance assembly language for coding the computationally intensive fragments, and AVS for visualization. Codes involved a mixture of data parallelism as well as task parallelism. Thus, developing software for these applications requires a software environment that can handle different programming languages and different programming paradigms.

Although, automatic compilers for sequential languages have been successful (to a limited extent) for vector machines, experience suggests that they fail for parallel machines. Conventional languages like C and FORTRAN have been extended to provide features for parallel programming such as process creation, message-passing and synchronization. Paral-

lelization of most of the significant codes has been limited to such languages. Although, packages like Express, PVM, P4, PICL, and LINDA provide some level of portability, the codes are typically too tied to low-level architectural details to achieve performance.

Distribution of data and interactions between different data elements is critical in achieving efficient parallelization of data parallel scientific and engineering applications. User defined distribution directives are provided in a number of efforts, including Data parallel C, Kali, Vienna Fortran, DINO, and Fortran D. These initial efforts have led to the development of High Performance Fortran (HPF). The decomposition and distribution directives of HPF are geared towards uniform machines and regular problems. Extensions are required for supporting loosely synchronous problems. The utility of these primitives for data distribution on heterogeneous machines is not so obvious; clearly, the need for exploiting data parallelism for heterogenous machines is limited. In its current form, HPF is not suitable for heteroproblems.

Coarse level task parallelism for a number of applications has been successfully supported on heterocomputers with packages like Express, PVM and AVS. Language effort to support task parallelism includes PCN, Mentat, Joyce, pC++, CC++, HPC++, Ada, Divacon, Jade, Natasha, Fortran M, ABCL, Actor, Argus, Concurrent Smalltalk, COOL, Eiffel, POOL-T, and Presto. Compilers for many of these languages are still in their infancy and experience with real applications has been limited.

The major task is to design and implement a language (or add directives in existing languages) specifying the task and data parallel program components and indicating how they should be decomposed onto the heterocomputer. Directives could also identify tasks suitable for SIMD machines and how to decompose a single task onto a heterogenous target machine.

References

[1] G. C. Fox, "The Architecture of Problems and Portable Parallel Software Systems," Technical Report, SCCS-134b, July 1991.

[2] Maher Kaddoura, Sanjay Ranka, and Albert Wang, "Array Decompositions for Parallel Machines with Non-uniform Computational Power," Technical Report, Syracuse University, June 1993.

PVM: Experiences, Current Status and Future Direction [*]

Adam Beguelin [§], Jack Dongarra[†‡], Al Geist [‡],
Robert Manchek[†], Steve Otto[¶], and Jon Walpole[¶]

[†]University of Tennessee
Department of Computer Science
107 Ayres Hall
Knoxville, TN 37996-1301

[‡]Oak Ridge National Laboratory
Mathematical Sciences Section
P. O. Box 2008, Bldg. 6012
Oak Ridge, TN 37831-6367

[¶]Oregon Graduate Institute
Computer Science Department
P. O. Box 9100
Portland, OR 97291-1000

[§]Carnegie Mellon University
School of Computer Science
5000 Forbes Avenue
Pittsburgh, PA 15213-3890

The computing requirements of many current and future applications, ranging from scientific computational problems in the material and physical sciences, to simulation, engineering design, and circuit analysis, are best served by concurrent processing. While hardware multiprocessors can frequently address the computational requirements of these high-performance applications, there are a number of integration aspects to concurrent computing that are not adequately addressed when conventional parallel processors are used to solve these problems.

The PVM (Parallel Virtual Machine) software package provides the software infrastructure for programming heterogeneous networks [4, 1, 3]. PVM provides mechanisms for configuring a virtual machine on a network, initializing processes on this network and communicating among these processes. PVM is a lightweight package intended for user installation. Nearly any Unix or Unix-like machine can be used as a processor in a virtual machine as long as the user has an account on the machine and it is accessible over a network. Several existing concurrent applications have been ported to execute on the PVM system, with encouraging results. For example, PVM execution speeds for molecular dynamics simulations (an application with a high volume of communication) using IBM RS/6000 workstations averaged only 30 percent slower than an iPSC/860 hypercube with a comparable number of processors. Another application calculates the electronic structure of a high-temperature superconductor at a rate of approximately 250 Mflops under the PVM system.

Applications that use a combination of shared memory machines, hypercubes, and scalar processors have been run under the PVM system, with corresponding increases in performance over any one multiprocessor. Preliminary experiments have shown promise in this type of computing environment. PVM virtualizes such a heterogeneous collection of computers into a distributed-memory, message-passing, parallel computer. PVM is becoming a spanning software technology for network computers, cluster computers, and tightly-coupled massively-parallel processors (MPPs), and significantly, vendors, including IBM, Convex, and Cray, are implementing versions of PVM on their platforms.

We are working to enhance significantly the functionality of PVM. Extensions to PVM along a number of dimensions are proposed. First, we are planning to add support for parallel and distributed processing in multi-user and multi-owner environments. This support will include the ability to capture idle cycles available on shared networks, to sensibly schedule multiple parallel jobs, and to integrate MPPs with networked personal workstations. Secondly, we will add a collection of tools for debugging, profiling and monitoring concurrent applications. Source level debugging will be supported using existing debugging systems that will be adapted for concurrent environ-

[*]This project was supported in part by the Defense Advanced Research Projects Agency under contract DAAL03-91-C-0047, administered by the Army Research Office, the Applied Mathematical Sciences subprogram of the Office of Energy Research, U.S. Department of Energy, under Contract DE-AC05-84OR21400, and by the National Science Foundation Science and Technology Center Cooperative Agreement No. CCR-8809615.

ments [2]. Profiling will concentrate on visual animation and display of program behavior, with emphasis on inter-component communication and synchronization. In addition, we will also develop tools for monitoring overall system load, resource availability, and network traffic. These facilities will permit reconfiguration and relocation of application components, and will provide administrative interfaces for general resource management. Finally, we will extend the PVM message passing system to support communication of multimedia data, including digital audio and video. The idea here is to give a simple and very portable interface for multimedia applications.

This new version of PVM will form the "kernel" of a Concurrent Processing Environment (CPE). Rather than build all the above capabilities directly into the kernel, we will take a modular approach. Interfaces are defined that allow the modules to be used independently in other environments, and allow the environment to coexist with related software systems. A distributed scheduler, for example, will be a separate module with a well-defined interface to the CPE kernel. This "open-systems" approach addresses heterogeneity at the system software level as well as at the operating system and hardware levels.

By hiding the complexity of concurrent processing systems and by presenting a uniform programming model we will encourage the development of parallel applications and system services. The CPE will also provide a runtime environment and target (virtual) machine for compilers such as HPF.

Despite our focus on heterogeneous multiuser networks, the project will also contribute to the process of integrating massively parallel processors (MPPs) with more common-place workstation networks. A prominent trend in MPP design has been the move towards cluster-oriented architectures. Examples of such systems are the Intel Paragon and TMC CM5. These systems are conceptually similar to workstation networks in that they are multi-user, network-based architectures with an operating system running on each node. In fact, such systems constitute a simpler (because they are homogeneous and do not support such complex notions of ownership) subset of the architectures considered in the proposed research. Furthermore, MPP vendors are already interested in ports of PVM to their platforms. Consequently, we expect our environment to become a spanning technology that will assist in the seamless integration of MPPs into heterogeneous networks.

Future users of our system will be able to run batch and interactive parallel applications unobtrusively on multi-user heterogeneous networks. These applications will be able to transfer audio and video data as well as conventional data, will enjoy fault-tolerant execution, and will have access to external visualization and performance monitoring packages. The system will support automatic redistribution of work, through dynamic process migration, in order to cope with reclaimed and newly available processors. This dynamic reconfiguration will be transparent to application programmers, who will program in terms of virtual, rather than physical, processors. Application programmers will not need to worry about the degree of physical parallelism, the location of processors, process migration, resource allocation or scheduling. Hence, the programming model based on PVM message passing, will be kept simple.

Not only will the application programmer's interface to our system be simple and transparent, but the execution of the system will also be transparent to other users of the machines on the heterogeneous network. A key requirement of a cycle harvesting system is that it be unobtrusive to the users of the computers it is using. Our system will place high importance on this characteristic, if necessary trading efficiency for unobtrusiveness. In this way, we hope to gain access to many more processor cycles than would otherwise be possible.

Acknowledgements

We would like to thank Jim Patterson of BCS for helpful discussions.

References

[1] A. L. Beguelin, J. J. Dongarra, A. Geist, R. J. Manchek, and V. S. Sunderam. Heterogeneous network computing. In *Sixth SIAM Conference on Parallel Processing*, 1993.

[2] D. Cheng. Proposal for a standard debugger server protocol. Technical report. To appear at the SuperComputing '93 workshop, "Debuggers for High Performance Computers."

[3] Jack Dongarra, Al Geist, Robert Manchek, and Vaidy Sunderam. Integrated PVM framework supports heterogeneous network computing. *Computers in Physics*, April 1993.

[4] A. Geist and V. S. Sunderam. Network-based concurrent computing on the PVM system. *Concurrency: Practice and Experience*, 4(4):293–311, June 1992.

Message Passing in the 1990's: Performance, Safety, Correctness[*]

Anthony Skjellum[†]

NSF Enginering Research Center
& Computer Science
Mississippi State University
Mississippi State, MS

Brian K. Grant

Department of Computer Science
& Engineering
University of Washington
Seattle, WA

Origins of Message Passing

First-generation message passing systems (*e.g.*, NX, Vertex, PICL, Express) were designed with vendor-specific goals, performance characteristics relative to their underlying hardware, and limited notions of safety (*i.e.*, tag management). Emerging from this era are common support for blocking and non-blocking point-to-point communication, global operations over the ensemble of processes (often processors), and basic process management. Typically, the point-to-point messaging primitives operated on user-supplied (*e.g.*, NX) or system-managed buffers (*e.g.*, Reactive Kernel). Users were to allocate and free message buffers, align data, convert data (as needed) to/from heterogeneous host processes, and guarantee that message contents aligned on sender and receiver. Originally, the recipient was required to know a message's size before it could be accepted; later probe mechanisms were provided more uniformly. Receipt selectivity was either on tag only, or on both tag and sender. Processes were typically named with hardware-oriented {node,pid} naming; the trend to limiting users to one process per processor increased rather than decreased during the 1980's. The software overhead of these systems was 50-200 times the latency of the underlying messaging networks. Transmission protocols were typically three-way, offering reasonable flow-control and reliability.

In parallel with the development of multicomputer message passing came the development of network file systems in the workstation environment and widespread use of workstation clusters. These developments created the need for heterogeneous data-transmission and simplified interprocess-

communication mechanisms. Sun's XDR service became the de facto standard for a machine-independent data representation, and nearly all communication systems were based on the Internet-standard TCP/IP Protocol Suite. Unfortunately, most XDR and TCP/IP implementations had high overheads and were not suitable for high-performance communication.

Evolution

PVM emerged as one of the most popular cluster message-passing systems in 1992, though PVM did not originally work on nodes of multicomputers (more recently, multicomputer vendors have offered both layered and native versions of PVM for multicomputer message passing). PVM's model and semantics closely resembled those of systems such as PICL and NX from the mid to late 1980's. PVM's main contribution was its broad interoperability across workstation platforms. Another attraction was the portability of its TCP- and XDR-based implementation. However, its programming paradigm offered no significant advantage over the paradigms of the earlier systems.

By way of contrast, the MPI standardization effort had its roots in other systems, particularly PARMACS and Zipcode, which included higher-level concepts in their programming models. Formalization of message-passing models, notions of correctness in loosely synchronous programming, and considerations of safety had become concerns of programmers building significant applications with message passing, which were ignored by the early systems and also by PVM. Furthermore, MPI was to incorporate concepts that would deliver higher performance to the user; these concepts were the product of experience with higher-level message systems (*e.g.*, invoices (aka buffer descriptors), powerful collective operations).

---

[*]Parallel Computing on a Network of Computers — A Minisymposium during Supercomputing '93, Invited Presentation.

[†]To whom correspondence should be addressed. e-mail: *tony@cs.msstate.edu*

Comparison of PVM and MPI

PVM provides the following types of services:

- Process management for clusters,

- Dynamic process creation,

- Dynamic group management,

- Point-to-point communication,

- Multicasts and barriers,

- Explicit data conversion capabilities for users.

Things to think about when choosing PVM:

- User specification of communication protocols,

- User management of buffers and data conversion,

- Close ties to XDR for data conversion,

- Excess data motion, even in absence of heterogeneity,

- Lack of full set of collective communication operations,

- Lack of group/context safety mechanisms found in Zipcode and MPI,

- Race conditions involving dynamic groups,

- Race conditions involving virtual machine management,

- Lack of thread safety,

- PVM does not support a model of parallel I/O,

- PVM's cluster software is extremely portable among Unix and Unix-like systems.

MPI provides the following types of services:

- Groups of processes,

- Communicators for group-scope message passing (group+context),

- Point-to-point operations with communicator scope,

- Collective operations with communicator scope,

- Virtual topology for logical process naming,

- Thread safety.

Importantly, the gather-scatter semantics of MPI provides the ability to:

- Optimize data motion when sending and receiving messages,

- Hide heterogeneous conversions from the user,

- Relieve the user of buffer management.

Group scope in MPI guarantees that special properties of hierarchies can be exploited:

- Homogeneous subgroups can avoid data conversions,

- Specialized communication modes can be exploited where available (*e.g.*, channels, local shared-memory clusters).

The collective operations allow the user to exploit high performance collective capabilities of certain architectures, while avoiding the need to develop collective calls from point-to-point calls on all systems (slow, error prone).

Things to think about when moving to MPI1:

- MPI1 process management is left to implementations,

- MPI1 does not enforce a model of parallel I/O,

- MPI1 does not guarantee interoperability between implementations,

- MPI1 will provide a stable core for future standardization efforts,

- A user-manual is under development,

- A coherent, useful subset is specified alongside the standard,

- Several (but not all) vendors have committed to implementing MPI1,

- A portable cluster implementation of MPI1 is under development.

Finally, MPI documents outline a logical programming paradigm for writing parallel libraries and applications in the safest possible way without explicit compiler support for parallelism.

SmartNet
Richard F. Freund

NRaD Code 423

freund@superc.nosc.mil

Attempts to better utilize clusters of workstations and heterogeneous High Performance Computing (HPC) systems for distributed computing have brought about the development of a variety of distributed resource management tools. However, tools such as Distributed Queuing Systems (DQS), Condor, LoadLeveler, Load Balancer, Load Sharing Facility (LSF - formerly Utopia), Distributed Job Manager (DJM) and Computing in Distributed Networked Environments (CODINE) have largely focused on load balancing and/or ad hoc optimization management techniques to maximize job throughput. While these techniques are effective in "soaking" extra CPU cycles and ensuring maximal busy time for each machine, they are not as effective in managing very heterogeneous configurations of networks and HPC machines. At NRaD we have developed a distributed resource management tool, SmartNet, that will make allocation decisions based on theoretical and experiential information of tasks that ensure near-optimal use of the heterogeneous resources.

SmartNet is a management scheme for near-optimal allocation of very heterogeneous HPC resources (both machines and) networks. Currently it is PVM-based, but it could be based on any or on multiple Distributed Computing Environments. SmartNet is specifically designed for very heterogeneous configurations, i.e., for those in which opportunistic load-balancing and greedy algorithms are insufficient as primary allocation paradigms. SmartNet makes automatic allocation decisions based on theoretical and experiential information about relative affinities of various tasks to different machines. It also includes effects of predicted network latencies.

The heart of SmartNet consists of:
a. an Expected Time to Compute (ETC) function which predicts performance of various tasks on different machines and networks. This predicted performance is based on theoretical and experiential information, as well as allowing for user input.
b. a Look Ahead/Look Back (LALB) strategizer function which near-optimally fits newly submitted tasks to the existing queue of currently executing and already allocated tasks.

The set of factors that are input to these functions include:

a.	Experiential and theoretical matching of processor to task

b.	Network latencies

c.	Data profiling

d.	LALB scheduling

e.	Secondary load-balancing, among task-suitable machines

f.	Predicted time to compute, at run time, with updates, upon completion, of actual times to experience tables.

The characteristics of SmartNet are:

a.	It makes near-optimal allocation decisions, based on matching of task (algorithm plus data) to processor.

b.	It is dynamically "tunable" for best performance, cost- effective performance, differing priorities among tasks, LANs/WANs, etc.

c.	SmartNet makes decisions 'on the fly' (and thus is only near- optimal).

d.	Since SmartNet updates its experience tables, it exhibits enhanced performance, over time, through 'learning'

e.	Flexible and dynamic 'reasoning'. Since SmartNet reasons about networks and machines at scheduling time, it has the capability to reason differently when confronted with different situations. For example, one time SmartNet may decide to use a remote computer because a high-speed network makes the small latency penalty worth the performance benefit. Another time,

faced with the same task and machine, but only a narrow bandwidth channel to the remote machines, it will decide to use the computationally inferior local machine, because of the relatively large latency penalty. This flexibility means that SmartNet exhibits resource robustness and evolutionary adaptation for enhanced configurations.

There is no other tool we know of which does automatic, LALB, configuration flexible, near-optimal assignment of heterogeneous tasks for a heterogeneous suite, based on theoretical and experiential matching of processor to task. The only basis of comparison would be against dissimilar systems, e.g., a system which uses merely load-balancing or one which uses only ad hoc matching. We intend to demonstrate concrete example(s) in which either load-balancing or ad hoc schemes are inadequate compared to SmartNet. We believe that SmartNet's predictive capability far exceeds, and thus its opportunity to do near-optimal allocation, far exceeds anything now available. Furthermore we will demonstrate that SmartNet expands gracefully to very large number of dissimilar resources and is also potentially useful in future planning for large networks.

Session 11:
Interconnection/Networks
Chair: Greg Papadopoulos

Designing Interconnection Networks For Multi-level Packaging

M. T. Raghunath*   Abhiram Ranade*

Computer Science Division,
University of California, Berkeley, CA 94720

Abstract

A central problem in building large scale parallel machines is the design of the interconnection network. Interconnection network design is largely constrained by packaging technology. We start with a generic set of packaging restrictions and evaluate different network organizations under a random traffic model. We identify families of networks (product of complete graphs, high degree deBruijn graphs) that we believe will be useful for multilevel packaging. Our results indicate that customizing the network topology to the packaging constraints is useful. Some of the general principles that arise out of this study are: 1) Making the networks denser at the lower levels of the packaging hierarchy has a significant positive impact on global communication performance, 2) It is better to organize a fixed amount of communication bandwidth as a smaller number of high bandwidth channels, 3) Providing the processors with the ability to tolerate latencies (by using multithreading) is very useful in improving performance.

1 Introduction

Interconnection network design is a central issue in building large scale general purpose parallel computers. The network takes up a significant fraction of the total cost; is often the hardest part of the system to engineer, and for many applications determines the final performance. The issues in designing a network range from the very high level: what topology should we use, to the most mundane: what should be the widths of the different channels. But each of these questions can make or break a network design. Each question is also more complex than it appears superficially: should we use hybrid network topologies (e.g. mesh at board level, and butterfly between boards)? Is it useful to have variable channel widths in different parts of the machine? Is it useful to duplicate (also called *dilate*) channels?

The interconnection network critically depends upon the communication behavior of the applications running on the parallel computer. For instance, if the application consists of multiplying dense matrices, it is

conceivable that a two-dimensional grid will be an appropriate interconnection network. However, our goal is to design networks to support general purpose parallel programming, so our design cannot be unduly influenced by the characteristics of a single program. For modeling general applications, it is customary to assume random communication patterns. In particular, we assume that every time a processor accesses shared data, the location accessed is randomly distributed over the entire address space. Similar models have been used by most studies of network design[6, 11, 13].

The choice of the interconnection network also depends upon the packaging technology available. In order to evaluate different network design alternatives, we need a model of packaging technology. A well explored packaging technology is VLSI, and it is possible to evaluate different networks layed out on a VLSI chip using Thompson's grid model [16]. The principal cost measure in this model is the layout area. It has been shown that for fixed layout area, most of the common networks such as hypercubes, multidimensional grids, butterflies etc. (with channel widths adjusted to equalize area requirements) have the same bandwidth for delivering messages with random destinations. Dally[7] argues that lower dimensional networks have better latencies.

The VLSI model is not adequate for large machines, since large parallel machines typically employ several levels of packaging, e.g. racks, boards and VLSI chips. To compare different network designs, we need a model that takes packaging hierarchies into account. Developing such a model is difficult because cost is a function of a large number of parameters, such as the number of wires at each level of the hierarchy, the size of the printed circuit boards, the number of boards, number of connectors etc. In addition to the costs associated with these parameters, there may also be technology specific constraints, e.g. standard printed circuit boards may be limited to a pin-count of 500, standard IC packages may have pin-counts of up to 250 etc. Further, advances in technology can significantly change the cost characteristics of each level of the hierarchy, or even the number of levels.

We would like to identify interconnection networks that are suitable for multilevel packaging technologies. Although the precise characteristics of existing or emerging packaging technologies are hard to model, a common characteristic of most technologies is a progressive increase in costs and decrease in capacities as we go up the packaging hierarchy. For instance, it is

*This work is supported by the Air Force Office of Scientific Research (AFSC/JSEP) under contract F49620-90-C-0029 and National Science Foundation Grant Number CCR-9005448. M. T. Raghunath is also supported by a fellowship from IBM Corp. This research was also supported in part by National Science Foundation under Infrastructure Grant Number CDA8722788.

© 1993 ACM 0-8186-4340-4/93/0011 $1.50

clear that as we proceed up the hierarchy, wires usually get longer with larger inter-wire spacings. Metal wires on VLSI chips may be a few millimeters long and spaced about 1 micron apart, whereas wires connecting different boards may be as long as 1 meter and spacing between wires on a cable connector may be as much as 1 mm. This results in a higher cost per wire at the higher levels of the hierarchy, and the higher cost translates into a reduction in number of wires available at the higher levels. Further the rate at which data can be transferred on a wire will usually decrease as we go up the hierarchy. In other words, packaging hierarchies exhibit the property of *packaging locality*, i.e. the connections within any unit of packaging are cheaper, denser, and faster than connections at higher levels. This in turn means that design of the interconnection network is more constrained by higher level restrictions than those at lower levels. This suggests that interconnection networks should be designed level-by-level, highest level first.

In this paper we consider a generic packaging technology with two levels, in which the processors in the parallel computer are organized into a number of *modules*. A larger number of levels might be more accurate (considered in [14]), but we feel that significant insights can be obtained with just two levels. We define a cost model for networks built using our two level technology, and then go on to define and compare a number of different interconnection networks. First we fix the high level (inter-module) network. As will be seen, this can be done analytically (section 3). Next, we consider possible lower level (intra-module) networks(section 4), and these, we compare using simulation. Our simulations assume a shared-memory model of interprocessor communication where accesses are directed to random locations (section 5), but we believe our observations also apply to other models requiring global communication.

Our results show that the networks used to connect modules must be substantially different from the ones considered customarily, e.g. multidimensional grids, hypercubes, butterflies, etc. We identify a new family of network topologies called n-hop networks which are important for the inter-module network. As it turns out, these topologies are also important in the case of three-level packaging hierarchies which we consider elsewhere [14]. As far as the overall network is considered, we find that a hybrid network (consisting of different networks at different levels, or having different channel widths at different levels) is likely to give better performance for fixed cost. Hybrid networks have so far received little attention in the literature.

Section 3.2 has a comparison of our work with other network design studies. Section 6 presents results of simulations for the case $N = 1024$ processors and $M = 32$ modules. Section 7 gives our conclusions. Detailed discussion of the simulation results is presented in appendix A.

2 A Two-Level Model of Packaging

In our model, a parallel computer consists of M *packaging modules*. Each module holds N/M processors (for a total of N), the corresponding fraction of total system memory, as well as some communication hardware. It is important to point out that we use the term *packaging module* in an abstract sense. What a *packaging module* physically corresponds to will depend on the scale of the machine; it could be a board, a rack or even a cabinet consisting of multiple racks. Further, a module itself will typically have a hierarchical structure, which we ignore for simplicity.

As mentioned earlier, it is difficult to model costs precisely, except in VLSI, where the layout area is a widely accepted metric. Informally, however, there is general agreement among hardware designers as to what the main costs are at higher packaging levels. In this paper we consider the cost to be a function of the following metrics, which most hardware designers would believe are among the most significant ones (in order of importance)[a]:

1. *Bisection Width:* This is the minimum number of wires that need to be cut in order to divide the network into two equal parts.

2. *Module Pin-count:* This is the number of wires leaving or entering each module.

3. *Number of Wire Bundles:* The wires connecting modules can be grouped into bundles, such that wires in each bundle connect the same pair of modules. The total number of bundles in a network is another indication of the difficulty of building the network: it is easier to assemble a network of a given bisection width if the wires are organized into a small number of fat bundles; as opposed to a large number of skinny ones.

The cost function may be strongly non-linear; at the extreme, there may even be hard constraints which cannot be overcome however much you are willing to pay, e.g. it may just be impossible, given a technology, to have a module pin-count of 2000. Further, it is hard to estimate precisely how the above metrics can be combined to yield a dollar cost for a particular design. We defer discussion of this to the next section.

In principle, these cost metrics could be used for the network at each level. In this paper we mainly focus on the cost of the inter-module network. For the intra-module network, we consider several candidates with widely varying costs. However, we feel that many of these candidates will be interesting since we expect the cost of the intra-module network to be dominated by the inter-module cost.

3 Inter-Module Network

The first observation is that for almost all networks the bisection width is a good first approximation for

---

[a]This is by no means an exhaustive list of possible cost measures. For instance, a network with long wires is harder to engineer electrically than a network with short wires. Many of the more modern parallel computers such as the CM-5 use asynchronous differential signaling with several bits being in transit on the same pair of wires at the same time. This overcomes some of the limitations imposed by long wires. Also see the paper by Scott and Goodman[15].

Inter-Module Topology	Module Pin-count	Bundles Per Module	Total Bundles
Complete graph	$\frac{4B}{M}\frac{M-1}{M}$	$M-1$	$M(M-1)/2$
2-hop Network	$\frac{8B}{M}\frac{\sqrt{M}-1}{\sqrt{M}}$	$2(\sqrt{M}-1)$	$M(\sqrt{M}-1)$
3-hop Network	$\frac{12B}{M}\frac{\sqrt[3]{M}-1}{\sqrt[3]{M}}$	$3(\sqrt[3]{M}-1)$	$\frac{3}{2}M(\sqrt[3]{M}-1)$
n-hop Network	$\frac{4nB}{M}\frac{\sqrt[n]{M}-1}{\sqrt[n]{M}}$	$n(\sqrt[n]{M}-1)$	$\frac{n}{2}M(\sqrt[n]{M}-1)$
Butterfly	$4B\log M/M$	4	$2M$
CCC	$6B\log M/M$	3	$3M/2$
Hypercube	$2B\log M/M$	$\log M$	$M\log M/2$
d-dim Toroid	$dB\sqrt[d]{M}/M$	$2d$	Md
3-dim Toroid	$3B/M^{2/3}$	6	$3M$
2-dim Toroid	$2B/\sqrt{M}$	4	$2M$
Ring	B	2	M

Table 1: Characteristics of topologies used to connect M packaging modules (Bisection width = B)

Inter-Module Topology	Module Pin-count	Bundles Per Module	Total Bundles
Complete graph	992	31	496
2-hop Network	1664	10	160
3-hop Network	2048	7	112
Butterfly	5120	4	64
CCC	7680	3	48
Hypercube	2560	5	80
3-dim Toroid	2560	6	96
2-dim Toroid	3072	4	64
Ring	8192	2	32

Table 2: Characteristics of different topologies used to interconnect 32 packaging modules ($B = 8192$)

the performance. So we could compare networks by holding their cost fixed and considering the bisection width attained for each network. Alternatively, we could hold the bisection width constant, and pick the network that has the least cost. Table 1 shows a comparison of standard and non-standard topologies (n-hop topologies, described in section 4.2) keeping the bisection width constant[b].

Unfortunately, we cannot pick a clear winner – the different topologies represent different tradeoffs between module pin-count and the number of bundles. Substituting absolute numbers for B and M can give us a better insight. Consider for example that we are designing a 1024 processor machine. A reasonable value of B for such a machine is 8192, corresponding to 8 bits of remote memory bandwidth per processor per cycle. We believe a reasonable value for M to be 32. Obviously, our conclusions will be different for dramatically different values of M. We discuss the issue of choosing M at more length in section 3.1. Table 2 gives the comparison. Note that for $M = 32$, networks such as toroids or the 2 or 3-hop networks will not have the same number of modules in each dimension because 32 is not a perfect square or a perfect cube. The numbers in the table for these networks correspond to the nearest power of 2 partitions.

As we go down the table we see that the pin-count increases while the number of bundles decreases. The relative weights of these two metrics would determine which of these networks has the lowest cost. However, we can prove the following (proof omitted here)[c]:

Claim 1 *The Complete graph has the lowest pin-*

count for a fixed bisection width.

Claim 2 *There is no other network with the same bisection width that has both lower pin-count and fewer bundles per module than the 2-hop network.*

We believe that at the higher levels of the packaging hierarchy the number of pins per module has a greater effect on cost than the total number of bundles. Therefore, we will consider the top rows of the table for further investigation. We first consider the complete graph since it achieves the minimum pin-count for a given bisection. However, as the table indicates, the complete graph also uses the maximum number of bundles. Some technologies may have constrains which prohibit such a large number of bundles. In such cases, we must use a topology that has fewer bundles, therefore, we also consider the 2-hop network.

3.1 Scalability

It is somewhat surprising that we chose the complete graph as a promising candidate; complete graphs are considered not to be scalable as an interprocessor network. The rationale for this belief, as we discussed earlier, is that they have very large number $O(M^2)$ of bundles. We note however, that we wish the network design to be scalable for large values of N rather than M. The number of modules is not directly related to the number of processors: as we build larger machines, we will have to build them using a taller hierarchy, involving larger modules at the top level. If we are building a network for a 100,000 processors, it is unlikely that the top level of the packaging hierarchy will consist of modules that contain 10 processors each. We feel that the number of modules M at any level will depend upon the technology, but not substantially on the number N of processors.

3.2 Comparison to Previous work

Most of the previous comparative studies of networks deal with *uniform networks*, i.e. a single network topology is used to connect together processors rather than customizing the topology to suit the different levels of the hierarchy. Further, almost none of the previous work has considered the possibility of

---

[b]All logarithms are to base 2.

[c]We do not know how to extend these tradeoffs to a family of networks. The closest result we have obtained is that family of n-digit deBruijn graphs are near-optimal, viz. there is no other network with the same bisection width that has lower pin-count and less than half the number of bundles of a deBruijn graph.

having communication channels of different widths at different levels of the hierarchy. As our results demonstrate, customizing network topologies and channel widths to packaging technology significantly improves performance.

Several of the existing and proposed parallel machines are based on hybrid networks that attempt to match the network to the packaging technology. For instance the CM-1 uses denser networks to connect the 16 bit-serial processors on a chip, while the entire machine can be considered a hypercube over these chips. The CEDAR system likewise organizes the machine into Omega network connected clusters, with each cluster consisting of several processors connected by a cross-bar network. Estimates of the communication performance of the CM family can be found in [5] and performance measurements of the CEDAR can be found in [2]. These measurements evaluate the performance of only single design point. In this paper we provide a comprehensive evaluation of a variety of design choices, albeit in an abstract setting.

The work closest to ours is that by Dandamudi [9]. He evaluated the performance of a number of hierarchical networks using the number of bundles as a cost measure. His motivation and approach are however very different from ours. His work is driven by the goal of trading off system performance to reduce the cost of the highest level connections ("Inter-Module" connections as per our terminology). For this he considers different interconnection networks for the highest level and evaluates their cost performance tradeoffs. On the other hand, as will become clear soon, the bulk of our study is concerned with how to design a lower level network ("intra-module" network) to efficiently exploit the maximum bandwidth provided by the inter-module interconnect.

Many researchers have examined the networks corresponding to the lower rows of table 1. Dally[7] has analyzed the class of multi-dimensional toroids using bisection width as the cost measure. Abraham and Padmanabhan [1] have analyzed the same class of networks (k-ary n-cubes) based on a constant pin-count restriction, and Agarwal [3] has analyzed the same class of networks under three different restrictions: constant bisection, constant channel width and constant pin-count. There are also a variety of studies analyzing the performance of networks like meshes, hypercubes[8], and multibutterflies[13] for random communication patterns. All of these studies primarily deal with *uniform networks*, where the topology is fixed before packaging is considered.

4 Intra-Module Networks
4.1 Inter-Module Topology: Complete graph

The only standard N processor network known to us that has a partitioning into M modules such that the interconnection between the modules is a complete graph is a Butterfly network. This occurs when M and N are powers of 2 and $M \leq \sqrt{N}$. Figure 1(a) shows a butterfly network connecting 16 processors to 16 memories and figure 1(b) shows how this network can be

partitioned into 4 modules, such that each module has 4 processors and 4 memories. Also note that the nodes in columns 2 and 3 have been reordered to make the connections between these columns local to the module. The numbers on the processors and memories are shown primarily to illustrate the reordering and do not carry any special significance.

Since we need to route access requests from the processors to the memories and the corresponding replies back from the memories to the processors, we need two separate butterfly networks. Therefore, each link in the figure should be interpreted as a pair of directed links. Note that the bundle of wires going between any two modules, A and B, actually consists of 4 different channels two in each direction. One channel carries access requests from the processors in module A to memories in module B, another carries requests from B to A. Similarly two channels carry responses from A to B and B to A respectively.

Although we started with a *dance-hall* type network, it is useful to associate each memory with a processor from a practical point of view. In this case, the implementation is simplified because each processor could use a single memory that is partitioned into private memory and shared memory. While the private memory would be accessed directly by the processor, the shared memory would be accessible to all the processors via the network. We represent this in figure 1(c) by drawing the processors and their associated memories adjacent to each other.

4.1.1 Basic butterfly network

The first network we consider is a butterfly connecting 1024 processors to 1024 memories; partitioned into 32 modules in the manner of figure 1(b).

A bisection width of $B = 8192$ implies that pin-count per module is 992 and that each bundle has 32 wires. Since each bundle has 4 channels, each channel will be 8 bits wide. Since the inter-module channels are 8 bits wide, we get a uniform network if we make the intra-module channels also 8 bits wide. We will call this network *Butterfly.8.8*. The first suffix stands for the intra-module channel width and the second suffix for the inter-module channel width.

4.1.2 Widening channels

The previous network used a uniform topology that did not take advantage of the differences in packaging hierarchy. In general, at the lower levels of the packaging hierarchy we can have more wires and also transfer bits across these wires at greater speeds. Both these characteristics permit us to increase the capacity of the networks at the lower levels of the hierarchy. Instead of separately modeling increased wire density and clock rates, we consider networks that keep the clock rate constant and just use higher wire densities. Accordingly, we consider networks with wider intra-module channels: *Butterfly.16.8* and *Butterfly.32.8*. Both networks have the same topology as *Butterfly.8.8*, but they have 16 and 32 bit wide intra-module channels respectively.

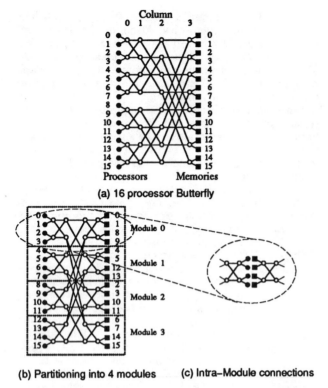

Column
0 1 2 3

Processors   Memories

(a) 16 processor Butterfly

Module 0
Module 1
Module 2
Module 3

(b) Partitioning into 4 modules   **(c) Intra–Module connections**

Figure 1: Butterfly Network and its partition

4.1.3 Dilation

Another method for utilizing more local wires is dilation. We consider the networks *Butterfly.8-2dil.8*, *Butterfly.8-4dil.8*, and *Butterfly.16-2dil.8*. The first network has 2 8-bit wide channels between nodes, the second has 4 8-bit wide channels and the third has 2 16-bit wide channels. If many messages need to go out in the same direction, they can be simultaneously sent along the dilated channels. The first network requires the same number of wires per routing node as *Butterfly.16.8* while the other two use the same as *Butterfly.32.8*.

In the case of network dilation, we do not dilate the channels connecting into the memories or the processors. If we dilate the channels connecting to the memories, we may have to use multi-ported memories or add some complicated circuitry to prevent multiple accesses from being made simultaneously.

4.1.4 Cross-bar

To establish an upper bound on the best performance achievable, we also consider the networks *Xbar.8.8*, and *Xbar.32.8*. Both networks connect the processors and memories to the inter-module channels using 32 by 32 cross-bars. In the first case both the input and output channels of the cross-bar are 8 bits wide. In the latter case the channels that connect to the processors and memories are 32 bits wide. The inter-module channels remain 8 bits wide as before.

4.2 Inter-Module Topology: 2-Hop Network

A 2-hop network is a product graph of two complete graphs[d]. The nodes in the graph can be thought of labeled using a pair of numbers (i, j) where each number ranges from $0..\sqrt{M}$. There are complete graphs between all nodes of the form $(*, j)\forall j$, and also between all nodes of the form $(i, *)\forall i$. We call this a 2-hop network because every pair of nodes is guaranteed to be connected by a shortest path of length at most 2. In general a n-hop network is a product of n complete graphs, each of size $\sqrt[n]{M}$. A complete graph interconnect is a 1-hop network in this sense. When the number of hops is $\log M$, the resulting topology is a hypercube.

Interestingly, it turns out that the starting point for generating a 2-hop inter-module network is also a butterfly. In fact, any butterfly network of size $N = 2^{(n+1)x}$ can be partitioned into 2^{nx} modules so that the interconnection between the modules is a n-hop network. A $2^{(n+1)x}$ butterfly will have $(n + 1)x$ columns. We separate these columns into $(n + 1)$ groups of x columns each and shuffle the rows such that the connections within each group form butterflies of size 2^x. Next we partition the network into 2^{nx} modules such that each module has 2^x rows and $(n+1)x$ columns. The edges that connect between the modules will form a n-hop network. Note that this construction only applies when the number of processors is of the form $2^{(n+1)x}$, and the number of modules is 2^{nx}. This construction can be easily extended to the case where the number of processors is not of the form $2^{(n+1)x}$, by building a network of size $2^{(n+1)x}$, partitioning it into 2^{nx} modules and connecting multiple processors to each network input.

We can also build a n-hop network when the number of modules M is not of the form 2^{nx}, but the numbers in table 1 will not apply directly. The table assumes that the n-hop network topology is a n-fold product of complete graphs of size $\sqrt[n]{M}$. If the nth root of M is not an integer, the sizes of the complete graphs that form the product will not be equal. The number of bundles and the pin-count will differ slightly from that shown in the table.

In our present case, we need to build a 2-hop network on 32 Modules. Since 32 is not a perfect square, we use the topology $K_4 * K_8$, where K_x denotes a complete graph on x nodes and $*$ denotes graph product. Figure 2 shows this graph. For the sake of simplicity, the figure only shows one of the 4 K_8s. The actual topology, will have 3 more K_8s, one each node of the K_4s.

As in the one-hop case, each edge in the figure will correspond to 2 pairs of channels, one in each direction. Of each pair of links, one will carry processor to memory traffic, and the other memory to processor

---
[d]Let $G_1 = (V_1, E_1)$ and $G_2 = (V_2, E_2)$ be two graphs. The product of G_1 and G_2, denoted by $G_1 * G_2 = (V, E)$ where $V = V_1 \times V_2$ and $E = \{((u_1, u_2), (v_1, v_2)) | ((u_1 = v_1) \land (u_2, v_2) \in E_2) \lor ((u_2 = v_2) \land (u_1, v_1) \in E_1)\}$.

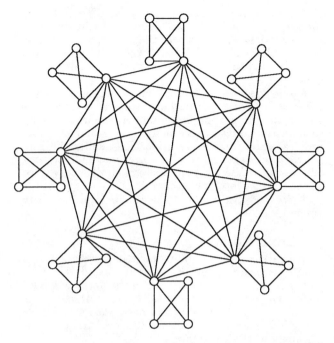

Figure 2: Inter-Module 2-hop Network (Only one of the 4 complete graphs on 8 nodes is shown)

traffic. In order to achieve a bisection width of 8192, the edges of the K_4 will have to be 256 bits wide (4 64-bit wide channels), and the edges of the K_8 will be 128 bits wide (4 32-bit wide channels).

4.2.1 Basic 2-hop network

The intra-module network of the basic 2-hop network is shown in figure 3. The processors are connected to the nodes on the left. Since there are 32 processors per module and only 8 inputs, we have to connect 4 processors to each input. This is done by building a 2 level tree as shown on the top node. The memories are also connected in a similar fashion. Processors and memories are paired as in the earlier network topologies, but this is not illustrated pictorially.

The channels between the column 2 and 3 correspond to K_4. They connect between modules that differ in their least significant 2 bits. The channels between column 5 and 6 correspond to K_8 and connect between modules that differ in their most significant 3 bits. All channels are 32 bits wide except those between columns 2 and 3, which are 64 bits wide.

As per our naming convention we call this network *2hop.32.64-32* since the intra-module channels are 32 bits wide and there are two kinds of inter-module channels, which are 64 and 32 bits wide.

4.2.2 Widening channels and dilation

Similar to the networks defined for the complete graph inter-module topology, we define the network *2hop.64.64-32*. This network is the same as the previous network except that all the intra-module channels

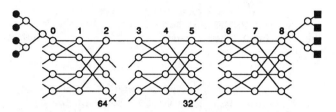

Figure 3: Intra-Module Network: Basic 2 hop network

are 64 bits wide, including those that connect to the processors and memories.

We also define the network *2hop.32-2dil.64-32* with a degree 2 dilation of the intra-module network.

4.3 Routing Algorithms

Our routing algorithms use cut-through routing [10], with adequate buffer space in each routing node. Buffer space is allocated on a per-message basis. We assume that all the wires in the network can transfer one bit per clock cycle and that each routing node imposes a single cycle pipeline delay on any message that does not suffer link or queue space contention. When a routing node's outgoing channels are wider than its incoming channels, the node cannot send messages in a pipelined fashion. We assume that these nodes wait for the entire message to come in before sending out any flits. For brevity, we omit a detailed description of the routing nodes.

For the cross-bar networks discussed earlier, we treat the entire cross-bar as a single routing node that imposes a single cycle pipeline delay. This assumption is overly optimistic, but it is justified since we study the cross-bar networks only to establish an upper bound on performance.

5 Traffic Model

We base our evaluation of network performance on a shared-memory model. The memory accesses made by a processor are assumed to be distributed randomly over the entire shared address space. Each access is sent over the network to the memory where the data resides, the access is performed and then returned to the processor. For simplicity, we assume that both the access requests and the responses are 128 bits long, inclusive of the data, memory/network addressing information, and control information. We consider two models:

Open-network model[12]: In each cycle of execution, each processor generates a message with a fixed probability of λ, independent of other processors and previous cycles of execution. The interval between accesses is geometrically distributed with mean $1/\lambda$.

Multithreading work-load model: The preceding model is unrealistic in that it allows each processor to have an unbounded number of outstanding requests. Instead, in the multithreading work-load model, each processor runs a fixed number of threads, each of which can have at most one outstanding request at any time. When a thread issues an access the processor switches to the next thread in round-robin order. The processor stalls when a thread is scheduled but its previous access has not completed. We assume a single cycle thread-switch time, in the manner of [4].

We consider two inter-access interval distributions for the multithreading work-load: geometric and periodic. In the geometric model the inter-access times are geometrically distributed similar to the open-network model. In the periodic model, the inter-access interval is a constant. If the processor is executing a tight inner loop, the interval between remote accesses is likely to be a constant and the periodic model attempts to capture this effect. In reality the distribution of accesses is likely to be somewhere in between. Note that in both the periodic and geometric models, the accesses are directed to random addresses and therefore will follow random paths in the network.

6 Simulation Results

6.1 Open-network

Figure 4 shows the results for the butterfly networks. The latencies are round-trip latencies, i.e., the time taken for the access request to go from the processor to the memory, make the access and return to the processor. The x-axis is the normalized load expressed as a percentage of the peak load. The curves extend along the x-axis until the point at which the corresponding generation rate no longer yielded a stable latency.

Figure 5 shows the results for the cross-bar networks. The graphs corresponding to *Butterfly.8.8*, *Butterfly.8-2dil.8* and *Butterfly.32.8* are included for comparison.

Figure 6 shows the results for the networks with a 2-hop network between modules. The graphs corresponding to *Butterfly.8.8*, and *Butterfly.32.8* are included to establish the relative performances.

Detailed discussion of the graphs can be found in appendix A

6.2 Multithreading work-load

The performance metric under this work-load model is the average processor utilization, as a function of number of threads and of the rate at which threads make memory accesses. Based on the bisection width of the networks we can see that the peak bandwidth that each network can support is 8 bits per processor per cycle. This corresponds to a mean access rate of one every 16 cycles, since each access is 128 bits long. We considered mean access intervals of both 16 and 32 cycles.

A mean access interval of 16 cycles can potentially saturate the bisection and corresponds to running the network at 100% load. Since message insertion is linked with the delivery of responses, trying to run the network at 100% load does not pose a problem. The processors themselves merely slow down until the injection rate matches the response rate. As the number of threads per processor increases, the processors become increasingly latency tolerant and are able to get more out of the network.

A mean access interval of 32 cycles corresponds to running the network at 50% load. In this case, since the network is lightly loaded, the processors should be able to achieve almost 100% utilization if they can successfully hide the network latency using multithreading.

Figure 7 shows the processor utilizations for the different networks when the mean access interval is 16 cycles. The graphs shows four lines corresponding to multithreading factors of 1, 2, 4, 8 and 16. Figure 7(a) shows processor utilizations under the geometric model and figure 7(b) corresponds to the periodic access model. Figure 8 shows similar curves for a mean access interval is 32 cycles.

A detailed discussion of the results is presented in appendix A.

7 Conclusions

We have considered interconnection network design from a packaging point of view and have developed a cost model for the highest level of the packaging hierarchy. We adopt a hierarchical network design strategy in which we design different networks for each level of the hierarchy starting at the top level and proceeding down to the lower levels.

We have identified a family of networks which are promising candidates for interconnecting the top levels of the hierarchy since they exhibit a reasonable trade-off between pin-count and number of bundles. We call this family n-hop networks. A n-hop network topology is a n-fold product of complete graphs.

Our hierarchical design strategy yields hybrid network architectures which exploit packaging locality better than network architectures which start with a uniform topology that is later partitioned into a packaging hierarchy. Our results show that we can get significant improvements in performance by exploiting packaging locality. We observed that increasing the connections local to a module by using either dilation or wider channels improved performance. It was better to increase the channel widths rather than use dilation, especially if our processors were capable of a high level of multithreading. With 8 threads per processor (geometric distribution of access intervals), we observed that increasing the intra-module channel width from 8 to 32 improved the processor utilization of the butterfly network from around 55% to almost 80%. Also the performance of the network with 32 bit wide intra-module channels came very close to that of the best possible cross-bar network.

All our results indicate that the performance improvement achieved by multithreading the processors is quite significant. Processor utilizations increased by about a factor of 2 with 4 threads and almost 3 with 8 threads when compared to the utilization with a single thread. Designing processors capable of running multiple threads and rapidly switching between threads is therefore useful for large scale parallel computers.

References

[1] S. Abraham and K. Padmanabhan. Constraint based evaluation of multicomputer networks. In

Proceedings of the International Conference on Parallel Processing, 1990.

[2] S. G. Abraham and E. S. Davidson. A Communication Model for Optimizing Hierarchical Multiprocessor systems. In *Proceedings of the International Conference on Parallel Processing*, pages 467–474, 1986.

[3] Anant Agarwal. Limits on Interconnection Network Performance. *IEEE Transactions on Parallel and Distributed Systems*, 2(4) u 412, October 1991.

[4] R. Alverson et al. The TERA Computer System. In *1990 International Conference on Supercomputing*, pages 1–6, 1990.

[5] *Connection Machine Model CM-2 Technical Summary*, 1987. Technical Report No: TR HA87-4.

[6] W. J. Dally. Wire-Efficient VLSI Multiprocessor Communication Networks. In *Advanced Research in VLSI*, pages 391–415, 1987.

[7] William Dally. *A VLSI Architecture for concurrent data structures*. PhD thesis, California Institute of Technology, 1986. Tech Report: 5209:TR:86.

[8] William J. Dally. Performance analysis of k-ary n-cube interconnection networks. *IEEE Transactions on Computers*, 39(6):775–785, June 1990.

[9] Sivarama Dandamudi. *Hierarchical Interconnection Networks for Multicomputer Systems*. PhD thesis, University of Saskatchewan, Canada, 1988. Department of Computational Science 88-18.

[10] P. Kermani and L. Kleinrock. Virtual Cut-Through: A New Computer Communication Switching Technique. *Computer Networks*, 3:267–286, 1979.

[11] C. P. Kruskal and M. Snir. The performance of multistage interconnection networks for multiprocessors. *IEEE Transactions on Computers*, C-32(12):1091–1098, December 1983.

[12] Gyungho Lee. A performance bound of multistage combining networks. *IEEE Transactions on Computers*, C-38(10):1387–1395, October 1989.

[13] Tom Leighton, Derek Lisinski, and Bruce Maggs. Empirical evaluation of randomly-wired multistage networks. In *International Conference on Computer Design*, 1990.

[14] M. T. Raghunath. *Interconnection Network Design Based on Packaging Considerations*. PhD thesis, University of California, Berkeley, 1993. In preparation.

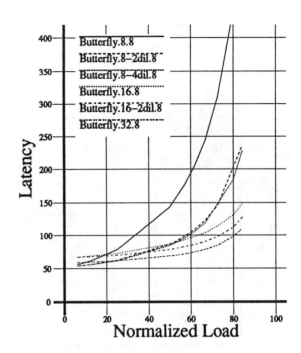

Figure 4: Open-Network Model; Butterfly Networks

[15] Steven L. Scott and James R. Goodman. The Impact of Pipelined Channels on k-ary n-cube Networks. To appear in IEEE Transactions on Parallel and Distributed Systems.

[16] C. D. Thompson. *A Complexity Theory for VLSI*. PhD thesis, Carnegie-Mellon University, 1980.

A   Discussion of results

We see that in all the open-network graphs, as the applied load increase, the latency initially increases gradually and as the network nears saturation, the latency increases rapidly.

The graphs for both geometric and periodic access patterns are similar to each other, except that the utilizations for the periodic model are higher. This is to be expected because of the absence of variance in the inter-access times.

Dilation versus wider channels

The data corresponding to *Butterfly.8.8*, *Butterfly.8-2dil.8* and *Butterfly.8-4dil.8* in figures 4 and 7 indicate that dilation of channels helps in improving performance. This improvement results from the reduced contention for the intra-module channels. Increasing the dilation from 2 to 4 does not seem to have much of an effect, indicating that a dilation factor of 2 is sufficient to eliminate most of the intra-module contention.

As opposed to dilation, widening the channels within a module affects the network performance in three different ways. First, it reduces the contention for intra-module channels. Secondly, it increases the

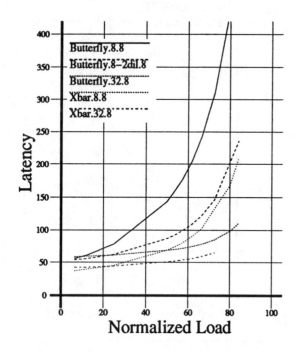

Figure 5: Open-Network Model; Cross-bar networks

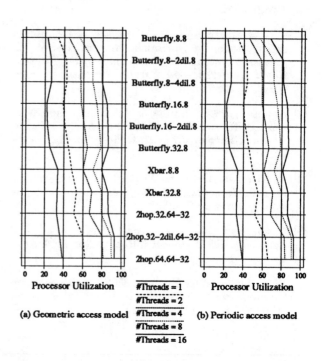

(a) Geometric access model
(b) Periodic access model

#Threads = 1
#Threads = 2
#Threads = 4
#Threads = 8
#Threads = 16

Figure 7: Processor utilization, mean access interval = 16 cycles

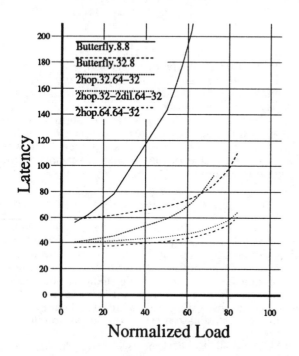

Figure 6: Open-Network Model; 2-hop networks

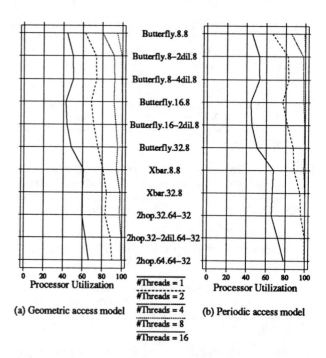

(a) Geometric access model
(b) Periodic access model

#Threads = 1
#Threads = 2
#Threads = 4
#Threads = 8
#Threads = 16

Figure 8: Processor utilization, mean access interval = 32 cycles

effective memory service rate. Thirdly it increases message latency because of the non-uniformity in channel widths[e]. It is clear that the first effect has a positive influence on network performance. The second effect also helps improve performance because conflicts between accesses at the memories have less of an effect. The third effect hurts network performance because it increases the latency.

When the load is small (in the open-network case) or there are few threads (multithreading), the performance of the networks with wider channels is slightly worse than *Butterfly.8.8*. This is because of the third effect mentioned above. But, when the load on the network is increased, the effects of reduced contention and the higher memory service rate become more predominant. In the long run we can expect all memories to receive approximately the same number of requests because the access distribution is random, but in the short run the access distribution can be uneven. A higher memory service rate helps to reduce the effect of this non-uniformity.

Cross-bar

The intra-module cross-bar network completely eliminates the possible contention for links within a module. It also has a lower minimum latency because we assume that it imposes only a single cycle pipeline delay as opposed to one cycle per stage in a multi-stage network.

In figure 5 we see that the graph for *Xbar.8.8* is approximately parallel to that of *Butterfly.8-2dil.8* indicating that both networks have similar performance with respect to contention. The graph for the cross-bar network is lower because of its lower minimum latency. This difference does not show up under the multithreading workload (figure 7) indicating that the effect of this difference in latency is small. The comparison between *Xbar.32.8* and *Butterfly.32.8* is similar. This indicates that providing extra local bandwidth either through dilation or wider channels is successful in eliminating almost all the contention for the intra-module channels.

2-hop Networks

The results for the 2-hop networks indicate similar relative behavior as the *Butterfly.*.** networks; dilation improves the performance over the base network, and widening channels is even better. However, the difference between dilation and wider channels is not as pronounced since the network initially has 32-bit wide memory channels. Increasing the channel width from 32 to 64 leads to a smaller marginal increase in performance.

Since the 2-hop and complete graph networks use different pin-counts and number of bundles, it is not really fair to compare them. However, since both

networks are based on the butterfly topology, the results indicate that, for a given bandwidth, it is better to build a smaller butterfly with wider channels and load each input of the butterfly with more processors. When there are fewer channels that are wider, it is easier to balance the load on them and achieve better utilization.

On the other hand, if we compare the two networks based solely on pin-count rather than bisection width, we should consider a complete graph network with double the pin-count, since a 2-hop network uses approximately twice the number of pins(table 1). In this case, the complete graph networks would have twice the bisection bandwidth. Therefore, it is reasonable to compare the performance of the 2-hop networks at 100% load with that of the complete graph networks at 50% load. Under this comparison, we can clearly see that the complete graph networks out-perform the 2-hop networks because the complete graph is optimal when pin-count is the only limitation.

Multithreading

It can be seen that all networks achieve significant improvement in processor utilization as the number of threads is increased. This demonstrates that multithreading is successful in masking the access latencies. Increasing the number of threads per processor corresponds to operating the network farther down the x-axis on the load-latency graphs of the open-network model. Though this increases the latency experienced by the messages, the processor is able to better overlap the latency with useful computation. It is important to note that even when the number of threads is small(2-4), there is a significant improvement in processor utilization in relation to the utilization corresponding to a single thread. As we increase the number of threads further, the processor utilizations improve, but the marginal increase per added thread diminishes because increasing the number of threads also increases the loading of the network which increases latency.

Performance at low network loads

The graphs corresponding to an inter access time of 32 cycles (figure 8) show that at high levels of multithreading, it is possible to get processor utilizations of almost 100%. Since the load never gets so high as to make the latencies increase dramatically, multithreading can completely hide the network latency. For the networks we evaluated we can see that about 4 threads can achieve this. Naturally, as we scale the machine to more processors we expect that we will need more threads, but we expect that the number of threads will only grow as $\log N$ since the network latencies will grow as $\log N$.

We also see that at low levels of multithreading, the effects due to non-uniform channel widths are more pronounced. Since the network load is small, the increase in latency due to non-uniform channel widths dominates the effects due to reduced contention and increased memory service rates.

---

[e]When a message transits through a node whose output channel is wider than its input channel, the message suffers a larger delay because it must be entirely buffered before it can be forwarded.

Optimal Fully Adaptive Wormhole Routing for Meshes

Loren Schwiebert and D. N. Jayasimha
Department of Computer and Information Science
The Ohio State University
Columbus, Ohio 43210–1277
Email: {loren, jayasim}@cis.ohio-state.edu

Abstract

A deadlock-free fully adaptive routing algorithm for 2D meshes which is optimal in the number of virtual channels required and in the number of restrictions placed on the use of these virtual channels is presented. The routing algorithm imposes less than half as many routing restrictions as any previous fully adaptive routing algorithm. It is also proved that, ignoring symmetry, this routing algorithm is the only fully adaptive routing algorithm that achieves both of these goals. The implementation of the routing algorithm requires relatively simple router control logic. The new algorithm is extended, in a straightforward manner, to arbitrary dimension meshes. It needs only $4n - 2$ virtual channels, the minimum number for an n-dimensional mesh. All previous algorithms require an exponential number of virtual channels in the dimension of the mesh.

Keywords: wormhole routing, mesh architectures, routing algorithms, deadlock freedom, optimality.

1 Introduction

Wormhole routing [6] has become the switching technique of choice in modern distributed-memory multiprocessors such as the Intel Paragon, the Symult 2010, the MIT J-machine, the Caltech MOSAIC and the nCUBE-2. Implementations of wormhole routing typically divide each message into packets, which are then divided into flits. The header flits of a packet contain the routing information and the data flits of the packet follow the header flits through the network in a pipelined fashion. All channels in the path are reserved from the time the header flits acquire the channel until the last data flit in the packet has traversed the channel. The pipelining of the flits makes the message latency largely insensitive to the distance between the source and destination, so there is lower message latency when there is little or no channel contention. Each channel has enough storage to buffer only a few flits, so wormhole routing requires significantly less hardware for buffering than packet

switching does. These two factors make wormhole routing an attractive switching technique for distributed-memory multiprocessors.

The most significant problems with wormhole routing are message latency and contention that can occur with even moderate network traffic. Since *all* the channel queues in the path from the source to the destination are held from the time they are acquired until the entire message has been transmitted (which is after the entire path has been established except for very short messages which fit in the intermediate channel buffers), performance degradation due to contention can be severe and message latency can be unacceptably high. A message that requires several channels can block many messages while being transmitted. These blocked messages can in turn block other messages, which further increases the message latency. The problems of latency and contention could be partially overcome by providing additional *physical* channels between nodes in the network. This is an expensive solution, however. A more cost-effective method is to allow multiple *virtual* channels to share the same physical channel [4]. Each virtual channel has a separate buffer, with multiple messages multiplexed over the same physical channel. Both latency and contention can be further reduced by utilizing the multiple paths between the source and destination. However, because channels are held until the message has been transmitted, a routing algorithm with no restrictions on the use of virtual or physical channels can result in deadlock [6].

The simplest routing algorithms are *deterministic (oblivious)* and define a single path between the source and destination. A message must wait for each busy channel in the path to become available. On the other hand, adaptive routing algorithms support multiple paths between the source and destination. Adaptive routing algorithms are either minimal or non-minimal. Minimal routing algorithms allow only shortest paths to be chosen, while non-minimal routing algorithms also allow longer paths. Adaptive routing algorithms, whether minimal or non-minimal, can be further differentiated by the number of shortest paths allowed. Adaptive routing algorithms that do not allow *all*

Table 1: **Overview of Adaptive Routing Algorithms for Meshes**

Author(s)	Fully Adaptive?	VCs for 2D Mesh	Comments
Chien & Kim [2]	Yes	6	Partially Adaptive for Higher Dimensions
Dally [3]	Yes	6	2D Mesh Only
Dally & Aoki [5]	Yes	n	2D Mesh with $n \times n$ nodes
Glass & Ni [8]	Yes	6	2D Mesh Only
Glass & Ni [9]	No	4	Roughly Half the Adaptiveness of Fully Adaptive
Jesshope, Miller & Yantchev [10]	Yes	8	Number of Virtual Channels is Exponential in Dimension of Mesh
Linder & Harden [11]	Yes	6	

messages to use *any* shortest path are called *partially adaptive*. Adaptive routing algorithms that *do* allow all messages to use any shortest path are called *fully adaptive*. While all fully adaptive routing algorithms allow a message to use any *physical* channel that is part of a shortest path, different restrictions are placed on the choice of *virtual* channels on that physical channel, so not all fully adaptive routing algorithms are equivalent. Some fully adaptive routing algorithms allow more adaptiveness than others by placing fewer restrictions on the choice of *virtual* channels.

Separate buffers are needed for each virtual channel. Furthermore, routing algorithms that require more virtual channels need additional router control logic and are usually more complex. The multiplexing and scheduling of the virtual channels on the physical channel is also more complicated. In addition, router latency and cycle time increase with the number of virtual channels [1], so fewer virtual channels is better. Decreasing the number of virtual channels needed for a given adaptiveness is accomplished by using a less restrictive routing algorithm. Conversely, a less restrictive routing algorithm has better performance relative to other routing algorithms when the same number of virtual channels is used.

2 Previous Work

Adaptive routing algorithms have been developed for mesh, torus and hypercube topologies. Torus and hypercube topologies can be characterized as k-ary n-cubes, where k is the radix and n is the dimension. For example, an 8D hypercube is a 2-ary 8-cube and a 16×16 torus is a 16-ary 2-cube. An n-dimensional mesh is similar to a torus, except a mesh does not have any wrap-around channels. Routing algorithms for only mesh topologies are reviewed here, because wormhole routing has been used

primarily on low-dimension meshes and the focus of this paper is on mesh topologies.

Many adaptive routing algorithms for meshes have been proposed [2, 3, 5, 8, 9, 10, 11]. Table 1 summarizes the main features of each algorithm. In the Table, VCs is used for number of bidirectional virtual channels per router.

Designing deadlock-free routing algorithms for wormhole routing was simplified by a proof that an acyclic channel dependency graph guarantees deadlock freedom [6]. Each node in the channel dependency graph is a virtual channel. A directed edge from one virtual channel to another means that a message could use the second virtual channel immediately after the first. Since the graph is acyclic, deadlock freedom can be proved by assigning a numbering to the edges of the graph, ensuring that virtual channels are used in always increasing or always decreasing order. A channel dependency graph is connected if there is a path from any source to any destination.

The proof in [6] is a necessary and sufficient condition for deterministic routing algorithms which can be characterized as functions of the form $R : C \times N \rightarrow C$, where the incoming channel, belonging to the set of channels C, and the destination, belonging to the set of nodes N, define an outgoing channel on which to route the message. Acyclicity of the channel dependency graph has also been used as a basis for developing adaptive routing algorithms defined by relations of the form $R : C \times N \rightarrow C^P$, where a set of channels, rather than a single channel, is defined on which the message can be routed. Requiring an acyclic channel dependency graph is overly restrictive for routing algorithms defined by relations of the form $R : N \times N \rightarrow C^P$, where the current node, rather than the incoming channel, and the destination define the set of channels on which the message can be routed [7]. Cycles may exist in the channel dependency graph if some subset of channels defines a connected subgraph with an acyclic *extended* channel dependency graph. An extended channel dependency graph is a dependency graph which arises from direct and indirect dependencies. Each edge in the channel dependency subgraph defines a *direct* dependency. An *indirect* dependency is a dependency between two channels in the connected subgraph that exists only because of the intermediate use of channels not in the subgraph.

A method of analyzing routing algorithms based on the permitted and prohibited turns from one virtual channel to another is presented in [9]. The dependencies between virtual channels are characterized as turns. The set of possible turns are defined by the topology and are given here for meshes. The turns can be 90° turns (i.e., a traversal from a virtual channel in one direction to a virtual channel in any orthogonal direction), 0° turns (i.e., a traversal from one virtual channel to another virtual channel in the same direction) and 180° turns (i.e., a traversal from one virtual channel to a virtual channel in the opposite direction). Clearly, 180° turns are not used for minimal routing. The *turn model* groups the turns into cycles and breaks all cycles by prohibiting some turns. This is equivalent to removing edges from the channel dependency graph. It is then necessary to show that cycles cannot be created from the remaining turns. This is done by providing a numbering of the edges in the channel dependency graph.

For the 2D mesh, the algorithms proposed in [2, 3, 11] all produce an equivalent fully adaptive minimal algorithm called double-y. This routing algorithm requires two virtual channels in each Y direction and one virtual channel in each X direction. This set of virtual channels has a total of sixteen 90° turns and four 0° turns. Double-y allows eight of the sixteen 90° turns and prohibits all 0° turns.

Double-y was improved upon in [8] by use of the turn model. It was shown that double-y, while being fully adaptive, still places unneeded restrictions on the routing. The Maximally Fully Adaptive (mad-y) routing algorithm, which makes better use of the virtual channels and hence improves adaptiveness, was proposed. In addition, it was shown that a fully adaptive routing algorithm with fewer virtual channels could not be produced, based on the assumption that a cycle is a necessary and sufficient condition for deadlock with adaptive routing algorithms. Thus it was argued that mad-y is the best possible fully adaptive wormhole routing algorithm for 2D meshes. Any reduction in virtual channels or routing restrictions results in an algorithm that is either not fully adaptive or not deadlock-free. In the next section it is shown that the proposed algorithm is more adaptive than mad-y.

The following conventions are used throughout the paper. Channels are assumed to be bidirectional. All channels, whether physical or virtual, are referred to as virtual channels. N, S, E and W are used to indicate the appropriate direction, with N–W used to indicate a turn from North to West, for example. The symbol VC_{nd} denotes virtual channel n in the d direction. For example, VC_{1N} is virtual channel one in the North direction. The channel number is omitted when there is a single virtual channel in that direction. When the term routing algorithm is used in the rest of the paper, it refers to a fully adaptive deadlock-free wormhole routing algorithm for meshes.

3 Optimal Minimal Routing

The requirement that the channel dependency graph be acyclic forces unnecessary restrictions on the routing algorithm. Since mad-y has this requirement, it is not the least restrictive routing algorithm for 2D meshes. A new routing algorithm, the Optimal Fully Adaptive routing algorithm, which has substantially fewer restrictions, is proposed. This new algorithm is first presented for the 2D mesh and then generalized to n-dimensional meshes.

A block diagram of the router with the extra virtual channels placed in the North and South directions is shown in Figure 1(a). The virtual channels in the North and South directions are differentiated by marking VC_{1N} and VC_{1S} with a single dash and VC_{2N} and VC_{2S} with a double dash. This configuration has a total of sixteen 90° turns and four 0° turns. *Unrestricted* turns are indicated by solid lines, *restricted* turns by dashed lines and *prohibited* turns by dotted lines. The term *permitted* turns is used to describe the combination of restricted and unrestricted turns. The constraints imposed by the Optimal Fully Adaptive routing algorithm, referred to as opt-y, can be summarized succinctly: a message that needs to route further in the West direction cannot use VC_{1N} or VC_{1S}. Opt-y has the following two sets of constraints (See Figures 1(b) and 1(c)):

- Two 90° turns, N–W using VC_{1N} and S–W using VC_{1S}, are prohibited.

- The 0° turns from VC_{2N} to VC_{1N} and VC_{2S} to VC_{1S} are allowed only when the message does not need to route further West.

The following restrictions arise solely from the previous constraints:

- The 90° turns W–N using VC_{1N} and W–S using VC_{1S} are allowed only when the message does not need to route further West. These turns are restricted only because the N–W turn from VC_{1N} and S–W turn from VC_{1S} are prohibited.

- The 0° turns from VC_{1N} to VC_{2N} and VC_{1S} to VC_{2S} are possible only when the message does not need to route further West, because VC_{1N} and VC_{1S} are not used until the message has completed routing West.

- VC_{1N} and VC_{1S} cannot be used by the router at the source if the message needs to route West.

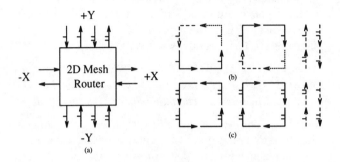

Figure 1: **Optimal Fully Adaptive Routing**

Several important properties are proved for opt-y:

- Opt-y is fully adaptive.

- Opt-y is deadlock-free.

- Opt-y requires only the minimum number of virtual channels.

- Opt-y places the fewest possible restrictions on the use of these virtual channels.

- Opt-y is the only algorithm to satisfy all four of the previous properties (except for algorithms symmetric to opt-y).

Theorem 1 *Opt-y is fully adaptive.*

Proof. Recall that with minimal routing, each routing step takes the message closer to the destination. If the source and destination vary in only one dimension, there is a single minimal path. Opt-y can use this path – the single virtual channel in the East and West directions or either virtual channel in the North and South directions. For a destination that is Northeast (Southeast) of the source, the message can route adaptively along the North (South) and East virtual channels. For a destination that is Northwest (Southwest) of the source, the message can route adaptively along VC_{2N} (VC_{2S}) and the West virtual channel. Once the message has routed completely West, it can use either of the North (South) virtual channels and switch between them. $\square$

A message can use VC_{1N} or VC_{1S} only when the destination is not West of the current node. Otherwise, it must choose one of the other virtual channels. This restriction depends on the current node, not the incoming channel, so opt-y has the form $R : N \times N \rightarrow C^p$. The result proved in [7] can now be used to show that opt-y is deadlock-free.

Using the terminology in [7], the routing algorithm is denoted R and the set of channels used by R is denoted C. There is some subset of channels, $C_1 \subseteq C$, that defines a routing algorithm $R_1 \subseteq R$, i.e., R_1 is the routing algorithm R restricted to using C_1. Since there are cycles in the channel dependency graph, it is not possible to provide a numbering of the channels that guarantees the channels are used in always increasing or always decreasing order. It is shown in [7] that any routing algorithm of the form $R : N \times N \rightarrow C^p$ is deadlock-free if it satisfies the following three conditions:

- The channel dependency graph defined by C_1 for R_1 is connected.

- The routing algorithm R_1 allows no cycles and is therefore deadlock-free.

- The additional channels $(C - C_1)$ of routing algorithm R do not introduce cycles in the extended channel dependency graph of C_1.

The idea behind the proof is that cycles are permitted if messages also have the possibility of switching to an acyclic path. The set of outgoing channels, C^p, always includes at least one channel in C_1, so a deadlock-free path is always available. In order for deadlock to be avoided, header flits cannot enter a virtual channel queue until the queue is empty. In addition, if all channels in C^p are busy, the output selection policy must either defer selecting a channel or choose a busy channel in $C_1 \cap C^p$. For the channel dependency graph in Figure 1, C_1 consists of all the virtual channels except VC_{2N} and VC_{2S}. Consequently, R_1 uses only the permitted 90° turns shown in Figure 1(b).

Lemma 1 *The channel dependency graph defined by C_1 for R_1 is connected.*

Proof. If the source and destination differ in a single dimension, the message can use the virtual channel in that direction to reach the destination. For destinations that are Northeast (Southeast) of the source, the message can be routed adaptively North (South) and East. For destinations that are Northwest (Southwest) of the source, the message must route completely West and then North (South). $\square$

Lemma 2 *The routing algorithm R_1 allows no cycles and is therefore deadlock-free.*

Proof. The proof of this lemma can be found in [9], where R_1 is described as the West-First routing algorithm. $\square$

Lemma 3 *The additional channels of routing algorithm R do not introduce cycles in the extended channel dependency graph of C_1.*

Proof. The only possibility for a cycle in C_1 is for an *indirect* dependency to be introduced by using VC_{2N} or VC_{2S}. R_1 is fully adaptive for all messages except messages whose destination is West of the source. Indirect dependencies that allow a use of the channels different from R_1 could arise in only two ways: (1) A message uses VC_W after using VC_{1N} or VC_{1S}. This cannot occur, since the routing algorithm, R, prohibits the use of VC_{1N} or VC_{1S} by any message that needs to route further West. (2) A message using some VC_W later uses another VC_W in a different row of the mesh. This is possible only because a message that is routed West can use VC_{2N} or VC_{2S} and later route West again. However, this indirect dependency does not cause a deadlock. It is sufficient to show that this indirect dependency does not create a cycle in the channel dependency graph for C_1. The channel dependency graph for C_1 has no dependencies from a channel in the East, North or South directions to a channel in the West direction, i.e., the West channels are always used before any other channel in C_1. The indirect dependencies create new dependencies only among the West virtual channels, however, these dependencies do not create a cycle. Since minimal routing is used, there are no cycles using only the West virtual channels and hence there are no cycles in the extended channel dependency graph of C_1. □

Theorem 2 *Opt-y is deadlock-free.*

Proof. The proof follows immediately by lemmas 1 – 3. □

4 Proofs of Optimality

Opt-y is optimal in two ways: (1) It requires the minimum number of virtual channels per router. (2) It requires the fewest restrictions on the use of the virtual channels. Two reasonable and standard assumptions are made when proving the optimality of opt-y. First, optimality applies only to the number of virtual channels at the interior nodes of the mesh. Nodes on the edges of the mesh need to be connected to other nodes in only two or three directions, so fewer virtual channels could be used for these routers. Second, all the nodes use the same routing algorithm.

The optimality proofs are greatly simplified by proving that *all* configurations with fewer than six virtual channels and *most* configurations with six virtual channels are either not deadlock-free or not fully adaptive. A version of this result is proved in [8] under the assumption that only acyclic routing algorithms are deadlock-free. A stronger result is proved in this paper, since no assumptions are made about the fully adaptive routing algorithm.

Note: The following conventions are used for figures showing deadlock configurations. In each figure, the routers are represented as circles, with the virtual channels

as edges connecting the routers. The source and destination routers of message i are labeled Si and Di, respectively. Virtual channels are labeled Mi to indicate that message i has acquired that channel. Since bidirectional channels are assumed, arrows are used to indicate in which direction the message is proceeding. Messages on the left side of a vertical channel are using VC_1 and messages on the right side are using VC_2. Messages above a horizontal channel are using VC_1 and messages below are using VC_2.

Theorem 3 *Deadlock-free fully adaptive wormhole routing on a 2D mesh requires a second virtual channel in two opposite directions: North and South or East and West.*

Proof. Consider the potential deadlock configuration shown in Figure 2(a). All four messages are waiting for a virtual channel in the North or West direction. If there is only one virtual channel in the North and West directions, then the routing algorithm is not deadlock-free. This applies to *any* fully adaptive routing algorithm. Similarly, Figure 2(b) shows a deadlock configuration if there is a single virtual channel in the North and East directions, Figure 2(c) shows a deadlock configuration if there is a single virtual channel in the South and West directions and Figure 2(d) shows a deadlock configuration if there is a single virtual channel in the South and East directions. At least two more virtual channels are needed to avoid all four deadlock cases and the virtual channels must be added in opposite directions. For example, the top two deadlock configurations can be avoided by adding a virtual channel in the North direction and the bottom two deadlock configurations can be avoided by adding a virtual channel in the South direction. □

Lemma 4 *At least two 90° turns must be prohibited to make the routing algorithm deadlock-free.*

Proof. A knot is a set of nodes that forms a cycle and no node in the set has a path to a node outside the set. A knot in the channel dependency graph is a sufficient condition for deadlock. Knots can occur when a set of messages all route in the clockwise or counter-clockwise directions, so it is necessary to prevent both of these knots. At least one 90° turn must be prohibited to prevent each knot, so at least two 90° turns must be prohibited. □

By theorem 3, opt-y requires only the minimum number of virtual channels for deadlock-free fully adaptive routing. The remainder of this section is used to show that opt-y has the fewest restrictions of *any* fully adaptive routing algorithm with six virtual channels, and that, ignoring symmetry, *all* other fully adaptive routing algorithms have more restrictions than opt-y.

Since at least two 90° turns must be prohibited by lemma 4 and opt-y prohibits only two, the only other routing algorithms that need to be considered are those that

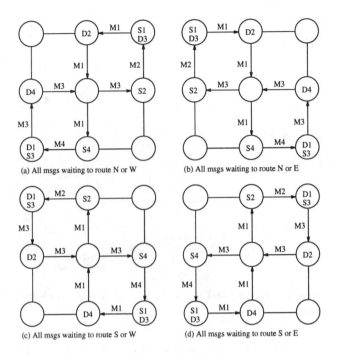

(a) All msgs waiting to route N or W

(b) All msgs waiting to route N or E

(c) All msgs waiting to route S or W

(d) All msgs waiting to route S or E

Figure 2: **Potential Deadlock Configurations**

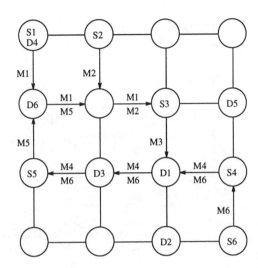

Figure 3: **Deadlock for Opt-y with E and W virtual channels**

prohibit only two 90° turns. Ignoring symmetry, there are only three such routing algorithms: North-Last, Negative-First and West-First [9]. In addition, by theorem 3, only configurations with a second virtual channel in the North and South or East and West directions need to be considered. Therefore, there are six different routing algorithms to consider. Opt-y, which uses West-First, is deadlock-free. A deadlock configuration is shown for each of the five remaining possibilities. Deadlocks arise regardless of whether or not 0° turns are permitted. **Note**: In some of the examples, deadlock can be avoided by prohibiting additional 90° turns. Such modifications are irrelevant, since the goal is to minimize the number of restrictions.

Lemma 5 *Opt-y is not deadlock-free if the restrictions shown in Figure 1 are applied to C_1, but the virtual channels are added in the East and West directions.*

Proof. The routing algorithm is fully adaptive only if the 90° turns N–W and S–W using VC_{2W} are unrestricted. A deadlock configuration is shown in Figure 3. □

Lemma 6 *The North-Last routing algorithm is not deadlock-free with only six virtual channels and two prohibited 90° turns.*

Proof. The turn model representation of the North-Last routing algorithm with the second virtual channel in the East and West directions is shown in Figure 4(a). Only the 90° turns are shown, since the 0° turns are not used

for showing deadlock. The deadlock configuration for this routing algorithm is shown in Figure 4(b). The turn model representation with the second virtual channel in the North and South directions is shown in Figure 5(a). The deadlock configuration for this routing algorithm is shown in Figure 5(b). □

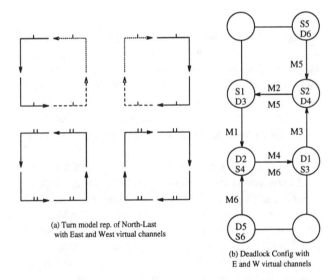

(a) Turn model rep. of North-Last with East and West virtual channels

(b) Deadlock Config with E and W virtual channels

Figure 4: **North-Last with E and W virtual channels**

Lemma 7 *The Negative-First routing algorithm is not deadlock-free with only six virtual channels and two prohibited 90° turns.*

Proof. The turn model representation of the Negative-First routing algorithm with the second virtual channel in the

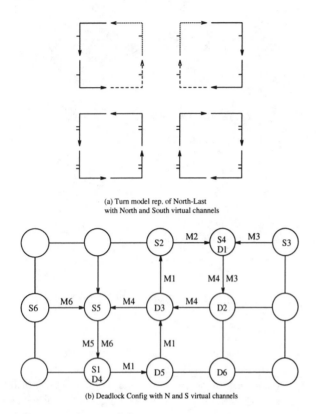

(a) Turn model rep. of North-Last
with North and South virtual channels

(b) Deadlock Config with N and S virtual channels

Figure 5: **North-Last with N and S virtual channels**

East and West directions is shown in Figure 6(a). Only the 90° turns are shown, since the 0° turns are not used for showing deadlock. The deadlock configuration for this routing algorithm is shown in Figure 6(b). The turn model representation with the second virtual channel in the North and South directions is shown in Figure 7(a). The deadlock configuration for this routing algorithm is shown in Figure 7(b). □

The only remaining possibility is to divide the restrictions between the virtual channels so that some are applied to VC_1 and the remaining to VC_2. However, a deadlock configuration is always possible, regardless of which two 90° turns are prohibited. This leads to theorem 4, which is proved for *symmetric* routing algorithms. Symmetry is preserved if the virtual channels are added in the X dimension with a corresponding set of restrictions and/or the restrictions are applied to VC_2 instead of VC_1.

Theorem 4 *Ignoring symmetry, opt-y prohibits fewer 90° turns than any other fully adaptive deadlock-free routing algorithm which uses only six virtual channels.*

Proof. By lemma 4, at least two 90° turns must be prohibited. Ignoring symmetry, there are only three such routing

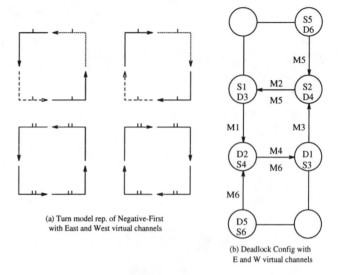

(a) Turn model rep. of Negative-First
with East and West virtual channels

(b) Deadlock Config with
E and W virtual channels

Figure 6: **Negative-First with E and W virtual channels**

algorithms [9]. Opt-y uses one of these. However, by lemma 5, it is not deadlock-free if the virtual channels are added in the East and West directions instead of the North and South directions. The other possibilities, North-Last and Negative-First, are both not deadlock-free (by lemma 6 and lemma 7, respectively). Since there are no other possibilities to consider, opt-y is the only deadlock-free fully adaptive routing algorithm that requires only six virtual channels and prohibits only two 90° turns. □

Theorem 5 *No routing algorithm using only six virtual channels per router can have fewer restrictions than those imposed by opt-y.*

Proof. By lemma 4 and theorem 4, it is clear that only the 0° turns need to be considered. Opt-y restricts the use of the 0° turns from VC_{2N} to VC_{1N} and from VC_{2S} to VC_{1S} to messages that do not need to route further West. Figure 8 gives an example where deadlock occurs when the restriction on the 0° turn from VC_{2N} to VC_{1N} is removed. A similar deadlock configuration can be constructed if the restriction on the 0° turn from VC_{2S} to VC_{1S} is removed. Since the restrictions on the other two 0° turns are a direct consequence of the prohibited 90° turns, opt-y cannot be made more adaptive. □

5 Comparison

Opt-y is compared with mad-y, the least restrictive of any previously proposed routing algorithm. Since mad-y also requires a second virtual channel in both the North and South directions, the virtual channel requirements are the same for both routing algorithms.

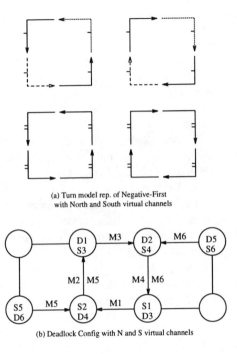

(a) Turn model rep. of Negative-First
with North and South virtual channels

(b) Deadlock Config with N and S virtual channels

Figure 7: **Negative-First with N and S virtual channels**

Mad-y is shown in Figure 9. Mad-y has the following two sets of constraints:

- Four of the sixteen 90° turns are prohibited.

- 0° turns from VC_{2N} to VC_{1N} and VC_{2S} to VC_{1S} are prohibited.

The following three restrictions arise solely from the previous constraints:

- 0° turns from VC_{1N} to VC_{2N} and VC_{1S} to VC_{2S} are allowed only when a message does not need to route further West and has not already routed East. The West-bound restriction is because a message cannot route West from VC_{2N} or VC_{2S}. The East-bound restriction is because a message never uses VC_{1N} or VC_{1S} after routing East.

- The two 90° turns N–E using VC_{1N} and S–E using VC_{1S} are allowed only when the message has not routed East. These turns are restricted only because a message cannot use VC_{1N} or VC_{1S} after VC_E.

- The two 90° turns W–N using VC_{2N} and W–S using VC_{2S} are allowed only when the message is not routed further West. These turns are restricted only because the turns from VC_{2N} or VC_{2S} to VC_W are prohibited.

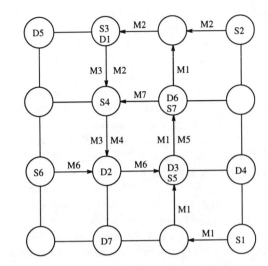

Figure 8: **Deadlock due to Fewer Restrictions**

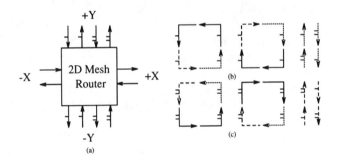

Figure 9: **Maximally Fully Adaptive Routing**

Mad-y allows four more 90° turns than double-y, but these turns are restricted so that a message uses them at most once. Additionally, a message can make at most one 0° turn, since a message cannot use VC_{1N} or VC_{1S} after switching to VC_{2N} or VC_{2S}. Finally, a message cannot make both a restricted 90° turn and a 0° turn. A message that makes a restricted W–N or W–S turn is no longer in VC_{1N} or VC_{1S}, so it cannot make a 0° turn. Similarly, a message that makes a restricted N–E or S–E turn never uses VC_{1N} or VC_{1S} again, so it cannot make a 0° turn. A message that makes a 0° turn cannot make a restricted turn to the East, because the message never uses VC_{1N} or VC_{1S} again. Similarly, a message can make a 0° turn only after routing completely West, so it cannot later make a restricted turn from the West.

For opt-y, only two 90° turns are prohibited and only two 90° turns are restricted. For mad-y, four 90° turns are prohibited and four 90° turns are restricted. Mad-y also prohibits half the 0° turns and restricts the other half. For opt-y, all the 0° turns are restricted, so none of the 0° turns are prohibited. Therefore, opt-y imposes *less than half* as many restrictions as imposed by mad-y.

Opt-y also makes much better use of the restricted turns. The 0° turns are restricted to messages that no longer need to route West, but messages can switch from either virtual channel to the other. This allows a message to make a 0° turn *more than once*. A message also has the possibility of making one of the restricted 90° turns *and* some 0° turns.

Not only does opt-y have fewer restrictions, the router control logic is simpler as well. This is because the routing relation of mad-y is of the form $R : C \times N \rightarrow C^p$, so the set of outgoing channels from which a message can choose depends not only on the destination but also on the incoming channel. Opt-y does not differentiate based on the incoming channel because the routing relation is of the form $R : N \times N \rightarrow C^p$. This simplifies the hardware required to choose the outgoing channel on which to route the message, since the choice is independent of the incoming channel.

6 Generalization

The Optimal Fully Adaptive routing algorithm can be extended to n-dimensional meshes in a straightforward manner. Minimal routing is still assumed. The routing algorithm needs only the minimum number of virtual channels. It is not proved that the routing algorithm imposes the fewest restrictions. The routing algorithm is generalized using the following steps:

- Assign a channel to each direction of each dimension.

- Number the dimensions in some order and add a second virtual channel to both directions of all dimensions except the first dimension.

- Allow a message to route along the second virtual channel at any time.

- For each dimension except the last, choose one of the two directions. Prohibit a message from routing on the first virtual channel until it has completed routing in the chosen direction of *all* lower dimensions.

- Allow a message to make a 0° turn between the virtual channels only after the message has completed routing in the chosen direction of *all* lower dimensions.

For example, consider a 4D mesh with dimensions XYZW and number the dimensions 1, 2, 3 and 4 respectively. The positive and negative directions in the Z dimension are called Up and Down respectively. The positive and negative directions in the W dimension are called In and Out respectively. Let the negative directions in the X, Y and Z dimensions be the chosen directions. A second virtual channel is added in both directions of dimensions Y, Z and W. A message can route adaptively in any dimension using virtual channel one once it has completed routing in the chosen direction of all lower dimensions. For example, a message can use VC_{1N} and VC_{1S} only after it has completed routing West. Similarly, a message can use VC_{1U} and VC_{1D} only after it has completed routing West and South. A message can use VC_{1I} and VC_{1O} only after it has completed routing West, South and Down. A message can route, without any restrictions, in the X dimension and in any direction using virtual channel two.

The Optimal Fully Adaptive routing algorithm is fully adaptive and deadlock-free for arbitrary dimension meshes. Furthermore, this algorithm uses only the minimum number of virtual channels. The proofs, given in [12], are extensions of the proofs for the 2D mesh.

Limited research has been done on wormhole routing for higher dimension meshes. For example, mad-y has been defined only for 2D meshes [8]. The partially adaptive routing algorithm proposed by Glass and Ni in [9], while requiring no additional virtual channels, allows only about $1/2^{n-1}$ of the paths provided by a fully adaptive routing algorithm for an n-dimensional mesh. Three virtual channels per physical channel are used by Chien and Kim in [2] to support partially adaptive routing for arbitrary dimension meshes. Jesshope, Miller and Yantchev propose a routing algorithm that is fully adaptive by dividing an n-dimensional mesh into 2^n regions and using separate virtual channels for each region [10]. Fully adaptive routing on arbitrary dimension meshes requires 2^{n-1} subnetworks with $n + 1$ levels per subnetwork and one virtual channel per level for each router using the routing algorithm proposed by Linder and Harden in [11]. Table 2 summarizes the number of virtual channels per router required by each routing algorithm.

It can be seen from Table 2 that there is a *dramatic* reduction in the number of virtual channels required by the Optimal Fully Adaptive routing algorithm compared to the algorithms proposed in [10, 11]. In addition, fully adaptive routing is possible using about *two-thirds* the virtual channels needed for partially adaptive routing using the routing algorithm proposed in [2]. The only adaptive algorithm that requires fewer virtual channels is the partially adaptive algorithm proposed in [9]. With less than twice as many virtual channels, the Optimal Fully Adaptive routing algorithm allows an average of 2^{n-1} times as many paths.

7 Conclusion

A deadlock-free fully adaptive routing algorithm has been proposed for wormhole routing on n-dimensional meshes. It has been proved for the 2D mesh that the routing algorithm requires the minimum number of virtual channels and places the fewest restrictions on the use of those

Table 2: **Virtual Channels per Router**

| Topology | Deterministic | Partially Adaptive | | Fully Adaptive | | |
	Dimension Order	Glass & Ni	Chien & Kim	Jesshope, Miller & Yantchev	Linder & Harden	Optimal Fully Adaptive
2D Mesh	4	4	6	8	6	6
3D Mesh	6	6	12	24	16	10
4D Mesh	8	8	18	64	40	14
nD Mesh	$2n$	$2n$	$6n - 6$	$n2^n$	$(n+1)2^{n-1}$	$4n - 2$

virtual channels. Ignoring symmetry, opt-y is the *only* fully adaptive routing algorithm for 2D meshes that satisfies both of these properties.

An important open problem currently under investigation is what constitutes a necessary and sufficient condition for deadlock freedom in adaptive routing algorithms. Designing optimal routing algorithms for arbitrary topologies would be greatly simplified by a necessary and sufficient condition for proving routing algorithms are deadlock-free. The necessary and sufficient condition proved in [6] applies only to deterministic routing. There is no known necessary and sufficient condition for adaptive routing relations of the form $R : C \times N \rightarrow C^p$ or $R : N \times N \rightarrow C^p$.

The routing algorithm requires only the minimum number of virtual channels for an n-dimensional mesh. It has not been shown that the proposed routing algorithm has the minimum number of restrictions for arbitrary dimension meshes. Proving optimality would require the examination of many possible routing algorithms. A necessary and sufficient condition for deadlock freedom would greatly facilitate the proof of this open problem by reducing the cases that need to be considered.

Acknowledgments

The authors would like to thank Dave Lutz, D. K. Panda, Kant Patel, and Shobana Balakrishnan for valuable discussions which have improved the quality of the paper.

References

[1] A. A. Chien. A Cost and Speed Model for k-ary n-cube Wormhole Routers. In *Hot Interconnects '93*, August 1993.

[2] A. A. Chien and J. H. Kim. Planar-Adaptive Routing: Low-cost Adaptive Networks for Multiprocessors. In *Proceedings of the 19th Annual International Symposium on Computer Architecture*, pages 268–277, 1992.

[3] W. J. Dally. Fine-Grain Message-Passing Concurrent Computers. In *Proceedings of the Third Conference on Hypercube Concurrent Computers*, volume 1, pages 2–12, 1988.

[4] W. J. Dally. Virtual-Channel Flow Control. *IEEE Transactions on Parallel and Distributed Systems*, 3(2):194–205, March 1992.

[5] W. J. Dally and H. Aoki. Deadlock-Free Adaptive Routing in Multicomputer Networks Using Virtual Channels. *IEEE Transactions on Parallel and Distributed Systems*, 4(4):466–475, April 1993.

[6] W. J. Dally and C. L. Seitz. Deadlock-Free Message Routing in Multiprocessor Interconnection Networks. *IEEE Transactions on Computers*, C-36(5):547–553, May 1987.

[7] J. Duato. On the Design of Deadlock-Free Adaptive Routing Algorithms for Multicomputers: Design Methodologies. In *Parallel Architectures and Languages Europe 91*, volume I, pages 390–405, 1991.

[8] C. Glass and L. Ni. Maximally Fully Adaptive Routing in 2D Meshes. In *International Conference on Parallel Processing*, volume I, pages 101–104, 1992.

[9] C. Glass and L. Ni. The Turn Model for Adaptive Routing. In *Proceedings of the 19th Annual International Symposium on Computer Architecture*, pages 278–287, 1992.

[10] C. R. Jesshope, P. R. Miller, and J. T. Yantchev. High Performance Communications in Processor Networks. In *Proceedings of the 16th Annual International Symposium on Computer Architecture*, pages 150–157, 1989.

[11] D. H. Linder and J. C. Harden. An Adaptive and Fault Tolerant Wormhole Routing Strategy for k-ary n-cubes. *IEEE Transactions on Computers*, 40(1):2–12, January 1991.

[12] L. Schwiebert and D. N. Jayasimha. Optimal Fully Adaptive Wormhole Routing for Meshes. Technical Report OSU-CISRC-4/93-TR16, The Ohio State University, 1993.

Efficient Collective Data Distribution in All-Port Wormhole-Routed Hypercubes[*]

D. F. Robinson, D. Judd, P. K. McKinley, and B. H. C. Cheng

Department of Computer Science
Michigan State University
East Lansing, Michigan 48824-1027
{robinsod,danjudd,mckinley,chengb}@cps.msu.edu

Abstract

This paper addresses the problem of collective data distribution, specifically multicast, in wormhole-routed hypercubes. The system model allows a processor to send and receive data in all dimensions simultaneously. New theoretical results that characterize contention among messages in wormhole-routed hypercubes are developed and used to design new multicast routing algorithms. The algorithms are compared in terms of the number of steps required in each, their measured execution times when implemented on a relatively small-scale nCUBE-2, and their simulated execution times on larger hypercubes. The results indicate that significant performance improvement is possible when the multicast algorithm actively identifies and uses multiple ports in parallel.

1 Introduction

The recent trend in supercomputer design has been towards *scalable* parallel computers, which are designed to offer corresponding gains in performance as the number of processors is increased. Many such systems, known as *massively parallel computers* (MPCs), are characterized by the distribution of memory among an ensemble of processing nodes. Each node has its own processor, local memory, and other supporting devices.

In parallel scientific computing, data must be redistributed periodically in such a way that all processors can be kept busy performing useful tasks. Because they do not physically share memory, nodes in MPCs must communicate by passing messages through a communications network. Some communication operations are *point-to-point*, that is, they involve only a single source and a single destination. Other operations are *collective*, in that they involve more than two nodes. Examples of collective communication include *multicast, reduction,* and *barrier synchronization*. The growing interest in the use of such routines is evidenced by their inclusion in many commercial communication libraries and in the *Message Passing Interface* (MPI) [1], an emerging standard for communication routines used by message-passing programs. Besides message-passing, collective communication operations are also important in implementing data-parallel languages, such as High Performance Fortran [2].

Communication performance depends on several characteristics of the network architecture, including the *network topology, routing algorithm,* and *switching strategy*. Network topologies of commercial and research MPCs vary widely and include the 2D mesh (Intel Paragon), 3D mesh (MIT J-machine), hypercube (nCUBE-2), 3D torus (Cray MPP), and the Fat Tree (Thinking Machines CM-5). Most routing algorithms used in commercial machines are deterministic, that is, the path between a particular source and destination is fixed. The predominant switching technique is *wormhole routing* [3], in which a message is divided into a number of *flits* that are pipelined through the network. The two salient features of wormhole routing are: (1) only a small amount of buffer space is required in each router, and (2) the network latency is almost distance insensitive if there is no channel contention among messages [4].

In wormhole-routed MPCs, communication among nodes is handled by a separate *router*. As shown in Figure 1, several pairs of *external channels* connect the router to neighboring routers; the pattern in which the external channels are connected defines the network topology. Usually, the router can relay multiple messages simultaneously, provided that each incoming message requires a unique outgoing channel. In addition, two messages may be transmitted simultaneously in opposite directions between neighboring routers.

A router is connected to the local proces-

[*]This work was supported in part by the NSF grants CDA-9121641, MIP-9204066, CDA-9222901, and CCR-9209873, by the Department of Energy under grant DE-FG02-93ER25167, and by an Ameritech Faculty Fellowship.

792

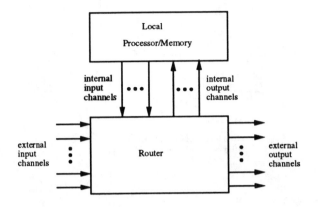

Figure 1. Generic MPC node architecture

sor/memory by one or more pairs of *internal* channels. One channel of each pair is for input, the other for output. The *port model* of a system refers to the number of internal channels at each node. If each node possesses exactly one pair of internal channels, then the result is a so-called "one-port communication architecture" [5]. A major consequence of a one-port architecture is that the local processor must transmit (receive) messages sequentially. Architectures with multiple ports reduce this bottleneck. In the case of an *all*-port system, every external channel has a corresponding internal channel, allowing the node to send to and receive on all external channels simultaneously.

In this paper, the specific problem of efficient multicast communication for all-port wormhole-routed hypercubes is addressed. Formally, a *hypercube* (or *n*-cube) consists of 2^n nodes, each of which has a unique n-bit binary address. For each node v, let v also denote its *n*-bit binary address, and let $\| v \|$ represent the number of 1's in v. A channel $c = (u, v)$ is present in an *n*-cube if and only if $\| u \oplus v \| = 1$, where $\oplus$ is the bitwise exclusive-or operation on binary numbers. The hypercube topology has been used in multicomputer design for many years [6]. The nCUBE-2 [7] is the first hypercube to support wormhole-routing, as does the recently announced nCUBE-3 [8].

The remainder of the paper is organized as follows. Section 2 illustrates the issues and problems involved in supporting efficient multicast communication in all-port hypercube systems. Section 3 gives new theoretical results· that provide the foundation for this work. Section 4 presents the new algorithms that have been produced to support multicast in all-port wormhole-routed hypercubes. Section 5 compares the algorithms using analysis, simulation, and implementations on a 64-node nCUBE-2. Finally, conclusions are presented in Section 6.

2 Background and motivations

Collective communication operations may be implemented in either hardware or software. However, most existing wormhole-routed multiprocessors support only point-to-point, or *unicast* communication in hardware. In these environments, all communication operations must be implemented in software by sending one or more unicast messages; such implementations are called *unicast-based*. A multicast operation may be implemented by sending a separate copy of the message from the source to every destination. An alternative is to use a *multicast tree* of unicast messages. In a multicast tree, the source node actually sends the message to only a subset of the destinations. Each recipient of the message forwards it to some subset of the destinations that have not yet received it. The process continues until all destinations have received the message. Using this approach, the time required for the operation can be greatly reduced.

Although implemented in software, unicast-based collective communication algorithms must exploit the underlying architecture in order to minimize their execution time. In a wormhole-routed system, the implementation should not only exploit distance-insensitive unicast latency [4], but must also avoid channel contention, that is, no two messages involved in the operation should simultaneously require the same channel. Avoiding channel contention depends on the underlying unicast routing algorithm of the MPC; hypercubes often adopt *E-cube routing*, in which messages are routed through dimensions in either ascending or descending order. Also, the implementation should involve no local processors other than those affected by the operation. For example, in a multicast, only source and destination processors should be required to handle the message. Finally, the implementation should account for the port model, which affects how fast nodes can send and receive messages.

The following (small-scale) example illustrates the issues and difficulties involved in implementing efficient multicast communication in hypercubes.

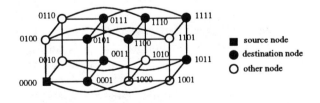

Figure 2. An example of multicast in a 4-cube

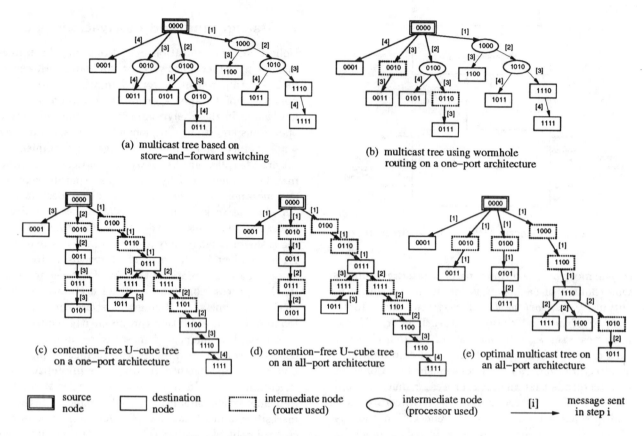

(a) multicast tree based on
store–and–forward switching

(b) multicast tree using wormhole
routing on a one–port architecture

(c) contention–free U–cube tree
on a one–port architecture

(d) contention–free U–cube tree
on an all–port architecture

(e) optimal multicast tree on
an all–port architecture

| source node | destination node | intermediate node (router used) | intermediate node (processor used) | [i] message sent in step i |

Figure 3. Unicast-based software multicast trees

Consider the 4-cube in Figure 2, and suppose that a multicast message is to be sent from node 0000 to eight destinations {0001, 0011, 0101, 0111, 1011, 1100, 1110, 1111}. (In this example and all subsequent examples, we assume that the E-cube routing algorithm resolves addresses from high order bits to low order bits. In the nCUBE-2, the opposite resolution strategy is used, but this difference does not affect any of the results presented.)

In early hypercube systems that used store-and-forward switching, the procedure shown in Figure 3(a) could be used. At step 1, the source sends the message to node 1000. At step 2, nodes 0000 and 1000 inform nodes 0100 and 1010, respectively. Continuing in this fashion, this implementation requires 4 steps to reach all destinations. In this example, five nodes (0010, 0100, 0110, 1000, and 1010) are required to relay the message, even though they are not destinations. Using the same routing algorithm in a one-port wormhole-routed network also requires 4 steps, as shown in Figure 3(b). In this case, however, only the *routers* at two of the non-destination nodes (0010 and 0110) are involved in forwarding the message. For example, the message may be passed from 0000 to 0011 in one

step; the message is relayed at node 0010 by the router, not the local processor. However, because the message must be replicated at nodes 0100, 1000, and 1010, the local processors at those nodes must still handle the message.

Figure 3(c) illustrates the result of using the *U-cube algorithm* [9] to solve the problem on a one-port wormhole-routed system. (U-cube, which was designed specifically for one-port wormhole-routed architectures, will be discussed further in Section 4.) The only local processors required to handle the message are those at destination nodes. Furthermore, on a one-port architecture, all messages are guaranteed to be contention-free [9]. Although common channels are used between the 0111-to-1011 path and the 0111-to-1100 path, these messages are sent sequentially, so contention does not arise. Details of avoiding contention in one-port architectures can be found in [9].

Although the algorithm used to construct the tree in Figure 3(c) still requires four steps, this approach is optimal for multicasting to 8 destinations on a one-port architecture. Specifically, $\lceil \log_2(m+1) \rceil$ is a tight lower bound on the number of steps required to reach m destinations on a one-port hypercube. Since the U-cube algorithm was designed specifically for one-port systems, however, it makes no attempt to take advantage of multiple ports. For example, if the algorithm were implemented on an all-port hypercube, it would still require four steps to complete the multicast in the above example, as illustrated in Figure 3(d), although some destinations are reached earlier than in Figure 3(c). Notice that three steps are required to reach destination node 1011, since that unicast message must traverse a channel in the path required to reach node 1100, thereby delaying its transmission.

Figure 3(e) shows a multicast tree that accounts for both wormhole routing and an all-port architecture. The algorithm requires only two steps, no local processors other than the source and destinations are involved, and contention among constituent messages is avoided. This particular tree, which is based on the methods presented in this paper, is optimal for multicast to the given set of nodes on an all-port architecture. In the next section, we develop the theoretical results necessary to guarantee that our new algorithms, presented in Section 4, are contention-free.

3 Theoretical foundations

In this section, we present new theoretical results that will serve as a basis for subsequent algorithms. First, we formally define terms related to dimension-ordered routing and subcubes. Then we present several theorems that are useful in determining that certain pairs of paths are guaranteed to be arc-disjoint (and hence, contention-free). Finally, we formally define contention in an all-port hypercube architecture, and present a related theorem.

3.1 Notation and definitions

Bitwise *and*, *or*, and *exclusive-or* are represented by symbols $\otimes$, $|$, and $\oplus$, respectively. Logical *and* and *or* are represented by $\wedge$ and $\vee$, respectively. We use N to represent the number of processors. Since n represents the dimensionality of the hypercube, $N = 2^n$. For each node, say x, the outgoing (and incoming) channels of node x are labeled 0 through $n-1$, where channel d connects node x to node $x \oplus 2^d$. We say that channel d is used to *travel* in dimension d.

The path from a source node u to a destination node v resulting from dimension-ordered routing is denoted $P(u,v)$. $P(u,v) = (u; w_1; w_2; \ldots; w_p; v)$ is the sequence of nodes visited on the path. Note that $p + 1 = \|u \oplus v\|$. Under E-cube routing, a unique shortest path is always taken. In particular, a message will always travel over the required dimensions in *de-*

scending (alternately, *ascending*) order. For example, the path from source node 0101 to destination node 1110 is $P(0101, 1110) = (0101; 1101; 1111; 1110)$. A unicast from node u to node v occurring at time step t is denoted $(u, v, P(u, v), t)$.

The following definition simplifies references to the initial channel in a dimension-ordered route, that is, the first dimension in which a message will travel.

Definition 1 $\delta(u, v)$ *represents the highest-ordered bit position in which u and v differ. Formally,* $\delta(u, v) = \lfloor log_2(u \oplus v) \rfloor$. *If $u = v$, then $\delta(u, v)$ is undefined.*

In order to specify a subset of the nodes of a hypercube, we may explicitly state some of the n address bits, and allow the other address bits to range over all possible values. We define a *subcube* to be such a subset of nodes, where the explicitly-stated address bits are the high order bits, and the free-ranging address bits are the low order bits.

Definition 2 *A subcube $S = (n_S, M_S)$ is defined by a dimensionality $n_S \in \{0 .. n\}$, and a mask $M_S \in \{0 .. 2^{(n-n_S)} - 1\}$. Informally, subcube S consists of those nodes whose highest-ordered $(n - n_S)$ bits have a value equal to M_S. Formally, for any node u, $u \in S$ iff $(u \gg n_S) = M_S$, where "$u \gg i$" indicates a right-shift of u by i bits.*

3.2 Basic results

This section contains lemmas that will be used to facilitate subsequent theorems. These lemmas are also useful in understanding later sections of the paper. Due to space limitations, proofs of all lemmas and theorems are omitted here, but can be found in [10].

Lemma 1 *Let $P(x, y) = (x; w_1; w_2; \ldots; w_p; y)$ be any E-cube path (For clarity, let $w_0 = x$ and $w_{p+1} = y$.), and let $(w_i \to w_{i+1}) \in P$ be any arc in $P(x, y)$. Let d be the dimension over which $(w_i \to w_{i+1})$ travels, $2^d = w_i \oplus w_{i+1}$. Then the following conditions hold:*

1. $\forall j \in \{1..i\}$, $\forall k \in \{0..d\}$, $w_j \otimes 2^k = x \otimes 2^k$

2. $\forall j \in \{i + 1..p\}$, $\forall k \in \{d + 1..n - 1\}$, $w_j \otimes 2^k = y \otimes 2^k$

3. $x \otimes 2^d \neq y \otimes 2^d$.

Lemma 1 characterizes the behavior of dimension-ordered routing in a hypercube. In particular, the lemma formalizes the notion that any unicast travels in a particular dimension at most once, and that the unicast travels in a strictly decreasing order of dimension.

Lemma 2 *For any three nodes x, y, z, and for any subcube S, if $x, z \in S$ and $x \leq y \leq z$, then $y \in S$.*

Lemma 2 states that the node addresses within any subcube are contiguous.

3.3 Arc-disjoint paths

In implementing a multicast algorithm, whenever the paths of two constituent unicast messages share an arc (channel), care must be taken to ensure that the paths do not attempt to use the shared arc simultaneously. Alternatively, when two paths have no arc in common, contention (between these two particular paths) is always avoided. Paths with no common arc are said to be *arc-disjoint*.

Each of the following theorems state sufficient conditions on two paths such that any two paths meeting these conditions are arc-disjoint. Each theorem is stated formally. Where needed for clarity, theorems are stated informally within a parenthetical block of text.

Theorem 1 *Consider any two paths $P(x, y)$ and $P(x, v)$ originating from a common source node. If $\delta(x, y) \neq \delta(x, v)$, then $P(x, y)$ and $P(x, v)$ are arc-disjoint. (Paths leaving a common source on different channels are arc-disjoint.)*

Theorem 2 *Consider any two paths $P(u, v)$ and $P(x, y)$. If there exists a subcube S such that $u, v \in S \wedge x, y \notin S$, then $P(u, v)$ and $P(x, y)$ are arc-disjoint. (A path with source and destination within subcube S is arc-disjoint from any path with source and destination outside S.)*

3.4 Contention

As previously stated, any two unicasts having arc-disjoint paths are contention-free. Unicasts whose paths share an arc may or may not contend for that arc, depending on the relative timing and communication latencies of the unicasts. Due to the nondeterministic characteristics of communication latency, we must establish necessary conditions for avoiding contention, such that when these conditions are met, it is *guaranteed* that contention will not occur.

In order to study contention between messages, the definition of the *reachable set* of nodes in a multicast implementation is needed [9].

Definition 3 *A node v is in the reachable set of node u, denoted R_u, if and only if one of the following holds:*

1. *$v = u$; or*

2. *There exists a unicast $(w, v, P(w, v), t)$ such that $w \in R_u$.*

The reachable set of a node u contains those nodes in the multicast that receive the message, either directly or indirectly, through node u. If the multicast is viewed as a tree of unicast messages, then R_u is the set of nodes in the subtree rooted at u. Using this definition, the characteristics of a multicast necessary to avoid contention between messages sent in different time steps, called *depth contention*, can be formally defined.

Definition 4 *A multicast implementation is contention-free if and only if its constituent unicasts are pairwise contention-free. For any two unicasts $(u, v, P(u, v), t)$ and $(x, y, P(x, y), \tau)$ where $t \leq \tau$, the two unicasts are contention-free if and only if either:*

1. *$P(u, v)$ and $P(x, y)$ are arc-disjoint; or*

2. *$(t < \tau) \wedge (x \in R_u)$.*

When viewing a multicast as a unicast tree, the second item in the above definition allows two unicasts to share an arc under the condition that either (1) one unicast is an ancestor of the other (this case occurs when $x \in R_v$), or (2) one unicast is an ancestor of a later sibling of the other. The latter case occurs when $(t < \tau) \wedge (x \in R_u)$, but $x \notin R_v$. From the above definition of contention-free unicast pairs, we can conclude that no two unicasts from a common source node will experience contention, as shown in the following theorem.

Theorem 3 *Any two unicasts $(u, v, P(u, v), t)$ and $(u, y, P(u, y), \tau)$ with a common source node are contention-free.*

4 Algorithms

In this section, we define several algorithms whose performance was compared on all-port hypercubes. The performance evaluation data are given in Section 5.

4.1 Algorithms based on dimension-ordered chains

We begin with a brief review of the U-cube algorithm [9]. This algorithm, designed for one-port architectures, produces multicast trees on such systems that are of minimum height and are guaranteed to be contention-free. The U-cube multicast algorithm relies on the binary relation "dimension order," denoted $<_d$, which is defined between two nodes a and b as follows: $a <_d b$ if and only if either $a = b$ or there exists a j such that $a \otimes 2^j < b \otimes 2^j$ and $a \otimes 2^i = b \otimes 2^i$ for all i, $j + 1 \leq i \leq n - 1$. A sequence $\{d_0, d_1, d_2, \ldots d_p\}$ of source and destination addresses in which all the elements are distinct and $d_i <_d d_j$ for all $0 \le i < j \le p$ is called a *dimension-ordered chain* [9]. A sequence $\{d_1, d_2, \ldots, d_m\}$ is called a d_0-*relative dimension-ordered chain* if and only if $\{d_0 \oplus d_1, d_0 \oplus d_2, \ldots, d_0 \oplus d_m\}$ is a dimension-ordered chain.

If address resolution is performed from highest (left) to lowest (right), then dimension order is the same as the usual increasing order. For example, dimension ordering of 10100, 00110, and 10010 results in the chain: 00110, 10010, 10100.

On the other hand, if addresses are resolved from lowest to highest, then a dimension-ordered chain is: 10100, 10010, 00110.

Figure 4 gives the U-cube algorithm. The source d_0 and the destination addresses are sorted into a d_0-relative dimension-ordered chain, denoted Φ, at the time when multicast is initiated. The source node successively divides Φ in half and sends a message to the first node in the upper half of the chain. That node is responsible for delivering the message to the other nodes in the upper half, using the same U-cube algorithm. At each step, the source deletes from Φ the receiving node and those nodes in the upper half. The source continues this procedure until Φ contains only its own address.

Algorithm 1: The U-Cube Multicast Algorithm [9]
Input: Dimension ordered address sequence
$\{d_{left}, d_{left+1}, \ldots, d_{right}\}$, where d_{left}
is the local address, and a message M.
Output: Send out one or more copies of message M
Procedure:
  repeat
    1. $x = \delta(d_{left}, d_{right})$, the position of the first bit difference
    2. let $d_{highdim}$ be the leftmost destination in the chain such that $\delta(d_{left}, d_{highdim}) = x$
    3. $center = left + \lceil \frac{right-left}{2} \rceil$
    4. $next = center$
    5. $D = \{d_{next+1}, d_{next+2}, \ldots, d_{right}\}$;
    6. Send a copy of message M to node d_{next} with the address field D
    7. $right = next - 1$
  until ($left = right$)

Figure 4. The *U-cube* multicast algorithm

Figure 5 gives an example of this method in a one-port 4-cube. The source node 0100 is sending to a set of eight destinations {0001, 0011, 0101, 0111, 1000, 1010, 1011, 1111}. Taking the exclusive-or of each destination address with 0100 and sorting the results produces the d_0-relative dimension-ordered chain $\Phi = \{0000, 0001, 0011, 0101, 0111, 1011, 1100,$

1110, 1111\}. (The reader will notice that this d_0-relative chain represents the same multicast operation examined in Figure 3.) The corresponding U-cube tree is shown in Figure 5. It takes 4 steps for all destination processors to receive the message.

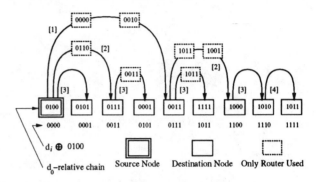

Figure 5. Multicast chain in a one-port 4-cube

It has been previously shown that message transmission in U-cube tree is contention-free regardless of startup latency and message length [9]. Furthermore, the U-cube algorithm achieves minimum time for a one-port architecture by requiring only $p = \lceil log_2(m+1) \rceil$ time steps for m destinations. For details of the theory behind the U-cube and the accompanying U-mesh algorithm, please refer to [9].

The *U-cube* algorithm, however, makes no attempt to parallelize message transmissions from a given sender. When executed on an all-port hypercube, the algorithm will often fail to take advantage of that architectural property. In the tree shown in Figure 3(d), for example, step 1 of the algorithm "mistakenly" selects node 0111 as the first destination to which the message is transmitted. This decision leaves node 0111 responsible for delivering the message to four nodes, all of which differ from 0111 in the highest dimension. Better message-forwarding decisions, shown in Figure 3(e), result in a tree of height two.

This observation leads to two simple variations on the U-cube algorithm. In fact, both algorithms differ from U-cube in a single statement, which determines the degree to which they exploit the all-port capability of the system. In the *Maxport* algorithm, a sender transmits (in parallel) to the maximum number of destinations permitted by the architecture and the specific destination set. Step 4 in the body of the main loop is $next = highdim$, rather than $next = center$, as in U-cube (Figure 4). This choice can sometimes lead to performance worse than U-cube, however. For example, if node 0000 is the source of a multicast to nodes 1001, 1010, and 1011, the resulting Maxport "tree" will require three steps, as shown in Figure 6(a). The U-cube solution shown in Figure 6(b) requires only two steps.

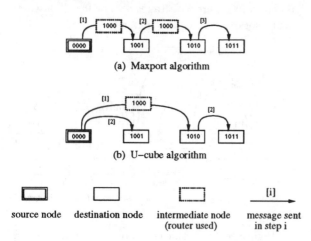

(a) Maxport algorithm

(b) U–cube algorithm

source node   destination node   intermediate node   message sent
                                    (router used)   in step i

Figure 6. Simple Maxport and U-cube comparison

Just as U-cube does not account for dimension, neither does Maxport account for the number of destinations for which each node is responsible. A simple modification to the algorithm solves the problem. As the name implies, the *Combine* algorithm exhibits characteristics of both the *U-Cube* and *Maxport* algorithms. This algorithm attempts to use multiple ports, but not at the expense of leaving a single node responsible for a large subset of the destinations. In order to obtain the *Combine* algorithm, step 4 in the body of the main loop is changed to $next = \max(highdim, center)$. The performance of all three algorithms is compared in Section 5.

4.2 An algorithm based on cube-ordered chains

In this section, we present an alternative approach to multicasting, in which the source node and destination nodes are considered as elements of subcubes.

Definition 5 *A chain $D = \{d_{first}, d_{first+1}, \ldots, d_{last}\}$ is a cube-ordered chain of dimension n iff*

1. *for all $d \in D$, $0 \leq d < 2^n$; and*

2. *for all subcubes $S = (n_S, M_S)$, where $n_S \leq n$ for all i, j, k where $first \leq i \leq j \leq k \leq last$, if $d_i, d_k \in S$, then $d_j \in S$.*

(A chain D is cube-ordered iff the nodes of D within any subcube are contiguous.)

Theorem 4 *If $D = \{d_{first}, d_{first+1}, \ldots, d_{last}\}$ is a dimension ordered chain, then D is also a cube-ordered chain.*

In the Maxport algorithm, for each participating node, say x, the unicasts originating at node x are transmitted on different outgoing channels. In this approach, the message is always forwarded to different subcubes; when node x receives the message over channel d, it also receives a list of destination nodes, D, which are in the same d-dimension subcube as x, say subcube S. In turn, x issues one unicast into each subcube *within S* which (1) does not contain x, (2) is maximal, and (3) contains at least one destination node. As will be shown later, it is possible to input any cube-ordered chain, not just a dimension-ordered chain, to Maxport and still be able to avoid contention among messages. An ordinary dimension-ordered chain may not be the most appropriate cube-ordered chain to use. In fact, performance increase may be gained by exchanging subcubes of the chain, where possible, so that source nodes (including intermediate source nodes in the multicast tree) always choose the most "crowded" destination node among available destination nodes.

Figure 7 shows the *weighted_sort* algorithm, which permutes a cube-ordered chain so that the most "crowded" node appears as the first node of each subcube. This is accomplished by exchanging subcube halves (these halves are themselves subcubes) so that the most populated half occurs first in the chain. Notice that the *cube_center* function is applied to a cube-ordered chain of addresses that are contained within a subcube of dimension n_S. This function returns the starting position of the second ($n_S - 1$) dimension subcube "half" of the input subcube. (If one of the ($n_S - 1$) dimension subcubes contains no destination nodes, then cube_center returns a value of $last + 1$.)

The weighted_sort algorithm, as shown, is a centralized algorithm with computational complexity $O(m^2)$, where m is the number of destination nodes. We have also developed a distributed version that has complexity $O(m \log_2 m)$. For details, please refer to [10]. To use the weighted_sort algorithm with Maxport, the list of destinations is first sorted according to dimension-order, then sorted using the weighted sort algorithm, and finally input to Maxport. Let us call the combination of these techniques the *W-sort* routing algorithm.

Figure 8 illustrates the behavior of the W-sort algorithm in a 4-cube. As shown in Figure 8(a), the set of destination nodes is $D = \{0, 1, 3, 5, 7, 11, 12, 14, 15\}$. (Their binary equivalents are given for reference.) Since the nodes of D are in ascending order, D is a cube-ordered address sequence, by Theorem 4.

```
Procedure: weighted_sort (D, first, last, n_S)
Input: Cube-ordered chain D = {d_first, d_first+1, ..., d_last}
    and a subcube size n_S.
Output: Upon exit, D is a weighted cube-ordered chain.
Procedure:
    if last - first ≥ 2 then
        center = cube_center(D, first, last, n_S)
        weighted_sort(D, first, center - 1, n_S - 1)
        weighted_sort(D, center, last, n_S - 1)
        if (first ≠ 0) ∧
            ((center - first) < (last - center + 1)) then
            /* swap subcubes */
            D = {d_center, d_center+1, ..., d_last,
                    d_first, d_first+1, ..., d_center-1}
        endif
    endif
endif
```

Figure 7. The *weighted_sort* procedure

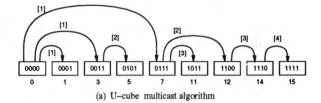

(a) U-cube multicast algorithm

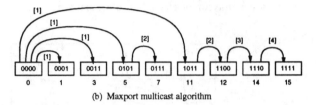

(b) Maxport multicast algorithm

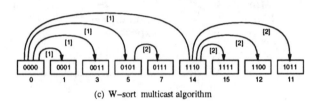

(c) W-sort multicast algorithm

Figure 8. Examples of multicast communication

Figure 8(a) shows the U-cube algorithm executed on an all-port architecture, which requires 4 time steps to perform the multicast. Each arc represents a unicast, and is labeled with the time step in which it occurs. In this example, intermediate routers are not represented. Notice that node 7 cannot send to nodes 11 and 12 during the same time step, since both unicasts require the same outgoing channel.

Figure 8(b) shows the Maxport algorithm applied directly to address sequence D. In this example, the Maxport algorithm also requires 4 steps to reach all destination nodes. Notice that all unicasts with a common source node are transmitted on different outgoing channels, and thus can be sent during the same time step in an all-port architecture.

Now, we consider rearranging the nodes in the destination address sequence before beginning the multicast. Applying the *weighted_sort* algorithm to address sequence D produces a new address sequence $D = \{0, 1, 3, 5, 7, 14, 15, 12, 11\}$. Subcube $S = (3, 1)$ contains destination nodes $\{11, 12, 14, 15\}$. The two halves of subcube S, $S_0 = (2, 10)$ and $S_1 = (2, 11)$, contain destination nodes $\{11\}$ and $\{12, 14, 15\}$, respectively. Thus, the *weighted_sort* algorithm interchanges S_0 and S_1, since S_0 contains fewer destination nodes than S_1. This interchange results in the more populated subcube (S_1) receiving the message first. Continuing recursively, the two halves of subcube S_1 are also interchanged. Figure 8(c) shows the resulting W-sort multicast, which requires only 2 steps.

Theorem 5 *The* weighted_sort *algorithm applied to a cube-ordered chain* $D = \{d_{first}, d_{first+1}, ..., d_{last}\}$ *results in* $\hat{D} = \{\hat{d}_{first}, \hat{d}_{first+1}, ..., \hat{d}_{last}\}$, *where:*

1. $\hat{D}$ is a cube-ordered chain;

2. $\hat{D}$ is a permutation of D; and

3. $\hat{d}_{first} = d_{first}$ (the source node remains in the first position).

Theorem 6 *The* W-sort *algorithm applied to a cube-ordered chain* $D = \{d_{first}, d_{first+1}, ..., d_{last}\}$ *results in a contention-free multicast from source node* d_{first} *to destination nodes* $\{d_{first+1}, d_{first+2}, ..., d_{last}\}$.

5 Performance evaluation

In order to understand the relative performance of the algorithms presented in Section 4, they were compared in three ways on destination sets in which the nodes are randomly distributed throughout the hypercube. First, we compared their performance in terms of the average and maximum number of steps required to reach the destinations. Second, we compared the algorithms by implementing them on an nCUBE-2 and measuring the average and maximum delay, across destinations, for messages of various sizes. Third, we simulated the performance of the algorithms using a simulation tool that has been validated against the nCUBE-2. Since we had access to a real system with only 64 nodes, simulation allowed us to compare the algorithms on larger systems.

5.1 Stepwise comparisons

Figures 9 and 10 plot the averages, among random sets of destinations, of the maximum number of steps needed to multicast data in a 6-cube and a 10-cube, respectively. For each point in a curve, 100 destination sets were chosen randomly. In addition to reducing the number of steps, the new algorithms "smooth out" the staircase behavior of the U-cube algorithm.

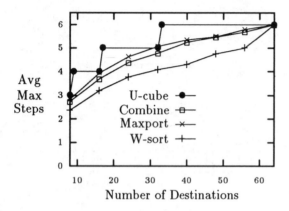

Figure 9. Stepwise comparisons on a 6-cube

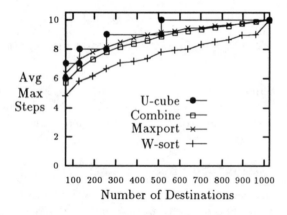

Figure 10. Stepwise comparisons on a 10-cube

5.2 Implementations on an nCUBE-2

Figures 11 and 12 plot the average and maximum, among destinations, of the measured delay between the sending of a 4096-byte multicast message and its receipt at the destination. For each point in a curve, 20 destination sets were chosen randomly in a 5-cube. These plots show that all the algorithms designed to take advantage of the multiport architecture offer some benefit over the U-cube algorithm. However, any advantage of among Maxport, Combine, and W-sort, is unclear. Interestingly, Figure 11 shows that the average delay for U-cube is actually worse for multicast than for broadcast. This anomaly occurs because the algorithm sometimes forces multiple messages out the same channel instead of taking advantage of multiple channels. In Figure 12, we see clearly the staircase behavior of U-cube. As predicted by the stepwise comparisons, the new algorithms tend to smooth the relative delays among various sized destination sets.

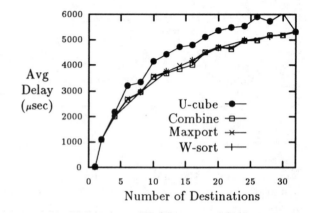

Figure 11. Average delay comparisons on a 5-cube

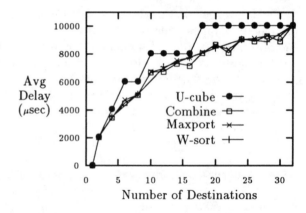

Figure 12. Maximum delay comparisons on a 5-cube

5.3 Simulations of larger systems

In order to compare the algorithm for larger hypercubes, we relied on simulation. As part of an earlier project [11], we have developed a CSIM-based simulation tool, called *MultiSim*, which can be used to simulate large-scale multiprocessors. In particular, MultiSim uses novel methods to efficiently simulate wormhole-routed systems. In addition, the simulator has been validated against an nCUBE-2 hypercube multicomputer [11].

Figures 13 and 14 plot the average and maximum, among destinations, of the delay between the sending of a 4096-byte multicast message and its receipt at the destination. For each point in a curve, 100 destination sets were chosen randomly in a 10 cube. These plots show that all the algorithms designed to take advantage of the multiport architecture offer advantages over the U-cube algorithm. For the larger systems, the advantage of W-sort becomes more obvious in both the average and maximum cases.

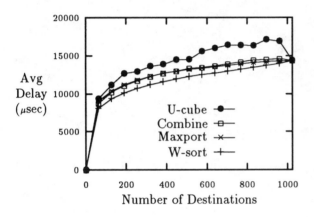

Figure 13. Average delay comparisons on a 10-cube

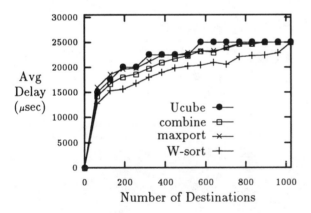

Figure 14. Maximum delay comparisons on a 10-cube

6 Conclusions

Efficient data distribution is critical to the performance of new generation supercomputers that use massively parallel architectures. In this paper, the problem of collective data distribution, specifically multicast in all-port wormhole-routed hypercubes, has been addressed. It has been demonstrated why the U-cube multicast algorithm [9], which is optimal for

one-port architectures, fails to take advantage of multiple ports when they are present in the system. New theoretical results regarding contention among messages in wormhole-routed hypercubes have been developed and used to design new multicast routing algorithms and to prove that these algorithms are contention-free. The algorithms were compared in terms of the number of steps required in each, their measured execution times when implemented on a relatively small-scale nCUBE-2, and their simulated execution times on larger hypercubes. The results indicate that significant performance improvement is possible when the multicast algorithm actively identifies and uses multiple ports in parallel.

References

1. S. Berryman, J. Cownie, J. Dongarra, and others, "Document for standard message-passing interface." in preparation, July 1993.

2. High Performance Fortran Forum, "Draft High Performance Fortran language specification." (version 1.0), Jan. 1993.

3. W. J. Dally and C. L. Seitz, "The torus routing chip," *Journal of Distributed Computing*, vol. 1, no. 3, pp. 187–196, 1986.

4. L. M. Ni and P. K. McKinley, "A survey of wormhole routing techniques in direct networks," *IEEE Computer*, vol. 26, pp. 62–76, Feb. 1993.

5. S. L. Johnsson and C.-T. Ho, "Optimum broadcasting and personalized communication in hypercubes," *IEEE Transactions on Computers*, vol. C-38, pp. 1249–1268, Sept. 1989.

6. C. L. Seitz, "The cosmic cube," *Communications of the ACM*, vol. 28, pp. 22–33, January 1985.

7. NCUBE Company, *NCUBE 6400 Processor Manual*, 1990.

8. R. Duzett and R. Buck, "An overview of the nCUBE-3 supercomputer," in *Proc. Frontiers'92: The 5th Symposium on the Frontiers of Massively Parallel Computation*, pp. 458–464, Oct. 1992.

9. P. K. McKinley, H. Xu, A.-H. Esfahanian, and L. M. Ni, "Unicast-based multicast communication in wormhole-routed networks," in *Proc. of the 1992 International Conference on Parallel Processing*, vol. II, pp. 10–19, Aug. 1992.

10. D. F. Robinson, D. Judd, P. K. McKinley, and B. H. C. Cheng, "Efficient collective data distribution in all-port wormhole-routed hypercubes," Tech. Rep. MSU-CPS-93-8, Department of Computer Science, Michigan State University, East Lansing, Michigan, Apr. 1993.

11. P. K. McKinley and C. Trefftz, "MultiSim: A tool for the study of large-scale multiprocessors," in *Proc. 1993 International Workshop on Modeling, Analysis and Simulation of Computer and Telecommunication Networks (MASCOTS 93)*, pp. 57–62, Jan. 1993.

Session 11:
Scheduling and Allocation
Chair: Fran Berman

A Scheduler-Sensitive Global Register Allocator *

Cindy Norris
norris@udel.edu

Lori. L. Pollock
pollock@udel.edu

Department of Computer and Information Sciences
University of Delaware
Newark, DE, 19716

Abstract

Compile-time reordering of machine-level instructions has been very successful at achieving large increases in performance of programs on machines offering fine-grained parallelism. However, because of the interdependences between instruction scheduling and register allocation, it is not clear which of these two phases of the compiler should run first to generate the most efficient final code. In this paper, we describe our investigation into slight modifications to key phases of a successful global register allocator to create a scheduler-sensitive register allocator, which is then followed by an "off-the-shelf" instruction scheduler. Our experimental studies reveal that this approach achieves speedups comparable and increasingly better than previous cooperative approaches with an increasing number of available registers without the complexities of the previous approaches.

1 Introduction

In order to exploit parallelism at both the multiprocessor and instruction level, supercomputers utilize pipelined, superscalar, or VLIW machines for the node processors. These machines achieve increased performance by overlapping the execution of low level machine instructions such as memory loads and stores, and integer and floating point operations. In order to exploit the available instruction level parallelism in programs and utilize the full potential of the node processors, the compiler includes an instruction scheduling phase which rearranges the code sequence to hide latencies and reduce possible run-time delays [13] [18] [10] [17].

Due to the interdependences between instruction scheduling and register allocation, which allocates registers to values so as to minimize the number of memory accesses at run-time [7] [6] [5] [16] [4] [12], the compiler writer faces the problem of determining which phase should run first to generate the most efficient final code. When register allocation is performed before instruction scheduling (postpass scheduling), the register allocator, in its attempt to reuse the same physical register to avoid spills, may add false dependences between otherwise independent instructions and restrict them from being reordered by the scheduler or scheduled in parallel. However, when instruction scheduling is performed before register allocation (prepass scheduling), the instruction scheduler, in its attempt to reorder instructions to maximize fine-grain parallelism, may lengthen the lifetime of values and thus increase the contention for registers and potential for register spilling. In addition, the spill code produced by the register allocator will not be scheduled in the final code. In effect, the lack of communication and cooperation between the instruction scheduler and the register allocator can result in generating code that contains excess register spills and/or a lower degree of instruction level parallelism than possible.

Only recently have there been strategies developed to introduce some communication of requirements between the scheduler and the allocator such that the two phases can cooperate to generate better code [11] [2] [15]. Experimental results from these groups indicate that the cooperative schemes indeed generate more efficient code than a conventional code generator that treats register allocation and instruction scheduling in isolation. However, strategies either focus on local register allocation, suffer from implementation and compile time expense or have not yet been validated experimentally.

In this paper, we present a simple strategy for cooperation between a global register allocator and an instruction scheduler which avoids both the compilation overhead of multiple invocations of the scheduler and the added implementation complexity of simultaneous allocation and scheduling. Our approach has

*This work was partially supported by NSF under grant CCR-9300212.

804

been to develop a *scheduler-sensitive* global register allocator(SSG), which executes first, followed by an "off-the-shelf" instruction scheduler. This overall organization of the phases has two advantages: (1) By keeping two separate phases, we avoid the complexities of attempting to perform register allocation and instruction scheduling simultaneously. (2) By applying the code scheduler after register allocation, spill code inserted during register allocation will be carefully scheduled along with the other instructions during normal execution of the scheduler.

The *scheduler-sensitive* global register allocator is a graph coloring allocator that takes into consideration the scheduler's objectives throughout each phase of its allocation. The potential for code reordering is reflected in the construction of the interference graph. Decisions on what to do when the allocator can not find a coloring are made with regard to both register allocation and scheduling goals. Our experimental studies show that this approach consistently outperforms postpass scheduling and has comparable performance to other cooperative approaches, performing better than previous methods for larger register sets.

We begin with a closer look at previous strategies for cooperative register allocation and instruction scheduling. A detailed description of our *scheduler-sensitive* global register allocator is then presented. The discussion of the experimental results is split into two sections, one focusing on comparing the relative performance of our different scheduler-sensitive register allocation strategies and one focusing on comparisons of our "best" strategy with the other cooperative approaches.

2   Previous Cooperative Strategies

Goodman and Hsu [11] have developed two separate cooperative strategies. In their cooperative postpass scheduling approach, the local register allocator runs first and uses information typically used by the scheduler, namely the data dependence dag, to guide the register allocator in making its allocation, while the scheduler is constrained by dependences added by the register allocator. The test results showed that dag-driven local register allocation significantly improved the performance of postpass code schedulings.

Alternatively, in their second approach, called integrated prepass scheduling, the instruction scheduler is executed first, but is constrained by a limit on the number of registers it has available and thus oscillates in its heuristic for scheduling based on whether the current number of live variables (i.e., variables that have been defined prior to or within this block and

which could be used later in the program execution) has reached the register limit. On highly pipelined machine models, the integrated prepass scheduling approach slightly outperformed the dag-driven register allocation approach.

Bradlee, Eggers, and Henry [2] developed a slightly modified version of integrated prepass scheduling (which they called IPS) in which they calculate the register limit in a different way, replace the local allocator with a global allocator, and invoke the scheduler again after allocation in order to better schedule spill code. Their version of integrated prepass scheduling showed greater speedups than those found by Goodman and Hsu.

Bradlee, Eggers, and Henry also developed a more integrated approach called RASE. A prescheduling phase is run in which the scheduler is invoked twice in order to calculate cost estimates for guiding the register allocator. A global register allocator then uses the cost estimates and spill costs to obtain an allocation and to determine a limit on the number of local registers for each block. A final scheduler is run using the register limit from allocation and inserting spill code as it schedules. Because the scheduler is invoked 3 to 4 times, RASE runs six times slower than postpass scheduling on average without significant improvement in the generated code quality over IPS. In addition, the final scheduler is complicated by simultaneously performing local register allocation with instruction scheduling.

Since submission of this paper, Pinter [15] has published an article describing a cooperative approach based on building a parallel interference graph and some heuristics for trading off between scheduling and register spilling. We are currently studying the relationship between her approach and the work presented here and look forward to her experimental results.

3   Scheduler-Sensitive Allocation

Our goal in developing a cooperative allocation and scheduling strategy has been to improve on Goodman and Hsu by addressing the problem of integrating *global* register allocation and scheduling. However, we wanted a simpler and less expensive scheme than RASE.

Our approach has been to experiment with various ways that a successful *global* register allocator can be made to cooperate with the scheduler without major modifications to either the allocator or the scheduler. Based on its demonstrated success, we selected the *optimistic allocator* (OA) developed by Briggs, Cooper, and Torczon [4] as our base allocator.

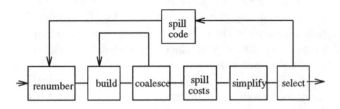

Figure 1: The Base Allocator (Optimistic Allocator)

```
if (P)              if (P)
   v = 3               v1 = 3
else                else
   v = 5               v2 = 5
.. = v ...          v3 = phi(v1, v2)
                    .. = v3 ...
```

Figure 2: Static Single Assignment applied to v

3.1 The Base Register Allocator

Like most global register allocators, OA is based on a graph coloring allocation method, namely, the method developed by Chaitin [6]. An interference graph is constructed in which the nodes represent candidates for physical registers, and edges connect nodes that must be assigned different physical registers because their values will coexist during program execution. Using no more than k colors where k is the number of available physical registers, the allocator attempts to find a k-coloring of the interference graph.

Figure 1 depicts the high level view of the base allocator, OA. The input to the RENUMBER phase consists of intermediate code generated using an unlimited number of virtual registers. In the first step of the RENUMBER stage, the Static Single Assignment (SSA) graph [8] is computed. This representation transforms the code so that each use corresponds to a single definition. To achieve this, virtual registers are renumbered and special functions called phi functions are inserted into the code. For example, in Figure 2, the use of variable v following the *if* statement is either a use of the definition of v in either the *then* or the *else* part. Each of these definitions is subscripted, and a phi function is inserted to indicate that the most recently executed definition is assigned to v3. There are a couple of advantages to rewriting the intermediate code in this form for register allocation and code scheduling. (1) Renumbering can decrease the number of definitions and uses within a single live range

[1] and thus less spill code would be inserted when a live range is spilled. (2) Renumbering eliminates antidependences within each basic block which gives the scheduler more flexibility in choosing instructions for parallel execution.

The RENUMBER stage also determines which values in the program can be *rematerialized*. A value can be rematerialized if it can be recomputed before its use because its operands are always available. A rematerializable value is a good candidate for spilling since the value can be rematerialized, and thus does not need to be stored and reloaded. The final step of RENUMBER eliminates the phi functions added during static single assignment.

The BUILD phase constructs the interference graph. The COALESCE phase eliminates copy statements if the operands of the copy do not interfere. This stage is particularly useful in eliminating the copies added by the RENUMBER stage.

The SPILL COSTS stage determines the costs that will be used in selecting which nodes should be spilled when a coloring can not be found. OA uses Chaitin's computation for the cost of spilling a node. The cost is equal to the sum of the number of uses and definitions of the corresponding live range where each use or definition is weighted by 10^d, d being the depth of the use or definition in the flow graph. This is an estimate of the number of loads and stores that will be executed if the node is spilled assuming that each loop is executed 10 times. This cost is divided by the *benefit* of spilling the node, that is, the number of interference edges incident on the node. An alternative to storing a value into memory is rematerializing the value. The spill cost of a rematerializable value is the number of uses of that value weighted by 10^d where d is the depth of the use, since rematerialization code will be inserted before each of these uses. This cost is divided by the benefit of rematerializing the value, which is computed the same as the spilling benefit.

The SIMPLIFY stage removes each node from the interference graph and pushes it onto a stack for coloring. Initially, nodes with degree less than the number of registers are removed from the interference graph since these nodes will certainly be colorable. Then, the node with the least spill cost is removed and pushed onto the stack. During the SELECT stage, each node is popped from the coloring stack and inserted into the interference graph along with its edges. The node is then assigned a color that is different from all of its neighbors. If the node is not colorable, it is pushed

---

[1] A live range is defined to be the set of definitions and uses where the definitions are all connected by common uses.

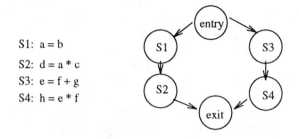

S1: a = b
S2: d = a * c
S3: e = f + g
S4: h = e * f

Figure 3: Data dependence DAG

onto a stack of nodes for which spill code is to be inserted.

The SPILL CODE stage inserts spill and/or rematerialization code into the intermediate code for each node that was not colored by the SELECT stage. The live range for a spilled variable is replaced by a set of smaller live ranges where each live range begins at the point of the load and ends with the use or begins at the point of the definition and ends with the store. The interferences and the set of edges that can be added must be recalculated, and thus the process begins again with the RENUMBER stage. If all nodes are colored during the execution of the SELECT stage, the process terminates.

3.2 A Dag Driven BUILD

The BUILD stage of SSG is significantly different from the BUILD employed by Briggs, Cooper, and Torczon [4] in OA. In their BUILD, the interferences are determined assuming that the given code order represents the final order of the instructions to be executed. In the context of local code scheduling, the interference graph should reflect whether two values interfere given any legitimate code reordering. For this reason, SSG builds the interference graph based on the data dependence DAG which reflects all legitimate code reorderings for each basic block. For example in Figure 3, if we assume that there are no future references to a or b, the variable a does not interfere with variables b and d. There is no ordering of the instructions in which a and b could be simultaneously live. Also, there is no legitimate ordering of the instructions which result in variables a and d being simultaneously live. However, the statements could be executed in the order: S1, S3, S2, S4 which would result in variables e and a being simultaneously live. Thus, the interference graph must reflect that a and e interfere.

A node in the interference graph is created for each

virtual register in the program, and edges are added by considering each definition as it is encountered during the forward scan. When a definition, $v_i = ...$ is encountered, an interference is added between v_i and any virtual register which is live both on entrance to and exit from the basic block. If a variable v_j is live on entrance to a basic block but not on exit, then an interference between v_i and v_j is added if not all uses of v_j are ancestors of v_i in the DAG. Similarly, for each previously encountered definition, v_k, within the basic block, an interference between v_i and v_k is added if all uses of v_k are not ancestors of v_i. The ancestor information can be easily determined by computing the transitive closure of the data dependence DAG.

Although the interference graph now reflects the maximum freedom of code reordering by the code scheduler, the increased number of interferences will make the register allocator's task more difficult as it will be less able to color the larger graph. The ideal situation would be to accurately predict the ordering that the scheduler would select and only include the interference edges that reflect that ordering. However, we want to avoid multiple invocations of the scheduler. An alternative is to remove interference edges from the graph built from the dependence DAG which correspond to code orderings that would be least likely selected by the code scheduler. In particular, an interference between two variables, v_i and v_j, can be eliminated by adding DAG edges which make all uses of v_i ancestors of the definition of v_j or vice-versa. Some interferences are impossible to eliminate by the addition of DAG edges either because one or both of the values are global or because adding edges would add a cycle to the DAG.

When adding DAG edges to reduce the number of interferences, three concerns must be addressed. First, it would be best to add edges which would not force the scheduler to schedule instructions in an order which it would not choose if those edges were not added. If edges are added from the uses of v_i to the definition of v_k, then these edges are said to be *scheduler-sensitive* if the scheduler would choose to schedule the instructions containing the uses before the instruction containing the definition anyway. Second, it is desirable to avoid adding edges to eliminate interferences when there are already sufficient registers available to meet the register demand. If the register demand of a basic block does not exceed the number of registers, then it is unnecessary to add DAG edges for that basic block. Third, it is desirable to add DAG edges in a way that adds the least amount of overhead at compile time.

The first concern is addressed by attempting to anticipate the instruction order selected by the scheduler. A significant factor used by the scheduler in determining the execution order of the basic block is the cumulative cost of nodes in the DAG. The cumulative cost of a node n in the DAG is the minimum number of cycles required to execute the subgraph of the DAG rooted at n. If the cumulative cost of all uses is much greater than the cumulative cost of the definition, then SSG assumes that the scheduler will choose to schedule the instructions containing the uses prior to the instruction containing the definition.

The second concern is addressed by estimating the register demand of a basic block. We estimate the demand as the sum of the number of variables live on entrance and the number of definitions within the basic block. Since this information is available before register allocation begins, DAG edges can be added to a basic block in the early phases before the interference graph is even built.

The third concern is addressed by adding DAG edges during the point in the allocation where doing so is cheapest in compile time. DAG edges can be added at three different points (in order of cost): prior to the BUILD, during the BUILD and during the SIMPLIFY stage. In order to decrease the cost of identifying the interferences that can be eliminated by DAG edges during the SIMPLIFY phase, we make the determination of whether an interference can be eliminated by adding DAG edges while we are identifying interference edges to be included in the interference graph. This information is readily available at this time and saved in an *edgeblock* matrix to be utilized when DAG edges are added during the SIMPLIFY phase.

3.3 Removing Interferences in BUILD

We identified and experimentally evaluated three strategies for adding DAG edges in the BUILD stage. Our first strategy, called *No Edges*, is to add no DAG edges in the BUILD phase. The advantage of this technique is that edges will only be added as necessary to avoid spilling a node in the SIMPLIFY phase. The disadvantage is that the interference graph will contain more interferences than if DAG edges were added in the BUILD, and in addition, all added DAG edges will be added during the SIMPLIFY phase where the compilation expense is higher.

Our second strategy, called *Before BUILD*, is to add DAG edges prior to actually constructing the interference graph in addition to adding DAG edges during SIMPLIFY. The DAG edges added at this point in the allocation are the cheapest edges in terms of compilation expense. Generally, after an edge is added, the transitive closure is computed in order to prevent the addition of edges forming a cycle. Also, the cumulative costs of nodes within the DAG can change, requiring the recomputation of those costs. The set of edges that we select to add to a DAG prior to building the interference graph does not require recomputation of either the transitive closure or the cumulative costs.

The *Before BUILD* strategy is to identify the blocks where the estimated register demand exceeds the number of available registers and add all edges from all n statement nodes, S_{1i}, $i = 1..n$, which use variable, v_k, to a statement node, S_2, which defines a variable, v_i, when the following conditions hold:

1. The cumulative cost of each S_{1i}, $i = 1..n$ is greater than the cumulative cost of S_2. This restriction adds only scheduler-sensitive edges, and also prevents the need to recompute cumulative costs.

2. The statement number of S_{1i}, $i = 1..n$ is less than the statement number of S_2 in the original sequential ordering of the basic block. This restriction prevents the need to recompute the transitive closure between the addition of edges because adding edges that meet this requirement does not create a cycle.

The disadvantage of this approach is that it may add unnecessary DAG edges. Estimating the register demand is an attempt to prevent the addition of unnecessary DAG edges, but our current estimate is an upper bound on the register demand, and the actual demand may be less.

Our third strategy, called *Before & During BUILD*, is to add DAG edges while the interference graph is being built in addition to adding edges prior to BUILD. The cheapest scheduler-sensitive DAG edges in terms of compile time expense are the ones we added before BUILD. However, there could still be scheduler-sensitive edges left in the DAG that do not cause a cycle, but are directed from a later statement to an earlier statement in the original code sequence, (ie., Condition 2 does not hold.). The transitive closure must be computed between the addition of edges to insure that future DAG edges will not create a cycle in the dependence graph. The transitive closure operation is performed incrementally for increased efficiency.

3.4 Weighted Spill Costs

The cost estimates for spilling a node and rematerializing a value can be made to be scheduler-sensitive by incorporating the time to execute instructions into the weights of the spill cost estimates. A memory access is generally several cycles slower than the time to execute an instruction to rematerialize a value. That is, the load instruction prior to the use of a variable that has been spilled will cause more delay than the rematerialization instruction prior to the use if the value were rematerialized. To reflect this, we use the original OA cost estimate for rematerializing a node, but we slightly modify Chaitin's spill cost estimate for spills into memory. Our scheduler-sensitive spill cost estimate, which we call *Weighted Chaitin*, weights the cost for a use by 10^d times the number of cycles required before a value for which a load is issued can actually be used. We do not change the weight on the definitions of spilled nodes.

3.5 Spill, Rematerialize, or Add Edges?

The interference graph is first simplified in the SIMPLIFY stage by removing each node which has less than k neighbors where k is the number of available registers. When no more nodes can be removed from the interference graph in this way, SSG first finds the node with the least spill cost and then has two choices: (1) it can remove a node from the graph with least spill cost or (2) it can add edges to one of the basic block DAGs in order to eliminate enough interferences to continue simplifying the graph. We have developed and experimentally evaluated three different strategies for selecting which DAG edges should be added at this point during the SIMPLIFY stage. We first describe the measure that is used in comparing different DAG edge candidates.

Any DAG edges which increase the cumulative cost of the root increase the minimum number of cycles required to execute the basic block. For this reason, the cost associated with each DAG edge is defined to be one plus the difference between the cumulative cost of the sink and the cumulative cost of the source. (One is added to account for issuing the sink instruction along this new path.) If this cost is nonpositive, then the cumulative cost of the root of the DAG will not be changed by adding the DAG edge. Note that a set of DAG edges, although generally small, is added to eliminate a single interference.

3.5.1 Removing interferences with *SpillNode*

The *SpillNode* strategy adds DAG edges to eliminate interferences with the node in the interference graph which has been identified to have the least spill cost. The objective of this strategy is to avoid spilling the node by adding DAG edges if possible, but otherwise to go ahead with the spill. Sets of DAG edges are added to eliminate an interference in order of increasing cost until there are no more edges to add or the

degree of any node in the interference graph becomes less than the number of available registers. If there are no more DAG edges that can be added to eliminate interferences with the spill node and no node has become colorable, then the spill node is simply removed from the interference graph and pushed onto the stack for coloring. By focusing on the spill node when adding DAG edges to eliminate interferences, this strategy avoids any cost of finding a better candidate for eliminating interferences. However, it may not be as important to add edges to reduce the degree of the spill node since it is the cheapest to spill anyway.

3.5.2 Removing interferences with *MaxNode*

The *MaxNode* method attempts to find a better interference graph node for which to eliminate interferences than the spill node. The node selected, the *MaxNode*, is the interference graph node which the *edgeblock* matrix identifies as having the greatest number of interferences that can be eliminated by adding DAG edges. This is not necessarily the node with the highest degree. A node may have a high degree, but it may be impossible to reduce the degree of the node by adding DAG edges. Again, the sets of DAG edges are added in order of increasing cost until there are no more edges to add or the degree of any node in the interference graph becomes less than the number of available registers. If there are not enough possibilities to eliminate interferences with the *MaxNode* so that the *MaxNode* will be colorable, then no DAG edges are added and SIMPLIFY removes from the interference graph the node with the least spill cost. By focusing on *MaxNode*, there is more potential for causing a node to become colorable than the *SpillNode* approach. However, there is a small cost incurred for identifying this node.

3.5.3 Adding the *CheapEdges* first

In contrast to the other two strategies, the *Cheap-Edges* strategy does not focus on a particular interference graph node. Instead, it selects sets of DAG edges that can eliminate interferences in order of cheapest to most expensive. Sets of DAG edges continue to be added until there are no more edges to add or the degree of a node in the interference graph becomes less than the number of available registers. If it is not possible to reduce the degree of any node in the interference graph so that it is less than the number of available registers, then SIMPLIFY removes from the interference graph the node with the least spill cost. This method has the potential of adding edges with the least cost, but the possibility that spilling a node is not considered in this method, so it may choose to add too many edges when spilling may have been more advantageous.

3.6 One More Modification

We found a slight modification to RENUMBER to cause a significant impact on the overall outcome. The final step of the RENUMBER stage is to eliminate phi functions by examining each operand of the phi function and either coalescing or inserting a copy. In order to prevent adding antidependences, the final phase of SSG's RENUMBER does not perform the coalescing; a copy statement is always inserted. These copy statements then may be removed by the COALESCE stage if they do not add an antidependence.

4 Evaluation of SSG Strategies

4.1 Experimental Framework

The performance of SSG has been compared to the performance of the Postpass scheduling approach where a conventional register allocator is followed by a scheduler based on the Gibbons and Muchnick [10] basic block scheduling algorithm. In order to do this comparison, the *optimistic allocator* of Briggs, Cooper, and Torczon [4] was implemented to perform the conventional register allocation. The registers are allocated using a *round robin* approach, because experimental results indicate round robin provides a better allocation in the context of code scheduling and global register allocation than a first fit approach [1].

The register allocators work with code written in iloc, a low-level intermediate code developed at Rice University for the development of optimizing compilers [3]. Iloc code is generated assuming an infinite number of virtual registers. SSG and OA both accept iloc code and the number of physical registers as input and map the virtual registers onto the set of physical registers, rewriting the code in terms of these real registers with spill code added as necessary. SSG may also reorder the code to reflect DAG edges added during register allocation.

The iloc code produced by Postpass and SSG is targeted for a hypothetical medium pipelined machine with pipelined functional units. For this machine, it is assumed that loads take 6 clock cycles, adds take 2, multiplies take 3, etc. A simulator/interpreter is used to determine the number of cycles required to execute the iloc code. For simplification, the register set is assumed to be general purpose, floating point operations

Strat	Number of Registers					
	10	15	20	25	30	Avg
ncc	1.050	1.228	1.253	1.200	1.169	1.180
ncs	0.960	1.186	1.246	1.195	1.162	1.150
ncm	1.039	1.218	1.183	1.123	1.132	1.139
nwc	1.115	1.232	1.262	1.200	1.169	1.196
nws	0.996	1.163	1.229	1.159	1.138	1.131
nwm	1.033	1.249	1.185	1.147	1.132	1.149
bcc	1.048	1.202	1.249	1.198	1.169	1.173
bcs	1.025	1.232	1.247	1.165	1.169	1.168
bcm	1.123	1.245	1.243	1.197	1.170	1.196
bwc	1.097	1.259	1.255	1.198	1.169	1.196
bws	1.135	1.261	1.252	1.186	1.168	1.200
bwm	1.152	1.263	1.247	1.197	1.170	1.206
bdcc	1.050	1.211	1.246	1.194	1.169	1.174
bdcs	0.948	1.205	1.247	1.192	1.169	1.152
bdcm	1.163	1.251	1.260	1.198	1.170	1.208
bdwc	1.124	1.254	1.255	1.194	1.167	1.199
bdws	1.101	1.248	1.248	1.196	1.169	1.192
bdwm	1.100	1.232	1.232	1.198	1.170	1.188

Table 1: Average Speedup of SSG over Postpass

are treated as integer operations, and structural hazards are ignored. The hypothetical machine contains a hardware interlock mechanism, and thus no-ops do not need to be inserted in order to enforce interlocks.

The speedup measurements for SSG were achieved by translating each of the first 12 Livermore Loops [14] into iloc intermediate code and performing classical local and global optimizations. The performance of SSG was evaluated by calculating the speedup of SSG followed by scheduling against OA (conventional) register allocation followed by scheduling. Speedup is defined as $totalcycles(Postpass)/totalcycles(SSG)$ where $totalcycles$ is the number of cycles required to execute the program after completing register allocation and scheduling.

In total, 18 different scenarios of scheduler-sensitive register allocation were studied. We refer to each of these strategies by a name xyz where x is either n for *No Edges*, b for *Before BUILD*, or bd for *Before & During BUILD*, y is either c for *Chaitin* or w for *Weighted Chaitin* spill costs, and z is either c for *CheapEdges*, s for *SpillNode*, or m for *MaxNode*. For example, ncm denotes the strategy of using *No Edges*, *Chaitin*, and *MaxNode* in combination. Table 1 presents the speedups over Postpass for each of the 18 different strategies assuming 10, 15, 20, 25 and 30 available physical registers.

4.2 Results

This section discusses the most prominent results of our experimental studies.

First, we found that adding edges before the construction of the interference graph increases the speedup over not adding edges before BUILD when used in conjunction with *SpillNode* and *MaxNode*. When DAG edges are added during the SIMPLIFY phase, these added DAG edges may eliminate interferences other than the one that the technique is trying to eliminate because these edges may also cause the uses of another value to become ancestors of a different, or the same, definition. Because SIMPLIFY does not account for elimination of these interferences, it may add more DAG edges than necessary to make a node colorable.

In contrast, the *CheapEdges* selection of DAG edges to add in SIMPLIFY and the *Before BUILD* strategy of adding DAG edges in BUILD try to add essentially the same edges, those with the cheapest cost throughout the entire DAG. Since *Before BUILD* adds these edges before the SIMPLIFY phase is reached, the cheap edges added during the SIMPLIFY stage generally will be of positive cost.

An important result of adding edges *Before BUILD* or *Before & During BUILD* is the subsequent reduction in the number of conflicts in the interference graph. We recorded the number of interferences in the interference graph during the first iteration of the SSG algorithm and noted that the *Before BUILD* strategy reduces the number of interferences in the interference graph by 21 % on average over *NoEdges*. The *Before & During BUILD* strategy reduces the number of interferences by 27 % on average. Thus, a large reduction in the number of interferences can be achieved by these two strategies, which causes a significant savings in the memory required to maintain the interference graph.

As we expected, using the *Weighted Chaitin* method for determining spill costs yielded a greater speedup than calculating spill costs by Chaitin's method, because *Weighted Chaitin* eliminates more references to memory by favoring rematerialization over spilling.

The *CheapEdges* parameter used in conjunction with *No Edges* provides a greater speedup than either *SpillNode* or *MaxNode*. *CheapEdges* will add DAG edges of positive cost only after all the negative cost edges have been added. Using *SpillNode* or *MaxNode* in conjunction with *No Edges* does not allow for eliminating interferences by adding these cheap DAG edges.

The *MaxNode* parameter used in conjunction with *Before BUILD* provides a greater speedup than either *SpillNode* or *CheapEdges*. Adding DAG edges via the

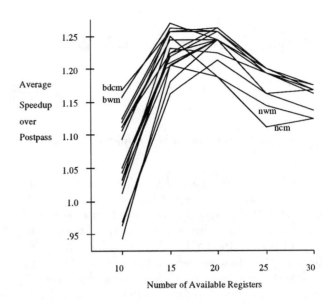

Figure 4: Average Speedup of SSG over Postpass

SpillNode strategy severely limits the number of DAG edges that can be added, because it will only add DAG edges that will eliminate interferences with the node with least spill cost. The *CheapEdges* strategy represents the other extreme in that it could eliminate interferences with any node in the interference graph with degree greater than the number of registers. Also, the least cost edges that *Cheap Edges* could add are a superset of the edges already added *Before BUILD*. The *MaxNode* strategy falls somewhere in between these strategies.

4.3   Choosing the Best Overall Strategy

Figure 4 graphically depicts the average speedups over Postpass for the 18 SSG strategies. The strategies that performed the worst and the best overall are labeled. Except for a few strategies with 10 available registers, all of the strategies outperformed Postpass. Although the performance of the different strategies varied widely for 10 registers, they all hovered around a speedup of 1.17 for 30 registers. Most of the speedups disregarding the 10 register case were between 1.10 and 1.26. The speedups for most of the strategies were the greatest for either 15 or 20 registers. The best average speedup achieved by any of the strategies was 1.26, which was attained by bwm for 15 registers.

The two strategies which provide the best average speedup over all numbers of registers were two *MaxNode* strategies, bdcm and bwm. In order to compare

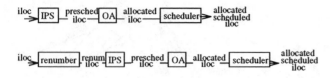

Figure 5: Overview of IPS Implementations

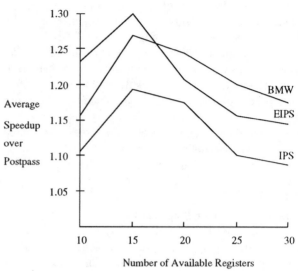

Figure 6: Avg Speedup of BMW, EIPS and IPS

scheduler-sensitive register allocation to other cooperative approaches, we selected the bwm strategy which is to add DAG edges *Before BUILD*, use *Weighted Chaitin* spill cost estimates, and select DAG edges to add during SIMPLIFY based on *MaxNode*. We chose bwm for the following reasons: (1) Adding DAG edges before the interference graph is constructed significantly reduces the size of the interference graph that is built. (2) The *Weighted Chaitin* spill cost estimate in general yielded an increase in speedup over Chaitin's spill cost calculation. (3) Although the bdcm strategy achieved a slightly higher average speedup over bwm, bdcm is more costly in terms of compile time, because adding edges during the BUILD can not be done as efficiently as adding edges before BUILD. Since BMW's are supposed to give great performance, we appropriately renamed bwm to BMW for the comparison against other cooperative approaches.

5   Comparison with Other Approaches

We implemented and compared the speedups over Postpass of our BMW strategy, Goodman and Hsu's Integrated Prepass Scheduler (IPS) algorithm with the improvements suggested by Bradlee, Henry and Eggers [2], and our Enhanced Integrated Prepass Scheduling.

The top portion of Figure 5 depicts the organization of the phases of our implementation of Bradlee's version of Goodman and Hsu's Integrated Prepass Scheduler (IPS) [2] [1] [11]. We chose to use IPS for comparison to SSG rather than the RASE method of Bradlee, Henry and Eggers [2] for several reasons: (1) Bradlee, Henry and Eggers reported little speedup in the RASE method over the IPS method except in the case of very large basic blocks. (2) The IPS method is simpler to implement than RASE due to the simultaneous local register allocation and scheduling phase in RASE.

We found that the performance of IPS can be increased by preceding IPS by the execution of the RENUMBER phase of OA, including the modification to RENUMBER used in SSG, and by using the

Weighted Chaitin spill cost estimate. The organization of the phases in this approach, which we call Enhanced IPS (EIPS), is depicted as the bottom portion of Figure 5. Figure 6 graphically depicts the average speedups over Postpass of BMW, EIPS, and IPS for different numbers of available registers. Both EIPS and BMW outperform IPS in all cases. Table 2 presents the speedups for each of the 12 Livermore loops for various numbers of available registers. The speedup of EIPS is greater than that of BMW for register set size of 10. The BMW strategy performs better than EIPS when register set sizes are 20 and 30.

It is also interesting to compare the percent increase in the number of interferences of EIPS and BMW over IPS. We recorded the number of interferences in the interference graph during the first pass of OA and during the first pass of BMW. On average, when OA is preceded by EIPS, then the number of interferences is 6 % greater than when preceded by IPS. The number of interferences in the interference graph in the first pass of BMW is on average 9 % greater than that of OA when preceded by IPS. These results show that the EIPS and BMW strategies differ very little from each other in the increase in the size of the interference graph over IPS, and on average do not increase the size of the interference graph significantly.

6   Conclusions

In this work, we set out to develop a cooperative global register allocation and instruction scheduling

	Number of Registers					
	10		20		30	
loop	EIPS	BMW	EIPS	BMW	EIPS	BMW
1	1.574	1.514	1.264	1.304	1.121	1.156
2	1.240	1.232	1.390	1.436	1.148	1.205
3	1.068	0.956	1.070	1.068	1.073	1.061
4	1.332	1.230	1.255	1.333	1.234	1.311
5	1.115	1.021	1.065	1.120	1.093	1.120
6	1.444	1.320	1.063	1.063	1.000	1.000
7	1.321	1.026	1.653	1.653	1.533	1.533
8	0.896	1.085	1.084	1.284	1.296	1.453
9	1.309	0.857	1.358	1.347	1.090	1.090
10	0.925	1.060	1.033	0.993	1.013	1.008
11	1.282	1.247	1.078	1.107	1.078	1.107
12	1.277	1.277	1.259	1.259	1.000	1.000
Avg	1.231	1.152	1.214	1.247	1.140	1.170

Table 2: EIPS and BMW Speedup over Postpass

environment with the dual goals of minimizing the amount of modification to each phase while providing speedups over uncooperative approaches which are comparable or better than previous cooperative, more complex approaches. In this paper, we described how we achieved these goals by examining how each key phase of a graph coloring register allocator could be made to be scheduler-sensitive. We experimentally identified which of 18 different scenarios of scheduler-sensitive register allocation gives the best overall speedups over uncooperative postpass scheduling. When experimentally compared with other cooperative approaches, our best scheduler-sensitive register allocation strategy yielded comparable speedups and better speedups with larger numbers of registers.

We believe that the major contribution of this work is that the scheduler-sensitive modifications to the register allocator can be easily incorporated into compilers for superscalar, superpipelined, or VLIW machines with no change to the instruction scheduler. These machines are being used increasingly to exploit instruction level parallelism in conjunction with coarser grain parallelism within supercomputer MIMD systems.

References

[1] D. G. Bradlee. *Retargetable Instruction Scheduling for Pipelined Processors*. PhD thesis, University of Washington, 1992.

[2] D. G. Bradlee, S. J. Eggers, and R. R. Henry. Integrating register allocation and instruction scheduling for RISCs. In *Fourth International Conference on Architectural Support for Programming Languages and Operating Systems*, pages 122–131, Santa Clara, CA, April 1991.

[3] P. Briggs, K. D. Cooper, and L. Torczon. R^n programming environment newsletter #44. Department of Computer Science, Rice University, September 1987.

[4] P. Briggs, K. D. Cooper, and L. Torczon. Rematerialization. In *Proceedings of the SIGPLAN '92 Conference on Programming Language Design and Implementation*, June 1992.

[5] D. Callahan and B. Koblenz. Register allocation via hierarchical graph coloring. In *Proceedings of the SIGPLAN '91 Conference on Programming Language Design and Implementation*, pages 192–203, Toronto, CANADA, June 1991.

[6] G. Chaitin, M. Auslander, A. K. Chandra, J. Cocke, M. E. Hopkins, and P. W. Markstein. Register allocation via coloring. *Computer Languages*, 6:47–57, January 1981.

[7] F. Chow and J. Hennessy. Register allocation by priority-based coloring. In *Proceedings of the SIGPLAN '84 Symposium on Compiler Construction*, June 1984.

[8] R. Cytron, J. Ferrante, B. Rosen, and M. Wegman. Efficiently computing static single assignment form and the control dependence graph. *ACM Transactions on Programming Languages and Systems*, 13(4):451–490, October 1991.

[9] Freudenberger and Ruttenberg. Phase ordering of register allocation and instruction scheduling. *Proceeding of International Workshop on Code Generation – Concepts and Techniques*, 1992.

[10] P. B. Gibbons and S. S. Muchnick. Efficient instruction scheduling for a pipelined architecture. In *Proceedings of the SIGPLAN '86 Symposium on Compiler Construction*, June 1986.

[11] J. R. Goodman and W. Hsu. Code scheduling and register allocation in large basic blocks. In *Supercomputing '88 Proceedings*, pages 442–452, Orlando, Florida, November 1988.

[12] L. J. Hendren, G. R. Gao, E. R. Altman, and C. Mukerji. A register allocation framework based on hierarchical cyclic interval graphs. In *International Workshop on Compiler Construction*, Paderdorn, GERMANY, October 1992.

[13] J. L. Hennessy and T. Gross. Postpass code optimization of pipeline constraints. *ACM Transactions on Programming Languages and Systems*, 5(3):422–448, July 1983.

[14] F. H. McMahon. *FORTRAN CPU Performance Analysis*. Lawrence Livermore Laboratories, 1972.

[15] S. S. Pinter. Register allocation with instruction scheduling: a new approach. In *Proceedings of the SIGPLAN '93 Conference on Programming Language Design and Implementation*, June 1993.

[16] T. A. Proebsting and C. N. Fischer. Probabilistic register allocation. In *Proceedings of the SIGPLAN '92 Conference on Programming Language Design and Implementation*, pages 300–310, San Francisco, CA, June 1992.

[17] S. Weiss and J. E. Smith. A study of scalar compilation techniques for pipelined supercomputers. In *Second International Conference on Architectural Support for Programming Languages and Operating Systems*, October 1987.

[18] H. Young. Evaluation of a decoupled computer architecture and the design of a vector extension. *Computer Sciences Technical Report 603*, 21(4), July 1985.

Self-Scheduling on Distributed-Memory Machines [*]

Jie Liu[†]
Department of Computer Science
Western Oregon State College
Monmouth, OR 97361-1314
liujie@cs.orst.edu

Vikram A. Saletore
Department of Computer Science
Oregon State University
Corvallis, OR 97331-3902
saletore@cs.orst.edu

Abstract

We present a general approach of self-scheduling a non-uniform parallel loop on a distributed-memory machine. The approach has two phases: a static scheduling phase and a dynamic scheduling phase. In addition to reduce scheduling overhead, using the static scheduling phase allows the data needed by the statically scheduled iterations to be prefetched. The dynamic scheduling phase balances the workload. Data distribution methods for self-scheduling are also the focus of this paper. We classify the data distribution methods into four categories and present partial duplication, a method that allows the problem size to grow linearly in the number of processors. The experiments conducted on a 64-node NCUBE show that as much as 79% improvement is achieved over static scheduling on the generation of a false-color image.

1 Introduction

Parallel computers are used to accelerate the execution of time-consuming scientific applications in which loops are the richest source of parallelism [9]. When there exists no data dependence between any pair of iterations in a loop, the loop is a *parallel loop*. For concurrent execution of a parallel loop, the iterations have to be assigned to processors. A specification on the assignment of iterations to processors is a *schedule*, which indicates for each iteration the processor executing the iteration. Since one of the main reasons of employing parallel computers is to reduce the execution time, schedules that render a short execution time is always desirable.

Loops can be found in many applications, and many methods have been proposed to parallelize a wide range of serial loops [8, 10]. Applications where parallel loops have variable iteration execution times are common [16]. In applications such as Monte Carlo calculations, sparse matrix computation, numerical partial differential equation, and image processing, iterations of a parallel loop have variable length execution times[3].

If the execution times of different iterations do not differ significantly, the loop is *uniform*, otherwise the loop is *non-uniform*. One of the difficult problems in concurrent execution of a non-uniform parallel loop is choosing a schedule that minimizes the total execution time of the loop.

To schedule a uniform parallel loop for maximum speedup, an equal number of iterations is assigned to each processor (assuming that processors start executing the loop at the same time). Since iterations of a non-uniform parallel loop have variable length execution times, assigning an equal number of iterations to each processor does not always result in each processor having an equal amount of work. Since the last finished iteration determines the finishing time of the entire loop, balancing workload among processors is a critical factor for performance. This paper discusses the scheduling of non-uniform parallel loops on distributed-memory parallel machines such as the NCUBE and Intel iPSC/2.

The next section presents related work. Section 3 discusses a general approach of implementing self-scheduling schemes on distributed-memory machines, classifies data distribution methods, and introduces new methods. Section 4 shows the experimental results obtained on a 64 processor NCUBE. We conclude this paper and list further research in Section 5.

2 Related Work

The multiprocessor parallel loop scheduling problem can be described as following.

---

[*]This research was supported in part by the National Science Foundation under grant CCR-9210568.

[†]Also with: Department of Computer Science, Oregon State University, Corvallis, Oregon.

Let $I = \{t_1, t_2, \cdots, t_N\}$ be the iteration space of a parallel loop, $e(t_i)$ be the execution time for iteration t_i, and $M = \{p_0, p_1, \cdots, p_{P-1}\}$ be the processor space. N, P, and $e(t_i)$ are positive integers. Further, $D = \cup d_i$, where d_i is a partition of I into P disjoint subsets $I_0^i, I_1^i, \cdots, I_{P-1}^i$, D is a set consists of all such partitions, and $|D| = P^{N-P} \times \frac{N!}{P!(N-P)!}$. The scheduling problem is to find an optimal partition d_o such that

$$\min_{d_i \in D} \left\{ \max_{k=0}^{P-1} \{ \sum_{t_j \in I_k^i} e(t_j) \} \right\} \geq \max_{k=0}^{P-1} \left\{ \sum_{t_j \in I_k^o} e(t_j) \right\}.$$

Except for some trivial cases, such as $P = 1$, $e(t_i)$ are constants, or $P = N$, the yes-no version of the multiprocessor parallel loop scheduling problem is NP-complete [1]; therefore, heuristic approaches have been considered to be the most powerful countermeasures. These heuristic approaches can be classified either as static scheduling or as dynamic scheduling.

In a static scheduling scheme, iterations are assigned to processors before computation. Static scheduling schemes incur no run time overhead. However, they are unable to respond to an imbalance in the workload among processors.

An imbalance in the workload is the problem a dynamic scheme is designed to alleviate. Dynamic scheduling schemes do not assign iterations to processors until the computation is underway. Dynamic scheduling schemes achieve a well balanced workload resulting from a high processor utilization; however, the cost is the additional run time scheduling overhead. In the presence of variable length iteration execution times, dynamic scheduling schemes are in principle superior in balancing the workload[10].

The common approach in the dynamic scheduling of parallel loops is the self-scheduling technique which maintains a global queue of tasks [10, 16, 17]. When a processor becomes idle, the processor removes the next task from the queue and executes it, i.e., processors "self-schedule" themselves as the program executes [12].

In *pure self-scheduling* (PSS) only one iteration is assigned to an idle processor. PSS balances the workload well. However, it does not always yield good performance because the cost of achieving this balanced workload may be so high that it offsets the benefit of balancing the workload. To reduce the high overhead, *chunk self-scheduling* (CSS) allocates a fixed k number of iterations (chunk) to an idle processor. The main drawback of CSS is its dependence on both chunk size

and the characteristics of an individual loop. Worse yet, even for the same loop, the execution time does not monotonically increase or decrease with chunk size because there is no optimal value of k for even the simplest cases [10].

Polychronopoulos and Kuck [10] presented *guided self-scheduling* (GSS). In GSS, $\frac{1}{P}$ of unscheduled iterations are assigned to a processor when it becomes idle. GSS reduces the scheduling overhead by assigning large number of iterations at the beginning. It achieves balanced workload by assigning a small number of iterations toward the end of scheduling process. However, in GSS, the first several chunks may contain too much work and cause an imbalance in workload. In addition, near the end of the scheduling process, GSS assigns many chunks of size one or two iterations. This turns GSS into PSS.

Tzen and Ni [17] proposed *trapezoid self-scheduling* (TSS) to improve GSS by reducing the number of synchronizations. TSS achieves this by linearly decreasing the number of iterations assigned to each processor. In *Factoring* [3], P consecutive chunks form a batch. The sizes of chunks in the same batch are the same. This size is determined using the *no-more-than-half* rule in implementation. The rule states that the chunk size of a batch is no more than half of the chunk size of the previous batch. It is shown in [7] that the no-more-than-half rule can be too conservative.

Liu, Saletore, and Lewis [6] introduced *Safe Self-Scheduling* (SSS). The basic principle of SSS is to assign each processor the largest number of consecutive iterations having a cumulative execution time just exceeding the average workload $\frac{E}{P}$, where $E = \sum_{i=1}^{N} e(t_i)$. Clearly, both $\frac{E}{P}$ and the execution time of a given number of iterations can only be estimated using the statistical information on the execution times of the tasks, the total number of tasks, and the number of processors. The arguments given in [6] are that it is possible to obtain approximations of these pieces of information. The execution times can be obtained through profiling utilities, and the probabilities of a particular execution times can be obtained through sampling [4]. In addition, a program that solves a particular problem usually runs many times to solve different instances of the same problem; therefore, information regarding the parameters used in SSS can be collected from the earlier runs and used to benefit the later runs.

The implementation of SSS given in [6] assigns $\alpha \times \frac{N}{P}$ iterations to each processor at compile time, where $0 < \alpha \leq 1$ (for most of applications we encountered, $0.5 \leq \alpha < 1$). At run time, an idle processor fetches more unscheduled iterations. The ith fetching processor is assigned a chunk of $\max((1-\alpha)^{\lceil \frac{i}{P} \rceil} \times \frac{N}{P} \times \alpha, k)$ iterations, where k is used to control granularity.

This implementation of SSS differs from Factoring in several ways. First, Factoring uses the no-more-than-half rule, i.e., $\alpha \le 0.5$ while in SSS, $0 < \alpha \le 1$. Second, SSS has two phases: a static scheduling phase and dynamic scheduling phase. In SSS, a processor starts to execute a parallel loop with statically assigned iterations and smooth out the uneven finishing times with a self-scheduling scheme. Third, the implementation given [6] assumes that little is known about the iteration execution times. When more information is available, the amount of iterations assigned to each processor can also vary to best fit SSS's basic principle. Fourth, SSS's static scheduling phase increases the affinity between an iteration and the processor that executes the iterations. This property not only further improves the performance of SSS by increasing the ratio of cache hit, but also is the key feature that allows an efficient implementation of a self-scheduling scheme on a distributed-memory machine [7, 15].

The benefit of processor affinity in loop scheduling is also demonstrated by the Affinity Scheduling introduced by Markatos and LeBlanc [9]. Affinity scheduling scheme divides the N iterations of a parallel loop into P chunks of $\lceil \frac{N}{P} \rceil$ each. The ith chunk is placed on the local work queue of processor i. When a processor becomes idle, it removes $\frac{1}{k}$ of the iterations from its local work queue and executes them. When a processor's work queue becomes empty, the processor finds the most loaded processor, removes $\lceil \frac{1}{P} \rceil$ of the iterations from that processor's work queue, and executes them.

The above schemes are all designed for shared memory multiprocessors. To realize the concept of self-scheduling on a distributed-memory machine is much more difficult. First, loop scheduling, by nature, is centrally controlled because each task must be executed once and only once; therefore, mechanisms must be imposed to ensure this. Second, since there is no shared memory to store the task queue used by a self-scheduling scheme, the queue, which is shared, has to be stored on one of the processors. This processor then has to assign the tasks to other processors. Third, for applications that manipulate large amount of data, the data has to be distributed. During dynamic scheduling phase, an iteration should be assigned to a processor that stores the data needed by the iteration. This is not a trivial problem, because data usually has to be distributed before the computation begins while iterations are assigned to processors during the computation. Worse yet, when data needed by an iteration is not stored on the processor to which the iteration is assigned, the data must be sent to the processor. An alternative is to keep reassigning the iteration to another processor until it is assigned to a processor that stores the data. Both approach are very expensive.

Rudolph and Polychronopoulos [13] implemented GSS on distributed-memory machines. They used a centralized scheduling technique that designated one processor to stored the task queue and to perform scheduling only. The data was replicated on every processors.

This straight forward approach has its problems. First, the centralized scheduling technique does not scale very well and the processor performing the scheduling soon becomes a bottleneck as the number of processors increases. Second, the problem size cannot be increased when more processors are available because data has to be replicated. Third, the data distribution method limits the granularity because if we allow an arbitrary assignment of array elements to processors, then the data structure describing the array distribution would have the same number of elements as the array.

Saletore, Liu, and Lam [15] presented the *Distributed Safe Self-Scheduling* (DSSS) for distributed-memory machines. They also introduced a multi-level scheduling technique easing the bottleneck effect caused by a centralized scheduling method.

DSSS also has two phases: a static scheduling phase and a dynamic scheduling phase. The data used in static scheduling phase is prefetched. The chunks assigned in dynamic scheduling phase have the same size. The data associated with a chunk is grouped into a block. Each block is then stored on one processor, which is designated as the owner of the block. The same block of data is then duplicated on a fixed number of other processors. In this way, an iteration can be assigned either to the designated processor or to a processor that stores a duplicated copy of the data needed by the iteration.

3 Distributed Self-Scheduling

In the following discussion, a *scheduling processor*, denoted as P_s, assigns iterations to other processors. A *working processor* requests iteration from P_s and executes iterations assigned to it. In this section, we first present a general approach of implementing a given self-scheduling scheme on a distributed-memory parallel computer. We assume that only one processor acts as P_s. The data distribution policies that correspond to different levels of data requirement are also discussed. Finally, we present a method for decentralizing the scheduling process using more than one processor act as P_s.

3.1 A general approach

We propose an approach that has two phases: a static scheduling phase and a dynamic scheduling phase. In this approach, chunks are calculated using the given self-scheduling scheme. The first P chunks are assigned to the P processors statically. The rest of the chunks are assigned to the processors dynamically. Including of the static scheduling phase reduces the scheduling overhead. More importantly, the data used by the iterations during the static scheduling phase can be prefetched based on the iteration assignment.

In the dynamic scheduling phase, processors are self-scheduled to achieve a balanced workload. The first finished processor in static scheduling phase becomes P_s[1] which assigns iterations to other processors during the dynamic scheduling phase.

Designating a processor as P_s is not necessary during the static scheduling phase because processors do not make any request for iterations during this phase. However, P_s is needed during the dynamic scheduling phase to store the shared information such as the loop index. To store the shared information on more than one processor incurs enormous overhead in maintaining the consistency of these pieces of information. Requiring P_s performing computation in the dynamic scheduling phase may result in a long delay in processing the requests for more work from the working processors.

3.2 Data distribution

One of the problems of scheduling a parallel loop in a distributed-memory environment is that an iteration must be assigned to a processor that stores the data needed to carry out the iteration. Otherwise, the iteration has to be re-assigned (hopefully) to a processor that stores the data, or message passing has to be invoked to bring in the data to the processor to which the iteration is assigned. Both methods are too expensive to be performed frequently. We propose to store data on more than one processors.

Based on how the data is stored and the amount of data stored on more than one processor, we classify the data distribution policies into four categories: (i) total replication, (ii) partial replication, (iii) partial duplication, and (iv) no duplication. *Replication*

---

[1]In practice, identifying the first finished processor is difficult. In our implementation, we always select processor 0 as P_s by assign less iterations during the static scheduling phase.

Table 1: The data distribution categories and the loop scheduling schemes

Data distribution	Scheduling schemes
total replication	GSS, TSS, Factoring, CSS
partial replication	SSS
partial duplication	DSSS
no duplication	Static scheduling schemes

refers to the situation when a piece of data is stored on all the processors. *Duplication* refers to the situation when a piece of data is stored on more than one processor but not all the processors. The data distribution methods and the self-scheduling schemes supported by the methods are listed as Table 1.

How to distributed the data to ensure that an iteration is always assigned to a processor that stores the needed data depends on how predictable a scheduling scheme assigns iterations to processors. For example, if we statically schedule a parallel loop, the assignment of iterations to processors is completely predictable. The data used by an iteration can be stored on the processor that executes the iteration; therefore no data needs to be duplicated. On the other hand, self-scheduling schemes such as GSS assign all the iterations at run time and an iteration can be assigned to any processor; therefore, the data needs to be replicated to all the processors. In a straight forward implementation of SSS on a distributed-memory machine, the assignment of iterations to processors in the static scheduling phase is known; therefore, the data used in this phase can be prefetched and the data used in the dynamic scheduling phase needs to be replicated.

3.2.1 Total replication

In total replication, all the data used by the entire loop is stored on every processor. This method should be used when only a fixed amount of data is needed by the entire loop. In addition, this amount is independent of the problem size and the data is usually not modified. Monte Carlo integration is an example of this case.

Total replication has to be used when all the iterations are assigned to processor at run time. For example, if a parallel loop is scheduled using CSS, the data has to be replicated to all the processors because an iteration can be assigned to any processor. In this case, total replication limits the problem size solvable to be the largest problem solvable on one processor. For instance, if for a particular machine, we can store 1 million integers on one processor, then regardless the

817

number of processors the machine has, the size of similar problems solvable on the machine cannot use more than 1 million integers. This method of distributing data has no scalability. Clearly, this is not acceptable because many scientific computations often scale with the available processing power.

3.2.2 Partial replication

In partial replication, only a part of the data is stored on all the processors. The rest of the data is partitioned into pieces and each piece is stored on a different processor. The data distribution that facilitates SSS is an example of partial replication.

Theorem 1 Let N be the problem size that can be solved using total replication and N' be the problem size that can be solved using partial replication. Assuming that $N' \times \beta$ amount of data is stored without duplication or replication and evenly distributed, where $0 < \beta \le 1$, then we have $N' = \frac{N}{\frac{\beta}{P}+1-\beta}$.

proof: For all the data stored on a processor, $\frac{N'}{P} \times \beta$ amount of data is stored on this processor only and $N'(1 - \beta)$ amount of data is replicated on the processor. Since the amount of memory used by both of these methods are the same, i.e.,

$$N = \frac{N'}{P}\beta + N'(1 - \beta) \qquad (1)$$

By solving N' from Eq.(1) we have

$$N' = \frac{N}{\frac{\beta}{P} + 1 - \beta} \qquad (2)$$

Since $\frac{\beta}{P} + 1 - \beta < 1$, it is always true that $N' > N$, i.e., we can always solve larger problems using partial replication than that of using total replication. For example, when $\beta = 0.9$, then 90% of iterations have their data stored on only one processor and the rest of the iterations have their data replicated. That is, if for a particular machine, we can store 1 million integers of data on one processor, then for a machine with 16 processors, the size of the similar problems solvable can use as many as 6.4 million integers when $\beta = 0.9$ and 9.14 million integers when $\beta = 0.95$.

3.2.3 Partial duplication

Partial duplication is similar to partial replication except that the replicated data is now duplicated to a *fixed k* number of processors. This "fixed k" is independent of the total number of processors. In partial duplication no data (needed by only a particular iteration) is stored on all the processors.

In order to implement the given scheduling scheme, we group the data used by a chunk of iterations and call it a block. Each chunk is calculated according the given self-scheduling scheme, which can be any self-scheduling scheme. The block of data associated with each chunk is stored on some fixed k number of processors, where $1 < k < (P - 1)$, assuming that one of the processors is P_s and it does not perform any computation during the dynamic scheduling phase. Each data block, although duplicated on more than one processor, is *owned* by only one processor which is responsible for updating its values. Every $P - 1$ consecutive chunks of iterations form a round or a batch. Chunk i of the $P-1$ chunks in a round is assigned to a designated processor i. This processor then owns the data of that chunk. A chunk does not have to be assigned to the designated processor during the dynamic scheduling phase. Rather, a chunk can be assigned to any processors that stores the data needed by the chunk. The information on this mapping of blacks of data to processors is stored on P_s.

During the self-scheduling phase, an idle processor sends a request to P_s for additional work. P_s first tries to assign the requesting processor a chunk whose associated data block is owned by the requesting processor. If that chunk in the current round has already been scheduled to another processor, P_s then assigns a chunk *within the same round* that has its data duplicated on the requesting processor. If all such chunks in that round have been scheduled, P_s then attempts to assigned a chunk from the next round in a similar fashion. To achieve a well balanced workload, large chunks are assigned before a small chunk. Since chunk sizes decrease in the later rounds, P_s always tries to schedule larger chunks in the current round before assigning chunks from the next round.

Theorem 2 Let N be the problem size that can be solved using total replication and N' be the problem size that can be solved using partial duplication. Assuming that $N' \times \beta$ amount of data is not duplicated, where $0 < \beta \le 1$, and the rest of data is divided into blocks according to the chunks determined by the given scheme. The data owned by a processor is duplicated on other $k-1$ processors. We have

$$\frac{N \times (P - 1)}{1 + k \times (1 - \beta)} < N' < \frac{N \times P}{1 + k \times (1 - \beta)}.$$

proof: The data stored on a processor comes from three parts. The first part is the data stored on the processor only and has an amount of $\frac{N' \times \beta}{P}$. The second part is the data owned by this processor but also duplicated on other processor. The amount of this kind is $\frac{N'(1-\beta)}{P-1}$. The third part, having an amount of $\frac{N'(1-\beta)}{(P-1)} \times (k-1)$, is duplicated on the processor. Since the amount of memory used by both of these methods are the same, i.e.,

$$N = \frac{N'}{p}\beta + \frac{N'(1-\beta)}{(P-1)} \times (k-1) + \frac{N'(1-\beta)}{(P-1)}$$

we have

$$N = \frac{N' \times \beta}{P} + \frac{k \times N'(1-\beta)}{(P-1)}$$

Clearly, by approximating (P - 1) with P , we then have

$$N > \frac{N' \times (\beta + k(1-\beta))}{P}$$

By approximating P with (P - 1), we then have

$$N < \frac{N' \times (\beta + k(1-\beta))}{P-1}$$

By solving N' we have

$$\frac{N \times (P-1)}{1 + k \times (1-\beta)} < N' < \frac{N \times P}{1 + k \times (1-\beta)}.$$

Theorem 2 reveals two important properties. First, assuming that each iteration needs a fixed amount of data, the problem size solvable using partial duplication is linear in the number of processors. This is an important property because it shows that by using partial duplication, a programmer can always solve larger problems by using more processors without being confining only to static scheduling schemes. Due to the importance of the property, we show it as a Corollary.

Corollary 1 For a parallel loop, if the amount of data needed by an iteration is independent of the problem size and the data is distributed using the partial duplication method, then the size of problem solvable is linear in the number of processor.

proof: From theorem 2 we have that the size of problems solvable on P processors $N' > \frac{N \times (P-1)}{k - \beta \times (k-1)}$, where N is the problem size solvable on one processor. Since both k and β are constants, so we have $O(N') = O(P)$.

The second property is that the selection of k reflects the trade-off between the size of problems solvable and the possibility of an idle processor having the data owned by a busy processor. A large k limits the size of problems because duplicated copies of data need additional memory space, while a small k decreases the chance of an idle processor having the data owned by a busy processor.

3.2.4 No duplication

No duplication refers to the situation where data used by one iteration is stored on only one processor. The only case where no duplication should be selected over others is when the parallel loop is statically scheduled. For applications where the execution times between iterations do not vary much, static scheduling schemes should be used in conjunction with this data distribution method. However, some applications that use static scheduling schemes may experience a poor processor utilization.

As mentioned before, when an iteration is assigned to a processor that does not have the required data the iteration can be re-assigned to a processor that has the data or message passing can be invoked to bring in the data to the processor. If the programmer determines to take these approaches, data does not need to be duplicated. Using either of these approaches may results in a scheduling overhead that is too high to demonstrate the benefit of balancing the workload. Unless loop size is small and the grain size is so large that the message passing overhead can be ignored, these approaches should be avoided.

It appears that this method can be used with Affinity Scheduling scheme [9]. The fact is that in Affinity Scheduling the data may not need be duplicated or replicated initially. However, when a processor executes iterations in another processor's work queue, the data needed by those iterations has to be sent to the processor on which the iterations are executed. This requires the data to be at least partially duplicated. However, the overhead of sending more iterations to an idle processor is higher than that of partial duplication. This is because, first, the messages are much larger because they contains data; second, the message preparation takes longer time because it has to pack and unpack data; third, for each of these messages there are two processors spending time on non computation tasks: the processor that is sending the message and the processor that is receiving the message. In addition, Affinity Scheduling requests an idle processor to obtain more iterations from the "most loaded" processor, an expensive operation to perform on distributed-memory machines.

3.3 Implementing Partial Duplication

To implement the operations in partial duplication efficiently, we propose to use three arrays. The array chunks[] stores the chunks. A chunk is defined by a starting iteration number and an ending iteration number. Chunk i starts from chunks[i] and ends at chunks[i + 1] - 1. The array flags[] has the same size as the array chunks[]. The value of flags[i] is set to false if chunk i has been scheduled and set to true otherwise. The array table[][] has $P - 1$ rows that store chunk numbers. Row i lists all the chunks that have their data stored on processor $i + 1$ in a no increase order in chunk sizes. The value of table[i][0] always indexes an element in the row. When processor $i + 1$ becomes idle, the value of table[i][table[i][0]] indicates the next chunk that will be assigned to processor $i+1$. However, before the chunk is assigned, P_s checks the corresponding element in array flags[] if the chunk has been assigned to another processor. If the chunk has been assigned, then table[i][0] is incremented to index the next element in row i. This process continues until an unassigned chunk is found or all the chunks in row i have been scheduled.

To determine on which processors a block of data is duplicated, we view the processors logically connected in a ring. The data owned by a processor is duplicated on its two neighboring processors. If a chunk whose data is owned by processor $i+1$, then the chunk number is stored in table[i][j] where $j \bmod k$ is equal to 1. A chunk that has it number stored in table[i][j] where $j \bmod k$ is not equal to 1 is duplicated on processor $i+1$. Given a chunk from chunks[c] to chunks[c + 1] - 1, its data is owned by processor $(c \bmod (P - 1)) + 1$.

The above described method of selecting on which processor a block of data should be duplicated is a simple one. The data does not need to be duplicated on the neighboring processors. Other assignment can be chosen as well. In addition, the data may also be stored on more than 3 processors. However, as k increases there is more flexibility in scheduling iterations at run time, but the storage requirement also increases proportionally.

An example of partial duplication

Let us study the scheduling of a parallel loop with 160 iterations on a 5 processors distributed-memory machine, i.e., $N = 160$ and $P = 5$. Assume that the chunks are calculated using SSS with $\alpha = 0.8$; the processors are logically connected in a ring; each block of

Table 2: The elements of array chunks[]

	values								
index	0	1	2	3	4	5	6	7	8
val.	117	126	135	144	153	155	157	159	160

data needed by a dynamically scheduled chunk is stored on three processors, i.e., $k = 3$. The data needed by a chunk is also duplicated on its owner's two neighboring processors.

The static scheduling phase

In static scheduling phase, there are 5 processors performing computation. A working processor executes $\lceil \frac{N}{P} \times \alpha \rceil = \lceil \frac{160}{5} \times 0.8 \rceil = 26$ iterations. Let P_s only execute half of what other processors execute, which is 13 in this example. That is, 117 iterations are scheduled statically. The data associated with these iterations is prefetched.

The dynamic scheduling phase

Dynamically scheduled chunks are stored in the array chunks[] as shown in Table 2. Information regarding which processor stores which block of data is stored on P_s in the array table[][] shown in Table 3. During the dynamic scheduling phase, an idle processor, say processor i, sends a requesting message to P_s for more iterations. P_s then checks table[][]'s $i - 1$ row and schedule the first unscheduled chunk in that row. P_s then increments table[i - 1][0] to index the next element in the row.

For example, when processor 1 finishes the iterations assigned to it during the static scheduling phase, it sends in a message to request for more iterations. P_s receives the message and checks the first row of table[][]. Since table[0][0] is 1, P_s then checks table[0][1] which has a value of 0. If chunk 0 has not been scheduled, then iterations from chunk[0] to chunk[1] - 1 are assigned to processor 1; the value of table[0][0] is changed to 2; and flags[0] is set to false. If chunk 0 is already scheduled, then P_s increments table[0][0] by 1 and checks the chunk indicated by table[0][table[0][0]].

3.4 Decentralizing control

So far, we have assumed that there is only one P_s. When the total number of processors increases, having only one P_s results in sequentialized task assignment to idle processors. Also, frequent requesting messages

Table 3: The elements of array `table[][]`

	values									
Columns	0	1	2	3	4	5	6	7	8	9
`table[0]`	1	0	3	1	4	7	5	8	0	0
`table[1]`	1	1	0	2	5	4	6	0	8	0
`table[2]`	1	2	1	3	6	5	7	0	0	0
`table[3]`	1	3	2	0	7	6	4	0	0	8

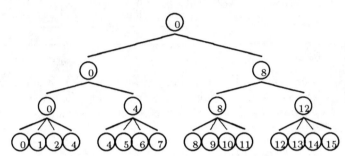

Figure 1: Grouping processors for decentralized control

sent by the idle processors to P_s may cause a bottleneck due to increased traffic.

To solve the sequentialized task assignment problem, more than one processor have to participate in scheduling. If these processors are spread evenly across the system, they may also relax the problem of bottleneck. But this can only be achieved at the increased cost in managing the system. We discuss a method that decentralizes the control by dividing recursively the processors into two or more groups of equal size until each group has only e processors. We call the resulting groups of e processors *leaf groups*. For each leaf group, there is one P_s and $e - 1$ working processors. P_s is responsible for two tasks. First, it assigns tasks to the working processors in the same group to balance the local workload. Second, it communicates with P_ss of neighboring groups to balance the global workload. The optimal value for e depends on both the hardware and the problem itself.

If we assume that the underlying architecture is a hypercube, then the division of processors into two groups of equal size can be performed by dividing the processors along a dimension. For example, for two leaf groups, the processors having most significant bit 0 of their binary addresses form the first group. The rest form the second group. In general, if $e = 2^l$ then all the processors with the rightmost l digits being 0 are P_ss. A P_s's parent processor can be obtained by

```
forall (i=0; i < 250000; i++)
    x = 1.0 + 3.0 * random(&R, &A, &C);
    y = (-3.0) + 7.0 * random(&R, &A, &C);
    z = (-1.0) + 2.0 * random(&R, &A, &C);
    if (sqr(z) + sqrt(sqr(x) + sqr(y) - 3.0) < 1.0)
        {
            /* estimate the weights and linear moments */
        }
```

Figure 2: Code for Monte Carlo Integration

flipping its right most bit that has a value of 1 into 0. Figure 1 gives an example of grouping a 4 dimensional hypercube where $e = 4$. A P_s's sibling P_s at level l can be obtained by flipping the l's most significant bit. Figure 1 shows that there are four P_ss. To improve efficiency, iterations can also be assigned to P_ss in static scheduling phase because no working processor is requesting for work during this phase.

4 Experimental Results

In this section, we present two experimental results. The first experiment uses Monte Carlo method to calculate weight and center of mass for an object. The data is distributed using total replication. The second experiment produces a false-color image. Both experiments are conducted on an NCUBE/7, a distributed-memory parallel computer with 64 processors.

4.1 Monte Carlo Integration

Monte Carlo integration is used to find the weight and the position of the center of mass [11] of a complicated shaped object. It is used when the limits of integration of the volume cannot easily be written in an analytically closed form. Using this method, integral of a function f over the multidimensional volume V, $\int f dV$, is approximated as $\frac{V}{N} \sum_{i=1}^{N} f(x_i)$ over N random points $x_1, x_2, \cdots, x_N$ selected over the volume.

The object in this experiment is defined by three simultaneous equations: $z^2 + \sqrt{x^2 + y^2 - 3} \leq 1$, $x \geq 1$, and $y \geq -3$. Assuming the object has a constant density ρ, we estimate the weight using $\int \rho dx dy dz$ and linear moments using $\int x\rho dx dy dz$, $\int y\rho dx dy dz$, and $\int z\rho dx dy dz$. The coordinates of the center of mass is then the ratio of the linear moments to weight.

The code showing in Figure 2, a parallel loop with one *if-then* statement, is used. In our experiment, the number of iterations, which is the same as the data points selected, is 250,000.

Table 4: Monte Carlo Integration

	Execution time (sec) & speedup in () Sequential execution time 118.962(sec)				
Schemes	4	8	16	32	64
SSS	41.0 (2.9)	17.6 (6.7)	8.3 (14.3)	4.2 (28.0)	2153 (55.3)
CSS	42.3 (2.8)	18.8 (6.3)	9.3 (12.8)	5.0 (23.8)	3051 (38.9)
Static	30.9 (3.9)	15.5 (7.6)	7.9 (15.1)	4.4 (26.8)	2270 (52.4)

Table 5: Generation of False-Color Image

	Execution time (sec) & speedup in () Sequential execution time 81.707(sec)				
Schemes	4	8	16	32	64
SSS(rep)	24.0 (3.4)	11.1 (7.4)	5.5 (14.9)	2.8 (29.5)	1.5 (54.1)
SSS(dup)	24.1 (3.39)	11.3 (7.2)	6.0 (13.6)	2.95 (27.7)	1.7 (48.1)
Static	23.9 (3.4)	13.7 (6.0)	8.5 (9.6)	5.0 (16.2)	2.609 (31.3)

Table 4 lists the results of three representative scheduling schemes. The schemes are SSS [6], CSS with 5 iterations assigned each time, and static scheduling (static chunk). When the number of processors is small, i.e., (smaller than 16 in this case), static scheduling performs the best. As the number of processors increase, SSS schemes performs better. In SSS α is calculated to be 0.88. In this test, the scheduling processor does not perform any computation.

4.2 Generation of False-Color Image

The color image produced by translating a matrix of data into a color presentation is called a false-color image. This technique is often used to display data that is not inherently imaging in nature such as the temperature distribution on a steel board.

In this experiment, each element of the matrix contains an integer ranging from 0 to 1000. Each point is then mapped to a color which is represented by a number ranging from 0 to 255. The computations among different pixels are different because the execution time of the function that maps a data value to its corresponding color differs according to the data value itself. We implemented static scheduling scheme and SSS. For SSS we tested replication and duplication of distributing the data used during the dynamic scheduling phase. The image tested has 512×512 pixels.

Table 5 shows the performances of different schemes. For SSS, a value of 0.55 was used for α and the data in self-scheduling phase is replicated in SSS(rep) and duplicated in SSS(dup), i.e., partial replication policy and partial duplication policy are used to distribute the data SSS(rep) and SSS(dup), respectively. The chunk sizes are calculated using SSS. The improvements in speedup in both SSS(rep) and SSS(dup) over static scheduling come from a better utilization of processors. The overhead of using partial duplication of data

is higher than that of using partial replication of data. This is because a slightly larger overhead is involved in assigning a chunk to an idle processor in partial duplication of data.

5 Conclusions

Self-scheduling schemes are used, essentially on shared memory machines, to schedule parallel loops with variable length iteration execution times not known at compile time. Parallel loops of this form can be found in many applications. With the increasing in the number of processors attached together in a parallel computer, memory tends to be distributed. This paper studies the problem of implementing the concept of self-scheduling of parallel loops on a distributed memory environment.

The approach introduced in this paper uses two phases: a static scheduling phase and a dynamic scheduling phase. In addition to reducing scheduling overhead, using static scheduling phase allows the data used by the statically scheduled iterations to be prefetched. The workload is balanced in the dynamic scheduling phase. Data distribution methods for self-scheduling are also the focus of the paper. We classify the data distribution methods into four categories. We also present *partial duplication*, a method that permits the problem size to grow linearly in the number of processors. To ease the bottleneck of a single processor as the scheduling processor, we have proposed and implemented a multi-level scheduling scheme for parallel loops.

Experiments results show that self-scheduling schemes perform better than static scheduling schemes when the number of processors is reasonable large. As much as 79% improvement is achieved over static scheduling scheme. The partial duplication method of data distribution allows self-schedule a parallel loops of much larger size without a great loss of efficiency.

Further investigations include automating self-scheduling using the method proposed in this paper in a base language such as CHARM [2], a machine independent MIMD parallel programming system. Data distribution methods for multi-level scheduling that maintain efficient iteration execution require more studies.

Acknowledgments

We would like to thank Bob Broeg for his efforts in enhancing the clarity of this paper. We thank Dr. Walter G. Rudd for supporting this research in part. We also thank Yiu B. Lam for testing some of the ideas presented in the paper. We sincerely thank the reviewers for finding of errors, suggesting of improvements, and offering of encouragements.

References

[1] Coffman E.G. (ed), "Computer and Job-shop Scheduling Theory," John Wiley and Sons, New York, 1976.

[2] Fenton W, Ramkumar B., Saletore V.A., Sinha A.B., and Kale L.V., "Supporting Machine Independent Programming on Diverse Parallel Architectures", in *Proc. of 1991 Int. Conf. on Parallel Processing*, 1991, pp. 193-201.

[3] Hummel S.F., Schonberg E., and Flynn L.E., "Factoring: A Method for Scheduling Parallel Loops," *Communications of the ACM*, Vol. 35, No. 8, August, 1992, pp. 90-101.

[4] Kant K. "Introduction to Computer System Performance evaluation," McGraw-Hill Inc., New York, 1992.

[5] Kishor S. T., "Probability and Statistics with Reliability, Queuing, And Computer Science Applications", Prentice-Hall, 1982.

[6] Liu J, Saletore V.A., and Lewis T.G., "Scheduling Parallel Loops with Variable Length Iteration Execution Times on Parallel Computers", in *Proc. of ISMM Fifth Int. Conf. on Parallel and Distributed Computing and Systems*, Pittsburgh, Pennsylvania, Oct. 1-3, 1992.

[7] Liu J. "Shceduling Parallel Loops on MIMD Computers", Ph.D dissertation, Department of Computer Science, Oregon State University, 1993.

[8] Lu L.C. and Chen, M., "New Loop Transformation techniques for Massive Parallelism," YALEU/DCS/TR-833, October, 1990.

[9] Markatos E.P. and LeBlance T.J., "Using Processor Affinity in Loop Scheduling on Shared-Memory," The University of Rochestor, Computer Science Department, TR 410, 1992.

[10] Polychronopoulos C. and Kuck D.J., "Guided Self-Scheduling: A practical Scheduling Scheme for Parallel Supercomputers", *IEEE Transactions on Computers*, VOL. 36, NO 12, December 1987.

[11] Press W.H., "Numerical Recipes in C: The Art of Scientific Computing," Cambridge University Press, New York, 1988.

[12] Quinn M.J., "Designing Efficient Algorithms for Parallel Computers," McGraw-Hill Book Company, 1987

[13] Rudolph D.C. and Polychronopoulos C., "An Efficient Message-Passing Scheduler Based on Guided Self scheduling", in *Proc. of the 3rd Int. Conf. of Supercomputing*, pp. 50-60, 1989.

[14] Saletore A.V., "A Distributed and Adaptive Dynamic Load Balancing Scheme for Parallel Processing of Medium-Grain Tasks", in *Proc. of The Fifth Distributed Memory Computing Conf.*, April 1990, pp. 994-999.

[15] Saletore V.A., Liu, J., and Lam B.Y., "Scheduling Non-uniform Parallel Loops on Distributed Memory Machines," in *proc. of Hawaii Int. Conf. on System Sciences,"* Jan. 5-8, 1993, Vol. II, pp. 516-525.

[16] Tang P., Yew, P. and Zhu C, "Impact of self-scheduling on performance of multiprocessor systems," in *Proc. of 1988 ACM Int. Conf. on Supercomputing*, July 1988, pp. 593-603.

[17] Tzen T.H. and Ni L.M., "Dynamic Loop Scheduling on Shared-Memory Multiprocessors", in *Proc. of Int. Conf. on Parallel Processing*, Vol. II, 1991, pp. 247-250.

Performance Analysis of Job Scheduling Policies in Parallel Supercomputing Environments

Vijay K. Naik
IBM T. J. Watson Research Center
P. O. Box 218
Yorktown Heights, NY 10598.

Sanjeev K. Setia*
Department of Computer Science
George Mason University
Fairfax, VA 22030.

Mark S. Squillante
IBM T. J. Watson Research Center
P. O. Box 704
Yorktown Heights, NY 10598.

Abstract

In this paper we analyze three general classes of scheduling policies under a workload typical of large-scale scientific computing. These policies differ in the manner in which processors are partitioned among the jobs as well as the way in which jobs are prioritized for execution on the partitions. Our results indicate that existing static schemes do not perform well under varying workloads. Adaptive policies tend to make better scheduling decisions, but their ability to adjust to workload changes is limited. Dynamic partitioning policies, on the other hand, yield the best performance and can be tuned to provide desired performance differences among jobs with varying resource demands.

1 Introduction

In recent years, distributed-memory parallel processing systems have matured to deliver excellent performance on many large-scale scientific applications, with the promise of a continued cost-effective growth in performance. These developments in both hardware and software technology make it clear that high-performance parallel systems will be an important supercomputing base. To fulfill this role and achieve the best overall performance, parallel computing systems, however, cannot be used in a fashion where the entire machine is dedicated to a single application, as is often the case. While many applications have exhibited good performance on distributed-memory systems, it is less clear how they will perform on a system that is shared by more than one job. Users of supercomputers expect their individual jobs to perform well. On the other hand, in a supercomputing environment, demands on the resources vary significantly among jobs and system resources must be judiciously distributed

among various jobs to achieve the best overall performance. This objective raises a number of fundamental resource management issues for parallel supercomputing environments which remain open [2]. The allocation of processors among the parallel programs submitted for execution, i.e., job scheduling, is one such issue and is the focus of our study.

Since the resource requirements may vary considerably among the jobs and since the demand on the resources may be unpredictable, in a supercomputing environment, efficient job scheduling that maximizes throughput while maintaining fairness among various jobs has always been a critical issue. In the case of supercomputers based on distributed parallel processing, this task is even more difficult because, in addition to managing the jobs, the scheduler must contend with managing a large number of powerful processors. Distributed parallel systems have traditionally provided only rudimentary facilities for allocating processors to arriving jobs. In particular, the policies most often used consist of *static partitioning* where the processors are divided into a fixed number of disjoint sets that are allocated to individual programs. This approach can lead to relatively low system throughputs and resource utilizations under nonuniform workloads [15, 8, 14], which is common at supercomputing centers. More recently, system implementations have incorporated scheduling schemes that provide some flexibility in regrouping processors into different partitions [3, 10]. *Adaptive partitioning* policies, where the number of processors allocated to a program is determined at job arrival and departure instants based on the current system state, have also been considered [12, 8, 14]. While these approaches outperform their static counterparts by tailoring partition sizes to the current load, the performance benefits can be limited due to their inability to adjust scheduling decisions in response to subsequent workload changes. A *dynamic partitioning* policy, where the size of the partition allocated to a program can be modified during its execution, alleviates these potential problems but at the expense of

---

*Research was partially supported by the National Science Foundation under grant CCR-9002351, while the author was at University of Maryland

increased overhead due to data migration and reconfiguration of the application.

A better understanding is needed of the tradeoffs involved with the above listed general classes of scheduling policies in parallel supercomputing systems executing large-scale scientific applications. Our objective in this paper is to determine a set of principles for the scheduling of large-scale scientific applications in distributed-memory supercomputing environments. We analyze the performance characteristics of the three general classes of scheduling policies described above under a job mix representative of large computational fluid dynamics applications. The analysis is based on steady-state performance measures from both the system and user viewpoints, as well as the transient behavior of these policies in response to sudden workload changes. Our results show that the system scheduling policy must distinguish between jobs with large differences in execution times. We also demonstrate the importance of adjusting processor allocation decisions as a function of the system load, including fluctuations in the job arrival process, in order to provide good performance for the entire workload.

In Section 2, we introduce our modeling analysis and evaluation methodology. Section 3 describes the scheduling policies considered. In Sections 4 and 5 we present our results and conclusions, respectively.

2 Models and Analysis

Current and expected near-future trends for supercomputing centers suggest environments in which jobs with very different resource requirements arrive at various intervals to systems consisting of large numbers of processors. Based on these trends, we define system and application models, as well as the performance evaluation methodology, used to investigate the issues raised in the introduction.

2.1 System and Workload

We consider a parallel supercomputing system that consists of $P = 512$ identical processors each having its own local memory module and delivering sustained execution rates of 100 MFLOPS in the computationally intensive sections of an application. It is assumed that the system processors can be partitioned arbitrarily and that the presence of other jobs in the system has a negligible performance impact on a running job. A general interconnection network supports information sharing among the processors. The network fabric is assumed to be such that every processor-pair is equidistant in the sense that, at the application level,

the same amount of time is spent transferring information between any pair of processors. We also assume that the network bandwidth is sufficient to prevent any performance degradation due to the presence of multiple jobs, which is supported by experience with recent parallel systems. The latency per message, as experienced at the application level, is assumed to be 5 μsec and the average achievable message transmission speed is assumed to be 100 MB/sec.

Arrivals to the system are representative of large-scale scientific applications, and are assumed to come from a Poisson source with mean rate λ. We consider a workload consisting of a mix of jobs with a wide variation in resource requirements, as suggested by recent studies of expected supercomputer applications [13]. Given this large variability in resource demands, the system can (coarsely) classify jobs as being either *small*, *medium* or *large*. We model this by probabilistically determining the class of a job upon its arrival, i.e., an arrival belongs to the small, medium or large job class with probability p_s, p_m and p_l, $p_s + p_m + p_l = 1$, respectively. The resource requirements of a job are chosen uniformly among a set of resource demands associated with the job's class (see Section 2.2).

While the primary resource requirements of most scientific applications are cpu cycles, memory and I/O, in this study we only consider job classification on the basis of cpu demand as this is a key job characteristic for such programs. Our methodology, however, is equally applicable when other job characteristics are used. We assume that the job stream consists of a large number of small jobs, fewer medium jobs, and even a smaller number of large jobs. The probabilities p_s, p_m and p_l were chosen to maintain a 320:8:1 ratio of small to medium to large jobs, which (approximately) represents the ratios of the different per-class mean execution times on a single processor.

2.2 Application Profile

To study job stream characteristics that are representative of actual supercomputing environments, we conducted a detailed analysis of several large computational fluid dynamics (CFD) applications. The parallel applications used in our study were the NAS parallel benchmarks [1] as well as the parallel versions of ARC3D [11] and INS3D-LU [16] which were originally developed at NASA Ames. The computations in these applications are typical of those most used in the aeronautics and automobile industry. While they represent only one class of industrial applications, the above CFD codes provide sufficient insight into the characteristics of the job stream(s) arriving at a typical supercomputing center.

The parallel applications were carefully analyzed for their properties on computation, communication, data dependencies, memory usage, data partitioning, load balancing and scalability. Algorithms were chosen that provide the best possible performance on a given number of processors. The resource requirements of each job represent the actual resource requirements of a complete parallel application. These were obtained by detailed measurement-based analysis of each application. We verified the predicted performance of our analysis, by implementing the applications on Victor V256 and on a network of RS/6000 workstations at IBM T. J. Watson Research Center. Not all applications considered in our study, could be executed on these systems because of memory and time constraints. The resource requirements for these applications were determined by analysis and simulation. We refer the interested reader to [6, 7, 5] for further details on the relevant analysis.

In the present study, a total of 23 different applications were chosen with grid sizes ranging from 4K through 100M. We assume that each parallel application is capable of executing on several processor configurations, but that there is a maximum number of processors, Max_{appl}, on which an application can be executed effectively. For each job, we determined Max_{appl} and the execution times for each possible processor configuration on which the job could be executed. Since each parallel application executes most efficiently on a certain number of processors for a given architecture, such an optimum number of processors may not be equal to Max_{appl}. The optimum number of processors were determined using the efficiency curves. When a job arrives at the system it requests the number of processors on which its performance is optimum, denoted by Req_{appl}.

Table 1 summarizes the characteristics of the 23 applications used in our study. For each job class,

Class	# of Jobs	PEs	Avg. *sec*	Min *sec*	Max *sec*
Small	15	32	412	4	2532
Medium	4	128	4545	1589	7698
Large	4	128	33771	18468	48688

Table 1: A summary of job characteristics.

we list the number of jobs comprising the class and the minimum, maximum and average execution times over all jobs of the class when executed on the specified number of processing elements (PEs). More detailed

job statistics can be found in [9, 14].

2.3 Performance Evaluation

Our analysis of the scheduling policies considered is based on two metrics that measure performance from different perspectives, namely from the system and user viewpoints. The first performance metric, denoted by $\overline{S}$, is mean job response time. Let J_n denote the nth job to leave the system, and define α_n and δ_n to be the arrival and departure times of J_n, respectively. We then have

$$\overline{S} = \lim_{n \to \infty} \frac{1}{n} \sum_{k=1}^{n} S_k \qquad (1)$$

where $S_n \equiv \delta_n - \alpha_n$. Note that system throughput is directly related to $\overline{S}$ by Little's result [4] and, given the above modeling assumptions, is equal to the job arrival rate λ. Thus, $\overline{S}$ measures performance from the *system* point of view.

Our second performance metric, denoted by $\overline{U}$, is the mean ratio of job response time to job service time. More formally,

$$\overline{U} = \lim_{n \to \infty} \frac{1}{n} \sum_{k=1}^{n} U_k \qquad (2)$$

where $U_n \equiv S_n/x_n$ and x_n denotes the service time of J_n on Req_{appl} processors. Note that queuing delays and not being allocated Req_{appl} processors both result in differences between the values of S_n and x_n. Thus, $\overline{U}$ reflects the performance perceived by the *user*.

In addition to these steady-state measures, transient values of S_n and U_n after different bursts of job arrivals are considered. We examine arrival bursts consisting of a single batch of small jobs, as well as a sustained increase in the job arrival rate. This allows us to compare how well the scheduling policies react to sudden changes in the system workload.

The above performance measures are obtained from a stochastic discrete-event simulation which was written using CSIM. A large number of simulation experiments were performed under a variety of workload conditions. In each case, steady-state performance measures are obtained using the regenerative method to within 5% of the mean at 95% confidence intervals. Our transient analysis consists of running the simulations long enough for the system to reach a steady-state condition under each scheduling policy, introducing an arrival burst, and then recording the desired performance metric (S_n or U_n) for subsequent job departures. By "steady-state condition" we mean that the performance estimator remains within 10% of its (previously obtained) steady-state value ($\overline{S}$ or $\overline{U}$) for at least 100 job departures prior to the arrival burst, and thus the 100 measures immediately preceding the burst are (somewhat) representative of the performance measure under steady state. Results for several different sample paths are obtained by repeating these transient simulation runs multiple times with different random number generator seeds.

3 Scheduling Policies

In this section we define the scheduling policies considered in our study, which were first introduced in [8]. We use $Avail_{sys}$ to denote the number of processors available when a job arrives and Min_{sys} to denote the minimum number of processors that the system may assign to a job.

3.1 Fixed Partitioning (FP)

This is the simplest scheduling policy considered, wherein the processors are divided at system configuration time into a fixed number of disjoint sets, or partitions, of equal size. We use $FP(x \times P/x)$ to denote the policy under which there are x partitions each of size P/x.

When a job arrives to the system, it is allocated a partition if one is available. Otherwise, the job waits in a system queue until a partition becomes free. A *first-come first-served* (FCFS) queuing discipline is used for the system queue.

3.2 Adaptive Partitioning (AP)

Instead of having fixed partitions, the AP policy adjusts the size of the partition allocated to a job according to the current system state. When a job arrival finds more than Min_{sys} idle processors, the system allocates to it a partition of size $\min(Req_{appl}, Avail_{sys})$. If fewer processors are idle, the job is placed in a FCFS system queue. When the execution of a job completes, the released processors are divided equally among the waiting jobs under the constraint that no job is assigned more than Req_{appl} or less than Min_{sys} processors. Any jobs remaining in the system queue must wait until additional processors become available due to subsequent job completions.

The AP policy adapts to changes in system load, as reflected by the system queue length. Under light traffic intensities, the number of processors allocated to a job tends toward that requested by the job, whereas at heavy loads the job partition size will be smaller than the job request.

3.3 Fixed Partitioning with Job Priorities (FPJP)

This policy is similar to the FP policy with the exception that the scheduler includes job class information in its allocation decisions. Each partition is designated as "belonging to" a certain class of jobs, and a separate queue is maintained for each job class. Access to a partition is prioritized on the basis of the partition's class, such that jobs of the same class have nonpreemptive priority over jobs of different classes. In addition, larger job classes cannot acquire partitions belonging to smaller job classes, while small jobs have nonpreemptive priority over medium jobs for large job partitions.

Upon the arrival of a large job, the system allocates to it a large job partition if one is available. Otherwise, the arriving job waits in a FCFS queue associated with the large job partitions. When the execution of a large job completes, the available partition is allocated to the job at the head of the large job queue. If this queue is empty and the system contains waiting small jobs, the partition is allocated to the job at the head of the small job queue. When this queue is also empty, the partition is allocated to the job at the head of the medium job queue, if any. The medium job class is handled in a similar manner subject to the policy constraints defined above.

A small job arrival is allocated any of the available partitions in the system, including those belonging to medium and large jobs. If no such partition is available, the job waits in a queue associated with the small job partitions. When the execution of a small job completes, the available partition is allocated to the job at the head of the small job queue. If this queue is empty, the partition remains free until a small job arrives.

We use $FPJP(x,y,z)$ to denote the policy under which x, y and z processors are allocated to partitions belonging to small, medium and large jobs, respectively. Various (fixed) subdivisions of the per-class x, y and z allocations are possible under FPJP.

3.4 Dynamic Partitioning (DP)

This policy is similar to the AP policy with the exception that the partition of processors allocated to a large or medium job can be modified during the job's execution. We therefore assume that these applications are capable of reconfiguring themselves in response to requests from the operating system in a cooperative manner. The system scheduler maintains a list of running jobs that can be reconfigured, which we call the *interruptible list*. After a medium or large job reconfigures itself, the job is removed from this list and is not eligible for reconfiguration until a certain time interval, denoted by T, has elapsed.

If an arriving job requests at most $Avail_{sys}$ processors, then the job is allocated a partition of size Req_{appl}. However, if $Req_{appl} > Avail_{sys} \geq Min_{sys}$ and the interruptible list does not contain a job whose partition size is greater than P/N, where N denotes the current number of jobs in the system, then the job arrival is allocated all of the available processors. Otherwise, the system scheduler notifies one or more of the jobs on the interruptible list with partitions larger than P/N to reduce their partition size to P/N, provided that $P/N \geq Min_{sys}$. To minimize the number of interrupted jobs, the system attempts to free up just enough processors so that the total number of available processors is close to $\min(Req_{appl}, P/N)$.

Upon the release of processors, including that due to a job completion, the available processors are divided equally among the waiting jobs, if any, under the constraint that no job receives less than Min_{sys} or more than Req_{appl} processors. If the number of available processors exceeds a policy parameter M and the interruptible list contains a job whose current partition size is less than P/N, then the system scheduler notifies that job to increase its allocation to $\min(P/N, S + M/2, Req_{appl})$, where S denotes the job's current partition size. Thus, at most half of the available processors are allocated to one of the large or medium jobs on the interruptible list. Note that the policy parameters M and T can be used to control the rate at which large and medium jobs are reconfigured.

When a job is notified by the scheduler to modify its partition size, the application initiates a reconfiguration at the next programmer-defined reconfiguration point, e.g., at the end of the current iteration. This reconfiguration is realized in two phases. In the first phase, the entire data set representing the current state is transferred from all processors in the old partition to a subset of Min_{sys} processors in the new partition. In the second phase, the data set is then redistributed from this subset to all processors in the new partition. This two-phase scheme is used for both increasing and decreasing the partition size. If the partition size is to be increased, the application adds the newly-acquired processors to its partition before commencing the first phase of reconfiguration, whereas if the partition size is to be reduced, the application releases the excess processors to the system scheduler at

the end of the first phase.

4 Results

In this section we consider the performance characteristics of job scheduling policies within the context of our modeling analysis, as described in Sections 3 and 2, respectively. Our main objective is to determine a set of principles for the scheduling of large-scale scientific applications in distributed-memory supercomputing environments. The performance measures of interest are mean job response time (i.e., $\overline{S}$), mean ratio of job response time to job service time (i.e., $\overline{U}$) and transient values of S_n and U_n. Our results, a portion of which follow, were obtained as described in Section 2.3. Additional results can be found in an extended version of the paper [9].

Throughout our experiments, we assumed that processors were allocated in units of 4 and that $Min_{sys} = 32$. The FP($x \times 512/x$) policies considered are those for which $x \in \{1, 2, 4, 8, 16\}$. Several FPJP(x,y,z) policies were considered, most notably those with $x \in \{128, 192, 256\}$, $y \in \{128, 192\}$ and $z \in \{128, 192\}$ such that $x + y + z = 512$. We also considered various subdivisions of the per-class partitions under FPJP, as well as different values for M and T under DP. The results presented in this section are for the parameters that provided the best performance.

4.1 System Performance

Our first set of results compares system performance under each of the different scheduling policies as measured by $\overline{S}$. We observe that the optimal partition size for the FP policies, i.e., that which provides the smallest $\overline{S}$, varies with the job arrival rate. When λ is small the FP(1×512) policy yields the best performance, but as system load increases, first the FP(2×256) policy and then the FP(4×128) policy provide the smallest $\overline{S}$. We also observe that the AP policy performs as well as the best FP policy for a given value of λ. These results, which are not shown in the interest of space, demonstrate that the system scheduling policy must reduce the number of processors allocated to each job with increasing system load. Similar trends have been observed under a different workload mix [8, 14], as well as under different system and application assumptions [12, 15].

In Figure 1, we plot $\overline{S}$ as a function of λ for the AP, FPJP(128,128,256), FPJP(128,192,192) and DP policies. Similar results for equation (1) taken over the individual small, medium and large job classes are plotted in Figures 2, 3 and 4, respectively. As noted

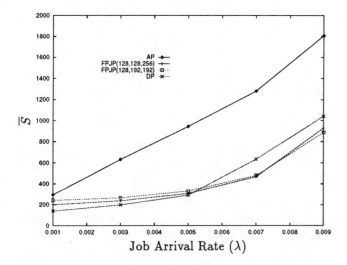

Figure 1: Mean System Performance as a function of λ under AP, FPJP and DP.

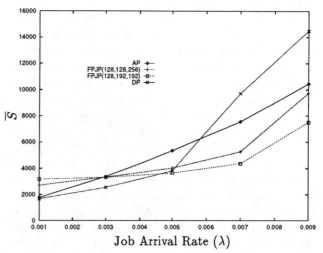

Figure 3: Mean System Performance of Medium Jobs as a function of λ under AP, FPJP and DP.

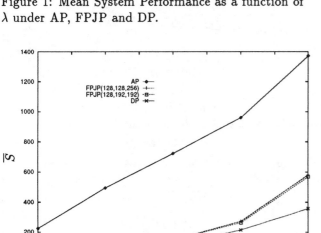

Figure 2: Mean System Performance of Small Jobs as a function of λ under AP, FPJP and DP.

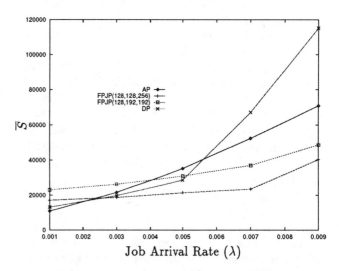

Figure 4: Mean System Performance of Large Jobs as a function of λ under AP, FPJP and DP.

above, the AP curves also illustrate the performance of the best FP policy for a given arrival rate. Moreover, since the FPJP results are for optimal subpartition sizes, and since the AP policy performs as well as the best FP policy, the FPJP curves represent the performance of a policy under which each of the per-class partitions are subdivided in an adaptive manner similar to the AP policy.

We observe that the AP policy performs poorly in comparison to the FPJP and DP policies, particularly for the small job class. This is because the AP policy does not distinguish between the different job classes in its allocation decisions. When λ is small, the policy

tends to allocate a large number of processors to each arriving job because the number of available processors is relatively large while the number of waiting jobs is relatively small. Allocating large partitions to medium and large jobs decreases their execution time, and hence their $\overline{S}$, but tends to increase the time small jobs must wait in the system queue for processors to become available. The performance impact of this behavior increases with λ, and even the response times of medium and large jobs suffer due to being executed on smaller numbers of processors. These results show that the system scheduling policy must distinguish between jobs with large differences in execution times when making allocation decisions.

The FPJP policies eliminate this behavior by restricting the maximum number of processors acquired by a medium and large job. In particular, these policies perform quite well across most λ ranges for each of the different job classes. Increasing the number of processors belonging to a specific class decreases $\overline{S}$ for that class at the expense of increasing response times for the other classes, as expected. Since small jobs can acquire partitions belonging to any class, and have nonpreemptive priority over medium jobs for large job partitions, $\overline{S}$ for small jobs is less sensitive to changes in the partition sizes for medium and large jobs.

We observe that the DP policy also eliminates the problems identified above for the AP and FP policies. In particular, the DP policy provides the best performance for small jobs. This is because the scheduler can interrupt a running medium or large job and allocate some of its processors to a newly arrived small job, thus reducing the time small jobs wait in the system queue. The DP policy also yields the best performance for medium and large jobs when λ is small because a relatively large number of processors are allocated to these job classes under light loads. This policy outperforms the FPJP policies for these loads because medium and large jobs can utilize processors that would otherwise be idle under the FPJP policies. As λ increases, however, the best performance for small jobs is obtained at the expense of a significant increase in the mean response time for medium and large jobs.

We note that the increase in $\overline{S}$ for these larger job classes at heavy system loads is not due to the reconfiguration overhead. In [9, 14] we provide reconfiguration statistics for large and medium jobs obtained from our simulations of the DP policy. While not insignificant, these overheads represent a relatively small fraction of the response times for medium and large jobs. The increase in $\overline{S}$ results from the fact that the average partition size for these classes at heavy system loads is much smaller than their partition sizes under the FPJP policies. When the traffic intensity is high the number of small jobs in the system tends to be large. This decreases the number of processors allocated to medium and large jobs under DP. We also observe that the average number of reconfigurations that reduce the size of a partition is somewhat greater than those which increase the partition.

4.2 User Performance

Our next set of results compares the performance of each of the different scheduling policies as measured by $\overline{U}$. From the user viewpoint, this is the measure of interest as it represents the response time relative to the inherent resource demands of the job. In Figure 5 we plot the values of equation (2) taken over the individual small, medium and large job classes under the DP policy as a function of λ. Similar results for the

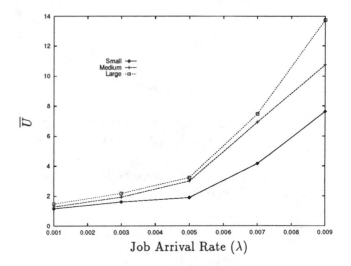

Figure 5: Mean User Performance for each Job Class as a function of λ under DP.

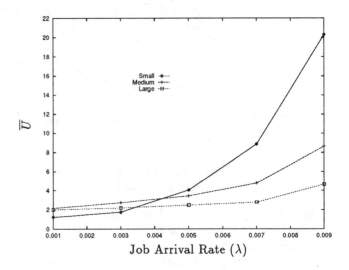

Figure 6: Mean User Performance for each Job Class as a function of λ under FPJP(128,128,256).

FPJP(128,128,256) policy are provided in Figure 6. Note that these curves illustrate a relative factor by which the service received by jobs changes with system load. We first observe that the values of $\overline{U}$ across all job classes are comparable when λ is small. Since contention for the processors is small under both policies at light loads, each job spends relatively little time waiting in the system queue for a partition and the number of processors it eventually receives is relatively close to Req_{appl}. As expected, $\overline{U}$ increases with system load. This is due to the fact that the number of jobs in the system increases with λ, thus increasing the time jobs spend waiting in the queue.

We note that the DP policy tends to reduce the amount of time a job spends in the system queue, at the expense of potentially increasing the job execution time by allocating it a relatively small number of processors. Since Min_{sys} is not too small ($Min_{sys} = 32$), the system queuing time is the dominant factor in the response time of small jobs. By reducing this factor, DP yields the best $\overline{U}$ for the small job class across all system loads. The job execution time, however, is a relatively important factor in the response time of medium and large jobs. Since the DP policy decreases the number of processors allocated to jobs with increasing λ, the job execution time becomes the dominant factor in the response time of medium and large jobs at heavier system loads. This explains the sharp increase in $\overline{U}$ for these larger job classes with increasing λ.

We observe that the converse is true under the FPJP policies where the $\overline{U}$ value for small jobs increases very sharply with system load (note the difference in scale with Figure 5) while its value for the large job class remains almost constant (increasing slightly at $\lambda = 0.009$). The FPJP policies restrict the minimum number of processors allocated to medium and large jobs, thus limiting the rise in execution times for these job classes. This is obtained, however, at the expense of increasing the amount of time jobs spend waiting in the system queue, which has a major impact on the response time of small jobs.

4.3 Transient Analysis

Our next set of results compares how well the scheduling policies react to sudden changes in the system workload. Bursts of increased arrival activity tend to be transitory in most supercomputing environments. To address this situation, as well as compare how quickly the effect of an arrival burst dissipates under the different policies, we consider the case where the job arrival rate remains fixed while the system incurs a one-time burst consisting of a single batch of small jobs. Several different batch sizes were examined. The following results are for a batch size of 10, as these highlight the trends exhibited for all of the batch sizes considered.

In Figure 7 we plot the values of U_{t+s} under the

DP policy for $0 \leq s \leq 400$ and $\lambda = 0.007$, where the arrival burst occurs at time δ_{t+100} and t represents a job departure that satisfies the steady-state condition (see Section 2.3). Results for several dif-

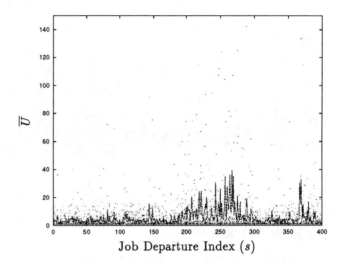

Figure 7: Transient User Performance as a function of Job Departure Index under DP with a Single Arrival Burst.

ferent sample paths were obtained by repeating the transient simulation runs 10 times with unique random number generator seeds. Thus, 10 different U_{t+s} data points are reported for each job departure index s. Each of these sample points are illustrated as dots in the figure. The dashed line depicts the average of the 10 data points for a given value of s. Similar results for the FPJP(128,128,256) policy are provided in Figure 8. We observe that the FPJP policy yields a significantly higher variance in the values of U_{t+s} than those obtained under DP, even in steady-state (i.e., $0 \leq s \leq 100$). We also find that the impact of the single burst under the DP policy has a smaller magnitude for both the sample points and their averages, and dissipates much more rapidly than under FPJP. Increasing the batch size magnifies these trends.

To further examine how well the policies react to sudden workload changes, we have also briefly considered the case where the burst consists of a sustained increase in the job arrival rate. Our preliminary simulation results suggest that the DP policy adapts more quickly than FPJP to the sudden change in workload. Moreover, the magnitude of performance degradation under the FPJP policy is much greater than that realized under DP.

Our results demonstrate that the DP policy tends to handle periods of low and high traffic intensities

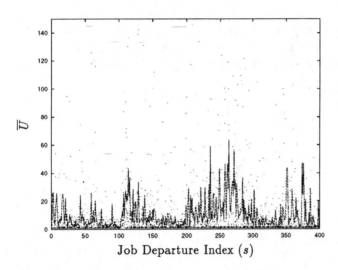

Figure 8: Transient User Performance as a function of Job Departure Index under FPJP(128,128,256) with a Single Arrival Burst.

better than the other scheduling policies considered. This is due to the fact that only DP can take advantage of idle processors during such periods of low activity by dynamically increasing the size of the partitions allocated to long-running jobs. Similarly, the DP policy reacts the fastest to any sudden burst in arrivals by quickly adjusting its current allocations of processors, whereas the other policies must wait until the jobs in execution depart before any changes in processor allocations are possible.

5 Conclusions

Current and near-future trends for supercomputing centers suggest environments in which jobs with very different resource requirements arrive at various intervals to systems consisting of large numbers of processors. In this paper we investigated the impact of these trends on general classes of job scheduling policies. Our main objective was to determine a set of principles for the scheduling of large-scale scientific applications in distributed-memory environments. We conclude by summarizing these scheduling principles and by briefly discussing how an actual implementation can be designed to incorporate these principles in its processor allocation decisions.

Our analysis demonstrates that the system scheduling policy should reduce the number of processors allocated to each job with increasing load, up to a minimum number of processors, in order to provide good performance for the entire workload. These processor allocation decisions should distinguish be-

tween jobs with large differences in execution times, where increasing the performance of a particular job class, from both the system and user viewpoints, tends to be obtained at the expense of decreasing the performance of the other classes. Our analysis further demonstrates the importance of having a scheduling policy that adapts appropriately to periods of low and high arrival activity, a common scenario in most supercomputing environments.

The DP policy is one approach that is capable of realizing all of these key scheduling objectives. Our results show that DP yields the best performance for small jobs while exhibiting poorer performance for the medium and large job classes. The converse is true under the FPJP policy. It is important to note, however, that the benefits of both the DP and FPJP policies can be obtained by appropriately choosing the minimum partition sizes on a per-class basis (instead of a single Min_{sys} value) under DP, as well as by adjusting the parameters that control the rate of reconfiguration. In this manner, the desired performance differences among the various job classes can be achieved under a judiciously parameterized DP policy, without imposing burdensome demands on the users or the system administrator.

Acknowledgements

We would like to thank Phil Heidelberger for fruitful discussions regarding the transient analysis of our study.

References

[1] D. Bailey, J. Barton, T. Lasinski, and H. Simon. The NAS Parallel Benchmarks. NASA Ames Research Center Technical Report No. RNR-91-002, 1991.

[2] R. Carter, C. Kuszmaul, and B. Nitzberg. System level requirements for multidisciplinary applications on highly parallel systems. In *Computational Aerosciences Conference*, 1992.

[3] *The Connection Machine CM-5 Technical Summary*, Thinking Machines Corp., Cambridge, Mass., 1992.

[4] J. D.. C. Little. A Proof of the Queuing Formula $L = \lambda W$. *Operations Research*, vol. 9, 1961.

[5] N. H. Naik, V. K. Naik, and M. Nicoules. Parallelization of a class of implicit finite difference

schemes in computational fluid dynamics. *Int. J. High-speed Computing*, vol. 5, 1993.

[6] V. K. Naik. Performance Effects of Load Imbalance in Parallel CFD Applications. In *Proceedings of the fifth SIAM Conference on Parallel Processing*, 1992.

[7] V. K. Naik. Scalability issues for a class of CFD applications. In *Proceedings of the Scalable High Performance Computing Conference*, 1992.

[8] V. K. Naik, S. K. Setia, and M. S. Squillante. Scheduling of Large Scientific Applications on Distributed Memory Multiprocessor Systems. In *Proceedings of the sixth SIAM Conference on Parallel Processing for Scientific Computing*, 1993.

[9] V. K. Naik, S. K. Setia, and M. S. Squillante. Performance Analysis of Job Scheduling Policies in Parallel Supercomputing Environments. IBM Research Report RC 19138, 1993.

[10] *Paragon^{TM} XP/S Product Overview*, Intel Corp., Beaverton, OR, 1991.

[11] T. H. Pulliam. Efficient Solution Methods for Navier-Stokes Equations. Lecture Notes for the von Karman Institute for Fluid Dynamics Lecture Series: Numerical Techniques for Viscous Flow Computation in Turbomachinery Bladings, 1986.

[12] E. Rosti, E. Smirni, G. Serazzi, L. Dowdy, and B. Carlson. Robust partitioning policies of multiprocessor systems. Technical report, Dept. of Computer Science, Vanderbilt University, 1992.

[13] R. Schreiber and H. D. Simon. Towards the teraflops capability for CFD. In H. D. Simon, editor, *Parallel CFD - Implementations and Results Using Parallel Computers*, MIT Press, 1992.

[14] S. K. Setia. Scheduling on Multiprogrammed Distributed Memory Parallel Computers. Ph.D. Dissertation, Department of Computer Science, University of Maryland, August 1993.

[15] S. K. Setia and S. K. Tripathi. A comparative analysis of static processor partitioning policies for parallel computers. In *Proc. of Intl. Workshop on Modeling and Simulation of Computer and Telecommunication Systems (MASCOTS '93)*, 1993.

[16] S. Yoon, D. Kwak, and L. Chang. LU-SGS Implicit Algorithm for Three-Dimensional Incompressible Navier-Stokes Equations with Source Term. AIAA Paper 89-1964-CP, 1989.

Session 11:
Minisymposium
Fernbach and Forefronts Awards

Session 11:
Minisymposium
Clustered Workstations
Chair: Ray Cline

Session 12:
Performance
Measurement and Debugging
Chair: Bart Miller

Adaptive Message Logging for Incremental Replay of Message-Passing Programs

Robert H. B. Netzer

Jian Xu

rn@cs.brown.edu

jx@cs.brown.edu

Dept. of Computer Science
Brown University
Box 1910
Providence, RI 02912

Abstract

Cyclic debugging executes a program over and over to track down bugs. However, for message-passing parallel programs, nondeterminacy makes cyclic debugging impossible without support of special tools. To provide repeatable executions, messages must be traced for later replay. Since parallel programs are long-running, providing fast response to debugging queries requires *incremental* replay, where reexecution is started from intermediate states instead of from the beginning. To support incremental replay, processes must be checkpointed periodically and the contents of some messages traced, but the time and space cost of saving these messages can be prohibitive. This paper presents an *adaptive* message logging algorithm that keeps these costs low by logging only a fraction of the messages. Our algorithm dynamically tracks dependences among messages to determine which cause *domino effects* and must be traced. The domino effect can force a replay to start arbitrarily far back in the execution, and domino-free replay allows any part of the execution to be quickly reexecuted. Experiments on an iPSC/860 hypercube indicate that our algorithm logs only 1–10% of the messages, a 1 to 2 order of magnitude reduction over past schemes which log every message. Our experiments also show that the resulting logs provide a small bound on the amount of reexecution needed to satisfy any replay request. Our new logging algorithm thus reduces the overhead of message logging while bounding the response time to replay requests.

1. Introduction

Repeated execution is a powerful debugging strategy, allowing enough information to eventually be collected to understand bugs. However, message-passing parallel programs can be nondeterministic, and obtaining repeatable executions requires special tools — bugs cannot always be reproduced by a simple reexecution.

This research was supported by ONR Contract N00014-91-J-4052 (ARPA Order 8225) and NSF grant CCR-9309311.

Obtaining repeatability requires tracing the execution's messages, using the trace to replay the program as needed. In previous work we developed an *adaptive* strategy that makes run-time tracing decisions, usually tracing only 0–10% of the messages, and reducing the cost of tracing by 1–2 orders of magnitude over past schemes which trace every message. However, this technique required reexecuting the program from the beginning, and can provide unacceptable response time to replay requests of long-running programs. In this paper we present a new scheme that integrates checkpointing and adaptive message logging to provide *incremental* replay, allowing the execution to be restarted from intermediate states. Our scheme adapts to the execution's message-passing patterns to log only the contents of messages that would substantially slow replay if not logged. Experiments on an iPSC/860 show that only 1–10% of the messages typically need to be logged, and that such a log is sufficient to quickly replay *any* part of the execution. Our scheme simultaneously lowers logging overhead while bounding the time required to satisfy a replay request.

Our approach to supporting incremental replay is to periodically checkpoint to disk the state of each process. We can then restart the execution of any process from one of its checkpoints instead of from its beginning. To satisfy message receive operations during the replay, we must also log the contents of some messages, and logging is a dominant cost of this scheme. We keep this cost low by not logging every message. When processes checkpoint independently of each other, we have the freedom to restart a process from any of its checkpoints, independently of where other processes are restarted. This freedom allows us to decide at run-time which messages need *not* be logged because they can be quickly recomputed (during the replay) by re-executing the processes that sent them. We log only messages whose recomputation would substantially slow replay by causing a *domino effect*. For example, a domino effect occurs when some part of a process (say p_1) must be re-executed to reproduce a message needed by another, but p_1 itself requires a message that causes part of a third process p_3 to be re-executed, and p_3 requires a message sent by an earlier part of p_1, requiring

p_1 to be restarted even further back. In the worst case this domino effect can continue indefinitely, requiring all processes to be restarted from the beginning of the execution. Our algorithm logs enough message to completely avoid any domino effect during replay.

Our main result is an algorithm that dynamically locates and logs domino-effect-causing messages. The algorithm tracks dependences between messages, and when a message is received that introduces a domino-effect-causing dependence, it is logged. No other messages are logged. By logging enough to provide domino-free replay, only a small amount of each process must be reexecuted to satisfy any replay request. Experiments show that in each process only one or two intervals between checkpoints usually need to be reexecuted. We also present a model to exactly characterize which messages lead to domino-causing dependences, and prove that logging the minimal number of messages to avoid these dependences is NP-hard. Our algorithm logs the first message at which such a dependence can be detected, and is thus an approximation. However, experiments show that it performs well.

This work is part of our larger effort on developing adaptive tracing strategies for debugging[7, 8, 14].

2. Motivation and Related Work

There are two parts to incremental replay of message-passing programs: inter-process communication (IPC) tracing, and checkpointing and message logging. IPC tracing records enough to ensure that replay is deterministic and exhibits the same computation as the original execution. Checkpointing and message logging saves a program's intermediate states so that replay of long-running programs can start from a checkpointed state (instead of the beginning). Although in this paper we address checkpointing and message logging, below we briefly describe past work on both problems.

In a message-passing program, variations in scheduling and message latencies can cause two executions of the same program on the same input to produce different results. Although this nondeterminacy may be intended, replaying an execution of such a program requires information about how its processes communicated during that execution. By tracing the order in which messages are delivered (but not their contents), a traced execution can be replayed from its start by forcing a reexecution to deliver messages in the same order[6, 11, 13]. Since IPC tracing is necessary for replay, we assume that such a scheme is always used in addition to checkpointing and message logging (and since message contents are not recorded, its overhead is much lower).

Although IPC tracing alone provides information sufficient for replay, it requires restarting the execution from its beginning, which is impractical for long-running programs — tool users expect fast responses to debugging queries. To achieve quick replay, checkpoints must be taken to periodically save the execution's intermediate states. In addition, the contents of certain messages must also be logged. For example, Figure 1 shows an execution where each process takes two checkpoints. If the checkpoints are always combined as shown to form *restart lines* for replay, then message $m2$ is *lost* — it was sent before the rightmost line but received after. Thus, when replay starts from this restart line, $p1$ will not regenerate the message, so its contents must be initially logged during execution (so the message receive can be satisfied from the log during replay). If the replay will always begin from either of the two lines shown messages $m1$ and $m3$ need not be logged since they will always be recomputed during any replay.

Checkpointing and message logging has been mainly studied in the context of fault tolerant computing [4, 10, 12] and global-state evaluation[1]. Two major schemes have been proposed: *coordinated checkpointing* and *independent checkpointing*. With a coordinated checkpointing, some process must initiate the checkpointing session and run an algorithm to coordinate all other processes in saving their states[1]. Messages that cross the line formed by the local checkpoints are also saved. Although coordinated checkpoints can be used for replay, their main disadvantage is that they force all processes to checkpoint at about the same time. Such a scheme does not adapt well to the execution's message passing patterns, but instead logs *all* messages in-transit at the time

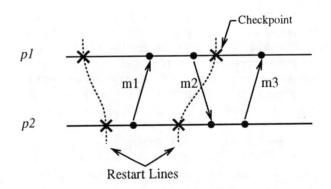

Figure 1. Example execution with checkpoints. The restart lines show ways to start replay. Message m2 is then "lost" and must be retrieved from the log.

of the checkpoint. If the coordinated checkpoint is initiated at an inopportune moment, many messages could be logged. This problem stems from the overly restrictive view that only consistent checkpoints can be taken. Replay *need not* start from a consistent checkpoint; any set of checkpoints can be combined for restart. The approach we outline in this paper exploits this observation by computing at run time how individual checkpoints are best combined to minimize the number of messages logged.

In contrast, independent checkpointing gives each process the autonomy to checkpoint independently of all others. The main disadvantage is the *domino-effect*. Since the checkpoints are no longer coordinated, replaying part of one process could require an earlier interval of another to also be re-executed. For example, if in Figure 1 the execution were started from the rightmost restart line, but $m2$ had not been logged, then process $p1$ cannot be started from the checkpoint but must be rolled back further so that $m2$ will be recomputed. In the worst case, the reexecution has to be started from the very beginning. To avoid the domino effect, each process must independently determine which messages to log. Most work on message logging has been in the fault tolerance community, where execution is restarted after a fault only from last consistent checkpoint[12], and old messages can be discarded. However, for debugging, replays are requested often (unlike failures), and they must complete quickly. Thus, we wish to be able to restart from *any* checkpoint, which need not be consistent. The fault tolerance results thus do not solve the replay problem. In the debugging community, previous work on independent checkpointing for replay simply traces the contents of all messages[3, 13], which can be prohibitively expensive.

Our work on adaptive logging exploits independent checkpointing by combining checkpoints for replay in ways that adapt to the particular execution being traced. This paper reports the first results on how to support trace-and-replay debugging with independent checkpointing without logging all messages. In Section 3 we present our model for representing program executions, and use this model in Section 4 to consider how checkpoints can be combined to minimize message logging but still avoid the domino effect. In Section 5 we present an adaptive logging algorithm that makes these decisions on-the-fly, and in Section 6 present experimental results that show our algorithm usually logs only $1 - 10\%$ of the messages.

3. Model

Our model is simply a notation for representing program executions. A *checkpointed program execution* is a pair, $P = \langle E, \xrightarrow{\text{RD}} \rangle$, where E is a finite set of *events*

and $\xrightarrow{\text{RD}}$ is the *replay dependence* relation defined over E.

An event represents the execution instance of a send, receive, or checkpoint operation. We assume a fixed number of processes exist during execution, and denote the set of all events in process p by E_p, and the ith checkpoint in process p as $C_{p,i}$. The *state interval* $S_{p,i}$ is all computation performed in process p between checkpoints $C_{p,i}$ and $C_{p,i+1}$ (and includes $C_{p,i}$ but not $C_{p,i+1}$).

The replay dependence relation, $\xrightarrow{\text{RD}}$, shows how events depend on one another *during a replay*. An event b is said to be *replay dependent* on an event a (i.e., $a \xrightarrow{\text{RD}} b$) iff a must be reproduced during re-execution before b can be re-executed, because a precedes b in the same state interval, or because a sequence of messages was sent from a (or a following event) to b (or a preceding event). The $\xrightarrow{\text{RD}}$ relation is identical to Lamport's happened-before relation[5] except that events in a state interval $S_{p,i}$ do *not* necessarily depend on events in $S_{p,i-1}$ (the previous state interval), even though they both belong to the same process. This definition reflects the independence during replay of a state interval on earlier ones; since $S_{p,i}$ can be re-executed starting from $C_{p,i}$, no events in earlier intervals in the same process need be executed. In Lamport's relation, an event is dependent on all earlier events in the same process. The $\xrightarrow{\text{RD}}$ relation is defined as the irreflexive transitive closure of the union of two other relations: $\xrightarrow{\text{RD}} = (\xrightarrow{\text{SO}} \cup \xrightarrow{\text{M}})^+$. The $\xrightarrow{\text{SO}}$ relation shows the order in which events in the same state interval execute. The ith event in a state interval in process p (denoted $e_{p,i}$) always executes before the $i + 1^{\text{st}}$ event in the same interval: $e_{p,i} \xrightarrow{\text{SO}} e_{p,i+1}$. Note that the last event in the interval is not ordered before the first event in the following interval by $\xrightarrow{\text{SO}}$. The $\xrightarrow{\text{M}}$ relation shows the message deliveries: $a \xrightarrow{\text{M}} b$ means that a sent a message that b received (and we write $a \xrightarrow{\text{M}} b$ to denote the message).

Figure 2 illustrates for an example checkpointed program execution the *execution graph*, an equivalent representation of $P = \langle E, \xrightarrow{\text{RD}} \rangle$. The events in E are the nodes of this graph, and $a \xrightarrow{\text{RD}} b$ iff a path exists from a to b in the graph. In our examples, we implicitly assume that intra-process edges are directed from left to right (but we omit the arrowheads from the figures). Note that there is no edge entering any of the checkpoints (denoted by the "×"s), indicating that the checkpoints are not replay dependent on any event.

4. Domino-Free Replay

Our goal is to be able to replay any single state interval in the execution. We can easily replay multiple intervals by simply concurrently replaying several single intervals at once (discussed in Section 5.2). To replay some interval $S_{p,i}$, we must restart the execution of process p from checkpoint $C_{p,i}$, and then ensure that the messages $S_{p,i}$ originally received (during execution) are reproduced (during replay). To reproduce a message we can either log it initially during execution (so we can retrieve it from the log during replay), or we can recompute its contents by also replaying the state interval that sent it. In this section we present results showing which messages need to be logged and which can be timely recomputed. We log only the *domino-effect* messages, which if not logged could cause arbitrarily many other intervals to be replayed (to recompute messages) when satisfying a replay request, thus slowing replay. We first define precisely which messages need to be reproduced to allow any state interval to be replayed, and characterize what domino-effect-free replay means. We then prove that by logging enough domino-effect messages, the replay of any state interval will never exhibit a domino effect. In Sections 5 and 6 we present an on-line algorithm for detecting and logging these messages and show its effectiveness.

To replay a state interval $S_{p,i}$, any message $a \xrightarrow{M} b$ on which an event in $S_{p,i}$ depends must either be recomputed during replay or be initially logged during execution. To recompute messages during replay, we must choose a *restart line*, checkpoints at which to restart each process (illustrated in Figure 2). Any message on which $S_{p,i}$ depends that is sent from the right of the restart line will be recomputed during replay (and thus need not be logged). Any message on which $S_{p,i}$ depends that crosses the line from left to right must initially be logged so it can be retrieved from the log during replay. Otherwise, it will be unavailable during replay, since its sender (which is to the left of the line) is not being re-executed. If $S_{p,i}$ does not depend on a message $a \xrightarrow{M} b$, it means that $S_{p,i}$ either depends in no way on the state interval X that sent the message, or that it depends only on events in X *before* $a \xrightarrow{M} b$ was sent.

Figure 2 illustrates these cases. If we wish to replay interval $S_{1,3}$, we need to reproduce messages m4 and m5. They can be either logged or recomputed. If we choose the restart line as shown, message m5 will be recomputed (by also replaying interval $S_{2,3}$), and message m4 will be logged (message m4 is a domino-effect message (described below) and is logged by our algorithm). Since $S_{2,3}$ is also being replayed, the message it requires (m7) must also be reproduced, and is recomputed by replaying $S_{3,2}$. Even though m6 crosses the restart line, it is *not* logged, since $S_{1,3}$ does not depend on m6 — it is received by $p3$ *after* $p3$ sends the message on which the other intervals depend (m7). In general, after a process is

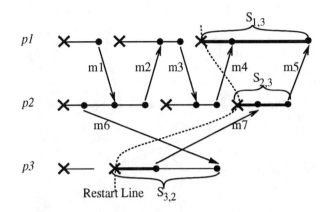

Figure 2. Restart line for replaying interval $S_{1,3}$. The "×"s indicate checkpoints. Only message m4 is logged, and only bold parts of state intervals are re-executed.

restarted, it may be stopped and then restarted from a later checkpoint to skip over receives of messages that are not needed. This start/stop replay allows us to avoid logging some messages that need not be reproduced (such as m6). The bold portions of processes $p1$, $p2$, and $p3$ in Figure 2 are re-executed to replay $S_{1,3}$.

To decide where to place the restart line, we attempt to log as few messages as possible as long as messages can be quickly recomputed. If we were to always recompute the messages on which $S_{p,i}$ depends, the *domino effect* may force arbitrarily many state intervals in the past to be re-executed[9]. Our approach is to log enough messages to provide *domino-free replay*. Figure 3 illustrates a domino effect when replaying $S_{1,3}$. If no messages are initially logged, we must replay all the state intervals in $p1$ and $p2$ to recompute message m4; interval $S_{2,2}$ requires a message from $S_{1,2}$, which requires a message from $S_{2,1}$, which finally requires a message from $S_{1,1}$. In general, the domino effect can force replay to start at the very beginning of the execution. The *domino-effect messages* cause this effect by introducing replay dependences from earlier state intervals in a process to later intervals.

Definition 4.1

A *domino dependence* is a replay dependence from an event in an interval $S_{p,i}$ to an event in a later interval $S_{p,j}$ in the same process ($j > i$).

The *domino-effect messages* are those messages that lie on any path in the execution graph that comprises a domino dependence.

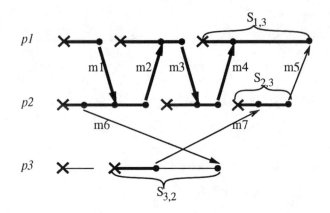

Figure 3. Domino effect when replaying interval $S_{1,3}$, causing $p1$ and $p2$ to start at the beginning of the execution. Domino-effect messages are in bold, and bold parts of state intervals must be re-executed.

Intuitively, the domino-effect messages are those causing replay dependences that make it impossible to replay $S_{p,i}$ without also re-executing earlier state intervals in the same process. Our goal is to provide *domino-free* replay.

Definition 4.2

We say that a state interval $S_{p,i}$ will have *domino-free replay* iff it can be replayed without reexecuting any previous state interval $S_{p,j}$ ($j < i$) in the same process.

The execution P will have domino-free replay iff all of its state intervals will have domino-free replay.

Theorem 1 states that logging enough domino-effect messages to break the domino dependences guarantees that replay is domino-free (proofs appear in the Appendix). In Section 6 we show that domino-free replay allows any state interval to be replayed by typically reexecuting at most one or two state intervals in each other process.

Theorem 1 (Domino-Free Replay Theorem)

We say that a replay dependence $a \xrightarrow{M} b$ is *broken* if the message $a \xrightarrow{M} b$ is logged. By logging enough domino-effect messages to break all domino dependences, the execution will have domino-free replay.

If we consider the execution graph, this theorem states that if we remove enough edges from the graph (by log-

ging messages) to break all paths from a state interval to future state intervals in the same process, then any state interval can be replayed with no domino effect.

Although the next theorem states that computing the minimal number of messages needed to provide domino-free replay is NP-hard, we present an on-line approximation algorithm in the next section that works by logging any message that completes a domino dependence.

Theorem 2 (Message-Logging Complexity Theorem)

Computing the minimal number of messages that must be logged to obtain domino-free replay is an NP-hard problem.

5. Adaptive Logging and Replay Algorithms

Theorem 2 shows that the problem of logging the minimal number of messages to provide domino-free replay is NP-hard. In this section, we present an on-line approximation algorithm, and discuss how to replay from the message log. Although we concentrate on replaying a single state interval, the replay scheme can be extended to replay multiple state intervals concurrently.

5.1. Adaptive Message-Logging Algorithm

We now present our message logging algorithm, shown in Figure 4. Our approach is to dynamically track the replay dependences among messages and checkpoints to determine which messages *complete* a domino-dependence, and log only these messages. A message completes a domino dependence if it is the first message that completes a path from an earlier state interval to a later interval in some process. To track dependences, each process keeps count of its current state interval and maintains a *replay dependence vector* (*RDV*). The *RDV* is

---

1: Send = the event that sent *Msg*;
2: if ($e \xrightarrow{\text{RD}}$ *Send* for any event e in any earlier state
3:   interval of process p) **then**
4:   /* *Msg* completes a domino dependence */
5:   log *Msg*;
6: else
7:   /* *Msg* does not complete a domino dependence */
8:   update this process' replay dependence vector(*RDV*)
9:   from the *RDV* piggybacked on *Msg*;

Figure 4. Adaptive message logging algorithm, invoked after receiving *Msg* in process p.

similar to a vector timestamp[2] (used to maintain the happened-before relation, discussed in Section 3), except that it is a vector of state interval indices, one per process. The current *RDV* for process p contains the index of the earliest state interval in every other process on which p has a replay dependence. Process p's *RDV* entry for p itself always contains its current state interval number. Each process appends its *RDV* onto outgoing message, and upon receiving a message, updates its *RDV* as described below. After taking a checkpoint, a process reinitializes its *RDV* by nullifying all components except the one for itself, indicating that the newly taken checkpoint is not replay dependent on any other event. At any point, the *RDV* shows the checkpoints that comprise the current restart line.

To determine whether a message completes a domino dependence, the algorithm in Figure 4 is invoked after each receive operation. When process p receives a message, it checks whether the sender is replay dependent on any previous state interval in p (lines $1-3$ in Figure 4). This check is performed by determining if the pth component of the piggybacked vector is less than the current state interval number of p. If so, then the sender depends on some event in an earlier interval of p; the message thus completes a domino dependence and is logged. Otherwise, the message can be reproduced during replay by properly choosing the restart line (discussed later) and is not logged. When the message does not complete a domino dependence, the *RDV* must be updated to reflect the new dependence it introduces; the *RDV* is updated by a component-wise minimum with the vector appended to the message (except that if an entry for one of the vectors is null, then the element from the other is used as the result). Updating *RDV*'s by a component-wise minimum ensures that they always show the current restart line.

To illustrate our algorithm, consider the execution of Figure 2, which is reproduced in Figure 5 with messages annotated with their piggybacked *RDV*'s. We consider why messages $m2$ and $m4$ are logged. When $p1$ takes its first checkpoint, $C_{1,1}$, its *RDV* is initialized to $[1,-,-]$. When $p1$ sends $m1$, it appends this *RDV* to the message. When $p2$ receives $m1$, the algorithm tests whether the second element of the piggybacked *RDV* is less than the current checkpoint interval number. It is not (since it is null), meaning that the sender does not depend on an earlier interval in $p2$, so message $m1$ is not logged. Consequently, $p2$'s *RDV* is updated to $[1,1,-]$ by taking a component-wise minimum with the piggybacked vector. The new *RDV* indicates the restart line needed for replaying interval $S_{2,1}$ up to the current event. When $p1$ receives $m2$, the first component of the piggybacked *RDV* is 1, less than $p1$'s current state interval number (2). The

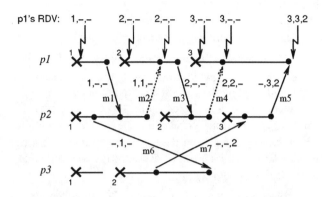

Figure 5. Message logging algorithm on example in Figure 2. Each dashed message completes a domino dependence and is logged. The replay dependence vector (RDV) piggybacked on each message is shown.

send event thus depends on an earlier state interval in $p1$ ($S_{1,1}$, by the dependence introduced by $m1$), so $m2$ is logged. Since $p1$ will not depend during replay on $m2$ (because it is logged), $p1$'s *RDV* is left unchanged.

Similarly, our algorithm logs $m4$, the message that completes the domino dependence from $S_{1,2}$ to $S_{1,3}$. Messages $m2$ and $m4$ (the dashed edges in Figure 5) are the only messages logged. After removing the dashed edges from the execution graph, we can see there is no path from an event in an earlier state interval to an event in a later interval of the same process. By Theorem 1, we can replay all state intervals with no domino effect. Note that although our algorithm logs the minimal number of messages in this example, in general it is not optimal when a domino-effect message lies on more than one path (where logging one message can break many domino dependences).

5.2. Execution Replay

We now outline how to replay a state interval using the message logs generated by our algorithm. Our algorithm guarantees that, for any state interval, all messages on which it depends have either been logged or can be regenerated during replay with no domino effect. The crux of replay is computing the proper restart line and determining which state intervals must be reexecuted. As discussed in Section 2, we must also ensure replay is deterministic by forcing messages to be delivered in the same order as during the original execution. Enforcing this order requires using the message dependence trace (which we assume is always recorded), and for this we rely on past schemes and do not address this problem here. We focus only on how to determine which state intervals need be replayed. We consider how to replay a single state interval, $S_{p,i}$, although multiple state intervals can easily be replayed concurrently using the same approach.

To determine where to start replay for $S_{p,i}$, the restart line is computed by constructing the execution graph and locating the earliest checkpoint in each process on which any event in $S_{p,i}$ depends. Process p itself is always restarted from checkpoint $C_{p,i}$. The execution graph is constructed from the message dependence trace, which shows to which event each message was delivered (discussed in Section 2).

Once the restart line is known, we must then compute which portions of the state intervals to the right of the line should be reexecuted. Recall that only those portions of intervals on which $S_{p,i}$ depends need be reexecuted (as illustrated in Figure 2), and this start/stop replay allows us to avoid logging messages that $S_{p,i}$ does not require (such as message m6 in Figure 2). We must reexecute at least part of each interval on which $S_{p,i}$ depends, and these parts can easily be computed by examining the execution graph; we find the last event in each interval from which a path to an event in $S_{p,i}$ exists (this event will always be a send). During replay each such interval is started from its checkpoint, and stopped (by setting a local breakpoint) at this send. Reexecuting all such intervals will ensure that all messages required by $S_{p,i}$ (and not logged) will be recomputed.

Note that sometimes a message will be recomputed that no interval requires (e.g., a message sent to an interval on which $S_{p,i}$ does not depend). These unneeded messages pose no problem since the mechanism for forcing the original message delivery order (to keep replay deterministic) will ensure that they are never delivered to the wrong receive operation.

To illustrate replay, suppose that interval $S_{1,3}$ in the example of Figure 2 is to be replayed. The restart line is shown, and consists of the earliest checkpoints on which $S_{1,3}$ depends. Note that m4 is logged, so $S_{1,3}$ does not depend on $C_{2,2}$ for replay. Replay is begun from the restart line, and all of interval $S_{2,3}$ is reexecuted, since $S_{1,3}$ depends on its last event (which sends m5). However, interval $S_{3,2}$ is stopped after sending m7, since $S_{1,3}$ depends on no subsequent events in this interval.

Although starting and stopping the replay incurs some overhead, it allows us to avoid logging unnecessary messages and further reduce run-time overhead. The experiments in Section 6 indicate that not many intervals usually need be reexecuted to satisfy a replay request, so

the starting and stopping cost should be low. In addition, skipping unneeded portions of the execution further reduces replay response time.

This method of replaying a single interval can be directly extended to replay multiple intervals concurrently (e.g., to replay up to some consistent global state). Given a set of intervals to be replayed, we form the restart line by computing a minimum over the restart lines for those intervals. Any message not logged on which one of the intervals depends will be regenerated.

6. Experimental Results

To measure the effectiveness of our adaptive message logging strategy, we analyzed executions of several message-passing programs. We measured the percentage of messages our algorithm logged, and the number of state intervals needing reexecution to satisfy a replay request. These measures indicate how well we adaptively reduce trace size, and how effectively domino-free replay keeps replay time low. We computed these measures as we varied the frequency with which each process takes a checkpoint. To compare the results as this frequency varied, we simulated our algorithm from a message trace of a single execution of each program. Since the test programs were nondeterministic, simulation was necessary to allow us to vary checkpoint frequency and still analyze the same execution (otherwise, different runs would produce different executions). Our experiments show that only $1 - 10\%$ of the messages were typically logged, a substantial reduction over past schemes which log the contents of every message. In addition, we found that only one to two state intervals in each process usually required reexecution to satisfy any replay request, indicating that logging the domino-effect messages is effective at keeping replay times low.

Our first experiment investigated what percentage of messages are typically logged. We analyzed five test programs (provided by colleagues) on a 128-node Intel iPSC/860 hypercube. Each program was run once on a 16-node subcube with an instrumented message-passing library to provide traces for simulation. These programs ran between 10 and 934 seconds and passed between 300 and 370,000 messages. Since the checkpoint frequency has an impact on our algorithm's performance (e.g., no messages are logged if no checkpoints are taken), we varied the period with which each process takes its checkpoint as we simulated the algorithm. We varied the period from 1% of the total execution time to 50% (taking a checkpoint every 1% results in 100 checkpoints per process). Data for checkpoint periods longer than 50% are omitted since then only two checkpoints are taken (per process) and the data for 50% is representative. Figure 6

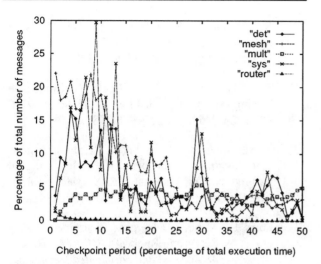

Figure 6. Percentage of messages logged for varying checkpoint intervals.

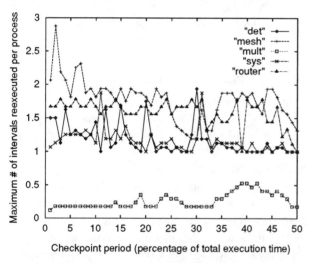

Figure 7. Maximum state intervals (per process) that must be reexecuted to satisfy any replay request.

shows the percentage of messages logged as the checkpoint period varies. For most cases, our algorithm logs less than 10% of the messages. The performance tends to improve as the checkpoint period increases, indicating the decreased likelihood of domino-effect messages as the number of distinct state intervals decreases. In practice, checkpoints should be taken as far apart as possible (to reduce checkpointing overhead), and the data points for small checkpoint periods do not represent cases that would appear in practice. We thus expect our algorithm to log typically 1 – 10% of the messages. For *router* (the longest-running program), less than 0.1% of the messages

were usually logged.

Our second experiment studied the response time of replaying a state interval using the message logs. We computed the maximum number of state intervals (per process) that required reexecution to satisfy any replay request (as discussed in Section 5.2). This maximum indicates at most how long a typical replay request will take, and shows how effectively domino-free replay keeps this time low. Figure 7 shows the results as the checkpoint period varies. In almost all cases, only 1 – 2 state intervals (per process) required reexecution, even when the checkpoint period was small (and thus when the execution was divided into many state intervals).

We conclude that our strategy of logging enough messages to eliminate the domino effect is effective. It not only requires logging a small percentage of messages, but the absence of domino effects results in (essentially) bounded replay time.

7. Conclusions and Future Work

In this paper we show how a checkpoint-and-replay scheme can *adaptively* decide which messages to log, instead of logging every message as proposed by past schemes. By formulating the problem in terms of reachability in a graph, we prove that only messages causing domino-dependences need be logged to provide domino-free replay. Although computing the minimal set of messages that must be logged is an NP-hard problem, we present an on-line approximation algorithm. Our algorithm tracks dependences among messages and logs the first message that completes each domino dependence. Experiments indicate that our algorithm typically logs only 1 – 10% of the messages. In addition, these logs are sufficient to replay any state interval in a process, and normally require only one or two additional intervals in each other process to also be reexecuted. Our work thus achieves both low message logging and quick replay.

Future work includes combining adaptive message logging with adaptive message dependence tracing, investigating adaptive checkpointing, and improvements to our on-line algorithm. First, we assumed that all dependences among messages were traced (e.g., by writing a trace for every message that shows to which event it was delivered). Netzer and Miller have shown how to significantly reduce the size of dependence traces (by 1 to 2 orders of magnitude) by tracing only *racing* messages, which can be located on-the-fly[7]. We wish to combine this approach with adaptive message logging. Second, we assumed that processes periodically take checkpoints. We are investigating how checkpointing *and* message logging can adapt to the execution. Finally, better on-line approximation algorithms for logging may exist.

Acknowledgements

We thank Prith Banerjee of the Univ. of Illinois for the router program, and Mark Hill of the Univ. of Wisconsin–Madison for the other test programs.

References

[1]   K. Mani Chandy and Leslie Lamport, "Distributed Snapshots: Determining Global States of Distributed Systems," *ACM Trans on Comp Syst* **3**(1) pp. 63-75 (Feb, 1985).

[2]   C. J. Fidge, "Partial Orders for Parallel Debugging," *SIGPLAN/SIGOPS Workshop on Parallel and Distributed Debugging*, pp. 183-194 Madison, WI, (May 1988). Also appears in *SIGPLAN Notices* **24**(1) (January 1989).

[3]   Arthur P. Goldberg, Ajei Gopal, Andy Lowry, and Rob Strom, "Restoring Consistent Global States of Distributed Computations," *ACM/ONR Workshop on Parallel and Distributed Debugging*, pp. 144-154 Santa Cruz, CA, (May 1991).

[4]   David B. Johnson and Willy Zwaenepoel, "Recovery in Distributed Systems Using Optimistic Message Logging and Checkpointing," *Proc. of the 7th Annual ACM Symp. on Principles of Dist Computing*, (1988).

[5]   Leslie Lamport, "Time, Clocks, and the Ordering of Events in a Distributed System," *CACM* **21**(7) pp. 558-565 (July 1978).

[6]   Thomas J. LeBlanc and John M. Mellor-Crummey, "Debugging Parallel Programs with Instant Replay," *IEEE Trans. on Computers* **C-36**(4) pp. 471-482 (April 1987).

[7]   Robert H.B. Netzer and Barton P. Miller, "Optimal Tracing and Replay for Debugging Message-Passing Parallel Programs," *Supercomputing '92*, pp. 502-511 Minneapolis, MN, (November 1992).

[8]   Robert H.B. Netzer, "Optimal Tracing and Replay for Debugging Shared-Memory Parallel Programs," *ACM/ONR Workshop on Parallel and Distributed Debugging*, pp. 1-11 San Diego, CA, (May 1993).

[9]   B. Randell, "System Structure for Software Fault Tolerance," *IEEE Trans. on Software Engineering* SE-1(2) pp. 220-232 (June 1975).

[10]   R. E. Strom and S. Yemini, "Optimistic Recovery in Distributed Systems," *ACM Trans. on Computer Systems* **3** pp. 204-226 (August 1985).

[11]   Kuo-Chung Tai and Sanjiv Ahuja, "Reproducible Testing of Communication Software," *IEEE COMPSAC '87*, pp. 331-337 (1987).

[12]   Y. M. Wang and W. K. Fuchs, "Optimistic message logging for independent checkpointing in message-passing systems," *IEEE Symp. on Reliable Distributed Syst.*, pp. 147-154 (Oct 1992).

[13]   Larry D. Wittie, "Debugging Distributed C Programs by Real Time Replay," *SIGPLAN/SIGOPS Workshop on Parallel and Distributed Debugging*, pp. 57-67 Madison, WI, (May 1988).

[14]   Jian Xu and Robert H.B. Netzer, "Adaptive Independent Checkpointing for Reducing Rollback Propagation," *IEEE Symp. on Parallel and Distributed Processing*, Dallas, TX, (Dec 1993).

Appendix. Proofs of Theorems

Theorem 1 (Domino-Free Replay Theorem)
    By logging enough domino-effect messages to break all domino dependences, the execution will have domino-free replay.

Proof. Let $\xrightarrow{RD'}$ be the replay dependence relation that results by removing all dependences broken by message logging. We will prove that for all state intervals $S_{p,i}$, there exists a restart line that passes through $C_{p,i}$, and one checkpoint in each other process, such that no message $a \xrightarrow{M} b$ crosses it left to right where $a \xrightarrow{RD'} x$ (for some x in $S_{p,i}$). That is, each message $a \xrightarrow{M} b$ crossing the line left to right is either logged or does not affect $S_{p,i}$. The existence of such a restart line implies that $S_{p,i}$ will have domino-free replay since no previous state intervals in the same process then need to be replayed.

To prove that such a restart line exists, consider the execution graph with edges corresponding to all logged messages deleted. Since all domino dependences are broken, this graph has no path from an event in any state interval $S_{p,i}$ to an event in a later interval $S_{p,j}$ ($j > i$) in the same process. Below we show that for each interval $S_{p,i}$, a restart line exists such that no path crosses the line left to right from any event a to an event in $S_{p,i}$.

Consider any state interval $S_{p,i}$. We construct its restart line by including $C_{p,i}$ and for each other process, q, the earliest checkpoint $C_{q,k}$ in q on which any event x in $S_{p,i}$ depends (i.e., $C_{q,k} \xrightarrow{RD'} x$). We claim that no path exists from an event a to the left of the line to any event x in $S_{p,i}$ (which must be to the right of the line, since the line contains $C_{p,i}$). To establish a contradiction, assume that such a path exists, and further assume that a is the only event in the path to the left of the line (i.e., the edge out of a crosses the line).

Case 1: a belongs to process p. In this case, a is in a state interval that precedes $S_{p,i}$, so the path from a to x is a domino dependence. However, the existence of this dependence contradicts the assumption that all domino dependences were broken by logging messages.

Case 2: a belongs to process q, where $q \neq p$. Recall that the restart line was constructed to contain $C_{q,k}$, the earliest checkpoint in q on which $S_{p,i}$ depends. However, the path from a to $S_{p,i}$ implies that $S_{p,i}$ depends on a, and because a is to the left of the restart line, $C_{q,k}$ is not the *earliest* checkpoint on which $S_{p,i}$ depends, a contradiction.

Thus, no path can exist from an event a to the left of the line to any event in $S_{p,i}$. QED

Theorem 2 (Message-Logging Complexity Theorem)
Computing the minimal number of messages that must be logged to break all domino dependences is an NP-hard problem.

Proof. We use a reduction from the vertex cover problem, known to be NP-complete: given an undirected graph, $G = (V, E)$, does G have a vertex cover with k or fewer vertices? A vertex cover is a subset V' of the vertices such that every edge is connected to some vertex in V'. Given G, we reduce the problem of determining whether it has a vertex cover with k or fewer vertices to the problem of determining whether all domino dependences in a program execution, P, can be removed by logging k or fewer messages.

From the graph G we construct P as follows. For every $v \in V$, P contains a two-process gadget, $gad(v)$, and two messages between $gad(a)$ and $gad(b)$ iff an edge exists between a and b in G, as illustrated in Figure 8. The right-most process performs two checkpoints; the left-most performs none. Each gadget consists of six message operations (three per process), and one message sent between its two processes. When two nodes a and b are connected, we construct a message from node 4 of $gad(a)$ to node 1 of $gad(b)$, and another message from node 5 of $gad(b)$ to node 6 of $gad(a)$ (or, we could construct them from node 4 of $gad(b)$ to node 1 of $gad(a)$, and from node 5 of $gad(a)$ to node 6 of $gad(b)$, and we

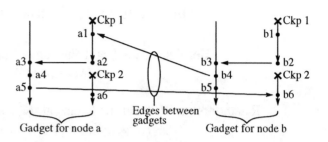

Figure 8. Gadgets, for nodes a and b, and intergadget messages (that exist iff a and b are connected in G).

arbitrarily pick one of these two directions). These messages introduce a path from state interval 1 (S_1) to state interval 2 (S_2) in the right-most process of the gadget for b. If a node has more than one connecting edge, we add additional events (just below nodes 1,4,5 and 6) to send and receive these messages. Thus, whenever an edge connects two nodes, there is a path from S_1 to a later interval (S_2) in some process.

We claim that G has a vertex cover of k or fewer vertices iff all domino dependences in P can be removed by logging k or fewer messages.

If Part. Assume that all domino dependences in P can be removed by logging k or fewer messages; i.e., by deleting k or fewer edges in P's execution graph, we remove all paths from S_1 to S_2 in any process. Let n be the number of deleted edges. We claim that these paths can be removed by deleting only the message inside each of n gadgets without deleting any inter-gadget messages. If a message from $gad(a)$ to $gad(b)$ is deleted, we can instead delete the message inside $gad(b)$ (or $gad(a)$), since it lies on more paths. Thus, we can assume that all paths from S_1 to S_2 in any process can be removed by logging n intra-gadget messages (one per gadget). G then has a vertex cover consisting of the nodes corresponding to these gadgets. These nodes form a vertex cover since we must have logged at least one message in each pair of connected gadgets.

Only-If Part. Assume G has a vertex cover of k or fewer nodes. We can delete k or fewer edges in P's execution graph and remove all paths from S_1 to S_2 in any process. Since gadgets are connected exactly when their corresponding nodes are connected, any two connected gadgets will have at least one of their messages logged. Deleting the edges corresponding to these logged messages will ensure no path exists from S_1 to S_2 in any process. QED

The Paragon Performance Monitoring Environment

Bernhard Ries (Intel European Supercomputer Development Center)
bernhard@esdc.intel.com

R. Anderson, W. Auld, D. Breazeal, K. Callaghan, E. Richards, W. Smith (Intel SSD)
{raya, auld, donb, karla, ericr, wds}@ssd.intel.com

Abstract

Parallel systems present a special challenge to debugging and performance analysis given the massive amounts of data and physically distributed state of the application. We describe an integrated toolset that provides an extensible and consistent programming environment for monitoring and visualizing the performance of parallel applications. It uses a scalable distributed monitoring system to gather performance data that drive profiling and graphical performance visualization tools. Performance data ara analyzed by both application and system oriented performance tools which are tied together by a common graphical interface.

1   Introduction

Modern scalable high-performance computing systems provide the high potential for sustained performance that is needed to solve Grand Challenge computing problems. To fully understand the performance behavior of such systems and to operate the machines near the high end of their performance range, new performance data-collection, analysis and visualization tools are needed. Some of the most challenging problems that have to be solved by an integrated performance environment are:

- Different categories of users require different types of performance tools. For example, system administrators are interested in observing the overall behavior of the system while application programmers need to focus on a specific application run. Thus, there is a need for both system and application performance analysis tools. The tools must be able to present information at different levels of detail: from low-level information on hardware and operating system statistics up to high-level metrics on program efficiency or speed.

- Monitoring the performance of massively parallel systems or applications can lead to very large amounts of performance data. Different techniques must be devised for the performance environment to be able to handle or reduce the amount of data that needs to be processed. Possible approaches include selective instrumentation techniques, data reduction and compression, and scalable presentation techniques. Many researchers agree that processors with at least the same processing power as those executing the application are needed to properly reduce and present performance data. This dilemma can be solved by using the high-performance computing system itself for performance analysis.

- The current trend towards multiprogramming in operating systems for scalable high-performance computers introduces new problems for application performance tools. In order to be an aid in tuning applications the tools must be able to distinguish system effects from application bottlenecks.

- Monitoring the performance of parallel applications necessarily introduces perturbation. The performance environment must strive to minimize the amount of intrusion and should try to filter out monitoring effects or provide the user with a measure of the intrusiveness of the measurements.

- The diversity of programming models available on scalable high-performance computing systems and the lack of programming model standards make it necessary for the tools to be highly flexible. Tools should be able to present the performance data in the context of the programming model being used but it should not be necessary to design a completely new performance environment for every new programming model.

This work was supported in part by the Advanced Research Projects Agency, Agreement Number MDA972-92-H-001 and the Intel Corporation.

This paper describes how these problems are addressed in the integrated performance monitoring environment developed by Intel and initially targeted for use on Intel Paragon systems. It consists of an instrumentation front-end, a distributed monitoring system and a set of graphical and command-oriented tools that can be used to analyze performance data.

The paper is organized as follows: in section 2 we describe related work, section 3 gives some background on the target system, an Intel Paragon running Paragon OSF/1. Section 4 gives a detailed description of the performance monitoring architecture. Section 5 describes future plans and extensions, and section 6 presents our conclusions.

2   Related Work

The field of performance monitoring and performance visualization for parallel machines has received a lot of attention lately. This has led to a large number of monitoring environments with different capabilities. The Pablo [16] project has implemented a system in which performance tools are built from individual modules that can be easily interconnected and reconfigured. The Pablo team has also developed a self-documenting trace-format that includes internal definitions of data types, sizes and names. The TOPSYS environment [3] is based on a distributed monitoring system that is used by multiple tools, including an on-line performance visualizer [4]. The IPS-2 system [11] takes a hierarchical approach to performance visualization and integrates both system and application based metrics. ParaGraph [10] is a tool that provides a large number of different displays for visualizing the performance of parallel application. We have tried to integrate the results of this work into our performance monitoring environment and will likely continue to exploit the results of this research.

3   The Paragon Multiprocessor

3.1   Hardware Architecture

The Paragon [6] hardware architecture consists of processing nodes based on the Intel i860XP microprocessor. Each processing node has one i860XP application processor, a second i860XP used for message-protocol processing and a Network Interface Controller (NIC) that connects the node to the communication network. Nodes are arranged in a two-dimensional mesh and are interconnected through a network that provides a full-duplex node to node bandwidth of 200 MB/s.

Each node board also contains hardware support for performance monitoring in the form of a special daughterboard that provides hardware counters. The counters are used to monitor bus ownership and information about communication traffic. In addition, the daughterboard implements a a 56-bit global counter that is driven from the global 10 MHz clock from the backplane. This counter is used to generate global time stamps that are accurate to 100 ns local to each node and 1 microsecond across all nodes in the system. This feature is of particular importance since many performance tools need highly accurate time stamps to generate correct results.

3.2   Operating System and Programming Model

The operating system and programming model supported by the target architecture have to be taken into account during the design of performance monitoring tools since the performance tools should be able to present the performance data in the context of the programming model being used.

The Paragon OSF operating system [19] is based on the Mach 3.0 microkernel technology and an extended OSF/1 server. Each node in the system runs a microkernel that provides core operating system functions like virtual memory management and task management. Other operating system services are handled by the OSF/1 server. The operating system provides a single system image with standard UNIX functionality. Multiprogramming is fully supported by the operating system - multiple users may log on to the machine and run applications at any time.

If all nodes in the machine were scheduled according to conventional UNIX scheduling policies, this would lead to non-deterministic load conditions for parallel application runs. To avoid this, partitions with different scheduling characteristics can be defined within the machine. In this way, the nodes in the system are logically divided into an I/O partition that contains nodes designated to communicate with peripheral devices, a service partition used for sequential jobs (shells, user commands etc.) and a compute partition that is used for parallel application runs.

The service partition normally uses conventional UNIX scheduling with dynamic load balancing through process migration. Gang scheduling is used within the compute partitions. This means that while a parallel job is executing, it has exclusive access to the set of nodes it uses. After a configurable time-interval, the entire job is suspended (rolled out) and a different job is resumed (rolled in). Thus, the perturbation of parallel application runs through other jobs in the system is minimized. Even so, the scheduling of applications must be taken into account when designing performance tools because the effects of gang scheduling must be filtered out by application level tools.

The Paragon supports a message passing programming model that is compatible with the NX/2 programming model available on previous generation Intel machines [14]. This model is also supported by the application level performance tools. However, support for other programming models such as shared virtual memory, High Performance Fortran (HPF) or thread models may be added in the

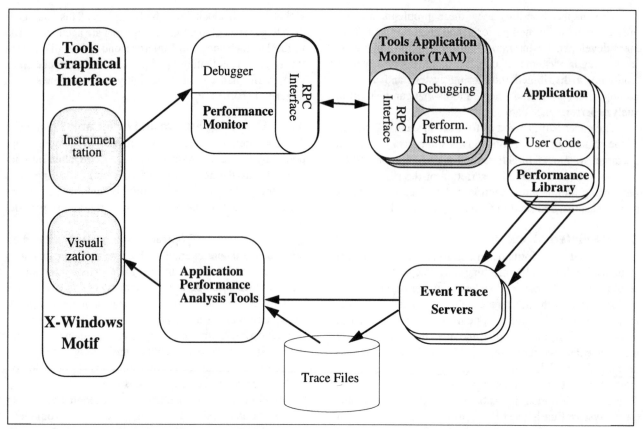

Fig. 1. Performance Monitoring Architecture

near future. Thus, the performance monitoring environment must be flexible enough to allow tools for new programming models to be added without undue implementation overhead.

4 Performance Monitoring Architecture

4.1 Overview

Figure 1 gives an overview of the Paragon Performance Monitoring Architecture. It consists of the following parts:

- The Tools Graphical Interface (TGI) is used as a front-end for instrumenting the parallel application and to visualize the performance data produced by the performance tools. It is based on X-Windows and the Motif toolkit.

- The Instrumentation Front End, which is part of the debugger, is used to parse user requests for performance instrumentation of a parallel application. It generates the commands that are then sent to the distributed monitoring system through an RPC interface.

- The Distributed Monitoring System consists of the

Tools Application Monitor (TAM), the performance library that is linked with the application program, and the event trace servers. The TAM is responsible for instrumenting the application with jumps to the performance libraries. The libraries produce trace data that are sent to the event trace servers. The servers perform post-processing tasks and write the performance data to file or send them directly to the application performance analysis tools.

- The application performance analysis tools interpret the trace data they receive from the event trace servers. Currently, we have implemented three tools. A modified version of ParaGraph allows detailed graphical animation of processor activity and message passing. Profiling tools (prof and gprof) can be used to examine performance at the statement and procedure level.

- The System Performance Visualizer (SPV) is designed to monitor the overall system usage by displaying parameters such as CPU utilization, bus usage and network traffic. Since this tool is not application oriented, there is no need for instrumentation. Instead, the data are directly generated by the hardware performance monitoring board.

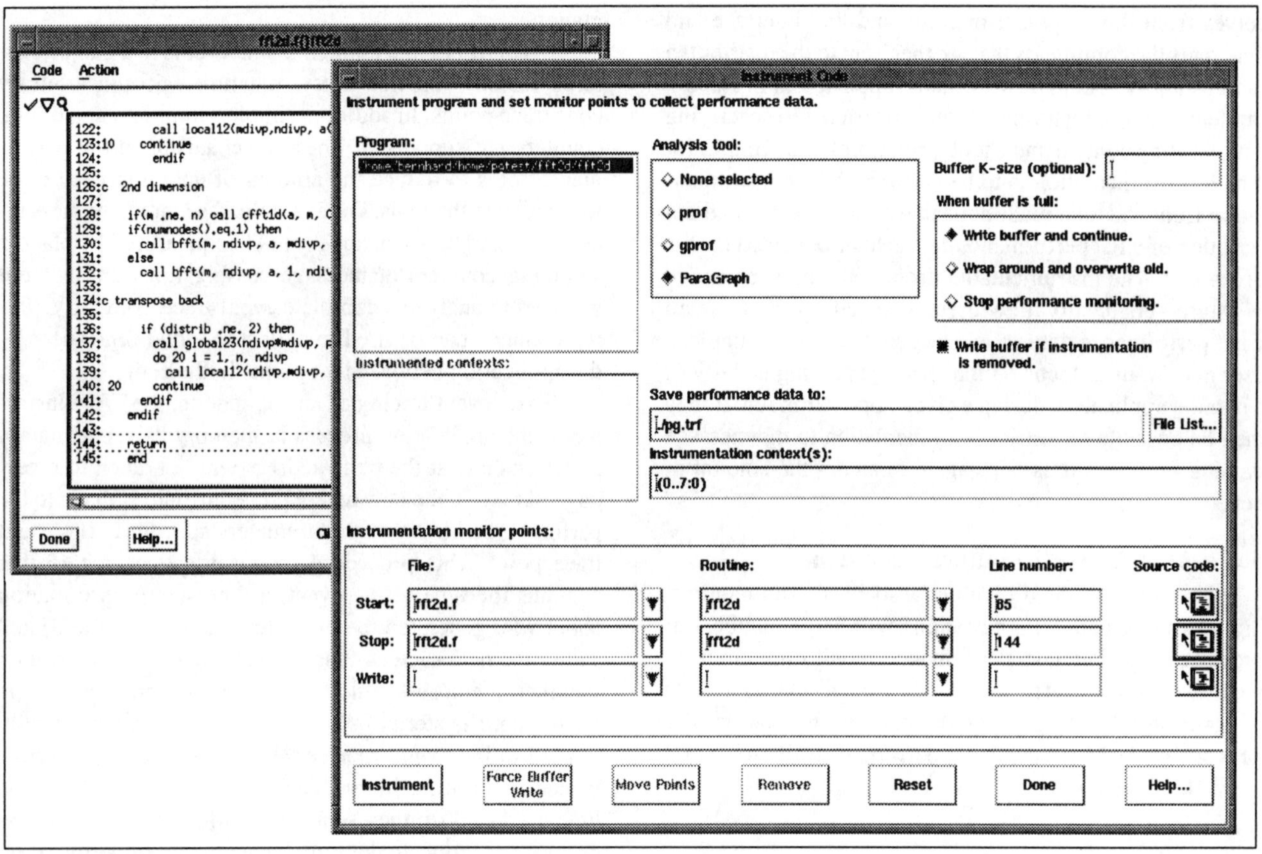

Fig. 2. Instrumenting an Application

As can be seen, the performance monitoring environment is closely integrated with the debugging functionality since many of the tasks necessary for performance monitoring are also needed for debugging (e.g. accessing symbol table information, instrumenting the application). In the following discussion we will focus on the performance monitoring aspects of the Paragon tool environment. A detailed description of the debugging interface and the techniques used in the Tools Application Monitor can be found in [1].

4.2 Tools Graphical Interface

The Tools Graphical Interface serves two purposes. On the one hand it is used for loading, starting and instrumenting an application. On the other hand it provides a common interface through which the user can operate the performance tools and display performance data. The fact that all tools share a common user interface that is based on the Motif style guide standard makes the functionality of the tool environment easily and obviously available to the user. Operating and learning the interface is further facilitated by an on-line help system that provides context-sensitive help. Most tools also provide a command-line interface since this may be preferable to a graphical interface in some cases.

The tasks of instrumenting and starting application runs are closely integrated with the debugging functionality available on the Paragon. To instrument an application for use with a particular performance tool, the user starts the application using the debugger. The next step consists of defining a monitoring context, i.e. a part of the parallel application for which tracing is to be enabled. Such a context (a set of processes and start and stop locations for tracing within those processes) can be defined through a point-and-click interface (see Figure 2). This allows the user to focus on the part of the application that is limiting the performance and to reduce the amount of performance data that is generated, a feature that is of particular importance for detailed performance measurements. For example, the profiling functionality could be used to find the parts of the application that consume the largest percentage of time and these parts could then be analyzed in detail using the ParaGraph tool. In the example shown in Figure 2, the user has chosen to instrument a particular section of code that is delimited by two line numbers for analysis using the ParaGraph tool.

4.3 Instrumentation Front End

The instrumentation front end parses commands it receives from the graphical or command-line interface and generates the commands that are then sent to the distributed monitoring system to instrument the application. In the first implementation, instrumentation is restricted to specifying a monitoring context and a tool (prof, gprof, ParaGraph) for which instrumentation is to be performed. The instrumentation front end then reads a file that contains a detailed description of what performance data is to be collected for the given tool. The instrumentation front end will be extended in future versions to allow users to specify in more detail what performance data should be gathered. For example, a user may want to focus on the message passing activity of a parallel application during a given application run. It may then be possible to restrict instrumentation to the message passing functions thus once again reducing the amount of generated performance data.

4.4 Distributed Monitoring System

To overcome the difficulties associated with monitoring massively parallel applications with large numbers of processes, the Paragon performance monitoring environment uses a distributed monitoring system that is able to perform high-level operations in parallel. It consists of a network of TAM processes, a performance library and a network of event trace servers.

4.4.1 Tools Application Monitor

The Tools Application Monitor is made up of a network of TAM processes arranged in the form of a broadcast spanning tree with one TAM process for every node used by the application. This makes it possible to broadcast monitoring requests to all nodes in an efficient manner. The instrumentation front-end communicates with the TAM network through an RPC interface based on the Mach Interface Generator (MIG). Communication within the TAM network also occurs by message-passing over Mach ports. For the purposes of performance instrumentation communication within the TAM network is downstream only since the performance data are sent to the application performance tools by way of the event trace servers (see below).

4.4.2 Performance Library

To instrument an application for performance measurements, the TAM modifies the application code to vector to a performance library. To minimize the data collection perturbation, the performance library is automatically linked with every application so that event traces can be gathered without incurring the overhead of context switches. The performance data that can be captured include event traces and counters as well as profiling infor-

mation:

Event traces and counters: The events that can be captured include function entry, function exit and arbitrary code trace points. In addition, simple, summing, and timing counters are supported. These mechanisms allow performance tools to reduce the amount of data that need to be forwarded to the tools. For example, the amount of messages exchanged between nodes could be measured by placing summing counters at message-passing functions without the need to analyze a complete event-trace. Similarly, timing counters can be used to collect the total time spent by the application between two points in the code.

To do event tracing of an application, the TAM instruments the application process in memory by replacing application code at the trace address with a branch to a new page of text. In the new text, a procedure call is made to the performance library with parameters specific to the event trace point. This procedure produces a trace record that contains the type of the event, a time stamp, information about who generated the event (e.g. node, process id) and additional data such as function parameters or data from a specified memory location. To minimize perturbation, the trace record is stored in a trace buffer that is periodically flushed to the event trace servers. In addition, the performance monitoring library can be configured to trace the time used to flush the event trace buffers in order to allow performance tools to determine the amount of perturbation introduced. Once the performance library procedure returns, the new text code executes the replaced instructions and jumps back to the event trace point and application execution continues.

Due to the complex programming model supported by the Paragon, tracing only events within the application code is not sufficient. Paragon applications may spawn multiple processes on every node. This means that context switch information has to be traced in spite of the fact that the gang scheduling policy ensures that an application has exclusive access to its processing nodes while it is scheduled. The context switch information is collected by the Mach kernel. Similarly, information about gang scheduling has to be gathered to enable the tools to correctly portray the application's performance information. This information is routinely gathered by the scheduler that is responsible for handling roll-in and roll-out events.

Profiling information: For profiling, a counter is set at each function exit and the performance library collects a statistical sample of the current program counter at each clock tick. To turn profiling on, the performance library sets up profiling buffers and then uses the OSF/1 AD profil() system call. When profiling is turned off, the performance library flushes and deallocates the profiling buffer. Profiling and event tracing can occur simultaneously. For example, the call graph information used by the gprof tool is

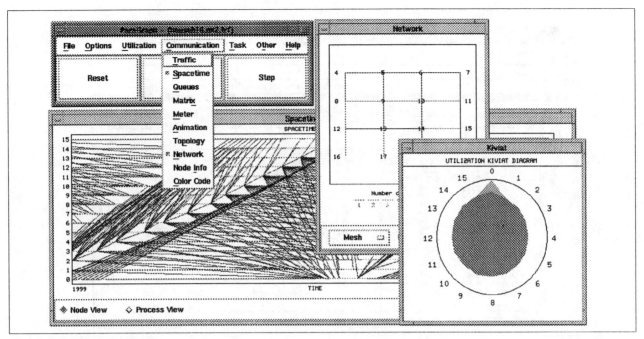

Fig. 3. ParaGraph Displays

derived from function entry traces while the time spent within routines is measured through statistical profiling.

4.4.3 Event Trace Server

The Event Trace Servers perform post-processing tasks on the performance data they receive from the performance library. One event trace server services a number of performance libraries. The exact ratio of servers to performance libraries is configurable and depends on the type of performance measurement being performed. For example, for profiling, one separate file with profiling information is generated for each profiled process so it may be desirable to also have one event trace server per process. Other performance tools (e.g. ParaGraph) operate on a single trace file that contains event trace information from all monitored nodes in the application. In this case, the event trace servers must merge event trace information from multiple performance libraries, and information about context switches and gang-scheduling into one trace. ParaGraph also requires the trace to be sorted in time order. In this case, a network of event trace servers arranged in a tree configuration may be more appropriate.

In the normal case, the output of the event trace servers consists of one or many trace files that can be interpreted by the application performance analysis tools. However, the trace servers may also forward their output directly to a tool for on-line visualization of an application's performance.

The Paragon performance monitoring environment supports event traces in the Pablo Self-Defining Data For-

mat[16]. SDDF is a trace description language that specifies both the data record structures and data record instances. The Pablo software supports both binary and ASCII trace representations and provides a flexible library of C++ classes to access and manipulate the data stored in SDDF files. It thus meets the goal to "standardize the interface routines to trace files and not the physical file itself" [12][13].

4.5 Application Performance Analysis Tools

The application performance analysis tools interpret the performance data gathered by the distributed monitoring system and report them back to the user. They either have a command-line interface that can be invoked from the graphical interface or directly use the functionality of the tools graphical interface to present graphical output. Currently, we have implemented three application performance tools but the design of the performance monitoring architecture makes it easy to integrate new tools into the framework.

4.5.1 ParaGraph

ParaGraph [10] is one of the most widely used tools for analyzing the performance of parallel applications. It can be used in a post-mortem fashion to visualize the performance data contained in a trace file generated during an application run. ParaGraph was originally written for use with the PICL Portable Instrumented Communication Library [7], which runs on a variety of message passing par-

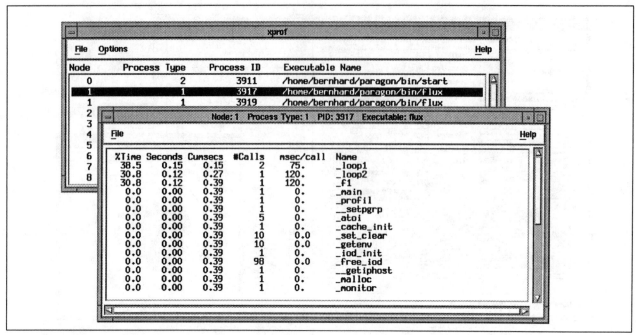

Fig. 4. Profiling Interface

allel architectures. In the mean time, many groups have adapted ParaGraph to other programming models and architectures [8][15][17]. The widespread use of ParaGraph was the prime motivation for providing the tool as part of the Paragon performance monitoring environment. ParaGraph is a graphical tool that provides a variety of displays to visualize the performance of a parallel application. The user can choose as many displays as will fit on the screen from three different types of displays. The utilization displays are concerned primarily with depicting processor utilization, communication displays can be used to visualize interprocessor communication, and the task displays provide a way of relating the events in the trace to source locations in the parallel programs. Figure 3 shows some of the displays generated by ParaGraph for a Householder transformation algorithm executed on 16 nodes. The general functionality of the tool has been left unchanged and will not be described any further. However, a number of important changes and enhancements have been made to the tool.

- ParaGraph has been integrated into the Tools Graphical Interface. Thus, the tool now has a standardized Motif interface that is easy to learn and consistent with the rest of the Paragon tool environment. As a side-effect, many new features were added to the user interface (e.g. the correct handling of expose and resize events, use of backing store, when available, to retain information when a window is obscured and re-exposed, customization of the interface through X-resources, the ability to interactively change the colors used for the

visualization, an on-line help facility and extended support for saving ParaGraph's screen layout).

- ParaGraph now supports the major features of the Paragon/NX programming model such as synchronous, asynchronous and interrupt-driven message passing and probe operations. Since the distributed monitoring system allows tracing of system calls, we can also trace file I/O and display I/O activity in ParaGraph's utilization displays. ParaGraph also supports multiple processes per node and takes gang-scheduling and task switch information into account when displaying performance data. The mapping of logical application nodes to physical nodes is also available through the distributed monitoring system and is used by ParaGraph to visualize the routing of messages through the physical network.

- The instrumentation front-end allows the user to specify a monitoring context in an on-line fashion. This makes it possible to focus on subsets of nodes and parts of an application's code without the need to recompile. ParaGraph fully supports traces that come from subsets of an application's nodes. In addition, the user can select a subset of the traced nodes for visualization. This provides a primitive zooming mechanism and enhances the scalability of the tool.

- ParaGraph now supports traces in the Pablo Self-Defining Data Format [16] instead of the PICL trace format. One of the drawbacks of this approach is that the Pablo routines do not allow random-access to

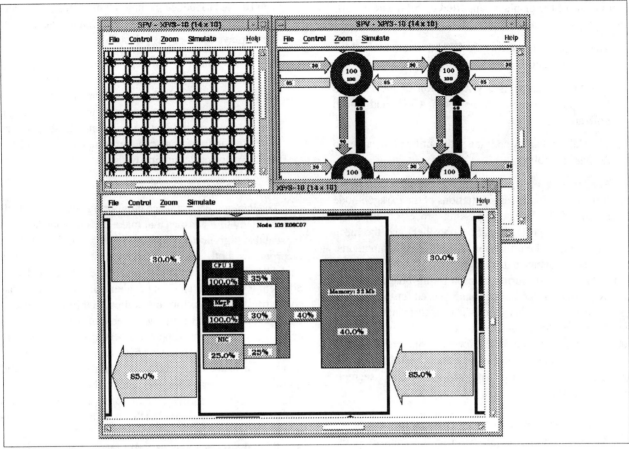

Fig. 5. System Performance Visualization

the trace file which forced us to drop ParaGraph's critical path analysis since it is based on scanning the trace file backwards. However, ParaGraph's critical path analysis seems to be of limited use since it provides little feedback as to where in the source-code the critical path is located. We plan to implement a true source-code oriented critical path analysis tool in the near future (see section 5).

4.5.2 Prof and Gprof

For profiling, the Paragon performance monitoring environment provides slightly modified versions of the well-known UNIX tools prof and gprof [9]. The tools are fully integrated with the distributed monitoring system as has been described above. Thus, the tools graphical interface and the instrumentation front-end can be used to specify a profiling context in the usual way, which results in instrumentation of the appropriate part of the application.

One file containing profiling data is produced per instrumented application processes and the files are stored in a common directory for analysis by the profiling tools. In addition to the standard command-line interface, the profilers can also be invoked through the tools graphical interface (see Figure 4).

4.6 System Performance Visualization

The application performance analysis tools described above allow the user to monitor the behavior and performance of parallel applications at different levels of granularity. They try to filter system effects out as far as possible. However, in many cases it is useful to monitor overall system usage without focusing on a specific application. The System Performance Visualization tool (SPV) serves this purpose.

One of the motivations for implementing this tool was the fact that the LED panel on previous generation Intel systems was often used as a primitive debugging and performance monitoring aid. SPV is a graphical tool that allows the user to visualize the Paragon front panel on a workstation but it also provides zooming capabilities that make it possible to display more detailed information such as CPU, mesh and memory bus utilization values. Colors that can be configured according to the user's wishes are used to represent different utilization values. Figure 5 shows some of the displays supported by SPV. The following displays are available:

- The CPU display shows the CPU utilization of all the nodes. Mesh utilization is not displayed.

- The Mesh display is a visualization of the Paragon front panel which shows both CPU and mesh utilization.

- The Values display adds the actual utilization values to the Mesh display.

- The Node display provides the greatest level of detail. It shows symbolic representations of the Paragon node boards (CPU, message passing processor, memory, bus and Network Interface Controller) and the mesh and displays the utilization values for all components.

The performance data displayed by SPV are generated by the hardware performance monitoring board and thus bypass the data collection mechanism used for the application performance analysis tools. The performance data collected by the hardware are sent periodically over the Paragon mesh to a daemon that forwards the information to the SPV tool. Thus, the display is pseudo real-time, i.e. the front panel information is displayed within a few seconds of the real Paragon front-panel.

5   Future Directions

We plan to further improve our performance monitoring environment in the near future. Areas that will be investigated include:

- New tools: The design of the performance monitoring architecture makes it relatively easy to add new tools to the environment. We plan to add tools that help relate performance bottlenecks to locations in the user. In many cases, simple table of numbers may be more effective than sophisticated graphical displays. Thus, a good candidate for addition to the tool environment is a critical path analyzer such as the one implemented within the IPS-2 system [18]. As new programming models emerge, the tools will have to be modified to support these programming models.

- It is not feasible to cover all the needs users have for performance tools. The Pablo system is very flexible in that it allows tools to be configured out of existing modules. We plan to integrate parts of our tool environment completely into the Pablo software. This will allow users to add new tools and displays to the existing performance monitoring environment. It will also make it possible to run different modules of the performance analysis tools in parallel to fully utilize the power of the parallel machine for performance analysis. Selective instrumentation techniques can

then be used to reduce the amount of performance data generated by tracing only the information needed for the displays the user has selected.

- We also plan to further modularize the tool environment. Currently, some of the features needed for performance analysis are implemented within the debugger (e.g. instrumentation, symbol table lookup). It would be desirable to implement these parts as separate modules that can be joined to form either performance or debugging tools.

6   Conclusions

The Paragon performance monitoring environment addresses many of the issues that make performance analysis for scalable high-performance computing a difficult task. It incorporates both system and application performance analysis tools which are able to present performance data at different levels of detail. The problems of monitoring massively parallel applications are addressed through a distributed monitoring system that is capable of using the power of the parallel system to perform performance analysis in parallel. At the same time we strive to minimize perturbation and measure the amount of perturbation introduced through monitoring. To some extent, the environment is able to support performance monitoring in a multiprocess and multiuser environment but this is a topic that needs further investigation.

Even though we have initially focused on implementing tools that support the NX message-passing programming model, we believe the monitoring environment is flexible enough to allow an easy implementation of tools for other programming models.

7   References

[1]   D. Breazeal, R. Anderson, W.D. Smith, W. Auld, and K. Callaghan. *A Parallel Software Monitor for Debugging and Performance Tools on Distributed Memory Multicomputers*. In *Proceedings of the Supercomputer Debugging Workshop 1992*, Dallas, Texas, October 1992. Los Alamos National Laboratory.

[2]   D. Breazeal, K. Callaghan, and W.D. Smith. *IPD: A Debugger for Parallel Heterogeneous Systems*. In *Proceedings of the ACM/ONR Workshop on Parallel and Distributed Debugging*, pages 216-218, Santa Cruz, CA, May 1991.

[3]   T. Bemmerl. *The TOPSYS Architecture*. In H.Burkhart, editor, *CONPAR 90 - VAPP IV*, volume 457 of *Lecture Notes in Computer Science*, pages 732-743. Springer-Verlag, Berlin, Heidelberg, New York, September 1990.

[4]   T. Bemmerl, O. Hansen, and T. Ludwig. *PATOP for Performance Tuning of Parallel Programs*. In H.Burkhart, editor, *Proceedings of CONPAR 90 - VAPP IV, Joint International Conference on Vector and Parallel Processing*, volume 457 of *Lecture Notes in Computer Science*, pages 840-851, Zurich, Switzerland, September 1990. Springer-Verlag, Berlin, Heidelberg, New York.

[5]   T.Bemmerl. *Programming Tools for Massively Parallel Supercomputers*. In *Proceedings of the CNRS-NSF workshop on Environments and Tools for Parallel Scientific Computing*, Saint Hilaire du Touvet, France, September 1992.

[6]   Intel Supercomputer Systems Division. *Paragon XP/S Product Overview*. Intel Corporation, 15201 N.W. Greenbrier Parkway, Beaverton OR 97006, 1992.

[7]   G.A. Geist, M.T. Heath, B.W. Peyton, and P.H. Worley. *A User's Guide to PICL, a portable instrumented communication library*. Technical Report ORNL/TM-11616, Oak Ridge National Laboratory, Oak Ridge, TN, October 1990.

[8]   I. Glendinning, S. Hellberg, P. Shallow, and M. Gorrod. *Generic Visualisation and Performance Monitoring Tools for Message Passing Parallel Systems*. In N.Tophan, R.Ibbett, and T.Bemmerl, editors, *Proceedings of the IFIP WG 10.3 Workshop on Programming Environments for Parallel Computing*, volume A-11 of *IFIP Transactions*, pages 139-149, Edinburgh, Scotland, April 1992. North-Holland.

[9]   S.L. Graham, P.B. Kessler, and M.K. McKusick. *gprof: a Call Graph Execution Profiler*. *ACM SIGPLAN Notices*, 17(6):120-126, June 1982.

[10]   M.T. Heath and J.A. Etheridge. *Visualizing the Performance of Parallel Programs*. *IEEE Software*, 8(5):29-39, September 1991.

[11]   J.K. Hollingsworth, R.B. Irvin, and B.P. Miller. *The Integration of Application and System Based Metrics in a Parallel Program Performance Tool*. In *Proceedings of the Third ACM SIGPLAN Symposium on Principles and Practice of Parallel Programming*, volume 26, no. 7 of *ACM SIGPLAN Notices*, pages 189-200, Williamsburg, Virginia, April 1991. ACM Press.

[12]   B.P. Miller and C. McDowell. *Summary of ACM/ONR Workshop on Parallel and Distributed Debugging*. *ACM Operating Systems Review*, 26(1):18-31, January 1992.

[13]   B. Mohr. *Standardization of Event Traces Considered Harmful or Is an Implementation of Object-Independent Event Trace Monitoring and Analysis Systems Possible?* In *Proceedings of the CNRS-NSF workshop on Environments and Tools for Parallel Scientific Computing*, Saint Hilaire du Touvet, France, September 1992.

[14]   P. Pierce. *The NX/2 Operating System*. In *Proceedings of the 3rd Conference on Hypercube Concurrent Computers and Applications*, pages 384-391. ACM, 1988.

[15]   D.T. Rover, M. B. Carter, and J. L. Gustafson. *Performance Visualization of SLALOM*. In *Proceedings of the Sixth Distributed Memory Computing Conference*, pages 543-550, Portland, Oregon, May 1991. IEEE, IEEE Computer Society Press.

[16]   D. A. Reed, R. D. Olson, R. A. Aydt, T. M. Madhyastha, T. Birkett, D. W. Jensen, B. A. Nazief, and B. K. Totty. *Scalable Performance Environments for Parallel Systems*. In *Proc. of the Sixth Distributed Memory Computing Conference*, pages 562-569, Portland,Ore, April 1991. IEEE.

[17]   M. van Riek and B. Tourancheau. *The Design of the General Parallel Monitoring System*. In N.Tophan, R.Ibbett, and T.Bemmerl, editors, *Proceedings of the IFIP WG 10.3 Workshop on Programming Environments for Parallel Computing*, volume A-11 of *IFIP Transactions*, pages 127-137, Edinburgh, Scotland, April 1992. North-Holland.

[18]   C.Q. Yang and B.P. Miller. *Critical Path Analysis for the Execution of Parallel and Distributed Programs*. In *Proceedings of the 8th International Conference on Distributed Computing Systems*, pages 366-375, San Jose, CA, June 1988. IEEE.

[19]   R. Zajcew, P. Roy, D. Black, C. Peak, P. Guedes, B. Kemp, J. LoVerso, M. Leibensperger, M. Barnett, F. Rabii and D. Netterwala. *An OSF/1 UNIX for Massively Parallel Multicomputers*. In *Proceedings of the Winter 1993 USENIX Technical Conference*, pages 449-468, San Diego, CA, January 1993. The USENIX Association.

Execution-Driven Tools for Parallel Simulation of Parallel Architectures and Applications (*)

David K. Poulsen and Pen-Chung Yew

Center for Supercomputing Research and Development
University of Illinois at Urbana-Champaign
Urbana, IL 61801

Abstract

EPG-sim is a newly-developed set of tools that performs execution-driven critical path simulation, trace generation, and simulation for serial, optimistically parallelized, and parallel application codes. These capabilities are integrated within a single framework through the use of intelligent source-level instrumentation. The ability to perform execution-driven simulations driven by optimistically parallelized codes, the ability to execute these simulations on parallel hosts, the use of source-level instrumentation, and the integration of the capabilities provided by EPG-sim are among the novel contributions of this work. EPG-sim has important uses in studying parallel architectures, parallelizing compilers, and parallel applications.

1. Introduction

Execution-driven simulation and tracing techniques have received considerable attention in recent years. Execution-driven techniques modify application codes by inserting additional *instrumentation* code. The resulting *instrumented codes* execute on a *host* machine using actual input data. Execution causes the generation of events reflecting the behavior of the original applications executing on a hypothetical *modeled* machine. Other event generation techniques include hardware monitoring, interrupt-based methods, pure simulation, and microcode-based methods [1]; these techniques can be used to study multiprogramming and operating system behavior in addition to application behavior. This paper concerns itself with execution-driven event generation techniques based on application code instrumentation, and tools resulting from the use of these techniques.

Execution-driven techniques have important uses in studying parallel systems. Parallel processor, memory system, and interconnect architectures can be modeled in order to study their parameters and the effect of varying these parameters on system or application performance. The effectiveness of parallelizing compilers, and of particular parallelizing transform techniques, can be evaluated. Dynamic profiling and analysis based on execution-driven techniques can be used to guide parallelizing compilers and to assess application parallelism and performance.

Execution-driven event generation may be used in *critical path simulation* (CPS), in *execution-driven trace generation* (ETG), to produce input for *trace-driven simulation* (TDS), or to drive *execution-driven simulation* (EDS). CPS directly executes instrumented serial codes such that they are implicitly, *optimistically parallelized* when executed on a uniprocessor host. This allows the potential parallelism and performance of these optimistically parallelized codes to be measured. ETG is merely the process of generating trace events via execution-driven techniques. TDS and EDS use these events to drive simulators, rather than using direct execution as in CPS.

The distinction between TDS and EDS is one of feedback. In TDS, no feedback (e.g., event timing or memory latency as determined by simulation) occurs that could affect subsequent event generation. In EDS, event generation and simulation are coupled so that feedback can occur. This feedback can be used to alter the ordering, timing, or latency of subsequently-generated events. In a simulated parallel code, the path of execution, and ordering and latency of events, may depend on the ordering and timing of preceding events [2]. In TDS, these dependences cannot be taken into account, limiting the accuracy of such simulations [3, 4]. EDS correctly models processor interactions. Another limitation of TDS is that traces, particularly those generated by non-execution-driven means, are biased to the particular system being traced, so they cannot be used arbitrarily in simulations of dissimilar systems (e.g., with different numbers of processors). EDS does not have

(*) This work was supported by the Department of Energy under grant No. DE FG02-85ER25001, the National Science Foundation under grant No. NSF MIP 89-20891, the National Security Agency, and an IBM Resident Study Fellowship.

such a limitation.

EPG-sim is a new set of instrumentation, tracing, and simulation tools that unifies and integrates execution-driven CPS, ETG, and EDS capabilities through the use of intelligent source-level instrumentation techniques. The tools have the ability to study serial, optimistically parallelized, or parallel codes, and the ability to model varying processor and system architectures. CPS, ETG, and EDS can be performed on uniprocessor or parallel hosts. EPG-sim provides a broader spectrum of capabilities than other tools described in the literature, since it supports all of these execution-driven techniques and provides good performance over a wide range of cost / accuracy tradeoffs. EPG-sim is robust, having the ability to simulate entire, full-size application codes using realistic input data, and is portable to different uniprocessor and parallel host machines.

This paper is organized as follows. First, background material on existing execution-driven systems is presented and EPG-sim is described in comparison to these systems. Next, the implementation of EPG-sim is described in detail. This includes information on source-level instrumentation, CPS, ETG, and EDS, and a brief discussion of accuracy issues. The last section of the paper presents experimental results that illustrate the functionality and usefulness of EPG-sim. A more extensive discussion of the systems, capabilities, and issues described in this paper can be found in [5].

2. Background

The design of EPG-sim addresses the need for an integrated set of tools that combines the best features of existing execution-driven simulation and tracing systems. The following paragraphs provide a brief survey of these systems and discuss the ways in which their capabilities are combined in EPG-sim.

Many execution-driven simulation and tracing systems have been described in the literature. MaxPar [6] is a CPS tool that measures the potential performance, parallelism, and behavior of optimistically parallelized codes given various architectural parameters. Other CPS tools have been used to measure program parallelism [7] and to perform dynamic dependence analysis [8]. ETG tools instrument serial codes for trace generation on uniprocessor hosts [1], or parallel codes for trace generation on parallel hosts [9, 10]. Examples of EDS systems include Tango [2], Proteus [11], and PEET [12]. These systems use serial or parallel codes to drive simulations that execute on uniprocessor hosts. Simulators exist that perform EDS for parallel codes on parallel hosts, but only for particular types of host architectures or modeled system architectures [13].

EPG-sim allows CPS, ETG, and EDS to be driven by serial, optimistically parallelized, or parallel codes. This can be done because of the extension of CPS instrumentation techniques to ETG and EDS. CPS executes on uniprocessor hosts and measures optimistically parallelized codes. ETG for serial codes executes on uniprocessor hosts, or for parallel codes on parallel hosts. In most cases, EDS for parallel codes executes on uniprocessor hosts. EPG-sim allows instrumented parallel codes to execute on uniprocessor or parallel hosts, and allows optimistically parallelized or parallel codes to drive parallel simulations.

Some CPS tools and most general EDS tools use machine-language-level instrumentation and event generation techniques. This results in processor models that are efficient but fairly architecture-specific. CPS tools that employ source-level instrumentation have used somewhat simplistic processor models. EPG-sim uses source-level instrumentation to implement a general, architecture-independent processor model that can model varying processor architectures at a reasonable level of detail. CPS is useful for low-cost, high-level architecture and application performance studies, but such simulators cannot model memory systems at a detailed level. EDS tools have the ability to model varying system architectures at varying levels of detail, limited only by the cost and complexity of the desired models. EPG-sim simultaneously supports modeling of varying processor and system architectures and combines CPS and EDS capabilities, resulting in a system that provides a wider range of cost / accuracy tradeoffs than other systems described in the literature.

3. Implementation

EPG-sim consists of a common set of instrumentation tools, a runtime library, and a set of parallel, discrete-event simulation tools (see Figure 1). The instrumentation tools use intelligent, source-level techniques and are implemented within a parallelizing compiler. The runtime library provides support for instrumented application codes and provides interfaces for tracing and simulation. The discrete-event simulation tools model varying parallel system architectures and implement EDS when coupled with instrumented codes. The following sections describe the various components of EPG-sim in more detail.

3.1 Source-level instrumentation

EPG-sim uses source-level instrumentation to generate events for CPS, ETG, and EDS. Source-level event generators are implemented by instrumenting application codes using tools based on the Parafrase-2 compiler [14],

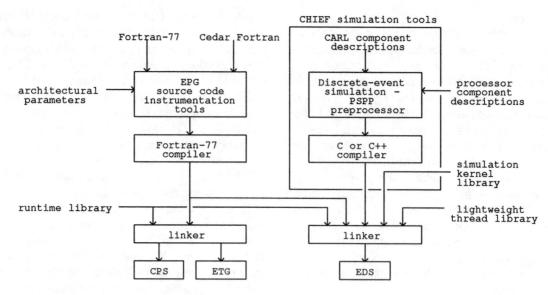

Figure 1 - EPG-sim Overview

developed at CSRD. Parafrase-2 supports Fortran-77 and Cedar Fortran [15], allowing both serial and parallel codes to be instrumented. The EPG (Execution-driven Program Generation) source code instrumentation tools are implemented as a set of passes within Parafrase-2. These tools perform instrumentation and constitute the front-end for EPG-sim. EPG handles source codes in a robust manner, with little or no user intervention, and produces efficient instrumented codes.

Events of interest are identified statically by EPG or by instrumenting to identify dynamic instances of events. Examples of events identified by EPG include: memory accesses, processor operations, task scheduling and dispatching operations, and static or dynamic data or control dependences. Dynamic dependence analysis is described in Section 3.2. Instrumentation is added for each event of interest to process that event at execution time. Examples of event processing include: generating traces, dispatching events to a simulator, histogramming or collecting statistics based on events, or performing direct simulation such as CPS (discussed in Section 3.2). Events may be associated with the value of simulation time at which they occur, or with the *static task* in the source code (a particular subroutine, loop, basic block, or statement) in which they occur. Histogramming allows profiles to be produced as a function of simulation time or of static tasks. Instrumentation may delay subsequent events in simulation time according to the occurrence of dynamic data or control dependences, feedback from EDS, or resource availability (e.g., processors, memory ports). The specific types of events identified and their corresponding instrumentation strategy varies according to the type of simulation being performed.

EPG uses a detailed, table-driven processor model that may be changed in order to model varying processor architectures. The table specifies the number of cycles of simulation time to assume for each individual arithmetic, logical, and assignment operation, and for overheads associated with variable access, array addressing, subprogram calls, loop startup, processor scheduling, and intertask or interprocedural memory access or synchronization. Fields in each table entry allow different values to be specified for scalar and pipelined vector operations. The processor model is flexible enough to describe varying architectures at a reasonably detailed level; however, implementation details like register and pipeline usage and conflicts are not modeled.

The processor model uses the notion of a task *grain size*, particularly when optimistically parallelizing codes. Task grain sizes include: subroutines, loop iterations (i.e., a DOALL / DOACROSS model of execution), basic blocks, statements, and individual operations. Tasks at the specified grain size are allowed to execute in parallel, completely or partially overlapping with the execution of other tasks, subject to their dynamic dependences or synchronization and resource availability. Operations within a particular task must execute serially. When performing optimistic parallelization, the number of simulated processors may either be *unconstrained*, allowing maximum parallelism in codes to be measured, or *fixed*, allowing the effects of processor scheduling policies to be observed. The processor scheduler is implemented as a runtime library routine that can be used to implement arbitrary scheduling policies. Scheduling strategies include round-robin, earliest available processor, and *near-optimal* [6], which attempts to maximize processor utilization.

3.2 Critical path simulation (CPS)

CPS in EPG-sim uses instrumentation to measure the minimum parallel execution time of optimistically parallelized codes, given various architectural and timing parameters. Variations on the techniques described here are also used to implement ETG and EDS, as discussed in the following sections. The techniques used are based on those used in MaxPar [6].

Minimum parallel execution time is measured by instrumenting to compute the earliest time at which each task could execute, given complete dynamic, interprocedural knowledge of data and control dependences, task grain size and associated serialization constraints, processor scheduling, resource constraints, and other parameters. Task completion times are determined by the timing of the serialized operations within them. An operation in a task may complete as soon as its dependences and serialization constraints are satisfied and the time for its operations and memory accesses has been assessed. Processor event timing is performed according to the model described in Section 3.1. In the most basic case, memory delays are also constant; more complex memory delay models are possible, as discussed below.

Dynamic data dependence analysis is accomplished by keeping track of times at which variables or array elements are available for reading or writing. These times are kept in *shadow variables* associated with each variable or array element. For a variable X, a *write shadow* twX stores the time at which X was last written, and a *read shadow* trX stores the time at which X was last read. If storage-related (anti and output) dependences are ignored, read shadows are not used. Dynamic interprocedural dependence analysis is implemented by passing appropriate shadows across subprogram call boundaries. To measure dynamic control dependences, tCOND shadows track times at which control dependences were satisfied.

Computations are performed using shadow variables to perform dynamic dependence analysis, determining the earliest time at which an operation could execute given its dynamic dependences. As an example, consider the addition operation C = A + B. For this operation, the instrumentation shown in Figure 2 is generated by EPG. The addition operation may begin as soon as anti and output dependences are satisfied for C (twC, trC), flow dependences are satisfied for A and B (twA, twB), and control dependences on the statement are satisfied (tCOND). The operation may complete as soon as its dependences are satisfied and the computation takes place (tOPS). Read shadows are updated according to the time

the operation completes in the event that subsequent anti dependences involving A or B are encountered. The instrumentation for an operation is dense; however, good execution-time performance still results.

```
C = A + B
twC = max (twC,trC,twA,twB,tCOND)
      + tOPS
trA = max (trA,twC)
trB = max (trB,twC)
```

Figure 2 - CPS Instrumentation Example

Operations within a task are performed serially, so for task grain sizes consisting of multiple statements, an artificial flow dependence is introduced between sequential statements to serialize them. This is done using an additional shadow variable, tTIME, in the max() expression in the instrumentation for each statement. When the number of processors is fixed, a runtime library processor scheduling routine is called at the beginning of each task to select a processor according to a specified strategy. An additional shadow term, tAVAIL, is added to the max() expression for the first statement in each task to delay the start of that task until the scheduled processor is available.

To measure the effect of varying intertask memory delay or synchronization overhead, the distinction between intertask and intratask memory accesses must be made. To do this, tasks are uniquely numbered, and the current task number is kept in tTASKid. A *synchronization write shadow* swX is associated with each write shadow twX. Whenever twX is updated, swX is set to the tTASKid of the task that wrote X; this allows the instrumentation to determine at execution time if a variable to be read was written in the same task. Whenever twX is accessed, a delay is added to twX if swX does not match the current tTASKid; this assesses the intertask delay. Similarly, a *synchronization read shadow* srX is associated with trX, is updated whenever X is updated, and is checked whenever trX is accessed. To measure the effect of varying interprocedural synchronization overhead this same technique is used, only invocations of subprograms, not tasks, are uniquely numbered, and tPROCid, pwX, and prX shadows, corresponding to the tTASKid, swX, and srX shadows, are used.

CPS executes on uniprocessor hosts. To perform simulations using parallel Cedar Fortran codes as input, EPG converts these codes into serial Fortran-77 codes that still generate correct parallel timing information. This is done by converting parallel loops into serial loops and using shadow variables (e.g., tTIME shadows) to keep track of times at which parallel tasks *would have* executed if they had been executed in parallel. The resulting instrumented codes execute serially, but their shadow variables reflect their simulated parallel execution.

3.3 Trace generation (ETG)

ETG is accomplished in EPG-sim through the use of variations on the CPS instrumentation techniques described in Section 3.2. ETG is supported for serial, optimistically parallelized, and parallel codes. When performing ETG, events of interest are instrumented to generate trace information. Events of interest typically include memory references, or entry to or exit from particular static tasks. Trace information generated includes virtual address, data (from actual program execution), the value of simulation time, and processor number. Traces can also be generated in symbolic form, for instance, including variable names and subscript expressions for memory references. The following instrumentation is added for each memory reference event:

```
call genevent(opcode,addr,pid,time).
```

The exact content and form of the trace output is determined by `genevent`, a runtime library interface routine that is reconfigurable to suit particular applications.

ETG is performed for optimistically parallelized codes simply by using CPS instrumentation and adding `genevent` calls. For serial or parallel codes, the CPS instrumentation is modified to disable dynamic dependence analysis and optimistic parallelization (read and write shadows are no longer used), and to enforce the serialization required by the program semantics (using `tTIME` shadows, see Section 3.2). This results in only explicit parallelism being exploited. ETG for serial or optimistically parallelized codes executes on uniprocessor hosts. ETG for parallel codes may execute on uniprocessor or parallel hosts. When performing ETG for parallel codes on uniprocessor hosts, techniques similar to those used in CPS for parallel codes are used to convert parallel applications into instrumented serial codes.

3.4 Execution-driven simulation (EDS)

EDS in EPG-sim utilizes the ETG techniques described in Section 3.3 to form execution-driven event generators. These event generators are coupled with parallel discrete-event simulators to implement EDS. The overall structure of an EPG-sim EDS is shown in Figure 1.

CHIEF [16] parallel discrete-event simulators are used to construct system models and to perform simulation. The CHIEF system is portable, allowing simulations to be executed on a variety of uniprocessor and parallel host machines. A CHIEF simulator consists of a simulation model and a kernel library that drives the simulation. Multiple simulation paradigms are supported through the use of different kernel libraries. Paradigms currently supported use standard parallel discrete-event simulation, Chandy-Misra, or Time-Warp techniques [17]. Since CHIEF simulation kernels support parallel discrete-event simulation, EDS in EPG-sim is supported on uniprocessor or parallel hosts. Because of the features of the execution-driven event generators used, EDS in EPG-sim can be driven by serial, optimistically parallelized, or parallel codes. This results in the ability to perform parallel simulation of optimistically parallelized codes on parallel hosts.

CHIEF simulation models are described and constructed using a hardware description language, CARL [18]. CARL, an extension of C, supports hierarchical, component-based modeling of parallel systems at a wide range of levels of detail, from high-level abstract models to detailed behavioral register-transfer-level models. This allows models to be constructed at a level of complexity (and corresponding execution time cost) appropriate to the desired degree of simulation detail. Because of the hierarchical, component-based nature of CARL, these models can be used to construct other, more complex models. Processor models are special components, also described in CARL, that interface with execution-driven event generators. System models described in CARL are compiled for use with a particular kernel through a preprocessor, PSPP.

An EPG-sim EDS consists of a system model, processor models, instrumented application codes to drive the processor components, and runtime library interface routines. A thread of execution in an instrumented application code is associated with each processor component in the simulation model. Each thread, when executed, generates the sequence of simulation events produced by its processor. A distinct thread per processor can be provided by executing a different set of application code routines on each processor (i.e., a MIMD model of execution), or by executing a single application code in SPMD fashion, using one thread per processor. The latter approach is suitable for Cedar Fortran codes with parallel loops. In this case, instrumentation restructures loops so that they self-schedule iterations. For the parallel DOALL loop shown in Figure 3, the code is restructured so that multiple threads may execute it simultaneously.

The lower part of Figure 3 shows the resulting self-scheduling code (omitting any event instrumentation). Each thread gets a unique processor assignment from the `getvpn` call. The first iteration number (`inum`) and total number of iterations (`icnt`) for the loop are passed to the `loop_entry` routine, which stores these values so they can be shared by all threads. The `loop_entry` and `loop_exit` calls also perform barrier synchronizations that enforce the semantics of the parallel loop. Each `next_iter` call self-schedules a loop iteration, leaving the index value for that iteration in a private, per-thread copy of the loop index variable (`I`). Other program variables (`A`, `B`, `C`) are shared among threads.

```
doall I = M, N, P
      C(I) = A(I) + B(I)
end doall
      . . .
call getvpn(pid)
inum = M
icnt = max((N - M + P) / P, 0)
call loop_entry(inum,icnt)
while (next_iter(I,P)) do
      C(I) = A(I) + B(I)
end while
call loop_exit
```

Figure 3 - Self-Scheduled Parallel Loops

In order for a processor component to produce simulation events based on its thread in an application code, a lightweight thread library is used to switch between each processor component and its application thread. At any given point in simulation time, each processor component needs to know the next event to be issued by its thread. To determine this, the processor component performs a lightweight context switch into its thread and executes instrumented application code until an event is generated. Runtime library interface routines capture this event and perform a lightweight context switch back to the corresponding processor component. This mechanism ensures that events among multiple processors are issued and simulated in the correct order, even when a single application code is executed in SPMD fashion, or when simulating the execution of optimistically parallelized codes. The next time a processor component performs a lightweight context switch into its thread, the processor component returns the time at which the simulation of the previous event for that thread completed. This execution-driven feedback mechanism allows the timing of simulated events to affect the order and timing of subsequent events.

3.5 Accuracy

EPG-sim provides a wide range of cost / accuracy tradeoffs for simulating parallel systems by providing both CPS and EDS capabilities and by allowing varying processor and system architectures to simultaneously be simulated. The use of execution-driven techniques rather than trace-driven techniques increases the usefulness and accuracy of the tools. While the functionality of EPG-sim is the focus of this paper, accuracy issues are discussed briefly here.

CPS is appropriate for high-level architecture and application studies. Dynamic, interprocedural dependence analysis allows CPS to uncover parallelism not identified via static compiler analysis. Additional parallelism can be identified that might only have been uncovered through the use of parallelizing transformations. The major limitations of CPS - the ability to extract optimistic, but not optimal, parallelism, and the inability to model complex memory system architectures - are inherent in the techniques used, and are not limitations specific to EPG-sim. Parallelism measured using CPS is not optimal for two important reasons. First, CPS determines the critical path of execution through codes as presented; the effects of arbitrary code restructuring cannot be measured. Second, since CPS executes on uniprocessor hosts, tasks are dispatched to the processor scheduler in serial execution order. Although these tasks may execute in a different logical order than their physical dispatch order, the dispatch order can affect the optimality of the task schedule.

CPS cannot easily model memory latency effects caused by memory contention, network contention, or cache coherence activity. Constant memory delays are usually assumed; however, instrumentation can distinguish between intratask and intertask memory accesses and assign different delays accordingly. Runtime routines can be used to model more complex memory delays, but the interaction of memory accesses between processors is still difficult to model. EDS can be used to overcome these limitations, since it allows arbitrary system models to be constructed at any level of detail or abstraction desired.

One accuracy concern that remains in EPG-sim EDS is the accuracy of the processor models. Both CPS and EDS in EPG-sim use the architecture-independent processor model described in Section 3.1. The processor model is general and less architecture-specific than that of previously reported CPS or EDS systems. Processor models implemented using source-level instrumentation are not appropriate for modeling details of internal processor behavior such as internal register and pipeline usage and conflicts or instruction-sequence-specific timing. Register usage effects can be approximated through more sophisticated source-level instrumentation. For instance, EPG-sim can suppress events due to scalar variable accesses to model register usage.

4. Experimental results

The preceding sections describe the components, capabilities, and implementation of EPG-sim. This section presents some example results, illustrating the functionality and efficiency of the tools. Simulation results are used to demonstrate some of the event types that can be identified, to give simple examples of the kinds of data that can be derived, and to compare the performance of various types of simulations. The examples are intended only to illustrate the usefulness of EPG-sim; no detailed attempts are made to discuss the architectural significance of the results obtained.

CPS for several Perfect Benchmarks (R) codes [19] was performed to illustrate the usefulness and efficiency of such simulations. Most experiments were performed with unconstrained numbers of modeled processors (speedup results for fixed numbers of processors and near-optimal processor scheduling are also presented). Local (intratask) memory accesses, and arithmetic and logical operations, took one cycle each. Global (intertask) memory access delays took one cycle for most experiments, or were varied as indicated. Tasks were defined to be loop iterations, and storage-related data dependences were ignored. The dataset sizes of the codes studied were reduced in order to decrease execution time. These types of reductions do not change the relative performance of simulations when compared to native application speed.

code	parallel	speedup	s(512)
QCD	6065688	5.17	3.97
MDG	17068897	29.72	26.29
TRACK	4169294	28.33	24.09
BDNA	158069	1777.24	378.15
OCEAN	245670	312.73	192.60
DYFESM	381842	132.08	98.76
ARC2D	83108	1804.36	348.35
FLO52	91962	357.71	199.55
TRFD	11927	41.23	37.36
SPEC77	27801229	25.50	1.91

Figure 4 - Perfect Code Optimistic Parallelization

Figure 4 shows the minimum parallel execution time for optimistic parallelization of various Perfect codes using unconstrained numbers of processors. The maximum speedup (or *inherent parallelism* [6]) of each code, compared to serial execution time as calculated during CPS, is also given, followed by the speedup for 512 processors using near-optimal processor scheduling. The unconstrained processor speedups represent the maximum parallelism of the codes. Fixing the number of processors shows that some codes require large numbers of processors in order to exploit this parallelism effectively. Even with a fixed number of processors, CPS is able to identify considerably more parallelism than current parallelizing compilers [20].

Figure 5 is a histogram for the Perfect code TRACK displaying the number of task instantiations against parallel execution time. The data are sampled in large buckets; each point accumulates a task instantiation count for a range of approximately 20,000 cycles of simulation time. The profile clearly indicates two distinct phases of computation within the execution of the code; the first has more irregular parallelism, whereas the second exhibits a more regular pattern. Profiles of this type can be used to identify phases of computation that have unusually high or low parallelism, or can be plotted against static tasks to indicate sections of application codes with particular parallelism characteristics.

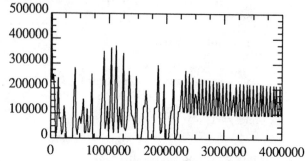

Figure 5 - TRACK Parallelism vs. Execution Time

Figure 6 shows speedup versus intertask communication overhead (global memory access delay) for various Perfect codes, normalized at zero overhead for each code to facilitate comparison. The decrease in speedup with increasing overhead indicates the relative sensitivity of each code's performance to this overhead. This decrease can also be interpreted as indicating the amount of intertask communication (or synchronization) in each code's critical path of execution. When parallel execution time, as opposed to speedup, is plotted against overhead (not shown), the increase in execution time is approximately linear in the amount of overhead; this explains the characteristic 1/x shape of the curves in Figure 6, and suggests that the effect of increased overhead is to lengthen the critical path of execution, not to cause other paths to become critical.

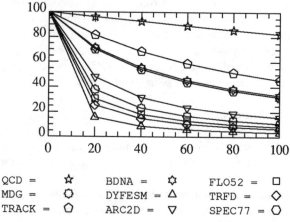

QCD = ☆	BDNA = ✿	FLO52 = □
MDG = ○	DYFESM = △	TRFD = ◇
TRACK = ⬠	ARC2D = ▽	SPEC77 = ○

Figure 6 - Speedup vs. Communication Overhead

Additional experiments using CPS on the Perfect code TRFD were performed to compare various versions of this code. Experiments were performed with parameters and assumptions as in the previous CPS experiments. Three versions of TRFD were studied: TRFD, the original code; TRFD-p, a functionally equivalent parallel version of TRFD [21]; and TRFD-s, a serial version of TRFD-p.

code	num	speed	cpu
TRFD	unc	41.23	1.06
TRFD	512	37.36	65.31
TRFD	128	26.74	17.31
TRFD	32	15.28	5.31
TRFD	16	9.59	3.31
TRFD-s	unc	893.33	5.00
TRFD-s	512	185.06	325.00
TRFD-s	128	55.49	85.25
TRFD-s	32	18.34	26.00
TRFD-s	16	9.91	16.25
TRFD-p	unc	30.94	2.75
TRFD-p	512	30.94	3.50
TRFD-p	128	30.94	3.00
TRFD-p	32	22.61	3.00
TRFD-p	16	13.16	3.00

Figure 7 - TRFD Parallelization

Figure 7 shows the maximum speedup for optimistic parallelization of TRFD and TRFD-s, or for explicit parallelization of TRFD-p, using unconstrained or fixed numbers of processors. The time to execute each simulation is also shown, in user cpu seconds on a SUN SPARCstation-2 model 4/75. All execution times are normalized so that the raw execution time of each uninstrumented code is 1.0. The data for TRFD corresponds to the data in Figure 4. The results for TRFD-s show that restructuring reveals significant additional parallelism that could not be identified in TRFD; however, more processors are required to exploit this parallelism. Much of the additional parallelism is created by eliminating induction variables and scalar data dependences. The results for TRFD-p show the effect of exploiting only the explicit parallelism in TRFD-s. There is still significant inherent parallelism in the restructured code that is not explicit in parallel loops in TRFD-p.

The execution time results in Figure 7 show that CPS is efficient for unconstrained or small fixed numbers of processors. Execution time increases linearly with the (fixed) number of processors since near-optimal processor scheduling employs a linear search algorithm to locate the most suitable processor to schedule. Round-robin processor scheduling can be used to overcome this limitation while still obtaining reasonable schedules. Execution times for TRFD-p are lower because only explicit parallelism is being measured; this requires less instrumentation since dynamic dependence analysis is not performed.

TDS and EDS for TRFD-p were performed to compare their accuracy and performance. In either case, events were generated considering only the explicit parallelism in TRFD-p, and events for scalar memory references were

suppressed to simulate register usage. The modeled machine used a dancehall architecture, uniform memory access delays, and processors with private caches connected by a crossbar. Experiments assumed 16 processors, one cycle processor to cache delays, one cycle cache hit delays, 100 cycle cache miss delays, and 100 cycle delays for cache invalidation messages. The cache coherence scheme used directories with pointer caches, unlimited processors per directory entry, and a simple three-state protocol. Memory and network contention were not modeled.

Figure 8 shows the results of various simulations of TRFD-p. Speedups compared to similar simulations with one processor are shown, along with average cache hit ratios and the time to execute each simulation (as in Figure 7). As expected, the speedups shown fall short of the ideal speedups predicted in Figure 7 (TRFD-p, 16 processors).

no.	speed	hit %	cpu
1	--	--	23.00
2	8.44	95.50%	53.25
3	8.44	95.50%	331.50
4	--	--	131.25
5	8.33	95.63%	378.75

Figure 8 - TRFD-p TDS and EDS

Line 1 in Figure 8 shows the time to perform EPG-sim ETG for TRFD-p assuming 16 processors. This time is longer than the time to perform the corresponding CPS (Figure 7, TRFD-p, 16 processors) due to the insertion of genevent calls at each memory reference. Lines 2 and 3 show the results for TDS using the traces generated in line 1. In line 2, the simulation used a straightforward model coded in C; in line 3, the EPG-sim EDS CHIEF model executed in TDS mode. As expected, lines 2 and 3 show the same simulation results, but varying execution times. Line 4 shows the time to perform the simulation in line 3 assuming all memory accesses are cache hits and with the cache components of the CHIEF model removed. The difference in execution times between lines 3 and 4 indicates the overhead of adding additional components to the CHIEF model.

Line 5 in Figure 8 shows the results of performing EPG-sim EDS for TRFD-p. This simulation produces slightly different results compared to TDS (line 3) due to the accuracy gained from allowing feedback during simulation. The differences are due primarily to differences in processor scheduling. TDS uses near-optimal processor scheduling, performed at ETG time, whereas EDS uses self-scheduling at execution time. While the difference in cache hit ratio is negligible, and the difference in speedup is only 1.3%, TRFD-p does not use any constructs that typically cause larger accuracy discrepancies [4].

The execution time required to generate events for EDS is the same as that required for ETG (line 1 in Figure 8) since the same instrumented code is executed in both cases. To make a fair comparison between execution times for TDS and EDS the time for ETG should be added to the TDS times. Considering this, the overhead of moving from EPG-sim TDS (line 1+3) to EDS (line 5) is not large. Most of the overhead incurred in moving from a straightforward C TDS (line 1+2) to an EPG-sim EDS is due to the introduction of CHIEF simulation models. This overhead is a strong function of the complexity of the CHIEF model, as illustrated by the difference in execution times between lines 3 and 4. While the overhead of using CHIEF models is large, using these models provides a wide range of cost / accuracy tradeoffs, allows simplified model construction and integration, and is necessary so that simulation events are correctly ordered.

CPS is a form of high-level execution-driven simulation that is useful in studying the parallelism of applications and the ability of architectures to exploit that parallelism. Basic CPS experiments, even with unconstrained numbers of processors, can produce useful performance information. CPS for entire Perfect codes using actual datasets is easily accomplished. Execution-time performance decreases by only three to five times (compared to native execution speed) when basic simulations for the Perfect codes are performed, despite the dense instrumentation required for these simulations. EDS incurs significant additional execution-time overhead, but allows system modeling at a considerably enhanced level of detail and accuracy. Most of this additional overhead is due to the use of CHIEF system models, while a smaller amount is due to the overhead of generating events to drive simulations. Some EDS performance is sacrificed in EPG-sim, when compared with other EDS systems (e.g., Proteus) in order to allow architecture-independent processor modeling and the integration of CPS.

5. Conclusions

Execution-driven techniques instrument application codes to generate events for simulation or tracing. These techniques are more accurate and versatile than trace-driven techniques and are preferable for studying parallel systems. Previously reported systems using execution-driven simulation and tracing techniques have numerous capabilities desirable in a general execution-driven system, including critical path simulation (CPS), trace generation (ETG), and simulation (EDS). CPS models the execution of optimistically parallelized codes on a hypothetical modeled system. This type of simulation reduces the dependence on parallel codes and hand parallelization when studying parallel architectures. EDS allows complex systems to be modeled in greater detail, with a correspondingly higher cost in execution time. The execution-driven capabilities described in the literature have been implemented using various source-level and machine-language-level approaches. The need exists for a general, flexible set of execution-driven tools, implemented within a single framework, that addresses all of these capabilities. Source-level instrumentation provides an attractive and functional way to accomplish this implementation and integration.

EPG-sim is a set of general-purpose execution-driven tools that performs parallel simulation and trace generation for studying parallel systems. These tools can model varying processor and system architectures, and can simulate the effects of serial, optimistically parallelized, or parallel codes being executed on modeled parallel systems. CPS, ETG, and EDS can be performed, and simulations can be executed on uniprocessor or parallel hosts. These capabilities are integrated into a single execution-driven system through the use of source-level instrumentation. EPG-sim is portable to different uniprocessor and parallel host machines, increasing the flexibility of the system. The ability to perform EDS with optimistically parallelized codes driving modeled parallel systems, the ability to execute these simulations on parallel hosts, the use of source-level instrumentation, and the integration and breadth of capabilities provided by EPG-sim are among the novel contributions of this work.

Source-level instrumentation provides many useful benefits: it allows the integration of the various capabilities of EPG-sim; and it provides intelligent and efficient instrumentation that is architecture independent, is tailored to specific types of simulation, and provides good execution-time performance. These features result in a system providing an exceptionally broad range of cost / accuracy tradeoffs, supporting the notion of paying in simulation complexity only for the level of detail required. The use of EPG to implement CPS has produced several useful features compared to other CPS systems. EPG instrumentation is robust and expandable, and it offers good performance, both in terms of performing instrumentation and in terms of simulation cost. EPG instrumentation models processor architectures in a detailed and less architecture-specific manner, allowing the effects of varying architectural and timing parameters on performance to be studied in greater detail. The ability to measure interprocedural synchronization overhead is a useful extension of previous CPS work.

Acknowledgments

The design of EPG-sim owes much to several other projects and individuals at CSRD, notably: Parafrase-2 (Bruce Leung, Mohammad Haghighat, and Dale Schouten), MaxPar (Ding-Kai Chen), CPAT (Paul Petersen), and CHIEF (Pavlos Konas). The authors also wish to thank Dr. Josep Torrellas, John Andrews, and Carl Beckmann for their interest in this paper and the tools it describes, and Merle Levy and Angeline Gliniecki for detailed, last-minute proofreading.

References

1. Stunkel, C. B., Janssens, B., and Fuchs, W. K., "Address Tracing for Parallel Machines", IEEE Computer, January 1991, pp. 31-38.

2. Davis, H., Goldschmidt, S., and Hennessy, J., "Multiprocessor Simulation and Tracing Using Tango", Proceedings of ICPP 1991, pp. II-99-106.

3. Bitar, P., "A Critique of Trace-Driven Simulation for Shared-Memory Multiprocessors", in Dubois, M., and Thakkar, S. (eds.), 16th ISCA Workshop on Cache and Interconnect Architectures in Multiprocessors, Boston: Kluwer Academic, 1989.

4. Goldschmidt, S. R., and Hennessy, J. L., "The Accuracy of Trace-Driven Simulations of Multiprocessors", Proceedings of SIGMETRICS 1993, pp. 146-157.

5. Poulsen, D. K., and Yew, P.-C., "Execution-Driven Tools for Parallel Simulation of Parallel Architectures and Applications", Center for Supercomputing Research and Development, University of Illinois at Urbana-Champaign, CSRD Report No. 1280, September 1993.

6. Chen, D.-K., Su, H.-M., and Yew, P.-C., "The Impact of Synchronization and Granularity on Parallel Systems", Proceedings of ISCA 1990, pp. 239-249.

7. Larus, J., "Parallelism in Numeric and Symbolic Programs", Third Workshop on Programming Languages and Compilers for Parallel Computing, August 1990.

8. Petersen, P., and Padua, D., "Dynamic Dependence Analysis: A Novel Method for Data Dependence Evaluation", Presented at the 5th Annual Workshop on Languages and Compilers for Parallel Computing, New Haven, CT, August 3-5, 1992.

9. Eggers, S., Keppel, D., Koldinger, E., and Levy, H., "Techniques for Efficient Inline Tracing on a Shared-Memory Multiprocessor", Proceedings of SIGMETRICS 1990, pp. 37-47.

10. Stunkel, C. B., and Fuchs, W. K., "TRAPEDS: Producing Traces for Multicomputers via Execution-Driven Simulation", Proceedings of SIGMETRICS 1989, pp. 70-78.

11. Brewer, E., Dellarocas, C., Colbrook, A., and Weihl, W., "Proteus: A High Performance Parallel Architecture Simulator", Laboratory for Computer Science, MIT, MIT/LCS/TR-516, September 1991.

12. Grunwald, D., Nutt, G. J., Sloane, A. M., Wagner, D., and Zorn, B., "A Testbed for Studying Parallel Programs and Parallel Execution Architectures", Technical Report, Department of Computer Science, University of Colorado, Boulder, April 28, 1992.

13. Reinhardt, S. K., Hill, M. D., Larus, J. R., Lebeck, A. R., Lewis, J. C., and Wood, D. A., "The Wisconsin Wind Tunnel: Virtual Prototyping of Parallel Computers", Proceedings of SIGMETRICS 1993, pp. 48-60.

14. Polychronopoulos, C. D., Girkar, M. B., Haghighat, M. R., Lee, C. L., Leung, B. P., and Schouten, D. A., "Parafrase-2: An Environment for Parallelizing, Partitioning, Synchronizing and Scheduling Programs on Multiprocessors", Proceedings of ICPP 1989, pp. II-39-48.

15. Hoeflinger, J., "Cedar Fortran Programmer's Handbook", Center for Supercomputing Research and Development, University of Illinois at Urbana-Champaign, CSRD Report No. 1157, October 1991.

16. Bruner, J., Cheong, H., Veidenbaum, A., and Yew, P.-C., "CHIEF: A Parallel Simulation Environment for Parallel Systems", Center for Supercomputing Research and Development, University of Illinois at Urbana-Champaign, CSRD Report No. 1050, November 1990.

17. Konas, P., and Yew, P.-C., "Synchronous Parallel Discrete-Event Simulation on Shared-Memory Multiprocessors", Presented at the 6th Workshop on Parallel and Distributed Simulations, Newport Beach, CA, January 1992.

18. Beckmann, C. J., "CARL: An Architecture Simulation Language", Center for Supercomputing Research and Development, University of Illinois at Urbana-Champaign, CSRD Report No. 1066, December 1990.

19. Berry, M., Chen, D.-K., Koss, P., Kuck, D., Pointer, L., Lo, S., Pang, Y., Roloff, R., Sameh, A., Clementi, E., Chin, S., Schneider, D., Fox, G., Messina, P., Walker, D., Hsiung, C., Schwarzmeier, J., Lue, K., Orszag, S., Seidl, F., Johnson, O., Swanson, G., Goodrum, R., and Martin, J., "The Perfect Club Benchmarks: Effective Performance Evaluation of Supercomputers", International Journal of Supercomputer Applications, Vol. 3, No. 3, Fall 1989, pp. 5-40.

20. Blume, W., and Eigenmann, R., "Performance Analysis of Parallelizing Compilers on the Perfect Benchmarks (R) Programs", IEEE Transactions on Parallel and Distributed Systems, Vol. 3, No. 6, November 1992, pp. 643-656.

21. Andrews, J. A., and Gallivan, K. A., "Analysis of a Cedar Implementation of TRFD", Center for Supercomputing Research and Development, University of Illinois at Urbana-Champaign, CSRD Report No. 1312, August 1993.

Session 12:
Panel
Moderator: Frederica Darema

What's in the Future for Parallel Architectures?

Panelists

David Douglas, Thinking Machines Corporation

Anoop Gupta, Stanford University

Olaf Lubeck, Los Alamos National Laboratory

David Maier, Oregon Graduate Center

Paul Messina, California Institute of Technology

Justin Ratner, Intel Corporation

Burton Smith, Tera Computers

Moderator

Frederica Darema, IBM Corporation

Abstract

For over a decade now parallelism has been in the forefront as the cost effective means of attaining high-performance computing capabilities. Progress in chip technology for processors and memories, and progress in high speed networks are enabling advancement in several frontiers of high-performance computing: from the more powerful parallel personal computers and workstations, to the massively parallel machines, to distributed computing. A significant derivative of the high computational power and network speed is the generation and exchange of vast amounts of data with the accompanying necessity to manage such data.

We have seen multiple approaches to parallelism, that have manifested themselves in terms of the parallel systems architectures, the base processors the systems are built upon, the networks interconnecting these processors. Experience has validated or invalidated the effectiveness of some of these systems. Experience has also shown that, though parallelism looks promising, an important factor for success is the development of suitable software.

So the questions still remain: What kinds of parallel systems should we build? What's the best parallel architecture? Is there only one, or there are multiple? Are the advances we see, exclusionary of each other, or are they complimentary and even symbiotic. How are the answers to such questions affected by the technology capabilities for the base processors, the interconnections, and the software developments? This panel will address these issues, and will provide opinions.

Session 12:
Minisymposium
Supercomputing Around the World

Supercomputing Around the World

David X. Kahaner
Office of Naval Research Asia
23-17, 7-chome, roppingi
Minato-ku, Tokyo 106 JAPAN
kahaner@cs.titech.ac.jp

Allen D. Malony
Dept. of Comp. and Info. Science
University of Oregon
Eugene, Oregon 97403-1202
malony@cs.uoregon.edu

Abstract

Many countries around the world now have high-performance computing programs underway. In the second of what we hope will be a continuing mini-symposium series, representatives from Singapore, Indonesia, Norway, The Netherlands, and Malaysia meet to speak on national and international high-performance activities.

1 Introduction

This mini-symposium offers an international perspective of high-performance computing activities by bringing together representatives from different parts of the world to discuss supercomputing endeavors in their respective countries. As remarked in the first mini-symposium, the potential of supercomputing knows no national bounds, and whatever the goals of supercomputing initiatives in different regions of the world - scientific, economic, even political - the exchange of information about these activities is of vital importance to achieving the success of supercomputing on a global scale. It is hoped that this mini-symposium will help to broaden international participation and exposure in Supercomputing conferences in the future. This year we welcome representatives from Singapore, Indonesia, Norway, The Netherlands, and Malaysia. The abstract of each speaker's talk is presented below.

Parallel Computing at the Institute for Systems Science, Singapore

Dr. Raghu Raghavan

**Manager for Parallel Processing Research
Institute for System Science
National University of Singapore
Heng Mui Keng Terrace
Kent Ridge, Singapore 0511
RAGHU@ISS.NUS.SG**

In contrast to the mainstream of parallel computing research in the United States, where performance is the main criterion and cost seemingly unimportant, the applications in the Asian context in general must aim at cost-effectiveness as a goal. In Singapore, there is a Supercomputing Center which functions mainly as a service center to encourage local industry to try a (NEC) supercomputer for their applications. At the Institute of Systems Science, we have a research program that has two distinct application areas in mind: (i) the modeling of continuous spatially extended systems, and (ii) mathematical programming applications for trade and transportation in a distributed environment. In addition, we have (iii) a theory program to serve partly as a rubric to cover the harder mathematical developments needed, as well as more long-term research, and (iv) a point of view on imaging applications that runs somewhat counter to present industry trends.

In (i) our present focus area is finite- or boundary-element models of parts of the human body for advanced medical applications. In (ii) we use a paradigm of topology-indpendent computation across a network, similar to the IBM 'postal model', or the Berkeley 'LogP' model to develop algorithms. In (iii) we have done some analysis for the branch-and-bound problem in the LogP model, and also obtained some results in inductive inference that point to an absolute advantage for a team of machines over a single one in learning. Finally in (iv) we continue to believe in the cost-effectiveness of hardware efficient on data-parallel algorithms, similar in spirit to the MasPar for a number of image-related applications.

Our platforms are: the SGI-Onyx currently with 4 processors for (i), a network of Sun SparcStation-10's connected by ATM-switched fiber for (ii), smart researchers for (iii), and a (sub-optimal) 8000-processor SIMD machine (WaveTracer Zephyr) as a testbed for ideas in (iv).

The program at ISS is just over a year old. The talk will describe the activities, the progress, and the plans in the above-mentioned areas.

Supercomputing In Indonesia

Mr. Suryadi Slamet

Computing Center
Nasantara Aircraft Industries Ltd.
JL Pajajaran 154
Bandung 40174, Indonesia
PT. Pindad (Persero)
JL. Gatot Subroto
Bandung 40285, Indonesia
HERU@OGAH.CS.UI.AC.ID

The need for computing power equivalent to what is now offered by supercomputers had been identified by some engineers in high-tech industries and oil companies in the middle of the 1980's in Indonesia. High performance computing was especially needed to solve problems in the areas of seismic processing and aerodynamics. Since then, a small number of installations, Convex and IBM 3090 with vector facilities, have been set up.

The government's program to promote research and development activities as well as high-tech industries such as aerospace has put the supercomputing program into high gear. The list of application programs that need a supercomputer keeps growing from seismic processing and aerodynamics to weather modeling, fluid dynamics, reservoir modeling, etc.

The plan to establish a national center for supercomputing has just been initiated. The center will be fully funded by the government; the facilities can be used by any institution that needs high performance computing. One of the two different types of machines, vector and massively parallel, is being considered as a candidate to be procured for the center.

Supercomputing and Massively parallel systems in Norway
Professor Trond Steihaug

Director
National MPP Center, Para//ab
University of Bergen
NORWAY
trond@ii.uib.no

A 34Mbits network Connecting the Norwegian Universities was established in early 1992. This infrastructure makes it possible to decentralize the computing resources, and yet make it available to the entire scientific community in Norway. On this background the National Supercomputing Board decided to establish three centers for supercomputing in Norway, in Bergen, Oslo, and Trondheim. The three centers have different emphasis in supercomputer architectures.

The most exiting development takes place in Bergen. Since 1985 researchers at the Deparment of Informatics have been involved with parallel computing on a variety of achitectures such as the iPSC1/2, Alliant, and MasPar MP-1 and MP-2. The National Supercomputing Board appointed Bergen as their MPP center and provided funding for the acquisition of a 108-node Intel Paragon with 98 compute nodes and 3 GigaBytes of memory.

The center in Trondheim has been running the main computing resource until now (a 4 processor Cray Y-MP), and the center will continue to build on their strength on vector technology and support this for scientific research. In Oslo they will concentrate on clusters of high-end workstations. In spring 1993 they started with 16 IBM RS/6000 systems (14 Model 580 and 2 Model 980).

In this talk we will review the development in Bergen and make a presentation of some of the activities at para//ab where the National MPP center is an integral part of the activities.

Supercomputing Research in Europe and the APPARC project

Prof.Dr. H. Wijshoff

Chairman of the APPARC project
Department of Computer Science
Leiden University
Niels Bohrweg 1
2333 CA Leiden
The Netherlands
harryw@cs.leidenuniv.nl

The APPARC project is a European wide effort, funded by the EC Esprit Agency DG XIII, to investigate performance critical applications of parallel architectures. Performance-critical applications typically involve manipulation of large, sparse discrete data objects. In our view, one of the major causes of low performance for these applications is the hardware memory organization in present-day high performance computers. Progress towards general applicability of high performance computing depends upon the removal of this memory performance barrier for the class of sparse computations. Hence, sparse computations and hardware memory architecture form the main technical themes of the APPARC project.

The nine research groups involved in the APPARC proposal have considerable expertise and strong links with leading research groups elsewhere in Europe and around the world. They are committed to collaboration in the interdisciplinary mode that will be necessary for the APPARC quest, and an extensive program of workshops and exchange of personnel is planned. The APPARC group intends to interact strongly with the industrial community by gathering information on the real computing challenges that industry is facing.

Supercomputing Initiative in a Developing Country: Malaysia

Associate Prof. Jamaludin Ibrahim

Dean, Faculty of Computer Science
and Information Systems
Universiti Teknologi, Malaysia
Jalan Semarak 54100
Kuala Lumpur, MALAYSIA
DFSKSM@UTMKL.BITNET

The ability to develop indigenous technology is an important factor in sustaining economic development in a developing country such as Malaysia. Low labor cost and initial dependence on foreign technology/design has given developing countries an initial advantage. However, manufacturing cost is rising and dependence on foreign technology is not a wise strategy to maintain competitive advantage in a global market place. At the same time, environmental issues are becoming more relevant in realizing a sustainable development. High technology development and environmental modeling are compute intensive. Supercomputing or High Performance Computing is required to solve many environmental and industrial design problems.

The Universiti Teknologi Malaysia is proposing to set up a national supercomputing center to provide the necessary tools for academic, research institutions and R&D departments in the industry. A survey was conducted and an implementation plan has been proposed. At the same time, the Malaysian Institute of Microelectronics Research (MIMOS) is setting up a national computer network infrastructure that links up various research, governmental and academic institutions. The talk also describes the need for supercomputing technology in Malaysia, problems encountered and a proposed plan of action.

Session 12:
Workshop
Chair: Jack Dongarra

MPI: A Message Passing Interface

The MPI Forum

This paper presents an overview of MPI, a proposed standard message passing interface for MIMD distributed memory concurrent computers. The design of MPI has been a collective effort involving researchers in the United States and Europe from many organizations and institutions. MPI includes point-to-point and collective communication routines, as well as support for process groups, communication contexts, and application topologies. While making use of new ideas where appropriate, the MPI standard is based largely on current practice.

1 Introduction

This paper gives an overview of MPI, a proposed standard message passing interface for distributed memory concurrent computers and networks of workstations. The main advantages of establishing a message passing interface for such machines are portability and ease-of-use, and a standard message passing interface is a key component in building a concurrent computing environment in which applications, software libraries, and tools can be transparently ported between different machines. Furthermore, the definition of a message passing standard provides vendors with a clearly defined set of routines that they can implement efficiently, or in some cases provide hardware or low-level system support for, thereby enhancing scalability.

The functionality that MPI is designed to provide is based on current common practice, and is similar to that provided by widely-used message passing systems such as Express [15], PVM [2], NX/2 [16], Vertex, [14], PARMACS [10, 11], and P4 [4, 13]. In addition, the flexibility and usefulness of MPI has been broadened by incorporating ideas from more recent and innovative message passing systems such as CHIMP [6, 7], Zipcode [17, 18], and the IBM External User Interface [8]. The general design philosophy followed by MPI is that while it would be imprudent to include new and untested features in the standard, concepts that have been tested in a research environment should be considered for inclusion. Many of the features in

MPI related to process groups and communication contexts have been investigated within research groups for several years, but not in commercial or production environments. However, their incorporation into MPI is justified by the expressive power they bring to the standard.

The MPI standardization effort involves about 60 people from 40 organizations mainly from the United States and Europe. Most of the major vendors of concurrent computers are involved in MPI, along with researchers from universities, government laboratories, and industry. The standardization process began with the Workshop on Standards for Message Passing in a Distributed Memory Environment, sponsored by the Center for Research on Parallel Computing, held April 29-30, 1992, in Williamsburg, Virginia [19]. At this workshop the basic features essential to a standard message passing interface were discussed, and a working group was established to continue the standardization process. Following this a preliminary draft proposal, known as MPI1, was put forward by Dongarra, Hempel, Hey, and Walker [5]. This proposal was intended as a discussion document, and embodies the main features that were identified in the earlier workshop as being necessary in a message passing standard. A meeting of the MPI working group was held at Supercomputing '92, at which it was decided to place the standardization process on a more formal footing, and generally to follow the format and organization of the High Performance Fortran Forum. Subcommittees were formed for the major component areas of the standard, and an email discussion service established for each. In addition, the goal of producing a draft MPI standard by July 1993 was set. To achieve this goal the MPI working group has met every 6 weeks for two days, and is presenting the draft MPI standard at the Supercomputing '93 conference in November 1993. These meetings and the email discussion together constitute the MPI forum, membership of which is open to all members of the high performance computing community.

This paper is being written at a time when MPI is still in the process of being defined, but when the main features have been agreed upon. The only major exception is the role played by communicator objects in handling process groups and communication contexts. This is discussed in Section 3.1, and at the time of writing (August 1993) is still an area of active discussion. The details of the syntax, and the language bindings for Fortran-77, Fortran-90, C, and C++, have not yet been considered in depth, and so will not be discussed here. This paper is not intended to give a definitive, or even a complete, description of MPI. While the main design features of MPI will be described, limitations on space prevent detailed justifications for why these features were adopted. For these details the reader is referred to the MPI specification document, and the archived email discussions, which are available electronically as described in Section 4.

2   An Overview of MPI

MPI is intended to be a standard message passing interface for applications running on MIMD distributed memory concurrent computers and workstation networks. We expect MPI also to be useful in building libraries of mathematical software for such machines. MPI is not specifically designed for use by parallelizing compilers. MPI does not contain any support for fault tolerance, and provides reliable communications (or fails the program). MPI is a message passing interface, not a complete parallel computing programming environment. Thus, issues such as parallel I/O, parallel program composition, and debugging are not addressed by MPI. (Though MPI does provide a portable mechanism which will allow its intrumentation and the collection of tracefiles for tools such as ParaGraph[9] or Upshot[12]). MPI does not provide support for active messages. MPI was designed to allow heterogeneous implementations and virtual communication channels. Finally, MPI provides no explicit support for multithreading, although one of the design goals of MPI was to ensure that it can be implemented efficiently for a multithreaded environment.

3   Details of MPI

In this section we discuss the MPI routines in more detail, and indicate some of the alternate suggestions that have been made for different aspects of the interface. Since the point-to-point and collective communication routines depend heavily on the approach taken to groups and contexts, and to a lesser extent on process topologies, we shall discuss groups, contexts, and

topologies first. These three related areas have generated much discussion within the MPI forum, and at the time of writing a consensus is only just beginning to emerge.

3.1   Groups, Contexts, and Communicators

This section explains the concepts of group and context, which are, in turn, bound together into abstract communicator objects.

3.1.1   Process Groups

A process group is an ordered collection of processes, and each process is uniquely identified by its rank within the ordering. For a group of n processes the ranks run from 0 to $n - 1$. This definition of groups closely conforms to current practice.

Process groups can be used in two important ways. First, they can be used to specify which processes are involved in a collective communication operation, such as a broadcast. Second, they can be used to introduce task parallelism into an application, so that different groups perform different tasks. If this is done by loading different executable codes into each group, then we refer to this as MIMD task parallelism. Alternatively, if each group executes a different conditional branch within the same executable code, then we refer to this as SPMD task parallelism (also known as control parallelism). The initial MPI specification will adopt a static process model, so that, as far as the application is concerned, a fixed number of processes exist from program initiation to completion. Since MPI says nothing about the way in which a program is started, it takes no stance on whether these processes are multiple instances of the same executable (the SPMD model), or instances of many executables (loose MIMD model), or something in between. However, the MPI draft will not preclude the subsequent addition or adoption of a more sophisticated, dynamic process model.

Although the MPI process model is static, process groups are dynamic in the sense that they can be created and destroyed, and each process can belong to several groups simultaneously. However, the membership of a group cannot be changed. To make a group with different membership, a new group must be created. This operation can be performed either locally (without synchronisation), or by a collective partitioning operation in the group to be split. In MPI a group is an opaque object referenced by means of a handle[1].

---

[1]In Fortran, a handle is an index into a table, while in C, a

MPI provides routines for creating new groups by listing the ranks (within a specified parent group) of the processes making up the new group, or by partitioning an existing group using a key. The group partitioning routine is also passed an index, the size of which determines the rank of the process in the new group. This also provides a way of permuting the ranks within a group, if all processes in the group use the same value for the key, and set the index equal to the desired new rank. Additional routines give the rank of the calling process within a given group, test whether the calling process is in a given group, perform a barrier synchronization with a group, and inquire about the size and membership of a group.

3.1.2 Communication Contexts

Communication contexts were initially proposed to allow the creation of distinct, separable message streams between processes, with each stream having a unique context. A common use of contexts is to ensure that messages sent in one phase of an application are not incorrectly intercepted by another phase. The point here is that the two phases may actually be calls to two different third-party library routines, and the application developer has no way of knowing if the message tag, group, and rank completely disambiguate the message traffic of the different libraries from one another and from the rest of the application. Context provides an additional criterion for message selection, and hence permits the construction of independent message tag spaces (see Section 3.3.1).

The user never performs explicit operations on contexts (there is no user visible context data type), however contexts are maintained within communicators on the user's behalf, so that messages sent through a given communicator can only be received through the correctly matching communicator. MPI provides a collective routine on a communicator to pre-allocate a number of contexts for use within the scope of that communicator, these can then be used by the MPI system, without a further synchronisation, when the user creates duplicates or sub-groups using the communicator. The program is correct, provided that these operations occur in the same order on all the processes which own the communicator. (This is the same criterion as for the other collective operations on a communicator.)

_____
handle will be a provided typedef.

3.1.3 Communicator Objects

The "scope" of a communication operation is specified by the communication context used, and the group, or groups, involved. In a collective communication, or in a point-to-point communication between members of the same group, only one group needs to be specified, and the source and destination processes are given by their rank within this group. In a point-to-point communication between processes in different groups, two groups must be specified. In this case the source and destination processes are given by their ranks within their respective groups. In MPI abstract objects called "communicators" are used to define the scope of a communication operation. Communicators used in intra-group and inter-group communication are referred to as intra- and inter-communicators, respectively. An intra-communicator can be regarded as binding together a context and a group, while an inter-communicator binds together a context and two groups, one of which contains the source and the other the destination. Communicator objects are passed to all point-to-point and collective communication routines to specify the context and the group, or groups, involved in the communication operation.

3.2 Application Topologies

In many applications the processes are arranged with a particular topology, such as a two- or three-dimensional grid. MPI provides support for general application topologies that are specified by a graph in which processes that communicate are connected by an arc. As a convenience, MPI provides explicit support for n-dimensional Cartesian grids. For a Cartesian grid periodic or nonperiodic boundary conditions may apply in any specified grid dimension. In MPI a group either has a Cartesian or graph topology, or no topology.

3.3 Point-to-Point Communication

3.3.1 Message Selectivity

MPI provides for point-to-point communication, with message selectivity explicitly based on source process, message tag, and communication context. The source and tag may be wild-carded, so that in effect they are ignored in message selection. The context may not be wild-carded. The source and destination processes are specified by means of a group and a rank. For intra-group communication the group and context are bound together in an intra-communicator, as discussed in Section 3.1.3. For inter-group communication the groups containing the source and destination processes are bound together with the context in an inter-communicator. Thus, a send routine is passed a handle to a communicator object, the rank of the destination process, and the message type to fully specify the context and destination of a message. A receive routine uses the same three things to determine message selectivity.

3.3.2 Communication Modes

A send operation can take place in one of three communication modes. A message sent in **standard** mode does not require a corresponding receive to have been previously posted on the destination process. A message sent in standard mode will still be delivered when the receive is posted sometime later. A message sent in **ready** mode requires that a receive have been previously posted on the destination process. If the receive has not been previously posted the outcome is indeterminate. In standard mode, the send can return before the matching receive has been posted. For a message sent in **synchronous** mode the send operation does not return until a matching receive has been posted on the destination process.

For each of the three communication modes, a send operation can either be locally blocking or nonblocking, so there are a total of six different types of send routine. A blocking send routine will not return until the data locations specified in the send can be safely reused without corrupting the message. A nonblocking send does not wait for any particular event to occur before returning. Instead it returns a handle to a communication object that can subsequently be used when calling routines that check for completion of the send operation.

A receive operation may also be locally blocking or nonblocking and either of these two types of receive may be used to match any of the six types of send. A blocking receive will not return until the message has been stored at the locations indicated by the receive. A nonblocking receive returns a handle to a communication object, and does not wait for any particular event to occur. The handle can be used subsequently to check the status of the receive operation, or to block until it completes. A nonblocking receive also returns a handle to a "return status object" which is used to store the length, source, and tag of the message. When the receive has completed this information can then be queried by calling an appropriate routine.

The 6 send and 2 receive routines described above form the core of the MPI standard for point-to-point communication.

3.3.3 User-defined Datatypes

MPI provides mechanisms to specify general, mixed (of different types), non-contiguous message buffers. This is done by allowing the user to define the datatype (which consists of a set of types and memory offsets) using MPI datatype-definition routines. Once the datatype is defined, it can be passed into any of the point-to-point or collective communication routines. The effect of this will be for data to be collected out of possibly non-contiguous memory locations, transmitted, and then placed into possibly non-contiguous memory locations at the receiving end. It is up to the implementation to decide whether the data of a general datatype should be first packed in a contiguous buffer before being transmitted, or whether it can be collected directly from where it resides.

User-defined datatypes as supported by MPI allow the convenient and (potentially) efficient transmittal of general array sections (in Fortran 90 terminology), and arrays of (sub-portions of) records or structures.

Since all send and receive routines specify numbers of data items of a particular type, whether built-in or user-defined, implementations have enough information to provide translations that allow an MPI program to run on heterogeneous networks.

3.4 Collective Communication

Collective communication routines provide for coordinated communication among a group of processes [1, 3]. The process group and context is given by the intra-communicator object that is input to the routine. The MPI collective communication routines have been designed so that their syntax and semantics are consistent with those of the point-to-point routines. In addition, the collective communication routines may be, but do not have to be, implemented using the MPI point-to-point routines. Collective communication routines do not have a tag argument. A collective communication routine must be called by all members of the group with consistent arguments. As soon as a process has completed its role in the collective communication it may continue with other tasks. Thus, a collective communication is not necessarily a barrier synchronization for the group. On the other hand, an MPI implementation is free to have barriers inside collective communication functions. In short, the user must program as if the collective communication routines do have barriers, but cannot depend on any synchronization from them. MPI does not include nonblocking forms of the collective communication routines. In MPI collective communication routines are divided into two broad classes: data movement routines, and global computation routines.

3.4.1 Collective Data Movement Routines

There are three basic types of collective data movement routine: broadcast, scatter, and gather. There are two versions of each of these. In the one-all case data are communicated between one process and all others; in the all-all case data are communicated between each process and all others. The all-all broadcast, and both varieties of the scatter and gather routines, involve each process sending distinct data to each process, and/or receiving distinct data from each process. All processes must send and/or receive buffers of the same type and length.

The one-all broadcast routine broadcasts data from one process to all other processes in the group. The all-all broadcast broadcasts data from each process to all others, and on completion each has received the same data. Thus, each process ends up with the same output buffer, which is the concatenation of the input buffers of all processes in rank order.

The one-all scatter routine sends distinct data from one process to all processes in the group. This is also known as "one-to-all personalized communication". In the all-all scatter routine each process scatters distinct data to all processes in the group, so the processes receive different data from each process. This is also known as "all-to-all personalized communication".

The communication patterns in the gather routines are the same as in the scatter routines, except that the direction of flow of data is reversed. In the one-all gather routine one process (the root) receives data from every process in the group. The root process receives the concatenation of the input buffers of all processes in rank order. The all-all gather routine is identical to the all-all scatter routine.

3.4.2 Global Computation Routines

There are two basic global computation routines in MPI: reduce and scan. The reduce and scan routines both require the specification of an input function. One version is provided in which the user selects the function from a predefined list, and in the second version the user supplies (a pointer to) a function. Thus, MPI contains four reduce and four scan routines.

4 Summary and Conclusions

This paper has given an overview of the main features of MPI, but has not described the detailed syntax of the MPI routines, or discussed language binding issues. These will be fully discussed in the MPI specification document, a draft of which is expected to be available by the Supercomputing 93 conference in November 1993.

The design of MPI has been a cooperative effort involving about 60 people. Much of the discussion has been by electronic mail, and has been archived, along with copies of the MPI draft and other key documents. Copies of the archives and documents may be obtained by netlib. For details of what is available, and how to get it, please send the message "send index from mpi" to `netlib@ornl.gov`.

Acknowledgements

Many people have contributed to MPI , so it is not possible to acknowledge them all individually. However, many of the ideas presented in this paper are the result of hours of deliberation with members of the MPI Forum. The following people have made important contributions to the success of the MPI Forum: Lyndon Clarke, Doreen Cheng, James Cownie, Jack Dongarra, Anne C. Elster, Jim Feeney, Sam Fineberg, Jon Flower, Al Geist, Ian Glendinning, Adam Greenberg, William Gropp, Leslie Hart, Tom Haupt, Don Heller, Rolf Hempel, Tom Henderson, Tony Hey, C. T. Howard Ho, Steve Huss-Lederman, John Kapenga, Bob Knighten, Rik Littlefield, Ewing Lusk, Arthur B. Maccabe, Peter Madams, Oliver McBryan, Dan Nessett, Steve Otto, Peter Pacheco, Paul Pierce, Sanjay Ranka, Peter Rigsbee, Mark Sears, Ambuj Singh, Anthony Skjellum, Marc Snir, Alan Sussman, Eric Van de Velde, David Walker, and Stephen Wheat.

References

[1] V. Bala, J. Bruck, R. Cypher, P. Elustondo, A. Ho, C.-T. Ho, S. Kipnis, and Marc Snir. Ccl: A portable and tunable collective communication library for scalable parallel computers. Technical report, IBM T. J. Watson Research Center, 1993. Preprint.

[2] A. Beguelin, J. J. Dongarra, G. A. Geist, R. Manchek, and V. S. Sunderam. A users' guide

to PVM parallel virtual machine. Technical Report TM-11826, Oak Ridge National Laboratory, July 1991.

[3] J. Bruck, R. Cypher, P. Elustondo, A. Ho, C.-T. Ho, S. Kipnis, and Marc Snir. Ccl: A portable and tunable collective communication library for scalable parallel computers. Technical report, IBM Almaden Research Center, 1993. Preprint.

[4] Ralph Butler and Ewing Lusk. User's guide to the p4 parallel programming system. Technical Report ANL-92/17, Argonne National Laboratory, October 1992.

[5] J. J. Dongarra, R. Hempel, A. J. G. Hey, and D. W. Walker. A proposal for a user-level, message passing interface in a distributed memory environment. Technical Report TM-12231, Oak Ridge National Laboratory, February 1993.

[6] Edinburgh Parallel Computing Centre, University of Edinburgh. *CHIMP Concepts*, June 1991.

[7] Edinburgh Parallel Computing Centre, University of Edinburgh. *CHIMP Version 1.0 Interface*, May 1992.

[8] D. Frye, R. Bryant, H. Ho, R. Lawrence, and M. Snir. An external user interface for scalable parallel systems. Technical report, IBM, May 1992.

[9] Heath, M. T. and J. A. Etheridge. 1991. "Visualizing the performance of parallel programs." Technical Report ORNL TM-11813. Oak Ridge National Laboratory.

[10] R. Hempel. The ANL/GMD macros (PARMACS) in fortran for portable parallel programming using the message passing programming model – users' guide and reference manual. Technical report, GMD, Postfach 1316, D-5205 Sankt Augustin 1, Germany, November 1991.

[11] R. Hempel, H.-C. Hoppe, and A. Supalov. A proposal for a PARMACS library interface. Technical report, GMD, Postfach 1316, D-5205 Sankt Augustin 1, Germany, October 1992.

[12] Virginia Herrarte and Ewing Lusk. Studying parallel program behavior with upshot. Technical Report ANL-91/15, Argonne National Laboratory, 1991.

[13] Ewing Lusk, Ross Overbeek, et al. *Portable Programs for Parallel Processors*. Holt, Rinehart and Winston, Inc., 1987.

[14] nCUBE Corporation. *nCUBE 2 Programmers Guide, r2.0*, December 1990.

[15] Parasoft Corporation. *Express Version 1.0: A Communication Environment for Parallel Computers*, 1988.

[16] Paul Pierce. The NX/2 operating system. In *Proceedings of the Third Conference on Hypercube Concurrent Computers and Applications*, pages 384–390. ACM Press, 1988.

[17] A. Skjellum and A. Leung. Zipcode: a portable multicomputer communication library atop the reactive kernel. In D. W. Walker and Q. F. Stout, editors, *Proceedings of the Fifth Distributed Memory Concurrent Computing Conference*, pages 767–776. IEEE Press, 1990.

[18] A. Skjellum, S. Smith, C. Still, A. Leung, and M. Morari. The Zipcode message passing system. Technical report, Lawrence Livermore National Laboratory, September 1992.

[19] D. Walker. Standards for message passing in a distributed memory environment. Technical Report TM-12147, Oak Ridge National Laboratory, August 1992.

Session 13:
Performance Bottlenecks
Chair: Mike Quinn

Analytical Performance Prediction on Multicomputers

Mark J. Clement and Michael J. Quinn
Department of Computer Science
Oregon State University
Corvallis, Oregon 97331-3202

Abstract

Multicomputers have the potential to deliver Gigaflop performance on many scientific applications. Initial implementations of parallel programs on these machines, however, are often inefficient and require significant optimization before they can harness the potential power of the machine. Performance prediction tools can provide valuable information on which optimizations will result in increased performance. This paper describes an analytical performance prediction model. The model is designed to provide performance data to compilers, programmers and system architects to assist them in making choices which will lead to more efficient implementations. Efficient performance prediction tools can provide information which will help programmers make better use of the power of multicomputers.

1 Introduction

One of the most important advances in high performance computing is the increasing availability of commercial parallel computers. These machines promise to provide solutions to many problems that require more computational resources than are available on conventional sequential processors.

Because larger numbers of processing elements can be efficiently connected when memory is physically distributed, multicomputers have become increasingly popular in the scientific computing community. In the near future several vendors may produce multicomputers capable of delivering teraflop performance. With these massively parallel computers, scientists will be able to attempt to solve several of the "Grand Challenge" class problems that are currently limited by the speed of conventional computers.

The potential computational power of even the current generation of multicomputers is often not delivered on scientific problems that seem to be good candidates for parallel execution. It is often difficult for a programmer to predict what effect modifications to the algorithm will have on performance. Parallel system architects are forced to make trade-offs in system features without being able to predict the effect those decisions will have on the performance of important applications. This research addresses these two problems through an analytical model which uses application source code and essential machine parameters to satisfy the needs of these two groups.

High level parallel languages are essential in making parallel processors feasible for large programming projects. They allow the program to be written in a machine independent manner, and abstract away the complexity of explicit message passing. The Dataparallel C language [9] provides a SIMD model of parallel programming with explicit parallel extensions to the C language. Because of the static nature of Dataparallel C, it is possible to perform detailed performance analysis at compile time. The Intercom tool [13] developed for Dataparallel C identifies communication points in a parallel program. Using the information provided by Intercom and compiler generated information on the number of computations performed, this model can effectively predict the performance of Dataparallel C programs. The concepts developed here can also be extended to other parallel languages.

Several of the current generation of multicomputers have features which make performance prediction possible for parallel applications. This paper presents and evaluates a new analytical model and analyzes the success of the model in predicting the performance of parallel algorithms on different hardware platforms that share these features. This kind of performance prediction tool should enable programmers and compilers to take advantage of more of the potential power of multicomputers and make solution of "Grand Challenge" problems feasible.

2 Motivation

We have mentioned that performance prediction is important in achieving efficient execution of parallel programs. We will now explain how to use performance prediction information and how to derive the specifications for this model. We have found that taking an analytical approach as opposed to a simulation based approach to performance prediction improves the utility of the model. This model can be used by programmers to help in performance debugging, by compilers to choose the best possible optimizations, and by system architects to balance the communication and computational speeds. We will examine the needs of these three groups and show how their needs have influenced the design of this model.

- During program development, it is important for the programmer to determine the effect that changes to the source code will have on the performance of the algorithm. If this performance prediction is difficult or time consuming, the programmer will not be likely to try very many different implementations of an algorithm. Since the performance prediction of our analytic model does not depend on sample runs of the code, it can provide rapid feedback to the programmer. Several performance prediction tools require the programmer to rewrite the algorithm in a simulation language or to define the data dependency relationships. We feel that this is too high of a price to expect a programmer to pay. For this reason, this analytical tool extracts all of the algorithmic information from the source code of the program.

- Performing optimization of compiled programs on multicomputers can be more difficult than optimizing for shared memory systems. Data distribution, message passing costs, memory access overhead, and overhead induced by parallelization must all be considered to achieve an efficient implementation. An effective optimizer must have a model of the machine which takes all of these features into account in order to make correct decisions in compiling a parallel program. The analytical nature of our model makes it a prime candidate for use by an optimizing compiler. If simulation runs are required to make a prediction, the model will consume too much time to be useful in searching for the optimal combination of optimizations for each of these features. This model does not require simulation runs and

has been shown to be effective in predicting the effects of optimizations on the performance of applications.

- Many parallel applications fail to achieve good performance on multicomputers because the systems are unbalanced. If the message passing time is too high compared to the time for a computation, then fine grain applications will never achieve good performance. System designers have little information about how balanced the communication and computation must be to perform acceptably on a target set of applications. Since this model does not require sample runs on the target architecture, system designers can use it to determine the effects of varying system parameters on a variety of parallel applications.

3 Performance Metrics

There are several ways of evaluating performance in a parallel environment. On a sequential machine, the principle performance goal is to minimize the execution time of an application. In a parallel environment it is also important to make efficient use of a large number of the available processors. In the best case situation, a parallel machine with p processors can reduce the execution time from the single processor time T_s to the parallel time $T_p = T_s/p$ for a speedup of p. If the parallel machine is not able to execute the algorithm significantly faster than a single node, then there is no reason to buy a parallel machine; it would be more cost effective for the algorithm to be run on a single processor. For this reason we will be using parallelizability, or relative speedup, as the performance measure which our model will predict.

Some research has suggested that scaled speedup is an important metric to use in evaluating parallel performance [8]. The scaled speedup metric measures the speedup attained when the problem size is scaled up along with number of processors. This metric is well suited to problems like weather prediction where the problem size can be easily varied. On problems where the problem size is fixed, or where the single processor execution time is unacceptable, relative speedup can be a better indicator [5]. Many scientific applications will require a drastic reduction in execution time before a computer solution will be practical. For these reasons, this research has concentrated on looking at the speedup attained on a fixed problem size when additional processors are added to the computation.

4 Developing the analytical model

An effective analytical model will incorporate features which have a dominant effect on performance and will ignore those features which have secondary effects. Several trends in modern distributed memory parallel systems permit us to make simplifying assumptions which lead to a more understandable model. We will use these assumptions to develop the parallel model used in this research. We have also identified several features in current multicomputers that need to be addressed if reliable performance prediction is to occur. These first order effects will be included in our model.

The time to execute the program on a single processor $T_{single} = T_s + T_p$ where T_s is the inherently sequential part of the algorithm and T_p is the parallelizable part of the algorithm. Several researchers [6] [16] have suggested the following form of a model for the parallel execution time of an algorithm:

$$\tau(p) = T_s + \frac{T_p}{p} + \sigma(p, topology)$$

where $\sigma(p, topology)$ is a function which estimates the communication overhead given the topology, and T_p is the time for the parallelizable part on one processor.

We have found that it is important to include a term for parallel overhead introduced by the emulation of virtual processors in Dataparallel C. Depending upon the choice of global or local variables, different optimizations are possible which result in variable overhead for virtual processor emulation. The number of times the compiler must set up a virtual processor emulation loop (N_o) can be used to estimate the parallelization overhead in the computation. The time spent in parallel overhead, T_o will be accounted for in our model.

The generalized form of the speedup for p processors can be expressed as:

$$S(p) = \frac{T_{single}}{\tau(p)} = \frac{T_s + T_p}{T_s + \frac{T_p}{p} + \sigma(p, topology) + T_o}$$

This reduces to Amdahl's law when $\sigma(p, topology) = 0$ and $T_o = 0$.

4.1 Trends in Floating Point performance

Traditionally, floating point arithmetic was so much more time consuming than integer arithmetic that the integer instructions were generally ignored in calculations of algorithmic complexity. The current generation of microprocessors exhibit floating performance that is equal to or greater than the integer performance. Many of the microprocessors used as compute nodes in multicomputers can execute two floating point operations (an add and multiply) in the same time that an integer instruction can execute. Several of the major multicomputer vendors are using this class of microprocessors for computational nodes. The Intel Paragon uses the i860 processor which has this feature [11]. The IBM POWERparallel machine uses RS/6000 technology which also has comparable times for floating point and integer instructions.

Since floating point and integer instructions take close to the same amount of time in these machines, it is possible for the model to estimate the number of computations through examining the parse tree generated by the compiler and counting the number of operations (N_{inst}).

4.2 Communication overhead

The $\sigma(p, topology)$ term incorporates overhead caused by communication between processors during the computation. In the general case, it accounts for effects caused by the topology dependent distance between processors, link bandwidth and message startup time for communications. For this analysis, we will assume that the machine uses cut-through or wormhole routing. With these circuit-switched routing schemes, the transfer time between any two nodes is fairly similar. Most modern parallel computers employ some form of circuit-switched technology to avoid the delay associated with store and forward routing. This simplifies the $\sigma(p, topology)$ term by allowing us to ignore distance considerations when estimating the communication cost for an operation.

One of the most significant contributors to communication overhead in the current generation of multicomputers is the message startup time ($T_{startup}$). We will define message startup time as the total time between when an application makes a call to the communication library and when data begins to be transmitted across the communication interface. This startup cost includes time spent in the communication library and system call overhead as well as the inherent time for the hardware to begin transmitting. As multicomputers have matured, they have added multitasking operating systems and more stringent error checking which have increased the overhead associated with starting a communication. Several researchers have noted that startup cost is the predominate factor in determining the total cost of communication [10] [17]. For this reason we will assume that overhead induced by limitation in actual bandwidth on the communication channels and link congestion are actually second order effects, and we will not consider them in our model. This makes the model much simpler, since it does not have to deduce the length of messages, but can just count the number of messages exchanged. Some applications which transmit large data sets will also see the the network bandwidth as a first order effect, but for many of the problems that we have dealt with it can safely be ignored. The Intercom tool can determine the number of communications $N_{communicate}$ from the source code. We will define the normalized startup cost $C_{startup}$ as the ratio $T_{startup}/T_{fp}$ (where T_{fp} is the time to execute a floating point instruction). The model will estimate the total number of cycles spent in communication to be $N_{communicate} * C_{startup}$.

4.3 Memory effects

Several researchers have noted that the memory hierarchy can have a significant impact on the performance achieved by a parallel program [7][18]. References to parallel (poly) variables in Dataparallel C are translated into structure accesses that will generally not be available in the on-chip cache. These uncached accesses will generally be limited to parallel code and have a significant effect on the performance of popular multicomputer processors including the iPSC/860 [15]. Using the number of uncached memory accesses extracted from the source code (N_m) and the number of cycles necessary to access an uncached memory location (C_m), the performance prediction tool can estimate the number of cycles spent waiting for uncached memory.

4.4 Compiler effects

Dataparallel C generates a standard C program as its output. The native C compiler then compiles the C code into an executable. The quality of the native C compiler can have a big effect on the number of machine instructions generated for each logical operation specified in the program. A constant for each compiler $C_{compile}$ can be determined through benchmarks or through extrapolating from results of the same compiler on other architectures. This compiler factor will be used to create a better estimate of the number of instructions executed in an application.

4.5 Applying the assumptions

Through applying the foregoing assumptions, we will develop an analytic model for predicting perfor-

mance on multicomputers with wormhole routing, relatively high message startup costs and similar floating point and integer instruction times. Using information extracted from the source code, the compiler estimates N_s and N_p, the number of operations in the sequential and parallelizable portions of the code. Dataparallel C has explicit information about which parts of the program will be executed in parallel and which parts are sequential so this division is not a complex process for the compiler. Let $T_s = C_{compile} * N_s * T_{fp}$ and $T_p = (C_{compile} * N_p + C_m * N_m) * T_{fp}$.

Our model of $\sigma(p, topology)$ involves only the startup cost $T_{startup}$ and the topology. We can express $\sigma'(p, topology) = \sigma(p, topology)/T_{fp}$ in terms of the normalized startup time. For a broadcast communication on a hypercube topology $\sigma'(p, topology) = N_{communicate} * C_{startup} * (1 + \log(p))$.

Using the dominant effects we have described here,

$$T_s = (C_{compile} * (N_s + N_p) + C_m * N_m) * T_{fp}$$

$$T_p = C_{compile} * N_s * T_{fp} +$$
$$\frac{(C_{compile} * N_p + C_m * N_m) * T_{fp}}{p} +$$
$$T_{fp} * \sigma'(p, topology) + T_{fp} * C_{compile} * N_o$$

With $S(p) = T_s/T_p$ the T_{fp} terms drop out and we are left with a speedup equation dependent only on the variables which are available to our prediction tool.

The terms N_s, N_p, N_m, N_o and $N_{communicate}$ can all be determined from the internal parse tree generated by the compiler. The term $C_{compile}$ can be determined through a sample program or through experience with the compiler on other processors. $C_{compile}$ describes the efficiency of the compiler in generating optimized code. The term $C_{startup}$ can be determined from a sample communication program or estimated from machine specifications. C_m is generally available as a system specification.

5 Experimental Results

Several experimental results are presented here to validate the concept of a analytical performance prediction model. One set of experiments was performed to determine if the tool could accurately predict the performance effects of changing the implementation of an algorithm on a fixed target machine. This kind of performance prediction information would be used by a programmer or compiler to optimize a program. Other experiments were performed to demonstrate that the tool could predict performance on different target machines for several different algorithms. This kind of prediction information would be useful to system designers in determining the effects of changing system parameters.

5.1 Source code variation

One of the challenges of programming in Dataparallel C is determining the parallel type to use for different variables. Dataparallel C has a notion of global (mono) variables which are kept consistent across all of the physical processors and local (poly) variables which may be different for every virtual processor. There is a complex set of rules for determining which parallel type to use for loop variables or array index variables to produce the best performance [9]. In some cases, the choice depends on the target architecture to be used by the application. If the compiler were able to predict the performance characteristics for each of the choices, it could automatically select the correct types and relieve the programmer of the task of variable type selection.

Matrix multiplication is often used as a benchmark on parallel machines. Several versions of the matrix multiplication algorithm have been implemented in Dataparallel C. As a test of the model we changed two of the loop indices in the "matrix2" implementation from parallel local variables to parallel global variables. The experiment was performed on the Intel iWarp array. The iWarp is connected in a mesh topology, uses wormhole routing, has a message startup latency of 470 cycles and has similar floating point and integer execution times. The prediction tool was able to accurately predict the performance of the original version and the new version called "matrix2+" . The results are shown in Figure 1.

5.2 Experimental results on different target machines

A second set of experiments were performed using two target architectures that exhibit the features we described in our model development. The experiment was performed on the Intel iWarp array and on an iPSC/860. The iPSC/860 uses the Intel i860 processor, is connected in a hypercube topology, uses wormhole routing, has a message startup latency of 5280 cycles and has similar floating point and integer execution times. Experiments were performed using three standard Dataparallel C applications. The experimental results show that the analytical model is successful in predicting performance for the two machines.

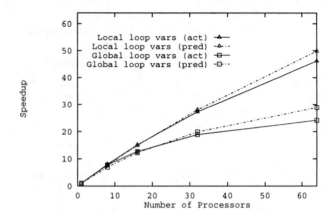

Figure 1: Experimental and predicted values results for 256x256 matrix multiplication on the iWarp array.

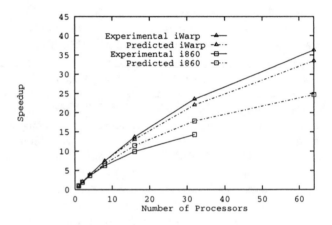

Figure 2: Experimental and predicted results for the shallow water atmospheric model.

5.2.1 Atmospheric model

This application was developed by the National Center for Atmospheric Research for benchmarking the performance of parallel processors [9]. The program solves a system of shallow water equations on a rectangular grid using a finite differences method. The model uses a two dimensional array of data elements that communicate with their nearest neighbors. The performance prediction tool is able to approximate the actual performance fairly accurately. More significantly, the tool was able to clearly differentiate between the performance to be expected on the two machines. The results are shown in Figure 2.

Performance information from an analytical model can allow a system architect to observe the effects of

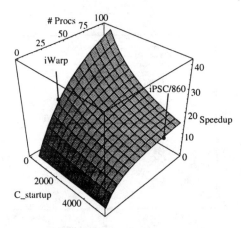

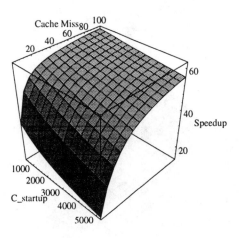

Figure 3: Speedup results for the shallow water atmospheric model with variable message startup cost. C_startup is the message startup time divided by the time for an arithmetic operation. A C_startup value of 470 corresponds to the iWarp processor and a value of 5000 approximates the iPSC/860.

Figure 4: Speedup results for the shallow water atmospheric model for 64 processors with variable message startup cost and cache miss penalty.

changing specific system parameters. In Figure 3 the message startup cost is varied for the shallow water atmospheric model to show the effect this parameter has on speedup. Figure 4 shows how cache miss penalty and message startup cost interact in predicted speedup results. Machines with large cache miss penalties will achieve larger speedup values for a given message startup cost. The performance in Mflops will be seriously degraded on machines with large values of C_m as is shown in Figure 5. Performance results from a large number of parallel applications should make the trade-offs much clearer to systems architects.

5.2.2 Ocean Circulation model

This program simulates ocean circulation using a linearized, two-layer channel model [9]. This application also uses nearest neighbor communication but in this case the two machines achieve nearly identical speedup results. This is due to a combination of grain size differences and differences in the number of accesses to uncached memory between the ocean circulation model and the shallow water model. It would be difficult for a programmer to guess that the two programs would perform this differently from perusing the source code. Again, the performance prediction tool was able estimate the speedup attained by the application. The results are shown in Figure 6.

5.2.3 Sharks World

Sharks world is included as an example of an application with few communications. The program simulates sharks and fish on a toroidal world [9]. As expected, both machines are able to achieve near linear speedup on this application. The predicted and actual results are shown in Figure 7.

6 Related Research

Several different approaches have been taken in modeling parallel systems and predicting performance. Most of the analytical models do not use application source code and so are limited in their accuracy. The simulation based prediction tools do not allow system architects to experiment with different trade-offs in system parameters.

Markov models have been used to approach the problem from a queueing theory direction. Kapelnikov describes a methodology used to build Markov processes, starting from the description of a program [12]. Building Markov processes requires more time and expertise than most programmers have available, especially for large programs.

Balasundaram et al. [2] have developed a performance estimator based on a training set approach. Their analysis focuses on determining the best data distribution for a given algorithm. System parameters are determined using training sets which are similar to the sample programs which could be used with this research to determine the startup cost. The training set

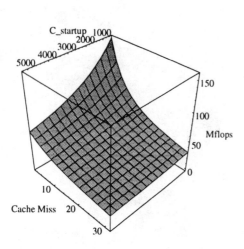

Figure 5: Mflops results for the shallow water atmospheric model for 64 processors and variable message startup cost and cache miss penalty. A processor speed of 10Mflops is assumed for each processing element.

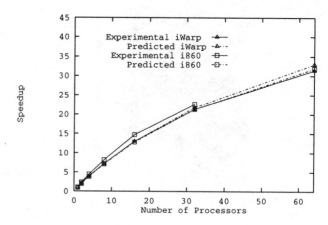

Figure 6: Experimental and predicted results for the ocean circulation model.

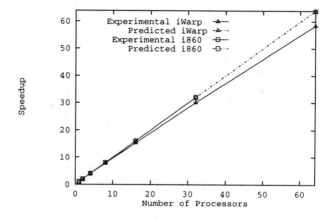

Figure 7: Experimental and predicted results for Sharks World simulation.

approach combines several of the effects that must be separated to allow for architectural experimentation. They also do not account for the cache miss penalty, which is important in the class of processors which we are studying here.

Morris has developed a data flow modeling language, which is used to model a computation [14]. The requirement that a programmer must rewrite the algorithm in a new language will not only limit the ease of use of this performance tool, but will limit the accuracy, since the real program will not be examined.

Born has developed an analytic model that relies on some statistical distribution of communication requests [3]. Traditional analytic models that do not use information from program source code give little insight into the performance of a machine on an actual application.

Annaratone has developed a tool that uses the communication/computation ratio to make decisions in parallelizing Fortran code [1]. The tool uses an initial run of the program to determine system and algorithmic parameters. This tool provides a good example of how performance prediction information can be used to optimize compiler translation of source code.

A static parameter based prediction tool was developed by Fahringer [4]. This tool uses a sample run on the target machine to determine model parameters for the system and algorithm. These parameters are then used to optimize the parallel implementation of Fortran 77 programs.

One principle difference between our model and

other research is that it allows for performance prediction without a training run on the target machine. It is important for system architects to be able to predict performance on future machines and other tools do not provide this functionality. Parallel computer purchasers can also benefit from being able to estimate the performance of their applications on machines with different system parameters.

7 Conclusions and Future Work

Predicted performance information can be useful in optimizing multicomputer system performance. In this paper we have examined several features of current multicomputers which make it possible to predict performance for these machines. An analytical multicomputer model was developed, which allows us to gather performance information with minimal programmer intervention. This model is particularly useful, since it does not require sample runs on an existing machine and can be used to predict performance on a hypothetical machine or one to which the user does not have access. Performance data from the model corresponds closely to actual data acquired from two commercial multicomputers.

Future work will concentrate on incorporating this simplified model into the existing Intercom tool and testing the tool on a wider range of applications. An attempt will be made to classify applications whose performance is accurately predicted by this analytical model. Additional analysis will also be performed to determine new model features which will allow performance prediction on a broader range of parallel programs and hardware architectures.

Much work is left to be done as far as generalizing the model to other applications and architectures, but this approach has the potential to provide much needed information to the multicomputer user community. Performance prediction tools can aid multicomputer users and designers in increasing parallel efficiency on these machines. High efficiency parallel execution will be essential if "Grand Challenge" problems are to be solved on multicomputers.

References

[1] M. Annaratone and R. Ruhl. Balancing interprocessor communication and computation on torus-connected multicomputers running compiler-parallelized code. In *Proceedings SHPCC 92*, pages 358–365, March 1992.

[2] V. Balasunderam, G. Fox, K. Kennedy, and U. Kremer. A static performance estimator to guide data partitioning decisions. *SIGPLAN Notices*, 26(7):213 – 223, July 1991.

[3] R. G. Born and J. R. Kenevan. Theoretical performance-based cost-effectiveness of multicomputers. *The Computer Journal*, 35(1):63–70, 1992.

[4] T. Fahringer and H. P. Zima. A static parameter based performance prediction tool for parallel programs. Technical Report ACPC/TR 93-1, University of Vienna Department of Computer Science, January 1993.

[5] H. P. Flatt. Further results using the overhead model for parallel systems. *IBM J. Res. Develop.*, 35:721 – 726, 1991.

[6] H. P. Flatt and K. Kennedy. Performance of parallel processors. *Parallel Computing*, 12:1 – 20, 1989.

[7] A. J. Goldberg and J. L. Hennessy. Mtool: An integrated system for performance debugging shared memory multiprocessor applications. *IEEE Transactions on Parallel and Distributed Systems*, 4(1):28–40, January 1993.

[8] J. L. Gustafson, G. R. Montry, and R. E. Benner. Development of parallel methods for a 1024-processor hypercube. *SIAM J. Sci. Stat. Comput.*, 9(4):609–639, July 1988.

[9] P. J. Hatcher and M. J. Quinn. *Data-Parallel Programming on MIMD Computers*. The MIT Press, Cambridge, Massachusetts, 1991.

[10] R. W. Hockney and E. A. Carmona. Comparison of communications on the intel ipsc/860 and touchstone delta. *Parallel Computing*, 18(9):1067 – 1072, 1992.

[11] Intel Corporation. *Paragon OSF/1 C Compiler User's Guide*, January 1993.

[12] A. Kapelnikov, R. R. Muntz, and M. D. Ercegovac. A methodology for performance analysis of parallel computations with looping constructs. *Journal of Parallel and Distributed Computing*, 14(2):105–120, February 1992.

[13] D. McCallum and M. J. Quinn. A graphical user interface for data-parallel programming. In *Proceedings of the 26th Hawaii International Conference on System Sciences*, pages 5–13. IEEE Computer Society Press, 1993.

[14] D. Morris and D. Evans. Modelling distributed and parallel computer systems. *Parallel Computing*, 18(7):793–806, July 1992.

[15] S. A. Moyer. Performance of the ipsc/860 node architecture. Technical Report IPC-TR-91-007, Instidute for Parallel Computation, School of Engineering and Applied Science, University of Virginia, May 17, 1991.

[16] D. Muller-Wichards. Problem size scaling in the presence of parallel overhead. *Parallel Computing*, 17(12):1361 – 1376, December 1991.

[17] T. von Eicken, D. E. Culler, S. C. Goldstein, and K. E. Schauser. Active messages: A mechanism for integrated communication and computation. Technical Report UCB/CSD 92/#675, Computer Science Division – EECS, University of California, Berkeley, CA 94720, March 1992.

[18] X. Zhang. Performance measurement and modeling to evaluate various effects on a shared memory multiprocessor. *IEEE Trans. Software Engineering*, 17(1):87 – 93, January 1991.

Hot Spot Analysis in Large Scale Shared Memory Multiprocessors

Karim Harzallah   Kenneth C. Sevcik

Computer Systems Research Institute
University of Toronto
Toronto, Ontario, Canada M5S 1A4

Abstract

Scalable multiprocessors that support a shared-memory image to application programmers are typically based on physical memory modules that are distributed. Consequently, the access times for a particular processor to various parts of physical memory differ. In this paper, we explore the implications of this non-uniformity in memory access times. In particular, we study the effect of hot-spots in hierarchical large scale NUMA multiprocessors. Hot-spot analysis is of interest because coordinated threads of parallel programs lead to hot spots whose impact on performance may be substantial or even dominant. We have developed an analytical model of access latencies and contention for shared resources in the interconnection network that links the processors and memory modules. Our objective is to provide a better understanding of non-uniform memory access times in scalable architectures. We show the extent to which a variable can be shared before it becomes a performance bottleneck, and assess the potential gain from replication of shared data items. We also demonstrate that the backoff value (after a memory request rejection) must be chosen carefully to balance memory access time and network utilization. Finally, we show that memory utilization is improved by allowing memory request buffering.

1   Introduction

Parallel applications can be most easily designed and expressed in terms of a (virtual) global shared memory. To support this image in a scalable system, however, physical memory modules are distributed and an interconnection network is used to carry read and write requests from processors to memory modules. In terms of access latency, each memory module can be considered "close" to some processors, but "distant" from others. Non-Uniform Memory Access (NUMA) architectures make it possible to build large-scale, parallel processing systems that provide a shared memory programming image. Existing commercial systems that can be classified as large scale NUMA include the BBN TC2000 [5], the CM5 from Thinking Machines Inc, and the KSR1 [8] from Kendall Square Research. Among the academic research prototypes, we find the MIT Alewife [3], the Stanford DASH [13], and the Hector multiprocessor at the University of Toronto [16].

Several studies have been conducted to understand and improve the performance of NUMA multiprocessors. Nanda et al. [14] compared the performance degradation resulting from contention for shared resources in the BBN GP 1000, the BBN TC2000, and the Sequent Balance 21000. They experimented with various workload models, and found that the interconnection latency is the largest source of delay. Their results also showed that, in the presence of widely shared locks, the queueing delay for locks is the most influential factor on performance.

Other work by Zhang and Qin [17] examined several analytical models to predict and evaluate the overhead of interprocessor communication, processor scheduling, process synchronization, and remote memory access where network contention and memory contention are considered. To support their models, they presented measurements collected from experiments done on the BBN GP 1000. In their treatment of the remote memory access delay, the authors assumed that accesses are uniformly distributed over the shared memory space, thus limiting the scope of potential NUMA applications to evaluate.

Sevcik and Zhou [15] have studied the performance benefits of large NUMA multiprocessors, and assessed their limitations. They introduced the notion of NUMA expansion ratio, which is a measure of how well an application is suited for the non-uniform characteristics of the architecture. Their approach involved both analysis and experimentation. They concluded that data reference locality is an important determinant of an application's performance in a NUMA system.

Another approach to evaluating the interaction between the hardware architecture and the policies managing it is to use off-line optimal analysis. Bolosky and Scott [7] used a trace-driven dynamic programming algorithm, and computed the policy decisions that would maximize the system performance for a given program execution. The off-line optimal analysis is interesting in that it provides a baseline against which to compare real policy behavior. The authors applied this technique to investigate migration and replication policies. Although the off-line analysis allows the investigation of a relatively large range of shared memory architectures, their model assumed that contention is not a major factor in performance, which is not the case for many real parallel applications.

Related work by LaRowe, Holliday, and Ellis [12] analyzed the memory system performance of local/remote NUMA machines. They explored the effectiveness of dynamic page placement, and in particular, dynamic multiple-copy page placement. Their analysis was based on approximate mean-value analysis techniques. They validated their model against experimental data obtained while running a synthetic workload.

The non-uniformity of memory access effect grows more significant as improvements in CPU speed continue to outstrip improvements in memory performance, forcing future processors to spend a larger fraction of their time waiting for memory [14] [6]. Previous studies have shown that ignoring the location of data in NUMA systems leads to a significant performance penalty [15] [1]. In this paper, we investigate the effect of a nonuniform traffic pattern consisting of a single hot spot. We analyze the performance impact of such contention, and consider, as one example architecture, the Hector system. Our analysis attempts to answer the following questions within the framework of our model:

- To what extent can a variable be shared before it becomes a bottleneck?

- What can be gained from replication?

- What impact does the backoff value after a memory request rejection have on performance?

- How much is performance improved by buffering memory requests at memory modules?

Our work is different from most previous work in that it replaces the assumption of uniformly distributed memory accesses with an assumption at the opposite extreme: all memory accesses in the system are directed to a single memory module (the "hot spot"). It captures the main features of a NUMA system, while still being simple to understand and to evaluate. Our hardware model involves a multiple level memory hierarchy reflecting the structure found in scalable architectures.

The rest of the paper is organized as follows. In Section 2, we describe the hardware model and the software model assumed for this study. Section 3 presents the analysis of the model. In Section 4, experimental results based on the model are discussed, and we summarize our findings in Section 5.

2 The System Model

We represent a multiprocessor architecture for supporting a shared-memory programming image as a number of processors interconnected in a hierarchical fashion: Each processor has a local memory module. The virtual global shared memory is supported by mapping portions of virtual memory into the physical pages of memory local to some processor. Under some conditions, a single virtual page may be replicated in several physical memory modules in order to localize read accesses for multiple processors. This architecture is generally applicable to several of the shared memory systems mentioned in Section 1. Our analytic approach is also sufficiently general to be relevant to several systems. For the sake of concrete experiments, we specialize the model and its analysis to reflect the Hector multiprocessor.

Hector is a hierarchical NUMA multiprocessor being developed at the University of Toronto [16]. The lowest level of the hierarchy consists of processing modules (PMs), each comprising of a MC88100 processor running at 16MHz, two distinct 16KB instruction and data caches, 16MB of memory, and various I/O interfaces. Multiple PMs are connected by a bus, forming a station. In the current configuration, every station is composed of four PMs. The stations, in turn, are connected by a unidirectional bit-parallel ring, called the local ring. At the next higher level of the hierarchy, communication between local rings is done via another unidirectional ring called the global ring. Every processor has hardware access to the memories of all processors in the system, forming a large distributed shared memory. The high level architecture of Hector is presented in Figure 1.

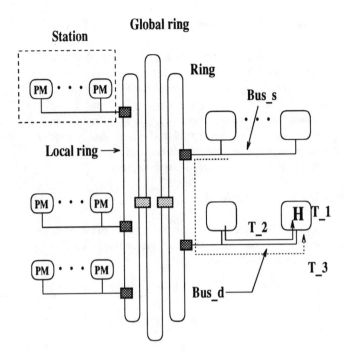

Figure 1: Hector: A hierchical shared memory multiprocessor

n	the number of stations in the system
k	the number of processors in each station
q	the number of requests that can be queued at a memory module
S_m	the number of cycles that a memory is busy serving a single request
S_r	the ring service time
S_b	the bus service time
C_i	the cost of a memory access from level i (relative to the memory), ignoring contention

Table 1: Model hardware parameters

We have abstracted away many of the system specific details of Hector in order to keep the model sufficiently general to be of use in the evaluation of other systems. The dimensions of the system are defined by n and k, where n is the number of stations in the system, and k is the number of processors per station making the total number of processors nk. The degree of buffering at each memory module is determined by q, the maximum number of requests that can be queued at a memory module. S_m, S_b, and S_r are the mean service times of the memory, the bus, and the ring (one full cycle) respectively. In the absence of contention, the memory access time varies with respect to the level from which the request is made. We denote by C_i the memory access time from level i. (In our study, $i = 1, 2, 3$ correspond to local, on-station, and off-station access costs respectively.) The model hardware parameters are summarized in Table 1.

2.1 The Software Model

Previous work [15] [1] has indicated that code and data placement is critical to good performance in NUMA systems. It is desirable that the data reside in the memory of the processor that is accessing it most frequently. This results in fewer remote accesses, and hence lower latency and less contention. Also, in proposed scalable systems, contention for memory access is a potential bottleneck. This is attributable to the fact that variables may be shared among most, if not all, the processors, or, in many cases, to false sharing, as has been observed by Bolosky, et al. [6]. In shared-memory multiprocessors, locks are commonly used to synchronize activities among processors. This use of synchronization variables often leads to widespread sharing. Unfortunately, this type of sharing can drastically impair performance in large-scale systems. This leads to the conclusion that if stringent measures are not taken to alleviate the contention, the overhead can sometimes offset any benefit from parallelism in programs. Motivated by the importance of the issue, we investigate the implications of traffic non-uniformity. Our workload model is thus a set of threads, each requiring access to the same memory module at the rate of one request every g clock cycles. A hot spot is therefore created simulating high demand for a lock, or a high degree of false sharing of a page, for example.

Although this extreme stress case workload is not a "real" parallel application, as it may not reflect the memory reference patterns of a real program, it is interesting in that it depicts the kernel of misbehaving applications that lead to poor performance. It captures some of the reference behavior of a certain class of programs and provides insight into the potential cost of memory latency in poorly designed applications.

The software model parameters are summarized in Table 2. Caches alleviate memory latency, but cannot eliminate first time references and reloads due to invalidations needed to maintain the consistency of the data. The parameter g is the average number of cycles between physical access attempts to the hot module from each processor. When a memory request is negatively acknowledged, it is retried after an interval of time, t_b cycles. For mathematical tractability, we will assume a constant backoff interval.

g	the number of cycles between successive memory requests
t_b	the backoff time

Table 2: Model software parameters.

3 Analysis of the Model

In this section, we develop an analytical model of a hierarchical NUMA shared memory multiprocessor. The model is based on simple equations describing the system interconnection network. A similar approach has been used elsewhere for treating the case where all memory modules are accessed symmetrically by the processors [15]. The model assumes that read and write requests to memory are serviced in the same amount of time. For our analysis we consider a 24-processor Hector prototype. The main measures of performance addressed are the hot spot memory module utilization and the memory access latencies incurred by processors at various locations relative to the hot spot. Traffic to a single hot spot has a global effect, so we will also examine the implications of contention on the communication bandwidth. Hence, the network utilization will be considered as a measure of performance as well.

3.1 Response Time Equations

The response time, T_i, of a memory request includes (1) the execution time between requests, g, (2) the time for a memory reference from the *ith* level of the memory hierarchy ignoring contention, and (3) the delays due to contention. The contention may occur along the communication path and at the memory module itself. The delays depend on the location of the issuing processor relative to the hot spot. Expressions for the various response times are given below:

$$T_1 = g + C_1 + D_1 \qquad (1)$$
$$T_2 = g + C_2 + D_2 + 2D_d \qquad (2)$$
$$T_3 = g + C_3 + D_3 + 2D_d + 2D_s + 2D_r \qquad (3)$$

where D_1, D_2, D_3 are the average memory contention delays incurred at the memory module by local, on-station, and remote requests respectively, and

D_d, D_s, and D_r are the latencies incurred by remote requests traveling across the network components. In Figure 1, H denotes the hot spot location, bus_d is the station bus where the hot spot is located, and bus_s represents any other bus. Local accesses do not use a bus, on-station accesses use only bus_d, and off-station accesses use the ring and bus_s in addition to bus_d. The factors of two account for the fact that a request crosses each network component both on the way to and on the way back from the hot spot.

3.2 Delay Equations

In order to determine the delays, we must first derive the utilizations of the various centers. Estimates of the utilizations are given by:

$$U_m = S_m\left[\frac{1}{T_1} + \frac{k-1}{T_2} + \frac{k(n-1)}{T_3}\right] \qquad (4)$$
$$U_d = 2S_b\left[\frac{k-1}{T_2} + \frac{k(n-1)}{T_3}\right]V_m \qquad (5)$$
$$U_r = S_r\frac{k(n-1)}{T_3}V_m \qquad (6)$$
$$U_s = 2S_b\frac{k}{T_3}V_m \qquad (7)$$

where V_m is the average visit count to the hot spot module per memory access. This permits us to estimate the delay in accessing memory as:

$$D_1 = (t_b + C_1 - S_m)R_m + D_m \qquad (8)$$
$$D_2 = (t_b + C_2 - S_m + 2D_d)R_m + D_m \qquad (9)$$
$$D_3 = (t_b + C_3 - S_m + 2D_d + 2D_r + 2D_s)R_m \\ + D_m \qquad (10)$$
$$D_m = S_m(1 - U_m)\sum_{i=1}^{q-1} iU_m^i \qquad (11)$$

where R_m is the average number of retries on the memory ($V_m = 1 + R_m$). The second term, D_m, is just the memory service time times the expected number of requests in queue. The expected delay at the bus and at the ring can be approximated by the product of the estimated queue length and the service time per request.

$$D_d = S_b\frac{U_d}{1 - U_d} \qquad (12)$$
$$D_r = S_r\frac{U_r}{1 - U_r} \qquad (13)$$
$$D_s = S_b\frac{U_s}{1 - U_s} \qquad (14)$$

3.3 Retry Equations

When a memory module cannot enqueue all the requests made to it, the remaining requests must be rejected and later retried. The probability of rejection can be approximated by the probability that the request queue at the memory module is full. Let P_B denote the probability that the qth slot of the buffer is occupied. If we assume a geometric queue length distribution, we can express P_B as a function of U_m, where U_m is the utilization of the memory.

$$P_B = 1 - \sum_{i=0}^{q-1}(1 - U_m)U_m^i = U_m^q$$

The probability of finding the buffer full on the second and successive tries is in fact dependent on previous events, and on the backoff value. To account for this dependency, we assign higher than P_B probability of rejection for the retries generated after a small backoff time. Let $H(i)$ denote the probability of rejection associated with the ith try. Assuming that an immediate retry fails with certainty, that in equilibrium a request fails with probability P_B, and that the dependence decays exponentially, we let

$$H(i) = P_B + (1 - P_B)e^{-i\frac{t_b}{S_m}} \quad (15)$$

$$\text{then,} \quad R_m = \sum_{j=1}^{\infty}\prod_{i=1}^{j} H(i) \quad (16)$$

3.4 Evaluation of the model

Since the utilizations are known only once the model has been evaluated, we solve the model by the iterative scheme shown below.

1. Set all utilizations to zero.

2. Estimate the number of retries from eqs. (15) and (16).

3. Evaluate the various delays D_i, $i = 1, 2, 3$, D_m, D_d, D_r, and D_s using eqs. (8), (9), (10), (11), (12), (13), and (14) respectively.

4. Calculate the response times T_1, T_2, and T_3, based on the new values of the delays using eqs. (1), (2), and (3) respectively.

5. Evaluate the utilizations from eqs. (4)-(7).

S_b	$=$	1	S_r	$=$	1	S_m	$=$	8
C_1	$=$	10	C_2	$=$	12	C_3	$=$	19
			t_b	$=$	12			

Table 3: The default values for model parameters (in cycles).

We iterate steps 2 through 5 until successive estimates of memory utilization, U_m, are sufficiently close, and then obtain performance measures from the final iteration.

To establish confidence in the robustness of our analysis, we modified our model to reflect our Hector prototype peculiarities such as limited buffering, priority of resource acquisition among the different classes of requests, and optimization of negatively acknowledged packets. We then validated our model with a detailed simulator proven to be quite accurate when compared against measurements obtained from experimentation on the prototype [11]. Our results [9] from simulation and analysis showed good agreement despite the assumptions made in deriving the model. We believe that the model captures the key features of the hierarchical structure, while making it possible to quickly study the effects of varying system parameters. Figure 2(a) shows validation of this model against a detailed simulation model of Hector. Figure 2(b) shows validation of the same model modified to reflect a KSR1 against measurement data from a 50 processor KSR1.

4 Results

Figure 3(a) shows how the system utilizations vary with the mean time between memory reference requests (g). The chosen range of g represents values likely to occur in practice. For moderate values of g (150-300 cycles between requests), the hot memory module is the system's bottleneck. As g gets smaller, the bus of the station accommodating the hot spot, bus_d, becomes the limiting factor of the system performance. As g decreases the probability for a request to be rejected becomes greater, causing the bus to be overloaded with retries. An important feature of the delay curves of Figure 3(b) is that there is a range of values of g (< 150) for which a small change in the mean time between memory reference requests produces a disproportionately significant increase in delays. Consequently, bursty memory requests should

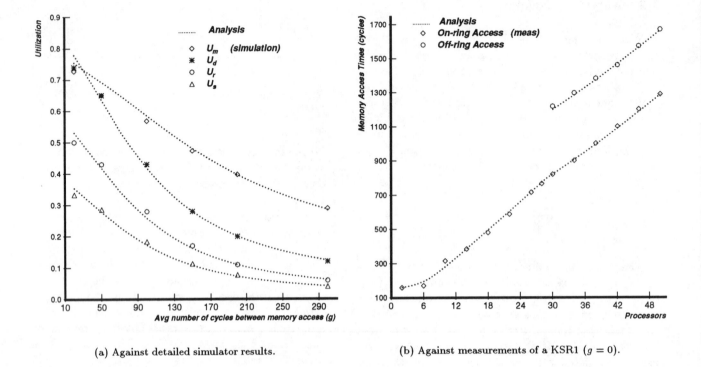

(a) Against detailed simulator results.

(b) Against measurements of a KSR1 ($g = 0$).

Figure 2: Validation.

be avoided as much as possible, as was previously observed by Anderson [4].

The latency curves of Figure 3(b) show that at low values of g, off-station requests suffer the most from contention. (This may not be the case in systems such as Hector where remote requests are given a higher priority over local ones. This priority in service has not been incorporated into this model.) For large values of g, the difference in latencies is primarily due to the physical path a request has to travel. On the other hand, the contention factors dominate for small values of g.

It is important to fully understand the interactions among the various model parameters. For instance, one can notice that a 60 percent variation in the utilization ($30 < g < 300$) of bus_d translates to a 500 percent change in memory access time for remote processors.

4.1 Eliminating Hot Spots Through Replication

When the hot spot memory module is frequently accessed, the local bus becomes the performance bottleneck. To avoid this problem, we consider replicating the data structure on two stations (two way replica-

tion). Such replication has an initial cost for creating the replica and ongoing costs for maintaining the consistency between the two copies. Here, we assess only the potential gain in order to determine whether further exploration of the possibility is justified in a particular situation or not. If we assume that each processor accesses the replica that is closest to it, and that for equidistant cases there is an equal probability of accessing either one, then an r-way replication scheme (where $r \leq n$), decrees new rates of access that affect equations (4),(5), and (6). The new equations describing the model with an r-way replication (established by arguments analogous to those in Section 3) are as follows:

$$
\begin{aligned}
U_m &= S_m[\frac{1}{T_1} + \frac{k-1}{T_2} + \frac{k(n-r)}{rT_3}] \\
U_d &= 2S_b[\frac{k-1}{T_2} + \frac{k(n-r)}{rT_3}]V_m \\
U_r &= S_r\frac{k(n-r)}{T_3}V_m
\end{aligned}
$$

The results of this section were obtained using the equations given in [10] which apply for two way replication.

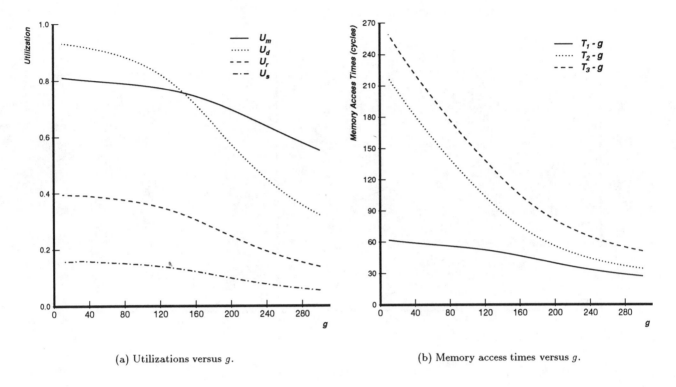

(a) Utilizations versus g.

(b) Memory access times versus g.

Figure 3: Model results.

The curves in Figure 4(a) show the change in utilizations as the reference frequency increases for a replicated hot spot. Replicating the hot spot reduces the contention at the memory level and along the communication network. In contrast to the single copy case in Figure 3(a), bus_d utilization remains below the memory utilization for the whole range of g values, suggesting that the number of retries indeed drops with replication. For small values of g, the utilizations of bus_s and of the *ring* are greater than those incurred with a single hot spot. This is due to an increase in the throughput of the requests as a result of replication. The benefits of reduced contention and latency gained from replication must be balanced against the cost of maintaining consistency of the replicas.

Replicating data allows a greater number of requests to be satisfied locally, thus removing some load from the ring and bus_d. It also indirectly decreases the number of retries, which has the effect of reducing the load on the network. However, this means that the requests can progress at a faster rate (because of the closed feedback loop in the model), resulting in a more highly utilized network, and subsequently leading to higher delays. In Figure 4(a) U_r and U_s are higher (for $g \leq 100$) than in the non-replicated case. Fig-

ure 4(b) plots the ratio of memory access times without and with replication for each of the three types of requests. The shape of the curves in Figure 4(b) illustrates how the memory access times involve delays that depend on the dynamic state of the network, which in turn depends on the rate of requests. For low values of g, the progress of the requests is limited by the observed delays rather than by the number of cycles between memory requests. Hence, the contention becomes more pronounced, translating into a declining relative gain (with respect to the non replicated case). Figure 4(b) also indicates that off-station accesses benefit the most from replication, because this type of access is the most sensitive to contention and thus gains the most from a strategy that alleviates memory congestion. As the access frequency increases, the relative gain improves to a maximum. It is interesting to note that the relative gain for local, on-station, and off-station access manifest maxima for different values of g. This is due to the fact that memory accesses from different levels exhibit different sensitivity to contention.

901

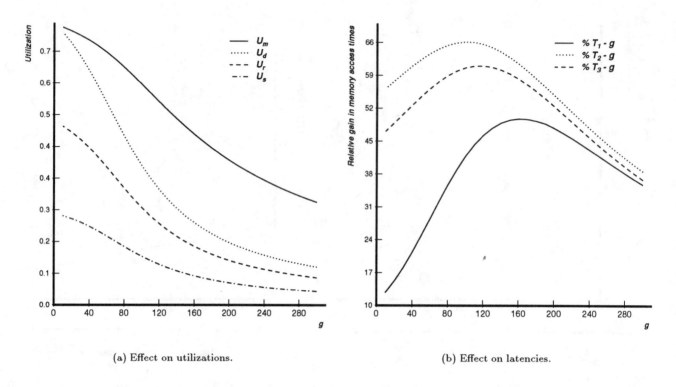

(a) Effect on utilizations.

(b) Effect on latencies.

Figure 4: Effects of 2-way replication.

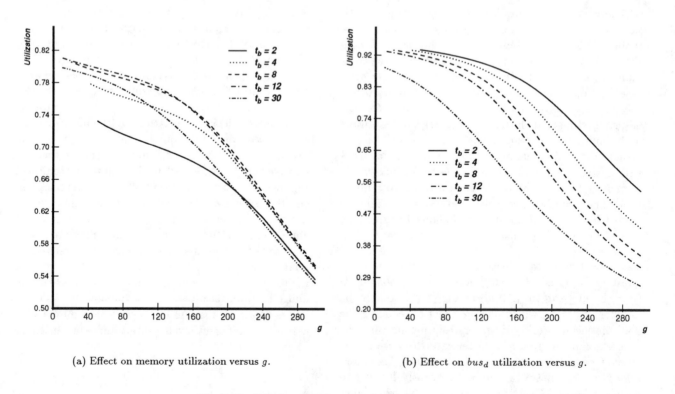

(a) Effect on memory utilization versus g.

(b) Effect on bus_d utilization versus g.

Figure 5: Effects of various backoff values, t_b.

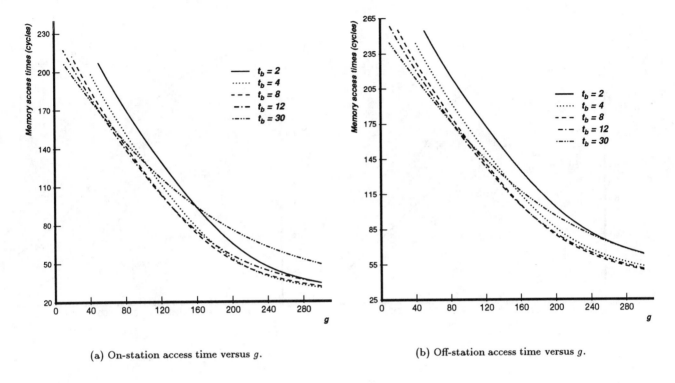

(a) On-station access time versus g.

(b) Off-station access time versus g.

Figure 6: Effects of various backoff values, t_b.

4.2 Impact of Backoff Values

In this section, we evaluate the effect of backoff values on system performance using our analytical model, and discuss the trade-offs between reduced traffic bandwidth and wasted cpu cycles. Figure 5(a) compares the system performance for backoff values of 2, 4, 8, 12, and 30 cycles. Intermediate values of backoff times achieve high memory utilization over all ranges of g, and in particular for low values. However, this does not necessarily correspond to minimizing the memory access time. The curves illustrating the utilization of bus_d for different t_b values show that large t_b results in more efficient use of bus_d, since a larger backoff value results in spreading out arrivals, thus reducing the contention. By using a large backoff value, we reduce network traffic, but this saving comes at the expense of increased memory access latency times for high values of g. (Similar results were obtained by Agarwal and Cherian [2].) For low values of g, the curves converge, which is expected since most of the requests are satisfied on their first try. Note that the memory utilization curves associated with $t_b = 30$ and $t_b = 4$ intersect when $g = 100$ (i.e., resulting in the same system throughput), yet one backoff value ($t_b = 30$) causes fewer retries which translates into a

25 percent of saving in bus utilization. The saving would be more significant with larger systems.

Figures 6(a), and 6(b) depict the effects of various backoff values on the on-station and off-station access times. Note that under heavy load the impact is qualitatively the same for both classes of requests. For light load, the access times for on-station and off-station accesses behave differently for corresponding backoff values.

4.3 Buffer Size Implications on Performance

Figure 7 shows the benefit of increasing the memory buffer size for various request frequencies. Extra buffers added to memory modules benefit the system the most during the critical phases of the lifetime of the applications (i.e., when the degree of contention is high). For instance, a buffer of size two improves the memory utilization (relative to utilization of a memory with a single buffer) only by 2 percent for $g = 300$, yet, the improvement is 8 percent when $g = 50$ cycles. Like other aspects of system design, memory buffer design is subject to the law of diminishing returns as Figure 7 illustrates.

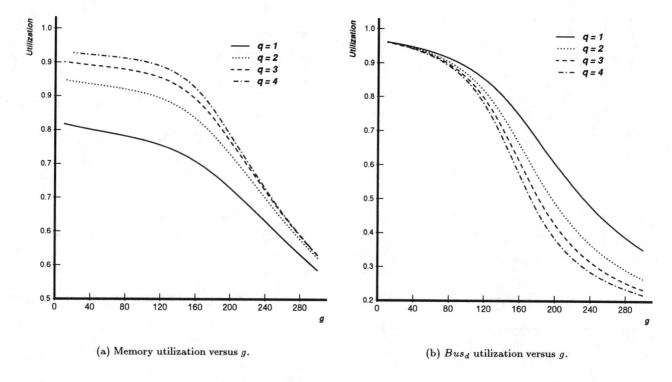

(a) Memory utilization versus g.

(b) Bus_d utilization versus g.

Figure 7: Effects of various memory queue lengths, q.

5 Conclusions

Memory allocation decisions are crucial to good performance in NUMA systems, and a model that provides insights into the design tradeoffs is valuable. In this paper, we have presented an analytical study of the performance of large scale NUMA multiprocessors in the presence of a single memory hot spot. We developed a simple model that captures the main features of this type of architecture, namely the non-uniformity of memory access times. Our results reveal that memory latency is very sensitive to the non-uniformity of memory requests. We show that, if measures are not taken to alleviate the contention, parallel applications can suffer long memory access delays.

Our analysis also assessed the potential gain from replication, and quantified the expected improvement in memory utilization and network bandwidth by allowing memory request buffering. Finally, we investigated the effect of the backoff value (after a memory request rejection) on the network bandwidth, which is a valuable resource in large-scale machines. The results indicate that varying the backoff value can result in a tradeoff between throughput and network utilization. We are currently investigating the benefit of adaptive backoff values on the overall system performance.

Our experiments confirm the need for developing new techniques to manage the distributed physical memory found in NUMA multiprocessors. Traditional methods that ignore non-uniform memory latency characteristics are bound to impose significant communication overhead on scalable parallel systems. The model developed in this paper provides some insight into the NUMA problem, and can help in the development of better approaches to NUMA memory management.

Acknowledgements: Our thanks to Songnian Zhou for feedback on an earlier draft of the paper, and to the University of Washington for access to their KSR-1 for our validation experiments. Thanks also to Hui Li for informative discussions on KSR architectural issues.

References

[1] R. L. Adema and C. S. Ellis. Duke university, computer science department. Technical report, Memory Allocation Constructs to Complement NUMA Memory Management, 1991.

[2] A. Agarwal and M. Cherian. Adaptive back-off synchronization techniques. In *16th International Symposium on Computer Architecture*, pages 396–406. ACM, May 1989.

[3] A. Agarwal, B. H. Lim, D. Kranz, and J. Kubiatowicz. April: A processor architecture for multiprocessing. In *17th International Symposium on Computer Architecture*. ACM, May 1990.

[4] T. E. Anderson. The performance of spin lock alternatives for shared-memory multiprocessors. *Transactions on Parallel and Distributed Systems*, 1(1), 1990.

[5] BBN. Inside the butterfly tc2000. Technical report, BBN Advanced Computers, Cambridge, MA, February 1990.

[6] W. J. Bolosky, M. L. Scott, R. P. Fitzgerald, R. J. Fowler, and A. L. Cox. NUMA policies and their relation to memory architecture. In *4th Intl. Conference on Architectural Support for Programming Languages and Operating Systems*, pages 212–221. ACM, April 1991.

[7] William J. Bolosky and Michael L. Scott. Evaluation of multiprocessor memory systems using off-line optimal behavior. Technical report, University of Rochester, Computer Science Department, September 1991.

[8] T. Dunigan. Kendall square multiprocessor: Early experiences and performance. Technical Report ORNL/TM-12065, Oak Ridge National Laboratory, March 1992.

[9] K. Harzallah and K. C. Sevcik. Evaluating memory system performance of a large scale NUMA multiprocessor. Technical Report 283, University of Toronto, CSRI, available for anonymous ftp from ftp.csri.toronto.edu, March 1993.

[10] K. Harzallah and K. C. Sevcik. Hot spot analysis in large scale shared memory multiprocessors. Technical Report 280, University of Toronto, CSRI, January 1993.

[11] M. Holliday and M. Stumm. Performance evaluation of hierarchical ring-based shared memory multiprocessors. Technical Report 1992–18, Duke University,Computer Science Department, 1992.

[12] R. P. LaRowe, M. A. Holliday, and C. S. Ellis. An analysis of dynamic page placement on a numa multiprocessor. In *Sigmetrics Conference on Measurement and Modeling of Computer Systems*, pages 23–34. ACM, June 1992.

[13] D. Lenoski, J. Laudon, K. Gharachorloo, A. Gupta, and J. Hennessey. The directory-based cache coherence protocol for the dash multiprocessor. In *17th International Symposium on Computer Architecture*, pages 148–159. ACM, May 1990.

[14] A. K. Nanda, H. Shing, T. Tzen, and L. M. Ni. Resource contention in shared-memory multiprocessors: A parameterized performance degradation model. *Journal of Parallel and Distributed Computing*, 12:313–328, 1991.

[15] K. C. Sevcik and S. Zhou. Performance benefits and limitations of large numa multiprocessors. Technical Report 256, University of Toronto, November 1991. also to appear in the proceedings of Performance '93, Rome, September 1993.

[16] Z.G. Vranesic, M. Stumm, D.M. Lewis, and R. White. Hector - a hierarchically structured shared-memory multiprocessor. *IEEE Computer*, January 1991.

[17] X. Zhang and X. Qin. Performance prediction and evaluation of parallel processing on a numa multiprocessor. *Transactions on Software Engineering*, 17(10):1059–1068, October 1991.

Performance on a Bandwidth Constrained Network: How much bandwidth do we need?

Bob Boothe

Computer Science Dept.
University Of Southern Maine
Portland, ME 04103

Abhiram Ranade

Computer Science Dept.
University of California
Berkeley, CA 94720

Abstract

In this research we approach the question of network design from the perspective of the applications and ask: How much network do we need? We answer this question, in the context of shared memory multiprocessors, for 4 scientific applications. We simulate their executions under infinite bandwidth assumptions and collect profiles of their varying bandwidth needs. These profiles are then fed into a performance model of how bursty traffic squeezes through a bandwidth constrained network. Our results suggest that networks should provide a remote memory bandwidth of 2–4 bits/operation and memory module bandwidths of 8–16 bits/op. The higher memory module bandwidth is needed because of hot spots in the traffic patterns. Further simulations show that these hot spots arise primarily because of randomness and not because of multiple accesses to a single location. Thus combining techniques will not be able to eliminate hot spots from these applications.

1 Introduction

We are interested in the design and performance of large shared memory multiprocessors. In these machines, the programmer is given an abstract model of the machine and is typically neither concerned with nor capable of controlling the precise layout and movement of data. Shared memory machines must therefore be designed to provide enough network and memory bandwidth to make the abstract model of shared memory work. In this paper we quantify through simulation and analysis the bandwidth demands that will be placed upon shared memory machines.

For large parallel machines, the network cost will be a crucial concern because the cost of the network grows faster than other costs as the machine is scaled. For example, on indirect networks, such as butterflys or fat-trees, $O(p \log p)$ routing nodes are used to connect p processors. On direct networks the cost increases superlinearly as well. On hypercubes the degree of the routing nodes grows as $O(p \log p)$, and on meshes the width of the channels must grow as $O(\sqrt{p})$ in order to maintain a fixed bisection bandwidth/processor. We have undertaken this research in order to establish network design goals by trying to answer the question: *How much bandwidth do we need?*

The main complication that arises in answering this question is that traffic is bursty. Applications pass through different computational phases, some of which do more or less computation or communication than others. Furthermore the communication is not spread evenly across the collection of memory modules. Some memory modules are likely to be subject to higher usage than others (a hot spot) either because of many parallel accesses to a single shared variable or simply due to random coincidence. This study of application behavior tells us how much bandwidth is needed, how bursty is the traffic, and how useful is special hardware for message combining.

1.1 Overview

The rest of this paper is divided into 6 sections. In Section 2 we summarize some relevant background topics such as bandwidth reduction with caching and latency tolerance through multithreading. In Section 3 we present our simulation model and the benchmark applications. In Sections 4, 5, & 6, we present our simulation results and analyze them in terms of remote memory bandwidth, hot spot memories, and the potential benefits of special combining hardware. And in Section 7 we summarize the main results and discuss their application to future network designs.

2 Background

In this section we summarize a few relevant results from previous research. These results are presented in order to help motivate the decisions made in the design of our simulated machine model.

2.1 Caching to reduce bandwidth

Caching provides a means of filtering out many remote references and thereby reducing the bandwidth demands on the network. Caching is effective if the extra traffic caused by bringing lines of data across the network and the extra coherency traffic is overshadowed by the reduction in references afforded by a high hit rate in the cache. For most applications caching is effective at reducing bandwidth demands and provides bandwidth reductions[5] ranging from a factor of 4 to a factor of 13.

However maintaining cache coherency is complicated, and in fact there exist proposed large shared memory machines (TERA[2]) that do not provide caching. Because the network will be a large fraction of the system cost for large machines, we expect that the cost and complexity of coherent caching will be justified by the savings in network cost that caching provides by reducing the bandwidth requirement. Thus in this research we focus on machines that provide caching of shared memory.

2.2 Long network latency

One main difficulty that arises in large parallel computers is the long latency for remote references. Long latencies are inevitable because the processors and memories are interconnected by packet switched networks in which messages are routed through the network across many nodes and links. Delays occur because of the physical limits of the nodes and links and because of congestion within the network.

For large machines, remote reference latencies will be hundreds of cycles. For instance, a remote read miss takes 101 processor cycles on the 64 processor DASH prototype[15] when there is no congestion. On a 1088 processor KSR1[13], a remote read miss takes 570 cycles. With congestion, latencies increase because messages are stalled and buffered many times as they progress through the network. Simulations of butterfly networks by Dally[8] show that latency due to congestion rises dramatically as network traffic is increased and that for a network operating at 50% of capacity, latency may be 3 times that of an unloaded network.

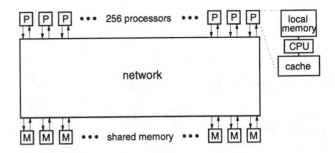

Figure 1: Model of parallel computer.

For our simulations of a 256 processor machine, we assume a remote reference latency of 200 cycles and that half of this latency is due to congestion in the network. Our results, however, are insensitive to the precise latency assumptions because we also simulate a mechanism for tolerating latency.

2.3 Multithreading to tolerate latency

If each processor has only a single thread of execution, it will be forced to stall on remote references in order to wait for their results. With long remote reference latencies, the processor will sit idle for long periods of time. In our simulations we have used a technique called *multithreading*[1, 5, 11] to keep the processors busy. Multithreading gives each processor several threads so that it can work on one thread while the other threads are waiting on remote references. This allows overlapping communication and computation and thus facilitates achievement of high processor utilization in the presence of long memory latencies.

3 Simulation setup

We have built a simulation system[4] that allows us to simulate our benchmark applications on an idealized parallel computer. These simulations are realistic in every respect (processor, latency, caching, multithreading) except that the network has infinite bandwidth. By simulating applications on an infinite bandwidth machine, we obtain an accurate picture of their varying bandwidth needs. We then use these simulation results along with a mathematical model to predict the performance of an arbitrarily constrained bandwidth network.

3.1 Simulated machine

Figure 1 shows the basic model of our simulated machine. There are 256 processors connected via a

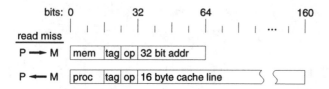

Figure 2: Messages caused by a read miss to an unmodified location.

App.	Description & Problem size
blkmat	blocked matrix multiply, 320 × 320
sor	successive over relaxation, 768 × 768 grid
ugray	ray tracing renderer, gears (7169 faces)
barnes	N-body simulation, 16384 bodies

Table 1: Parallel Applications

network to an equal number of memory modules. Each processor module consists of a CPU, some local memory, and a cache. The shared memory space is randomly interleaved across the memory modules in order to avoid uneven usage of the memories. The rationale is the same as that for randomizing memory addresses to avoid stride problems across a set of memory banks[21]. Our interleaving granularity is a cache line.

For the CPU we assume a typical pipelined RISC processor. We have used the instruction set and timing of the MIPS R3000[12], with one major modification: we assume that the processor has hardware that allows rapidly context switching between a small number of threads. For the simulations presented in this paper, the number of threads per processor is 2, 3 or 4, depending upon the application. We used a switch-on-miss multithreading policy[5]: the processor context switches whenever a shared memory read misses in the cache.

Each processor is equipped with a 64K byte cache for shared memory.[1] The caches have a 16 byte line size and are 4 way set-associative. Cache coherency is managed with an invalidation based directory protocol[7]. The line size and invalidation based protocol were selected so as to help minimize bandwidth usage[6, 17].

The network is treated as a black box, with the goal of this research being to determine its bandwidth parameters.

Although we are studying shared memory machines, the network itself is a simple message passing system. Messages are sent automatically from the processors when cache misses occur, and other messages are sent by the memories modules in order to return results and to maintain cache coherency. Figure 2 shows the messages that are needed to service a read miss to an unmodified location. The first message contains four fields: **mem** = the memory bank destination for routing, **tag** = a message tag to be used

in the result message, **op** = the operation (read), and the address to be read. The result message is similar and returns the 16 bytes cache line that is being read. These messages sizes are at the small end of the spectrum of possible implementations. For instance, we have assumed that the only routing information needed is the number of the destination memory bank or processor, and we have assumed that the return address can be generated as the message is routed[10]. Also, we have used 32 bit addresses, whereas a large parallel machine will likely support a larger address space. The important point with respect to this study is that a simple read miss will cause a total of 224 bits (7 words) of network traffic. If the actual messages in a particular implementation are larger, then our results should be scaled up accordingly.

3.2 Applications

Table 1 lists the applications used in this study. Blkmat and sor are simple applications; ugray[3] and barnes[23] are complex. We would have liked to have more benchmark applications, but unfortunately most available benchmarks have been written for and have inputs suitable only for smaller machines than we are interested in. For this study, simulating large systems is crucial because hot spots arise, for instance, when all or many processors reference a single shared variable, and this hot spot congestion becomes noticeable only when there are many processors.

Table 2 shows a few basic parameters and results from our simulations. The simulation were for the first 20 million cycles of parallel execution (except in the case of blkmat which completed execution sooner). The simulated machine has a latency of 200 cycles and multithreading was used to help hide that latency. The multithreading level (number of threads per processor) for each application is shown. These levels were chosen separately at the best level for each application. At the chosen levels, some cycles are still lost to memory latency and some are also lost to synchronization. These idle cycles are reflected by the processor utilization figures. Barnes for instance has only 72% utilization because there are many stall cycles due to synchronization. However for large parallel ma-

---
[1] A real processor would also have caches for local memory and instructions, but we don't explicitly model these because they should have very high hit rates. We treat all local and instruction accesses as cache hits.

Application	Simulation Length (cycles)	Multithreading Level	Processor Utilization	Cache Hit Rate	Average Remote Memory Bandwidth (bits/op)
blkmat	1.8 M	2	93%	65%	0.98
sor	first 20 M	4	94%	99%	1.24
ugray	first 20 M	3	88%	88%	1.68
barnes	first 20 M	2	72%	85%	0.59

Table 2: Simulation parameters and basic results.

chines, these utilizations all indicate good speedups.

4 Remote memory bandwidth

The last column in Table 2 shows the average remote memory bandwidths used by the benchmark applications. This is simply the sum total of all traffic divided by the execution time. In this table and throughout this paper all bandwidth results are normalized by the number of processors, the processor cycle time, and the number of operations/cycle that the processor can execute. Results are thus expressed in terms of bits/operation. As an example, consider the case where each processor has a remote read miss every 100th cycle. A remote read miss causes 224 bits of traffic as shown in Figure 2, and since the MIPS R3000 executes one operation per cycle, the average remote memory bandwidth would be 2.24 bits/op. The average remote memory bandwidths of the applications range from 0.59 to 1.68 bits/op.

Measurements of traffic on the 32 processor DASH prototype[15] provide similar results. They measured remote memory bandwidths of 0.33, 0.97, and 2.38 bits/op for the barnes, water, and locus applications respectively.[2] Our simulation of barnes shows higher remote memory bandwidth than DASH because we have used more processors, and for this application the proportion of communication increases with the number of processors[22].

4.1 Performance model for bursty traffic

The average remote memory bandwidth results give an optimistic view of the demands on the network because traffic will be bursty rather than uniformly spread out. Applications pass through different computational phases, some of which have higher bandwidth needs than others. Also the cache increases the burstiness of traffic because at the start of a phase

[2]These numbers were derived from network utilization results presented in their paper.

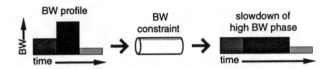

Figure 3: High bandwidth phases will slow down as they squeeze through the bandwidth constrained network.

there may be many misses and high traffic; while at the end of a phases most data will be cached and there will be fewer misses and lower traffic.

In this section we develop a performance model for bursty traffic in a bandwidth constrained network. The basic idea is illustrated in Figure 3. We start with a bandwidth profile of an application. This is obtained from simulations, and it shows the varying bandwidth needs of the application as a function of time. For most applications the bandwidth will not be uniform. Instead, the applications will have different phases with different bandwidth needs as shown in the figure. The network of a real machine will have a maximum bandwidth capacity, which is represented in the figure by the pipe labeled *BW constraint*. For our performance model, we assume that during phases when an application needs less bandwidth than is available, it will execute at full speed. But during phases when the bandwidth needs exceed the network bandwidth capacity, we assume that execution slows down and makes progress at the rate as which messages squeeze through the network.

Figure 4 formally specifies our performance model. This model is much more accurate than simply looking at the average bandwidth over the entire run of the execution, but it is still optimistic. Under some adverse traffic patterns there may be some links of the network or memory modules that are more heavily used than others. These will be bottlenecks and could further slow down the execution of the machine. Hopefully, such bottlenecks will be rare when data is spread randomly across the machine as we have assumed.

$$\text{slowdown} = \frac{\sum_{i=1}^{n} t_i \max\left(1, \frac{\text{bw}_i}{\text{bw}_{\text{net}}}\right)}{\sum_{i=1}^{n} t_i}$$

Squeeze Performance Model

n = number of phases
t_i = duration of phase i
bw_i = bandwidth needed in phase i
bw_{net} = bandwidth available

Figure 4: Performance model of an application having phases with varying bandwidth needs being executed on a machine with limited network bandwidth.

4.2 Simulation results

In practice, applications do not exhibit long uniform phases as suggested by the squeeze performance model. The processors are all semi-independent systems which issue occasional messages into the network. Together they form a very bursty system. At some particular point in time, there might be a large burst of new messages resulting from random coincidence. However, this burst will not slow down the machine if on subsequent cycles there is a compensating lull in new traffic. On a small time scale the network and its buffering serve to smooth out the traffic.

To take into account this natural smoothing of the traffic, we have gathered our simulation data over intervals of 100 cycles. Much shorter sample intervals would be pessimistic since they would report bursts of traffic that could be smoothed out by a real network, and likewise much longer sample intervals would be optimistic since they would smooth over long bursts of traffic that on a real network *would* have a performance impact. We chose the value of 100 cycles because it is half of the expected 200 cycle network latency. This latency will consist of both physical delays and congestion delays with perhaps half of the latency due to each. The congestion delay is caused by the jostling of messages as they move through the network, and this is the period in which small bursts of traffic are smoothed out.

Figure 5 shows a snippet from the remote memory bandwidth profile of sor. This snippet is for 100,000 cycles, whereas the applications were simulated for 20,000,000 cycles. The vertical bars in this graph

bw	blkmat	sor	ugray	barnes
32				
16				
8	1.01	1.01		
4	1.02	1.07		
2	1.13	1.29	1.02	
1	1.37	1.85	1.71	1.01

Table 3: Slowdown factors under various bandwidth limits.

each represent a sample interval of 100 cycles. During each interval, the sizes of all messages sent into the network were added together to give a single sample value: the remote memory bandwidth total for that interval. These sample values were then normalized to bits/op.

This bandwidth profile graphically show both the short term and long term burstiness of traffic, but the entire 20,000,000 cycle profiles are far too large to be included. We therefore present the complete bandwidth profiles by sorting the sample intervals. The sorted profiles are shown in Figure 6. Sorting the samples allows drawing a compact graph that more clearly shows the fraction of time the applications operate at various bandwidth levels. For example, when running sor the network sits idle (or nearly idle) for 54% of the time. For 12% of the time (the interval of sorted samples from 54% to 66%) the bandwidth is between 0 and 1 bits/op, and the rest of the time it is higher. About 10% of the time it is higher than 4 bits/op. The other applications exhibit less variance in their bandwidth profiles.

These sorted profiles can be used to easily visualize and compute the performance loss that will result when the applications are run on a machine with a bandwidth constrained network. For blkmat, for example, if the network has a bandwidth capacity of 1 bit/op, 85% of the program execution has bandwidth needs less than this, and will be unimpeded, but the remaining portion will be slowed down, much of it by about a factor of four.

Table 3 shows the precise slowdowns of the applications under various bandwidth limits. These were calculated by applying the squeeze performance model to the bandwidth profiles. Blkmat, for instance, under a bandwidth of 1 bit/op will slow down by a factor of 1.37.

Using this table, one can choose an appropriate bandwidth level such that the cost of increasing the network bandwidth is warranted by the increase in performance. Clearly it is not worth doubling the size and cost of the network just for a 1% or 2% per-

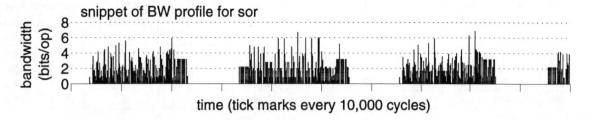

Figure 5: Snippet of the remote memory bandwidth profile of sor.

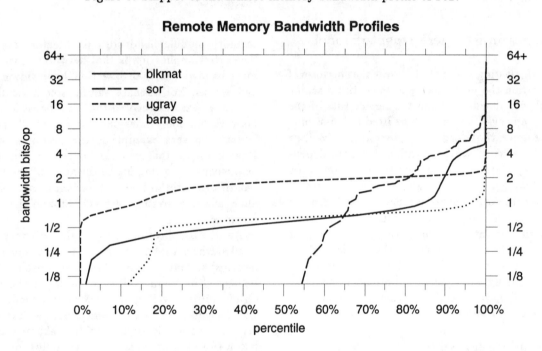

Figure 6: Sorted profiles of the applications' remote memory bandwidth usage.

formance increase. Thus the proper remote memory bandwidth of the network is from 2 to 4 bits/op.

5 Hot spot memory modules

The next part of the bandwidth picture concerns how evenly references are spread across the memory modules. If a particular memory module is getting more traffic than other modules, it is dubbed a *hot spot*. A hot spot become a problem when traffic directed to it exceeds its capacity. At this point messages to it will be delayed and will back up into the network.

Not only will messages to the hot spot be delayed, but as congestion backs up into the nodes of the network, messages destined for other memories can get blocked as well. The congestion quickly compounds and can spread across the network in a process called *tree saturation*[18].

Hot spots occur for several reasons. We classify hot spots into three categories which we call *location, layout,* and *random*. Location hot spots occur when there are many accesses to a particular shared variable, such as a shared counter. They are called location hot spots because they involve a single location. Layout hot spots occur when data is spread across the machine in a regular fashion, but because of the particular access patterns of the applications, some memory modules are much more highly utilized than others. This is analogous to the stride problem for vector computers, and can be diminished by randomly interleaving addresses across the memory modules. We have done this randomization of addresses in our simulations to avoid layout hot spots, but this accentuates the third category of hot spots which are due simply to random variation. At various points in time, simply through random chance, some memory modules will be more heavily utilized than others.

bw	blkmat	sor	ugray	barnes
32	1.01	1.08	1.02	1.01
16	1.03	1.19	1.05	1.03
8	1.25	1.55	1.36	1.10
4	2.23	2.41	2.65	1.77
2	4.44	4.26	5.31	3.49
1	8.88	8.02	10.61	6.97

Table 4: Slowdowns factors based on hot spot memory module bandwidth.

App.	Avg. BW	Network BW	Network over design factor	Memory Module BW	Memory Module over design factor
blkmat	0.98	4	4	16	16
sor	1.24	4	3	32	26
ugray	1.68	2	1.2	16	10
barnes	0.59	1	1.7	8	14

Table 5: Over design factors for the network and memory modules.

5.1 A pessimistic performance model

For a long lasting hot spot, it is clear that because of tree saturation the performance of the entire machine will be slowed down to match the service rate of the hot spot memory. However a short lived hot spot may only slow down those processors directly involved, or possibly because of synchronization and data dependencies, the delays may propagate to other processors as well.

Our model takes a pessimistic outlook and assumes that hot spots will slow down the entire machine. During each sample interval, the most heavily accessed memory module thus determines the machine slowdown for that interval. The total slowdown is calculated by applying the squeeze performance model to the links and traffic directly entering and exiting the hot spot memory module.

5.2 Simulation results

Figure 7 shows the simulation results for the hot spot memory module bandwidth. These are typically a factor of 4 to 8 larger than the remote memory bandwidths, and thus hot spots are an important part of the traffic picture.

Table 4 shows the application slowdowns computed using our performance model. Based on these results we can say that the network needs a memory module bandwidth of 16 bits/op. We should qualify this by restating that this is a pessimistic model and that it assumes either rapid onset of tree saturation or propagation of delays to processors not directly involved in the hot spot. We performed additional simulations with a sample interval of 500 cycles in order to gauge how sensitive our results are to this assumption. These simulation, which are probably optimistic, suggest that a memory bandwidth of 8 bits/op is adequate. Thus our conclusion is that memory module bandwidth should be from 8 to 16 bits/op.

Compared to our results in Section 4 indicating a remote memory bandwidth of 2 to 4 bits/op, the memory module bandwidth is a factor of 4 higher. The direct implication is that networks having higher local bandwidths than bisection bandwidths are advantageous. For instance the fat tree network in the CM-5[14] was designed so that the lowest level of the network has four times the bandwidth of the upper levels. Another example is the networks of M. T. Raghunath[19] that provide higher local bandwidths as a means of getting high utilization of the bisection bandwidth. A third example is mesh networks that allow adaptive routing of traffic around the hot spot memories.

Another implication of the higher memory module bandwidths is that the memory modules must be over designed so that they have far more capacity than will be needed on average. We can calculate this over design factor by dividing our performance model's bandwidth suggestions by the average bandwidths actually used by the applications. Table 5 shows this calculation (for each application individually) for both the network and the memory modules. The network and memory module bandwidths used in this table were taken from Tables 3 & 4 at levels that allowed achieving slowdowns ≤ 1.10. The network over design factors are moderate and range from 1.2 to 4. The memory module over design factors are much larger and range from 10 to 26.

Such large over design factors are required to service the hot spots in the memory access patterns. These hot spots arise because of the inevitable non-uniformity of the random message distribution. An analogous problem is the random distribution of n balls into n buckets. On average each bucket will receive 1 ball, but the worst case bucket will receive $\Omega(\log n / \log \log n)$ balls.

6 Location hot spots

The elimination and reduction of location hot spots has been the subject of a large body of research[9, 10, 16, 18, 20, 24]. These involve either hardware combin-

Hot Memory Module Bandwidth Profiles

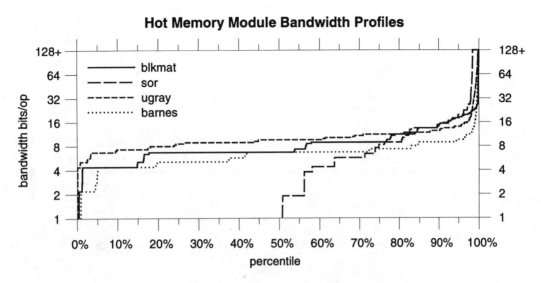

Figure 7: Sorted profiles of the applications' hot memory module bandwidth usage.

ing of messages or software combining trees. Hardware support is typically for fetch-and-add operations, from which many highly parallel synchronization techniques can be built[10]. Software techniques have been devised for barriers and synchronous reductions[16, 24].

Despite the large amount of research on combining techniques, there has been little previous work done on measuring how beneficial combining would be for real applications. This is partly a chicken and egg problem because without hardware support, programmers have little incentive to use fetch-and-add like operations. Although it has been suggested that fetch-and-add is useful even if not combined because it is a simple atomic operation that can be performed quickly at the memories[16]. We have provided such a non-combining fetch-and-add operation in our simulation system, but the applications use it only a few times.

In general, ordinary memory requests, such as several reads to a single location, can also be combined. In this section we determine an upper bound on the benefits of hardware combining. Our simulations count the total number of accesses to each individual memory location during a sample interval. We then use these numbers as our upper bound on combining. In other words, we assume that all references to a single location during a sample interval can be combined. This is optimistic for two reasons. First, combining of different reference types (such as a read, a fetch-and-add, and a write) is very complex and unlikely to ever be implemented. And second, our sample interval of 100 cycles is long enough that in a real network messages will often pass through the routing nodes before their potential combining partners arrive.

Figure 8 shows the number of accesses to the hottest

(most heavily used) location during each sample interval. As before, the samples are sorted from lowest to highest. Using ugray as an example, the lowest 15% of the intervals show a hot location access count of 1. This means that no location was referenced more than once during these intervals. After these, the rest of the intervals all the way up to the 96th percentile show a maximum count of 2. These two accesses might be combined, but such limited combining has little benefit and is not the motivation for combining hardware.

Chances for combining large numbers of accesses are rare. For example intervals with 10 or more messages directed to a single location occur during only 3% of the intervals for sor, 0.3% of the intervals for ugray, and 0.2% of the intervals for barnes. For sor most of these hot spots are due to barriers and could be eliminated with either a special purpose barrier network as on the CM-5[14] or with software barriers[16, 24]. Since serious location hot spots are so infrequent, we do not believe that hardware combining is justified.

We should note that two of the applications were modified after the initial run of these simulations. Sor showed an unexpected hot spot which was caused by all processors resetting a shared flag when only one processor needed to reset it. This was easily amended. For ugray, there was a problem with contention for a single lock that guarded a free list. This lock was a bottleneck, but had not been noticed before because ugray had never previously been run with so many processors. The bottleneck was eliminated by using a parallel free list.

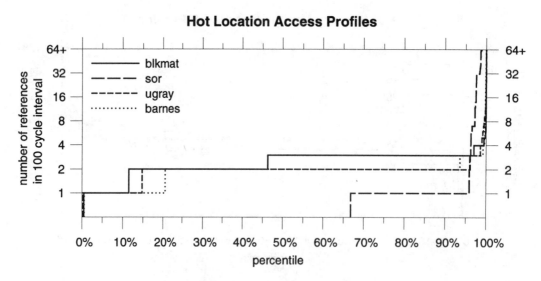

Figure 8: Sorted profiles of the applications' hot location access counts.

7 Summary

Our simulation results and performance model have shown that in order to support the four applications that we have studied, the networks for large shared memory cache coherent multiprocessors should provide a remote memory bandwidth of 2–4 bits/op and a memory module bandwidth of 8–16 bits/op. The higher bandwidth requirement at the memory modules is needed to accommodate random hot spot traffic.

Table 6 shows the results of calculations based on applying our bandwidth design goals to a variety of network topologies for a 256 processor machine. First, the link widths were calculated so that the networks would provide either a remote memory bandwidth of 4 bits/op or a memory module bandwidth of 16 bits/op. The larger of these two link widths was then selected and used for calculating the total wire count (which is a rough estimate of network cost). For these calculations we have assumed that the network and processor cycle times are the same, and that the processor executes 1 operation/cycle. The key observation to be made is that all of the networks except for the butterfly provide more local bandwidth than bisection bandwidth, and this extra local bandwidth is beneficial because it provides the higher bandwidth needed by the hot spot memory modules.

Acknowledgments

We would like to thank David Culler for his many comments and suggestions that helped improve the presentation of this research. This work was sup-

ported by the Air Force Office of Scientific Research (AFOSR/JSEP) under contract F49620-90-C-0029 and NSF Grant Number 1-442427-21936. Computing resources were provided by NSF Infrastructure Grant number CDA-8722788.

References

[1] Anant Agarwal, Beng-Hong Lim, David Kranz, and John Kubiatowicz. APRIL: A Processor Architecture for Multiprocessing. In *The 17th Annual Int. Symp. on Computer Architecture*, pages 104–114, 1990.

[2] Robert Alverson, David Callahan, Daniel Cummings, et al. The TERA Computer System. In *1990 Int. Conf. on Supercomputing*, pages 1–6, 1990.

[3] Bob Boothe. Multiprocessor Strategies for Ray-Tracing. Master's thesis, U.C. Berkeley, September 1989. Report No. UCB/CSD 89/534.

[4] Bob Boothe. Fast Accurate Simulation of Large Shared Memory Multiprocessors. Technical Report 92/682, Computer Science Division, University of California, Berkeley, 1992.

[5] Bob Boothe and Abhiram Ranade. Improved Multithreading Techniques for Hiding Communication Latency in Multiprocessors. In *The 19th Annual Int. Symp. on Computer Architecture*, pages 214–223, May 1992.

[6] Robert Francis Boothe. *Evaluation of Multithreading and Caching in Large Shared Memory Parallel Computers*. PhD thesis, University of California at Berkeley, June 1993.

[7] L. M. Censier and P. Feautrier. A New Solution to Coherence Problems in Multicache Systems. *IEEE Transactions on Computers*, C-27(12):1112–1118, December 1978.

Network	Routing Nodes	Links[3] per Node	Link Width if constrained by:		Total Wires
			Remote Memory Bandwidth	Memory Module Bandwidth	
Ring	256	4	128	4	65536
2-D Torus	256	8	8	2	8192
3-D Torus	256	12	4	1.3	6144
Butterfly[4]	1024	8/2	2	8	36864
Fat-Tree[5]	120	24/4	8	4	15360
Hypercube	256	16	2	1	4096

Table 6: Example networks and the link widths they need to meet the bandwidth design goals.

[8] William J. Dally. Virtual-Channel Flow Control. In *The 17th Annual Int. Symp. on Computer Architecture*, pages 60–68, 1990.

[9] Susan R. Dickey and Richard Kenner. Hardware Combining and Scalability. In *Proc. of the 1992 ACM Symposium on Parallel Algorithms and Architectures*, pages 296–305, 1992.

[10] Allan Gottlieb, Ralph Grishman, Clyde P. Kruskal, Kevin P. McAuliffe, Larry Rudolph, and Marc Snir. The NYU Ultracomputer — Designing a MIMD, Shared-Memory Parallel Machine. In *Conf. Proc. of the 9th Annual Symposium on Computer Architecture*, pages 27–42, 1982.

[11] Anoop Gupta, John Hennessy, Kourosh Gharachorloo, Todd Mowry, and Wolf-Dietrich Weber. Comparative Evaluation of Latency Reducing and Tolerating Techniques. In *The 18th Annual Int. Symp. on Computer Architecture*, pages 254–263, 1991.

[12] Gerry Kane. *MIPS RISC Architecture*. Prentice Hall, 1989.

[13] Kendall Square Research Corporation. *Kendall Square Research Technical Summary*, 1992.

[14] Charles E. Leiserson, Zahi S. Abuhamdeh, David C. Douglas, Carl R. Feynman, Mahesh N. Ganmukhi, Jeffrey V. Hill, et al. The Network Architecture of the Connection Machine CM-5. In *Proc. of the 1992 ACM Symposium on Parallel Algorithms and Architectures*, pages 272–285, 1992.

[15] Daniel Lenoski, James Lauden, Truman Joe, David Nakahira, Luis Stevens, Anoop Gupta, and John Hennessy. The DASH Prototype: Implementation and Performance. In *The 19th Annual Int. Symp. on Computer Architecture*, pages 92–103, 1992.

[16] John M Mellor-Crummey and Michael L. Scott. Algorithms for Scalable Synchronization on Shared-Memory Multiprocessors. *ACM Transactions on Computer Systems*, pages 21–65, February 1991.

[17] Brian Walter O'Krafka. *Design and Evaluation of Directory-Based Cache Coherence Systems*. PhD thesis, U. C. Berkeley, January 1992.

[18] G. F. Pfister and V. A. Norton. "Hot Spot" Contention and Combining in Multistage Interconnection Networks. In *Proc. 1985 Int. Parallel Processing Conf*, pages 790–797, 1985.

[19] M. T. Raghunath and Abhiram Ranade. Customizing Interconnection Networks to Suit Packaging Hierarchies. Technical Report UCB/CSD–93–725, Computer Science Division, University of California, Berkeley, CA 94720, January 1993.

[20] Abhiram Gorakhanath Ranade. *Fluent Parallel Computation*. PhD thesis, Yale University, May 1989.

[21] B. Ramakrishna Rau, David W. L. Yen, Wei Yen, and Ross A. Towle. The Cydra 5 Departmental Supercomputer: Design Philosophies, Decisions and Trade-offs. *Computer*, January 1989.

[22] Jaswinder Pal Singh, John L. Hennessy, and Anoop Gupta. Implications of Hierarchical N-Body Techniques for Multiprocessor Architecture. Technical Report CSL-TR-92-506, Stanford University, 1992.

[23] Jaswinder Pal Singh, Wolk-Dietrich Weber, and Anoop Gupta. SPLASH: Stanford Parallel Applications for Shared-Memory. *Computer Architecture News*, pages 5–44, March 1992.

[24] Pen-Chung Yew, Nian-Feng Tzeng, and Duncan H. Lawrie. Distributing Hot-spot Addressing in Large-Scale Multiprocessors. In *Int. Conf. on Parallel Processing*, pages 51–58, 1986.

---

[3] All of these network calculations are based on using pairs of unidirectional links to provide bidirectional routing. For the butterfly and fat-tree networks, two numbers are given for links per node. The first value applies to the routing nodes and the second value applies to the processor and/or memory nodes.

[4] This butterfly network calculation is based on 2 by 2 switches.

[5] This fat-tree calculation is based on 4 by 4 switches and on decreasing by a factor of 2 the total number of links at each higher level in the tree.

Session 13:
Panel
Moderator: Gary Montry

Massively Parallel vs. Parallel Vector Supercomputers: A User's Perspective

Gary Montry, Moderator
Southwest Software
11812 Persimmon NE
Albuquerque NM 87111

David H. Bailey
NAS Facility
MS T045-1
NASA Ames Research Center
Moffett Field CA 94035

Eugene D. Brooks III
Computation Organization
Lawrence Livermore National Lab
P.O. Box 808 L-66
Livermore CA 94551

David W. Forslund
CDO/ACL
Mail Stop B287
Los Alamos National Lab
Los Alamos NM 87545

Robert J. Harrison
Mail Stop K1-90
Battelle Pacific Northwest Lab
P.O. Box 999
Richland WA 99352

Don Heller (form. w/ Shell Oil)
Center for Research on Par. Comp.
Rice University
P.O. Box 1892
Houston TX 77251

Tom Kraay
Boos Allen
1953 Gallows Road
Suite 600
Vienna VA 22182

David H. Bailey

Highly Parallel Supercomputing: Promise and Challenge

There is a general consensus that vector-parallel computing technology will ultimately give way to highly parallel, distributed memory systems -- the only question is when. So what is the current status of highly parallel computing?

Performance:

Promise: Superior performance (10-50 Gflop/s) on certain very large, highly localized, highly tuned, idealized applications; superior performance/cost on a wide range of applications. Challenge: Less than full vector-parallel systems on most other applications.

Programming models and languages:

Promise: Virtual shared memory (VSM) on some new systems; standardized languages such as HPF and PVM. Challenge: Significant tuning still required with VSM; initial implementations of HPF likely not very efficient; no good programming model yet for asynchronous applications.

Operating systems:

Promise: Improved robustness and reliability. Challenge: Still poor compared to conventional systems.

I/O subsystems:

Promise: RAID disks and HiPPI interfaces. Challenge: I/O remains a bottleneck in some cases.

© 1993 ACM 0-8186-4340-4/93/0011 $1.50

Overall Assessment:

Considerable progress has been made, but more effort needs to be made in all four areas to bring this technology into the mainstream of scientific computing. Thus it appears that vector-parallel computing will continue to play an important role in the field.

Eugene D. Brooks III

In the past, analysts comparing computer systems were faced with systems composed of hairball bit serial processors, systems composed of large numbers of microprocessors which lacked enough memory bandwidth to support their pipelined floating unites, and conventional multiprocessor vector processing systems which passed three pipes to memory for each processor. We spent a lot of time evaluating whether or not the new alternative technologies would overtake vector processing as the way to produce the fastest system for scientific computing. To make this comparison at this point, however, is a red herring. Massively parallel systems which are composed of processors possessing honest vector capability are appearing on the market now and these systems are acquiring single node vector processing speeds which rival those of conventional supercomputers. The notion of using vector processing to amortize memory and floating point unit latency is orthogonal to the notion of using many processors to achieve more speed than can be obtained with a single processor.

David W. Forslund

Solving Large-scale Problems on a Very Large MPP System

In the fall of 1992, a complete hardware configuration of a 1024 node CM-5 with 4096 vector units was installed in the Advanced Computing Laboratory at Los Alamos. The successful evolution of the system into a production environment solving Grand Challenge and industrial problems at the 10+ Gflop level required work on a variety of fronts including efficient use of the vector hardware and communications network, stable system operation and high speed data storage. Although far from mature, such systems are routinely used today to successfully solve previously unsolvable problems in science and industry.

Robert J. Harrison

Ab Initio Quantum Chemistry on Massively Parallel Computers

One of the missions of the Molecular Science Software Group, part of the Molecular Science Research Center at Pacific Northwest Laboratory, is to make available on high performance computer systems current models of the electronic structure of molecules and solids. The objective of this is to enable the study of systems large enough, and with sufficient accuracy, to be able to construct detailed descriptions of environmentally important chemical processes. This is particularly challenging for several reasons. First, computational chemistry codes contain many numerically intensive components including not just standard linear algebra operations (e.g., matrix diagonalization) but also many operations specific to this application area, which is formulated algebraically rather than numerically (i.e., we do not use grids). Secondly, our applications are very hard to express in data parallel models, requiring use of a MIMD message passing paradigm, which we are now beginning to abandon in favor of a globally addressable distributed data environment. Finally, there is continuing rapid development of algorithms with improved scaling of computational expense with system size.

Our major problems (in common with almost all other disciplines) in this effort are lack of standardized (i.e., portable) language support for MIMD program development, the poor I/O performance of MPP systems, and the generally immature and non-robust operating systems and environments of these machines.

Don Heller

The Shell Oil Company, the U.S. subsidiary of the Royal Dutch/Shell Group, first made a study of parallel computers and their possible application to geophysical computing in 1969. When it became apparent that single-chip microprocessors would make it economically feasible to build, maintain and deploy a reliable parallel computer, a research group was formed in 1981 to survey the technology and initiate or obtain a suitable computer system. In 1984 we became nCube's first customer with a 512-node nCube-1, and we now have three nCube-2 systems in production (256, 128 and 32 nodes). The next generation of systems is under consideration.

The primary goal was to use parallel computers for selected geophysical application programs in the corporate setting. In this respect we have been successful, including requisite network and job support.

We have also built parallel versions of several petroleum reservoir simulators, but these have not been put into use. Some of the factors separating the two application classes will be discussed.

Parallel computers can be made to work in practice, but one must be careful about the job mix, expectations, and competition from simpler systems.

Tom Kraay

Several traditional recursive algorithms have been reduced to explicit expressions for the ith element. A famous example is the list of Fibonacci numbers. When such is the case, MPP systems excel at requirements for computing the first n elements when n is large.

On the other hand, other lists are recursively computed because an analytic expression for a general element does not exist. In this case, vector computers can easily outperform MPP systems.

Recently, a sorting apparatus was patented using an algorithm for which this is true. The method has been deemed by many as the fastest known means of sorting an arbitrary list since each record is only read once, there are no numerical comparisons, and no rearrangement of data is necessary.

As the algorithm is explained, it becomes intuitively obvious that the entire sorting process is best accomplished by a heterogeneous architecture consisting of an MPP preprocessor and a vector post-processor. This is an ideal example of how a hybrid of the two architecture topologies could outperform an implementation of the same process on either one exclusively.

Session 13:
Minisymposium
Gbit Testbeds
Chair: Charlie Catlett

Other titles from
IEEE Computer Society Press

Current Research in Decision Support Technology
edited by Robert W. Blanning and David R. King

This tutorial presents recent studies on DSS and identifies research issues of current interest that offer significant promise for further development. The areas covered explore the use of expert systems in DSS construction, recent research on logic modeling and integration, and group DSS and the determination of the organizational impact of DSS on understanding organizational information processing and decision-making.

Sections: Introduction, Advanced Decision Modeling and Model Management, Knowledge-Based Decision Support, Organizational Issues in DSS Development.

256 pages. 1993. Hardcover. ISBN 0-8186-2807-3. Catalog # 2807-01 — $45.00 Members $35.00

Groupware:
Software for Computer-Supported Cooperative Work
edited by David Marca and Geoffrey Bock

Investigates the task of designing software to fit the way groups interact in specific work situations and emphasizes the technical aspects involved in the development of software within the bounds of strong social and organizational factors. The book provides a guide to the computer-supported cooperative work field, highlights key trends and ideas, and covers the perspective of work as a cooperative and social endeavor being done by groups, not just individuals.

Sections: Introduction, Groups and Groupware, Conceptual Frameworks, Design Methods, Enabling Technologies — System-Related, Enabling Technologies — UI-Related, Computer Supported Meetings, Bridging Time and Space, Coordinators, What Makes for Effective Systems.

592 pages. 1992. Hardcover. ISBN 0-8186-2637. Catalog # 2637-01 — $75.00 Members $45.00

Information Systems and Decision Processes
edited by Edward A. Stohr and Benn R. Konsynski

This book focuses on DSS and vital issues in the application of information technology to decision making, and introduces some promising new directions for research. It contains the collaborative studies of DSS researchers and explains the potential opportunities and problems in the application of information systems to the decision process in organizations.

Sections: Review and Critique of DSS, Decision Processes, Behavioral Decision Theory and DSS, Group Decision Support Systems, Organizational Decision Support Systems, Technology Environments to Support Decision Processes, Model Management Systems, Research Challenges, Research Approaches in ISDP.

368 pages. 1992. Hardcover. ISBN 0-8186-2802-2. Catalog # 2802-04 — $45.00 Members $35.00

Fault-Tolerant Software Systems:
Techniques and Applications
edited by Hoang Pham

A collection of 12 papers investigating the rapidly growing field of software fault-tolerant computing. It provides a concise overview of the latest theories and techniques to reveal the recent directions of research, and to stimulate more research in this field.

Papers: Definition and Analysis of Hardware and Software Fault-Tolerant Architectures, An Environment for Developing Fault-Tolerant Software, Assuring Design Diversity of N-Version Software, Modeling Execution Time of Multi-Stage N-Version Software, Performance Analysis of Real-Time Software Supporting Fault-Tolerant Operation, Reliability Analysis Fault-Tolerant Systems.

128 pages. 1992. Softcover. ISBN 0-8186-3210-0. Catalog # 3210-05 — $35.00 Members $25.00

▼ **To order call toll-free: 1-800-CS-BOOKS** ▼

▼ **Fax: (714) 821–4641** ▼

10662 Los Vaqueros Circle   **Los Alamitos, CA   90720-1264**   **Phone: (714) 821–8380**

Other titles from
IEEE Computer Society Press

Codes for Detecting and Correcting Unidirectional Errors
edited by Mario Blaum

This collection of papers presents state-of-the-art theory and practice for codes that correct or detect unidirectional errors. The text begins with a selection of four papers providing an introduction to the field that includes applications. It also features key papers demonstrating the best results in each subject related to unidirectional errors.

Sections: Unidirectional Errors, Codes for Detecting Unidirectional Errors, Codes for Correcting Unidirectional Errors, Codes for Correcting *t*-Symmetric Errors and Detecting All Unidirectional Errors, Codes for Correcting and Detecting Combinations of Symmetric and Unidirectional Errors, Codes for Detecting and/or Correcting Unidirectional Burst Errors, Codes for Detecting and/or Correcting Unidirectional Byte Errors.

224 pages. 1993. Hardcover. ISBN 0-8186-4182-7. Catalog # 4182-03 — $44.00 Members $35.00

The Cache Coherence Problem in Shared-Memory Multiprocessors:
Hardware Solutions
edited by Milo Tomasevic and Veljko Milutinovic

Provides an insight into the nature of the cache coherence problem and the wide variety of proposed hardware solutions available today. Its chapters discuss the shared-memory multiprocessor environment, the cache coherence problem and solutions, directory cache coherence schemes, and scalable schemes for large multiprocessor systems, and evaluate different hardware coherence solutions.

Sections: Introductory Issues, Memory Reference Characteristics in Parallel Programs, Directory Cache Coherence Protocols, Snoopy Cache-Coherence Protocols, Coherence in Multilevel Cache Hierarchies, Cache Coherence Schemes in Large-Scale Multiprocessors, Evaluation of Hardware Cache Coherence Schemes.

448 pages. 1993. Hardcover. ISBN 0-8186-4092-8. Catalog # 4092-01 — $62.00 Members $50.00

Bridging Faults and IDDQ Testing
edited by Yashwant K. Malaiya and Rochit Rajsuman

Includes an overview and 17 key papers on recent developments and the major issues regarding bridging faults and the use of IDDQ testing. Some of the selections presented in this text discuss analytical models, test generation procedures, and fault coverage under various situations. Other articles cover the basics of bridging faults and reveal the limitations of conventional logic testing.

Papers: Detecting I/O and Internal Feedback Bridging Faults, Limitations of Switch-Level Analysis for Bridging Faults, IDDQ Benefits, A New Approach to Dynamic IDDQ Testing, High-Quality Tests for Switch-Level Circuits Using Current and Logic Test Generation Algorithms, Constraints for Using IDDQ Testing to Detect CMOS Bridging Faults, Fault Location with Current Monitoring, Built-In Current Testing.

136 pages. 1992. Softcover. ISBN 0-8186-3215-1. Catalog # 3215-05 — $35.00 Members $25.00

Readings in Computer-Generated Music
edited by Dennis Baggi

This tutorial contains 12 articles that cover applications of computer technology to music and focus on the significant effort towards improving musical quality at the levels of tools, compositional strategies, representational models, and abstract methodologies. Its topics range from compositional models and languages to express music, to systems for sound modeling and interpretive performance.

Papers: Formula – A Programming Language for Expressive Computer Music, Tonal Context by Pattern Integration Over Time, Sound Synthesis by Dynamic Systems Integration, AlgoRhythms: Real-Time Algorithmic Composition for a Microcomputer, Composition Based on Pentatonic Scales: A Computer-Aided Approach, An Expert System for the Articulation of Bach Fugue Melodies.

232 pages. 1992. Hardcover. ISBN 0-8186-2747-6. Catalog # 2747-01 -- $45.00 Members $35.00

▼   **To order call toll-free: 1-800-CS-BOOKS**   ▼

▼   **Fax: (714) 821–4641**   ▼

10662 Los Vaqueros Circle   Los Alamitos, CA   90720-1264   Phone: (714) 821–8380

Other titles from
IEEE Computer Society Press

Software Engineering:
A European Perspective
edited by Richard H. Thayer and Andrew D. McGettrick

Concentrates on the areas in which Europe excels such as formal methods, high-integrity systems, integrated software support environments, software quality management, and national and multi-national government initiatives. Its text contains a glossary of more than 1400 system/ software engineering terms, an annotated bibliography with 25 entries describing the European approach, a glossary of information sources with 270 entries, and a list of publicly available software engineering standards used in Europe with more than 100 entries.

Sections: Background and Issues, Life Cycle Development Models/Processes, Requirements Analysis and Specifications, Software Design and Methodologies, High-Integrity Systems, Formal Methods, Software Project Management, Software Quality Management, Software Development Environments, Glossary of Terms, Software Engineering Standards.

696 pages. 1993. Hardcover. ISBN 0-8186-9117-4. Catalog # 2117-01 — $79.00 Members $64.00

Software Management, 4th Edition
edited by Donald J. Reifer

This newly updated tutorial provides both the novice and experienced manager with the materials necessary to comprehend and use the basic theories, concepts, techniques, and tools of software management. Includes both original material and reprints focusing on these four topics: general background information, the five basic functions of general management, advanced management topics, and support material for teachers.

Sections: Software Process, Project Management, Planning Fundamentals, Organizing for Success, Staffing Essentials, Direction Advice, Visibility and Control, Risk Management, Metrics and Measurement, Software Engineering Technology Transfer, Support Material.

664 pages. 1993. Hardcover. ISBN 0-8186-3342-5. Catalog # 3342-01 — $79.00 Members $64.00

Software Reengineering
edited by Robert S. Arnold

Explores software reengineering concepts and processes, tools and techniques, capabilities and limitations, risks and benefits, research possibilities, and case studies. Key sections of the text present, evaluate, and examine several examples of real-life reengineering projects, reengineering and CASE tools, data reengineering, processes for finding reusable parts, and metrics for measuring source codes.

Sections: Software Reengineering: Context and Definition, Business Process Reengineering, Strategies and Economics, Reengineering Experience and Evaluation, Technology for Reengineering, Data Reengineering and Migration, Source Code Analysis, Software Restructuring and Translation, Annotating and Documenting Existing Programs, Reengineering for Reuse, Reverse Engineering and Design Recovery, Object Recovery, Knowledge-Based Program Analysis.

688 pages. 1993. Hardcover. ISBN 0-8186-3272-0. Catalog # 3272-01 — $79.00   Members $64.00

Computer-Aided Software Engineering (CASE), 2nd Edition
edited by Elliot Chikofsky

This popular technology series on CASE describes new information on its technology, its background, and its evolution. The papers presented in this text illustrate the present state of CASE, how its concepts have fared over time, and how it looks as a technology for the future.

Sections: CASE Environments and Tools: Overview, Evolution of Software Development Environment Concepts, Role of Data Browsing Technology in CASE, Role of Assistants and Expert System Technology in CASE, Role of Prototyping in CASE, Tailoring Environments (Extension, Meta-Specification, Generation), Issues of Evaluating Tools and Managing CASE, Bibliography.

184 pages. 1993. Softcover. ISBN 0-8186-3590-8. Catalog # 3590-05 — $35.00 Members $25.00

▼   **To order call toll-free: 1-800-CS-BOOKS**   ▼

▼   **Fax: (714) 821–4641**   ▼

10662 Los Vaqueros Circle   Los Alamitos, CA   90720-1264   Phone: (714) 821–8380

Color Plates

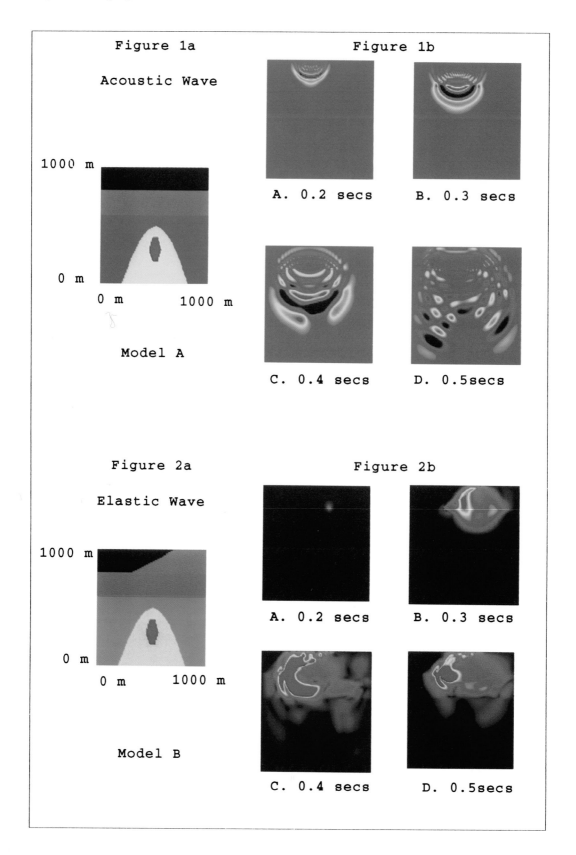

Figure 1a

Acoustic Wave

1000 m

0 m

0 m   1000 m

Model A

Figure 1b

A. 0.2 secs

B. 0.3 secs

C. 0.4 secs

D. 0.5 secs

Figure 2a

Elastic Wave

1000 m

0 m

0 m   1000 m

Model B

Figure 2b

A. 0.2 secs

B. 0.3 secs

C. 0.4 secs

D. 0.5 secs

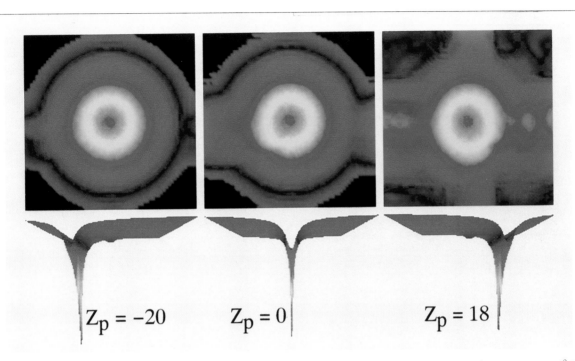

Figure 6: Plotted is the negative logarithm of the muon-position probability density (*top*) and the scalar-component $A^0(\vec{r}, t)$ of the muon's interaction with the time-dependent electromagnetic field (*bottom*) for projectile positions of $z_p = -20, 0,$ and $18\lambda_c$. The muon density was computed for a grazing impact parameter collision of $^{197}Au + ^{197}Au$ at energies of $2GeV$ per nucleon in the collider frame of reference.

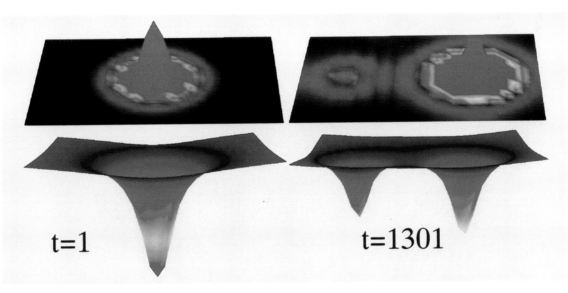

Figure 7: Coulomb potential (*bottom*) and muon-position probability density (*top*) at times $t = 1, 901,$ and $1301\tau_c$ and internuclear distance $R = 2.5, 19.9,$ and $52.9fm$.

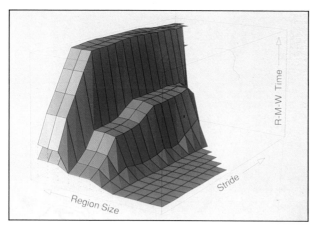

Figure C-1: KSR1 2-node physical and performance profile (Fig. 5). The projection is taken from point {-2.5, -1.7, +0.5}.

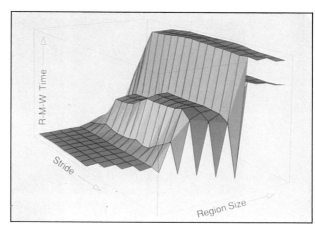

Figure C-2: KSR1 2-node physical and performance profile (Fig. 5). The projection is taken from point {-2.5, +1.7, +0.5}.

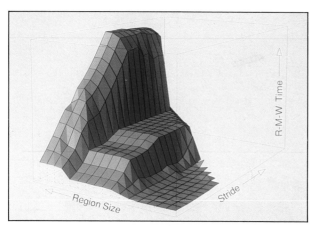

Figure C-3: KSR1 1-node physical and performance profile (Fig. 4). The projection is taken from point {-2.5, -1.7, +0.5}.

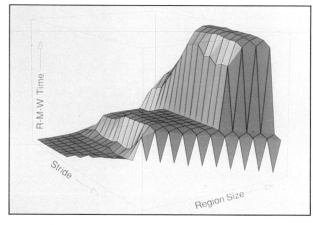

Figure C-4: KSR1 1-node physical and performance profile (Fig. 4). The projection is taken from point {-2.5, +1.7, +0.5}.

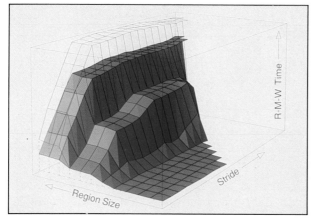

Figure C-5: KSR1 2-node physical and performance profile (Fig. 5). Cache misses satisfied in local ring:0 are shown.

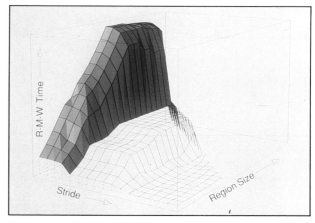

Figure C-6: KSR1 1-node physical and performance profile (Fig. 4). The effect of misses with page replacement is shown.

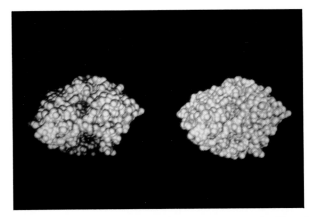

Figure 1: Molecule rendered with (left) and without (right) depth cueing.

Figure 3: Cross section of acetylcholinesterase enzyme in molecular surface representation.

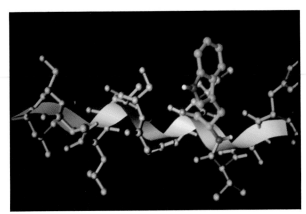

Figure 2: Typical polypeptide segment with one amino acid residue colored and a ribbon model superimposed.

Figure 4: Streamlines of the electric field of acetylcholinesterase converging near the entrance to the active site.

Multi-CPU Plasma Fluid Turbulence Calculations on a CRAY Y-MP C90,
V.E. Lynch et al., page 308.

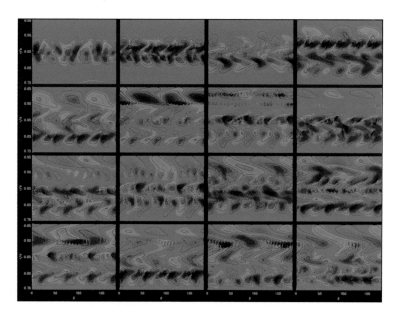

Figure 8: Color contours of the plasma density as a function of radius (vertical axis in each frame) and poloidal angle (horizontal axis) are shown as the nonlinear production calculation advances in time.

A Visualization Environment for Supercomputing-Based Applications in Computational Mechanics, C.J. Pavlakos et al., page 550.

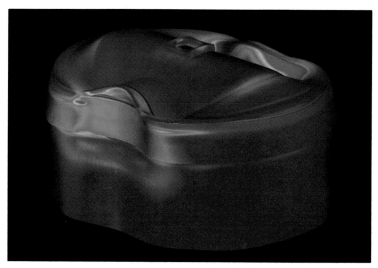

Figure 7: Visualization of equivalent plastic strain on a finite element model of a prototype joint (489,000 elements).

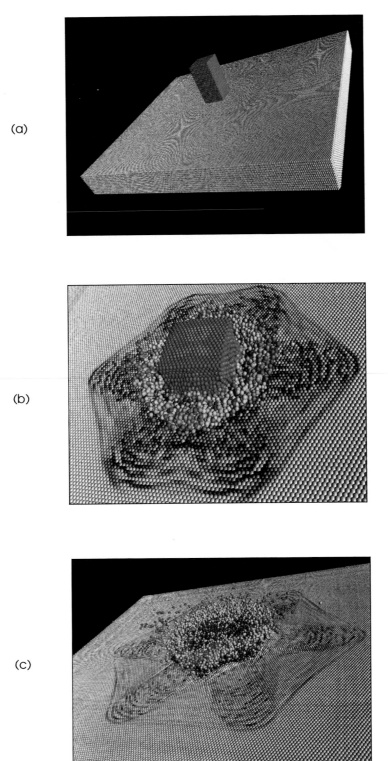

Figure 6: An impact simulation with 1014000 particles. Colors indicate kinetic energy with bright colors indicating high energy

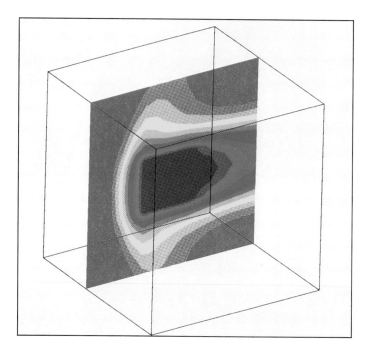

Figure 3: Mach number contours around a supersonically
moving body predicted by the 3-D BGK code.

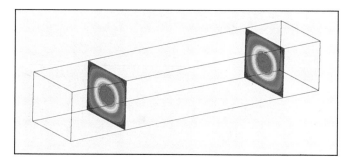

Figure 4: Velocity contours in a square duct
predicted by the 3-D BGK code.

Figure 1: Electrostatic field consisting of two charges, volumetrically ray traced using the vector to scalar converter.

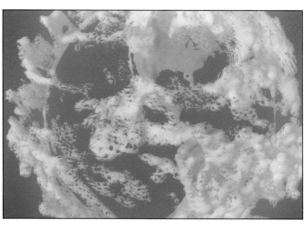

Figure 2: The percent cloudiness field rendered using wind velocities to advect the texture coordinates given to this 3D texture.

Figure 3: The vector filter algorithm applied to the wind field. Upper winds are in red, surface winds are in cyan.

Figure 4: A flow volume weaving through an aerogel substance.

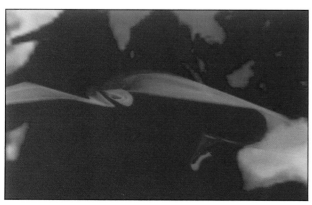

Figure 5: The flow volume algorithm applied to the global climate data set.

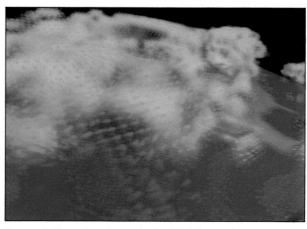

Figure 6: The clouds and wind fields rendered using the textured splats algorithm.

Fast Data Parallel Polygon Rendering, F.A. Ortega et al., page 709.

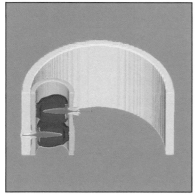

Figure 2: Image of oil well perforator with 355, 948 small polygons. Rendered in 0.5 seconds on a 512 node CM-5 partition.

Figure 5: Closeup image of original polygon edges. Note the small similarly sized polygons.

Figure 6: Closeup image of merged polygon edges. Note the different sized polygons.

VASE: The Visualization and Application Steering Environment,
D.J. Jablonowski et al., page 560.

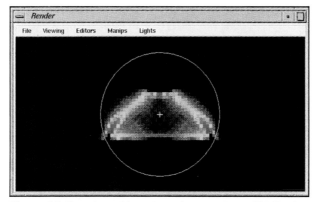

Figure 11: Rendered topology image from IRIS Explorer.

Author Index

IEEE Computer Society

IEEE Computer Society Press Publications

Monographs: A monograph is an authored book consisting of 100-percent original material.

Tutorials: A tutorial is a collection of original materials prepared by the editors, and reprints of the best articles published in a subject area. Tutorials must contain at least five percent of original material (although we recommend 15 to 20 percent of original material).

Reprint collections: A reprint collection contains reprints (divided into sections) with a preface, table of contents, and section introductions discussing the reprints and why they were selected. Collections contain less than five percent of original material.

Technology series: Each technology series is a brief reprint collection — approximately 126-136 pages and containing 12 to 13 papers, each paper focusing on a subset of a specific discipline, such as networks, architecture, software, or robotics.

Submission of proposals: For guidelines on preparing CS Press books, write the Managing Editor, IEEE Computer Society Press, PO Box 3014, 10662 Los Vaqueros Circle, Los Alamitos, CA 90720-1264, or telephone (714) 821-8380.

Purpose

The IEEE Computer Society advances the theory and practice of computer science and engineering, promotes the exchange of technical information among 100,000 members worldwide, and provides a wide range of services to members and nonmembers.

Membership

All members receive the acclaimed monthly magazine *Computer*, discounts, and opportunities to serve (all activities are led by volunteer members). Membership is open to all IEEE members, affiliate society members, and others seriously interested in the computer field.

Publications and Activities

***Computer* magazine:** An authoritative, easy-to-read magazine containing tutorials and in-depth articles on topics across the computer field, plus news, conference reports, book reviews, calendars, calls for papers, interviews, and new products.

Periodicals: The society publishes six magazines and five research transactions. For more details, refer to our membership application or request information as noted above.

Conference proceedings, tutorial texts, and standards documents: The IEEE Computer Society Press publishes more than 100 titles every year.

Standards working groups: Over 100 of these groups produce IEEE standards used throughout the industrial world.

Technical committees: Over 30 TCs publish newsletters, provide interaction with peers in specialty areas, and directly influence standards, conferences, and education.

Conferences/Education: The society holds about 100 conferences each year and sponsors many educational activities, including computing science accreditation.

Chapters: Regular and student chapters worldwide provide the opportunity to interact with colleagues, hear technical experts, and serve the local professional community.